Better Homes and Gardens®

NEW COMPLETE GUIDE TO GARDENING

SUSAN A. ROTH

Writer and Principal Photographer

Better Homes and Gardens® Books
Des Moines, Iowa

Better Homes and Gardens® Books
An imprint of Meredith® Books

New Complete Guide to Gardening
Writer and Principal Photographer: Susan A. Roth
Project Editors: Anne Halpin, Kay Sanders
Contributing Editor: Veronica Fowler
Associate Art Director: Tom Wegner
Contributing Graphic Designer: Ernie Shelton
Copy Chief: Angela K. Renkoski
Copy Editor: Barbara Feller-Roth
Proofreaders: Mary Pas, Kim Catanzarite
Illustrator: Neil Shigley
Contributing Photographers: Karen Bussolini, David Chinery, Stephen Cridland, DeGennaro Associates, Michael A. Dirr, Derek Fell, Ed Gohlich, Karlis Grants, Bill Holt, Saxon Holt, William Hopkins, Sr., Brent Isenberger, Jon Jensen, Mike Jensen, Gene Johnson, Jim Kascoutas, Balthazar Korab, Peter Krumhardt, Maris/Semel, Barbara Martin, Elvin McDonald, E. Alan McGee, Eric Roth, William Stites, Perry Struse, Judy Watts. Photographs courtesy of: Netherlands FlowerBulb Information Center, Reemay
Indexer: Kathleen Poole
Electronic Production Coordinator: Paula Forest
Editorial and Design Assistants: Susan McBroom, Jennifer Norris, Karen Schirm, Barbara A. Suk
Production Director: Douglas M. Johnston
Production Manager: Pam Kvitne
Assistant Prepress Coordinator: Marjorie J. Schenkelberg
Researchers: Marcia Eames-Sheavly, Erin Hynes, Pamela K. Peirce, Patricia R. Schwartz

Meredith® Books
Editor in Chief: James D. Blume
Design Director: Matt Strelecki
Managing Editor: Gregory H. Kayko
Executive Garden Editor: Cathy Wilkinson Barash

Director, Sales & Marketing, Retail: Michael A. Peterson
Director, Sales & Marketing, Special Markets: Rita McMullen
Director, Sales & Marketing, Home & Garden Center Channel: Ray Wolf
Director, Operations: Valerie Wiese

Vice President, General Manager: Jamie L. Martin

Better Homes and Gardens® Magazine
Editor in Chief: Jean LemMon
Executive Garden Editor: Mark Kane

Meredith Publishing Group
President, Publishing Group: Christopher M. Little
Vice President and Publishing Director: John P. Loughlin

Meredith Corporation
Chairman of the Board: Jack D. Rehm
President and Chief Executive Officer: William T. Kerr

Chairman of the Executive Committee: E.T. Meredith III

Cover photograph: Hollyhocks by William Stites

All of us at Better Homes and Gardens® Books are dedicated to providing you with the information and ideas you need to enhance your home and garden. We welcome your comments and suggestions about this book. Write to us at: Better Homes and Gardens Books, Garden Editorial Department, 1716 Locust St., Des Moines, IA 50309–3023.

For nearly 50 years, *Better Homes and Gardens®* gardening books have provided wisdom to generations of gardeners. The various editions of our original ringbound *Garden Book* have sold more than 4½ million copies.

At Better Homes and Gardens® Books, we think that this is our best, most complete gardening book yet. That's why we titled it the *New Complete Guide to Gardening.* In creating this book, author and photographer Susan A. Roth traveled from coast to coast, talking with gardeners and photographing their gardens. She contacted researchers, gathering the most up-to-date information on lawn and plant care, gardening techniques, and landscape plants. Then, veteran book editor Anne Halpin helped compile all this knowledge into an easy-to-use, information-packed book that is a wonderful marriage of no-nonsense gardening how-to and beautiful ideas.

Within this book, you'll find help in landscaping your property, with page after page of at-a-glance information as well as illustrations focusing on topics ranging from shade gardening to designing a garden for winter color. You'll also find 9 chapters chock-full of information on growing and an extensive encyclopedia of the best plants available. Last, but not least, you'll get the nitty gritty of plant care—everything from the right way to plant a tree and prune your shrubs to how to water your lawn.

A writer and photographer specializing in gardening and landscaping, Susan Roth is the author and editor of numerous gardening books. Both her writing and photography have won several awards from the Garden Writers Association of America. A skilled and passionate gardener, Susan became hooked at age 8 when she planted a peach pit in her California backyard and watched it germinate and grow into a fruit-bearing tree. Since then, she has gardened in Connecticut, Indiana, and upstate New York. Susan now lives and gardens with her husband, Mark Schneider, on Long Island on a hilly, half-acre site, where they attempt to organize their eclectic collection of old favorites and rare plants into rock gardens, mixed borders, woodland shade gardens, and perennial borders to grace their property.

To quote author Pearl Buck, "The secret of joy is contained in one word—excellence. To know how to do something well is to enjoy it." The *New Complete Guide to Gardening* is your guide to making gardening one of the greatest joys in your life.

CONTENTS

CHAPTER 1
DEVELOPING THE RIGHT LANDSCAPE PLAN 6

CHAPTER 2
SOLVING LANDSCAPE CHALLENGES 66

CHAPTER 3
TREES & SHRUBS 120
Deciduous Trees Encyclopedia   142
Deciduous Shrubs Encyclopedia   170
Evergreen Trees & Shrubs Encyclopedia   203

CHAPTER 4
VINES & GROUNDCOVERS 234
Vines & Groundcovers Encyclopedia   242

CHAPTER 5
ROSES 266
Roses Encyclopedia   276

CHAPTER 6
PERENNIALS, ORNAMENTAL GRASSES, & FERNS 286
Perennials Encyclopedia   296
Ornamental Grasses Encyclopedia   334
Ferns Encyclopedia   342

CHAPTER 7
ANNUALS 346
Annuals Encyclopedia   354

CHAPTER 8

BULBS 380

Bulbs Encyclopedia   388

CHAPTER 9

FRUIT & NUTS 408

Fruits Encyclopedia   428
Nuts Encyclopedia   443

CHAPTER 10

VEGETABLES 446

Vegetables Encyclopedia   462

CHAPTER 11

HERBS 492

Herbs Encyclopedia   496

CHAPTER 12

SOIL BUILDING, PLANTING, & PROPAGATING 506

CHAPTER 13

GARDEN TOOLS & MAINTENANCE 532

CHAPTER 14

STARTING & MAINTAINING LAWNS 560

HARDINESS ZONE AND FROST DATE MAPS 574

INDEX 576

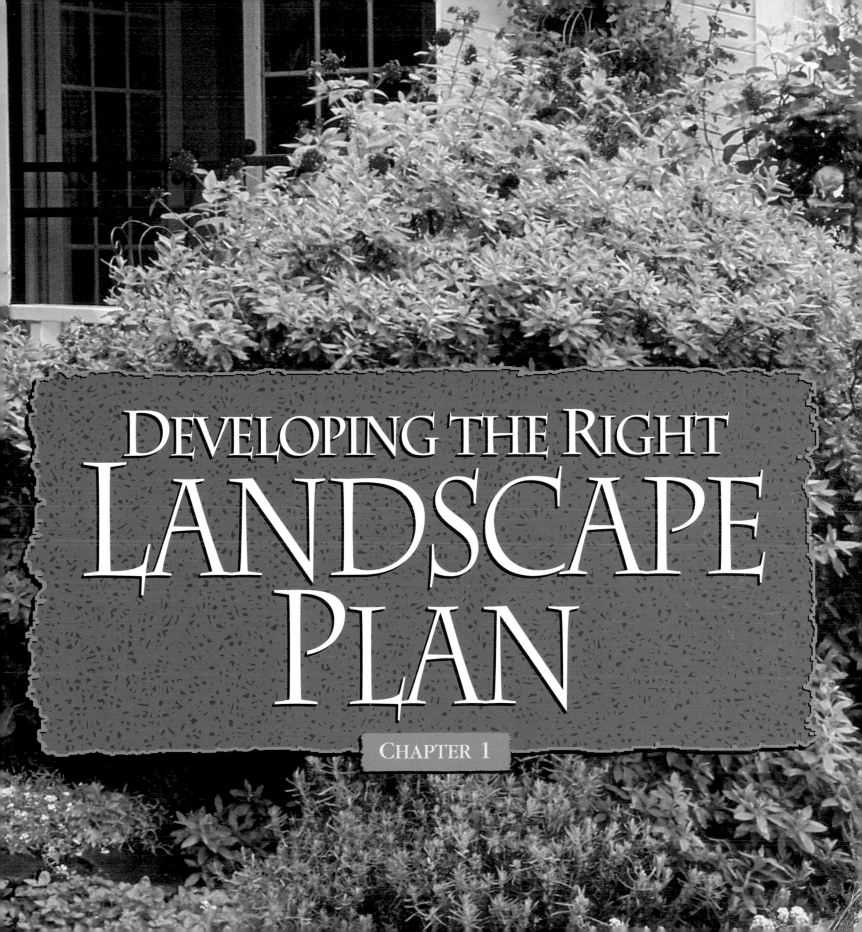

Developing the Right Landscape Plan

Chapter 1

ASSESSING YOUR EXISTING LANDSCAPE

Photo by Jim Kascoutas

Lay tracing paper over an enlarged photograph of your site and sketch in your proposed additions. This strategy helps you visualize your landscaping ideas before you implement them.

The plantings that surround your home contribute dramatically to your home's value and appearance. The layout of the walkways, driveway, and outdoor living areas also plays an important role in your landscape design. Ideally, the landscape design

Photo by Jim Kascoutas

The first step to an effective landscape design is to plot out your existing landscape and assess its strengths and weaknesses.

creates a setting that complements and enhances your home's architecture. Good landscaping also solves problems; you can modify sun, slow wind, block unsightly views, and create lovely vistas with plants.

When attractively implemented and well-maintained, landscaping increases a home's value by 10 to 40 percent, according to real estate appraisers. Yet most homeowners feel helpless when it comes to designing a landscape. The skimpy landscape installed by the builder, however

inadequate and inappropriate, often is left unchanged for years, and it can become overgrown and unsightly.

GETTING STARTED

Even if you started with a good landscape design and appropriate plantings, time changes things. Just as you redecorate your home's interior from time to time, painting the walls and buying new furniture, your home's landscape needs renovation every 15 to 20 years to keep plantings in scale and to compensate for trees growing larger and casting shade in once-sunny areas.

Where you live determines to a large degree how much you use your outdoor living space, the functions the plants in your landscape serve, and which types of plants you can grow. In the Southeast, for example, you will want deciduous trees that cast shade, but are arranged to enhance rather than block breezes. In the Northern Plains, you'll want to position evergreen trees to block strong winter wind, but allow the warming sun to penetrate. Gardeners along the coast will need a windbreak of salt-tolerant trees and shrubs to shelter areas for gardens.

The first step in developing a landscape plan is to assess the site as it currently exists.

REGIONAL DIFFERENCES

Before beginning to landscape or garden in earnest, you need to assess the general climate in your region and the specific elements that affect the plant-growing environment surrounding your home. Although each region has predictable climate trends, the immediate area surrounding your home can have several small microclimates of colder or warmer temperatures, fluctuating wind patterns, or differing soil.

If you don't already know, determine the following:

■ Hardiness zone for plants for your region. (See page 578 for map.)
■ Soil type (clay, sand, loam, etc.) in each garden area.
■ Soil pH (measure of acidity and alkalinity) for each garden area.
■ Sun exposure for various parts of your property. This shifts throughout the year as deciduous trees lose their leaves and the sun's angle changes.
■ Drainage patterns on your property, such as fast-draining slopes or low wet spots with poor drainage.
■ Length of the growing season—the period of time between the last frost in spring and the first frost in fall.
■ Location of any frost pockets or microclimates of colder or warmer temperatures.
■ Direction of prevailing winds.

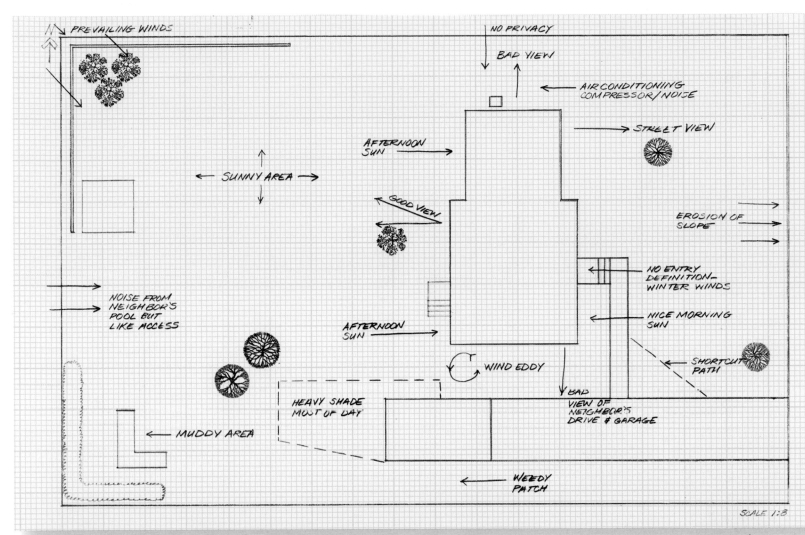

PREVAILING WINDS

NO PRIVACY

BAD VIEW

AIR CONDITIONING COMPRESSOR/NOISE

AFTERNOON SUN

STREET VIEW

SUNNY AREA

GOOD VIEW

EROSION OF SLOPE

NOISE FROM NEIGHBOR'S POOL BUT LIKE ACCESS

NO ENTRY DEFINITION— WINTER WINDS

NICE MORNING SUN

AFTERNOON SUN

WIND EDDY

SHORTCUT PATH

HEAVY SHADE MOST OF DAY

BAD VIEW OF NEIGHBOR'S DRIVE & GARAGE

MUDDY AREA

WEEDY PATCH

SCALE 1:8

Topography, microclimates, quality of the view, and other factors are mapped on this tracing paper drawing.

You can learn these climate and soil details by observation and through soil testing and research.

SURVEYING YOUR LANDSCAPE

Once you understand the growing conditions on your property, the next step is to make a plot plan to help evaluate the site's potential. Size up how much space you have by studying your property survey, then redraw the property's dimensions and the house's location in a larger size on big sheets of graph paper. Use a scale that allows enough room to draw your entire property — such as 1 inch of graph paper equals 4 feet of landscape (¼ scale), or 1 inch of graph paper equals 8 feet of landscape (⅛ scale).

Add to your emerging plot plan all existing structures, such as garages, tool sheds, decks, patios, driveways, and walkways. Mark all windows and doors of the house. Indicate existing trees and planting beds. A scale rule or a template of landscape symbols (available at most art supply stores) might be helpful in drawing these. Use a professional-type tape measure, or stakes and a long rope marked in 1-foot lengths, to take accurate measurements before marking these items on the plan. Mark the plot plan with the direction north, then indicate any drainage, soil, or exposure extremes.

This accurate view of your existing property is the starting point for change. When you know what you want your new or renovated landscape to be and the kinds of plants you can grow, you can use this plot plan to test your ideas on paper (see pages 12–13).

ASSESSING YOUR LANDSCAPE NEEDS

Stately evergreens add a vertical element to this border and provide a screen from neighboring property. Evergreens also can muffle sounds such as traffic noise.

One person may consider leaf raking a burdensome chore, while another considers it a pleasant activity and a good excuse to be outdoors. Because lifestyles, tastes, budgets, and enthusiasm for gardening differ widely, it follows that there are as many ideas of the perfect garden and landscape as there are people. So no one can design the best landscape plan for you without knowing you well. And no one knows your family better than you.

To avoid ending up with a new landscape that is not quite what you had in mind or that doesn't meet your family's needs, plan ahead by asking yourself and your family some important questions about your lifestyle. Does your family spend a lot of time outdoors? Would they spend more if you built an attractive deck, added a swimming pool, or created a flower-filled setting for dining or reading and relaxing?

HOW DO YOU USE YOUR PROPERTY?

Consider how you want to use the property surrounding your house. It can serve many functions if you plan it right. Is it a place for adults to lounge, children to play, or both? Do you like to sit outdoors on a warm evening and eat and cook outdoors, or are you strictly indoor folks? Do you want to indulge in a gardening passion such as growing roses, heirloom vegetables, or cut flowers? Or, are your main goals simply to beautify your home's surroundings and create attractive views both indoors and outdoors?

Even if you aren't an avid gardener, you may want a lovely view that can be enjoyed from indoors every day of the year. Your special view may vary from a flower-filled garden seen every morning from the breakfast table to a dramatically silhouetted weeping cherry viewed from your bedroom window as the foliage changes through the seasons. These special sights are important and bring pleasure throughout the year.

LANDSCAPING THAT SOLVES PROBLEMS

Ask yourself practical questions, because good landscaping also solves problems. Do you need more privacy from the street or neighbors? Do you need room for more cars to park off the street? Is the house too shaded by overgrown trees and shrubs, or is it too hot and sunny in summer? Is the lawn too large to mow yourself?

Sometimes you get so accustomed to the things you see around you every day that you stop noticing what's before your eyes. So walk around your property and pretend it belongs to someone else. Take a critical look at the landscaping from all angles—from the street, as you approach the house from the front walk and driveway, and perhaps even from your neighbors' yards.

Take a comprehensive look to determine if the trees and shrubs are out of scale with the house, if the colors of the flowers clash with the paint on the house, if the fence style is in keeping with the architecture of the house. Are there eyesores, such as trash cans, rubbish piles, or swing sets, that should be hidden?

HOW MUCH TIME DO YOU HAVE?

Finally ask yourself how much time you realistically can spend maintaining the yard and gardens. Keep in mind that a lawn needs regular attention once or twice a week from spring through fall, but groundcover plantings require hardly any attention. Flower gardens demand concentrated maintenance in spring and fall and only minimal care during summer. Informal shrub plantings are practically care-free, needing pruning only once every few years, but formally sheared hedges require a lot of effort several times a year. Some shade trees are messier than others, but most create work only for several weekends in autumn.

If your time is limited, consider low-maintenance groundcovers and informal shrub plantings. Consider hiring help for mowing or fall and spring cleanup, so you can use your time and energy for gardening or other activities you really enjoy.

Key to a successful landscape is determining how you want to use it. This new patio, carved out of a steep slope, created space for the family's small children to play and an ideal spot for dining outdoors.

GATHERING AND SKETCHING IDEAS

You'll find inspiration and a wealth of practical how-to information on garden design and plant material in this book. Use it as a guide to ascertain what you want in your landscape and how to get it. Inspecting gardens up close offers another source of ideas; you see what others have done with their landscapes. Enjoy a weekend visiting a public garden or going on a garden tour and talking to the owners.

Browsing through gardening and home-oriented books and magazines also can be inspirational. Clip out magazine photos of gardens that you like and study them or show them to a landscape designer if you decide to get professional help.

The illustrated plant encyclopedia sections of Chapters 3 through 11 are a complete reference to the best plants available to implement your landscaping and gardening dreams. The encyclopedias also will help you identify plants that you see in other gardens.

MAKING A PLAN

When planning changes to your property, keep the entire landscape in mind, so that each part works in concert with the others. Check local building codes early on. And consider the ultimate size of trees and shrubs when you position and plant them. Sometimes it's difficult to imagine how tall a small

A good plan is the beginning of a landscape tailored to your needs and desires. A professional designer worked with the homeowners to transform this backyard from boring to delightful.

HIRING A PROFESSIONAL

There are times when you may need professional help to design or install your landscape. Use the information in this chapter to guide you in developing an eye for landscape detail. With an enriched sense of landscape design, you can do a better job yourself or find a professional whose ideas you can trust.

When hiring help, keep in mind that qualifications and talents vary widely. Check out anyone you hire to work on your landscape as you would any professional you hire. Ask for references; most importantly, go see some of his or her finished work. That's the best way to judge if the person you hire has the kind of knowledge and skill level you need.

Seek out a landscape or garden designer or a landscape architect, not a landscape maintenance company, to do design work for you. A garden designer often knows more about plants than a landscape architect, who is certified in site planning, surveying, and other engineering aspects of landscaping. A designer or an architect will create a planting plan for you, but may or may not actually install the design, though either one usually can recommend a company to do the installation for you. For an extra fee, a designer usually will supervise an installation. A design-build firm both designs and installs the landscape.

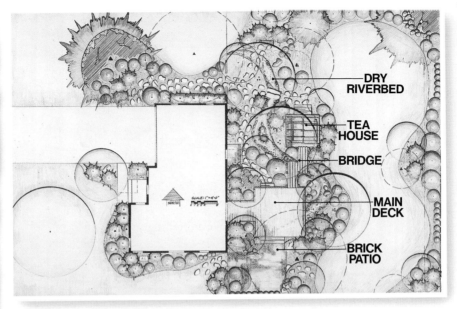

This landscape plan, prepared by a professional designer, served as the blueprint for the major backyard remodeling at far left. The drawing was the culmination of a long planning process. Ideas flowed, and the designer revised the plan several times.

DRY RIVERBED

TEA HOUSE

BRIDGE

MAIN DECK

BRICK PATIO

sapling can become; in a few years it may be towering over your house.

TEST YOUR PLAN ON PAPER

Once you've decided what you want in your landscape, test the design on paper. Lay a sheet of tracing paper over the plot plan of your existing property and secure it with masking tape. Sketch in the changes that you'd like to make, using the mature size of the plants. By drawing in the canopy of a mature tree on your plan, you can gauge where to position the trunk.

Anything goes at this point. Let your dreams and imagination guide you. Create a large wraparound deck, move or widen the front walk, add additional parking space, or cut down an overgrown Norway spruce and replace it with an herb garden.

If you have trouble visualizing your proposed plot plan in three dimensions, take a snapshot of your landscape (a panoramic camera is a great help). Lay tracing paper over the photo and draw in your proposed

landscape. This bubble diagram then can be translated into a plot plan with accurate measurements. Make variations until the result pleases you.

If drawing isn't your best skill, try a landscape design program on your computer. You'll still need to have accurate measurements, but the program assists you in drawing and provides a full-color, three-dimensional view of your future landscape. Most landscape design software is fun to toy with, but features differ, so choose carefully to justify the expense. Used with the design and plant information in this book, landscaping software will paint a picture of your dream landscape. Then it's up to you to realize the dream.

All that really matters is that whatever you do with your yard pleases you and fulfills your intentions. You can enjoy your landscape and garden every day, both from outside and inside your house, if you plan it correctly.

OUTDOOR ROOMS

Garden rooms can flow into each other. Here a large lawn leads onto a brick patio surrounded with flowers.

Garden designers often talk about "outdoor rooms," with each room having a floor, walls, and a ceiling. If you think of your property in terms of spaces that can be divided literally or figuratively into rooms, you've taken the first step in designing a functional landscape.

DESIGNING A ROOM IN THE GREAT OUTDOORS

Think of your outdoor rooms as having the following structures:

■ FLOOR: Lawn, groundcover plantings, mulch, and paving materials such as bricks, flagstones, or decking form the garden floor, carpeting the ground with color and texture and dressing up bare earth.

■ WALLS: Masonry walls, wooden or iron fences, the sides of buildings, and living walls such as hedges, shrubbery, and trellised vines form walls. The vertical plants and structures define spaces, create enclosure and privacy, and often cast shade and block wind.

■ CEILING: The sky is the ultimate ceiling, but trees and overhead structures such as arbors, pergolas, and umbrellas create more intimacy and cast shade, create shadow patterns, and block views from above.

Designing a garden as a series of rooms is an excellent way to make a large, rambling plot more livable. It also allows you to create different areas for different purposes. You can keep the kids' swing set separated from your perennial garden and have an informal picnic area away from a more formal rose garden.

This intimate garden space conveys the sense of being in an outdoor room. Fencing and vines form the walls. Paving stones and plants create an intriguing floor.

Photo by Ed Gohlich

DESIGNING FOR SMALL SPACES

The concept of garden rooms works well for a large property, but what if you've got a postage-stamp-size yard? To turn a small space into an intimate garden room, follow these guidelines:

■ Eliminate the lawn entirely and install a paved sitting area with a walkway of the same material. The walkway should wind through planting areas.

■ Plant fine-textured shrubs in the background and a few bold-textured shrubs in the foreground to create the illusion of distance.

■ Add a few low-walled terraces, raised beds, or a berm to bring dimension to a flat area.

■ Create the illusion of additional space beyond the immediate area with a path that seems to lead to another part of the garden.

■ Follow a simple color scheme of pastels throughout the garden to create a restful ambience.

■ Rely on long-blooming plants and those with colorful foliage to bring continual color to an area.

■ Position a specimen tree, a statue, a bench, or a fountain at the far side of the garden to draw the eye into the distance.

■ Establish privacy with a row of columnar flowering or evergreen trees or a tall lattice fence and an overhead arbor.

■ Grow vines on walls, trellises, and fences or even twining into trees to save space but create the feeling of lush growth.

■ Choose dwarf, slow-growing, and compact trees and shrubs that won't quickly overgrow the planting area.

Choosing a Style

Designing your landscape demands some of the same knowledge and skills as decorating the interior of your home. You create a mood and style with the colors, textures, shapes, sizes, and placement of the plants and structures you choose. When considering where plants will look good, you also have to keep in mind their preferred growing conditions. Also remember that plants are not static; most change with the seasons and grow larger over the years.

DEFINING GARDEN STYLE

Although style can be a difficult concept to discuss, it's easiest to just think of it as an overall sense of design that creates a mood. Gardens usually are designed in one of three broad styles: formal, informal, or natural.

A formally designed landscape can be imposing and serene at the same time. This style relies on straight lines and symmetrical plantings along with elegant touches such as sculptures and garden ornaments. Hedges often are sharply pruned into flat walls.

Formal landscapes may be predominantly green or touched with color, but the colors usually are understated and secondary to the garden's structure. A geometric knot garden of herbs, an English-style double border, and a pristine rose garden are suited to formal landscapes.

An informal landscape is almost the opposite of a formal one. Curves and color abound. Plantings are usually asymmetrical, although that doesn't mean they are not balanced or planned. Plants often are allowed to grow into their natural shapes. Cottage gardens, ornamental grasses, and mixed borders of small trees, shrubs, and flowers are at home in informal landscapes.

A natural landscape is an informal landscape that tries to mimic nature. Woodland, prairie, and meadow gardens are examples of natural styles. Although a natural garden may border on untamed chaos, it's most attractive if the gardener's taming hand appears from time to time to keep the plantings under control. Natural landscapes look best when designed and planted with some basic design principles in mind, but breaking the rules is to be expected.

Symmetrical and orderly design give this formal rose garden an ambiance of elegance and serenity. It invites visitors to take a leisurely stroll.

A GARDEN STYLE TO MATCH YOUR HOUSE

Landscapes look best if they complement a home's architecture. Here are suggestions to match garden to house:

■ **BUNGALOW OR COTTAGE:** A split-rail fence or picket fence painted to match the house's shutters or trim. Small flowering trees for a large house. One tall shade tree to emphasize the charm of a small house. Flagstone path and patio or weathered deck if house has natural-colored wood siding. Informal hedges, mixed borders, and natural or cottage gardens.

■ **VICTORIAN:** Wrought-iron fence or Gothic picket fence to match home's gingerbread trim. Dramatic trees, such as a weeping beech, in scale with building's size. Herringbone brick walks, circular patio, elaborate fountain and statuary. Flower-filled gardens and formal hedges.

■ **WILLIAMSBURG COLONIAL:** Formal front with wide brick walkway (basket-weave pattern), symmetrical plantings, formal hedges. Tall shade trees at each side for balance. Brick patio or wooden deck with railings and finials to match house architecture, painted to match house trim. Deck stained the same color as the house. Herb and flower beds in geometric patterns. Natural gardens in distant areas.

■ **WOOD-SIDED CONTEMPORARY:** Large trees in scale with house. Flagstone or brick walkways and patio (jack-on-jack or traditional pattern) or deck made of wood to match the house. Deck with clean, simple design lines. Informally pruned shrubs, mixed border plantings, and natural gardens.

■ **BRICK FEDERAL:** Brick walkway (pinwheel pattern) and walls in matching color. Wrought-iron gates. Wood fence stained to match house trim or shutters. Brick patio or deck with railings stained to match house trim. Tall trees for scale. Formal or informal hedges and gardens. Pastel flower colors to harmonize with red brick (avoid red, magenta, or bright pink).

Photo by Stephen Cridland

Lush, tumbled plantings, abundant color, and asymmetrical but balanced design characterize this informal garden.

Natural gardens may capitalize on woodland and other wild settings, or they can be created from scratch.

THE RIGHT SHAPE

Ornamental gardens look wonderful anywhere—bordering a front walk, fronting the street, lining the driveway, beside a patio, or surrounding the front lawn. Even vegetable and herb gardens can be silhouetted and highlighted against the solid backdrop.

The minimum size for an ornamental garden that has a progression of color from spring through fall is 12 feet long by 3 feet wide. Inexperienced gardeners might wish to start small, then make the garden larger as they become more accomplished in following years. Keep the garden's width in proportion to its length. Generally, small plots look balanced if they are three times as long as they are wide. However, even extra-long gardens need be only 8 to 12 feet wide.

When laying out your garden, remember that you'll need access to the plants in the rear to tend them. Traditional borders have a 3-foot-wide path between the garden and the background hedge, which lets you get to the tall plants in the back. This 3-foot alley also fosters air circulation and prevents the hedge from shading plants at the rear.

Most people can reach 3 to 4 feet into the garden from any side, so an 8-foot-wide bed or border is the largest you can tend without stepping directly in the garden. If you must step in the garden, plan to place discreet stepping-stones among the plants so you won't tramp on emerging growth or compact the soil.

Design beds, borders, and lawn areas so their size and shape complement each other. Here the wide, curving lawn balances the borders while leading visitors on a stroll through the garden.

You want your garden to be large enough to make a visual impact yet small enough to maintain in the time you have available. It also should mesh attractively with the rest of your landscape. The size, shape, and position of beds and borders should be carefully planned. If you carve a garden from your lawn—either from the center or around the edges—be sure the remaining lawn has a pleasing shape so it enhances the landscape's design.

For your pleasure, position the gardens where you can see them throughout the day from indoors and out. Don't feel bound by tradition and relegate the garden to the backyard.

designed to be beautiful enough for the front yard (see pages 52–55).

TRADITIONAL SHAPES

Garden borders are intended to be viewed from only one side. A border generally is planted against a garden wall, hedge, fence, or a side of the house.

Although a garden bed may abut a walkway or patio, it lacks a structural background and generally is viewed from all sides. A bed in the middle of a lawn, called an island bed, poses some real design challenges (see pages 28–29).

Borders are easier to design than beds because the plants can be

CURVES AND ANGLES

Style helps determine whether your garden has straight sides and sharp corners or curving outlines. Curves look more casual and informal than straight lines. Although straight-sided beds and borders are intrinsically formal, they appear less imposing if the plants are arranged in flowing drifts rather than rows.

Before digging a new garden plot or remodeling an old one, lay out the proposed border with a garden hose or flexible rope, rearranging the lines until you get a shape that looks attractive. Try making the front edge bend gently inward and then flare dramatically outward and perhaps back again. Avoid numerous sharp curves in favor of a few gentle sweeps. Sculpt a pleasing overall outline, one that balances the outward curves with the inward curves. For a garden that outlines the perimeter of the yard, avoid placing two outward curves opposite each other; this looks pinched.

DEFINING EDGES

No matter what the shape and style of your garden, if it is edged by lawn, you should carefully define that edge. This often is done with an edging tool—usually a half-moon edger, which cuts a sharp, troughlike edge around the boundary between lawn and garden. The edge must be recut once or twice a year to keep it sharp and curtail grass roots. Without this labor-intensive maintenance, lawn grass creeps into the garden, creating a weed problem. Another option to stop the spread of grass is a physical barrier such as a vinyl lawn border or a brick mowing strip.

Grass sets off the overall garden to perfection, but sometimes it so closely matches the color of garden plant foliage that it blurs the garden's edges. You can highlight plants better and stop the lawn from invading by edging the garden with a decorative brick mowing strip, flagstone border, or gravel path. Stones and masonry

used this way contrast effectively with flowers and foliage and give the garden a definite shape and structure while allowing foreground plants to spill onto the stonework.

You also can edge the front of the border using low-growing plants with foliage texture and color that contrast vividly with the green grass. Lamb's-ears is a favorite edger; its broad, silver-furred leaves form flat rosettes that stand out boldly from the lawn. Dwarf lavender or blue fescue are other gray or silvery choices. 'Palace Purple' coralbells, with its stand-out, maple-shaped, reddish purple leaves, offers another exquisite choice for edging. Or, consider edging with long-blooming annuals, such as sweet alyssum, wax begonias, or impatiens.

Edging plants can form a continuous strip along the garden's front border for a formal effect; however, a combination of various low-growing plants is more pleasing. Alternate clusters of different types of plants to create a subtle edge, but one that clearly states: The garden begins here.

Lamb's-ears, with its attractive silvery green foliage, spills onto the adjacent lawn, giving a soft edge to the garden.

EDGING PLANTS

Aligned along the front of a garden, low edging plants mark the boundary between garden and lawn or garden and walkway. They serve as an attractive filler that collars the planting. Edging plants that border a lawn are most effective if the leaf color or texture (or both) contrasts strongly with the grass or if the plants are long-blooming. Use groundcovers as edging plants to define a walkway; don't use them to define a lawn, because they may become invasive.

ANNUALS
Begonia × semperflorens-cultorum (wax begonia)
Impatiens wallerana (impatiens)
Lobelia erinus (edging lobelia)
Lobularia maritima (sweet alyssum)
Senecio cineraria (dusty-miller)
Tagetes tenuifolia (signet marigold)

GROUNDCOVERS
Ajuga reptans (bugleweed)
Liriope muscari 'Variegata' (variegated lilyturf)
Lysimachia nummularia 'Aurea' (moneywort)

HERBS
Lavandula angustifolia 'Munstead Dwarf' (English lavender)
Thymus vulgaris 'Argenteus' (thyme)

ORNAMENTAL GRASSES
Carex morrowii 'Variegata' (Japanese sedge)
Festuca ovina var. *glauca* (blue fescue)

PERENNIALS
Alchemilla spp. (lady's-mantle)
Geranium spp. (cranesbill)
Heuchera micrantha 'Palace Purple' (purple-leaf coralbells)
Hosta spp. (dwarf hosta)
Iberis sempervirens (edging candytuft)
Lamium maculatum (spotted dead nettle)
Pulmonaria saccharata (Bethlehem sage)
Stachys byzantina 'Silver Carpet' (lamb's-ears)

OTHER PRINCIPLES OF LANDSCAPE DESIGN

The landscape surrounding your home consists of two different parts: the hardscape and the softscape. The hardscape consists of the man-made structures in the garden including fences, paving, decking, patio furniture, window boxes, and ornaments. The softscape encompasses all the plant material: lawn, shrubs, trees, and flowers.

Hardscape materials are permanent landscape additions and do not change with the seasons, grow larger, or suddenly die, as plants do. They give a garden year-round structure, creating a constant against which you can arrange the plants of the softscape. Compared to plants, the hardscape is considered low-maintenance, although most structures require some upkeep and repair or replacement over the years.

The handsome green fence defines this garden, providing a contrasting background with the snow that shows off the exfoliating bark of the 'Heritage' birch and other plants.

CREATING THE BONES OF THE GARDEN

The hardscape and the woody plants (trees and shrubs) of the softscape combine to create the garden's year-round structure, sometimes referred to as the garden's bones. When the bones are well-designed, the landscape looks good throughout the year, even as the flowers and foliage change with the seasons. Thus, it pays to lay out the garden bones carefully.

Here are some general guidelines:
■ Create axes or sight lines by framing an uninterrupted view through a gate or pair of trees. Line up gates, paths, and stairs so one view leads into another.
■ Use linear plantings or structural elements, such as a row of trees, straight walks, and geometric beds, to create a strong axis in a formal garden. Use bold curves and repeated groupings in an informal garden to create the axis and lead the eye.
■ Place a focal point (such as a specimen plant, garden ornament, or bench) at the end of the sight line to emphasize the line of sight and draw the eye along the axis.
■ Use fences, walls, patios, and decks of an attractive material and color that are in proportion to the

house and landscape to create a pleasing visual structure.

■ Create mystery by hiding part of the garden around the bend of a walkway or path. Or, design a special place beyond a gate for visitors.

■ Group evergreens together and deciduous shrubs together in masses or drifts to form pleasing patterns and rhythms. This structure will be most obvious in winter.

■ Place deciduous shrubs in front of taller evergreens so the evergreen foliage forms a constant backdrop to the changing seasonal look of the shrubbery.

■ Locate a weeping tree or a tree with a dramatic silhouette as a focal point in an open setting where its structure can be appreciated; don't crowd it.

■ Layer plants according to height in a grouping: Choose one or more small flowering trees, several shrubs beneath and beside the trees, and a carpet of groundcovers and perennials beneath these larger plants.

■ Group three or more tall, conical or pyramidal evergreens in a staggered planting (rather than a straight row) to block the view of a neighbor's driveway, yard, or storage area.

■ Balance the size of the house with equally weighty plantings—either proportionally tall plants or wide planting beds, or both.

Concrete statues serve as focal points in this formal garden, directing the eye down the straight sight line. A parade of vine-entwined arches further emphasizes the axis.

COMBINING PLANTS EFFECTIVELY

When choosing plants for your landscape, consider the visual attributes, such as texture and the color of flowers and foliage, of each plant.

The plants surrounding this striking entrance offer a contrast of size, color, shape, and texture.

SIZE

Over the years, woody plants (trees and shrubs) grow steadily until they reach their mature size. Herbaceous plants (perennials and ornamental grasses) mature within a few years. Choose plants whose mature size fits the space available.

SHAPE

Plants mature into predetermined shapes unless you alter the shape with pruning. Some plants grow tall and straight, some are wide and spreading or arching, some are dense and rounded, and others are tall with long, weeping branches.

Plants of different sizes and shapes grouped together create contrast. Select plants with shapes that combine well with the shapes of their neighbors to attractively fill the space. A flower garden of only daisy shapes is redundant and boring; enliven it with clumps of tall, spirelike flowers to break the monotony. Keep in mind that spikes and spires often dominate a scene, so plant them judiciously.

Consider foliage shapes as well. Tall, sword-shaped leaves create the same vertical drama flower spires do; they effectively contrast with rounded or feathery leaves and flowers.

On a larger scale, consider the silhouettes of trees and shrubs in your landscape. They may be upright and vase-shaped, narrow and columnar, rounded, spreading, or weeping. See pages 38–41 for information on using trees and shrubs effectively in the landscape.

TEXTURE

A plant's texture—fine, medium, or bold—depends somewhat upon the roughness or smoothness of its leaves and petals. It also depends upon the size of the leaves, flowers, and branches. Most bed and border plants are medium-textured, so you need to concentrate on including the fine- and bold-textured ones when planning for appealing contrasts. Small, delicate leaves and flowers give a plant a fine texture and a restful appearance. Plants with small leaves and flowers, such as sweet alyssum, thread-leaved coreopsis, and white gaura, lend an airy effect to the area where they're growing. Fine-textured plants look smaller than they actually are and seem to recede, giving the illusion of space.

Plants with large flowers and wide, flat, smooth leaves, such as rose mallow, hosta, and canna, have a bold texture that commands attention and looks tropical and lush. Their dramatic texture seems insistent, grabbing your attention and stirring excitement. Because they are so imposing, bold-textured plants work well where seen from a distance.

When used in quantity, they make spaces appear smaller.

When designing a garden, try to mix various textures, using bold plants as focal points among fine- or medium-textured ones, but don't overdo the contrast. The way you associate fine-, bold-, and medium-textured plants gives your garden character. Use texture poorly and the garden becomes either too busy or boring. Texture used well renders your garden pleasantly stimulating, quietly serene, or jazzy and exciting.

DENSITY AND VISUAL WEIGHT

Some plants are loose and open; others are dense and compact. Loosely branched plants have a weightless, airy quality that makes a garden seem graceful and natural. Dense plants look heavy and anchored to the ground. Small, dense plants have the same visual weight as large, airy plants. Evergreens have the same density and visual weight throughout the year; deciduous trees and shrubs are dense when they are fully leafed, but are airy and less weighty in winter when leafless.

LEAF COLOR

The leaves of most plants are green—from pale emerald to deep blue-green and all shades and hues between. However, some leaves are golden, silvery, reddish purple, or spotted and striped with bright variegations. Evergreen leaves contribute unchanging color all year, although some evergreens take on richer red hues in winter. Deciduous leaves change with the seasons: soft green in spring, dark green in summer, and often fiery red, orange, or rich golden yellow in autumn.

When combining plants, strive for a contrast of texture and color. The smooth leaves of trout lilies are emphasized by the finer, smaller, bright green leaves of sweet woodruff.

FLOWER COLOR

Flowers splash the landscape with every color in the rainbow, sometimes in such profusion that they obliterate any foliage effect. But most garden flowers often are fleeting, lasting only a few weeks, as in the case of most trees, shrubs, and perennials. Annuals usually bloom for months on end, supplying steady color to complement the changing show of other flowers. (For more on color, see pages 30–37.)

COLOR OF BERRIES AND BARK

Berries, which usually ripen in autumn, are most often seen in shades of red, purple, or yellow and contribute color to the fall and winter garden. Bark comes in natural earthy colors, but may be unexpectedly red, gold, or green, dramatizing the winter landscape. Endow your landscape with year-round interest by selecting plants that supply color in winter. (See chart on page 37.)

In summer, the foliage and bold, white flowers of the Korean dogwood contrast nicely with the fine texture of the fountain grass.

COMBINING PLANTS EFFECTIVELY
continued

COMBINING PLANTS

Combining plants successfully depends upon whether their design attributes work together to create a balanced and harmonious scene that's in scale with the surroundings. When selecting plants for your yard, try to think of them as a community of plants rather than as individual specimens. Choose plants that grow well together and have shapes, sizes, colors, and textures that complement one another.

Balance is an important consideration in garden design. This large Japanese maple balances the large form of the house. Balance also works on a much smaller scale in the garden, where one perennial or shrub is in proportion to another.

The following tips will help you design effective plantings:

■ Create impact by massing several identical shrubs or perennials together into a large drift or an irregular, teardrop-shaped cluster. This strategy looks more attractive than the spotty effect produced by polka-dotting plants here and there or the restless look generated by using many different plants.

■ Create restfulness by combining shrubs and trees with complementary shapes. For example, plant low, horizontally spreading shrubs on both sides of a tall, arching shrub. Their branches should not interfere with one another, as they should occupy different spaces in the garden.

■ Create balance by giving the same visual weight to all sides of the garden. You can balance a mass of dense, weighty shrubs with a single, large specimen on the opposite side of the garden. Both plantings have the same visual weight although their actual volumes differ.

■ Create harmony with colors that look good together, then repeat and echo the colors throughout the landscape. Use those colors in various plants and in the hardscape. Link different areas by using the same building materials from one area in another. Unify further by repeating shapes.

■ Create rhythm by repeating drifts of the same plant throughout the garden or using different plants with the same shape.

■ Create contrast by combining plants with different textures and colors. Remember, too much contrast is disturbing; too little is boring. Use bold-textured plants sparingly because they can be overpowering. Maximize contrasts—and excitement—by juxtaposing plants with different colors, textures, and forms. To avoid too much contrast, generate combinations in which only one or two of the ingredients differ.

The plants you put together create a visual comparison of color, texture, shape, and size. The contrast, whether strong or subtle, gives your garden its personality and allure. By grouping plants into eye-appealing contrasts, you have begun to design an effective garden.

PLANTING IN DRIFTS

Once you determine which shapes, colors, and color combinations please you, envision them in groups. Each group should consist of several all-of-a-kind plants. The result is eye-catching beauty.

Avoid planting flowers or other plants singly in polka-dot fashion, even if carefully color-coordinated, because the result usually looks weak and amorphous. An exception to this rule is big, dramatic plants, which have so much character they look grand planted alone as a focal point among contrasting forms.

For impact, you should group at least three (and always an odd number) of any plant. If space allows, plant five or more of a kind. Arrange the groups in a drift. The goal is to make the drifts look as though they were planted by the wind, not you. For the best effect, stagger the plants within the drift; don't plant them in lines or rows. Odd numbers of plants work best because it's too

These hostas create rhythm in the garden with their undulating shape through the bed. Rhythm also can be created by repeating the same shape, plant, or color.

easy to plant an even number in straight lines.

Where there's room, repeat drifts of the same plants throughout the garden to establish continuity and rhythm. This technique is especially important in formal gardens, where repetition creates a sense of calm and elegance.

Arrange annuals and spring-flowering bulbs in bold drifts; you can buy many plants or bulbs for little money. When making large drifts of perennials, use plants grown in quart-size containers rather than 1- or 2-gallon pots. The smaller plants spread more quickly, so they fill in the drift better than larger plants. In the end, you get more for your money by purchasing perennials in smaller pots. Another cost-saving measure is to buy dormant, or bare-root, plants from a mail-order company. Usually small, these plants are inexpensive and grow quickly.

Create your garden by arranging your selected plants in various-size,

overlapping drifts. Keep the low plants in the foreground, put taller plants behind them in the midground, and place the tallest plants in the background. However, avoid setting plants out by height in rigid rows. Instead, allow drifts of shorter and taller plants to weave about in a casual display.

Remember that you will be cutting off tall stalks of faded flowers, so a tall flowering plant may become short after it finishes blooming. You might position a soaring plant in the midground if it blooms before or after the plants behind it.

Tall plants with airy clusters of lacy flowers, such as gaura and coralbells, would be lost in the midground. They work well in the foreground, where they form a dainty scrim through which you can see and enjoy the bolder flowers behind them.

A drift of 'Peach Blossom' astilbe is pleasing to the eye, forming an undulating wave of soft color.

COMBINING PLANTS EFFECTIVELY
continued

surrounding a deck or patio. Mixed borders look attractive throughout the year because they include a variety of plant types that provide an everchanging display of flowers, berries, foliage, and bark. Whether deciduous (losing their leaves in fall)

leave enough growing space for them to mature. Use tall shrubs in the background, medium-size ones in the midground, and low growers in the foreground. Combine shapes that work well together. For example, you can use a low, spreading shrub to

This mixed border is especially attractive in early spring with shrubs, such as the vibrant 'PJM Compact' rhododendron, fragrant viburnum, and daffodil bulbs in bloom.

DESIGNING MIXED BORDERS

When combining plants in your landscape, group them into beds and borders. Don't scatter them about the lawn. Probably the most successful planting scheme is a mixed border consisting of small flowering trees, deciduous and evergreen shrubs, and a groundcover underplanting. Bulbs, flowering perennials, and annuals can be planted in front of the shrubs or between shrub groupings.

You can locate a mixed border anywhere on your property—as the border around the perimeter of a central lawn, next to the house foundation, along property lines, or

or evergreen, woody plants give the garden year-round structure.

Designing a satisfactory mixed border takes some skill. You must carefully integrate the herbaceous and woody plants into a pleasing combination. Planting a row of flowers in front of the shrubs or mixing the flowers and shrubs randomly in the border won't create a pleasing structure. Your goal is to arrange the woody plants in groups within the mixed border to form an attractive layout, one that looks good even in winter.

Shrubs and small trees can consume one-half to two-thirds of the space in the border. Group shrubs together in strategic positions, in widely spaced drifts, being sure to

nestle beneath the arching branches of a vase-shaped shrub. A single columnar shrub can serve as a punctuation mark among a group of rounded ones.

Plant masses of perennials, bulbs, annuals, and ornamental grasses between the shrub groupings. Consider shape, size, and vigor when making your choices. For example, tall lilies look good emerging from behind a group of rounded Bumald spirea, and mounds of impatiens fill in prettily beneath the arching boughs of a vase-shaped viburnum. A groundcover unifies the plantings.

Because shrubs and trees grow much larger than perennials, be sure the border is deep enough to accommodate layers of plants—

The benefit of mixed borders is that they look good all year. In this border, bulbs provide spring color, perennials provide bursts of summer flowers, shrubs change color in fall, and evergreens provide greenery even in winter.

12 to 15 feet deep is not too much. Curve the garden's outlines, taking care that the border forms an appealing shape around the yard. The garden will look balanced if you group shrubs in the widest parts of the border. You also might place a small tree such as a flowering dogwood or crabapple behind the shrubs to provide height and dimension. Plant the border's narrow inward curves with herbaceous plants or low, spreading shrubs.

Because so many shrubs bloom in spring, you might choose spring bulbs to bloom with the shrubs. Fill in the rest of the border with summer-blooming perennials and annuals, which will take over after the shrubs and bulbs finish flowering. Plant a few fall-blooming perennials and ornamental grasses to complement the reds and golds of the fall foliage and berry display.

Summer-flowering shrubs can be combined with any of the modern shrub roses; both are wonderful additions to a mixed border. Give these large growers plenty of space to mature, and you'll be rewarded with months of bright blossoms and often brilliant fall berries. Groundcover roses work well in the foreground of a mixed border, but they need plenty of growing room.

COMBINING PLANTS EFFECTIVELY
continued

Herbaceous borders are another garden classic. True herbaceous borders, found in many English estate gardens, consist solely of perennials with perhaps a few roses.

CREATING A FLOWER BORDER

Considerably scaled down, but using the design principles of the great English estate gardens, an English-style perennial border overflows with glorious flowers from spring through fall. You can rely on herbaceous perennials (basically those without woody growth) as the garden mainstays; include clumps of spring-blooming bulbs for early color and annuals for summer-through-fall continuity. In large borders, old garden roses might be used as shrubs or climbers.

Design your herbaceous border along the edge of a lawn or walkway that is bordered by a hedge. Privet, yew, boxwood, and Japanese holly are all effective hedge plants. For a traditional effect, the hedge should be sheared into a neat green wall 4 to 5 feet tall. An informally pruned hedge works almost as well and requires less maintenance, but you must allow enough room for the hedge to grow to its ultimate size.

You're in luck if a tall, brick or stone wall borders your garden. Use the wall as a wonderful backdrop for the flowers and train climbing roses and vines to grow up and over it.

Create the border with a straight or gently curved front edge, making its depth proportional to its length. Grand English borders are as long as 150 feet and as wide as 12 feet. You can create an effective display with a border 20 to 25 feet long and 4 to 6 feet wide. Include a narrow path at the back of a deep border so you can easily tend the plants in the rear. (See page 18.)

Gertrude Jekyll, a famous English garden designer of the early 19th century, often planted a border with cool blues, lavenders, and pinks at one end, hot yellows and oranges in the center, cool colors toward the far end, and masses of purple and lavender flowers at the far end, creating a feeling of great distance. White flowers punctuated the border throughout.

You can follow a similar scheme in your border or apply the color rules discussed on pages 30–33. Whatever color scheme you choose, don't be skimpy with the plants. The formality of the English garden demands that you closely follow the design rules laid out on pages 22–27.

CREATING A DOUBLE BORDER

A double border is a formal English garden design in which two long, straight, herbaceous borders run along both sides of a wide gravel or lawn path. The borders need not be mirror images, but flowers and flower combinations are repeated from one side of the border to the other, blending the whole garden into a balanced picture. The borders should be backed by formally clipped hedges or stone or brick walls, although a fence is a more American backdrop.

You can create a double border along the side of your property, as a separate garden room, or along the property's main axis, perhaps extending from a door or sitting area. You might wish to edge the length of both borders with a uniform edging plant, such as clipped boxwood. Or, choose one of Ms. Jekyll's other favorite edgers—coralbells, edging candytuft, or lamb's-ears.

Because hedges or walls enclose it, this type of garden becomes a separate room with an inviting path that leads you among the garden riches. The path allows you to stroll slowly along the border, enclosed within the intimacy of the living walls of greenery and flowers. You might wish to place a garden bench—a stone or teak bench is traditional—in an alcove at the end of the border or in a cutout along its length.

DESIGNING AN ISLAND BED

Like a tropical island surrounded by a surging sea, an island flower bed stands in isolation enveloped by an expanse of lawn. This positioning departs from the conventional arrangement of flowers and shrubs in plots backed by a hedge, wall, or fence beside the house. On a large property, the expansive lawn may mean that the flower border around the property perimeter is far away. An island bed can bring flowers closer while providing continuity by echoing border plantings. On a small property, one or more island beds provide additional growing space if the borders aren't sufficient to indulge a gardening hobby.

Position the island bed off-center in the lawn, making it an oval, kidney shape, or other curving, irregular shape that fits the contours and size of the lawn and border plantings. Be certain the island bed is large enough to visually anchor the landscape and balance the spaces of the open lawn. A small island looks puny and lost if surrounded by a sea of lawn. When designing the island bed, move back from it, perhaps at a window inside the house or the front door, so you can gauge the proportions better.

Because an island bed will be viewed from all sides, great care must go into its planning. Position the tallest plants in the center of the bed and scale down the plant heights toward the outer edges. Place one or more types of edging plants around the perimeter. This planting strategy ensures that no plant hides another. The narrower your bed, the shorter the tall flowers in the center should be. Usually the tallest plant should be no more than half the bed's width so the planting won't look off-balance or top-heavy.

You may wish to create a sense of balance and rhythm by repeating drifts of flowers and plant combinations throughout the bed. Rather than arranging the drifts directly opposite each other, repeat them from one side to the other, perhaps in a triangular placement— one repetition on one side and two on the opposite side—to create an effective rhythm.

An island bed has no immediate backdrop. Its background may be a distant view or the plantings that border the property. But this borrowed background will play a part in how the island bed looks. Stroll your proposed site to view it from all angles, considering how the distant backdrop will work with the garden.

In a classic garden design, a double border is laid out to be enjoyed by those strolling down a central path. The two chairs echo the two sides of the border.

You might consider planting an evergreen screen to give the garden more intimacy or to hide a distracting view to the street.

Large island beds can be turned into mixed borders, with shrubs and small trees in the middle and groundcovers, flowers, and low plants at the edges. This paints a more interesting winter scene than a garden planted only with herbaceous plants.

In a tree-studded front yard or backyard, where lawn struggles to grow in the shade, an island bed makes a perfect solution. A large island bed could flow around and under the trees, creating an oasis in the grass. The lawn is transformed into a lovely shade garden filled with ferns, shade-loving perennials and annuals, and even shrubs and small trees if the area is large enough.

Island beds are surrounded by lawn. They are designed to be attractive when viewed from all sides.

Photo by Gene Johnson

USING COLOR EFFECTIVELY

These 'Admiration' pansies and 'Wonderland' sweet alyssum have the same flower color. This creates a pleasing monochromatic effect that emphasizes the contrast in flower size and texture.

The first thing you notice about a flower invariably is its color. And you probably consider flower color first when selecting a plant for your garden. But don't forget to think about the colors of other plant parts when choosing what to grow. Some plants—including perennials, annuals, ornamental grasses, and both deciduous and evergreen trees and shrubs—have colorful foliage. Many trees and shrubs produce ornamental berries. Others have attractively colored bark. It pays to choose and combine colors in your gardens and landscape as carefully as you select clothing colors.

Your garden will look prettier and be more fun to create if you plan it to reflect a color scheme. It can be simple and monochromatic, such as an all-white or all-pink garden, or a festive, multicolored affair, such as a red, white, and blue garden or a hot-colored garden of yellow, gold, orange, and scarlet flowers. Your garden's color scheme might even change through the seasons if it relies heavily on perennials, perhaps emphasizing yellows and white in spring, pinks and blues in summer, and purples and violets in autumn.

TOO MUCH OF A GOOD THING

Too much color in a garden can be as much of a problem as too little. A riot of flower colors creates a restless look. Add colored or variegated foliage to the mix and the effect can be uncomfortably chaotic. Instead of creating a happy marriage, adjacent colors may constantly argue and nag at each other like a bickering couple. If some thought is given to choosing compatible colors, the flowers will complement each other, making their neighbors more attractive by the company they keep.

THE COLOR WHEEL

Even though the colors in your garden probably will not match the precise colors of the color wheel, by understanding how these 12 colors relate to one another you can begin to approach garden design with an artist's imagination.

Red, yellow, and blue are the primary colors of the color wheel. These are pure, vibrant hues. When mixed in varying amounts, and with black and white, they become all the other colors of the universe. A half-and-half mixture of any of the three primary colors creates the three secondary colors: red and yellow produce orange, blue and yellow make green, and red and blue yield violet. Equal amounts of a primary and one of its neighboring secondary colors create an intermediate color: red-orange, yellow-orange, yellow-green, blue-green, blue-violet, and red-violet. These 12 colors, which are arranged like 12 slices of a pie, form the basic color wheel.

Sophisticated versions of the color wheel incorporate more intermediary colors and may even include gradations in lightness and darkness of these colors.

Mix white with any color and you get a tint, or pastel version, of that color. Pastel colors, because they are paler, seem less commanding than the full hue (pure color). Add black and you create a shade, a darker version of that color. The darkness of a shade gives it a deep rich hue. Add both white and black, or gray, and the result becomes a dusky version called a tone. Tones are subtle, subdued colors that help to blend darker and brighter hues.

Because so many plant pigments contribute to the color of a flower or leaf, rarely will you encounter a pure hue. More likely you'll find your garden's palette created of tints, shades, and tones of secondary and intermediary colors.

Colors also change with the light striking them. When seen in overcast light, pastel colors intensify. In brilliant sunshine, pastels may seem to fade to nothingness; in shade, they light up the shadows. Intense colors become brilliant in full sun; dark colors appear gloomy in the shade.

Neighboring colors affect one another, too. Yellow-green may look sickly next to blue, but it can take on a healthy glow placed beside orange. To use clashing colors in your garden, separate them with neutral colors. White flowers are time-honored peacekeepers, but often pastels work well, too. Foliage plants with gray or silvery leaves add pizzazz to a garden while helping to harmonize clashing flower colors.

Understanding color theory by studying the color wheel, which consists of 12 pure hues, can help you design an artistic garden. Complementary colors, which make a strong, bold statement when combined, are opposite each other on the color wheel. Analogous colors, which make a softer statement when combined, are adjacent to each other.

Red

Red-Violet

Red-Orange

Violet

Orange

Blue-Violet

Yellow-Orange

Blue

Yellow

Yellow-Green

Blue-Green

Green

WORKING WITH COLOR

Here are some guidelines to follow when designing with color:
■ Hot, bright colors, such as yellow and orange, visually advance and seem closer than they are, carrying well over a distant view. Hot colors are usually attention-getting and exciting.
■ Cool colors, such as blue and lavender, recede and seem farther away than they are. They are not easy to see from a distance. Cool colors are restful and soothing.
■ White and pastels lighten up shady areas and seem to pop right out of the shadows. They shimmer and glow at dusk.

■ Dark colors, such as red and purple, look gloomy when planted in shade and are hard to see.
■ Combinations of analogous colors (those side by side on the color wheel) are soothing and pleasing.
■ Combinations of complementary colors (those opposite each other on the color wheel) are bold and exciting.
■ Groups of plants with white or cream-colored flowers or silver or gray foliage are neutral, effectively separating warring flower colors and enhancing harmonious ones.

■ Green foliage can serve as a blender or neutralizer. Surrounding bright, hard-to-mix scarlet with lots of green makes the brightness easier on the eyes.
■ Contrasting colors work best if you either deepen or soften one of the colors. Then, use lots of the softer, deeper color or less of the brighter color. For example, when planning a blue and orange scheme, use deep blue-violet instead of pure blue, or use peach or salmon instead of bright orange.

DESIGNING WITH COLOR

Choose the colors of your landscape plants to complement the colors of your house. The orange-peach of these 'Fashion' azaleas, brown trunks of the cedars, and deep green of the euonymus create a rich palette that enhances the terra-cotta of the house walls and buff tones of the window trim.

A flower garden's color scheme is probably the easiest part of the garden to design. All you need to do is think of flowers in terms of color combinations. Ask yourself which colors will be next door or in the neighborhood when each plant is in bloom. By thinking this way, you can compose a rich collection of colors that will combine into a satisfying garden picture.

Although you certainly will wish to include your favorite colors, the results will be more successful if you consider a few guidelines before deciding upon a color scheme for your garden. Because you see your garden within the context of your entire landscape rather than in isolation, be sure it forms a pleasing whole by choosing colors that:

■ Look good with the color of siding and shutters or trim of your house
■ Complement the colors of flowering trees and shrubs that figure prominently in your landscape
■ Combine well with the foliage colors of prominent landscape shrubs and trees
■ Work with the hardscape (bricks, stones, wood) in your yard and garden.

Once you begin thinking about all the elements that provide color in your landscape, you may decide to forgo yellow and red tulips, for example, in favor of pastel pink and white ones, because those colors will look better with the hot pink crabapple trees that dominate your front yard in May. If the bricks of your house are sandy yellow, you might want to play up the warm tones with yellow and orange flowers rather than pink and lavender ones.

Red, magenta, and scarlet are too dark for and clash with a red brick walkway or house, but pale blue, creamy white, and pastel pink complement and contrast with the red bricks.

Some colors may work better in specific garden sites than others. See Working With Color on page 31 for some guidelines used by garden designers to create successful color combinations.

Once you decide upon a color scheme, you can plan the garden in any of several ways. Be systematic and sit down with the encyclopedia sections of chapters 4 through 11 in this book, a dozen or so seed and nursery catalogs, and a pencil and paper. Start drawing your garden, carefully selecting perennials, annuals, bulbs, and grasses in the colors that carry out your scheme from spring through fall. A less exacting (but

An all-yellow flower garden glows like beams of sunshine. This annual garden includes rudbeckia, celosia, and marigolds.

more expensive) approach may work out just as well: Simply purchase only those plants you see at the nursery with blossoms in your chosen colors. Because nurseries usually display only blooming annuals and perennials, relegating out-of-bloom specimens to the back lot, it's wise to plant the garden over a period of months. Visit the garden center once a month, purchasing perennials as they go into bloom. Leave spots in your garden so that you can include later-blooming plants during the course of the year.

THE COLOR GREEN

When considering "garden color," most people think of flower color and overlook foliage. But green, the color of leaves, is a color, too, and an important one in the garden. Too often, green is considered a background color that highlights flower colors. It isn't given its due as a color.

Green foliage comes in many shades, tints, and hues: kelly green, blue-green, chartreuse, lime green, and more. In variegated plants the green may be striped, streaked, spotted, or splashed with creamy white, silver, golden yellow, or pink.

Foliage colors can enhance or detract from flower color combinations. Foliage plants, such as hostas and ornamental grasses, can be used as strong color components among bright flowers. Yellow-green leaves look warm and cheerful with yellow, orange, and scarlet flowers, whereas blue-greens do a wonderful job of enhancing pink and magenta flowers. Remember that flowers are often fleeting, but foliage remains to beautify your garden throughout the growing season.

Create long-lasting color and textural contrasts by relying on combinations of plants. Here bold-textured, blue-green hostas grow through a sea of fine-textured, dark green ferns.

DESIGNING WITH FOLIAGE

How you use foliage in your garden is as important as how you use the flowers. Many garden designers believe that you should choose a perennial primarily for its leaves and secondarily for its flowers, because the leaves contribute to the garden's picture much longer than the flowers. If you have a difficult time convincing yourself to do this, at least give the leaves a serious second consideration. You might avoid plants with uninteresting or tattered-looking leaves or locate them away from center stage.

Many perennials feature beautifully textured or colored leaves. Astilbe and columbine, for instance, have lovely, fernlike leaves that create a delicate, refined look. Others, such as hosta and rodgersia, have big, bold leaves that create drama and dynamic contrast. Some leaves are striped or splashed with gold or silver variegations; others are washed all over with deep purple or steely blue-green. And some plants are treasured for their felted, silvery leaves.

PLANNING FOR COLOR IN FALL AND WINTER

Part of the art—and science—of designing a landscape is to achieve an ever-changing sequence of colors that begins in spring and doesn't finish until the end of fall or even into winter. Most of us think of garden color as something to enjoy in spring and summer, when flower gardens are in bloom. Careful planning can stretch the season of bloom for flower gardens, but there are other sources of color and interest besides perennials, bulbs, and annuals. Your landscape also can come alive in fall and winter with beautiful berries, fiery foliage, and colorful bark. Consider these other sources as well when planning a landscape with multiseason color.

RELY ON A VARIETY OF PLANTS

Deciduous trees and shrubs often have dazzling fall foliage, and some have colorful berries, bark, or branches that add interest in winter. In spring and summer, you are distracted by the flowers and

Maidenhair tree

BEST TREES FOR FALL COLOR

The following trees give an excellent and reliable show of fall color.

RED OR SCARLET
Acer × *fremanii* 'Autumn Blaze'
  (Freeman maple)
Acer palmatum 'Bloodgood'
  (Japanese maple)
Acer rubrum 'October Glory' and
  'Red Sunset' (red maple)
Acer saccharum 'Bonfire'
  (sugar maple)
Amelanchier spp. (serviceberry)
Cornus spp. (dogwood)
Prunus × 'Okame' (Okame cherry)
Prunus serrulata (Japanese
  flowering cherry)
Quercus spp. (northern red oak,
  southern red oak, Nuttall's oak,
  scarlet oak, Shumard oak)

MIXED RED, ORANGE, AND GOLD
Acer circirnatum (vine maple)
Acer griseum 'Gingerbread'
  (paperbark maple)
Acer saccharum (sugar maple)
Franklinia alatamaha (Franklin
  tree)
Lagerstroemia indica (crape myrtle)
Liquidambar styraciflua
  (sweet gum)
Nyssa sylvatica (black gum)
Oxydendrum arboreum (sourwood)
Parrotia persica (Persian parrotia)
Pyrus calleryana 'Bradford'
  (Bradford pear)
Sorbus alnifolia
  (Korean mountain ash)

Stewartia pseudocamellia
  (Japanese stewartia)

ORANGE, YELLOW, OR GOLD
Acer × *fremanii* 'Celebration'
  (Freeman maple)
Acer palmatum (Japanese maple)
Acer platanoides (Norway maple)
Acer truncatum (Shantung maple)
Betula spp. (birch)
Cercidiphyllum japonicum
  (katsura tree)
Cladrastis lutea (yellowwood)
Fraxinus pennsylvanica (green or
  red ash)
Ginkgo biloba (maidenhair tree)
Liriodendron tulipifera
  (tulip tree)

PURPLE
Fraxinus americana 'Autumn
  Applause', 'Autumn Purple', and
  'Royal Purple' (white ash)
Liquidambar styraciflua
  'Burgundy' (sweet gum)
Pyrus calleryana 'Redspire'
  (Callery pear)
Ulmus parvifolia 'Athena'
  (lacebark elm)

BEST SHRUBS FOR FALL COLOR

Although fall color can vary from year to year and from one sun exposure to another, these shrubs are the most reliable when it comes to a colorful foliage display.

YELLOW

Aesculus parviflora (bottlebrush buckeye)
Clethra alnifolia (summer-sweet)
Hamamelis virginiana (common witch hazel)
Hibiscus syriacus (rose-of-Sharon)
Ilex spp. (possum haw, winterberry)
Lindera benzoin (spicebush)
Rhododendron mucronulatum (Korean rhododendron)

RED TO WINE RED

Berberis koreana (Korean barberry)
Cornus sericea (red-osier dogwood)
Cotoneaster spp. (cotoneaster)
Deutzia gracilis 'Nikko' (dwarf slender deutzia)
Enkianthus perulatus (white enkianthus)
Euonymus alatus (winged euonymus)
Hydrangea quercifolia (oakleaf hydrangea)
Itea virginica 'Henry's Garnet' (Virginia sweetspire)

Rhododendron arborescens (sweet azalea)
Rhododendron vaseyi (pink-shell azalea)
Rhus spp. (sumac)
Viburnum spp. (viburnum)

RED, YELLOW, ORANGE, AND PURPLE

Aronia spp. (chokeberry)
Berberis thunbergii (Japanese barberry)
Cotinus spp. (smokebush, smoke tree)
Cotoneaster divaricatus (spreading cotoneaster)
Fothergilla spp. (fothergilla, witch alder)
Stephanandra incisa 'Crispa' (cutleaf stephanandra)

RED AND YELLOW

Cotoneaster lucidus (hedge cotoneaster)
Enkianthus campanulatus (red-vein enkianthus)
Itea virginica (Virginia sweetspire)
Rhododendron calendulaceum (flame azalea)

ORANGE TO GOLD

Hamamelis × *intermedia* (hybrid witch hazel)
Rhododendron spp. (swamp azalea, plum-leaved azalea, royal azalea)
Spiraea × *bumalda* (Bumald spirea)

Viburnum

foliage—you may not notice the attractive form of a tree or shrub until the leaves drop in autumn. Evergreens are green—or golden or blue-green—all year.

Ornamental grasses are green in summer, then reach a peak in fall, developing attractive seed heads and, in some cases, changing color. Many grasses can remain in the garden all winter. Groundcovers may be green or have colorful leaves; some bloom, some produce colorful berries, and some are evergreen.

PLANNING FOR COLOR IN FALL AND WINTER

continued

FLOWERS DURING THE OFF-SEASONS

Many plants bloom in fall and some even bloom in winter, but are not well-known or available at the garden center, because nurseries have a difficult time selling

Photo by Eric Roth

out-of-bloom plants during the spring gardening frenzy. Order these off-season bloomers from a catalog or ask your nursery to make a special order if your choices aren't in stock.

Favorite fall-blooming perennials include blue and purple New England asters and golden and rusty-colored chrysanthemums. Less-well-known fall bloomers include blue-flowered autumn sages, bright yellow hybrid goldenrods, and mauve or white Japanese anemones. The ornamental grasses are at their best this time of year, when the seed heads turn into glistening feathers. They are especially eye-catching when they are backlit by the setting sun.

Many cool-season annuals, such as sweet alyssum and edging lobelia, get a second wind after summer's heat has passed and bloom right through light frosts. In frost-free climates, these and other cool-season annuals, such as snapdragons, pansies, and pot marigolds, can be planted in fall to bloom all winter.

Autumn crocus, saffron crocus, and winter daffodil bloom in September and October. They bring unexpected color beneath shrubs and in rock gardens. Other small bulbs, such as snow crocus, Siberian squill, and snowdrops, bloom in late winter, bringing a carpet of color to the garden floor, especially where they have naturalized in a lawn that is still dormant.

A surprising number of shrubs and some trees, such as Franklin tree and crape myrtle, bloom in autumn or from winter into early spring. Plant these late—or early—bloomers in prominent locations where you can see them from inside or when going to and from the house. An enchanting winter-blooming shrub is Chinese witch hazel and its smaller hybrids. When blooming in January or February, these large shrubs light up the garden with sunny yellow flowers and perfume the air with a sweet fragrance. (See page 41 for lists of fall- and winter-blooming shrubs and shrubs with beautiful berries.)

A garden can be pleasing all year around. In the photo above, 'Autumn Joy' sedum sparkles in the fall sunshine. At right, ornamental grasses remain standing through the winter, adding texture, volume, and soft color.

FIERY FOLIAGE AND BRIGHT BERRIES

Although your landscape may not brim with flowers in October, it can sizzle with foliage and berries. Red and gold fall leaves look lovely with a background of dark green evergreens, and after deciduous leaves drop, the evergreens remain all winter to contribute lively color. Most berries look showiest in autumn, when they ripen. Some may be eaten by birds, but other berries and fruits are less tasty and hang on to add bright visual notes during the snowy months.

EVERGREENS IN WINTER

Winter comes alive with color, albeit more subtle than during the growing season, if you employ evergreens in your landscape. Needle-leaved evergreens, such as pines and spruces, bring solidity and texture to the landscape. Choose tall types as screens, specimens, and windbreaks and dwarf forms for foundations and borders.

Needle-leaved evergreens come in an array of colors, not just basic green. Choose blue-green spruces or golden false cypresses to contrast with dark green yews. The shiny, green leaves of many broad-leaved evergreens, such as *Leucothoe* 'Scarletta' and Japanese andromeda, take on deep reddish tones when the weather turns cold.

BEAUTIFUL BARK

The bark of deciduous trees and shrubs can bring surprising splashes of color to a winter landscape. The gleaming, white trunks of many birches are showy throughout the year, but especially in winter. Other trees feature a colorful patchwork of peeling or shining, metallic bark that is less apparent in summer when shaded by leaves, but demands to be noticed in winter.

Shrubs of red-twig dogwood bring Christmasy cheer to the garden and look especially wonderful planted in a mass that intensifies the color.

TREES AND SHRUBS WITH DECORATIVE BARK

COLORFUL PEELING BARK
Acer griseum (paperbark maple)
Betula nigra (river birch)
Hydrangea quercifolia (oakleaf hydrangea)

CORAL-RED BARK
Acer palmatum 'Sango-Kaku' (coral-bark maple)
Cornus sericea (red-osier dogwood)

COLORFUL MOTTLED BARK
Chionanthus retusus (Chinese fringetree)
Cornus spp. (kousa dogwood, Cornelian cherry)
Parrotia persica (Persian parrotia)
Pinus bungeana (lace-bark pine)
Platanus spp. (sycamore)
Stewartia pseudocamellia (Japanese stewartia)
Ulmus parvifolia (lacebark elm)

GOLDEN BARK
Cornus sericea 'Flaviramea' (golden-twig dogwood)
Salix alba 'Tristis' (golden weeping willow)

GREEN BARK
Acer palmatum 'Aoyagi' (green-bark maple)
Kerria japonica (Japanese rose)
Laburnum × *watereri* (golden-chain tree)
Poncirus trifoliata (hardy orange)

WHITE BARK
Betula spp. (paper birch, white-bark birch)
Populus spp. (poplar)

GLEAMING METALLIC BARK
Prunus spp. (ornamental cherry)

Prunus mackii

Betula nigra

USING TREES IN THE LANDSCAPE

When selecting a tree, consider its attributes during all four seasons of the year. This crabapple tree provides beautiful blossoms in spring, attractive, green foliage in summer, changing leaf color in fall, and a lovely silhouette of branches in winter.

Select trees for your home's landscape with great care and thought. After all, they will be around for decades to come, either enhancing your home or creating problems in your yard. Take time to find just the right tree for just the right spot.

The beauty trees bring to our gardens is without compare. Trees create overhead structure to both block and frame views of the sky, a neighbor's house, or distant scenery. We feel right at home in a neighborhood where streets are lined with tall trees, and those trees cool the pavement and muffle traffic sounds. A tall tree's large size brings a serene feeling of peace, calm, and permanence to a landscape.

Trees around our homes can help to moderate extremes of sun, wind, and temperature.

DECIDUOUS TREES

Trees that lose their leaves in fall and stay bare during winter are called deciduous. Their leaf color, while predominantly green during the growing season, may be many shades of green, green variegated with creamy markings, or richly hued purplish-red or bronze. Fall color is another matter, especially in the cold regions where many shade and flowering trees turn into spectacles of flaming colors in autumn.

The tallest deciduous trees in our landscape are called shade trees, because their leafy branches cast cooling shade. Smaller trees, those that naturally grow on forest edges, are more likely to produce showy flowers than are the shade trees—we term them small flowering trees. Both types can produce wonderful displays of fall foliage.

STREET-TREE SMARTS

Street trees must endure adverse growing conditions—air pollution, soot, scant compacted soil, alkaline soil, road salt, heat, drought, and vandalism. Many trees in urban settings live only 15 to 20 years, at best. If you select tree species adapted to adverse urban conditions, and give them more care, they can live longer. Urban foresters suggest these trees for street-tree use:

SMALL TREES FOR PLACING UNDER POWER LINES
Acer buergerianum (trident maple)
Acer campestre (hedge maple)
Acer tataricum (Tatarian maple)
Acer tataricum ssp. *ginnala* (Amur maple)
Acer truncatum (Shantung maple)
Crataegus spp. (hawthorn)
Malus spp. (crabapple)
Syringa reticulata (Japanese tree lilac)

TALL TREES ___ ___
Acer rubrum ___
Aesculus × *carnea* ___ (red horse chestnut)
Betula nigra 'Heritage' (river birch)

Carpinus betulus 'Fastigiata' (fastigiate European hornbeam)
Fraxinus americana (white ash)
Fraxinus pennsylvanica (green ash)
Ginkgo biloba 'Princeton Sentry' (maidenhair tree)
Gleditsia triacanthos var. *inermis* (thornless honey locust)
Gymnocladus dioica (Kentucky coffee tree)
Koelreuteria paniculata (golden-rain tree)
Liquidambar styraciflua (sweet gum)
Liriodendron tulipifera (tulip tree)
Nyssa sylvatica (black gum)
Phellodendron amurense 'Macho' (Amur cork tree)
Platanus × *acerifolia* 'Bloodgood' (London plane tree)
Quercus spp. (oak)
Sophora japonica (Japanese pagoda tree)
Sorbus alnifolia (Korean mountain ash)
Tilia cordata (small-leaved linden)
Tilia tomentosa (silver linden)
Ulmus parvifolia (lacebark elm)
Zelkova serrata (Japanese zelkova)

CONIFERS

These widely adapted needled evergreens hail from some of the harshest environments on the planet: spruces and firs cling to boulders on windswept northern mountaintops; bald cypresses rise from the murky waters of southern swamps with their branches dripping Spanish moss; and loblolly pines tower over expanses of golden grass-lined savannas on the edges of the Great Plains.

No matter where you live, there are probably many conifers suited to your garden's growing conditions and landscape needs. Beautiful and adaptable tall plants solve problems and provide year-round color and structure to your garden.

Not all evergreens are actually green. Many garden forms feature scales and needles in shades of blue-green that range from gray to steely blue, or golden hues that include golden yellow, chartreuse, or lime green. Some conifers have variegated foliage—the leaves may be flecked with creamy white or circled with golden bands. Full sun brings out the best coloration on both golden and blue conifers, but gold-hued ones also can be more easily burned by hot sun, especially in winter.

These conifers make wonderful additions to most landscapes, creating a welcome color accent that endures throughout the year. Be cautious, however, about overdoing the effect. Yellow-foliaged plants can look anemic, especially if too many are planted. They are effective when set off against dark green conifers or broad-leaf evergreens, where they mimic sunbeams in a winter garden. Blue-needled conifers look even bluer when combined with shrubs and perennials featuring pastel pink, lavender, or blue flowers.

It is essential to take the mature height and width of a tree into account at planting time. Although they looked fine when they were small, these spruces grew into massive trees that are out of scale with the house and cast gloomy shade all year.

CHOOSING THE RIGHT LOCATION

Before going tree shopping, take time to evaluate the location you have in mind for a tree: Determine if a tree really should go there; determine what tree is best for that spot. All too often, large-growing trees crowd homes, walks, gardens, and other buildings, because whoever planted them years ago didn't have the foresight to imagine how large that tree would get a decade or two in the future.

Because conifers normally grow into large trees that cast shade throughout the year, be careful to place them correctly on your property. Placed too close to the house, conifers cast a gloomy shade throughout the year. In foundation plantings, their ultimate size can engulf a house.

Stand in the location you selected for a tree and ask these questions:
■ How far will its branches reach in 15, 20, 25 years? Will they interfere with the house or other trees?
■ How tall will the tree be in 15, 20, 25 years? Will it grow into power lines, an overhang, or other trees?
■ Where will the tree cast shade during the morning and afternoon? Is the shade in a welcome place?
■ Will the tree's roots have plenty of growing room or will they be constricted by pavement?

After answering these questions, search the tree encyclopedia, which begins on page 142, for a tree with a suitable size and shape and one that will perform the functions you have in mind.

USING SHRUBS IN THE LANDSCAPE

A mix of shrubs—spirea, viburnum, cotinus, and weigela lends a variety of colors and forms to this border.

Shrubs are the mainstay of most home landscapes, creating easy-care plantings for most situations. Many favorite deciduous shrubs bloom in spring or summer and then display brightly changing foliage and gleaming berries in autumn. Shrubs with golden, purplish, or variegated leaves bring contrast to the garden for months. Evergreen shrubs also may flower and fruit, and have colorful leaves, but are loved for the year-round greenery.

Here are some design tips for using shrubs in your landscape:

■ Choose low to medium-height evergreen and deciduous shrubs for foundation plantings so they won't grow too large and obscure the house. And, you won't need to prune them so often to keep the window views visible. (See pages 70–71.)

■ Place low-spreading or groundcovering shrubs in front of taller shrubs to act as a "facing" to create a layered design.

■ Arrange tall upright evergreen shrubs in a staggered row to create an informal privacy screen—in a straight row for a more formal wall-like effect. (See pages 78–79.)

■ Plant evergreen shrubs that respond well to pruning in rows to create a formal sheared hedge that divides the landscape into garden rooms. (See pages 14–15.)

■ Cluster shrubs in mulched beds under trees to create a lovely shade garden or woodland effect.

■ Design a mixed border of shrubs, small trees, and perennials, clustering several identical shrubs together for best effect.

■ Locate deciduous shrubs in front of taller evergreens in a border so the year-round greenery backdrops changing flowers and foliage.

SHRUBS WITH SHOWY FLOWERS

* denotes a flower is fragrant.

LATE WINTER- AND EARLY SPRING-BLOOMING

Chimonanthus praecox (wintersweet)

Corylopsis spp.(winter hazel)

Corylus avellana 'Contorta' (Harry Lauder's walking stick)

Daphne spp. (daphne)

Hamamelis spp. (witch hazel)

Rhododendron mucronulatum (Korean rhododendron)

SPRING-BLOOMING

Aronia spp. (chokeberry)

Buddleia alternifolia 'Argentea' (silver fountain buddleia)

Calycanthus floridus (sweet shrub)

Chaenomeles spp. (flowering quince)

Cytisus spp. (broom)

Deutzia spp.(deutzia)

Enkianthus spp. (enkianthus)

Forsythia spp. (forsythia)

Fothergilla spp. (fothergilla)

Genista spp. (woadwaxen)

Kerria japonica (Japanese rose)

Philadelphus spp. (mock orange)

Rhododendron spp. (azalea)

Spiraea spp. (spirea)

Syringa spp. (lilac)

Viburnum spp. (viburnum)

Weigela florida (old-fashioned weigela)

SUMMER-BLOOMING

Aesculus parviflora (bottlebrush buckeye

Buddleia globosa (globe butterfly bush)

Cotinus spp. (smokebush)

Hypericum spp. (St.-John's-wort)

Indigofera kirilowii (kirilow indigo)

Itea spp. (sweetspire)

Potentilla fruticosa (shrubby cinquefoil)

Rhododendron viscosum (swamp azalea)

Rosa spp. (shrub rose)

LATE SUMMER- AND FALL-BLOOMING

Abelia × grandiflora (glossy abelia)

Buddleia davidii (butterfly bush)

Caryopteris × clandonensis (bluebeard)

Clethra alnifolia (summer-sweet)

Lespedeza thunbergii (bush clover)

Rhododendron arborescens (sweet azalea)

Syringa 'Pocohontas'

SHRUBS WITH SHOWY BERRIES

* denotes an evergreen.

BLACK

Aronia melanocarpa (black chokeberry)

Mahonia spp. (holly grape)

Osmanthus heterophyllus (holly . osmanthus)

Viburnum tinus (Laurustinus viburnum)

BLUE, PURPLE, OR LAVENDER

Callicarpa spp. (beautyberry)

Symplocos paniculata (sapphire berry)

Viburnum spp. (nannyberry, withe-rod, black haw)

CORAL OR ORANGE

Euonymus europaeus (European spindle tree)

Ilex verticillata 'Aurantiaca' (winterberry)

Pyracantha coccinea 'Soleil d'Or' (fire thorn)

Symphoricarpos × chenaultii (Chenault coralberry)

RED

Aronia arbutifolia (red chokeberry)

Aucuba japonica (Japanese laurel)

Berberis spp. (barberry)

Cotoneaster spp. (cotoneaster)

Ilex spp. (holly)

Nandina domestica (heavenly bamboo)

Photinia spp. (photinia)

Pyracantha coccinea (fire thorn)

Rhus spp. (sumac)

Skimmia japonica (Japanese skimmia)

Viburnum spp. (linden, leatherleaf, tea viburnum, cranberry bush)

WHITE OR SILVERY GRAY

Callicarpa japonica 'Leucocarpa' (Japanese beautyberry)

Myrica pensylvanica (bayberry)

Symphoricarpos albus (snowberry)

YELLOW OR GOLD

Ilex verticillata 'Winter Gold' (winterberry)

Viburnum opulus 'Xanthocarpum' (European cranberry bush)

Pyracantha 'Mohave'

USING VINES AND GROUNDCOVERS IN THE LANDSCAPE

Whether you're planting a vine to soar above your head or a pretty groundcover to carpet the ground at your feet, these sprawling plants provide an element in the garden that few other plants can: They add a distinct sense of dimension wherever they are planted.

Walk under a vine trained over an arbor or a pergola and you'll get a sense of being enveloped by the garden. Groundcovers draw your eye downward to themselves and their neighbors, encouraging you to experience every inch of your garden.

A white arbor covered with a luxuriant trumpet vine creates a welcoming entrance to a home or garden.

Photo by Ed Gohlich

Sweetly scented sweet woodruff is a lovely flowering carpet in dappled sun or shade. It blooms in mid to late spring at the same time as many azaleas and rhododendrons.

Low growing shrubs, such as Juniperuis horizontalis, make excellent groundcovers. Their coarse texture is much more interesting than grass.

VINES

Vines are among the most versatile and underappreciated of plants. Vines soften harsh walls, camouflage unattractive board and chain-link fences, and, if grown on an overhead structure, create shade and privacy. A vine planted against the sunny side of a house wall can provide considerable cooling insulation during summer. You can grow a clinging vine, such as climbing hydrangea, up a sturdy tree to create a wild, natural look and provide overhead flowers. Annual vines or vines such as clematis, which have sparse growth, can be allowed to grow into shrubbery for added dimension and interest.

One of the great advantages of growing vines in a garden is that they take up little ground space. You can tuck several between shrubs in a foundation planting or mixed border and let them grow up a wall, fence, or trellis to create a vertical effect. In small gardens or narrow areas between buildings, a vine provides lovely effects at eye level and overhead while taking up a fraction of the space of a tree or shrub.

GROUNDCOVERS

Sometimes referred to as "living mulch," groundcovers serve a number of practical and aesthetic roles in landscapes. As a living mulch, a groundcover fills in to form a dense planting that discourages weeds, holds moisture, prevents erosion, and is easier to care for than a lawn. And as if these good works were not enough, groundcovers look beautiful; they dress up the garden by creating a living carpet of foliage and flowers beneath taller plants.

Think of a groundcover planting like the carpet in a well-decorated room; without it the floor would be bare and the setting sterile-looking. Trees, shrubs, flowering perennials, and bulbs can grow through most groundcovers—just the way pieces of furniture rest on a rug.

Groundcovers play an important role in most types of landscapes.

They are useful lawn substitutes in low-maintenance landscapes. In fact, many groundcover plants flourish in sites hostile to lawn grass—such as deep shade or hot, dry slopes. Groundcovers used as lawn substitutes make environmental sense, because they consume less energy, water, fertilizer, and pesticides to keep them well groomed.

Using Roses In The Landscape

Climbing roses add instant romance to a landscape, especially when trained over an arbor.

Photo by Stephen Cridland

Old garden roses are becoming more and more popular in today's gardens for their luscious scent and their ease of culture. Unlike most modern roses, which are best grown by themselves, old garden roses combine well with perennials, bulbs, and ornamental grasses. (Annuals planted beneath roses should be planted carefully to avoid harming the roses' shallow root systems.) Old-fashioned roses also team well with flowering shrubs, such as hydrangea, spirea, and mock orange.

Old garden roses look perfect in country and cottage gardens, because their exuberant growth gives them a casual, unkempt air. The lankier types, such as the cabbage roses, excel when tied up to cascade from a pillar, fence, gate, or an arch.

Because roses flower in early to midsummer, you can highlight their blossoms with companion plants that bloom at the same time. Lavender, blue, purple, pastel pink, or white flowers suit the colors of all old garden roses. Rambler roses, which can be trained to climb a tree or low building, share the romantic air of old garden roses.

Bourbon, Portland, and hybrid perpetual roses—as well as the modern English roses that resemble old garden roses—repeat their bloom in midsummer and early fall, so provide blooming companions for them, too. Try using neighboring plants with colored foliage so you'll get multiseasonal interest out of the same plants. Silver-leaved plants, such as artemisia and lamb's-ears, and purple-foliaged plants, such as 'Burgundy Glow' ajuga, 'Palace Purple' coralbells, and smokebush, also fit into the color scheme.

Plan the garden to include plenty of flowers that bloom both before and after the roses. Clematis vines are tried-and-true companions to climbing roses. The two share the same space, intertwining without smothering each other, and the satiny blossoms of

COMPANION PLANTS FOR ROSES

SPRING-FLOWERING
Ajuga reptans (bugleweed)
Alchemilla spp. (lady's-mantle)
Galium odoratum (sweet woodruff)
Heuchera spp. (coralbells)
Iberis sempervirens (edging candytuft)
Myosotis scorpioides (forget-me-not)
Viola cornuta (horned violet)

SUMMER-FLOWERING
Artemisia schmidtiana 'Silver Mound' (silver mound mugwort)
Cerastium tomentosum (snow-in-summer)
Coreopsis rosea (pink coreopsis)
Geranium spp. (cranesbill)
Lamium maculatum (spotted dead nettle)
Lavandula angustifolia (lavender)
Nepeta × *faassenii* (catmint)
Santolina chamaecyparissus (lavender cotton)
Stachys byzantina (lamb's-ears)

LATE-SUMMER- AND FALL-FLOWERING
Ceratostigma plumbaginoides (leadwort)

'Silver Charm' rose and 'Hidcote' lavender

clematis provide a luscious contrast to the roses. You can design a complete garden picture with spring-flowering bulbs and perennials to form skirts of flowers under the rosebushes; then you can add annuals, late-summer- and fall-blooming perennials, lilies, and ornamental grasses to provide the main garden interest in the months after the majority of the roses fade.

FORMAL ROSE GARDENS

Napoleon's wife, the Empress Josephine, attempted to collect every type of rose then known. Her garden was laid out in a geometric design of beds and walkways. Josephine's garden inspired today's formal rose gardens, where modern roses are arranged in rows within beds. Often the beds are curved, with walks laid out in concentric circles. Such a style makes it easy to care for these high-maintenance plants, providing access for pruning and allowing for adequate air circulation.

You can make your formal rose garden far more beautiful than the norm with just a little effort. Plant each bed with only one rose cultivar to avoid the spotty look that results from mixed floral colors and varying plant heights. Feature a different-colored rose in each bed and plan the colors in neighboring beds to look good together. If your aim is to grow perfect rose flowers, choose hybrid tea roses, whose elegant, high-centered flowers bloom individually on tall stems. If you want the most color impact, select floribunda roses, whose smaller flowers bloom in lavish clusters. Grandiflora roses grow quite tall and should be used where their height is appropriate.

A tree rose in the center of the bed can be a dramatic focal point. Place a garden ornament such as a gazing

globe, sculpture, or sundial at the center where paths converge. Or, frame the entrance with an arch or a pergola planted with large-flowered climbers or rambler roses. You also can grow them on a trelliswork fence that surrounds the garden.

Because hybrid tea and floribunda roses are admired solely for their flowers—not for their foliage and form, which is sparse and leggy— you'll want to partially camouflage the bushes. One option is to follow the style of Victorian gardens by outlining each bed with a clipped boxwood hedge, which gives the

garden year-round structure and form. You can substitute similar-looking dwarf Japanese holly in northern regions where boxwood is not hardy.

Flowering plants and silver-foliaged plants make lovely, although less traditional, edgings. Lavender's needlelike, gray leaves and fragrant flower spikes make a wonderful contrast to the globular rose flowers. Catmint looks similar to lavender although it is softer and more floppy. Santolina has tight whorls of scaly, silvery gray leaves. Clipped, it makes a low, formal edging that reflects the beauty of any rose you grow.

FAVORITE FRAGRANT ROSES

FLORIBUNDAS
'Angel Face' deep lavender-mauve
Guy de Maupassant ('Meisocrat') white and pink bicolor
'Intrigue' ('Jacum') deep purple-plum
'Singin' in the Rain' ('Mcivy') copper

HYBRID TEAS AND GRANDIFLORAS
'Blue Moon' lavender-blue
'Dolly Parton' deep red with orange tones
Double Delight ruby-red and white bicolor
Jardins de Bagatelle ('Meimafri') creamy white
'Marco Polo' ('Meipaleo') yellow
Perfume Beauty ('Meinicin') deep pink
'Roslyn Carter' coral-red
The McCartney Rose ('Meizeli') fuschsia
'Tiffany' medium pink with yellow
Yves Piaget ('Meivildo') pink

OLD GARDEN ROSES
'Celestial' (Alba rose) pale blush pink
'Comte de Chambord' (Portland rose) medium mauve-pink
'Fantin-Latour' (Centifolia rose) pale blush pink
'Ispahan' (Damask rose) medium pink
'Madame Alfred Carriere' (Noisette rose) white
'Madame Isaac Pereire' (Bourbon rose) deep rose pink
'Reine des Violettes' (Hybrid Perpetual rose) lavender-mauve
'Sombreuil' (Tea rose) antique white

SHRUB ROSES
Abraham Darby ('Auscot') peachy pink and yellow
Graham Thomas deep yellow
'Hansa' crimson-purple
'Othello' ('Ausslo') burgundy
'Sarah van Fleet' china pink

'Graham Thomas' rose

USING PERENNIALS IN THE LANDSCAPE

Photo by William Stites

A profusion of brightly colored perennials leads you down this garden path.

Perennials can find a suitable place in almost any area of your landscape. The mainstay of the flower garden, perennials were traditionally planted in formal borders in front of a hedge or fence. But they also bring joy to cottage gardens, bob between the grasses in meadow gardens, fill in the spaces between shrubs and in mixed borders, and frolic in the dappled light beneath the trees in woodland and shade gardens. Some perennials spread aggressively and make good groundcovers or soil stabilizers.

When planning your perennial garden, try to select a balanced assortment of spring-, summer-, and fall-blooming plants. Although most perennials put on their floral show for only two to three weeks, some bloom for six, eight, or even twelve weeks. By relying on these long bloomers, you will achieve a flower-filled scene that changes from month to month, even in a small space.

Another way to achieve impact and succession of color is to group plants of different heights and bloom seasons closely together, interplanting taller specimens to rise right out of lower ones and including late bloomers to take the place of early bloomers. This strategy provides more weeks of color out of the same garden spot than you would get if everything were planted in tidy, separate locations.

For the best effect, choose low plants with a spreading habit to weave around the stems of more upright specimens. Snow-in-summer, for example, forms a frothy cascade of snowy white flowers in early summer and then remains quietly gray the rest of the year. This creeping plant could be allowed to wander around and under clusters of upright plants, such as gayfeather and purple coneflower, that also do well in poor, dry soil.

Sedum 'Autumn Joy'

LONGEST-BLOOMING PERENNIALS

The following perennials bloom for an exceptionally long time. Although most perform better if deadheaded, those with an asterisk (*) must be cut back or deadheaded after each flush of flowers to promote reblooming.

6 TO 8 WEEKS

Achillea × 'Coronation Gold' (fern-leaf yarrow)
Achillea × 'Moonshine' (moonshine yarrow)
Aquilegia × *hybrida* 'McKana Hybrids' (columbine)
Aster × 'Alma Potschke' (Michaelmas daisy)

Aster novae-angliae (New England aster)
Campanula carpatica (Carpathian bellflower)
Centaurea montana (mountain bluet)
Cimicifuga spp. (bugbane)
Coreopsis verticillata (thread-leaved coreopsis)
Echinacea purpurea 'Bright Star' (purple coneflower)
Geranium endressii 'Wargrave Pink' (cranesbill)
Geranium × 'Johnson's Blue' (cranesbill)
Geranium sanguineum (bloody cranesbill)
Heliopsis helianthoides (false sunflower)
Helleborus niger (Christmas rose)

Hemerocallis hybrids (daylily)
Lavandula angustifolia 'Munstead' (lavender), herb
Monarda didyma 'Cambridge Scarlet' (beebalm), herb
Oenothera speciosa (showy primrose)
Oenothera tetragona 'Fireworks' (sundrops)
Phlox maculata 'Miss Lingard' and 'Omega' (Carolina phlox)
Phlox paniculata 'Mt. Fuji' (garden phlox)
Physostegia virginiana 'Vivid' (obedient plant)
Rudbeckia fulgida 'Goldsturm' (orange coneflower)

ORNAMENTAL GRASSES

No garden should be without ornamental grasses. Their streamer-like leaves form fine-textured fountains that add a restful aspect while combining well with shrubs, perennials, annuals, and bulbs.

Many grasses are green, but some, such as blue wild rye or blue oat grass, are dusky blue or blue-gray. Others, such as Bowles golden grass are shades of golden green. Zebra grass and variegated Japanese silver grass have boldly striped or banded leaves; purple fountain grass bears dusky, reddish purple blades.

Grass flowers take on many attractive forms—open sheaves, foxtails, feathery plumes, and bottlebrushes in subtle, earthy colors. As the seed heads ripen, colorful bristles and long hairs develop on the seeds, creating a wonderful, light-catching effect; the seed heads shimmer in the light of the autumn and winter sun.

In late autumn, grasses dry into tall sheaves of leaves and seed heads that can stand through the winter like a huge dried flower arrangement. They bleach to soft hues of straw, wheat, and almond. Dried grasses fill the garden with their magnificent presence at a time when other perennials have shriveled and died to the ground.

A unique quality of grasses is the sound they bring to the garden. The slightest breeze creates a symphony of rustling sounds as evocative as a babbling brook or lapping waves.

Use grasses as textural contrasts to bolder-leaved plants. Their linear foliage emphasizes and contrasts well with round leaves and more solid-looking plants. Use them as specimens in mixed borders or plant them in drifts or masses. Low grasses, such as blue fescue and ribbon grass, make excellent groundcovers; medium-sized fountain grass and blue oat grass fit into both formal and informal flower borders; and tall grasses, such as Japanese silver grass, ravenna grass, and pampas grass, work well as specimens or in natural landscapes.

For about six weeks after they are cut back in late winter, grasses are not showy. To fill this void in a grass-filled garden, plant spring-flowering bulbs, such as crocus, glory-of-the-snow, daffodils, tulips, and alliums. Their dying foliage will in turn be hidden by the emerging grass.

Photo by Mike Jensen

Ornamental grasses give a casual look and feel to a border as they bloom in late summer.

Veronica × 'Blue Peter' and 'Icicle' (speedwell)
Veronica longifolia 'Lavender Charm' (speedwell)

10 WEEKS
Aster × *frikartii* 'Monch' and 'Wonder of Staffa' (Frikart's aster)
*Dicentra eximia 'Alba' (fringed bleeding-heart)
Gaillardia × *grandiflora* 'Baby Cole' (blanketflower)
Hemerocallis 'Stella de Oro', 'Lemon Lollipop', 'Penny's Worth', and 'Happy Returns' (daylily)
*Nepeta × *faassenii* 'Dropmore' (catmint)
Perovskia atriplicifolia (Russian sage)
*Phlox paniculata 'Sandra' (garden phlox)

**Platycodon grandiflorus* (balloonflower)
Rudbeckia nitida 'Autumn Glory' (shining coneflower)
Salvia × *superba* (hybrid salvia)
**Scabiosa caucasica* 'Butterfly Blue' (pincushion flower)
Sedum 'Autumn Joy' (showy stonecrop)
Stokesia laevis (Stokes' aster)

12 WEEKS OR MORE
**Achillea millefolium* 'Appleblossom' and 'Fire King' (common yarrow)
Anthemis 'E.C. Buxton' (golden marguerite)
Aster × 'September Ruby' (aster)
Campanula portenschlagiana (Dalmatian bellflower)
Campanula poscharskyana (Serbian bellflower)

Coreopsis grandiflora 'Sunray' and 'Early Sunrise' (coreopsis)
Coreopsis verticillata 'Moonbeam' and 'Zagreb' (thread-leaved coreopsis)
*Dendranthema × *rubellum* (hybrid chrysanthemum)
Dicentra eximia 'Luxuriant', 'Zestful', and 'Bountiful' (fringed bleeding-heart)
Gaura lindheimeri (white gaura)
*Phlox paniculata 'Eva Cullum' and 'Franz Shubert' (garden phlox)
Verbena bonariensis (Brazilian verbena)
Veronica longifolia 'Sunny Border Blue' (speedwell)

Aster × *frikartii*

USING ANNUALS IN THE LANDSCAPE

Annuals are valuable because they bloom all summer long if you deadhead them regularly to prevent them from forming seeds. In a mixed flower garden, annuals provide a reliable source of blossoms to carry on between waves of flowering perennials and summer bulbs.

For the best effect, plant annuals in drifts just as you would perennials. Try planting large patches of one type of annual between drifts of perennials to provide a continual show.

Follow the basic rules of garden design discussed earlier in this chapter. Choose colors, textures, and forms that look good together. Combine spiky flowers with daisylike ones, for example, and plant in large drifts rather than in ones and twos.

Annuals also work well in window boxes and planters, providing flowers for months in a limited amount of space. Trailing annuals, such as nasturtium, verbena, and edging lobelia, tumble over the sides of containers, giving them a soft appearance. They also can spill artfully out of hanging baskets in a shower of blossoms.

Dahlberg daisies, sweet alyssum, and moss roses paint this backyard with perky color from spring until frost. There's an informal gaiety to the palette of colors and jumble of textures in this garden.

Verbena 'Peach Blossom' and Petunia integrifolia tumble over the top of a retaining wall, softening its edges.

FRAGRANT ANNUALS

These flowers not only look pretty, they also smell good. Some perfume the air around them; others share their scent only if you come close.

Clarkia amoena (farewell-to-spring)
Cleome hasslerana (spider flower)
Dianthus chinensis (China pink)
Erysimum cheiri (wallflower)
Heliotropium arborescens (heliotrope)
Lathyrus odoratus (sweet pea)
Lobularia maritima (sweet alyssum)
Matthiola incana (stock)
Nicotiana alata (flowering tobacco), species form is fragrant at night
Pelargonium spp. (scented geranium)
Petunia × *hybrida* (petunia)
Phlox drummondii (annual phlox)

Sweet pea is an old-fashioned favorite.

Many annuals last well when cut and used in flower arrangements. Because cutting them back usually serves to promote more bloom, annuals such as zinnia, cosmos, and larkspur form the reliable mainstay of flowers in a cut-flower garden. Stocks, sweet peas, and pinks add delicious fragrance to arrangements. (See pages 102–103 for suggested annuals to grow in cutting gardens.)

BEYOND PETUNIAS

Impatiens, petunias, and marigolds are the most popular flowers around—perhaps too popular, because we see them grown everywhere. These favorites serve us well, but the world of annuals also includes many more plants that are just as easy to grow. Many lesser-known annuals, such as Swan River daisy and black-foot daisy, are delicate to look at, being dainty of both flower and form, and a snap to grow. Try these softer-looking flowers instead of the more flamboyant annuals when you want to create a lovely texture in your garden that will complement—not compete with—other plants.

UNUSUAL ANNUALS TO GROW

Try one or more of these annuals to add interest to your garden:

Brachycome iberidifolia (Swan River daisy)
Brassica oleracea, Acephala group (flowering cabbage and kale)
Dyssodia tenuiloba (Dahlberg daisy)
Hypoestes phyllostachya (polka-dot plant)
Melampodium paludosum (melampodium)
Moluccella laevis (bells-of-Ireland)
Nigella damascena (love-in-a-mist)
Perilla frutescens (perilla)
Ricinus communis (castor oil plant)
Sanvitalia procumbens (creeping zinnia)
Scaevola aemula (fanflower)
Tithonia rotundifolia (Mexican sunflower)
Torenia fournieri (wishbone flower)

Photo by Bill Holt

Fanflower, with its unique flowers, is a conversation piece in any garden. It is also an excellent plant for a container.

USING BULBS IN THE LANDSCAPE

Spring-blooming bulbs, such as these Spanish squill, can be planted under deciduous trees. The bulbs flower before the leaves of the trees come out and shade the plants below.

Photo by William Stites

Combine bulbs with early-spring-blooming perennials for greater lushness and impact. Purple grape hyacinths are even more cheering when set against yellow marsh marigolds.

Many bulbs bloom early in spring, before perennials and annuals fill the garden, so their color is especially welcome. What's more, bulbs are generally easy to grow, and they can serve a variety of purposes in the garden. Here are some considerations for designing effective bulb plantings.

BULB COMBINATIONS

Hardy bulbs look best planted in large groups rather than individually. They will look lost if planted polka-dot style. Bulbs with large flowers, such as tulips and daffodils, work well in flower beds

BULBS FOR NATURALIZING

These early-blooming bulbs perform well in a lawn, where they reseed and increase in number, spreading into drifts. The trick to keeping bulbs blooming year after year is to avoid mowing their leaves until at least six weeks after they bloom. This may entail mowing only areas of lawn around the patches of bulbs if the lawn becomes straggly looking.

Chionodoxa luciliae (glory-of-the-snow)
Crocus chrysanthus (snow crocus)
Crocus × vernus (Dutch crocus)
Fritillaria meleagris (checkered lily)
Galanthus nivalis (snowdrops)
Ipheion uniflorum (spring starflower)
Iris reticulata (reticulated iris)
Scilla siberica (Siberian squill)

Photo by Elvin McDonald

Among the earliest of all bulbs to bloom, snowdrops earn their name for their ability to burst through snow and ice.

and mixed borders and under deciduous trees. Small-flowered bulbs, such as crocuses and snowdrops, look pretty grouped in rock gardens, under shrubs, and naturalized in a woodland or lawn.

Because the foliage of large-flowered, spring-blooming bulbs becomes unsightly and disappears by early summer, you'll need to decide when planting bulbs what will take their place in summer. They can share essentially the same garden spot with later-blooming perennials or annuals. The perennial or annual foliage grows around the dying bulb leaves, providing a succession of foliage and flowers. Be sure that whatever you use to overplant bulbs is shallow-rooted so you will not damage the bulbs when planting.

Useful interplanting companions include daylilies, ferns, or hostas with narcissus, Dutch hyacinths, or other spring bloomers. Most annual flowers would also be good choices. You might tuck bulbs into the soil under groundcovers such as lamb's-ears, whose gray foliage makes a lovely springtime partner for bulb flowers. And bulbs look wonderful growing out of expansive evergreen groundcovers such as pachysandra, English ivy, and myrtle. Bulbs also combine well with early-blooming perennials, such as bleeding-hearts, violets, barrenworts, primroses, and lungworts, and are often combined with cool-season annuals and biennials, such as pansies and forget-me-nots.

BULBS IN LAWNS

Small, early-blooming bulbs, such as snowdrops, starflower, Siberian squill, and snow crocus, can be planted in large swaths in a lawn, where they will bloom and spread year after year in happy compatibility with the grass. These naturalized bulbs are colorful in any climate, but are especially welcome in the still-brown, warm-season lawns of the South and Southwest. To keep the bulbs flourishing, don't mow the lawn until six weeks after the bulbs have bloomed. This allows their foliage to mature and nourish the bulbs for next year's blossoms.

Glory-of-the-snow naturalizes well in a lawn, thriving even in the dappled shade of evergreen trees. Look closely and you can see variations in the size of the white star in the center of the blossoms.

BULBS FOR CUT FLOWERS

Most bulbs are excellent cut flowers, their blossoms making long-lasting bouquets. (Don't cut the foliage if you want the bulbs to rebloom the next year.) If you don't want to rob your flower border of the blossoms, grow bulbs in a separate cutting garden. Choose tulips, daffodils, and Dutch hyacinths for spring arrangements and lilies and gladiolus for summer.

A cutting garden needn't be limited to summer-blooming annuals and perennials. Spring-blooming bulbs, such as the tulips shown here, extend the cut-flower season.

USING EDIBLES IN THE LANDSCAPE

Most of this Colorado front yard is devoted to growing edible plants. A small apple tree is planted for shade. Replacing lawn, vegetables and herbs grow in abundance, arranged as beautifully as a flower garden.

If the idea of having your landscaping be useful as well as beautiful appeals to you, consider creating an edible landscape. Instead of selecting purely ornamental plants for the shrub borders, flower beds, and foundation plantings around your home, grow plants that produce a harvest. Many edible plants are so beautiful that they can double as ornamentals in the landscape.

Edible landscaping honors the environment because it doesn't use resources on purely decorative plants. It makes sense to grow edible plants in the front yard or flanking the front walkway if that's where the sun shines.

Locating rows of vegetables in your front yard does not make an edible landscape. To be a true edible landscape, the edibles must be incorporated into your garden's design so that they actually double as ornamentals. Look at edible plants the same way you look at ornamentals. Consider their color, form, height, texture, and other visual qualities. Choose good-looking edible plants and combine them with standard ornamentals, following the basic rules of landscape design while striving to meet the crops' cultural needs.

FRUITS AND NUTS

Some of our most scrumptious fruits grow on decorative trees, bushes, or vines. Here are some attractive ways to incorporate these favorites into your garden:

■ Use a tall, lacy-leaved pecan or walnut tree in the front lawn instead of a maple or oak to cool the house, then gather the luscious nuts in autumn.

HERBS

Herbs are naturals in an edible landscape. Many feature highly aromatic, silvery gray leaves that provide a lovely contrast to green-leaved plants, and they have a pleasing aroma when warmed by the sun, brushed in passing, or crushed underfoot. Herb flowers often provide a softening effect.

VEGETABLES

Vegetable plants often have attractive leaves or fruits with color and texture that combine well with ornamentals. Those grown for their delicious leaves may be difficult to include in an edible landscape, because once they reach harvest size and you pluck them from the garden, they'll leave an empty space. Your design should allow you to grow lettuce, spinach, and Swiss chard among the flowers without leaving

■ Plant several semidwarf apple or peach trees in place of a magnolia or dogwood so you can enjoy their glorious spring flowers, but also reap sweet-scented, tree-ripened fruits in summer.

■ Plant blueberries, elderberries, bush cherries, currants, or filberts as a hedge to create privacy or as decorative specimens in a foundation planting and enjoy a bonus crop of delicious fresh fruits and nuts.

■ Use leafy, vining fruits, such as grapes and kiwis, to cover arbors and pergolas to create shade and privacy both before and after harvest.

■ Edge a flower or shrub border with alpine strawberries for a pretty foliage effect and fresh fruit for your cereal in the morning.

A living fence made from espaliered dwarf apple trees acts as a garden divider and privacy screen while offering its harvest of crisp fruit.

Photo by Stephen Cridland

■ Edge a flower bed with parsley to enjoy the beauty of its curly, emerald-green leaves.

■ Grow thyme in a rock garden or as paving plants in a patio or walk where its dainty, fragrant leaves look pretty and can be conveniently harvested.

■ Tuck parsley, sage, or rosemary into a container garden along with annual flowers to enjoy the lovely foliage contrast.

■ Plant a drift of gem-colored purple basil to provide a stunning contrast to pastel pink or blue blossoms in a flower garden.

■ Grow a swath of golden oregano as a groundcover under shrubs or tall flowers.

Most herbs are too beautiful to hide in the bed behind the garage. In this container for all to see, the emerald foliage of curly-leaved parsley sets off 'Antique Shades' pansies.

nasty-looking gaps after harvest. Fruiting plants, such as eggplants and peppers, remain even after you reap their harvest, so they pose fewer placement problems.

■ Incorporate pepper plants among the flowers. They display shiny, green leaves on strong stalks and provide gleaming spots of color from the various stages of the ripening pods.

■ Use a few rhubarb plants in the back of a perennial border. Harvest the new stalks in spring and allow subsequent growth to mature into dramatic, leathery leaves to create a bold statement among more subdued plants.

■ For an attractive foliage effect, include purple cabbages, ornamental kales, and purple mustards among annual flowers in the midground of a bed or border.

■ Plant a row of asparagus in a sunny site so its tall, lacy foliage is a leafy background for a bed of shorter flowers.

■ Arrange scarlet runner beans, purple hyacinth beans, pole beans, and climbing peas on a fence or trellis to enjoy their decorative flowers, leaves, and pods.

This combination of 'Red Giant' mustard and curly parsley is pretty enough to eat. The pansy flowers also are edible. Toss them in a salad or use them as a garnish.

DESIGNING HERB GARDENS

garden. Or, plant a collection of fragrant herbs that yield a sweet-smelling dried harvest if you like to make your own potpourris and sachets. A history buff might enjoy researching and duplicating an authentic medieval knot garden.

blocks or squares to bring order to the beds. A dooryard location allows you daily enjoyment. A large clay pot containing your favorite culinary herbs is a pretty and practical addition outside your kitchen door.

Herbs grown for cooking can be arranged in delightful patterns in a garden, rather than set in rows. In this beautiful garden, several varieties of thyme and sage share space with a stone cat.

H erb gardens possess a special charm all their own. As you create an herb garden, combine plants into attractive plots built upon designs that reflect tradition or highlight a specific theme.

DESIGN CHOICES

Y ou might choose your favorite culinary herbs for a kitchen

Another option is to simply combine a variety of attractive and useful herbs to fit a particular space in your home's landscape. With careful planning as well as knowledge of each herb's cultural needs, your herb garden will have a pleasing and practical design.

A circular shape is a favorite for herb gardens, either designed in concentric circles or wagon-wheel style, with triangular blocks of different herbs planted between each spoke. Or, mark off the garden in

To enhance the subtle beauty of your herb plants, try edging the beds with a border of bricks, cobblestones, or a wattle fence to give it definition, a year-round structure, and a rustic look. You can mimic the gardens of the medieval and Renaissance periods by defining the beds with low, formally clipped hedges. Lavender makes a traditional and sweet-smelling hedge. Silvery germander is another good choice.

Instead of lawn, create one or more paths to meander between raised beds or separate garden areas. Bricks, wood chips, pea gravel, paving stones, or cobblestones are favorites for covering pathways.

Most circular herb gardens, as well as those of other designs, include a sundial, garden statue, or birdbath as a focal point. A traditional bee skep woven of straw adds a lovely and historical touch to a small garden, especially if you plant your beds with bee-attracting herbs, such as thyme and beebalm. But any rustic-looking, found object brings a bit of history and whimsy to your garden. Small wooden or stone benches for relaxation are also a must.

Where to place herbs in your garden design depends on their size and growth habits. Creeping thyme, for example, is low-growing, but eventually spreads into a dense mat that covers a substantial area. Lemon balm reseeds profusely, and mints spread rapidly via underground runners. See the encyclopedia section of Chapter 11, starting on page 496, for help in deciding what to plant where.

Sundials make traditional additions to herb gardens. This metal one adds height to a bed of lemon thyme and echoes the colors of the Russian sage in the background.

Thyme spills over a garden wall, bringing a splash of color and offering its scented leaves at an easy height for harvesting.

Herbs perform admirably planted in containers of well-drained soil and can be conveniently located for the family chef beside a sunny kitchen door. Here parsley, lemon thyme, and rosemary, grow companionably.

USING CONTAINER PLANTS IN THE LANDSCAPE

This container garden blends flower colors, plant shapes, and heights to create the abundant feel of a garden. The variety of pot shapes and sizes contributes to the eye-catching vignette.

Photo by William Stites

There are many good reasons to garden in planters and containers rather than directly in the ground. Maybe you don't have much room for a garden, want to dress up your deck or front stoop with flowers, or want to grow a tropical tree that spends the winter on the sunporch. Perhaps you need to contain an aggressive plant or hope to protect a precious one from slugs or deer. Or, you might enjoy the cheerful appearance of window boxes full of flowers decorating the front of your cottage.

It's surprising how many plants are suited to potted life. Annual flowers are a cinch, of course, but bulbs, miniature roses, small shrubs, such as azaleas, and even small trees, such as amur maple or flowering crabapple, are suitable for container culture.

Container gardening is a landscaping style unto itself, with a unique set of considerations. The container and the soil are important decisions. And because plants in containers are more vulnerable to drying and temperature fluctuations and have only modest root room, they tolerate less neglect.

DESIGNING CONTAINER GARDENS

Containers and window boxes don't need to be boring. Create a miniature garden in a large container by stuffing it with lots of different plants instead of a couple of geraniums or petunias. There is only one rule to follow: Choose plants that like the same growing conditions. For greater visual variety, group different pots together, such as a container of mixed succulents and one of tropical foliage plants with containers of pastel flowering annuals. Here are some design principles to consider when choosing plants for your container garden so the result is really striking:

■ Use cascading plants or vines to drape over the edges of the container.

■ Place a tall, upright plant in the center or off-center to give the arrangement height.

■ Choose several billowy, fine-textured plants as a graceful filler.

■ Create a color scheme just as you would for a flower garden in the ground. A simple combination of two or three colors works best.

■ Combine and contrast fine- and bold-textured foliage for effect.

■ Contrast plants with silver or bronze leaves with green-leaved plants for long-lasting and easy-care color.

For example, you can fashion a potted kitchen herb garden by your back door by combining your favorite culinary herb plants in a large terracotta pot. Include an upright rosemary for height. Use creeping thyme to drape over the container's edge. Add chamomile and oregano to provide fine foliage texture and daisylike flowers. Include lavender for purple flowers and silver leaves.

Combine a variety of plant shapes and colors in a container. This planter has trailing variegated-leaved ivy, purple coleus, and the fresh green plumes of ferns contrasting with tall, spiky foliage, yet the composition is harmonious.

It's easy to embellish a difficult site when you garden in containers. Containers planted with flowers and foliage enliven the edge of this swimming pool.

PLANTS TO GROW IN CONTAINERS

PLANTS FOR HEIGHT
✓ *Canna* × *generalis* (canna lily)
Celosia argentea (cockscomb)
Cleome hasslerana (spider flower)
✓ *Cosmos bipinnatus* (cosmos)
Fuchsia × *hybrida* (fuchsia; use tree form)
Nicotiana spp. (flowering tobacco)
Pennisetum setaceum 'Rubrum' (purple fountain grass)
Perovskia atriplicifolia (Russian sage)
✓ *Salvia farinacea* (mealy-cup sage)

PLANTS FOR FILLER
Athyrium nipponicum 'Pictum' (Japanese painted fern)
Begonia × *tuberhybrida* (tuberous begonia)
Brachycome iberidifolia (Swan River daisy)
Brassica oleracea (flowering cabbage and kale)
Caladium × *hortulanum* (fancy-leaved caladium)
Centaurea spp. (dusty-miller)
Coleus × *hybridus* (coleus)
Festuca ovina var. *glauca* (blue fescue)
Heliotropium arborescens (heliotrope)
Heuchera micrantha 'Palace Purple' (purple-leaf coralbells)
Hosta spp. (hosta)
Impatiens wallerana (impatiens)
Liriope muscari 'Variegata' (blue lilyturf)
Melampodium paludosum (blackfoot daisy)
Pelargonium × *hortorum* (zonal geranium)
Polystichum acrostichoides (Christmas fern)
Salvia officinalis (garden sage)
Tagetes patula (French marigold)
Viola × *wittrockiana* (pansy)
Zinnia angustifolia (narrow-leaf zinnia)

PLANTS FOR CASCADING
Dyssodia tenuiloba (Dahlberg daisy)
Hedera helix (English ivy)
Hypoestes phyllostachya (polka-dot plant)
Lantana camara (lantana)
✓ *Lobelia erinus* (edging lobelia)
Pelargonium peltatum (ivy geranium)
Petunia × *hybrida* (petunia)
Rosmarinus officinalis var. *prostratus* (trailing rosemary)
Scaevola aemula (fanflower)
Thunbergia alata (black-eyed Susan vine)
Tropaeolum majus (nasturtium)
Verbena × *hybrida* (verbena)
Vinca major (large periwinkle)

USING CONTAINER PLANTS IN THE LANDSCAPE

continued

earthy look. But consider their disadvantages: They are heavy, breakable, and expensive. And, they dry out quickly and may not survive winter freezing. If terra-cotta appeals to you, consider plastic look-alikes.

ask local landscapers to give you the big, black plastic pots trees come in.
■ Big pots, especially clay ones, are heavy when filled with soil and water. To move them more easily, rest them on a frame with casters.

Planter boxes decorate the edge of a deck railing, creating a softer, more inviting look. This box is planted with blue salvia, petunias, flowering tobacco, and ivy geraniums.

CHOOSING CONTAINERS

There are all types of containers in many different sizes and colors and a huge range of prices.

Here are some tips to help you sort through the possibilities:
■ Unless you are growing a plant that likes soggy soil, such as horsetail, use a pot with drainage holes at the base. If you have a beautiful pot that lacks drainage holes, put the plants in a smaller plastic pot and conceal it in the decorative container. Put a brick or other support under the inner pot so the drainage water has a place to go, but be careful not to create a sump (a low spot into which water drains and sits, creating an environment that fosters root rot).
■ Terra-cotta pots are a standard, perhaps because they have a classic,

■ Soil dries out more slowly in plastic pots than in clay. Clay is a good choice if you have a habit of overwatering, but many gardeners prefer to use plastic.
■ Large pots dry out more slowly than small ones. For small vegetables and flowers, the pot should be at least 12 inches in diameter. For large vegetables and flowers, a 2½- to 5-gallon pot is best. For trees and shrubs, the container should be at least 3 feet wide and high. In almost all cases, bigger is better.
■ In a hot, sunny climate, choose light-colored pots. They absorb less heat than dark pots, keeping the roots cooler. Wooden containers stay cooler than others.
■ To save money if you don't care what the pot looks like—when vegetable gardening, for instance—

POTTING MIXES

Plants grow best in good soil. That holds doubly true for plants in pots, where the soil is subject to more drying, heating, cooling, and leaching of nutrients. Because there are no standards for what can be sold as potting soil, you can't be sure that any bag of potting medium you buy will make your plants happy.

You can mix your own potting soil or buy it. The goal is a medium that holds water well so you don't have to water constantly, drains well so roots get enough oxygen, supports plants so they don't flop over, and provides a slow-release source of phosphorus and potassium.

Potting mixes usually contain some of the following ingredients in varying proportions: compost or leaf mold, peat moss, sand, soil (garden loam or commercial potting soil), perlite, vermiculite, bonemeal, granite dust, greensand, langbeinite, sulfur, or limestone.

If you buy a soilless mix—one that contains materials such as perlite, vermiculite, and peat, but no actual soil or sand—add 1 part good, loamy, crumbly garden soil or commercial potting soil per 5 parts soilless mix. The soil is a buffer against changes in nutrient levels and pH.

FERTILIZING CONTAINER PLANTS

The slow-release nutrients you add to a soil mix don't include nitrogen or micronutrients, so you

A SIMPLE SOIL-MIX RECIPE

Container gardeners often develop their own secret recipes for the growing medium for their pots. If you're an inexperienced container gardener, try this recipe. The soil in the mix holds nutrients and water and buffers changes in pH and nutrients. The organic matter improves texture and holds water and nutrients. The sand, perlite, or vermiculite encourages good drainage; however, sand is heavy and may make moving large containers difficult.

- 1 part good loamy garden soil or commercial topsoil
- 1 part organic matter (peat moss, leaf mold, compost)
- 1 part sand, perlite, or vermiculite
- ¼ part bonemeal or rock phosphate (for phosphorus)
- ¼ part greensand, granite dust, or langbeinite (for potassium)

need to provide those once the plant is growing in the pot. Use a liquid high-nitrogen fertilizer, such as a mix of fish emulsion and seaweed, or a liquid chemical fertilizer, such as 10-20-20. Apply it once a week using a quarter-strength solution. You can either apply the diluted fish emulsion or seaweed to the soil or foliar feed by spraying it onto the leaves. Never foliar feed plants in full sun.

If you don't want to fertilize every week, try adding controlled-release fertilizer pellets to the potting soil. These come in different nutrient combinations—some are designed for annuals and others for vegetables—and are formulated to last anywhere from 30 to 120 days.

Exercise your imagination when choosing containers for flowers. Balakan geraniums spill from this old baby carriage for a whimsical effect. The geraniums actually are growing in a plastic pot concealed in the carriage.

WATER, WATER, WATER

Plants in containers require frequent watering. During hot and windy weather, they may need a drink twice a day. The rule of thumb is to water when a finger stuck in the soil finds it dry.

A few tricks conserve water and save you time spent watering.
- ◻ Apply an inch of mulch to the soil surface.
- ◻ Keep potted plants out of the wind.
- ◻ Use plastic pots, either alone or as liners for clay pots.
- ◻ Line a clay pot with plastic sheeting before filling it with soil; punch a drainage hole in the plastic.
- ◻ Use a self-watering pot, which has a reservoir at the base, for especially sensitive plants.
- ◻ Add a water-holding material, called polymer beads or hydrogel, to the soil mix. Because polymer beads wick water out of the pot if too

close to the surface, keep them 3 to 4 inches below the soil line.
- ◻ Install a drip watering system. The small tubes that feed into each pot are nearly invisible; you can set a timer to turn on the system automatically. You also can add a fertilizer attachment, eliminating another task.

Because most of the water your potted plants drink comes from the faucet rather than the sky, find out if the water is acidic or alkaline. You can test it yourself with litmus paper, which is inexpensive, or ask the water company for the information. If the pH is below 5.0, add a teaspoon of finely ground limestone per gallon of potting soil. If the pH is above 8.5, use the same amount of sulfur. Either mix the additive into the soil each time you repot or sprinkle it on the surface every year and water it in.

USING DECKS AND PATIOS IN THE LANDSCAPE

connect the house and outdoor living area with an overhead structure to create a ceiling.

DOING IT RIGHT

Make the outdoor living area large enough to handle your

then be designed to lead down to ground level. Put stairs in accessible locations and include 3-foot-tall railings on the deck and stairs for safety if the deck and stairs are high off the ground. Railings must be strong enough for people to lean on and raised off the deck so leaves and

A well-designed and decorated deck makes an ideal spot for morning coffee or an after-work drink. A deck extends outdoor living space most efficiently if it's located directly off a frequently used room.

A deck or patio located beside your home gets the most use. It invites you to step out the door and spend a few minutes reclining in the sun or relaxing in the shade. A convenient location off the kitchen makes cooking and eating outdoors a breeze. A deck or patio that's at the same level as the house extends your living area, especially if sliding doors open onto the space. You can further

family and the number of guests you expect to entertain. If you throw large outdoor parties, provide sufficient room for people to move about and mingle and for the amount of outdoor furniture you'll need.

DECK DETAILS

Decks are usually raised off the ground to house level to avoid stepping down when walking from indoors onto the deck. Stairs must

litter can be swept under them. Space rail posts far enough apart that young children cannot get their heads stuck, but use a spacing that's aesthetically pleasing and consistent from post to post and rail to rail. Built-in benches often can take the place of safety railings on low decks. Local building codes usually dictate these measurements and safety features.

Deck planks may be laid parallel with the house for a traditional look

TAKE A SEAT

Here's the minimum space you'll need to comfortably hold a table and chairs for the following number of people:

- Table for two: 6×8-foot area
- Table for four: 8×8-foot area
- Table for six: 10×10-foot area
- Table for eight: 8×12-foot area

or diagonally for a contemporary appearance.

Redwood, cedar, and cypress are rot-resistant woods often used for decks; they weather to a beautiful silvery gray, but can be stained. Pressure-treated pine costs less and lasts twice as long as these other woods, but is not as good-looking; use it for all supports in contact with the ground, if not for the deck floor. Pressure-treated wood is slightly green when new, but weathers to light gray. It can be stained or painted after it ages, but a sealant is recommended as a onetime application immediately after installation.

No matter what kind of wood it's built from, decking can be left natural or stained gray, tan, or brown, whichever looks best with your home's paint. Paint or stain railings to match or make them a contrasting color, such as white or dark green, that goes with your home's trim.

PATIO MATERIALS

Flagstone, fieldstone, and brick make beautiful patios; poured concrete, concrete blocks, or interlocking pavers look less attractive, but are less expensive. To beautify an aging concrete patio, use it as the base for an overlay of pebbled paving stones, bricks, or flagstones.

Paving materials come in many different colors and can be laid in any of numerous patterns to complement any style of garden. Use a material that fits your budget and matches your home's architecture. Here are some tips to keep in mind:

- Bricks can be embedded in mortar or concrete for permanence and to prevent the growth of weeds between them. Bricks also can be laid at less cost in a 2-inch base of sand and left unmortared. In poorly drained areas or in climates with severe winters, lay 3 to 5 inches of crushed rock beneath the sand.
- Brick colors vary from pale pink to deep brick-red and tan. Choose a color that harmonizes with the exterior of your home.
- Brick can be laid in any of numerous patterns, from simple to complex. The pattern's texture influences the style of the garden.
- Concrete is inexpensive and can be easily laid in any shape. A textured finish is less slippery than a smooth finish. Beautify concrete by adding a heavy aggregate, by dividing it into sections with strips of pressure-treated wood, or by coloring, stamping, or topping it with colored stones.
- Precast, interlocking concrete pavers are easy to install and come in many shapes, textures, and colors that mimic brick and cobblestone, but cost less. Choose a style carefully; some look too fake or industrial.
- Quarried flagstones, such as granite, sandstone, bluestone, and slate, are cut into uniform pieces and are flat-surfaced and easy to install. These look most formal.
- Fieldstones look more rustic than flagstones because they are not uniformly shaped and have an uneven surface; they must be fitted together and partially buried to make a surface flat enough for walking.

PAVING PLANTS FOR PATIOS

These low-growing, fine-textured plants thrive in hot, dry conditions between paving stones. Most tolerate being lightly walked on. Tuck them among stepping-stones, flagstones, and patio blocks to soften masonry and create a cottage feel.

ANNUALS
Brachycome iberidifolia (Swan River daisy)
Dyssodia tenuiloba (Dahlberg daisy)
Eschscholzia californica (California poppy)
Lobelia erinus (edging lobelia)
Lobularia maritima (sweet alyssum)
Portulaca grandiflora (moss rose)

HERBS
Mentha requienii (Corsican mint) needs cool, moist conditions
Thymus praecox subsp. *arcticus* (mother-of-thyme)
Thymus pseudolanuginosus (woolly thyme)

PERENNIALS
Ajuga reptans (bugleweed)
Campanula carpatica (Carpathian bellflower)
Cerastium tomentosum (snow-in-summer)
Phlox subulata (moss pink)
Sedum acre (goldmoss sedum)

Plants tucked among paving stones soften hard edges and often give off delightful scents when tread upon.

USING WALKS AND PATHS IN THE LANDSCAPE

colonial one. Herringbone set on edge (which takes twice as many bricks) creates an intricate, gingerbready appearance that's perfect with a Victorian home. Flagstones can be formal if evenly cut. Irregularly cut flagstones or natural fieldstone are informal.

The brick pattern changes in each leg of this front walk, which helps emphasize the change in direction as visitors make their way to the front door.

A walkway leading from the street or driveway to the front door creates a welcome entrance for your home. Choose a paving material that matches your home's style and color.

DESIGNING WALKWAYS

Brick walks suit almost any home if the color and pattern reflect the home's style. Choose running bond for a contemporary house and basket-weave or herringbone for a

Design the walkway so it allows easy movement between the street or driveway and the front door. Don't make the common mistake of locating the walk right next to the house in a straight line from the driveway. This placement is inconvenient, because visitors must walk past parked cars, and the area beside the house is too narrow to plant. Balance the position of the walk with the size of the house by locating the walk farther into the yard, where visitors would naturally walk or where passengers from a car can easily get to it. Allow the walk to

wind toward the front door, making a gradual curve or turning a right angle, to create a sense of anticipation as you approach.

GARDEN PATHS

Both formal and informal gardens benefit from paths that direct viewers through the garden. A path—even if you don't walk on it—leads your eye, directing you to look at the scene you so carefully crafted. Formal gardens call for straight paths with sharp corners along the front of the border. The path provides a place to walk and allows foreground plants to spill forward. (With a lawn border, edges must be neater and floppy plants are in danger of being mowed.) Paths may intersect at right angles or lead to a strong focal point, such as a bench or statue set in an alcove or cutout.

Informal gardens call for curving paths that might duck behind a large shrub or a corner of the house, creating a bit of mystery. The path should meander in a seemingly unstudied fashion, but actually point the way to pretty focal points of intense color or interest.

Choose a path surface to match your garden's style. Mulch and wood chips look good in wildflower and natural landscapes; use more formal materials in traditional settings. Choose straight-edged flagstones for formal gardens and fieldstones for a country mood. Brick paths work in almost any style garden, as does dark-colored gravel. Avoid white gravel, because its brightness captures your attention, detracting from the flowers. Be sure to give gravel an edging to hold it in place. Lay an undercoating of landscape fabric beneath so the stones don't work their way into the soil and disappear.

PATH AND WALKWAY DESIGN GUIDELINES

■ Make a walkway to the front door 48 to 60 inches wide to allow two people to walk side by side and to balance the size of the house.

■ Build walkways to the rear entrance or back of the property 24 to 36 inches wide; a wider walkway may confuse visitors.

■ Consider a grade less than 3.5% "flat"; break up a steeper grade with level walk areas and pairs of steps .

■ Allow a garden path to wander a bit. Locate a large plant at a curve to block the view and create a sense of mystery.

A path through a garden can be constructed of stepping-stones or another informal natural material rather than with bricks or flagstones. A boardwalk makes an attractive walk in a seaside location. Choose wood chips, pine needles, crushed stone, crushed seashells, or gravel for flat areas or gentle slopes. Shredded bark holds best on a steep slope; it may be stabilized by laying rot-resistant logs (such as cedar) horizontally across the slope to mark off steps. For neatness and to keep the materials in place, include a wood, brick, metal, or stone edging. In a natural setting, allow edging plants to spill over the sides of the path.

A lawn path is a classic choice. For easier maintenance, make the path only as wide as one or two passes with your lawn mower.

USING OTHER STRUCTURAL ELEMENTS IN THE LANDSCAPE

Structures such as fences and the naked branches of deciduous trees endure throughout the year, forming landscape features in winter.

Fences, walls, arbors, and gates serve both practical and aesthetic functions in a landscape. They can provide privacy or an invitation to enter a specific area; be a backdrop for plantings or a foreground for pretty views beyond; and give a sense of enclosure or mark off a wide-open space.

TYPES OF STRUCTURES

A tall fence or wall provides privacy and security and even acts as a windbreak (see pages 76–77 for privacy fencing and fence styles; pages 82–83 for windbreaks). It also creates a feeling of enclosure and intimacy. Where the grade changes, a stone wall can be set into a slope to create a retaining wall; the wall can be built with planting pockets for growing rock garden plants. An overhead structure, such as an arbor or a pergola, moderates the sun, blocks an overhead view, and provides a place to grow vines.

A gate, of course, can keep people and pets in or out, but also provides a destination at the end of a path; left ajar, it is a friendly invitation that welcomes visitors into the garden. Gates, walls, pillars, or decorative, curved fences can frame the entrance to a driveway or walkway and fashion a formal or dramatic statement. But these structures also serve the practical purpose of signaling the entrance's exact location, so drivers know where to turn into the driveway and pedestrians can find the front walk.

FENCES AND WALLS

A lthough most fences and walls are placed along property borders, they can be used anywhere in the landscape to create garden rooms, provide screening, or direct traffic. Fences and walls give a garden year-round structure. As a result, they become important landscape design elements. (See pages 20–21 for more on creating a good bone structure in your garden.) Be sure to choose a material, style, and color that match the architecture of your home.

On a flat, dimensionless property with a wide-open backyard, for example, you might locate flower beds in the middle of the sunny area. Surrounding the beds with a 3-foot-

GARDEN ACCESSORIES

Although plants or plant groupings often create focal points in a garden, structures and accessories, such as birdbaths, benches, gates, and statues, make strong, permanent focal points. Locate focal points judiciously and don't use too many in one garden.

Benches should match your garden's style. Teak benches with wide or straight backs and armrests are traditional in English gardens, though the shape of the bench is more important than the actual wood. Less expensive versions may be made of oak or pine. Grapevine and cedar-log furniture possess a rustic charm that enhances a country flower or herb garden.

Statuary that seems cute in a cottage garden may look tacky in a more formal setting, so choose carefully. A stone bunny or frog peeking out from beneath a hosta leaf adds a whimsical charm that enhances the appeal of a country setting, but looks inappropriate in a formal rose garden. In formal settings, avoid cuteness and go for drama. Choose a large, graceful urn or tall figurine to make a grand statement.

tall picket or rail fence gives the garden a sense of permanence and turns the space into a flower-filled garden room. Gates or openings in the fence direct traffic. The low height of the fence allows you to see the flowers on the other side.

A wall around a patio that leads off the house emphasizes the feeling of an outdoor room because it marks boundaries. Choose a low wall that allows you to see out over the yard if there is a pleasing vista beyond and if you wish to catch the breeze. A tall wall or fence surrounding a small patio can create a wonderful sense of intimacy, enhancing the feeling of an outdoor room because you cannot see over the walls. A tall wall also traps heat and blocks wind, a desirable asset in many climates (see pages 82–83). Be sure to balance the floor space with the wall's height, so you enjoy a pleasant sense of enclosure, not one of confinement.

Add an arbor over part or all of a deck or patio or over an entry gate to create a ceiling for your outdoor room. The structure casts some shade—how much depends upon the thickness and closeness of the crosspieces and whether or not vines cover it. A vine-covered arbor will moderate the sun, but remember that an arbor extending off the side of a house may restrict your view from indoors.

A fence or wall can be placed strategically to hide unsightly but necessary objects such as electric and water meters, air-conditioning units, and vent pipes. You can erect screening to create an outdoor room to park bikes, hide trash cans, or hold gardening equipment. Choose an attractive material so the screen will be a garden asset that adds to the outdoor decor.

When viewed from the house, this picket fence provides a sense of enclosure and privacy. When viewed from the street, it serves as a foreground to landscape plantings and emphasizes the charming railing around the porch.

Solving Landscape Challenges

Chapter 2

YARD SOLUTIONS: CREATING A WELCOMING FRONT ENTRANCE

Featuring an irregular flagstone walk that widens into a patio planted with paving plants, this nontraditional design gives a colonial home a new and appealing look.

The entry landscaping is the first part of your home that most visitors see, and it makes a lasting impression. Ideally, the design should enhance your home; create a welcome, comfortable feeling; and help visitors find the front door. They shouldn't have to wonder which door to use or where to park their cars.

DESIGN POINTERS FOR ENTRYWAYS

Here are some ways to make your entrance inviting:
■ For an appealing, informal effect, position the front walk so it follows a gently curving path from the street or driveway and across part of the front lawn.
■ For a formal effect, lay out the walk in a straight line from the street or at a right angle to the driveway.
■ Make the walk to the main entrance at least 4 feet wide and the walk to the backdoor or service entrance 2 to 3 feet wide. Partially hide a secondary entrance at the front of the house with a small tree or large shrub.
■ Design large areas on each side of the walk near the house, street, or driveway and fill them with low shrubs, groundcovers, and perennials.
■ Avoid lining up a row of shrubs or planting a hedge on each side of the

Planting areas close to an entrance create a sense of welcome when they are filled with low shrubs, groundcovers, perennials, and pots brimming with annuals.

walk, which creates cramped, tunnel-like walls.

■ Create a landing at least 6×6 feet at the front door; extend the landing at least 1½ feet on each side of the doorjamb so there's plenty of room for visitors to stand.

■ Create a patio-like landing, vestibule, or courtyard in front of the main entrance to add drama. This area can be enclosed with a low wall or fence to create a transition from outdoors to indoors.

■ Where there's a circular driveway in front of a home, inlay a decorative pattern of brick, cobblestone, or flagstone in the pavement to soften the look of the driveway and create an entrance landing.

■ Locate flower planters on the front landing or at wide points in the walk.

■ Add an arbor to the front of the house and over the landing; grow flowering vines on it.

DECORATIVE DRIVEWAYS

Expanses of asphalt and concrete near the house can look unattractive; if your budget allows, consider paving your driveway with bricks, cobblestones, or bricklike interlocking pavers so the drive becomes a landscape asset. You can also inlay these materials in a gravel, asphalt, or concrete driveway. This treatment is effective used in the following places:

■ To create a sense of welcome at the entrance to the driveway from the street
■ To mark additional parking spaces at the side or end of the driveway
■ To create an entry court on a circular driveway near the home's front door
■ To indicate the walkway to the front entrance on a straight driveway
■ To create a place for passengers to alight on firm ground along one side of a narrow driveway
■ To create a decorative edging along the driveway

YARD SOLUTIONS: CREATING A WELCOMING FRONT ENTRANCE

Shrubs in your front yard don't all have to hug the house. The landscape will be more interesting and inviting if you let your plantings spill out into the spot traditionally reserved for lawn.

To many people, landscaping in front of a house means foundation planting of yew, arborvitae, or rhododendron and an expanse of lawn. The tradition of foundation planting began when houses were built with high foundations that needed to be hidden. But most houses today aren't built that way, and new houses often have siding right down to the ground. It's no longer necessary to have evergreen foliage camouflaging the concrete foundation throughout the year. This means landscaping out front can be more interesting. When you design plantings for the front of your house, think about the entire front yard, not just the foundation area.

ALTERNATIVES TO FOUNDATION PLANTINGS

Depending upon your home's style, choose a traditional, formal design or an informal, casual look for your front yard. A traditional design relies heavily on evergreen plants, such as boxwood, yew, and holly; evergreen groundcovers, such as pachysandra and myrtle; and upright accent plants, such as arborvitae or false cypress—all symmetrically planted along the house's foundation. Informal designs rely less on evergreens, especially formally clipped ones, and feature more varied and colorful plants.

If you want to break away from traditional designs, you will discover that the area usually relegated to foundation planting and front lawn can provide a newfound garden space for growing a collection of wonderful plants. For example, you can plant a deep mixed border of evergreen and deciduous shrubs interspersed with masses of perennials and spring bulbs along the foundation instead of just a row of evergreens. Underplant shrubs and perennials with an evergreen groundcover or spread an attractive and dressy mulch. Don't be afraid to include deciduous flowering shrubs and even small trees where there's room.

Whichever style you select, be sure to choose shrubs whose natural size won't be too large for their position. All too often foundation shrubs get out of control and grow up to conceal the windows, making the house dark and damp. To save yourself from constant pruning chores, choose low-growing shrubs and dwarf or slow-growing versions of tall evergreens.

CREATE A LIVABLE FRONT YARD

If your property is small or if the best sun is in the front, don't feel shy about turning the front yard into usable outdoor living and garden space. Give yourself some privacy from the street with a hedge, screen, or fence, then turn that useless lawn area into an outdoor living space by incorporating a porch, deck, or patio that links to the

OTHER PLACES FOR PLANTS OUT FRONT

Here are some other places to consider for gardening:
- Grow flowers in the grassy strip between the sidewalk and street.
- Plant a mixed border or small bed next to the entrance of the driveway.
- Plant flowers around the mailbox and train vines up the post.
- Grow vines up a lamppost.
- Mount window boxes on porch railings or on or just below windowsills; fill them with flowers and trailing vines.
- Make a small dooryard garden by the front door.
- Plant shrubs, ornamental grasses, or substantial perennials such as peonies along the driveway.

BEST SHRUBS FOR FOUNDATION PLANTINGS

These shrubs look good in a foundation planting or mixed border in front of a house. Most are low-growing; some are dwarf or slow-growing versions of larger plants. None need a lot of pruning. Plants with * are listed in the groundcovers encyclopedia.

DECIDUOUS SHRUBS

Berberis thunbergii var. *atropurpurea* 'Crimson Pygmy' (dwarf red barberry)

Callicarpa dichotoma (purple beautyberry)

Clethra alnifolia 'Hummingbird' (dwarf summer-sweet)

Cotoneaster adpressus (creeping cotoneaster)

Cotoneaster apiculatus (cranberry cotoneaster)

Cotoneaster divaricatus (spreading cotoneaster)

Cotoneaster horizontalis (rockspray cotoneaster)

Daphne spp. (daphne)

Deutzia gracilis 'Nikko' (dwarf slender deutzia)

Fothergilla gardenii (dwarf fothergilla)

Hydrangea macrophylla (French hydrangea)

Hypericum spp. (St.-John's-wort)

Itea virginica (Virginia sweetspire)

Lespedeza thunbergii (bush clover)

Potentilla fruticosa (shrubby cinquefoil)

Spiraea nipponica 'Snowmound' (spirea)

Stephanandra incisa 'Crispa' (cutleaf stephanandra)

Syringa meyeri (dwarf Korean lilac)

EVERGREEN SHRUBS

Buxus microphylla (littleleaf box)

Buxus microphylla var. *koreana* (Korean box)

Cephalotaxus harringtonia 'Prostrata' (Japanese plum yew)

Chamaecyparis lawsoniana 'Minima Glauca' (dwarf Lawson false cypress)

Chamaecyparis obtusa 'Nana', 'Nana Gracilis', 'Nana Lutea', and 'Filicoides' (dwarf Hinoki false cypress)

Chamaecyparis pisifera 'Filifera Aurea Nana' (dwarf golden Sawara false cypress)

Chamaecyparis pisifera 'Juniperoides' (golden Sawara false cypress)

Cotoneaster dammeri (bearberry cotoneaster)

Cotoneaster salicifolius (willowleaf cotoneaster)

Daphne cneorum (garland flower)

Daphne odora (winter daphne)

Gardenia jasminoides (gardenia)

Ilex cornuta 'Burfordii Nana' (dwarf Chinese holly)

Ilex crenata 'Hetzii', 'Green Lustre' and 'Golden Gem' (Japanese holly)

Ilex × *meserveae* (blue holly)

Juniperus chinensis 'Gold Coast' and 'Old Gold' (dwarf Chinese juniper)

Juniperus conferta (shore juniper)

Juniperus horizontalis (creeping juniper)

Juniperus procumbens var. 'Nana' (dwarf Japanese garden juniper)

Juniperus scopulorum 'Welchii' (Rocky Mountain juniper)

Leucothoe spp. (leucothoe)

Microbiota decussata (Russian cypress, Siberian cypress)

Nandina domestica 'Compacta' and 'Harbour Dwarf' (dwarf heavenly bamboo)

Pieris japonica 'Valley Rose' (Japanese pieris)

Pinus mugo (Mugo pine)

Pinus strobus 'Nana', 'Blue Shag', and 'Soft Touch' (dwarf Eastern white pine

Pittosporum tobira 'Wheeler's Dwarf' (dwarf Japanese pittosporum)

Prunus laurocerasus 'Otto Luyken' (dwarf cherry laurel)

Raphiolepis indica (Indian hawthorn)

Rhododendron carolinianum (Carolina rhododendron)

Skimmia japonica (Japanese skimmia)

Taxus baccata 'Repandens' (dwarf spreading English yew)

Taxus cuspidata 'Densa' (dwarf Japanese yew)

Yucca smalliana (Adam's needle)

---

front door or front walk. Use the property borders for flower gardens. Instead of a hedge, plant a mixed border of various shrubs or an edible landscape of berry bushes. (See pages 52–53 for more on edible landscaping.)

You can be extremely casual by planting a flower- and vegetable-filled cottage garden in your front yard, as long as you anchor it to the house and landscape with an appropriate fence along the street and provide enough shrubs and trees for year-round structure. (See page 100 for information on designing a cottage garden.) Plant both the lawn and street sides of the fence for the best effect.

YARD SOLUTIONS:
MAKING THE MOST OF A BACKYARD

If your garage is bursting with gardening paraphernalia, consider building a toolshed. This one is attractive enough to serve as a focal point for the whole backyard.

Your backyard is a world of possibilities. If an area away from the house offers a superb view—of a lake, a mountain, or even a flower garden—locate a sitting area there, too. This may be a small patio or deck, a gazebo, or an open, level area of gravel or mulch where you can put a table and chairs, a bench, or a hammock. Place a bench on the edge of the lawn, along a wooded path, or under a tree to invite visitors to sit and enjoy the garden. Such intimate settings make perfect garden retreats for someone in search of peace and quiet.

A BACKYARD FOR OUTDOOR LIVING

People who enjoy the outdoors appreciate having an inviting area in their backyard and garden for relaxing, barbecuing, and entertaining. And many homeowners simply love to putter around outside and indulge a gardening hobby. When it comes to designing a functional backyard, you must first consider what your family's needs will be—and those needs will change as your family changes. If you have young children, you'll want a safe place that's visible from indoors

where you can locate a swing set or sandbox. As the children get older and lose interest in those play areas—and as you simultaneously gain more free time—you may want to turn that area into a vegetable or cut-flower garden.

You may wish to visually divide your backyard into several garden rooms. Locate outdoor living areas and flower gardens close to the house, where you can enjoy them from indoors and out. Locate utilitarian areas, such as a vegetable garden and an outdoor recreation area, off to the side or behind an attractive low hedge or fence.

CAMOUFLAGE TACTICS

Here are additional ways to hide a shed, compost pile, or other undesirable view:

- Install a decorative fence or lattice panels.
- Plant a hedge or screen of tall shrubs.
- Plant tall ornamental grasses.
- Grow leafy or flowering vines on trellises.
- Espalier fruit trees on the wall of a shed or garage.
- Plant a row of tall sunflowers.
- Distract attention from the problem: Put in a path leading in another direction with a focal point at the end.
- If the eyesore can be seen from a deck or patio, position chairs or benches to face away from the problem.

MAKE ROOM FOR OUTDOOR UTILITY AREAS

If you are a serious gardener or simply short on garage storage space, you may wish to dedicate an out-of-the-way part of your yard as an outdoor utility area. Here you can keep a compost pile and store tools and garden equipment—or anything else that may detract from the garden's appearance—if you screen the area with a hedge or fence. Add an attractive gate that's wide enough for a wheelbarrow, and you're in business.

A tool- or garden shed provides a convenient alternative to garage storage for all the various gardening tools you may need. Choose an attractive shed that matches your home's architecture and blends with the style of your garden. A custom-designed shed can be a handsome garden addition. It need not be screened off, but can be designed to fit into its own garden setting. If your shed is more utilitarian than beautiful, screen it with plantings or fences. Locating the shed in a convenient spot can save you a lot of steps when you are carrying out your gardening chores.

A simple bench on a wood chip path is surrounded with flowers and other plantings, turning a neglected backyard into a retreat.

Make way for play. A corner of this backyard is reserved for children's recreation. Site a play area where it can be observed from the house.

YARD SOLUTIONS: CREATING PRIVACY

A SENSE OF ENCLOSURE

Solid fences, hedges, and screen plantings block views and create privacy while offering a pleasing sense of enclosure and intimacy. If you don't have the patience to wait

■ For a two-story house on a small or narrow property, plant a screen of narrow or columnar evergreens, which legally can grow taller than the 6-foot fence limit.
■ Where space is not a problem, plant an informal hedge or a mixed

Large lots need a sense of enclosure and defined boundaries. This extensive shrub border not only provides privacy, it also creates visual interest in what otherwise would be a vast expanse of lawn.

Increasingly, yards and gardens are becoming important places for outdoor living. As with the inside of your home, you want your outdoor rooms to be private from the neighbors. The larger your property, the more likely you'll already have a natural sense of seclusion, but landscaping may be necessary to create privacy on both large and small properties.

for a hedge or screen planting to mature, you can create instant privacy by erecting a solid fence. But a fence won't work in all cases, because fence height is limited along property lines, and fences may be ineffective on sloping ground.

Here are some other ways you can create privacy:
■ For a one-story house on a small or narrow lot, erect a solid fence on the property border; usually 6 feet tall is the zoning limit. Soften with vines.

border of tall and medium-size shrubs—the deeper the better. Use evergreens for year-round privacy, add deciduous shrubs for variety.
■ To give a patio or deck privacy and block a view from a neighboring second-story window, erect an arbor or overhead structure above the sitting area. Enclose part of the area with a lattice screen if desired.
■ To block a view from or onto higher ground, use a strategically located, medium-size or tall tree.

■ To screen the street or other unattractive area from view, plant a hedge or screen of medium-size to tall evergreens along the street (where fence height is usually restricted to 4 feet). In cold climates where roads are salted in winter, choose salt-tolerant types.

■ To enclose and separate one garden area from another, use a decorative fence or wall, or plant a hedge. Include a gate.

ROAD-SALT-TOLERANT TREES

In climates where roads are salted in winter, the salty runoff can damage nearby trees. These trees tolerate the salt and make the best choices for screens or street trees along salted roadways:

DECIDUOUS TREES
Acer platanoides (Norway maple)
Acer tataricum subsp. *ginnala* (Amur maple)
Fraxinus pennsylvanica (red ash)
Ginkgo biloba (maidenhair tree)
Liquidambar styraciflua (sweet gum)
Quercus nigra (water oak)
Robinia pseudoacacia (black locust)
Ulmus parvifolia (lacebark elm)

CONIFERS
Juniperus virginiana (Eastern red cedar)
Pinus flexilis (limber pine)
Pinus parviflora (Japanese white pine)
Pinus thunbergiana (Japanese black pine)

Even in small areas, a private nook can be carved out by erecting a fence and planting trees, shrubs, and vines to muffle sounds and mask undesirable views.

CHOOSING A WALL OR FENCE

Constructed walls and fences look best when they match or complement your home's building materials and style. A brick home acquires a sense of permanence and becomes more elegant when a brick wall defines the garden space.

Choose a stucco wall if your house is built of stucco. Choose a quaint picket fence for a cottage or shingled colonial home, but avoid using such an informal fence for a formal home. Custom-designed fences add elegance to any property and are usually built from sturdier and longer-lasting materials than ready-made types.

Gates vary in height, but usually match the height of the fence or wall. Add an enticing arbor over the gate to support a vine. Or, craft the gate with a circular peephole or add another decorative element. Wrought-iron gates look fine in a brick or stucco wall.

YARD SOLUTIONS: CREATING PRIVACY
continued

WALL STYLES

Walls can be freestanding to provide privacy and divide spaces, or set into a slope to create a retaining wall where the grade changes. Walls may be made of brick, concrete, fieldstone, cut stone, concrete block, or adobe (in arid climates). Stone costs more than brick, but it looks most natural in many settings. A dry-laid fieldstone wall offers numerous crevices for growing rock garden plants.

Angle a retaining wall slightly backward for best stability. Unless the soil is sandy, include weep holes to prevent water and ice from forcing stones out of alignment; install a drainage pipe along the wall's base.

Plant low-spreading shrubs and groundcovers at the top of the retaining wall so they creep and cascade over the wall. Vines, too, can soften the appearance of stone or masonry.

FENCE STYLES

Fences come in all styles—from rustic split rail to Japanese bamboo panels. A fence makes a year-round design statement in your garden, so choose it with care. A tall, lattice fence around a patio provides a firm hold for twining vines such as clematis and honeysuckle while allowing the breeze to enter. Solid board fences along a property border provide the most privacy, but they can look rigid and imposing; soften them with vines and foreground plantings, if necessary.

FENCE AND WALL STYLES

The type of fence or wall you choose should depend largely on what is regionally appropriate and what matches the architectural style of your house.

An adobe wall looks appropriate in the desert Southwest, where it matches Santa Fe-style architecture.

A freestanding fieldstone wall divides this yard into garden spaces.

A tall, narrow-slatted wooden fence blocks this side yard from the sidewalk in front, creating a useful, private area.

A tall, white board fence reflects light into a shady garden while creating privacy from the neighbors.

A solid wooden fence with locking gates attached to brick pillars provides security in a busy neighborhood.

FENCE TIPS

When installing a fence, keep in mind these points:

■ Local zoning regulations may restrict fence and wall heights; limits are often 6 feet on a property border and 4 feet on the street. A fence located inside your property border rather than on it can be as tall as you like, however.

■ On uneven ground, level the top of the fence along its entire length; don't slant the sections with the grade. Camouflage the uneven fence bottom with plants.

■ On hilly ground, level one or more sections of fence along their top lengths, then lower or raise the adjoining sections to accommodate the grade change.

■ Use pressure-treated posts for the longest wood life.

■ Be sure gates are wide enough to allow a wheelbarrow, lawn mower, and other maintenance equipment to pass through.

Allow fences to weather to a natural gray or paint or stain them. Usually white or a neutral earth color—gray, brown, or green—is best. Extra-dark green stain makes a fence recede and forms a lovely foil for blooming plants during the growing season while providing valuable color during winter. White fences reflect light back into the garden, which helps dispel shade, but can be too bright and prominent in sunny locations. A more daring choice is to paint or stain the fence a color that matches the house's trim, such as blue or red; this works best in a small cottage garden or with a contemporary design.

YARD SOLUTIONS: CREATING PRIVACY
continued

Marking the property border and providing an effective barrier, this informal azalea hedge needs little pruning and offers springtime blossoms.

HEDGE AND SCREEN PLANTINGS

Hedges and screens create living walls that mark boundaries and create enclosure and privacy. A hedge can be either formally sheared into flat walls or informally pruned so that it has a fluffy, irregular outline, if it is pruned at all.

A formal hedge usually needs less space than an informally pruned one. A screen planting is similar to a hedge except it is made up of a row of closely spaced trees or tall shrubs, usually left unpruned. Good plants for screens, especially in limited spaces, are many of the columnar and upright conifers. Sometimes columnar deciduous trees are used for screens. A tall screen can double as a windbreak if strategically located.

BUILDING A BERM

A berm is an artificial mound of soil that creates a contour and gives height to a garden. By berming soil in certain areas of your

EVERGREENS FOR SCREENS AND TALL HEDGES

Plant a living fence to create year-round privacy. Needle-leaved evergreens make excellent tall screens or hedges for a property border or garden boundary.

Use evergreens as windbreaks to slow down cold winter winds in open areas. In a narrow area, choose columnar cultivars; where there's more room, wider pyramidal types are fine. Place individual plants in a line or in staggered rows, spacing them at about ⅓ their mature width.

Those marked with * can be clipped for a formal hedge; those marked with ** tolerate part shade.

*Calocedrus decurrens
  (incense cedar)
Chamaecyparis spp. (false cypress)
**Cryptomeria japonica
  (Japanese cedar)
* ** × Cupressocyparis leylandii
  (Leyland cypress)
Cupressus arizonica var. *glabra*
  (smooth Arizona cypress)
*Juniperus chinensis 'Hetzii
  Columnaris' (Chinese juniper)
Juniperus scopulorum
  (Rocky Mountain juniper)
Juniperus virginiana
  (Eastern red cedar)
Metasequoia glyptostroboides
  (dawn redwood)
*Pinus spp. (pine)
* **Podocarpus macrophyllus
  (yew pine)
Pseudotsuga menziesii
  (Douglas fir)
Sequoiadendron giganteum
  (giant sequoia)
* **Taxus spp. (yew)
Thuja occidentalis (arborvitae)
Thuja plicata (Western red cedar)
* **Tsuga spp. (hemlock)

Hedges don't have to be neatly clipped, low rectangles. This evergreen arborvitae hedge allows the trees to keep their natural shape, creating a more casual look.

property—along the street, for instance—you can use the added height to advantage in creating privacy. A berm should be large enough and wide enough to look solid and natural; all too often berms are skimpy, ineffectual, and fake-looking mounds. Give the top of the berm a slight depression so it catches and holds water, allowing it to soak in rather than run off.

Keep these facts in mind when building a berm:

■ Minimum size for a berm should be 2½ feet high and 4 feet wide. An increase in height demands a proportional increase in width.

■ Changing the grade by building a berm can change drainage patterns. You might wish to include a drainage swale at the base of the berm to channel water.

■ In an area of heavy or sandy soil, a berm built of good topsoil provides a well-drained place to grow plants that otherwise would fail.

■ Avoid placing a berm on a downhill side of the house, as it will create a frost pocket.

■ A berm close to the house can act as a windbreak and provide insulation in cold climates; be sure it does not cause drainage problems along the house foundation, however.

BEST HEDGE SHRUBS

The following shrubs work well as hedge plants. Some of these shrubs work well in either type of hedge. Those recommended as formal hedges respond well to shearing; those recommended for informal hedges need little pruning to form a dense barrier, if closely planted.

FORMAL CLIPPED HEDGES

Abelia × *grandiflora* (glossy abelia)
Berberis koreana
   (Korean barberry)
Berberis thunbergii
   (Japanese barberry)
Buxus spp. (boxwood)
× *Cupressocyparis leylandii*
   (Leyland cypress)
Euonymus alatus
   (winged euonymus)
Ilex crenata (Japanese holly)
Ilex glabra (inkberry)
Ligustrum spp. (privet)
Lonicera nitida
   (boxleaf honeysuckle)
Osmanthus heterophyllus
   (holly osmanthus)
Photinia × *fraseri*
   (red-tip photinia)
Podocarpus macrophyllus
   (yew pine)
Ribes alpinum (Alpine currant)
Taxus spp. (yew)

INFORMAL HEDGES

Berberis koreana
   (Korean barberry)
Clethra alnifolia (summer-sweet)
Cornus alba (Tartarian dogwood)
Cornus sericea
   (red-osier dogwood)
Cotoneaster lucidus
   (hedge cotoneaster)
Cotoneaster multiflorus
   (many-flowered cotoneaster)
Euonymus alatus
   (winged euonymus)
Forsythia × *intermedia*
   (showy border forsythia)
Hibiscus syriacus (rose-of-Sharon)
Ilex verticillata (winterberry)
Lonicera spp. (bush honeysuckle)
Myrica cerifera (wax myrtle)
Myrica pensylvanica (bayberry)
Ribes alpinum (Alpine currant)
Rhododendron spp.
   (azalea and rhododendron)
Spiraea spp. (spirea)
Stephanandra incisa 'Crispa'
   (cutleaf stephanandra)
Syringa spp. (lilac)
Viburnum spp. (viburnum)

YARD SOLUTIONS: LANDSCAPING FOR CLIMATE CONTROL

Hot or cold winds can effectively be blocked by strategically planting trees. At the house near right, the wind blows unchecked, harming plants and making living uncomfortable for the inhabitants. At the house far right, evergreens are grouped to divert wind away from the dwelling.

The general climate of the region where you live influences the types of plants you can grow and the way you use your garden. Each region is known for its general climate characteristics. For instance, the Deep South is hot and humid during the long summer months with rain evenly spread throughout the year; the Pacific Northwest is cool, cloudy, and rainy in winter with long dry spells in summer. Athough you can't influence Mother Nature on a large scale, you can design and plant your property to moderate some of your climate's most extreme characteristics, making your home and garden feel more comfortable while you're conserving energy and saving on heating and cooling bills.

UNDERSTANDING MICROCLIMATES

Different areas of your property experience different patterns of sun, shade, wind, moisture, and frost. One garden area close to the house may be sheltered from the wind by the building and lie in shadow most of the day; it provides a perfect place to grow broad-leaved evergreens that might perish in another location. A low-lying area feels cooler than the top of the slope, and in fact plants there are susceptible to frost because cold air flows downhill and collects in this frost pocket. These small areas with markedly different growing conditions are called microclimates.

A summer breeze feels refreshing and cool, but a winter wind feels uncomfortable and frigid. Full sun is too hot in summer in most climates, but brings welcome warmth in winter. You can modify the microclimates in your garden by directing airflow and wind and by blocking or capturing sunshine at different times of the year. Experts at the U.S. Department of Energy estimate that proper planting and landscaping can cut a

MODIFYING MICROCLIMATES

Here are some planting tips for modifying the microclimates around your home:

- Plant deciduous trees on the south side of the house to block hot summer sun and allow in warming sun in winter.
- Plant evergreen or deciduous trees on the west side of the house to block hot summer sun; winter sun comes from the southwest, so the evergreens will not block it.
- Plant evergreens on the north side of the property to block prevailing winter winds; the trees will not block sun in this location.
- Prune lower branches from deciduous trees on the south side to allow the winter sun to shine beneath them; even leafless branches cut out some sunlight.
- The farther a tree is from the house, the taller it must be to effectively moderate hot sun on the roof and a patio near the house. Place a 15-foot-tall tree 10 feet from the house; place a 40-foot-tall tree 30 feet from the house.
- Use an overhead trellis or an overhang to block summer sun from windows and outdoor living areas; a 3-foot-deep overhang is usually sufficient to block hot summer sun from a window, but still allow in warming winter sun.

home's heating bill by as much as 30 percent and its air-conditioning bill by 50 to 75 percent. That means you can be more comfortable and save money, too.

THE NEED FOR TREES AND LAWN

Trees are nature's air-conditioners. They cool surrounding areas three ways: by casting shade, by evaporative cooling (water lost and evaporated from their leaves removes heat from the air), and by creating air currents that result from differences in air temperature between shaded and nonshaded areas. Scientists claim that a single large tree can provide as much cooling as five 10,000-Btu air-conditioners. Trees also muffle noise and remove pollutants from the air.

Areas of lawn are cooler than paved areas because the moisture lost from the grass blades cools the surrounding air. Pavement and buildings also absorb heat during the day and cool slowly during the night, keeping the area warmer at night than it would otherwise be; this may be an advantage in winter, but is usually a disadvantage in summer. The color of paving affects its temperature; dark colors absorb more heat, but light colors can reflect a glare. On a 90-degree day, the surface temperature of an unshaded blacktop driveway may be 140 degrees Fahrenheit; it raises the nearby air temperature by at least 5 degrees Fahrenheit. A light-colored concrete surface would be much cooler, however.

In hot climates any garden area will be cooler than a paved area, so it makes sense to reduce areas of pavement or to keep those areas shaded.

THE SUN'S ANGLES

The sun's angle changes throughout the year as the earth turns on its axis. Thus, the shadow cast by a building or tree changes in length; it is longest in winter and shortest in summer. At a latitude of 40 degrees (about equal to New York City and Denver), the sun's maximum angle is about 26 degrees in mid winter and 72 degrees in midsummer; farther north, the angle is even lower in winter and higher in summer; farther south, it is less angled.

In summer, when the sun is high in the sky, it rises in the northeast and sets in the northwest; the hottest sun comes from the west in the afternoon. In winter, when the sun is lower in the sky, it rises in the southeast and sets in the southwest; the warmest winter sunshine comes from the south between the hours of 9 a.m. and 3 p.m. For a cooling effect, shield the house from that hot afternoon sun in summer. For the greatest warming effect in winter, leave the southern exposure open and unblocked by trees during winter.

When positioned correctly, a deciduous tree casts cooling shade on the outdoor living areas, roof, and windows in summer, but allows sun to warm these areas in winter after its leaves fall off. Generally speaking, for the greatest energy-saving benefits throughout the year, you can position deciduous trees on the west and south sides of your home. The distance trees should be located from the house depends upon their height, especially on the south side. If a tree is planted too far away, the summer shadow falls short of the house and patio. If located too close to the south side, the tree casts shade in winter when it isn't welcome.

YARD SOLUTIONS:
LANDSCAPING FOR CLIMATE CONTROL
continued

BLOCKING THE WIND

Constant wind or periodic high winds during storms take their toll on landscape plants. Winter wind accompanied by full sun quickly desiccates evergreens, burning their leaves. A light breeze in summer may feel pleasantly cool, but a hot wind in a desert area or a strong wind anytime makes outdoor living uncomfortable, if not impossible.

A windbreak—a structure or planting that is wider than it is tall—slows or redirects wind. It can save gardens in windy areas and protect your home from frigid winter blasts. A windbreak affects the wind's velocity: It slows wind somewhat on the windward side, creates a windless protected area on the leeward side, and creates a protected area of lessened wind speed beyond the

Cold air tends to settle in low areas, creating especially frigid places called frost pockets. Placing plants on the slopes leading to these frost pockets blocks cold air, making a warmer microclimate for plants below.

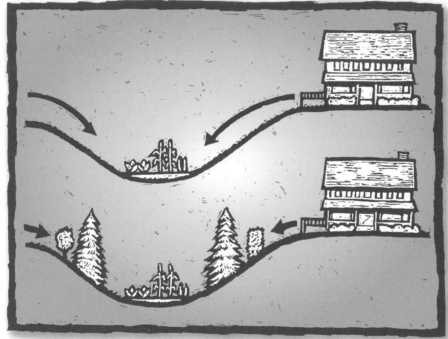

An extra-solid windbreak, such as a tall fence, isn't as effective as a less dense windbreak that allows some air through. A too-solid windbreak compresses the air and causes turbulence on the leeward side; the less dense break diverts much of the wind and slows down the rest.

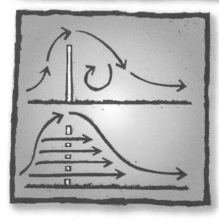

"lee," or windless pocket. A 6-foot-tall fence can be an effective windbreak, but if you need higher protection, choose a living hedge or screen.

CHANNELING THE WIND

Just as air movement can be blocked, it can be channeled. In hot, arid climates or humid climates, you can make your outdoor living area more comfortable by channeling air movement to create a cooling breeze. An opening in a windbreak allows blocked air to flow through the opening at a faster speed; this is undesirable when trying to stop wind, but desirable when trying to increase a breeze. Fortunately, winter and summer winds usually come from different directions, so summer's cooling breeze won't turn into a frigid blast in winter.

Create a wind funnel by planting two rows of deciduous or evergreen trees and shrubs in converging lines, or a "V" shape. Locate the wide opening of the "V" facing the direction of the prevailing summer breeze. Locate the opening at the tip of the "V" near the outdoor living space. Use other plantings to direct air to circulate around the house. As the funnel narrows, the air flows faster, acting as a natural air-conditioner and dehumidifier.

MODIFYING A FROST POCKET

Cold air flows like water—downhill along the surface of the ground. Low-lying areas will actually catch and hold cold air; those cold pockets can be frosty in spring and fall when higher areas are frost-free. Walls and windbreaks stop air movement and catch cold air, creating frost pockets on high ground. Don't plant tender annuals and vegetables or early-blooming trees such as magnolias and apricots in frost-prone microclimates or you may lose them to unexpected freezes.

Here's how you can warm up a frost pocket:

■ Create a barrier uphill from the frost pocket to stop airflow.

■ Make an opening—such as a gate in a fence or wall—to funnel trapped cold air out and downward.

ENERGY-CONSERVING TIPS

■ **COLD CLIMATES:** Plant an evergreen windbreak on the north and northwest sides of the property to reduce heating costs. Leave the south side of the house open to winter sun. Locate outdoor living areas on the south side of the house and use large areas of paving here to retain heat and extend the seasons for outdoor living in spring and fall. Use a blacktop driveway for best snow and ice melt.

■ **TEMPERATE CLIMATES:** Conserve energy by shading the house with deciduous trees in summer and allowing in winter sun. Locate an evergreen windbreak on the north and northwest sides of the property. Channel summer breezes around the house. Locate outdoor living areas on the east and north sides of the house and pave with a medium-colored material; shade these areas with overhead structures or deciduous trees.

■ **HOT, ARID CLIMATES:** Create windbreaks to stop hot winds and make outdoor living areas more comfortable.

Channel cool breezes around the house with clusters of tall, native trees and use trees to shade parking areas and the house roof. Keep paved areas to a minimum or shade them with overhead structures and trees to reduce heat buildup. Locate outdoor living areas on the east and north sides of the house and include an enclosed courtyard to trap cool air and to block hot wind. Use a medium-colored paving material to reduce both heat and glare. Shade west and south windows with a 3-foot-deep overhang.

■ **HOT, HUMID CLIMATES:** To reduce air-conditioning costs, use high-pruned deciduous shade trees on the south and west sides of the house to create summer shade yet not block breezes. Create wind channels to encourage summer breezes to flow around the house and dissipate muggy air. Locate outdoor living areas on the east and north sides of the house. Use light-colored paving to minimize heat. Use a 3-foot-deep overhang on south-facing windows.

CREATING EFFECTIVE WINDBREAKS

Here are some rules of thumb for establishing good windbreaks:

■ A windbreak effectively slows wind for a distance of 5 to 15 times the height of the windbreak on the leeward side.

■ A solid windbreak is less effective than one that lets some air pass through because it compresses the air and causes turbulence on the leeward side.

■ A dense windbreak slows wind speed the most, but over a shorter distance than a looser windbreak, which slows it less, but for a longer distance.

■ Wind speed is slowed most—up to 50 percent—closest to the leeward side of the windbreak, for a distance 2 to 3 times the windbreak's height.

■ Locate the windbreak perpendicular to the prevailing winds; in most regions, wind usually comes from the northwest and west in winter and from the southwest in summer, but it differs depending upon your microclimate.

■ Test the prevailing winds by erecting 5-foot-tall poles with a cloth flag tied at the top in various locations around your property. Observe these for several weeks each season and note where the wind comes from.

■ To dramatically slow winter wind, plant a dense evergreen windbreak close to the house on the north side.

■ To slow wind modestly from any direction, plant a windbreak of evergreen or dense deciduous trees in a shelterbelt 100 to 300 feet upwind from the house.

■ Be sure the windbreak is dense at the bottom to prevent wind from being channeled underneath. If tall evergreens become thin at the bottom, fill the gaps with shrubs.

■ A windbreak at the top of a hill can prevent cold air from descending and protects plants lower down from frost.

■ A dense windbreak at the bottom of a slope traps cold air and creates a frost pocket.

YARD SOLUTIONS: SHADE GARDENING

which have evolved to prosper in low light by developing delicate, thin leaves that efficiently absorb whatever sun falls on them—and the happy outcome will be a lush, beautiful shade garden.

A shade garden doesn't have to be boring. This shade garden combines colorful perennials, including pink-flowered astilbe, with a selection of hostas for a garden that's as pretty as any in full sun.

Many gardeners curse the shade, because it seems that anything they try to grow there languishes: Lawn grass grows thin and weak, and the most common and most popular shrubs and flowers flop. This sorry situation results from the all-too-common mistake of trying to grow sun-loving plants in a shady site. Choose shade-loving plants—

When planted and designed with the growing conditions in mind, a shady garden site can offer a cool welcome on a hot summer's day. Filled with alluring flowers and soft foliage spread out beneath a high canopy of leafy boughs, a shade garden can be the most beautiful spot on your property. All you need to achieve this is a palette of shade-loving plants and the know-how to properly grow them.

DEFINING SHADE

In learning to garden in the shade, keep in mind that all shade is not created equal. Figure out exactly which type of shade you're dealing with, because the type of shade determines which plants grow best.

Deep shade is all-day shade where no direct sun reaches the ground; this often occurs under heavily foliaged trees. Deep shade may be dry or moist depending upon whether the trees are surface-rooted or deep-rooted. Fewer plants thrive in this type of shade, especially if dry, than in brighter conditions.

Part shade or half shade means shade for part of the day with direct sunlight during the other part. Many sun-loving plants bloom well in half shade because they receive from four to six hours of direct sun each day, though they may not perform as well as in all-day sun. Morning shade followed by afternoon sun may be too hot for many shade plants, causing them to wilt in the heat. But the cooler morning sun with afternoon shade is good for many shade-loving plants.

Light shade or filtered shade occurs under a tree canopy of open-branched trees where spots of sunshine filter to the ground in a constantly shifting play of shadows. A wide selection of plants prospers in filtered shade.

Open shade occurs on the north side of a building where no direct sunlight falls, but where light may be reflected to the ground from surrounding walls. Open shade often remains damp, unless the building creates a rain shadow and blocks rainfall from reaching the ground.

MODIFYING SHADE

You can turn a densely shaded situation into a lightly shaded one, where you'll have a wider choice of plants, by thinning out a few tree branches. Cut branches off right at the trunk or remove side branches where they fork into a "Y". Don't leave behind unsightly stubby branches, which will sprout unnatural-looking new growth. You may have to remove or thin out branches every few years to maintain light shade conditions.

GARDENING IN DRY SHADE

Many shaded locations are cool and damp, but some are actually dry. Upon close examination you may discover that certain shady spots in your yard harbor poor, dry soil because the trees' surface roots suck up all the available moisture and nutrients. A thick canopy of tree leaves may worsen the problem, acting like an umbrella and deflecting rain from the ground beneath. Lack of moisture, not lack of light, often proves to be the culprit when shade-loving plants fail to thrive in their preferred light conditions.

HELP FOR COMPACTED SOIL

Dry, root-clogged soil feels and looks hard and compacted; when you try to dig a hole with a trowel or shovel, it can't easily penetrate the ground. If you discover that the soil in your potential shade garden is hard and compacted, try digging in lots of organic matter, such as rotted manure or compost, as long as you don't interfere with major tree roots. If tree roots prevent your digging a planting hole for a shade-loving shrub or perennial, you can sever all interfering roots smaller than an inch in diameter without harming the tree.

Where digging will tamper with tree roots, spread a layer of topsoil no more than 4 inches deep over the ground. Cover this layer with a 2-inch-deep mulch of chopped-up leaves, which will decompose into a rich humus. Anything deeper may smother the roots. Earthworms move into the decomposing leaves, further speeding the decomposition, and also burrow into the harder subsoil beneath the topsoil, making it more amenable to gardening. Where shallow-rooted trees pose a problem, you will be waging a continual battle and need to thickly replenish the mulch each year.

When gardening in the dry shade under a tree, water regularly and deeply during summer. Where you might usually apply an inch of water a week to satisfy your garden's needs, when gardening in the dry soil beneath maples, beeches, and sycamores you may need to apply 2 inches of water—1 inch for the trees and 1 inch for the flowers.

Broad stone steps give a rock garden look to this difficult growing area. Groundcovers and perennials that tolerate dry shade beautify the ground beneath shallow-rooted maples.

YARD SOLUTIONS: SHADE GARDENING
continued

Not all shade is created equal. A wide variety of plants will thrive in dappled shade, which also includes a fair amount of sun. In hot climates, especially, a little shade helps conserve moisture and prevents plants from burning up in direct sun.

Variegated leaves, such as those found on these hostas, 'Thomas Hoag' and Hosta undulata variegata, add interest in just about any garden, but are particularly important in shade gardens, where it's harder to find colorful plants with showy blooms.

This tree, at various times of day, casts shade on a patio or the lawn. Use this ever-changing play of light and shade to cool your favorite sitting spot or to create the ideal conditions for plants that thrive in light shade.

DESIGNING A SHADE GARDEN

A shade garden can be dressed up from head to toe with appropriate plants. Small, flowering trees arch above your head while shrubs—especially shade-loving broad-leaved evergreens with their glossy, dark green leaves—bloom at eye level. A carpet of perennials, ferns, and groundcovers provides foliage and flowers near the ground. Woodland wildflowers flourish in shade gardens and can turn a shady nook into a wondrous place in spring. (See pages 106–107 for more about woodland gardens.)

Shade lovers don't usually bloom as abundantly as sun worshipers, perhaps as an energy-conserving measure, but you can enjoy a host of flowers in the shade by choosing the right kinds. However, your shade garden will rely upon an assortment of beautiful foliage plants for much of its allure. You can brighten up the shadows in a shade garden with a few clever tricks:

■ Grow lots of plants with white-variegated leaves or white or pastel flowers, which seem to glow in the dark shadows.

■ Avoid dark red or purple flowers, because these colors recede into the dimness.

■ Brighten open shade along buildings by painting the walls light-reflecting white or a pastel color.

■ Use masses of golden-leaved plants and those with yellow flowers to create the impression of a beam of sunshine scattered across the garden floor.

■ Include garden statuary, furniture, or other ornaments to add interest and a focal point to a foliage garden.

■ Contrast plants with finely divided, fernlike leaves with those featuring big, tropical-looking leaves to add excitement and drama.

YARD SOLUTIONS: SHADE GARDENING

continued

SHADE-LOVING PLANTS

These plants prosper in light or half shade. Plants marked with * also do well in difficult deep shade.

ANNUALS

Begonia × semperflorens-cultorum (wax begonia)

Coleus × hybridus (coleus)

Impatiens wallerana (impatiens)

Lobularia maritima (sweet alyssum)

Torenia fournieri (wishbone flower)

Viola × wittrockiana (pansy)

BROAD-LEAVED EVERGREENS

Aucuba japonica (Japanese laurel)

Buxus sempervirens (common boxwood)

Camellia japonica (camellia)

Daphne cneorum (garland flower)

Euonymus japonica (evergreen euonymus)

Gardenia jasminoides (gardenia)

Ilex spp. (holly)

Illicium floridanum (Florida anise)

Kalmia latifolia (mountain laurel)

Leucothoe fontanesiana (drooping leucothoe)

Lonicera nitida (boxleaf honeysuckle)

Magnolia grandiflora (Southern magnolia)

Mahonia aquifolium (Oregon holly grape)

Nandina domestica (heavenly bamboo)

Osmanthus heterophyllus (holly osmanthus)

Photinia × fraseri (red-tip photinia)

Pieris spp. (pieris)

Pittosporum tobira (Japanese pittosporum)

Prunus laurocerasus (cherry laurel)

Raphiolepis indica (Indian hawthorn)

Rhododendron spp. and hybrids (azalea and rhododendron)

Skimmia japonica (Japanese skimmia)

Viburnum rhytidophyllum (leatherleaf viburnum)

BULBS

Agapanthus hybrids (lily-of-the-Nile)

Begonia × tuberhybrida (tuberous begonia)

Caladium × hortulanum (fancy-leaved caladium)

Galanthus nivalis (snowdrop)

Hyacinthoides hispanica (wood hyacinth)

Leucojum aestivum (summer snowflake)

Lilium martagon (Martagon lily)

Lycoris squamigera (resurrection lily)

CONIFERS

Abies concolor (white fir)

Calocedrus decurrens. (incense cedar)

Cedrus atlantica (Atlas cedar)

Cephalotaxus harringtonia (Japanese plum yew)

Chamaecyparis spp. (false cypress)

Cryptomeria japonica (Japanese cedar)

Picea glauca (white spruce)

Pinus flexilis (limber pine)

Podocarpus macrophyllus (yew pine)

Sciadopitys verticillata (umbrella pine)

Taxus spp. (yew)

Thuja plicata (Western red cedar)

Tsuga canadensis (Canada hemlock)

DECIDUOUS SHRUBS

Abelia × grandiflora (glossy abelia)

Aesculus parviflora (bottlebrush buckeye)

Callicarpa spp. (beautyberry)

Calycanthus floridus (sweet shrub)

Cephalanthus occidentalis (buttonbush)

Clethra alnifolia (summer-sweet)

Corylopsis spp. (winter hazel)

Daphne × burkwoodii (Burkwood daphne)

Dirca palustris (leatherwood)

Euonymus alatus (winged euonymus)

Fothergilla gardenii (dwarf fothergilla)

Hamamelis spp. (witch hazel)

Hydrangea macrophylla (French hydrangea)

Hydrangea quercifolia (oakleaf hydrangea)

Ilex decidua (possum haw)

Ilex verticillata (winterberry)

Itea japonica (Japanese sweetspire)

Kerria japonica (Japanese rose)

Lindera benzoin (spicebush)

Lonicera fragrantissima (winter honeysuckle)

Paeonia suffruticosa (tree peony)

Philadelphus coronarius (sweet mock orange)

Rhododendron hybrids (Knap Hill, Exbury, and Mollis hybrid azaleas)

Rhododendron spp. (native azalea)

Salix purpurea (purple osier)

Sorbaria sorbifolia (Ural false spirea)

Symphoricarpos spp. (snowberry)

Viburnum plicatum forma *tomentosum* (double file viburnum)

Weigela florida (old-fashioned weigela)

DECIDUOUS TREES

Acer palmatum (Japanese maple)

Acer pensylvanicum (striped maple)

Aesculus glabra (Ohio buckeye)

Amelanchier spp. (serviceberry)

Carpinus caroliniana (American hornbeam)

Catalpa bignonioides (catalpa)

Celtis occidentalis (common hackberry)

Cercidiphyllum japonicum (Katsura tree)

Cercis canadensis (Eastern redbud)

Cornus florida (flowering dogwood)

Cornus mas (Cornelian cherry)

Halesia carolina (Carolina silverbell)

Magnolia × soulangiana (saucer magnolia)

Nyssa sylvatica (black gum)

Oxydendrum arboreum (sourwood)

Parrotia persica (Persian parrotia)

Stewartia pseudocamellia (Japanese stewartia)

Styrax japonicus (Japanese snowbell)

FERNS

*Adiantum pedatum (maidenhair fern)

*Athyrium nipponicum 'Pictum' (Japanese painted fern)

*Cyrtomium falcatum (Japanese holly fern)

*Dryopteris marginalis (marginal shield fern)

Osmunda cinnamomea (cinnamon fern)

Polystichum acrostichoides (Christmas fern)

Polystichum munitum (Western sword fern)

ORNAMENTAL GRASSES

Carex elata 'Bowles Golden' (golden sedge)

Carex morrowii (Japanese sedge)

Chasmanthium latifolium (sea oats)

Hakonechloa macra 'Aureola' (Japanese wind grass)

PERENNIALS AND BIENNIALS

Aconitum spp. (monkshood)

Alchemilla mollis (lady's-mantle)

Anemone × hybrida (Japanese anemone)

Astilbe spp. (astilbe)

Begonia grandis (hardy begonia)

*Cimicifuga spp. (bugbane)

Corydalis lutea (yellow corydalis)

*Dicentra spp. (bleeding-heart)

Digitalis purpurea (foxglove)

Eupatorium coelestinum (hardy ageratum)

Helleborus niger (Christmas rose)

Hemerocallis fulva (tawny daylily)

*Hosta cultivars (hosta)

Lamium maculatum (spotted dead nettle)

Ligularia spp. (ligularia)

Liriope muscari (blue lilyturf)

Lunaria annua (honesty)

Myosotis sylvatica (woodland forget-me-not)

Phlox stolonifera (creeping phlox)

Primula spp. (primrose)

*Pulmonaria saccharata (Bethlehem sage)

VINES AND GROUNDCOVERS

Actinidia kolomikta (Kolomikta vine)

*Aegopodium podagraria 'Variegatum' (bishop's weed)

*Ajuga reptans (bugleweed)

Akebia quinata (five-leaf akebia)

*Arctostaphylos uva-ursi (bearberry)

*Asarum caudatum (British Columbia wild ginger)

*Bignonia capreolata (cross vine)

Campsis radicans (trumpet creeper)

Ceratostigma plumbaginoides (leadwort)

*Chrysogonum virginianum (goldenstar)

Clematis × hybrida (hybrid clematis)

Clematis maximowicziana (sweet autumn clematis)

Cobaea scandens (cup-and-saucer vine)

Convallaria majalis (lily-of-the-valley)

Epimedium spp. (bishop's hat)

Ficus pumila (creeping fig)

Galax urceolata (galax)

*Gaultheria procumbens (checkerberry)

Gelsemium sempervirens (Carolina jasmine)

*Hedera helix (English ivy)

Hydrangea petiolaris (climbing hydrangea)

Jasminum nudiflorum (winter jasmine)

Juniperus conferta (shore juniper)

Liriope spicata (creeping lilyturf)

Lonicera × heckrottii (goldflame honeysuckle)

Lysimachia nummularia (creeping Jenny)

*Mazus reptans (mazus)

Pachysandra terminalis (Japanese spurge)

*Parthenocissus quinquefolia (Virginia creeper)

Polygonum aubertii (silver lace vine)

*Saxifraga stolonifera (strawberry begonia)

Thunbergia alata (black-eyed Susan vine)

Trachelospermum jasminoides (confederate jasmine)

Vinca minor (myrtle)

YARD SOLUTIONS: COPING WITH POOR SOIL

LIFE ON THE LEAN SIDE

Many attractive trees, shrubs, perennials, and groundcovers, notably ones hailing from the Mediterranean, thrive in sharply draining soil and get by with little in the way of nutrients. Other drought-tolerant plants, such as the perennial sunflowers native to the prairies of the Great Plains, have extensive root systems that penetrate deeply into the ground in search of moisture. Still other plants, such as the sedums and stonecrops, have fleshy leaves or roots that store water to use later in periods of drought.

By choosing these well-adapted plants for poor-soil situations, you are ahead of the game in all respects. Your garden can be a delightful display of easy-care flowers and foliage designed in any style you wish. Create a formal border to frame a lawn, a terraced hillside with plants spilling over the retaining walls, or an alpine-style rock garden. As long as you choose the right plants for the growing conditions, you'll be rewarded with easy-care beauty in an otherwise difficult site.

COUNTERACTING POOR SOIL

Poor soil is usually naturally dry, and you may need to water frequently even if you install appropriate plants. If you don't want to use a lot of irrigation water, you may wish to turn your garden into a water-conserving Xeriscape garden (see pages 94–95). Otherwise, here are a few ways to combat poor soil conditions:

■ Spread an inch or two of organic matter across the soil surface when preparing a new bed and work it into the top 6 inches or so of the soil.

■ Cover exposed soil with 3- to 4-inch-thick organic mulch and renew it every year. The mulch reduces evaporation from the soil surface and slowly breaks down into vital organic matter to replenish the soil.

■ Water newly installed plants throughout their first growing season—even if they are drought-tolerant types—to help them establish good root systems.

■ Water during dry periods by letting the sprinkler run slowly and for a long time to allow water to soak several feet into the ground. This encourages roots to go deeper once surface water is depleted.

■ Apply a slow-release, organic-based fertilizer twice a year—once in early spring and again in midsummer—to compensate for the soil's low-nutrient content.

Many plants actually prefer impoverished soil, such as this grouping of sedum, silver-leaved artemisia, and society garlic.

Poor, sandy, or gravelly soil stresses most plants because it is infertile, lacking in nutrient-rich, water-holding organic matter. Rain and irrigation water run right though sandy soil, and fertilizer leaches away quickly. Although you can dramatically improve poor soil's water-holding capacity by working in copious amounts of organic matter such as rotted manure, leaf mold, or compost, the effort is enormous. It is far easier to design a garden using plants adapted to the tough growing conditions.

PLANTS FOR POOR SOIL

The following plants perform well in infertile or sandy and gravelly soil, which stunts many ornamentals:

ANNUALS

Brachycome iberidifolia (Swan River daisy)
Calendula officinalis (pot marigold)
Centaurea cyanus (cornflower)
Dianthus chinensis (China pink)
Eschscholzia californica (California poppy)
Gaillardia pulchella (annual blanket flower)
Gazania rigens (treasure flower)
Gomphrena globosa (globe amaranth)
Helianthus annuus (sunflower)
Helichrysum bracteatum (strawflower)
Lobularia maritima (sweet alyssum)
Lupinus texensis (Texas bluebonnet)
Melampodium paludosum (blackfoot daisy)
Papaver spp. (poppy)
Petunia × *hybrida* (petunia)
Portulaca grandiflora (moss rose)
Tithonia rotundifolia (Mexican sunflower)

BULBS

Crocus chrysanthus (snow crocus)
Muscari botryoides (grape hyacinth)
Tulipa saxatilis (tulip)

DECIDUOUS SHRUBS

Caryopteris × *clandonensis* (bluebeard)
Cytisus × *praecox* (Warminster broom)
Elaeagnus umbellata (autumn olive)
Genista tinctoria (common woadwaxen)

Hypericum frondosum (golden St.-John's-wort)
Ilex decidua (possum haw)
Lespedeza thunbergii (bush clover)
Myrica pensylvanica (bayberry)
Potentilla fruticosa (shrubby cinquefoil)
Symphoricarpos albus (snowberry)
Weigela florida (old-fashioned weigela)

DECIDUOUS TREES

Acer campestre (hedge maple)
Acer saccharinum (silver maple)
Fraxinus pennsylvanica (red ash)
Populus alba (white poplar)
Robinia pseudoacacia (black locust)
Zelkova serrata (Japanese zelkova)

EVERGREEN TREES AND SHRUBS

Juniperus chinensis (Chinese juniper)
Juniperus scopulorum (Rocky Mountain juniper)
Juniperus virginiana (Eastern red cedar)
Nandina domestica (heavenly bamboo)
Picea glauca (white spruce)
Picea orientalis (Oriental spruce)
Pinus rigida (pitch pine)
Rosa rugosa (rugosa rose)
Yucca smalliana (Adam's needle)

PERENNIALS

Acanthus spp. (bear's breeches)
Achillea spp. (yarrow)
Asclepias tuberosa (butterfly weed)
Aurinia saxatilis (basket-of-gold)
Cerastium tomentosum (snow-in-summer)
Coreopsis verticillata (thread-leaved coreopsis)
Echinacea purpurea (purple coneflower)
Gaura lindheimeri (gaura)

Gypsophila spp. (baby's-breath)
Helianthus angustifolius (fall sunflower)
Heliopsis helianthoides (false sunflower)
Lavandula angustifolia (lavender)
Liatris spicata (gay-feather)
Nepeta spp. (catmint)
Oenothera speciosa (showy primrose)
Perovskia atriplicifolia (Russian sage)
Rudbeckia fulgida (orange coneflower)
Santolina chamaecyparissus (lavender cotton)
Sedum spp. (stonecrop)
Stachys byzantina (lamb's-ears)
Thymus spp. (thyme)

VINES AND GROUNDCOVERS

Arctostaphylos uva-ursi (bearberry)
Campsis radicans (trumpet creeper)
Cobaea scandens (cup-and-saucer vine)
Epimedium spp. (bishop's hat)
Ipomoea × *multifida* (cardinal climber)
Ipomoea tricolor (morning glory)
Jasminum nudiflorum (winter jasmine)
Juniperus conferta (shore juniper)
Juniperus horizontalis (creeping juniper)
Wisteria floribunda (Japanese wisteria)

Rugosa rose

YARD SOLUTIONS: WORKING WITH POORLY DRAINED SITES

Instead of draining a wet site, landscape it with plants that prefer having their feet wet. Many types of iris, including this yellow-flag iris, grow and bloom best in wet soil.

A unique and beautiful assortment of plants prefers soggy soil. Some plants even flourish in standing water and are undaunted by periodic flooding. Some of these plants are quite adaptable to ordinary moist garden conditions, although they grow even more vigorously in a soggy site.

ASSESSING WET SOILS

Wet conditions can bring problems, such as flooded basements, standing water, or soggy soil. Heavy, compacted soil drains slowly to begin with. Combine slow-draining soil with a high natural water table, a sloping site where water runs off quickly, or an incorrectly graded site, and that spells trouble.

If poor drainage causes continual flooding in your basement or standing water close to the house, you may need to install drainage pipes to channel away water. You can take on small projects yourself or call in a professional if the problem is serious. A certified landscape architect usually can correct serious drainage and

INSTALLING DRAINAGE PIPES

To channel subsurface water away from the house or from where it collects and makes an area soggy, lay drainage pipes in a drainage ditch (drainage swale) along the base of a foundation, wall, or patio—wherever water collects. Rather than using tiles, these days most landscapers use perforated flexible plastic drainpipe.
1. Dig a trench 4 inches wider than the drainpipe and about 1 foot deep.
2. Slope the entire length of the trench so that it gradually lowers, at a rate of ⅛ of an inch or more for every foot of horizontal run.

3. Lay 2 inches of gravel at the bottom of the trench.
4. Lay the perforated pipe with holes positioned at the bottom of the trench to prevent clogging.
5. Cover the pipe with 2 inches of gravel.
6. Fill the trench with soil and lay down sod if the trench is in a lawn or plant appropriate garden plants.
7. Discharge the drainpipe into a basin, dry well, natural or man-made pond, or sewer. Perforated pipe may be connected to nonperforated pipe to channel water through areas where soggy soil is not a problem.

PLANTS FOR WET OR BOGGY SITES

The following plants will beautify a wet or boggy site with their flowers and foliage. Plants marked with * tolerate boggy soil or standing water, especially in spring; others do best in constantly wet to damp soil.

ANNUALS

Mimulus × *hybridus* (monkey-flower)

BULBS

Lilium canadense (Canada lily)
Zantedeschia aethiopica (calla lily)

DECIDUOUS TREES

Acer negundo (box elder)
Acer rubrum (red maple)
Acer saccharinum (silver maple)
Amelanchier arborea (downy serviceberry)
Betula nigra (river birch)
Carpinus caroliniana (American hornbeam)
Catalpa bignonioides (common catalpa)
Celtis occidentalis (common hackberry)
Larix laricina (American larch)
Nyssa sylvatica (black gum)
Platanus occidentalis (sycamore)
Quercus alba (white oak)
Quercus bicolor (swamp white oak)
Quercus nigra (water oak)
Quercus nuttallii (Nuttall's oak)
Quercus palustris (pin oak)
Salix alba 'Tristis' (golden weeping willow)
Ulmus americana (American elm)

EVERGREENS

Chamaecyparis thyoides (Atlantic white cedar)
Ilex glabra (inkberry)
Magnolia grandiflora (Southern magnolia)
Magnolia virginiana (sweet bay)
Pinus elliottii (slash pine)
Pinus taeda (loblolly pine)
Taxodium distichum (bald cypress)
Thuja occidentalis (arborvitae)

PERENNIALS AND FERNS

Bergenia spp. (bergenia)
Caltha palustris (marsh marigold)
Chelone spp. (turtlehead)
Cimicifuga spp. (bugbane)
Dryopteris spp. (wood fern)
Eupatorium purpureum (Joe-Pye weed)
Filipendula rubra (queen-of-the-prairie)
Iris ensata (Japanese iris)
Iris laevigata (blue flag iris)
Iris pseudacorus (yellow flag)
Iris sibirica (Siberian iris)
Matteuccia pensylvanica (ostrich fern)
Myosotis sylvatica (woodland forget-me-not)
Osmunda cinnamomea (cinnamon fern)
Osmunda regalis (royal fern)
Primula japonica (Japanese primrose)
Rodgersia spp. (rodgersia)

SHRUBS

Aronia arbutifolia (red chokeberry)
Callicarpa dichotoma (purple beautyberry)
Calycanthus floridus (sweet shrub)
Cephalanthus occidentalis (buttonbush)
Clethra alnifolia (summer-sweet)
Cornus alba (Tartarian dogwood)
Cornus sericea (red-osier dogwood)
Dirca palustris (leatherwood)
Hamamelis vernalis (vernal witch hazel)
Ilex decidua (possum haw)
Ilex verticillata (winterberry)
Itea virginica (Virginia sweetspire)
Rhododendron atlanticum (coast azalea)
Rhododendron viscosum (swamp azalea)
Salix discolor (pussy willow)
Salix purpurea (purple osier)
Viburnum nudum (withe-rod)
Viburnum trilobum (American cranberry bush)

VINES AND GROUNDCOVERS

Arctostaphylos uva-ursi (bearberry)
Bignonia capreolata (cross vine)
Campsis radicans (trumpet creeper)
Mazus reptans (mazus)

grading problems. Keep in mind that anytime you regrade the soil, even slightly, drainage patterns can change, often to the detriment of your home and garden.

Wet or boggy sites that don't threaten your home or your comfort need not be drained and can be transformed. Let nature guide you. You can create a lovely wetland garden in that otherwise soggy spot by planting water-loving trees, shrubs, perennials, and ferns.

Consider plants that like wet feet to adorn the edges of a natural pond or stream bank. Plant groups of appropriate shrubs interspersed with ferns and perennials in a natural arrangement anywhere the ground is wet—to enhance rather than fight the site Mother Nature created.

YARD SOLUTIONS: CREATING A WATER-CONSERVING LANDSCAPE

You can have a lush-looking garden even while using little water. Lavender, creeping thyme, and sedum thrive in hot, dry conditions.

No matter where you live, conserving water makes sense. In arid areas of the country, especially the West, scarce rainfall limits gardening endeavors, and only extensive irrigation allows you to create a traditional landscape and lawn. The population boom in the Sunbelt means that more people than ever are now competing for the same scarce water. Conservation has to be the name of the game in these areas.

Even in traditionally water-rich areas of the country, water is becoming a precious resource due to periodic droughts and increasing populations.

Almost 50 percent of the water consumed by households is used not for drinking, washing, and bathing, but for irrigating lawns and gardens and filling swimming pools. And much of this water is wasted because of overwatering or runoff. This costly waste of natural resources can be greatly reduced by using water-conserving gardening practices. Water consumption in the garden can easily be reduced to 25 percent of the water bill if you know how, and without sacrificing the beauty of your property.

XERISCAPE GARDENS

A Xeriscape is the trademarked term for a landscape designed for low water use. Many people think this fancy term translates into an unattractive and barren landscape where gravel replaces lawn and cactus replaces shrubs.

But in reality a Xeriscape garden can be as beautiful and colorful as a traditional landscape if you follow the same design principles you would use in any garden.

The difference lies mainly in choosing drought-tolerant plants to carry out your design and then following other water-conserving practices.

LOW-WATER-USE PLANTS

Plants that tolerate drought are the mainstay of the Xeriscape garden. A wide selection of exotic and native plants can fill that bill. Many hail from Mediterranean countries and adapt well to arid coastal conditions. Others tolerate the dry, windswept areas of mountain regions; still others are desert dwellers. Native plants from your region of the country should adapt well to a Xeriscape if you live in an arid or desert region; you can find them at specialty nurseries.

Many drought-tolerant plants have small, fine-textured leaves or are

XERISCAPING BASICS

You can conserve water and probably reduce your water bill by half if you follow these easy and logical gardening guidelines:

■ Reduce lawn size or eliminate lawn entirely by instead planting groundcovers and beds of low shrubs and flowers.

■ Seed or sod lawns with low-water-use turf grasses.

■ Do not plant shrubs and trees in lawns, but in independent planting beds that can be watered separately.

■ Choose drought-tolerant landscape plants.

■ Locate drought-tolerant shade trees to cool hot exposures and reduce water needs.

■ Prepare the soil before planting by adding water-holding organic matter.

■ Mulch well to reduce evaporation.

■ Irrigate only when and where needed and apply the correct amount of water.

■ Use drip irrigation where practical.

■ Combine plants that have the same water needs into large planting areas and use separate irrigation zones keyed to each area's water requirements.

covered with gray or silvery hairs as a water-conserving measure. Some boast large, succulent, waxy stems and leaves for storing water. Thorns often protect them from animals.

Although these drought-tolerant plants perform perfectly well with a minimum of water, they often fail if planted in heavy clay, even if it is dry, because clay soil does not hold much oxygen. These plants need loose, oxygen-rich soil. When planning a Xeriscape in heavy clay soil, try creating large, raised berms, at least 2 feet high, of well-drained soil on top of the clay and use these as planting beds. The plants will thrive and the berms will create interesting contours in the garden.

DESIGNING A XERISCAPE

To create a pleasing Xeriscape, follow the same rules of scale, proportion, and plant placement that you would in any other type of garden. The textures and colors of drought-tolerant plants combine well to create a beautiful design. Though they do not possess the bright green lushness of tropical and temperate plants, their spare, silvery look has a beauty of its own. These plants blend with the natural landscape around your home and give your garden a sense of place.

SENSIBLE GROUPINGS

Some Xeriscape experts like to separate suitable plants into several groups—extra-low water use, low water use, and moderate water use. It helps to use these groupings in areas where drought is serious, because a major principle in Xeriscaping—and traditional gardening, too—is to group plants with the same water needs into the

same plantings. Keep those with higher water requirements near the house, where they are easily observed and watered. Use the most drought-tolerant ones farthest from the house.

NONPLANT FEATURES

You can dress up your garden and make it more interesting and livable by adding natural features such as large boulders, dry stream beds made of polished river rocks, and other features in keeping with the look of your Xeriscape. Driftwood and other pieces of weathered wood are traditional ornaments. Create a stone patio and walkways from local flagstones to blend with the boulders and other rocks.

In arid or seashore regions, large areas of crushed granite, gravel, or stones can blanket the dusty earth with compatible textures and earth tones where you do not want a lawn or groundcover plantings. Avoid white gravel; it looks too bright and unnatural and also reflects heat and light onto plants, causing burning. Give these stony areas an interesting shape, and they'll become easy-care design assets.

LAWN IN A XERISCAPE

Many Xeriscapes eliminate lawn, because traditional lawn grasses drink up water. You need not forgo a lawn altogether if it serves a practical purpose. Reduce the lawn to a small but functional size—the size you need for sunbathing, playing ball, or other activities—then plant it with a drought-tolerant grass.

Kentucky bluegrass, the thirstiest lawn grass, is widely planted in the Midwest and West where there is not enough rain to sustain it; constant

irrigation is needed to keep it green. Bluegrass is the most popular turf grass in the Northeast, too. You can achieve that same bright green appearance by planting tall, turf-type fescue, which needs only about half the water of bluegrass to stay green.

That brilliant green turf can look artificial and jarring in an arid or desert garden. In Xeriscapes that rely

on silver-toned, small-leaved natives and Mediterranean plants, one of the native turf grasses, such as buffalo grass, makes a better choice. These slow-growing, drought-resistant native grasses are a dusky blue-green or gray-green color that looks better with the silvery hues of many Xeriscape plants. Surviving on rainfall alone or an occasional watering, these native grasses need mowing only once or twice a year, if at all—another resource-saving advantage.

Waterwise landscapes not only don't require much water, they don't require much maintenance. In this landscape, traditional lawn is replaced with no-fuss junipers, rugosa roses, and lavender.

YARD SOLUTIONS: CREATING A WATER-CONSERVING LANDSCAPE

continued

XERISCAPE PLANTS

The following plants are widely adapted for Xeriscape gardens across the country. If you live in an arid or desert region, seek out locally grown native plants from a specialty nursery in addition to any of these plants that will grow in your region. Plants marked with * grow in dry shade.

ANNUALS

Brachycome iberidifolia (Swan River daisy)
Calendula officinalis (pot marigold)
Cleome hasslerana (spider flower)
Cosmos spp. (cosmos)
Eschscholzia californica (California poppy)
Gaillardia pulchella (annual blanket flower)
Helianthus annuus (sunflower)
Helichrysum bracteatum (strawflower)
Nigella damascena (love-in-a-mist)
Papaver spp. (poppy)
Portulaca grandiflora (moss rose)
Sanvitalia procumbens (creeping zinnia)
Tagetes spp. (marigold)
Verbena × hybrida (verbena)
Zinnia angustifolia (narrow-leaf zinnia)

BULBS

Allium spp. (ornamental onion)
Crocus spp. (crocus)
Tulipa spp. (tulip)

DECIDUOUS SHRUBS

*Abelia × grandiflora (glossy abelia)
Berberis spp. (barberry)
Buddleia spp. (butterfly bush)
Caryopteris × clandonensis (bluebeard)
Cytisus spp. (broom)
Genista spp. (woadwaxen)
*Hibiscus syriacus (rose-of-Sharon)
*Kerria japonia (Japanese rose)
Kolkwitzia amabilis (beautybush)
*Lonicera spp. (bush honeysuckle)
Myrica pensylvanica (bayberry)
Philadelphus spp. (mock orange)
Potentilla fruticosa (shrubby cinquefoil)
Rhus spp. (sumac)
Ribes alpinum (Alpine currant)
Rosa rugosa (rugosa rose)
Symphoricarpos spp. (snowberry)
Syringa spp. (lilac)
Tamarix spp. (tamarisk)
Vitex agnus-castus (chaste tree)

DECIDUOUS TREES

Acer tataricum subsp. *ginnala* (Amur maple)
*Aesculus glabra (Ohio buckeye)
Amelanchier spp. (shadblow)
Celtis occidentalis (common hackberry)
Elaeagnus angustifolia (Russian olive)
Fraxinus pennsylvanica (green ash)
Gleditsia triacanthos var. *inermis* (thornless honey locust)
Gymnocladus dioica (Kentucky coffee tree)
Koelreuteria paniculata (golden-rain tree)
Lagerstroemia indica (crape myrtle)
Quercus macrocarpa (bur oak)

Robinia pseudoacacia (black locust)

Sophora japonica (Japanese pagoda tree)

Sorbus aucuparia (European mountain ash)

Ulmus parvifolia (lacebark elm)

Ulmus pumila (Siberian elm)

EVERGREENS

Juniperus × media 'Pfitzerana' (Pfitzer Chinese juniper)

Juniperus scopulorum (Rocky Mountain juniper)

Juniperus squamata 'Blue Star' (Blue Star juniper)

Juniperus virginiana (Eastern red cedar)

Mahonia aquifolium (Oregon holly grape)

Mahonia bealei (leatherleaf mahonia)

Pinus aristata (bristlecone pine)

Pinus banksiana (Jack pine)

Pinus edulis (Pinyon pine)

Pinus flexilis (limber pine)

Pinus mugo (Mugo pine)

Pinus nigra (Austrian pine)

Pinus ponderosa (Ponderosa pine)

Pinus rigida (pitch pine)

Pinus sylvestris (Scotch pine)

Yucca smalliana (Adam's needle)

GROUNDCOVERS

Aegopodium podagraria 'Variegatum' (bishop's weed)

Ajuga reptans (bugleweed)

Arctostaphylos uva-ursi (bearberry)

Juniperus conferta (shore juniper)

Juniperus horizontalis (creeping juniper)

Juniperus sabina (savin juniper)

Liriope spicata (creeping lilyturf)

Rosmarinus officinalis var. *prostratus* (creeping rosemary)

Stachys byzantina 'Silver Carpet' (lamb's-ears)

Thymus serpyllum (wild thyme)

ORNAMENTAL GRASSES

Cortaderia selloana 'Pumila' (dwarf pampas grass)

Elymus arenarius 'Glaucus' (blue wild rye)

Festuca amethystina (sheep's fescue)

Festuca ovina var. 'Glauca' (blue fescue)

Helictotrichon sempervirens (blue oat grass)

Panicum virgatum (switch grass)

Phalaris arundinacea 'Picta' (ribbon grass)

PERENNIALS

Acanthus mollis (bear's breeches)

Achillea spp. (yarrow)

Armeria maritima (sea thrift)

Asclepias tuberosa (butterfly weed)

Aurinia saxatilis (basket-of-gold)

Belamcanda chinensis (blackberry lily)

Calamintha nepeta (calamint)

Cerastium tomentosum (snow-in-summer)

Coreopsis verticillata (thread-leaved coreopsis)

Echinacea purpurea (purple coneflower)

Euphorbia polychroma (cushion spurge)

Gypsophila spp. (baby's-breath)

Helianthus angustifolius (swamp sunflower)

Heliopsis helianthoides (sweet oxeye)

Iris × germanica (bearded iris)

Lavandula angustifolia (English lavender)

Liatris spicata (gay-feather)

Nepeta spp. (catmint)

Oenothera berlandieri (showy primrose)

Perovskia atriplicifolia (Russian sage)

Rudbeckia fulgida (orange coneflower)

Sedum spp. (stonecrop)

Stachys byzantina (lamb's-ears)

Verbena canadensis (clump verbena)

VINES

Campsis radicans (trumpet creeper)

Cobaea scandens (cup-and-saucer vine)

Euonymus fortunei (wintercreeper)

Ipomoea tricolor (morning glory)

Lonicera sempervirens (trumpet honeysuckle)

Parthenocissus quinquefolia (Virginia creeper)

Parthenocissus tricuspidata (Boston ivy)

Polygonum aubertii (silver lace vine)

Pyracantha coccinea (firethorn)

Rosa banksiae (Lady Banks rose)

Thunbergia alata (black-eyed Susan vine)

Wisteria sinensis (Chinese wisteria)

YARD SOLUTIONS: GARDENING ON A SLOPE

TURNING A PROBLEM INTO A PLUS

Unless you envision a swimming pool or a croquet court, your difficult slope can become a garden asset. You can modify the slope somewhat, making it more friendly.

IDEAS FOR SLOPE LANDSCAPING

Here are some good ways to take advantage of a sloping property and minimize problems:

■ Build a raised deck to hang over a steep slope; this will give you flat outdoor living space and a fine view.

■ Design a viewing garden at the bottom of the slope to be seen from the top of the slope.

■ Plant the slope with groundcovers, trees, and shrubs for an easy-care design solution.

■ Terrace the slope into several flat levels with retaining walls and use the terraces for flower gardens.

■ Turn the slope into a natural-looking rock garden by installing large boulders and outcroppings of native rocks.

By leveling part of a slope and terracing the rest, a peaceful retreat has been carved out of this landscape.

Steep slopes can be the nemesis of gardeners. Rain and irrigation water run off rather than slowly percolating through the soil, and they may even cause erosion and drainage problems. If the slope is really steep, it may be difficult to even get a footing. Digging planting holes is challenging if not impossible. The steeper the slope of a lawn area, the more difficult—and even dangerous—it is to mow.

Once properly planted, the vertical rise makes a becoming and special way to show off plants, and the hilly terrain creates a natural mood and gives a special dimension to a garden.

From the bottom of a hill you can look up at the undersides of tree branches and enjoy them from an entirely different perspective. This is the best way to view Carolina silverbell or Japanese snowbell, for instance, because their lovely, bell-like, white blossoms dangle in clusters from the undersides of their branches.

Some plants are best viewed from above; from the top of a slope you can look down on them. The display of blossoms and berries of double-file viburnum, which decorate the tops of the shrub's flat, horizontal branches, look most spectacular when seen from a higher vantage point.

Weeping trees look especially magnificent planted on a slope, where their branches cascade in a waterfall effect. Low, spreading plants can be made to tumble down a hillside, too, spilling their way to the bottom. Positioning plants according to height becomes an easier task, because the rise of the slope allows short plants to stand above taller ones farther down the slope.

MODIFYING A SLOPE

A slope may need to be regraded if its existing contours have been changed during home construction, resulting in serious erosion or drainage problems. Builders might have sliced into hillsides without properly regrading or retaining the land when putting in a home. You may need a professional landscape architect to correct the situation.

The most time-honored way to deal with a steep slope is to divide it into several level terraces so it resembles a giant staircase. You can define and hold the terraces in place with any number of materials. Landscape timbers are most economical and can look quite attractive. Stone or brick walls cost more, but make more exciting choices. Whichever you choose, be sure the material matches your home's construction and design.

Keep several factors in mind when terracing the hillside. Make the terraces as deep as you can and the retaining walls no more than about 3 feet tall, if possible, for the best aesthetic effect. Be sure to install drainage pipes behind the retaining walls to prevent the walls from breaking due to pent-up water pressure or built-up ice, which forces stones out of place.

Give yourself access to a slope, whether it is terraced or not, by creating a path with a set of wide stairs that invites you to climb to the top. Creating a staircase that goes from terrace to terrace invites people into the garden and allows you easy access for planting and maintenance. The path and stairs may wind up the hill, zigzagging back and forth on an extra-steep hill, or carve a straight track on a gentle slope. Use the same material as in the retaining walls to create the stairs or make them

inexpensively from landscape timbers or cedar logs to define the rise of the stairs and simply cover the treads with whatever material you use to mulch the garden.

USING RAILROAD TIES AND LANDSCAPE TIMBERS

Authentic railroad ties are rarely used in landscaping because they are treated with creosote, a preservative that is toxic to people and plants. Instead, landscape timbers, which measure 8 feet long and either 6×6, 6×8, or 8×8 inches around are used for retaining walls and stairs; they are made of pressure-treated pine and are nontoxic, long-lasting, and uniform.

A preservative is forced deep into pressure-treated wood and lasts longer than painted-on preservative. According to the Environmental Protection Agency, pressure-treated wood is not toxic to plants, and the preservatives do not leach into the soil; however, some people still prefer to use a naturally rot-resistant wood when building raised vegetable gardens.

When sawing pressure-treated wood, wear a face mask to prevent inhaling or ingesting the dust particles, which can prove harmful. Also, do not burn pressure-treated wood; it releases toxic fumes.

PREVENTING EROSION

Slopes sometimes present erosion problems because of fast water runoff. You can slow the water by terracing, but short of that there are other tactics to take. Select deep-rooted plants that bind the soil. Most groundcovers work wonders at controlling erosion; they are deep-rooted and their spreading branches

and leaves stop water from running downhill faster than does grass. Good choices include English ivy, cotoneaster, bearberry, myrtle, broom, wintercreeper, and creeping junipers.

INSTALLING PLANTS

Planting on a slope can be difficult. Be sure to position trunks of trees and shrubs so they grow straight toward the sky. This poses a problem if they have a large root ball. You need to create a small, level terrace around the planting hole to properly bury the root ball while keeping the trunk straight. Create a basin to catch irrigation water over the terrace. Hold the terrace and root ball in place with logs or rocks until the tree is established.

When planting groundcovers on a slope, be sure to mulch well until the groundcover fills in to keep down weeds and slow down water runoff. Shredded bark mulch holds well on a slope, binding itself into a dense erosion-resistant mat.

Steps are an important part of gardening on a slope, providing easy access to different levels and giving structure to the landscape.

SPECIAL GARDENS: DESIGNING A COUNTRY COTTAGE GARDEN

Country gardens are appealing because of their easy, casual look that bespeaks a gardener who loves flowers more than fuss.

Traditionally, cottage gardens were practical; the plants grown in them served primarily as food, medicines, dyes, and fibers. The beauty of their flowers and foliage came as an afterthought. However, your cottage garden can celebrate the abundance of flower color, texture, and fragrance as the first consideration.

GETTING STARTED

A cottage garden's country feel comes from informally arranging appropriate flowers and herbs in combination with rustic or romantic structures, and perhaps whimsical sculpture or found objects, in a seemingly unstudied design.

You will want to plan the lines and bones of the garden to give it an appealing design; perhaps you can lay it out in raised beds filled with a lush mix of plants. Whether in the city, suburbs, or actual country, you can lend a country feel to your garden by surrounding it with a picket or split-rail fence, rose-draped arbor, or fieldstone wall. A gazebo creates a romantic getaway where you can relax and enjoy the garden surrounded by perfumed flowers. The garden's unplanned look gives it its friendliness and invites you to enjoy its welcoming charm.

You can locate your cottage garden in the traditional manner along the walk to your home's front door, or place it anywhere else on your property where it gets full sun. Use the side of your house, garage, barn, or toolshed as one garden wall, enclosing the other sides with a rustic fence or stone wall. Embellish the garden's entrance with a gate or an arbor.

A path leading from the gate through the garden is a must, whether it takes you to the kitchen or front door or to a bench under an apple tree. Although tradition calls for a functional, straight path, you can be creative and lay out a meandering walkway with plants spilling over the edges if you wish. Just keep the paving simple. Gravel or used bricks make suitable and inexpensive choices. Or, you could lay down cobblestones or stepping-stones and interplant them with fragrant paving plants, which are low, rock garden plants. (See page 61 for a list of paving plants.)

Cottage garden flowers include perennials, bulbs, and self-seeding annuals, often planted together with herbs and vegetables. If you want a bit of order in your garden, you can arrange perennials in random patches. Surround them with self-sowing annuals; each year, the annuals' serendipitous arrangements bring delightful surprises to the garden. Tuck culinary herbs and vegetables wherever you find spaces or plant them to edge a path. Imagine a pretty frill of curly parsley creating a scalloped edging along the walk or pastel green leaf lettuces thriving in the shade beneath the daisies.

Because disorder characterizes cottage gardens, you might even mix the seeds of your chosen annuals together and scatter them over prepared soil and wait for the results. So much for design! Just take care to select an assortment of spikes and daisies and fluffy flower heads so the garden boasts a pleasing variety of contrasting shapes. Include flowers that bloom at different seasons, so the garden will be in constant bloom from spring through fall.

The fence and gate of a cottage garden demand to be embellished with flowering vines. Climbing roses add a romantic note and aren't so heavy that they'll topple the fence. Ramblers are traditional, but large-flowered climbers work wonderfully, too. Other cottage garden choices include honeysuckle, wisteria, and clematis, or annuals such as morning glories and moonflowers. You might even try your hand at training grapes, gourds, or cucumbers along the fence.

It's important to tame the chaos of the flowers and give your eye a place to rest by creating a focal point in the garden. You might do this with a bench or small tree placed in a prominent location. A crabapple or other fruit tree would be appropriate. And don't forget the old-fashioned

roses, the kinds that look as if they belonged in a Victorian oil painting; they make a good choice where a shrub is called for.

Every cottage garden deserves a garden ornament to enhance its charm and provide a focal point among the flowers. You can't err with a birdbath or gazing globe (a reflecting metal ball on a pedestal), but be cautious when it comes to statuary. Stone bunnies and frogs may look cute peeking from beneath the leaves, but painted dwarves and Snow White might be too whimsical.

AN EASY-CARE PATIO GARDEN

A patio or deck provides the perfect viewing spot for your country garden and expands your home's living space to include the outdoors. By trading in some of your lawn for bricks or flagstones, you will also be considerably reducing your yard maintenance chores.

Locate the patio directly off the house, with access through the kitchen door or sliding glass doors from the living room or dining room. Physically linking the patio to the house not only makes the patio a convenient extension of your home's living space, but it also visually anchors the patio to the landscape. A patio located away from the house may look as if it's floating in space unless a large garden or structure links it with the rest of the yard.

Be sure your patio has enough room for people to move around easily and to hold a table and chairs as well as lounge furniture. Keep the patio in scale with the rest of the landscape; the usual rule of thumb is to make the patio no more than one-third the size of the yard. (City gardeners can effectively pave over an entire small yard, leaving perimeter planting borders.)

Just because it's made of brick or stones doesn't mean that your patio need be a sterile place. To give it a country look, bring the flower garden right up to the patio to soften its edges. But don't stop there; use the patio itself as another place to grow flowers. Group clay, wooden, or cement planters brimming with annual flowers into focal points around the edges of the patio, flanking the door to the house, and beside a prominent piece of furniture. You can even plant the spaces between the paving stones with paving plants.

Paving plants grow happily between the cracks in pavement. Most tolerate being lightly walked on; those that don't will do well and look pretty if planted in an out-of-the way crack at the patio's side. Paving plants added to the spaces between the flagstones in your patio sprawl delightfully over the stones, softening their appearance and creating a romantic, slightly disheveled look. You might wish to design the patio with extra-large spaces and planting pockets to enhance this look.

Almost any type of paving works in a patio garden as long as it is laid in an informal pattern. But the more weathered it looks, the better it blends with the garden. Flagstones or rubble should be of varying sizes and shapes and placed irregularly, not in rigid patterns. When laying bricks, choose a busy, old-fashioned-looking design such as basket weave rather than the more formal straight-lined patterns. And choose used paving bricks, not new, bright red ones, if you can.

A patio can be mortared or mortarless, but if you want to grow paving plants, be sure the stones or bricks are unmortared. A mortarless patio is easier and less expensive to install than a mortared patio and better survives the stress of freezing and thawing in cold climates.

A mortared brick patio, however, looks more romantic and old-fashioned than a mortarless one, especially if you use mortar that contrasts with the color of the bricks. For instance, used, soft pink paving bricks combined with light gray mortar creates a weathered look that perfectly reflects the romance of a cottage garden.

Rustic touches give a garden a country-cottage look. Rough stone, an old pump, willow furniture, and a rugged arbor are hallmarks of the style.

SPECIAL GARDENS: CUTTING GARDENS

Laid out in neat rows, this garden of tulips is easily maintained. And the tulips are easy to harvest for bouquets. Annuals will replace the tulips after their spring season is complete.

The major drawback in picking flowers from the garden for indoor use is that you rob your outdoor display of its beauty. You might have to choose between the pleasure of seeing the irises blooming at the curve of your front walk as you go to and from the house and enjoying them in a vase on the hall table. The ideal situation, of course, is to not

A cutting garden can be informally planted in a cottage-garden style, so that flowers snipped for bouquets won't be missed.

PLANTS FOR DRYING

The plants listed here dry well, either left on the plant in the garden or when cut and hung upside down in a cool, airy spot.

ANNUALS
Celosia argentea (cockscomb)
Gomphrena globosa (globe amaranth)
Helichrysum bracteatum (strawflower)
Limonium sinuatum (statice)
Lunaria annua (money plant)
Moluccella laevis (bells-of-Ireland)
Nigella damascena (love-in-a-mist)

ORNAMENTAL GRASSES
Briza media (quaking grass)
Chasmanthium latifolium (sea oats)
Miscanthus sinensis (Eulalia grass)
Pennisetum alopecuroides (fountain grass)

PERENNIALS AND BIENNIALS
Achillea filipendulina (fern-leaf yarrow)
Achillea millefolium (common yarrow)
Artemisia ludoviciana 'Silver King' (Western mugwort)
Gypsophila paniculata (baby's-breath)
Lavandula angustifolia (lavender)
Sedum × telephium 'Autumn Joy' (Autumn Joy sedum)

FLOWERS FOR CUTTING GARDENS

The flowers listed here last well when they are cut and used in flower arrangements:

ANNUALS

Antirrhinum majus (snapdragon)
Calendula officinalis (pot marigold)
Callistephus chinensis (China aster)
Celosia argentea (cockscomb)
Centaurea cyanus (cornflower)
Cleome hasslerana (spider flower)
Consolida ambigua (rocket larkspur)
Cosmos bipinnatus (cosmos)
Eustoma grandiflora (lisianthus)
Heliotropium arborescens (heliotrope)
Lathyrus odoratus (sweet pea)
Matthiola incana (stock)
Nigella damascena (love-in-a-mist)
Papaver spp. (poppy)
Pelargonium × *hortorum* (zonal geranium)
Petunia × *hybrida* (petunia)
Salvia farinacea (mealy-cup sage)
Tagetes spp. (marigold)
Viola × *wittrockiana* (pansy)
Zinnia elegans (common zinnia)

BULBS

Spring-blooming

Allium aflatunense (Persian onion)
Convallaria majalis (lily-of-the-valley)
Narcissus hybrids (daffodil, narcissus)
Tulipa hybrids (tulip)
Zantedeschia aethiopica (calla lily)

Summer-blooming

Freesia × *hybrida* (freesia)
Gladiolus hybrids (gladiolus)
Lilium hybrids (lily)
Polianthes tuberosa (tuberose)
Zantedeschia aethiopica (calla lily)

Late-blooming

Amaryllis belladonna (belladonna lily)
Dahlia × *pinnata* (dahlia)

PERENNIALS

Spring-blooming

Dicentra spectabilis (bleeding-heart)
Helleborus spp. (Christmas and Lenten roses)
Phlox divaricata (wild blue phlox)

Summer-blooming

Achillea filipendulina (fern-leaf yarrow)
Alstroemeria spp. (Peruvian lily)
Asclepias tuberosa (butterfly weed)
Astilbe × *arendsii* (astilbe)
Coreopsis grandiflora (coreopsis)
Delphinium × *elatum* (delphinium)
Dianthus barbatus (sweet William)
Digitalis purpurea (foxglove)
Gypsophila paniculata (baby's-breath)
Iris × *germanica* (bearded iris)
Leucanthemum × *superbum* (Shasta daisy)
Lupinus hybrids (lupine)
Paeonia lactiflora (peony)
Phlox paniculata (garden phlox)

Late-blooming

Aconitum carmichaelii (monkshood)
Aster novae-angliae (New England aster)
Dendrathema × *grandiflorum* (garden chrysanthemum)
Echinacea purpurea (purple coneflower)
Rudbeckia fulgida (orange coneflower)

---

have to choose, but to have enough blossoms to go around. The best way to assure this is to design a separate cutting garden intended to produce cut flowers.

A GARDEN FOR INDOOR PLEASURE

Part of the pleasure in growing a cutting garden brimming with flowers is being able to harvest blossoms from the garden to use as luxurious indoor bouquets. If you like crafts, you can grow everlasting flowers especially for drying and fashioning into long-lasting wreaths and arrangements. You might enjoy using the seedpods and fruits that ripen in fall as unusual additions to your creations.

There are two schools of thought when it comes to creating a cutting garden. One school favors setting out flowers in rows with paths in between, similar to the way you might lay out a vegetable garden. You are, after all, growing the flowers as a crop intended for harvesting. The second school favors a cottage garden style planted with enough abundance that the flowers you clip for bouquets won't be missed.

In either case, you will want to choose flowers—both annuals and perennials—that last well when cut or are especially good for pressing or drying.

SPECIAL GARDENS: MEADOW AND PRAIRIE GARDENS

Creating a meadow is not as easy as scattering seed and standing back for spectacular results. But for large, sunny areas, meadows—especially those with a broad path mowed through them—are a wonderful landscape device.

Many people mistakenly believe that they can turn their lawn into a breathtaking meadow or prairie of bright flowers and swaying grasses by simply scattering handfuls of flower seeds over the grass and not mowing it. Unfortunately, it doesn't happen that way. Even wildflower seeds need assistance to produce satisfactory results, and the mat-forming roots of lawn grasses compete with the flowers, eventually crowding out any that do sprout.

DOING IT RIGHT

A beautiful, self-sustaining meadow garden can be yours if you start it and maintain it correctly. Begin with understanding Mother Nature's methods. Meadows of grasses and flowers occur naturally only in open, sunny areas in regions such as the Northeast, Southeast, and Pacific Northwest where forests predominate. Meadows may be wet or dry, depending upon local soil conditions. They gradually revert to forests unless grazing or mowing keeps trees and shrubs from taking over. In the Midwest and Plains states, where rainfall is insufficient to support a forest, vast, open prairies of deep-rooted grasses and flowers occur. Grazing, periodic fires, and drought keep the prairie from reverting to scrub.

You can plant a meadow or prairie garden of native wildflowers and grasses that reflects the habitat in your area. You can even improve a bit on the balance of nature by including more flowers in proportion to grasses than would occur naturally, as long as you don't ignore planting grasses altogether.

Grasses form an important component of natural meadows and prairies and ought to be included in all meadow gardens. Clump-forming meadow grasses stabilize the soil and create a neutral background for the changing show of colorful flowers. And grasses are beautiful in their own right. They offer a seductive display of linear foliage, which sways and undulates in the breeze, and a refreshing, green color that changes to tawny earth shades in autumn.

To create a natural and self-sustaining meadow of grasses punctuated by clusters of colorful flowers, you need to sow the right mixture of wildflowers and grasses— one designed for your region. The seed mix should rely mostly on native or naturalized perennials if it is to bloom abundantly year after year. Experienced gardeners find that regardless of the claims on the package label, most annuals in meadow garden seed mixes do not

MEADOW GARDEN BASICS

These are the basic steps toward creating a successful, self-sustaining meadow or prairie garden:

■ Strip off lawn grass or remove all other vegetation and weeds, roots and all.

■ Till the soil to prepare a seedbed.

■ Choose a seed mixture of perennial and annual wildflowers and native grasses appropriate to your region. Sow at twice the recommended rate on the package.

■ Water the planting regularly during its first growing season, as you would any garden area.

■ Control weeds by hand-pulling or selective herbicide application during the first two years.

■ Mow or cut the meadow to a height of 6 inches every year in late winter.

■ Where ticks are a problem, create a 6-foot-wide mowed path through the garden, if you wish to stroll through it.

NATIVE WILDFLOWERS FOR MEADOW AND PRAIRIE GARDENS

These sun-loving wildflowers and grasses can be easily naturalized in a grassy field or meadow, either by starting them from seed or planting container-grown plants. Those marked with * do best in moist or wet meadows. Those marked with ** are non-natives that will do well in a meadow without being invasive.

ANNUALS

**Cleome hasslerana* (spider flower)
Consolida ambigua (rocket larkspur)
Cosmos bipinnatus (cosmos)
Cosmos sulphureus (yellow cosmos)
Eschscholzia californica (California poppy)
Eustoma grandiflora (lisianthus)
Gaillardia pulchella (annual blanket flower)
Helianthus annuus (sunflower)
Lupinus texensis (Texas bluebonnet)
**Nigella damascena* (love-in-a-mist)
***Papaver rhoeas* (corn poppy)
Phlox drummondii (annual phlox)

GRASSES

Bouteluoa gracilis (blue grama)
Brizia media (quaking grass)
Chasmanthium latifolium (northern sea oats)
Elymus arenarius 'Glaucus' (blue wild rye)
***Festuca ovina* (sheep's fescue)
Molinia caerulea (moor grass)
Panicum virgatum (switchgrass)

PERENNIALS

Aquilegia canadensis (wild columbine)
Asclepias tuberosa (butterfly weed)
Aster spp. (fall aster)
Baptisia australis (wild blue indigo)
Boltonia asteroides (white boltonia)
**Chelone glabra* (turtlehead)
***Chrysanthemum leucanthemum* (oxeye daisy)
Coreopsis spp. (coreopsis)
Echinacea purpurea (purple coneflower)
**Eupatorium purpureum* (Joe-Pye weed)
**Filipendula rubra* (queen-of-the-prairie)
Gaillardia × grandiflora (blanket flower)
Helenium autumnale (sneezeweed)
Helianthus angustifolius (fall sunflower)
Heliopsis helianthoides (false sunflower)
**Liatris* spp. (gay-feather)
Lupinus spp. (lupine)
**Monarda* spp. (beebalm)
Oenothera tetragona (sundrops)
**Physostegia virginiana* (obedient plant)
Rudbeckia spp. (coneflower)
Solidago spp. (goldenrod)

These wildflowers, Calliopsis tinctoria and annual blanket flower (Gaillardia pulchella), are ideal for prairie plantings.

reseed well, so a garden based on annuals puts on a poor display after the first year. Because it may take the perennials two years to bloom, many mixes contain annuals to create a first-year display while the permanent perennials get established. Just be sure your mix has a good number of perennials along with annuals.

DESIGN FOR BEAUTY

A meadow or prairie garden succeeds best as a landscape feature if sited in full sun on a large property where its somewhat wild nature takes on the aspect of a country pasture.

Check local ordinances if you plan to plant the meadow in your front yard, because some communities have restrictions about lawn mowing and may decide your meadow is actually an unkempt lawn. If you set off the meadow with a rustic fence and mow a wide path through it to a bench, shed, or old apple tree, the meadow integrates better into the rest of the landscape, becoming both more intentional and natural, while taking on the delightful appearance of the field of flowers you intended.

SPECIAL GARDENS: WOODLAND GARDENS

T he delicate blossoms of wild blue phlox, great white trillium, Virginia bluebells, and scores of other enchanting woodland wildflowers can be yours to enjoy without hiking into the wild. All you need is a wooded site and a humus-rich soil where you can copy the forest environment.

Where lawn or other traditional plantings refuse to grow, woodland flowers and other shade-loving plants create a restful, cooling garden. Purple moss pink carpets this woodland grove.

PLANTING AND DESIGNING THE WOODLAND

F orest plants occur in horizontal layers from the sky to the ground, with canopy trees overhead, understory trees and shrubs in between, and wildflowers, ferns, and mosses on the ground. The forest

Two naturals for the humus-rich, moist soil of a woodland garden are Celandine poppy and Virginia bluebells.

floor has a 4- to 8-inch-deep layer of loose, humus-rich soil consisting of rotted leaves and twigs above a more solid soil. The humus and the soil underneath are acidic, varying from very acid (pH 4.0 to 5.0) to slightly acid (pH 6.0 to 6.9). This rich, acid soil is the key to growing a successful woodland wildflower garden, but if you don't have it, you can create it.

Site your proposed woodland garden where overhead trees cast dappled shade throughout the day and where the soil is loose and crumbly. This may be in a natural woodland, in a small grove or group of trees, or even under one large, deep-rooted, wide-spreading tree.

Evaluate the soil by feeling it; if you can scrape the humus off the surface of the ground with your hands, it is an excellent site for a woodland garden. If the soil is hard, compacted, and root-filled, defying a trowel, you'll have to improve it. Poor soil results when tree leaves have been raked off and carted away year after year instead of being allowed to rot naturally into leaf mold, or when the surface roots of the trees overhead have compacted and dried out the soil.

You can refurbish poor soil by spreading chopped leaves and twigs over the soil in a deep layer. Dust the leaves with compost activator and keep them moist to speed up decomposition. The rotting leaves encourage earthworms, which burrow deeper into the soil, loosening up the lower layers. You may have to repeat this procedure for several years until the humus becomes deep enough to plant in.

Once you've selected your site, clear out undesirable underbrush, invasive vines, and small saplings, but leave behind good-looking shrubs in strategic places beneath the canopy trees. Trim off low-hanging branches and open up the canopy by thinning the trees so that dappled light falls below.

Lay out a path to meander among the trees and give it a wood chip surface. The path gives structure to the garden, beckons you to explore, and protects the delicate plants from being trampled. You might edge the path with stones or logs, but leaving it unedged looks most natural.

Do not dig deeply or turn over the soil in a woodland site. Cultivating destroys the soil layers and disrupts the trees' root systems. Dig small, individual holes for flowers and ferns. You can dig planting holes for shrubs and small understory trees such as dogwoods and azaleas, but do not excavate large areas or cut through large tree roots; plant somewhere else.

Woodland wildflowers are spring-blooming, ephemeral plants. Most bloom before the overhead canopy of leaves has blocked out significant sunlight, then they die to the ground by midsummer. If you add a generous amount of ferns to your garden, their lovely foliage sustains the garden in summer and fall, after the ephemerals disappear for the year.

Arrange wildflowers and ferns in groups under the trees and along the path edges, but don't set them out in rows. Take your cues from nature and don't worry about leaving open space between the groups. Plant spreading types so they can roam freely and fill in to become dramatic swathes. Plant tap-rooted types here and there so the ground-covering plants weave beneath taller plants in a pleasing way.

Woodland plants always have a protective covering of humus over their roots, and so should yours. After planting, apply a loose covering of shredded leaves or humus around the wildflowers; don't leave the soil exposed to drying sun and wind.

NATIVE WOODLAND PLANTS

The following plants grow wild in the woodlands of North America and are easy to obtain from wildflower nurseries. The one marked with * is a European species that has naturalized here:

BULBS
Camassia leichtlinii (camas)
Erythronium americanum (trout lily)
Trillium grandiflorum (white trillium)

FERNS
Adiantum pedatum (maidenhair fern)
Athyrium filix-femina (lady fern)
Dryopteris marginalis (marginal shield fern)
Matteuccia pensylvanica (ostrich fern)
Osmunda cinnamomea (cinnamon fern)
Osmunda regalis (royal fern)
Polystichum acrostichoides (Christmas fern)
Polystichum setiferum (soft shield fern)

PERENNIALS AND HERBACEOUS GROUNDCOVERS
Aconitum spp. (monkshood)
Chrysogonum virginianum (goldenstar)

Cimicifuga simplex (Kamchatka bugbane)
Dicentra eximia (fringed bleeding-heart)
**Galium odoratum* (sweet woodruff)
Iris cristata (crested iris)

White Trillium

Mertensia virginica (Virginia bluebells)
Phlox pilosa (Carolina phlox)
Phlox stolonifera (creeping phlox)
Polemonium caeruleum (Jacob's ladder)
Polygonatum biflorum (Solomon's seal)
Tiarella spp. (foamflower)
Viola spp. (violet)
Waldsteinia fragrariodes (barren strawberry)

SHOPPING FOR WILDFLOWERS

Woodland wildflowers, unlike meadow plants, are not easily propagated by seeds, so you'll need to purchase grown plants. Because they mature slowly from seed, woodland plants are expensive. Beware of bargain wildflowers,

because they are probably wild-gathered. Unscrupulous suppliers may collect wildflowers then sell them, ravaging their native habitat.

Not only is gathering wildflowers unethical and often illegal, the resulting plants usually die in your garden because they were mistreated

and shocked during gathering. Nursery-propagated ones will be most likely to flourish. Please do not gather wildflowers yourself, but purchase them only from suppliers who assure you their plants are nursery-propagated.

SPECIAL GARDENS: WATER GARDENS

This water garden attracts wildlife and offers a place to grow interesting aquatic plants such as tropical water lilies.

A pool with aquatic plants, no matter its size, becomes the focal point of a garden, drawing visitors to its edge. Add a small fountain or waterfall, and you can enjoy the music of moving water. You can even stock the pool with goldfish or koi.

The best water gardens are built with a flexible PVC liner, which allows you to create a pond that best fits your garden site. You can use the liner for streams, waterfalls, and shelves to hold aquatic plants. Prefabricated pond shells are often hard to install and don't allow much leeway in design. For a formal setting, choose a raised concrete pool.

A waterfall or cascade will look quite real if it is built from irregularly shaped rocks. A fountain spray looks artificial, but is good in a formal pool. Both require a submersible electrical pump to recirculate the water. Be sure to choose a pump with enough power to handle the volume of water you need to recirculate to the height and distance your design calls for.

CONSTRUCTION ADVICE

Creating a garden pond or pool with a PVC liner is not difficult, but it takes strength and some construction know-how. Dig the pool to at least 18 inches deep, 3 feet if extra large. Haul away the excavated dirt. (Check local building codes; deep ponds may require a safety fence.) You'll have to haul in capstones and pea gravel. Take great care to install the liner correctly and to smooth and fold it in place. You'll need a spirit level to make the base of the pool perfectly level to prevent the liner from showing. Follow the manufacturer's instructions and consult a detailed book on water gardening before beginning.

One of the most common design problems is finishing the edges so the pool looks real. Here are some hints:

■ Camouflage the edge of the pool with stones and boulders, not a ring of flat capstones or bricks.

■ Hide the pond liner by stacking edging stones on a perimeter shelf 12 inches wide and 6 inches below the water level in front of the liner; fold back the liner and tuck it between the top stones of the stack and the capstones. (This also creates crevices for fish and frogs.)

■ Design a shallow bank of pea gravel that extends over the liner around the pond edge and under the water. (This makes a shallow area for birds.) The bank should be 6 inches deep and 24 inches wide and extend to slightly beyond the water's edge,

The gravel area near the edge of a contoured pond is a haven for birds. The gravel anchors a potted water plant at its proper depth below the surface of the water.

MAKE A TUB GARDEN

You can create a small water garden for a water lily and a few bog plants in any watertight container such as a washtub or ceramic or fiberglass garden pot. Whiskey-barrel halves and clay pots are good if they are waterproofed. To do this, insert a plastic liner inside them.

Plant the tub garden with submerged pots of aquatic plants. You can even add a few goldfish. Top off the container every week with fresh water and enjoy it close at hand on a deck or patio.

AQUATIC PLANTS

Include some of these popular aquatic plants in your garden pool:

EDGE PLANTS

Caltha palustris (marsh marigold): shiny, yellow buttercups in early spring. Heart-shaped leaves to 1 foot. Zones 5–7.

Cyperus isocladus (dwarf papyrus): whorls of long leaves atop 2½-foot stems. Wheat-colored flowers in summer. Zones 9–10; overwinter indoors.

Iris pseudacorus (yellow flag): showy, yellow flowers in early summer. Sword-shaped leaves to 4 feet. Zones 4–10.

Iris versicolor (blue flag): showy, light to deep blue flowers in summer. Sword-shaped leaves to 3 feet. Zones 4–10.

Myriophyllum aquaticum (parrot's-feather): Beautiful whorls of feathery, blue-green leaves float below surface and rise above it. Zones 6–10.

Pontederia cordata (pickerel rush): Spires of purple or white flowers in summer. Lance-shaped leaves, 2 to 3 feet tall. Zones 3–10.

FLOATERS

Eichhornia crassipes (water hyacinth): spikes of pale lavender flowers in midsummer. Shiny leaves and trailing roots. Zones 9–10, can be a pest in natural sites. Safe in colder areas because it dies over winter.

Pistia stratiotes (shellflower): Pale green leaves form lovely rosettes floating on surface. Zones 9–10, where it can be a pest in natural sites. Safe in colder areas because it dies over winter.

SUBMERGED PLANTS

Myriophyllum spp. (water milfoil): Fine-textured, hairlike, green to reddish leaves cloak long stems. Zones 5–10.

Vallisneria americana (eel grass): Pale green leaves form clumps of ribbons. Zones 4–10.

WATER LILIES

Nymphaea spp. (tropical water lilies): fragrant, showy, satiny purple, blue, pink, yellow, or white flowers on tall stems above water. Day- or night-blooming. Round leaves float. Best in hot weather. Overwinter tubers in frost-free area.

Nymphaea spp. (hardy water lilies): lovely, small, floating blossoms in white, pink, peach, red, or white. Lightly scented. Round leaves float. Zones 3–10.

WATER GARDEN ECOLOGY

Aquatic plants come in several forms: floating, submerged, and edge. Water lilies are their own type because they float, but are rooted to the pond bottom. All grow best with six or more hours of full sun daily.

Floating plants are not anchored in the soil; their roots dangle in the water and their leaves float freely on the water surface. They often shade the surface and thus reduce algae growth and evaporation.

Submerged plants root in the soil at the bottom of a pond, and their leaves and stems remain below water level. Sometimes called oxygenating plants, these beneficial plants give off a lot of oxygen and use up carbon dioxide and dissolved nutrients, which discourages algae.

Edge plants, often called bog or marginal plants, must have their roots in constantly wet soil or submerged underwater. Their leaves either rise above the water or float on the surface. Grow edge plants in dark-colored, 2- to 10-gallon plastic pots of regular garden soil. Set the pots on a perimeter shelf or on submerged stones or bricks, so the soil surface is 2 to 4 inches below the water surface. Fertilize the potted plants once a year with tablets.

For the best pond ecology, have about 50 to 70 percent of the water surface covered by aquatic plants and add goldfish. The combination of fish and plants in the water garden keeps it healthy. All you'll need to do is fill it with water, clean out leaf litter, and thin aquatic plants if they become too vigorous.

One of the primary joys of water gardening is growing water lilies.

sloping the gravel toward the center.
■ Create a lawn edge by extending the liner and gravel away from the pond and adding an inch of soil, then sod, above the waterline.

Don't build an artificial pond in a wet site. You might be able to excavate a wet site to hold natural water, but don't line it with plastic, which could heave and buckle. Locate a lined pond in a well-drained site and plan for overflow in case of heavy rain. To form a catch basin, create a lowered edge in a selected place, add gravel fill to the area, and channel the water with drainage pipe so that any overflow moves downhill and away from the pond.

SPECIAL GARDENS: ROCK GARDENS

Rock garden plants do best in the special microclimate created by careful placement among stones and boulders. A rock garden is also an ideal solution to landscaping a problem slope.

Ideally, a rock garden should look like a slice of a natural, rocky landscape. Alpine rock gardens resemble a windswept mountain peak complete with rugged, lichen-coated rocks and boulders, bun- or matlike flowering alpine plants, and twisted evergreens stunted by harsh growing conditions. Woodland rock gardens made of mossy rocks and boulders demand ground-hugging wildflowers such as trilliums, violets, and ferns; desert rock gardens feature cactus and other succulents as well as desert annuals such as California poppies.

ROCK GARDEN PLANTS

ANNUALS
Brachycome iberidifolia (Swan River daisy)
Dianthus chinensis (China pink)
Eschscholzia californica (California poppy)
Gaillardia pulchella (annual blanket flower)
Lobelia erinus (edging lobelia)
Lobularia maritima (sweet alyssum)
Melampodium paludosum (melampodium)
Nigella damascena (love-in-a-mist)
Sanvitalia procumbens (creeping zinnia)
Verbena × *hybrida* (verbena)
Zinnia angustifolia (narrow-leaf zinnia)

BULBS
Allium spp. (ornamental onion)
Crocus spp. (crocus)
Cyclamen spp. (cyclamen)
Fritillaria spp. (checkered lily)
Iris danfordiae (Danford iris)
Iris reticulata (reticulated iris)
Scilla siberica (Siberian squill)
Sternbergia lutea (winter daffodil)
Tulipa spp. (species tulip)

DWARF CONIFERS
Chamaecyparis pisifera var. *filifera* 'Sungold' (Sawara false cypress)
Chamaecyparis thyoides 'Ericoides' (false cypress)
Juniperus conferta (shore juniper)
Juniperus horizontalis (creeping juniper)
Juniperus procumbens var. 'Nana' (dwarf Japanese garden juniper)
Juniperus scopulorum 'Skyrocket' (Rocky Mountain juniper)
Picea abies 'Nidiformis' (bird's-nest spruce)
Picea glauca 'Conica' (dwarf Alberta spruce)
Picea orientalis 'Whittgold' (Oriental spruce)
Picea pungens var. *glauca* 'Globosa' (Colorado blue spruce)
Pinus mugo 'Mops' (Mugo pine)
Pinus strobus 'Soft Touch' (Eastern white pine)
Pinus sylvestris 'Hillside Creeper' (Scotch pine)

PERENNIALS
Aquilegia flabellata (fan columbine)
Arabis caucasica (wall rockcress)
Aurinia saxatilis (basket-of-gold)
Campanula portenschlagiana (Dalmatian bellflower)
Cerastium tomentosum (snow-in-summer)
Corydalis lutea (yellow corydalis)
Dianthus plumarius (cottage pink)
Geranium spp. (cranesbill)
Gypsophila repens (creeping gypsophila)
Heuchera spp. (coralbells)
Iberis sempervirens (edging candytuft)
Phlox subulata (moss pink)
Scabiosa caucasica (pincushion flower)
Sedum kamtschaticum (Kamtschatka stonecrop)
Thymus pseudolanuginosis (woolly thyme)

SITING THE ROCK GARDEN

An open, steeply or gently sloping, north- or east-facing site is best for alpine plants; woodland and desert plants are less choosy. Or, you can create a mound or hill from a fast-draining soil mix. Flat ground can work, too, as long as the soil drains well, but it is less visually interesting, and the plants may be more difficult to see.

The most important visual element in a rock garden is the rocks. They should look natural. You can achieve a natural look by following two rules: Choose rocks all of the same type and position them so they look as if they were arranged by nature's hand, not yours. Use the largest rocks you or several people can handle for the most natural look. You might even wish to consider hiring a professional landscaper who can move boulders and large rocks with a small forklift or backhoe.

Porous rocks, such as limestone, sandstone, shale, and tufa, work best for alpine plants, because they absorb water, keeping the roots cool and moist. Choose nonporous rocks such as marble, basalt, and granite for desert rock gardens. Woodland rock gardens do well with either rock type, depending upon other growing conditions.

Position the largest rocks first to create the rock garden's structure, then add more rocks for balance. Partially bury the rocks so that at least a third of each rock is underground, so they look like a natural outcropping; don't place them directly on top of the soil. Tilt the rocks slightly backward so they funnel water back into the soil. Align stratified rocks in the same plane, so they project from the side of a hill or out of flat ground as if they were

exposed by erosion. Group rounded rocks in a flat area at the base of a slope to imitate a boulder field left behind by an ancient glacier.

Most rock garden plants are sensitive to poor drainage and perish in any soil that is not fast-draining, although this does not necessarily mean they prefer dry soil. They do best in moist but well-drained soil with a low to moderate nutrient content, and will rot in rich or damp soil. Amend all but gravelly soil before installing the rocks to make it more fast-draining, then fill in around the rocks with a soil mix made from ⅓ coarse sand, fine gravel, or stone chips; ⅓ peat or composted leaves; and ⅓ loamy soil.

PLANTING ROCK GARDENS

True alpine plants are native to mountainous regions above the tree line and are adapted to harsh growing conditions. They form neat buns and mats of foliage and grow slowly, but often produce gorgeous flowers. Alpine plants may be difficult for all but specialty gardeners to grow. Saxatile plants—those that flourish in stony and rocky soil—are easier for most gardeners to grow and adapt well to rock gardens. Once you have mastered them, you can move on to growing more esoteric specialty plants.

Be sure to choose plants that are in scale with the size of your rock garden and the rocks in it. Plant a small rock garden with fine-textured small plants and very dwarf conifers. A large-scale garden can accommodate larger dwarf conifers. Arrange plants naturally so they spill down the hillside and nestle around the rocks. In nature, alpine and

saxatile plants grow right next to a rock, enjoying extra water from runoff and a bit of shade from the rock's small shadow. Position your plants accordingly, planting the root ball directly at the base of a rock.

Dwarf conifers add dimension and year-round greenery to a rock garden, where they imitate the contorted specimens found on windswept mountain peaks. Choose columnar, rounded, and spreading shapes to add interest to the garden, but position them artfully to avoid the look of a collection.

Apply a mulch of fine gravel or pebbles to keep the crowns of water-sensitive rock garden plants dry to prevent rotting. The gravel top dressing also keeps dirt from splashing on the tiny plants and discourages weeds, which can quickly overrun these slow-growers. The top dressing also gives that final, natural-looking touch to the rock garden.

Rock garden plants are excellent candidates for landscaping next to steps. This rock garden in miniature contains bellflower, pansies, and sweet alyssum.

SPECIAL GARDENS: GARDENING TO ATTRACT BIRDS

Bird's love water—to bathe in and to drink. One of the best time-tested ways to attract birds is to set up a simple birdbath in your backyard.

Wildlife is a natural benefit in a garden. Songbirds are particularly welcome because they bring movement and soothing sounds to the garden. Although birds are common in gardens, you can encourage more of them to visit or take up residence by turning your yard into a specially planted garden designed to provide the creature comforts of food, shelter, and water.

PROVIDING BIRD FOOD

The easiest way to attract songbirds to your garden is to put out seed in feeders; squirrel-proof ones are a good idea if you don't want to share the seed with them. Locate the feeder near a shrub or tree—one that provides a safe perch for birds flying to and from the feeder—but far enough away that squirrels can't use it for a launching pad. Be sure to locate the feeder in a fairly open place, however, so cats and other predators cannot hide nearby waiting to attack. Also, spilled seed from the feeder can attract mice and rats, so a location away from the house is a good idea.

Feeders set on the ground will attract cardinals, finches, grackles, jays, juncos, mockingbirds, sparrows, and titmice. Hanging feeders lure chickadees, finches, sparrows, titmice, warblers, and woodpeckers. Mount a platform-type feeder on a post for chickadees, finches, flickers, grackles, jays, mockingbirds, nuthatches, sparrows, titmice, and wrens. In winter, put up suet feeders for chickadees, flickers, mockingbirds, nuthatches, titmice, and woodpeckers.

In addition to seed mixes, birds enjoy such foods as grains, fruit, nuts, peanut butter, and crushed eggshells and sand for grit.

NATURAL BIRD FOOD

Besides bird feeders, you can provide food for birds naturally. Include plants that provide nuts, seeds, nectar, and berries, and birds will flock around. These natural food sources make economical wildlife meals and won't give out when you go on vacation. Select perennials and shrubs so the garden blooms and fruits continuously from spring through fall, to provide a food source that lasts through winter.

PLANTS THAT PROVIDE FOOD FOR SONGBIRDS

For a natural source of food to feed the songbirds in your garden throughout the year, include as many of these beautiful plants as possible in your yard. They will provide a steady supply of seeds, nuts, and berries to feed a variety of birds. Allow the perennial and annual flowers to go to seed; their seedpods will attract cardinals and finches.

ANNUALS

Cosmos spp. (cosmos)
Eschscholzia californica (California poppy)
Ornamental grasses
Portulaca grandiflora (moss rose)
Tagetes erecta (African marigold)
Zinnia elegans (common zinnia)

PERENNIALS

✓ *Aster* spp. (aster)
Coreopsis spp. (coreopsis)
Echinacea purpurea (purple coneflower)
✓ *Echinops ritro* (globe thistle)
✓ Ornamental grasses
✓ *Rudbeckia* spp. (coneflower)
Scabiosa caucasica (pincushion flower)
Solidago spp. (goldenrod)

SHRUBS

Callicarpa spp. (beautyberry)
Cotoneaster spp. (cotoneaster)
Ilex × *meserveae* (hybrid holly)
Ilex verticillata (winterberry)
Juniperus spp. (juniper)

Ligustrum spp. (privet)
Lindera benzoin (spicebush)
Myrica pensylvanica (bayberry)
Rhus spp. (sumac)
Rosa rugosa (Rugosa rose)
Sambucus canadensis (American elderberry)
Symphoricarpos spp. (snowberry)
Viburnum dilatatum (linden viburnum)
Viburnum opulus (European cranberry bush)
Viburnum trilobum (American cranberry bush)

TREES

Acer spp. (maple)
Amelanchier spp. (serviceberry)
Betula spp. (birch)
Cornus spp. (dogwood)
Crataegus spp. (hawthorn)
Fagus grandifolia (American beech)
Ilex spp. (holly)
Liquidambar styraciflua (sweetgum)
Malus spp. (crabapple)
Nyssa sylvatica (black gum)
Picea spp. (spruce)
Pinus spp. (pine)
Quercus spp. (oak)
Sorbus spp. (mountain ash)

VINES AND GROUNDCOVERS

Euonymus fortunei (wintercreeper)
Lonicera spp. (honeysuckle)
Parthenocissus spp. (Virginia creeper, Boston ivy)
Pyracantha spp. (firethorn)

Attract birds to your garden year-round by providing a variety of food sources. Crabapples, even when covered with snow, are favorites of many birds.

PROVIDING WATER

A simple birdbath—a shallow basin of water—can lure more birds to your garden than can a feeder. If you can provide water in winter by using a small heater in the birdbath, you'll be gratified by the number of birds that come to drink and bathe. Often birds must fly long distances to get water; they will remember where your birdbath is and visit it daily. Some birds, especially robins, really enjoy splashing in the birdbath and are fun to watch.

Water can come from other sources, too. A small natural or artificial pond with a shallow edge or rocks and boulders with hollows that hold pools of water look at home in natural-style gardens. Pools and ponds also attract toads and frogs, who gobble up insects such as mosquitoes and other annoying pests.

SPECIAL GARDENS: GARDENING TO ATTRACT BIRDS
continued

PROVIDING SHELTER AND NESTING SITES

Birds need shelter from the wind, rain, and cold and a secure location for a nest. Evergreen trees make ideal protected places,

Water can be provided for birds in a variety of places. This rock pool provides the perfect shallow water that birds prefer.

especially in winter. Include conifers or tall, broad-leaved evergreens as specimens in your landscape or plant them as a hedge or windbreak.

Some birds nest in tall trees; others prefer sites near or on the ground. A dense planting of shrubs or a natural thicket of wild brambles or shrubs in wooded areas or in the borders and foundation planting around your home provides the perfect nesting site. Birdhouses, while providing homes for nesting birds, also double as garden ornaments.

To make your landscape more bird-friendly, let the grass grow a little higher, let flowers form seedpods,

and let shrubs assume their natural forms; prune only to remove dead and damaged wood.

HUMMINGBIRD HABITS

At least one species of hummingbird is likely to visit your garden at some time during the year. Some just pass through on their migratory route to and from South and Central America; others may arrive in spring and remain until fall. Of the 340 species, only 10 occur north of the Mexican border and only the ruby-throated hummingbird settles east of the Mississippi River. Hummers are less common in the Plains states, common in the Western states, and live year-round in the Sunbelt.

Unique among birds, hummers' special wing structure allows them to hover and fly backward. They're fast, too, flying at speeds between 25 and 50 mph and dive-bombing during mating rituals at 60 mph. When hovering above a flower, their wings beat up to 80 times a second.

PLANTS FOR HUMMINGBIRD FOOD

Red attracts hummingbirds like a magnet. Though they visit flowers of other colors—orange and pink most often—they'll investigate anything red they encounter, including red clothes hanging on the line. Their long, narrow bills and needlelike tongues allow them to get nectar from tubular flowers unreachable by bees or butterflies.

In return for the nectar, they pollinate the flowers. When a hummingbird buries its head deep inside a flower, pollen brushes onto its head and is carried to the next blossom. Hummers visit nectar-laden flat flowers, but prefer tubular shapes

CREATING A HUMMINGBIRD GARDEN

A garden designed especially to attract hummingbirds comes alive with their iridescent colors and eye-catching movement. Hummingbirds get much of their nourishment from flower nectar. You can make the garden natural or formal. Hummingbirds have evolved as pollinators to many of our lovely wildflowers, so you may wish to plant the garden with native plants. These needs, however, must be met:
- Nectar sources from red tubular flowers
- Supplemental food sources from hummingbird feeders
- Suitable water supply, such as fountain or water spray
- Sunlight for warmth
- Open space for flight
- Dense plantings for nesting and shelter
- Absence of insecticides

where there's no other competition for nectar.

Be sure to plant lots of flowers—a single hummingbird needs to visit hundreds of flowers a day to fuel its high metabolism. Choose annuals, such as red salvia and fuchsia, that bloom all season and perennials that open sequentially so your hummers never find themselves without food.

Arrange the flowers in beds and borders around a large, sunny lawn so the birds can get to them easily. Do not block the flowers with tall foliage or structures that impede the birds' hovering and flight. You'll enjoy seeing hummers close up at window boxes or hanging baskets near a patio or window. Avoid using insecticides, because hummers eat insects.

HUMMINGBIRD FEEDERS

Include at least one hummingbird feeder in your garden. This supplemental food source helps with their high-calorie diet needs and supplies emergency food in case of flower failure. Suspend the feeder in the shade of a tree or porch and keep it filled. Small feeders may need replenishing once or twice a day.

You can purchase a commercial mixture or make your own. Combine 1 part sugar to 5 parts water and boil it to dissolve the sugar and kill bacteria and mold. (Don't use honey, which can be toxic to hummers.) Refrigerate the mixture for up to one week. Clean the feeder weekly or sooner if you see algae or mold.

Since hummingbirds can be quite territorial and sometimes aggressive, separate feeders out of sight of one another (or by at least 6 feet). The more feeders you have, the more birds your garden can support.

WATER NEEDS OF HUMMINGBIRDS

Hummingbirds need water, but will not drink or bathe in water as deep as in most birdbaths. They prefer to dart in and out of the spray from a waterfall or fine-spray sprinkler and drink dewdrops and water that settle in a cupped leaf or indentation of a rock. Provide them with a shallow basin, or better yet with an artificial garden pool and fountain or trickling waterfall.

SHELTER AND NESTING SITES FOR HUMMINGBIRDS

Most yards with trees and shrubs provide enough shelter for hummingbirds. A hummingbird might build its thimble-size nest on a tree limb, light fixture, or tangle of vines.

Spider webs and bits of bark and leaves camouflage the nest, but the nest is so tiny, you'll probably never notice it anyway.

PLANTS TO ATTRACT HUMMINGBIRDS

ANNUALS
Antirrhinum majus (snapdragon)
Consolida ambigua (rocket larkspur)
Fuchsia × hybrida (fuchsia)
Lantana spp. (lantana)
Lobelia erinus (edging lobelia)
Nicotiana spp. (flowering tobacco)
Pelargonium × hortorum (zonal geranium)
Pelargonium peltatum (ivy geranium)
Petunia × hybrida (petunia)
Phlox drummondii (annual phlox)
Salvia splendens (red salvia)

BULBS
Canna × generalis (canna lily)
✓ *Dahlia pinnata* (dahlia)
✓ *Gladiolus* hybrids (gladiolus)

PERENNIALS AND BIENNIALS
Alcea rosea (hollyhock)
Aquilegia spp. (columbine)
Asclepias tuberosa (butterfly weed)
Dianthus barbatus (sweet William)
Dicentra spp. (bleeding-heart)
Digitalis spp. (foxglove)
Heuchera spp. (coralbells)
Monarda didyma (beebalm)
Penstemon spp. (beard-tongue)
Pulmonaria spp. (lungwort)

SHRUBS
Buddleia davidii (butterfly bush)
Chaenomeles speciosa (flowering quince)
Hibiscus syriacus (rose-of-Sharon)
Kolkwitzia amabilis (beautybush)
Lonicera tatarica (tatarian honeysuckle)
Symphoricarpos chenaultii (Chenault coralberry)
Weigela florida (old-fashioned weigela)

TREES
Aesculus glabra (Ohio buckeye)
Albizia julibrissin (silk tree)
Crataegus phaenopyrum (Washington hawthorn)
Liriodendron tulipifera (tulip tree)
Malus floribunda (Japanese flowering crabapple)
Robinia pseudoacacia (black locust)

VINES
Campsis radicans (trumpet creeper)
Ipomoea spp. (cardinal climber, morning glory)
Lonicera sempervirens (trumpet honeysuckle)
Phaseolus coccineus (scarlet runner bean)

Hummingbirds prefer tubular flowers and the color red, making this fuchsia an ideal flower for attracting the tiny bird.

SPECIAL GARDENS: GARDENING TO ATTRACT BUTTERFLIES

Provide the right environment and the right plants and you can attract butterflies, such as this tiger swallowtail, to your garden.

Butterflies, like hummingbirds, add beauty, color, and movement to a garden. And, like the tiny birds, they feed on nectar-rich flowers. But butterflies prefer flat heads or narrow spikes of numerous tiny flowers, which offer a landing platform or perch to hold onto when feeding. Flowers in the daisy family are butterfly favorites and are sure to attract butterflies anywhere. Although hummingbird flowers are rarely fragrant, butterfly flowers often emit a heady perfume.

BUTTERFLY PLANTS

Though the flowers that attract butterflies are bright and colorful, the butterflies see them quite differently than we do, because they detect only the ultraviolet color patterns in the flowers. These patterns are invisible to human eyes, but draw a clear road map to the nectar source for butterflies and bees. When designing your garden to attract butterflies, plant large masses of individual flowers, rather than single flowers scattered here and there. This large splash of blossoms beckons butterflies by sight and smell.

· Locate your garden in full sun and protect it from strong winds with a fence or living windbreak. Butterflies appreciate a natural, meadowlike garden of flowers and grasses, but won't turn up their feelers at a formal garden if the right flowers are present.

WATER FOR BUTTERFLIES

Butterflies need water, but prefer to drink from mud puddles rather than from deeper water. Often they congregate around a water source. You can easily supply this needed water by filling a shallow basin with clean sand and keeping it flooded. Sink the basin in a sunny spot in the garden. Because butterflies are cold-blooded, they need to bask in the sun to warm up enough to fly. Provide them with flat rocks for sunning, though they will also light on stone or brick walls, paths, patios, or even deck railings.

PROVIDING FOOD FOR CATERPILLARS

The butterflies that we so delight in, with their languid, fluttering flight and lovely colors, do have a less agreeable side.

This winged form is just one stage of their life cycle; the other is a caterpillar stage. A butterfly's main mission in life is to mate and lay eggs, which hatch into caterpillars. Usually living for about two weeks, the female butterfly lays eggs on the undersides of a host plant—usually a different type of plant than it feeds on for nectar. The eggs hatch in a few days into tiny larvae, which mature into caterpillars. The caterpillars live for several weeks, growing ever larger and eating the foliage or flowers of the host plant. When the caterpillar stops feeding, it goes through a metamorphosis, forming a saclike chrysalis with a pupa inside. The pupa transforms itself from a caterpillar into a winged butterfly to continue the life cycle. Depending upon the type of butterfly and the climate, some butterflies go through several generations in a single season before hibernating or migrating for winter.

To keep the most butterflies in your garden, you need to supply a food source for the caterpillars, because most butterflies fly no more than several hundred yards from where they emerged from their chrysalis.

Fortunately, only two of the butterfly species we admire so much for their elegant appearance have caterpillar stages that are destructive to garden plants. The other types feed on weeds or trees and shrubs that easily withstand the feeding injury. Eastern black swallowtails, gorgeous butterflies with long, iridescent tails and bright, eyelike spots, come from bright-striped, green-and-yellow caterpillars that munch on plants in the carrot family, notably parsley, dill, and carrots, but also the pretty roadside weed Queen-Anne's lace. You can attract and keep this butterfly in your garden by planting plenty of parsley and dill; perhaps they will leave some for you

Attracting butterflies to your garden also means tolerating the damage they can do as larvae. This caterpillar will turn into a gorgeous black swallowtail, but only after devouring a considerable amount of parsley.

PLANTS TO ATTRACT BUTTERFLIES

Plants marked with * also serve as host plants for caterpillars.

ANNUALS AND HERBS

Ageratum houstonianum (flossflower)

**Anethum graveolens* (dill)

**Antirrhinum majus* (snapdragon)

Consolida ambigua (rocket larkspur)

Coreopsis tinctoria (golden coreopsis)

Cosmos bipinattus (cosmos)

Dahlia × hybrida (annual dahlia)

Dianthus chinensis (China pink)

Felicia amelloides (blue daisy)

Foeniculum vulgare (fennel)

Gaillardia pulchella (blanket-flower)

Helichrysum bracteatum (strawflower)

Heliotropium arborescens (heliotrope)

Lantana spp. (lantana)

Lobularia maritima (sweet alyssum)

**Petroselinum crispum* (parsley)

Petunia × hybrida (petunia)

Phlox drummondii (annual phlox)

Sanvitalia procumbens (creeping zinnia)

Schizanthus pinnatus (butterfly plant)

Tagetes spp. (marigold)

Tithonia rotundifolia (Mexican sunflower)

**Tropaeolum majus* (nasturtium)

Verbena × hybrida (verbena)

Zinnia spp. (zinnia)

BULBS

Allium spp. (ornamental onion)

Lilium spp. (lily)

PERENNIALS AND BIENNIALS

Achillea spp. (yarrow)

✓ **Alcea rosea* (hollyhock)

Anemone × hybrida (Japanese anemone)

Asclepias tuberosa (butterfly weed)

Aster spp. (aster)

Aubrieta deltoidea (false rockcress)

Aurinia saxatilis (basket-of-gold)

Baptisia australis (wild blue indigo)

**Borago officinalis* (borage)

Coreopsis spp. (coreopsis)

Dianthus spp. (sweet William)

Echinacea purpurea (purple coneflower)

Eupatorium purpureum (Joe-Pye weed)

✓ *Gaillardia × grandiflora* (blanket flower)

Helianthus spp. (sunflower)

Iberis sempervirens (edging candytuft)

✓ *Monarda didyma* (beebalm)

Phlox spp. (phlox)

Primula spp. (primrose)

Rodgersia spp. (rodgersia)

✓ *Rudbeckia* spp. (coneflower)

Salvia spp. (sage)

Scabiosa caucasica (pincushion flower)

Sedum spp. (stonecrop)

Solidago hybrids (goldenrod)

**Trifolium pratense* (red clover)

**Viola* spp. (violet)

SHRUBS

Abelia × grandiflora (glossy abelia)

Buddleia davidii (butterfly bush)

**Lindera benzoin* (spicebush)

Rhododendron spp. (azalea and rhododendron)

TREES

**Liriodendron tulipifera* (tulip tree)

**Robinia pseudoacacia* (black locust)

VINES

Aristolochia macrophylla (Dutchman's pipe)

Ipomoea tricolor (morning-glory)

Wisteria floribunda (Japanese wisteria)

---

to eat, too. The caterpillar stage of the European cabbage white butterfly, a delightful, little, bright white butterfly, feeds on cabbage family plants, zonal geraniums, and a few other garden flowers.

Remember that spraying your entire property with insecticides usually destroys the caterpillar stages of the beautiful butterflies you are hoping to enjoy. It's better for your plants, the butterflies, and the environment to use insecticides only when a serious pest occurs and then only on the affected plants. You can handpick destructive caterpillars off your flowers and vegetables if you wish to spare the butterflies. You can also plant plenty for both you and the caterpillars, covering your share with fine netting to prevent egg-laying.

If you are serious about butterfly gardening, you can consult a good field guide to determine which species are most likely to frequent your area, then plant the specific host and nectar plants to attract them. Meanwhile, planting masses of the flowers listed above will get your garden started on the road to becoming a mecca for butterflies.

SPECIAL GARDENS: MAKING GARDENING FUN FOR CHILDREN

activity is to make it fun and rewarding. Gardening can be that, if you go about it right by presenting the activity as play, not as work. Patience comes with age, so start out with gardening activities that bring successful results in a few weeks, such as starting fast-germinating seeds of flowers or vegetables or

Photo by Perry Struse

Daisy chains are a time-honored favorite garden craft. They are as simple as making slits in the stem of one flower, inserting the stem of another, slitting that stem, inserting yet another, and continuing the chain.

Getting your children, grandchildren, or other favorite young people involved in gardening is an excellent way to share quality time together, to teach some basic biology, and to instill a respect for nature and the environment. The experience might even be the beginning of a lifelong hobby that several generations can share. The key to getting children involved in any

planting transplants that are quick to flower or set fruit.

A CHILD'S EDIBLE GARDEN

Growing something a child can actually eat and serve to grown-ups creates special pride. So set aside a small plot where your child can grow some salad or vegetable crops or herbs for teas and flavoring. You can do the heavy work of turning the soil, but even preschoolers can help

FUN GARDENING ACTIVITIES FOR CHILDREN

■ Plant seeds of moonflower vines and watch the large, fragrant, white flowers unfurl at dusk each evening.

■ Carve the child's name or initials in the skin of a developing pumpkin or winter squash; at harvest time scar tissue will have made permanent letters.

■ Plant a flower garden to attract butterflies and then identify the butterflies that arrive for the feast.

■ Taste-test different varieties of homegrown tomatoes, beans, or bell peppers to see which each family member prefers.

■ Put cut daisy stems in water colored with food coloring to explain how plants take up water and nutrients.

■ Talk about plant names and discuss the difference between descriptive common names and scientific botanical names. Then make up some common names of your own for odd-looking or odd-acting plants such as lamb's-ears, snow-in-summer, pussy willow, and naked ladies.

■ Create a secret garden or maze with tall shrubs and vines and put a child-size bench or chair there for a private retreat and playhouse.

■ Grow a "garbage" garden started from seeds and cut tops of vegetables that you bought at the grocery store and ate for lunch or dinner.

smooth it and pick out stones and weeds. Help the child sow the seeds or plant the transplants and mark the rows with colorful drawings of the crop. Place the drawing on a stake and cover it with a taped plastic bag to keep it waterproof.

The garden need be no more than a 4×4-foot patch with two or three short rows. Be sure that the rows are narrow enough that your child can reach inside and apply mulch so weeds don't overtake the garden. If you don't have a place for a separate garden, designate part of a row in your garden for your child.

Choose vegetables your child likes to eat. Growing a vegetable the child detests doesn't guarantee a change of attitude about eating it. It's best to allow children to grow their favorites. Leaf lettuce, spinach, radishes, carrots, green beans, and cherry tomatoes are all easy to grow and can be harvested in a few weeks. Young children can best hold and plant large seeds, such as beans and cucumbers. Carrot and lettuce seeds are small and may be difficult for small children to plant without help.

Mint and parsley are foolproof to grow from transplants, and children like their flavor. Mint can be invasive, so use this to teach a lesson and figure out how to contain it. Alpine strawberries are also easy and fun to grow, and the flavor of the ripe berries is intense and sweet. The tiny berries easily can be harvested each morning for a cereal garnish.

Make the garden fun to be in and to look at by growing vining crops, such as cucumbers and pole beans, on a tall tepee made from lashing together four to six bamboo stakes. Your child also can use the tepee as a fort, for hiding out in the garden, or for watching the crops grow. You

might also want to put a scarecrow together from old clothes and sheets.

A CHILD'S FLOWER GARDEN

Children love pretty flowers, especially if they smell good, are brightly colored, or are huge and tower over their heads. You can cut the flowers for bouquets and use them to decorate the dinner table. Zinnias and marigolds are easy to grow from seed and are large and colorful.

Favorite fragrant plants include lily-of-the-valley, paper-white narcissus, dianthus, honeysuckle, roses, sweet peas, China pinks, scented geraniums, and herbs. Huge, showy flowers to grow include 'Southern Belle' hibiscus, sunflowers, hybrid clematis, hybrid iris, dahlias, Joe-Pye weed, and Oriental lilies. Fun flowers to grow include snapdragons, hollyhocks, moneyplant, nasturtiums, and Johnny-jump-ups.

GARDENING CHORES

Teach your child that a garden must be nurtured and cared for if it is to flourish. Give your child responsibility for the garden, just as you would for a pet. Don't let all the responsibility fall back on your shoulders, but don't be a nag either. Present the chores as something you can enjoy doing together while gaining a sense of accomplishment.

Although some of the chores may be too difficult for a young child to perform alone, you can do most together. You can drag the hose and sprinkler, but let your child turn on the faucet. Then set a timer as a reminder to turn it off. You can do most of the hoeing, but have your child help. Get a small, child-size

Photo by Brent Isenberger

hoe. Appropriate-size tools will be easier to handle and take care of.

The companionable act of gardening with your child brings untold rewards. It teaches responsibility, builds your child's self-esteem, and passes down knowledge from one generation to the next. You'll be creating happy memories and sowing the seeds for a healthy crop of future gardeners.

A small garden and pint-size tools allow children to take a sense of pride and ownership in a garden of their very own.

TREES & SHRUBS

CHAPTER 3

ABOUT TREES

ANATOMY OF A TREE

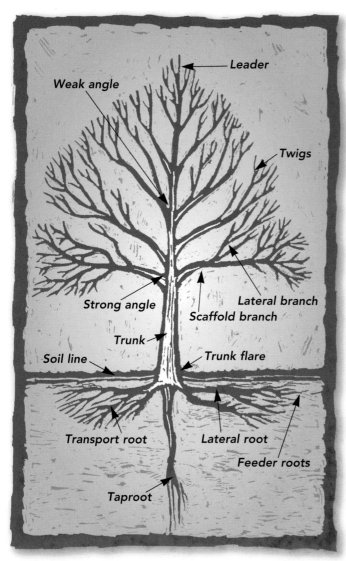

Leader

Weak angle

Twigs

Strong angle

Lateral branch

Scaffold branch

Trunk

Soil line

Trunk flare

Transport root

Lateral root

Feeder roots

Taproot

Like nothing else in your garden, trees define the landscape. Whether they're towering shade trees, stately evergreens, or delightful flowering trees, they create the bones of your garden.

DEFINING A TREE

Trees have a single main trunk that grows directly from the ground. The trunk of a healthy tree has a flare around the base where the tree emerges from the ground and from which the main anchoring roots grow. The main trunk is called the leader. Most trees have a single leader, but in some the trunk naturally divides into multiple leaders. The main branches that radiate from the trunk are called scaffold branches.

Some types of trees have taproots that grow straight down for many feet and stabilize the tree. All trees, whether they have taproots or not, send out four to 10 stout lateral roots that radiate from the trunk and support the tree; these are located within the top 2 to 4 feet of the soil. From these roots grow numerous transport roots, which are ¼ to 1 inch in diameter and spread parallel to the ground in all directions. Tiny feeder roots, which are about the size of a pencil lead and less than 2 inches long, grow from the transport roots and usually occupy the top 6 inches of soil. The feeder roots actually absorb most of the tree's nutrients and water from the soil. Because they are close to the soil surface, feeder roots are sensitive to drought and mechanical injury.

Tree roots extend well beyond the canopy, or drip line, of the tree, often to a distance three times its diameter. When a tree is dug from the nursery field and is balled and burlapped, it loses up to 95 percent of its roots and goes into transplant shock. It does not grow vigorously again until some of the lost roots regenerate. Regardless of a tree's size, its roots grow about 18 inches a year, so a small tree may recover faster than a large one.

Trees come in two basic types: deciduous (trees that lose their leaves each year) and evergreen (trees that don't lose their leaves each year).

Evergreen trees retain their leaves all year. They are classified as broad-leaved or coniferous. Broad-leaved evergreens, such as hollies, have flattened leaves and may have showy flowers. Conifers have needlelike leaves and bear cones.

DECIDUOUS TREES

Deciduous trees are valued for their large, leafy branches, which provide refreshing shade in summer. After their leaves drop in autumn, warming sun can stream through their branches. Shade trees, which include the oaks and maples so common in our yards, are among the tallest trees in the landscape and constitute the forest's canopy trees.

All deciduous trees bloom, but most of the large shade trees do not have showy or colorful flowers, although fall foliage colors can be outstanding. Any flowers a shade tree possesses are a bonus, not the main reason for growing it.

Many small trees, such as dogwoods and crabapples, have eye-catching flowers. Indeed, gardeners often classify them as small flowering trees. A number of these lovely trees also treat us to a show of glossy berries in autumn and winter. Generally, they are the understory trees that grow naturally along the edges of a woodland.

Deciduous shade trees have an

Deciduous trees such as this sugar maple, left, lose their leaves in autumn and remain leafless all winter. New foliage grows in spring. Many deciduous trees put on a beautiful fall color show before their leaves drop.

Most conifers, such as this oriental spruce (Picea orientalis 'Whittgold'), right, grow into tall spirelike trees with a central trunk and whorls of branches covered with bundles of needle- or scalelike leaves.

enormous quantity of leaves— a quantity you can best appreciate in autumn when they drop to the ground and you have to rake them. These leaves perform a valuable environmental service. They produce oxygen from carbon dioxide, continually refreshing the air we breathe. Leaves also trap dust and other pollutants and muffle sound. An acre of trees removes about 13 tons of dust and gases from the atmosphere each day.

CONIFER CHARACTERISTICS

Tall and aristocratic pines, spruces, and firs are the denizens of the forest primeval and lend an aura of drama to our gardens. Although the most familiar conifers are the ones we use as Christmas trees, conifers include a variable group of trees, 500 species in fact.

By definition, conifers bear flowers and seeds in conelike structures. Seed-bearing cones usually have woody scales, but may have fleshy scales and resemble berries in a few species. Most conifers grow into extremely tall trees with spirelike trunks and symmetrical whorls of

branches. Resin passages flow throughout their tissues.

The vast majority of conifers have narrow evergreen leaves shaped like needles or flat scales. A handful of conifers are deciduous—most notably bald cypress, larch, and dawn redwood. These deciduous conifers drop all their foliage in autumn. They grow new foliage each spring.

The needles of evergreen conifers do not live forever—the oldest ones drop every year. Most needles stay on the tree for three to five years, then yellow and drop, but younger needles remain green during the annual leaf drop.

Leaves of conifers, such as this Pinus resinosa, are shaped like needles or scales and often are arranged in bundles or whorls around the stems.

ABOUT SHRUBS

Shrubs, like trees, are classified either as deciduous plants, which lose their leaves each year, or evergreens. Both types are valuable additions to landscapes, gracefully bridging the gap between large trees and small landscape features, such as annual and perennial flowers and lawn.

Broad-leaved evergreen shrubs keep their leaves through the winter months. Here Japanese pieris relieves the winter doldrums with its early-blooming blossoms and shiny green foliage.

DECIDUOUS SHRUBS

Probably the most useful and easiest-to-care-for plants in our gardens are deciduous shrubs. We may think of shrubs as small versions of trees, but by definition shrubs are multitrunked woody plants. It's their multiple-stem nature, not their size, that defines them. Shrubs vary in size and shape, from low and spreading to tall and vase-shaped.

Deciduous shrubs lose their leaves in autumn and remain leafless and dormant throughout winter, surging into new growth in spring. Most of our garden favorites display decorative blossoms for about two weeks in spring or summer; a few may bloom longer or during winter or fall. Many deciduous shrubs put forth showy fruits that provide another season of color, usually in late summer and autumn. Some even hang on to their berries through winter, brightening the landscape and providing food for birds. As with deciduous trees, the leaves of deciduous shrubs can turn striking colors in autumn before dropping to the ground. Although leafless in winter, many deciduous shrubs embellish their surroundings and grab attention with colorful bark or interesting branching patterns.

EVERGREEN SHRUBS

There are good reasons for planting evergreen shrubs. Their dense, bushy habit and four-season foliage make them perfect plantings for areas that need to be softened or disguised with greenery throughout the year. They are the favorite choice as foundation plants—those plants used around the house to soften its angles and give it an established look. Evergreens also are a good choice for hedges where privacy or screening a view are paramount goals.

Many favorite garden shrubs are broad-leaved evergreens. By definition, they bear flattened leaves that remain green throughout the dormant season. Broad-leaved evergreens are available in a large assortment of sizes and shapes, from dwarf varieties of boxwood that are less than 1 foot tall to majestic rhododendrons that reach 20 feet in height. There's a host of landscape choices in between—low and trailing plants, compact and rounded shrubs, and horizontally spreading shrubs. They are practical plants that perform many landscape functions and possess a variety of attributes. Some have glossy green or variegated foliage; others present showy flowers or colorful fruit. Broad-leaved evergreen shrubs include boxwood, rhododendrons, azaleas, camellias, and hollies.

While conifers naturally grow into trees, their dwarf forms can be used like shrubs in a landscape, because they are small and often bushy. More and more frequently, showy dwarf conifers are stealing the spotlight from their larger, more ordinary cousins. Fascinating forms and variations in color are turning dwarf conifers into the darlings of plant collectors and connoisseurs. Gardeners with limited space also are finding dwarf conifers an excellent alternative to large conifers.

Photo by J. Watts

Gardeners love deciduous shrubs for their cold-hardiness and colorful blossoms. 'Anthony Waterer' spiraea delivers its raspberry pink blossoms in midsummer.

DWARF CONIFERS

*Dwarf white pine
(Pinus strobus 'Soft Touch')*

Slow-growing conifers, which are compact mutations of normal plants, often are called "dwarf conifers." Their ultimate size, however, is relative. A "normal" white pine may grow to 70 feet tall in 50 to 100 years; the dwarf form 'Nana' reaches only 10 feet in that time. It is a dwarf because its mature size is smaller than the species, although it grows rather large given enough time. Some experts separate dwarf conifers into categories to help distinguish them according to their ultimate size. The following categories are used in the encyclopedia starting on page 142:

■ **LARGE:** the normal size of the mature species

■ **INTERMEDIATE:** slow-growing, semidwarf or compact plants, maturing at one-half the size of the species

■ **DWARF:** slow-growing, reaching less than 10 feet tall in 10 years and usually maturing at one-tenth the size of the species

■ **MINIATURE:** extremely slow-growing, reaching less than 3 feet tall in 20 years

SITING AND BUYING TREES AND SHRUBS

Before you shop for a tree or shrub, evaluate the site where you plan to grow it. Ask yourself if the site is suitable and decide what size plant will work best when it reaches maturity.

LOCATING A TREE

All too often, large-growing trees are crowded beside houses, walks, gardens, and other buildings, because the people who planted them didn't have the knowledge or foresight to imagine how large that tree would grow a decade or two in the future.

To avoid future problems, stand in the location you have in mind for a tree and ask yourself these questions:
■ How far will the branches of the tree reach in 15, 20, or 25 years? Will the branches interfere with the house, garage, or other trees?
■ How tall will the tree be in 15, 20, or 25 years? Is the top likely to grow into power lines, an overhang, or other trees?
■ Where will the tree cast its shade during the morning and afternoon? Will the shade be in a welcome place or an unwelcome place?
■ Will the tree's roots have plenty of growing room or will they be constricted by pavement?

After answering these questions, search through the encyclopedia starting on page 142 for a tree with the size and shape you desire, one that will perform the functions you have in mind. (See Chapter 1 for more information about using trees in the landscape.)

CHOOSING A LOCATION FOR SHRUBS

Deciduous shrubs have varying needs for sun and shade depending upon the species. Most broad-leaved evergreens appreciate some shade. The best location receives dappled, light shade throughout the day. Also acceptable is a location with morning sun and afternoon shade, so the plant is not exposed to the hot afternoon sun. Some broad-leaved evergreens, such as those with small leaves, do perform well with full sun. Sun also is needed for the best leaf coloration in broad-leaved evergreens that take on red hues in winter.

Beware of locating broad-leaved evergreens where they receive shade

The gardener layered color and texture in this garden vignette. Planted along a stone wall, azalea bushes form a focal point.

Photo by William Stites

in summer and full sun in winter. This can happen if evergreens are sited beneath a deciduous tree. What seems like a perfect situation in summer turns into a disastrous situation in winter. A more advantageous location would be the north or east side of a building, where the shadow of the building provides protection. A location shaded by tall conifers also is suitable.

Full sun in winter burns the leaves of broad-leaved evergreens. Leaves lose moisture during sunny but freezing weather, and because the groundwater is frozen, the roots are unable to take up water to replace that lost by the leaves. The leaves then dehydrate and burn. The problem caused by winter sun is worst in the coldest part of a plant's growing range. In the North, soil and groundwater freeze early and remain frozen. A blanket of snow that reflects the sunlight further complicates the problem.

In general, broad-leaved evergreens grow and thrive in humus-rich, acid soil. For more information about the soil needs and optimum planting conditions for specific shrub species, consult the encyclopedia starting on page 170.

CHOOSING A HEALTHY TREE OR SHRUB

Don't automatically purchase the tallest tree or shrub on the nursery lot. A large plant may not have a root system that's big enough to support it. Research shows that large trees suffer more from transplant shock than small ones because they lose a larger percentage of their roots when they are dug from the field. It may take several years for a sizable (expensive) tree to recover from the shock and begin growing. By that time a smaller (and less expensive) tree may have caught up with it.

Photo by Peter Krumhardt

Shop for a tree with healthy green leaves, even growth, and a root ball in proportion to the topgrowth.

Unfortunately, many modern nursery practices, if carried out improperly, can mean that the healthy-looking tree or shrub you brought home declines after you plant it in your landscape. To choose a healthy plant at the garden center, look for the following indications:

■ Healthy topgrowth that is in proportion to the root ball

■ A trunk that does not rock back and forth in loose soil in the container or root ball

■ A smooth trunk without any open wounds or deep scars

■ Branches evenly spaced around the trunk

■ A dominant leader (main trunk) with an undamaged growing point

■ A healthy root ball that does not show exposed, encircling roots above soil level near trunk

■ A trunk that is centered in the container

PLANTING TREES AND SHRUBS

When planting a balled-and-burlapped tree or shrub, dig a hole only as deep as the root ball to avoid the soil settling later. Remove or fold back the burlap; chemically treated burlap does not rot and will hinder root growth.

After all the effort put into selecting the correct tree or shrub for your property, invest the time and energy necessary and plant it properly. An improperly planted tree or shrub may seem to thrive for many years, but then it will slowly and unexpectedly decline and eventually die. The reason for the premature death often is hidden underground in the way roots grow. Purchase a plant with a healthy root ball, then follow the planting steps outlined here to ensure the plant's long-term survival.

Trees and shrubs are sold as bare-root, container-grown, or balled-and-burlapped specimens. Each requires a different planting method, but all need the same type of planting hole and aftercare.

HOLE PREPARATION

The most recent planting recommendations, based on years of professional arborists' research, say to dig a hole twice as wide as the root ball and just as deep. If you dig a hole that's too deep and refill it with loose soil, the soil compacts and the tree may sink, causing root problems. Position the root ball of the tree in the planting hole so that the top of the root ball is at ground level. If your soil is heavy, position the tree slightly higher. You can test the level of the root ball by laying a board or shovel handle across the hole before refilling it.

Refill the planting hole with the soil dug from it. Press the soil gently around the root ball, but do not stamp it with your feet. Experts no longer advise "improving" the backfill with peat, compost, or other organic matter, because this creates a pocket of soil with a different texture and structure. Often the new roots are reluctant to grow beyond the improved area. Instead, they circle around inside the improved pocket. If your soil is extremely poor, it's advantageous to improve a large planting area or bed rather than only the planting hole.

After backfilling, create a berm, or dam, of soil around the perimeter of the planting hole to hold water. Periodically flood this area so water can slowly sink in and moisten the root ball. Remove the berm after the first growing season. It's crucial to keep the root ball of the newly planted tree moist while the tree is acclimating to the new location. Do not allow it to suffer drought for the first two to three years after planting.

Spread a 2- to 3-inch-deep layer of organic mulch around the tree to keep the soil cool and moist. Do not pile mulch up against the trunk. This is a common practice in some areas, but mounding the mulch encourages trunk rot and rodent damage.

PLANTING A BALLED-AND-BURLAPPED TREE OR SHRUB

Garden centers commonly sell balled-and-burlapped trees and shrubs, which adapt well to transplanting if they have a healthy root ball. Unfortunately, not all balled-and-burlapped trees do, because they were mishandled in the nursery field where they were grown.

Two situations result in a root ball with too much soil and not enough root. The seedling tree may have been planted too deep, as often happens with mechanical planting machines. Or, soil may have been inadvertently mounded up around the stems of field-grown trees during mechanical cultivation. When such trees are dug mechanically for balling, the roots are deeper than they should be; the machine digs to a specified depth and severs the roots, resulting in a root ball containing loose soil on top and too few roots beneath.

Check for this condition before purchasing a balled-and-burlapped plant. Pull back the burlap and stick your fingers into the top of the root ball. The roots should be at the soil surface. If you discover more than an inch or two of loose soil above the root ball, assume the plant was not properly dug and don't buy it.

Whether or not you suspect the balled-and-burlapped plant has been dug too deep, unwrap the top of the burlap and scrape off any loose soil to reveal the root ball's correct planting depth. That way you can avoid planting the tree or shrub too deep and ultimately suffocating the roots. When the tree is in the planting hole, remove as much burlap as possible, any ties and wrapping, and the wire basket, if present. If these are not removed, they prevent the plant's roots from growing beyond the burlap, and the plant becomes stunted and dies.

Untreated burlap decays in about a year in moist soil, but chemically treated burlap and artificial burlap (made with plastic fibers) do not rot readily. Artificial and treated burlap, which are difficult to distinguish from the real thing, often are used to wrap root balls. They take years to rot and will kill a plant if left around the planted root ball.

THE LATEST TREE-PLANTING METHODS

Research shows that many of the tried-and-true methods for planting a tree are not actually in the tree's best interest. Although some landscapers still practice the old methods, there are better ways to plant a tree to ensure its long-term survival.

■ **NEW METHOD:** Dig a wide planting hole no deeper than the tree's root ball so the soil won't settle.

■ **OUTDATED METHOD:** Planting holes were once dug deep and wide. If the loosened soil at the bottom of the hole packed down, the tree sank and the roots suffered.

■ **NEW METHOD:** Refill the planting hole with the soil removed from the hole. This encourages the roots to grow readily beyond the planting hole.

■ **OUTDATED METHOD:** Lots of organic matter was added to backfill soil that went into the planting hole. Researchers now know that new roots often do not grow beyond the improved soil in the hole. Instead, the roots circle around and around and compete with each other for available water and nutrients.

■ **NEW METHOD:** After the tree is in the planting hole, pull back and entirely remove the burlap wrap from balled-and-burlapped trees.

■ **OUTDATED METHOD:** Burlap was left on the root ball to eventually rot. Natural burlap does rot readily in moist ground, but new synthetic materials, which are difficult to distinguish from natural burlap, will not rot. If left in the ground, synthetic burlap prevents root expansion.

■ **NEW METHOD:** Stake a new tree only if it cannot stand by itself, is top-heavy, or is in a windy, exposed site. If you do stake a tree, make the ties loose and leave the stakes and ties in place for only one year.

■ **OUTDATED METHOD:** New trees were rigidly staked so they couldn't move, and they were left staked for several years. According to the most recent research, unstaked trees that can sway in the wind form stronger trunks that better resist breakage.

■ **NEW METHOD:** Prune only broken or wayward branches at planting time. Do not routinely prune branches to compensate for roots lost during transplanting.

■ **OUTDATED METHOD:** In the past, up to one-third of the branches were routinely removed to compensate for lost roots. However, researchers showed that hormones produced by the buds and leaves encourage root regeneration.

■ **NEW METHOD:** Do not wrap tree trunks unless the trees are planted in areas that will be exposed to reflected sun and heat from expanses of concrete or paving. You also may wrap to prevent injury to the bark during transport and planting. Remove any unnecessary wrap from trees after planting or after the trees have leafed out. If a wrap is necessary, let it remain on the tree for no more than one year.

■ **OUTDATED METHOD:** Tree trunks often were wrapped for several years to prevent injury from sunscald and insects. Research shows that the wrap can actually harbor insects and hold in dampness, promoting disease. A tight wrapping, or materials used to secure wrapping, can cut into the expanding tree trunk and strangle it.

PLANTING TREES AND SHRUBS

continued

PLANTING A CONTAINER-GROWN TREE OR SHRUB

More and more frequently, nurseries are growing trees and shrubs in containers rather than in the ground. Convenient as this method may be for the nursery, it often results in root habits that later spell disaster for the plant. If the plant is not centered in the container, the roots may grow in a "J" or hooked manner. If a tree or shrub is left in the container too long, the roots may circle around and around inside the container. Once planted, these deformed roots eventually girdle, or strangle, the trunk and cut off the plant's nutrient and water supply from the roots. You must take measures to counteract these problems at planting time.

Before purchasing, look to see if a large girdling root is bulging from the soil near the trunk. Stick your fingers into the soil near the trunk to feel for large circling roots near the surface. Is the trunk off center in the container? Pull the root ball from the container and look for a mass of circling roots. Do not purchase a tree or shrub if any of these tests reveal hooked or girdling roots.

Handle the plant by lifting the container—not the trunk—to avoid damaging the trunk and roots. Before removing the tree or shrub from the container, wet the root ball, then slide it out or cut the container's edges to free it. Before planting, use a sharp knife to slice off a 1- to 2-inch shell of roots from around the entire perimeter of the root ball. This helps redirect new roots so they grow outward instead of circling around as if they were still in the container. Use your fingers to loosen the roots exposed by the slices. Completely sever any large root that bulges up and circles around the trunk. Untangle and redirect smaller, more pliable roots.

PLANTING A BARE-ROOT TREE OR SHRUB

Small, bare-root trees and some shrubs can be bought by mail order or at the nursery in late winter or early spring. These dormant plants must be kept cool and moist and be planted as soon as possible. Protect the roots until planting time by keeping them covered with moist material or heeling them in the ground in a temporary spot until you can prepare the permanent site.

Photo by Peter Krumhardt

Generally sold by mail-order nurseries, bare-root trees and shrubs must be planted immediately before the roots dry out. Bare-root plants are lightweight and easy to plant, and they are inexpensive.

Position the bare-root tree or shrub in the planting hole at the same level it was growing in the nursery. Close inspection should reveal a line at the bottom of the trunk where the bark becomes darker; that's the soil line where the roots and trunk diverge.

STAKING KNOW-HOW

Controversy surrounds the simple act of tree staking. Because research shows that trees allowed to sway in the wind actually grow stronger trunks and roots, the once universal practice of staking is now limited. The following are the rules for staking newly planted trees:

■ Stake if the tree is top-heavy and likely to blow over in a strong wind.

■ Stake if the planting site is exposed to constant wind or strong gusts.

■ Stake if the trunk is weak and cannot stand upright.

■ Stake if the tree is planted in a public location where it could be damaged by pedestrians, vandals, or dogs.

■ For their first winter, stake new upright evergreens that are more than 3 feet tall. Because they retain foliage in winter, newly planted evergreens can be easily toppled by snow or wind.

Trees may be anchored with one, two, or three stakes; the number depends upon the tree's size and weight. A tree with a 3-inch-diameter trunk needs two stakes; a larger tree needs three stakes; a smaller tree needs only one. Choose sturdy, 8-foot-tall stakes such as pressure-treated 2×2s or fence posts made of cedar or metal.

Place the first stake on the windward side of the tree, driving it 18 inches into the ground alongside the root ball—not into the root ball. If you are using two stakes, place

Position the tree in the planting hole and fold back or remove the burlap. Refill the hole with the same soil removed from it. Build a dam around the top of the root ball to hold water. Drive two stakes on both sides of the root ball and secure them with ties threaded through pieces of garden hose. Leave the stakes in place for only a year.

This tree was left staked too long. As the trunk expanded, the guy ties became embedded in the trunk and girdled it, cutting off the tree's supply of water and nutrients. If the tight wire is removed before it strangles the tree, the trunk will have a weak spot at that point and may break during a storm.

the second stake exactly opposite the first. If you are using three stakes, place them equidistantly around the trunk.

To stake a weak tree that cannot stand by itself, position ties along the trunk at a height just above where the trunk begins to sway. Use heavy-duty wire or special plastic ties. Be sure to thread the wire through a piece of rubber or UV-resistant garden hose to prevent the tie from gouging the bark. Trees are commonly killed by wounds from wire ties, ties that are too tight, or ties that have been left in place too long. Remove the ties after one year. If ties are left on longer, the expanding

trunk grows around them and the wire girdles the tree.

Sometimes trees are attached to short, almost ground-level stakes with long guy wires. Although this method holds the tree securely, the stakes and wires are difficult to see, and people can easily trip over them. Use this method only in garden beds. Tall stakes are a safer choice where people might walk.

PLANTING TREES AND SHRUBS

continued

To determine how to space shrubs in a border, add their mature widths together and then divide by half. Plant the shrubs so their trunks are that distance apart.

SPACING RULES FOR SHRUBS

All too often, inexperienced gardeners—and many experienced ones, too—plant shrubs too close together and too close to buildings. That's an unnecessary waste of dollars and effort. Too many shrubs are purchased and the planting area quickly becomes overcrowded. Always remember that the young shrub you purchase at the garden center grows larger each year until it matures, just as a young child grows until reaching full adult size.

When choosing shrubs for your home landscape, try to match the space you are attempting to fill with the mature size of the shrub you're considering. Spacing shrubs according to their mature size means that in three to five years the branches will be touching slightly. If you force a large-growing plant such as a forsythia into a small space beside the front door, you will constantly have to prune it to keep the doorway accessible.

When mass-planting all-of-a-kind shrubs, space the trunks of each shrub at a distance equal to or greater than its mature width. For example, space shrubs that grow 5 feet wide at least 5 feet apart. This is called 5-foot-on-center spacing. If plants are slow-growing, space them more closely so they will achieve a fuller-looking effect sooner, but expect to remove every other one sometime in the future or to do a lot of pruning. Try not to line up the shrubs rigidly, but stagger them for a less regimented appearance.

In a shrub border where you're arranging different types and sizes of shrubs, you'll need to make more complicated spacing calculations. Add the width of the two different shrubs together and then divide by two. The result is the distance you should allow between the two trunks, or centers. If the shrubs are slow growers, space them more closely. Be sure to combine various shapes in a compatible design. For example, position a low-spreading shrub in front of a tall, vase-shaped one so their forms complement each other.

PLANTING A HEDGE

You'll find it easiest to plant bare-root hedge plants in a long trench. Large balled-and-burlapped or container plants can be planted in individual holes. Space plants for a sheared, formal hedge in a straight line 12 to 18 inches apart, depending upon the shrub's ultimate size. A formal hedge should be uniform. To achieve uniformity, run wire along several stakes to mark the center of the hedge. Mark each planting site with a stake before digging and install the plants so they abut the wire.

Shrubs suitable for sheared, formal hedges respond to repeated clipping by forming dense, twiggy growth. Shearing can mutilate leaves and turn stems into ugly stubs, so it's best to choose small-leaved shrubs that show less marring than large-leaved types.

Space plants for an informal hedge 24 to 36 inches apart in a single or staggered line so they grow into a thick barrier. Use a single line where space is limited and a staggered row where you have ample space. Exact spacing is not as important as with a formal hedge.

Informal hedges appear more graceful and natural than clipped, formal hedges, but they take up more space. To minimize pruning, choose shrubs that naturally grow dense and reach the height and width you need for screening. Where you have lots of room, many kinds of wide-spreading flowering shrubs make excellent informal hedges. Where space is limited, choose a cultivar that grows narrow and upright without pruning. You don't need to regularly clip an informal hedge, but you may need to occasionally thin branches and make rejuvenating pruning cuts as for nonhedge shrubs (see page 140).

Privet, top, is favored for creating a dense, formal hedge because it responds well to shearing. Bridal-wreath spirea, bottom, creates a lovely, informal flowering hedge behind a flower garden.

PLANTING A HEDGE

There are three patterns for planting a hedge. To be sure your hedge is straight, mark the center with a line tied to two stakes. Dig planting holes or a trench, according to the type of hedge plants you have.

To plant bare-root shrubs as a formal hedge, fist dig a trench then make equidistant mounds to hold the plants.

To plant balled-and-burlapped shrubs as a formal hedge, dig individual holes spaced equally apart

To plant an informal hedge, stagger the planting holes on both sides of the center line to produce a fuller effect.

CARING FOR TREES AND SHRUBS

By providing some basic and consistent care, you can improve the chances that your trees and shrubs will grow into spectacular specimens. That basic care is easy and quick.

WATERING

Although trees and shrubs have deep roots and use less water than a lawn, they, too, suffer during drought. If a spring-flowering shrub becomes water-stressed in summer when it is forming next year's flower buds, you'll notice the effects from the stress when it produces a poor show of blossoms the following year. So it pays to water—and water deeply—during periods of drought.

Trees and shrubs fare better if they are well watered when freezing weather arrives. Plants that are drought-stressed in autumn are less cold-hardy, and once the ground freezes they cannot rehydrate themselves. Provide a good soaking, if nature doesn't, in fall as leaves are dropping. (See pages 542–545 for more information on watering.)

FERTILIZING

Trees and shrubs benefit from fertilizer. Supplying a tree with the big three nutrients—nitrogen, phosphorus, and potassium (see pages 512–513)—usually is enough. Trees growing in alkaline or sandy soil may need micronutrients such as iron and manganese as well.

Because most feeder roots are near the soil surface, you can feed a tree by simply broadcasting fertilizer granules beneath the tree's canopy. Trees growing in lawns benefit from the fertilizer spread on the lawn and generally need no additional feeding. Do not apply "weed and feed" products to lawn areas that encompass trees, however, because the herbicide may harm the trees. For trees not growing in a fertilized lawn, apply a controlled-release, high-nitrogen fertilizer at a rate of 3 to 6 pounds of actual nitrogen per 1,000 square feet of tree canopy. Apply fertilizer such as 5-10-5 or 10-6-4 in early spring, when the roots are actively growing.

If a lawn tree needs a boost, do not broadcast the fertilizer, because more than 3 pounds of nitrogen per 1,000 square feet of ground can cause excessive lawn growth. Instead, call a professional arborist to do a deep-root feeding, a method in which a high-pressure hydraulic device injects liquid fertilizer 4 to 12 inches into the ground (below the grass roots). The fertilizer should be injected in a 3-foot grid pattern beginning 3 feet from the trunk and extending 3 feet beyond the canopy. This is the most efficient way to deliver potassium and phosphorus to tree roots. Unlike nitrogen, these elements do not readily move through the soil.

An alternate method is to use granular fertilizer. Drill 12-inch-deep holes 18 to 24 inches apart, beginning 3 feet from the trunk and extending 3 feet beyond the canopy. Fill the holes with enough granular fertilizer to equal 3 to 6 pounds of actual nitrogen per 1,000 square feet, keeping the fertilizer 4 inches below the soil surface. Top the holes with a soil amendment or grass plugs.

Flowering shrubs respond to fertilizer by blooming more freely and producing strong stems and foliage. Spread rotted manure or aged compost over the shrub roots each year or feed with a fertilizer such as 5-10-5. Don't overfertilize; you can burn the shrub's roots. A 4- to 5-foot-tall shrub needs only ¼ to ½ cup of fertilizer sprinkled evenly on the soil in a circle extending outward from the branches. Read label directions. Azaleas, hollies, and other acid-loving plants need a specially designed fertilizer.

Apply the plant food in early spring to stimulate healthy, new growth. Fertilizer applied in late summer or fall stimulates growth that may not harden properly before winter and may be injured by cold temperatures.

If you garden organically, apply compost or a balanced organic fertilizer once a year during growing season. Distribute it evenly around the drip line of trees and shrubs.

MULCHING

Mulching a planted shrub may be the best thing you can do to ensure its health. Spread an organic mulch, such as pine bark or shredded leaves, several inches thick under the shrub's limbs to keep the roots cool and moist and to discourage weeds. Plastic sheeting and landscape fabric mulches discourage weeds in shrub beds, but have many drawbacks. See pages 522–525 for complete information on organic mulches and weed barriers.

Planting trees and shrubs in beds, rather than as individual specimens in a lawn, keeps them healthy, and they are easier to care for. When you site a tree in a mulched bed or a bed of groundcovers and shrubs, you avoid injuring the trunk when mowing (a leading cause of tree death).

An arborist treats a very tall tree for pests by injecting an insecticide into the base of the trunk.

HANDLING PEST AND DISEASE PROBLEMS

Unfortunately, deciduous and evergreen trees and shrubs can fall prey to insects and diseases. Some pests do only minimal damage, but others can destroy the plant unless they're controlled. Today the accepted practice is to use pesticides only when necessary to control active pests rather than to routinely apply pesticides as a preventative.

You may be able to spray small trees and shrubs yourself with a hose-end sprayer or a powerful compression sprayer. However, you should call a licensed professional applicator to apply pesticides to large trees. A professional has the powerful hoses necessary to reach tall treetops. Extra-tall trees may have to be treated for pests by injecting the insecticide into the base of the trunk; the tree's circulatory system carries it to the tips of the branches. This exacting procedure needs to be carried out by a skilled professional arborist.

See pages 546–559 for more information on controlling pests and diseases and applying pesticides and fungicides.

These dogwoods and azaleas are planted in a large mulched bed, which creates a healthy environment and makes them easier to care for.

SOIL SOLUTIONS

In general, broad-leaved evergreens do best in moist, humus-rich, acid soil. Their roots may be shallow, so they dry out easily in sandy soil. They are easily damaged in a waterlogged site. However, some hollies and other broad-leaved evergreens prefer light soil.

Avoid planting azaleas, rhododendrons, mountain laurels, camellias, and other acid-loving plants in heavy or neutral to alkaline soil. Instead, improve the entire planting area by deeply turning in copious amounts of organic matter. Alternatively, in poorly drained sites or other improbable locations, plant in a raised mound of improved soil.

Create a gently sloping mound of wood chips large enough to contain the roots of the mature plant and then bury the root ball at the appropriate level above the soil. Or better yet, create an entirely new raised planting area from a truckload or two of wood chips to create a border for a collection of these shrubs. The wood chips eventually decay into a humus-rich soil, but will continue to provide the perfect, well-drained, moist medium.

PREVENTING DAMAGE

The following practices help keep mature trees and shrubs healthy:

■ Avoid damaging trunks with the lawn mower or string trimmer. Trunk injury can kill trees. To protect them, place trees and shrubs in groundcover beds or garden borders, or ring them with organic mulch.

■ Remove stakes, ties, and trunk wraps that can strangle the trunk as it grows.

■ Do not dig extensively under a tree's canopy. This can harm the feeder roots. Never sever a root larger than your finger. Avoid digging a trench for utilities or any other reason closer than 3 feet from a trunk. Locating the trench outside of the drip line is even better. To prevent tree damage from machinery during construction, fence off the area under the tree's canopy. Heavy equipment can compact the soil.

■ Do not change the soil level beneath the tree's canopy, because that's where the roots are. If the surrounding level must be changed, build a retaining wall at the canopy edge and don't change the grade inside the wall.

■ Protect newly planted conifers from strong wind and sun in winter, especially the first year after planting. Erect a burlap windbreak or protect with cut boughs from Christmas trees.

■ Gently shake or sweep heavy snow off branches of evergreens to prevent them from breaking under the weight.

■ Do not apply dormant oil to blue-gray conifers; the oil dissolves the colorful waxy coating.

PRUNING TREES AND SHRUBS

Behind nearly every beautiful tree and shrub is a gardener who knows what to prune—and what not to prune. Correct pruning not only creates a beautiful plant, it also keeps it at its healthiest, prevents damage from storms, and helps it fit into the landscape. But incorrect pruning can do more harm than good.

BASIC TREE PRUNING

To maintain healthy, attractive trees and shrubs, some routine maintenance is called for. Be sure to make all pruning cuts at the branch collar, the ridge of bark where the branch joins the trunk (see illustration at right), not flush with the trunk and not so far away that a branch stub is left. For tall trees or extensive pruning, hire a professional arborist. Choose one who is a member of the American Society of Consulting Arborists or a similar professional group to be certain you're hiring the most knowledgeable caretaker. Bad pruning can do more damage than none at all. To prune a mature tree:
■ Remove any sprouts that emerge from the tree's base.
■ Correct weak branch crotches—those that emerge at V-shaped angles rather than at stronger, more horizontal angles.
■ Remove multiple leaders that form on trees that normally have only one leader.

■ Remove crossed branches that rub against each other.
■ Thin out the crowns of dense, heavy trees to allow wind to pass through the branches rather than risk them breaking. Never head back branches by cutting them back to stubs; this encourages growth more prone to storm damage.

PRUNING CONIFERS

Tall conifers sometimes need to be pruned to control their size, remove a broken limb, or replace a damaged leader. When used as a screen or hedge in a small space, these evergreens may need regular pruning (or shearing) to keep them dense and compact. Dwarf conifers require no more pruning than the removal of an occasional damaged branch.

Understanding how a conifer grows helps you determine how to prune it. Many conifers, especially pines, produce a single flush of new growth once a year; the flexible, new green stems and emerging needles are called candles. Other conifers, such as yews, grow continually from spring through summer.

Most conifers have a tall central leader or main stem. If insects or an ice storm damages the leader, you'll need to train a side branch as a replacement to prevent the tree from being deformed.

When the leader is gone, usually two or more side branches grow upward and the tree loses its natural pyramidal shape.

You can train a new terminal shoot from a side branch. Choose the strongest of the side shoots beside the lost leader. Wrap insulated wire, such as stereo speaker wire, around the shoot and gently bend the reinforced shoot into an upright

HOW TO PRUNE A TREE LIMB

For the sake of safety and preserving the tree's health, never prune a large limb all in one piece. Instead, cut off the limb in stages to control its fall and prevent the bark from ripping. (If the limb is very large, cut off side branches first.)

To remove the limb, make an undercut several inches away from the trunk (Cut 1, below). Cut slightly more than halfway through the limb. Make a second cut on the top of the limb, sawing until the limb snaps in half (Cut 2). Cut off the remaining stump, angling the cut slightly (Cut 3). This leaves the bark ridge and branch collar intact, promoting healing of the wound.

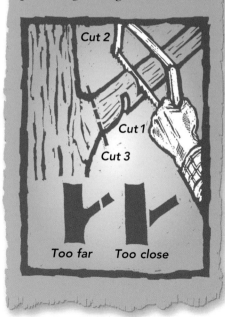

Cut 2
Cut 1
Cut 3

Too far   Too close

To shorten and slow the growth of a long branch of a conifer without disfiguring it, cut the central branch where it forks into side branches.

position. Continue wrapping the wire about a foot down the main trunk. If necessary, rewrap the new terminal and the top of the trunk the next year to continue guiding the growth straight upward. Most conifers will not produce new growth from old wood. This means that if you cut back a branch to a point where it has no side branches or needles, you have essentially killed the branch. New needles or branches will not grow from the leafless branch. Yews and a few other conifers are an exception to this rule; these are noted in the encyclopedia section starting on page 204.

Large conifers can be reduced in size by selectively thinning the branches as new growth begins or by pinching the candles. Do not head

back or shear the tree. Cut all the long limbs where they naturally fork, maintaining the tree's natural layering and pyramidal shape (long branches at the bottom and shorter ones at the top). Do not cut off the top of the leader. The pruned tree should have a natural shape and the cuts should be barely noticeable.

If you like to cut greens for indoor decoration, it will do no harm to thin pines and similar conifers in winter. Make those cuts judiciously so the cut ends are camouflaged by side growth.

Many conifers have an attractive skirt of ground-sweeping branches. If possible, allow enough room in your garden so these low branches have ample space to grow, although you can cut off the branches if they're in the way. Most pines—especially multitrunk ones—look attractive even with their lower limbs removed, and often these lower limbs die naturally. However, stiff, symmetrical trees, such as spruces, look unattractive when the lower limbs are removed.

Decide for yourself whether or not a particular tree's shape and silhouette will be disfigured by removing the lower limbs. Remember that a limb removed will not grow back. Instead of cutting off the lower limbs, consider creating a mulch ring around the perimeter of the low branches to ease lawn-mowing and weeding chores.

THINNING TO CONTROL SIZE

Although most homeowners unwittingly shear yews and other evergreen shrubs into balls and cubes, thinning cuts are the best way to prune evergreen shrubs. Thinning results in lovely, dense shrubs that keep their desired size forever; shearing causes shrubs to slowly

PINCHING EVERGREEN TREES AND SHRUBS

To slow and control a plant's growth and encourage it to become bushier and fuller, try pinching its tips.

■ **BROAD-LEAVED EVERGREENS** Most broad-leaved evergreens produce one flush of growth a year, in spring. The young stems burst from the buds, elongating rapidly with a collection of tiny, new leaves arranged along their lengths. At this time, before the new leaves fully expand, you can pinch the new growth, snapping off part of its length. Pinching controls the plant's growth and encourages it to branch and become denser.

■ **CONIFERS** To keep a conifer more compact and slow its growth, you can prune the candles. Before the needles fully elongate and the wood hardens, break off part of the candle with your fingers (a process called pinching) or cut back the candle with shears to control the length of the resulting growth. This does not mar the needles that grow from the remainder of the candle.

PRUNING TREES AND SHRUBS

continued

grow larger because you cut only partway into the exterior foliage. Shrubs that have insufficient room to grow can be thinned to control their size. Because a thinned evergreen forms new growth in its interior, you can cut back the interior repeatedly to keep the shrub at the desired size.

Thin evergreen shrubs in the following way: Use pruning shears (the one-handed kind, not two-handed hedge shears) to cut back the long branches. Cut a branch by reaching into the shrub's interior and holding the branch with one hand. Using the other hand, clip just beyond a point where the branch forks into side branches. Repeat these cuts throughout the shrub, letting the shrub's natural shape guide you.

When you are finished thinning, the shrub should look fluffy and have an uneven exterior. It should not look pruned, except that it will be smaller and somewhat less dense than before. This is the best way to reduce a shrub's size because it looks natural and does not stimulate excessive new growth.

PRUNING FLOWERING AND DECIDUOUS SHRUBS

Terminal buds at the tip of each branch secrete hormones that keep the growth of a shrub or tree under control. If that dominant bud is injured or removed, side branches begin to grow excessively. That's why shearing cuts, which head back all the terminal buds from many branches, result in a rebound of excessive growth that soon needs pruning all over again. The growth is dense and twiggy on the shrub's exterior and the interior becomes bare and leafless. A thinning cut, however, removes the terminal bud,

Formally sheared hedges, like the one below, need trimming several times a year. Clip them with manual shears, left, or electric shears, being careful to taper the sides so the hedge is wider at the bottom than at the top. This allows all the leaves to receive ample sunlight and prevents loss of lower limbs and a bare-bottomed hedge.

These identical yews were pruned using two methods. The shrub on the left was thinned with hand shears, giving it a fluffy appearance. The shrub on the right was sheared with hedge shears, creating a flat, uniform surface.

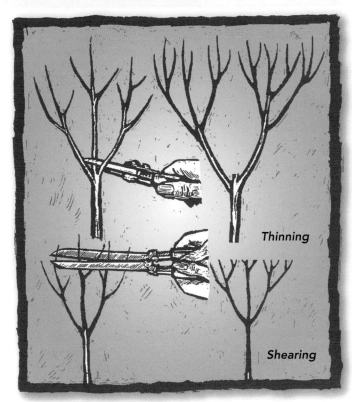

Thinning

Shearing

Thinning cuts, made with hand shears, should be made where the main branch forks into side branches. Shearing cuts, made with hedge shears, should be made straight across all new growth.

For the most natural appearance when pruning, cut just past the point where the main branch forks into side branches. Do not leave a stub.

but allows buds on side branches to become dominant and suppress excessive growth. New growth is controlled and the shrub's interior remains leafy.

Don't make the common mistake of using hedge shears to cut back (shear) flowering shrubs by clipping all around the shrub's edges. Too often, homeowners hack shrubs into balls and cubes by shearing back all the growth—but this just stimulates more growth while creating an unattractive shrub. Use this type of pruning only for formal hedges.

Most flowering shrubs look best if allowed to assume their natural, graceful outlines. Their shape can be maintained or spruced up with thinning cuts made in the shrub's interior. Some deciduous shrubs benefit from annual pruning, but many others perform beautifully for years with no pruning. Most flowering deciduous shrubs, such as forsythia, weigela, and lilac, produce new stems or canes from their bases every year. This new growth added to the old growth can turn a shrub into a thicket of tangled stems. As older stems age, they flower less and eventually die. Your pruning goal should be to remove the oldest stems to make way for new, more free-flowering growth.

SHEARING A HEDGE

Formal hedges that are meant to create tall or low walls of greenery must be sheared several times a year to keep them neat and wall-like. Here's where the two-handed hedge shears—either manual or electric—come into play. Follow these steps for a new hedge:

1. Spring of the first year: Cut back hedge plants to a height of 3 inches to encourage dense, new growth.
2. Spring of the second year: Before new growth begins in spring, shear the top and sides into flat walls. Keep the base wider than the top; the bottom branches need to receive sunlight to retain their leaves.
3. Summer of the second year: Shear off half the length of the new stems before they harden. Shear once more if growth is excessive.
4. Each year thereafter: Before new growth begins in spring or just after it begins, shear the top and sides, maintaining a slight taper from top to bottom. The new growth will cover the sheared stubs. Fast-growing hedge shrubs may need to be sheared two or even three times during the growing season. Rejuvenate old hedges that have grown too tall by cutting them to the ground in early spring.

Incorrect shape   *Correct shape*

PRUNING TREES AND SHRUBS
continued

REJUVENATING SHRUBS

Old deciduous shrubs that form multiple stems need to be rejuvenated from time to time even if they are regularly thinned. Every year, cut back the oldest stems and any dead ones to a height of 2 inches.

REJUVENATING A YEW OR ARBORVITAE

Most conifers will not resprout from bare wood. Yews and arborvitae are the exception. You can cut back a severely overgrown yew or arborvitae to the bare trunk, and it will recover into a beautiful specimen. Recovery may take several years, however, and the operation is not for the faint of heart. But if you're willing to take the chance, use a saw and loppers to cut the tree down to its skeleton just as new growth begins, in late winter or early spring. Then watch it regrow.

Photo by David Chinery

Photo by Saxon Holt

Pruning for rejuvenation is best done on flowering shrubs when they are dormant. All the deadwood on this deutzia has been cut out and a third of the stems are cut back. The process is repeated for two subsequent years.

Saw them off with a handheld pruning saw or clip them with lopping shears.

It's easiest to remove the branches in two steps: Cut the top part of the branch and pull it out of the shrub from the top; next cut the remainder of the stem about 2 inches from the ground and pull it out from the bottom. The oldest stems will be thick and have tough-looking bark; dead stems have dried, split bark and are brittle and brown in the center. Leave young, healthy, stout stems, but remove weak and spindly ones. If you do this every year, the shrub always has stems of all ages and will flower prolifically.

Severely overgrown, neglected, or badly pruned shrubs can be cut completely to the ground in late winter to rejuvenate them. New canes will grow from the ground. You can selectively remove the new growth, keeping the strongest stems and removing the weakest. If you prefer not to take such drastic measures, cut back one-third of the old stems each year for three consecutive years.

Shrubs won't be harmed if they are not pruned every year. Although some benefit from annual pruning, others require thinning the stems at ground level only every three or four years.

If broad-leaved evergreens become overgrown and too large for their space in the landscape, instead of pulling them out, rejuvenate them by cutting the stems back severely. Although this drastic procedure results in unattractive plants for several years, if you can tolerate their unsightly appearance, your reward will be healthy, good-looking, and much smaller plants.

In late winter or early spring, cut all the main stems back to ground level or to lengths that are several feet long, using lopping shears or a pruning saw. Rhododendron and mountain laurel recover better if you cut back only one-third of the stems each year for three consecutive years. That way, the remaining stems and foliage can fuel the rejuvenation.

TIMING IS EVERYTHING

Prune flowering shrubs when they are not budding so you won't diminish the shrub's flower display. Spring-flowering shrubs bloom on old wood—that is, wood and flower buds that formed the previous year, usually during summer. Summer-flowering shrubs bloom on new growth—that is, wood formed during the same season.

Prune spring-flowering shrubs immediately after they bloom. That way the resulting new growth produces flower buds for the next year. Prune summer-flowering shrubs in late winter or early spring by thinning back the branches or cutting them completely to the ground. The pruning stimulates new growth that blooms that same year.

DEADHEADING

You may wish to deadhead, or remove faded blossoms, from some flowering shrubs unless they produce colorful berries late in the year. Deadheading prevents seed formation, allowing the plant to channel energy into new vegetative growth, and it improves the plant's appearance. It also encourages better blooming the next year. Some plants tend to bloom well only in alternate years unless deadheaded, because seed formation slows the following year's flower bud production.

Plants that benefit from deadheading include lilac, rhododendron, azalea, camellia, mountain laurel, and pieris. These tend to form large flowers and seed heads, which are easily removed. Snap off the faded flower heads between your thumb and forefinger, taking care not to injure the buds at the base of the old blossoms. It's not too late to deadhead when the stem tissue has hardened and seedpods are beginning to form, but at that time you must cut off the seedpods carefully with pruning shears.

Many shrubs, such as rhododendron, mountain laurel, and lilac, bloom better the following year if faded blossoms are removed before they set seed. To deadhead a rhododendron, above, pinch off the developing cluster of seedpods between your thumb and forefinger. Be careful not to injure the new side shoots on either side.

Deciduous Trees

DECIDUOUS TREES

ACER SPP.
Japanese Maple

Grown for their beautiful foliage and silhouettes, small slow-growing Japanese maples *(Acer palmatum)* and cutleaf maples *(A. palmatum* var. *dissectum)* are the stars of any garden, any season of the year. The leaves of the species are divided into five to seven sharply pointed, toothed lobes that radiate

ACER PALMATUM 'ORNATUM'

from the center like fingers of a hand. In cutleaf or threadleaf forms, the fingers are deeply divided into feathery or lacy patterns. Leaves may be light green, gold, blood red, burgundy, or variegated. Spring foliage may be reddish. Fall brings a magnificent show; green-leaf types turn gold or yellow; purple- and red-leaf forms turn brilliant red or scarlet, and gold-leaf forms turn orange-yellow to yellow. Trunk bark is smooth gray marked with darker striations, and twigs are shiny pea green, purplish-black, or coral-red. Upright, vase-shaped cultivars reach 15 to 30 feet tall and wide. Cutleaf forms are usually weeping and mounded to 5 to 10 feet tall and twice as wide.

Also of Japanese origin, the full-moon maple *(A. japonicum)* is similar to Japanese maple. The rounded leaves have seven to 13 shallowly cut lobes. Trees are rounded to 30 feet tall and wide.

Vase-shaped and rounded Japanese and full-moon maples are excellent shade trees for small gardens, patios, and borders. Use weeping cutleaf forms as magnificent specimens in borders, foundations, and lawns; locate to cascade over water. Purple-leaf forms contrast beautifully with blue-green conifers, and golden forms stand out against dark green.

Site: Full sun to part shade, red-leaf forms need ample sun. Protect from hottest afternoon sun, especially in the South. Humus-rich, moist, slightly acid, well-drained soil essential. Japanese maple, zones 5 to 8, protect from extreme heat. Full-moon maple, zones 6 to 9.

How to Grow: Plant container or balled-and-burlapped plants in spring or fall. Mulch beneath branches to keep soil cool and moist. Protect from wind. Prune out dead wood and twigs from interior. Thin lightly in winter to reveal trunks and branching pattern. Verticillium wilt can kill trees suddenly.

Cultivars and Similar Species: Over 200 Japanese maple cultivars. Upright forms: 'Bloodgood', very popular red-leaf; 'Sango-Kaku' (coral-bark maple), coral-red twigs, lime-green leaves, brilliant yellow fall color, 15 feet tall, zones 6 to 9; 'Aoyagi' (green-bark maple), pea-green young branches, bright green leaves, yellow fall color; 'Butterfly', white-pink-and-green variegated leaves, bushy to 10 feet.

Cutleaf forms: *A. p.* 'Dissectum Atropurpureum', burgundy-red deeply cut leaves in spring, burgundy-green in summer, red in fall; 'Crimson Queen', bright crimson new growth, deep red in summer, scarlet in fall; 'Filigree', light yellow-green leaves, gold fall color; 'Ornatum', older cultivar, finely cut

leaves, green-red in summer, crimson in fall; 'Red Pygmy', garnet-red linear leaflets; 'Viridis', light green leaves, green branches, yellow fall color.

Full-moon maple: 'Aureum' (golden full-moon maple) chartreuse leaves, gold fall color, excellent in light shade; 'Aconitifolium', large green leaves, mahogany-red fall color, 30 feet.

ACER SPP.
Trifoliate Maple

The trifoliate maples are small, tough, slow-growing trees with three-lobed leaves. They make pretty landscape plants for a border, patio, or courtyard in difficult growing conditions. Amur and hedge maples also can be massed as a privacy screen or windbreak.

ACER GRISEUM

Amur maple's *(Acer tataricum* subsp. *ginnala)* narrow leaves have dark green tops and light green undersides, and turn deep red to scarlet in fall. The yellowish white flower clusters are very fragrant and ripen into showy, winged, papery, red fruits. This rounded, multitrunk tree grows 15 to 20 feet tall and wide. Hedge maple *(A. campestre)* has 3- to 5-lobed rounded leaves, corky bark, and yellow foliage color in late fall. Rounded and low-branched; to 35 or more feet tall.

The bark of paperbark maple (*A. griseum*) is shiny cinnamon-brown and peels in large papery curls. Trunk bark of old trees looks like smoothly polished brass. The jagged-edged, three-lobed leaves are dark green and change in late fall to rich chestnut-brown or russet-red. Upright to oval; 20 to 40 feet tall, 15 to 25 feet wide.

Site: All best in full sun. Paperbark maple and amur maple tolerate part shade, although fall color is best in sun. Amur maple best in well-drained fertile soil, but tolerates most soils and even high pH. Hedge maple tolerates poor, sandy, and alkaline soil, and heat and urban conditions. Paperbark maple grows best in well-drained, humus-rich soil; pH 5 to 7 and needs plentiful moisture, but tolerates clay soil.

Amur maple, zones 3 to 6; hedge maple, zones 5 to 8; paperbark maple, zones 5 to 7.

How to Grow: Plant balled-and-burlapped or container trees in spring or fall, spacing 20 feet apart. Amur and hedge maples can be clipped into a dense hedgelike screen or windbreak; space 10 feet apart for a hedge. Prune when dormant; remove lower branches to walk beneath tree and to reveal attractive bark. Amur maple may cause a weed problem and suffer from verticillium wilt.

Cultivars and Similar Species: Amur maple: 'Flame', excellent red fall color; 'Red Rhapsody', brilliant red fall color; 'Red Wing', very showy red fruits; 'Compacta', bushlike.

Hedge maple: 'Queen Elizabeth', upright to oval, fast-growing, gold fall color.

A. maximowiczianum (Nikko maple) similar to paperbark maple with three-parted compound leaves, zones 5 to 7.

Hybrids of the two: 'Gingerbread', flaky cinnamon-colored bark, brilliant red and orange fall color, pest- and heat-resistant, faster growing, zones 5 to 8; 'Cinnamon Flakes', similar with late red fall color.

ACER SPP.
Tall Shade-Tree Maple

These tall maples make excellent shade trees for a lawn or street, but be sure to select the right one for your climate. Do not plant them under power lines, because they grow too tall. Use Norway maple and silver maple only in areas of extreme cold, drought, or poor soil where other shade trees do not do well.

Norway maple (*Acer platanoides*) is valuable in the Northern Plains, Midwest, and Mountain states where many other shade trees have a difficult time. Its extremely dense shade, surface roots, and habit of spreading seedlings everywhere makes it undesirable where other trees do well.

The ridge-barked tree is covered with beautiful clusters of chartreuse flowers in early spring before young leaves emerge. The large leaves are shiny dark green with five sharp-pointed lobes and turn brilliant yellow in very late fall in the North; colors poorly in the South. Round and dense; to 50 feet tall and wide.

ACER RUBRUM 'AUTUMN FLAME'

Red maple (*A. rubrum*) is named for the mist of red flowers that cover the silver-barked tree before the leaves appear in early spring. It's native to eastern North America. The dark green leaves have red petioles and gray-green undersides. Fall color appears early and varies from bright yellow to red and every shade between, often on the same leaf. Pyramidal when young, rounded with age; to 60 feet tall and 45 feet wide.

Silver maple (*A. saccharinum*) is a fast-growing native of stream banks in eastern North America. It is one of the best shade trees for poor soil areas, however, the wood is damaged easily by ice and wind. Older trees can be hazardous. Leaves are deeply cut into five jagged lobes and are light green on top with silver undersides, creating a lovely flashing light in a breeze. Foliage turns light yellow in mid autumn. Misty greenish yellow to red flowers open in very early spring. Trunk bark is smooth gray when young; rough and flaky with orange patches with age. Upright to oval with slightly pendulous branches; 50 to 80 or more feet tall and 80 feet wide.

Sugar maple (*A. saccharum*), native from Canada to Georgia and west to Texas, is renowned for its magnificent fall color and delicious sugary sap. Leaves are broad and sharply lobed and medium green. In mid autumn leaves exposed to full sun turn scarlet to orange-red; shaded ones turn orange to gold or bright yellow. The strong central trunk has a rough brown bark. Upright and oval to 80 feet tall and 60 feet wide.

Site: All need full sun; sugar maple also grows in part shade; variegated forms need part or light shade in the South. Norway maple grows well in sandy to heavy, acid to alkaline soil; tolerates poorly drained compacted soil and road salt, but best with moderate to plentiful moisture. Red maple best in acid, fertile site with plentiful moisture, but does well in wet conditions and clay or rocky soil. Silver *continued*

Deciduous Trees

ACER SPP.
(continued)

maple best in deep, fertile, acid soil with plentiful moisture, but performs well in wet or dry soil and withstands flooding. Sugar maple needs fertile, well-drained, slightly acid soil. Plant fast-growing and weak-wooded silver maple well away from buildings in case of storm damage.

Norway maple, zones 4 to 7, tolerates air pollution and urban conditions; red maple, zones 3 to 9, tolerates air pollution; silver maple, zones 3 to 9, tolerates heat and drought; sugar maple, zones 3 to 7.

How to Grow: Plant bare-root trees in early spring or balled-and-burlapped plants in spring, summer, or fall, giving plenty of growing room. Prune when dormant. Consider cabling older silver maples or thin crowns to reduce wind resistance; improper pruning can make even more susceptible to damage; needs regular pruning to remove storm-damaged wood.

Surface roots can disrupt pavement and lawns. Dense shade of Norway maple interferes with lawn growth; choose a groundcover suited to dry shade or apply attractive organic mulch. Seedlings of silver and Norway maples create a weed problem; Norway maple threatens natural areas.

Diseases include anthracnose during rainy years on silver maple; verticillium wilt serious on all these maples. Insect pests include: Aphids on Norway maple, scale on silver maple, borers and leaf hoppers on red maple. Leaf scorch a problem on Norway and red maples during hot, windy weather in exposed sites, but not on improved cultivars. Chlorosis affects red, silver, and sugar maple in alkaline soil due to manganese deficiency. Sugar maple sensitive to road salt and dry, compacted soil.

Cultivars and Similar Species: Norway maple: 'Cleveland', upright, 50 feet tall, 25 feet wide; 'Columnare', 35 feet tall, 15 feet wide; 'Crimson King', 40 feet tall, 35 feet wide, maroon-red foliage all summer; 'Crimson Century', 25 feet tall, 15 feet wide, color similar to 'Crimson King'; 'Royal Red', hardy, slow-growing, glossy maroon-red leaves all season, red-bronze fall color; 'Deborah', 65 feet tall, 55 feet wide, oval, straight trunk, red new growth, yellow in fall; 'Fairview', similar to 'Deborah' but faster growing; 'Emerald Luster' ('Pond'), round, 65 feet tall, 60 feet wide, strong branches, vigorous growth; 'Drummondii', light green leaves edged white; 'Emerald Queen', oval, 75 feet tall, 65 feet wide, fast-growing; 'Summershade', 75 feet tall 65 feet wide, extremely heat-, wind- and insect-resistant; 'Superform', oval to rounded, 45 feet tall, 40 feet wide, straight trunk; 'Oregon Pride' ('Bailpride'), leaves deeply cut and lacy, to 40 feet tall and wide. *A. truncatum* (Shantung maple), similar but with purplish new growth, orange fall color, heat- and drought-tolerant maple for Southwest and Plains.

Hybrids of the two: 'Norwegian Sunset' ('Keithsform'), compact, upright oval to 40 feet tall, 30 feet wide, purplish new growth, orange-red fall color; 'Pacific Sunset' ('Warrenred'), upright to rounded, 35 feet tall, 30 feet wide, purplish new growth, bright red fall color, more dense and spreading.

Red maple: North and Northeast—'Autumn Flame', early long-lasting, red fall color; 'Red Sunset', dense and upright to 50 feet tall, 35 feet wide, bright red fall color; 'Karpick', narrow oval to 35 feet tall, 20 feet wide, red twigs, golden yellow and red fall color. South—'Red Sunset'; 'October Glory', excellent crimson leaves in late fall; 'Legacy', dense, strong branches, heat- and drought-tolerant, red to yellow-orange fall color; 'Steeple' ('Astis'), dense oval column, fast-growing, heat- and drought-tolerant, yellow and orange fall color. Upper Midwest—'Northwood', orange-red fall color, oval shape, 70 feet tall, 50 feet wide; 'Northfire' ('Olson'), oval to 50 feet tall, fiery orange-red fall color; 'Autumn

Spire', broadly columnar to 50 feet tall, 25 feet wide, scarlet fall color; 'Ruby Frost', strong branches, drought-tolerant, good fall color. Midwest—'Northfire' and 'Red Sunset'. Southwest—'Caddo', heat- and drought-tolerant, yellow-orange and red fall color, 70 feet tall.

A. × fremanii (Freeman maple), hybrid of red and silver maples, oval to 50 feet tall, 40 feet wide, deeply cut leaves, acid to slightly alkaline soil, excellent shade tree in upper Midwest and Plains, zones 4 to 7: 'Autumn Blaze' ('Jeffersred'), brilliant red fall color, upright oval branching, storm- and drought-tolerant, nearly seedless; 'Armstrong', columnar to 60 feet tall, 25 feet wide, deeply cut leaves, yellow-orange fall color; 'Celebration' ('Celzam'), seedless, oval to 65 feet tall, 40 feet wide, strong branches, gold early fall color; 'Scarlet Sentinel' ('Scarsen'), narrowly oval to columnar, fast-growing, 45 feet tall, 25 feet wide, yellow-orange to orange-red fall color.

Silver maple: 'Silver Queen', seedless, deeply cut leaves; 'Skinneri', cutleaf form, strong horizontal branches; 'Northline', slow-growing, good in prairie region.

Sugar maple: North—'Majesty', oval to 70 feet tall, 45 feet wide, vigorous, red and orange early fall color; 'Green Mountain', oval to 65 feet tall and wide, thick, dark green leaves tolerate heat, drought, sunscald and dry wind, fall color golden yellow in alkaline soil, red in acid. Midwest—'Majesty'; 'Green Mountain'; 'Bonfire', red fall color in acid and slightly alkaline soil; 'Legacy', thick leaves resistant to heat and wind, yellow-orange fall color. 'Green Mountain'; 'Sweet Shadow', lacy cut leaves, yellow fall color. South—'Legacy', dense oval to 50 feet tall 35 feet wide, thick dark leaves resist heat and wind; red, pink, and orange fall color; 'Steeple', dense, oval column.

A. negundo (box elder), craggy, picturesque North American tree with compound leaves. Flourishes in wet or dry sites and in alkaline soil, zones 2 to

8, withstands flooding, but is weak-wooded and messy. Useful only in the Plains and Mountain states for shade.

AESCULUS SPP.
Horse Chestnut, Buckeye

A hybrid of the disease-prone horse chestnut and the native red buckeye, red horse chestnut (*Aesculus × carnea*) is both more beautiful and less disease-prone than its parents. In late spring, 6- to 8-inch-tall spires of showy pink or rose-red flowers

AESCULUS × CARNEA

project upward like candles from the branches. Leaves are bold-textured and palmately compound, divided into five to seven shiny, dark green leaflets. Spiny green husks fall to the ground in autumn and split open to reveal shiny brown nuts, which are poisonous if eaten. The tree is broadly round; 30 to 40 feet tall. Makes a dramatic lawn or border tree. Don't use near street. Use red horse chestnut in native plant or naturalistic gardens, or as a small specimen or screen.

Native to stream banks and rivers of the Midwest, Ohio buckeye (*A. glabra*) leafs out early in spring, well before most other plants. It has bright green, five-fingered leaves. Fall color develops early and varies from bright yellow to golden orange. Greenish yellow flowers bloom in mid spring in 4- to 7-inch-tall spires. Prickly fruit drops to the ground in fall and splits open to reveal shiny brown buckeye (poisonous nut). The tree has a rugged character, with furrowed, corky, gray bark. Rounded tree, with low ascending branches; to at least 30 feet tall. Use Ohio buckeye as a shade tree in difficult cold parts of Midwest and Mountain states. Use in naturalistic sites and moist areas.

Site: Plant red horse chestnut in full sun, Ohio buckeye in full sun to light shade. Moist, humus-rich, well-drained soil; red horse chestnut adapts to any pH, Ohio buckeye needs slightly acid soil. Plentiful, even moisture. Red horse chestnut hardy in zones 5 to 8, tolerates drought better than horse chestnut; Ohio buckeye, zones 3 to 8, tolerates heat and drought better than other chestnuts.

How to Grow: Plant balled-and-burlapped trees in spring or fall. Ohio buckeye is taprooted and may be difficult to transplant. Constant litter problem from fallen flowers, twigs, leaves, and nuts. Locate in groundcover planting to absorb the mess. Difficult to grow grass under Ohio buckeye unless lower branches are pruned. Neither tree needs much pruning; prune in late winter.

Can suffer from leaf scorch and mildew during drought and from leaf blotch and anthracnose during wet weather, but not as severely as horse chestnut.

Cultivars and Similar Species: Red horse chestnut: 'O'Neil Red', 10- to 12-inch-tall, bright red flower clusters; 'Briotii', 10-inch-tall, deep rose-red flowers, smaller tree. *A. hippocastanum* (horse chestnut), white flowers marked with red, susceptible to leaf scorch, mildew, and drought injury, messy upright tree, zones 4 to 8; 'Baumannii', double flowers, no nuts, less messy. *A. pavia* (red buckeye), native

multistemmed, rounded tree or shrub, to 25 feet tall, slender spires of red spring flowers attract hummingbirds, moist, partly shady site, zones 6 to 9.

Buckeye: *A. flava* (yellow), Midwest native, rich gold to pumpkin orange fall color, upright to 60 feet tall, with ascending lower branches, zones 3 to 8.

ALBIZIA JULIBRISSIN
Silk Tree, Mimosa

This is one of the cold-hardiest trees in the pea family, and it brings a tropical appearance to northern climates. Silk tree leafs out very late in spring, producing lovely, fernlike, bright green leaves just when you suspect the tree might be dead.

ALBIZIA JULIBRISSIN

Foliage remains green until frost. The real show comes in late summer, when the light to bright pink powder-puff flowers bloom for a month or more, turning the tree into a tropical wonder. Wide, flat, brown pods hang onto the tree all winter and look messy. Trunks are light brown and smooth-barked. Tree is broad-spreading and flat-topped with horizontal branches; to 30 feet tall. Silk tree casts light shade and is useful on patio. Provides late-summer color.

continued

ALBIZIA JULIBRISSIN
(continued)

Site: Full sun. Well-drained soil; tolerates acid or alkaline soil and road salt. Zones 6 to 9; tolerates drought and urban and seashore conditions.

How to Grow: Plant container or balled-and-burlapped plants in spring, summer, or fall. Self-sown seedlings can be a problem.

Prune in early spring to remove deadwood. Shorten long horizontal branches to reduce possibility of breakage. Mimosa webworm and wilt can be serious. Mature trees can die suddenly from wilt; grow resistant cultivars.

Cultivars: 'Rosea', deep pink flowers; 'Charlotte' and 'Tyron', new wilt-resistant cultivars.

AMELANCHIER ARBOREA (AMELANCHIER CANADENSIS)
Shadblow, Downy Serviceberry

Multitrunked, this native tree turns the leafless woods into a mist of lacy white flowers for a week in early spring. Flowers are joined by

AMELANCHIER ARBOREA

the new leaves, which emerge a downy gray and mature to dark green. They're rounded, with fine teeth, and turn yellow, orange, red, and purplish red in early fall. Small berries, which

taste like blueberries, ripen from red to purplish black in early summer and can be used for preserves and pies, if you get to them before the birds do. The bark is dark gray or pink-gray, smooth and sinewy when young, becoming scaly when old. Open and upright form; usually to 25 feet tall, can reach 50 feet. Serviceberry is lovely in naturalistic gardens, along the edge of woodland, or massed in informal borders.

Site: Full sun to part shade. Humus-rich, well-drained, moist, fertile soil best; pH 5 to 7.5. Average to wet conditions. Zones 3 to 8.

How to Grow: Plant balled-and-burlapped plants in spring or fall. May need two or more trees to ensure pollination and fruit set. Needs little pruning. May train to develop single or several strong trunks. Usually pest-free, but scale, mites, leaf spots, and fire blight sometimes are serious.

Cultivars and Similar Species: 25 species native to North America; hybridize freely, making identification difficult. 'White Pillar', columnar, large flower clusters, orange-red fall color. *Amelanchier laevis* (Allegheny serviceberry), similar but slightly larger flowers, smooth reddish new leaves, slender nonsuckering clump, to 40 feet tall; 'Snowcloud', large flower clusters, scarlet fall color. *A. × grandiflora* (apple serviceberry), natural hybrid of the two, with showier flowers, single trunk; 'Autumn Brilliance', oval shape, brilliant scarlet fall color; 'Cumulus', abundant white flowers, yellow-orange fall color, oval shape; 'Robin Hill', pink buds open to white flowers, yellow and red fall color; 'Lamarkii', disease-resistant. *A. alnifolia* (Saskatoon), 5- to 8-foot-tall shrub with superior edible fruit, zones 2 to 8; 'Pembina' and 'Smokey' self-fertile.

BETULA SPP.
Birch

The tough native river birch *(Betula nigra)* grows naturally along streams and in swampy areas from New England to Florida and throughout the Midwest. It also adapts well to urban conditions. The beautiful bark on its slender multiple trunks—most outstanding in the cultivar 'Heritage'—peels off the trunks and large branches in curling,

BETULA PENDULA

papery sheets. Bark on seed-grown trees is variable, peeling to reveal gray-brown, red-brown, cinnamon-brown, or salmon patches. The dark green, triangular, toothed leaves turn yellowish in late autumn and are borne on graceful, slightly pendulous branches. Pyramidal to oval when young, rounded with age, and often multitrunked; 30 to 40 or more feet tall. Especially attractive in winter landscape. Locate clump in prominent position in mixed border, foundation, or lawn. Striking planted as grove.

Native from coast to coast as far north as Labrador and Alaska and southward to New England, paper or canoe birch *(B. papyrifera)* has gleaming, creamy white, peeling bark that develops when the tree is about 15 feet tall. The bark remains white, although marked with black, even on old trees. Leaves are dark green and triangular with small teeth, cast a light shade, and exhibit excellent yellow fall color. Trees are most effective when grown as a single-trunked specimen, where the trunk becomes stout and white. Pyramidal when young, becoming irregular to oval when mature; 50 to 70 feet tall and half as wide. Use paper birch as single specimen in lawn or border, sited where it can be appreciated in winter.

European white birch *(B. pendula* or *B. alba),* a popular clump birch, has beautiful white bark and a graceful outline. Unfortunately, the tree is susceptible to insects and, unless grown in the far North, often dies when it reaches maturity, its most beautiful stage.

Site: Give river birch full sun. Paper birch, full sun in the North; provide light afternoon shade in the South. Humus-rich, moist but well-drained, acid (pH of 6.5 or lower) soil best. River birch tolerates clay and wet or periodically flooded sites, also withstands drought once established. River birch hardy in zones 4 to 9; best birch for South and Midwest. Paper birch, zones 2 to 5; to Zone 7 in mountain or coastal areas with cool summers; better in Midwest than European birch. European birch, zones 3 to 5.

How to Grow: Plant balled-and-burlapped trees, river birch in spring, summer, or fall; paper birch in spring or fall. Although river birch casts light shade, dense surface roots may make gardening underneath difficult. Vigorous paper birch trees resist insects better; mulch to keep soil cool and moist, water during drought.

Train to single or multiple trunks. Remove lower limbs to reveal trunks. Prune river birch in late summer; bleeds heavily if pruned in early spring. Prune paper birch in winter or fall; bleeds if pruned in spring. Late spring pruning also allows entrance to borers.

River birch is resistant to bronze birch borers and less troubled by other insects than most birches; leaf spot is problem in wet years. Chlorosis due to iron deficiency in alkaline soil. Paper birch is less susceptible to insects than European birch, but heat- and drought-stressed trees may suffer from borers or leaf miners. Larvae of luna moths feed on the leaves.

Cultivars and Similar Species: River birch: 'Heritage' ('Cully'), superior, fast-growing, with showy creamy white and cinnamon-brown bark, better yellow fall color, disease-resistant leaves, immune to bronze birch borer, 50 feet tall. *B. albo-sinensis* (Chinese red birch), orange-red or orange-brown peeling bark; zones 5 to 8. *B. lenta* (sweet birch, cherry birch), best yellow fall color of native birches, shiny brown-black bark when young, resistant to bronze birch borer; zones 4 to 7.

Paper birch: *B. maximowicziana* (monarch birch), similar Asian species with yellow-white peeling bark at maturity, large heart-shaped leaves, less susceptible to borers and more drought-tolerant, zones 5 to 7. *B. ermanii* (Erman birch), Asian species with creamy to pinkish white peeling bark, zones 6 to 7. *B. jaquemontii* (white-barked Himalayan birch), chalk white peeling bark, zones 5 to 7. *B. platyphylla* var. *japonica* 'Whitespire' (Whitespire birch), desirable cultivar, highly resistant to bronze birch borers and moderately resistant to leaf miners if grown from cuttings, more drought-tolerant than other white birches; nonpeeling chalk white bark develops when tree is 15 feet tall, multiple trunks, zones 4 to 7.

CARPINUS CAROLINIANA
American Hornbeam, Blue Beech, Ironwood

This small to medium-size, multitrunked native tree makes an excellent shade tree for small gardens.

CARPINUS CAROLINIANA

The oblong leaves are pale green in spring, but deepen to dark green in summer and change to red-orange in fall. The smooth, light gray bark is pretty in winter. Wide spreading, rounded to flat-topped; 20 to 30 feet tall and wide. Use as shade tree in small gardens, as patio tree, or as understory tree in shade or woodland gardens.

Site: Part shade best; tolerates heavy shade. Humus-rich, moist, well-drained, acid to alkaline soil; tolerates wet site and flooding. Zones 3 to 9.
How to Grow: Plant balled-and-burlapped or container plants in spring. May be damaged in ice storms. Train to multiple trunks; prune in late winter. Usually pest-free.
Similar Species: *Carpinus betulus* (European hornbeam), similar but larger and single-trunked, with numerous symmetrical, slender branches, pyramidal when young, rounded with age, 40 to 60 feet tall and wide, yellowish fall color, withstands heavy pruning for hedge, zones 5 to 7; 'Fastigiata', symmetrical oval, to 35 feet tall; 'Columnaris', dense, spirelike.

CATALPA BIGNONIOIDES
Common Catalpa, Indian Bean

In early to midsummer, 10-inch-tall spires of purple-and-yellow-speckled white flowers that *continued*

Deciduous Trees

CATALPA BIGNONIOIDES
(continued)

resemble those of the horse chestnut decorate the branches of this southeastern native. Large, 4- to 8-inch-long, heart-shaped, green leaves

CATALPA BIGNONIOIDES

give the tree a bold texture. Pencil-thin pods develop by autumn and hang on through winter. Rounded to irregular form; 30 to 40 feet tall and wide. Valued for flowers and bold texture in difficult sites. Use with groundcover where tree litter isn't a problem. Contrast with fine-textured plants.

Site: Full sun to part shade. Best in humus-rich, moist soil, but tolerates extremes: wet, dry, and alkaline conditions. Zones 5 to 9; withstands hot, dry climates and urban conditions; good in Midwest, Plains, and Mountain states.
How to Grow: Plant small balled-and-burlapped trees in spring, summer, or fall. Brittle wood may break in storms. Litter of small twigs and pods poses cleanup problem.

Train to central leader for first 12 feet. Shorten branches on mature trees to reduce weight and prevent breakage. Prune when dormant.

Verticillium wilt, leaf spot, and mildew may be problems; worms of catalpa sphinx may defoliate trees.
Cultivars and Similar Species: 'Aurea', yellow-green leaves. *Catalpa speciosa* (northern catalpa), similar, with larger leaves and pods, flowers two weeks earlier, zones 4 to 9.

CELTIS OCCIDENTALIS
Common Hackberry

A member of the elm family, common hackberry makes a good substitute for the American elm in the Midwest. The oval, pointed leaves have tiny teeth along their edges and

CELTIS OCCIDENTALIS

are medium green, tuning yellowish in fall. The gray trunk bark is corky and deeply furrowed with odd, wartlike projections. Tiny berries ripen in autumn and attract birds and wildlife. Pyramidal when young, becoming broad-topped and arching with age; 40 to 50 or more feet tall and wide. An excellent shade tree for difficult sites. Good street tree if not planted under power lines.

Site: Full sun to part shade. Best in rich, moist soil, but tolerates extremes from wet to dry, acid to alkaline, clay to sand. Zones 3 to 8; adapted to heat, wind, cold, and dryness. Good in

Plains, Midwest, and Mountain states.
How to Grow: Plant bare-root trees in early spring or balled-and-burlapped trees in spring, summer, or fall. Care-free. Prune to develop strong branch angles. Prune when dormant. May be affected by witches'-broom, gall, mildew, and scale, but is immune to Dutch elm disease.
Cultivars and Similar Species: 'Prairie Pride', thick leaves, immune to witches'-broom, uniform oval crown. *Celtis laevigata* (sugar hackberry), rounded with pendulous branches, to 40 feet tall, toothless leaves, smooth beechlike bark with many warty projections; good in South, zones 6 to 9. *C.* × 'Magnifica', hybrid of the two, insect-resistant, large, glossy, dark green leaves, zones 5 to 8.

CERCIDIPHYLLUM JAPONICUM
Katsura Tree

D ainty, elegant, and heart-shaped, the leaves of this multitrunked Asian tree emerge reddish purple in spring, mature to blue-green, then turn exquisite shades of burnt orange,

CERCIDIPHYLLUM JAPONICUM

gold, and apricot in autumn. Shaggy gray-brown bark on older trees offers winter interest. Pyramidal when young, maturing to broad-spreading and flat-topped; 40 to 50 feet tall and

20 to 40 feet wide. Locate katsura tree where it can be appreciated close up, in lawn or near patio. This tree should be planted more often.

Site: Full sun in zones 5 to 7; part shade in zones 8 and 9. Rich, moist, well-drained soil; either acid or alkaline, but best fall color in acid site. Plentiful moisture, especially when young; ample moisture in zones 8 and 9. Hardy in zones 5 to 9.
How to Grow: Plant balled-and-burlapped or container trees in spring. Care-free. May be trained to single trunk, but more distinctive when multitrunked. Thin and shorten branches to reduce possibility of breakage. Pest-free.
Cultivars: 'Pendula', weeping tree, to 20 feet tall. *Cercidiphyllum japonicum* var. *magnificum* 'Pendulum', weeping tree, to 50 feet tall.

CERCIS CANADENSIS
Eastern Redbud

Native to the forest edges from New Jersey to Florida and west to Texas, this charming small tree

CERCIS CANADENSIS

blooms in early spring on leafless branches. The rose-pink to magenta, sometimes white, pea-shaped flowers appear in clusters directly from the main branches. Large, heart-shaped,

dull green leaves emerge reddish purple and change to yellowish before dropping in fall. Bark is a beautiful, smooth gray. Rounded to flat-topped, multitrunked tree; 20 to 40 feet tall. Lovely patio, border, or woodland edge tree. Combine with dogwoods. Best with dark background to show off blossoms.

Site: Full sun to light shade. Best in moist, well-drained, deep soil; tolerates acid or alkaline conditions. Doesn't do well in wet sites. Plentiful moisture. Zones 4 to 9; not cold-hardy where summers are cool, such as in Pacific Northwest.
How to Grow: Plant balled-and-burlapped or container plants in spring or fall. Usually short-lived by tree standards.

Allow to form multiple trunks. Prune crossed branches when dormant or immediately after flowering. Prune as little as possible; wounds may allow disease organisms to enter. Verticillium wilt, canker, leaf spot, leafhoppers, and caterpillars.
Cultivars and Similar Species: 'Forest Pansy', red-purple leaves most vivid in spring but fade to green if summer nights are hot; 'Alba', white flowers; 'Silver Cloud', white variegated leaves, sparse flowers. *Cercis occidentalis* (western redbud), 12 feet tall, tolerates alkaline soil, best redbud for Pacific Northwest. *C. chinensis* (Chinese redbud), shrubby, to 12 feet tall, profuse early, larger, deep pink flowers, zones 6 to 9; 'Avondale', profuse flowers, performs in Northwest. *C. canadensis* var. *texensis* (*C. reniformis*) 'Oklahoma', smaller, glossy leaves, deep magenta flowers, 20 feet tall, best redbud for Southwest, zones 6 to 9.

CHIONANTHUS VIRGINICUS
White Fringe Tree, Old-Man's-Beard

Honey-scented blossoms appear on this tree for two weeks in

late spring just before or as the leaves emerge. Individual flowers have four 1-inch-long, straplike petals, but are borne in large clusters and in such quantity that a blooming tree looks like a cloud come to earth. Leaves are oval and shiny dark green, about 4 to 8 inches long with pale undersides,

CHIONANTHUS VIRGINICUS

and turn yellowish in late fall. Sprays of pretty blue fruit appear on female trees in late summer and fall and attract birds. Rounded and multistemmed; 15 to 20 feet tall and 20 to 30 feet wide. Fringe tree is low-branched; plant in a mixed border or mass as a screen. It's native from New Jersey to Florida and east to Texas,

Site: Full sun to light shade. Best in rich, moist, acid soil, but tolerates average to dry conditions. Zones 5 to 9; tolerates air pollution.
How to Grow: Plant balled-and-burlapped plants in spring or fall. Some trees are self-fertile, but usually a female and male tree are needed for berry set; nurseries don't sell trees by sex, however. Male trees have showier flowers, but lack fruit. Prune when dormant or immediately after flowering to develop attractive shape. Sometimes troubled by scale.
Similar Species: *Chionanthus retusus* (Chinese fringe tree), more *continued*

CHIONANTHUS VIRGINICUS
(continued)

refined appearance with smaller, earlier leaves and snow white flowers one week later in late spring, attractive peeling gray-brown bark, no fall color, zones 6 to 9.

CLADRASTIS LUTEA (CLADRASTIS KENTUKEA)
Yellowwood

This native flowering tree is almost extinct in the wild but is being grown more in gardens. In early summer, long, wisteria-like clusters of fragrant, white flowers drip from the

CLADRASTIS KENTUKEA

branches. The 1-foot-long leaves are compound and divided into seven to 11 leaflets. Their bright green color stands out against darker greens and turns soft yellow and apricot in fall. Even in winter, the tree shines because of its smooth, silvery bark, which resembles the European beech. Round-headed; 30 to 50 feet tall and wider than tall. Use for shade in lawn or bordering small or large properties. Deep-rooted, accommodates other plants beneath its branches.

Site: Full sun. Deep, fertile, well-drained, acid to alkaline soil. Drought-tolerant once established. Zones 4 to 8.
How to Grow: Plant small balled-and-burlapped trees in spring or fall. Don't plant in exposed, windy site. Doesn't bloom until at least 10 years old; may bloom heavily in alternate years. Slow-growing. Prune in summer (bleeds in winter and spring) to develop single trunk with wide crotch angles; cable to prevent storm damage. Shorten branches to reduce weight. Usually pest-free, but leafhoppers and verticillium may be troublesome.
Cultivars: 'Rosea', pale rose-pink flowers; 'Sweetshade', vigorous growth, resistant to leafhoppers, brighter yellow fall color.

CORNUS SPP.
Dogwood

Pagoda dogwood (*Cornus alternifolia*), an East Coast native, bears fragrant, lacy, white flowers that put on a pretty show in late spring. Leaves are glossy dark green and turn

CORNUS FLORIDA

purplish red in autumn. Blue-black berries provide food for wildlife. The purple twigs and gray trunk bark are attractive in winter. Spreading horizontal form; grows 20 feet tall and 35 to 40 feet wide. Architectural effect of pagoda dogwood's branching

pattern is lovely in formal or naturalistic gardens and as patio or accent tree. 'Argentea' lights up shady sites all summer.

Native to forest edges from southern Maine to Florida and west to Kansas, the beautiful flowering dogwood (*C. florida*) is stunning year-round. The white or pink blossoms, which consist of four showy bracts, open gradually. If weather remains cool, the flowers last for at least three weeks. Oval, dark green leaves turn red or purplish red in early autumn. Red berries, which ripen in late summer, attract birds. Spreading horizontally in an undulating pattern, the branches make handsome tiers that add grace to the winter landscape. Horizontally spreading; to 20 feet tall in North and much taller in South. Flowering dogwood is a magnificent small flowering tree for borders, patios, and woodland edges.

Blooming for four or more weeks, beginning a month after our native dogwood, Kousa dogwood (*C. kousa*), an Asian species, brings beautiful creamy white blossoms to the early summer garden. In late summer, strawberry-like red fruit dangles from the branches. Fall color is spectacular dark red, and the bark is an attractive mottled mixture of gray, brown, and creamy white. Upright to vase-shaped when young, eventually horizontally spreading; 20 to 30 feet tall and wide. An excellent small tree for summer flowers and year-round interest in lawn or border, or to shade patio.

When the misty, dark yellow flowers of Cornelian cherry (*C. mas*) bloom on leafless branches for about three weeks in late winter and early spring, they light up the garden, because this is when most plants are dormant. Glossy, bright red berries ripen in summer and are quickly eaten by birds. Foliage is glossy green and remains green through autumn. The exfoliating gray-and-tan bark heightens the beauty of the bare winter silhouette. Rounded, multitrunked, low-branched tree; 20 to 25 feet tall. Use Cornelian cherry in a mixed border with evergreen background. Makes a good screen.

Site: Pagoda and flowering dogwood, full sun to part shade; in South, part shade, preferably in afternoon. Give Kousa dogwood full sun, and Cornelian cherry full sun to light shade. Humus-rich, well-drained, moist soil is best for dogwoods. Flowering dogwood prefers acid pH. Kousa dogwood best in fertile, acid, well-drained, sandy loam. Cornelian cherry tolerates most soils. All best with plentiful moisture; Kousa somewhat drought-tolerant. Pagoda dogwood is hardy in zones 4 to 7; flowering and Kousa dogwood and Cornelian cherry, zones 5 to 8; pink and red flowering dogwood less cold-hardy and heat-resistant. Kousa dogwood tolerates heat and drought of Midwest and upper South better than flowering dogwood.

How to Grow: Plant balled-and-burlapped plants in spring or fall; Cornelian cherry also can be planted in summer. Mulch all dogwoods to keep soil cool and moist. Avoid injuring trunk of flowering dogwood with lawn mower or string trimmer; irrigate during drought but avoid wetting leaves. Kousa usually needs more than one tree in close proximity to set fruit.

Pagoda dogwood and Cornelian cherry need no regular pruning; prune when dormant if needed. Remove water sprouts and low branches of flowering dogwood, which allow access to anthracnose fungus; prune when dormant or in summer. Prune lower branches of Kousa dogwood when dormant to reveal bark.

Pagoda somewhat susceptible to twig blight. Borers serious for flowering dogwood, especially on stressed or injured trees. Anthracnose fungus is spreading in Northeast and Middle Atlantic states, often killing trees. Control with properly timed fungicide applications, by planting in open, sunny site so foliage dries quickly, and by applying low-phosphorous, high-calcium fertilizer. Kousa dogwood is somewhat susceptible to borers; not infected by anthracnose. Cornelian cherry pest- and disease-free.

Cultivars and Similar Species: Pagoda dogwood: 'Argentea', lovely white-and-green leaves. *C. controversa* (giant dogwood), similar but much larger Asian species, 35 to 50 feet tall, disease-free, zones 6 to 8, variegated form available.

Flowering dogwood: For best flower bud hardiness, select locally grown trees. White flowers—'Cloud Nine'; 'Springtime'; 'Gold Nugget', green leaves with gold margins; 'Cherokee Princess'; 'Cherokee Daybreak', green leaves with creamy white margins; 'Sterling Silver', white-and-green variegated leaves. Pink to rose-red flowers—'Cherokee Chief', deep pink-red growth; 'Cherokee Sunset', green leaves variegated with rose and yellow; 'Rubra', pale to medium pink; 'Purple Glory', dark pink flowers, purple foliage.

Kousa dogwood: *C. kousa* var. *chinensis*, larger flowers, free-flowering; 'Elizabeth Lustgarten', weeping to 10 or more feet tall; 'Milky Way', floriferous, bushy; 'National', vase-shaped, large flowers and fruit; 'Summer Stars', showy for at least six weeks; 'Rosabella' ('Satomi'), deep rose-pink flowers; 'Gold Star', golden leaves with golden yellow central blotch; 'Snowboy', green leaves with creamy white edges. *C.* × *rutgersensis* (stellar dogwood), hybrids with *C. florida*, bloom time halfway between the two species, anthracnose- and borer-resistant; 'Aurora', large, overlapping white bracts, full bushy tree; 'Constellation', delicate, separate, starry bracts, narrow tree; 'Celestial', overlapping white bracts; 'Ruth Ellen', early blooming, horizontal branches, lovely white, starlike bracts; 'Stellar Pink', broad pale pink bracts, rounded tree; 'Galaxy', rounded, slightly overlapping, white bracts, upright.

Cornelian cherry: 'Golden Glory', pyramidal, to 15 feet tall, 8 feet wide, heavy-flowering; 'Aurea', golden leaves; 'Elegantissima', pink-flushed green leaves with yellow margins.

CRATAEGUS VIRIDIS 'WINTER KING'

Winter King Green Hawthorn

This award-winning cultivar of a native tree brightens the landscape from fall throughout winter with clusters of gleaming scarlet berries. Trunk bark on mature trees

CRATAEGUS VIRIDIS 'WINTER KING'

is rough and flakes to reveal orange patches. Late spring brings a profusion of lacy, white flowers. Summer features fine-textured, scalloped, glossy, green leaves, which, unlike most hawthorns, are disease-free. Flat-topped and horizontally spreading; to 30 feet tall and wide. Excellent with evergreen background to show off berries. Plant as a specimen or in small groves.

Site: Full sun. Almost any well-drained soil. Drought-tolerant. Zones 5 to 8; good in Midwest. Tolerates wind and urban conditions. *continued*

CRATAEGUS VIRIDIS 'WINTER KING'
(continued)

How to Grow: Plant balled-and-burlapped trees in spring or fall. Provide good air circulation. Prune when dormant to thin branches and remove water sprouts. Resistant to fire blight, fungal leaf spot, and insects that plague most hawthorns.

Cultivars and Similar Species: *Crataegus* × 'Vaughn', hybrid with disease-resistant leaves, masses of long-lasting, orange-red fruit; 'Princeton Sentry', upright branching for tight spaces, excellent fruit, few thorns. *C. laevigata* 'Crimson Cloud' (English hawthorn), shrubby, to 20 feet tall and half as wide, thorny, disease-resistant foliage, crimson flowers, scarlet berries.

C. phaenopyrum (Washington hawthorn), rounded, to 25 feet tall and wide, thorny, latest-flowering hawthorn, early summer white flowers, red berries all winter, scarlet and purple fall color, less susceptible to disease than other hawthorns, zones 4 to 8; 'Presidential', large, long-lasting berries.

ELAEAGNUS ANGUSTIFOLIA
Russian Olive

Beautiful, 3-inch-long, lance-shaped, silver leaves on Russian olive trees add light and brightness to a landscape. Dense and bushy, the thorny branches bear inconspicuous, yet sweetly fragrant, pale yellow flowers in spring. Sweet yellow berries covered with silvery scales appear in late summer and early fall, attracting birds. Small, round, multistemmed tree to 20 feet tall and wide. Lovely used as screen or windbreak. Makes attractive specimen tree in border.

Site: Full sun. Best in light to sandy, well-drained soil. Tolerates alkaline soil and drought, and seashore and urban conditions. Zones 3 to 7, performs poorly in southern heat and humidity.

ELAEAGNUS ANGUSTIFOLIA

How to Grow: Plant bare-root plants in early spring or balled-and-burlapped plants in spring, summer, or fall. Birds spread seeds and plant can become pest, spreading to wild areas. Check to see if this is a problem in your area.

Prune to single trunk if desired. Shorten branches to reduce weight and breakage. Responds to heavy pruning; can be trained to hedge. Verticillium wilt can be serious. Susceptible to leaf spot and aphids.

Cultivars: 'Red King', bright, rusty red fruit. *Elaeagnus commutata* (silverberry), suckering shrub, silvery leaves, zones 2 to 6.

FAGUS SYLVATICA
European Beech

This long-lived, slow-growing tree is an aristocrat among shade trees. Long, smooth-edged, arrow-shaped leaves emerge silvery green in spring, mature to glossy dark green, and turn golden brown in fall. The massive, stout trunks of mature trees and their low, spreading branches are covered with smooth, silvery bark and look magnificent in the winter landscape. Edible nuts are enclosed in prickly husks. Pyramidal to rounded; 50 to 60 feet tall and 35 to 45 feet wide. Use European beech as a lawn or specimen tree on large property or in park.

Site: Full sun to part shade. Moist, well-drained, acid soil. Hardy in zones 5 to 8.

How to Grow: Plant balled-and-burlapped trees in spring or container trees in spring, summer, or fall. Mulch soil; shallow roots and the dense shade cast make it impossible to grow garden or lawn under branches.

Train to single leader; multiple leaders may break when large. Lower branches may be left to form beautiful rounded form or pruned off to better reveal trunk. Prune when dormant. Leaf spot, mildew, canker, and beech bark disease can be problems.

FAGUS SYLVATICA

Cultivars and Similar Species: *Fagus sylvatica* var. *purpurea*, seed-grown purple-leaf form with variable color. 'Asplenifolia' (fern-leaf beech), delicately cut leaves; 'Dawyckii', columnar, to 60 feet tall, 30 feet wide; 'Dawyck Purple', columnar, purple leaves; 'Dawyck Gold', golden leaves on narrow, columnar tree; 'Pendula', magnificent weeping tree to 60 feet tall; 'Riversii' (purple or copper beech), dark purple leaves all summer; 'Purpurea Pendula', purple leaves, weeping form grafted to standard, 10 to 15 feet tall; 'Tricolor' ('Roseo-marginata'), bright rose-red new growth, maturing to purple with pink-and-cream-splashed margins; 'Rohanni', similar to 'Riversii' but with wavy-edged leaves. *F. grandifolia* (American beech), pewter gray bark, edible beechnuts, pointed, tooth-edged leaves, light yellow to golden bronze fall color, native tree that should be used more, especially in the South, zones 4 to 9.

FRANKLINIA ALATAMAHA (GORDONIA ALATAMAHA)
Franklinia, Franklin Tree

Now extinct in the wild, this Southeastern native woodland tree was named after Benjamin Franklin. Valued for its unusual bloom season, franklinia produces white camellia-like flowers throughout late summer and fall. Flowers first appear while the 6-inch-long, narrow leaves

FRANKLINIA ALATAMAHA

are still glossy green and continue when the foliage is wine red and gold. The slim trunks and branches of this open-branched tree are covered with a tight, sinewy, dark gray bark with light striations. Pyramidal to rounded, multitrunked tree; 20 to 30 feet tall and 15 to 20 feet wide. Plant in a border or woodland where winter silhouette and late-season flowers can be seen from indoors.

Site: Full sun to light shade; flowers best in full sun with moist conditions. Humus-rich, moist, well-drained, acid soil. Plentiful moisture. Hardy in zones 5 to 8.
How to Grow: Plant balled-and-burlapped or container trees in spring. Difficult to grow unless soil and light conditions are met. Needs no pruning. May suffer from wilt disease.
Cultivars: No cultivars of this rare tree are available.

FRAXINUS PENNSYLVANICA
Green or Red Ash

Highly adaptable, this fast-growing, large shade tree features lustrous, dark green compound leaves composed of five to nine pointed leaflets with jagged edges. Foliage turns beautiful yellow in early fall. The tree is somewhat coarse-textured, especially when leafless, and the trunk has furrowed,

FRAXINUS AMERICANA

ash gray bark. Pyramidal, with ascending branches when young, becoming upright and spreading; 50 to 60 feet tall and half as wide. Seedless forms make excellent shade trees for lawns, parks, and streets in areas where cold, poor soil, and drought preclude other large trees.

Site: Full sun. Adapts to most soils; tolerates infertile soil, drought, salt, and alkaline conditions. Zones 2 to 9; excellent in Plains and Midwest.
How to Grow: Plant balled-and-burlapped trees in spring, summer, or fall. Fruiting trees pose serious litter and seedling problem; choose nonfruiting forms, not seedling-grown, unnamed trees.

Train to single leader and develop strong scaffold branches. Remove lower limbs as tree matures. Prune in fall or winter. Leaf rust, leaf spot, and stem canker are common. Dieback may be serious, especially with white ash. Borers, scale, leafhoppers, leaf miners, sawflies, fall webworms, and galls are common.

Cultivars and Similar Species: 'Marshall's Seedless', insect-resistant, to 40 feet tall; 'Emerald', seedless, 40 feet tall, golden yellow fall color, adapts to hot, dry climates; 'Lednaw' ('Aerial'), columnar, to 30 feet tall, seedless; 'Newport', superior form, seedless, oval to upright, to 50 feet tall; 'Patmore', seedless, disease-resistant, erect oval, to 50 feet tall; 'Summit', columnar, to 50 feet tall, seedless, golden yellow fall color; 'Urbanite', pyramidal, to 50 feet tall, seedless, urban-tolerant; 'Wandell' ('Skyward'), narrow pyramid, to 35 feet tall, deep bronze-red fall color. *Fraxinus americana* (white ash), 50 to 80 feet tall and wide, early yellow, orange, or maroon fall color, more beautiful than green ash, but less adaptable and more prone to disease, zones 4 to 9; 'Rosehill', disease-resistant, seedless, 60 feet tall, fiery bronze-red fall color; 'Autumn Applause', deep red to mahogany fall color, seedless; 'Autumn Purple', deep purple fall color, seedless; 'Royal Purple', purple fall color, Zone 3; 'Champaign County', dense crown, bronze fall color, seedless.

Deciduous Trees

GINKGO BILOBA
Ginkgo, Maidenhair Tree

This gorgeous tree from China has unusual fan-shaped, bright green leaves that turn brilliant yellow in late fall and are borne on short spurs along the horizontal branches. The tree is open and airy, casting only light shade. Mature trees have a

GINKGO BILOBA

beautiful rough bark and a picturesque framework of massive, irregular branches. The form of this slow-growing tree is variable among seed-grown trees—it's best to purchase named cultivars with known traits. Varies from pyramidal to broad and spreading; to 80 feet tall and 30 to 80 feet wide. Ginkgo makes a stately shade tree for gardens and lawns; use columnar forms as street trees, except under power lines.

Site: Full sun. Deep, well-drained soil; pH adaptable; tolerates road salt. Zones 4 to 8; tolerates urban conditions and heat.
How to Grow: Plant balled-and-burlapped trees in spring, summer, or fall. Plant only male trees; females produce messy, foul-smelling fruit, but not until at least 20 years old. Train to single trunk with strong scaffold branches. Remove suckers. Prune in late winter. Pest- and disease-free.

Cultivars: 'Autumn Gold', broadly conical, to 50 feet tall, 30 feet wide, male, excellent golden fall color; 'Magyar', upright, branching, to 50 feet tall, male; 'Princeton Sentry', narrow pyramid, to 65 feet tall, male; 'Saratoga', broad, dense, and compact cone, 25 to 40 feet tall, male; 'Mayfield', narrow, to 60 feet tall, 20 to 25 feet wide, male; 'Lakeview', narrow, to 50 feet tall, 30 feet wide, male; 'The President', upright, to 60 feet tall, male.

GLEDITSIA TRIACANTHOS VAR. INERMIS
Thornless Honey Locust

Graceful and fast-growing, this shade tree has delicate foliage

GLEDITSIA TRIACANTHOS 'SUNBURST'

which casts light shade, perfect for gardening beneath. The compound leaves have as many as 100 small, rounded, bright green leaflets, which turn yellow in early autumn and clean up easily when they drop. The tiny spring flowers are highly fragrant. The species has vicious branched thorns and long, dark brown seedpods, but most cultivars are thornless and seedless. Broad spreading; 35 to 70 feet tall and wide. This is an excellent street, lawn, or garden tree, because grass can grow in its shade. Don't use under power lines.

Site: Full sun. Performs well in most soils, but best in rich, moist site. Tolerates drought, pH 6 to 8, and road salt. Zones 4 to 9, but performs poorly in heat and humidity of the South.
How to Grow: Plant balled-and-burlapped or container trees in spring, summer, or fall. Seedpods are serious litter problem; use seedless forms. Prune when dormant to control size; bleeds in spring. Thin overly vigorous new growth on young trees back by one-third in midsummer.

Insects and diseases are often serious. Webworms defoliate trees. Spider mites, borers, leaf spot, mildew, and rust are common.
Cultivars: 'Moraine', dark green leaves, fruitless, zigzagging trunk, excellent resistance to webworms; 'Shademaster', seedless, slightly pendulous branches, straight trunk, dark green leaves; 'Sunburst' ('Suncole'), bright yellow new growth at branch tips all summer, broadly pyramidal, highly susceptible to webworms; 'Ruby Lace', deep ruby red new growth, turning bronze-green in summer, highly susceptible to webworm; 'Skyline ('Skycole'), broadly pyramidal, straight trunk, dark green leaves, excellent golden fall color; 'Christie', rounded, rapid growing; 'Continental', narrow, seedless; 'Trueshade', rounded with horizontal branches, golden fall color; 'Imperial', 30 to 35 feet tall, good street tree.

GYMNOCLADUS DIOICA
Kentucky Coffee Tree

Native to moist, rich soils of the Southeast, Midwest, and Middle Atlantic states, this is a tough tree that should be grown more often in problem sites. The large, doubly compound leaves are 3 feet long and 2 feet wide, and composed of hundreds of leaflets. Leaves emerge pinkish purple in late spring, mature to dark blue-green, and turn pale yellow in fall. In early spring, fragrant, showy panicles of fluffy, greenish

GYMNOCLADUS DIOICA

white flowers bloom on female trees; flowers of male trees are less showy. Female trees produce 10-inch long, reddish brown seedpods containing large seeds that may be poisonous when raw; the Colonists roasted and used them as a coffee substitute. The tree is picturesque in winter. Its craggy silhouette features silvery twigs and unique, rough, deeply furrowed, dark brown bark with curled ridges on the trunk and branches. Tree is oval with ascending branches; 50 to 70 feet tall and 40 to 50 feet wide. Best as a shade tree on large properties; locate where winter silhouette can be seen against the sky.

Site: Full sun. Best in humus-rich, moist soil, but tolerates pH 6 to 8 and drought. Zones 4 to 7; good in urban conditions.
How to Grow: Plant balled-and-burlapped trees in spring, summer, or fall. Messy tree throughout the year; locate where this isn't a problem. Bleeds in spring; prune in midsummer. Usually pest- and disease-free.
Cultivars: Seedless male forms may be available.

HALESIA CAROLINA (HALESIA TETRAPTERA)
Carolina Silverbell

The bell-shaped, 1-inch-long, translucent white blossoms of this beautiful native tree dangle in clusters from the undersides of its outstretched branches for two weeks in mid to late spring along with the newly emerging, bright green leaves. Leaves are 3 to 5 inches long and oval with pointed tips. They're dark yellow-green in summer, turning

HALESIA MONTICOLA

yellow before dropping in early fall. Shrubby and broadly rounded with low, horizontal to ascending branches; 20 to 30 or more feet tall and 35 feet wide. Carolina silverbell is delightful along the edge of a woodland, to shade a patio, or as an understory tree in a shade garden.

Site: Full sun to part shade. Humus-rich, moist, well-drained, acid soil. Plentiful moisture. Zones 5 to 9.
How to Grow: Plant balled-and-burlapped trees in spring or fall. Easy to grow in right location. Prune lower limbs and train to single trunk when young, if desired. Prune immediately after flowering. No pest problems. Becomes chlorotic in alkaline soil.

Cultivars and Similar Species: Pink-flowered forms sometimes available. *Halesia monticola* (mountain snowbell), similar but taller with central leader.

KOELREUTERIA PANICULATA
Golden-Rain Tree

Named for its showy yellow flowers—an unusual color for a tree—golden-rain tree is a welcome

KOELREUTERIA PANICULATA

sight when it blooms in midsummer. The large flower panicles consist of tiny, starlike flowers that ripen into attractive brown seedpods shaped like Japanese lanterns. Its large leaves are composed of seven to 15 coarse, jagged-lobed leaflets, which emerge purplish red in spring, mature to bright green in summer, and often turn golden orange in autumn. Rounded form; 30 to 40 feet tall and wide. Use golden-rain tree in a lawn, to shade a patio, or as a street tree, except under power lines.

Site: Full sun. Adapts to range of soil types, including high pH. Drought-tolerant. Zones 5 to 9; withstands heat and urban conditions.
How to Grow: Plant balled-and-burlapped trees in spring, summer, or fall. Self-sown seedlings a problem if sited in garden; best in lawn where seedlings can be mown. *continued*

Deciduous Trees

KOELREUTERIA PANICULATA
(continued)

Lower limbs may die from lack of light; prune off if needed when dormant. Pest- and disease-free.

Cultivars and Similar Species: 'September', flowers in late summer or early fall, zones 6 to 9. *Koelreuteria bipinnata* (Chinese flame tree), late-summer flowers, pink seedpods, zones 7 to 9.

LABURNUM × WATERERI
Golden-Chain Tree

Long, wisteria-like chains of golden yellow flowers dangle from the branches of the golden-chain tree in mid spring, creating a beautiful sunny sight. The bright green leaves are

LABURNUM × WATERERI 'VOSSII'

made up of three pointed leaflets and drop with little color change. The olive green bark on the trunk and branches makes the tree attractive in winter. Upright to oval; 15 feet tall and about 12 feet wide. Lovely small tree for spring border or foundation planting; effective planted in groups.

Site: Full sun with light afternoon shade. Humus-rich, moist, well-drained soil best, tolerates high pH. Zones 5 to 7.

How to Grow: Plant balled-and-burlapped plants in spring or fall. Usually short-lived. Seeds are highly poisonous if eaten.

Prune growths from trunks to develop main leader. Prune after flowering; bleeds in spring. Twig blight can be serious. Aphids and mealybugs sometimes troublesome.

Cultivars and Similar Species: 'Vossii', superior cultivar with 2-foot-long flower clusters. *Laburnum alpinum* 'Pendulum', weeping, 10 feet tall, 1-foot-long flower clusters.

LAGERSTROEMIA INDICA
Crape Myrtle

Flowering from July to September, the lovely crape myrtle produces large clusters of brilliant white, pink, purple, or lavender flowers held above its glossy green leaves. This multistemmed tree has gorgeous bark, which peels to reveal a mosaic of gray and creamy patches; hybrids have

LAGERSTROEMIA INDICA 'TUSKEGEE'

even more colorful bark. Fall color also is excellent, ranging from shades of gold and scarlet to dark maroon and red. Cold-hardy hybrids of this southern favorite are now available, extending the tree's adaptability farther north. Upright to spreading; 15 to 25 feet tall and half as wide. Plant crape myrtle in borders, along

foundation, or as a patio tree, where it can be appreciated all year.

Site: Full sun best. Well-drained, moist soil. Zones 7 to 9; heat-tolerant.
How to Grow: Plant balled-and-burlapped or container plants in spring, summer, or fall. Withstands heavy pruning and blooms on new growth; can be cut to ground and treated as shrub where winter cold harms tops. Don't head back branches to stumps (pollarding), because it turns this graceful tree into a monstrosity. Older types suffer from mildew, black soot fungus, aphids, and scale.
Cultivars and Similar Species: *Lagerstroemia fauriei*, rust-brown bark, white flowers, 25 feet tall, zones 6 to 9.

Hybrids of the two: mildew-resistant, top-hardy in zones 7 to 9, root-hardy in Zone 6. Semidwarf, 5 to 12 feet tall—'Acoma', white flowers, silvery gray bark, red-purple fall color, dense shrub; 'Hopi', light pink flowers, gray bark, rounded shrub, orange-red fall color; 'Zuni', lavender flowers, light brown-gray bark, orange-red to dark red fall color, multitrunked large shrub. Intermediate, 12 to 20 feet tall—'Apalachee', light lavender, cinnamon-brown bark, columnar, orange fall color; 'Comanche', coral-pink flowers, light orange-brown bark, purple-red fall color, rounded; 'Osage', light pink, chestnut-brown bark, red fall color, open-branched; 'Tuscarora', dark coral-pink, mottled light brown bark, orange-red fall color, narrow. Large, 20 to 35 feet tall—'Natchez', white flowers, mottled cinnamon-brown bark, orange to red fall color; 'Muskogee', lavender-pink flowers, gray-tan bark, red fall color; 'Tuskegee', dark pink flowers, mottled tan-and-gray bark, orange-red fall color, horizontal branches.

LARIX KAEMPFERI
Japanese Larch

Unusual for a conifer, this tree drops all its needles in autumn, after turning gold or pumpkin orange.

LARIX DECIDUA

The 1-inch-long needles appear in tufts on short spurs, emerging bright green in spring and maturing to blue-green. The tree has a massive central trunk and wide-spreading, strong, heavy branches. Cones are 1½ inches long, shaped in a rosette. Pyramidal with slightly pendulous, horizontal branches; to 70 to 90 feet tall, 5 to 40 feet wide. Best as a specimen or screen on a large property.

Site: Full sun. Well-drained, acid soil, plentiful moisture. Zones 4 to 6; does not tolerate heat and urban conditions.
How to Grow: Plant balled-and-burlapped plants in spring or fall, allowing room for ultimate plant width. Twigs and cones may be a litter problem.

Do not remove lower branches; allow skirt of branches to form near ground. Forms new leader if injured. Japanese beetles, gypsy moths, sawflies, aphids, and larch casebearers can be serious.
Cultivars and Similar Species: *Larix decidua* (European larch), needles are bright green in spring, soft green in summer, yellow in fall, 75 feet tall, zones 4 to 6; 'Pendula', irregularly weeping, to 60 feet. *L. laricina* (American larch, tamarack), native to boggy areas of the North, blue-green needles turn gold in fall, zones 2 to 6.

LIQUIDAMBAR STYRACIFLUA
Sweet Gum

The beautiful, glossy, dark green leaves of the sweet gum tree are star-shaped, with five to seven pointed lobes, and up to 7 inches across. Fall usually brings a multitude of hues on the same tree: yellow, scarlet, and deep purple. The bark, too, is magnificent: silvery twigs and young branches may have corky ridges, and the trunk is deeply furrowed. Flowers are inconspicuous, but produce 1-inch-wide, spiny, tan

LIQUIDAMBAR STYRACIFLUA

balls (gumballs) that remain on the tree over winter and drop in spring. A member of the witch hazel family, sweet gum is native from New England south to Florida and west to Texas, and is named after the aromatic resin that bleeds from bark wounds. Narrow and pyramidal with slightly pendulous branches when young, rounded with age; 65 to 70 feet tall and 40 to 50 feet wide. Excellent shade tree for lawns, gardens, and parks if planted in groundcover so gumballs don't pose a nuisance. Or, choose a nonfruiting form.

Site: Full sun to part shade. Humus-rich, moist, acid soil best. Plentiful moisture. Zones 5 to 9.

How to Grow: Plant balled-and-burlapped or container trees in spring, summer, or fall. Fruit poses cleanup problem.

Prune when young to develop strong, well-spaced branches. As tree matures, remove lower limbs to emphasize straight trunk. Usually pest- and disease-free. Larvae of luna moths feed on leaves.
Cultivars: 'Burgundy', broadly columnar, to 40 feet tall, long-lasting purple-red fall color; 'Rotundiloba', rounded leaves, fruitless, narrowly pyramidal, yellow and purple fall color; 'Gold Dust' ('Goduzam'), gold-and-green variegated leaves, pink and burgundy fall color; 'Corky', fruitless, extremely corky young branches; 'Festival', conical, 40 feet tall, 15 to 20 feet wide, peach, pink, and yellow fall color, Zone 6; 'Palo-Alto', pyramidal, 40 feet tall, orange-red fall color, Zone 6.

LIRIODENDRON TULIPIFERA

LIRIODENDRON TULIPIFERA
Tulip Tree, Yellow Poplar

A cold-hardy member of the magnolia family, this large, native forest tree looks stately throughout the year. The spring foliage is bright green, matures to dark green, and changes to brilliant yellow in late autumn. Leaves are 3 to 8 inches across and almost *continued*

Deciduous Trees

LIRIODENDRON TULIPIFERA
(continued)

square in outline, with several shallow lobes. Late-spring flowers resemble 2-inch tulips with pretty, yellowish green petals marked with orange. They're high up in the tree, however, and not easy to see. With age, this fast-growing tree forms a massive, straight central trunk with several large horizontally spreading scaffold branches covered with furrowed, gray-brown bark. Pyramidal when young, becoming wide-spreading and rounded with age; 70 to 90 feet tall and 35 to 50 feet wide. Lovely shade tree for large lawn, park, or natural landscape.

Site: Full sun to part shade. Humus-rich, well-drained, moist soil. Plentiful moisture. Zones 5 to 9.
How to Grow: Plant balled-and-burlapped trees in spring. Keep well watered, especially when young. Needs good soil and plenty of room for roots.

Train to strong central leader with evenly spaced branches; multitrunked trees prone to storm damage. Aphids and leaf spot may be serious.
Cultivars: 'Majestic Beauty' ('Aureo-marginatum'), leaves with irregular, wide, bright golden green margin; 'Arnold' ('Fastigiatum'), narrow with upright branches, 60 feet tall, 15 to 20 feet wide.

MAGNOLIA SPP.

Saucer Magnolia, Star Magnolia
Saucer magnolia (*Magnolia × soulangiana*) blooms before the leaves emerge in early spring; the satiny, cup-shaped flowers are 5 to 10 inches across and composed of nine white, pink, purple, or bicolored petals surrounding a prominent yellow center. They bloom with early rhododendrons and daffodils. The smooth, light green leaves are

MAGNOLIA × SOULANGIANA

6 inches long with a bold texture, and turn golden brown in fall before dropping. The smooth, gray bark and fur-covered buds make this open-branched tree lovely in winter. Rounded and low branched; 20 to 30 feet tall and wide.

A star magnolia (*M. stellata* or *M. tomentosa*) in full bloom is a welcome sight at the end of winter. Fragrant flowers composed of a dozen or more straplike white or pale pink petals cloak bare branches in early spring. Late frosts, however, often ruin the flowers. Leaves are dull green and turn yellowish in autumn. Gray-barked branches are decorated with furry, silver buds in winter. Multistemmed; 15 to 20 feet tall.

Both are lovely early-blooming small trees for borders, foundation plantings, patios, and lawns.

Site: Full sun to part or light shade. Humus-rich, deep, acid, moist soil. Plentiful moisture. Zones 5 to 9.
How to Grow: Plant balled-and-burlapped or container plants in spring or fall. Although the trees themselves are cold-hardy, the early blossoms are often frost-killed in warm areas. Locate in cold spot to delay bloom. Avoid southern exposure, which encourages early frost-prone bloom.

Prune immediately after blooming, if necessary. Responds well to heavy corrective pruning. Allow to form several trunks with low, spreading branches. Usually problem-free, but may suffer from mildew, leaf spot, and scale.
Cultivars and Similar Species: Saucer magnolia: 'Alexandrina', large early flowers, white inside, rose-purple to pink outside; 'Rustica Rubra', rose-red outside, white inside; 'Lennei', enormous late flowers, purple outside, white inside; 'Brozzonii', 10-inch white flowers. *M. acuminata × denudata*: 'Elizabeth', 7-inch, creamy yellow flowers; 'Butterflies', 4- to 5-inch butter yellow flowers; 'Yellow Lantern', lemon yellow flowers; 'Yellow Bird', light yellow flowers, late-blooming.

Star magnolia: 'Centennial', double white flowers, tinged pink; 'Rosea', pale pink; 'Royal Star', pink buds, double white flowers, late-blooming; 'Waterlily', bushy, pink buds, many-petaled white flowers, late-flowering. *M. × loebneri* (Loebner magnolia), early-blooming, flowers when young, fragrant, 12-petaled, white flowers, 40 feet tall, zones 5 to 9; 'Leonard Messel', dark pink; 'Merrill', starlike white flowers, fast-growing, oval, 25 feet tall; 'Spring Snow', late-blooming, may escape frost; 'Ballerina', fragrant, white flowers, 30 petals, late-blooming.

Kosar hybrids: Late-blooming small trees with lilylike flowers escape frost; 'Ann', deep purple, earliest of the group; 'Jane', latest of the group, red-purple outside, white inside; 'Susan', red-purple inside and out.

MALUS FLORIBUNDA

Japanese Flowering Crabapple
This beautiful tree, which resembles an apple tree with small fruit, blooms in mid spring. Showy clusters of deep pink flower buds decorate the branches as the new leaves emerge and open to 1-inch-wide, pink-tinged white flowers that turn the tree into a cloud of

blossoms. Flowers are fragrant and remain showy for two weeks if weather is cool. Pea-size, yellow fruit ripens in autumn and hangs on during winter, providing decoration and food for birds and squirrels. This tree is a parent of many hybrid crabapples. Older cultivars had a reputation for being disease-prone and dropping messy fruit, but newer cultivars don't

MALUS FLORIBUNDA 'SNOWDRIFT'

have these problems. They're highly desirable, featuring colorful blossoms, disease-resistant green or purplish foliage, and showy red, orange, or gold fruit that dries on the tree and isn't messy. Rounded to broad-spreading; 15 to 25 feet tall and wide. Cultivars may be rounded to vase-shaped. Lovely flowering tree for border, lawn, or garden; plant older varieties away from walkways and patios to avoid mess from fallen fruit.

Site: Full sun. Best in loamy, well-drained, acid soil; tolerates heavy soil. Zones 3 to 7 best, some hardy to Zone 8; good in Midwest and North.
How to Grow: Plant balled-and-burlapped or container plants in spring, summer, or fall. Seedlings may become weed problem.
  Prune to remove suckers and water sprouts during winter. Train to single leader with evenly spaced branches. Susceptible to scab, mildew, and fire blight; some crabapples are highly susceptible; others are more resistant. Diseases usually worse in the South.
Cultivars and Similar Species: More than 500 named cultivars. Select improved, disease-resistant types with persistent fruit, such as the following: 'Adams', red buds, red flowers fading to pink, glossy red fruit, 20 feet tall; 'Centurion', red buds, rose-red flowers, red fruit, 20 feet; 'Jewelberry', red buds, pink and white flowers, golden yellow fruit, 8 to 12 feet; 'Calloway', white flowers, large persistent red fruit, 20 feet, good in South; 'Donald Wyman', red-pink buds open white, small, red fruit, 25 feet; 'Harvest Gold', red buds, pink flowers fading to white, light yellow fruit on red stems, 20 feet, road-salt tolerant; 'Louisa', pink flowers, golden yellow fruit, weeping, 15 feet; 'Prairifire', crimson buds, purple-red flowers, reddish young leaves, dark red fruit, 20 feet; 'Red Jade', deep pink buds, white flowers, bright red fruit, weeping tree, 15 feet; 'Snowdrift', pink buds, white flowers, orange-red fruit, 20 feet; 'Sugar Tyme', pale pink buds, white flowers, small red fruit, 18 feet; *Malus baccata* (Siberian crabapple), fragrant white flowers, small persistent glossy red fruit, zones 3 to 7; choose disease-resistant cultivars. *M. × zumi* 'Calocarpa', large white flowers, large glossy red fruit, disease-resistant, 15 feet tall, 25 feet wide.

METASEQUOIA GLYPTOSTROBOIDES
Dawn Redwood

Dawn redwoods grew 20 million years ago, and until the 1940s, they were thought to be extinct. Seeds eventually were gathered from a grove of 1500 trees found in China, and the seeds were distributed throughout the world. Now dawn redwoods grace arboretums, streets, parks, and homes. This fast-growing (3 feet of new

METASEQUOIA GLYPTOSTROBOIDES

growth a year is common), conical tree has a single straight trunk with a fluted, buttressed base covered with shredding, reddish brown to bright orange bark. Feathery, bright green foliage emerges in early spring and turns reddish brown or orange in late fall. Brown, 1-inch cones cascade from the branches and persist through winter. Grows to 80 to 120 feet tall and only 20 to 40 feet wide. Beautiful planted in groups on a large property. Can be used for a screen or street tree, except under power lines. Allow space for mature size.

Site: Full sun. Best in moist, well-drained, slightly acid soil. Zones 5 to 8; best with year-round moisture.
How to Grow: Plant container or balled-and-burlapped trees in spring or fall, spacing to 10 feet apart for a screen, 30 feet for a specimen. Does not tolerate drought as well as other conifers. Avoid planting in frost pockets; late frost can damage new growth. Do not remove lower branches. Forms a new leader if it is injured. May be sheared in midsummer for a hedge. Japanese beetles sometimes a problem.
Cultivars and Similar Species: 'National', narrow pyramid; 'Sheridan Spire', narrow pyramid.

Deciduous Trees

NYSSA SYLVATICA
Black Gum, Sour Gum, Pepperidge, Tupelo

An outstanding and dependable native tree for fall color, the black gum has 3- to 6-inch-long, oval leaves that are glossy dark green in summer. They turn to yellow, then to orange, scarlet, and deep red to maroon before dropping in late autumn. The

NYSSA SYLVATICA

tree is slow-growing with a strong central leader and horizontal to slightly pendulous branches. Flowers appear with the new foliage, but are not noticeable. Blue berries ripen in fall on female trees, but may be quickly eaten by birds. Trunk bark is dark gray to black and roughly checkered. Pyramidal when young, becoming irregular to rounded; 30 to 50 feet tall and 20 to 30 feet wide. A good tree for lawn, borders, native plant gardens, and street planting, except under power lines and in polluted areas.

Site: Full sun to half shade. Best in moist to wet, humus-rich, acid soil; tolerates drier conditions, but not alkaline soil. Zones 5 to 9.
How to Grow: Plant small balled-and-burlapped or container trees in early spring; taproot makes transplanting large trees difficult. Easy to grow. As tree matures, remove lower limbs to reveal straight trunk; prune in fall. Usually pest- and disease-free. Larvae of luna moths feed on leaves.
Cultivars: Look for cultivars with superior fall color.

OXYDENDRUM ARBOREUM
Sourwood, Sorrel Tree

This graceful native tree is decked out in midsummer with 10-inch-long clusters of fragrant, creamy white flowers that resemble nodding sprays of lily-of-the-valley. The flowers ripen to buff-colored seedpods, which remain decorative from late summer through autumn. Leaves are glossy dark green and turn shades of yellow, maroon, and scarlet in early to mid

OXYDENDRUM ARBOREUM

fall. The gray-black trunk bark is deeply furrowed and blocky. Pyramidal with ascending branches; 25 to 30 feet tall and 15 to 20 feet wide. Use as specimen or group in border, lawn, or native plant garden; wonderful planted in groups along edge of woodland.

Site: Full sun to part shade; flowers and fall color best in sun. Moist, well-drained, fertile, acid soil. Tolerates some drought. Zones 5 to 9.

How to Grow: Plant small container or balled-and-burlapped trees in spring; large trees are difficult to transplant. Allow tree to branch low to ground. Usually pest- and disease-free.
Cultivars: None available. Buy trees grown from local seed source.

PARROTIA PERSICA
Persian Parrotia

Noted for its outstanding fall color, patchwork bark, and pretty winter flowers, Persian parrotia is a tree for all seasons. A member of the witch hazel family, the wide-spreading tree produces clusters of

PARROTIA PERSICA

dark red flowers on bare branches in late winter or early spring. These are followed by reddish new growth, which matures to 5-inch-long, wedge-shaped, glossy, dark green leaves that turn brilliant shades of gold, orange, and scarlet in late autumn. The dark reddish brown bark on the trunk and main branches flakes off to reveal green, silver-gray, and cream patches (especially attractive in winter). Single to multitrunked, rounded to spreading, and low-branched; 30 to 40 feet tall and at least as wide. Unusual specimen for border or garden.

Site: Full sun to light shade. Well-drained, humus-rich, slightly acid to alkaline soil. Tolerates dryness once established. Zones 6 to 9; good in heat of the South.
How to Grow: Plant balled-and-burlapped trees in early spring or fall. Mulch under tree, because shade is too dense to grow lawn or garden. Allow to branch low to ground; don't thin. Japanese beetles may be a problem.
Cultivars: 'Vanessa', columnar, red leaf tips; 'Biltmore', excellent fall color.

PHELLODENDRON AMURENSE
Amur Cork Tree

With a stout trunk, a few rugged and craggy main branches, and orange-yellow twigs, amur cork tree creates a picturesque silhouette

PHELLODENDRON AMURENSE

throughout the year. The 10-inch-long, compound, aromatic leaves are composed of 11 pointed leaflets, which are glossy dark green on top and light blue-green on the underside. They turn yellow to bronze in early fall. Flowers are inconspicuous. Female trees produce black fruit that drop to the ground and bear a strong turpentine scent. A deeply ridged and furrowed, corky, grayish brown bark cloaks the short, stout trunks of older trees. Broad-spreading to rounded and

open-branched; 30 to 45 feet tall and wide. An interesting specimen for lawn, border, or park.

Site: Full sun. Well-drained, acid to alkaline soil. Drought-tolerant. Zones 4 to 7.
How to Grow: Plant balled-and-burlapped or container trees in spring, summer, or fall. Fruit of female trees is messy; plant male type. Prune during dormancy. Usually pest-free, but can develop leaf scorch in hot, dry conditions.
Cultivars: 'Shademaster', fruitless form, 30 to 35 feet tall; 'Macho', fruitless, 25 to 30 feet tall; upright to spreading.

PISTACIA CHINENSIS
Chinese Pistachio

Valued for outstanding and dependable fall color, especially in the South, Chinese pistachio puts on a flaming red-and-orange show in late autumn. Leaves are rich green, 8 inches long, and compound, with 10 to 12 oval to lance-shaped leaflets, which give the tree an airy quality.

PISTACIA CHINENSIS

Greenish flowers appear at the shoot tips before the leaves appear in spring and aren't showy. Female trees produce showy clusters of red peppercorn-like fruit, which ripen to bright blue and usually are eaten by

birds. In winter, the mottled gray bark flakes off to reveal attractive salmon-orange inner bark. Rounded; to 35 feet tall and wide. Excellent lawn, garden, patio, or street tree, especially in the South.

Site: Full sun. Moist, well-drained, acid to alkaine soil. Tolerates drought. Zones 7 to 9; good in South and Southwest. Tolerates urban conditions.
How to Grow: Plant balled-and-burlapped or container plants in spring, summer, or fall. Easy to grow. Prune when young to develop strong central leader. Pest- and disease-free.

PLATANUS × ACERIFOLIA 'BLOODGOOD'
London Plane Tree

This hybrid of an American and an Asian species of sycamore is a significant improvement over each of them. The large, maplelike, dark

PLATANUS × ACERIFOLIA 'BLOODGOOD'

green leaves cast pleasant shade, but have no fall color, turning brown in autumn before dropping. The tan bark exfoliates to reveal white and gray patches. Older trees are impressive, with ghostly white bark and a massive trunk and scaffold branches. Fruit is a curious, burrlike, tan ball composed of tightly packed seeds; *continued*

PLATANUS × ACERIFOLIA 'BLOODGOOD'
(continued)

develops in fall and hangs on into winter. Pyramidal when young, becoming rounded and open; 50 to 60 feet tall and 30 to 40 feet wide. A popular street and city tree, it is overplanted in some areas. Locate where it will be silhouetted against the sky and where the bark will be appreciated in winter.

Site: Full sun to part shade. Best in fertile, deep, moist soil; tolerates dry, poor, and alkaline soil. Zones 6 to 9; withstands heat, drought, pollution, and urban conditions.

How to Grow: Plant balled-and-burlapped trees in spring, summer, or fall. Fallen fruit needs to be cleaned up in spring. May be heavily pruned. As trees mature, remove lower branches up to 20 feet to reveal trunk. Highly resistant to anthracnose fungus, which infects other sycamores. Susceptible to mildew, borers, and lace bugs.

Cultivars and Similar Species: 'Columbia', pyramidal, anthracnose- and mildew-resistant, deeply lobed leaves; 'Liberty', pyramidal, mildew- and anthracnose-resistant, five-lobed leaves; 'Metroshade' ('Metzam'), fast-growing, new growth cinnamon color, 100 feet tall, 80 feet wide, mildew- and anthracnose-resistant, good street tree. *Platanus occidentalis* (sycamore, American plane tree, buttonwood), fast-growing native, to 150 feet tall, ghostly white-gray-and-tan bark, leaves susceptible to anthracnose and mildew; moist to wet soil, best in native landscape, zones 5 to 9.

PONCIRUS TRIFOLIATA
Trifoliate Orange, Hardy Orange

A cold-hardy cousin to the orange tree, trifoliate orange brings both beauty and security to your garden.

Armed with lethal, 2-inch-long, green thorns, it makes an impenetrable barrier. In spring, highly fragrant, star-shaped, white flowers cover the branches. Sour-tasting, citruslike, 2-inch, bright gold fruits decorate the branches in autumn and winter. The three-part, shiny green leaves turn yellow in fall and drop to reveal the fruit and green-barked branches. Oval; usually 10 to 15 feet tall, but can grow taller. Plant as unusual and attractive specimen in garden, or use as security hedge. Locate so it's visible in winter.

PONCIRUS TRIFOLIATA

Site: Full sun to part shade. Moist, well-drained, acid soil. Dry to moist conditions. Zones 6 to 9.

How to Grow: Plant bare-root or balled-and-burlapped plants in spring. Plant away from pedestrians and where children play. Responds to heavy pruning immediately after blooming; may be pruned into dense hedge. Usually pest- and disease-free. May become chlorotic if pH is above 7.5.

PRUNUS SPP.
Purple-Leaf Plum, Ornamental Cherry

Tiny, fragrant, pale to dark pink flowers sparkle all over the purple-leaf plum (*Prunus × cerasifera* 'Atropurpurea') in early spring and are

PRUNUS × 'OKAME'

soon joined by the colorful, newly unfolding leaves. The glossy, oval leaves emerge vivid purple-maroon and mature to a duller bronze-purple by midsummer—some cultivars keep their bright color better. Small, purple fruit ripens in midsummer and attracts birds. Tree is rounded to vase-shaped with ascending branches; 15 to 30 feet tall and as wide. Use it as a purple accent in a border or foundation planting.

Possibly possessing the most beautiful bark of any tree, Amur chokecherry (*P. maackii*) is a cold-hardy tree featuring glistening, metallic, golden bark with light-colored horizontal bands. It blooms in late spring, producing dangling clusters of tiny, white flowers. The black summer fruit attracts birds. The rounded single or multitrunked tree grows to 30 feet tall. A magnificent specimen, especially in cold areas; plant where it can be seen in winter.

Blooming for about three weeks beginning in late winter, Okame cherry (*P. × 'Okame'*) brings welcome color to bleak gardens. The dark pink buds open to small, starry, clear pink blossoms that are produced in great numbers. The fine-textured leaves are dark green and turn bright yellow and orange in fall. Rounded to vase-shaped; 25 to 30 feet tall. Plant this earliest-blooming cherry where you can see it from indoors.

Oriental cherry *(P. serrulata)* is a tree for all seasons. Large clusters of white or pink, single or double flowers hang from the limbs in mid spring. Oval to lance-shaped leaves emerge with a reddish tinge and mature to dark green, then turn red or scarlet in fall. Bark is glossy, deep reddish brown. Most cultivars are vase-shaped to rounded; to 25 feet tall. A dramatic spring-flowering tree for mixed borders and Japanese-style gardens.

Higan or weeping cherry *(P. subhirtella* var. *pendula)* puts on a show in early spring when its leafless, cascading branches burst forth with a shower of small single or double pink blossoms. Leaves are lustrous, dark green and remain green well into fall, dropping with little color change. Grows rapidly to 20 to 40 feet tall and 15 to 30 feet wide, and creates a wonderful winter silhouette. Excellent planted in garden near a pond, where it can cascade over water, or on top of a slope or wall. Locate where you can see it from indoors.

Site: Full sun. Moist loam best, but tolerates any average, well-drained soil and a range of pH. Purple-leaf plum is hardy in zones 4 to 9; one of cold-hardiest purple-leaf plants. Amur chokecherry is hardy in zones 3 to 7, okame cherry in zones 7 to 9, Oriental cherry in zones 5 to 8.

How to Grow: Plant bare-root in early spring, or balled-and-burlapped or container plants in spring or fall. Trees tend to be short-lived. Prune immediately after flowering. Borers, scale, aphids, tent caterpillars, canker, and leaf spot can be serious problems. Weeping cherry is more pest-tolerant than other cherries.

Cultivars and Similar Species: Purple leaf plum: 'Thundercloud', deep purple foliage; 'Newport', early light pink flowers, dark purple foliage; 'Mt. St. Helens', rounded, with strong trunk, light pink flowers, rich purple leaves all summer; 'Krauter's Vesuvius', dark purple-black foliage, light pink flowers. *P. × cistena* (purple-leaf sand cherry), white flowers, red-purple leaves, shrubby to 7 feet tall, good hedge, zones 3 to 8.

Amur chokecherry: *P. serrula* (paperbark cherry), pyramidal to rounded, 20 to 30 feet tall, gleaming dark red-brown bark, zones 5 to 8. *P. sargentii* (sargent cherry), single pink flowers before leaves, gleaming reddish bark, red and yellow fall color, 30 or more feet tall, zones 5 to 9.

Okame cherry: *P. mume* (Japanese apricot), early-blooming, single, pink flowers; double and dark pink-, red-, and white-flowered, and weeping cultivars available; zones 7 to 9. 'Hally Jolivette', hybrid, shrubby to 15 feet tall, semidouble pink and white flowers open over three weeks in early spring, often grafted to *P. serrula* for tree form and shiny red bark, zones 5 to 8.

Oriental cherry: 'Amanogawa', 20 feet tall, 5 feet wide, double, light pink flowers; 'Kwanzan', bright pink, double, late flowers, strong vase shape if grafted; 'Shirofugen', blush pink blossoms fading to white, flat-topped and wide-spreading; 'Mt. Fuji', white, fragrant, double flowers; 'Tai Haku', large, single white flowers, broad vase. *P. × yedoensis* (Yoshino or Potomac cherry), showy, early, pink-buds, single white blossoms; 'White Fountain', 12 to 15 feet tall, weeping, white flowers, gold fall color, zones 5 to 8; 'Akebono', ('Daybreak') soft pink flowers.

Weeping cherry: 'Yae-shirdare-higan' ('Pendula Plena Rosea'), double, dark pink, long-lasting flowers; 'Wayside Weeping', zones 4 to 8; 'Autumnalis', semidouble, pink flowers bloom in early spring and again lightly in autumn, less weeping.

PSEUDOLARIX KAEMPFERI

PSEUDOLARIX KAEMPFERI (PSEUDOLARIX AMABILIS)
Golden Larch

This pine family member is a deciduous conifer. The new needles in spring are light green, maturing to soft green in summer and yellow to russet-gold in autumn before dropping. The 2½-inch-long needles are flattened and spiral around the stems of new growth and short spurs of older wood. Branches spread horizontally and droop somewhat, creating a graceful, open silhouette reminiscent of a cedar. Cones are 3 inches long and borne on the upper branches, ripening to red-brown in autumn, but not lasting through winter. Broadly pyramidal; to 50 feet tall and 40 feet wide. Ultimately needs a large site, but grows so slowly it may be used in smaller gardens for years. Use as a specimen silhouetted against the sky.

Site: Full sun. Moist, well-drained, deep, acid, sandy loam. Does not tolerate alkaline conditions. Zones 5 or 6 to 8; does well in the South.
How to Grow: Plant container or balled-and-burlapped trees in spring or fall, allowing room for ultimate size. Protect from wind. Do not remove lower branches or the top. Usually pest-free.
Cultivars: Only the species is sold.

PYRUS CALLERYANA 'BRADFORD'

Callery Pear, Bradford Pear

Extremely popular, this tree decorates streets across the country with its fluffy clusters of small, white flowers in early spring and its gorgeous long-lasting, red, purple, orange, and scarlet foliage in late fall. The lustrous, dark green leaves appear when the flowers begin to fade and are oval and 4 to 5 inches long. The tiny fruit that develops in

PYRUS CALLERYANA 'BRADFORD'

summer is highly attractive to birds. The tree has a formal oval shape, which lends itself to street boulevards, but seems stiff and unattractive in gardens. 'Bradford' is prone to storm breakage due to crowded, narrow crotch angles; other newer cultivars make better choices. Uniform and oval; 30 to 50 feet tall and 20 to 35 feet wide.

Use Callery pear as a lawn or border tree in large gardens for early blossoms, shade, and wonderful fall color. Blossoms smell bad; locate away from house.

Site: Full sun to part shade. Tolerates light to heavy soil. Moderate moisture best, but is highly drought-tolerant. Zones 4 or 5 to 8; tolerates air pollution and urban conditions. Good in the Midwest.

How to Grow: Plant balled-and-burlapped or container trees in spring, summer, or fall. Large limbs may tear out during wind and ice storms; choose better cultivars. Prune when young to develop strong crotch angles. Suffers slightly from fire blight in the South.

Cultivars and Similar Species: 'Aristocrat', 40 feet tall, broadly pyramidal, strong central leader, less cold-hardy; 'Autumn Blaze', strong, wide crotch angles and wide crown, early fall color, cold-hardy; 'Chanticleer', pyramidal-oval, to 35 feet tall with stronger branches and central leader, good street tree; 'Redspire', dense, narrow pyramid, to 35 feet tall and 15 feet wide, strong branches, purple-red fall color.

Northern Series, cold-hardy to Zone 4—'Burgundy Snow', heavy-blooming, white flowers with burgundy centers, pyramidal, to 40 feet tall; 'Metropolitan', broad crown, to 45 feet tall, strong crotch angles; 'Frontier', narrow and upright, to 35 feet tall by 20 feet wide, most cold-hardy; 'Valiant', shorter and compact to 30 feet tall by 20 feet wide, crimson fall color.

Pyrus betulifolia 'Southworth' ('Dancer'), birch-leaf pear, birchlike silvery leaves flutter in slightest breeze, flowers and form similar to 'Bradford' without breakage problem, yellow fall leaves, zones 5 to 8. *P. salicifolia* 'Silver Frost' ('Pendula') (weeping willowleaf pear), white flowers, narrow silvery leaves, graceful weeping shape, to 25 feet tall, susceptible to fire blight, zones 5 to 9. 'Silver Frost' makes handsome specimen in border.

QUERCUS SPP.

Oak

Many oaks are excellent shade trees. The best ones for home landscapes are described here.

The oblong leaves of sawtooth oak (*Quercus acutissima*), an Asian species, emerge golden green, mature

QUERCUS PALUSTRIS

to dark green, and turn bright yellow to golden in late autumn, often persisting through winter. Golden catkins decorate the tree in spring and form numerous acorns in fall. Bark is deeply ridged and furrowed, becoming corky with age. Pyramidal when young, becoming rounded with low branches; 35 to 45 feet tall and about as wide. Use as a shade or lawn tree; should be grown more.

Water or possum oak (*Q. nigra*), a fast-growing native species, is very popular as a street or shade tree in the South. The dull, blue-green leaves are shaped rather like slightly lobed paddles and remain green through fall before dropping in early winter. The acorns are ½ inch long, and brown-and-black striped with shallow caps. The rough-barked silhouette is tall and massive. Upright to round; 50 to 80 feet tall and half as wide. Good shade or street tree, except under power lines. Good in wet areas.

Another native, pin oak (*Q. palustris*) has a tall, straight trunk and horizontal branches, with drooping lower branches. Its pleasing shape has made it a popular lawn tree. The yellow-green catkins bloom along with the emerging foliage. Deeply cut, narrow leaves are deep green when properly grown. Fall color is yellow or bronze, then brown, before leaves drop in late autumn, although they may persist through winter. Produces heavy crops of small, light brown acorns. Strongly pyramidal; 60 to 70 or more feet tall and 25 to 40 feet wide. Good lawn tree; allow plenty of room for skirt of pendent branches.

The native willow oak *(Q. phellos)* features tidy, narrow, dark green leaves that give it a much finer texture than most oaks. Leaves may turn red or yellow in fall in cold climates and are partially evergreen in warm ones. Produces copious amounts of ½-inch acorns. Rounded to pyramidal, with weeping lower branches; 50 to 90 feet tall and 40 feet wide. An excellent shade tree for lawn and gardens.

Native from Canada to Pennsylvania and east to Iowa, the northern red oak *(Q. rubra)* is one of the best oaks for fall color and one of the fastest-growing and longest-lived. The leaves, which are 4 to 8 inches long and cut with deep, sharp points, emerge pink-red in spring, mature to dark green with grayish undersides, and turn maroon-red to bright red in fall. Trees bear large acorns and have dark bark with smooth ridges and white stripes. Upright, with horizontal branching; to 70 feet tall and wide. Use as lawn, garden, or woodland tree.

Site: Oaks grow best in full sun. Sawtooth, pin, and willow oaks do best in rich, moist, acid, well-drained soil. Water oak best in moist to wet soil. Red oak does best in well-drained, light, acid soil and is drought-tolerant.

Sawtooth oak hardy in zones 5 to 9; heat-tolerant and performs well in the South. Water and willow oak, zones 6 to 9. Pin oak hardy in zones 5 to 8; performs poorly in soil of the Plains and the Midwest; tolerates pollution. Red oak hardy in zones 3 to 9; tolerates urban conditions.

How to Grow: Plant balled-and-burlapped or container trees in spring, summer, or fall. Pin oak is best planted in spring or fall, willow oak in spring.

Acorns may pose a litter problem, but provide food for wildlife. Water oak is weak-wooded compared to other oaks. Willow oak has strong wood, and the small leaves are easy to rake.

Train oaks when young to develop a central leader and evenly spaced branches. Prune off lower limbs of water oak as trees mature to reveal the bark. Lower branches of pin oak may be removed, but those above often droop lower as a result. Do not prune red oak in spring, which could allow entrance of oak wilt fungus by beetles.

Sawtooth, willow, and red oak may become chlorotic in alkaline soil; pin oak in neutral to alkaline soil. Water oak may suffer from mistletoe, aphids, scale, and borers. Gall and gypsy moth caterpillars may threaten pin oak. Gypsy moth caterpillars may bother red oak, and oak wilt is an increasing and serious problem for this species.

Cultivars and Similar Species:
Sawtooth oak: 'Gobbler', heavy yield of acorns relished by wildlife.

Water oak: *Q. macrocarpa* (bur oak), slow-growing, to 80 feet tall, straight trunk and twisting scaffold branches, blunt-lobed leaves, drought-tolerant, zones 3 to 9, excellent as shade tree or windbreak in the Plains; 'Boomer', upright, with spreading branches and vigorous growth.

Pin oak: 'Crownright', branches less pendulous, narrow shape.

Willow oak: Choose locally grown trees in the North to ensure hardiness.

Northern red oak: *Q. coccinea* (scarlet oak), similar, with more reliable fall color, not as widely available, zones 5 to 9. *Q. shumardii* (Shumard oak), looks similar, native to the Midwest and South Central states, performs well there in poorly drained or dry soils, zones 5 to 8. *Q. nuttallii* (Nuttall's oak), fast-growing, red fall color, pyramidal, tolerates wet soil and urban conditions of the South and Midwest, zones 5 to 8.

ROBINIA PSEUDOACACIA
Black Locust

This native tree was used to build ship masts and still is used for fence posts. The blue-green foliage is lovely and lacy, with 15 rounded leaflets, and casts a light shade that's easy to garden under. In good years, clusters of fragrant, creamy white flowers dangle from the branches,

ROBINIA PSEUDOACACIA

almost blanketing the foliage in late spring and early summer. The zigzagging branches and furrowed, light brown bark give the tree winter character. Branches are slightly thorny. Varies from narrow with tall, straight trunk, 75 feet tall, to irregular branching, to fan-shaped, 45 feet tall, depending on origin of tree. Excellent tree for difficult sites and for casting light shade on patio or garden.

Site: Full sun. Best in moist, fertile soil, but performs well in poor, infertile, dry sites. Zones 4 to 9.

How to Grow: Transplant balled-and-burlapped trees in spring, summer, or fall. Trees may sucker and send up sprouts at great distances from trunk; remove immediately. Shallow-rooted and can topple in strong storms.

Train to develop tall single leader when young; multiple trunks become weak with age. Prune in fall *continued*

ROBINIA PSEUDOACACIA
(continued)

or winter. Old trees develop brittle branches. Can drop-crotch mature trees to reduce height and prevent storm damage. Borers and leaf miners can be serious in some areas.

Cultivars and Similar Species: 'Bessoniana', oval, good street tree, almost thornless, few flowers; 'Frisia', golden yellow leaves all season; 'Umbraculifera', densely rounded to umbrella-like, 15 feet tall, rarely flowers, thornless.

SALIX ALBA VAR. 'VITELLINA'
Golden Weeping Willow

An old-fashioned favorite for planting beside a pond, this beautiful tree features bright gold

SALIX ALBA

branchlets that weep gracefully from massive scaffold branches. The leaves are narrow and lance-shaped, to 4 inches long and ½ inch wide. They emerge bright yellow-green early in spring, mature to dark green with silver undersides, and turn golden yellow in late autumn. Rounded and weeping; 50 to 70 feet tall and wide. Plant beside a pond, lake, stream, or river, and in wet sites where weeping shape can be reflected in water.

Site: Full sun. Needs moist to wet site. Zones 3 to 9.

How to Grow: Plant balled-and-burlapped or container trees in spring or fall. Drops continual litter of leaves and small branchlets. Weak-wooded. Prune in fall. Subject to storm damage, especially if crown is uneven. Brace large, heavy, old branches. Allow branchlets to sweep ground. Numerous disease and insect problems, including twig blight, gall, canker, aphids, borers, and sawflies.

Cultivars and Similar Species: The species is an upright tree with golden brown stems. *Salix matsudana* (Hankow or Peking willow), moist soil, zones 5 to 9; 'Tortuosa' (corkscrew willow), gnarled and contorted branches and twigs, twisted leaves, best trained to single trunk, to 30 feet tall, zones 4 to 9; 'Scarlet Curls', curly leaves, red twigs and branches, semipendulous, to 18 feet tall, zone 5 to 9. 'Golden Curls', hybrid, slightly twisted, golden stems and slightly curled leaves, to 30 feet tall, Zone 4.

SOPHORA JAPONICA
Japanese Pagoda Tree, Chinese Scholar Tree

Hardy and a summer-bloomer, this tree is becoming a favorite shade tree for lining streets and beautifying urban settings. The dark, shiny, bright green leaves are divided into numerous, small, pointed leaflets, which give it a fine-textured, airy appearance. Large panicles of small, creamy white flowers decorate the tree for several weeks in late summer. The leaves remain green until late fall, when they drop with no color change. The 4- to 8-inch-long brown seedpods may hang on the tree all winter. Rounded; 50 to 75 feet tall and wide. Lovely lawn tree and good street tree, except under power lines.

SOPHORA JAPONICA 'REGENT'

Site: Full sun. Best in fertile, moist soil; tolerates drought once established. Zones 6 to 9; tolerates air pollution, heat, and urban conditions.

How to Grow: Plant young balled-and-burlapped trees in spring or fall. Needs cleanup of leaves, pods, and flowers throughout year.

Train to develop tall trunk. Large scaffold branches may need bracing or cabling to prevent storm damage, or reduce weight by thinning secondary branches. Prune in late summer. Leafhoppers, mildew, and twig blight are sometimes problems.

Cultivars: Cultivars are better than seed-grown trees, which are slow growing and variable. 'Princeton Upright', fast-growing, compact, to 50 feet tall, upright branching; 'Regent', rapid-growing, early-blooming, oval crown, to 50 feet tall, insect-free.

SORBUS ALNIFOLIA
Korean Mountain Ash

Beautiful throughout the year, this little-known tree is gaining in popularity due to its disease resistance and showy qualities. Flattened 3-inch-wide clusters of white flowers bloom in late spring, contrasting with the bright green foliage. The 4-inch-long oval leaves have small teeth along

SORBUS ALNIFOLIA

their edges and resemble beech leaves, but turn red and gold in autumn. Large clusters of cherrylike, rose-red or scarlet berries ripen before the leaves change color, but persist well into winter, adding to the autumnal and winter landscape. Trunks are silvery and beautiful, like beech bark. Upright to pyramidal; 40 to 50 feet tall and 20 to 30 feet wide. Large, flowering shade tree for lawn, border, or garden.

Site: Full sun. Well-drained soil; adapts to most pH levels. Plentiful moisture. Zones 4 to 7; doesn't withstand air pollution.

How to Grow: Plant balled-and-burlapped or container trees in spring or fall. Easy-care. Resistant to borers. May suffer from scab and fire blight in hot, humid areas, otherwise highly disease-resistant.

Cultivars and Similar Species: 'Redbird', narrow, upright column, to 25 feet tall, copious red berries, gold fall color; *Sorbus aucuparia* (European mountain ash), once popular but grown only in the North, highly susceptible to fire blight, scab, borers, and numerous pests in the South, 35 feet tall, white early summer flowers, showy orange to red fall berries, fernlike, dark green leaves with fiery fall color, zones 3 to 7. *S. rufoferruginea* 'Longwood Sunset',

resembles European mountain ash, but is disease-resistant, orange berries, burgundy fall color, zones 4 to 7.

STEWARTIA PSEUDOCAMELLIA
Japanese Stewartia

A charming, small, flowering tree, Japanese stewartia brings four seasons of beauty to the garden. The flaky bark that cloaks the trunk and branches is a lovely patchwork of reddish orange, tan, and apricot and is especially showy in winter when not shaded by the dense foliage. In

STEWARTIA PSEUDOCAMELLIA

midsummer, 2- to 3-inch-wide, camellia-like, yellow-centered, white flowers are sprinkled all over the tree. Autumn brings a fiery show of gold, red, or purple foliage. Oval to vase-shaped, open-branched; to 30 feet tall and 20 feet wide. Plant in prominent location in border or foundation planting, especially where it can be seen from indoors in winter.

Site: Light afternoon shade best. Humus-rich, moist, acid soil. Plentiful moisture. Zones 6 and 7.

How to Grow: Plant container or balled-and-burlapped trees in spring or fall. Good soil is essential. Prune lower branches to reveal trunk. Pest- and disease-free.

STYRAX JAPONICUS

Similar Species: *Stewartia monadelpha*, metallic, orange bark, white flowers with violet centers, zones 6 to 8.

STYRAX JAPONICUS
Japanese Snowbell

This excellent small tree blooms in early summer, when spring's wealth of flowers has passed, making it a welcome addition to the garden. Dainty, bell-shaped, white blossoms hang in clusters from the outstretched branches and, combined with the fine-textured, dark green leaves, create a beautiful white-and-green effect. Leaves turn yellowish to rusty red in fall. Rounded to spreading, with horizontal branches; 20 to 30 feet tall and wide. Use as patio or border tree. Excellent planted on slopes so flowers can be seen from beneath.

Site: Part shade. Humus-rich, moist, acid, well-drained soil. Plentiful moisture. Zones 6 to 8.

How to Grow: Plant balled-and-burlapped or container trees in spring or fall. Shallow rooted; choose plants that tolerate dry shade for underneath. Prune to develop single leader, if desired. Borers may pose problems; otherwise pest- and disease-free. *continued*

STYRAX JAPONICUS
(continued)

Cultivars and Similar Species: 'Carillon', smaller with pendulous branches; 'Pink Chimes', pale pink flowers; 'Sohuksan', larger flowers and leaves. *Styrax americanum* (American snowbell), rounded and shrubby, to 10 feet tall, narrow-petaled white flowers in late spring, zones 6 to 9. *S. obassia* (fragrant snowbell), small, white, bell-shaped flowers in early summer, 8-inch round, dark green leaves with velvety, silver-green hairs on undersides, to 25 feet tall, zones 6 to 8.

SYRINGA RETICULATA (SYRINGA AMURENSIS VAR. JAPONICA)
Japanese Tree Lilac

Producing huge clusters of creamy white flowers for two weeks in early summer, this tree-size lilac puts on a spectacular show. Unfortunately, the flower's aroma may not please

SYRINGA RETICULATA

everyone. Leaves are broadly heart-shaped and up to 5 inches long, dark green on top and gray-green underneath. They turn yellowish in fall. The bark is beautiful—shiny red, like a cherry tree—on the trunk and branches. Older trunks become gray

and scaly. Rounded, multistemmed; 20 to 30 or more feet tall and 25 feet wide. Especially valuable flowering tree for borders and streets in cold climates. Showy when seen from distance.

Site: Full sun. Well-drained, loose, slightly acid soil. Plentiful moisture. Zones 3 to 7.

How to Grow: Plant balled-and-burlapped or container trees in spring or fall. May bloom in alternate years unless spent flowers are removed.

Prune to reveal trunk bark and to train to single leader, if desired. Thin out weak wood from tree's center. Doesn't suffer from mildew, borers, or scale as do many other lilacs, except in warm areas.

Cultivars and Similar Species: 'Ivory Silk', larger flowers, blooms heavily even when young. *Syringa reticulata* var. *mandschurica*, extremely similar, Zone 2. *S. pekinensis* (Pekin lilac), smaller flowers, beautiful peeling bark, needs good soil.

TAXODIUM DISTICHUM
Bald Cypress

Although native to the swamps of the South, the beautiful bald cypress thrives much farther North and grows in average moisture conditions. It forms a beautiful and graceful tree of large proportions. If grown near water or on a swampy site, gnarled, woody "knees" push up through the ground from the tree's wide-spreading root system. The straight trunk is covered with shredding, reddish bark and may form dramatic buttresses at its base. Unlike most conifers, bald cypress is deciduous, dropping needles and branchlets in autumn, making it "bald" in winter. The billowy branches feature fine-textured needles, which resemble yew foliage, are flattened, narrow and pointed, and about ½ inch long. New needles

TAXODIUM DISTICHUM

emerge bright yellow-green in late spring and mature to soft gray-green; fall color is effective golden brown. The round cones are 1 inch around and mature to dark brown. Columnar; to 60 feet tall and 25 feet wide, or taller. Plant as a specimen or in a grove; best near water or on a wet site on a large property. Fast-growing.

Site: Full sun. Deep, moist, acid, sandy loam. Needs plentiful moisture; thrives in a wet or swampy site and also tolerates average moisture. Zones 4 to 9; wind-resistant; tolerates midwestern conditions.

How to Grow: Plant container or balled-and-burlapped trees in spring or fall, spacing 20 to 25 feet apart for specimen, 15 to 20 feet for grove. May look unattractive when young, but becomes stately with age. Prune to remove competing leaders when young. Twig blight and spider mites sometimes troublesome. Becomes chlorotic in alkaline soil.

Cultivars and Similar Species: 'Shawnee Brave', bronze-orange fall color; 'Monarch of Illinois', wide-spreading. *Taxodium distichum* var. *nutans* (pond cypress), similar with light brown bark, leaves more scalelike; 'Prairie Sentinel', 60 feet tall and 10 feet wide, regular horizontal branches, soft-textured green in summer, rich red-brown in fall.

TILIA CORDATA 'GREENSPIRE'

TILIA CORDATA
Small-Leaved Linden, Littleleaf Linden

Small, heart-shaped, bright green leaves with lighter undersides form a dense coat on this uniformly shaped tree. The last linden to bloom, in midsummer, it produces fragrant, yellow-cream flowers in 3-inch clusters attached to spoon-shaped, pale green bracts, which give the tree a soft two-toned effect. Flowers ripen into round, pea-size, yellow fruit. Fall color is a poor yellow, and trunk bark is ridged and furrowed gray-brown. Pyramidal when young, becoming oval to rounded; 60 to 70 feet tall and 40 feet wide. Popular street or lawn tree. Shape can be too formal for some gardens.

Site: Full sun. Fertile, moist, well-drained soil; adapts to acid or alkaline conditions. Zones 3 to 8; tolerates air pollution.
How to Grow: Plant balled-and-burlapped trees in spring, summer, or fall. Aphids may drop honeydew on cars parked beneath street trees.

Train to single main leader and widely spaced scaffold branches; thin branches to reduce overcrowding. Prune when dormant. Fewer problems than other lindens, but aphids and Japanese beetles may cause problems.

Cultivars and Similar Species:
'Greenspire', extremely popular street tree, uniform pyramidal shape, to 50 feet tall, 35 feet wide; 'Fairhaven', straight trunk, uniform branches, slightly larger leaves; 'Chancellor' ('Chancole'), pyramidal, to 50 feet tall, 20 feet wide, golden yellow fall color; 'Corinthian' ('Corzam'), columnar, to 45 feet tall, 15 feet wide, smaller, shiny leaves; 'Glenleven', pyramidal and more open, to 50 feet tall, 35 feet wide, fast-growing, larger leaves, golden yellow fall color.

Tilia americana (basswood, American linden), pyramidal with ascending branches, to 80 feet tall, 8-inch leaves, spicy-scented flowers, best in native landscape; 'Redmond', compact, tight pyramid, to 70 feet tall, large, glossy leaves.

T. tomentosa (silver linden), dark green leaves with hairy silver undersides, creating shimmery effect, pyramidal to rounded, to 70 feet tall, silver bark, zones 5 to 8; 'Green Mountain', improved, rapid-growing, heat- and drought-tolerant; 'Sterling Silver', neat shape, to 50 feet tall, 40 feet wide, soft gray new growth, resists Japanese beetles and gypsy moths; 'Satin Shadow' ('Sashazam'), broadly pyramidal, to 50 feet tall, 40 feet wide, uniform, silvery, resists Japanese beetles and gypsy moths. Enjoy silver linden on slopes—you can look up at leaves.

ULMUS SPP.
Elm

The beloved American or white elm (*Ulmus americana*) once graced the streets of many towns, cities, and college campuses, but Dutch elm disease, a fungus spread by an imported bark beetle, wiped out the elms in many areas. The tree's silhouette is unmistakable—its tall trunk splits into several stout trunks that branch upward and outward to form a wide-spreading, fountainlike canopy. The 3- to 6-inch-long oval to oblong leaves have toothed edges and are glossy dark green in summer, turning yellowish to bright yellow in fall. Strongly vase-shaped, with ascending branches; to 80 feet tall and 60 feet wide. Excellent lawn and street tree because of arching shape. Plant only disease-resistant cultivars.

ULMUS AMERICANA

Although not a substitute for the American elm, lacebark or Chinese elm (*U. parvifolia*) is a beauty in its own right. The bark on trunk and branches is mottled, flaky, and colorful, usually a fine-textured patchwork of orange, tan, and gray. Flowers, which bloom in late summer, aren't showy. Leaves are dark glossy green, to 3 inches long with toothed edges, and turn yellowish to reddish purple in late autumn. Rounded to slightly vase-shaped; to 50 feet tall and wide. Excellent city and street tree, lovely as shade tree in lawn or garden on large property.

Site: Full sun. Fertile, humus-rich, moist but well-drained, acid to alkaline soil. American elm tolerates wet soil. Chinese elm performs well in poor and alkaline soil and in drought. American elm is hardy in zones 2 to 9. Chinese elm in zones 5 to 9; both tolerate unfavorable urban sites. *continued*

ULMUS SPP.
(continued)

How to Grow: Plant balled-and-burlapped or container trees in spring, summer, or fall. Plant American elm 500 feet from another elm to avoid pests. Chinese elm is a dense tree and may be susceptible to wind damage.

Remove lower limbs of American elm while young to encourage high branching and a single leader as long as possible. Remove deadwood immediately to avoid bark beetles that carry Dutch elm disease. Train Chinese elm to a single leader when young. Thin crowded branches every few years, if needed, to reduce wind resistance. Prune both types when dormant.

American elm is susceptible to wilt, canker, leaf spot, mildew, phloem necrosis, as well as incurable Dutch elm disease. Troublesome insects include aphids, Japanese beetles, elm bark beetles, borers, gypsy moths, scales, and elm leaf beetles. To limit damage from Dutch elm disease, separate elms as directed above, remove bark, which harbors beetles, from stacked wood cut from diseased trees, and institute pesticide program to control beetles. Infected trees may be saved for a time with fungicide injections. Chinese elm is highly resistant to Dutch elm disease, elm leaf beetles, and Japanese beetles.

Cultivars: American elm: The following cultivars are highly resistant, although not immune, to Dutch elm disease—'American Liberty', vase shape; 'Princeton', uniform vase shape, to 70 feet tall, resistant to leaf beetles; 'Delaware', vigorous, broad-spreading, to 80 feet tall. Disease-resistant hybrids: 'Accolade' ('Morton'), 'Danada', 'Washington', 'Jefferson', 'Cathedral'.

Chinese Elm: 'Athena' ('Emer I'), compact, rounded head, to 50 feet tall and wide, bronze-burgundy fall color, colorful, flaking bark, drought-tolerant, Zone 5; 'Drake', rounded, to 35 feet tall, almost evergreen leaves; 'Milliken',

rounded and spreading, to 50 feet tall and wide, colorful, flaking bark; 'Emerald Vase' ('Allce'), shaped like American elm, 70 feet tall, drought- and beetle-resistant, yellow fall color, colorful, flaking bark; 'King's Choice', shaped like American elm, fissured bark; 'Dynasty', hybrid, vase-shaped, red fall color. 'Pathfinder', immune to Dutch elm disease, colorful bark.

U. pumila (Siberian elm), tough, drought- and disease-resistant, cold-hardy, fast-growing, brittle wood, messy, weedy, lacks ornamental value; plant only improved cultivars in difficult cold, dry regions of the Plains and the Mountain states, zones 2 to 9.

ZELKOVA SERRATA
Japanese Zelkova

Resembling the American elm, this graceful tree can fill a landscape niche. Bark is mottled like the lacebark elm, but it's not as colorful. The elmlike leaves emerge pale green

ZELKOVA SERRATA 'GREEN VASE'

in spring, mature to dark green, and turn russet-orange to deep purplish red in mid fall. Vase-shaped with ascending branches; 50 to 80 feet tall and wide. Excellent for street, lawn, patio, or garden on large property.

Site: Full sun. Humus-rich, moist, well-drained soil best; performs well in

poorer soil and alkaline conditions. Tolerates drought once established. Zones 6 to 9; tolerates air pollution and urban locations.

How to Grow: Plant balled-and-burlapped trees in spring, summer, or fall. Not weak-limbed, as was once thought. Train while young to develop evenly spaced branches. Resistant to Dutch elm disease, elm leaf beetles, and Japanese beetles.

Cultivars: 'Village Green', fast-growing, broadly spreading to 50 to 60 feet, rusty red fall color, cold-hardy to Zone 5; 'Green Vase', fast-growing, graceful, fountain-shaped, to 70 feet tall, orange-brown to rust-red fall color; 'Halka', fast-growing, most like the American elm in shape, to 50 feet tall.

DECIDUOUS SHRUBS

ABELIA × GRANDIFLORA
Glossy Abelia

This fine-textured, semievergreen shrub with arching branches adds interest to the garden all year. The glossy, dark green leaves turn russet or bronze-red in autumn; they

ABELIA × GRANDIFLORA

remain that color through winter in mild areas, but drop off in cold areas. Even when bare of leaves in winter, the red twigs bring lovely color to the garden. Clusters of small, funnel-shaped, white flowers bloom at the branch tips from midsummer until frost, surrounded by rust-colored calyxes, which give the flowers a pink tinge. Rounded form; to 6 feet tall and 5 feet wide. Lovely as specimen or massed in mixed borders, combined with trees and broad-leaved evergreens. Can be used as clipped or unclipped hedge.

Site: Full sun to light or half shade. Fertile, humus-rich, well-drained, acid soil best. Plentiful moisture. Zones 6 to 9 in East and Northwest; evergreen in zones 7 to 9; semievergreen in zones 6 and cooler parts of 7.
How to Grow: Plant balled-and-burlapped or container plants in spring or fall, spacing 4 feet apart. Softwood cuttings root easily. Tops may die in severe winters, but will resprout from the base and bloom the same year. Blooms on new growth; prune long branches for shape in early spring. Prune deadwood annually. Rejuvenate by cutting to ground in late winter. Usually pest-free, but leaf spot can be a problem.
Cultivars and Similar Species: 'Sherwood', finer-textured foliage, mound to 3 feet tall and 4 to 5 feet wide; 'Francis Mason', new leaves bright green maturing to variegated green-and-yellow, pale pink flowers, sun-tolerant gold shrub for South; 'Edward Goucher', hybrid 4 feet tall; larger, lilac-pink flowers, not as graceful as the species.

AESCULUS PARVIFLORA
Bottlebrush Buckeye

Native to the South, this shrub deserves greater use in gardens. It forms an architectural mass of bold stems, leaves, and midsummer flowers. The leaves grow on long, red petioles and are divided into five to seven leaflets arranged to form a rounded outline more than a foot across. Dark green on top and grayish on the undersides, the leaves turn yellowish green to bright yellow in autumn. Multistemmed and suckering, this shrub has a layered architectural appearance because its stout gray-brown stems twist and branch irregularly. For several weeks in midsummer, feathery, 8- to 10-inch-tall, white bottlebrushes decorate the shrub. Smooth, brown nuts may follow, but usually only a few develop. Upright; to 12 feet tall and spreading to form a colony 10 to 15 feet wide. Forms a handsome mass in border plantings, shady areas under trees, and naturalistic settings. Use only in large gardens.

AESCULUS PARVIFLORA

Site: Full sun to full shade. Best in humus-rich, acid soil. Moderate to plentiful moisture. Zones 4 to 9.
How to Grow: Plant balled-and-burlapped or container plants in early spring before they leaf out, spacing to allow for rapid growth. Plant seed as soon as it drops to ground. Allow plenty of growing space.
 Little pruning needed. May cut to ground in late winter to renew. Not seriously troubled by leaf diseases that attack other species of *Aesculus*.
Cultivars: Late-summer-blooming cultivars sometimes are available.

ARONIA ARBUTIFOLIA 'BRILLIANTISSIMA'

ARONIA ARBUTIFOLIA
Red Chokeberry

Showy all year, red chokeberry greets spring with a show of round, pink flower buds and downy new leaves. For two weeks in mid spring, lacy masses of tiny pink-centered, white flowers cover the shrub. The small, oval leaves are dark green and leathery during summer and turn red, orange, and violet-pink in autumn. The real show is in winter, however, when dangling clusters of glossy, red berries, which rival those of the better-known winterberry, decorate the plant. Berries last through winter because they're seldom eaten by birds. Native to eastern North America, red chokeberry spreads by suckers. Vase-shaped to upright; to 10 feet tall; may spread to form a large colony. Tends to look leggy; camouflage lower stems with low shrubs, perennials, or ornamental grasses. Species is showiest when massed; good naturalized in native plant garden. 'Brilliantissima' makes good specimen in a shrub border.

Site: Full sun to half shade. Adaptable. Wet to dry, fertile to infertile, acid soil. Zones 4 to 9.
How to Grow: Plant balled-and-burlapped or container *continued*

ARONIA ARBUTIFOLIA
(continued)

shrubs in spring or fall, spacing 5 feet apart. Softwood cuttings root easily. Divide suckers in fall or remove them to control spread. May be aggressive in fertile, moist site.

Rarely needs pruning. Renew by cutting to ground in late winter. Usually pest- and disease-free, although a member of the rose family. Chlorosis is a problem in alkaline soil; leaf spot is a problem in too much shade.

Cultivars and Similar Species:
'Brilliantissima', more flowers, larger and shinier red berries, 6 to 10 feet tall; *Aronia melanocarpa* (black chokeberry), native, white flowers in spring, glossy green summer foliage turns wine red and orange in fall; black berries in fall attract birds; spreads by suckers so may be invasive; best in naturalistic or wildlife garden; *A. melanocarpa* var. *elata* and 'Autumn Magic', superior fall color, larger berries.

BERBERIS SPP.
Barberry

Japanese barberry *(Berberis thunbergii)* is a dense shrub with shiny, spoon-shaped, 1-inch-long, bright green leaves that turn scarlet in autumn. Its many magnificent colored-leaf forms, which include purple, gold, and variegated cultivars, make an outstanding contribution to mixed borders throughout the summer. All forms develop teardrop-shaped red berries on thorny, zigzagged, arching stems. Berries are attractive in fall, ripening along with the brilliant orange and red fall foliage, and decorate the branches well into winter. Yellow flowers bloom with the new foliage and may go unnoticed. Rounded; to 5 feet tall and wide.

Probably the showiest deciduous barberry, Korean barberry *(B. koreana)* is decorated in mid

BERBERIS THUNBERGII 'ROSE GLOW'

spring with bright yellow flowers dangling in 3-inch or longer clusters from the undersides of its thorny, reddish stems. Spiny-toothed, 3-inch-long, oval leaves appear with the flowers and are larger than most barberry leaves. Foliage turns bright red in autumn. Teardrop-shaped, glossy, red berries cluster on the branches in fall and winter. Rounded and dense; to 6 feet tall and wide.

These thorny shrubs make excellent barriers and security hedges, either pruned or unpruned. Use colored-leaf forms in mixed borders with perennials, grasses, and taller shrubs.

Site: Full sun to half shade for Japanese barberry, sun to part shade for Korean barberry. In purple-leaf and golden forms, sun develops best color. Japanese barberry needs well-drained average to sandy soil; drought-tolerant. Give Korean barberry average to fertile, well-drained soil, average moisture. Japanese barberry is hardy in zones 4 to 9; withstands hot, dry summers and urban conditions. Korean barberry, zones 3 to 8; best in North.

How to Grow: Plant balled-and-burlapped or container shrubs in spring or fall, spacing 3 or more feet apart. Dense, thorny growth may be difficult to clean of litter and fallen tree leaves.

Korean barberry may form colonies from root suckers; dig out suckers if necessary.

Prune lightly as needed to control shape. All deciduous barberries are outlawed in Canada because they're an alternate host for black stem rust of wheat. Rust isn't usually a problem with *B. thunbergii*, but new strains of fungus may be attacking it.

Cultivars and Similar Species:
Japanese barberry: 'Kobold', dwarf to 2 feet tall, 3 feet wide; 'Sparkle', glossy, green leaves, arching branches, 5 feet tall, good fall color; 'Erecta', upright and columnar, good for hedge; 'Aurea', bright gold leaves, slow-growing to 3 to 4 feet tall, few berries; 'Bonanza Gold', dwarf, golden leaves, to 1½ feet tall and 3 feet wide; resistant to sunscald. *B. thunbergii* var. *atropurpurea* (purple barberry or red barberry), burgundy-purple leaves, gold-tinged purple flowers; 'Crimson Pygmy' ('Atropurpurea Nana'), dwarf to 3 feet tall, 3 to 4 feet wide, burgundy-purple leaves; 'Rose Glow' ('Rosy Glow'), dwarf to 3 feet tall and wide, new leaves rose-pink mottled with maroon; mature growth maroon; 'Harlequin', new foliage mottled cream, pink, and purple; compact to 4 feet tall; 'Gold Ring', purple leaves with yellow edge during summer.

Korean barberry: *B. vulgaris* (common barberry), similar, brought to North America by Colonists for its edible fruit, and naturalized; highly susceptible to wheat rust; don't plant in wheat-growing areas; zones 2 to 8.

BUDDLEIA DAVIDII
Butterfly Bush, Summer Lilac

Older cultivars of butterfly bush tend to be large, ungraceful plants redeemed only by beautiful, late-summer flowers that attract butterflies. New cultivars are more compact and bloom longer—blossoms begin in May in the South and July or August in the North and continue through fall. Leaves are softly hairy, coarse-textured, long, pointed, and green on top with silvery undersides. Lightly scented flowers appear in long, tapered sprays at branch tips in

BUDDLEIA DAVIDII

purple, blue, lavender, pink, and white. Fountain- to vase-shaped; to 15 feet tall and 8 feet wide if unpruned; dwarf and pruned specimens 5 to 8 feet tall.

Use in back or midground of cottage gardens and informal mixed borders, depending on size. Hide stems with bushy, rounded plants.

Site: Full sun in North; full sun to part shade in South. Average to sandy, fertile to infertile, well-drained soil. Average moisture best; tolerates drought. Zones 5 to 10; tops die to ground in zones 5 and 6.
How to Grow: Plant container shrubs in spring, summer, or fall, allowing plenty of room between other tall plants. Softwood cuttings root easily. Extra-fertile soil may encourage leaf growth instead of flowers. Provide 4- to 6-inch-deep winter mulch to protect roots in northern climates.

Blooms on new growth. Each year prune in early spring before growth begins; prune to woody framework in mild climates or cut back to ground, depending on desired height. In northern areas, cut to ground annually

in winter or early spring. The species described below bloom on old growth; thin old growth immediately after blooming. Usually problem-free, but spider mites and nematodes may be troublesome in Southeast.
Cultivars and Similar Species: Compact: 'Black Knight', vivid, dark purple-black flowers; 'White Profusion', huge, white flowers; 'Opera', huge, lavender-pink flowers; 'Empire Blue', large, blue flowers, strong stems; 'Royal Red', large, wine red flowers; 'Pink Delight', clear pink flowers.

Buddleia davidii var. *nanhoensis*, 3 to 5 feet tall, numerous small flower heads; 'Nanho White', white flowers; 'Nanho Blue', small, true blue flowers; 'Nanho Purple'; small, dark purple flowers; 'Nanho Petite Plum', reddish purple; 'Nanho Petite Indigo', lilac-blue, narrow gray-green leaves. 'Lochinch', hybrid, lavender flowers, silver leaves. *B. alternifolia* 'Argentea' (silver fountain buddleia), large shrub with narrow, silver leaves and lavender-blue flowers in late spring; may be pruned into small tree if staked; zones 4 to 8.

CALLICARPA DICHOTOMA
Purple Beautyberry

Unusual and eye-catching when in fruit, purple beautyberry dazzles onlookers with glistening clusters of violet-purple berries that line its arching stems. The berries ripen among the leaves in autumn and are showiest when decorating the bare branches in winter. Flowers are small, misty, lilac-pink clusters, which bloom between the leaves along the lengths of the horizontally arching stems in late summer and fall. Arranged in a flat plane, leaves are light chartreuse green and may turn yellow in fall before dropping. Rounded; 3 to 4 feet tall and wide. Lovely planted in mixed borders or massed with taller plants. At its best in fall and early winter, so combine with plants that have interest at other times.

CALLICARPA DICHOTOMA 'ISSAI'

Site: Full sun produces best berries; performs well in light shade, where berries may last longer. Tolerates almost any kind of soil, from heavy clay to sandy loam. Average to wet conditions. Zones 5 to 8; tolerates urban and seashore conditions.
How to Grow: Plant balled-and-burlapped or container plants in spring or fall, spacing 3 feet apart. Propagate from softwood cuttings. Fruit may be eaten by birds; fruit will last without fading if protected from winter sun.

Bears flowers and fruit on new growth; responds well to annual hard pruning before new growth begins. May be cut to 6 inches from ground in late winter, annually or every three years. Stem canker and leaf spot rare problems. Rabbits may devour new spring growth.
Cultivars and Similar Species: 'Issai', fruit ripens early.

Callicarpa japonica, similar with deep purple fruit; 'Leucocarpa', white berries. *C. americana* (French mulberry, American beautyberry), 8 feet tall, open shrub, native to Southeast, tolerates dry shade, abundant violet to magenta persistent fruit, prune lightly, zones 7 to 9. *C. bodnieri* 'Profusion', 8 feet tall, vase-shaped, abundant violet purple persistent fruit, zones 6 to 9.

Deciduous Shrubs

CALYCANTHUS FLORIDUS
Sweet Shrub, Carolina Allspice

A dense, aromatic shrub native to the Southeast, sweet shrub makes an interesting addition to a shrub border. Its unusual, reddish brown flowers resemble 2-inch water lilies and emit a haunting, fruity fragrance that can perfume a garden in spring and

CALYCANTHUS FLORIDUS

early summer. The rare yellow-flowered form is much prettier. The oval, 2- to 5-inch-long, pointed leaves are rough to the touch, dark green on top, hairy and gray-green on the undersides, and fragrant if crushed. Fall color develops late and varies from yellow-gold to golden brown from year to year. When broken, the bark and wood exude a spicy cinnamon-like fragrance. Brown seed capsules ripen in fall. Rounded; 7 to 12 feet tall and wide.

A pleasant, green form in cottage or heirloom garden, or large shrub border. Locate near path or window where fragrance can be appreciated.

Site: Full sun to shade. Tolerant of many soils, acid to alkaline, average to wet. Best in rich, fertile, moist site. Zones 5 to 9.
How to Grow: Plant balled-and-burlapped and container shrubs in spring or fall, spacing 5 feet apart.

Collect seed when capsules change from green to brown, and sow immediately. Fragrance may vary; best to purchase when in bloom and select for fragrance. May spread by suckers; dig up unwanted suckers.

Flowers bloom on both old and new wood. Prune only for shaping, immediately after blooming. Pest- and disease-free.
Cultivars: A creamy yellow-flowered form sometimes is available; also 'Edith Wilder', long-blooming with highly fragrant flowers.

CARYOPTERIS × CLANDONENSIS
Bluebeard

C reating a mist of bright blue flowers and fine-textured silvery leaves in late summer and fall, this shrub is one of the finest of the late-season bloomers. The fragrant, fringed flowers attract bees, butterflies, and sometimes hummingbirds. Rounded to

CARYOPTERIS × CLANDONENSIS

3 feet tall and wide. Bluebeard is lovely in mixed borders combined with perennials, dark green shrubs, and grasses. Combines well with pink, yellow, and white flowers.

Site: Full sun best; tolerates part shade. Average to poor, well-drained soil. Moderate moisture best; tolerates

drought. Zones 4 to 8; tops die to ground in zones 4 to 6.
How to Grow: Plant container plants in spring or summer, spacing 3 feet apart. May self-sow, not weedy.

Blooms on new growth. Prune annually by cutting into live wood about 6 inches from ground in spring when buds are breaking. Flowers best if pruned hard every year, even where tops are not winter-killed. Usually pest- and disease-free.
Cultivars: 'Blue Mist', light blue; 'Heavenly Blue', deep blue; 'Dark Knight', dark purple, fragrant; 'Longwood Blue', deep bright blue; 'Worcester Gold', gold leaves, blue flowers.

CEPHALANTHUS OCCIDENTALIS
Buttonbush

G rowing in the wild in wet places in the Northeast and South and east to Texas, this bush produces delightful, perfectly round, white flower heads for two to three weeks in midsummer. The flowers are fragrant and attractive to bees. By summer's

CEPHALANTHUS OCCIDENTALIS

end, the flower heads ripen to red, gumball-like seed heads that eventually turn brown. The oval, pointed leaves are glossy green and emerge in late spring, turning somewhat yellow in fall. Usually rounded; 5 to 7 feet tall, although may grow much taller in wet site, forming a wide colony. Charming naturalized in wet places or beside ponds. Eye-catching in shrub border.

Site: Full sun to part shade. Heavy to average, fertile, acid soil. Moist to wet conditions; tolerates standing water. Don't allow to dry out. Zones 4 to 10.
How to Grow: Plant container shrubs in spring or fall, spacing 5 feet apart. Softwood or hardwood cuttings root easily. Spreads by suckers to form colony; you may need to dig out unwanted plants. Leafs out late and may appear dead.

Every few years, cut back to near ground in early spring before growth begins to rejuvenate. Usually pest-free.
Cultivars: Only the species is grown.

CHAENOMELES SPECIOSA
Flowering Quince

Valued primarily for its showy early to mid-spring blossoms, this shrub has a fascinating, craggy outline in winter when devoid of leaves. Its thorny branches zigzag and form a dense, twiggy mass. Almost 2 inches across, the round satin-petaled flowers are scarlet, red, pink, or white with yellow centers and open in spring before the leaves mature. Leaves unfold bronze-red, mature to glossy dark green and drop in fall without changing color. The bitter yellow-green fruit is about 2 inches across and makes fine preserves. Upright to spreading; 6 to 10 feet tall and wide. Hybrids aren't as tall.

Plant where early flowers are appreciated; combine with plants that are attractive the rest of year. Cut branches can be forced easily.

Site: Full sun. Light to heavy soil. Moderate water best; drought-tolerant. Zones 4 to 9.
How to Grow: Plant balled-and-burlapped or container plants in spring,

CHAENOMELES SPECIOSA 'CHAJUBAI'

summer, or fall, spacing 4 to 5 feet apart. Propagate from softwood cuttings. Difficult to clean of litter and fallen leaves.

Blooms on old wood. Best unpruned; thin selectively to control size and shape. Rejuvenate by cutting to ground immediately after flowering. Apple scab can be serious, especially in wet years. Fire blight can be a problem. Aphids often troublesome in spring.
Cultivars and Similar Species:
Chaenomeles japonica, spreading shrub, to 3 feet high and 5 feet wide, orange to red flowers, blooms in late winter, before *C. speciosa*, but not as attractive; 'Orange Delight', orange to orange-red, low, spreading. *C.* × *superba*, superior hybrid of the two species; 'Cameo', double, peachy-pink flowers, thornless, low, spreading; 'Chajubai', white flowers, low, spreading; 'Jet Trail', white, low, compact, nearly thornless; 'Pink Beauty', rose-pink flowers, tall; 'Texas-Scarlet', brilliant watermelon red, low, compact, nearly thornless; 'Nivalis', white, tall.

CHIMONANTHUS PRAECOX
Wintersweet

Blooming at any other time of year, wintersweet would be unremarkable, but it draws admiring glances in winter when 1-inch-long, transparent, yellow mopheads with purple centers unfurl on bare

branches and scent the yard with their sweet perfume. Blossoms open over a long period of time in November and December in the South, and January and February in the northern part of its range. A single cut branch can perfume an entire room. The graceful, 2- to 5-inch-long leaves are blue-green and pointed, with the feel of fine

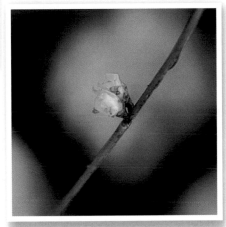
CHIMONANTHUS PRAECOX

sandpaper. They drop with little color change in autumn. The wood is aromatic; in its native Japan, twigs are cut to scent linen cupboards. Open and spreading; to 8 feet tall. Plant near a walk frequented in winter.

Site: Full sun best; tolerates light shade. Acid to alkaline, well-drained, fertile soil. Plentiful moisture. Zones 7 to 9.
How to Grow: Plant bare-root or container plants in spring. Cuttings are difficult to root. Sow fresh seeds in spring when capsules change from green to brown. Plant near a south- or west-facing wall to give winter protection. May not bloom until mature.

Blossoms form at leaf axils on young branches that grow from mature old wood. Grows slowly and flowers best if left unpruned. Cut out old stems at ground if they become weak. Usually pest-free. *continued*

Deciduous Shrubs

CHIMONANTHUS PRAECOX
(continued)

Similar Species: *Chimonanthus praecox* var. *luteus*, deep yellow flowers without purple centers. *C. praecox* var. *grandiflorus*, 2-inch flowers, bright yellow with red centers, less fragrant, leaves to 9 inches.

CLETHRA ALNIFOLIA
Summer-Sweet, Sweet Pepperbush

Named for the sweet fragrance of its late-summer flowers and the black seed capsules that resemble peppercorns, this native shrub is a garden standout for much of the year. Blooming for a month or more in late summer, 6-inch-long spires of creamy white and sometimes pink flowers perfume the garden with a sweet, spicy scent. Fall brings pointed, toothed, bright golden yellow leaves,

CLETHRA ALNIFOLIA

which are dark, glossy green during the growing season. The seed capsules and strong stem structure provide winter interest. Summer-sweet is native to wet areas from Maine to Florida and east to Texas. Upright and oval; 4 to 10 feet tall and 4 to 6 feet wide. Plant specimens or groups in shrub borders or naturalize in wet

spot or along pond or stream. Locate where scent can be appreciated.

Site: Full sun to half or light shade. Moist to wet, fertile, acid soil. Doesn't tolerate drought. Zones 4 to 9; tolerates salt spray and seashore conditions.

How to Grow: Plant balled-and-burlapped or container plants in spring, summer, or fall, spacing 5 feet apart. Cuttings taken in summer root easily. Mulch heavily to keep soil cool and moist. Leafs out late in spring. Slow to establish, but eventually begins to spread by suckers. If it spreads too much, dig up and divide, saving youngest plants.

Blooms on new growth. Thin in late winter to prevent sap bleeding by cutting out oldest and weakest stems at ground level. Spider mites may attack if soil is too dry.

Cultivars and Similar Species: 'Hummingbird', compact, rounded plant, 2 to 3 feet tall and 4 to 6 feet wide, heavy-flowering; 'Rosea', light pink flowers fade to white; 'Pink Spire', pink, nonfading flowers; 'Fern Valley', vivid pink, extremely fragrant flowers, vigorous plant.

CORNUS SERICEA (CORNUS STOLONIFERA)
Red-Osier Dogwood

The gleaming red-barked stems of red-osier dogwood cheer up any winter landscape. When planted in a mass, the multiple red stems are breathtaking. Stem color is brightest on young branches and intensifies with cold weather. Summer bark is greenish red. Lacy, white flower heads bloom in early summer, followed by clusters of white berries, which birds gobble. Leaves are handsome green with prominent veins and may be beautifully variegated. Fall color varies from purplish to reddish and can be outstanding. Broad and rounded; 7 to 9 feet tall, spreading to 10 or more

CORNUS SERICEA

feet. Best planted in groups in large garden. For winter enjoyment, plant shrubs against a dark green winter background within view of a window.

Site: Full sun for best bark color; tolerates light shade. Fertile, acid, moist soil best; tolerates wet or swampy soil. Don't allow to dry out. Zones 3 to 8.

How to Grow: Plant bare-root plants in early spring or container or balled-and-burlapped plants in spring, summer, or fall. Space 3 to 4 feet apart for quick mass effect. Spreads by stolons and can be invasive.

Cut stems to 2 inches from ground in spring just as growth begins when two or three years old to encourage new growth. Thereafter cut one-third to all of oldest stems each year; flowers and fruit form only on older stems. Stem canker, leaf spot, and mildew can be serious.

Cultivars and Similar Species: 'Flaviramea', golden yellow twigs; 'Silver and Gold', yellow twigs, white-and-green variegated leaves, to 7 feet tall, withstands heat and humidity better than variegated forms of *Cornus alba*; 'Nitida', bright pea green stems; 'Cardinal', bright orange-red twigs, disease-resistant; 'Gouchaultii', green leaves with creamy yellow borders splashed with pink, blood-red stems; 'Isanti', compact to 3 feet tall, bright red stems; *C. alba* (Tartarian dogwood), almost identical to *C. sericea*, but usually more upright; 'Argenteo-marginata' ('Elegantissima'), gray-green leaves with creamy white margins; 'Siberica', bright coral-red stems; 'Spaethii', bright yellow-bordered leaves; 'Aurea', soft yellow leaves.

CORYLOPSIS GLABRESCENS
Winter Hazel

Blooming a bit earlier than forsythia and in a softer shade of yellow, winter hazel brings welcome color to the late-winter and early-spring garden. The lightly fragrant flowers bloom in long clusters that dangle from the undersides of the outstretched bare branches. Bark is a warm, glistening brown, a pretty covering for the dramatic winter silhouette of zigzagging, horizontal branches. Large, round, toothed, pointed leaves are blue-green, turning yellowish to clear yellow in fall. Broad spreading; 8 to 15 feet tall and wide.

CORYLOPSIS GLABRESCENS

Plant large species as specimens, allowing horizontal branches plenty of growing room. Combine with vertical plants for best effect. Mass smaller species in shrub and mixed borders. Combines beautifully with Korean azalea, whose lavender-pink flowers bloom at the same time, and with a dark green evergreen background.

Site: Full sun to half or light shade. Fertile, acid, moist soil. Plentiful moisture best, especially in full sun. Zones 5 to 9.
How to Grow: Plant balled-and-burlapped or container plants in spring or fall, spacing according to mature size. Softwood cuttings root easily. Early flowers can be damaged by late freezes.
   Thin immediately after flowering, but only to control size. Be careful to retain natural shape. Usually pest-free.
Cultivars and Similar Species: *Corylopsis pauciflora* (buttercup winter hazel), 4 to 6 feet tall, daintier looking and denser plant; zones 6 to 9. *C. spicata* (spike winterhazel), fragrant, brighter yellow flowers, 6 to 8 feet tall, new foliage purplish; zones 6 to 9. 'Winterthur', probably hybrid of *C. pauciflora* and *C. spicata* with dainty form and fragrant flowers. *C. veitchiana* (Veitch winter hazel), yellow flowers with dark red anthers, zones 6 to 9.

CORYLUS AVELLANA 'CONTORTA'
Harry Lauder's Walking Stick, Corkscrew Hazelnut

Admire this unusual shrub in winter when its oddly twisted branches—as crooked as the cane of legendary vaudeville comic Harry Lauder—create a dramatic silhouette. A dark background and a frosting of snow on the branches turn this shrub into a living sculpture. Pendulous golden catkins decorate the branches in late winter before the leaves unfold. The summer foliage is coarse, dark green, heavily veined, twisted, and obscures the shrub's strange branches. Fall color is golden brown, and the nuts are edible filberts. Upright to rounded, with twisted, pendulous branches; 8 to 10 feet tall and wide. Use as single specimen planted against wall or evergreen to best highlight winter silhouette.

CORYLUS AVELLANA 'CONTORTA'

Site: Full sun. Humus-rich, moist, well-drained, acid to neutral soil. Plentiful moisture. Zones 4 to 8.
How to Grow: Plant balled-and-burlapped and container plants in spring or fall. Nursery plants are grafted. Remove suckers from rootstock.
   Prune to single trunk or several main trunks if desired. Thin out selected branches in winter if needed. Japanese beetles may disfigure leaves.
Cultivars and Similar Species: 'Rotzeller' (red-leaf filbert), normal branching, leaves red-purple in spring, bronze in summer, scarlet in fall, pink catkins, edible nuts, 15 to 20 feet tall.

COTINUS COGGYGRIA
Smokebush, Smoke Tree

Maturing into a huge shrub or multitrunk tree, smokebush often is cut to the ground to keep it a small focal point and to produce the most colorful foliage for a mixed border. The rounded, smooth-margined, 3-inch leaves grow in lovely whorls around the stems. Leaves are blue-green in the species, but burgundy to reddish purple in the popular cultivars. Smoky plumes of flowers and feathery flower stalks appear in early summer, changing from pink to gray as they age and persist through fall. Male plants *continued*

COTINUS COGGYGRIA
(continued)

COTINUS COGGYGRIA 'ROYAL PURPLE'

produce showier flowers than female plants. Fall color of orange, yellow, red, and scarlet often is outstanding. Upright and wide-spreading; 12 to 15 feet tall and wide, if left unpruned.

Purple-leaf forms are gorgeous when backlit. Combines well with pink, lavender, and pastel yellow flowers. Leaf form contrasts beautifully with ornamental grasses.

Site: Full sun. Well-drained, average to rocky soil. Moderate moisture. Zones 5 to 8.
How to Grow: Plant balled-and-burlapped or container plants in spring or fall, spacing according to desired plant size. Softwood cuttings root easily. Must have well-drained site.

For foliage effect in border, select three canes to grow from ground, allowing them to branch above 2 or 3 feet. Every spring, when growth is just beginning, prune these canes back to just above two lowest buds. For large shrub or tree and flowers, train to single trunk or multiple trunks and don't prune. Usually pest-free, but scale, verticillium, and leaf spot can be troublesome.
Cultivars and Similar Species: *Cotinus coggygria* var. *purpureus* (purple smokebush), purple-red leaves in

spring, turns bronze-green in summer; 'Royal Purple', dark purple all summer, red-purple in fall, pink flowers, compact plant; 'Velvet Cloak', dark purple all summer, brilliant red-purple in fall; 'Notcutt's Variety', dark crimson-maroon, purple-pink flowers.
C. obovatus (American smoke tree), upright shrub or low-branched tree, to 20 feet tall; blue-green summer foliage; yellow and red fall color, weak wood.

COTONEASTER SPP.
Cotoneaster

With its fine-textured flowers, foliage, and fruit, the low-spreading to cascading cranberry cotoneaster *(Cotoneaster apiculatus)* is a popular landscape subject. Dainty pink flowers decorate the branches in early summer, but the berry show in fall is more eye-catching. Tiny, red berries line the stems, ripening while the leaves are green, but persisting on the bare stems into winter. The oval, blunt-tipped leaves change color late, turning bronze-red to purple. The plant is semiprostrate to cascading

COTONEASTER HORIZONTALIS

with branches in a herringbone pattern. Low and spreading; to 3 feet tall and 6 feet wide. Excellent cascaded over low walls and massed to cover slopes; a good groundcover.

Spreading cotoneaster *(C. divaricatus)* is an attractive, large shrub with upright branches in a fishbone pattern; it is attractive most of the year. The 1-inch-long leaves are fine-textured, oval, and dark green. Fall color is a spectacular combination of yellow, red, and purple that lasts for a month or more. Tiny, rose-pink flowers bloom in early summer. Tiny, egg-shaped, red berries provide color from late summer into winter. Rounded; 5 to 6 feet tall, 6 to 8 feet wide. Use in shrub borders, informal hedges, or foundation plantings.

A unique branching structure adds to the charm of rockspray cotoneaster *(C. horizontalis)*. The branches form a single plane in a horizontal fish-bone pattern that highlights the leaves, fruit, and flowers. Dainty pink flowers line the branches in early summer. Leaves are fine textured and glossy, dark green, turning red-purple in late fall. From late summer through fall, ¼-inch red berries stud the branches. Low and spreading; 2 to 3 feet tall and 5 to 8 feet wide. Locate along walkway or foundation, or in rock garden. Can be espaliered against wall.

Many-flowered cotoneaster *(C. multiflorus)* is the showiest cotoneaster in bloom. Its long, arching branches are covered with clusters of ½-inch white flowers that look like a snowfall in late spring. Unlike other cotoneasters, this one has soft gray-green new foliage that matures to blue-green or gray. The ½-inch, red berries put on a spectacular display in autumn against the green leaves, which drop with little color change in late fall. Broad and rounded; 8 to 12 feet tall, 12 to 15 feet wide. Gray leaf color contrasts well with green shrubs in summer. Lovely planted as single specimen in shrub border.

Site: Full sun best; cranberry cotoneaster tolerates half shade. Fertile, moist but well-drained soil with plentiful moisture best. Cranberry cotoneaster tolerates heavy to sandy, acid to alkaline conditions—the most tolerant cotoneaster. Many-flowered cotoneaster suffers if soil is not well-drained. Cranberry cotoneaster is hardy in zones 5 to 8; good performer in Midwest, Mountain states, and Northeast. Spreading and rockspray cotoneaster, zones 5 to 8. Many-flowered cotoneaster, zones 4 to 7.

How to Grow: Plant container plants in spring or fall; cranberry cotoneaster also can be planted in summer. Space spreading cotoneaster 4 feet apart, rockspray 3 or more feet apart, many-flowered 8 feet apart. All root slowly from softwood cuttings.

Layered branches of cranberry cotoneaster mound upon themselves, creating a tangle that catches litter and leaves and is difficult to clean. Rockspray cotoneaster may be trained to grow up and spread across a wall with minimal tying; branches press against the wall. Plant at least two many-flowered cotoneasters for best fruit set.

Prune only if needed to control size, by thinning out selected branches in late winter; avoid destroying natural shape and branching pattern. Responds well to hard renewal pruning.

Mites troublesome if soil is too dry. Fire blight occasionally is a problem in the South. Rockspray also may be troubled by leaf spot. Spreading and many-flowered cotoneasters usually not bothered by pests and diseases that attack other species.

Cultivars and Similar Species: Cranberry cotoneaster: 'Blackburn', more compact. *C. adpressus* (creeping cotoneaster), low-growing with dense branches, to 1½ feet tall and 6 feet wide, rooting along ground; ½-inch, dark red berries, long-lasting, red fall foliage; ½-inch leaves with wavy margins; *C.a.* var. *praecox*, 3 feet tall and 6 feet wide, ½-inch fruit.

Spreading cotoneaster: *C. lucidus* (hedge cotoneaster), erect shape makes good hedge; pink flowers, red berries, showy red and yellow fall color; zones 2 to 6.

Rockspray cotoneaster: 'Variegatus', white-edged leaves, beautiful textural effect, slow-growing; 'Perpusillus', smaller leaves.

Many-flowered cotoneaster: *C. m.* var. *calocarpus*, larger, showier fruit; this is the usual form sold.

CYTISUS × PRAECOX
Warminster Broom

Native to southern Europe and the Canary Islands, broom tolerates poor, dry soil and wind. Cut and tied in bundles, the nearly leafless, wandlike, green-bark stems make excellent crude brooms, hence their common name. Pealike flowers appear in early spring, practically obscuring the branches with their creamy yellow brilliance. Tiny leaves appear after the flowers, but almost go unnoticed. The green stems carry on most of the photosynthesis and look stunning in the winter landscape.

CYTISUS × PRAECOX

Rounded and arching; to 5 feet tall and 7 feet wide. Effective massed on slopes or areas of poor soil to control erosion. Also makes a fine single specimen in a border.

Site: Full sun. Average to sandy and rocky, infertile soil. Moderate moisture. Drought-tolerant. Zones 6 to 9; tolerates wind and seashore conditions.

How to Grow: Difficult to transplant. Plant container plants in spring, spacing 4 feet apart. Take cuttings in summer. May be short-lived, especially if soil isn't well-drained. Self-sown seedlings may be a nuisance.

Cut back all stems by one-third their length, without cutting into old wood, immediately after flowering to prevent seed formation and encourage new growth and better bloom. Usually pest- and disease-free.

Cultivars and Similar Species: 'Albus', white flowers; 'Allgold', bright yellow; 'Hollandia', light pink-maroon; 'Zeelandia', pale yellow-and-red flowers look pink. *Cytisus × kewensis* (Kew broom), zones 6 to 9, pale yellow flowers on horizontally spreading stems, to 10 inches tall and 3 feet wide. *C. scoparius* (Scotch broom), loose and mounded, 6 to 8 feet tall, green branches, yellow flowers, zones 6 to 9; weedy in Northwest; 'Lena', crimson-and-yellow flowers; 'Moonlight', pale yellow, dense, mounding shape; 'Lilac Time', red-purple; 'Minstead', white flowers with lilac and deep purple.

DAPHNE SPP.
Burkwood Daphne, February Daphne

A hybrid between the deciduous garland daphne and the evergreen Caucasian daphne, Burkwood daphne (*Daphne × burkwoodii*) is semievergreen, holding its fine-textured whorls of oblong, blue-green leaves until early winter. Flowers give off a sweet, pervasive perfume, are white or pale pink, and are borne in 2-inch-wide clusters at the branch tips in mid spring. The red berries that ripen in summer and the foliage are poisonous. Probably most outstanding in its variegated forms, Burkwood daphne makes *continued*

DAPHNE SPP.
(continued)

DAPHNE × BURKWOODII 'CAROL MACKIE'

an elegant addition to most gardens. Rounded; 3 to 4 feet tall and 4 to 5 feet wide.

Holding its leaves through fall and into winter in warmer areas, February daphne (*D. mezereum*) is a semievergreen, early-blooming shrub. In late winter or early spring, its flowers bring color and fragrance to the awakening garden. Giving off a pervasive, spicy-sweet fragrance, the clusters of small flowers vary from mauve-pink to red-purple. By midsummer, it sets a heavy crop of tiny red fruit. The fruit and leaves are poisonous to people, although birds devour them. Leaves are 1 to 3 inches long and blue-green. Upright; 3 to 5 feet tall and wide.

Use these daphnes as specimens in shrub borders or foundation plantings, where the early bloom and fragrance will be appreciated.

Site: Full sun to half or light shade. Average to sandy, moist but well-drained soil; plentiful even moisture. Burkwood daphne tolerates slightly alkaline soil. Burkwood hardy in zones 4 to 7, February daphne in zones 3 to 7.

How to Grow: Plant young, container shrubs in early spring or fall. Mulch well to keep soil cool. Do not prune.

Daphnes may die suddenly for no apparent reason. Death probably results from temporary water-logged soil. Scale and virus diseases may trouble February daphne.

Cultivars and Similar Species: Burkwood daphne: 'Carol Mackie', green leaves with creamy margins, pale pink flowers, outstanding, 3 feet tall; 'Somerset', deeper pink flowers, fast-growing wide mound to 4 feet tall. *D. caucasica* (Caucasian daphne), a parent of *D. × burkwoodii*, abundant, tiny, sweet-scented, white flowers in spring and fall, sporadically at other times, leathery leaves; full sun to part shade; long-lived. *D. giraldii* (Giraldi daphne), 3 to 4 feet tall, vanilla-scented yellow flowers in late spring, zones 2 to 7.

February daphne: 'Alba', white flowers, yellow fruit; 'Ruby Glow', red-purple flowers. *D. genkwa* (lilac daphne), upright deciduous plant, to 8 feet tall, lilac flowers in early spring before leaves, no fragrance, but especially beautiful; zones 6 to 9.

DEUTZIA GRACILIS 'NIKKO'
Dwarf Slender Deutzia

This outstanding cultivar offers a beautiful show of white spring flowers, a graceful cascading and mounding shape, and deep red to burgundy fall color. Upright clusters of five-petaled white flowers line the arching stems in late spring for about two weeks, resembling a mound of snow. The medium-textured, dull green leaves are slender and pointed, 1 to 3 inches long, with fine teeth along their edges and turn color in late fall. Mounding; to 2 feet high with lower branches spreading to 5 feet wide. 'Nikko' offers several seasons of interest and makes an excellent facer shrub, groundcover, or rock garden plant. Use to cascade over low wall.

DEUTZIA GRACILIS 'NIKKO'

Site: Full sun to light shade; afternoon shade best in hot areas. Fertile, humus-rich soil and plentiful moisture. Zones 5 to 8.

How to Grow: Plant container plants in spring, summer, or fall, spacing 3 feet apart. Softwood cuttings root easily. Branches may root along ground, forming natural layers that can be dug up and separated. Easy to care for. Blooms on short side stems. Pruning usually not needed with 'Nikko'. Usually pest- and disease-free.

Cultivars and Similar Species: *Deutzia scabra* (slender deutzia), upright to 3 feet tall and 4 feet wide, sometimes larger, showy, white flowers, no fall color, prune oldest stems to ground every year, zones 6 to 8. *D. × magnifica* (showy deutzia), large shrub to 10 feet tall, the showiest white flowers of the deutzias in late spring and early summer. *D. × hybrida* 'Montrose', 'Pink Pompon', and 'Pink-a-Boo', 6-foot-tall shrubs, large clusters of double, pink flowers.

DIRCA PALUSTRIS
Leatherwood

Blooming in early spring just before its leaves emerge, leatherwood's small, two-lipped, pale yellow blossoms announce winter's end with quiet beauty. The light green, almost chartreuse, foliage color subtly contrasts with other shrubs during the growing season and changes to a luminous clear yellow in fall. The 1- to 3-inch-long, rounded to oval leaves obscure the red berries that ripen in summer. The extremely flexible stems can be twisted and tied (like leather) and are used for

DIRCA PALUSTRIS

basketmaking. Oval to rounded; 3 to 6 feet tall and wide. Native to eastern North America, this shrub deserves wider use in gardens. It is lovely in shade, woodland, or native plant gardens. Naturalize along a stream, pond, or wet site.

Site: Full sun to full shade; leaf color best in shade. Humus-rich, fertile, moist soil best. Adapts to average to wet soil. Zones 4 to 8.
How to Grow: Plant bare-root or container plants in spring or fall, spacing 3 feet apart. Sow seed when ripe. Best in light shade. Prune, if needed, immediately after flowering. Scale is sometimes a problem.
Similar Species: *Edgeworthia papyrifera* (paperbush), a Japanese shrub with fragrant pale gold or apricot blossoms in clusters on bare branches in very early spring; zones 8 and 9.

ELAEAGNUS UMBELLATA
Autumn Olive

Although they aren't particularly showy, the late-spring, pale yellow flowers are borne in such abundance that their sweet fragrance permeates the air. Young leaves are silvery and oblong with wavy margins. Leaves mature to bright green with silver-flecked undersides, giving a pretty two-toned effect, and drop with little color change. The silvery berries eventually turn red in fall, creating a show on the thorny stems. The berries attract wildlife, ripening late and lasting through winter. Autumn olive thrives in poor soil because it can fix soil nitrogen. Upright to spreading; 12 to 18 feet tall and wide. Use as a screen, barrier, or windbreak; plant in wildlife garden. Avoid planting

ELAEAGNUS UMBELLATA

in wild areas or near unmaintained or natural areas that allow this shrub to self-sow and become a weed problem.

Site: Full sun to light shade. Moist but well-drained, acid, average to sandy or heavy soil. Zones 5 to 9; tolerates seashore conditions.
How to Grow: Plant bare-root or container plants in spring, summer, or fall, spacing 6 feet or more apart. Softwood and hardwood cuttings root easily. Birds can spread seeds and turn plant into a noxious weed. Prune

immediately after flowering to control size and keep dense. Responds well to hard pruning. Usually disease free.
Cultivars: 'Cardinal', grows to 12 feet tall and fruits heavily; 'Ellagood', 15 feet tall, abundant fruit; 'Titan', 12 feet tall and 6 feet wide; good hedge.

ENKIANTHUS CAMPANULATUS
Red-Vein Enkianthus

Noted for its flowers and fiery autumn color, red-vein enkianthus deserves a prominent place in the garden. This slow-growing shrub's slender, layered branches spread horizontally with a graceful

ENKIANTHUS CAMPANULATUS

upturn, which makes a pretty silhouette in winter. The rich blue-green leaves sport red petioles and form lovely whorls around the stems, but the best show comes in fall when the leaves turn luminescent orange-red and gold. In late spring, clusters of dainty, creamy yellow, bell-shaped flowers with red stripes, which have an overall pale orange appearance, dangle from the branches, standing out against the greenery. Upright; usually about 8 feet tall, but can reach 15 feet tall and 10 feet wide with age. Use as focal point or specimen in border or foundation planting. Plant *continued*

ENKIANTHUS CAMPANULATUS
(continued)

in groups in large garden. Combines well with rhododendrons and azaleas. A background of evergreens shows off fall foliage especially well.

Site: Full sun to light shade; develops best fall color with sun. Humus-rich, acid, moist soil. Plentiful moisture. Zones 5 to 8.
How to Grow: Plant balled-and-burlapped or container plants in spring or fall, spacing 6 or more feet apart. Keep well-mulched. Doesn't need pruning, except to control size. If needed, thin immediately after flowering; be careful to maintain shape. Mites may be a problem in poor soil or dry conditions.
Cultivars and Similar Species: 'Red Bells', red flowers; 'Weston Pink Strain', pink to rose-pink flowers; 'Showy Lantern', solid pink flowers; 'Albiflorus', white flowers. *Enkianthus perulatus* (white enkianthus), pure white blossoms in mid spring, red fall color, tiered branches, 6 feet tall, zones 6 to 8.

EUONYMUS ALATUS
(E. ATROPURPUREA)
Winged Euonymus, Winged Spindle Tree, Burning Bush

Admired for its dependable bright red or rose-pink fall color, winged euonymus also offers interest in other seasons. The elliptical leaves are 1 to 3 inches long with fine teeth along the margins. They emerge bright green in early spring, accompanied by clusters of chartreuse flowers. Red fruit, hidden beneath the leaves, is eaten by birds. When bare of foliage, the bark and stems catch the eye. Corky wings extend along the horizontal branches and make wonderful shelves for catching and holding snow. Dark gray bark is mottled with creamy white and light gray. Spreading and flat topped; 10 to 15 feet tall and wide.

EUONYMUS ALATUS

Use as clipped or informal hedge or screen, specimen shrub, small tree, or mass in shrub border. Surface roots of old specimens may compete with garden plants; select companion plants that do well in dry shade.

Site: Full sun to shade; fall color tends toward pink in shade. Average to humus-rich, well-drained, moist soil. Plentiful moisture. Zones 4 to 8.
How to Grow: Plant balled-and-burlapped shrubs in spring, summer, or fall, spacing 3 to 4 feet apart for clipped hedge and 5 to 7 feet apart for informal planting. Softwood cuttings root easily. Mulch heavily, especially in hot, dry sites.
Tolerates heavy pruning, but looks best if thinned rather than sheared when used in informal situations. It can be trained into small, multiple-trunked tree. Spider mites can be a problem if plants are water-stressed. Rarely troubled by scale, as are most euonymus.
Cultivars and Similar Species: 'October Glory', brilliant red fall color; 'Compactus', dense, to 10 feet tall and wide, corky wings not as pronounced; 'Rudy Haag', compact, slow-growing, 5 or more feet tall; pink-red fall color; 'Monstrosus', prominent corky wings.
Euonymus bungeanus (winterberry euonymus), reddish pink and scarlet fruit, ornamental in fall and winter, yellow fall color, attractive bark, tall

shrub or multitrunk small tree, to 20 feet tall, zones 4 to 7. *E. europaeus* (European spindle tree, European euonymus), reddish fall color, showy pink-and-orange fall fruit, zones 4 to 7; 'Red Cap', abundant, persistent, showy fruit, winged branches; 'Aldenhamensis', especially showy and large fruit in long clusters.

FORSYTHIA × INTERMEDIA
Border Forsythia

Forsythia's greatest asset—and it's a big one—is the brilliant show of yellow blossoms that mark the beginning of spring. This sunny display of four-petaled blossoms decorates the lengths of the leafless, arching branches, clothed in golden-brown bark. If blossoms at this time of the year weren't so welcome,

FORSYTHIA × INTERMEDIA

forsythia wouldn't be so popular, because it's rather ungainly, with branches that arch gracefully and also shoot up at awkward angles. Leaves are coarse—3 to 5 inches long and pointed with jagged teeth—and remain green well into fall, turning slightly purple before dropping. Arching to vase-shaped; to 10 feet tall and 10 to 12 feet wide.

Use as informal hedge, or plant in mass or as specimen in border. Allow enough room to accommodate unpruned branches for best effect. Plant weeping forsythia to trail over a wall, cascade down a slope, or espalier against a wall.

Site: Full sun for best bloom; tolerates half sun. Average to humus-rich, well-drained soil. Plentiful moisture. Water during dry spells. Zones 4 to 8, to Zone 9 in West. Flower buds often killed during winter in zones 4 and 5; in Midwest and North, use cultivars bred for cold-hardiness of flower buds.
How to Grow: Plant bare-root shrubs in early spring, or balled-and-burlapped shrubs in spring, summer, or fall, placing slightly lower than was growing to encourage many new stems. Space 4 to 5 feet apart for informal mass, farther to allow full shape to develop. Softwood cuttings root easily.

Blooms on previous year's growth. Every few years, immediately after flowering, cut out oldest and weakest stems just above a strong shoot near the ground. Leave lower stems on outer portions of bush for natural effect. Cut back stems to 6 inches above ground to renew. Don't shear into straight lines; this destroys graceful, arching shape. Sometimes stem gall, aphids, mites, and leaf spot occur, but none are serious.
Cultivars and Similar Species: 'Spectabilis', the common golden yellow cultivar sold, to 10 feet tall and wide; 'Goldleaf', lime-green spring leaves, bright gold in summer, best in shade; 'Karl Sax', 1-inch-long, deep yellow flowers, arching branches; 'Lynwood', masses of bright gold flowers; 'Tremonia', cutleaf foliage, light yellow flowers; 'Minigold', dwarf to 4 feet tall by 5 feet wide; 'Winterthur', early-blooming, compact hybrid to 6 feet tall, pastel yellow flowers, cold-hardy; 'Meadowlark', bright yellow flowers, bronze and yellow fall color, 9 feet tall, zones 3 to 8; 'New Hampshire Gold', mounding to 5 feet tall, zones 3 to 8; 'Northern Gold', golden yellow blossoms, zones 3 to 8. *Forsythia mandshurica* 'Vermont Sun', to 8 feet tall, early bright yellow flowers,

zones 4 to 8. *F. suspensa* var. *sieboldii* (weeping forsythia), 6 to 8 feet tall and twice as wide with weeping vinelike branches that root along ground, golden flowers not as showy as border forsythia, zones 6 to 8. *F. ovata* (early forsythia), stiff shrub, 4 to 6 feet tall, bright yellow flowers bloom earlier than other forsythia, zones 5 to 7; 'Mini', 2 to 3 feet tall; 'Robusta', 8 feet tall, primrose yellow, mahogany-red fall color; 'Tetragold', 4- to 6-foot-tall mound, golden yellow. *F. viridissima* (green-stem forsythia), stiff and upright, to 6 feet tall, bright yellow flowers with green tinge two weeks later than border forsythia, zones 6 to 8.

FOTHERGILLA GARDENII
Dwarf Fothergilla, Dwarf Witch Alder

This multistemmed native shrub tips its branches with 2-inch-long, creamy white bottlebrushes for two weeks in early spring before or as its leaves emerge. Sparkling in the sun, the abundant blossoms smell like honey. The leather-textured leaves are

FOTHERGILLA GARDENII

rounded to oval, smooth-edged, coarsely veined, and green on top with lighter undersides. Fall color is a bonfire of bright yellow, orange, and red. This low shrub forms a dense mound of crooked stems, which

create winter character. Rounded, 3 to 5 feet tall and wide. Use as specimen or mass-plant in groups. Naturalize in open woodland garden. Combines well with redbud trees.

Site: Full sun to light shade; best blossoms and fall color with at least half sun. Humus-rich, acid, moist, well-drained soil. Moderate moisture. Zones 5 to 9.
How to Grow: Plant balled-and-burlapped or container plants in spring or fall, spacing 3 feet apart. Separate suckers in spring. Take softwood cuttings in early summer. May sucker and form colonies.

Needs no pruning; allow multiple twiggy stems to develop. Don't remove outer lower stems; they add to natural appearance. Remove broken branches during winter. Trouble-free.
Cultivars and Similar Species: 'Blue Mist', 3 to 3½ feet tall, lovely blue-green leaves, good fall color. *Fothergilla major (F. monticola)* (large fothergilla, witch alder), upright to 10 feet tall, 3-inch leaves, 2-inch bottlebrush flowers a bit later than dwarf fothergilla, excellent fall color, tolerates dry site.

GENISTA TINCTORIA
Common Woadwaxen, Dyer's Greenweed

Like the related brooms (*Cytisus* spp.), woadwaxen species also have beautiful green-barked stems that create a spiky evergreen effect in the garden. The summer leaves are barely noticeable against the prominent bark. Flowers are bright yellow and two-lipped like members of the pea family. Common woadwaxen produces bright golden flowers in late spring and early summer and sporadically thereafter on upright, unbranched, thornless stems. An invaluable plant for areas with poor soil and hot sun, thornless common woadwaxen is the most cold-hardy of the commonly grown genistas. Upright stems form a clump 2 to 3 feet tall and wide. *continued*

GENISTA TINCTORIA
(continued)

GENISTA TINCTORIA

Mass-plant in areas of poor soil and on slopes to control erosion.

Site: Full sun. Best in neutral to alkaline, sandy to rocky, well-drained, low-fertility soil; tolerates slightly acid, average soil if well-drained. Drought-tolerant. Zones 3 to 8.
How to Grow: Plant container plants in spring or fall, spacing 2 feet apart. Take cuttings in late summer; will root by spring. Don't fertilize; avoid fertilizer runoff from other plants.

Blooms on new growth. Needs no routine pruning as this ruins natural shape. Cut back to several inches from ground in spring to renew, if needed. Scale can be problem in warm climates.
Cultivars and Similar Species: 'Royal Gold', profuse golden blossoms; 'Flore Plena', double flowers, semiprostrate plant. *Genista lydia*, 1 foot tall with cascading branches to 5 feet wide, forming solid mass of gold when in full bloom in early summer, zones 6 to 9. *G. pilosa* (silkleaf woodwaxen), cascades of golden blossoms in late spring, silvery leaves, cascading stems to 1½ feet tall to 4 feet wide, zones 5 to 8; 'Vancouver Gold', 1 foot tall, 3 feet wide, floriferous; 'Lemon Spreader', soft lemon yellow flowers.

HAMAMELIS SPP.
Witch Hazel

Unfurling the ribbonlike petals of its mop-head blossoms on warm days in mid to late winter, then curling them tightly on cold days, hybrid witch hazel *(Hamamelis × intermedia)* is a wonderful winter-blooming shrub that commands attention when little else is in bloom. Clusters of fragrant flowers line the bare branches and bloom for a month or more, beginning in January in the South and in March in the North. The shrub grows to 20 feet tall and is gracefully vase-shaped with coarse, rounded, dull green leaves with wavy margins. Fall color varies from dull yellow-gold to deep red-orange.

HAMAMELIS × INTERMEDIA
'ARNOLD PROMISE'

Blooming in fall—sometimes with its yellow fall foliage and sometimes on bare branches after the leaves drop—the native common witch hazel *(H. virginiana)* perfumes the air with haunting, sweet fragrance. Blossoms are pale yellow with dark centers and not individually showy, but they're eye-catching in quantity. Witch hazel astringent is distilled from the bark and roots. In winter, a mature shrub is attractive, with an irregular branching habit and smooth, silvery gray bark. Rounded; to 30 feet tall and wide.

Plant witch hazels so they can be seen from indoors or along walks (to enjoy fragrance). Flowers look best with evergreen background.

Site: Full sun to part or light shade. Fertile, humus-rich, acid soil. Plentiful moisture. Zones 5 to 9.
How to Grow: Plant balled-and-burlapped or container plants in spring, summer, or fall. Take softwood cuttings in spring. Easy to grow. May flower heavily in alternate years.

Needs no pruning except to remove broken branches. Remove suckers from base of grafted plants. Usually problem-free, although Japanese beetles may eat leaves.
Cultivars and Similar Species: Hybrid witch hazel: 'Arnold Promise', showiest cultivar; large golden yellow blossoms with red calyx, long-blooming; 'Diane', copper-red flowers, excellent orange-red fall color, vase-shaped to 15 feet tall; 'Jelena', orange flowers with red base, orange-red fall color. 'Ruby Glow', coppery red flowers, orange-red fall color.

H. mollis (Chinese witch hazel), fragrant yellow blossoms with red centers, three weeks earlier than hybrid, compact to 15 feet tall, zones 5 to 9; 'Pallida', lemon yellow, intensely fragrant flowers with dark centers, shiny leaves, 15 feet tall; 'Brevipetala', extra-large, fragrant yellow blossoms. *H. vernalis* (vernal witch hazel), dense native shrub, moist to wet sites; small, yellow to red, fragrant flowers in late winter to early spring, zones 5 to 7; 'Carnea' and 'Superba', orange flowers with red bases.

HIBISCUS SYRIACUS
Rose-of-Sharon, Shrub Althaea

Valued for late-summer blossoms that resemble 2- to 4-inch-wide hollyhocks, this tall shrub is an old-fashioned favorite with a new, better image because of recent hybridizing work. Older forms grow into leggy specimens and set copious amounts of seeds that cause a weed problem. The new triploid hybrids have none of these bad traits. Hybrids grow into compact, densely branched, 8-foot-tall plants with 5- to 6-inch flowers that bloom from early summer into fall. They don't set seeds, so they're not weedy. Flower colors include white, red, lavender, purple, pink, and violet, with doubles and bicolors common. Shiny dark green leaves are coarsely toothed, pointed, and three-lobed, and turn bright yellow in fall. Older forms grow to 12 feet tall and 10 feet wide.

Plant rose-of-sharon in the back of a shrub, mixed border, or foundation planting. Sometimes planted as screen or hedge, but best as a specimen.

HIBISCUS SYRIACUS 'APHRODITE'

Site: Full sun to part shade. Best in humus-rich, moist, well-drained soil, but adapts to most soils. Zones 5 to 9; tolerates air pollution and hot weather.
How to Grow: Plant balled-and-burlapped or container plants in spring, summer, or fall. Softwood cuttings root easily. Older cultivars self-sowing and weedy. May suffer dieback or twig-kill in coldest regions.

Blooms on current season's growth. Prune hard each spring to encourage new floriferous growth. May cut back annually to 2 feet for 4-foot blooming height, if desired. Japanese beetles

may eat flowers; leaf spot may occur in wet years; aphids and whiteflies sometimes are problems.
Cultivars and Similar Species: 'Blue Bird', pale lavender-blue flowers with red base; 'Blushing Bride', double, pale pink; 'Collie Mullens', double, lavender; 'Red Heart', white with red center.

Tetraploids: 'Diana', large, pure white; 'Helene', 6-inch white flowers with extra petals and crimson eye; 'Minerva', lavender with red eye; 'Aphrodite', deep pink with red eye.

HYDRANGEA SPP.
Hydrangea

Hydrangeas come in a variety of forms. Smooth hydrangea (*Hydrangea arborescens* 'Grandiflora') practically is obliterated by snowball clusters of creamy white flowers in midsummer. Grandiflora's blossoms turn green to bright white to coppery pink for a beautiful changing show from early summer well into fall. The plant forms a rounded mound of unbranched upright stems, which often are weighed down by the heavy flowers. Rounded; 3 to 5 feet tall and wider than tall. Sends up suckers and can colonize an area. Use in mixed border for summer color.

The voluptuous, rose-pink or bright blue globelike flowers of the French hydrangea (*H. macrophylla*) make a happy statement when they burst into midsummer bloom. These Victorian-style blossoms can be so large that they weigh down the shrub's flexible stems. For a dramatic effect, choose a globe-shaped hortensia version of the French hydrangea. For an airy look, go for the lace-cap hydrangea; the flat-topped flower clusters have a center of tiny, blue or pink fertile flowers surrounded by a perimeter of showy 2-inch infertile flowers.

Micronutrient aluminum, a chemical available in acid soil and unavailable in neutral to alkaline soil, influences

HYDRANGEA ARBORESCENS 'ANNABELLE'

the flower color of French hydrangea, although some cultivars tend toward one color or another. The more acid the soil, the bluer the flowers.

Grows 2 to 8 feet tall and wide, depending on cultivar. Excellent summer color in mixed borders, cottage gardens, and shade gardens. Lacecaps look better planted in drifts in woodland settings than hortensias.

The latest of the hydrangeas to bloom, peegee hydrangea (*H. paniculata* 'Grandiflora') is a large shrub or small tree that produces pointed clusters of creamy white flowers, which are 1 to 1½ feet long, at its branch tips. These weigh down the branches, forming a lovely weeping effect. The showy clusters open greenish white and mature to creamy white, then age to a beautiful shade of old rose. Upright to weeping; 15 to 20 feet tall and half as wide. Best as single specimen in mixed border; combine with lower plants that complement the weeping shape.

Oakleaf hydrangea (*H. quercifolia*), a southern native, has huge, bluntly lobed leaves that turn deep wine-red in fall. In early summer, green flower buds form; by midsummer they open into 1-foot-long, cone-shaped bundles of four-petaled, snowy white blossoms. The clusters dry *continued*

HYDRANGEA SPP.
(continued)

on the bush, changing from creamy white to chartreuse and finally to rosy brown by autumn. The clusters last through winter. The shiny cinnamon-colored bark peels off in papery shreds. Spreads irregularly and forms large colonies; 6 or more feet tall. Best in informal or naturalistic landscapes. Plant in shade garden, woodland, or informal shrub border.

Site: Light to half shade best for smooth and French hydrangea; smooth hydrangea tolerates full sun only if constantly moist. Protect French hydrangea from hot afternoon sun. Give peegee hydrangea full sun to part shade. Oakleaf hydrangea best in light to full shade; full sun if moist. Best in humus-rich, fertile, well-drained soil. Plentiful moisture. In acid soil (pH 5 to 6.5), French hydrangea flowers are blue; in pH 6.5 and above, flowers are pink. For blue flowers in alkaline soil, add 14 ounces of aluminum sulfate mixed with 1 gallon of water to soil; for pink flowers in acid soil, add lime to soil at rate of 1 pound per 10 square feet. Peegee hydrangea tolerates any well-drained soil with a pH below 7. Oakleaf hydrangea tolerates heavy soil. Smooth hydrangea hardy in zones 4 to 9. French hydrangea, zones 6 to 9, evergreen, in very mild climates; good seashore plant; some lace-caps hardy through Zone 5. Peegee hydrangea, zones 4 to 8; tolerates urban sites. Oakleaf hydrangea, zones 5 to 9; flower buds may be killed and plant size limited in zones 5 and 6, but plant valued for bark and foliage effect.

How to Grow: Plant container plants in spring or fall. Space smooth and French hydrangeas 3 feet apart, peegee 6 or more feet apart, and oakleaf 5 feet apart. Softwood cuttings root easily. May divide mature colonies of smooth hydrangea in fall.

In mild climates, smooth hydrangea may rebloom on new growth if flowers are cut at base after they fade. A hard winter and late frost may kill flower buds of French hydrangea and prevent blooming. Cut flowers of peegee hydrangea when they fade to improve winter appearance, if desired. Keep oakleaf hydrangea well-mulched.

Annual hard pruning is best for smooth hydrangea; can cut to ground in late winter or early spring before growth begins; blossoms on current season's growth.

French hydrangea blooms on year-old growth and on older wood. Flowers well if not pruned, but judicious pruning improves flowering. In fall or early spring, prune shoots that flowered during previous summer (or cut dried flower heads in fall) back to strong, fat flower buds. Cut weak and old stems to ground. (Cutting flowers for fresh or dried arrangements serves same purpose.) Cut to ground to rejuvenate, but plants will not flower that year.

Peegee hydrangea blooms on new growth. Produces largest blossoms if pruned yearly in early spring before growth begins. (Cutting stems for fresh or dried flower arrangements serves same purpose.) Cut back main branches to just above lowest pair or two of buds. If left unpruned, flowers are more numerous but smaller.

Oakleaf hydrangea blooms on previous season's growth. Does not need regular pruning; thin or cut out weak growth in spring or after flowering, if needed.

Hydrangeas usually have no pest and disease problems.

Cultivars: Smooth hydrangea: 'Annabelle', 12-inch globes on stronger stems, 4 feet tall, widely available.

French hydrangea: Hortensia—'Nikko Blue', large, early-blooming, deep blue flowers, 6 feet tall; 'All Summer Beauty', large blue flowers, 3 to 4 feet tall; 'Forever Pink', large, rose-red flowers may change to blue, 3 feet tall; 'Ami Pasquier' and 'Bottstein', low-growing, remain pink regardless of pH; 'Pink Elf' ('Pia'), 1½ feet tall and 2 feet wide, pink flowers; 'White', pure white; 'Pink 'n Pretty', bright pink, compact; 'Red 'n Pretty', red, compact. Lacecap—'Blue Billow', abundant, blue to turquoise lace-cap flowers, low mound, cold-hardy buds; 'Blue Wave', rich blue, Zone 5, 6 feet tall; 'Blue Bird', pastel blue to pH 7, Zone 5; 'Mariesii', pink; 'Mariesii Variegata', blue flowers, leaves variegated with creamy white, 3 feet tall; 'Lanarth White', white perimeter surrounds blue sterile flowers. *H. aspera*, peeling bark, large or small leaves, flattened mauve, blue, or pale pink heads, 15 feet tall.

Peegee hydrangea: 'Grandiflora Webb's', larger flower clusters; 'Tardiva', blooms in early to late fall, smaller clusters than 'Grandiflora', to 20 feet tall; 'Praecox', blooms three weeks earlier than 'Grandiflora', with smaller flowers, 15 feet tall.

Oakleaf hydrangea: 'Snow Queen', huge, white flowers on sturdy stems; 'Snowflake', 15-inch, double-flowered clusters; 'Sikes Dwarf', 2½ feet tall, 4 feet wide; 'Alice', large, white flowers, late-blooming.

HYPERICUM FRONDOSUM
Golden St.-John's-Wort

A graceful summer-blooming plant with spreading branches, golden St.-John's-wort produces clusters of 1-inch, buttercup-like flowers in June and July. The blue-green leaves are long and narrow and last through fall before turning chestnut brown. Three-part brown capsules and dried leaves decorate the red-brown branches through winter. The mounded plant grows to 1½ feet tall and 5 feet wide and has arching branches. Excellent for easy-care summer color. Use as a specimen in mixed borders or foundation plantings, or mass-plant in large garden.

Site: Full sun to part shade. Thrives in poor, sandy, acid to alkaline soil with good drainage; tolerates average soil if well-drained. Moderate moisture best; drought-tolerant. Zones 5 to 9; most

HYPERICUM FRONDOSUM

St.-John's-worts do poorly in the heat and humidity of the South.

How to Grow: Plant container plants in spring, summer, or fall, spacing 3 to 4 feet apart. Take cuttings in midsummer. Sow seeds when capsules ripen. Cut to ground in late winter if stems are winter-damaged. Regrows and blooms on new wood the same year. Usually trouble-free, but may become diseased in hot, humid areas.

Cultivars and Similar Species: 'Sunburst', tetraploid, doesn't die to ground, best hardy hypericum, showy 2-inch, bright golden yellow flowers, 2-inch-long, blue-green leaves, red-orange fall color, moundlike, to 4 to 5 feet tall, often mistakenly listed as cultivar of *Hypericum patulum*. *H.* × *moserianum* (gold flower), compact to 2 feet tall, golden flowers all summer, best choice for South, zones 5 to 9. *H. calycinum* (Aaron's-beard), dark green, semievergreen leaves, 3-inch, golden yellow blossoms with large bushy centers all summer on arching stems to 1½ feet tall, stoloniferous, forms good groundcover, zones 6 to 9. 'Hidcote', hybrid of unknown origin; 3 to 4 feet tall; 3-inch flowers June until frost, zones 6 to 9. *H. patulum* (goldencup St.-John's-wort), semievergreen, 2-inch, golden flowers in midsummer, 3 feet tall, spreading, zones 7 to 9. *H. prolificum* (shrubby St.-John's-wort), dense and

upright, to 4 feet tall and wide depending on climate; 1-inch, bright yellow flowers all summer; zones 4 to 8.

ILEX SPP.
Possum Haw, Winterberry, Deciduous Holly

The native southeastern and south-central swamp holly or possum haw *(Ilex decidua)* makes quite a show in the winter garden, where its abundant scarlet berries are displayed on silvery-barked horizontal or weeping branches. A large shrub or small multitrunk tree, possum haw has rounded to oblong 1½- to 3-inch-long leaves with small, rounded teeth. Leaves are glossy dark green on top with pale undersides and turn yellow in late fall. The orange to scarlet berries, borne singly or in clusters of two or three along the lengths of the branches, ripen in fall while the leaves are still green. They look stunning with the yellow fall foliage and even more attractive in winter on the bare branches. Unless birds eat them, the berries remain showy through winter. Upright; to 20 feet tall and 10 feet wide. Use as specimen, screen, or hedge. Looks best with dark background in winter.

Winterberry *(I. verticillata)*, another native, shines when covered with berries in fall and winter, but takes a backseat in other seasons. Glossy, bright red to scarlet berries form singly or in clusters of three along the stems, standing out against the green foliage in fall and the gray stems in winter. The berry show is best in autumn. Birds can strip the plants overnight and temperatures below 10°F turn berries black. This suckering multistemmed shrub has an open, spreading shape, which is more compact in the cultivars. Insignificant white flowers bloom between the leaves in early summer. Leaves are up to 3 inches long and tapered, varying from dull green to

ILEX DECIDUA

glossy dark green in the best cultivars and may turn buttery yellow or remain green until blackened by frost. Upright to rounded; 6 to 10 feet tall and wide. Excellent mass-planted as informal hedge or screen in distant view. Plant in groups to intensify berry show.

Site: Full sun to light shade; winterberry needs sun for best berries. Possum haw best in humus-rich to sandy, acid soil; tolerates poorer soil and higher pH (up to 7.0) than other hollies. Needs plentiful moisture; tolerates wet to swampy site. Give winterberry humus-rich to heavy, wet to swampy, acid soil; tolerates pH up to 6.75. Possum haw hardy in zones 5 to 9; performs well in stressful conditions of Midwest and Plains. Winterberry, zones 4 to 9.

How to Grow: Plant balled-and-burlapped or container shrubs in spring or fall. Space possum haw 4 to 8 feet apart, according to use; space winterberry 5 feet apart. Possum haw needs a male *I. decidua* or *I. opaca* pollinator planted within several hundred feet to ensure berries on female plants; winterberry also needs male pollinator. Use fertilizer designed for acid-loving plants if leaves appear pale and chlorotic. Mulch well.

Prune possum haw to reveal bark on lower trunks if used as specimen. Prune as needed to create full hedge. Winterberry needs no *continued*

ILEX SPP.
(continued)

pruning; occasionally troubled by powdery mildew and leaf spot. Possum haw usually trouble-free.

Cultivars and Similar Species: Possum haw: 'Red Cascade', larger fruit, silvery weeping branches; 'Warren's Red', excellent cultivar, bright red fruit, upright; 'Sentry', columnar; 'Council Fire', bushy, orange-red fruit; 'Red Escort', rounded form, glossy leaves, male used for pollination.

Winterberry: 'Afterglow', compact, good summer foliage, long-lasting, orange-red fruit, tolerates drier site; 'Aurantiaca', good orange fruit persists well; 'Cacapon', glossy, dark red berries in dense clusters, long-lasting; 'Winter Red', copious large, bright red berries remain longer than others, but can be leggy at 10 feet tall and 8 feet wide; 'Red Sprite' ('Compacta' and 'Nana'), rounded dwarf, to 4 feet tall, abundant, large, red berries; 'Sparkleberry', long-lasting, abundant, brilliant red berries, 12 feet tall and wide; 'Winter Gold', bright gold berries. Male pollinators—'Early Male' pollinates 'Red Sprite', 'Sunset', and 'Sparkleberry'; 'Jim Dandy' (dwarf male) pollinates 'Red Sprite', 'Cacapon', 'Aurantiacum', and 'Afterglow'; 'Apollo' pollinates 'Winter Gold' and 'Sparkleberry'; 'Late Male' pollinates 'Winter Red'. 'Harvest Red', hybrid, wine-colored fall foliage, small red berries, well-shaped plant, zones 3 to 9; use 'Raritan Chief' as pollinator.

I. serrata (Japanese winterberry), Asian species with ¼-inch, brilliant red berries and fine-toothed leaves, 4 to 8 feet tall; 'Sundrops', pale yellow fruit.

INDIGOFERA KIRILOWII
Kirilow Indigo

If you want something unusual, try this elegant shrub. It begins to bloom in early summer and continues for many weeks, producing 4-inch spikes of 1-inch-long, two-lipped,

INDIGOFERA KIRILOWII

rose-pink flowers that resemble small wisteria blossoms. The bright green compound leaves have a lacy texture and silky finish that lasts all summer and fall. Rounded to spreading; 3 to 4 feet tall if unpruned and not winter-killed; to 1½ feet if cut back or winter-damaged. Use as groundcover in poor soil or in mixed border where flowers and foliage provide color and texture.

Site: Full sun. Average, well-drained soil; tolerates alkalinity and moist or dry conditions. Zones 5 to 7; tops often winter-killed in zones 5 and 6. Thrives in heat.

How to Grow: Plant balled-and-burlapped or container plants in spring, summer, or fall, spacing 2 to 3 feet apart. Don't fertilize. Blooms on new growth. Remove winter-killed branches in early spring or cut to ground each year to renew. Pest-free.

Similar Species: *Indigofera gerardiana* (*I. heterantha*) (Himilayan indigo), rose-purple flowers, 10 feet tall.

ITEA VIRGINICA
Virginia Sweetspire

More showy in the garden than in the wild, this East Coast native attracts attention for months. Slender, 3-inch clusters of fragrant, creamy white blossoms decorate the tips of the arching branches for two weeks in early summer. The pointed, glossy, dark green leaves stand out against maroon stems and change to alluring colors in fall—bronze-yellow in shade and glowing hues of red and orange in sun. Fall color develops early and lasts for several months in the North and all winter in the South. Mounded; to 5 feet tall. Lovely specimen in border or foundation; plant in masses in large garden. Naturalize along woodland edge or beside a pond or stream.

ITEA VIRGINICA

Site: Full sun to shade; flowering and fall color best with at least half sun. Cool, humus-rich, moist soil. Tolerates wet sites. Zones 6 to 9.

How to Grow: Plant container plants in spring or fall, spacing 4 feet apart. Take semihardwood cuttings. Mulch soil well.

Does not need regular pruning. Renew by cutting to ground in late winter. No serious pests or diseases.

Cultivars and Similar Species: 'Henry's Garnet', red-purple foliage in fall lasts into winter, 6-inch flower spikes; 6 feet tall and 8 feet wide; 'Saturnelia', fall color red, orange, pink, and yellow. *Itea japonica* (Japanese sweetspire), fragrant, bright white flowers, red fall color, suckering and fast-growing; 'Beppu' ('Nana'), scarlet to crimson fall color, spreading to 5 feet.

KERRIA JAPONICA
Japanese Rose

This graceful shade-lover is best known in its variegated and double-flowered forms. The species blooms in mid spring, producing single, 1- to 2-inch, golden yellow flowers that resemble yellow wild

KERRIA JAPONICA 'PICTA'

roses or buttercups. Double-flowered blossoms resemble little pompons. The lance-shaped leaves are bright green with jagged edges and retain their color until they drop in late fall. The slender, shiny, pea green stems are attractive and form a twiggy mass; they add color to winter gardens. Vase-shaped to arching, suckering shrub; to 5 feet tall and 6 feet wide. The variegated-leaf forms are pretty plants with subtle variegations and single flowers, adding sparkle to shady spots. Use in shade garden or shrub border.

Site: Light to full shade. Well-drained, humus-rich, moist soil. Plentiful moisture. Zones 5 to 9.
How to Grow: Plant container or balled-and-burlapped shrubs in spring, summer, or fall, spacing 4 feet apart. Suckers may be divided in spring or fall. Cuttings root easily in summer or fall. Some branches of variegated forms may revert to all green; cut them out at ground level. Flowers fade quickly in too much sun.

Blooms on previous year's growth. Prune annually immediately after flowering, remove shoots that flowered at ground level or cut them back to strong side branch. Remove dead branches. Renew by cutting to ground after flowering. Usually pest-free.
Cultivars: 'Picta' ('Argenteo-marginata', 'Variegata'), gray-green leaves with irregular, creamy white margins, single, yellow blossoms, slow-growing; outstanding contrast in shaded site; 'Aureo-variegata', green leaves with yellow margins, single, yellow flowers; 'Pleniflora', double, pomponlike flowers; upright, lanky plant.

KOLKWITZIA AMABILIS
Beautybush

This large, old-fashioned shrub is a sight to behold when it blooms in early summer. Bell-shaped, ½-inch-long flowers that resemble foxglove are pale pink with yellow-speckled

KOLKWITZIA AMABILIS

throats and transform the plant into a pink fountain. The rest of the year, the plant recedes into obscurity. Leaves are oval and pointed, 1 to 3 inches long, and dull green, sometimes turning reddish before dropping in fall. The multiple stems form a dense stand, and exfoliating gray-brown bark may look unkempt in winter. Vase-shaped; to 10 feet tall. Locate where it has plenty of room and can be enjoyed when in bloom but will go unnoticed rest of year.

Site: Full sun. Average to humus-rich, well-drained soil. Moderate to plentiful moisture; withstands drought once established. Zones 5 to 8.
How to Grow: Plant balled-and-burlapped or container shrubs in spring, summer, or fall; allow plenty of space. Blooms on old wood. Once established, cut oldest and weakest side branches off main branches; cut just after flowering to keep vigorous. Leave low branches near outer edges for vase shape. To renew, cut all stems to ground immediately after flowering. Usually pest- and disease-free.
Cultivars: 'Pink Cloud', abundant clear pink flowers.

LESPEDEZA THUNBERGII
Bush Clover

A standout in the late summer and fall garden, bush clover blooms when little else is in flower. Individual rosy purple flowers are ½ inch long,

LESPEDEZA THUNBERGII 'GIBRALTAR'

but grow in clusters along the long, arching stems, turning the plant into a fountain of color in late summer and fall. The three-part, blue- *continued*

LESPEDEZA THUNBERGII
(continued)

green leaves have a lovely, fernlike texture. Upright to mounded; reaching 3 to 6 feet tall in one season after cut to ground. Use as a specimen in a mixed border. Combines beautifully with yellows, golds, lavenders, and purples of common fall flowers.

Site: Full sun. Average to sandy, well-drained soil. Tolerates poor, dry soil and drought. Zones 6 to 8.
How to Grow: Plant container plants in spring, summer, or fall, spacing 3 to 4 feet apart. Dies back to ground during winter in cold climates; treat like herbaceous perennial. Don't fertilize.

Blooms on current season's growth. Remove winter-killed branches (or entire tops) in spring when growth begins or cut back hard to keep tidy even where not winter-killed. Usually pest-free.
Cultivars and Similar Species: 'Alba', bright white flowers, upright; 'Gibraltar', floriferous, rose-purple, weeping mound. *Lespedeza bicolor* (shrub bush clover), dark green leaves, rose-purple flowers in mid- to late summer, 6 to 8 feet tall, not as showy, tops are cold-hardy in Zone 6.

LIGUSTRUM OVALIFOLIUM
California Privet

One of the handsomest of the many privets used for hedges, California privet boasts lustrous, oval, dark green leaves 1 to 2½ inches long. The foliage is evergreen in the warm parts of its range and deciduous in the cold parts. In early to midsummer, 2- to 4-inch, upright clusters of fragrant, bright white flowers decorate the plants, creating a pretty green-and-white effect. Shiny black berries nestle among the leaves in fall and may remain after leaves drop. Dense and upright to rounded; 10 to 15 feet tall. Excellent for a

sheared formal hedge, property marker, or as background to formal flower garden. Use unpruned as an informal screen.

LIGUSTRUM VULGARE 'LODENSE'

Site: Full sun to half shade. Average to fertile, moist to dry soil. Moderate moisture; tolerates dryness once established. Zones 6 to 9.
How to Grow: Plant bare-root or balled-and-burlapped shrubs in early spring, spacing according to use: 1½ to 2 feet for pruned hedge, farther for screen. Softwood cuttings root easily. Easy to care for.

Shear as needed to keep tidy if used as formal hedge. Tolerates heavy pruning. Usually trouble-free, but may be infected by twig blight and powdery mildew, and infested with aphids, mites, or mealybugs.
Cultivars and Similar Species: *Ligustrum obtusifolium* (border privet), broadly horizontal, nodding clusters of malodorous white flowers, blue-black berries with white bloom, zones 4 to 8; *L. o. regelianum*, to 5 feet tall with horizontal branches. *L. vulgare* (European privet), upright and spreading, to 15 feet tall and wide, dark green leaves, shiny black berries persist all winter, zones 4 to 8; 'Lodense', 4 feet tall, easily maintained as low hedge; 'Variegatum', creamy white-edged leaves, showy.

LINDERA BENZOIN
Spicebush

All parts of this East Coast native release a spicy wintergreen aroma when crushed or broken. Although not showy, the small clusters of yellow blossoms that decorate the slender, shiny, dark brown stems in late winter or early spring attract attention because they appear so early. Oval to oblong, green leaves turn clear, bright yellow in late fall and make an outstanding show. Scarlet berries line the stems in fall after the leaves drop, but may be eaten by

LINDERA BENZOIN

birds. Loose, open, rounded shrub; to 12 feet tall and wide. Naturalize in woodland or native plant garden; use as a specimen in shrub border or as a caterpillar host in butterfly garden.

Site: Full sun or light to part shade; dense and floriferous in full sun. Well-drained, moist, slightly acid to slightly alkaline soil best. Zones 5 to 9.
How to Grow: Plant balled-and-burlapped or container plants in spring or fall, spacing at least 5 feet apart. Cuttings are difficult to root. Berries appear on female plants. Locate male plant near several female plants for best berry display. May be difficult or slow to establish. Does not need regular pruning. Caterpillars of

swallowtail butterflies feed on foliage, but do no serious damage.
Cultivars: Usually only the species is available.

LONICERA FRAGRANTISSIMA
Fragrant Honeysuckle, Winter Honeysuckle

Blooming for up to a month in late winter or early spring, fragrant honeysuckle is aptly named. Loved for its pervasive, sweet, lemony scent rather than for its ordinary looks, this shrub is a favorite in the South, where it begins to bloom in January. The creamy white blossoms are pretty but not showy.

LONICERA FRAGRANTISSIMA

They bloom among rounded, dull blue-green to dark green leaves on tall, slender, shiny-barked stems, which form a tangled mass. Foliage lasts through fall and drops in early winter with little color change. The dark red berries are hidden beneath the summer foliage. Irregular to rounded; 6 to 10 feet tall and wide. Use as a privacy screen or plant single specimen where fragrance can be enjoyed.

Site: Full sun to part shade. Fertile, moist but well-drained soil; avoid wet sites. Plentiful moisture; tolerates drier soil than other honeysuckles. Zones 5 to 9.

How to Grow: Softwood cuttings root easily. Not as weedy as other honeysuckles. Thin by cutting out oldest canes at ground every two or three years after flowering; retain natural vase shape. Cut to ground immediately after flowering to renew. May be troubled by aphids, sawflies, scale, caterpillars, and fall webworms. Leaf blight, powdery mildew, and leaf spot occasional problems.
Similar Species: *Lonicera tatarica* (Tatarian honeysuckle), rounded to heart-shaped, blue-green leaves; red, pink, or white spring flowers, red summer berries spread by birds make it a pesty weed, zones 3 to 8; numerous cultivars available.

MYRICA PENSYLVANICA
Bayberry

Native along the coastline of the East, this tough shrub withstands salt spray and salty, sandy soil. In harsh conditions, the handsome plant develops a windswept character. Bayberry has leathery, oblong, blunt-

MYRICA PENSYLVANICA

tipped, 4-inch-long leaves that are lustrous dark green with lighter undersides. The leaves contain oil glands that release a resinous scent when crushed. Deciduous to semievergreen, leaves eventually drop with no color change in the South and may turn deep red in the North before dropping in early winter. Waxy gray fruit forms showy, dense clusters along the stem of the female plant and is attractive in fall and through winter. Wax from the berries is used for making fragrant bayberry candles. Flowers are inconspicuous and bloom in early spring before the leaves emerge. Dense and rounded; 5 to 12 feet tall. Spreads by suckers to form colonies. Naturalize in seashore garden or mass-plant in areas of poor soil. Looks best with evergreen background in winter.

Site: Full sun to half shade. Average to sandy, well-drained, infertile, acid soil. Tolerates drought. Tolerates heavy soil if well-drained. Zones 4 to 9; withstands seashore conditions and direct salt spray. Choose plants propagated and grown in your climate to ensure cold-hardiness.
How to Grow: Plant container plants in spring, summer, or fall, spacing 5 feet apart. Cuttings are difficult to root. Collect seeds in fall; remove wax and plant outdoors. Need male shrub to pollinate female shrubs for berry production.
    Does not need regular pruning. Remove dead branches in summer. Renew by cutting to ground. Usually pest-free.
Similar Species: *Myrica cerifera* (wax myrtle), similar, to 35 feet tall, zones 6 to 9.

PAEONIA SUFFRUTICOSA
Tree Peony

Extremely showy when in bloom, tree peonies have an exotic, architectural character at other times. The magnificent flowers measure up to 12 inches across and are fragrant, with huge, satiny, red, pink, rose, white, or yellow petals surrounding prominent yellow stamens. Leaves are blue-green, deeply cut, and scattered around the twisted, gnarled *continued*

Deciduous Shrubs

PAEONIA SUFFRUTICOSA
(continued)

stems. Tree peonies are revered plants in China and Japan, having been cultivated since ancient times. Open, irregular shape; to 5 feet tall and wide. Include as a specimen in a mixed border or foundation planting. Don't crowd.

PAEONIA SUFFRUTICOSA

Site: Full sun or dappled shade most of day, with protection from hottest afternoon sun, is best. Flowers fade quickly in full sun, last longest in light shade. Humus-rich, fertile, well-drained, moist soil. Plentiful moisture. Best in zones 6 and 7. In Zone 8, plant in cool site; in Zone 5, protect in winter.
How to Grow: Plant bare-root plants in fall or container plants in spring, summer, or fall; be sure graft union is 4 inches below soil level. Protect from winter sun, which can desiccate plants in cold climates. Stake double flowers.
   In fall, prune dead flower stalks to where new shoot has formed. Remove deadwood in summer. Botrytis and anthracnose fungus can disfigure plants.
Cultivars: Many cultivars available in single, semidouble, and double forms.

PHILADELPHUS CORONARIUS

PHILADELPHUS CORONARIUS
Sweet Mock Orange

Long cultivated for the sweet fragrance that resembles orange blossoms, mock orange produces four-petaled, white flowers, which bloom for two weeks in early summer. The plant looks uninteresting the rest of the year. Leaves are rounded and dark green, and drop with little color change in fall. Bark on the many leggy stems is exfoliating and reddish orange. Rounded to arching; 10 to 12 feet tall and wide. Best when in bloom; use as background hedge or screen.

Site: Full sun to light shade. Humus-rich, fertile, moist soil best, but tolerates poorer conditions. Plentiful to moderate moisture best; tolerates drought. Zones 4 to 7.
How to Grow: Plant balled-and-burlapped or container plants in spring, summer, or fall, spacing at least 5 feet apart. Softwood cuttings root easily.
   May become leggy and unattractive if not properly pruned. Prune immediately after flowering by removing older canes at base and cutting back individual branches to create full shape. Usually pest-free.
Cultivars and Similar Species: 'Aureus', bright yellow leaves in spring, yellow-green in summer, sparse

flowers. *Philadelphus × lemoinei* (Lemoine mock orange), single or double, fragrant, white flowers; tidy, small leaves, 5 feet tall, zones 4 to 8; 'Avalanche', fragrant flowers, 3 feet tall. *P. × virginalis*, showy, fragrant, semidouble flowers, 8 feet tall, 6 feet wide; zones 5 to 8; 'Minnesota Snowflake', large, double, fragrant flowers, 8 feet tall, zones 4 to 8; 'Natchez', 2-inch, single, fragrant flowers; 'Dwarf Snowflake', 3 to 4 feet tall, dense, fragrant double blossoms, zones 4 to 8; 'Bouquet Blanc', fruity fragrance; 'Snow Velvet', 3-inch, semidouble, scented blossoms.

POTENTILLA FRUTICOSA
Shrubby Cinquefoil

Native to northern regions of North America, this tough shrub withstands cold and drought while looking delicate and pristine. One-inch-wide, buttercup-like flowers deck the graceful, arching branches all summer. The fine-textured leaves are divided into almost linear lobes and

POTENTILLA FRUTICOSA 'GOLDFINGER'

are silky gray-green in spring, maturing to dark green and turning yellow-green in fall. When devoid of leaves, the plant shows off its shiny, brown, shredding bark on slender, upright stems. Rounded and dense; to 4 feet tall and wide. Attractive as single specimen or mass-planted in borders and foundation plantings. Use as low hedge. Suited to Xeriscape.

Site: Full sun. Average to light or gravelly, well-drained soil. Moderate moisture. Tolerates drought and alkalinity. Zones 2 to 7; best where summers aren't too hot. Excellent in Midwest, Plains, and Mountain states.
How to Grow: Plant balled-and-burlapped or container plants in spring, summer, or fall, spacing 3 feet apart. Softwood cuttings root easily. Flowers fade in extremely hot weather.

Each year in late winter, cut back one-third of stems at ground level to renew if plant begins to look ragged. Spider mites may be troublesome. Leaf spot may occur if too humid and moist.
Cultivars: Superior ones include 'Yellow Gem', mounded to 1½ feet tall and 3½ feet wide, yellow flowers, gray-green leaves and red stems; 'Goldfinger', bright yellow, 1½-inch flowers, blue-green leaves; 'Katherine Dykes', soft yellow flowers, gray-green leaves; 'Abbotswood', white flowers, blue-green leaves; 'Princess' ('Blink'), delicate pink flowers; 'Sunset', orange blossoms; 'Tangerine', orange-tinged yellow blossoms; 'Sutter's Gold', 1-foot mound, yellow blossoms; 'Klondyke', 2-foot mound, bright yellow flowers.

RHODODENDRON SPP.
Native Azalea

Native primarily to mountainous or coastal regions of the East Coast, flowers of this lovely group of azaleas are less flashy than hybrid azaleas, but possess a charming beauty, and most have good fall color. These azaleas look at home in woodland and naturalistic gardens, but also beautify spring borders. Coast azalea and swamp azalea are perfect naturalized along a stream or in a wet site. Locate fragrant types where their scent can be enjoyed.

Coast azalea (*Rhododendron atlanticum*) grows naturally in pine barrens from New Jersey to Georgia. Tubular, pinkish white flowers with flared faces and long, curling stamens bloom as the leaves unfold and smell sweet. Forms a round, 3- to 6-foot-tall, spreading shrub.

RHODODENDRON ATLANTICUM
CHOPTANK RIVER STRAIN

Florida flame azalea (*R. austrinum*) blooms in mid to late spring when new leaves appear. The tubular flowers have flared faces and long spidery stamens and are golden yellow, cream, orange, or near red, in clusters of eight to 15 flowers. Less fragrant than other species. Rounded, loosely branched; to 8 to 10 feet tall.

Pinxterbloom azalea (*R. periclymenoides*) possesses fragile-looking clusters of pale pink to violet-pink or white scentless flowers in mid to late spring just before or with the new leaves. Blossoms have long tubes, flared faces, and graceful long stamens and bloom in clusters of up to a dozen. The bright green leaves turn yellowish in autumn. Native to rocky slopes and woodlands from Massachusetts to North Carolina. From 2 to 8 feet tall and wide-spreading.

Pink-shell azalea (*R. vaseyi*) bears clusters of short-tubed, flat-faced, clear white to rose-pink flowers with long curling stamens on naked branches in spring. Leaves are smooth and shiny, not fuzzy like other deciduous azaleas, and turn brilliant light red to bronze-purple in fall. Forms a rounded 6 to 8 feet tall shrub.

Plum-leaved azalea (*R. prunifolium*) is the latest bloomer of the group, blooming for about four weeks in July and August. Rare in its native Alabama and Georgia habitat, this shrub brings glowing color to gardens when few other shrubs are in bloom. The long tubular flowers, which flare open into wide stars with long stamens, usually appear in clusters of five. Typically orange-red, they vary from salmon to scarlet to blood red. Leaves turn a lovely mix of pale orange and deep orange-red in fall. Spreading to rounded; 5 to 7 feet tall and wide.

Site: All are best in light to half shade with protection from hot sun. All need humus-rich, moist, well-drained, acid (pH 4.5 to 5.5) soil and plentiful moisture. Florida flame azalea tolerates full sun in moist sites and pinxterbloom azalea grows in full shade and also tolerates dry or rocky soil in shade.

Coast azalea, zones 5 to 8. Florida flame azalea, zones 6 to 9; excellent in the South. Pinxterbloom azalea, zones 5 to 8. Plum-leaved azalea, zones 6 to 9. Pink-shell azalea, zones 4 to 9.
How to Grow: Plant container shrubs in spring, summer, or fall, spacing 4 feet apart. Keep soil mulched to protect shallow roots. Needs no pruning. Remove deadwood as needed. Usually pest-free.
Cultivars and Similar Species: Coast azalea: Choptank River strains are natural hybrids with *R. viscosum*. 'Choptank River Belle', pinker buds open to fragrant, pink-flushed flowers in June; 'Choptank River Duchess', deep rose-pink buds open to fragrant, white flowers with deep pink backsides in late May; 'Marydel', Choptank River selection, deep pink buds and pinkish white, fragrant flowers. *continued*

RHODODENDRON SPP.
(continued)

Swamp azalea or swamp honeysuckle (*R. viscosum*), white flowers in midsummer with a spicy sweet, clovelike fragrance; dull orange fall color, native to coasts and wetlands up and down East Coast; 'Pink Mist', white, tinged-pink, fragrant. *R. arborescens* (sweet azalea), blooms in between *R. atlanticum* and *R. viscosum*, pervasive spicy sweet fragrance, white flowers with red or pink stamens; red fall color; 15 to 20 feet tall in moist site.

Mountain-dwelling flame azalea (*R. calendulaceum*) similar to Florida flame azalea with yellow or scarlet, scentless blossoms for two weeks in early summer; fall color orange, red, and gold; full, bushy plant; zones 5 to 8, best where cool.

Rose-shell azalea (*R. prinophyllum/ R. roseum*) is similar to pinxterbloom azalea, but with fragrant later-blooming clove-scented pink flowers; tolerates higher pH; zones 3 to 6. Piedmont azalea (*R. canescens*) has fragrant white flowers with pink tubes; shade tolerant, zones 7 to 9.

Pink-shell azalea: 'Pinkerbell', deep pink; 'White Find', clear white.

Plum-leaved azalea: 'Sweet September', soft pink, blooms in September; 'Cherry Bomb', orange-red, July; other hybrids with various colors available from specialty growers. Cumberland azalea (*R. bakeri*) native to the Southeast with orange to red blossoms in early summer; quite shade tolerant, 3 to 8 feet tall with horizontal branches, zones 5 to 8.

RHODODENDRON SPP.
Asian Azaleas

Unlike the American species, deciduous azaleas native to Asia have flat-faced, not tubular flowers. They are equally charming, however, and make excellent shrubs for spring borders and naturalistic gardens. Gorgeous as a single specimen in a

RHODODENDRON MUCRONULATUM

shrub border or foundation, these shrubs can be mass-planted to great effect in large gardens. They combine well with daffodils.

Blooming on bare branches just as winter turns into spring, Korean rhododendron's *(Rhododendron mucronulatum)* bright rose-purple to soft lavender blossoms create a glorious show of color. Individual blossoms are 1½ inches wide. The 5-pointed bells are speckled with a darker hue and borne in clusters of 3 to 6 at the branch tips. The pretty pointed, elliptical leaves turn yellow-bronze with crimson overtones in late fall. The bark is yellowish brown and shiny. Shrubs are upright; to 4 to 8 feet tall and wide.

Royal azalea's *(R. schlippenbachii)* sheer-as-silk flowers are pastel pink with brown-speckled upper petals. The flat-faced blossoms create an unparalled display in early to mid spring, just as the leaves unfold. Whorled leaves are rounded to spoon-shaped, dark green in summer, turning yellow, orange, and pink-orange in late fall. Upright and open-branched; 4 to 6 feet tall and wide.

Site: Light to half shade; full sun okay in the North. Shade during blooming prolongs blossoms. Humus-rich, fertile, moist soil. Korean azalea needs acid (pH 4.5 to 5.5) soil; royal azalea tolerates higher pH (acid to neutral) than other azaleas. Plentiful moisture.

Korean azalea, zones 5 to 7; royal azalea, zones 5 to 8.

How to grow: Plant balled-and-burlapped or container shrubs in spring, spacing 3 feet apart. Locate Korean azalea in a cold spot in the garden to prevent premature, frost-prone blossoms. Needs no pruning. Thin branches immediately after blooming to control size if needed. Flower buds of royal azalea may be injured in Zone 5; protect from winter wind and frost pockets. Usually pest-free, but mites may trouble royal azalea in a hot sunny site.

Cultivars: Korean azalea: 'Cornell Pink', pure bright pink blossoms; 'Shrimp Pink', warm pink; 'Knight's Light Purple', light lilac; 'Cama', soft pink fading to white; 'Album', white.

RHODODENDRON HYBRIDS
Hybrid Azalea

The large-flowered deciduous Knap Hill, Exbury, and Mollis azaleas, developed in England, are complex hybrids between several

EXBURY AZALEA

North American species and several Asian species with earlier hybrids. Well-grown plants are a magnificent sight in mid to late spring when the flowers practically obliterate the leaves. Lovely in the spring border combined with scillas and other late bulbs, but unremarkable the rest of the year. Upright and open shrubs, 4 to 10 feet tall and 4 to 6 feet wide.

The large flower trusses of the Knap Hill and Exbury azaleas have 20 or 30 flowers per cluster; individual flowers are 2 to 3 inches across and open-faced with speckled and blotched petals. A rainbow of colors include pastels and rich, dark hues. Some selections are highly fragrant, others are scentless. Leaves are long and pointed, somewhat coarse, with variable fall color. Mollis azaleas have smaller trusses and flowers and usually bloom in hot colors.

Site: Full sun to light shade. Humus-rich, moist, well-drained, acid (pH 4.5 to 5.5) soil. Plentiful moisture. Zones 5 to 8.
How to Grow: Plant balled-and-burlapped or container plants in spring or fall, spacing 6 or more feet apart. Keep well-mulched. Do not allow to dry out. Pruning not needed, but branches can be thinned immediately after blooming to control size. Mildew often seriously disfigures foliage.
Cultivars and Similar Species: Named cultivars are numerous but expensive. Often unnamed seedlings are sold by color; less expensive, but less desirable because their traits are unknown.

Northern Lights hybrids: hybrids of Mollis azaleas and *Rhododendron prinopyllum* bred at the University of Minnesota; selected for cold-hardiness of flower buds in a lovely range of colors; fragrant, compact to 6 feet, zones 3 to 8; well-suited to the Northeast and northern Midwest, adaptable elsewhere.

RHUS TYPHINA
Staghorn Sumac

Offering a dramatic architectural beauty throughout the year, this native shrub is best in informal or natural settings because it runs a bit wild by sending up thickets of suckering stems. The 2-foot long, featherlike, bright green leaves are divided into 11 to 31 leaflets and grow in dramatic whorls at the stem-tips. Fall color is outstanding red and scarlet. Conelike, green flowers ripen on female plants into 8-inch-tall, fuzzy, seed-bearing, red clubs, which are quite showy from late summer through winter, but are especially striking in the winter landscape when displayed on the stark gray stems. The stout twigs are velvety and hairy, resembling stag horns. Upright; to 20 to 25 feet tall and wide. Best massed in a large, informal or naturalistic garden. Beautiful in autumn against an evergreen background. Cutleaf sumac makes a good specimen.

RHUS TYPHINA 'LACINIATA'

Site: Full sun to part shade. Average to rocky or sandy, well-drained soil. Drought-tolerant. Zones 3 to 8.
How to Grow: Plant bare-root plants in early spring, or balled-and-burlapped plants in spring, summer or fall, spacing 10 or more feet apart for a mass planting, farther from other tall plants. Take stem cuttings in late winter. Propagate cutleaf forms from root cuttings. Plant where suckering, spreading habit is not a problem.

Leafs out late in spring; don't assume it's dead.

Prune to remove deadwood, infected stems, and unwanted suckers. Select new suckers to replace infected stems. Cut to ground in late winter to rejuvenate. Stem canker and dieback may be serious.
Cultivars and Similar Species: 'Dissecta' (cutleaf sumac), finely dissected, fernlike leaves, red fruit; 'Laciniata', deeply divided leaves, but not as deep as 'Dissecta', red fruit. *Rhus glabra* (smooth sumac), similar but with smooth leaves and twigs and brighter red clubs; zones 3 to 9; 'Laciniata', finely cut leaves, may suffer from mildew. *R. copallina* (shining sumac), pale yellow-green flowers in late summer, colorful, red fruit, compound leaves, scarlet fall color, zones 4 to 9; *R. aromatica* (fragrant sumac), pale yellow flowers in spring before hairy, three-lobed, fragrant leaves, orange to scarlet in fall, red, berrylike fruit in late summer, zones 3 to 9; 'Gro-Low', 2 feet high, groundcover for erosion control.

RIBES ALPINUM

RIBES ALPINUM
Alpine Currant

A dense, twiggy habit and small, maplelike leaves make this adaptable plant a fine choice for a tough situation. Flowers are yellow green and inconspicuous *continued*

RIBES ALPINUM
(continued)

on female plants, but subtly noticeable on male plants, blooming with the new leaves. Most cultivated plants are males; they are more immune to leaf diseases. Yellowish fall color is not showy. Rounded; 3 to 5 feet tall. Excellent informal or sheared hedge.

Site: Full sun to shade. Average to light, well-drained soil; tolerates alkaline soil. Moderate moisture. Zones 3 to 7; good in the Plains and Mountain states where summers are hot and dry.
How to Grow: Plant container plants in spring, summer, or fall, spacing 2 to 3 feet apart for a hedge. Take softwood cuttings. Cannot be legally planted in areas of white pine forest, because plants in the genus *Ribes* can carry white pine bluster rust, although this species does not.

May be sheared at any time because flowers are not a concern. Leaf spot, rust, aphids, mites, and worms may be troublesome.
Cultivars: 'Aureum', yellowish leaves, best in sun; 'Green Mound', compact, to 3 feet.

SALIX SPP.
Pussy Willow, Purple Osier

One of the first signs of spring are the silver, furred buds of pussy willow (*Salix discolor*), which delight children and adults with their silky feel. Flowers mature into yellow bottlebrushes just as the new leaves emerge. The narrow leaves are dark green on top with gray-white undersides, giving them a sparkling appearance. In winter, the bare, smooth, dark brown branches, with their large buds, look pretty combined with rough-textured plants. Upright; to 18 feet tall and 6 to 8 feet wide. Use this native shrub in natural areas, perhaps as a hedge.

SALIX PURPUREA

Showy in winter with gleaming reddish purple stems, the purple osier or basket willow (*S. purpurea*), from Eurasia, has long been grown in American gardens. The stems are flexible and used to make baskets. Narrow, silver-blue leaves are 4 inches long and a fraction of an inch wide, giving the plant a wonderful, fine texture during the growing season. Flowers and fruit are inconspicuous. Rounded; 8 to 10 feet tall, usually pruned to remain lower. Naturalize in a moist spot in the garden or use as a specimen or hedge in a formal garden. Locate where stems can be seen from indoors in winter.

Site: Give pussy willow full sun, purple osier full sun to half shade. Pussy willow best in average to humus-rich, moist to wet soil; purple osier in similar, but more fertile soil. Both hardy in zones 3 to 9.
How to Grow: Plant bare-root or container plants in spring or fall, spacing pussy willow 4 to 5 feet apart and purple osier 3 to 5 feet. May take softwood cuttings of purple osier. Cut pussy willow stems for indoor use just as buds enlarge, but keep out of water.

Prune pussy willow back hard each spring to encourage new, vigorous growth and flowering, but retain shrub's shape while harvesting stems for indoor display. May cut to the ground to renew.

Each year in late winter, cut back all purple osier stems to within 1 inch of old wood, about 2 to 3 feet from the ground, to develop a "stool" from which branches develop. This produces colorful branches each year. Harvest stems for decoration or basketmaking.

Pussy willow is usually pest-free. Purple osier is subject to a number of insects and leaf diseases.
Cultivars and Similar Species: Pussy willow: *S. caprea* (goat willow), upright, small tree, to 15 to 25 feet tall, purplish brown twigs with large buds, larger male catkins in early spring, dry to wet site; 'Weeping Sally' ('Pendula'), lovely weeping tree with pendulous branches on grafted trunk, silver catkins, shiny narrow foliage, 6 to 8 feet tall, 4 to 5 feet wide. *S. chaenomeloides* (Japanese pussy willow), 12 to 15 feet tall, 3-inch, silvery catkins, red buds on glossy stems in winter, rapid grower, zones 4 to 9. *S. melanostachys* (black pussy willow), black catkins, red stems, zones 4 to 9.

Purple osier: 'Nana' ('Gracilis'), 5 feet tall, fine-textured; 'Pendula', weeping mound, to 2 or 3 feet tall, useful as a groundcover if not grafted; sometimes grafted to use as a small weeping tree; 'Streamco', 10 to 15 feet tall, weeping, purple stems root at the ground to form dense thicket; bred for stabilizing stream banks. *S. alba* 'Britzensis' (coral embers willow), brilliant orange-red stems, to 4 to 5 feet if cut back each year, otherwise becomes a tree.

SAMBUCUS RACEMOSA
European Red Elder

The cutleaf and gold-leaf forms of this vigorous shrub and its relatives offer a bright feathery grace unequaled by other shrubs. The lush leaves are divided into seven feathery leaflets and may be further cut into a fine-textured lace. Dome-shaped clusters of lacy, white flowers bloom in early summer and ripen into tight clusters of shiny, red berries in midsummer. European red elder attracts birds, which feed on the berries and nest in the dense foliage. Vase-shaped; to 9 to 12 feet if unpruned, 4 to 5 feet if pruned annually. Plant in wildlife garden to attract birds or in an edible landscape. Lovely along a woodland edge, in a mixed border, or used as a fast-growing hedge. Cutleaf forms are most ornamental. Gold-leaf forms are striking in mixed border with a dark green background.

SAMBUCUS RACEMOSA 'PLUMOSA-AUREA'

Site: Full sun to light afternoon shade. Gold-leaf forms need protection from hottest sun, especially in the South. Fertile, well-drained but moist soil best; green forms tolerate dryness, but growth not as beautiful or vigorous. Zones 3 to 8.
How to Grow: Take hardwood or softwood cuttings. New plants may die back, but usually recover rapidly and grow vigorously once established.
  Tolerates heavy pruning. Best to cut back to 6 inches tall every year to encourage showiest growth. For a taller plant, prune back to woody framework each year. Borers can kill stems.
Cultivars and Similar Species: 'Sutherland Gold', cut, golden leaves, lime green in shade; 'Plumosa-Aurea', cut, chartreuse leaves, yellow flowers, red berries; 'Laciniata', ferny, green leaves; 'Tenuifolia', needlelike leaves. *Sambucus nigra* (European elder), 10 to 20 feet, five-leaflet compound leaves,

6-inch, lacy, white, flat flower clusters in early to midsummer, needs light shade; 'Albo-Variegata', green leaves with creamy edges, white flowers, black berries; 'Marginata', silver-edged leaves; 'Aureo-marginata', yellow-edged leaves; 'Purpurea' (*S. nigra* var. *porphyrophylla* 'Guincho Purple'), dusky purple leaves, pink flowers. *S. canadensis* (American elderberry), creamy white flowers.

SORBARIA SORBIFOLIA (SPIRAEA SORBIFOLIA)
Ural False Spirea

This cold-hardy shrub deserves to be more widely grown. It blooms in midsummer, producing upright, feathery, white plumes that resemble the flowers of the perennial astilbe. The foot-long, feathery leaves are bold and ornamental, emerging with a reddish cast early in spring, turning green in summer, and

SORBARIA SORBIFOLIA

dropping in fall with no color change. Clump-forming multistemmed shrub; 6 to 10 feet tall and wide. Needs growing space. Best in a mass planting because of suckering tendency. Use for erosion control on a bank. Can be invasive.

Site: Full sun to light shade. Best in fertile, humus-rich, moist soil; tolerates a drier site, but growth is stunted. Zones 3 to 8.

How to Grow: Plant balled-and-burlapped plants in spring, summer, or fall, spacing 4 feet apart. Take softwood or hardwood cuttings. Remove old flower heads to improve appearance. Blooms on new growth; prune heavily in early spring. Usually pest-free.
Cultivars: Only the species is grown.

SPIRAEA SPP.
Spirea

Bumald spirea (*Spiraea japonica* 'Bumalda') is a popular shrub that offers gardeners a neat, compact shape, fine-textured, blue-green foliage with good fall color, and pretty blossoms in summer. The 1-inch, toothed leaves emerge pinkish red in

SPIRAEA THUNBERGII

early spring, mature to green, and turn red-orange in fall. Flat clusters of rose-pink blossoms decorate the plants in early to midsummer, longer if deadheaded. In winter, the plant is a twiggy, fine-textured mass of red-brown stems. The colored-leaf forms with gold or lime green leaves are popular, but overuse does not detract from their beauty. Rounded mound; 2 to 3 feet tall and 5 feet wide. Use as a specimen or plant in groups in a mixed border or foundation planting. Combine gold-leaf forms   *continued*

SPIRAEA SPP.
(continued)

with purple-leaf plants for long-lasting color.

The first of the spireas to bloom, in very early spring Thunberg spirea (*S. thunbergii*) decks its slender twigs and branches with clusters of tiny, snow white flowers before the leaves emerge. After blossoms fade, the narrow, light yellow-green leaves provide a nice color and textural contrast to other shrubs. Foliage turns yellowish orange to bronze in late fall. Arching; to 3 to 5 feet tall and wide. Makes an attractive informal hedge or screen. Use as a specimen in the shrub border.

Site: Full sun; Bumald spirea also tolerates light shade. Average to humus-rich, moist but well-drained soil. Thunberg spirea prefers more fertile soil. Plentiful moisture. Both hardy in zones 4 to 9.

How to Grow: Plant bare-root shrubs in late winter or early spring; balled-and-burlapped or container plants in spring, summer, or fall. Space Bumald spiraea 3 to 4 feet apart and Thunberg 4 feet apart. Suckering plants may be dug up and divided in early spring. Take softwood cuttings of Thunberg in early summer. Remove blossoms of Bumald spirea as they fade to promote continuous flowering through summer.

Bumald spirea blooms on new growth. May be cut nearly to the ground to renew. Cut out oldest stems at ground level, annually in early spring to encourage best bloom and control size and suckering.

Thunberg spirea blooms on old wood. Thin oldest stems and weakest new growth at ground level annually, immediately after blooming, to maintain arching shape; never shear. Cut to ground to renew.

Bumald spirea subject to many insects and diseases, including fireblight, powdery mildew, leaf spot, caterpillars and aphids; usually not seriously troubled. Aphids sometimes trouble Thunberg spirea.

Cultivars and Similar Species: Bumald spirea: Other cultivars of *S. japonica*—'Anthony Waterer', semiupright to 3 feet, 5-inch, carmine red flowers, some leaves variegated with yellow; plant is variable; 'Froebelii', similar to 'Anthony Waterer', but brighter pink flowers and a bit taller; 'Crispa', crinkled leaves, 2 to 3 feet; 'Goldflame', 2 to 3 feet, new growth orange-gold, maturing to light green in summer, copper-orange in fall, pink early-summer flowers; 'Limemound', lemon yellow new growth matures to lime green, orange-red in fall, mounded to 3 feet. *S. japonica*, the species, 4 to 5 feet tall, rose-pink summer flowers, ½-inch, toothed, blue-green leaves, plant quite variable; 'Shibori' ('Shirobana'), rose-pink, white, and pink flower clusters on the same plant, 3-to-4-foot mound; 'Norman', deep rose-red flowers, burgundy fall color, 3-foot mound. *S.* × 'Goldmound', golden new leaves, golden-green in summer, pink flowers early summer; sunburns in heat of the South; zones 4 to 8.

Thunberg spirea: *S.* × *vanhouttei* (bridal-wreath), vase- or fountain-shaped shrub, to 7 feet tall with cascades of 2-inch clusters of white flowers in mid spring with the tulips, dainty, wedge-shaped, blue-green leaves, no fall color, rust fungus often disfigures leaves; zones 3 to 8; 'Renaissance', rust-resistant. *S. prunifolia* 'Plena' (bridalwreath), old-fashioned shrub covered with tiny, double, white flowers before the leaves in early spring, glossy, green leaves with reddish fall color; rust fungus often disfigures leaves; zones 5 to 9. *S. nipponica* 'Snowmound', white flowers covering dense 3- to 4-foot mound in early summer.

STEPHANANDRA INCISA 'CRISPA'

Cutleaf Stephanandra, Lace Shrub

Admired for its lovely, fine-cut leaves and tidy low shape, cutleaf stephanandra is an attractive and useful shrub. The three-lobed, triangular leaves are about 1 inch long and emerge reddish in spring, mature to bright green in summer, and turn red-purple or

STEPHANANDRA INCISA 'CRISPA'

orange-red in autumn. Flowers are pastel yellow-green and, while not showy, add a note of texture and color in early summer. Winter reveals an entrancing tangle of slender, reddish, arching, and zigzagging branches that look pretty set off by snow. The arching stems root where they touch the ground, forming a dense growth. Cascading mound; 2 to 3 feet tall and wide. Excellent shrub for the foreground of a border or foundation planting. Mass plant on banks for erosion control.

Site: Full sun to light shade. Fertile, moist, well-drained soil with a pH of 6.0 to 7.5. Plentiful moisture. Zones 5 to 8.

How to Grow: Plant balled-and-burlapped or container plants in spring, summer, or fall, spacing 3 feet apart. Softwood and hardwood cuttings root easily. Twigs may be winter-killed in the North. Prune out deadwood and thin lightly in spring. Usually pest- and disease-free.

Cultivars: The species grows to 4 to 7 feet high and much wider; much less common than 'Crispa'.

SYMPHORICARPOS ALBUS
Snowberry

Grown for its snow white berries, which last from fall through winter, snowberry is a garden curiosity rather than a showpiece. The berries form in clusters along the stems and persist from fall through winter. Leaves are oval to lobed, 2 inches long, and dark blue-green on top and hairy underneath. Tiny, bell-shaped, reddish white flowers bloom in summer, but are inconspicuous

SYMPHORICARPOS ALBUS VAR. LAEVIGATUS

because they occur on the shrub's interior. Rounded to spreading; 4 to 6 feet tall and wide. Use this suckering shrub as a bank cover to control erosion or grow it for its interesting fruit.

Site: Full sun to part shade. Average to poor, well-drained soil with a pH of 6.0 to 7.5. Tolerates heavy soil and drought. Zones 3 to 6.

How to Grow: Plant balled-and-burlapped or container shrubs in spring, summer, or fall, spacing 3 feet apart. Softwood cuttings root easily in early summer. Grows rapidly, but must be pruned. Best to prune to the ground every few years in early spring. Powdery mildew may infect leaves, and fungal diseases may infect stems and berries; destroy infected parts. Aphids and scale sometimes troublesome.

Similar Species: *Symphoricarpos albus* var. *laevigatus*, taller plant, larger berries. *S. × chenaultii* (Chenault coralberry), lovely fine-textured shrub with tiny pink flowers in summer, ¼-inch, pink-and-white berries in clusters in fall and winter; zones 5 to 8; 'Hancock', rose-red berries, low-spreading; to 2 feet tall and 6 feet wide, small leaves.

SYMPLOCOS PANICULATA
Sapphire Berry, Asiatic Sweetleaf

With the brightest, truest blue of any berry, a sapphire berry plant in full fruit in autumn becomes a jewel of the landscape. Unfortunately, birds can strip the plant of its berries in a few days. Fuzzy, fragrant, creamy white flowers in 3-inch clusters look

SYMPLOCOS PANICULATA

lovely combined with the bright green leaves in early summer. Foliage drops with no color change. Tall, open, multistemmed shrub or small tree; 15 to 20 feet tall and 10 to 20 feet wide. Plant in groups in a naturalistic or wildlife garden. Use as a tall background hedge or a small specimen tree.

Site: Full sun best for shrub form; tolerates light shade, but grows more open and treelike. Average to heavy, well-drained, acid to neutral soil. Plentiful moisture. Zones 6 to 8.

How to Grow: Plant container shrubs in spring, summer, or fall, spacing 8 to 10 feet apart or 3 feet for a hedge. Take softwood cuttings in early summer. Plants self-sow and easily transplant. May need cross-pollination from another shrub to set fruit; plant several shrubs.

Prune to remove deadwood. Prune to a tree shape if desired. Renew shrubs by cutting a third of the stems to the ground each year for three years. Occasionally troubled by leaf spot or insects, but never serious.

Similar Species: *Symplocos tinctoria*; similar native species, berries less showy, rarely cultivated.

SYRINGA SPP.
Lilac

There's room in any garden for the small, tidy Meyer or dwarf lilac *(Syringa meyeri)*. Common lilacs grow tall and rangy, but this dense shrub is always pretty, neat, and floriferous—even when young. The fragrant, tiny violet or violet-pink flowers are borne in 3- to 4-inch-long, densely packed clusters that smother the shrub with color in mid spring. New leaves open purplish and mature to 1- to 2-inch-long, wavy-edged, bright green ovals that turn yellowish in autumn. Rounded and broad; 5 to 6 feet tall and 8 to 12 feet wide. Excellent informal hedge or specimen. Nice winter silhouette.

Brought to the new world by the settlers, the common lilac (*S. vulgaris*) is loved for its romantic *continued*

SYRINGA SPP.
(continued)

SYRINGA VULGARIS

fragrance. A well-grown specimen is gorgeous in bloom in mid spring, but is not distinctive the rest of the year. Often it grows into a tall, straggly plant with blossoms only at the top of the bush. In humid climates, the wedge-shaped, velvety green leaves become disfigured in late summer by mildew. Flowers may be single or double and form in dense pyramidal clusters in shades of pink, lavender, lilac, purple, blue, magenta, white, and rarely yellow. Single-flowered types produce more flower heads, but the double-flowered heads are fuller and showier. Common lilacs tend to sucker prolifically, forming a thicket of stems that require constant pruning. Upright; to 20 to 25 feet tall. Mass-plant as a tall screen or border background, or use as a specimen in a shrub border.

Site: Full sun. Meyer lilac prefers average soil, common lilac moist, humus-rich soil; both with pH 7.0 to 8.0 (apply lime where soil is acid). Meyer lilac best with moderate moisture; tolerates drought. Meyer lilac, zones 4 to 8, does well throughout country, tolerates heat and drought. Common lilac, zones 3 to 7, in Zone 8 carefully select cultivars, needs winter chill for best performance.

How to Grow: Plant bare-root plants in early spring; container or balled-and-burlapped plants in spring, summer, or fall. Space common lilac 8 feet apart. Cuttings are difficult to root except commercially. Older common lilac shrubs may be grafted onto privet; privet suckers must be removed.

Meyer lilac does not need regular pruning; if needed, thin to control size immediately after blooming. Carefully remove faded flowers of common lilac to promote better bloom and reduce mildew. Cut out one-third of the oldest branches and any weak, thin canes and suckers each year immediately after blooming. To rejuvenate, cut all stems to 1 foot from the ground and select the strongest ten new stems.

Meyer lilac does not suffer from mildew as does common lilac. Powdery mildew often serious for common lilac in the East, less of a problem in the West where not humid. Scale insects and borers also common.

Cultivars and Similar Species: Meyer lilac: 'Palibin' (*S. palibiniana*), purple-red buds open to pale pink flowers, shorter plant. *S. microphylla* (littleleaf lilac), similar with hairy, 1-inch-long leaves, fragrant flowers in dense 2-inch clusters; sometimes available as a small grafted tree; zones 5 to 7. *S. patula* (dwarf Korean lilac) resembles a small common lilac with fragrant, 3-inch, pale lilac-purple flower clusters in late spring; 2-inch, mildew-resistant leaves, yellow fall color; zones 3 to 8; 'Miss Kim', smaller plant with pale ice blue flowers. *S. × persica* (Persian lilac), 4 to 8 feet tall, violet flowers, zones 4 to 8.

Common lilac: 2,000 named cultivars. The French hybrids are 200 heavily scented cultivars bred in France, most with double blossoms; plants do not sucker as freely, grow 8 to 15 feet tall, 6 to 12 feet wide. Common or French lilacs—'Belle de Nancy', double, pink flowers; 'Katherine Havemeyer', double, lavender-pink; 'Madame Lemoine', double, white; 'Annie Shiach', purple; 'Ami Schott', cobalt blue; 'Ludwig Spaeth', deep purple; 'Monge', purple; 'Michael Buchner', medium blue; 'Primrose', creamy yellow; 'Sensation', purple-red edged with white. Low-chill lilacs for zones 8 to 9—'Angel White', white; 'Big Blue', purple-blue; 'Blue Skies', light blue; 'Lavender Lady', lavender.

S. × hyacinthiflora, cold-hardy hybrid developed in Manitoba, compact, nonsuckering, free-flowering, fragrant, blooms earlier than common lilac; 'Mount Baker', 10- to 12-foot mound of single, white blossoms, excellent cultivar; 'Excel', soft pink; 'Assessippi', pale lavender; 'Esther Staley', lavender-pink; 'Maiden's Blush', light pink; 'Pocahontas', dark purple. *S. × prestoniae*, cold-hardy to Zone 2, tall, late-blooming; 'Miss Canada', red buds opening pink; 'Donald Wyman', wine-red; 'Isabella', pink.

TAMARIX RAMOSISSIMA
Five-Stamen Tamarisk, Odessa

This seashore plant creates a graceful, feathery texture on a tough site. The scalelike foliage is

TAMARIX RAMOSISSIMA

light apple green or blue-green, dropping in autumn after turning yellow. Tiny, rose-pink flowers are borne in airy, 1- to 3-foot-long terminal clusters that last for a month or more in early to midsummer, then bloom sporadically through fall. Plants look coarse and ungainly in winter when bare of leaves. Spreading and vaselike; to 10 to 15 feet tall and wide. Best used in seashore gardens.

Site: Full sun. Well-drained, light, acid soil best; tolerates sandy soil. Zones 4 to 9; salt-tolerant.

How to Grow: Plant container plants in spring, summer, or fall, spacing 8 or more feet apart. Take softwood or hardwood cuttings; fresh seed germinates immediately. Do not fertilize. Blooms on new growth. Cut to the ground in late winter every year, or every few years, to keep small; will flower that same year. Mildew, scale, and stem canker a problem; root rot if grown too wet.

Cultivars and Similar Species: 'Summer Glow', deep pink flowers, silver-blue leaves; 'Rosea', rose-pink, late-flowering. *Tamarix parviflora* (small-flowered tamarisk), similar but flowers in late spring and early summer on previous year's growth; prune after flowering; zones 5 to 9.

VIBURNUM SPP.

Viburnum

Nothing equals Korean spice viburnum *(Viburnum carlesii)* when it comes to perfuming the spring garden. The flowers produce an intense, sweet clove fragrance. This is a semisnowball type of viburnum, with the flower clusters opening into half-spheres made up of tightly packed, funnel-shaped flowers. Bright pink buds open to pale pink flowers that mature to white. Leaves are oval, 1 to 4 inches long, slightly hairy and dull green. Fall color is not dependable, but in good years is wine red. Rounded and stiff; to 5 or more feet tall and wide. Use in foundation planting or mixed border where the scent can be enjoyed.

Extremely showy when in bloom in late spring and again in fall when the fruit is fully colored, the large linden viburnum *(V. dilatatum)* attracts attention throughout the year. The blossoms drape the branches with creamy white lace, appearing in dense, flat, 3-to-5-inch-wide clusters atop the foliage—pretty to look at, but not to smell. The leaves are shiny, rounded, and dark green. They change to deep red in autumn. In fall, tiny, red berries form flat clusters that turn the shrub into a beacon of color, especially when accompanied by the fall leaves. Berries last through fall and often well into winter. Upright; to 8 to 10 feet tall and 6 to 8 feet wide. Use this large shrub in a border, as an informal screen or hedge, or against a wall. Plant more than one for best berry display. Locate away from house because of bad-smelling flowers.

VIBURNUM DILATATUM 'ERIE'

Valued for flowers and berries, the American cranberry bush *(V. trilobum)* is a plant for all seasons. The showy 4-inch, flattened flower clusters consist of tiny, fertile flowers surrounded by a ring of infertile, 1-inch, pure white flowers. The fertile flowers produce cranberry-size fruits that ripen in autumn into glossy, translucent, red berries that last well into winter. Berries have a musky, sweet taste and may be made into preserves. Leaves are toothed, three-lobed, and deep green like maple leaves. Fall color is light to dark red. Upright and spreading; to 8 to 12 feet tall and wide. Use as specimen shrub or massed in borders; makes fine screen or unpruned hedge. Plant in edible landscape or wildlife garden.

Double file viburnum *(V. plicatum* forma *tomentosum)* is a horizontally spreading shrub that looks elegant throughout the year. The branches are covered in late spring with pairs of flattened, creamy white flower clusters consisting of lacy, fertile flowers surrounded by a ring of infertile, showy, white flowers. Red berries decorate the branches in midsummer, but birds eat them. Leaves are also arranged double file along the branches, are glossy green with prominent veins, and turn reddish purple in autumn. Spreading; to 8 to 20 feet tall and 10 to 25 feet wide. Plant this large shrub as a specimen where its horizontal branches contrast with upright shapes. Looks lovely planted at the bottom of a slope or staircase, where the flowers can be seen from above.

Black haw *(V. prunifolium)*, a native, grows into a large, treelike shrub that is lovely on the edge of a woodland garden. Creamy white flowers bloom in late spring in 2- to 4-inch, lacy clusters that stand out against the glossy, dark green foliage. The oval, toothed leaves have a leathery texture and turn deep purple to scarlet in late autumn. The berry show is magnificent. In late summer the tiny berries, which grow in large clusters, ripen with a series of color changes: from pale green to yellow, to pink, to blue, and finally to black. They are then eaten by birds. Stiff and upright; to 15 feet tall and *continued*

VIBURNUM SPP.
(continued)

VIBURNUM TRILOBUM

12 feet wide. Use as shrub or small tree in a naturalistic or wildlife garden.

Site: Korean spice and double file viburnum best in full sun to part shade; linden in full sun to half shade; cranberry bush best in full sun, but tolerates half shade; black haw, full sun to light shade. Korean spice, linden, and cranberry bush like average to fertile, moist but well-drained, slightly acid soil; plentiful to moderate moisture. Double file viburnum best in humus-rich, moist but well-drained soil with plentiful moisture. Black haw prefers average to humus-rich soil, and tolerates drought. Korean spice viburnum hardy in zones 4 to 8; linden and double file viburnum, zones 5 to 8; cranberry bush, zones 2 to 8; black haw, zones 3 to 9.

How to Grow: Plant bare-root shrubs in early spring; balled-and-burlapped or container shrubs in spring, summer, or fall. Space Korean spice 3 to 4 feet apart, linden 5 feet apart, cranberry bush 4 to 5 feet apart, and double file and black haw 8 to 10 feet apart.

Korean spice and cranberry bush are easy to grow; double file is easy if kept moist. Plant two linden viburnum near each other for best fruit set; black haw also needs a pollinator.

Korean spice viburnum does not need regular pruning. To control size, thin immediately after blooming. Prune linden to remove deadwood and to control size in late winter, thinning carefully to maintain shape. Prune older cranberry bush by removing a third of the stems at ground level each year for three years. Do not prune double file regularly; rejuvenate old specimens by cutting to the ground in spring. Black haw rarely needs pruning; can be trained to tree form.

The Korean spice viburnum species is susceptible to mildew and leaf spot; many of the hybrids and related cultivars are not. Borers sometimes bother linden and double file viburnum. Cranberry bush may suffer aphids and borers; susceptible to twig blight in warm, humid areas. Scale and borers may trouble black haw.

Cultivars and Similar Species: Korean spice viburnum: 'Aurora', dark red buds open pink and turn white with excellent fragrance; 'Compactum', 3 feet tall, disease-resistant, dark green leaves. *V. × carlcephalum,* 6 to 10 feet tall, shiny, dark green leaves turn reddish purple in fall, 5-inch semisnowballs of fragrant, white flowers open from pinkish white buds. *V. ×* 'Cayuga', 5-inch white flower clusters from pink buds, highly fragrant, disease-resistant, small, dark green leaves. *V. × juddii* (Judd viburnum), open, rounded shrub, to 6 to 8 feet, 3-inch white flower clusters from pink buds, highly fragrant, disease-resistant. *V. ×* 'Eskimo', 4-inch, white snowball-like heads of tubular flowers, dark semievergreen foliage, horizontal branches, red to black berries in late summer; disease-resistant; 4 to 5 feet tall, zones 6 to 8. *V. × burkwoodii* 'Mohawk', fragrant, semisnowball-like, white flowers open from dark red buds, compact growth, glossy, dark green leaves turn orange-red in fall, zones 5 to 8, resistant to mildew and leaf spot.

Linden viburnum: 'Erie', 10 to 12 feet tall, red fall berries turn coral in winter, but are long-lasting, yellow to orange-red fall color; 'Catskill', compact, small leaves, good fall color, long-lasting dark red berries; 'Iroquois', dark scarlet, large, long-lasting fruit, dark green leaves, rounded, dense, 9-foot shrub, orange-red to maroon fall color; 'Oneida', flowers heavily in spring and sporadically all summer, dark red, long-lasting berries, pale yellow and orange-red fall color; 'Xanthocarpum', yellow or gold berries.

Cranberry bush: 'Compactum', upright to 6 feet, good flowers and fruit; 'Bailey', smaller dwarf than 'Compactum' with deep red fall color; 'Wentworth', late-ripening, long-lasting large berries, good red fall color. *V. opulus* (European cranberry bush), similar, leaves more toothed, little fall color, zones 3 to 8; 'Roseum' (European snowball), snowball-like flower clusters made entirely of sterile flowers, no fruit; 'Compactum', 5 feet, flowers and fruits well, Zone 4; 'Xanthocarpum', yellow fruit; 'Onondaga', compact with dark red new growth, purple-tinged summer leaves; 'Notcutt', large berries, maroon-red fall color.

Double file viburnum: 'Mariesii', popular cultivar, horizontal branching, showy flowers held high above the leaves, to 8 to 10 feet tall and 12 feet wide; 'Shasta', compact and floriferous, to 6 feet tall, 12 feet wide, larger snow white flowers; 'Shoshoni', dwarf form of 'Shasta', 4 feet tall and 6 feet wide, heavy fruiting; 'Summer Snowflake', flowers from summer through fall; 'Pink Beauty', flowers pink in cool climates. *V. plicatum* (Japanese snowball), sterile, 4-inch-wide, white flower clusters in double ranks on upright growth; 'Watanabe', 4 to 6 feet tall, white snowballs all summer.

Black haw: *V. rufidulum* (southern black haw), similar, with glossier, leathery leaves, to 8 feet tall, native to the Southeast, zones 5 to 9. *V. lentago* (nannyberry), native to the Southeast, more pointed leaves, forms a lower, suckering shrub. *V. cassinoides* (withe-rod), similar, but more shrubby, to 6 feet, pink and bright blue berries in fall, rich purple fall foliage, shade to sun, wet to moist soil, zones 3 to 6.

VITEX AGNUS-CASTUS
Chaste Tree

This late-blooming, large shrub brings violet-blue flowers to the garden in late summer. Tall spires of tiny blossoms stand up from the branches, contrasting with the silvery foliage. The aromatic leaves, which appear in late spring, consist of five to seven leaflets arranged like the fingers of a hand and are dark gray-green on top and silver-gray on the undersides.

VITEX AGNUS-CASTUS

They drop with little color change in autumn. Trunk bark is light gray-brown and corky. Rounded shrub or multistemmed small tree; to 10 feet tall and wide in the North, to 20 feet tall in South. Excellent in a border or foundation planting.

Site: Full sun. Well-drained, average to sandy soil; tolerates drought. Zones 6 to 9; may die to ground in zones 6 and 7. Thrives in heat.
How to Grow: Plant container shrubs in spring, summer, or fall, spacing 5 to 10 feet apart. May die back in exceedingly cold winters; wait until new growth appears, then cut out dead portions or cut to ground. Can train to a small multitrunk tree in the South.
  Remove deadwood annually. Regrows rapidly and blooms the same year if cut back hard in spring. Blooms on new growth. Thin previous year's growth on mature shrubs in spring to encourage vigorous growth and bloom. Usually pest-free and disease-free.
Cultivars and Similar Species: 'Alba', white flowers; 'Rosea', pink; 'Abbeville Blue', deep blue. *Vitex agnus-castus* var. *latifolia*, wider leaves, larger flowers.

WEIGELA FLORIDA (W. ROSEA)
Old-Fashioned Weigela

Blooming in late spring and early summer, when most of spring's dazzle is spent, weigela blooms in such abundance that the flowers can bend the arching stems toward the ground. The funnel-shaped, 1-inch-long, pink, rose-red, or white blossoms appear in clusters along the stems, contrasted with the lush foliage. Leaves are oval and pointed, 3 to 4 inches long, and hold their green color through late fall, dropping with little color change. Plants may bloom again lightly in fall. Vase-shaped to rounded with long,

WEIGELA FLORIDA 'VARIEGATA'

arching branches; to 6 to 9 feet tall and 9 to 12 feet wide. Use this somewhat ungainly shrub in informal gardens, as a specimen in a shrub border, or mass-plant as an informal hedge. Cultivars with purple or variegated foliage make excellent contrast to green shrubs in summer. Use purple foliage plants with red-flowered weigelas.

Site: Full sun to half shade. Best in well-drained, humus-rich soil with a pH of 6.0 to 7.5. Moderate moisture. Tolerates poor, dry site. Zones 5 to 9; some cultivars to Zone 4.
How to Grow: Plant bare-root shrubs in early spring, balled-and-burlapped or container plants in spring, summer, or fall, spacing 4 to 5 feet apart. Softwood cuttings root easily. Easy to grow.
  Prune immediately after flowering every year or few years; remove at ground level branches that flowered to keep shrub vigorous and in good form. Usually pest-free and disease-free.
Cultivars: 'Pink Princess', bright lavender-pink flowers, purple-edged leaves, Zone 4; 'Bristol Ruby', red flowers fading to purple, long-blooming; 'Java Red', compact to 4 feet, purple-red new leaves, maturing to red-flushed green, deep red flower buds open dark pink; 'Vanicek', deep crimson-red flowers, Zone 4; 'Variegata', green leaves with wide, irregular, yellow or white edge, rose flowers; 'Variegata Nana', 3 feet, white-edged leaves, pink flowers; 'Minuet', dwarf to 3 feet, purple-tinged leaves, profuse light rose-purple flowers, Zone 3; 'Red Prince', red flowers do not fade to purple; 'Tango', compact to 2 feet, wine-purple leaves, red flowers, Zone 4; 'Candida', white flowers, light green foliage; 'Bristol Snowflake', pink-tinged white flowers.

EVERGREEN TREES AND SHRUBS

ABIES CONCOLOR
White Fir

The most adaptable and among the prettiest of the firs, white fir is an elegant, stiffly symmetrical evergreen. Its soft gray-green to silvery blue-green needles *continued*

Evergreens

ABIES CONCOLOR
(continued)

ABIES CONCOLOR 'CANDICANS'

curve upward and are 1½ to 2½ inches long. Immature cones are purplish and mature to 5-inch-long, light brown cones. White fir is native to the mountains of the West. Densely conical; to 35 to 50 feet tall and 15 to 30 feet wide. Locate as a specimen in a lawn or border where branches can sweep to the ground. Makes a lovely contrast with dark evergreens and pastel-flowered shrubs and trees.

Site: Full sun to part shade. Moist, well-drained, sandy loam. Does poorly in wet or clay conditions. Tolerates some drought; other firs generally need cool, moist soil and low humidity. Zones 4 to 8; best in the North and Pacific Northwest where cool. *Abies concolor* is best fir for Midwest and East.
How to Grow: Plant container or balled-and-burlapped trees in spring or fall, spacing according to mature size. Keep soil cool with mulch. Most firs are grafted to rootstocks of *A. fraseri* or *A. balsamea,* therefore performing poorly in the South and Midwest; firs grafted to *A. firma* perform better in the South and Midwest.

Tends to form a double leader when young; remove weakest one. Do not

remove lower branches; do not remove top. Will not resprout from old, leafless wood. No major pests or diseases.
Cultivars and Similar Species: Large: 'Candicans', bright silver-blue, narrow and upright; 'Violacea', silvery blue.

Dwarf: 'Compacta', bright blue, to 3 to 4 feet tall and wide.

A. firma (Momi fir), only fir that does well in heavy soil and heat; needles are dark green on top, light green on undersides, to 50 feet, zones 5 to 8. *A. balsamea* (balsam fir), shiny, dark green needles, strong balsam fragrance, narrow pyramid, to 50 to 75 feet tall and 20 to 25 feet wide, zones 2 to 6; best in the North. *A. homolepis* (Nikko fir), attractive, pale green needles, dense, to 30 to 50 feet tall; zones 5 and 6. *A. koreana* (Korean fir), compact, to 15 to 30 feet tall, rich green needles with silver undersides, beautiful red-and-chartreuse male and female young cones, zones 5 to 7; 'Horstmann's Silberlocke', silvery effect from twisted needles that expose silver undersides, compact; 'Aurea', dwarf, compact, golden form. *A. nordmanniana* (Nordmann fir), black-green needles, tiered, downward-sweeping branches, 60 feet tall, zones 5 to 7. *A. fraseri* (Fraser fir), narrow pyramid to 40 feet, glossy, dark green needles, good in high elevations of the South and in the North, moist well-drained acid soil, favorite Christmas tree, zones 3 to 7. *A. lasiocarpa* (Rocky Mountain fir, alpine fir), pale blue-green needles, gray to chalk white bark, narrow pyramid, tolerates dry heat and light soil; 'Glauca', silver blue; 'Compacta', nice, blue dwarf.

AUCUBA JAPONICA
Japanese Laurel

Bold-textured, 4- to 8-inch-long, glossy, oval, dark green leaves give aucuba a lush tropical look. The popular variegated forms with gold-spotted leaves bring exciting color to the garden. In autumn, large, glossy, red berries form on female plants and

last through winter. Upright shrub; to 8 feet tall and 6 feet wide. Excellent shrub for shady gardens. Use boldly speckled cultivars with caution—they can be gaudy. Types with subtle variegations or narrow leaves are elegant in the garden.

AUCUBA JAPONICA

Site: Part, light, or heavy shade. Protect from hot afternoon sun during the growing season and full sun in winter. Well-drained, moist, humus-rich soil. Moderate moisture best; tolerates some dryness. Zones 7 to 9.
How to Grow: Plant container or balled-and-burlapped shrubs in spring or fall, spacing 3 to 6 feet apart. Suffers from winter burn in coldest parts of its range. Female plants need a male nearby to set berries.

Cut back stems every few years before growth starts to maintain size and shape. Stem dieback due to a fungal infection may be a problem.
Cultivars: 'Crotonifolia', leaves finely speckled with gold, may be male or female; 'Salicifolia', fine-textured, narrow green leaves with toothed margins, female plant; 'Mr. Goldstrike', bold, gold-splashed leaves, male plant; 'Variegata', bright gold flecks and spots on dark green leaves, female. 'Crassifolia', large, green leaves, male plant; 'Macrophylla', large, green leaves, female plant.

BERBERIS JULIANAE
Wintergreen Barberry

Lustrous, dark green leaves on this handsome barberry are long and narrow—about 3 inches long and ½ inch wide—with spiny margins. Showy, yellow flowers bloom in mid spring, followed by blue-black berries.

BERBERIS JULIANAE

The evergreen leaves may take on bronze or wine-red hues during winter. Mounded shrub; 6 to 8 feet tall and wide. Excellent barrier or hedge.

Site: Full sun to light shade. Moist, well-drained, slightly acid soil, zones 6 to 9.
How to Grow: Plant container or balled-and-burlapped shrubs in spring or fall, spacing 3 feet apart for a hedge, 5 feet for a specimen. Protect from winter sun and wind, especially in the North, as leaves may burn. Avoid pruning—it disfigures the plant. Renew by cutting to within several inches of the ground. Pest- and disease-free.
Cultivars and Similar Species: 'Nana', smaller and dense; 'Spring Glory', new growth bright red. *Berberis verruculosa* (warty barberry), handsome, low mound, to 5 feet, fine-textured, hollylike, spiny evergreen leaves, thorny stems, showy yellow flowers, blue-black berries; part shade. *B.* × *mentorensis* (Mentor barberry), semievergreen hybrid, between the deciduous *B. thunbergii*

and the evergreen *B. julianae*, has fine-textured, leathery, blue-green leaves with a few spines, leaves turn reddish and drop in early winter in cold areas, small yellow flowers in mid spring; tolerates hot, dry climates, zones 5 to 9.

BUXUS SEMPERVIRENS
Common Boxwood

Neat and tidy, the oval leaves of common boxwood are no more than 1 inch long and half as wide. Dark green on top with light or yellow-green undersides, they grow in pairs, densely cloaking the square stems. Tiny, white flowers bloom in spring and give off a distinctive scent. Rounded to broad-spreading; to 15 or

BUXUS SEMPERVIRENS

more feet tall and wide. This slow-growing shrub often is used to create elegant walled gardens in the South. Grow as formal or informal hedge, low edging, or in foundation plantings.

Site: Full sun to part or light shade; afternoon shade in the South. Fertile, moist, acid to slightly alkaline, well-drained soil. Zones 6 to 8.
How to Grow: Plant container or balled-and-burlapped shrubs in spring or fall, spacing 3 feet apart for a hedge, 5 or more feet for a specimen. Protect from winter wind and sun. Mulch well to protect shallow roots.

Pruning boxwood can be an art form. Thin branches in spring to maintain fluffy appearance or shear for formal effect. Leave unpruned for a magnificent cloudlike effect. Blight, leaf spot, mealybugs, mites, and scale insects can be problems. Root rot occurs in poorly drained sites, causing yellow top growth.
Cultivars and Similar Species: 'Elegantissima', green leaves with creamy margins, upright; 'Suffruticosa' (edging box), dense, compact, and low-growing; 'Vardar Variety', Zone 4. *Buxus microphylla* (littleleaf box), leaves slightly shorter and narrower, rounded shrub, to 4 feet tall and wide, turns yellow-green in winter. *B. m.* var. *koreana* (Korean box), leaves less than ½ inch long, loose, open shape, zones 5 to 8; 'Wintergreen', stays bright green in winter; 'Green Mountain', upright shape, good for hedges. Hybrids— 'Green Gem', rounded dwarf with good green color, Zone 5; 'Antarctica', dark green all year, oval to 5 feet, Zone 4; 'Green Mountain', cone-shaped, to 5 feet, good green color all year, Zone 5.

CALOCEDRUS DECURRENS
Incense Cedar

Popular in the Pacific Northwest, this fast-growing native tree is tough and adapts to many climates. In the mountains of the West Coast, it grows as a broadly conical tree, but cultivated types usually form a narrow column with deeply furrowed, reddish bark and short side branches, which are strong and don't break under snow. The graceful fans of scalelike, lustrous, emerald green foliage emit a spicy fragrance when crushed and during hot weather. The distinctive cones are tapered, ¾-inch-long cylinders with several scales that ripen and release seeds in fall. Columnar; to 30 to 50 feet tall and 10 feet wide. Stiff and formal. Use a single plant as a strong upright accent, *continued*

Evergreens

CALOCEDRUS DECURRENS
(continued)

but best planted in groups because of narrow shape. An excellent tall screen.

CALOCEDRUS DECURRENS

Site: Full sun to part shade. Best in moist, deep, well-drained acid soil; tolerates heavy and infertile soil. Plentiful moisture best; tolerates drought. Zones 5 to 8; tolerates heat and humidity and urban conditions.
How to Grow: Plant container or balled-and-burlapped trees in spring or fall, spacing 5 to 6 feet apart for a screen, 12 feet for a specimen. Occasional deep watering when young encourages deep roots and future drought-resistance. Needs no pruning; do not remove lower limbs or top. May be sheared for a hedge. May suffer from heart rot and mistletoe.
Cultivars: 'Columnaris', the commonly grown form.

CAMELLIA JAPONICA
Camellia

Leathery, glossy, green foliage and waxy flowers in shades of pink, red, and white have made this a favorite warm-climate shrub, but new cold-hardy hybrids are now thriving in gardens farther north. Oval leaves are about 5 inches long, 1 inch wide, and taper to a point. This open-branched shrub blooms for about six weeks in late winter and early spring, boasting numerous 3- to 5-inch-wide flowers with a circle of showy, yellow stamens in their centers. Flowers may be single, semidouble, or fully double, and some have ruffled petals. They are excellent for cutting. Dense pyramidal shrub or small tree; to 15 feet tall.

Use camellia as a specimen in foundations or borders, mass-plant in an open woodland, or espalier against a wall. The hybrids and *Camellia sasanqua* make best landscape plants because they are denser.

CAMELLIA JAPONICA

Site: Best in part shade; tolerates full shade and full sun. Fertile, humus-rich, moist, acid soil. Plentiful moisture. Zones 7 to 9.
How to Grow: Plant container or balled-and-burlapped shrubs in spring or fall, spacing 5 feet apart for a mass planting, 10 or more feet for a specimen. Remove unsightly faded flower heads immediately. Mulch to protect shallow roots. Prune to thin, if needed to control size, after flowering. Spider mites sometimes troublesome.
Cultivars and Similar Species: More than 2,000 cultivars; favorites include: 'Pink Perfection', double, shell pink; 'Debutante', pale pink, peony form; 'Elegans', rose-pink, 5-inch, anemone form; 'Tomorrow', large, semidouble, red; 'Purple Dawn', purplish red double.

C. sasanqua (Sasanqua camellia), 2- to 3-inch flowers in late fall and early winter, dense shrub, to 25 feet, zones 7 to 9; 'Bonanza', deep red; 'Sparkling Burgundy', ruby-rose; 'Daydream', white and pink; 'Yuletide', scarlet. Cold-hardy hybrids with *C. oleifera* (tea-oil camellia) and *C. sasanqua:* 'Winter Series', lustrous small leaves, brown bark, single, double, or semidouble, lavender, pink, rose, or white flowers in autumn, rounded and dense, to 20 feet, hardy to Zone 6. Spring-blooming, cold-hardy hybrids with *C. japonica* will be available.

CEDRUS SPP.
Cedar

A bit open and angular when young, Atlas cedar (*Cedrus atlantica*) ages well, becoming a grand specimen with upreaching top branches, low-sweeping, horizontally spreading lower branches, and a massive trunk. Similar to the Lebanon cedar, Atlas cedar is more open and sparsely branched and has a taller crown. Needle color varies

CEDRUS DEODARA 'AUREA'

from dark green to blue-green. The ¾- to 1½-inch-long, stiff needles form dense tufts along the upper sides of branches. The popular blue Atlas cedar has silvery blue needles. The blocky, ornamental female cones are blue-green, 3 inches long with a concave tip, and take two years to ripen. Slow to moderate growth. Stiff and pyramidal when young, becoming irregular and flat-topped with age; to 60 feet tall and 30 to 40 feet wide, can reach 120 feet with great age.

Deodar cedar (*C. deodara*) is an elegant favorite in hot, dry climates. Graceful when young, it forms a dense, broad pyramid, with semipendulous branches and leader, which identifies the tree from a distance. Older trees develop a picturesque, spreading, flat top with the lower branches sweeping the ground and then reaching upwards. The sharp-pointed, bluish green needles are 1½ to 2 inches long—the longest of the cedars—and have a soft, feathery look. Large, egg-shaped, 3- to 4-inch tall female cones take two years to mature and are bluish maturing to red-brown. Fast-growing. Pyramidal; to 50 to 80 feet tall and 30 to 40 feet wide.

The North African cedar-of-Lebanon (*C. libani*) matures into a magnificent specimen. Its massive lower trunk branches into several leaders that nod near their tips and have tiers of wide-spreading horizontal branches that sweep the ground. Young trees are bright green, and mature trees are dark gray-green. The stiff, sharp-pointed needles are ¾ to 1½ inches long and borne in dense tufts. In fall, yellow-brown male cones and purplish female cones decorate the branches. Slow-growing; pyramidal when young, becoming irregular with horizontal branches with age; to 50 feet tall and wider than tall, 80 or more feet with great age.

Elegant specimens for large properties. Locate where ground-sweeping branches have room and where silhouette can be appreciated.

Site: Atlas cedar likes full sun to part shade; deodar and Lebanon cedars need full sun. Atlas cedar best in fertile, moist, acid, well-drained soil, but tolerant of any well-drained soil, including alkaline. Give deodar well-drained, average to dry soil. For Lebanon cedar, deep, well-drained, fertile soil is best. All three tolerate drought when established. Atlas cedar hardy in zones 6 to 9; good in the South. Deodar cedar, zones 7 to 9; tolerates wind, heat, and drought, best cedar for the South, good in the Southwest. Cedar-of-Lebanon, zones 5 to 7, Zone 8 in the West; best with dry air; does not tolerate air pollution.

How to Grow: Plant container or balled-and-burlapped trees in spring or fall, allowing space for mature spread. Branches may break under heavy snow. Purchase named cultivars of deodar cedar; seedling trees variable in form.

Shorten long branches of young Atlas cedars when new growth begins to harden to encourage side branching and later strength. Remove multiple leaders when young. Remove lower limbs to reveal bark, if desired. Spread of deodar cedar may be controlled by cutting back new growth on side branches by half. Branches up to 12 inches around resprout if pruned back, but will not resprout from leafless wood. Do not prune cedar-of-Lebanon.

Weevils, tip blight, borers, and root rot occasional problems for Atlas cedar. Deodar cedar may suffer weevils, canker, or cold damage. Cedar-of-Lebanon usually problem-free.

Cultivars and Similar Species: Atlas cedar: 'Glauca' (blue Atlas cedar), silvery blue; 'Glauca Pendula', silvery blue needles, weeping branches, stake for an upright trunk; 'Aurea Robusta', yellowish new needles, bluish inner needles; 'Fastigiata', upright branches, dense form, silvery blue needles.

Deodar cedar: Large—'Aurea', yellow needles turning golden-green; 'Albospica', new growth ivory turning yellow, inner needles bright green;

'Gold Cone', narrower form, golden needles; 'Klondike', lime green in summer, golden in winter; 'Sander's Blue', powder blue new growth darkens to gray-blue; 'Shalimar', cold-hardy in Zone 6. Intermediate—'Aurea Pendula', weeping form of 'Aurea'; 'Pendula' ('Prostrata'), grows along the ground or drapes if trained; 'Kashmir', silvery blue-green, 20 feet tall, more cold-hardy. Dwarf—'Snow Sprite', compact and mounding, ivory new growth turning yellow, part shade.

Cedar-of-Lebanon: Intermediate—'Pendula', narrow, irregular column, long, weeping branches if staked, dark green needles. Dwarf—'Sargentii', spreading mound to 6 feet tall. *C. libani* subsp. *brevifolia* (Cypress cedar), similar, with smaller needles and cones, shorter stature, slow-growing. *C. libani* subsp. *stenocoma*, pyramidal and stiff, dark green; cold-hardy to Zone 5.

CEPHALOTAXUS HARRINGTONIA
Japanese Plum Yew

Resembling a yew with pointed needles, this small, dark green

CEPHALOTAXUS HARRINGTONIA 'PROSTRATA'

conifer makes an excellent shade-tolerant choice for a foundation planting—and it is *continued*

Evergreens

CEPHALOTAXUS HARRINGTONIA
(continued)

reportedly deer-proof. The 1- to 2-inch-long needles are flat, shiny, and dark green with a bold texture and are arranged in two ranks along the stems, forming a V-shaped pattern. Fruit is oval, olive-brown, 1-inch-long, naked seeds. Varies from a spreading, 6-foot-tall shrub to a pyramidal, 25-foot-tall tree.

Site: Full sun to full shade. Tolerates most moist, well-drained soils, sand to clay; withstands heavier soil than yews. Zones 6 to 9; excellent in the South; tolerates more heat than yews.
How to Grow: Plant container or balled-and-burlapped plants in spring or fall, spacing according to use and cultivar size. May suffer from winter-burn in full sun in the North. Slow-growing, rarely needs pruning. May be sheared if desired. Resprouts from old, leafless wood if cut back hard. Mites sometimes troublesome.
Cultivars and Similar Species: 'Fastigiata', narrow and upright to 8 feet tall and 6 feet wide, needles spirally arranged; 'Prostrata', spreading, to 2 to 3 feet tall and wide. *Cephalotaxus harrington* var. *drupacea*, large, spreading, bushy mound. *C. fortunei*, upright and rounded, to 10 to 20 feet tall, 3-inch-long needles.

CHAMAECYPARIS SPP.
False Cypress

In its native Northwestern habitat, Lawson false cypress (*Chamaecyparis lawsoniana*) grows into a massive tree. But most garden subjects are dwarf forms with colorful foliage. The deep green, gray-green, or golden scalelike leaves are arranged in flattened sprays held in vertical or horizontal planes, creating a soft, layered appearance. Small blue-green cones ripen to reddish brown.

Pyramidal to conical; the species can be 60 feet tall and 30 feet wide, but cultivars are smaller. Use colorful forms as specimens for year-round foliage in foundation plantings or shrub borders. Use the species and subdued types as screens or hedges.

Nootka false cypress or Alaska cedar (*C. nootkatensis*) is native to the coast of Alaska and the Pacific Northwest. It's a tall, slow-growing timber tree, especially popular in gardens for its graceful weeping and dwarf forms. Scalelike leaves are usually dark blue-green to gray-green, and branches are slightly pendulous. Conical; to 40 or more feet tall and 15 to 20 feet wide. Makes a graceful, dramatic specimen in lawn or border. Use as a screen instead of hemlock.

CHAMAECYPARIS OBTUSA 'AUREA'

Hinoki false cypress (*C. obtusa*) features elegant, scalelike, glossy, dark green leaves with white crosses on the undersides. The trunk bark of older specimens becomes reddish brown and shredded. Pyramidal; to 50 feet tall and 20 feet wide; cultivars smaller. Species makes an excellent screen. Use the colorful cultivars as accents in a shrub border or foundation.

The species form of Sawara false cypress (*C. pisifera*) is rarely grown in gardens, but its many cultivars are

popular. The Filifera types have pendent branches with a stringy, threadlike texture. Plumosa types have a plumed effect. Squarrosa types have soft-to-the-touch, pointed needles that are billowy and mosslike. Numerous cultivars exist. Pyramidal; to 60 feet tall and 20 feet wide; cultivars smaller. Dwarf forms are excellent in foundation plantings and mixed borders. Combine colors carefully.

Site: Lawson best in full sun to part shade, Nootka and Sawara need full sun; Hinoki best in full sun to afternoon shade. Humus-rich, well-drained, moist, acid to neutral soil is best. Lawson performs poorly in heavy soil. Nootka and Sawara like plentiful moisture. Lawson false cypress hardy in zones 5 to 8; performs poorly in the East, best in the West where cool and moist. Nootka false cypress, zones 5 to 7; tolerates heat and humidity; good in the Midwest. Hinoki and Sawara, zones 5 to 8; best in humid areas.
How to Grow: Plant container or balled-and-burlapped trees in spring or fall. Space Lawson cypress 3 feet apart for a 10-foot-tall dense hedge; space other types 8 to 10 feet apart for screen, 6 to 20 feet apart for specimen use, depending on cultivar size. Protect dwarf and colored-leaf forms from winter wind and sun to prevent burning. Older inner foliage may turn brown without dropping; remove by hand if unsightly.

New shoots do not grow if pruned into bare wood. New growth of Lawson may be sheared for a hedge; top at 10 feet. Hinoki is best left unpruned. False cypress does not resprout from leafless wood, but resprouts from older wood containing foliage.

Roots of Lawson false cypress highly susceptible to phytopthora fungus. Nootka usually pest-free. The others may get mites if too hot and dry.
Cultivars: Lawson: Many cultivars. 'Oregon Blue', blue needles, resistant to phytopthora; 'Ellwoodii', columnar, dense, feathery needles, gray-green in

summer, steel-blue In winter; 'Golden King', rounded when young, becoming pyramidal, to 35 feet tall, golden color; 'Pendula Glauca', upright if staked, arching and weeping, blue-green branches; 'Lanei', golden, upright and compact; 'Dragon Blue', upright and compact, bright blue-gray; 'Minima Glauca', rounded 3-foot shrub, dense blue-green needles.

Nootka: Tall—'Glauca', blue-green foliage; 'Glauca Pendula', blue-green, weeping; 'Variegata', blue-green needles with yellow variegations; or 'Variegata', white-splashed foliage, slightly weeping; 'Aurea', new growth tinged gold, pyramidal; 'Pendula', graceful weeping curtains of dark green branches, to 25 feet; 'Green Arrow', extremely narrow column; 'Sullivan', weeping, dense and full, shade-tolerant. Dwarf—'Compacta Glauca', narrow pyramid to 6 to 10 feet, blue-green; 'Globosa', rounded.

Hinoki: Large—'Crippsii', broadly pyramidal, golden yellow new growth, bright green interior. Intermediate—'Aurea', outer portions of fans gold, inner foliage dark green; 'Tetragona Aurea', brilliant yellow, narrow pyramid with tufted branches. Dwarf—'Nana', slow-growing, rounded, to 3 feet tall, eventually larger, dark green tufted sprays; 'Nana Lutea', similar to 'Nana', but with golden new growth; 'Kosteri', irregular pyramid with twisted, layered branches, tufted, light green foliage; 'Nana Gracilis', pyramid, to 10 feet tall, dense, tufted, dark green foliage in sculptural, twisted fans; 'Filicoides', irregular pyramid, to 10 feet, long, pendulous, green foliage clusters.

Sawara: Filifera type—'Filifera', slow-growing, green, to 10 feet; 'Filifera Aurea', bright yellow, excellent texture, faster-growing, to 20 feet; 'Filifera Aurea Nana', similar but slow-growing, to 5 feet; 'Golden Mop', bright gold-yellow all year, slow-growing mound, to 3 feet. Squarrosa—'Boulevard', deep silver-blue in light shade, dense dwarf pyramid, useful when young. Plumosa—'Plumosa', full-size tree; 'Plumosa Aurea', dwarf, golden yellow outer needles; 'Plumosa Nana', pillowlike globe to 5 feet tall and twice as wide; 'Juniperoides', compact, conical, to 10 feet, with soft, feathery, creamy yellow new growth maturing to light green.

COTONEASTER SPP.
Cotoneaster

A gracefully arching and cascading low shrub, bearberry cotoneaster (*Cotoneaster dammeri*) is an all-seasons plant. The oval leaves are lustrous dark green, about 1 inch long, and may take on an attractive purplish tinge during winter or drop off in the coldest areas. Small, white flowers with red anthers decorate this groundcovering plant in late spring and are followed by tiny, bright red berries in autumn. Grows to 2 feet tall and 6 feet wide. Plant as a facing shrub, fast-growing groundcover on a slope, or to cascade over a wall.

COTONEASTER DAMMERI

The leathery leaves of willowleaf cotoneaster (*C. salicifolius*) measure up to 4 inches long and about ½ inch wide, and are beautifully textured with a netting of veins. Winter's cold may tinge leaves purplish. In spring, 2-inch-wide, flat clusters of tiny, creamy flowers decorate limbs. Small, red berries ripen in fall and usually look showy all winter. Arching shrub; to 10 to 15 feet tall and 8 to 12 feet wide; low-growing cultivars most popular. Use the species as a border shrub; plant low-growing types as groundcovers, facing shrubs, or on a fence, or let cascade over a wall.

Site: Full sun. Cotoneaster tolerates most well-drained soils; willowleaf needs moist, well-drained acid to neutral soil. Both hardy in zones 6 to 9.
How to Grow: Plant container or balled-and-burlapped shrubs in spring or fall, spacing 3 feet apart for groundcover types, 4 to 6 feet apart for specimens, depending upon ultimate size. Fallen leaves may be difficult to clean from branches. Cut back selected branches as needed to control size. Bearberry suffers fewer pests and diseases than other cotoneasters, especially in the South, but still susceptible to lacebugs, scale, mites, and fire blight. Willowleaf susceptible to leaf spot, canker, scale, and spider mites, but less prone to fire blight.
Cultivars: Bearberry cotoneaster: 'Coral Beauty' ('Royal Beauty'), vigorous, heavy berry set; 'Lowfast', 1 foot tall.

Willowleaf cotoneaster: 'Emerald Carpet', compact, whiter flowers, good fruit set; 'Repens' ('Repandens'), trailing to weeping, to 2 feet tall and 6 feet wide, good purple winter color; 'Scarlet Leader', low-growing, to 3 feet high, red-purple winter color.

CRYPTOMERIA JAPONICA
Japanese Cedar

This outstanding tree and its numerous cultivars are the best conifers for the South. The species grows into a tall tree with branches all the way to the ground. The short, glossy needles are arranged spirally in plumelike clusters along slightly pendulous, spreading branches, which create a distinctive texture. The leaves are awl-shaped, four-sided, slightly twisted scales and are ¼ to ¾ inch long. Bright green to blue- *continued*

CRYPTOMERIA JAPONICA
(continued)

CRYPTOMERIA JAPONICA

green during the growing season, they turn bronze-blue to reddish in winter. Bark on the tall, straight trunk is red-brown and shredding. The round, 1-inch cones are dark brown. Pyramidal to conical; 50 feet tall and 25 feet wide, taller with age. Use as a specimen, a screen, or plant in groves.

Site: Full sun at the coast; part to light shade in the North and inland. Deep, fertile, moist, acid soil. Plentiful moisture; suffers during drought. Zones 6 to 9; best with high humidity.
How to Grow: Plant container or balled-and-burlapped trees in spring or fall, spacing 10 to 12 feet apart for screen; 25 to 35 feet for grove or specimen, depending on cultivar size. Protect from wind, especially in winter; foliage may burn in winter in coldest areas. Remove dead inner needles if they don't fall naturally.

May be pruned as a hedge if thinning cuts are made into wood containing foliage; do not shear. Branch dieback, leaf blight, and leaf spot sometimes troublesome.
Cultivars: Purchase named cultivars; unnamed seedlings are variable and ungainly.

Large: 'Elegans', burgundy-plum winter color; 'Yoshino', bright blue-green in summer, no inner dead foliage, resists fungus, cold-hardy, needs no pruning; 'Angelica', vigorous, fine, dense foliage, cold-hardy and less susceptible to winter burn; 'Benjamin Franklin', dense, good screen, rich green with no inner dead foliage, resists wind, salt spray, and fungus; 'Lobbii', long, deep green needles, dense, compact and sculptured; 'Sekkan Sugi', new growth creamy yellow, matures to dark yellow, slightly weeping.

Intermediate: 'Elegans Nana', soft, feathery,1-inch, green needles turn red-brown in winter, 3-foot globe; 'Globosa Nana', 3-foot dome, blue-green in summer, rusty red in winter; 'Jindai Sugi', compact, light green all year, slow-growing column, to 10 feet.

× CUPRESSOCYPARIS LEYLANDII
Leyland Cypress

Fast-growing, this graceful conifer is a naturally occurring hybrid of *Chamaecyparis nootkatensis* and

× *CUPRESSOCYPARIS LEYLANDII*

Cupressus macrocarpa. Soft, scalelike leaves are pressed into ropelike bunches along the stems, forming flattened, feathery fans like the Nootka cypress. Growth is dense, with branches to the ground. Columnar to narrowly pyramidal; grows as much as 3 feet a year to 65 feet tall and 15 feet wide; taller with age. It makes an effective, fast-growing screen, windbreak, or pruned hedge, even in part shade. Where disease and pest problems are serious, substitute *Juniperus chinensis* 'Spartan' or *Thuja plicata* 'Hogan'.

Site: Full sun to part shade; tolerates full shade, but is less dense. Best in fertile, moist site, but adapts to most soils, acid or alkaline. Plentiful moisture best. Zones 6 and 7 to 9; heat- and salt-spray-tolerant; good in the South and along the seashore.
How to Grow: Plant container or balled-and-burlapped trees in spring or fall, spacing 3 feet apart for hedge, 6 feet for screen, farther for specimen use. Young trees susceptible to winterkill in Zone 6. Container plants transplant better than balled-and-burlapped.

Remove multiple leaders when young to prevent breaking apart in winter storms with maturity. Shear in early summer for a hedge. Bagworms and canker are serious in some areas.
Cultivars and Similar Species: 'Castlewellan', new growth golden yellow, bronze in winter, 20 feet; 'Emerald Isle' ('Moncal'), dense, dark green, 25 feet; 'Naylor's Blue', bright gray-blue in summer, especially blue in winter, loose-branching, to 35 feet; 'Contorta', twisted branches; 'Silver Dust', subtle creamy variegations. *Cupressus macrocarpa* (Monterey cypress), distinctive, picturesque, flat-topped dark green conifer native to the West Coast, canker serious, zones 8 to 9 in the West; use along the coast; use cultivars in mixed borders; 'Golden Pillar', dwarf, slender cone with vertical fans, golden outer foliage, chartreuse inner foliage; 'Golden Cone', dwarf, cone-shaped, intense gold foliage.

Evergreens

CUPRESSUS ARIZONICA VAR. GLABRA
Smooth Arizona Cypress

The braided-looking branches of this fast-growing, dense tree consist of tiny, pointed scales pressed against the stems. Their color varies from gray-green to blue-green, with

CUPRESSUS ARIZONICA VAR. *GLABRA* 'BLUE ICE'

the blue cultivars being the most beautiful and popular. The trunk bark is shiny, reddish brown, and peels off in flakes. The round cones are about 1 inch around. Pyramidal; to 35 feet tall and 15 to 20 feet wide. Use as a specimen or screen, especially in difficult hot, dry locations. Good replacement for Rocky Mountain juniper where disease is a problem.

Site: Full sun. Well-drained, heavy to light, alkaline to acid, dry soil; drought-tolerant. Zones 7 to 9; good in the South and Southwest; thrives in heat. May be short-lived in the East unless carefully sited.
How to Grow: Plant container or balled-and-burlapped trees in spring or fall. Space to 6 feet apart for screen, 12 to 15 feet for specimens. Remove competing leaders when young. Resents heavy pruning or shearing. Bagworms may be a problem; less susceptible to blight than junipers.

Cultivars and Similar Species: 'Carolina Sapphire', blue needles, popular in the South; 'Blue Ice', powder-blue needles, reddish twigs, narrow and conical to 30 feet or taller and 8 feet wide; 'Blue Pyramid', compact pyramid, to 20 feet and 10 feet wide, outstanding gray-blue.

DAPHNE SPP.
Garland Flower, Winter Daphne

Probably the most popular of daphnes, the sweet-smelling garland flower *(Daphne cneorum)* becomes a mound of color when in full bloom in mid spring. Tight clusters of flower buds tipping the branches are deep pink, opening to rose-pink, four-petaled flowers. The fine-textured, evergreen leaves are shiny, dark green on top and gray-green on the

DAPHNE ODORA 'VARIEGATA'

undersides, growing on low-spreading branches that form a neat mound throughout the year. Rounded and compact; to 2 feet tall and twice as wide. Use in rock gardens, to cascade over walls, or as a groundcover. Excellent massed along a walk.

Winter daphne *(D. odora)* is the most fragrant. It has a sweet, lemony scent. The small, rose-purple blossoms appear in tight, 1-inch-wide clusters at the stem tips in late winter and early

spring. The leathery, dark green, shiny leaves are oval, about 2 to 3 inches long, and create a fine texture throughout the year. Rounded, dense shrub; to 3 to 4 feet tall and wide. Excellent in foundation plantings or shrub borders near walkways.

Site: Give garland flower full sun to half shade; winter daphne light to part shade. Garland flower needs sandy, well-drained soil with even moisture; must have perfect drainage. Winter daphne needs well-drained, moist, acid to alkaline soil. Garland flower, zones 4 to 7; winter daphne, zones 7 to 8.
How to Grow: Plant container or balled-and-burlapped shrubs in spring or fall, spacing 3 feet apart. Mulch garland flower well to keep soil cool. Protect from winter sun and wind. Protect winter daphne from snow-load in winter; may be short-lived.

Do not prune. Sudden death may result from poor drainage or drying out. Insects and diseases rarely a problem.
Cultivars: Garland flower: 'Pygmae Alba', white flowers; 'Ruby Glow', purple-pink; 'Eximia', blood red buds open rose-pink.

Winter daphne: 'Alba', creamy white flowers; 'Aureo-marginata', leaves edged with yellow or cream, petals creamy white with purplish undersides; 'Variegata', more pronounced yellow variegation, pale pink flowers.

EUONYMUS JAPONICA
Evergreen Euonymus

Grown for its beautiful year-round greenery, evergreen euonymus features a dense covering of 1- to 3-inch oval leaves with slightly toothed edges and a waxy, dark green sheen. The greenish white flowers bloom in early summer, but they are barely noticeable among the leaves. Nonshowy, orange-and-pink fruit develops in late summer. Upright to oval shrub; to 10 feet tall   *continued*

Evergreens

EUONYMUS JAPONICA
(continued)

EUONYMUS JAPONICA

and half as wide. Effective as screen or single shrub. Use as informal or formal hedge. Use dwarf forms for edging.

Site: Full sun to full shade; grows more loosely in shade. Tolerates heavy clay and sandy soils. Moderate moisture. Zones 8 to 9; tolerates seashore conditions.
How to Grow: Plant container or balled-and-burlapped shrubs in spring or fall, spacing 2 to 4 or more feet apart, depending on cultivar. Can be heavily pruned. Mildew, leaf spot, aphids, and scale sometimes problems.
Cultivars: 'Grandifolia', upright dense growth, good for sheared hedge; 'Microphylla', tiny leaves on dwarf plant, to 2 feet high; 'Microphylla Variegata', tiny, white-margined leaves, dwarf plant to 2 feet; 'Aureo-marginata', gold-edged leaves; 'Aureo-variegata', leaves blotched with yellow in centers; 'Silver King', dark green leaves with silvery white margins; 'Moness' ('Silver Princess'), white-margined leaves, dwarf plant to 3 feet.

GARDENIA JASMINOIDES
Gardenia

Pure white, waxy blossoms on the gardenia can perfume the entire garden when they bloom in summer. The many-petaled flowers are 2 to 3 inches across, larger in some cultivars. Blooming is heaviest early in summer, but sporadic blossoms appear throughout the season. The pointed leaves are lustrous, leathery, dark green, about 2 to 4 inches long and half as wide. The rounded shrub grows 4 to 6 feet tall and wide. Plant in foundation plantings, borders, and shade gardens. Locate where fragrance will be enjoyed.

GARDENIA JASMINOIDES

Site: Full sun to part shade. Humus-rich, moist, acid soil. Plentiful moisture. Hardy in zones 8 to 10.
How to Grow: Needs summer heat and constant moisture; mulch to keep soil moist. Feed monthly during growing season with acid fertilizer, fish emulsion, or blood meal.

Control size with selective pruning after blossoming ceases. Highly susceptible to nematodes, which may limit where it can be grown. Scale insects, mealybugs, whiteflies, and sooty mold also are problems.
Cultivars and Similar Species: 'August Beauty', dense upright form, to 5 feet tall and 3 feet wide, blooms spring through fall; 'First Love' ('Aimee'), upright form, 6-inch blossoms; 'Mystery', upright shrub, 5-inch flowers all summer; 'Radicans', dwarf to 1 foot tall and 2 to 3 feet wide, small leaves and flowers; use as groundcover; 'Radicans Variegata', same as 'Radicans', but with white-margined, gray-green leaves; 'Veitchii', flowers freely during the growing season, 4 feet tall; 'White Gem', single flowers, dwarf to 2 feet.

ILEX SPP.
Holly, Inkberry

Beloved as a cut green for winter holiday decorations, English holly (*Ilex aquifolium*) features glossy, dark green, spiny-edged leaves. Female trees produce clusters of glossy red berries that cling to the tree's branches throughout winter. This handsome pyramidal tree grows to 20 or more feet tall and 10 feet wide; it tolerates air pollution and urban conditions. Excellent in a formal landscape; allow plenty of room to mature. Plant as a screen or hedge.

ILEX AQUIFOLIUM

Chinese holly (*I. cornuta*) grows slowly and produces copious amounts of berries without being pollinated by a male plant. The fruit, which is showy all winter, may be bright red, light red, orange-red, or yellow. The spiny, dark green leaves are shiny. Rounded shrub; to 10 feet or more tall and wider than tall. Excellent shrub for mixed borders and foundation plantings, hedge, or security barrier.

The small, oval, dark to bright green leaves of Japanese holly (*I. crenata*) are about 1 inch long and have no spines. Japanese holly has the neat, fine-textured appearance of boxwood. Black berries develop in fall. Dense, rounded shrub to 10 feet tall and wide. Excellent in foundation plantings or as a hedge behind a formal flower border.

ILEX CRENATA 'HETZII'

Inkberry (*I. glabra*) is a native similar to Japanese holly, but with a medium texture and a more open shape. The fall fruit is glossy, black, and larger and showier than that of the Japanese holly. Upright to rounded, open shrub; to 8 feet tall and 10 feet wide. Use as an evergreen hedge or massed in the landscape. Excellent in problem soils.

The cold-hardy, tough hybrid blue or Meserve hollies (*I. × meserveae*) are hybrids of Chinese and English holly. Their shrublike size, neat, dark, glossy, blue-green leaves, and abundant bunches of long-lasting red berries have made them extremely popular. The berries remain showy all winter. Rounded to pyramidal; 15 feet tall and wide. Excellent in foundation plantings and as a background hedge.

Yaupon (*I. vomitoria*), an East Coast native holly, is easy to grow, fine-textured, and features striking scarlet berries and silvery gray bark. The berries ripen in fall and remain showy into spring. Upright to irregular large shrub or small tree; 15 to 20 feet tall. Use as a hedge, screen, or small tree in a foundation or shrub border.

Site: English holly grows in full sun to light shade; needs shade in the South. Chinese holly best in full sun to part shade. Inkberry and yaupon are fine in full sun to full shade. Blue holly best in half to light shade; tolerates full sun, but may dry out in summer in the South and winter in the North.

English holly prefers well-drained but moist, average to sandy, acid soil, with ample moisture. Chinese holly needs light, humus-rich, well-drained, acid soil; best with even moisture, but drought-tolerant. Japanese and blue holly best in average to light, well-drained, humus-rich, acid soil; blue holly needs moderate to plentiful moisture. Give inkberry moist, acid soil; tolerates wet conditions. Yaupon grows in average to light, acid to alkaline soil; tolerates wet to dry conditions.

English holly is hardy in zones 7 to 9; extra care needed in Southeast; tolerates air pollution. Chinese holly and yaupon also zones 7 to 9, but perform well in South; yaupon tolerates seashore conditions. Japanese holly, zones 6 to 8; tolerates urban conditions. Inkberry, zones 5 to 9. Blue holly, zones 5 to 8.

How to Grow: Plant container or balled-and-burlapped shrubs in spring or fall, spacing 2½ to 3 feet apart for sheared hedge; allow plenty of room for specimens, spacing according to ultimate size. Mulch hollies well to protect the shallow roots. Best fruit set occurs on female English, blue holly, and yaupon plants if pollinated by a male plant located no more than 100 feet away. Fertilize in late winter if berry set is poor. Protect from wind and sun in winter to prevent burned foliage. Inkberry may send up suckers.

Do not remove lower limbs of English holly; allow to branch to the ground; may be thinned or sheared in winter to control size; rejuvenate by cutting trunk to ground and selecting a new leader. Chinese holly may be thinned or sheared during dormancy, but shearing disfigures leaves until new growth fills in. Japanese holly responds well to thinning or shearing; for formal hedge, shear in late winter and again in midsummer; for informal hedge, thin as needed every year or more. Inkberry tolerates heavy shearing; cut back hard or to the ground when dormant to renew. Blue holly may be thinned when dormant. Yaupon withstands heavy pruning; leave unpruned for a picturesque plant; remove lower limbs to reveal bark.

English and blue holly troubled less by leaf miners, mites, and scale insects than are other hollies. Chinese holly may have problems with scale insects and leaf spots. Mites can trouble Japanese holly in dry areas. Inkberry and yaupon usually problem-free.

Cultivars and Similar Species: English holly: 'Argenteo-marginata', dark green leaves edged white, red berries; 'Ciliata Major', new growth purple, mature leaves bronze-green with long, curved spines, red berries; 'Gold Coast', gold-edged leaves, male; 'Sparkler', uniform pyramid, abundant bright red berries; 'Bacciflava', gold berries. 'Nellie R. Stevens', pyramidal, to 20 feet, orange-red fruit, fast-growing to 20 feet, mostly spineless, excellent in South; pollinate with 'Edward J. Stevens'.

Chinese holly: 'Burfordii', abundant red fruit, leaves have single small spine at tip, dense tree or shrub, to 20 feet; 'Burfordii Nana', slow-growing, to 8 feet, dark red berries, less fruitful; 'D'or', similar to 'Burfordii', but with yellow berries; 'Rotunda', spiny leaves, dense, to 4 feet tall, 6 feet wide, red berries; 'Rotunda Nana', smaller leaves. 'China Girl' hybrid, heavy set of red berries, bright green leaves, rounded, to 10 feet tall and wide, heat-tolerant, zones 6 to 9; pollinate with 'China Boy'.

continued

Evergreens

ILEX SPP.
(continued)

Japanese holly: 'Compacta', slow-growing, compact and rounded to 6 feet; 'Convexa', vase-shaped shrub, small, convex leaves, heavy berry set; 'Green Lustre', rounded, to 2 by 3 feet; 'Golden Gem', low and spreading, small, gold leaves; 'Hetzii', rounded, to 2 feet tall, 4 feet wide, shiny, convex, large leaves; 'Microphylla', small leaves, fast-growing, upright form.

Inkberry: 'Viridis', fast-growing, with upright stems; 'Compacta', small leaves, slow-growing and compact, but eventually becoming large; 'Ivory Queen', showy, white berries, intermediate size.

Blue holly: 'Blue Prince', 12-foot pyramid, lustrous leaves, purplish stems; 'Blue Princess', broad shrub, generous fruit set, slow-growing; 'Blue Maid' ('Mesid'), broad pyramid, hardy, large, red berries; 'Blue Stallion' ('Mesan'), no spines, good pollinator, pyramidal; 'Golden Girl' ('Mesgolg'), broad pyramid, yellow berries.

Yaupon: 'Nana', small leaves, slow-growing, 3- to 4-foot mound, eventually larger, red berries; 'Stoke's Dwarf', male, forms 4-foot mound of tiny leaves; 'Pendula', weeping form.

JUNIPERUS SPP.
Juniper, Red Cedar

The wild form of Chinese juniper (*Juniperus chinensis*) is rarely found in North American gardens, but popular dwarf or compact cultivars are. Foliage usually includes needlelike and scalelike leaves, ranging in color from green to blue-gray, but many cultivars exhibit golden needles. The cones are small, waxy, blue globes. The cultivars vary from compact trees to wide-spreading shrubs; most of the shrubs are now considered hybrids with *J. sabina* and are classified as *J. × media*. The species is conical; to 60 feet tall and 20 feet wide; cultivars

JUNIPERUS SCOPULORUM 'SKYROCKET'

are smaller and vary in size and shape. Excellent near foundations, in borders, and for hedges and screens.

Rocky Mountain juniper or western red cedar (*J. scopulorum*), a western native, looks similar to the native eastern red cedar (*J. virginiana*), but does not grow as large and retains its attractive color through winter. The scalelike leaves are green to blue-green; multiple trunks are covered with shredding, reddish bark. Its many cultivars make beautiful additions to dry gardens. Narrow pyramid; to 40 feet tall; cultivars shorter. Use for fine-textured vertical effect in a border or foundation planting; effective dense screen or hedge. Blue cultivars provide great color. 'Skyrocket' may be difficult to use effectively; groups of three make a nice statement.

The adaptable eastern red cedar (*J. virginiana*) is an underrated landscape subject because it is so common in the wild throughout the East. Leaves may be scalelike or needlelike and are dark green in summer, turning brown or yellowish in winter—improved cultivars have better winter color—and emit a cedar fragrance when crushed. The trunk features shredding, reddish brown bark. Female trees have attractive, waxy, blue, round cones that provide

food for wildlife. Pyramidal to columnar; 50 feet tall and 10 to 20 feet wide. Use as a windbreak, screen, or specimen in difficult sites.

Note: Low, spreading groundcover junipers are covered in Chapter 4.

JUNIPERUS VIRGINIANA

Site: Full sun. Chinese juniper grows best in moist to dry, well-drained soil; tolerates alkaline soil and drought. Rocky Mountain juniper best in average to sandy, well-drained, moist to dry soil; drought-tolerant; performs poorly in heavy soil. Eastern red cedar adapts to any well-drained soil, including sandy, gravely, or clay, acid or alkaline, and tolerates salt; best with moist conditions, but drought-tolerant.

Chinese juniper, zones 4 to 9; Rocky Mountain, zones 3 to 6; best in the West and North, performs poorly in the Southeast because of high humidity; eastern red cedar, zones 3 to 9, tolerates seashore conditions.

How to Grow: Plant container or balled-and-burlapped plants in spring or fall, spacing according to use and cultivar size. Do not overwater Chinese juniper. Narrowest forms of Rocky Mountain may need to be wrapped with twine in winter to prevent branches from opening and splitting under snow and ice. Do not plant eastern red cedar near apple orchard or crab apples.

Do not shear; thin to control size and maintain natural appearance. Resprouts from old, leafless wood if cut back hard to rejuvenate. Remove competing leaders of Rocky Mountain, if needed. Lower limbs of eastern red cedar may be removed as tree ages.

Some Chinese juniper cultivars suffer from juniper blight (phlomopsis) in some areas; others are totally blight-free; root rot develops in the West if overwatered. Juniper blight and cedar apple rust serious for Rocky Mountain juniper in some areas. Eastern red cedar usually problem-free; mites may occur in dry site. Cedar apple rust disfigures cedar trees, but seriously harms nearby apples, crab apples, and hawthorns.

Cultivars and Similar Species: Chinese juniper: Intermediate—'Hetzii Columnaris', green column, to 30 feet tall; 'Mountbatten', silvery green pyramid, to 20 feet; 'Wintergreen', rich green pyramid, to 15 feet; 'Torulosa' (Hollywood juniper), scalelike, green leaves, upright with twisted branches, to 25 feet; 'Blue Point', broad pyramid, to 12 feet tall, 8 feet wide, dense, blue-green foliage; 'Spartan', dense, green pyramid, to 15 feet tall, 5 feet wide; 'Robusta Green', loose and upright, to 15 feet tall, 6 feet wide, tufted, bright green needles; 'Mint Julep', mint green leaves, compact, upward arching branches, fountainlike to 5 feet tall, 7 feet wide. Dwarf—'Gold Coast', golden stem tips all year, compact spreading shrub, to 3 feet tall, 5 feet wide.

J. × *media* 'Hetzii', upright, spreading, to 15 feet tall and wide, scalelike, blue-green leaves; 'Old Gold', golden all year, spreading mound to 3 feet tall, 5 feet wide; 'Gold Star', gold-tipped branches, 4 feet tall, 6 feet wide; 'Pfitzeriana', scalelike, green leaves, wide-spreading branches at 45-degree angles, 6 feet tall, 12 feet wide; 'Pfitzeriana Aurea', golden stem tips in summer turn green in winter; 'Pfitzeriana Glauca', silver-blue; 'Ramlosa', dark green, like 'Pfitzeriana', but compact, to 4 to 5 feet tall and 6 to 8 feet wide; 'Seagreen', light green new growth, maturing to bright green, arching, vase-shaped, to 5 feet tall, 5 feet wide.

Rocky Mountain: 'Blue Heaven', blue year-round, pyramidal, to 20 feet, disease-resistant; 'Blue Trail', silver-blue column, to 18 feet; 'Medora', blue-green, narrow, dense column, adapted to cold and drought; 'Sutherland', silvery green column, to 18 feet; 'Wichita Blue', bright blue pyramid, to 20 feet, disease-prone; 'Skyrocket', extremely narrow column, to 15 feet tall, 2 feet wide, silver-blue all year, splits under snow and ice; 'Moonglow', intense silver blue, dense pyramid, to 20 feet; 'Silver Spreader', silver-gray, low, wide-spreading, to 3 feet tall, 6 feet wide; 'Winter Blue', steel blue, mounded to 2 feet tall, 4 feet wide.

Eastern red cedar: 'Cupressifolia', dark green foliage, dense, broad pyramid; 'Idyllwild', dark green, broad, informal pyramid, to 15 feet; 'Manhattan Blue', dark blue-green, dense, compact pyramid, to 12 feet tall, 7 feet wide; 'Princeton Sentry', blue-green, narrow column, to 25 feet; 'Emerald Sentinel', emerald green column, to 15 feet.

KALMIA LATIFOLIA
Mountain Laurel

Mountain laurel brings the East Coast woodlands into beautiful bloom for weeks in early summer. The 4-inch-long, oval, leathery leaves grow in whorls around the stems. Clusters of pink flower buds open into 4- to 6-inch heads of crown-shaped, white or pale pink blossoms. Cultivars offer brighter blossoms in shades of deep pink and red. Old plants form picturesque, gnarled trunks. Rounded to irregular shrub; 6 to 15 feet tall and wide. Plant in groups in shady borders or naturalize in woodlands.

Site: Full sun to full shade; most floriferous with sun. Well-drained, humus-rich, moist, acid soil. Plentiful moisture. Zones 5 to 9.

KALMIA LATIFOLIA

How to Grow: Plant container or balled-and-burlapped shrubs in spring or fall, spacing 3 to 5 feet apart, depending upon cultivar size. Leaves may turn yellow or burn in winter in too much sun. Mulch well to protect shallow roots. Remove flower clusters as they fade to promote good blooming next year.

Thin stray branches immediately after blooming, if needed. Cut to ground to rejuvenate. May be troubled by leaf spot, whiteflies, scale insects, borers.

Cultivars: 'Carousel', flowers banded with cinnamon-purple; 'Elf', dwarf with pink buds, white flowers; 'Heart's Desire', red buds open red with white margin; 'Olympic Wedding', pink buds, flowers banded with maroon; 'Ostbo Red', red buds open pink; 'Pink Surprise', medium pink buds and flowers; 'Raspberry Glow', burgundy buds, dark pink flowers; 'Sarah', red buds, red-pink flowers; 'Snowdrift', white flowers, compact plant.

LEUCOTHOE FONTANESIANA
Drooping Leucothoe

Native to streamsides in East Coast woodlands, drooping leucothoe is also a popular landscape evergreen. The leathery, lance-shaped leaves are 2 to 5 inches long and shiny, dark green with lighter undersides, arranged in a single plane *continued*

Evergreens

LEUCOTHOE FONTANESIANA
(continued)

LEUCOTHOE FONTANESIANA

along stems. Forms a low, spreading bush of long, unbranched, arching stems. New growth is often reddish; leaves may take on purple or red hues in cold months. In late spring, long clusters of bell-shaped, creamy white flowers blossom along stems and give off pleasant fragrance. Grows 3 to 6 feet tall and wide. Not usually eaten by deer. Excellent low shrub for massing in borders or naturalistic site, or for facing taller shrubs in borders. Mixes well with azaleas and rhododendrons.

Site: Part to full shade best; tolerates full sun in evenly moist soil. Well-drained, moist, humus-rich, acid soil. Plentiful moisture. Zones 5 to 9; best in shady, cool, moist situation.
How to Grow: Plant container or balled-and-burlapped shrubs in spring or fall, spacing 3 to 4 feet apart. Mulch well to retain soil moisture. Protect from winter sun in North. Prune in early spring, only if crowded or too large, by removing oldest stems at ground level and allowing new growth to fill in. Leaf spot and root rot can be serious.
Cultivars and Similar Species: 'Scarletta', new growth rich red,

matures to dark green, turns burgundy in winter; compact shape. 'Girard's Rainbow', new growth variegated pink, white, and copper; 'Nana', dense dwarf, to 2 feet tall and 6 feet wide; 'Lovita', small leaves. *Leucothoe axillaris* (coast leucothoe), similar, 2 to 4 feet tall and twice as wide, with zigzagging branches and white flowers, zones 6 to 9. *L. keiskei*, ground-hugging plant, new growth bright red, turning dark green in summer, rich red to burgundy in fall and winter, large, nodding, white flower clusters in summer, zones 6 to 9.

LIGUSTRUM JAPONICUM
Japanese Privet, Wax-Leaf Privet

This serviceable, dense shrub finds a niche in many southern gardens. The oval, deep green leaves, which are 2 to 4 inches long and half as wide, have a lustrous, waxy coating and contribute quietly to the garden all year. Small, fragrant, white flowers bloom in 6-inch-tall clusters in mid- to late summer (not everyone likes their aroma). Shiny, black berries ripen in fall and last through winter. Upright; to 15 feet tall and 6 to 8 feet wide.

LIGUSTRUM JAPONICUM

Site: Full sun to full shade. Tolerates most soils, except soggy ones. Zones 7 to 9; tolerates seashore conditions.

How to Grow: Plant container or balled-and-burlapped shrubs in spring or fall, spacing 3 feet apart for formal hedge, 5 to 6 feet for informal hedge or screen, and farther for specimen. Easy to grow. Responds well to shearing or thinning during dormancy, but looks best when thinned for a natural appearance. May be trained into a small, multitrunk tree by removing lower branches. Aphids, scale insects, whiteflies, and sooty mold can be troublesome.
Cultivars: 'Variegatum', deep green leaves edged creamy yellow to white; 'Korea Dwarf', small leaves 1 to 2 inches long, slow-growing; 'Rotundifolium', rounded leaves, dense, compact plant; 'Suwannee River', hybrid, compact mound, to 3 to 4 feet.

LONICERA NITIDA
Boxleaf Honeysuckle

Tiny, rounded leaves on this fine-textured evergreen to semievergreen honeysuckle are ½ inch long and densely cloak the

LONICERA NITIDA 'BAGGESEN'S GOLD'

stems. Tiny, slightly fragrant, white flowers blossom in spring, followed in late summer by small, purple fruit. Dense, rounded shrub; to 5 feet. Usually not troubled by deer. Useful as a sheared or informal hedge or background planting. Gold-leaf form is an excellent contrast in a border.

Site: Full sun to part shade; gold form has best color in full sun. Moist to dry, loamy soil. Zones 7 to 9.

How to Grow: Plant container or balled-and-burlapped shrubs in spring or fall, spacing 2 to 3 feet apart for a hedge, 5 feet apart for a specimen. Responds well to shearing and pruning. Remove dead inner twigs and branches, if needed. Renew by cutting to the ground in early spring. Aphids are sometimes a problem.

Cultivars and Similar Species: 'Baggesen's Gold', golden leaves and layered branches. *Lonicera pileata* (privet honeysuckle), often confused with *L. nitida*, but leaves are slightly larger, plant is lower and more spreading with horizontal branching, to 3 feet tall, shade-tolerant, zones 6 to 9.

MAGNOLIA SPP.
Southern Magnolia, Sweet Bay

The southern magnolia or bull bay (*Magnolia grandiflora*), the grand dame of southern trees, is revered for its plate-size, creamy white

MAGNOLIA GRANDIFLORA

flowers that emit a heady, lemony perfume. The cupped flowers bloom heavily in early summer and sporadically through the rest of the growing season. Bold-textured, oblong leaves are up to 10 inches long, shiny, dark green on top with light green or rusty undersides. Conelike seedpods ripen in autumn, splitting to reveal red-fleshed seeds. Low-branched columnar to pyramidal tree; to 60 to 80 feet tall and about half as wide. Use in a lawn or as screen or hedge.

Sweet bay (*M. virginiana*), a graceful, summer-blooming East Coast native, is evergreen in the South and semievergreen in the North. Spring growth is silvery and matures into 5-inch-long, oblong, dark green leaves with silvery undersides that flash in the breeze. Creamy white, 3-inch flowers dot the tree for a month or more in early summer, making a pretty statement and emitting a sweet, lemony scent. Cucumber-like fruit with orange-red seeds ripen in autumn. This shrub or multistemmed, open-branched tree grows to 50 feet tall in the South, 20 feet in the North. Use it as an understory tree in a wooded site or shade garden. Makes a good screen where evergreen.

Site: Southern magnolia, full sun to part shade; sweet bay, half to full shade. Humus-rich, moist but well-drained, acid soil. Plentiful moisture; both tolerate wet site; sweet bay tolerates swampy sites. Southern magnolia hardy in zones 7 to 9; hardy cultivars to southern Zone 6; sweet bay, zones 5 to 9.

How to Grow: Plant container or balled-and-burlapped trees in spring or fall, spacing according to mature size. Allow room for southern magnolia to mature. Seed-grown trees may not flower for years; best to purchase a named cultivar of southern magnolia. Pods and old leaves drop in late fall, creating litter. Protect both species from full winter sun and wind in northern parts of their range. Sweet bay suffers chlorosis in alkaline soil.

Southern magnolia most attractive if lower limbs are removed. Sweet bay needs no pruning. Both usually pest- and disease-free.

Cultivars and Similar Species: Southern magnolia: 'Majestic Beauty' ('Monila'), huge flowers and leaves; 'St. Mary', slow-growing, compact, to 20 feet, flowers heavily when young, leaves have rusty undersides; 'Samuel Sommer', 14-inch-wide flowers, fast-growing to 50 feet, leaves have rusty undersides; 'Little Gem', shrubby and slow-growing to 20 feet, small leaves with rusty undersides, 4-inch flowers bloom on young plants; 'Edith Bogue', compact pyramid, leaves have light rust on undersides, branches withstand ice storms, Zone 6; 'Bracken's Brown Beauty', compact, to 30 feet, small leaves have rusty undersides, 6-inch flowers, southern Zone 6; Spring Grove series, cold-hardy to Zone 6.

Sweet bay: *M. v.* var. *australis*, large-growing southern type; 'Henry Hicks', remains evergreen in the North.

MAHONIA BEALEI

MAHONIA AQUIFOLIUM
Oregon Holly Grape

Neither a holly nor a grape, Oregon holly grape is named for its large, spiny, green leaves that resemble English holly and its blue fruit that looks like grapes. The leaves are actually 12-inch-long *continued*

Evergreens

MAHONIA AQUIFOLIUM
(continued)

compound structures made up of 3-inch-long leaflets arranged in rows along a central rib. The shiny, leathery foliage is reddish when young and takes on purplish tones in winter. Bunches of golden flowers make a splash in mid spring, ripening in summer into clusters of dusky, blue berries that attract birds. Native to the moist woodlands of the Pacific Northwest, this evergreen finds a home in shady gardens. Varies from upright, open shrub to rounded and spreading; 4 to 6 feet tall. Makes a dramatic, bold-textured element in mixed borders.

Site: Light to full shade best in the North, shade or sun in the South. Humus-rich, moist, acid soil with plentiful moisture. Zones 5 to 9.
How to Grow: Plant container or balled-and-burlapped shrubs in spring or fall, spacing 3 to 4 feet apart. Protect from desiccating wind and sun, especially in winter. Mulch well to protect shallow roots. May get leggy with age; remove older bare stems to make room for new growth. Rust, leaf spot, scale insects, aphids, and whiteflies sometimes troublesome.
Cultivars and Similar Species:
'Compacta', 2 to 3 feet tall. *Mahonia bealei* (leatherleaf mahonia), blue-green leaves, fragrant, yellow flowers in late winter and early spring, blue berries in summer, zones 6 to 9. *M. repens* (creeping mahonia), groundcover spreading by stolons, 10 inches tall.

NANDINA DOMESTICA
Heavenly Bamboo

A relative of the barberry, this shrub is not a true bamboo, but its leaves and unbranched, straight stems are reminiscent of bamboo plants. New growth is often reddish purple and matures to blue-green compound leaves that consist of 4-inch-long, lance-shaped leaflets. The foliage, which may be semievergreen in cold climates, takes on reddish hues in winter. One-foot-long clusters of white flowers bloom at the stem tips in early summer and ripen into huge clusters of red berries in autumn; the berries look spectacular all winter and into spring. Plants spread by stolons into large clumps. Grows 6 to 8 feet tall; lower, compact forms more common. Use to contrast bolder plants in shade gardens. Plant as a specimen or in masses.

NANDINA DOMESTICA

Site: Full sun to full shade. Best in humus-rich, moist but well-drained soil. Tolerates poor, dry soil under trees. Zones 7 to 9; adapts to both humid and arid regions.
How to Grow: Plant container or balled-and-burlapped shrubs in spring or fall, spacing 2 to 4 feet apart depending upon cultivar size. May become chlorotic in alkaline soil. The species becomes leggy unless pruned; compact cultivars need less pruning. Prune oldest canes to ground level every year or two in late winter. Head back oldest canes so they are shorter than the inner canes to make a denser-looking plant and to hide lower parts of bare stems, if desired. Mildew may be a problem where humid.
Cultivars: 'Compacta', slow-growing to 5 to 6 feet, finer-textured leaves, reddish in winter; 'Harbour Dwarf', 18 inches tall, bronze-red in winter; 'Moyer's Red', leaves red in winter, 8 feet tall; 'Nana Purpurea', 18-inch mound, red-purple in winter; 'Fire Power', dense, 2-foot mound, brilliant red leaves in winter; 'Moon Bay', red stems, foliage fiery red in winter; 'Wood's Dwarf', 18-inch mound, orange-red winter color.

OSMANTHUS HETEROPHYLLUS
Holly Osmanthus, False Holly, Holly Olive

Often mistaken for holly, this shrub has similar spiny leaves, sometimes with pretty variegations. The shrub forms a dense evergreen mass. Inconspicuous flowers bloom in late summer and fall and emit a

OSMANTHUS HETEROPHYLLUS 'GULFTIDE'

powerful fragrance reminiscent of jasmine. The blue-black fruit is hardly noticeable. Rounded and upright shrub; to 10 or more feet. An excellent slow-growing hedge or barrier that forms an impenetrable mass. Use variegated forms as specimens to brighten shade gardens.

Site: Full sun to light shade. Heavy clay to average, well-drained, fertile soil. Tolerates slightly alkaline soil. Zones 7 to 9.

How to Grow: Plant container or balled-and-burlapped shrubs in spring or fall, spacing 3 to 4 feet apart for a hedge, farther for a specimen. Protect from winter wind. May be pruned for a formal hedge. Pest- and disease-free.

Cultivars and Similar Species: 'Gulftide', twisted, spiny leaves, dense and compact, to 6 feet; 'Variegatus', cream-edged, green leaves, compact, to 5 feet; 'Goshiki', new growth variegated with orange maturing to cream. *Osmanthus fragrans* (sweet olive), dense, 10-foot-tall shrub, fine-toothed leaves, fragrant, small, creamy flowers in summer, zones 8 and 9.

PHOTINIA SERRULATA

PHOTINIA × FRASERI
Red-Tip Photinia, Fraser Photinia

Common as a hedge in the Southeast and Southwest, photinia offers color all year. Spring growth is glossy, bright red and matures to 4-inch-long, lance-shaped, deep green leaves. Smaller flushes of growth in summer add splashes of red. The 6-inch clusters of white flowers have an offensive odor. Clusters of red berries, which ripen to black, look attractive from fall through winter. Upright shrub or small multistemmed tree; to 15 feet tall. Bold textured, colorful hedge, screen, or specimen; locate carefully because of flower odor.

Site: Full sun to full shade. Acid to alkaline, well-drained soil. Drought-tolerant, but best with plentiful moisture. Zones 8 and 9.

How to Grow: Plant container or balled-and-burlapped shrubs in spring or fall, spacing 4 to 5 feet apart for hedge, farther for specimen. Easy to grow. Prune flowers before they open to avoid odor. If foliage turns yellowish, fertilize with nitrogen.

Prune when young to encourage bushiness. Thin or shear annually before new growth begins for a hedge and for most colorful new growth. Sometimes troubled by leaf spot; provide good air circulation.

Similar Species: *Photinia serrulata* (Chinese photinia), parent of *P. × fraseri*, new growth less colorful, blooms earlier, zones 7 to 9. *P. glabra*, finer-textured leaves, new growth red, flowers smaller, later, zones 8 and 9.

PICEA SPP.
Spruce

Norway spruce *(Picea abies)*, an extremely popular European native, flourishes in cold climates. A young tree is stiffly pyramidal, but becomes graceful as it ages. Needles are stiff, dark green, ½ to 1 inch long, and bluntly pointed. The tree retains its lower branches all the way to the ground. Decorative, purple-red cones appear in spring and mature to 6-inch-long, brown cones. Pyramidal; reaches 60 feet tall and 30 feet wide. Allow room for full-size and dwarf types to grow to their mature sizes. Use large and intermediate types as windbreaks or specimens on large properties. Do not plant in front of a house; the tree overpowers the landscape.

Similar to the Norway spruce, white spruce *(P. glauca)* is a pale green

PICEA ORIENTALIS 'AUREA-SPICATA'

North American native. The cones are pale brown cylinders. Ultimately a large tree, white spruce forms a broad, dense pyramid when young and becomes spirelike with ascending branches when mature. The dwarf Alberta spruce is a popular dwarf form with feathery needles and a uniform shape. Pyramidal to columnar; to 60 feet tall by 20 feet wide. Site large trees carefully; use as specimens or screens. Use smaller types in borders and foundation plantings.

The most beautiful of the spruces, Serbian spruce *(P. omorika)* is a favorite among conifer afficionados. Its short, drooping branches curve upwards at their tips, giving the tree a distinctive form. Dark blue-green on top and gray-white on the underside, the needles are densely arranged on the upper surface of the branches and have a subtle two-tone effect. Young cones are blue-gray and mature to 2-inch-long, brown cylinders. Pyramidal with weeping branches; 60 feet tall and 25 feet wide. Excellent vertical accent in a border.

The elegant oriental spruce *(P. orientalis)* has a wonderful texture and glossy color. Extremely dark green and glossy, blunt-tipped needles are the shortest of the spruces and overlap, giving the tree a *continued*

Evergreens

PICEA SPP.
(continued)

dense, neat appearance. As on other spruces, the branches are somewhat ascending and the short branchlets become pendulous on mature trees. Young, red-purple cones add decoration in spring and mature to dangling brown cones in fall. Broadly conical; to 60 feet tall and 30 feet wide. Gorgeous texture and lustrous color. Use as a large specimen. Use golden forms to contrast with dark green evergreens.

PICEA PUNGENS

Colorado spruce (*P. pungens* var. *glauca*) is an extremely dense tree that forms a perfect pyramid. The stiff needles are about 1 inch long and may be dark green, gray-green, or blue-green in the species. Blue forms (Colorado blue spruce) may be blue-gray to steel blue to powder blue. Cones mature to light brown cylinders. Pyramidal, 60 feet tall and 25 feet wide. The stiff shape makes it difficult to integrate trees into the garden. Use as a specimen on large properties away from the front of the house. Don't crowd with other plants that could shade lower limbs. Use intermediate and dwarf types in borders and foundation plantings.

Site: Full sun best for Norway, oriental, and Colorado spruce; white and Serbian fine in full sun to part shade.

Give Norway spruce well-drained, moist, acid soil; best with plentiful moisture. White spruce best in moist loam, but tolerates poorer conditions, including drought. Serbian and Colorado spruce best in deep, fertile, well-drained soil with even moisture. Serbian tolerates acid or alkaline conditions; Colorado somewhat drought-tolerant. Oriental spruce, average to poor, rocky soil; good drainage a must.

Norway and Colorado spruce are hardy in zones 3 to 7; Colorado tolerates dry climates. White spruce, the most heat-tolerant, zones 2 to 8. Serbian spruce, zones 4 to 8, tolerates heat, humidity, and dry air. Oriental, zones 4 or 5 to 8, better than Norway spruce in Midwest and South.

How to Grow: Plant balled-and-burlapped trees in spring or fall, allowing plenty of room to reach mature size. Large trees transplant well.

Norway spruce does not tolerate wet soil. Protect dwarf Alberta spruce from wind, drought, and hot sun to prevent mites; provide good air circulation to prevent fungus. Mulch Serbian spruce to keep soil cool and moist. Can die for no apparent reason; probably from extreme soil moisture. Protect Oriental spruce from drying winter wind. Colorado spruce does not root well in heavy soil; can blow over in storms.

Prune spruces in early spring, cutting into new growth halfway, to encourage density, if desired. Remove lower branches if they die naturally, but tree looks best if branches are left to reach the ground.

Mites, aphids, bagworms, sawflies, borers, budworms, canker, and spruce gall may afflict spruces.

Cultivars and Similar Species: Norway spruce: Large—'Acrocona', pink young cones in spring, wide pyramid; 'Cranstonii', open pyramid with long, intertwining branchlets; 'Inversa', central leader with weeping branches;

'Reflexa', spreads on the ground with upward-reaching branch tips. Intermediate—'Clanbrassiliana Stricta', compact, broad pyramid; 'Hillside Upright', dark green, narrow pyramid. Dwarf—'Nidiformis' (bird's-nest spruce), dense and low-spreading, may burn in winter, dark green, reaches 5 feet tall and 7 feet wide in 50 years; 'Tabuliformis' (tabletop spruce), similar to bird's-nest spruce, but won't burn in winter; 'Pumila', mounded to globe-shaped, hardy.

White spruce: Large—'Caerulea', blue-green needles. Intermediate—'Densata' (Black Hills spruce), broad pyramid, heavy needles, moderate growth, suffers from mites if dry, good ornamental in the North, 30 feet tall with age; 'Pendula', light gray-green, narrow, weeping pyramid. Dwarf—'Conica' (dwarf Alberta spruce), fine-textured, light green needles, dense cone, slow-growing, but old plants reach 20 feet tall; 'Rainbow's End', similar to 'Conica', but creamy yellow growth in summer contrasts with green older needles, upright, narrow; 'Arneson's Blue', extremely blue with patches of green, conical. Miniature—'Gnom', bun-shaped, tiny needles.

Serbian spruce: Large—'Pendula', variable form with pronounced weeping habit. Intermediate—'Pendula Bruns', narrow and weeping. Dwarf—'Nana', dense, globose when young, becoming broadly pyramidal.

Oriental spruce: Intermediate—'Atrovirens', dark green; 'Aurea-spicata', creamy new growth turns bright yellow, then green; 'Skylands', new growth brilliant creamy yellow darkening to rich gold, slender. Dwarf—'Shadow's Broom', bird's nest shape, dark green; 'Gowdy', dense and narrow, dark green; 'Whittgold', golden new growth, green interior, dense cone.

Colorado spruce: Tall—'Bizon Blue', brilliant blue, dense; 'Fat Albert', pale silvery blue, dense pyramid; 'Koster', silver-blue to blue; 'Fastigiata', narrow. Intermediate—'Moerheim', irregular growth, not as stiffly symmetrical, blue all year; 'Foxtail', narrow, twisted branches with tufted ends, blue; 'Pendula', blue needles, weeping shape, central trunk; 'Procumbens', low, spreading across the ground. Dwarf— 'R. H. Montgomery', broad pyramid, blue; 'Globosa', rounded, blue.

PIERIS SPP.
Fetterbush, Japanese Pieris

Fetterbush (*Pieris floribunda*) is a neat southern native, ideal for small sites. Spires of green flower buds decorate it all winter, opening in early spring to slightly nodding clusters of bell-shaped, white flowers. Leaves are glossy, dark green, 3 inches long, with slightly scalloped edges. Low, rounded shrub grows 3 to 6 feet tall and wide. Perfect in woodland or shade gardens, or as edging or facing shrub.

PIERIS FLORIBUNDA

Japanese pieris (*P. japonica*) shines throughout the year. The glossy, evergreen foliage on the shrub forms whorls of leaves at the branch tips, which are topped in winter with clusters of beadlike, light green or red flower buds. The buds open in late winter or early spring into 6-inch-long pendulous clusters of white, pink, or rose-red, bell-like flowers, which remain showy for up to six weeks.

The new growth is eye-catching rusty red, bright red, or multicolored. Leaves mature to shiny dark green and may turn deep burgundy in winter. This upright shrub grows to 8 feet tall and 3 or 4 feet wide. Excellent for shade gardens, borders, and foundations. Combines well with rhododendrons, azaleas, and pines.

Site: Half to full shade. Japanese pieris tolerates full sun in the North if soil remains moist; needs shade in the South. Humus-rich, moist but well-drained, acid to slightly acid soil. Fetterbush needs excellent drainage; Japanese pieris needs plentiful moisture. Fetterbush hardy in zones 5 to 7; Japanese pieris in zones 6 to 8.
How to Grow: Plant container or balled-and-burlapped shrubs in spring or fall, spacing 3 to 4 feet apart. Protect from full sun in winter. Deadhead immediately after flowering to improve blooming next year.

Fetterbush needs no pruning. Selectively thin long branches of Japanese pieris to shape, if needed; cut back hard in spring to renew. Fetterbush develops stem rot if soil is not properly drained. Japanese pieris may be troubled with lacebug in overly sunny site; fetterbush not bothered.
Cultivars: Fetterbush: 'Millstream', compact mound to 18 inches tall and 4 feet wide.

Japanese pieris: 'Dorothy Wycoff', red flower buds open to red-tinged white flowers, compact plant; 'Purity', late-blooming, white flowers, compact, to 4 feet; 'Red Mill', outstanding, red new growth, long-lasting, white flowers, dense and bushy; 'Valley Rose', pastel pink flowers, bronze-tinged new growth, compact, to 4 feet; 'Valley Valentine', red buds, pink flowers, colorful new growth, 7 feet tall; 'Variegata', white-margined leaves, white flowers, slow-growing, to 5 feet; 'Forest Flame', new growth pink, turns

cream, finally green, 7 feet, Zone 5; 'Spring Snow', upright, pure white flower clusters, dwarf to 2 feet.

PINUS SPP.
White Pine

Needles of the white pines are arranged in clusters of five. As a group, these are graceful trees with fine-textured needles. They perform well in gardens and landscapes where they make excellent specimens and effective screens.

Limber pine (*Pinus flexilis*) is a beautiful tree native to western North America. Dense, fine-textured, slender, blue-green needles are 3 inches long and may be twisted, giving the tree a soft, fluffy texture. Bark is rough and dark gray. The branches are so flexible the current year's growth can bend in half without breaking. Trees are pyramidal; to 45 feet tall and 30 feet wide.

Korean pine (*P. koraiensis*) matures into an outstanding, somewhat formal specimen. Thick, 3½- to 4½-inch-long stiff needles are glossy dark green with white stripes, creating an overall gray-green color. Blue-needled forms are the most beautiful. Trees are loosely pyramidal, well-branched to the ground, and grow 40 feet tall.

Japanese white pine (*P. parviflora*) is open with tiered branches decorated with narrow, 2½-inch-long, twisted, blue-green needles clustered in tufts at the branch tips. Bark on older trees becomes scaly and dark gray. Trees are dense and conical, becoming wide-spreading and flat-topped with age; to 25 to 50 feet tall and wide.

Eastern white pine (*P. strobus*) features horizontally spreading branches and 2- to 3-inch-long light green to bluish green needles. Although widely planted, its common occurrence does not lessen *continued*

Evergreens

PINUS SPP.
(continued)

its beauty. Bark on old trunks is deeply furrowed and gray-brown. Pyramidal tree; to 50 to 80 feet tall and 20 to 40 feet wide.

PINUS STROBUS

Himalayan pine (*P. wallichiana*) has sharp-pointed, 6-to 8-inch-long needles arranged in semipendulous cascades on branches that cloak the tree to the ground, creating a soft, fluffy effect. Needles are gray-green with white stripes, giving the tree a silvery sheen. Forms a broad pyramid; 30 to 50 feet tall and wide.

Site: White pines do well in full sun to part shade in well-drained soil with moderate moisture. Eastern white pine tolerates dry soil, but not poorly drained soil, road salt, air pollution, or seashore conditions. Limber pine tolerates salt spray and wind, a rocky site, and drier soil than other white pines, but is less drought-tolerant than black pines.

Limber pine, zones 3 to 7, good in the West and Midwest. Korean pine, zones 4 to 7, to Zone 8 in the West. Japanese white pine, zones 5 to 9, tolerates salt and seashore conditions. Eastern white pine, zones 3 to 9, short-lived in heavy soil in the Southeast.

Himalayan pine, zones 5 to 8, hardiness varies with seed source.

How to Grow: Mulch soil of eastern white pine, Japanese white pine, and Himalayan pine to keep cool and moist. Retain limbs of all pines all the way to the ground; remove lower limbs if they die naturally. Cut back limbs only to a fork in the branch to control size; pines do not resprout from leafless wood. Shear eastern white pine annually when "candles" form to maintain as a tall hedge or screen. Shelter Himalayan pine from wind; to prevent die-back of lower branches, water during drought and do not shade lower branches.

Limber pine may get white pine blister rust. White pine blister rust and white pine weevils often serious on eastern white pine; becomes chlorotic in alkaline soil. Himalayan white pine resists white pine blister rust.

Cultivars and Similar Species: Limber pine: 'Vanderwolf's Pyramid', long, blue-green, twisted needles, fast-growing, narrowly pyramidal; 'Glauca Pendula', tall and wide-spreading, weeping, blue needles; 'Extra Blue', pyramidal, blue needles; 'Temple', upright and open-branched, short, blue-green needles.

Korean pine: 'Glauca', blue-gray needles, 25 feet; 'Silveray', silvery gray needles, 25 feet. *P. cembra* (Swiss stone pine), shorter, greener needles, more dense and conical becoming flat-topped; zones 3 to 7.

Japanese white pine: 'Glauca', silvery blue-green, tufted needles, slow-growing, intermediate size; 'Brevifolia', dwarf, slow-growing, blue-green.

Eastern white pine: Tall—'Hillside Winter Gold', light yellow in winter; 'White Mountain', silvery powder blue needles, vigorous. Intermediate—'Pendula', magnificent weeper, support to desired height then allow to weep, best on wall or fence; 'Fastigiata', columnar when young, broadens with age. Dwarf—'Nana', compact dwarf mound, to 2 to 3 feet tall and wide; 'Horsford Dwarf', light green bun, to 1 foot; 'Blue Shag', 3-foot globe, blue.

Himalayan pine: 'Zebrina', yellow-banded needles; 'Glauca', blue needles; 'Frosty', silvery needles; 'Morton', most cold-hardy, Zone 4.

PINUS SPP.
Three-Needled Pine

These tough but beautiful pines feature bundles of three needles. They are more tolerant of adverse growing conditions than white pines.

Lace-bark pine (*Pinus bungeana*) is a rare and outstanding pine featuring multiple trunks covered with a patchwork of green, pink, and cream bark. The best coloring develops when sun strikes the trunks. Needles are sharp-pointed, glossy dark green, and 3 inches long. Trees are slow-growing; pyramidal when young, becoming open and flat-topped; 30 to 50 feet tall and wide.

PINUS BUNGEANA

Loblolly pine (*P. taeda*) is a fast-growing, straight-trunked southern pine that adapts to adverse conditions, providing effective screen where other evergreens do poorly. Dark yellow-green needles are 6 to 10 inches long. Bark is dark gray, deeply furrowed and ridged. Pyramidal when young, open-branched and rounded with age; to 45 feet tall and half as wide.

Longleaf pine *(P. palustris)* has tufts of bright green 8- to 16-inch-long needles and orange-brown bark. Slash pine *(P. elliottii)* has yellow-green 8- to 10-inch-long needles. Both are narrow southern natives that grow to 80 to 90 feet tall.

Plant lace-bark pine as a slow-growing, eye-catching specimen where the bark can be admired up close. Use loblolly and other native southern pines in groves for a wooded effect and to shade azaleas and camellias, or in a staggered line for a quick screen.

Site: Full sun and average to moist, well-drained soil. Loblolly pine also performs well in part shade and in acid clay soil, and tolerates poor drainage. Lace-bark pine tolerates alkalinity. Slash pine tolerates poorly drained soil.

Lace-bark pine hardy in zones 5 to 9; loblolly pine, zones 7 to 9; longleaf pine, zones 7 to 9; slash pine, zones 8 to 9.

How to Grow: Cut back limbs only to a fork in the branch; pines do not resprout from leafless wood. Remove lower branches of lace-bark pine to reveal trunks and do not remove multiple trunks. Lace-bark pine branches may break under snow or ice load. Loblolly pines may get pine beetles and heart rot.

Cultivars: Lace-bark pine: 'Rowe Arboretum', tight pyramid, glossy green foliage.

Loblolly pine: 'Nana', dense and round to 15 feet tall.

PINUS SPP.
Red and Black Pine

Extremely tolerant of adverse growing conditions such as dry, sandy, or gravely soil, as well as salt spray or air pollution, these pines are no less beautiful because of their tough constitution. They have stiff needles in bundles of two.

Picturesque Japanese red pine *(Pinus densiflora)* has several irregular trunks and horizontal branches that feature bright red-orange bark. Bright green needles are slightly twisted, 3 to 4 inches long, and arranged in tufts. Trees are irregular to flat-topped; can reach 60 feet tall and wide.

PINUS DENSIFLORA 'OCULUS-DRACONIS'

Gardeners often think Mugo or mountain pine *(P. mugo)*, a slow-growing, compact, shrubby pine, is smaller than it actually is because plants often are sheared in the nursery to look dense and compact. This pine grows 2 to 4 inches a year and usually becomes broad-spreading; to 10 to 15 feet tall and wide. Dwarf forms average 2 to 6 feet in height. Seed-grown plants are variable and less compact than named cultivars. Rigid, dark green needles are 1 to 2 inches long and slightly curved.

Red pine *(P. resinosa)* is a cold-tolerant native conifer hailing from northcentral and northeastern United States and Canada. Brittle, 6-inch-long, dark green needles are arranged in dense tufts. Bark on older trunks is reddish brown and broken into diamond-shaped plates. Trees are rounded and heavily branched; to 50 feet tall.

Scotch pine *(P. sylvestris)* becomes open and craggy with age and is a favorite picturesque small landscape tree. The stiff, twisted needles are 1 to 3 inches long and vary from yellow-green to blue-green, sometimes turning yellowish green in winter. Bark is orange-brown to red-brown on the upper trunks and gray to red-brown and fissured at the bottoms of old trunks. Grows open and wide-spreading with an irregular flat top; 30 to 60 feet tall, 30 to 40 feet wide.

The small, attractive Japanese black pine *(P. thunbergiana)* has long been a favorite for seashore planting. The shiny, dark green needles are 2½ to 4½ inches long. Prominent silvery buds make it easy to identify. Bark is dark gray to black and fissured into plates. Trees are irregular and open, growing 35 to 60 feet tall.

Austrian pine *(P. nigra)* has dark green, 5-inch-long, sharp, stiff needles, furrowed mottled bark, and reaches 60 to 100 feet tall. Loses lower branches with age.

Virginia pine *(P. virginiana)* is native to the eastcentral United States and endures adverse conditions. Irregularly branched, it features stout, 2- to 3-inch-long, twisted, deep green needles that may be yellowish in winter. Pyramidal to flat-topped; 15 to 40 feet tall and 10 to 30 feet wide.

Cultivars of Japanese red pine make excellent slow-growing pines for small yards if located to dramatize their silhouettes and allowed space for their wide spread. Mugo pine and dwarf forms of Scotch pine are excellent in a foundation planting or mixed border. Use very dwarf forms in rock gardens. Red pine is excellent windbreak in the North. Use Japanese black, Virginia, Austrian, and similar pines to stabilize dunes on East Coast and as screens.

Site: Best in full sun and well-drained soil with moderate moisture. Japanese red pine needs slightly acid soil. Mugo pine best in deep, moist, loamy soil; tolerates alkaline soil and part shade. Red pine needs acid soil. *continued*

Evergreens

PINUS SPP.
(continued)

Red, Virginia, Japanese black, and Scotch pines perform well in sandy or gravely soil, and tolerate drought. Austrian pine tolerates salt spray, light and heavy soils, and alkalinity.

Japanese red pine hardy in zones 5 to 7. Mugo pine, zones 3 to 7, heat-tolerant. Red pine, zones 3 to 6, best in cold climates. Scotch pine, zones 3 to 8. Japanese black pine, zones 6 to 9; tolerates heat and salt spray, good seashore and high-desert plant. Austrian pine, zones 4 to 8. Virginia pine, zones 5 to 9, tolerates seashore conditions.

How to Grow: Cut back limbs only to a fork in the branch; pines do not resprout from leafless wood. Prune lower limbs to reveal trunk of Japanese red pine; do not remove multiple trunks. Japanese black pine can be sheared and trained to emphasize the cloudlike branching. Keep Mugo pine compact by shearing new growth as "candles" expand.

Pine needle scale and sawfly larvae can be serious on Mugo pine. Scotch pine suffers from pine wilt and blue stain fungus spread by nematodes, and from European pine shoot beetle, Diplodia tip blight, and Zimmerman pine moth. Pinewood nematodes carried by longhorn beetles and blue stain fungus carried by black turpentine beetles kill mature Japanese black pines (20 years and older). Austrian pine gets Diplodia tip blight on mature trees (15 to 20 years old); dothistroma needle blight can be serious; resists oak root rot fungus. Check locally to see if pest problems preclude planting these pines in your area.

Cultivars and Similar Species: Japanese red pine: Intermediate— 'Umbraculifera' (Tanyosho pine), multistemmed with flattened top, naturally forming "cloudlike" shape, to 15 to 30 feet tall and wide; 'Heavy Bud', similar to 'Umbraculifera', but with large buds, light green needles,

more cold-hardy; 'Oculus-draconis' (dragon's-eye-pine), green needles with wide, bright yellow bands; 'Pendula' ('Prostrata'), grows along the ground or weeps if grafted to a standard. Semidwarf—'Soft Green', more dwarf than 'Umbraculifera'.

Mugo pine: Intermediate—*P. m.* var. *pumilio*, prostrate to 10 feet wide. *P. m.* var. *mugo*, mounded to 3 to 5 feet tall and much wider. Semidwarf—'Big Tuna', pyramidal and dense. Dwarf—'Mitsch's Mini', very dwarf, brown buds; 'Gold Spire', gold new growth matures to green; 'Aurea', light green in summer, gold in winter, compact to 3 or more feet; 'Mops', globe-shaped, 3 feet tall and wide; 'Paul's Dwarf', 1-inch needles, very dwarf, mounded to 1½ feet.

Red pine: 'Quinobeguin', globe shape, short needles, dwarf.

Scotch pine: Tall—'Arctic', blue-green needles, bright yellow in winter, Zone 2; 'Austrian Hills', good in cold, dry climate; 'East Anglia', straight stems, nonyellowing needles. Intermediate—'French Blue', bright blue-green needles all year, compact and uniform; 'Aurea', light green in summer, bright yellow in winter; 'Fastigiata', columnar to 25 feet tall and 4 feet wide. Dwarf—'Beuvronensis', dome-shaped, small shrub; 'Glauca Nana', blue-green, neat rounded pyramid, 6 to 8 feet tall; 'Hillside Creeper', prostrate, spreads to 10 feet.

Japanese black pine: 'Thunderhead', silver buds form showy, bright white "candles" from fall through winter, vigorous and upright; 'Majestic Beauty' ('Monina'), resists smog damage.

Austrian pine: 'Arnold Sentinel', columnar to 25 feet. Use *P. heldreichii* var. *leucodermis* (Bosnian pine) as a slow-growing substitute for *P. nigra*; tolerates dry and alkaline soil, pyramidal to 45 feet tall, diplodia-resistant, zones 2 to 6.

Virginia pine: 'Wates Golden', light green in summer, bright gold in winter. *P. banksiana* (jack pine), similar northern native, pyramidal to shrubby,

to 50 feet tall, sandy or clayey, acid soil, good coastal plant, zones 2 to 6. *P. edulis* (pinyon pine), southwestern native, bushy and stiff, to 15 to 20 feet, good in a Xeriscape and high desert; several serious insects in landscape situations; zones 5 to 7, to 8 in the West; good in the West and Midwest.

PITTOSPORUM TOBIRA
Japanese Pittosporum

The rounded leaves of this southern favorite densely decorate the stems, creating an appealing textural effect. The most

PITTOSPORUM TOBIRA 'VARIEGATA'

popular type has variegated leaves with creamy white edges and gray-green centers. White flowers bloom in 2-inch clusters in late spring and have a wonderful orange-blossom scent. Compact rounded to spreading shrub; 10 feet tall and twice as wide. Use as hedge or screen. Variegated forms are excellent in foundation plantings and shade gardens.

Site: Full sun to full shade; most compact in sun. Well-drained sandy to clay, acid to alkaline soil; moderate moisture. Zones 8 and 9; tolerates seashore and hot, dry conditions.

How to Grow: Plant container or balled-and-burlapped shrubs in spring or fall, spacing 3 to 4 feet apart for hedge, much farther for a specimen. Usually easy to grow. Responds well to heavy pruning in spring; looks best when pruned with thinning cuts. Cut back hard in spring to renew. Leaf spot and mealybugs may be troublesome.

Cultivars: 'Variegata', gray-green leaves with creamy edges; 'Cream de Mint', slow-growing, dense mound, to 2 feet tall, mint green leaves with creamy edges; 'Wheeler's Dwarf', compact, slow-growing, to 3 feet tall.

PODOCARPUS MACROPHYLLUS

PODOCARPUS MACROPHYLLUS
Yew Pine

Popular in the South, this useful evergreen has a bold, feathery texture. The waxy needles are dark, glossy green with two white bands on the undersides, 2 to 3 inches long and almost ½ inch wide, and are arranged spirally around the stems. Yellow catkins bloom in spring and ripen into berrylike red or blue fruit. Oval and upright; to 20 to 30 feet tall and 10 to 15 feet wide. Excellent clipped hedge or screen. Use dwarf forms in foundation plantings. Use unpruned as specimen. May be espaliered.

Site: Full sun to light shade. Best in moist, well-drained, fertile soil, but

does well in sandy loam or clay if it is not wet. Does not tolerate alkaline conditions. Zones 8 and 9; tolerates heat and salt spray.

How to Grow: Plant container or balled-and-burlapped plants in spring or fall, spacing 4 to 5 feet apart for a hedge or screen, 10 to 15 feet for specimen. Protect from wind and winter sun in Zone 8 to prevent winter injury to stem tips. May be sheared in spring and again in midsummer for a formal effect. Thin as needed for a tree shape. Usually pest-free; may get root rot in wet site.

Cultivars: *Podocarpus macrophyllus.* var. *maki*, dwarf, shrubby and upright, to 10 feet tall, most common form.

PRUNUS LAUROCERASUS
Cherry Laurel, English Laurel

The oblong, 6-inch-long leaves of this European shrub are shiny dark green with tiny teeth scattered along the edges, giving them a medium to bold texture. Stems emit a cherry fragrance if crushed. Extremely fragrant, 6-inch-long spires of tiny, starlike,

PRUNUS LAUROCERASUS 'OTTO LUYKEN'

white flowers bloom among the leaves in mid spring; these ripen to blue-black berries. Dense, spreading; to 20 feet tall and slightly wider. Excellent screen or hedge. Use dwarf forms in foundation plantings and massed in shady sites.

Site: Full sun to full shade. Humus-rich, moist soil; must be well-drained; moderate moisture. Zones 7 to 9; tolerates seashore conditions.

How to Grow: Plant container or balled-and-burlapped plants in spring or fall, spacing 4 to 6 feet apart for hedge or screen, much farther for specimen. Protect from winter sun and wind in the North. May be heavily pruned by thinning. Leave unpruned where it has sufficient growing room. May be cut back hard in spring to renew. Leaf spot common, especially if watered overhead; may get root rot in poorly drained soil; whiteflies sometimes troublesome.

Cultivars and Similar Species: 'Otto Luyken', smaller leaves, compact, to 4 feet tall; 'Mt. Vernon', slow-growing, to 2 feet; 'Nana', dense, slow-growing, to 5 feet, good sheared hedge; 'Schipkaensis', smaller leaves, slow-growing, vase-shaped, zones 6 to 9; 'Zebeliana', narrow leaves, dense, spreading shrub, to 5 feet.

P. caroliniana (Carolina cherry laurel), similar with longer leaves and more treelike shape, southern native, zones 7 to 9; 'Bright 'n' Tight', compact, upright, to 10 feet, good screen.

PSEUDOTSUGA MENZIESII
Douglas Fir

A timber tree in the West, Douglas fir can reach 200 feet in the wild, but is smaller in home landscapes, where it grows into a fine-textured, majestic spire with horizontal branches. Lower branches are somewhat downswept and upper branches upturned. The dark green to blue-green needles are 1½ inches long with a strong camphor scent and arranged in two horizontal ranks. Cones emerge rose-red and mature to cinnamon-brown with whiskerlike spines. Trunk bark is reddish with deep fissures. Narrow pyramid; 50 to 80 feet tall and 15 to 25 feet wide. Attractive, fast-growing tree *continued*

Evergreens

PSEUDOTSUGA MENZIESII
(continued)

PSEUDOTSUGA MENZIESII 'GLAUCA'

for a specimen, screen, or grouping. Makes a good cut Christmas tree.

Site: Full sun. Well-drained, deep, moist, acid to neutral soil. Best in zones 3 to 6; grows in cool areas of zones 7 and 8. Trees from Pacific Coast seed sources do best where moist or humid; the bluer forms from the Rocky Mountains tolerate more dryness.
How to Grow: Plant container or balled-and-burlapped trees in spring or fall, spacing 10 feet apart for a screen, farther for a specimen. Protect from strong wind. Do not remove lower branches or the top. New growth may be sheared for a hedge. Canker, twig blight, budworms, gypsy moths, tussock moths, and root weevils can be problems.
Cultivars: Large: 'Blue', the color of a Colorado blue spruce; 'Carnifix Weeping', weeping branches, twisted leader, dark green; 'Pendula', weeping branches, twisted leader, green; 'Glauca', blue-green, slower-growing, more cold-hardy.
   Dwarf: 'Fletcheri', flat-topped globe, blue-green; 'Loggerhead', dense, low-spreading, with a bird's-nest shape, dark green.

QUERCUS VIRGINIANA
Live Oak

Like most oaks, this awesome southern native is extremely long-lived and becomes picturesque and craggy with age. Horizontally spreading branches often drip with Spanish moss, adding to its romantic appearance. Leaves are leathery and usually 3 inches long and 1 inch wide with smooth edges. New leaves

QUERCUS VIRGINIANA

emerge bright olive green in spring and mature to dark green on top with gray-green woolly undersides. Older leaves drop when new leaves emerge. Flowers are long, yellowish catkins that decorate the tree in spring. Trunk bark is black and heavily textured in large blocks. Clusters of 1-inch, dark brown to black acorns ripen in late summer. Broad-spreading, rounded tree; to 50 to 80 feet tall and 60 to 100 feet wide. Plant as a street tree or specimen on a large property. Used to line drives on estates and plantations.

Site: Full sun. Adapts to most soil types and moisture conditions. Hardy to southern Zone 7, but best in zones 8 and 9 where it cannot be damaged by ice storms; withstands coastal conditions.

How to Grow: Plant balled-and-burlapped trees in spring or fall, allowing room for ultimate spread. Do not allow English ivy or other heavy vines to grow too high into trees; extra weight could topple trees during hurricanes. Train to a single leader when young. Remove deadwood when older. Root rot may be troublesome.
Cultivars: Only the species is grown.

RHAPHIOLEPIS INDICA
Indian Hawthorn

Easy adaptability and a dense covering of beautiful, rounded leaves and showy flowers make this tolerant shrub a popular addition to home and public landscapes. The 4-inch flower clusters, which bloom abundantly from late winter into early summer, are made up of small, individual, white or pink fragrant flowers. These are followed by blue-black berries. The leathery leaves are

RHAPHIOLEPIS INDICA

about 2 inches long, dark green, and may turn purplish in winter. Rounded mound; to 4 feet tall and 6 feet wide, sometimes larger. Excellent foundation shrub. May be massed in a border or used to create a low hedge or barrier.

Site: Full sun to light shade, denser in sun. Best in moist, slightly acid to neutral soil; tolerates drought. Zones 8 and 9; tolerates seashore conditions.

How to Grow: Plant container or balled-and-burlapped shrubs in spring or fall, spacing 2 to 3 feet apart for a hedge, farther for a specimen. Provide more shade in desert areas. If needed, pinch or cut back individual branches after flowering to increase density and control size. Leaf spot can be problem, especially if watered overhead.

Cultivars and Similar Species: Plants commonly sold as *Rhaphiolepis indica* may be the similar *R. umbellata* or hybrids of the two. 'Ballerina', rose-pink flowers, reddish winter foliage, 2 feet tall; 'Charisma', pale pink, 3 feet tall; 'Enchantress', rose-pink flowers from late winter into summer, compact, to 4 to 5 feet tall, susceptible to leaf spot; 'Majestic Beauty', pink flowers in huge clusters, tall plant, to 10 to 15 feet, leaf-spot-resistant; 'Indian Princess', 3-foot, broad mound, light pink flowers fade to white; 'Spring Rapture', rose-red flowers from winter into spring, 3 to 4 feet tall and wide; 'Springtime', loose-branched, open mound, to 5 feet tall, pink flowers winter into spring.

RHODODENDRON SPP.
Evergreen Azalea

The gorgeous, large-flowered Southern Indica azaleas (*Rhododendron × indicum*) are synonymous with springtime in the South. They bloom in mid spring with the dogwoods, creating an ethereal sight. Flowers come in shades of white, pink, lavender, orange-red, rose-red, purple, and cream. Leaves are tidy. Rounded shrubs grow 6 to 10 feet tall and wide. Excellent under pines and dogwoods in a lightly shaded, naturalistic garden. Include in borders as specimens or in groups.

Thousands of cold-hardy, evergreen azaleas (*R. hybrida*) have been bred by noted plant breeders over the past half-century. These plants have tidy leaves and produce masses of flowers that blanket the plants with color in early, mid, or late spring, depending on the cultivar. The five-petaled blossoms form a flaring trumpet and may be single, fully double, or hose-in-hose (a type of double with two single flowers, one inserted within the other). Some cultivars are overused; seek out more unusual types from specialty growers. Although the foliage is evergreen, in coldest areas the innermost leaves often change color and drop in fall; only leaves near the stem tips remain through winter. Generally rounded to spreading shrubs; to 4 to 8 feet tall and wide, depending upon cultivar.

RHODODENDRON × INDICUM

Some are lower or ground-hugging. Use as specimens or mass-plant in foundation plantings, borders, shade gardens, and informal hedges. Naturalize in an open woodland. Use groundcover types in rock gardens.

Site: Give Southern Indica azaleas part to light shade, hardy hybrids half to light shade. Well-drained, moist, humus-rich, acid soil. Plentiful moisture. Southern Indica azaleas hardy in zones 8 and 9, hardy hybrids in zones 5 to 9, depending on cultivar.

How to Grow: Plant container or balled-and-burlapped shrubs in spring or fall, spacing 4 to 10 or more feet apart depending upon ultimate size. Mulch well to protect shallow roots. Prune with thinning cuts to control size immediately after blooming, if necessary. Petal blight can afflict Southern Indica azaleas; lacebugs, mealybugs, root weevils, and petal blotch can trouble hardy hybrids.

Cultivars: Southern Indica: 'Fielder's White', white; 'Formosa', rose-purple; 'George Lindley Tabor', light orchid-pink with white variegations; 'Pride of Mobile', bright pink; 'White Grandeur', pure white, double; 'Southern Charm', deep rose; 'Phoenicia', lavender; 'Brilliant', watermelon red; 'Duc de Rohan', salmon pink. Imperial series—sun-tolerant, lush foliage, mounded and dense, to 5 feet; 'Countess', deep salmon pink with crinkled edges, part shade; 'Duchess', double, bright to soft pink; 'Princess', rich pink; 'Queen', double, pink.

Cold-hardy hybrids: *R. mucronatum* 'Delaware Valley White', pure white, zones 7 to 9. Glen Dale hybrids—large plants with large pastel flowers often streaked with other colors, size and shape variable with cultivar, zones 6 to 9; 'Glacier', bright white flowers, excellent foliage; 'Aphrodite', pale rose-pink; 'Ben Morrison', coral-pink with white edges and red blotch; 'Fashion', coral-red, late-blooming; 'Buccaneer', orange-red; 'Trophy', light lavender-pink. Gable hybrids—layered branches, small leaves, zones 7 to 9; 'Rose Greeley', single and hose-in-hose, white flowers with chartreuse blotch; 'Purple Splendor', red-violet frilled with dark blotch, single and hose-in-hose, low to medium height, spreading; 'Stewartsonianum', bright true red. Kurume hybrids—masses of small flowers, compact, dense, layered plants with small leaves, zones 7 to 8; 'Coral Bells', coral-pink, hose-in-hose; 'Pink Pearl', double, soft pink; 'Hino-crimson', brilliant orange-red; 'Hino-degiri', brilliant magenta-rose. Satsuki or Macrantha hybrids—early summer-blooming, low-growing to 2 feet with very large striped or flecked *continued*

Evergreens

flowers, zones 7 to 9; 'Pink Gumpo', light pink; 'White Gumpo', white; 'Red Gumpo', rose-pink. Robin Hill hybrids—similar to Satsuki, but more cold-hardy, zones 5 to 8. North Tisbury hybrids—low or groundcovering plants with summer-blooming, small flowers, zones 6 to 8, sun to part shade; 'Pink Pancake', salmon pink; 'Red Pancake', orange-red.

RHODODENDRON SPP.
Evergreen Rhododendron

Not as flashy as many hybrid rhododendrons, Carolina rhododendron (*Rhododendron carolinianum*) is a choice native that provides delicate effect in a woodland garden. It features 3-inch clusters of pale pink to pale rose-purple or white flowers at its branch tips in mid to late spring. The leathery, medium-textured, 3-inch-long leaves are dark green on top with brown scales on the undersides. This species has been hybridized with other small-leaved species to yield a wealth of refined rhododendrons, perfect for smaller gardens. Rounded, open shrubs are 3 to 5 feet tall and wide. Carolina is excellent naturalized in open woodland or included in a shrub or mixed border. Small-leaved types work well as specimens or massed in borders and foundation plantings. Use very dwarf types in rock gardens.

Catawba rhododendron (*R. catawbiense*), a native Appalachian species, and its hybrids make a bold statement both in and out of bloom. They are among the most popular landscape plants in areas with acid soil. Individual, bell-shaped blossoms are lilac- to rose-purple with green marks on their interiors, and form dramatic clusters (called trusses) of up to 20 blossoms in mid to late spring. Bold-textured, 6-inch-long, 2-inch-wide, oblong leaves are dark green on top and light green on the undersides. The leaves droop and curl during cold weather to conserve water. The Catawba species has been used extensively in hybridizing and has yielded a huge selection of cultivars in a range of colors. Open, rounded shrub; to 6 to 10 feet or more tall and wide. Use as an understory plant in a woodland garden, as a specimen, or mass in border.

RHODODENDRON YAKUSIMANUM

Growing to enormous size in the wild, the rosebay rhododendron (*R. maximum*) needs plenty of growing space in a home landscape. Blossoms appear in early summer and vary from pale to rose-pink or white with dull green or orange speckles. The flower clusters may have as many as 25 blossoms, but may be partially obscured beneath the maturing new leaves. Mature leaves measure 8 inches long and are lustrous, dark green with rusty undersides. Old specimens of this fast-growing evergreen become picturesque, with twisted, gnarled trunks. Rounded, open shrub; to 10 to 30 feet tall and wide, depending upon climate. Excellent for naturalizing in a moist woodland, including in a border or as a screen on large property. Coarse texture best contrasted with fine-textured plants.

The unique-looking and slow-growing, Yaku rhododendron (*R. yakusimanum*) forms a neat, rounded mound of dense stems and dark evergreen leaves. The oblong leaves cup downward and measure 3 to 4 inches long. They unfold with a white, fuzzy coating and have a thick, tan felt on the undersides. The felt is so thick that inexperienced gardeners may worry there is something wrong with the plant. Tight, showy clusters of white or pink blossoms, which open from pink or rose-red buds, decorate the mounds in late spring. Rounded and dome-shaped; to 3 feet tall and 5 feet wide. Compact and slow-growing, an ideal plant for foundations, mixed borders, and rock gardens.

Site: Carolina rhododendron, full sun to part shade; Catawba, full sun to shade, half shade usually best; rosebay, light to full shade; Yaku, part to light shade. Well-drained, humus-rich, moist, acid soil with plentiful moisture. Carolina hardy in zones 5 to 7, Zone 8 where cool in summer. Catawba, zones 4 to 7; rosebay, zones 5 and 6, Zone 7 with shade and moderate temperatures; Yaku, zones 6 and 7, warmer Zone 5 with winter protection, Zone 8 where temperatures are mild.

How to Grow: Plant container or balled-and-burlapped shrubs in spring or fall, spacing 4 to 10 feet or more apart depending on ultimate size. Remove faded flower clusters to promote better bloom next year. Protect Carolina and rosebay from winter sun and wind in the North. Keep soil mulched to protect shallow roots. Catawba fails in heavy or neutral to alkaline soil.

No regular pruning needed. Rejuvenate Carolina by cutting back dramatically in late winter. Renew

Catawba and rosebay by cutting back one third of the branches each year for three years in late winter.

May be bothered by black vine weevils, borers, scale insects, whiteflies, leaf spot, crown rot, and petal blight. Rosebay and Yaku usually less troubled than other rhododendrons.

Cultivars and Similar Species:
Carolina rhododendron: *R. c.* var. *album,* large white flowers. Hybrids—'Dora Amateis', white-spotted with green; 'Purple Gem', small plant, abundant small trusses of light purple flowers. Hybrids with early-blooming *R. dauricum*—tough, sun-tolerant, cold-hardy, compact, floriferous, early spring-blooming, perform well from North to South and in Midwest; 'PJM', rose-purple blossoms, dark burgundy-black winter foliage; 'Elite', lavender-pink, later-blooming; 'April Snow', pure white, double, green winter leaves; 'Olga Mezitt', clear pink, dark leaves in winter; 'Princess Susan', magenta, dark winter leaves; 'Thunder', dark purple, black-mahogany winter leaves. Many more compact, small-leaved hybrids available.

Catawba: Thousands of cultivars; 'Album', white with yellow-green flare. Iron-clad rhododendrons, hardy to Zone 4, reliable from North to South and in Midwest; 'Roseum Elegans', lavender-rose-pink; 'Nova-Zembla', crimson-red; 'Sappho', white blotched with purple; 'Catawbiense Album', white, late; 'Boule de Neige', white, compact. Dexter hybrids—hardy to Zone 5, tall, with enormous flower clusters; 'Scintillation', pink with yellow throat; 'Gigi', rose-red with deep red spots; 'Mereley Cream', creamy with yellow blotch; 'Vulcan', bright red. Leach hybrids—hardy to Zone 5, large flowers; 'Janet Blair', pale pink with brown speckles; 'Rio', salmon pink with yellow throat; 'Hindustan', frilly flowers, orange-flushed pink; 'Bravo', brilliant deep pink.

Rosebay: *R. m.* var. *album,* white flowers. *R. m.* var. *purpureum,* rose-purple. *R. m.* var. *roseum,* pink. David

Leach hybrids—early- to midsummer-blooming, large but compact plants, flowers stand above the foliage; 'Summer Glow', red buds, pink flowers; 'Summer Snow', white; 'Summer Summit', pink buds open white with pink blotch; 'Summer Solace', white with chartreuse splotch.

Yaku: 'Yaku Prince', deeper pink flowers; 'Yaku Princess', low and compact, pink buds open white, heat-resistant; 'Yaku Queen', pale pink with dark pink exteriors; 'Yaku Sunrise', rose-violet; 'Oliver', pure white; 'Bashful', rose-pink; 'Ken Janeck', light pink fading to white.

SCIADOPITYS VERTICILLATA
Umbrella Pine

Quite a conversation piece in a garden, this eye-catching tree forms an intense, dark green pyramid that branches to the ground with a distinctive texture. The thick, glossy, flattened needles are up to 5 inches long, forming dense whorls at the branch tips. The 4-inch-long, oblong

SCIADOPITYS VERTICILLATA

cones are green ripening to brown. Trees are extremely slow-growing and therefore rare and costly. Usually not touched by deer. Varies from a narrow cone to a broad pyramid; to 25 to 30 feet tall and 15 to 20 feet wide, or larger. Excellent specimen for

a mixed border or foundation. Allow room for mature growth since the tree becomes more valuable as it ages.

Site: Full sun to light shade, with some afternoon shade in the North, light shade in the South. Fertile, moist, acid soil; tolerates wet site. Zones 5 to 8.
How to Grow: Plant container or balled-and-burlapped trees in spring or fall, spacing 15 feet apart. Protect from wind and strong winter sun. Prune to remove competing leaders when young. Do not remove lower branches. Usually pest-free.
Cultivars and Similar Species: 'Aurea', tall, golden needles; 'Wintergreen', tall, more cold-hardy, Zone 4, and darker blue-green all winter; 'Richie's Cushion', dwarf, dense mound.

SEQUOIADENDRON GIGANTEUM (SEQUOIA GIGANTEA)
Giant Sequoia, Giant Redwood

Maturing to an ancient age and growing to a mammoth size in the wild, giant sequoia can reach 250 to 300 feet tall, with a massive, reddish brown trunk unobscured by lower branches (grows much smaller in cultivation). Native to California, it adapts to the East Coast. Pointed blue-green needles are $\frac{1}{8}$ to $\frac{1}{2}$ inch long and spiral around the stems in three ranks, forming whiplike, plumy branches. Egg-shaped cones are brown, about 1 inch long. Dense, narrow pyramid, 60 to 100 feet tall. Locate in groves or as specimens on a property where they have room to grow and their ultimate height will not overpower a home or landscape.

Site: Full sun. Deep, fertile, moist, well-drained, acid to slightly alkaline soil. Plentiful moisture. Zones 7 to 9; 6 with protection. Best with moist air in the East or West. *continued*

Evergreens

SEQUOIADENDRON GIGANTEUM
(continued)

SEQUOIA SEMPERVIRENS

How to Grow: Plant container or balled-and-burlapped trees in spring or fall, allowing space for ultimate size. Foliage may burn in winter; protect from wind. Remove suckers from base. Remove lower limbs when they die. May be sheared for a hedge. Needle blight and canker are rare problems.
Cultivars and Similar Species: 'Pendulum', pendulous branches close to the trunk; 'Hazel Smith', bluish needles, more cold-hardy. *Sequoia sempervirens* (redwood, coast redwood), more slender, but even taller; dark green, ½-inch-long, yewlike needles with two white bands, borne in two ranks; deeply furrowed and ridged, reddish bark; native to the Pacific Northwest; best with coastal conditions in the West; Zones 7 to 9; 'Majestic Beauty', denser branching; 'Santa Cruz', pale green needles, more weeping branches; 'Soquel', rich green, downward-sweeping branches.

SKIMMIA JAPONICA
Japanese Skimmia

Valued for its long-lasting, brilliant red berries, this slow-growing, low evergreen makes an excellent choice for a small-scale garden or foundation planting. The shiny, oblong leaves, which are whorled around the ends of the branches, are bright green and measure 3 to 5 inches long and ¾ to 2 inches wide. The red flower buds form dense clusters at the stem tips and are showy all winter; they open creamy white in early spring. Flowers and buds on male plants are larger and showier than on female plants, but the female plants produce

SKIMMIA JAPONICA

abundant red berries. The berries ripen in fall and last all winter and may be present when the spring flowers bloom. Stems are reddish purple and emit a spicy fragrance when crushed. Broad-spreading; to 2 to 3 or more feet tall and twice as wide. Excellent low shrub for foundations, facing taller shrubs, foreground of borders, and naturalizing in a shady site.

Site: Part to full shade. Well-drained, humus-rich, moist, acid to neutral soil; plentiful moisture. Zones 7 and 8; provide shelter in cool parts of Zone 7.
How to Grow: Plant container or balled-and-burlapped shrubs in spring or fall, spacing 3 to 4 feet apart. Female plants need male nearby for pollination and berries. Protect from winter sun and wind; foliage may discolor in winter sun. Thin immediately after blooming to control size if needed. Mites may cause problems.
Cultivars and Similar Species: 'Rodgersii', female clone, large, red fruit, compact; 'Rodgersii Nana', male, compact and slow-growing. *Skimmia japonica* subsp. *reevesiana*, similar, but more open with more pointed leaves and self-fertile flowers so all plants produce berries, zones 6 to 8.

TAXUS SPP.
Yew

A small to medium-size tree or large shrub, English yew *(Taxus baccata)* is native to Europe and a popular landscape plant in English gardens. The flat, 2-inch-long, sickle-shaped needles are dark green and waxy, and spiral around the stems. Multitrunked and wide-spreading; to 45 feet tall and 20 feet wide; cultivars smaller.

TAXUS CUSPIDATA 'CAPITATA'

Japanese yew *(T. cuspidata)* and hybrid yew *(T. × media)* are more cold-hardy and adaptable to more regions than the English yew. The Japanese yew is usually a small to medium-size tree or a large shrub. Needles are ½ inch long, dark green on top and yellow-green beneath and arranged loosely in two rows. It is multistemmed with upright to spreading branches; to 40 feet tall and wide.

Hybrid yew is usually a spreading, medium-size shrub with similar needles arranged in two ranks on each side of the stems, which are olive-green, not brown. Upright to spreading; reaches 3 to 20 feet tall depending upon cultivar. Both have berrylike red fruit on female plants, shredding, red-brown bark, and light green new growth that contrasts with the darker older needles.

Yews are excellent for foundations, hedges, screens, and mixed borders, especially in shade. Avoid shearing into stiff shapes, but prune naturally for best effect. Overused and thus taken for granted. Dark green color contrasts beautifully with light greens and golden greens of other plants.

Site: Full sun to full shade; golden forms need some sun. Fertile, moist, well-drained, acid to alkaline soil. Soil must be well-drained. English yew, zones 6 and 7, and cool areas of 8. Japanese yew, zones 4 to 7; hybrid yew, zones 5 to 7.
How to Grow: Plant container or balled-and-burlapped plants in spring or fall, spacing 3 feet apart for hedge, 5 to 10 feet for screen, 4 to 5 feet for mass plantings, farther for specimen, according to cultivar size and form. Plant on a raised bed to ensure good drainage in heavy-soil areas. Protect from winter wind to prevent yellowing of needles. Berrylike red fruit contains a single poisonous seed; needles and twigs are poisonous to livestock.

Yews respond well to thinning or shearing techniques. They grow continually throughout the season and do not put out a single flush of spring growth as do most conifers. Overgrown plants can be cut back severely into old wood in spring; they slowly regrow into shapely plants. Root weevils, twig blight, mealybugs may be problems.
Cultivars: English yew: Intermediate— 'Amersfoort', short, stubby needles like

a boxwood, open, conical shape, Zone 5; 'Fastigiata' (Irish yew), dense, broad column with rigid, upright branches, black-green needles; 'Fastigiata Robusta', narrow column; 'Standishii', lovely, golden needles, shape similar to Irish yew, but slower-growing. Semidwarf—'Adpressa Fowle', dense, short, rounded, dark green needles, stiff horizontal branches, slow-growing, broad cone. Dwarf—'Repandens', gracefully arching habit, 3 feet tall and at least twice as wide, hardy to Zone 5 if sheltered; 'Washingtonii', slow-growing, new growth bright gold, maturing to light green.

Japanese yew: Large—'Columnaris', fast-growing, narrow pyramid; 'Capitata', broad, slow-growing pyramid, to 40 feet. Intermediate— 'Nana', spreading branches, slow-growing, to 15 feet tall and 30 feet wide. Dwarf—'Aurescens', compact to 1 foot tall and 3 feet wide, does not winter-burn; 'Green Wave', low mound of arching branches; 'Low Spreading', low and fast-growing; 'Densa', low-spreading to 4 feet tall, 8 feet wide.

Hybrid yew: Intermediate—'Brownii', dense and rounded, to 10 feet tall and wide; 'Hicksii', broad column with upright branches, excellent hedge, fast-growing. Semidwarf—'Tauntonii', green year-round, low-spreading, to 3 feet tall, tolerates cold, wind, and heat; 'Densiformis', dense and mounding, to 4 feet tall and 6 feet wide, good for hedges and shearing; 'Viridis', slow-growing column with bright gold new growth and light green mature growth. Dwarf—'Everlow', slow-growing, 1½ feet tall and 5 feet wide, good winter color; 'Flushing', dense, dark green, slender column, slow-growing, to 4 feet tall, 1½ feet wide.

THUJA SPP.
Arborvitae

Rather ordinary looking, arborvitae or eastern white cedar (*Thuja occidentalis*) is so widely planted that it is a cliche as a vertical accent in a

foundation planting or aligned as a screen. What it lacks in beauty, however, it makes up in utility. It is easy to grow. Shiny, scalelike leaves are bright green on top, light green underneath and are pressed tightly against the branches, forming flat horizontal fans. Foliage may bronze in winter. Usually has a single trunk (sometimes a multiple trunk) with fibrous gray-brown bark and short branches all the way to the ground. Columnar; to 40 feet tall, 15 feet wide.

THUJA OCCIDENTALIS

Giant arborvitae or western red cedar (*T. plicata*) is a beautiful, hardy plant native to the Pacific Northwest where it thrives in gardens. The graceful, rich green foliage turns bronze in winter. Trees are fast-growing and often have multiple trunks with branches to the ground. Narrow pyramid; to 60 feet tall and 20 feet wide. Use as a tall screen in the East or West. Use as a specimen in the West. Good tree if you have problems with deer.

Site: Eastern white cedar needs full sun; giant aborvitae, full sun to part shade. Deep, fertile, moist but well-drained soil. Tolerates wet conditions and alkaline soil; giant arborvitae also tolerates acid soil. Eastern *continued*

Evergreens

THUJA SPP.
(continued)

white cedar, zones 3 to 7, best in the East. Giant arborvitae, zones 4 to 7; best in the East and Northwest.

How to Grow: Plant container or balled-and-burlapped trees in spring or fall, spacing 3 to 5 feet apart for hedge or screen, much farther for specimen. Ice and snow may bend and break the tall forms; especially troublesome with multiple trunks.

For a specimen, remove multiple trunks that occur in the nursery and train to central leader when young. For a natural-looking hedge, allow plants to grow 12 inches taller than ideal hedge height, then cut back tops by 18 inches and thin the side branches in late winter. Eastern white cedar does not resprout from old wood; giant arborvitae develops new shoots if old wood is cut back severely. Bagworms may trouble eastern white cedar.

Cultivars and Similar Species: Eastern white cedar: Large—'Affinity', narrow pyramid, yellow-green foliage, good screen; 'Pyramidalis', fast-growing, narrow cone, choose one with a single trunk; 'Nigra', pyramid, dark green all year, good hedge. Intermediate— 'Techny', pyramidal, green all year, good hedge; 'Emerald', dense, narrow pyramid, bright green all year, foliage in vertical sprays; 'Hetz's Wintergreen', narrow pyramid, light green, resists snow damage; 'Elegantissima', narrow, gold-tipped new growth, strong central leader, good in the North; 'Sunkist', upright, gold-orange foliage. Dwarf—'Ericoides', dense globe, tiny, needlelike leaves, yellow-green in summer, brownish in winter; 'Danica', excellent dwarf globe, bright green, holds shape in winter; 'Rheingold', conical, deep gold in summer, copper in winter, gets open and floppy with age; 'Hetz Midget', compact dwarf globe, rich green in summer, bronze in winter.

Giant arborvitae: Large—'Atrovirens', pyramidal, shiny dark green foliage.

Intermediate—'Zebrina', green foliage banded with yellow, looks overall yellow from a distance; 'Stoneham Gold', broad cone, gold new growth, dark green mature growth. Dwarf— 'Cuprea', globe, light yellow tips on deep green needles; 'Giganteum', hybrid with *T. plicata* and *T. occidentalis*; zones 5 to 7.

TSUGA CANADENSIS
Canada Hemlock, Eastern Hemlock

Native to the northeastern woodlands, this graceful, fine-textured evergreen is a beloved landscape tree. The dark green needles have two white stripes on their undersides and are about ⅔ inch long with blunt tips. They are arranged in two ranks along the

TSUGA CANADENSIS

branches. Limbs spread horizontally and cascade slightly. The small, brown cones mature in autumn. Pyramidal; to 75 feet tall and 30 feet wide. Use as a specimen, hedge, or screen in sun or shade. Naturalize in a grove.

Site: Full sun to light shade. Humus-rich to sandy, moist, well-drained, acid to alkaline soil. Plentiful moisture. Zones 3 to 8.

How to Grow: Plant container or balled-and-burlapped trees in spring or fall, spacing 6 to 15 feet apart for hedge or screen, 25 feet for specimen. Mulch to keep soil cool. Perishes during drought. Protect from wind in sunny locations and dry sites.

Most graceful if lower limbs are left to the ground, but may be removed. Responds well to thinning or shearing during late winter if used as a hedge. Remove multiple leaders formed by shearing at the nursery if growing as a tree. Woolly adelgids are killing forest and landscape trees in the Northeast and Mid-Atlantic region. (All American species are susceptible; Japanese species may be immune.) Professionally applied and properly timed horticultural oil and pesticide sprays offer good control. Mites serious in dry sites.

Cultivars and Similar Species: Large— 'Albospica', white-tipped foliage, some shade. Intermediate—'Jeddeloh', spreading mound with a bird's-nest center, spiraling branches to 5 feet tall and wide; 'Gentsch White', white-tipped new growth, flat-topped globe, part shade, shear lightly to encourage white growth; 'Pendula', upright and weeping, variable; 'Sargentii', weeping mound, 15 feet tall and 30 feet wide. Dwarf—'Beehive', tight globe, tiny needles; 'Cole's Prostrate', creeping for rock gardens, provide shade to prevent sunburn on exposed silvery stems; 'Aurea Compacta', stiff, upright pyramid, bright gold, part sun. *Tsuga caroliniana* (Carolina hemlock), more open tree with longer, pointed, radially arranged needles, less susceptible to woolly adelgid, but not immune, zones 4 to 7. *T. heterophylla* (western hemlock), similar to Canada hemlock, but needs moister atmosphere and cooler summers, good in zones 6 to 8 in the Northwest. *T. sieboldii* (southern Japanese hemlock), long, rounded needles, open, graceful shape, tolerates clay soil, drought, and urban conditions; zones 5 or 6 to 8.

VIBURNUM SPP.
Leatherleaf Viburnum
Laurustinus Viburnum

Leatherleaf viburnum *(Viburnum rhytidophyllum)*, a handsome, commanding plant, is one of the few evergreen viburnums and has a distinctive texture. Its leaves are narrow and about 8 inches long. The tops are shiny, dark green, puckered and crinkled in a quilted pattern due to their prominent veins. The undersides are woolly white, creating a striking contrast. Flattened, creamy

VIBURNUM RHYTIDOPHYLLUM 'ROSEUM'

yellow flower heads are 4 to 8 inches across and bloom from mid to late spring. Showy, red berries develop in summer and ripen to black. Rounded to oval shrub, 10 feet tall and 8 feet wide. Use this bold plant as an accent in a large shrub border or as an informal screen or hedge. Contrast with fine-textured plants.

The oval, 3-inch evergreen leaves of laurustinus viburnum *(V. tinus)* are lustrously dark and have a finer texture than other viburnums. Pink flower buds open to 2- to 4-inch-wide, flattened clusters of white flowers from late winter through early spring. Berries are an unusual metallic blue and quite showy until they ripen to black at summer's end. Upright to

rounded; 6 to 12 feet tall, 5 to 8 feet wide. An attractive informal hedge or screen. Use as specimen in a border.

Site: Leatherleaf viburnum thrives in sun to part or full shade; laurustinus viburnum in light to full shade. Well-drained but moist, average to fertile, slightly acid to alkaline soil; moderate moisture. Leatherleaf hardy in zones 6 to 8; laurustinus, zones 8 and 9.

How to Grow: Plant container or balled-and-burlapped shrubs in spring or fall, spacing 4 to 6 feet apart for hedge or screen, farther for specimen, depending upon ultimate size. Plant two leatherleaf plants to ensure best berry set. Foliage may become winter-tattered in northern areas or plant may be killed to ground. Protect from full sun in winter. Laurustinus also prone to winter injury if not hardened off in fall; avoid pruning, fertilizing, and unnecessary watering in late summer and autumn.

Control size of leatherleaf by pruning with thinning cuts immediately after flowering, if needed. Cut to ground in late winter to rejuvenate. Prune laurustinus every few years in midsummer if used as a hedge. Both usually pest- and disease-free.

Cultivars and Similar Species: Leatherleaf: 'Roseum', pink flower buds open yellowish. *V. lantana* (wayfaring tree), coarse tree, red summer berries; 'Mohican', leathery, dark green, semievergreen leaves, creamy white spring flowers, brilliant red fall berries turn black. *V. × rhytidophylloides*, hybrid of the two, semievergreen, better choice for the Midwest; zones 5 to 8; 'Willowwood', red berries in autumn; 'Allegheny', red berries, rounded, dense form, semievergreen.

Laurustinus: 'Eve Price', pink flowers, compact plant with smaller leaves; 'Compactum', dense and slow-growing, smaller leaves, to 5 feet; 'Robustum', larger leaves. *V. davidii*, mounded to 3 feet tall, glossy, 5-inch-long, pointed leaves with prominent veins, white flowers and blue berries; zones 7 to 9.

YUCCA SMALLIANA
(Y. FILAMENTOSA)
Adam's Needle

Native to the southeastern United States, this unusual evergreen (often known as *Yucca filamentosa*) is loved for the architectural effect

YUCCA SMALLIANA 'BRIGHT EDGE'

created by its 2-foot-long, sword-shaped, gray-green leaves, which grow in a dramatic, stemless rosette. The leaves are succulent with curly fibers along the margins and sharp points at the tips. A 3- to 5-foot-tall stalk of 3-inch, bell-shaped, white flowers emerges from the center of the rosette in midsummer, adding to the drama. Grows to 4 feet tall and wide. Use as a year-round accent in Xeriscape, rock, desert, or seashore gardens. May be grouped in a dry area for dramatic effect.

Site: Full sun. Well-drained sandy or gravely soil. Moderate moisture. Drought-tolerant. Zones 5 to 9.

How to Grow: Plant container plants in spring or fall, spacing 3 to 4 feet apart. Cut down old flower stalks and old dead leaves. Use a gravel or stone mulch. No pruning needed. May develop root rot in overly moist site.

Cultivars: 'Ivory Tower', 6-foot flower spikes; 'Bright Edge', green leaves with bright gold edge.

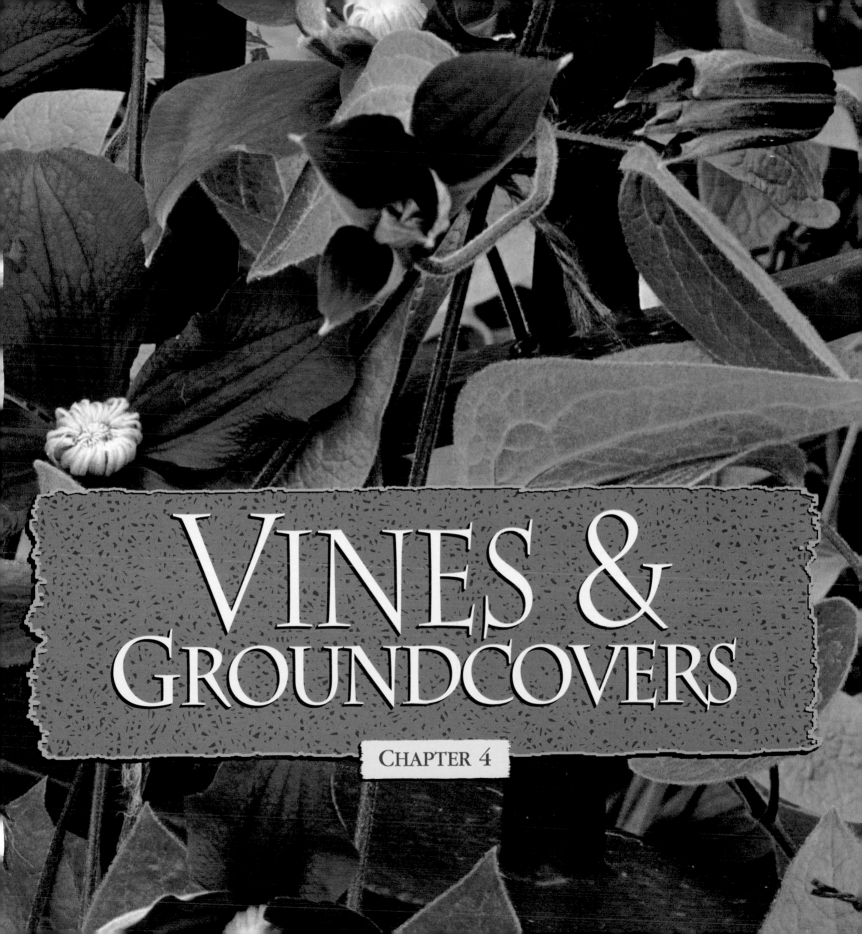

VINES & GROUNDCOVERS

CHAPTER 4

HELPING VINES GROW

Known for their exuberant growth and ability to solve a host of landscape problems, vines and groundcovers belong in every garden. Adorning walls and trellises with a tracery of branches and blossoms or blanketing the garden floor with lush foliage and flowers, these ornamentals are indispensable for giving a finishing touch to a garden or landscape.

PLANTS FOR A SINGLE PLANE

Vines and groundcovers grow mostly in a single plane— groundcovers spread horizontally, and vines spread vertically. Some vines, such as English ivy, also behave like a groundcover, scrambling across the ground and rooting in the soil. But once they encounter a vertical object, such as a tree, they change direction, climbing up with great speed.

Most vines and groundcovers are easy to grow, but their competitive habits sometimes transform them from garden friends into garden thugs. If allowed to grow out of control, these vigorous plants threaten nearby plants and invade garden areas and even uncultivated areas where you never intended them to take up residence. But if you know how to tame them, vines and groundcovers perform a host of useful functions in the garden.

HOW VINES CLIMB

Gardeners refer to "training vines," as though a gardener educates a vine to do its appointed job. Usually it's the gardener who needs to be trained. Vines need support to flourish. The gardener must recognize what the vine needs and provide correct support.

Vine roots stay grounded, but the leaves and blossoms reach toward the sun. In the natural environment, they climb into trees or shrubs or scale up rocks and cliff faces. In the garden, they climb walls and fences or grow on trellises and poles. Vines climb by many methods. Observe how a vine grows, because its climbing method

CLIMBING METHODS OF VINES

TENDRILED
Ampelopsis spp. (porcelain-berry, pepper vine)
Asarina scandens (climbing snapdragon)
Bignonia capreolata (cross vine)
Clematis spp. (clematis)
Cobaea scandens (cup-and-saucer vine)
Passiflora spp. (passion flower)

TWINING
Actinidia spp. (hardy kiwi, kolomikta vine)
Akebia quinata (five-leaf akebia)
Aristolochia macrophylla (Dutchman's pipe)

Campsis radicans (trumpet creeper)
Celastrus scandens (American bittersweet)
Gelsemium sempervirens (Carolina jasmine)
Ipomoea spp. (morning glory, moonflower, cardinal climber, cypress vine)
Jasminum spp. (jasmine)
Lonicera spp. (honeysuckle)
Mina lobata (crimson starglory)
Thunbergia alata (black-eyed Susan vine)
Trachelospermum jasminoides (Confederate jasmine)
Wisteria spp. (wisteria)

CLINGING
Campsis radicans (trumpet creeper)
Euonymus fortunei (wintercreeper) trails or climbs
Ficus pumila (creeping fig)
Hedera helix (English ivy) trails or climbs
Hydrangea anomala subsp. *petiolaris* (climbing hydrangea)
Parthenocissus tricuspidata (Boston ivy)

GRABBING
Pyracantha spp. (firethorn)

CLAMBERING OR LEANING
Rosa spp. (climbing and rambler roses)

Vines climb their supports in a variety of ways. This 'Heavenly Blue' morning glory, an annual vine, twines around a sturdy handrail.

indicates how it can be "trained" to grow in the spot of your choice.

Vines may be annual or perennial. Perennial vines may be herbaceous or woody, and woody ones may be deciduous or evergreen. Regardless of its growth habit, a particular vine moves vertically by one or several of the following methods: twining, clinging, grabbing, or clambering:

■ TENDRILED VINES have threadlike tendrils that grow from leaf axils or leaf tips and tightly grasp corkscrew-fashion around a narrow support. Or, they have long leaf stems (petioles) that twist around and grab an object in the same manner as a tendril.

■ TWINING VINES have pliable stems and trunks that twine around a sturdy object in a spiraling stranglehold.

■ CLINGING VINES have aerial rootlets that form along the stems and branches and cling to a rough surface. Some clinging vines have adhesive disks that are called holdfasts. These disks form at the ends of tendrils and cling to smooth or rough surfaces.

■ GRABBING VINES, sometimes called hook climbers, have thorns or long, barbed hooks that grab onto or tangle with a support, often another plant.

■ CLAMBERING OR LEANING VINES have long, pliable canes and branches that sprawl and clamber over an object, leaning on or drooping over it.

HOW TO TRAIN VINES

Clamps made especially for vines help them climb a masonry wall. Insert the clamps in the mortar.

Gently weave twining stems where you want them to grow.

Fasten wires or strings to a wall or fence to create a support system for a climbing vine.

SUPPORTING AND CONTROLLING VINES

Photo by E. Alan McGee

Wisteria, a twining vine, is among the most beautiful of climbing plants. But plant wisteria with caution. Unless it is kept well pruned each fall, it quickly will get out of control.

Some vines, such as large-flowered clematis, are delicate, well-mannered plants that seldom get out of hand. Others, such as wisteria and trumpet creeper, are so vigorous they can strangle trees and topple arbors. But with good maintenance and care, even the most aggressive vines can be important assets to your landscape.

VINE SUPPORTS

A twining vine, such as honeysuckle, cannot grow on a masonry wall, because it has nothing to twine around. Climbing hydrangea, however, happily scales the wall, hoisting itself up with clinging holdfasts. If you want a honeysuckle to decorate the wall, you need to provide something for it to twine around. A trellis, a piece of wire mesh, or a sturdy wire grid (see box on page 239) are solutions.

Clematis can climb a mailbox, lamppost, or tree trunk only if a gardener provides strings, wires, or a mesh cage for the vine's leaf petioles to grab onto. Black vinyl bird netting—the kind used to keep birds off fruit plants—makes an almost invisible and long-lasting support for clematis and other tendriled vines when attached to a wall or fence or wrapped around a tree trunk. You can make a mesh cage around the lower part of a tree trunk to encourage a twining or grabbing vine to move upward. Once the vine climbs up the lower trunk and into the branches, it's on its own.

Clambering types of vines such as climbing roses, or those that grab by thorns, such as firethorn, need to be tied in place to create a vertical effect. Provide a trellis, post, mesh, or wire grid and use garden twine, strips of cloth, or lengths of old panty hose as ties to position the vine.

Clinging vines such as hydrangea may not want to cling at first. It helps to tie them in place when you plant them. Tie the newly planted vines to nails driven into a wall to provide an anchor or use twine to temporarily hold the vines against a tree trunk.

Vines often need to be given some gentle direction by the gardener. You can unwrap the pliable new growth of a young, twining vine if it heads off where you don't want it, then rewrap it on the trellis, lattice fence, or mesh where it belongs. Be sure to do so gently and to twine the stems in the same direction they were growing.

VINE PRUNING

Woody perennial vines may need to be pruned for any number of reasons: to keep them from getting too large, to encourage blooming, and to remove top-heavy growth that can pull away from a support during windy or stormy weather. Specific pruning needs and techniques are described in the encyclopedia entries starting on page 242. But here's a general rundown on how to go about it.

The best time to prune is in late winter when the vine is leafless. The vine may be a tangle of branches then, but its structure is easy to see. You'll need handheld clippers, lopping shears, or a small pruning saw, depending upon the size of the vine. You'll also need a ladder.

Lift the tangle and try to remove deadwood. You can tell deadwood from live by scratching the bark: Deadwood is brown inside and brittle; live wood is green inside and usually not brittle. (Live clematis vines are always brittle.) Next follow each branch back to its origin at a main branch or trunk. Cut back the side branches to a foot or so from the main trunk, removing individual large branches as you see fit. Do not cut the main trunk, but cut away suckers from its base. New growth will sprout from the shortened branches and from the main trunk.

VINE TAKEOVER TACTICS

Vines look attractive decorating brick buildings and shingled houses, but this adornment sometimes comes at a cost. Although recent research proves that vines actually damage buildings much less than is commonly thought, in some instances vines can harm a structure.

Clinging vines growing on brick or masonry buildings do not trap moisture or cause mortar to crumble. Research shows that vines such as English or Boston ivy harm mortar only on buildings where the mortar already was unsound. The vines actually keep a building's walls and foundation drier. The vines provide insulation during winter and summer, saving on heating and cooling.

A vine growing on a shingled building creates several problems. Clinging vines damage siding when the vine is removed or pruned when it's time to repaint. When the vine is pulled off, it can take loose shingles with it, and it leaves remnants of its rootlets and holdfasts, which must be scoured off before painting. Some twiners, such as wisteria, have such strong growing tips they can pry up siding and roofing shingles.

To avoid potential damage, grow vines on trellises held away from the wall, on overhead arbors, or on pergolas instead of directly on the house. But remember that those romantic, vine-covered English cottages have stood for centuries without the vines destroying them.

Weigh the look against any extra maintenance you might have to do.

When extra-vigorous vines grow high into trees, they can cause damage. Heavy vines, such as English ivy, that drape a tree's branches make the tree top-heavy, which is dangerous in a storm. The vine's foliage, which catches a load of rain, ice, or snow, or acts like a sail in a strong wind, can cause the tree to topple. Twining vines, such as wisteria and bittersweet, can literally strangle a tree with their enormous twining trunks. Any vine covering a tree's branches blocks sunlight from the tree's leaves, causing its decline. Routine hard pruning can keep a vine from getting out of control and harming the tree.

ESCAPEES

Some non-native ornamental vines have escaped cultivation, becoming nuisances in natural woodlands. The plant that ate the South—kudzu—is an escaped vine that engulfs anything—trees, shrubs, houses—and has proved impossible to eradicate. Oriental bittersweet and Japanese honeysuckle are troublesome pests in some areas of the country where the climate allows their seeds to readily germinate in the wild. Birds eat the berries, fly into the woods, and while sitting on a tree branch "deposit" the seeds, which land near the base of the tree. The seeds germinate, perfectly positioned for climbing, and the new vines twine their way up and over the tree, smothering it in the process.

Be responsible and do not plant such vines in regions where they pose a threat to the landscape. The encyclopedia section starting on page 242 includes warnings about vines that can become nuisances.

HOW TO BUILD A WIRE GRID FOR HOLDING A TWINING OR GRABBING VINE TO A WALL

To create a vine-covered wall, you'll need to provide a permanent support for twining and tendriled vines such as clematis and passion flower. You also will need to tie clambering vines or vines that climb by thorns, such as roses and pyracantha, to help them climb. Here's how to create a pattern of crisscrossing wires that will form an 8-inch grid suitable for most grabbing or twining vines:

1. Use galvanized #18 wire, which will not rust and is long-lasting. Choose a dark color that blends well with most surfaces.

2. Use galvanized #12 screw hooks or eye hooks. Screw hooks are better because the hook will be 1 inch from the wall when it is driven in. This holds the wires an inch from the wall, allowing the vines more room to maneuver. In mortar or brick walls, use a drill with a mortar bit to make a hole for a plastic screw holder, then screw the hook into it.

3. Measure and mark an area to be covered by the vine so that the area is a multiple of 8 inches in both width and height.

4. Space the hooks in straight lines at 8-inch intervals across the top and bottom of the area to be covered. Attach the wires to the screw hooks in vertical lines from top to bottom. Pull the wires taut. Bend the hooks closed with pliers.

5. Space the hooks on the left and right sides of the pattern at 8-inch intervals. Position the top hooks 8 inches below and 8 inches toward the exterior of the hooks at the ends of the top row and 8 inches above and to the exterior of the hooks at the ends of the bottom row. Attach the wires and pull them taut. Bend the screw hooks closed with pliers.

PLANTING AND CARING FOR GROUNDCOVERS

Photo by Maris/Semel

By definition, a groundcover is any type of plant that covers the ground with dense, relatively low growth when planted en masse. Groundcovers must grow fairly quickly to achieve this ideal. Like vines, these highly competitive plants have several techniques to help them rapidly cover soil. Observe how individual groundcovers grow, because that will tell you how to keep them under control.

GETTING ESTABLISHED

To start a large swathe of a groundcover and get it established, turn over the soil in the entire planting area, rake it free of weeds, and improve the soil with organic matter (see Chapter 12). Once you've prepared the planting bed, install the young plants. Depending upon the type of plant, you will be planting bare-root plants (usually rooted cuttings), quart- or gallon-size container-grown plants, or flats of young plants (usually cuttings rooted in soil).

Spacing the young plants properly is crucial in getting a groundcover to fill in quickly. (See the encyclopedia starting on page 242 for the proper spacing for specific groundcovers.) Usually a year or two of growth will be needed to achieve the desired thick cover. Larger plants can be spaced farther apart than rooted cuttings. For the sake of economy, you can space plants farther apart than is recommended, but it will take an additional year or two for the plants to develop into a thick cover, and you will need to control weeds during that time.

Cuttings of English ivy, myrtle, mondo grass, and pachysandra—the most popular evergreen groundcovers—should be spaced about 8 to 10 inches apart "on center" (that is, from the center of one plant to the center of the next). By doing a little math, you can determine how much of the groundcover you'll need to cover a large area. Measure in inches the length and width of the area you wish to plant. (Measure in feet if the plants should be spaced a certain number of feet apart.) Then insert the measurements in the following formula: (width divided by spacing per plant) × (length divided by spacing per plant). The result is the number of plants needed.

After setting plants in the ground, water them well, then apply a 3- to 4-inch layer of organic mulch (see pages 522–525), such as wood chips or shredded bark, to keep weeds from encroaching. Hand-pull any

Groundcovers, such as this flowering bugleweed and the emerald green pachysandra, are good low-maintenance choices for shady areas where grass doesn't thrive.

To eventually achieve a thick, lush covering, groundcover plants must be correctly spaced. These periwinkle plants are planted at 10-inch intervals.

weeds that appear; these will probably germinate from seeds in the soil where the mulch is thin. Reapply mulch every year until the groundcover has filled in enough to deter any weeds.

MAINTAINING A HEALTHY GROUNDCOVER

Maintenance on an established groundcover is usually minimal. Fertilize once a year in spring according to the plant's needs. Hand-pull any weeds, usually tree and vine seedlings, that appear. Water during drought according to the plant's needs. Gently rake off fallen tree leaves or debris from the top of the planting. Do not remove leaves that settle beneath the branches or foliage unless they are unsightly. These will decay and nourish the groundcover. The last step is to edge the groundcover to prevent it from encroaching into the lawn or other garden areas.

REINING IN

The very quality that makes a groundcover plant successful— its ability to quickly cover ground and form a thick blanket—can make it a pest. You'll need to keep an eye on aggressive groundcovers and prevent them from invading areas where they're not welcome. Groundcovers such as bugleweed, English ivy, pachysandra, and wintercreeper, when used in beds under trees and shrubs, easily invade a lawn.

There are several methods for controlling a groundcover, depending on the way it grows. A groundcover that spreads by rhizomes, such as pachysandra, can be stopped with a physical barrier placed underground. Use steel or vinyl lawn edging. One that spreads by stolons or runners, such as myrtle or English ivy, will migrate over the edging and colonize on the other side. Control these plants by trimming the runners several times a year.

Many landscape maintenance workers routinely edge the border between the groundcover bed and the lawn with a half-moon edger or other tool, creating a trough that can't be crossed by the groundcover roots or the grass roots. This trough outlines the shape of the beds and lawn and keeps them neat. As the beds are edged, any groundcover rhizomes or runners are severed. A brick or stone edging or mowing strip also can mark the outline of the beds, but it may or may not prevent the groundcover from crossing onto the lawn. However, you can use the decorative edging as a guide to quickly trim the groundcover when it crosses the edge.

REJUVENATION

Some evergreen groundcovers suffer "winterburn" during severe winters. The foliage looks brown and scorched from a combination of full sun and severely cold weather. When this happens, rejuvenate the groundcover by mowing it with a lawn mower set on its highest setting—usually 4 inches. The mowing cuts back the stems, removes brown leaves, and stimulates fresh, new growth.

Some groundcovers, such as mondo grass, creeping lilyturf, and wintercreeper, should be rejuvenated this way every year, even if they have not been winterburned. The mowing improves the plants' appearance and, in the case of wintercreeper, keeps it desirably low.

HOW GROUNDCOVERS SPREAD

Most groundcovers spread by one of the following methods:

■ **RHIZOMES:** Underground stems that travel long distances near the soil surface and send up new topgrowth along their length.

■ **RUNNERS:** Aboveground stems that stretch along the soil surface a great distance from the main plant, sending out roots and topgrowth along their length.

■ **STOLONS:** Aboveground stems that arch away from the main plants and form roots and new plants where the tips meet the soil.

■ **LONG BRANCHES** that grow in a horizontal or an arching manner; these may or may not send down roots where they touch the ground.

Vines & Groundcovers

ACTINIDIA KOLOMIKTA
Kolomikta Vine

Grow this deciduous twining vine for its brightly variegated heart-shaped leaves, not for its inconspicuous but fragrant flowers. The leaves, which open purple, mature to bright green marked with large splashes of pure white and pink; male vines produce the most colorful foliage. The grapelike berries, which form on female plants if pollinated by

ACTINIDIA KOLOMIKTA

a male vine, are edible and ripen in early fall. Vines reach 20 feet. Train kolomikta vine to cover an arch or arbor or to twine around a fence. Provides colorful accent all season.

Site: Full sun to part shade; best color in sun. Fertile, moist soil best; tolerates clay soil and thrives in alkaline site. Hardy in zones 4 to 8.
How to Grow: Plant bare-root or container-grown plants in spring. Take cuttings from semi-mature stems in midsummer. Needs only light pruning in late winter. Usually pest-free. Attracts cats, who may shred leaves.
Cultivars and Similar Species: 'Arctic Beauty', colorful leaves. *Actinidia arguta* (hardy kiwi), rampant grower; produces edible fruits.

AEGOPODIUM PODAGRARIA 'VARIEGATUM'
Bishop's Weed, Goutweed

This groundcover's lovely foliage belies the plant's beastly nature—if conditions are right, the creeping rootstocks spread like wildfire through

AEGOPODIUM PODAGRARIA 'VARIEGATUM'

a garden. The leaves are variegated with bright white borders surrounding green centers. Lacy white flowers appear above the foliage in early summer. Some gardeners keep bishop's weed from becoming invasive by planting it where the spreading roots can be contained by a brick walk, stone wall, or house foundation. Foliage grows 1 foot tall; flower stalks 18 to 20 inches. The white-and-green leaves look lovely in a shade garden. Combine with big blue-leaf hostas or cover large areas in naturalistic gardens.

Site: Full sun to full shade. Leaves may burn in full sun if soil is dry. Any soil type; grows and spreads rapidly in rich, moist soil and slowly in compacted or dry soil. Best in average soil with even moisture. Hardy in zones 4 to 9.
How to Grow: For rapid coverage space container-grown plants or divisions 1 to 2 feet apart. Divide in spring by cutting rootstocks into

segments containing sprouting buds. Usually invasive; keep in place with lawn edging or curbing, or plant in naturalistic area. Resprouts even from tiny root left in soil, so it's difficult to eradicate once planted. Cut off faded flower stalks for best appearance. Cut back dead leaves and stems in late fall or winter. Dig out plants that revert to all-green. Usually pest-free.
Similar Species: All-green form spreads even more aggressively and should be avoided.

AJUGA REPTANS
Bugleweed, Carpet Bugle

Gardeners love this ground-hugging, rapidly spreading perennial for its beautifully textured foliage and spikes of lavender-blue (sometimes white or pink), late-spring flowers that grow 4 to 12 inches tall. Prominent veins give the shiny, dark green, semievergreen leaves a quilted appearance; leaves grow 3 inches high. Several outstanding cultivars

AJUGA REPTANS 'BURGUNDY GLOW'

with variegated or colored leaves and purple, pink, or white flowers bring months of color to a shady spot. Excellent carpeting groundcover beneath shrubs or trees in mixed borders or combined with taller perennials in shaded border or naturalistic garden.

Site: Light to full shade; tolerates full sun if kept moist. Bronze-leaf types need some sun. Fertile, well-drained, moist soil; moderate to plentiful, even moisture. Hardy in zones 4 to 9.

How to Grow: Plant container-grown plants anytime, spacing 12 to 18 inches apart. Seeds don't come true to type. Divide anytime during growing season. Spreads rapidly; may invade lawn areas if planted as edging. Remove spent flowers to prevent seeding and improve appearance. Leaves brown if soil dries. Clean up winter-damaged foliage in early spring. Crown rot is troublesome, particularly in the South. Provide air circulation; apply fungicide.

Cultivars and Similar Species: 'Pink Beauty', green leaves, pink flowers; 'Alba', green leaves, white flowers; 'Atropurpurea', dark bronze-purple leaves, blue flowers; 'Burgundy Glow', white-pink-rose-and-green-variegated foliage, blue flowers; 'Bronze Beauty', bronze leaves, blue flowers; 'Gaiety', dark bronze-purple leaves, lilac flowers; 'Silver Beauty', gray-green leaves edged white, blue flowers. *Ajuga pyramidalis*, more upright; spreads slowly. *A. genevensis*, hairy, dark green leaves, upright to 12 inches tall, blue, pink, or white flowers; spreads slowly.

AKEBIA QUINATA
Five-Leaf Akebia, Chocolate Vine

Because it forms a heavy drapery of stems and greenery, this vigorous, twining vine needs an extra-strong support. Its palmately compound leaves have five rounded leaflets, each 1 to 3 inches long, on reddish stems. Leaves remain lustrous and green well into winter in the North and are evergreen in the South. Demure sprays of small, dusky maroon or lavender flowers are more notable for their spicy vanilla or chocolate scent than for their appearance. Female and male flowers appear in separate clusters on the

AKEBIA QUINATA

same plant. In areas with long growing seasons, purple, sausage-shaped pods form in late summer. Vines grow to 30 or more feet tall; may grow 15 feet tall the first growing season. Refined and elegant appearance. Provides quick privacy screen on trellis. Beautifies unattractive chain-link fence. Use to create shade over pergola or gazebo. Combine with other flowering vines such as clematis, large-flowered climbing roses, or moonflowers.

Site: Full sun to full shade; grows most rampantly in sun. Control growth by planting in shade. Any well-drained soil; most vigorous in fertile, moist site. Semievergreen in zones 4 to 6; evergreen in zones 7 to 9. Can be invasive, especially in warmer parts of its range.

How to Grow: Plant container-grown plants several feet apart along fence or trellis for quick cover. Take stem cuttings in summer; sow seeds outdoors when fresh, or cold-stratify at 40° to 45°F for one month. To keep in bounds, prune hard each year after flowering, especially in small settings. Renew by cutting back to ground if it becomes overgrown. When used as a groundcover, akebia can climb into shrubs and trees. Has escaped cultivation through self-seeding and become a pest in the South. Usually free of pests and disease.

Cultivars: 'Alba', white flowers and fruits. 'Rosea', pale lavender flowers. *Akebia trifoliata* is similar, but with leaves divided into three leaflets; it's slower growing and less cold-hardy.

AMPELOPSIS BREVIPEDUNCULATA 'ELEGANS'
Tricolor Porcelain-Berry, Variegated Amur Ampelopsis

Distinguished by lovely, deeply lobed, green leaves mottled with pink and creamy white, this variegated version of porcelain-berry is much less invasive and troublesome than the green-leaved species. Its inconspicuous flowers bloom on new growth in midsummer, followed by berries. As they ripen, the pea-size fruits change from light green to

AMPELOPSIS BREVIPEDUNCULATA 'ELEGANS'

turquoise to lavender and finally to deep purple or porcelain blue. Clusters often contain berries at all color stages and are showy in early and mid fall. Birds may strip the vines of berries. The open-growing vine needs only a light or medium support for its tendrils to grasp and rapidly reaches to 20 feet high. Plant to climb a trellis, drainpipe, or fence. Colorful leaves liven dull areas. *continued*

AMPELOPSIS BREVIPEDUNCULATA 'ELEGANS'
(continued)

Site: Full sun to part shade; vigorous in sun. Not particular about soil; does well in heavy and rocky soil. Average moisture. Hardy in zones 5 to 9.

How to Grow: Plant bare-root or container-grown plants in spring. Take stem cuttings in late summer. Sow fresh seeds. Best in a warm, sheltered site. Can be pruned to the ground in late winter to renew without harming berry production. Do not plant the green-leaved species, which grows rampantly in the Northeast; it's a noxious weed that is choking native woodlands. 'Tricolor' and 'Elegans' come true from seed. Although they can escape to woodlands, these vines don't choke out native vegetation. Japanese beetles can be a problem.

Cultivars: 'Tricolor', similar or identical to 'Elegans'. *Ampelopsis brevipedunculata* var. *heterophylla*, rampant pest; do not plant. *A. arborea*, peppervine or porchvine, lovely, native, semievergreen vine with pink berries that ripen to dark purple; zones 7 to 9.

ARCTOSTAPHYLOS UVA-URSI
Bearberry, Kinnikinick

This shrubby evergreen groundcover makes an excellent low groundcover in a harsh climate, because it's native to northern parts of all the continents in the Northern Hemisphere. Nodding clusters of small, urn-shaped, pink-tinged white flowers decorate branches in mid spring, followed by abundant, tiny red berries in summer. Berries persist through winter if not eaten by birds—or bears. Fine-textured, lustrous green leaves are neat and tidy, and take on a bronze-purple hue for winter. Named cultivars make superior garden plants compared to the wild species.

ARCTOSTAPHYLOS UVA-URSI

Grows 6 to 12 inches tall; spreads wide with time, rooting as it goes. Use bearberry for beautiful color and texture as large-scale groundcover on difficult sites, such as slopes or erosion-prone areas.

Site: Full sun to part or light shade. Best in infertile, sandy soil. Tolerates acid to alkaline conditions. Average moisture; drought-tolerant once established. Hardy in zones 2 to 7. Tolerates seashore conditions.

How to Grow: Plant only container-grown plants—bare-root plants are difficult to establish—in spring, spacing 1 to 2 feet apart. Rooted branches may be separated and dug up like sod from main plant, but can be tricky to establish. May be desiccated by winter sun and wind; best under snow cover in coldest areas. May be slow to establish, but grows rapidly after first few years. Mulch new groundcover plantings to keep out weeds. Usually pest-free, but leaf spot, mildew, rust, and galls sometimes troublesome.

Cultivars: 'Massachusetts', flat-growing plant, pink flowers, vigorous, pest-resistant. 'Point Reyes', large, green leaves; heat-tolerant. 'Vancouver Jade', pink flowers, deep red winter foliage, vigorous, pest-resistant. 'Wood's Red', large, red fruits, reddish winter foliage, award-winner.

ARISTOLOCHIA MACROPHYLLA (A. DURIOR)
Dutchman's Pipe, Pipe Vine

Old-fashioned and fast-growing, this deciduous vine once was a mainstay for shading country porches. The fleshy, heart-shaped, dark green leaves hang flat and may be 6 to 12 inches long, forming a heavy drapery that provides plenty of deep shade. Leaves turn yellow-brown in autumn. Small, scentless, yellow-and-tan flowers shaped like a curved, wide-mouthed pipe peep from beneath the leaves and are best seen when the vine grows on a trellis or arbor. This native

ARISTOLOCHIA MACROPHYLLA

plant can grow 10 or more feet a year, and can reach 25 feet. Train it on a trellis, chain-link fence, pergola, or gazebo for dense screen. Coarse texture suited to large spaces.

Site: Full sun if given plentiful moisture; tolerates drought if shaded. Best grown in eastern or northern exposures in any well-drained soil. Hardy in zones 4 to 8.

How to Grow: Plant bare-root or container-grown plants in spring. Take cuttings in midsummer. Sow fresh seeds in fall. May be slow to establish, but once it does, it grows rapidly. Pinch side branches to promote branching. Prune back side branches to near main trunk to control size. Stout woody trunks require heavy support. Wind may taller leaves. Aphids and mites are sometimes troublesome.

ASARINA SCANDENS (A. BARCLAIANA)
Climbing Snapdragon, Chickabiddy

This dainty but fast-growing annual vine is loved for its fine-textured flowers and arrowhead-shaped leaves. Blossoms are ½-inch-long, furry, deep violet tubes with lighter throats. Though small, the blossoms appear in quantity, putting on a charming show from midsummer until frost. Climbing snapdragon climbs by wrapping its petioles (leaf stems) around a support in the same manner as clematis. It reaches 8 to 10 feet tall. Grow on a trellis or wire support. Use to twine into other vines or shrubs or to cascade over edge of a container or hanging basket.

ASARINA SCANDENS

Site: Full sun best; tolerates half sun. Fertile, moist soil; even moisture best. Evergreen perennial in zones 9 to 11; grown as annual elsewhere.
How to Grow: Sow seeds indoors four to six weeks before last frost date, taking care to keep young vining plants from tangling; transplant outdoors after frost danger has passed. May self-sow in the garden. Needs thin trellis, string, or wire support. Usually pest-free.
Similar Species: *Asarina erubescens* (creeping or trailing gloxinia) doesn't climb; use to cascade over edges of containers and window boxes.

ASARUM CAUDATUM
British Columbia Wild Ginger

Several species of wild ginger are native to North America, but British Columbia wild ginger is the most popular for gardens, because it's evergreen in most climates. The

ASARUM EUROPAEUM

4-inch-wide leaves are glossy, dark green, and rounded to heart-shaped. Flowers of all wild gingers are purplish brown urns that hide under the leaves in spring and often go unnoticed. Plants grow to about 6 inches high. All gingers spread by underground rhizomes to form beautifully textured, dense mats. Wild ginger gets its name from the gingerlike fragrance emitted from its crushed leaves. Brings beautiful texture to naturalistic shade or woodland garden. Combines well with ferns. Excellent groundcover under shrubs in formal shade gardens.

Site: Light to full shade. Humus-rich, slightly acid soil. Spreads best with abundant moisture, but tolerates drought once established. Hardy in zones 4 to 8; evergreen in warmest regions and in North when protected by snow.
How to Grow: Plant container-grown plants or bare-root rhizomes 1 inch deep, spacing 1 foot apart. Divide in spring or fall. Invasive if not divided or pulled back occasionally. Becomes discolored in too much sun. Slugs may be a problem, but usually pest-free.
Cultivars and Similar Species: *Asarum europaeum* (European wild ginger), almost identical, smaller, glossier leaves; slow spreader; zones 4 to 8. *A. canadense* (Canada wild ginger), native to eastern North America, rapid spreader, furry, 6-inch, heart-shaped, dull green deciduous leaves; roots used as ginger substitute by colonists; zones 3 to 7. *A. shuttleworthii* (southern wild ginger), native to southeastern North America, glossy, mottled, dark-and-light-green leaves; evergreen in South; zones 4 to 8; 'Calloway', foliage mottled silver and green.

BIGNONIA CAPREOLATA
Cross Vine

Native to the South, cross vine blooms in an unusual color and emits an unusual fragrance. Trumpet-shaped blossoms open in profusion for a month in mid to late spring. Blooms are coppery orange to buff brown and smell like curry or mocha. The oval, pointed leaves are evergreen to semievergreen, glossy, dark green in summer and purplish red in cold weather. The vines climb to 30 to 50 feet high on tendrils equipped with adhesive disks and roots along the ground. Cut stems reveal a pulpy center in a cross shape, thus the common name. Attractive for arbor, fence, or in a tree. Attaches to masonry and wood. Not dense enough for screen. *continued*

BIGNONIA CAPREOLATA
(continued)

BIGNONIA CAPREOLATA

Site: Full sun to full shade; best flowering in sunny site. Fertile, moist, well-drained soil. Tolerates wet site. Hardy in zones 6 to 9.
How to Grow: Plant in spring or fall. Cuttings taken in early summer root easily. Prune heavily to control rampant growth. Usually problem-free.
Cultivars: 'Atrosanguinea', dark reddish purple flowers.

CAMPSIS RADICANS
(BIGNONIA RADICANS)

Trumpet Creeper, Trumpet Vine

A deciduous vine native to the Southeast, trumpet vine grows rapidly and climbs high into trees on thick, twining, gray trunks and aerial rootlets. Clusters of large, trumpet-shaped, scarlet-orange flowers bloom for at least six weeks in mid- through late summer, attracting hummingbirds. The large, glossy, feathery, dark green leaves have hairy undersides. Climbs 30 to 40 feet high. Excellent summer color in large-scale gardens. Allow to climb mature sturdy trees, posts, and pergolas. Tolerates urban conditions.

CAMPSIS RADICANS

Site: Full sun to part shade; flowers best in sun. Grows in any soil, but poor soil tames rampant growth. Tolerates dry to wet site. Hardy in zones 4 to 9.
How to Grow: Plant bare-root or container-grown plants in spring. Propagate by severing root suckers or take cuttings in early summer. Flowers on new wood; prune side branches to near main trunk in spring. Destructive to masonry and wood shingles; best planted on sturdy tree or heavy arbor or pergola. Underground roots send up suckers far from main plant and can be a nuisance. Contact with foliage may cause skin rash. Usually pest-free.
Cultivars and Similar Species: 'Flava', yellow blossoms. *Campsis grandiflora* (Chinese trumpet vine), tender Asian species with huge peach-pink trumpets; zones 7 to 9. *C.* × *tagliabuana* 'Madame Galen', large, showy, coral-red blossoms; reaches 30 feet high and is less destructive than *C. radicans;* zones 5 to 9.

CELASTRUS SCANDENS
American Bittersweet

This uncommon native American vine shows spectacular gold-and-orange berries and yellow foliage in autumn. Prized for decorative arrangements, the berries remain showy for a month after leaves drop. Bittersweet climbs to 20 feet or more by twining stems. It bears pointed, dark green leaves during the growing season. Train on a fence or trellis or to climb a sturdy tree; best in naturalistic landscape.

CELASTRUS SCANDENS

Site: Full sun to part shade. Average soil. Drought-tolerant. Hardy in zones 3 to 8.
How to Grow: Plant bare-root or container-grown plants in spring, 2 feet apart for quick cover. Take softwood cuttings. Plant male vine with several female vines to ensure fruit set. Can strangle small shrubs and trees; prune hard each spring or fall. Sometimes beset by aphids, scale insects, mildew.
Cultivars and Similar Species: Oriental bittersweet *(Celastrus orbiculatus)* is spread by birds from gardens to woodlands in Northeast and is rampant pest; often mislabeled as American bittersweet. American bittersweet bears long clusters of berries near branch tips; Oriental bittersweet has round leaves; berries form clusters of three in leaf axils along entire length of stems.

CERATOSTIGMA
PLUMBAGINOIDES
Leadwort, Plumbago

Slow to start in spring, this lovely ground-covering perennial makes its statement late in the growing season. Vivid blue flowers begin to open in late summer and continue well into fall. When petals drop, they leave red calyxes, adding a pretty contrast to the show of blue flowers. As the weather cools, the olive-green, egg-shaped leaves turn rich bronze-red before dropping. Plants grow 8 to 12 inches tall and spread to 18 inches wide. Excellent groundcover to combine with spring and fall bulbs, tall perennials, or shrubs in mixed border or shade garden.

CERATOSTIGMA PLUMBAGINOIDES

Site: Full sun to part or light shade; afternoon shade in South. Average, well-drained soil. Moderate moisture. Hardy in zones 6 to 9, to Zone 5 with winter mulch.
How to Grow: Plant bare-root or container-grown plants in spring, spacing 18 inches apart. Take cuttings in early summer; divide in spring if centers become bare. Cut back woody stems in late winter to stimulate new growth. Doesn't compete well with shallow tree roots. May develop root rot in wet soil.
Similar Species: *Ceratostigma willmottianum*, similar flowers and foliage, but grows as open subshrub, 2 to 3 feet tall, lacks fall color; zones 8 to10.

CHRYSOGONUM VIRGINIANUM
Goldenstar, Green-and-Gold

Woodland clearings are the native site of this wildflower found from Pennsylvania to Louisiana. The 1-inch, five-petaled, long-stalked, starlike, golden yellow flowers smother the ground-hugging plants in spring, and bloom, though less profusely, through summer and fall, as

CHRYSOGONUM VIRGINIANUM

long as the weather isn't too hot. The tidy, triangular, green leaves are hairy with scalloped edges and form a thick mat that remains evergreen in mildest areas. Plants grow 6 to 10 inches tall and 12 to 24 inches across. Goldenstar makes a beautiful and unusual groundcover for a semishady spot in a wildflower garden, mixed border, beside a shady walk, or under taller perennials. Flower color may be brassy; combines well with hot colors and foliage plants such as hostas.

Site: Full sun to full shade; shade needed in southern zones. Fertile, well-drained, moist soil. Plentiful moisture, especially in sun. Hardy in zones 5 to 9.
How to Grow: Plant bare-root or container-grown plants in spring, spacing 12 inches apart. Divide goldenstar in spring or fall every two or three years. Self-sows, but rarely

becomes weedy. Sometimes suffers from mildew if too shady.
Cultivars: *Chrysogonum virginianum* var. *australe*, compact to 6 inches tall, spreads rapidly but flowers are smaller. 'Springbrook', 3 to 5 inches tall, small flowers. 'Allen Bush', long-blooming, 8 inches tall. 'Pierre', clump-forming, long-blooming.

CLEMATIS SPP. AND HYBRIDS
Clematis

The popular hybrid clematis (*Clematis × hybrida*) produces showy, open-faced flowers that range in size from saucers to dinner plates. Petal-like sepals of purple, lavender, white, pink, red, blue, and bicolored are arranged around a center of golden or reddish brown stamens. Many cultivars bloom nonstop from early summer to fall. Others produce two flushes of bloom—in early summer and in late summer or early fall. Seedpods that resemble silky golden pinwheels appear in late summer and fall. The woody,

CLEMATIS × HYBRIDA 'VILLE DE LYON'

slender, deciduous vines climb in a unique way: petioles (leaf stems) twist around a support, hoisting the vines into trees and onto fences. Vines grow 8 to 12 feet, depending upon cultivar.

In addition to the hybrids, there are numerous species worthy of *continued*

CLEMATIS SPP. AND HYBRIDS
(continued)

attention. One of the few evergreen species, Armand clematis (*C. armandii*), features leathery, dark green leaves divided into three narrow leaflets, each with three prominent veins. The vine makes a handsome year-round cover, but it's especially fetching in early spring when masses of almond-scented, waxy, 2-inch, white flowers begin to bloom. The show lasts for a month in spring and is followed in late summer by a display of plumelike seedpods. Vines grow 20 to 30 feet high. Like other clematis, Armand clematis climbs by twining leaf petioles and needs a narrow support.

CLEMATIS ARMANDII

Masses of tiny, four-pointed, white to creamy white stars blanket sweet autumn clematis (*C. maximowicziana, C. dioscoreifolia,* or *C. paniculata*). Sweetly scented flowers are followed by fluffy, silvery seedpods. Triangular leaflets are glossy, remaining green until late fall. This Asian vine grows rapidly, climbing a fence in a summer. Reaches 20 to 30 feet.

Gorgeous, fragrant anemone clematis (*C. montana*) is a standout in late spring, when 2-inch-wide white or pink flowers resembling anemones or dogwood, blanket the stems for several weeks. The blossoms possess a haunting fragrance reminiscent of vanilla. The silky plumes of seedpods festoon the vine in mid- and late summer. Climbs 20 to 30 feet high.

CLEMATIS MONTANA VAR. 'RUBENS'

Masses of golden, bell-shaped, 2-to-4-inch-wide blossoms cover golden clematis (*C. tangutica*) in early summer and again in late summer or early autumn, with sporadic blooming in between. Long, plumey seedpods also decorate the vine from midsummer through fall. The foliage is lovely and fine-textured. Climbs to 15 to 20 feet.

Enjoy clematis for their colorful flowers and vertical accent; hybrids are not dense enough for screen planting, though many species are. Train on trellis, arbor, lattice, or chain-link fence or decorate a shed, pergola, or gazebo. Provide mesh tube for support around lamppost or mailbox. Allow to naturalize, growing into shrubbery and trees. Plant on north side and provide twine lead so vine grows toward light and across shrub. Combine with climbing roses.

Species clematis can be used to cover a wall (with wire support).

Site: Hybrid clematis and anemone clematis grow best with tops in full to half-day sun and with roots in shade. East exposures are good. Armand clematis thrives on a south-facing wall at northern extremes of its range. Sweet autumn clematis likes part to light shade; best with northern or eastern exposure, but likes heat. Golden clematis needs more sun than the others; full sun is best.

Clematis grows best in rich, organic, well-drained soil with pH of 6.5 to 7.0. Needs plentiful moisture. Water deeply each week during growing season. Sweet autumn clematis tolerates most well-drained soils; somewhat drought-tolerant, but best with ample moisture. Hybrids are hardy in zones 4 to 8, Armand clematis in zones 7 to 9, sweet autumn clematis in zones 4 to 9 (performs well in both North and South), anemone clematis in zones 6 to 8, and golden clematis in zones 4 to 8.

How to Grow: Plant well-rooted, container-grown plants, rather than rooted cuttings, in spring, in large, well-prepared hole. Space 5 feet apart. Position crown 2 inches below the level it was growing in its container to promote branching. Cut back to 18 inches at planting to promote branching. Difficult to propagate by softwood cuttings.

Needs sturdy, narrow support; wire mesh or lattice is ideal. Tie trunk to bottom of support. Keep soil cool with mulch and shade; avoid piling mulch against stems. Fertilize every spring. Hybrids that bloom in spring on old growth and again in late summer on new growth should be pruned annually by removing deadwood in spring, then cutting back hard in summer after flowering. Hybrids that bloom nonstop bloom on new wood: Prune each year in early spring to 12 to 18 inches from ground, just above a pair of buds.

Fungus-wilt disease serious, but rarely bothers vigorous vines. Rabbits and deer can destroy young plants; enclose base in partially buried, wire-mesh cylinder. Japanese beetles a problem.

Aphids sometimes bother Armand clematis. Sweet autumn clematis may get spider mites in hot, dry site. Anemone clematis may suffer from wilt and Japanese beetles. Small-flowered species like golden and sweet autumn clematis do not suffer much from wilt.

Armand clematis may lose leaves at base; camouflage with shrubs or perennials. Prune tops every several years immediately after blooming.

Pinch stem tips of sweet autumn clematis to promote branching and denser growth. Can grow so high that bloom is unnoticed overhead; prune to ground each spring to control growth and promote flowering near eye level, if needed. Reseeds, can get weedy. Climbs best on wire or fine lattice.

Anemone clematis needs pruning only to control size. Blooms on previous season's growth; prune immediately after flowering every few years by cutting off tangle of side branches close to main trunk. If tops are winter-killed, vines won't flower.

Prune golden clematis in late winter to control size, if desired. The top may winter-kill in cold climates, but vine regrows from roots and blooms in summer and fall.

Cultivars and Similar Species: Large-flowered hybrids: 'Allanah', 7-inch, ruby flowers with brown centers; 'Candida', 12-inch pure white flowers with yellow centers; 'Comtesse de Bouchard', 5-inch mauve flowers with creamy stamens; 'Etoile de Violette', 4-inch dark purple flowers with bold yellow centers; 'General Sikorsky', 7-inch, medium blue flowers with gold centers; 'H.F. Young', 6 to 8-inch blue flowers with creamy stamens; 'Miss Bateman', 5-inch creamy blossoms, chocolate-red stamens; 'Nelly Moser', 8-inch white flowers with pink stripes and dark centers; 'Niobe', 5-inch ruby flowers; C. × jackmanii (Jackman clematis), 5-inch, four-sepaled purple flowers with green centers.

Armand clematis: 'Appleblossom', pale pink; 'Snowdrift', large, pure-white flowers.

Sweet autumn clematis: *C. virginiana* (virgin's bower), Northeastern native, blooms earlier, looks more delicate; zones 4 to 7. *C. drummondii*, similar Southwestern native; zones 6 to 8.

Anemone clematis: Forma *grandiflora*, 3- to 4-inch white flowers; var. *wilsonii*, white, heavily perfumed. *C.m.* var. *rubens*, rosy pink flowers with reddish new growth; 'Odorata', heavily scented; zones 6 to 8.

Golden clematis: *C. texensis* (scarlet or Texas clematis), scarlet, urn-shaped flowers in summer and fall, climbs to 10 feet tall; dies to ground each year; zones 5 to 8; 'Duchess of Albany', bright pink. *C. alpina* (alpine clematis), flaring bell-shaped blossoms early to midsummer, needs no pruning, zones 3 to 9; 'Willy', pale pink; 'Helsingborg', light blue.

COBAEA SCANDENS
Cup-and-Saucer Vine, Cathedral Bells

Although this tropical vine is a perennial, it's grown as an annual in most gardens. It starts growing rapidly when hot weather sets in,

COBAEA SCANDENS

hoisting itself skyward with tendrils that grow from the tips of its leaves. Vines can reach 20 to 30 feet high in a single season. In earlier times, the vine frequently was used to conceal the outhouse. The 2-inch, cupped

blossoms open creamy white and turn deep violet. They're set off by flat, green calyxes, creating a cup-and-saucer effect. Blossoms appear from midsummer through fall, and have a musk and honey scent. Use in summer to camouflage chain-link fence or other eyesore. Elegant on arbor or lattice fence.

Site: Full sun and warm exposure, best in northern climates; needs afternoon shade in southern climates. Average to poor, well-drained soil. Plentiful moisture. Perennial in zones 9 to 11; annual elsewhere.
How to Grow: Sow seeds outdoors when soil has warmed, or start indoors two to four weeks before last frost date. May self-sow. Needs strong support such as trellis or wire fence. Fertilize only when first planted; later fertilization produces much growth but few flowers. Susceptible to aphids and spider mites.
Cultivars: 'Flore Albo', creamy white flowers.

CONVALLARIA MAJALIS
Lily-of-the-Valley

Valued for its delicious fragrance and dainty form, lily-of-the-valley is popular in bridal bouquets and is a charming, low-maintenance groundcover. The broad green leaves resemble tulip leaves, but remain attractive until late summer. Slender stems emerge in mid spring to bear 12 to 20 tiny, bell-shaped, waxy white flowers. Plants grow 6 to 10 inches tall and spread widely. Best used as groundcover in naturalistic garden, under shrubs, or in woodland or shade garden. Excellent cut flower.

Site: Light shade; sun in cool-summer areas. Humus-rich, acid to neutral, moist soil. Apply manure or compost in late fall. Hardy in zones 3 to 7; performs poorly in milder climates. *continued*

CONVALLARIA MAJALIS
(continued)

CONVALLARIA MAJALIS

How to Grow: Plant rhizomes in fall or early spring 1 to 2 inches deep, 4 to 6 inches apart. Divide in fall when leaves yellow, or in late summer when stands become crowded. Creeping rootstocks spread to form thick stands and may be invasive. Foliage yellows early if soil dries. Stem rot and leaf spot sometimes troublesome.

Cultivars: 'Rosea', light pink; 'Plena', double-flowered white.

EPIMEDIUM × VERSICOLOR 'SULPHUREUM'
Bishop's Hat, Barrenwort

Grown more for its striking foliage than its dainty flowers, this ground-covering plant thrives in conditions that daunt other perennials. The arrow-shaped, toothed, olive-green leaves grow on wiry stems that emerge from the ground. Foliage is tinged with red when young, turning deep crimson in fall. Evergreen in warm climates and semievergreen in colder areas, the leaves look attractive in winter even if they turn brown. Sprays of nodding, ¾-inch, soft yellow flowers with short spurs create a delicate effect in early to mid spring.

Plants grow 8 to 12 inches tall and spread to 12 inches across. Effective edging for beds, borders, walks, and paths. Use in shade or woodland garden with ferns and flowering perennials. Use as groundcover beneath trees and shrubs.

EPIMEDIUM × VERSICOLOR 'SULPHUREUM'

Site: Light to full shade. Best in fertile, humus-rich, moist soil, but tolerates poor, dry soil in full shade. Hardy in zones 5 to 8.

How to Grow: Plant bare-root or container-grown plants in spring, spacing 12 inches apart. Divide woody rhizomes in spring after flowering or in fall; reproduces readily from small sections. Cut back all foliage in early spring, especially if winter-tattered, to encourage new growth and reveal flowers. Usually problem-free.

Cultivars and Similar Species: 'Cupreum', orange-yellow flowers. *Epimedium grandiflorum*, oval, 1-inch, green leaves that turn red in fall, pink-and-white flowers; 'Rose Queen', large raspberry-pink flowers; 'White Queen', white flowers. *E. pinnatum*, hairy leaves, yellow flowers with brown spurs. *E. × youngianum* 'Roseum', red-tinged, heart-shaped new leaves turning green, crimson spurred flowers; 'Niveum', snow-white flowers; *E. × rubrum*, rosy red-and-white flowers, foliage red-tinged in spring, green in summer. Many others.

ERICA CARNEA
(E. HERBACEA)
Spring Heath, Winter Heath

Blooming in late winter or early spring depending on the cultivar, spring heath brightens the garden with slender, heatherlike sprays of tiny, bell-shaped, pink, lavender, or white flowers and fine-textured foliage. A low, spreading woody plant with needlelike evergreen foliage, spring heath is showy throughout the year. It grows 18 to 24 inches high and wide. Mass on slopes to create fine-textured groundcover. Combines well with heather and dwarf conifers.

ERICA CARNEA 'SILBERSCHMELZE'

Site: Full to half sun; best with eastern exposure to protect from winter sun and wind. Well-drained, even sandy soil, rich in organic matter and low in nutrients. Moderate moisture. Hardy in zones 5 to 7; best in cool, moist climate on East Coast or Pacific Northwest.

How to Grow: Plant container-grown or bare-root plants in spring, spacing 12 to 18 inches apart. Take cuttings from new growth; apply rooting hormone. Finicky plants need proper exposure and soil to perform. Will rot in soggy sites. Prune stems hard after flowering. Don't fertilize; overfertilizing promotes lush growth susceptible to winter injury. Can be winter-killed if exposed to drying winter sun and wind;

protect with cut evergreen boughs in harsh climate. Usually pest-free.

Cultivars: Early winter to early spring bloom: 'Silberschmelze', white flowers, tall; 'Winter Beauty', lavender-pink flowers, tall; 'King George', deep pink flowers, medium height.

Midwinter to spring bloom: 'Praecox Rubra', ruby flowers, medium height.

Late winter to early spring bloom: 'Ann Sparkes', pink flowers, gold leaves, medium height; 'Myreton Ruby', red-purple flowers, low; 'Pink Spangles', pink flowers, low to medium height; 'Porter's Red', red-purple flowers, medium height; 'Ruby Glo', ruby-red flowers, low; 'Springwood Pink', pink flowers, low to medium height, easy to grow; 'Springwood White', white flowers, low to medium height, easy to grow; 'Vivelli', magenta flowers, dark green leaves turning black-green in winter, tall.

EUONYMUS FORTUNEI
Wintercreeper

Varying in form from a shrub to a vine, wintercreeper is grown for its rounded, leathery, evergreen leaves, which may be dark green,

EUONYMUS FORTUNEI VAR. *RADICANS*

variegated, or brightly colored. Certain cultivars make dense groundcovers or climbers that scale a wall or tree. Vines cling tightly to surfaces with

EUONYMUS FORTUNEI 'SILVER QUEEN'

aerial roots, or they root as they spread across the ground. Flowers are creamy or greenish and modest, and may be followed by creamy husked pods with orange seeds. As a vine, it climbs 40 feet; as a groundcover, it grows 2 to 24 inches tall and spreads wide, depending on cultivar. Durable, evergreen groundcover in sunny or shady sites; controls erosion. Excellent in formal settings or informal shade and rock gardens. Gives winter interest to a wall.

Site: Full sun to shade; variegated forms need part sun. Average well-drained soil. Moderate moisture; tolerates drought once established. Hardy in zones 5 to 9; good in East, West, and Midwest.

How to Grow: Plant container-grown plants or bare-root cuttings in spring or fall. Space 18 to 24 inches apart for groundcover. Take cuttings in summer; roots readily. Can become invasive; cut back yearly to keep in bounds. Groundcover types can be mown (set mower blade high) in spring to make uniform. May need to weed plants until they fill in. Leaf spot and mildew are problems where air circulation is poor. Scale insects can be serious; control with horticultural oil.

Cultivars and Similar Species: 'Coloratus', oval leaves 1 to 2 inches wide, dark green top and burgundy undersides, turns overall maroon in winter sun; 'Emerald 'n' Gold', dark green leaves edged with gold in summer, purplish green and pink leaves in winter, forms loose, shrubby, 2-foot-tall groundcover; 'Emerald Gaiety', low, vining groundcover, green leaves edged in creamy white in summer, turning pink in winter; 'Kewensis', tiny green leaves, forms tidy groundcover and climbs well, though leaves become larger; 'Silver Queen', white-and-green variegated leaves, low shrubby form. *Euonymus fortunei radicans*, 1-inch, glossy green leaves, forms shrubby bush if pruned, sprawls if not pruned, can climb if given opportunity; 'Variegatus', green-and-white variegated leaves. *E. vegetus*, 2-inch, oval, dark green leaves can form 5-foot-tall shrub, will climb if given opportunity; fruits heavily.

FICUS PUMILA (F. REPENS)
Creeping or Climbing Fig

Dainty of leaf and form, this tenaciously clinging vine climbs by aerial rootlets, creating a beautiful tracery of greenery on a wall. Leaves are dark green on top, lighter and

FICUS PUMILA

hairy on the undersides. The juvenile form of the vine, which is preferred, clings flat to a wall, bearing heart-shaped, inch-long leaves. *continued*

FICUS PUMILA (F. REPENS)
(continued)

Mature fruiting plants develop oblong, leathery leaves that are 2 to 4 inches long on branches that jut about 1 foot from a wall and bear 2-inch, inedible, light green fruits. Vines climb 25 to 50 feet high. Use on unpainted brick or stucco walls. Lovely when used to soften walled courtyard gardens where space is limited.

Site: Part to light shade. Best on north or east wall; foliage may burn in hot exposure. Average to humus-rich, well-drained soil. Keep moderately moist. Hardy in zones 9 to 11; best where humid.

How to Grow: Plant rooted cuttings or container-grown plants in spring, spacing 10 feet apart. Cut back newly planted vines to encourage new growth to cling. Take cuttings in spring. Slow to climb, but will become vigorous. Damages wood and paint. Prune severely every few years to control and keep plant juvenile. For appearance, cut out mature branches if they form. Root-rot nematode and Texas root rot are problems in the Southwest.

Cultivars and Similar Species: 'Minima', small leaves, remains juvenile longer; 'Variegata', white-and-green variegated leaves.

GALAX URCEOLATA (G. APHYLLA)
Galax

A native woodland plant that grows in the southern Appalachian Mountains, galax forms a 6-inch-high mat that eventually spreads 12 to 18 inches. Foliage is beautifully textured evergreen. Heart-shaped to rounded, lustrous, 3-inch, green leaves are slightly cupped, with toothed edges, and turn burnished reddish bronze in fall and winter, if exposed to sun. The plant, which spreads slowly, sends up

GALAX URCEOLATA

clusters of white flowers in slender vertical tapers in early summer. Makes charming, small-scale groundcover in shade garden. Locate under evergreens or on north side of building to provide year-round shade.

Site: Full shade in summer and light shade in winter. Humus-rich, acid soil. Keep moist, but not wet. Hardy in zones 5 to 8; best in cool, moist areas.

How to Grow: Plant "starts" in spring or fall, spacing 8 to 10 inches apart. Divide in spring or fall. May be difficult to establish; control competing weeds. Foliage can be damaged if exposed to full sun in winter. Usually pest-free.

GALIUM ODORATUM (ASPERULA ODORATA)
Sweet Woodruff

This rapidly spreading, ground-covering herb produces a carpet of fine-textured, bright green foliage and tiny, starlike white flowers. Blossoms appear for about a month in spring, a perfect backdrop for bulbs and woodland wildflowers to grow through it. The narrow leaves whorl around upright low stems, creating a swirled effect that contrasts with bolder foliage. Grows 6 to 8 inches tall and spreads by underground runners to cover large areas.

Deciduous in cold climates, sweet woodruff hangs onto its hay-scented leaves through winter in the warmest areas. Excellent groundcover for shade and woodland gardens and mixed borders; plant beneath shrubs and taller, shade-loving perennials such as hostas, ferns, and astilbes.

GALIUM ODORATUM

Site: Light to dense shade. Fertile, humus-rich, moist soil best; less rapid spreading in poor or heavy soil. Keep moist. Hardy in zones 4 to 8.

How to Grow: Plant divisions or container-grown plants in spring, spacing at least 1½ feet apart. Divide by cutting mat into sections in spring or fall. Prevent from invading lawn with edging or lawn border. Usually pest-free, but can suffer from root- or crown-rot fungus in poorly drained site.

GAULTHERIA PROCUMBENS
Checkerberry, Wintergreen

When broken or crushed, the leaves and berries of this native woodland plant release the pungent aroma of wintergreen. Leathery green and rounded, the leaves are about 1½ inches across and form a dense mat along creeping stems. Small, urn-shaped, white flowers peek from under the leaves in spring. Even showier are the bright red berries, which measure about ½ inch in diameter and make a lovely display from late summer through winter. Plant makes a 2-inch-high mat, spreading to 10 to 12 inches. Use as small-scale groundcover in shade or woodland garden.

GAULTHERIA PROCUMBENS

Site: Light to full shade; flowers and fruits best in light shade. Humus-rich, acid soil. Enjoys moist to boggy conditions. Hardy in zones 3 to 7. **How to Grow:** Plant container-grown plants or sodlike transplants in spring, spacing 12 inches apart. Divide creeping stolons in spring or take cuttings from new growth. Keep weeded; doesn't spread aggressively. Usually pest-free.

GELSEMIUM SEMPERVIRENS
Carolina Jasmine, Yellow Jessamine

Native to the Southeast, this vine forms a mass of twining, slender stems cloaked with glossy, pointed, evergreen leaves. Clusters of scented, yellow, 1½-inch-long, trumpet-shaped flowers bloom profusely in late winter and early spring, continuing sporadically into fall. Climbs to 20 feet. All plant parts are poisonous. Train to cover wall, trellis, or archway. Will climb into trees; lovely in

GELSEMIUM SEMPERVIRENS

dogwood or redbud. Combines well with blue flowers of wild phlox.

Site: Full sun to part to light shade. Average to humus-rich soil. Moderate moisture; drought-resistant once established. Hardy in zones 7 to 9, performs well in South and Southwest. **How to Grow:** Plant container-grown plants in spring or fall, spacing 5 to 10 feet apart for dense cover. Take stem cuttings in spring. Tie to supports to direct growth. Every few years, prune severely after first flush of blossoms to tame growth. Mulch to keep roots cool. Usually pest-free. **Cultivars:** 'Pride of Augusta', double flowers.

HEDERA HELIX
English Ivy

Attractive but sometimes invasive, this evergreen plant works as a groundcover or vine. As a vine, the whiskerlike holdfasts along the stems cling to wood, rock, bark, brick, concrete, or metal. As a groundcover, roots form along the lengths of the stems. English ivy grows in two distinct life-cycle phases or forms: juvenile and mature. Juvenile plants are vining with dark, glossy, green, three-to-five-lobed leaves with white veins. Adult growth forms at the tops of climbing juvenile vines, which

become bushy with triangular leaves and produce flowers and berries. Can climb 40 to 50 feet on rough surfaces; spreads equally far as groundcover. Groundcover dense enough to replace lawn, even under shallow-rooted trees. Variegated cultivars look pretty on wall or tree trunk. Deep roots help control erosion on banks.

HEDERA HELIX 'GOLDHEART'

Site: Part to full shade. In cold areas, leaves may burn during winter in full-sun locations. Use as vine on north- or east-facing walls. Best in fertile, humus-rich, moist soil, but tolerates poorer conditions. Hardy in zones 6 to 9. **How to Grow:** Plant rooted cuttings in spring, spacing 2 to 3 feet apart for quick cover. Take cuttings from new juvenile growth in spring. Don't allow to climb too far into trees; weight of vines can topple trees, and dense growth can smother them. Invasive as groundcover; trim back twice a year to control. Protect from winter sun and wind to prevent leaf scorch. Aerial roots can damage wood and masonry. Mites troublesome in hot, dry locations. **Cultivars and Similar Species:** 'Baltica', tolerates severe winter conditions, hardy groundcover under snow to Zone 4, as vine to Zone 6; 'Buttercup', new growth golden-green; 'Goldheart', prominent gold center with green edge; 'Glacier', *continued*

HEDERA HELIX
(continued)

variegated creamy white and gray-green; 'Needlepoint', tiny green leaves, slow-growing, less invasive. *Hedera algeriensis (H. canariensis)* (Algerian ivy); zones 9 to 11, large, thick, glossy green leaves.

HYDRANGEA ANOMALA SUBSP. PETIOLARIS
Climbing Hydrangea

Slightly fragrant, lacy, white flower clusters in early summer to midsummer make an elegant show on this outstanding vine. Leaves are large, glossy, and dark green with serrated edges. The vine forms a sturdy gnarled trunk covered with red-brown exfoliating bark, which is particularly showy in winter. It climbs 60 to 80 feet. Gorgeous on a brick or masonry wall. Best allowed to climb into a tree.

HYDRANGEA ANOMALA
SUBSP. *PETIOLARIS*

Site: Full sun to shade; best on north- or east-facing walls. Provide shade in South. Deep, rich, well-drained, moist, acid soil; grows best with plentiful moisture, especially in South. Hardy in zones 5 to 7.
How to Grow: Plant container-grown plants in spring. May need to tie in place until vine gets started, then requires no help. Sow fresh seeds. Take stem cuttings from nonflowering growth in late spring. May be difficult to get established; grows slowly at first, then takes off dramatically. Climbs trees without harming them. Damages wooden structures; may loosen mortar. Top-heavy vines can pull away from support; prune right after flowering to thin dense growth by cutting side branches back to about 6 inches from main trunk. Usually pest-free.
Similar Species: Japanese hydrangea vine *(Schizophragma hydrangeoides)*, similar but blooms later, lighter green, coarsely toothed leaves; zones 6 to 7.

IPOMOEA × MULTIFIDA

IPOMOEA SPP.
Cardinal Climber, Morning Glory

Cardinal climber *(Ipomoea × multifida)* attracts hummingbirds and butterflies with tubular, 1-inch, bright red flowers which bloom from summer until frost, remaining open day and night. Leaves are decorative, deeply cut into sharp fingers that look like tiny palm leaves. This annual vine climbs to 12 feet by twining stems.

The showy tubular flowers on the morning glory *(I. tricolor)* bloom profusely among heart-shaped leaves from midsummer to frost. Flowers open in morning, close in midafternoon, lasting but one day

IPOMOEA TRICOLOR

each. Blossoms of the species are purplish blue with white throats and red-tipped buds. More commonly grown is the hybrid 'Heavenly Blue'. Other hybrids and species are white, pink, red, purple, lavender, chocolate, or bicolored. The twining annual vine climbs to 8 to 10 feet high or long.

Use either vine to decorate fences, trellises, arbors, mailboxes, and lampposts. Include cardinal climber in a hummingbird garden

Site: Full sun. Average to poor soil. Even moisture. Cardinal climber is an annual vine useful in most climates. Morning glory is a cool-season annual in zones 2 to 11.
How to Grow: Nick seedcoat, then sow seeds outdoors after frost danger. May self-sow, but the poisonous seeds of morning glory seedlings are inferior. Provide support for twining stems. Cardinal creeper is usually problem-free. Canker, leaf spot, and rust may be troublesome for morning glory.
Cultivars and Similar Species:
I. × multifida: I. coccinea (red morning glory), scarlet flowers with yellow throats, heart-shaped leaves.
I. quamoclit (cypress vine), half-hardy perennial grown as annual, lacy leaves and small, flared, tubular scarlet flowers in summer open at night and morning.
I. tricolor: 'Heavenly Blue', 5-inch sky-blue flowers with white center; 'Tricolor

Mix', blue, rose, pink flowers.
I. purpurea, 2- to 2½-inch indigo, maroon, or white flowers; 'Early Call Mix', 4-inch red, pink, blue, chocolate, and violet flowers, good in short-summer areas. *I. × nil*, 'Scarlet O'Hara,' red flowers; 'Scarlet Star,' deep pink and white bicolored flowers. *I. alba* (moonflower), huge, fragrant, night-blooming white flowers. *I. batatus* 'Blackie', purple-black lobed leaves, reaches 10 feet tall, good for foliage contrast on fence or in container, troubled by Japanese beetles.

JASMINUM SPP.
Common Jasmine, Poet's Jasmine, Winter Jasmine

Cultivated since ancient times because of its intensely perfumed flowers, common jasmine (*Jasminum officinale*) is cherished in the South. A weakly twining vine or semiclimbing shrub, the stems are green and look pretty in winter.

JASMINIUM POLYANTHUM

Clusters of small, propeller-shaped, pink-tinged, white flowers bloom heavily in early summer and continue lightly through autumn, perfuming the air with a sweet fragrance. The deciduous to semievergreen leaves are deeply divided into five to nine delicate leaflets with neat points.

Winter jasmine (*J. nudiflorum*) brings color to lifeless gardens in mid to late winter. Yellow flowers appear singly along the stems. Long-lived flowers have no scent, open on warm days beginning in January in the South. The deep green stems look pretty when leafless in winter and the three-parted leaves provide texture from spring through fall. Winter jasmine is a sprawling shrub used as a climber or groundcover. Arching branches root along the ground, forming a deep thicket of ground-covering stems. As a shrub, it reaches 3 to 4 feet tall and twice as wide; it can be trained to 10 to 15 feet high on walls.

Drape winter jasmine over retaining walls or let cascade down banks to control erosion. Train summer jasmine to climb like a vine to 30 feet or allow to sprawl as ground-covering shrub. Both are lovely on walls or fences.

Site: Summer jasmine needs full sun. Evenly moist, average, well-drained soil for best flowering; rich soil produces fewer flowers. Hardy in zones 7 to 9; deciduous in zones 7 and 8; evergreen in Zone 9. Winter jasmine likes full sun to light shade. Average to poor, well-drained soil. Somewhat drought-tolerant. Hardy in zones 6 to 9.

How to Grow: Plant container-grown plants in spring or fall. Space summer jasmine 5 to 10 feet apart, winter jasmine 3 feet apart. Take stem cuttings in summer or fall; roots easily if treated with rooting hormone.

Tie the summer species to trellis or wire support for vining effect; plant against warm wall for best flowering. Easy to cut back and control. May need winter protection in coldest zones. Prune in fall after flowering ceases.

Winter jasmine blooms on old wood; prune immediately after blooming. Rejuvenate and keep in bounds by cutting to 6 inches from ground every

three or four years. Both species are usually problem-free.

Similar Species: *J. officinale: J.o. 'Affine'* has larger, pink-tinged flowers. *J. polyanthum*, evergreen, clusters of pink buds, heavily scented, blossoms from spring through fall, twines to 10 feet high; zones 9 to 10.

J. nudiflorum: 'Aureum', leaves blotched with yellow. *J. mesnyi* (primrose jasmine), larger, clear yellow flowers in spring and summer on climbing plant; zones 7 to 9.

JUNIPERUS SPP.
Shore Juniper, Creeping Juniper, Savin Juniper

Native to the seashores of Japan, low and dense shore juniper (*Juniperus conferta*) sends out long horizontal branches that root along

JUNIPERUS CONFERTA 'BLUE PACIFIC'

the ground, making an excellent evergreen groundcover. The sharp-pointed needles are bright bluish green in summer, but may turn yellow-green or bronze-green in winter. Dark blue, berrylike cones with a waxy coating make a pretty addition to the greenery during winter. Shore juniper grows 1 to 1½ feet high, spreading 6 to 9 feet wide.

Creeping juniper (*J. horizontalis*) is the most popular ground-hugging juniper. It's native to the *continued*

JUNIPERUS SPP.
(continued)

JUNIPERUS HORIZONTALIS

northeastern shores and slopes of North America. The needles are mostly the scalelike adult form, creating soft feathery green, blue-green, or steel-blue ropes on wide-spreading, trailing branches. Needles may turn plum in winter. The blue cones rarely appear on garden plants. Creeping juniper grows 1 to 2 feet high; spreads to form large mats 4 to 8 feet wide.

Broadmoor savin juniper (*J. sabina* 'Broadmoor'), a low, spreading cultivar of a normally vase-shaped shrub makes a good choice for a tough site. The horizontally spreading branches are wide-reaching, but tend to mound up in the center, giving a mass planting an undulating appearance. The needlelike foliage is bright green and feathery during the growing season, but may become yellowish green in winter. (Can easily be distinguished from *J. horizontalis* in winter, because the latter turns plum colored.) The foliage emits an unpleasant odor if crushed. Plants are ground hugging to 1½ feet tall and spread to cover a 5-foot area.

Shore juniper is excellent for stabilizing slopes, banks, and sand dunes. Use creeping and Broadmoor savin juniper as groundcover over large areas on difficult slopes or hot, dry sites. All three create lovely texture as groundcover in front of taller shrubs and trees. Use shore juniper to drape over low wall.

JUNIPERUS SABINA

Site: Full sun best; shore juniper tolerates half shade better than other junipers. Shore juniper and Broadmoor savin juniper need average to sandy, well-drained soil. Shore juniper tolerates heavy soil only if well drained; it thrives in seashore conditions and tolerates salt spray. Creeping juniper tolerates road salt and a wide range of soil from sandy and gravelly to heavy and slightly alkaline. All three tolerate drought, but do best with moderate moisture. Shore juniper is hardy in zones 6 to 8 and is popular in the South. Creeping juniper is hardy in zones 2 to 9, tolerating hot, dry conditions; good in the South and West. Broadmoor savin juniper is suited to zones 3 to 8.

How to Grow: Plant container-grown plants in spring or fall, spacing 5 feet apart. Cuttings are difficult to root. To suppress weeds, mulch groundcover plantings until filled in. Cut back long branches as needed to control spread.

Dieback can be problem for shore junipers in heavy, soggy soil.

Juniper blight can be serious for creeping juniper; spider mites may be troublesome. Broadmoor is blight-resistant, but juniper twig blight can be a serious problem with the species and some cultivars.

Cultivars and Similar Species: Shore juniper: 'Blue Pacific', low, trailing, to 1 foot tall, dense, deep blue-green needles, excellent form; 'Emerald Sea', dense, prostrate to 1½ feet high, bright green needles hold color in winter; 'Silver Mist', silvery blue-green needles in summer, somewhat plum-colored in winter. *J. procumbens* var. 'Nana' (*J. chinensis* var. *procumbens* 'Nana'), dwarf Japanese garden juniper, 1-foot-high, beautiful mounded groundcover, sharp-pointed, blue-green needles, tolerates poor soil and drought.

Creeping juniper: 'Douglasii' (Waukegan juniper), steel-blue foliage, silvery purple-plum in winter, 1 to 1½ feet tall, less troubled by twig blight; 'Wiltonii' ('Blue Rug'), ground-hugging, to 6 inches tall, silver-blue foliage, turns pale purple in winter; 'Bar Harbor', 1 foot tall, blue-green needlelike and scalelike foliage, purple in winter, salt-spray tolerant; 'Blue Chip', blue foliage, 10 inches tall, plum-tipped in winter, best in North; 'Emerald Spreader', ground-hugging to 6 inches tall, emerald-green foliage; 'Plumosa' (andorra juniper), 2 feet tall, dense blue-green to gray-green needlelike foliage, purple in winter, upturned branchlets; 'Plumosa Compacta', dense, 18 inches tall, gray-green foliage turning bronze-purple in winter.

Broadmoor savin juniper: 'Arcadia', 1 foot tall, scalelike, bright green leaves, blight-resistant; 'Buffalo', 8 to 12 inches tall, makes dense feathery mat, bright green all year; 'Tamariscifolia', short, feathery blue-green to green needles, affected by blight; 'Tamariscifolia-No Blight', blue-green needles, blight-resistant.

LIRIOPE SPICATA
Creeping Lilyturf

This grassy-leaved evergreen plant spreads rapidly by creeping rhizomes, creating a low-maintenance lawn in areas where a grasslike texture and height is important, but where there is little or no foot traffic. The ½-inch-wide, dark green leaves form tight clumps of foliage. In late summer, tight clusters of lavender or white flowers form in the centers of the clumps, barely showing above the leaves, followed by black berries in fall. Grows 8 to 10 inches tall. In hot climates, makes attractive groundcover for small or large areas.

OPHIOPOGON JAPONICUS

Site: Part to light shade; more shade in hottest climates. Fertile, humus-rich, well-drained soil best; spreads rapidly in light, sandy soil. Water during dry spells. Hardy in zones 6 to 9, but not fully evergreen in zones 6 and 7. Best used as groundcover only in zones 8 and 9. Salt-tolerant.
How to Grow: Set out divisions or potted plants in spring or early fall, spacing 8 to 12 inches apart for groundcover. Divide in spring to increase plants. Mow or shear to height of 3 to 4 inches every year in late winter or early spring to encourage luxurious new growth. Can be invasive; use lawn edging to keep in bounds. May be troubled by slugs and snails.
Cultivars and Similar Species:
Ophiopogon japonicus (mondo grass): similar, ⅛-inch-wide leaves; zones 7 to 9, space 8 to 12 inches apart.
Liriope muscari (big blue lilyturf): grows much larger and does not spread.

LONICERA SPP.
Goldflame Honeysuckle, Japanese Honeysuckle, Trumpet Honeysuckle

Shrubby goldflame honeysuckle (*Lonicera × heckrottii*) is perfect for decorating a trellis or fence, because it produces large numbers of flowers from summer through fall. Its fragrant, two-lipped flowers are bicolored with deep rose exteriors and yellow interiors. The blue-green leaves emerge purple-red. Evergreen in warm

LONICERA × HECKROTTII

climates; they drop without changing color in late autumn in the North. The slender, twining stems are an attractive purple-red and climb to 10 feet or more.

Introduced to North America from Asia in the 1870s, Japanese honeysuckle (*L. japonica*) is both a valued ornamental and a rampant pest. Its clusters of trumpet-shaped, fragrant, creamy white flowers turn butter yellow as they age and appear from early through late summer. The slender, reddish brown stems climb by twining to 15 to 30 feet high. Semievergreen in warm climates, the small, oval, green leaves drop with no color change in fall in the North. The black berries that follow the flowers are relished by birds, who spread the plant to woodlands, where it has smothered acres of native plants in the South and Middle Atlantic states.

A native species, trumpet honeysuckle (*L. sempervirens*) climbs by long, twining stems, which are

LONICERA SEMPERVIRENS

covered with blue-green evergreen to semievergreen leaves. Stems grow 10 to 25 feet high. The trumpet-shaped, orange-red flowers bloom from summer through fall. They are scentless, unfortunately, but they do attract hummingbirds. Translucent red berries may appear in fall.

Grow goldflame and trumpet honeysuckles on a trellis, wire grid, or fence. Combine with clematis and climbing roses. Japanese honeysuckle quickly makes thick groundcover for bank or unsightly area. Plant on trellis or fence in North for good screen.
continued

LONICERA SPP.
(continued)

Site: Honeysuckles grow in full sun to part shade; full sun is best for goldflame. Grows best in rich to average, well-drained soil and plentiful moisture. Japanese honeysuckle is most vigorous in moist, fertile soil; poorer soil allows better control. Trumpet honeysuckle is drought-tolerant, but blooms best with plentiful moisture. Goldflame and trumpet honeysuckles are hardy in zones 4 to 9. Japanese honeysuckle grows in zones 5 to 9, but do not plant in the East in zones 6 to 9 where it is a noxious weed. Better behaved and not a threat in zones 4 to 5.

How to Grow: Plant bare-root or container-grown plants in spring, spacing 3 feet apart. Take cuttings in summer. Goldflame is a weak climber; may need to be tied in place. Keep roots shaded and cool with mulch or low plantings. Prune out oldest branches every year after initial flowering. Prune side branches of Japanese honeysuckle back hard to main trunk and branches in late winter. Prune back long side shoots of trumpet honeysuckle to 6 to 8 inches in early spring to control growth and increase bloom. Prune lightly in summer if it becomes unruly. Keep roots shaded and cool with mulch or low plantings.

Aphids may be serious problem for goldflame and trumpet honeysuckles, especially in spring. Japanese honeysuckle usually trouble-free.

Cultivars and Similar Species: Japanese honeysuckle: 'Halliana' (Hall's honeysuckle), larger, pure white flowers; 'Aureo-reticulata', gold-veined leaves, less vigorous. *L.j.* var. 'Purpurea', purple-tinted foliage, maroon flowers with white inside. *L. periclymenum* (woodbine honeysuckle), fragrant, especially in evenings, two-lipped, creamy-white flowers blushed with maroon bloom all summer, to 20 feet tall, not a pest, native to Europe, semishade best, zones 5 to 9. *L. periclymenum* var. *serotina*, dark purple flowers, yellowish inside.

Trumpet honeysuckle: 'Superba', larger flowers; 'Magnifica', deep red-orange; 'Sulphurea' ('Flava'), clear yellow. *L. × brownii* (Brown's honeysuckle), 8 feet high, deep reddish orange blossoms summer through fall; 'Dropmore Scarlet', very floriferous; zones 3 to 9.

LYSIMACHIA NUMMULARIA
Moneywort, Creeping Jenny, Creeping Charlie

Named for its dime-size leaves that clasp the low, creeping stems, moneywort roots at the nodes as it spreads across the ground, forming an effective groundcover. Cup-shaped, yellow flowers dot the stems between the leaves in late spring, then off and on throughout summer. Plants grow 4 to 8 inches tall; 24 inches wide. Naturalize along ponds, stream banks, or in shade

LYSIMACHIA NUMMULARIA 'AUREA'

gardens under tall sturdy perennials, such as Siberian iris, ferns, and hostas. 'Aurea' combines well with gold-variegated hosta and lilyturf.

Site: Full sun to part shade. Humus-rich, moist to wet or boggy soil. Tolerates dry site in shade. Hardy in zones 3 to 8.
How to Grow: Plant bare-root or container-grown plants in spring. Divide in spring or fall; take cuttings in

summer. Invasive; may colonize lawns. Perishes in dry site. Usually pest-free.
Cultivars: 'Aurea', chartreuse spring leaves darken to lime-green.

MAZUS REPTANS
Mazus

This valuable groundcover thrives in moist, shady sites, producing carpets of early flowers and evergreen foliage to beautify the garden throughout the year. Flowers measure almost 1 inch long, large for a plant that hugs the ground. They're tubular with showy, spotted lower lips. Most commonly lavender, a handsome

MAZUS REPTANS

white form also is available. Flowers appear for two months from mid spring through early summer. Lance-shaped, 1-inch-long, toothed leaves are attractive after flowers pass. Plants grow 2 inches tall and 12 inches wide. Good groundcover in naturalistic gardens, along streams and ponds, or in woodlands beneath taller plants. Withstands light foot traffic; plant between pavers in shady, moist site or as lawn substitute.

Site: Full sun to full shade. Humus-rich, moist to boggy soil. Plentiful moisture, especially in sun. Hardy in zones 5 to 8.

How to Grow: Plant bare-root or container grown plants in spring, spacing 1 to 2 feet apart. Divide in early spring every three or four years to rejuvenate. Plant away from lawn, because it can be invasive. May not survive snowless winters in North; provide winter protection if needed. Usually pest-free.
Cultivars: 'Albus', white flowers.

MICROBIOTA DECUSSATA

MICROBIOTA DECUSSATA
Russian Cypress, Siberian Cypress

Resembling a creeping juniper, this feathery branched conifer is one of the few needle-leaved evergreens that grows well in part shade. Its flattened sprays of scalelike leaves are bright green during the growing season and turn coppery brown in winter. Native to Siberia, this prostrate plant grows naturally on mountain peaks above the tree line. Grows to 12 inches high, spreading many feet wide. Excellent groundcover beneath deep-rooted, lightly shading trees. Combines well with other conifers.

Site: Full sun to part shade. Fertile to average, well-drained soil. Moderate moisture. Zones 2 to 8; best where summers are cool.
How to Grow: Plant container-grown plants in spring or fall, spacing at least

5 feet apart. Cuttings difficult to root. Prune in early spring to keep in bounds. Doesn't tolerate heavy pruning; plant where fast-spreading plant is welcome. Usually pest-free.
Cultivars and Similar Species: 'Vancouver', improved variety.

MINA LOBATA
(IPOMOEA LOBATA)
Crimson Starglory, Exotic Love, Spanish Flag

Large, matte-green leaves on this annual vine are three-lobed and form a dense cover that makes a quick screen. Sprays of delicate flowers bloom in summer and fall on arching reddish stems. The flower buds are scarlet, but open to bright orange tubes that gradually fade to creamy white, creating a lovely color effect. Vine grows rapidly to 10 feet. Train on arbor, trellis, or picket fence.

MINA LOBATA

Site: Full to half sun. Average to poor, well-drained soil. Even moisture. Tender perennial. Hardy in zones 10 and 11; grown as annual elsewhere.
How to Grow: Sow seeds indoors in peat pots to facilitate transplanting; plant outside after frost danger has passed. Produces leaves and few flowers in fertile site. Protect from hot midday sun, which causes leaves to yellow. Usually pest-free.

PACHYSANDRA TERMINALIS
Japanese Spurge

This evergreen groundcover is an indispensable landscape plant in many parts of the country. Rapidly covering ground with whorls of toothed, glossy, dark green leaves, pachysandra flourishes in shade, forming a uniform green blanket that

PACHYSANDRA TERMINALIS

crowds out most weeds. It even does well in dry, compacted soil beneath maples and beeches if mulched. Small spires of creamy white flowers bloom in early spring, a pretty contrast to the foliage, although they often go unnoticed. Pachysandra spreads by long, underground runners, which can be stopped by a lawn edging or barrier, although the aboveground stems can drape over the barrier and root on the other side. Grows 8 to 10 inches tall; spreads to form extensive mat. Excellent evergreen groundcover for large areas beneath trees or as low-maintenance lawn substitute, especially in formal gardens.

Site: Light to full shade; more shade in hottest areas. Fertile, humus-rich, moist, acid soil best. Tolerates dry shade. Best with plentiful moisture. Hardy in zones 3 to 8; does not do well in hot locations. *continued*

PACHYSANDRA TERMINALIS
(continued)

How to Grow: Plant divisions or rooted cuttings in spring or fall. Space 6 to 10 inches apart. Mulch to prevent weeds during establishment. Divide or take cuttings from mature growth in early summer to increase plants. Leaves yellow in too much sun. Provide more nourishment and moisture in poor growing conditions under densely shaded trees by annually applying organic mulch. Can be invasive; control by edging border between lawn and groundcover. No need to rake fallen tree leaves from beneath groundcover; remove only leaves smothering foliage. Usually pest-free, but leaf-blight fungus, scale insects, and mites may be troublesome.

Cultivars and Similar Species: 'Variegata' and 'Silver-edge', lovely gray-green leaves with creamy white edges, slow spreader, excellent for brightening shady site; 'Green Carpet', superior, more compact, glossy leaves; 'Green Sheen', extremely glossy leaves, more sun-tolerant. *Pachysandra procumbens* (Allegheny spurge), beautiful, dull green to bluish green mottled leaves may be deciduous or evergreen, depending on climate and exposure, showy spikes of fragrant white or pinkish flowers in early spring, native woodland plant excellent for shade gardens, zones 4 to 9, needs humus-rich, moist soil and shade.

PARTHENOCISSUS QUINQUEFOLIA
(AMPELOPSIS QUINQUEFOLIA)
Virginia Creeper, Woodbine

Fast-growing, this native woodland plant has rounded leaves with five fingerlike leaflets. Deciduous leaves emerge bronze in spring, mature to rich green, and turn scarlet in early fall where exposed to sun. Inconspicuous flowers are followed in fall by blue-black berries, which are eaten by birds. Trailing along the ground and rooting as it goes, or twining into trees and shrubs where it also clings by aerial tendrils, Virginia creeper forms a loose groundcover or vine. It can climb 50 feet or spread as far on ground. Climbs brick, stone, or tree trunks, but may damage masonry and wood. Tolerates pollution and city and seashore conditions.

PARTHENOCISSUS TRICUSPIDATA

Site: Full sun to shade. Tolerates most soils, even poor, compacted sites and sandy sites. Best with plentiful moisture. Hardy in zones 3 to 9.

How to Grow: Plant container-grown plants in spring, spacing 3 to 4 feet apart for groundcover or wall cover. Roots readily from cuttings in summer. Prune annually once established. May be confused with poison ivy, which has three leaflets, not five. Can grow 10 or more feet in single year and may become invasive or weedy because birds spread seeds. Prevent from climbing high into trees or into shrubs; it can smother them. Usually pest-free.

Cultivars and Similar Species: *Parthenocissus quinquefolia* var. *engelmannii* has smaller, more ornamental leaves, tidier growth. *P.q. saint-paulii* has smaller leaves, numerous clinging tendrils, best for climbing walls. *P. tricuspidata* (Boston ivy) has glossy, three-lobed, toothed leaves; excellent clinging vine; zones 4 to 8.

PASSIFLORA CAERULEA
Blue Passion Flower

Hardy blue passion flower features exotic-looking, 4-inch, blue-pink-and-white flowers composed of a symmetrical arrangement of showy

PASSIFLORA ALATA

stamens held flat against rings of petals and sepals. The flowers emit a slight fragrance. Leaves are five-lobed and semievergreen to evergreen. The vine climbs by tendrils to 15 to 30 feet. Train on trellis or fence or where unusual flowers can be appreciated.

Site: Full sun. Deep, well-drained loam. Moderate moisture; somewhat drought-tolerant. Hardy in zones 8 to 10.

How to Grow: Plant container-grown plants in spring or fall, spacing 5 or more feet part. Roots readily from cuttings in summer. Rampant grower; prune yearly in fall or late winter. May die back to ground in Zone 8 during coldest winters. Nematodes may be troublesome in Zone 9.

Similar Species: *Passiflora incarnata* (wild passion flower), 2-inch pinkish-white flowers with purple stamens and edible yellow fruits; native vine; zones 7 to 9. Some tropical species can be grown as annuals: *P. alata*, fragrant, red-purple-and-white flowers; *P. edulis*, white-and-purple flowers, edible fruits.

PAXISTIMA CANBYI (PACHISTIMA CANBYI)
Canby Paxistima

Native to the Appalachian Mountains, this ground-covering evergreen creates an effective fine-textured carpet of low, upright to arching stems decorated with narrow, glossy, dark green leaves with toothed edges. The leaves turn bronze during the winter months. Flowers are inconspicuous. Unlike most

PAXISTIMA CANBYI

groundcovers, paxistima grows slowly and isn't invasive. Grows to 12 inches tall and spreads 3 to 5 feet wide. Use to create low hedge or groundcover beneath taller shrubs. Effective for year-round color and structure.

Site: Full sun to half shade. Fertile, moist, acid to neutral, well-drained soil. Plentiful moisture. Hardy in zones 4 to 7; performs poorly where hot.
How to Grow: Plant container-grown plants in spring or fall, spacing 2 to 18 inches apart. Take cuttings in summer, treat with rooting hormone. Arching stems root where they touch ground and can be dug up and separated. Protect from winter sun in North to prevent foliage from burning. Usually trouble-free, but may be infested with euonymus scale disease or leaf spot.

Similar Species: *Paxistima myrtifolia*, 3 feet tall, native to Pacific Northwest and grown there in native gardens, zones 5 to 8; 'Emerald Cascade', larger leaves (1½ inches long), cascading branches, to 1 foot tall.

POLYGONUM AUBERTII
Silver Lace Vine, Silver Fleece Vine

An old-fashioned twining vine, silver lace vine becomes a froth of pearly-white foam when it blooms in late summer. Leaves are coarse and arrow shaped, bright green when mature, light green tipped with red when young. A rampant grower, silver lace vine can grow 20 feet in a single season, eventually reaching to 30 feet high. Excellent for camouflaging chain-link fence. Use to cover pergola or arbor.

POLYGONUM AUBERTII

Site: Full sun to light shade. Adapts to most soils; tolerates dry soil and city conditions. Average moisture best. Hardy in zones 4 or 5 to 8. May die to ground in severe winters.
How to Grow: Plant container-grown plants in spring or fall, spacing 10 feet apart. Take cuttings in summer. Tie to support. Prune severely every spring to control size. Spreads by underground stems and may be difficult to eradicate. Japanese beetles may be troublesome.

PYRACANTHA COCCINEA
Firethorn, Pyracantha

A thorny, long-branched, sprawling shrub, firethorn usually is grown like a clambering vine and fastened to a fence or wall. There it can effectively show off its large, flat clusters of white flowers in early summer and its gorgeous bunches of red, orange, scarlet, and occasionally yellow berries from early fall well into winter. Leaves are narrow, 1½ inches long, and glossy dark green. They're

PYRACANTHA × 'MOHAVE'

evergreen in the South and semievergreen in the North. Grows 5 to 13 feet tall and wide, largest in warm climates. Excellent plant for fall and winter interest. Locate on wall or fence far enough from walkway that thorns won't snag clothing.

Site: Full sun. Average to sandy, well-drained soil. Tolerates heat and drought; performs well in arid areas if irrigated. Hardy in zones 6 to 9; a few cultivars hardy in Zone 5.
How to Grow: Plant container-grown plants in spring, spacing at least 5 feet apart. Take cuttings of new growth in spring, treat with rooting hormone. Tie to wire grid or trellis to train against wall or fence. Plant where there is good air circulation to discourage disease. Prune regularly immediately *continued*

PYRACANTHA COCCINEA
(continued)

after flowering to keep in bounds. Remove old, withered berries with a broom, to protect your hands from thorns. Fireblight can be serious; scab fungus can infect leaves and cause defoliation. Choose resistant cultivars. Aphids, scale insects, and lacebugs sometimes troublesome.

Cultivars and Similar Species: 'Aurea', yellow berries; 'Lalandei', deep orange berries, hardy in Zone 5, susceptible to scab; 'Lanlandei Thornless', less thorny; 'Kasan', orange-red berries, compact growth, hardy in Zone 5, susceptible to scab; 'Monrovia', bright orange berries; 'Teton', hybrid, upright growth, orange-yellow berries, fireblight- and scab-resistant, hardy in Zone 5; 'Mohave', red-orange fruit, hybrid, fireblight- and scab-resistant, nearly evergreen. *Pyracantha koidzumii* (Formosa firethorn), similar, but more rounded, evergreen leaves, zones 7 to 9. 'San Jose', bright red berries. 'Shawnee', bright yellow to pale orange berries, fireblight- and scab-resistant. 'Soleil d'Or', hybrid, golden-yellow berries.

RUBUS CALYCINOIDES
(RUBUS PENTALOBUS)
Creeping Rubus

This ground-hugging plant has an attractive pebbly texture created by the network of veins that decorate the leathery leaves. Evergreen to semievergreen, the leaves have three to five lobes, like maple leaves, and take on coppery red hues in winter. The white flowers are barely noticeable in early summer and are followed by salmon-pink to purple fruits. Rubus spreads by runners to form a dense 2-inch-tall mat that eventually covers a large area, but it isn't invasive. Use for contrast of texture as groundcover under conifers and ornamental grasses or other fine-textured plants.

RUBUS CALYCINOIDES

Site: Full sun to full shade; grows taller and is less dense in full shade. Average, well-drained soil. Hardy in zones 5 to 8.
How to Grow: Plant rooted cuttings or container-grown plants in spring, spacing 1 to 2 feet apart. Cuttings taken anytime during growing season root readily. Cut back runners to control. Usually problem-free.
Cultivars: 'Emerald Carpet' (Taiwan creeping rubus).

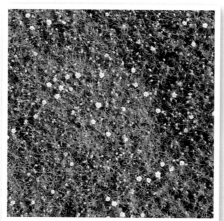

SAGINA SUBULATA

SAGINA SUBULATA
Scotch Moss

A flowering plant, this moss look-alike isn't a true moss. The velvety cushion of bright green leaves forms mats and hummocks about an

inch high, dotted in summer with tiny white flowers, which are borne singly. Use between paving stones and in small gardens for velvety carpet. Tolerates light foot traffic.

Site: Full sun in cool-summer areas; part shade where hot. Golden forms more tolerant of sun and hot weather. Fertile, humus-rich, moist soil. Plentiful moisture. Hardy in zones 3 to 9.
How to Grow: Plant small container-grown plants or divisions from flats in spring, spacing 3 inches apart for quick cover. Divide in spring by pulling up small sections and replanting. Keep weed-free. Can self-sow and become weedy. If it becomes too hummocky, cut out raised areas and press cut edges into soil to smooth planting. Slugs and snails serious in some areas.
Cultivars and Similar Species: 'Aurea' (Irish moss), golden green. *Arenaria verna*, also called Scotch moss, almost identical, but with flowers in clusters; also available in golden form.

SARCOCOCCA HOOKERIANA VAR. *HUMILIS*

SARCOCOCCA HOOKERIANA VAR. HUMILIS
Dwarf Sweet Box

Clusters of white flowers appear in spring on this shrubby, broad-leaved evergreen. The flowers would go unnoticed if not for their sweet, pervasive fragrance. Dwarf sweet box makes an unusual groundcover in a shady location, forming a dense cover of pointed, glossy, 2-inch-long, dark green leaves. These ripen into black berries. Dwarf sweet box spreads slowly by underground runners to cover a 6- to 8-foot-wide area and isn't aggressive. Grows 1½ feet tall. Beautiful groundcover for small or medium-size areas in woodland or shade garden. Combines well with rhododendrons and azaleas.

Site: Light to full sun throughout year. Best on north side of building. Fertile, moist, humus-rich soil. Plentiful moisture. Hardy in zones 6 to 9.
How to Grow: Plant container-grown plants in spring or fall, spacing 2 to 3 feet apart. May be increased by division. Protect from winter sun to keep foliage from burning. Usually pest-free.
Similar Species: *Sarcococca ruscifolia* (sweet box), very similar, but with red berries, more sharply pointed leaves.

SAXIFRAGA STOLONIFERA (S. SARMENTOSA)
Strawberry Begonia, Strawberry Geranium

Neither a begonia nor a geranium, this plant grows as strawberries grow, by sending out runners that form new plants at the tips. The rounded leaves are fleshy and hairy, with handsome scalloped margins and silver veins. Foliage is evergreen to semievergreen, depending on the climate. Airy 12-inch-tall spikes of white flowers dance above the leaves in spring. Plant forms a mat of foliage 2 to 3 inches tall. Perfect for covering small or large areas in shade gardens. Sometimes grown as a houseplant.

Site: Light to full shade. Rich, moist, well-drained soil. Plentiful water. Hardy in zones 6 to 9; performs poorly where hot and dry.

SAXIFRAGA STOLONIFERA

How to Grow: Plant container-grown plants in spring or fall, spacing 1 to 2 feet apart. Propagate by separating rooted plantlets. Moderately aggressive; easy to control by pulling out unwanted plants. Slugs may be troublesome.

THUNBERGIA ALATA
Black-Eyed Susan Vine

This annual vine can quickly cover a fence in a sheltered corner with its 1- to 2-inch-wide, five-petaled

THUNBERGIA ALATA
'SUSIE ORANGE WITH BLACK EYE'

blossoms, which bloom from midsummer until frost. Flowers usually are yellow or orange with dark eyes. Also available are blossoms in white

and buff, and ones without dark eyes. The plant climbs by twining and holds the flowers well away from its 3-inch-long, arrow-shaped leaves. Vines can climb 6 to 10 feet high. Use for bold color on fence, wall, or trellis, as screen or groundcover, and in containers and hanging baskets.

Site: Full sun or light shade. Fertile, well-drained soil. Plentiful water. Warm-season annual in zones 2 to 9; perennial in zones 10 and 11; frost kills top but not roots. Avoid reflected heat.
How to Grow: Sow seeds indoors, at 70° to 75°F, six to eight weeks before last frost. In mild-winter areas, sow in garden in early spring. Space 12 to 18 inches apart. Provide support for climbing. Red spider mites and aphids sometimes cause problems.
Cultivars: 'Susie' series, orange or yellow with dark eyes, or mixed with and without dark eyes. 'Angel Wings', 2-inch white flowers, yellow centers, lightly fragrant.

TRACHELOSPERMUM JASMINOIDES
Confederate Jasmine, Star Jasmine

Fragrant flowers grace this twining plant which forms an effective evergreen vine or groundcover. The oval leaves are lustrous dark green on top, pale green on their undersides, and opposite one another along the stems. The sweet-scented white flowers bloom profusely in early summer and sporadically thereafter. Climbs to 6 feet high as a vine; spreads wide as a groundcover. Elegant screen on lattice fence; for wall cover, train on lattice trellis. Use as groundcover in shady garden.

Site: Part to full shade. Average to rich, well-drained soil. Plentiful moisture. Suited to zones 8 and 9. *continued*

TRACHELOSPERMUM JASMINOIDES
(continued)

TRACHELOSPERMUM JASMINOIDES

How to Grow: Plant container-grown plants in spring or fall, spacing 5 feet apart for vine and 3 feet apart for groundcover. Take cuttings in early summer. Needs support to climb. May be troubled by whiteflies, scale insects, and mites.

Similar Species: *Trachelospermum asiaticum (Rhynchospermum asiaticum, yellow star jasmine)* similar, fragrant, yellowish white flowers; zones 8 to 9.

VINCA MINOR
Myrtle, Common Periwinkle

Indispensable as an evergreen groundcover, myrtle can carpet large areas. Its beauty would be better appreciated if the plant weren't so commonly grown. The trailing stems, which root as they grow, feature 1- to 2-inch-long, glossy, dark green leaves and form a thick mat 6 inches high, spreading to cover a large area. In spring, beginning about the time daffodils bloom, five-petaled, 1-inch-wide, lavender-blue flowers decorate the plants. These bloom for about a month. Myrtle looks elegant blanketing the ground beneath shrubs, trees, bulbs, and perennials. Nice in large-scale formal gardens; also works well in small, informal shade gardens and woodland settings. Performs well under shallow-rooted trees such as maple and beech.

VINCA MINOR

Site: Full sun to full shade; shade best where summers are hot. Average to rich, well-drained soil. Best in zones 4 to 7; grows farther south with plenty of shade and moisture.

How to Grow: Plant rooted cuttings in spring or fall, spacing 10 inches apart for quick cover. Cuttings root well with or without rooting hormone; may be stuck directly in garden if kept moist and shaded. Divide clumps in spring to increase plants. Takes several years to get well established as weed-smothering blanket. Apply mulch to stop weeds when first planted; apply high-phosporous fertilizer and keep well-watered during first year or two. Thereafter, easy to care for. Usually trouble-free, but stem-dieback fungus can be a problem.

Cultivars and Similar Species: 'Bowles' ('Bowlesii' and 'Bowles' Variety'), larger, deeper blue flowers that bloom heavily in spring and lightly in summer, dense, more compact growth; 'Sterling Silver' ('Argenteo-variegata'), white-splashed dark green leaves, slow grower; 'Alba', white flowers; 'Gertrude Jekyll', small white flowers, dainty ½-inch leaves; 'Atropurpurea' ('Rubra' and 'Purpurea'), dark magenta-purple flowers; 'Aureo-variegata', yellow-splashed leaves; 'Aurea', all-gold leaves; 'Albo-variegata', green-and-gold leaves, white flowers. *Vinca major* (large periwinkle), larger leaves and longer stems, mounds to 2 feet tall; zones 8 to 10 or as annual, best in shade, variegated form popular in containers.

WALDSTEINIA FRAGARIOIDES
Barren Strawberry

Native to the northeastern states and Canada, this tough groundcover, which spreads by rooting runners, forms a beautiful, thick evergreen mat of strawberry-like leaves and thrives in many garden conditions. The glossy, bright green leaves are made up of three wedge-shaped leaflets that turn bronze in winter, but green up again in spring. Abundant sprays of 5-inch, bold yellow flowers bloom in mid spring

WALDSTEINIA FRAGARIOIDES

and are followed by dry, hairy fruits that attract little attention. Forms mat about 6 to 8 inches deep and spreads to cover large area. Excellent, low-maintenance groundcover for planting under trees and shrubs and in shade gardens. Combines well with bulbs, ornamental grasses, and perennials.

Site: Full sun to full shade; flowers most abundantly in sun. Tolerates dry, sunny sites. Average to humus-rich, well-drained soil. Moist to dry conditions. Hardy in zones 4 to 7.
How to Grow: Plant rooted cuttings or small plants in spring, spacing 12 inches apart. Mulch well to prevent weeds until established. Usually pest-free.
Similar Species: *Waldsteinia ternata* (*W. sibirica*), native to Siberia, three oval-shaped leaflets, yellow flowers. *Duchesnea indica* (Indian strawberry, mock strawberry), similar in appearance, but with showy, tiny, strawberry-like fruit, semievergreen, zones 5 to 9.

WISTERIA FLORIBUNDA
Japanese Wisteria

Romatic and old-fashioned, wisteria vine can perfume an entire garden with its sweet fragrance when its mid to late spring blossoms are open. Sweet-pealike flowers bloom in dramatic 1- to 2-foot-long clusters and usually are vibrant bluish purple, but also come in purple, pink, violet, mauve, rose, and white. Individual blossoms of Japanese wisteria usually open first at the base of the cluster, progressing toward the tip; flowers begin blooming as plants are leafing out. The large, pinnately compound leaves are divided like huge feathers into seven to 11 leaflets. They emerge silvery green in spring, turn rich green in summer, and may turn yellow in fall. Long, velvety seedpods often hang on leafless vines over winter. This deciduous, twining vine is an aggressive grower that forms heavy, gnarled trunks, which can grow 8 to 10 inches in diameter, like those of a small tree, and can climb to 40 feet tall. Although wisteria has no adhesive discs to damage surfaces, growing tips of the strong, twining branches can pry up siding and roof shingles unless kept pruned.

WISTERIA FLORIBUNDA 'VIOLACEA-PLENA'

If not properly sited and controlled, wisteria can become a tree- or house-smothering pest, especially in the South. When properly trained, nothing equals its beauty and fragrance. Gorgeous, fragrant vine for covering arbor, gazebo, or pergola. Drape on house wall or along porch or roofline. Also may be used to ascend strong, dead tree or telephone-type pole.

Site: Full sun best; tolerates light shade in South and Southwest. West- or south-facing walls are excellent choices. Fertile to poor, well-drained soil. Average to plentiful moisture. Mature plants are drought-tolerant. May grow too rampantly in rich, moist site. Hardy in zones 5 to 9.
How to Grow: Plant bare-root or container-grown plants in spring; cover graft union so top forms own roots. Propagate by cuttings taken in early summer or by layering branches; seed propagation is slow. Tie to support for first several years; self-supporting thereafter. Train to main trunk with framework of side branches, depending on site and support. Gently twist brittle branches when training according to direction of growth: Chinese wisteria grows counterclockwise; Japanese wisteria grows clockwise. Provide extremely sturdy support, such as cedar 2×2s or 2×4s. Train to surface of

support; avoid allowing to twine around tree trunks or slender supports. When grown on house, provide separate support several feet from wall for air circulation and ease of pruning. Prune lightly every few months from spring through summer to control vigorous growth; prune side branches heavily (back to several buds from main branches) in late winter every year. (Flower buds form in summer at base of previous season's growth.) Prune off suckers from base of trunk. May send out invasive suckers 15 to 20 feet from main trunk. Train as freestanding weeping tree by tying trunk to 1½-inch diameter, 4-foot-tall pipe; support side branches for several years. Flower buds may be injured by late frosts and freezes. Vines may not bloom until seven to 10 years old; inexpensive seedling-grown plants may not bloom at all; purchase named cultivars propagated by cuttings. Needs no fertilizer, but superphosphate may encourage blooming. Usually pest-free.
Cultivars and Similar Species: 'Ivory Tower', white flowers, extremely fragrant; 'Violacea Plena', double, reddish violet flowers; 'Rosea', rose-pink flowers; 'Carnea', pale pink flowers; 'Alba', white flowers; 'Longissima', long violet flower clusters; 'Royal Purple', deep violet flowers. 'Plena', double, lilac flowers. *Wisteria sinensis* (Chinese wisteria), 1 foot long, slightly fragrant, lilac-blue flower clusters, all flowers in cluster open about the same time (before leaves), zones 6 to 9, extremely vigorous to 100 feet; 'Alba', white flowers; 'Jako', long white flowers, fragrant clusters.

Less aggressive native vines:
W. frutescens (American wisteria), 2- to 5-inch-long clusters of lilac flowers in summer on new growth, climbs to 40 feet tall, zones 7 to 9.
W. macrostachya (Kentucky wisteria), lilac-purple flowers, 6-inch clusters in early summer, zones 5 to 9.

ROSES

CHAPTER 5

ABOUT ROSES

Universal favorites, roses are the best-loved flowers of all time. Their history, rich in legend and lore, makes fascinating reading. Despite their sometimes temperamental nature, roses bring pleasure to gardeners as a single gorgeous blossom handed to a friend or as a breathtaking bouquet.

Although often grown in flower gardens, roses are actually small, woody shrubs. Unlike perennial flowers, they do not die to the ground at the end of the growing season, but they may lose all their foliage and go dormant during winter.

There are many different kinds of roses; they vary from large shrubs to small bushes and climbers. Whatever their size and shape, roses fall into two main categories: old garden roses and modern roses.

OLD GARDEN ROSES

The roses of yesteryear, collectively called old garden roses, were once grown by the European aristocracy. Although they went out of fashion for more than a century, old garden roses survived through the years in cottage gardens.

Now old cultivars are enjoying a deserved resurgence of popularity. They are being propagated and reintroduced from plants found growing in abandoned gardens. Usually large, these garden-worthy shrubs and climbers boast luxuriant clusters of highly fragrant flowers. Most old roses make handsome specimens even when out of bloom. They have a heavy cloak of leaves in summer; berrylike, bright red rose hips from fall into winter; and colorful thorny branches when the leaves are gone.

Many old garden roses bloom lavishly once a year, but others repeat their bloom. They may have single blossoms—clusters of five-petaled flowers with whorls of showy, yellow stamens in their centers—or double blossoms, with so many petals that the open flowers weigh down the branches.

Unlike the long petals of the high-centered modern rose, the central petals of a double-flowered old garden rose are short, forming a tightly folded center when fully open. The cup-shaped flower has a voluptuous appearance.

Most old-fashioned varieties emit a rich, sensual fragrance that is strong enough to perfume an entire garden. Pastel pink, crimson, and rose red, often with mauve or lavender overtones, are the most prevalent floral colors, although white and rich purple roses also exist.

Old garden roses have a long history. Three roses—the gallica rose *(Rosa gallica),* alba rose *(R. alba),* and damask rose *(R. damascena)*— are among the most ancient plants still cultivated. Grown in the Far and Near East during Biblical times, these roses probably were carried to Western Europe by crusaders. The blood of the gallica rose, and perhaps the damask and alba roses, flows somewhere in the family tree of every known old garden or modern rose.

An iron fence serves as the perfect support for this vigorous 'Bloomfield Dainty', a hybrid musk rose.

Photo by Jon Jensen

Most roses are in their glory in late spring to early summer, when they put out a flush of blossoms. Some bloom just once; others—depending on the cultivar—continue to flower through the summer and into autumn.

During the Renaissance, roses became prized plants in the royalty's grand ornamental gardens and were no longer confined to apothecary cloistered gardens. The gardeners of the British, French, and Dutch aristocracy collected and hybridized roses during the 18th and 19th centuries, developing several dozen groups, many of which still can be found today. Cultivars in each group of old garden roses descend from the same species and bear a family resemblance to the group.

THE MODERN ERA

The era of the modern rose began when the first hybrid tea rose was introduced in 1867. Bred from a tea rose and a hybrid perpetual rose, the hybrid tea rose seemed to be the ultimate in roses, featuring large, elegant, high-centered, fragrant blossoms that bloomed repeatedly from early summer through fall on reasonably cold-hardy plants.

All the groups of roses developed after 1867 are termed modern roses.

Previous groups and new hybrids within those groups are termed old garden roses. Modern roses include hybrid teas, grandifloras, floribundas, polyanthas, ramblers, climbers, and the latest group—English roses, which offer old-garden-rose character.

Combine old garden roses with perennials, bulbs, ornamental grasses, and flowering shrubs. Modern roses, however, grow best in separate beds because their root systems can't compete with other plants and their foliage is prone to disease.

'Camaieux' gallica rose grows into a 4-foot-tall bush that blooms in June. The fragrant double blossoms are white and streaked with crimson.

Photo by William Stites

PLANTING AND CARING FOR ROSES

Roses—especially modern types—need special care. Although their topgrowth is woody and permanent, they can be injured by cold weather. In general, old garden roses are easier to care for and more disease-resistant than modern roses, which are finicky and not long-lived.

Each group of old garden and modern roses differs a little in its pruning and cultural needs (see encyclopedia entries, pages 276–285, for specific instructions).

PLANTING BARE-ROOT ROSES

Most often, roses, whether old or modern, arrive in your garden as dormant, bare-root plants, but they can be purchased as potted, container-grown specimens. You can purchase bare-root roses at a local nursery or order them by mail. A bare-root rose looks stark, with stubby, thorny stems and stiff roots growing in opposite directions from a rough knob. The knob is the graft union, where the roots and main stem were grafted together. (Many old garden roses are grown on their own roots and do not have a graft union.)

Here are the basics for planting bare-root roses: About an hour before planting, soak the roots of the rose in a bucket of water. Dig an 18-inch-deep and -wide planting hole. Mix a quart of organic matter, such as well-rotted compost or manure, with the excavated soil and shape it into a low mound in the bottom of the hole.

Place the rose on the mound. If you live where temperatures drop below 20 degrees Fahrenheit, be sure the graft union is 1 to 2 inches below soil level to prevent cold injury. In warm climates, the graft union should be just above soil level.

Refill the hole, firming the soil with your hands and encircling the plant with a dam of soil several inches high. Fill the dam with water and allow it to soak in. Mound soil over the stems to form a dome about 6 inches high. The dome will keep the stems from drying out until the plant is rooted. Gradually remove the excess soil as the leaves open.

Roses growing in containers can be planted like a shrub (see Chapter 3).

CARING FOR AND FEEDING ROSES

Roses, especially modern types, perform best in fertile, moist soil. Most roses need full sun, but some old garden types tolerate a bit of shade, although they may have fewer flowers.

If rainfall is insufficient, modern roses need to be watered deeply several times a week during the growing season; old garden roses need deep watering once a week. (Water less during autumn to harden off the plants.) A good rule of thumb is to water deeply when the soil is dry to a depth of 3 inches. Use drip irrigation or a soaker hose to avoid wetting the foliage and encouraging black spot disease. If you must use an overhead sprinkler, water in the morning so foliage dries quickly.

Roses perform poorly if the soil dries out, so apply a heavy mulch to keep the soil cool and moist. Effective mulches include cocoa hulls, aged manure, composted leaves, bark chips, and shredded bark. Roses are heavy feeders and should be fertilized regularly. Feed newly planted roses a month after planting. Begin feeding established roses when they start to leaf out in spring. To keep hybrid modern roses growing and blooming, feed them every two to three weeks from spring through summer. Old garden roses need only an annual feeding in spring.

There are a number of ways to feed roses. The easiest is to apply a granular, slow-release, inorganic fertilizer designed especially for roses. If you prefer organic methods, you can rely on well-rotted manure or periodic dousings with fish emulsion. In cold climates, stop applying nitrogen fertilizer six weeks before the expected first frost in autumn. This will help the bush harden off before the weather turns cold. You also can apply phosphorous, in the form of superphosphate, and potassium, in the form of greensand or kelp meal, to help roses harden off for winter.

PLANTING BARE-ROOT ROSES

To plant a bare-root rose, first soak it in a bucket of water for an hour to rehydrate the plant.

Prepare an 18-inch-deep planting hole with a mound of soil in the middle to support the roots. Plant the rose at the correct depth, depending on the climate.

Mound soil over the base of the stems to prevent the newly planted rose from drying out. Form a dam of soil around the plant to collect water. Water well.

When the plant begins to grow, gradually remove the mound of soil and mulch well.

PRUNING ROSES

PRUNING MODERN ROSES

To keep modern roses healthy and blooming well, prune them in late winter or early spring. First shorten the canes. Make all cuts with sharp shears.

Cut at an angle facing away from the center of the shrub. As the stem on the right shows, cut just above outward-facing buds. The cut on the left stem is too far from the bud.

Thin the plant to three to five of the thickest, most vigorous canes.

Pruning roses correctly is essential for their health and lush bloom. Proper pruning prevents disease, keeps the shrub attractive and shapely, and encourages the longest possible flowering with the largest blooms.

Different types of roses require different pruning techniques. Modern roses, ramblers, large-flowered climbers, shrub, and old garden roses have varied growth habits and respond differently to pruning. Here's the correct way to prune each type:

PRUNING MODERN BUSH ROSES

Prune modern hybrid roses while they are still dormant in late winter or early spring, two weeks before the last expected frost. Shorten healthy canes to 8 to 24 inches tall, depending upon the vigor of the particular cultivar, and cut out weak or damaged canes. Make cuts with lopping shears or handheld shears, cutting at an angle just above outward-facing buds. Cut off all canes except the three to five thickest and darkest green ones—these are the most vigorous ones.

Although you should perform the major pruning when roses are dormant, keep in mind that every time you cut off a fresh or faded flower you actually prune the bush and influence its growth. You must remove the faded blossoms properly to stimulate new growth and thus more flowers.

When cutting a flower, use sharp handheld shears and cut at an angle just above the first large leaf, one with five leaflets. New growth emerges from the axil of this leaf and produces more blossoms. If you cut too high, weak growth results.

TRAINING RAMBLER ROSES

Rambler roses—rampant climbers that flower once a year—bloom on old wood from the previous season. They'll be most vigorous and floriferous if you cut off entire canes soon after they finish blooming. This encourages healthy new growth, which can reach 20 feet in a season.

If you don't remove the rambler's year-old canes after blooming, they will rebloom on side branches (called laterals) the next year, but the flowers may not be as lush. Without pruning or training, your rambler eventually will turn into a thorny, impenetrable thicket with dead canes on the inside and flowers only on the edges.

Tie the new shoots to a trellis, fence, or arbor. Strips of old pantyhose make excellent flexible plant ties. You might tie any older canes off to the side to make room for the new canes; this also makes the laterals bloom better. In fact, fastening the stems in a horizontal position produces maximum bloom.

TRAINING LARGE-FLOWERED CLIMBERS

Large-flowered climbing roses grow much less vigorously than ramblers and produce flowers throughout the growing season. They grow tall by adding height to the previous year's wood, so you must not prune them the first few years, except to remove spent flowers and damaged wood. Secure all the new growth to its support with twine or pantyhose strips. Only when the climber gets as tall as you want should you begin pruning. Prune during the dormant season to guide the climber's shape and to remove old or damaged wood.

Climbing roses, such as this Rosa moschata 'Plena', add a spectacular vertical element to a garden. They need proper pruning each year to bloom well.

PRUNING SHRUB AND OLD GARDEN ROSES

These roses, grown for their full, beautiful shapes and decorative flowers, should be pruned only lightly, as you would most other flowering shrubs. Prune repeat-flowering types when dormant in late winter and once-flowering shrubs after they finish blooming in early summer. Use lopping shears (not hedge shears) to cut out the oldest, nonproductive wood and weak, flimsy canes. (Old canes are thick and dark brown, often with split bark.) Cut old canes at ground level, then shorten remaining canes by one-third to one-half their length. Clip side shoots to two to five growth buds.

A pruning technique practiced by many rose aficionados will transform your shrub roses into a spectacle of head-to-toe blossoms. Cut back the main canes to different lengths, leaving the tallest ones in the middle and the outer canes shorter. This gives the shrub a beautiful vase shape with blossoms at all levels instead of just at the top.

TRAINING RAMBLER ROSES

Rambler roses bloom on the previous year's wood and can become a tangled mass. Prune as soon as they stop blooming for the season.

Cut off the year-old canes that have produced flowers. This encourages new growth that blooms the following year.

Tie the new shoots, which can reach 20 feet in one season, to the support as they grow.

SPECIAL CARE FOR ROSES

Treat your roses well, and they will delight you for years with their fragrance and color. In colder climates, they need to be shielded from the ravages of winter. In all climates, they need diligent protection from the pests and diseases that can mar their beauty.

WINTER CARE

Although old garden roses and some shrub roses defy even the frigid winters of the far North, most modern bush roses are too tender to tolerate winter's worst.

In Zone 5 or colder, you should protect rosebushes from winter cold; the graft union is especially sensitive to freezing. Cut back the rose to a height of about 2 feet after freezing temperatures have blackened the foliage. Then make an insulating mound of soil, wood chips, or sawdust around the stems. If you use soil, don't dig it up from around the rose's roots, but bring it from elsewhere. Remove the protective mound in early spring when the ground thaws. Prune as needed; any part of the rose that protruded above the protective mound may be dead.

Ramblers are usually cold-hardy, but tender, large-flowered climbers may be more trouble than they're worth in northern climates. You must lower them from the support and insulate the entire length of the stems and the graft union. Usually this means partially digging up the roots on one side of the plant so you can tip it to the side. Then you must bury the stems under soil or wood chips until spring. It helps in handling the rose to loosely tie the canes into a bundle before lowering them.

ROSE PESTS AND DISEASES

Roses, especially modern ones, suffer from a variety of insects and diseases. The most troublesome pests include aphids, Japanese beetles, rose chafers, borers, thrips, leafhoppers, and mites.

Some rose growers use chemical pesticides to control bugs; others succeed with an organic approach. Try hosing mites and aphids off the plants with a strong stream of water each morning. Contact sprays of insecticidal soap or pyrethrin also work well. Use traps (placed well away from the roses) to lure Japanese beetles away from the plants.

Black circles surrounded by yellow rings characterize black spot, a fungus that often disfigures leaves and weakens plants, defoliating those most susceptible. Some modern cultivars are more resistant than others. Although black spot occurs on some old garden roses, it rarely damages the plants significantly.

PROTECTING ROSES FOR WINTER

Protect rosebushes in colder regions by cutting back the canes and mounding the stubs with at least 8 inches of soil, mulch, or other protective materials.

To protect climbing roses from cold, dig up the roots on one side of the plant and tilt canes to the ground. Pin canes to the ground and cover with mulch or soil.

Photo by William Stites

Black spot is most common in hot, humid areas and on foliage that stays wet for hours. Because the spores overwinter on infested leaves, a thorough garden cleanup goes a long way toward preventing the disease. Avoid wetting leaves when watering, because the spores germinate in a film of water. Spraying with a baking soda solution may help prevent black spot (see box at right).

Powdery mildew causes curled leaves and disfigured flowers, coating them with a white powder. Fungicidal soap and sulfur sprays may slow or prevent the fungus, as will increased air circulation. Hosing off the leaves once a day stops spores from germinating. Hose the leaves in the morning so they can dry quickly. Lingering wetness encourages black spot.

Roses vary widely in disease resistance. Choosing disease-resistant cultivars, such as this 'James Mason', a modern gallica, helps avoid many rose problems.

ALBA ROSES

Alba roses are among the oldest known roses in cultivation, originating about 200 A.D. Noted for their strong, rich rose attar perfume, the refined-looking semidouble or double flowers of alba roses open flat and may be white or shades of pink. Blossoms appear in early summer and

SEMI PLENA ALBA ROSE

are set off against lovely blue-green foliage. Showy rose hips develop on cultivars with the fewest petals. Stems are studded with a scattering of thorns. The slender upright bushes grow 4 to 6 feet tall.

Use alba roses in background of flower borders or as hedges. Or, train as climbers on fences or pillars.

Site: Full sun to half shade. Tolerates poor soil, but performs best in fertile, moist site. Cold-hardy; zones 3 to 9.
How to Grow: Plant bare-root or container-grown plants in spring. Little pruning needed; remove old canes of mature shrubs every year immediately after flowering for best blooms. Albas are easy to grow and disease-resistant.
Cultivars: 'Semi Plena', white, semidouble, cultivated for perfume; 'Celestial', delicate pink, semidouble; 'Felicite Parmentier', pink fading to cream, double, green button center; 'Queen of Denmark', rose-pink, double.

BOURBON ROSES

Bourbon roses are one of the few repeat-flowering old roses. These Victorian roses, with their heady fragrance, feature globular flowers that open to buttonlike centers nestled between neatly interlocked petals. Colors include white, pink, and purple. Intermittent blossoms follow the profuse spring bloom; some cultivars bloom almost constantly. Leaves and stems resemble modern roses, but flowers, scent, and overall growth are traits of old-fashioned roses. Plants grow 5 to 6 feet tall, varying from bushy to spreading.

Use strong, vigorous shrubs as specimens or hedges. Peg those with trailing stems to ground or train on pillars to encourage greater flowering.

MADAME ISAAC PEREIRE BOURBON ROSE

Site: Full sun. Fertile, well-drained soil rich in organic matter. Keep well watered. Hardy in zones 6 to 9, colder with winter protection.
How to Grow: Plant shrubs in spring. Prune mature plants when dormant, shortening main branches by one-third and others by two-thirds. Deadhead and encourage repeat bloom by cutting back laterals by one-third.

Remove older wood at ground level every few years. Fertilize after each bloom flush to encourage repeat flowering. Suffers from black spot much more than other old roses.
Cultivars: 'Boule de Neige', little white flowers all summer; 'Zephirine Drouhin', deep rose-pink, thornless, train as climber; 'Madame Isaac Pereire', dark raspberry-purple, intense fragrance; 'Louise Odier', warm pink.

CANADIAN ROSES

This group of diverse roses, which includes shrubs and climbers, was bred by the Canadian Department

JOHN CABOT CANADIAN CLIMBER

of Agriculture to withstand Canada's tough growing conditions. No other modern rose equals the Canadian roses for cold-hardiness and long season of bloom. Hybrid teas and other bush roses cannot withstand Canadian winters, except in coastal British Columbia and Nova Scotia and on the borders of the Great Lakes, and then only with elaborate winter protection. The Canadian roses flourish where others freeze, blooming with abandon throughout the summer.

Canadian roses are excellent garden shrubs for Canada and the northern United States.

Site: Full sun. Fertile, moist, well-drained soil high in organic matter. Keep well watered and mulched. Hardy in zones 2 or 3 to 8.

How to Grow: Plant bare-root or container-grown plants in spring. Don't plant grafted plants; insist on own-root specimens to ensure cold-hardiness. Prune according to type of rose, cutting out deadwood in spring. Needs no winter protection. If exceptionally cold, winter will kill roses to the ground. Roses will regrow from roots. Climbers don't need winter protection. Generally resistant to black spot and powdery mildew.

Cultivars: Shrubs: 'Cuthbert Grant', red; 'Morden Armorette', dark pink; 'Morden Blush', light pink; 'Henry Hudson', light pink; and 'J.P. Connell', yellow.

Climbers: 'John Cabot', red; 'William Baffin', dark pink; 'Louis Jolliet', pink.

CENTIFOLIA ROSES

These sumptuous roses, sometimes called cabbage roses because their whorled petals and lush,

PAUL RICAULT CENTIFOLIA ROSE

rounded blossoms resemble cabbage heads, were immortalized in Dutch Masters paintings and Victorian fabrics and wallpapers. Like most old-fashioned roses, they flower only once a year, producing their fragrant,

luxurious flowers on arched thorny branches. Cabbage roses may be pink, rose, violet, and, rarely, white. Plants grow 4 to 6 feet tall, upright to bushy, some arching.

Use centifolia roses in mixed borders or cottage gardens; train types with long, flexible canes to pillars, arches, or fences.

Site: Full sun. Fertile, well-drained, moist soil. Keep well watered and mulched. Hardy in zones 3 to 9; winter protection needed in zones 3 and 4.

How to Grow: Plant bare-root or container-grown plants in spring. Prune out old wood immediately after flowering if needed; blooms best on older wood. Clip off faded blossoms. Susceptible to black spot and mildew. Plant in full sun; avoid wetting foliage.

Cultivars: 'Tour de Malakoff', purple-crimson, arching stems; 'De Meaux', light rose, compact dwarf plant; 'Paul Ricault', deep rose-pink, opening flat; 'Juno', blush pink; 'Fantin-Latour', clear pink, opens flat.

CHINA AND TEA ROSES

China roses arrived in France on trading ships from the Orient during the late 1700s and sparked immediate enthusiasm. They were the first continuous flowering roses seen in Europe. The clusters of small, fragrant flowers darken alluringly instead of fading as they age.

Tea roses, so named because their foliage smells like tea or, perhaps, because they were shipped in tea crates, arrived from China in the 1830s. These continuous flowering roses with high-centered buds and large flowers stirred excitement because they bloomed in colors not seen: yellow, red, and apricot-orange.

Neither China nor tea roses can survive cold winters, but they make admirable plants for gardens in Texas, southern California, and the Deep

OLD BLUSH CHINA ROSE

South, blooming almost year-round. China and tea roses are parents of modern roses. Most are small, bushy plants 3 to 4 feet tall; some are lanky and reach 7 feet.

Prune severely to maintain as small shrubs or train as climbers on pillars or fences.

Site: Full sun. Fertile, moist, well-drained soil best. Drought-tolerant. China roses hardy in zones 6 to 10; tea roses in zones 7 to 10.

How to Grow: Plant bare-root or container-grown plants in spring. Cut back by one-third when out of bloom to encourage new growth; prune to shape and remove deadwood. These roses are disease-resistant and thrive on neglect, but to encourage abundant bloom, pinch off faded flowers to prevent hip formation.

Cultivars: China: 'Old Blush', pink semidouble; 'Louis Phillipe', deep crimson, double; 'Madame Laurette Messiny', salmon pink, semidouble.

Tea: 'Fortune's Double Yellow', apricot, yellow, pink blend, climber; 'Marie van Houtte', cream to yellow; 'Monsieur Tilier', copper to pink; 'Sombreuil', creamy white.

Noisette roses, bred from China and tea roses: clusters of constantly blooming, fragrant, pastel flowers; zones 8 to 10.

DAMASK ROSES

Damask roses produce sprays of fragrant flowers noted for their rich damask fragrance, a source of attar of roses, used in perfumery. Blossoms come in clear shades of

MADAME HARDY DAMASK ROSE

pink or white and may be semidouble to double. Foliage is light green. Thorny stems may bend under the flowers' weight. Plants grow larger and taller than gallicas, reaching 4 to 6 feet.

Site: Full sun. Fertile, well-drained, moist soil; keep well watered and mulched. Hardy in zones 4 to 9; winter protection needed in Zone 4.
How to Grow: Plant bare-root or container-grown plants in spring. Easy to care for. Thin the old canes every few years, immediately after blooming. Cut back hard every five years to reinvigorate. Double blossoms may hang onto bush and rot; immediately clip faded flowers. Peg floppy lateral branches of some types to ground or low fence to encourage profuse bloom.
Cultivars: 'Madame Hardy', pure white double with green button center; 'La Ville de Bruxelles', lavender-pink, large, flat, double; 'Ispahan', medium pink, fragrant; 'Autumn Damask', repeats in fall, one of few early old roses that reblooms.

ENGLISH ROSES

Introduced in the early 1970s by British nurseryman David Austin, this new group of roses combines the wide color range and continuous flowering of modern roses with the heady fragrance, sumptuous flower form, and attractive shrub character of old-fashioned roses.

These revolutionary roses came from hybridizing modern climbers, floribundas, and hybrid teas with the two oldest known roses: gallicas and damasks. The bushy plants grow 3 to 6 feet tall, with flowers in shades of red, pink, white, and yellow.

KATHRYN MORLEY ENGLISH ROSE

Although not a class of old garden roses because they originated so recently, English roses can be considered old-fashioned roses for purposes of garden design. Their graceful growth habit makes them wonderful plants to include in a mixed border, cottage garden, or fragrance garden, but unlike old roses, they bloom all summer and fall. Several dozen varieties are available in England; fewer are available here.

Site: Full sun to part shade. Fertile, moist soil. Keep well watered and mulched. Hardy in zones 4 or 5 to 9; various types behave differently in different regions; too new for complete evaluation.
How to Grow: Plant bare-root or container-grown plants in spring. Prune for shape, removing weak, twiggy, and old unproductive wood, cutting remainder back by one-third to one-half when dormant. Remove faded blossoms by cutting above first five-leaflet leaf. Foliage generally resists diseases. Usual rose insect pests can be troublesome.
Cultivars: 'Abraham Darby', apricot-pink; 'Charmian', rose-pink; 'Constance Spry', pink, once-blooming climber; 'Cottage Rose', pink; 'Fair Bianca', white; 'Gertrude Jekyll', bright pink; 'Graham Thomas', yellow; 'Heritage', soft pink; 'Mary Rose', medium pink; 'Red Coat', scarlet, single; 'Wenlock', crimson.

FLORIBUNDA ROSES

Derived from crossing hybrid teas with polyantha roses, floribunda roses combine the best qualities of the two groups: high-centered blossoms borne in profuse clusters from early summer through fall. Flowers come in all colors; most are single (5 to 12 petals) or semidouble (13 to 25 petals). Some are double (25 to 45 petals), and some are fragrant. "Decorative floribundas" produce masses of clustered 2- to 3-inch flowers in bursts from early summer through fall. "Large-flowered floribundas" are compact plants with larger, long-stemmed flowers that rival hybrid tea blossoms. Floribundas grow on 2- to 3-foot-tall bushes. They are attractive in formal and mixed borders, and work well as hedges and in mass plantings.

SHOWBIZ FLORIBUNDA ROSE

Site: Full sun. Fertile, well-drained, moist soil; keep well watered and mulched. Slightly more cold-hardy than hybrid teas, floribundas are suited to zones 5 to 9; need winter protection in zones 5 and 6.

How to Grow: Plant bare-root or container-grown plants in spring with bud union 2 inches below soil level to encourage own roots. Pruning not as critical as with hybrid teas; cut back canes to within 6 inches of ground every three years to renew vigor. Remove suckers from understock. Easier to care for than hybrid teas. Fertilize twice monthly during blooming season; withhold fertilizer one month before frost. When cutting flowers and deadheading, make cut just above first five-part leaf below entire cluster for best reblooming. Slightly more resistant than hybrid teas, but pesticide program needed.

Cultivars: Decorative: 'Betty Prior', hot pink, single; 'Europeana', dark crimson; 'Rose Parade', pink; 'Bahia', orange; 'Fashion', coral-pink; 'Vogue', coral.

Large-flowered: 'Cherish', pink; 'Apricot Nectar', apricot; 'Saratoga', white; 'Angel Face', mauve.

GALLICA ROSES

The oldest known cultivated rose is *Rosa gallica*, prized by the ancient Greeks and Romans. Called the apothecary's rose in medieval Europe, petals of these fragrant flowers retain their perfume even when dried.

Gallica roses have light green foliage and bloom once in early summer, producing single or semidouble flowers followed in

CHARLES DE MILLS GALLICA ROSE

autumn by a profusion of showy, round red hips. Double-flowered forms don't produce rose hips. Flowers, which may be crimson, pink, purple, lavender, and even striped, bloom mostly on old wood. These handsome, dense, vase-shaped shrubs grow 3 to 5 feet tall and wide, with nearly thornless branches, and become showier with age. Use gallicas as low hedges, in mixed borders, or in cottage or herb gardens.

Site: Full sun. Tolerates poor, gravelly soil, but fertile conditions are best. Hardy in zones 4 to 9.

How to Grow: Plant bare-root or container-grown plants in spring. Own-root plants form thickets; grafted ones won't. Thin out old wood of mature plants immediately after blooming to

encourage new growth for next year's flowers. Don't prune faded flowers. Resistant to pests and diseases.

Cultivars: *R. gallica*, pink-red, semidouble with yellow center; 'Charles de Mills', dark crimson-maroon, large, flat, double; 'Rosa Mundi', semidouble, pale pink and crimson striped; 'Cardinal de Richelieu', dark purple, small, double; 'Belle de Crecy', bright pink changing to lavender, double.

GRANDIFLORA ROSES

Representing the best characteristics of its parent hybrid tea and floribunda roses, the first grandiflora rose, 'Queen Elizabeth', was introduced in 1954. Now several colors are widely grown. The long-stemmed, hybrid-tealike flowers form abundant clusters from early summer through fall on bushes 5 to 6 feet tall.

LOVE GRANDIFLORA ROSE

Flowers are midway in size between hybrid teas and floribundas. Use grandifloras as background plants in flower gardens or plant behind hybrid teas in rose beds.

Site: Full sun. Fertile, well-drained, moist soil; keep well watered and mulched. Slightly more cold-hardy than hybrid teas; zones 5 or 6 to 9; winter protection is needed in zones 5 and 6.

continued

Grandiflora Roses
(continued)

How to Grow: Plant bare-root or container-grown plants in spring. Usually grafted to hardy rootstock. Remove all but five strongest canes in spring, after buds break, and prune laterals back to three buds. Remove suckers. Fertilize twice monthly during blooming season; withhold fertilizer one month before frost. Cut fresh or faded flower clusters just above first five-leaflet leaf for best reblooming. Continual pest control necessary.

Cultivars: 'Queen Elizabeth', pink; 'Sundowner', copper; 'Love', red with white reverse; 'Prominent', orange; 'Arizona', bronze; 'John S. Armstrong', red.

Hybrid Musk Roses

Musk-scented, these shrub roses were bred in England in the early 1900s. They are noted for their profusion of large clusters of highly scented flowers, which resemble a

VANITY HYBRID MUSK ROSE

long-lost musk rose ancestor. Bearing single or semidouble flowers in shades of pink, apricot, or yellow, hybrid musks bloom heavily in spring and fall with scattered blossoms in summer. Plants grow 4 to 6 feet tall with arching canes and make attractive landscape shrubs. Train arching types as climbers or peg for groundcover.

Site: Full sun to part shade. Fertile, well-drained, moist soil; keep well watered and mulched. Most are hardy only in zones 6 to 9; some cultivars are more cold-hardy.

How to Grow: Plant bare-root or container-grown plants in spring. Cut out older canes when dormant. Clip off faded blossoms, cutting laterals back by one-third. Fertilize twice every month and keep well watered for repeat bloom. Disease-resistant.

Cultivars: 'Belinda', rose-pink with white center, single; 'Ballerina', pink with white center, single; 'Bloomfield Dainty', soft yellow aging to creamy pink, single; 'Felicia', pink, single; 'Bubble Bath', pink, double; 'Cornelia', apricot-copper, double; 'Daybreak', primrose yellow, double; 'Moonlight', creamy white, semidouble.

Hybrid Perpetual Roses

These stunning roses were all the rage when first introduced to Victorian gardens because they were the first large-flowered roses that bloomed repeatedly. Hybrid perpetual roses feature large, fully double, rounded flowers at the ends of their canes. The fragrant blossoms bloom in spring and again in fall. The upright, narrow plants grow 3 to 5 feet tall. These fine, cold-hardy, fragrant roses deserve to be rediscovered by today's gardeners. Train to a pillar or along a low fence.

Site: Full sun. Fertile, moist, well-drained soil high in organic matter. Cold-hardy, zones 4 to 9.

How to Grow: Plant bare-root or container-grown plants in spring. Prune during dormancy by removing old

ULRICH BRUNNER FILS
HYBRID PERPETUAL ROSE

wood and cutting back main stems no more than one-half and lateral branches to one-third their length. Prune again after first flowering to encourage repeat bloom. Suffers from black spot.

Cultivars: 'Reine Des Violettes', purest purple of all roses, almost thornless; 'Baroness de Rothschild', soft pink, cup-shaped; 'General Jacqueminot', cherry red, double, yellow center; 'Androise de Lyon', deep pink with purple and violet.

Hybrid Tea Roses

Introduced by a French breeder in 1867, 'La France' was the first hybrid tea rose. It featured a silvery pink blossom with deep pink reverse. This new plant marked the era of the modern rose. Hundreds, maybe thousands, of cultivars exist today.

Blossoms of hybrid tea roses have characteristic high-centered, tapered buds that gently unfold into double flowers of 20 to 50 petals. Colors include bold reds, purples, oranges, golds, pastels, or whites—every color but blue. Flowers form singly at the tips of long stems. Fragrance depends on the cultivar.

MODERNA HYBRID TEA ROSE

Unfortunately, the perfection in flower form isn't equaled by the plant itself. Bushes grow 2½ to 5 feet tall and are leggy with sparse foliage; they host numerous insects and diseases. Hybrid teas often are grown for exhibition blooms or cut flowers rather than garden appearance. Plant hybrid teas in formal beds and camouflage bottoms of leggy plants with low hedges or other plants.

Site: Full sun. Fertile, well-drained, moist soil. Keep deeply watered and mulched; don't allow to dry out. Hardy in zones 5 to 9, depending on cultivar; needs winter protection in zones 5 and 6.
How to Grow: Plant bare-root or container-grown plants in spring with bud union at or below soil surface, depending on climate. Remove all but three to five strongest canes in spring just after buds break. Prune remaining canes to 1 to 2 feet tall, cutting to outward-facing bud. Remove suckers from understock. Fertilize twice monthly during blooming season; withhold fertilizer one month before frost. When cutting flowers, make cut just above first five-part leaf for best reblooming. Even well-grown plants seldom live more than 10 years. Aphids, spider mites, Japanese beetles, and rose chafers may be serious. Powdery mildew, black spot, and rust

may defoliate bushes; worse where foliage gets wet. Continual pest control program needed for quality flowers.
Cultivars: Hundreds of cultivars. Most popular are: 'Peace', yellow and pink; 'Mr. Lincoln', red; 'Double Delight', red blend; 'Garden Party', white; 'Tropicana', orange; 'Royal Highness', pink; 'First Prize', pink.

LADY BANKS ROSE

Popular in antebellum days, the Lady Banks rose, *Rosa banksiae* 'Lutea,' is regaining popularity in modern southern gardens because of its romantic color and durable good looks. Blanketed with small, soft yellow, slightly fragrant double blossoms in late spring and early summer, this rampant climber has

LADY BANKS ROSE

evergreen leaves and almost thornless stems that can climb to 20 feet. The Lady Banks is a beautiful rose for pillars, arbors, fences, and trees; essential in period southern gardens.

Site: Full to part sun. Fertile, moist soil best; tolerates poor conditions. Hardy in zones 8 and 9; tolerates light salt spray.
How to Grow: Plant bare-root or container-grown plants in spring. Take stem cuttings in early summer. Each year, prune hard immediately after

blooming; prune lightly later in summer if it becomes too large. Provide wire or trellis support and tie in place to keep sprawling stems upright and climbing. Usually pest- and disease-free.
Cultivars: 'Normalis', single white; 'Albo-Plena', double white; 'Lutescens', single yellow.

MEIDILAND PINK LANDSCAPE ROSE

LANDSCAPE ROSES

Lots of color with little care—that's what you get when you make space in your garden for one or more landscape roses. These tough-as-nails roses are relatively new to the market, but are quickly blanketing the country with bloom. Use them as hedges, groundcovers, or specimens, especially where other, more tender roses have failed. There are two major groups of landscape roses. The French-bred Meidiland roses and the German-bred Flower Carpet roses. Both types look stunning covering a bank or weeping over a wall. All varieties display sprays of flowers from early summer through fall.

Hedge types reach 3 to 4 feet tall and 2 to 3 feet wide. Groundcover types spread 5 to 6 feet across with arching canes that are 2 to 3 feet in height. The groundcover *continued*

LANDSCAPE ROSES
(continued)

roses make excellent bank covers and can be trained to weep over walls.

Site: Full sun. Fertile, well-drained, moist soil; keep well watered and mulched. Hardy in zones 4 to 9.

How to Grow: Plant bare-root or container-grown plants in spring. Space groundcover types 3 to 4 feet apart; hedge types 2 to 3 feet apart. Cut back every few years to renew. Remove sprays of faded flowers to encourage rebloom; remove deadwood. Generally disease-free.

Cultivars: Meidiland: 'Bonica', double, fragrant, pale pink blossoms; 'Meidiland Pink', pink single with white center; 'Alba', tiny, white, double flowers in profuse clusters; 'Scarlet Meidiland', deep red, double; 'White Meidiland', large, white, double flowers in clusters; 'Pearl Meidiland', pale pink, double; 'Red Meidiland', red single with white center.

Flower Carpet: 'Flower Carpet Pink', lipstick pink, double flowers that cover the plant; 'Flower Carpet White', pure white, blooms all summer; 'Flower Carpet Appleblossom', white with pink center.

LARGE-FLOWERED CLIMBING ROSES

Elegant, these roses often are sports of modern bush varieties with the same names. The climbers have long, supple canes that can be trained to fences or trellises. Climbing roses don't really climb because they can't entwine, so the gardener needs to tie them to supports. Large-flowered climbers usually bloom heavily once in spring and sporadically through fall. They grow 7 to 10 feet tall. Train climbing roses to adorn a wall, pillar, arch, fence, or trellis.

MADAME GEORGE STAECHELIN
LARGE-FLOWERED CLIMBER

Site: Full sun. Fertile, well-drained, moist soil; keep mulched and well watered. Hardy in zones 5 to 9; best in warmer zones where they can reach greater heights. Winter protection is needed in zones 5 to 7.

How to Grow: Plant bare-root or container-grown roses in spring. Remove oldest and weakest canes at bases while dormant, leaving total of five to eight newest, strongest canes. Cut side branches back to three buds. Cut faded flowers as for hybrid teas. Tie canes to supports; horizontal canes produce most flowers. Fertilize twice monthly until one month before frost. Partially dig up roots, tilt plant, and lay canes on ground, burying with soil to overwinter in cold climates. Pests and diseases are same as for hybrid teas.

Cultivars: 'Climbing Peace', yellow and pink; 'Climbing Golden Dawn', yellow; 'New Dawn', silvery pink; 'Elegance', yellow; 'Madame George Staechelin', shell pink; 'Climbing American Beauty', red; 'Don Juan', red; 'America', coral pink; 'Blaze Improved', red; 'White Dawn', white.

MINIATURE ROSES

Growing from 6 to 18 inches tall with diminutive flowers and leaves to match, miniature roses seem like tiny versions of their big sisters. Indeed, the flowers of some minis have high centers, like hybrid tea roses; others produce sprays of decorative blossoms like floribundas. These petite beauties are becoming more and more popular, with new cultivars available every year. They are delightful in window boxes or containers, or as edging of a flower border or formal rose garden.

NEW BEGINNING MINIATURE ROSE

Site: Full to half sun. Fertile, well-drained, moist soil; keep well watered and mulched. Hardy in zones 5 to 9; winter protection needed in zones 5 and 6.

How to Grow: Plant bare-root or container-grown roses in spring; they need at least 1 cubic foot of soil in container. Prune when dormant, removing all but six of the strongest new canes and cutting these back by one-half. Fertilize twice monthly until one month before frost. Keep containers well watered. Prune faded blossoms. Same pests and diseases as hybrid teas, but spider mites are especially troublesome.

Cultivars: 'Child's Play', white with pink edges; 'Small Miracle', white; 'Jitter Bug', orange; 'New Beginning', orange-red; 'Pinstripe', red-and-white;

'Charm Bracelet', golden yellow; 'Cartwheel', pink-and-white; 'Little Sizzler', dark red.

MOSS ROSES

Moss roses, named for the eye-catching mossy spines covering their flower buds and stem tips, were hybridized between 1850 and 1870. The mossy spines vary from soft to

RED MOSS ROSE

bristlelike and emit a resinous fragrance; the cabbage-shaped flowers emit a rich perfume. Although most moss roses bloom abundantly only once a year, autumn brings attractive red hips that are set off by the mossy stem tips. Plants grow more stiff and upright than centifolia roses, reaching 6 feet tall. Grow them in cottage gardens.

Site: Full sun. Fertile, well-drained, moist soil; keep well watered and mulched. Hardy in zones 4 to 9.
How to Grow: Plant bare-root or container-grown plants in spring. Prune as for centifolias. These are easy-care roses. Blossoms susceptible to botrytis blight fungus; avoid wetting flowers and foliage.
Cultivars: 'Comtesse de Murinais', rich pink, changing to white; 'Salet', bright pink, rebloomer; 'Perpetual White Moss', white, double, rebloomer; 'Marchal de Voust', mauve turning purple, compact shrub; 'Hunslet Moss', rose-pink.

POLYANTHA ROSES

Low-growing and compact, polyantha shrubs grow to 2 feet tall. They originated in the late 19th century as hybrids between *Rosa multiflora,* an American rose with clusters of prolific small blossoms, and *Rosa chinensis,* a tender Chinese rose with repeat bloom. Polyanthas feature dense clusters of dainty white, pink, orange, red, or yellow flowers borne in waves from late spring through fall. They have neat, fine-textured leaves and make excellent low-maintenance landscape plants for the front of a mixed border. Or, use them for a low hedge or in a cottage garden.

THE FAIRY POLYANTHA ROSE

Site: Full sun. Fertile, well-drained, moist soil; keep well watered and mulched. Hardy in zones 4 to 9; need winter protection in Zone 4.
How to Grow: Plant bare-root or container-grown plants in spring. Cut off faded flower clusters by pruning lateral branches back about one-third their length for repeat bloom. Keep well watered and fertilize twice monthly for repeat bloom. Not badly troubled by insects and diseases.
Cultivars: 'The Fairy', pink; 'Margo Koster', salmon-orange; 'China Doll', pink-and-white; 'Cecile Brunner', pale pink; 'Nathalie Nypels', rose-pink.
    Climbers: 'Climbing Cecile Brunner', pink; 'Climbing Margo Koster', salmon-orange.

PORTLAND ROSES

Also called damask perpetual roses, Portland roses feature blossoms on short stems with foliage

JACQUES CARTIER PORTLAND ROSE

closely nestled just beneath the flowers. The garden value lies in their repeat show of richly fragrant, old-rose-type blossoms. Plants grow to 4 feet in height. They are well suited to small gardens and mixed borders.

Site: Full sun. Fertile, well-drained, moist soil; keep well watered and mulched. Hardy in zones 5 to 9.
How to Grow: Plant bare-root or container-grown plants in spring. Prune mature plants when dormant, shortening main branches by one-third and others by two-thirds. Deadhead and encourage repeat bloom by cutting back laterals about one-third. Remove older wood at *continued*

PORTLAND ROSES
(continued)

ground level every few years. Fertilize regularly to encourage repeat bloom. Keep well watered. Disease- and pest-resistant.

Cultivars: 'Jacques Cartier', rich pink with green eye; 'Comte de Chambord', bright pink changing to mauve; 'Sidone', rose-pink; 'Delambre', red.

RAMBLER ROSES

Romance—that's what rambler roses with their untamed look and abundance of fragrant flowers bring to any garden. Bouquets of small blossoms open in breathtaking profusion, putting on a show for several weeks in early or midsummer. Although they don't actually climb, the long, pliable canes can be coaxed easily to clamber over an archway or

VEILCHENBLAU RAMBLER

trellis, along a fence, or up and over a roof or arbor. Some types can be encouraged to scale a tree, where their thorns help hold them. Ramblers grow 20 to 50 feet tall, and they are delightful in cottage gardens.

Site: Full sun. Fertile, moist, well-drained soil high in organic matter. Keep mulched and well watered.

Wichuraiana ramblers are hardy in zones 4 to 9; Multiflora ramblers in zones 5 or 6 to 9; Sempervirens ramblers in zones 6 to 9; Noisette ramblers in zones 7 to 10.

How to Grow: Plant container-grown or bare-root plants in spring. Ramblers bloom on year-old wood; cut off flowering canes at base immediately after blooming and tie up new growth. Keep canes tied to support. Fertilize before and after blooming. Powdery mildew may be a problem if air circulation is poor.

Cultivars: Wichuraiana: 'Etain', salmon-pink; 'Ethel', lilac-pink; 'Lady Gay', rose-pink; 'Jersey Beauty', yellow, single.

Multiflora: 'Gold Finch', golden aging cream; 'Apple Blossom', pastel pink; 'Bobbie James', creamy white, semidouble; 'Bleu Magenta', deep purple-blue aging to violet; 'Trausendschon', pink, semidouble; 'Veilchenblau', purple-violet aging lilac-blue.

Sempervirens: 'Princess Louise', creamy blush pink; 'Felicite Perpetue', pink buds opening creamy.

Noisette: 'Claire Jacquier', yellow, repeats; 'Madame Alfred Carriere', pearl pink, continuous bloom.

REDLEAF ROSE

Unusual for a rose, this beautiful shrub is grown more for its foliage than for its flowers. The leaves of the redleaf rose (*Rosa glauca* syn. *R. rubrifolia*) are a dusky gray-purple with reddish edges and a silvery sheen along the veins, making a striking accent amid garden greenery. The small, single, rose-pink blossoms have starry white centers and sparkle against the dark leaves for two months in spring and early summer. In the fall, the foliage turns orange and scarlet, accompanied by eye-catching clusters of cranberry-size red hips. The vase-shaped shrubs grow 6 to 8 feet tall and wide.

REDLEAF ROSE

Use redleaf rose for foliage color contrast in shrub or mixed borders; the shrub looks elegant combined with pink, blue, and lavender flowers.

Site: Full sun. Fertile, well-drained soil rich in organic matter. Hardy in zones 2 to 8.

How to Grow: Plant bare-root or container-grown shrubs in spring. Blooms on old wood. Prune out oldest canes after blooming. Easy to care for. Disease-free and pest-resistant.

Cultivars: 'Carmenetta', larger flowers.

RUGOSA ROSES

Among the most beautiful and certainly the toughest of the shrub roses, *Rosa rugosa* and its cultivars produce fragrant flowers all summer. The large single or semidouble flowers feature prominent clusters of yellow anthers in their centers and may be pink, rose-red, or white. These ripen into large, glossy, red rose hips that cling to the stout, thorny stems from autumn well into winter. The crinkled texture of the disease-resistant leaves gives them wonderful garden impact, especially when they turn brilliant shades of orange to gold in autumn. Plants grow 4 feet tall and 6 feet wide, with stout, arching canes. *Rosa rugosa,* sometimes called the beach rose, is native to Japan and Siberia, but has naturalized along North America's eastern seaboard. Many cultivars are available, and the species has been used extensively in hybridizing modern shrub roses.

RUGOSA ROSE

Rugosa roses are excellent seaside and Xeriscape plants, beautiful in mixed borders; attractive year-round.

Site: Full sun. Tolerates poor, dry soil. Hardy in zones 2 to 9. Tolerates wind and salt spray.
How to Grow: Plant container-grown plants in spring, summer, or fall. May be grafted, but best to purchase plants on own roots. Easy to care for. Cut out 3- or 4-year-old canes each fall. Remove suckers from grafted plants. Don't remove faded flower if hips are desired. Foliage of species is highly disease-resistant; some cultivars susceptible to black spot. Japanese beetles may be troublesome.
Cultivars: 'Blanc Double de Coubert', double white, no hips, considered finest white landscape rose; 'Frau Dagmar Hartopp', 2 to 3 feet tall, silvery pink; 'Therese Bugnet', deep red changing to rosy pink, fragrant, red winter stems; 'Pink Grootendorst',

clusters of small pink flowers with unique "pinked" edges; 'Hansa', reddish purple, double.

SHRUB ROSES

This catch-all category includes large-flowered, tall, bushy, modern roses that don't fit neatly into other categories. Most, however, are tough performers with repeat bloom, cold-hardiness, and ease of care that makes them ideal for low-maintenance gardens. They may be low-growing to tall, depending on type and cultivar. Excellent for mass planting or in shrub and mixed borders.

DORTMUND SHRUB ROSE

Site: Full sun. Fertile, well-drained, moist soil; keep mulched and well watered. Hardy in zones 4 and 5 to 9, depending on cultivar.
How to Grow: Plant bare-root or container-grown shrubs in spring. Easy to care for. Remove deadwood yearly. Cut back and thin canes every few years to renew. Generally disease-resistant; usual rose pests may be troublesome.
Cultivars: 'Carefree Beauty', pink, semidouble; 'Golden Wings', yellow, single; 'Sparrieshoop', light pink, single; 'Fred Loads', orange, single; 'Dortmund', red, single, climber; 'Nearly Wild', pink, single.

GENE BOERNER TREE ROSE

TREE ROSES

Elegant tree roses are actually "standards" featuring an eye-level ball of foliage and flowers atop a tall straight stem. These creations come from grafting a bush-type rose to a tall, sturdy trunk and rootstock. Almost any type of rose can be made into a standard, but typically hybrid teas, grandifloras, and floribundas are used. Most are up to 5 feet tall. Use them in a formal setting as a focal point or to frame an entrance.

Site: Full sun. Fertile, well-drained, moist soil; keep mulched and well watered. Hardy in zones 5 to 9; needs winter protection in zones 5 to 7.
How to Grow: Plant container-grown plants in spring with bud union at or below soil surface depending on climate. May be planted in decorative pots or in ground. Prune out old and weak canes when dormant, but prune selectively to keep symmetrical shape. Remove suckers. Stake trunk to keep straight. Where temperatures fall below 28°F, protect graft union in winter by partially digging up plant, tipping it over, laying it on ground, and burying with soil until spring. Pests and diseases are same as for hybrid teas.
Cultivars: Almost any bush-type rose can be made into a tree rose.

PERENNIALS,
ORNAMENTAL
GRASSES & FERNS

CHAPTER 6

ABOUT PERENNIALS AND BIENNIALS

Perennials, such as this peony, die to the ground at the end of the growing season, but they resprout in spring to decorate the garden year after year.

Color that comes back year after year—that's what perennials, and to some degree biennials, deliver. Available in a nearly infinite variety of colors, shapes, and textures, these hardy plants often multiply, filling a garden with beauty.

PERENNIALS DEFINED

A perennial is any plant that lives for three or more years; many live much, much longer. The garden flowers that are termed perennials technically should be called herbaceous perennials because they lack the woody stems and branches of shrubs and trees, which are called woody perennials. Most herbaceous perennials die to the ground during winter, but their roots remain alive and send up new growth in spring. The tall tops of some perennials die in fall and the plants develop ground-hugging rosettes of leaves that survive the winter. A few perennials, such as bergenia and epimedium, are herbaceous, but have evergreen or semievergreen leaves. A few plants that gardeners classify as perennials, such as edging candytuft, are actually extra-low woody plants.

Most perennials bloom for two to three weeks at a specific time of the year, and their foliage remains until frost. Some cherished perennials, such as threadleaf coreopsis and fringed bleeding-heart, are long-blooming, producing flowers for eight to 12 weeks. Others, such as garden phlox and delphinium, can be encouraged to rebloom by cutting back the first flush of flowers after the blooms fade and before they set seed. Many perennials with a relatively short flowering period contribute lovely foliage texture and color to the garden long after their flowers fade. Some are grown just for their beautiful foliage alone.

FERNS

Ferns are primitive, nonflowering plants. Fern "leaves," called fronds, usually are divided into "leaflets," called pinnae. The fronds arise from underground rhizomes, which are modified stems that contain buds and roots. New fronds are tightly curled into structures called fiddleheads or crosiers, which unfurl in spring. They are covered with silvery hairs and come in a range of colors.

Ferns reproduce by spores, not seeds, and have two life-cycle stages. Spores are enclosed in clusters of tiny cases called sori, which usually form on the undersides of the fronds. Some ferns produce spores only on modified fronds called fertile fronds, which become brown from the spore cases. Each fertile frond ripens about a million spores, but only a few spores germinate into the tiny stage of a fern

Surrounded by infertile fronds, the curled fertile fronds are covered with brown spore cases, called sori.

called a prothallium. This small, heart-shaped structure contains male and female parts and fertilizes itself if given the proper moisture conditions. The prothallium gives rise to the mature fern plant.

Most ferns inhabit cool, moist woodlands, so provide dappled to full shade; deep, humus-rich, acid soil; and plentiful moisture. Ferns that grow in bogs tolerate poorly drained garden soil. They also flourish in some sun if the roots remain damp. Other ferns tolerate drought if they are shaded. Ferns that grow in rock outcroppings in forests or on dry slopes prefer well-drained, somewhat alkaline soil that mimics the limestone rock of their natural setting.

Many perennials spread, forming larger clumps every year. Some fast-growing plants need to be dug up and divided every few years or the plants lose vigor. Aggressive spreaders must be continually hacked back or they take over the garden. A few perennials, such as peony and gas plant, grow happily for 10 to 50 years without needing division.

Perennials are cold-hardy to different degrees; some can't survive winters north of Washington, D.C.; others flourish in Minnesota and the Dakotas. Some thrive in the hot, humid summers of the South; others wilt and flop in those conditions. The perennials listed in the encyclopedia starting on page 296 are rated according to the U.S. Department of Agriculture hardiness zones.

BIENNIALS DEFINED

Living for only two years, biennials germinate from seed the first year and put all their energy into growing foliage and strong root systems. They

Foxglove is a biennial, a flower that completes its entire life cycle in two years. Self-sown seedlings often make biennials permanent additions to the garden.

often live through the winter as a rosette of ground-hugging leaves; the next growing season, they send up flowering shoots, set new seed, and die once the seeds ripen. But biennials can be unpredictable, not always adhering to this ideal life cycle. Some behave as short-lived perennials, flowering for perhaps two or three years in a row before dying.

Many biennials, such as foxglove and hollyhock, reseed themselves so successfully that they seem to be perennial in your garden; they'll appear year after year. Usually seeds germinate the same season they ripen and fall to the ground, so flowers appear the next year, producing successive years of bloom. You can help them along by shaking the seed heads over the ground where you want the plants to grow.

ORNAMENTAL GRASSES

Most ornamental grasses (and grasslike plants such as sedges and rushes) are perennials and live for many years, although a few are annuals or tender perennials that are treated like annuals in northern climates. Ornamental grasses fall into two general groups: cool-season grasses and warm-season grasses, depending upon what time of year they actively grow.

Cool-season types begin growth in late winter or early spring and bloom in late spring or early summer. They are usually evergreen in warm climates; the leaves and stems may die to the ground in winter in cold climates. These grasses often suffer during hot summer weather, but they perk up in autumn and begin to grow again. Most prefer moist growing conditions.

Warm-season grasses don't begin growth until the weather warms up in mid to late spring, and they are undaunted by summer heat. Many tolerate drought. Flowers appear in late summer or fall, and seed heads ripen in autumn. The leaves often turn lovely colors in autumn, then bleach to warm, earthy shades of beige, tan, and straw during winter. Although dead, the stems and dry leaves usually stand in place all winter unless flattened or broken by strong wind or deep snow.

Cool-season and warm-season grasses are placed in two additional categories: clump-forming bunch grasses and running rhizomatous grasses. Bunch grasses form tufts that grow larger year after year, but they stay where you plant them. Running grasses spread by stolons (aboveground stems) or rhizomes (underground stems). Such grasses can be invasive and spread over a large area; some are pests that are difficult to eradicate because they will sprout from even a tiny piece of root left in the ground.

Ornamental grasses are especially easy to maintain if you provide individual plants with their preferred growing conditions. Most need full sun, but a significant few, such as the lovely Japanese wind grass (*Hakonechloa macra* 'Aureola'), brighten shady sites. Although many grasses tolerate average or poor, sandy soil, most grow best in fertile, humus-rich, moist soil.

PLANTING PERENNIALS

The roots of container-grown perennials may continue to grow in a circle unless you untangle them. Cutting ½ inch into the root ball with a weeding claw encourages new roots to grow out into the soil.

Although perennials are usually sold in nurseries in quart or gallon containers, they also may be purchased bare-root, especially from mail-order nurseries. Perennials are best planted in spring or fall when weather conditions are least stressful.

PLANTING BARE-ROOT PERENNIALS

Mail-order companies often ship bare-root plants. Sometimes they ship plants that were grown in containers, then removed from the container and the root ball wrapped in newspaper. Bare-root plants are shipped at the proper planting time in spring. Unpack them immediately. If they look dry, soak them in lukewarm water for about half an hour. If you can't plant promptly, moisten the packing material (usually sphagnum moss or wood shavings), then rewrap. Seal the plants in plastic bags and store in a cool, dark place.

At planting time, protect bare-root plants from drying sun and air by wrapping them in a moist towel. Lay plants in the shade until you pop them into their planting holes.

Many gardeners have puzzled over the mess of roots discovered amid the packing materials of bare-root plants and wondered which end is up. Careful inspection should reveal remnants of dried stalks or new, little shoots that mark the crown (growing point) where the stems will grow. Observe the plant's root system and determine if it seems to spread out or grow down.

PLANTING FERNS

Many of the ferns grown in North American gardens are native plants, and unscrupulous growers dig them from the wild, pot them up, and sell them to unsuspecting gardeners. This is unethical and often illegal. Please do not purchase wild-collected ferns or dig them yourself. Collecting ruins native plant populations, robbing our natural landscape of its beauty. And unless properly dug, plants collected from the wild often perish. You'll have the best results with ferns that were propagated and grown in a nursery.

Purchase ferns grown in containers much like flowering plants and plant them the same way. Before planting, enrich the soil with well-rotted compost or manure, but do not add other fertilizer. Fern roots grow close to the soil surface and are easily burned by chemical fertilizer. Apply a deep mulch of shredded leaves or wood chips to conserve moisture. Keep the soil appropriately moist during the growing season. Because new fiddleheads often are formed in fall and over winter, provide a light, protective winter mulch of shredded leaves and be sure the fern is well watered as winter approaches.

Most ferns thrive if you give them the shady, cool, moist conditions found in their native habitats.

PLANTING ORNAMENTAL GRASSES

Plant bare-root and container-grown ornamental grasses as you would perennials. Running grasses, such as bamboo and ribbon grass, need special handling to prevent their long rhizomes from spreading around your landscape and perhaps colonizing your neighbor's property.

The best way to control an aggressive rhizomatous grass is to plant it within some type of deep, sturdy barrier. You can create a barrier from 1/16-inch-thick fiberglass sheeting like that used to cover greenhouses. Such a barrier should last 10 years. Available at home improvement stores or greenhouse suppliers, the fiberglass sheeting is sold in rolls that are 4 feet wide and 50 feet long.

Dig a 2- to 3-foot-deep trench around the planting to be contained. Light soil requires deeper barriers than heavy soil. Cut the fiberglass to fit the trench. Place it in the trench so that it extends 2 inches above the soil level. (This prevents rhizomes from "walking" over the top of the barrier.) Be sure to overlap the cut ends by 2 feet to prevent rhizomes from sneaking through the junction. Refill the trench with soil and press the soil in place.

Dig a hole twice as wide and deep as the roots. Hold the plant in the hole, fanning the roots either outward or downward according to their growth habit. Fill in soil under and around the roots. Position the crown at the same depth it was previously growing, usually with the bottom of the crown an inch below the soil surface. Build a ring of soil over the root ball to act as a dam, then flood it with water to give the plant a drink. Settle the soil around the root ball.

PLANTING CONTAINER-GROWN PERENNIALS

Container-grown plants can be put in the ground any time of year they're available. To remove the plant from its container, first water it, then turn it upside down, holding your hand over the root ball to catch the plant as it slides out. If the plant won't budge, whack the bottom and sides of the container with a trowel to loosen the roots or cut the side of the container to free the plant.

Roots of container-grown plants frequently encircle the surface of the root ball. Unless you interfere, the roots may keep growing around and around even after planting. Lay the plant on its side on the ground. Holding it at the top with one hand, firmly rake the entire surface of the root ball with a weeding claw. Cut into the root ball with the tines of the weeding claw to sever the entangling roots. The cut roots will branch out and grow into the surrounding soil.

Dig a hole wider and deeper than the container. Fill the bottom of the hole with at least an inch of soil. Place the plant in the hole so the crown is at the same soil level as it was in the pot. Refill the hole with soil. Firm the soil. Build a dam around the plant; flood it with water.

PLANTING BARE-ROOT PERENNIALS

Inspect the roots and observe how they grow, either in a spreading fashion or straight down, and plant accordingly.

Position the plant in a prepared hole, making sure the roots have good contact with the soil. The crown (the part where the stems meet the roots) should be level with the soil surface.

Fill the hole and build up a small ring of soil to act as a dam to collect water.

CARING FOR PERENNIALS

As with any plant, perennials have their likes and dislikes. Some are more adaptable than others, however. For the best results, provide a perennial with its preferred growing conditions, paying attention to soil type and sun exposure. Water if rainfall is scarce. Mulch the soil well to retain moisture, slow down weeds, and keep the flowers and foliage free of dirt. Fertilize once or twice a year, depending upon your soil conditions and the plants you are growing.

Once you've provided the best growing conditions possible, there's little else you can do for your plants. Perennials are not difficult to grow, but they will be most rewarding if you take a few steps to ensure that they look and perform their best.

STAKING

Some perennials need to be staked so they grow straight and tall instead of flopping onto their neighbors. Staking also prevents plants from being broken by the wind and rain or weighted to the ground with heavy blossoms. The staking method should depend on the form of the plant. The best stakes are inconspicuous and easy to install; green or brown materials look best. Position the stakes early, before the plants need them, so the foliage

STAKING PERENNIALS

Perennials can be staked several ways, depending on how they grow and how many plants must be staked.

This simple stake consists of a bamboo pole or wooden stake driven into the ground. A single plant is tied to the stake with soft string or fabric. This method works well for extra-tall plants. This staking strategy costs little or nothing.

This looped stake can be purchased from garden specialty stores and catalogs. It sturdily holds a single stem, especially one that has only one large flower.

Plants with numerous stems can be supported by driving several poles or stakes into the ground and connecting them with natural-color twine or string. Such a support system works well for floppy plants that grow in clusters such as yarrow and asters.

Grow-through supports are positioned over a plant while it is young and not blooming. Stems and leaves grow through it, camouflaging the support. This type of support works especially well for shrublike perennials such as peonies.

grows up and around the stake, camouflaging it.

Tall plants with slender, unbranched flower stalks, such as foxglove and delphinium, call for individual stakes to support each stem. Drive a bamboo or wooden stake into the ground beside the stem and loosely fasten the stem to the stake with a loop of green garden twine, strips of old panty hose, or paper-wrapped twist-ties. As the plant grows, add more ties at 1-foot intervals. The length of the stake should be about three-quarters of the plant's ultimate height. You can purchase plastic-coated metal stakes with locking loops on the ends to quickly and easily support individual stems; although expensive, they last for years and are easy to use.

Clump-forming plants with many bushy, branched stems, such as aster, shasta daisy, and chrysanthemum, can be supported with a ring of twine that's attached to three to five stakes placed around the clump's exterior. As the plants grow, add higher rings of twine at 1-foot intervals. The stems and flowers bend outward and rest on the twine, covering it naturally. Or, you can purchase metal rings with legs to serve this purpose. Install them early so the plants grow up through the rings. As another alternative, support the plants with small, twiggy branches cut from shrubs and trees, a strategy called pea staking or brush staking.

Another staking device is a metal support that consists of a round grid of 3-inch mesh supported by three legs. These plant supports come in various sizes and heights. Place the support over floppy, bushy plants when they are young. The stems grow up through the mesh and are held beautifully and inconspicuously apart to show off individual flowers.

CARING FOR ORNAMENTAL GRASSES

Ornamental grasses—especially the tall, deciduous kinds—produce a substantial volume of leaves and stems, which must be cut back and cleaned up once a year. You can remove the dried foliage in late winter or very early spring before new growth begins, or cut it back in fall. Dormant grasses allowed to stand throughout winter brighten the landscape and provide shelter and seeds for birds and other wildlife. However, in arid parts of the country where brushfires are a serious danger, grasses should be cut as soon as they become dry.

For most grasses, you can use a hedge shears to chop through the foliage, cutting warm-season grasses back to within a few inches of the ground and cutting cool-season grasses back to two-thirds their size. Tackle extra-tough grasses or large plantings with a string trimmer or its saw-blade attachment.

Some tall grasses flop over if they don't get enough sun, have been overfertilized, need to be divided, or simply because it's their nature. You can set them upright again by staking.

Grasses are heavy, so they need a strong support. In midsummer, drive one or two metal pipes or wooden stakes deep into the ground at the back of the grass. Tie a tight belt of twine around the grass at the middle, then secure the grass to the stake. The stakes and ties will be inconspicuous because the leaves will cascade fountain style over the twine. Support less weighty grasses with wire hoops, stout twigs, or branches, as you would for flowering perennials.

At some point, most clump-forming grasses need to be divided to improve their appearance. Running grasses should be divided to control their growth. After five to 10 years, a clump-forming grass develops a dead center. New growth appears only from an actively growing ring around the perimeter of the clump; this situation is readily apparent in spring. The dead center looks unattractive and causes the grass to flop.

The best time to divide a grass is just before or as it begins active growth. This means late winter, early spring, and fall for cool-season grasses and early to mid spring for warm-season grasses. To divide grasses in summer, you must cut back the foliage to about a third of its height. Mulch and regularly water the transplants to reduce stress and water loss.

Clumps of large, tall grasses and established stands of running grasses are extremely difficult to divide because they have dense, deep, woody root stalks or rhizomes that are quite heavy.

Dig up the clump—or cut out a section of running grass—keeping some soil around the roots. When the root ball is excavated, cut it into as many sections as you want, discarding dead portions. A small grass, such as fescue, can be divided with the thrust of a sharp shovel, but you will need an ax or even a chain saw to cut the root ball of a large, tough grass such as *Miscanthus*. Keep the divisions moist and shaded until ready to replant. Plant as soon as possible.

Hedge shears work well for cutting back the dried stalks of ornamental grasses in early spring.

Stake tall grasses to keep them from flopping by tying them around the middle with twine secured to wooden or metal stakes.

CARING FOR PERENNIALS
continued

CUTTING BACK AND PINCHING

You can help tall, lanky plants grow more compactly and possibly avoid the need for staking by pinching them. In spring, when summer bloomers such as balloonflower or milky bellflower are about 8 inches tall, break off the growing tip of each stem by snapping it between your fingers or cutting it with handheld shears.

Late-summer and fall-blooming plants, such as asters, can be cut back twice. To make them bushier and lower, cut them back by half—first when they're 4 inches tall and again at 16 inches tall. Chrysanthemums need to be pinched at two-week intervals until midsummer for prolific fall blooming and to keep them compact; simply use your fingers to break off the tips of the stems above the first or second set of leaves.

You also may wish to cut back some perennials after they bloom to neaten them or reduce their height. If a plant's foliage looks shabby from mildew or exhausted after blooming, cut it back to the base as long as you see evidence of new growth. The new stems will produce healthy, fresh foliage. Use a hedge shears to cut back masses of fine-textured stems and faded flowers.

Pinch or rub off side flower buds or branches of perennials such as peony, chrysanthemum, and hibiscus to channel the plant's energy into a few large blossoms rather than numerous small ones. Remove the extras while they are mere suggestions of buds. This disbudding practice creates larger, showier blossoms.

DEADHEADING

After perennials bloom, cut off faded flowers or flower stalks unless they will produce decorative seed heads. Deadheading keeps the garden tidy and directs the plant's energy into its roots and leaves rather than into seed formation. Cut leafy flower stems just above the foliage for a neat appearance; cut off leafless stems at ground level.

Removing spent flowers encourages more flowers; for example, pinching off the blossoms of balloonflower and coreopsis as they fade encourages more flowers to appear on the same stems, lengthening the bloom period. Cutting off the entire spent flower head of garden phlox or delphinium encourages side branches with a flush of new flowers a month after the first. If you don't know whether a plant will rebloom after deadheading, try it.

DIVIDING PERENNIALS

Most perennials, with a few exceptions, slowly decline in vigor unless they're divided every few years. Plant division rejuvenates the plant, and it provides more plants. Replant the divisions near one another so they make a dramatic drift. Or, plant them in a different location and establish a new bed.

As a general rule of thumb, divide spring-blooming plants immediately after they flower. Divide summer and fall bloomers in early spring when they have about 3 inches of topgrowth. However, in the South, Southwest, and Midwest, it's advantageous to divide spring and summer bloomers in fall so they can readjust during cool weather rather than when it's hot. Wherever you live, divide plants at least four weeks before stressful weather arrives, so their root systems can regrow.

Some plants, such as shasta daisy and chrysanthemum, have shallow, fibrous root systems. Once the clump is dug up, you can pull it apart into many sections with your hands. Other plants, such as astilbe, have tough, woody roots that grow in a tangled mass. Study the topgrowth to locate individual crowns, then drive the blade of a spade between the crowns, cutting the clump into sections.

PINCHING PERENNIALS

Many plants become bushier and sturdier and have bigger blooms if you pinch off the ends of the stems.

In late spring or early summer, use your thumb and forefinger to simply pinch off the last inch or so of the stem.

The plant responds by sending out more shoots, creating a bushier, fuller plant with more blossoms.

To minimize the damage to the root systems of fleshy-rooted plants such as daylily and hosta, use garden forks to divide them. Insert the forks back-to-back in the middle of a clump, then press the handles outward, prying the clump in two.

Fast-growing plants need to be divided more frequently than slow growers. A plant's appearance tells you when it needs dividing. A clump

To divide daylilies, use garden forks and your hands to gently pry the root clumps apart.

FERN CARE

When provided with their preferred growing conditions, ferns are practically care-free. Almost no pests and diseases, except for slugs, trouble them. To keep them tidy, cut off old brown fronds from deciduous and evergreen ferns in late winter or early spring. Take care not to damage emerging fiddleheads by walking on them or breaking them with a rake or other tool.

Like perennials and grasses, ferns can be divided to increase your collection. In early spring as the fiddleheads are emerging, dig up clumps with multiple crowns. Gently pull apart individual crowns. Take care not to damage the fiddleheads, because new ones will not form. Plant immediately, spreading out the roots and keeping the crown at the same level at which it was growing. Keep the soil moist until the fern gets established.

Ferns that spread by runners to form large stands are divided more easily, because they don't have crowns. Dig up sections of the stand containing fronds and roots and transplant in new locations.

resembling a doughnut, with active growth on the outer edges and a dead center, needs to be divided.

Before replanting the divisions, replenish the nutrients in the soil. Fork over the soil and work in organic matter and superphosphate. Plant divisions as soon as possible to protect them from drying air and sun. If you can't replant immediately, "heel in" the divisions in a temporary site or a pot—covering the roots lightly with moist soil—until you can plant. Water newly planted divisions and mulch the soil well.

WINTER PROTECTION

In climates where the soil alternately freezes and thaws in winter, perennials can be heaved out of the ground, exposing the roots to cold and drought. This is less of a problem where snow insulates the soil for months than it is where snowfall is sporadic.

Protect perennials from frost heaving by covering with evergreen boughs, oak leaves, or a thick mulch applied in early winter after the soil freezes. The cover keeps the soil frozen and the plants anchored in the ground. Remove the cover in late winter; cut back the dead tops in early spring. The tops help hold snow and mulch in place.

CUTTING BACK PERENNIALS

Cutting back perennials after they finish blooming keeps them full, bushy, and attractive. How you cut them back depends on the type of plant.

Cut back faded flowers with tall, leggy stalks by trimming the stalk as close to the base of the plant as possible.

Shear off faded flowers of bushy plants with hedge shears.

Cut back individual flowers of large clusters as they fade.

ACANTHUS SPINOSUS VAR. SPINOSISSIMUS

Spiny Bear's Breeches

Grown as much for its bold-textured evergreen leaves as for its flowers, spiny bear's breeches brings sculptural beauty to the garden throughout the year. The 2-foot-long evergreen leaves are lustrous green and deeply divided with lethal-looking white spines along the edges. These spines are less sharp than the vicious ones tipping the less conspicuous

ACANTHUS SPINOSUS VAR. SPINOSISSIMUS

bracts surrounding the flowers. Mauve-and-white tubular flowers bloom on tall, dramatic stalks for a month in early summer. Plants are 3 to 4 feet tall in bloom, 3 feet wide.

Spiny bear's breeches is dramatic in the midground of beds and borders where foliage clumps can be admired, but tall flower stalks won't block other plants. Locate where large stand is desired because plant spreads.

Site: Full to half sun. Average to sandy soil. Drought-tolerant; avoid winter wetness. Hardy in zones 6 to 10. Best where summers are hot and dry, but tolerates humidity.
How to Grow: Plant container-grown plants anytime, spacing 3 feet apart. Divide in spring; keep well-watered until established.

Handle with leather gloves. Remove winter-tattered leaves in early spring. Very invasive; dig out unwanted plants, taking care to get all root pieces. Snails and slugs may be problems.
Similar Species: *Acanthus mollis,* spineless leaves, white-and-purple flowers, zones 8 to 10; does poorly in humid South.

ACHILLEA SPP.

Yarrow

The flat, bright yellow flowers and fine-textured green foliage make fern-leaf yarrow (*Achillea filipendulina*) a sure winner for any perennial garden. The flowers, which have a spicy, herbal scent, will continue to appear all summer long if you remove them as they fade. The popular cultivars listed below bloom longer and need less staking than the species. Plants grow 3 to 4 feet tall and 2 feet wide.

ACHILLEA FILIPENDULINA 'CORONATION GOLD'

Use fern-leaf yarrow in mid- or background of flower border or herb garden. Excellent cut or dried flower; cut the flowers after pollen is visible or they will wilt.

Common yarrow (*A. millefolium*) is a native European wildflower that has naturalized in North America, where it

ACHILLEA MILLEFOLIUM 'THE BEACON'

decorates the roadsides with pretty, flat heads of tiny, white flowers from mid- to late summer. The lacy, dark green, silky-haired foliage forms a ground-hugging mat and is reputed to have medicinal qualities for healing wounds. Plants grow 1 to 3 feet tall. The species is invasive and is best naturalized in a meadow or herb garden. Cultivars with brightly colored flowers are less aggressive and make beautiful additions to informal borders or cut-flower gardens.

Throughout the summer moonshine yarrow (*A.* × 'Moonshine') produces 2- to 3-inch flower heads in soft primrose yellow. Leaves are deeply dissected and gray-green, creating a shimmery effect. Compact and floriferous, this popular perennial can be finicky unless given the correct growing conditions. Grow in informal borders; lovely when combined with blue and violet flowers.

Site: Full sun. Average to sandy soil. Extremely drought-tolerant; does poorly in wet, heavy soil. Fern-leaf and common yarrow are suited to zones 3 to 9; moonshine yarrow is hardy in zones 3 to 8, performs poorly in hot, humid areas.
How to Grow: Plant container-grown plants in spring, spacing fern-leaf and common yarrow 2 feet apart, moonshine

Perennials

yarrow 1 foot apart. Divide mature clumps of fern-leaf yarrow every three or four years in spring or fall; divide common and moonshine yarrow every two or three years in spring. Take stem cuttings of fern-leaf and common yarrow in midsummer. Germinate seeds at 70°F; seed-grown plants may vary in color.

Fern-leaf and common yarrows may need staking, especially if grown in rich soil. Remove faded flowers to encourage long blooming. Root rot may occur in wet soil. Powdery mildew sometimes troubles common yarrow. Moonshine yarrow is susceptible to fungus diseases where summer humidity is high and afternoon rainstorms are common.

Cultivars and Similar Species: Fern-leaf yarrow: 'Gold Plate', 6-inch golden yellow flowers, sturdy 4- to 5-foot-tall stems; 'Parker's Variety', 4-inch bright yellow flowers, sturdy 3½-foot stems; 'Coronation Gold', hybrid with numerous 3-inch golden yellow flowers, gray-green leaves, sturdy 3-foot-tall stems, no staking.

Common yarrow: 'Rosea', pale pink flowers; 'Cerise Queen', bright rose-pink flowers, 18 inches tall; 'Fire King', dark red flowers, 2 feet tall; 'The Beacon', scarlet flowers, 2 feet tall; 'Lilac Queen', lilac flowers; 'Snowtaler', white flowers; 'Galaxy Hybrids', larger flowers fading from bright to soft shades, red, pink, salmon; 'Summer Pastels', seed-grown, color-coordinated mix of cream, apricot, and scarlet flowers.

ACONITUM CARMICHAELII (A. FISCHERI)
Monkshood

Named for the hooded flowers that resemble a monk's cloak, this blue-flowered perennial produces valuable color for the fall flower garden. The attractive, dark green leaves are palmately lobed, resembling those of a delphinium. All plant parts, especially the leaves and roots, are deadly poisonous if eaten, so exercise

ACONITUM NAPELLUS

extreme caution when growing any species of *Aconitum*. Grows 2 to 3 feet tall and 3 feet wide. The vertical spires of monkshood flowers make a pretty contrast with daisylike autumn flowers. Use it in borders and shade gardens.

Site: Full to half shade. Humus-rich, moist, fertile soil; needs plentiful moisture. Hardy in zones 3 to 7. Grows best where nights are cool; does poorly in Southeast because summer nights are warm.

How to Grow: Plant container-grown plants in spring, or bare tuberous roots in fall, spacing 3 feet apart. Needs no division and resents disturbance. Needs abundant moisture in full-sun locations. May need staking. Crown rot or mildew are sometimes troublesome.

Cultivars and Similar Species: 'Arendsii', 4 feet tall, amethyst blue flowers; *A. c.* var. *Wilsonii*, 6 feet tall, lavender-blue flowers. *A. napellus* (common monkshood), 3 to 4 feet tall, deeply divided leaves, dark blue flowers, late summer. *A.* × *cammarum* (bicolor monkshood), late summer; 'Bicolor', blue-and-white flowers, 3 feet tall; 'Bressingham Spire', violet-blue flowers, 3 feet tall.

ALCEA ROSEA
Hollyhock

This beloved cottage garden flower is a biennial, producing clumps of heart-shaped, rough-textured leaves the first year from seed and tall flower stalks the next year. The 5-inch flowers unfurl from tightly wrapped buds beginning at the bottoms of the stalks and progressing toward the tops, producing a summer-

ALCEA ROSEA

long display. Hollyhocks sometimes behave as short-lived perennials and also self-sow. Self-sown plants often differ from the parent. Flowers may be single, double, or semidouble and come in yellow, white, rose, pink, red, lavender, and almost black. They may be ruffled or fringed. Old-fashioned types can reach 12 feet tall; modern hybrids grow 2 to 8 feet tall and 18 inches wide. Use hollyhocks for vertical effect in the background of informal gardens.

Site: Full sun. Fertile, well-drained soil; water and fertilize regularly. Zones 3 to 8; set out nursery-grown plants each fall in zones 9 to 11.

How to Grow: Sow seeds in early summer and transplant to permanent location early the next spring; start seed of annual types indoors in winter for summer bloom. When *continued*

ALCEA ROSEA
(continued)

flowering ceases, cut off stalks and separate daughter plants near plant base, replanting to perpetuate fancy hybrids. Plants usually need staking. Rust fungus, Japanese beetles, and spider mites disfigure foliage, but not flowers; pest control needed.
Cultivars: 'Chater's' series, doubles in yellow, white, pink, scarlet, or mixed, 6 to 8 feet tall; 'Indian Spring', mixed colors, singles, 6 feet tall; 'Powderpuff Mixed', double flowers in white, red, pink, yellow, copper, maroon ruffles.

ALCHEMILLA MOLLIS
Lady's-Mantle

This old-fashioned medicinal herb is one of the most beautiful foliage plants you can add to your garden. The gray-green leaves are rounded and somewhat wavy with tiny scallops decorating the edges. A

ALCHEMILLA MOLLIS

velvety covering of fine hairs makes the leaves soft to the touch. The hairs also hold shimmering beads of water on dewy mornings. Fluffy sprays of lime-green flowers bloom in early summer. Plants grow 1 to 2 feet tall and 18 inches wide.

Lady's-mantle makes an excellent groundcover or edging. Use it in herb, cottage, or informal gardens where it can sprawl along a walkway. Cut flowers can be used fresh or dried.

Site: Full sun in cool climates; half to light shade elsewhere. Best in fertile, moist soil; tolerates dry soil in full shade. Hardy in zones 4 to 8; needs more shade and moisture in hotter climates.
How to Grow: Plant container-grown plants in spring, spacing 18 inches apart. Division needed infrequently; divide in early spring before flowering. Readily self-sows.

Deadhead to avoid reseeding and promote second bloom. Cut back in midsummer to renew if foliage looks tired from too much heat or sun. Fungus diseases can be troublesome in Southeast because afternoon showers cause wet foliage overnight.
Similar Species: *Alchemilla vulgaris*, greener flowers, leaves less hairy; *A. alpina* (alpine lady's-mantle), smaller plant, deeply lobed leaves with silvery white margins, green flowers, zones 3 to 7.

ANEMONE × HYBRIDA
Japanese Anemone

A hybrid between several wild species, Japanese anemone is one of the most elegant flowers of late summer and fall, if not the entire flowering season. The clusters of single or semidouble, shallow-cupped, white, rose, or pink flowers feature green buttonlike centers surrounded by a ring of yellow stamens and open from silver-furred buds held on strong, wiry stems. Foliage is bold and palmately lobed, forming handsome, dark green clumps. Plants are 3 to 5 feet tall in bloom; 2 to 3 feet wide.

Japanese anemones are beautiful with asters and ornamental grasses in formal or informal gardens, and they make excellent cut flowers.

ANEMONE × HYBRIDA 'MARGARETE'

Site: Full sun to half or light shade. Best in moist, deep, fertile soil; performs well in heavy and alkaline soils. Suited to zones 5 to 9.
How to Grow: Plant container-grown plants anytime, spacing 2 feet apart. Divide in spring; take root cuttings in fall. Forms large, somewhat invasive clumps. Tall stems occasionally need light staking. Generally pest- and disease-free.
Cultivars: 'Honorine Jobert', white, single flowers; 'Queen Charlotte', pink, semidouble, 3 feet tall; 'Margarete', pink, double, 3 feet tall; 'Whirlwind', white, semidouble, 2 to 3 feet tall; 'September Charm', silvery mauve flowers, single, 3 feet tall.

ANTHEMIS TINCTORIA
Golden Marguerite

Golden marguerite's yellow-petaled, yellow-centered daisies bloom abundantly throughout summer on long stems perfect for cutting. The bushy plants have lacy, green leaves with woolly, white undersides and a scent like a chrysanthemum. Plants grow 2 to 3 feet tall and 2 feet wide. An excellent plant for borders and informal gardens with poor soil, also for cut-flower gardens.

ANTHEMIS TINCTORIA

Site: Full sun. Average to poor soil. Hardy in zones 3 to 9; tolerates hot, dry conditions, but performs poorly in the hot, humid Southeast.

How to Grow: Plant bare-root or container-grown plants in spring, spacing 18 inches apart. Divide every two years in spring to prevent clumps dying out in centers. Take stem cuttings in summer.

Needs staking if grown in rich soil. Cut off faded flower stems to promote continual bloom; cut back hard after flowering ceases to promote dense branching. Short-lived in heavy soil. Usually trouble-free.

Cultivars: 'Beauty of Grallagh', larger, deeper colored flowers; 'E.C. Buxton', white flowers with yellow centers; 'Moonlight', extremely large, soft yellow flowers; 'Pale Moon', extremely large, extremely pale yellow flowers; 'Wargrave', creamy white flowers with yellow centers; 'Perry's Variety', golden-orange flowers.

AQUILEGIA × HYBRIDA
Hybrid Columbine

A charming, late spring to early summer bloomer, hybrid columbine displays clusters of intricate 3- to 4-inch flowers on wiry stems. The rounded petals form a shallow cup set against showy pointed sepals. Decorative, straight spurs with hooked tips shoot back 2 to 6 inches from the bases of the sepals and resemble a bird's claw, explaining the plant's botanical name, which means eagle. Flowers usually are bicolored and come in all colors of the rainbow. Fernlike, bright green to gray-green leaves create lovely mounds. Plants grow 2 to 3 feet tall and half as wide.

AQUILEGIA × HYBRIDA 'MCKANA HYBRIDS'

For best effect, plant columbines in the garden front despite their height. Mass-plant in naturalistic settings.

Site: Full sun to part shade in mild climates; part to light shade in hot ones. Humus-rich to average, well-drained, moist soil. Moderate moisture. Best in zones 3 to 8; also does well in zones 9 to 10 on Pacific Coast.

How to Grow: Space container-grown plants 1½ feet apart. Plants usually live only three or four years and need no division. Remove faded flowers to discourage self-sowing, which produces offspring of different and sometimes inferior colors and forms. Apply winter mulch in coldest regions. May rot in damp soil.

Leaf miners can disfigure foliage in midsummer and are worse on hybrids than species; cut off and destroy infested leaves and fertilize to stimulate attractive new foliage growth.

Cultivars and Similar Species: Long-spurred hybrids: 'McKana Giants' and 'Dragonfly', flowers in pastel shades; 'Star Hybrids', long-spurred, bicolored flowers. 'Biedermeier Hybrids', short spurred and compact; 'Hensol Harebell', nodding, short-spurred, purple flowers, does well in full shade. *Aquilegia canadensis* (wild columbine), wildflower native to East Coast, small red-and-yellow flowers on tall stems, attracts hummingbirds. *A. caerulea* (Colorado columbine), Rocky Mountain native, blue-and-white flowers; 'Kristall', white flowers. *A. flabellata* (fan columbine), low with fan-shaped leaves, clusters of nodding, short-spurred, blue-and-white flowers.

ARABIS CAUCASICA (ARABIS ALBIDA)
Wall Rockcress

This alpine plant forms a silvery mat of spoon-shaped, toothed leaves that look attractive throughout the year. Fragrant, four-petaled, white

ARABIS CAUCASICA 'SNOWCAP'

or rose-pink flowers blanket the plant in early spring, making a pretty combination with small bulbs. Grows 10 inches tall and 18 inches wide. Plant rockcress to creep from crevices in a rock garden or dry wall.

Site: Full sun. Fast-draining, lean, alkaline soil. Moderate moisture. Best in cool climates; zones 4 to 7. *continued*

Perennials

ARABIS CAUCASICA
(continued)

How to Grow: Plant container-grown plants anytime, spacing 1 foot apart. Divide every two or three years in early fall. Take stem cuttings in summer. Cut back flower stems after flowering to prevent straggliness. Root or crown rot may occur in a damp location or hot, humid climate.

Cultivars and Similar Species: 'Variegata', white flowers, white-edged leaves; 'Flore Pleno', double, white flowers; 'Snowcap', white flowers; 'Spring Charm', soft rose flowers; 'Rosabella', rose-pink flowers. *Arabis aubrietoides*, green leaves, purple flowers.

ARTEMISIA LUDOVICIANA VAR. ALBULA
Western Mugwort

Forming ribbons of silver through a garden, this Southwestern native provides months of gleaming color.

ARTEMISIA × 'POWIS CASTLE'

Unlike most artemisias, the aromatic leaves of this species are lance-shaped, not finely cut; the 3-foot stems are upright and covered with woolly, white hairs. Inconspicuous white flowers bloom in fall. Plants spread to 3 feet. Western mugwort provides excellent contrast to white,

pink, blue, and lavender flowers in informal flower gardens.

Site: Full sun. Average to poor, sandy soil. Allow soil to dry between waterings; drought-tolerant. Hardy in zones 4 to 9; best artemisia for the South.

How to Grow: Plant container-grown plants anytime, spacing 2 to 3 feet apart. Divide every year in spring or fall to control aggressive spreading. Pull unwanted sprouts and attached runners in spring or control by planting in old buckets with bottoms removed and sunk in garden. Cut back in midsummer if weather causes floppiness. May get root rot in damp site.

Cultivars and Similar Species: Most often sold as almost identical 'Silver King' (3 feet tall, deep silver) or 'Silver Queen' (2½ feet tall, silver-gray, jagged-edged leaves), but they're often mixed up and mislabeled. *Artemisia* × 'Powis Castle', deeply cut silver leaves, compact, 2 to 3 feet tall, heat-tolerant, zones 5 to 8. *A.* × 'Valerie Finnis', broadly cut silver leaves, 2 feet tall, zones 5 to 8. *A. absinthium* 'Lambrook Silver', silvery filigreed leaves, zones 3 to 9. *A. schmidtiana* 'Silver Mound' (silver mound mugwort), forms silky, 1- to 2-foot mound of finely cut silvery leaves, not aggressive, flops unattractively in mid- or late summer where hot and humid, cut back to renew, zones 3 to 7.

ASCLEPIAS TUBEROSA
Butterfly Weed

Native to prairies and dry fields across much of North America, butterfly weed blooms for a month in midsummer, attracting monarch and swallowtail butterflies to its orange, red, or gold flowers. The showy, flat heads of small, urn-shaped flowers ripen into 3-inch-long, greenish purple seedpods, which split open to reveal silky-haired seeds in late fall. The upright stems hold their linear leaves in horizontal rungs, giving the plant a

ASCLEPIAS TUBEROSA 'HELLO YELLOW'

somewhat stiff appearance. Plants grow 2 to 3 feet tall and form 1- to 2-foot-wide clumps. Butterfly weed is effective in informal, butterfly, meadow, and cut-flower gardens.

Site: Full sun. Average to infertile sandy soil. Moderate water. Drought-tolerant. Zones 4 to 9.

How to Grow: Plant small container-grown plants in spring, spacing 8 inches apart. Don't divide. Sow fresh seed in fall; may bloom the following summer.

Difficult to transplant because of brittle taproot. Emerges in late spring; take care not to damage hidden crowns. Cutting flowers encourages reblooming a month later. Yellow aphids sometimes disfigure plants in summer.

Cultivars and Similar Species: 'Gay Butterflies', seed-grown mix of several colors; 'Hello Yellow', yellow flowers.

ASTER SPP.
Michaelmas Daisy, Fall Aster, Frikart's Aster

Most of the graceful late bloomers we call Michaelmas daisies or fall asters are hybrids between New England (*Aster novae-angliae*) and New York (*A. novi-belgii*) asters and several other species. Billowy masses of small, yellow-centered, lavender, purple, blue, pink, or white blossoms form clouds of color for a month or two in late summer and fall, beginning anytime between mid-August and mid September, depending on the cultivar. The small, linear leaves covering the upright stems are fine-textured, but otherwise unremarkable. Height varies by cultivar, from 8-inch spreading dwarfs to 4- to 5-foot-tall types. Excellent for late summer and fall color in back of borders or meadows. The fine texture combines well with other fall bloomers. Good cut flower.

ASTER × FRIKARTII 'MONCH'

Lovely, but little-known, Frikart's aster (*A. × frikartii*) may be the finest of all asters. Resulting from a cross between an Italian and a Himalayan species at a German nursery, this fine perennial has been popular in England for many years. Lavender-blue daisies with yellow centers that are 3 inches wide begin blooming in July and continue into October. Plants have a delicate, airy look and are not marred by mildew, as are other asters. Plants grow 3 feet tall and wide. This aster is excellent combined with yellow flowers in beds and borders.

Site: Full sun is best; tolerates part or light shade. Fertile, well-drained but moist soil. Plentiful moisture. Michalemas daisy is hardy in zones 4 to

8, Frikart's aster in zones 5 to 8; best where cool and moist.

How to Grow: Plant container-grown plants in spring or fall, spacing Michaelmas daisy 1½ to 3 feet apart, Frikart's aster 3 feet apart. Divide by removing and replanting outside portions of clumps in spring to keep plants vigorous; divide Michaelmas daisy every two years, Frikart's aster every three or four years.

Pinch tall Michaelmas daisies when 6 inches tall and once more in early summer to encourage compact growth and more bloom. Stake tall and medium-height types. Both need winter mulch in colder zones. Fertilize Frikart's aster sparingly.

Mildew and rust often troublesome for Michalemas daisy; avoid wetting foliage, but water with drip or soaker hose so soil doesn't dry out. Choose disease-resistant cultivars. Spray for mildew. Frikart's aster may rot over winter if soil remains wet.

Cultivars and Similar Species: Michaelmas daisy: dozens of cultivars; tall ones often incorrectly called New England asters and shorter ones, New York asters; 'Alma Potschke', magenta-pink flowers, 3½ feet tall, mildew-resistant; 'Mount Everest', white flowers, 3 feet tall; 'Harrington's Pink', clear pink flowers, 4 to 5 feet tall, late blooming; 'Treasure', violet-blue flowers, 4 feet tall; 'Crimson Brocade', 3 feet tall, crimson-red flowers; 'Eventide', semidouble purple flowers, 3 feet tall; 'September Ruby', cerise flowers, disease-resistant, 3½ feet tall; 'Professor Kippenberg', lavender-blue flowers, 12 inches tall; 'Marie Ballard', 4 feet tall, powder blue flowers; 'Hella Lacy', large, violet-blue flowers, 4 to 5 feet tall; 'Purple Dome', purple flowers, mildew-resistant, 18 inches tall.

Frikart's aster: almost indistinguishable are 'Monch', light lavender-blue, sturdy plant; 'Wonder of Staffa', darker lavender-blue, prone to flopping.

ASTILBE SPP.
Astilbe

Thriving in shady spots, these long-lived perennials bring both foliage and floral beauty to the garden. The foot-long, feathery plumes of *Astilbe × arendsii's* tiny flowers stand above the foliage and come in a range

ASTILBE × ARENDSII 'GLOW'

of colors, including white, pink, rose, lavender, peach, and red. Flowers bloom for about a month beginning in early summer to midsummer, depending on the cultivar. Leaves are divided into pointed leaflets with toothed edges and are glossy dark green or bronze. Flowers are 2 to 3 feet tall, foliage clumps 1 to 2 feet tall and twice as wide.

The dramatic fall astilbe (*A. taquetii* 'Superba') brings color to the back of the border or naturalistic garden. Tall spires of mauve-pink blossoms tower above clumps of handsome, deeply cut, dark green foliage and last for a month or so during late summer. Its flowers grow 4 feet tall, plants form clumps 2½ to 3 feet wide. Excellent for late color in shaded borders and naturalistic gardens.

Site: Light to part shade; tolerates sun in cool regions and if constantly moist. Deep, humus-rich, moist, *continued*

Perennials

ASTILBE SPP.
(continued)

well-drained soil; keep moist to wet during growing season. Hardy in zones 4 to 8, but performs poorly in arid and hot, humid regions.

How to Grow: Plant bare-root plants or container-grown plants in spring. Plant *A. × arendsii* ½ inch deep and 1½ to 3 feet apart; fall astilbe 2 inches deep and 3 feet apart. Divide every three or four years in spring or fall.

Cut faded flower stalks or leave for naturalistic look. Feed heavily. Leaves scorch and shrivel if soil dries. Plants rot in winter-wet soil. Japanese beetles and spider mites can be problems.

Cultivars and Similar Species: *A. × arendsii:* Early—'Rheinland', bright pink flowers, 30 inches tall; 'Red Sentinel', red flowers, bronze leaves, 30 inches tall; 'Europa', pale pink flowers, 18 inches tall; 'Deutschland', bright white flowers, 20 inches tall. Midseason—'Amethyst', lilac-violet flowers, 40 inches tall; 'Bridal Veil', creamy white flowers, 36 inches tall; 'Fanal', dark crimson flowers, bronze leaf, 30 inches tall; *A. × rosea* 'Peach Blossom', light pink, 24 inches tall. Late season—'Avalanche', white flowers, 40 inches tall; 'Fire', salmon-red flowers, 36 inches tall; 'Glow', ruby-red flowers, 36 inches tall. *A. chinensis* 'Pumila' (dwarf Chinese astilbe), fast-spreading dwarf, makes attractive groundcover, stiff, narrow plumes of densely packed, mauve-pink flowers for a month in late summer, tolerates dry shade, zones 3 to 8. *A. simplicifolia* (star astilbe), undivided, deeply lobed, dark, glossy leaves; loose, nodding spires of white or pink flowers cover the compact leafy mounds in midsummer to late summer; 'Sprite', bronze-green foliage, pink flowers, 15 to 18 inches tall; 'Bronze Elegans', rose-pink flowers, bronze foliage, 18 inches tall; 'Aphrodite,' salmon-red flowers, 14 inches tall.

Fall astilbe: 'Purple Lance', dark rose-purple flowers, 3 to 4 feet tall.

AURINIA SAXATILIS
(ALYSSUM SAXATILE)
Basket-of-Gold

This sunny flower blooms from early through mid spring, making a wonderful bulb companion. The tight, rounded clusters of four-petaled, golden yellow flowers are held just above the foliage, completely

AURINIA SAXATILIS

blanketing its 2- to 5-inch-long, mat-forming, gray, spoon-shaped leaves. Plant spreads rapidly into cascading evergreen clumps 8 to 12 inches high and 12 inches wide. Arrange it so plants can spill over a wall. Compact forms work well as border edging.

Site: Full sun. Average to sandy, well-drained soil. Drought-tolerant. Hardy in zones 3 to 7; performs poorly in heat and humidity. Use as a biennial in South, planting in fall and discarding after blooming.

How to Grow: Plant container-grown plants in spring, spacing 12 to 18 inches apart. Take stem cuttings in summer. Cut back hard after flowering for compactness and for possible reblooming. Resents transplanting. May rot in winter-wet soil. Flops in rich soil.

Cultivars: 'Citrina', pale lemon yellow flowers, 10 inches tall; 'Compacta', golden yellow flowers, 6 inches tall, compact; 'Sunny Border Apricot',

apricot flowers, 10 inches tall; 'Dudley Neville Variegated', apricot-buff flowers, white-variegated leaves; 'Variegata', gold-edged leaves.

BAPTISIA AUSTRALIS
Wild Blue Indigo, Blue False Indigo

Easy-to-grow, this native wildflower slowly forms an impressive, bushy clump of upright stems cloaked with handsome blue-green leaves, which are divided into three smooth-edged leaflets. Spires of two-lipped, light to deep blue flowers appear for several weeks in early summer and attract butterflies. Flowers ripen into lovely, inflated, dark brown seedpods that rustle in the wind. Plants grow 3 to 6 feet tall and as wide.

BAPTISIA AUSTRALIS

Use baptisia for vertical contrast with peony, iris, and shasta daisy in the early summer border. Seedpods are excellent in dried arrangements; cut in midsummer when brown.

Site: Full sun in North; part shade in South. Best in fertile, humus-rich, deep, well-drained soil, but tolerates wide range of soil types. Drought-tolerant. Hardy in zones 3 to 9.

How to Grow: Plant container-grown plants in spring, spacing 3 feet apart. Rarely needs division. Sow fresh seeds. Plant in permanent location; taproots make transplanting difficult. May need light staking. Deadhead flowers before seed-set to encourage more blossoms. Generally pest- and disease-free.
Similar Species: *Baptisia alba*, white flowers, nodding seedpods, 2 to 3 feet tall, rich soil.

BERGENIA CORDIFOLIA
Heart-Leaf Bergenia

Admired more for its bold-textured clumps of cabbagelike leaves than for its pink flowers, bergenia brings architectural beauty to a flower garden. The 12-inch-long, round to

BERGENIA CORDIFOLIA 'SILVER LIGHT'

heart-shaped green leaves have a leathery texture and gleam like polished wood. Evergreen in most climates and semievergreen in the coldest ones, the leaves often take on magnificent reddish hues in fall and winter. Stalks of dark-centered, waxy, pink or white flowers bloom just above foliage in late winter and early spring. Grows 12 inches tall and 18 inches wide; spreads by rhizomes into large clumps. Bergenia is excellent for year-round effect as a border or path edging in a rock or informal garden.

Site: Full sun to part shade; afternoon shade in South. Tolerates various soil types, even alkaline, but best in humus-rich, moist soil. Moderate moisture best, but tolerates dry shade. Zones 3 to 8; foliage may be damaged by harsh winters if not snow-covered.
How to Grow: Plant container-grown plants in spring, spacing 2 feet apart. Divide rhizomes every four years, replanting fairly deep. Remove spent flower stalks. Cut off winter-tattered foliage. Slugs can be troublesome.
Cultivars and Similar Species: 'Perfecta', rose-red flowers on tall stems. *Bergenia crassifolia*, smaller oval leaves, light lavender-pink flowers; zones 4 to 8. *B. purpurascens*, oval leaves with deep red undersides, magenta flowers; zones 4 to 9.
   Hybrids: 'Bressingham White', white, 18 inches, late bloomer; 'Purpurea', dark pink flowers, purple-flushed leaves; 'Evening Glow', reddish purple flowers, maroon leaves in winter; 'Silver Light', white flowers flushed pink; 'Bressingham Ruby', rose-pink flowers, leaves with maroon undersides, deep ruby winter color.

BOLTONIA ASTEROIDES 'PINK BEAUTY'

BOLTONIA ASTEROIDES
White Boltonia

Forming a frothy stand of yellow-centered white, lilac, or purple asterlike flowers for four to six weeks in late summer and fall, compact cultivars of this lanky North American wildflower can be an asset to any flower garden. Leaves are blue-green and willowlike on tall, sparsely branched stems, which form a loose, rounded clump. Plants grow 3 to 7 feet tall and 3 to 4 feet wide.
   Use boltonia in the back of the border to contrast with fall bloomers of bolder-texture, such as stonecrop, Japanese anemone, chrysanthemum, and ornamental grasses. Hide bare bottoms of stems with other plants.

Site: Full sun to light shade. Fertile, moist, but well-drained soil. Drought-tolerant once established, but size is reduced. Hardy in zones 4 to 9; better in hot summer areas than asters.
How to Grow: Plant container-grown plants in spring, spacing 3 feet apart. Divide in spring every three or four years, separating rosettes. Take stem cuttings in summer. Stake in part shade. Not susceptible to mildew as are asters.
Cultivars: Preferred over the species are 'Snowbank', white flowers, compact to 4 feet tall; 'Pink Beauty', pale lilac-pink flowers, 3 to 4 feet tall.

CAMPANULA SPP.
Bellflower, Harebell

Popular and long-blooming, Carpathian bellflower (*Campanula carpatica*) features tidy, low mounds of toothed, bright green leaves from spring through fall. From early summer to midsummer and sporadically through fall, the plant sends up stems topped with 2-inch-wide, bowl-shaped flowers. Like most bellflowers, this one has blue or white blossoms and spreads readily into lovely clumps. It grows 9 inches tall and 12 inches wide. This bellflower is excellent in the foreground of the garden, as edging along a walk, or in a rock garden.   *continued*

CAMPANULA SPP.
(continued)

CAMPANULA CARPATICA

Blooming profusely from early summer to midsummer, the tall, stiff stems of clustered bellflower (*C. glomerata*) hold dense clusters of 1-inch bell-shaped, purple or violet flowers with pointed petals. Leaves are spear-shaped and hairy. Plants

CAMPANULA GLOMERATA 'JOAN ELLIOT'

grow 1 to 3 feet tall and 18 inches wide and spread rapidly to form open clumps. Plant clustered bellflower in groups in informal gardens for beautiful early summer flowers that combine well with pink and rose-colored flowers.

Milky bellflower (*C. lactiflora*) is tall and forms a loose bush of slender, gray-green leaves topped with large panicles of bell-shaped, milky blue flowers with white centers. Blossoms appear in midsummer and carry on for several weeks, reblooming readily if stems are cut back after the first flush. Their pale color looks lovely when backlit by the sun or viewed in the moonlight. Plants grow 3 to 5 feet tall and 3 feet wide. Milky bellflower is a graceful, long-blooming plant for informal and naturalistic gardens.

Spires of bell- to saucer-shaped, 1½-inch flowers on tall, straight stems make peach-leaf bellflower (*C. persicifolia*) a valuable addition to any flower garden. Blossoms open from the top of the stalk downward, beginning in July and continuing through August if cut back. The clumps of evergreen, rounded basal leaves grow larger every year, but are not invasive. Narrow with rounded teeth, the leathery leaves lining the flower stems look no more like peach leaves than do those of other bellflowers. Plants grow 1 to 3 feet tall, 2 feet wide. Plant peach-leaf bellflower in large groups for vertical effect in formal and informal gardens. It is also a long-lasting cut flower.

The exuberant, mat-forming, blue-flowered Dalmatian bellflower (*C. portenschlagiana*) looks especially alluring cascading from a wall or spilling around boulders in a rock garden. It also works well spreading beneath shrubs and taller perennials. The 1-inch-wide, upward-facing, bell-shaped flowers form an intense, lavender-blue blanket that conceals the evergreen foliage for three or four weeks in late spring and early summer. It may rebloom sporadically through fall. Plants grow 4 to 6 inches tall and spread to 24 inches or more. Dalmatian bellflower looks best in

CAMPANULA PORTENSCHLAGIANA

rock gardens, walls, mixed borders, naturalistic gardens, and informal gardens. Or, use it to edge a walk.

Site: Carpathian, milky, and peach-leaf bellflower thrive in full sun to part shade. Give clustered bellflower full sun in the North, partial shade in the South. Dalmatian bellflower grows in full sun to light shade.

Carpathian bellflower needs well-drained, average to sandy soil, moist but not wet. The other species need average to humus-rich, well-drained, neutral to alkaline soil, kept moist, but not soggy. Dalmatian bellflower must have excellent drainage.

Carpathian and clustered bellflowers are hardy in zones 3 to 8. Milky bellflower is suited to zones 5 to 7. Peach-leaf bellflower grows best in zones 3 to 6, is short-lived in zones 7 and 8. Dalmatian bellflower is hardy in zones 4 to 8 and performs better in the South than most other campanulas.

How to Grow: Plant container-grown campanulas or bare-root milky bellflower plants in spring. Space Carpathian and Dalmatian bellflowers 12 inches apart, clustered bellflower 18 inches apart, milky bellflower 3 feet apart, and peach-leaf bellflower 2 feet apart. Divide Carpathian, clustered, peach-leaf and Dalmatian bellflowers in spring, every three years. Milky bellflower resents division; instead take cuttings in spring. Take cuttings of Dalmatian bellflower in summer.

You must deadhead Carpathian bellflower to prolong blooming. Mulch in summer to keep roots cool. May self-sow, but is rarely weedy.

Clustered bellflower can be invasive; dividing it every two years helps control it. Cut back flower stalks after flowering to encourage rebloom.

After milky bellflower blossoms fade, cut back stems to just below lowest leaves to encourage reblooming. This species self-sows and becomes weedy if not deadheaded. Pinch back stems when 6 inches tall to increase bushiness and stem strength. Requires staking to prevent leaning toward the sun and flopping on nearby plants.

Peach-leaf bellflower also self-sows. It reblooms if you cut back faded flower stalks to several inches above the basal mat of foliage.

Campanulas are short-lived in poorly drained soil or drought conditions. Snails and slugs may be troublesome.

Cultivars and Similar Species:
Carpathian bellflower: 'Alba', white flowers; 'Blue Clips', 6 to 8 inches tall, flowers; 'White Clips', 6 to 8 inches tall, white; 'Wedgewood Blue', 6 inches tall, sky blue; 'Wedgewood White', 6 inches tall, white.

Clustered bellflower: 'Joan Elliott', dark violet flowers, early flowering, 18 inches tall; 'Alba', white, 24 inches tall; *C. g.* var. *Acaulis,* light violet-blue, 15 inches tall.

Milky bellflower: 'Alba', white flowers, 3 to 4 feet tall; 'Loddon Anna', pale pink, 4 feet tall; 'Pouffe', pale blue flowers, 18 inches tall, no staking.

Peach-leaf bellflower: 'Telham Beauty', pale china-blue flowers, 3 to 4 feet tall; 'Alba', white, 30 inches tall; 'Blue Gardenia', double, deep silvery blue, 36 inches tall.

Dalmatian bellflower: 'Resholt', dark violet flowers. *C. poscharskyana* (Serbian bellflower), similar spreading habit, but less invasive, blooms mid spring and sporadically through fall, flowers face upward, flat stars, leaves smaller on shorter stems and with more pointed tips, drought-tolerant; 'Alba', white flowers, zones 3 to 7.

CENTAUREA MONTANA
Mountain Bluet, Perennial Cornflower

The unusual cobalt blue flowers of mountain bluet are rounded with ragged-edged petals that radiate from a central, reddish purple center, creating a spidery effect. Overlapping scales beneath the flowers have a shingled appearance, enhancing each flower. Blossoms first appear at the stem tips, usually blooming from June into July, but will continue for months

CENTAUREA MONTANA

if deadheaded. The lance-shaped foliage is covered with whitish hairs when young, but matures to bright green. Grows 1½ to 2 feet tall and spreads to form large colonies.

Mountain bluet works best in informal or naturalistic gardens where neatness doesn't count. The blue flowers combine wonderfully with yellow, orange, and pink flowers.

Site: Full sun. Average to sandy, infertile, well-drained soil. Moderate moisture; drought-tolerant. Hardy in zones 3 to 8; best where cool.

How to Grow: Plant container-grown plants in spring, spacing 1 foot apart. Divide every three years in fall.

Deadhead regularly to extend blooming and prevent weedy self-seeding. Cut stems back to the ground when new growth appears at base for late-summer and fall reblooming. May need staking to control floppiness. Spreads aggressively in fertile soil; divide regularly to control. Root rot can develop in heavy, moist soil.

Cultivars and Similar Species: 'Alba', white flowers; 'Rosea', pink flowers; 'Violetta', violet flowers. *Centaurea macrocephala* (Armenian basket flower), thistlelike, golden yellow blossoms in early summer, 3 to 4 feet tall, zones 3 to 7.

CERASTIUM TOMENTOSUM
Snow-in-Summer

When in full bloom in late spring and early summer, this mat-former creates quite a sight. The dainty, 1-inch-wide, snow white flowers have five notched petals and bloom in such profusion that they literally obscure the leaves for three or four weeks. When not in bloom,

CERASTIUM TOMENTOSUM

snow-in-summer creates a beautiful effect with its ground-hugging, tiny, woolly, white leaves. Plants are 6 inches tall in bloom; spread to form 24-inch-wide mats. *continued*

CERASTIUM TOMENTOSUM
(continued)

Plant snow-in-summer as groundcover beneath taller perennials in a well-drained, sunny border or arrange to spill from cracks and crevices in rock wall or garden.

Site: Full sun. Average to sandy, infertile soil. Moderate water; drought-tolerant. Hardy in zones 2 to 7; performs poorly where hot and humid.
How to Grow: Plant container-grown plants in spring; divide in spring or fall every two years. Shear back hard after flowering. Spreads by underground runners and can become invasive, especially in fertile soil; plant away from less vigorous low plants. Usually pest-free; may suffer root rot in moist site.
Cultivars and Similar Species: 'Yo Yo', compact and less invasive. *Cerastium biebersteinii*, leaves are larger, flowers are slightly taller.

CHELONE LYONII
Pink Turtlehead

A native wildflower, pink turtlehead makes its home in wet meadows and flourishes in gardens, forming

CHELONE LYONII

impressive clumps where its growing conditions are met. A late-summer bloomer, turtlehead produces tight clusters of rose-purple, snapdragon-like flowers at the tips of its sturdy stems for about a month. The tubular flowers resemble the head of a turtle with its mouth open. The 6-inch-long pointed leaves have small teeth along the edges and are dark green. Grows 2 to 3 feet tall and 18 inches wide.

Grow turtlehead in moist borders or let it naturalize in a bog garden or along a stream or pond.

Site: Full sun in boggy site; part shade in moist site. Fertile, acid, moist or boggy soil. Don't allow to dry out. Hardy in zones 3 to 8.
How to Grow: Plant container-grown plants or dormant roots in spring, spacing 2 feet apart. Divide in early spring. Take cuttings in spring or early summer. Needs staking only if too shady. Pinch in early summer to make bushier and produce more flowers. Usually pest- and disease-free if given sufficient moisture.
Cultivars and Similar Species: *Chelone glabra*, pink-tinged white flowers, 3 to 4 feet tall, half as wide, zones 4 to 9. *C. obliqua*, deep pink flowers late summer to fall, 2 to 3 feet tall and half as wide, zones 3 to 9; 'Alba', white flowers.

CIMICIFUGA SIMPLEX
Kamchatka Bugbane

This Russian woodland wildflower captivates gardeners in late fall, blooming for several weeks in September and October, when most flowers are long gone. The arching, wandlike inflorescenses rise above the foliage and are densely packed with tiny, white flowers made up of minuscule petals and long, decorative stamens, creating the feathery appearance of bottlebrushes. The flowers look especially engaging when backlit by the low rays of the autumn sun. The compound, toothed leaves are handsome all season,

CIMICIFUGA SIMPLEX

making bold, dark green clumps that grow larger each year, but are never invasive. The several available cultivars are showier than the species and are preferred for most gardens. Plants are 3 to 4 feet tall when in bloom; 3 feet wide.

Plant bugbane in large stands in flower borders and woodland settings. Combines well with late asters, Japanese anemones, and monkshood.

Site: Full sun only if constantly moist; light to full shade best, especially in South. Humus-rich, deep, moist, acid soil. Abundant water. Hardy in zones 3 to 8.
How to Grow: Plant bare-root or container-grown plants in spring, spacing 4 feet apart. Rarely needs division. Keep constantly moist or leaf margins will brown and plants will become stunted. Usually needs no staking. Usually pest-free.
Cultivars and Similar Species: 'White Pearl' ('The Pearl'), 2-foot-long, dense, white flower spikes. *Cimicifuga racemosa* (snakeroot, black cohosh), mid- to late summer bloomer, foliage clumps 3 feet tall, flower wands 2 feet long and upright to 6 feet, may need staking, native wildflower, zones 3 to 8. *C. r.* var. *atropurpurea*, dark purple foliage.

COREOPSIS SPP.
Coreopsis, Tickseed

Native to the grasslands and roadsides of the Midwest, coreopsis is a popular garden flower because of its extended blooming season. *Coreopsis grandiflora* has daisylike, 2-inch-wide flowers with golden yellow petals and orange-yellow centers. They bring hot color to the garden from early to late

COREOPSIS GRANDIFLORA

summer, if faded flowers are removed. Flowers open from knoblike buds on long, wiry stems that stand well above the clump of basal foliage. Deeply cut into oblong or lanceolate segments, leaves form tufts near the base of the plant and are scattered partway up the flowering stems. Plants are short-lived, usually surviving for only several years; self-sown seedlings don't come true to type. Grows 2 to 3 feet tall; 1½ to 2 feet wide. A charming plant in informal and formal gardens; allow to self-seed in meadow plantings and cottage gardens. Excellent cut flower.

Thread-leaved coreopsis (*C. verticillata)* is one of the easiest and longest-blooming perennials for sunny gardens, blooming from midsummer into fall. Leaves are divided into threadlike segments, cloaking upright stems that form wide-spreading bushy plants. The 2-inch-wide, daisylike flowers have narrow, bright yellow petals and small, dark yellow centers, covering plants with sunny stars for an engaging, fine-textured effect. Grows 2 to 3 feet tall and spreads rapidly by rhizomes to 3 or more feet wide. Thread-leaved coreopsis offers fine texture contrast to bolder flowers and foliage. 'Moonbeam' combines well with almost any flower color.

Site: Full sun. Thread-leaved coreopsis also tolerates part shade. Average to sandy, well-drained, infertile soil. Moderate moisture. Drought-tolerant. Thread-leaved coreopsis is suited to zones 3 to 9. *C. grandiflora* is hardy in zones 5 to 9; blooms longest when cool.
How to Grow: Plant container-grown or bare-root plants in spring. Space *C. grandiflora* 1 foot apart, thread-leaved coreopsis 1½ feet apart. Divide *C. grandiflora* every spring for longevity; divide thread-leaved coreopsis every few years in spring or fall.

C. grandiflora may flop and sprawl if soil is rich and fertile; stake with ring support to hold flower stems. Deadhead regularly for long bloom and to prevent self-seeding, cutting back flowering stems for best appearance. Do not fertilize. Shear off faded flowers of threadleaf coreopsis when blooming becomes sparse to encourage another flush of flowers. May be invasive in fertile, moist soil. Late to emerge in spring.

C. grandiflora often troubled by mildew, also occasionally bothered by leafspot, aphids, and cucumber beetles. Root rot can occur in winter-wet soil. Rabbits may nibble thread-leaved coreopsis; otherwise, pest-free.
Cultivars and Similar Species: 'Early Sunrise', 1½ to 2 feet tall, early flowering, double; 'Sunray', double, 2-inch flowers, 2 feet tall; 'Goldfink', deep yellow, extremely floriferous, 9 inches tall, dense ground-covering foliage; 'Baby Sun', single, bright yellow, 20 inches tall.

Thread-leaved coreopsis: 'Zagreb', 15-inch dwarf, golden yellow flowers; 'Golden Shower', 2½-inch bright golden yellow flowers, 2 to 3 feet tall, long-blooming; 'Moonbeam', popular hybrid with pastel yellow flowers, long-blooming, 18 inches tall.

C. rosea (pink coreopsis), similar-looking, pink flowers with yellow centers, 12 to 15 inches tall, not drought-tolerant, performs poorly if dries out, zones 4 to 8.

CORYDALIS LUTEA
Yellow Corydalis

Yellow corydalis is a carefree plant that blooms from spring until frost. It's a delightful addition to rock

CORYDALIS LUTEA

gardens, informal beds, and naturalistic plantings. Loose sprays of lacelike, blue-green leaves divided into rounded lobes form low mounds that remain evergreen through winter in mild climates. Sprays of ½-inch-long, tubular, spurred, pastel yellow blossoms are produced from spring until hard frost without deadheading. Grows 15 inches tall and 8 inches wide. Tuck into crevices of rock wall, between stones in rock gardens, or between pavers in patios or walkways.

continued

CORYDALIS LUTEA
(continued)

Site: Light to full shade. Gravelly to fertile, well-drained soil; tolerates alkaline sites and drought, but best if moist. Suited to zones 5 to 7.

How to Grow: Plant container-grown plants in spring, spacing 1 foot apart. Divide or transplant seedlings in fall. Needs no deadheading. Reseeds vigorously, easy to transplant when small. Usually pest-free.

Similar Species: *Corydalis cheilanthifolia*, fernlike, bronze-tinged leaves, spires of yellow spring flowers, zones 5 to 7.

DELPHINIUM × ELATUM
Delphinium

One of the most glamorous—and finicky—perennials, delphinium brings striking tall spires of flowers to summer borders where the climate suits and gardeners are willing to fuss.

DELPHINIUM × ELATUM

The efforts are worth it when the dramatic blossoms begin to unfold at the bottoms of the spires. Flowers are rounded in outline and spurred; often a central small ring of petals rests among the outer petals, creating a "bee" in a contrasting color. The boldly cut, maplelike leaves form handsome, dark green clumps that send up several spikes so dense with blossoms that they topple from their own weight if not staked. Classic delphiniums grow as much as 7 feet tall, but shorter strains are easier to grow and more durable during foul weather. Colors are cool: alluring shades of true blue, lavender, purple, pink, white, and bicolors, including pastels and intensely saturated hues. Plants are usually short-lived, surviving five years in the Pacific Northwest and Northeast and only two or three years elsewhere. Plants grow 3 to 7 feet tall; 1 to 3 feet wide.

Delphiniums are elegant at back of border or formal gardens. Also traditional along fences in cottage gardens. Delphiniums combine well with iris, peonies, daylilies, shasta daisies, and lilies.

Site: Full sun in most climates; light shade in hottest areas, where adapted. Fertile, deep, slightly acid to alkaline soil rich in organic matter. Keep evenly moist with ample water. Hardy in zones 2 to 7; best where summers are moist and cool to warm—not hot—and winters are cold.

How to Grow: Plant container-grown plants in spring, taking care to place crown at soil level because planting too deeply causes crown rot. Space tall types 3 feet apart. Divide every other year for best longevity or take cuttings from basal growth in spring. Easily grown from commercial seed. In areas with hot summers or mild winters, plant in fall and remove after flowering finishes in summer.

Thin young plants to three shoots when 6 inches tall, mature plants to four or five shoots. Tall types must be individually staked, beginning when 1 foot tall, to prevent brittle stems from breaking. Plant in location sheltered from wind. Fertilize monthly during bloom season. Mulch heavily to keep soil cool. For repeat bloom, cut spent flower spikes just below lowest blossom; when new growth is 6 inches tall, remove spent flower stalk at ground.

Slugs, snails, mites, and mildew are problems; use pest control program.

Cultivars and Similar Species: Mid-Century hybrids—mildew-resistant, 4 to 5 feet tall; 'Ivory Towers', white flowers; 'Moody Blues', light blue; 'Rose Future', pink; 'Ultra Violet', dark blue-violet; 'Magic Fountains', mixed colors, dwarf to 3 feet tall.

Pacific hybrids—4 to 5 feet tall, huge single to semidouble flowers; 'Black Knight', deep violet flowers with black eye; 'Astolat', lavender to pink with dark eye; 'Blue Bird', mid blue with white eye; 'Galahad', all white; 'Summer Skies', sky blue with white eye.

Blackmore and Langdon—mixed colors with extremely large flower spikes; 'Connecticut Yankee', heavily branched, 2½ to 3½ feet tall, 'Blue Fountains', blue, white, or mauve flowers, Zone 8.

DENDRANTHEMA × GRANDIFLORUM
'RED HEADLINER'

DENDRANTHEMA SPP. (CHRYSANTHEMUM SPP.)
Chrysanthemum, Garden Mum, Hybrid Chrysanthemum

Late-blooming and long-blooming, these flowers are the mainstay of many fall gardens—the blossoms even withstand a light frost. Garden mums (*Dendranthema × grandiflorum,*

Chrysanthemum × morifolium) come in a variety of flower types, including tight buttons, single daisies, doubles, and pompons. Colors include rust-reds and copper-oranges as well as bright yellow and gold, and lavender-pink and white. Shapes vary from low mounds to tall, loose types, but garden favorites are the cushion mums, which form a neat mound less than 2 feet tall. Some gardeners plant potted blooming mums in fall and treat them as annuals, but the display is softer and more natural when mums grow as perennials. Garden mums may be 8 inches to 3 feet tall and wide. Arrange mums in drifts in foreground or midground of formal and informal beds and borders.

Hybrid chrysanthemum (D. × rubellum) is a cold-hardy, daisy-type mum that forms a compact mound, with blossoms of rose-pink or yellow from midsummer into fall. Grows 1 to 2 feet tall and 3 feet wide.

Site: Full sun. Fertile, humus-rich, moist, well-drained, acid soil. Plentiful moisture. Garden mums hardy in zones 5 to 9; hybrid chrysanthemum in zones 4 to 9.

How to Grow: Plant bare-root or small container-grown plants in spring, spacing garden mums 1 foot apart, hybrid chrysanthemum 3 feet apart. Divide garden mums every two or three years, hybrid mum every three or four years in spring to keep vigorous.

Fertilize garden mums monthly in summer. Pinch stem tips every two weeks from spring through midsummer (July 15 in North, August 1 to August 15 in South) to promote bushiness and delay bloom until fall. Mulch in summer to keep soil cool and moist; mulch loosely in winter after soil freezes to prevent alternate freezing and thawing. Cut back old stems in early spring.

Hybrid chrysanthemum spreads rapidly in light soil; avoid overfertilizing. Pinch in early summer to promote compactness and later blooming; shear after summer flush of blossoms wanes to promote fall bloom.

Garden mums may develop root rot in wet sites; aphids and spider mites often serious. Hybrid chrysanthemum usually trouble-free.

Cultivars: Many cultivars of garden chrysanthemum available. Choose cold-hardy mums, not tender florist types, as garden perennials. Hardy types produce overwintering rosette of foliage. In northern areas, select early-blooming types; in southern areas, select late-blooming types.

Hybrid chrysanthemum: 'Clara Curtis', bright pink; 'Mary Stoker', apricot-yellow.

DIANTHUS SPP.

Sweet William, Garden Pinks

Garden pinks are delightful, often spicily fragrant flowers with fringed petals. Sweet William (Dianthus barbatus), an old-fashioned cottage garden flower is a biennial or short-lived perennial, but sometimes

DIANTHUS PLUMARIUS

it's treated as an annual because it blooms so quickly from seed. Like other members of the pinks family, sweet William flowers have contrasting eyes. Unlike other members, the flowers are only lightly scented. They make up for the lack of scent by being borne in large, flat-topped clusters atop bushy plants with 3-inch-long, glossy, lance-shaped, dark green leaves. The bloom season lasts from early summer to midsummer. Flower colors include white, shades of pink, red, purple, and multicolors. The plant self-sows prolifically, but it may not come true to type. Plant grows 1 to 1½ feet tall; 1 foot wide. Mass plant in formal gardens or scatter about a cottage garden and allow to self-sow. Long-lasting cut flower.

The charming maiden pink (D. deltoides) produces a blanket of lightly scented, ¾-inch flowers with sharp-toothed (pinked) petals in such profusion that they totally obscure the foliage. The flowers bloom on branched stems for two months in spring and early summer, reblooming if sheared. Cultivars are available as named selections or mixed seed strains in shades of pink, magenta-red, and white, all marked with a crimson ring at the flower's center. The grasslike, 4- to 6-inch-long green leaves grow on creeping stems that form a thick, evergreen mat that takes on a rosy flush during cool weather. The 6-inch-high foliage spreads into 24-inch-wide mats; flower stems grow 8 to 12 inches tall. Charming in front of informal gardens.

The petals of the cottage pink (D. plumarius) are deeply fringed or plumed—rather than pinked—inspiring their botanical name. A beloved cottage garden flower, this pink is extremely fragrant, possessing an intense clove perfume. Flowers are borne in pairs or clusters on wiry stems and may be single, semidouble, or double, in pink, rose, magenta, or white, often with a contrasting eye. Blooming is in late spring and early summer and sporadically until frost if deadheaded. *continued*

DIANTHUS SPP.
(continued)

The extremely narrow, 1- to 4-inch-long, gray-green leaves have conspicuous veins and form a mat that grows into a loose, 12-inch-wide hummock. Foliage grows 6 inches tall and flower stalks to 24 inches.

Site: Sweet William needs full sun in most areas; some afternoon shade helpful in South. Give maiden pink full sun to light or half shade. Plant cottage pink in full sun. Sweet William and cottage pink prefer rich, humus-rich, well-drained, alkaline soil; maiden pink best in average to sandy alkaline soil. Give sweet William plentiful moisture, maiden and cottage pinks moderate moisture. Hardy in zones 3 to 9. Sweet William lives longest with cool summers and mild winters. Maiden pink performs well in the South.

How to Grow: Plant container-grown plants in spring, spacing sweet William 1 foot apart, maiden pink 18 inches apart, and cottage pink 10 inches apart. Divide sweet William every two or three years or take cuttings in spring to maintain selected cultivar. Divide maiden pink in early spring if plants aren't too woody; better to propagate by stem cuttings broken at node after blooming ceases. Divide cottage pink every two or three years in late summer by cutting back plants, separating into sections, and replanting deeply. May take cuttings in summer.

Add lime to soil where soil is neutral or acid. Remove flowering stems of sweet William at ground level after flowers fade to reduce self-seeding and promote possible repeat bloom. Maiden pink self-sows and may be somewhat weedy in tidy gardens. Shear back drastically in early spring before growth starts. Shear after flowering to prevent seeding, for neatness, and to promote rebloom. To prevent center of mat from dying out, sift sand into middle of plant in spring and fall.

Cover with evergreen boughs in winter in coldest areas. Shear back cottage pink drastically in early spring before growth starts and again after flowering to prevent seeding, for neatness, and to promote rebloom.

Sweet William is usually pest-free. Red spider mites sometimes trouble maiden and cottage pinks during hot, dry summers. Crown rot or root rot common if grown too wet. Rabbits may eat plants.

Cultivars: Sweet William: 'Newport Pink', rich coral-pink flowers; 'Blood Red', darkest red flowers, 15 inches tall; 'Scarlet Beauty', scarlet flowers; 'Pink Beauty', soft pink flowers; 'White Beauty', white flowers.

Maiden pink: 'Zing', scarlet flowers; 'Zing Rose', rose-red flowers, 6 inches tall; 'Albus', white flowers, 6 inches tall; *D. gratianopolitanus* (cheddar pink), single, pink to rose flowers with fringed petals, bearded throats, rich, spicy clove fragrance, flowers 6 to 10 inches tall above mat of evergreen gray-green foliage that spreads to 3 feet, may rot in winter-wet soil, top-dress with pea gravel, deadhead faded flowers, cutting at nodes to promote reblooming, zones 3 to 9, best with cool to mild summers; 'Bath's Pink', soft pink flowers with red eye; 'Flore-Pleno', double, light pink flowers; 'Tiny Rubies', double, light crimson-pink flowers, 4 inches tall; 'Rose Queen', double, rose flowers, 6 inches tall.

Cottage pink: 'Essex Witch', semidouble, range of pink, white, or salmon; 'Spring Beauty', double, mixed pink, rose, salmon, white.

DICENTRA SPP.
Bleeding-Heart

Native to forest floors from New York to Georgia, fringed bleeding-heart *(Dicentra eximia)* is a beguiling wildflower that decorates shady gardens from early spring through fall with pink flowers and gray-green foliage. The fernlike leaves form a vase-shaped clump from which arises graceful, upright stems of

DICENTRA SPECTABILIS

dangling, 1-inch-long, heart-shaped blossoms. Unlike many spring-blooming woodland flowers, fringed bleeding-heart doesn't die to the ground by summer; it stays attractive until frost. If conditions are cool and soil is moist, flower stalks continue sporadically throughout summer and more profusely in fall, especially so with the hybrids. Plants grow 9 to 18 inches tall and 15 inches wide. Fringed bleeding-heart is beautiful in shade and woodland gardens.

Common or old-fashioned bleeding-heart *(D. spectabilis)* was collected in China and introduced to England in 1842, where it became immediately popular. One of the earliest perennials to bloom, bleeding-heart blossoms begin in mid spring and continue for four or more weeks, accompanying tulips and spring-flowering trees and shrubs. Its arching sprays are strung with dancing, white-tipped, pink hearts laced through the large clumps of boldly cut, ferny, green foliage. Long-lived and nearly foolproof to grow in the right conditions. Plants usually go dormant during summer after hot weather arrives, but may remain green all summer in cool, moist climates. Grows 2 to 3 feet tall; 3½ feet wide. Gorgeous in cottage gardens and formal borders. Combine with low ferns or hostas, which will fill in bare spots left when plants go dormant. Charming cut flower.

Site: Fringed bleeding-heart grows in light to full shade; light shade best for common bleeding-heart, but it tolerates full sun if kept moist. Humus-rich, fertile, well-drained but moist soil. Even moisture for fringed bleeding-heart, plentiful water for common species. Fringed bleeding-heart hardy in zones 3 to 9, common bleeding-heart in zones 2 to 9.

How to Grow: Plant container-grown fringed bleeding-heart in spring, spacing 12 inches apart. Divide clumps every three years in fall. Plant dormant roots or container-grown plants of common bleeding-heart in spring, spacing 2 to 3 feet apart. No division necessary; propagate from cuttings.

Fringed bleeding-heart self-sows prolifically, but flower colors may not come true to type. Easy to weed out or transplant as desired. Common bleeding-heart may go dormant in summer if dry; mulch soil to keep cool and moist and prolong summer foliage.

Fringed bleeding-heart may rot in winter-wet soil; aphids may trouble common bleeding-heart.

Cultivars and Similar Species: *D. formosa* (western bleeding-heart), similar appearance, but spreads by rhizomes, blooming begins in mid spring, more drought-tolerant, but less tolerant of heat and humidity.

Hybrids: 'Luxuriant', deep rose-pink flowers (not red as advertised), 15 inches tall, blue-green leaves, floriferous, zones 3 to 7; 'Snowdrift', white flowers, 15 inches tall.

Common bleeding-heart: 'Alba', pure white flowers, less vigorous, pale green leaves; 'Pantaloons', pure white flowers, more vigorous than 'Alba.'

DIGITALIS PURPUREA

DIGITALIS PURPUREA
Foxglove

A tall biennial or short-lived perennial from grandmother's garden, foxglove self-sows to perpetuate itself year after year. Pendulous, trumpet-shaped, 1- to 2-inch-long blossoms borne on spectacular, one-sided spikes begin opening from the bottom of the spike upward in late spring to early summer, lasting for about four weeks. Flowers are lavender with spotted throats in the species, but white or shades of pink, lavender, purple, or yellow in the cultivars. Leaves are downy, forming large basal rosettes and climbing partway up the flower stalks. Plants are 2 to 5 feet tall when in bloom. Foxgloves are lovely massed for vertical effect in borders and in cottage and shade gardens.

Site: Part shade best. Fertile, humus-rich, moist, acid soil. Plentiful moisture. Zones 4 to 9.

How to Grow: Plant container-grown plants in spring, spacing 1 foot apart. Sow seeds in summer for next year's bloom.

Don't allow to dry out. Cut off stalks of ripened seedpods and shake out seeds where new plants are desired, or allow to self-sow. May need individual stakes. Sometimes troubled by powdery mildew, aphids, mealybugs, and Japanese beetles.

Cultivars and Similar Species: 'Alba', ivory-white flowers; 'Apricot Beauty', apricot-orange; 'Excelsior Hybrids', flowers borne all around spike in pink, mauve, yellow, and white, 4 to 5 feet tall; 'Foxy', mixed colors, 2½ feet tall.

Perennials in zones 3 to 8: *Digitalis* × *mertonensis* (strawberry foxglove), short-lived, rose-pink flowers, 3 to 4 feet tall; *D. grandiflora* (yellow foxglove), yellow flowers with brown throats, hairy leaves, 2 feet tall.

ECHINACEA PURPUREA
Purple Coneflower

This long-blooming prairie wildflower is closely related to *Rudbeckia*, the orange coneflower that it resembles in shape, but not color. Its big daisylike flowers consist of

ECHINACEA PURPUREA 'MAGNUS'

broad, somewhat reflexed, purplish pink, mauve, or white petals—which can be up to 4 inches long. The petals surround a raised, rusty-orange center, creating a startling color combination. Flowers bloom profusely on branched stems in midsummer and sporadically until frost. The rough-textured, arrow-shaped, dark green leaves measure 4 to 8 inches long and cloak upright stems 2 to 4 feet tall. Plants spread about 2 feet. *continued*

Perennials

ECHINACEA PURPUREA
(continued)

The orange centers allow this cool-colored flower to combine well with yellow and orange flowers. Use in midground of formal and informal plantings, naturalize in meadow and butterfly gardens, or combine with ornamental grasses.

Site: Full sun best; tolerates part to light shade. Average to infertile, well-drained soil. Moderate moisture; drought-tolerant. Hardy in zones 3 to 8.
How to Grow: Plant dormant roots or container-grown plants in spring, spacing 2 feet apart. Divide in spring or fall every four years if needed.

Allow flowers to dry into seed heads, which look lovely standing in winter. Don't fertilize. Needs staking only in rich, moist soil. Japanese beetles and caterpillars may be a problem.
Cultivars and Similar Species: 'Magnus', deep rose-mauve flowers, broad, horizontal petals, 3 feet tall; 'Bright Star', large, old-rose-colored petals, maroon centers, 3 to 4 feet tall; 'Bravado', extra-large, mauve-pink flowers, horizontal petals, 2 feet tall; 'Crimson Star', crimson flowers, 2 feet tall; 'White Swan', creamy white flowers, 2½ feet tall; 'White Luster', large, pure white flowers, 3 feet tall. *Echinacea pallida* (pale coneflower), 4- to 6-inch flowers with spidery, drooping, pale mauve petals.

EUPATORIUM SPP.
Mist Flower, Hardy Ageratum, Joe-Pye Weed

A welcome sight in autumn when it produces lavender-blue flowers, mist flower or hardy ageratum *(Eupatorium coelestinum)* cools autumn's otherwise hot color scheme. The dense, 4-inch heads of misty flowers resemble a looser and taller version of the popular annual ageratum. Leaves are triangular and coarsely toothed on leggy, upright, mahogany-colored stems. Plants grow 2 to 3 feet tall and spread by stolons into large stands. Best grown in informal or naturalistic gardens because of tendency to roam and flop.

EUPATORIUM COELESTINUM

Stunning in size, form, and color, Joe-Pye weed *(E. purpureum, E. fistulosum)* is a late-summer- to fall-blooming wildflower native to moist meadows. Better known as a garden plant in England than here in its homeland, Joe-Pye weed deserves wider planting in informal, large-scale gardens. The handsome, coarsely serrated, foot-long leaves are glossy, dark green and arranged in whorls. The upright, stout stems are hollow and mottled purple. Numerous tiny, reddish purple flowers make up rounded, compound inflorescences that measure 1½ feet across. The purple-foliaged cultivar makes an arresting sight from spring through fall. Plants grow 4 to 7 feet tall and 3 feet wide. Grow them in large borders, bog and butterfly gardens, and naturalistic gardens.

Site: Mist flower thrives in full sun to light shade, Joe-Pye weed in full sun. Average to fertile, moist soil. Mist flower prefers moderate moisture; Joe-Pye weed likes plentiful moisture and tolerates boggy conditions. Mist flower is hardy in zones 6 to 10, Joe-Pye weed in zones 4 to 8.
How to Grow: Plant container-grown plants in spring or fall, spacing mist flower 18 inches apart. Joe-Pye weed is best planted in spring, 3 feet apart. Divide mist flower every one or two years. Joe-Pye weed seldom needs division.

Mist flower emerges in late spring; be cautious not to uproot. Spreads aggressively in fertile, moist site; remove unwanted plants yearly to contain. Cut back once or twice in summer to promote compactness and tidier nature. May need staking. Mulch well. Pinching back Joe-Pye weed in early summer controls height, but reduces flower size.

Powdery mildew and aphids sometimes trouble mist flower; Joe-Pye weed is usually pest-free.
Cultivars: Mist flower: 'Alba', white flowers; 'Cori', clear blue flower; 'Wayside Variety', dwarf to 15 inches tall, crinkled leaves.

Joe-Pye weed: 'Atropurpureum', purple flowers, leaves, and stems; 'Gateway', 5 feet tall, large, rounded, dark mauve flower heads; 'Bartered Bride', pure white flowers.

FILIPENDULA RUBRA
Queen-of-the-Prairie

Magnificent and eye-catching, this plant produces fluffy, foot-tall panicles of tiny, rich pink to peach flowers from early summer to midsummer. Cut into jagged, dark green leaflets, the handsome, dark green foliage resembles astilbe, to which it's related. A tall, strong-stemmed plant, queen-of-the-prairie is a North American wildflower native to moist meadows and prairies. It grows 6 to 8 feet tall; 4 feet wide. Queen-of-the-prairie is a back-of-border plant for large-scale gardens or naturalized in moist meadows or along streams.

FILIPENDULA RUBRA

Site: Full sun, if kept wet, to part shade. Deep, fertile, moist soil. Plentiful moisture; tolerates boggy conditions. Zones 3 to 8; best in areas with cool, moist summers.

How to Grow: Plant container-grown plants in spring, spacing 3 feet apart. Divide tough rootstocks in spring. Rarely needs staking. Cut off faded flowers. Spider mites and mildew can be troublesome if soil is too dry.

Cultivars and Similar Species: 'Venusta', deep carmine-pink flowers, 4 feet tall; 'Venusta Alba', white. *Filipendula ulmaria* (queen-of-the-meadow), creamy white flowers, leaves with hairy white undersides, 3 to 6 feet tall, zones 3 to 9.

GAILLARDIA × GRANDIFLORA
Blanketflower

From early summer to mid fall, blanketflower brightens gardens with its 3-inch-wide, single or semidouble, daisylike flowers, which are banded with bright colors like an Indian blanket. Rounded, russet or dark burgundy centers surrounded by two-toned gold-and-maroon petals with jagged notches at their tips make an impact. Leaves are 6 inches long, gray-green, toothed, and resemble dandelion foliage. A hybrid between an annual and a perennial species, this plant compensates for its long-blooming season by being short-lived, often living only two or three years. Grows 2 to 3 feet tall and 2 feet wide.

Use in cottage and informal gardens. The bicolored blossoms are difficult to combine with other flowers; couple with other hot-colored flowers or their pastel versions.

GAILLARDIA × GRANDIFLORA

Site: Full sun. Fertile, sandy, well-drained soil. Tolerates seashore conditions. Allow to dry between waterings; drought-tolerant. Hardy in zones 2 to 10; heat-tolerant.

How to Grow: Plant container-grown plants in spring, spacing 1½ feet apart. Divide in spring, replanting root sections that show new growth. Self-sown seeds may not come true. Take stem cuttings in summer. Deadhead to prolong blooming. Sometimes powdery mildew and leaf hoppers attack. Crown rot may occur if too wet; root rot in winter in heavy soil.

Cultivars and Similar Species: 'Goblin', 4-inch, red flowers with yellow-edged petals, dwarf to 12 inches tall; 'Golden Goblin', pale yellow flowers, 12 inches tall; 'Baby Cole', 3-inch, yellow flowers with red-banded petals, dwarf to 8 inches tall; 'Burgundy', solid wine-red flowers; 'Aurea Pura' and 'The Sun', solid golden yellow flowers; 'Monarch Mix', seed-grown, variable mix of solids and bicolors.

GAURA LINDHEIMERI
White Gaura

An airy plant for creating a veil of flowers to soften a bold design, gaura is only recently gaining recognition in American gardens. Native to Louisiana, Texas, and Mexico, gaura has long been loved in British gardens for its loose, open wands of flowers, which bloom well above the foliage. Individual blossoms, which are 1 inch wide and made up of four clawed petals, open a few at a time from the bottom of the wiry stems upward. The stems elongate all season—each plant produces 10 to 12 stalks and a continual crop of flowers from late spring until a hard freeze. Flowers open white, but fade to pink.

GAURA LINDHEIMERI

Willowlike, gray-green leaves are held close to the stems and may turn dramatically red in late autumn. Plants grow 3 to 7 feet tall and 3 feet wide.

Despite its height, use gaura near the front of border to create soft, see-through effect. Wonderful in informal and naturalistic gardens.

Site: Full sun to part shade. Deep, sandy, well-drained soil; tolerates clay if well-drained. Even moisture best, but is drought-tolerant. Zones 5 *continued*

GAURA LINDHEIMERI
(continued)

to 9; tolerates heat of South and Southwest. In cool areas may not begin bloom until late summer.

How to Grow: Plant container-grown plants in spring, spacing 2½ feet apart. Forms deep taproot; division is difficult and rarely needed. May sprawl in fertile, moist soil. Self-seeds to point of weediness. Cut back, if desired, in midsummer to control size and promote new flowering. Usually pest-free.

Cultivars: 'Whirling Butterfly', shorter, to 3 feet tall, doesn't set seed.

GERANIUM SANGUINEUM
Bloody Cranesbill, Hardy Geranium

Modest-looking, but useful, hardy geraniums are foolproof to grow. With handsome leaves and pretty flowers, this diverse group—they're relatives of the bedding geranium—can solve many problems by weaving between more flamboyant plants. Bloody cranesbill, with its dark-veined magenta flowers, is perhaps the brightest of the cranesbills, but its softer-colored cultivars are easier to combine with other flowers. It forms low mounds of deeply divided, hairy leaves, which turn red in autumn, and its open-faced, five-petaled, 2-inch-wide flowers bloom all summer. Plants are 1 foot tall in bloom and spread aggressively as a groundcover.

Use clump-forming cranesbills in flower borders and spreading types as groundcovers. Bloody cranesbill is too invasive for formal borders, but lovely as a companion to old roses, shrubs, or perennials in mixed borders. Mass-plant as a groundcover under high-branched trees.

GERANIUM ENDRESSII 'WARGRAVE PINK'

Site: Full sun to light shade; afternoon shade in South. Average to fertile, moist soil; tolerates dry shade. Zones 4 to 8.

How to Grow: Plant bare-root or container-grown plants in spring, spacing 2 to 3 feet apart for groundcover. Divide in spring or fall when desired. Invasive; locate thoughtfully. Cut back foliage in midsummer if floppy; fresh leaves will grow. Usually pest-free.

Cultivars and Similar Species: 'Album', pure white flowers; 'Purple Flame', purple. *Geranium sanguineum* var. *striatum* (Lancaster geranium), prostrate, dark-veined, pale pink flowers, blooms summer and fall. *G. endressii* 'Wargrave Pink', notched, salmon-pink petals, flowers all summer, shiny divided leaves, 18 inches tall. *G. himalayense*, large, violet-blue flowers with red-purple veins and centers, deeply divided foliage turns red in fall, 15 inches tall; 'Johnson's Blue', hybrid with clear blue flowers.

GYPSOPHILA PANICULATA
Baby's-Breath

Just as baby's-breath makes an invaluable lacy filler between large flowers in floral arrangements, it can be used to create a cloudlike effect in flower gardens. Blooming from early to midsummer, the huge branched panicles contain about a thousand minuscule white flowers. The narrow, gray-green leaves that decorate the stems beneath the flowers further add to the softened effect. Plants grow

GYPSOPHILA PANICULATA

3 to 4 feet tall and wide. Use baby's-breath in midground of border to create veil around bolder plants. Essential plant in cutting gardens.

Site: Full sun. Fertile, well-drained, alkaline soil. Best kept moist, but tolerates drought. Zones 3 to 9.

How to Grow: Plant container-grown plants in spring, spacing 3 feet apart and setting graft union 1 inch below soil level. Take cuttings after flowering; large, fleshy root resents disturbance. Cut back immediately after blooming to encourage fall bloom. Staking needed to hold up flower-laden stems. Apply lime annually to acid soils. Usually pest-free.

Cultivars: 'Bristol Fairy', white flowers, 30 inches tall; 'Pink Fairy', double, pink flowers, 18 inches tall; 'Pink Star', large, double, pink flowers, 18 inches tall; 'Perfecta', white, individual flowers twice as large, 4 feet tall; 'Compacta Plena', double flowers, dwarf to 18 inches tall. *Gypsophila repens*, trailing plant, pink spring and summer flowers, for rock gardens; 'Alba', white; 'Rosea', pale pink.

HELENIUM AUTUMNALE

HELENIUM AUTUMNALE
Sneezeweed

A native of moist meadows, this eye-catching American wildflower got its common name because it was used as a snuff substitute. The abundant, 2-inch, hot-colored flowers bloom on tall, bushy plants, beginning in midsummer and continuing for two months. Petals are wedge-shaped with notched ends, and they curve down and away from the domed central disc. Colors include clear yellow petals with matching centers, or shades of orange, red, and mahogany with contrasting dark centers. The lance-shaped leaves have winged bases and clasp sturdy, winged stems. Plants grow 5 feet tall.

Plant in groups in midground to background of beds and borders or naturalize in moist meadow plantings.

Site: Full sun. Average to heavy, infertile, moist to wet soil. Best with plentiful moisture, but tolerates some drought. Zones 3 to 8; grows weak and lanky in heat and humidity.
How to Grow: Plant container-grown plants in spring, spacing 3 feet apart. Divide every year or two in early spring. Pinch in late spring to reduce height and delay flowering. Keep moist or plant may lose lower leaves. Needs staking only if grown in fertile soil. Cut back after flowering. Don't overfertilize. May be troubled by rust or leaf spots.
Cultivars: 'Moorheim Beauty', rusty orange-red petals, brown centers, 3 to 4 feet tall; 'Butterpat', yellow flowers; 'Rubrum', mahogany-brown flowers; 'Wyndley', coppery brown flowers, 3 feet tall; 'Brilliant', deep rusty scarlet flowers, 3 feet tall; 'Sunball', yellow flowers with green centers, heavy flowering, 4 feet tall; 'Red-Gold Hybrids', mixed copper, red, gold, and yellow flowers.

HELLEBORUS ORIENTALIS
Lenten Rose

This delightful plant is a must-have because it blooms in late winter, seeming to push up through the melting snow. A tuft of showy yellow-

HELLEBORUS ORIENTALIS

tipped stamens decorates the nodding, buttercup-like, pure white, rose, or maroon flowers. Blossoms, which are sometimes spotted, remain good-looking into late spring because the petals are actually bracts that remain colorful as seeds ripen. The foot-wide, deeply divided leathery leaves are evergreen and make attractive stands throughout the year. Foliage clumps are 18 inches tall and 2 feet wide. Lenten rose is an excellent year-round plant for shade gardens.

Site: Light to full shade during growing season and in winter. Fertile, humus-rich, moist, well-drained soil essential. Plentiful moisture. Zones 4 to 9.
How to Grow: Plant container-grown plants in spring, spacing 2 feet apart. Self-sows readily. Cut off winter-tattered foliage to show off flowers better. Easy to grow if soil and light are right. Usually pest- and disease-free.
Cultivars and Similar Species: *Helleborus niger* (Christmas rose), winter-blooming, pure white flowers age to rose, zones 3 to 8. *H. foetidus* (stinking hellebore), apple green flowers, only roots smell bad, zones 6 to 9.

HEMEROCALLIS HYBRIDS
Daylily

Easy-to-grow and indispensable, daylilies are the mainstay of many gardens. Extensive breeding has brought us hundreds of cultivars in a range of sizes, colors, and flower shapes, as well as four- to six-week

HEMEROCALLIS 'STELLA DE ORO'

blooming seasons beginning anytime from early summer to fall. Some cultivars even rebloom. Daylily's strap-shaped, bright green leaves emerge in early spring. The flowers are truly amazing—huge, trumpet-shaped affairs in every color, but blue and true white, sporting long, curving continued

HEMEROCALLIS HYBRIDS
(continued)

stamens. Throats are often a contrasting color such as light green or creamy yellow, and petals may be prettily ruffled. Individual flowers last only a day, but each flower scape produces numerous blossoms. Foliage clumps grow 1 to 3 feet tall; flower stalks 1 to 5 feet, depending upon cultivar.

Plant in groups in beds and borders and for erosion control.

Site: Full sun to half shade. Tolerates almost any soil, but best in fertile site. Drought-tolerant once established, best with plentiful moisture. Zones 3 to 9.
How to Grow: Plant tuberous roots or container-grown plants in spring, spacing 2 feet apart. Divide in spring every three to five years. Remove faded flowers daily if not self-cleaning. Cut off flower stalks after flowering ceases. Easy to grow and usually trouble-free.
Cultivars and Similar Species: Cultivars are too numerous to list. Rebloomers include 'Stella de Oro', orange-yellow flowers, 18 inches tall; 'Happy Returns', pastel lemon yellow flowers, 18 inches tall; 'Country Club', pink flowers with green throat, 18 inches tall; 'Diamond Anniversary', peach-pink flowers, 3 feet tall; 'Haunting Melody', fuchsia-rose flowers, ruffled, 3 feet tall; 'Jenny Sue', pale peach flowers, ruffled, 2 feet tall; 'Paul Bunyan', light gold flowers, 3½ feet tall; *Hemerocallis fulva* (tawny daylily), orange flowers, European wildflower naturalized in North America.

HEUCHERA SANGUINEA
Coralbells

Grown for its charming flowers and neat clumps of evergreen foliage, coralbells deserves a spot in most gardens. The loose, airy, clusters of ½-inch-long, bell-shaped blossoms rise on wiry stems held above clumps of rounded gray-mottled leaves with

HEUCHERA MICRANTHA 'RACHEL'

scalloped lobes. Blossoms appear for one to two months beginning in early spring. Foliage clumps are 8 inches high and 12 inches wide; flower stalks are 10 to 12 inches tall.

Coralbells is an elegant edging for formal gardens; lovely in clusters in a shade garden. Use purple-leaf cultivars as edging; makes a beautiful contrast with grass and gravel paths.

Site: Light to part shade. Humus-rich, well-drained, neutral to slightly alkaline soil. Moderate moisture. Zones 3 to 8.
How to Grow: Plant bare-root or container-grown plants in spring, spacing 1 foot apart. Divide in early spring every three years, or take stem cuttings in late fall. Remove flower stalks as they fade to encourage further blooming. Apply lime annually where soil is acid. Dig up and reset plants with leggy, woody bases protruding from ground. Usually pest- and disease-free.
Cultivars and Similar Species: Named varieties are usually hybrids attributed indiscriminately to *Heuchera sanguinea* or *H.* × *brizoides*, with profuse, ⅛-inch flowers, rounded lobed foliage, to 2 feet tall. 'Pretty Polly', pale pink; 'Freedom', rose-pink; 'Coral Cloud', coral-pink; 'June Bride', profuse pure white flowers; 'Matin Bells', red; 'Chatterbox', deep rose-pink; 'Bressingham Hybrids', seed-grown, large-flowered mix; 'Cherry Splash',

cherry red flowers, white-and-gold-splashed leaves. *H. micrantha* 'Palace Purple' (purple-leaf coralbells), magnificent 12-inch clumps of heavily veined, maplelike, evergreen, bronze-purple leaves with purplish rose undersides, tiny, white flowers in airy clusters on wiry stems, zones 4 to 8, seed-grown plants vary in color (select cutting-propagated plants or individual plants for best color). 'Rachel', smaller, deep purple leaves, pink flowers; 'Pewter Veil', mottled silvery leaves.

HIBISCUS MOSCHEUTOS
Rose Mallow, Swamp Rose Mallow

Rose mallow's startlingly large, saucer-shaped flowers measure 6 to 12 inches across and are composed of red, pink, or white petals that are crinkled like tissue paper. Blossoms form in clusters at the top of tall plants

HIBISCUS MOSCHEUTOS 'DISCO BELLE'

beginning in late summer and continuing until frost. The 8-inch, broadly oval leaves are dark green on top with downy white undersides. Native to marshy areas in eastern North America, rose mallow adapts to moist gardens, forming long-lived clumps that don't spread. Plants grow 5 to 8 feet tall.

Excellent for damp or wet spots in borders or naturalized in bog gardens or along a stream. Plant it in groups.

Site: Full sun to light shade. Fertile, humus rich, moist to wet soil. Constant moisture. Zones 5 to 9.

How to Grow: Plant container-grown plants in spring, spacing 3 feet apart, or sow seeds in spring. Division not necessary, but divide in spring if desired. Moisture availability influences height. Needs no staking. Emerges late in spring; avoid digging up. Japanese beetles and aphids often troublesome.

Cultivars: 'Southern Belle' series, 10-inch-wide pink, red, white blossoms, 4- to 6-foot-tall plants; 'Anne Arundel', 9-inch-tall pink flowers; 'Lord Baltimore', 12-inch red flowers, 4 to 6 feet tall; 'Lady Baltimore', pink flowers with red centers, 4 feet tall.

HOSTA SPP. AND HYBRIDS
Hosta, Plantain Lily

Spectacular foliage plants, hostas have leaves that are often heavily veined or puckered. Leaf color ranges from emerald green to frosty blue-gray to golden yellow and may be variegated in patterns. The leaves arise

HOSTA 'GOLDEN TIARA'

from the ground, forming lush clumps that vary in size from diminutive dwarfs to knee-high giants. Many types produce lovely spikes of lilylike

lavender, purple, or white flowers in mid- or late summer, but their foliage alone is enough to satisfy discerning gardeners. Hostas with bright variegations or yellow-green foliage are as eye-catching as flowers and their effect lasts the entire growing season. Plants grow 6 inches to 3 feet tall and wide, depending on cultivar.

Plant hostas in groups and as specimens in shade and woodland gardens. They combine well with fine-textured plants such as ferns and astilbes. Use dwarf types as edging or border plantings in formal and informal gardens; use large types as specimens.

Site: Light to full shade best. In general, green hostas prefer light to half-shade; gold and variegated types, light to three-quarters shade; and blues, light to half or full shade. Deep, fertile, humus-rich, moist soil. Plentiful moisture best, but tolerates average conditions. Some types tolerate dry shade. Zones 3 to 9.

How to Grow: Plant bare root or container-grown plants in spring, spacing 1 to 3 feet apart, depending on cultivar. Needs no division, but mature clumps may be divided in spring. Cut off faded flower spikes. Slugs and snails can be very troublesome; a monthly control program is usually recommended. Some types are slug-resistant.

Cultivars and Similar Species: Hundreds of wonderful cultivars available; too numerous to list.

IBERIS SEMPERVIRENS
Edging Candytuft

For two months beginning in early spring, rounded, 1-inch-wide clusters of white flowers cover the plant, turning it into a snowy mound. Even out of bloom, edging candytuft is a winner—its evergreen leaves,

IBERIS SEMPERVIRENS

which are arranged in whorls around procumbent stems, make attractive hills of dark green foliage. Grows 9 to 12 inches tall; 1½ feet wide.

Edging candytuft forms attractive mounds in rock gardens and walls. Use compact forms as edging for formal borders. Combines beautifully with tulips.

Site: Full to half sun. Average, well-drained, neutral to alkaline soil. Moderate moisture. Zones 3 to 9.

How to Grow: Plant container-grown plants in spring, spacing 6 to 12 inches apart. Needs no division. Take stem cuttings in summer. Cut back by one-third after flowering to keep plants compact and tidy. Cut back by two-thirds every few years to reduce woodiness and promote new growth. Clubroot may be troublesome.

Cultivars: 'Autumn Snow', blooms in spring and again in autumn, 9 inches tall; 'Snowflake', large leaves and flowers, 7 to 8 inches tall, later-blooming; 'Snowmantle', 12 inches tall, very sturdy mounds; 'Purity', white flowers, 8 inches tall; 'Little Gem', 6 inches tall; 'Alexander's White', early blooming, 10 inches tall.

IRIS SPP.
Iris

Crested iris (*Iris cristata*) is a graceful, native wildflower with small, sweetly fragrant, blue, lavender, or white flowers with yellow crests. It blooms in mid spring. Low, sword-shaped leaves provide a subtle vertical

IRIS CRISTATA

accent the rest of the growing season. Crested iris grows 4 to 8 inches tall and spreads by creeping rhizomes to form a dense groundcover. Plant it in drifts in woodland or shade gardens.

The elegant Japanese iris (*I. ensata, I. kaempferi*) features blossoms that look like flying birds. It blooms later than other irises, usually with huge, flat flowers in midsummer. Blossoms may be white, blue, purple, reddish purple, or lavender-pink with yellow crests and often are marbled or veined with a contrasting color. Leaves grow broad and sword-shaped to 2 feet long with a prominent midrib. Plants reach 3 to 4 feet tall and as wide. Japanese iris is gorgeous in naturalistic gardens along streams and ponds or in more formal settings.

Bearded iris (*I. × germanica*) brightens borders from spring to midsummer with its showy, lightly fragrant blossoms, which come in every

color. New reblooming types produce flowers again in fall. The elegant flowers consist of three upright, arching petals, called standards, rising above three reflexed petals, called falls. A stripe of dense yellow hairs creates a beard down the centers of the falls. The broad, sword-shaped, gray-green or bright green leaves grow in flat fans and make a bold contrast to the usual forms of foliage found in the garden. Plants grow 6 inches to 4 feet tall and wide. Use dwarf types in the foreground of beds and borders, taller types in mid ground. Best planted in clusters of a single color.

IRIS ENSATA

More delicate looking than the bearded iris, Siberian iris (*I. sibirica*) blooms in late spring or early summer, opening its graceful, beardless, yellow-crested blossoms in succession over several weeks. Flowers may be purple, blue, lilac, or white. The narrow, lancelike leaves form graceful, vase-shaped clumps that make a soft vertical statement among other plants. Plants grow 2 to 4 feet tall and wide. Siberian iris is lovely in borders, informal settings, and bog gardens.

Site: Give crested iris part to heavy shade; full sun in constantly moist soil. Japanese iris likes full sun to part shade, bearded iris needs full sun, and Siberian iris full sun to light shade.

Plant crested iris in neutral, humus-rich soil with even moisture. Japanese and Siberian irises prefer humus-rich, acid, moist to wet or boggy soil; Japanese iris even enjoys standing water. Bearded iris needs fertile, well-drained, alkaline soil and moderate moisture; drought-tolerant when established.

Crested iris is hardy in zones 3 to 9; Japanese iris in zones 4 to 9 (performs poorly where hot and dry); bearded iris in zones 3 to 10; Siberian iris in zones 3 to 9 (does well in the South).

How to Grow: Plant rhizomes or container-grown plants in spring. Space crested iris 15 inches apart. Plant Japanese iris 1 inch deep; space plants 1 to 2 inches apart. Plant bearded iris rhizomes half-buried; space plants 1 to 4 feet apart depending on cultivar. Plant Siberian iris rhizomes 1 inch deep; space plants 2 feet apart.

Divide crested iris in early fall if desired (not usually needed); divide Japanese iris in fall every three to four years; divide bearded iris every four years in mid- to late summer (fall in mild climates) by pulling apart and cutting rhizome clumps into healthy segments with one leaf fan apiece and cutting back leaves to one-third. Siberian iris rarely needs division.

Do not allow soil to dry for Japanese iris; will not tolerate alkaline soil. Remove individual flowers as they fade.

Carefully remove individual bearded iris flowers as they fade; cut back flower scapes after flowering finishes. Tall types may need individual staking. Do not cover rhizomes with mulch and keep free of debris.

Siberian iris needs no staking; remove flower stalks before seed sets.

Slugs often trouble crested iris. Thrips may infest Japanese iris flowers; otherwise pest-free.

Soft rot troubles bearded iris in heavy soil; remove yellowing leaves as soon as noticed to prevent spread. Iris borers can be serious; do not leave old leaves to overwinter.

Siberian iris is long-lived and usually pest-free.

Cultivars and Similar Species: Crested iris: 'Alba', white flowers; 'Shenandoah Sky', light blue; 'Abbey's Violet', deep violet-blue flowers with prominent white-and-yellow crests.

Japanese iris: Numerous cultivars. 'Eleanor Parry', reddish purple flowers; 'Gold Bound', pure white flowers with gold bands; 'Ise', palest blue flowers with deep purple-blue veins; 'Nikko', pale purple flowers with purple veins, 30 inches tall; 'Pink Frost', light pink flowers; 'Kagari Bi', rose-pink flowers with silver veins; 'Moriah', deep blue flowers, veined white; 'Royal Banner', burgundy flowers; 'Emotion', white flowers with blue edge.

Bearded iris: Thousands of cultivars available. Bearded irises may be classified as miniature (4 to 10 inches tall), dwarf (10 to 15 inches tall), intermediate (15 to 28 inches tall), and tall (more than 28 inches tall). Dwarf types bloom in mid and late spring, intermediate types in late spring and early summer, and tall types in early and midsummer. *I. pumila* sometimes used as name for dwarf types.

Siberian iris: Numerous cultivars. 'Caesar', deep blue-purple flowers; 'Caesar's Brother', deep purple; 'Cambridge', pale blue; 'Pembina', deep blue; 'Snow Queen', pure white; 'Papillon', light blue; 'Perry's Blue', medium blue; 'Sparkling Rose', rose-wine flowers.

LAMIUM MACULATUM
Spotted Dead Nettle

The foliage of this vigorous, sprawling groundcover provides months of shade-brightening color. The species features heart-shaped, scalloped-edged, green leaves striped with white down their centers.

LAMIUM MACULATUM 'PINK PEWTER'

Cultivars are showier, displaying large silver blotches or an overall golden color. From mid spring through summer, whorls of rosy lavender or white-hooded flowers bloom above the leaves on short spikes. Plants grow 8 to 12 inches tall; spread to 24 feet.

A wonderful groundcover for shade gardens, lamium combines well with tulips, hostas, ferns, and other tall shade perennials.

Site: Full to part shade. Average to humus-rich, moist soil. Plentiful moisture is best, especially in sunny spots. Lamium tolerates dry shade. Zones 3 to 8.

How to Grow: Plant bare-root or container-grown plants in spring, spacing 1 to 2 feet apart. Divide in fall. Take stem cuttings in summer. Cut back in midsummer if plants become straggly. May smother small woodland flowers. Slugs and leaf spot or root rot are sometimes troublesome. Bare spots result if plants repeatedly dry out.

Cultivars: 'Chequers', resembles species, but with white-striped leaves; 'White Nancy', white flowers, silver leaves edged green; 'Beacon Silver', rose-lavender flowers, silver leaves edged green; 'Pink Pewter', pale pink flowers, silvery leaves; 'Aureum', soft yellow leaves with white veins, pink flowers.

LEUCANTHEMUM × SUPERBUM (CHRYSANTHEMUM × SUPERBUM)
Shasta Daisy

This hybrid of two European daisies was created by the American plantsman Luther Burbank during the late 19th century. He sought to create a large-flowered daisy with long, strong stems for cutting. The result is the beloved shasta daisy, a perennial noted for its floriferous nature. Blossoms appear lavishly in June and July and continue into fall if plants are deadheaded. The 2- to 3-inch, yellow-centered, white flowers may be single, double, or semidouble and make excellent cut flowers.

LEUCANTHEMUM × SUPERBUM 'MARCONI'

Unlike the leaves of most mums, these are coarsely toothed, not lobed, and dark green. Leaves are larger near the ground and form a clump beneath the sparsely foliaged flowering stems; a rosette of evergreen basal leaves overwinters. Plants grow 6 to 36 inches tall, 18 inches wide.

Plant in masses in a formal border, as an edging, or midborder plant, depending upon height. Scatter them in a cottage garden. Tall types make the best cut flowers. *continued*

Perennials

LEUCANTHEMUM × SUPERBUM
(continued)

Site: Full sun in most areas, part shade where summers are hot and dry; doubles do best in part shade. Deep, fertile, well-drained neutral to alkaline soil, moderate moisture. Hardy in zones 4 to 9.

How to Grow: Plant container-grown plants in spring, spacing 2 feet apart. Divide every other year in early spring. Deadhead regularly or cut back after first flush to promote reblooming. Mulch over winter in the North. Stake tall cultivars with rings. Short-lived in winter-wet soil. Aphids and verticillium wilt troublesome.

Cultivars and Similar Species: Singles: 'Alaska', large, white, 20 inches; 'Snow Lady', early, pure white blossoms, 6 to 8 inches; 'Starburst', 6-inch blossoms, early, 3 feet; 'Little Princess', large flowers, compact, to 12 inches; 'Snowcap', pure white, 10 to 12 inches; 'Polaris', white, 36 inches.

Doubles: 'Aglaya', frilly, 28 inches; 'Marconi', early, 36 inches; 'T.E. Killen', large flowers, sturdy, to 30 inches; 'Cobham Gold', creamy yellow petals with gold centers, 15 to 18 inches.

LIATRIS SPICATA
Gay-Feather, Blazing-Star

Once an obscure wildflower native to moist meadows, gay-feather now grows in many gardens. Its slender bottlebrushes of rose, purple, or white flowers, which bloom from midsummer to fall, attract bees and butterflies. Unlike many spiked flowers, gay-feather's blossoms begin opening from the top of the spike downward. Leaves are narrow and arranged in whorls around the tall stems, emphasizing the vertical, feathery effect. Grows 3 feet tall and 2 feet wide.

Gay-feather makes a striking vertical effect in formal borders and in naturalistic plantings. Combines well

LIATRIS SPICATA 'KOBOLD'

with ornamental grasses. Good cut flower; remove tops of spikes as flowers fade.

Site: Full sun. Average to sandy, humus-rich soil. Keep moist in growing season. Zones 3 to 9.

How to Grow: Plant bare-root or container-grown plants in spring, spacing 2 feet apart. Divide clumps of fleshy roots every three or four years in fall, if crowded. May need staking to maintain straight spikes. Cut off faded spikes to promote rebloom. Easy-care and long-lived. Root-knot nematodes may be troublesome in South.

Cultivars and Similar Species: 'Kobold', 2½ feet tall, early-blooming, stiff spikes of dark violet-purple flowers; 'Floristan White', white flowers, 3 feet tall; 'August Glory', purple-blue, 3 to 4 feet tall. *Liatris pycnostachya* (Kansas gayfeather), 4 to 5 feet tall, needs staking in gardens, best in meadow.

LIRIOPE MUSCARI
Blue Lilyturf

Plants that tolerate dry shade are few and far between; this one takes those adverse conditions in stride, forming fountainlike clumps of glossy, dark green or variegated evergreen leaves. Leaves are 2 inches wide and 1 to 2 feet long. Plants striped with silver or gold make

beautiful color and textural contrasts in shady spots. Even though the foliage is its selling point, dense spikes of purplish blue flowers, which resemble grape hyacinth and arise from the middle of the clumps in late summer, are a pretty sight. Clumps grow to 1 to 1½ feet tall; 2 feet wide.

Use lilyturf as a small-scale groundcover or edging. It is also effective as a specimen or in drifts in shade gardens. Combines well with ferns and hostas.

LIRIOPE MUSCARI 'VARIEGATA'

Site: Half to full shade. Humus-rich to average, well-drained soil. Regular water is best, though plants are drought-tolerant. Zones 6 to 9; performs well in both humid and dry climates.

How to Grow: Plant bare-root or container-grown plants in spring, spacing 8 to 12 inches apart for groundcover. Division not needed for years, but clumps may be divided in spring. Cut back foliage to 2 inches in late winter to remove winter-tattered leaves and promote lush new growth. Slugs and snails often troublesome.

Cultivars: 'Majestic', violet flowers; 'Monroe White', showy, bright white flowers; 'Royal Purple', deep purple flowers; 'Variegata', green leaves with creamy white margins, bright lavender flowers; 'Silvery Sunproof', leaves almost white in sun, yellow green in shade, lavender flowers.

LUPINUS HYBRIDS
Lupine

Hybrid lupines form stately clumps of silky-haired, matte green leaves. The leaves may be a foot across and are rounded in outline, but cut into many fingerlike lobes. Dense spikes of pealike flowers rise above the foliage for a month or more in early summer. Flowers come in a variety of colors and may be bicolored. The best-known lupines are the 'Russell Hybrids', which were bred in England during the first half of this century and caused a

LUPINUS HYBRID

sensation when first exhibited. They offer a wide color range and dense flower spikes on tall plants. Newer hybrids grow more compactly with shorter, denser spikes. Unfortunately, all hybrid lupines are finicky and short-lived in most areas of North America. Plants grow 3 feet tall and wide.

Mass plant in formal borders for elegant flowers and foliage or plant as specimens in informal gardens.

Site: Full sun best; tolerates some shade. Humus-rich, acid, well-drained soil. Plentiful moisture. Zones 4 to 9. Performs poorly in hot-summer areas; grow as fall-planted, cool-season annual in Zone 6 and southward.
How to Grow: Plant container-grown plants in spring or fall, spacing 2½ feet apart. Avoid plants with encircling distorted taproots. Take stem cuttings in fall and overwinter in cold frame. Taproot resents disturbance. Mulch to keep soil cool. Deadhead spent spikes to ensure strong plants and promote possible second bloom. Stake tall types. Aphids, powdery mildew, slugs, and crown rot are sometimes troublesome.
Cultivars: 'Russell Hybrids', 3 feet tall in bicolors and shades of white, cream, pink, red, blue, yellow, orange, and purple; usually sold unnamed. 'Gallery Hybrids', 15 to 18 inches tall with blue, pink, red, yellow, and white flowers. 'Minarette', 18 to 24 inches tall, mixed colors.

MYOSOTIS SCORPIOIDES
Forget-Me-Not

Forget-me-not produces coiled clusters of tiny, pale blue flowers with paler centers and yellow eyes from spring though late summer. Stems are a bit floppy, and roots are stoloniferous, creating a loose, spreading plant with fuzzy leaves. Grows 6 to 8 inches tall; spreads to 18 inches wide.

Naturalize in woodland, along a stream, or in a bog garden. Sow seeds of woodland forget-me-not in autumn over bulb beds.

Site: Light to part shade best; full sun if soil stays constantly moist. Humus-rich, fertile, moist to wet soil. Provide plentiful moisture; thrives in boggy site or shallow water. Zones 3 to 8.
How to Grow: Plant container-grown plants in spring, spacing 1 foot apart. Divide in spring or fall. Individual plants may be short-lived, but abundantly self-sow. Mildew and spider mites may

MYOSOTIS SCORPIOIDES

attack if conditions are too dry; leaf rot a problem in South.
Cultivars and Similar Species: 'Semperflorens', compact to 8 inches tall, extremely floriferous medium blue flowers. *Myosotis sylvatica* (woodland or garden forget-me-not), erroneously called *M. alpestris*, biennial or short-lived perennial often treated as cool-season annual, azure blue flowers with yellow eyes in spring and sporadically through summer, upright to 2 feet tall, cultivars often globular 8-inch mounds; 'Royal Blue Compact', deep blue flowers, compact; 'Indigo Blue', blue flowers; 'Victoria Alba', white flowers, compact; 'Rosea', pink; 'Sapphire', bright blue, compact.

NEPETA × FAASSENII
Catmint

This outstanding aromatic plant in the mint family is one of the showiest of the family. It produces billowing masses of small, lavender-blue blossoms for several weeks in early summer—at the peak of rose season—and again in fall if cut back. When out of bloom, the narrow, wedge-shaped, 1½-inch-long, gray-green leaves and gently cascading stems make a striking contrast with neighboring green leaves and colorful flowers. Be sure you're *continued*

Perennials

NEPETA × FAASSENII
(continued)

NEPETA × FAASSENII

getting the real thing when you purchase this catmint; *Nepeta mussinii,* one of its parents and a much less showy plant, often is mislabeled as *N. × faassenii.* Grows 1 to 1½ feet tall; 2 feet wide.

Catmint is a classic edging for rose gardens; use it to border formal flower and herb gardens. Combines well with red, purple, pink, pale yellow, and white flowers.

Site: Full sun best; tolerates half shade. Average to sandy, well-drained soil. Moderate moisture. Zones 3 to 8.
How to Grow: Plant container-grown plants in spring, spacing 18 inches apart. Divide in spring or fall every three years. Sterile; won't self-sow. In spring, cut back new growth by half when 6 inches tall to encourage branching. Shear halfway after spring bloom to discourage floppiness and encourage rebloom. Performs poorly in heavy soil; rots in damp soil. *N. × faassenii* more tolerant of moisture and part shade than *N. mussinii.* Usually pest-free, but cats may roll on plants.
Cultivars and Similar Species: 'Blue Wonder', 6-inch spikes of lavender-blue flowers, compact mound, 10 to

15 inches tall; 'White Wonder', white flowers; 'Snowflake', white, compact, low-spreading. 'Six Hills Giant' (*N. gigantea*), covered with soft violet-blue flowers, 3 feet tall. 'Dropmore', smaller, more linear, much grayer leaves and prettier lavender flowers than species, to 2½ feet tall, needs ringed support.

OENOTHERA SPP.
Evening Primrose, Sundrops

Logic doesn't apply to the common names of plants in this genus— some night bloomers go by the name sundrops, and some day bloomers are called evening primroses. The showy primrose or Mexican evening primrose (*Oenothera speciosa, O. berlandieri*), a spectacular Midwest wildflower produces 2- to 3-inch-long, bowl-shaped, translucent, pale pink flowers with white centers and showy yellow stamens. Flowers open at sunrise and close into furled blossoms at sunset. Blooming begins in midsummer and lasts into fall. White-flowered forms open at night and may age to pink

OENOTHERA SPECIOSA

after pollination. Plants are low and somewhat sprawling, covered with hairy, 1- to 3-inch-long, lobed, gray-green leaves. Grows 1 to 2 feet tall; 1½ feet wide. Plant showy primrose in

informal and naturalistic gardens where its aggressive tendencies are more welcome.

Common sundrops (*O. tetragona, O. fruticosa*), an eye-catching species native to eastern North America, is a day bloomer, opening clusters of silky, saucer-shaped, canary yellow flowers each morning from early to midsummer. Lance-shaped green leaves cloak hairy, reddish stems and

OENOTHERA TETRAGONA

turn dark red in fall. Plants form evergreen rosettes that overwinter. They grow 18 to 36 inches and form large stands, spreading by underground roots. Sundrops look stunning combined with blue flowers in informal gardens.

Site: Full sun. Average to infertile soil. Moderate moisture; drought-tolerant. Showy primrose is hardy in zones 5 to 8; tolerates arid conditions and heat and humidity. Sundrops is hardy in zones 4 to 8.
How to Grow: Plant bare-root or container-grown plants in spring, spacing 2 to 3 feet apart. Divide as needed: showy primrose in spring, sundrops in spring or fall.

Spreads by stoloniferous roots and can be rampant in fertile soil. In late fall, cut back frost-killed stems and remove undesired plants to keep in bounds.

Showy primrose is usually pest-free; spittlebugs may trouble sundrops.
Cultivars and Similar Species: Showy primrose: 'Rosea', slender, prostrate grower, light rose-pink flowers; 'Alba', day-blooming, white flowers; 'Siskiyou', more floriferous and compact, to 3 inches tall, spreads less; *O. rosea*, upright flower buds open pink, age to deep rose.

Sundrops: 'Fireworks', 18 inches tall, red stems, red flower buds, bright yellow flowers; 'Highlight', fragrant, bright, pure yellow flowers all summer, 15 inches tall; 'Lapsley', large yellow flowers, 18 inches tall; 'Yellow River', large yellow flowers, green stems, 18 inches tall.

PAEONIA LACTIFLORA
Chinese Peony, Garden Peony

Cultivated in China more than 1,400 years ago, this sacred, fragrant flower has been a beloved perennial in North America and Europe for about 150 years. Breeding has created hundreds of cultivars in a

PAEONIA LACTIFLORA

range of colors, forms, and bloom times. The stunning, long-stemmed flowers in shades of white, red, pink, purple, or yellow, are 4 to 8 inches across. Single types have five large petals surrounding a showy center of

yellow stamens. Semidouble types have four to eight rings of petals with showy stamens visible. Double types form huge balls of petals. Japanese types are similar to singles, but with fringelike, yellow, pollenless staminodes in the center. These four types can be separated further into early, midseason, and late bloomers.

Peonies form bushy bundles of gorgeous, glossy, dark green leaves cut into bold leaflets, and they grow slowly into large, long-lived clumps. Even after their short bloom period, the attractive leaves remain green well into fall, when they may turn gleaming maroon. Plants grow 14 inches to 3 feet tall and as wide.

Peonies are spectacular as specimen plants in formal or informal gardens, or planted in drifts in large gardens. Excellent cut flower.

Site: Full sun; afternoon shade in South. Deep, humus-rich, fertile, moist soil. Plentiful moisture. Hardy in zones 2 to 8; in South grow early-season plants, single, and Japanese types for performance and disease resistance.
How to Grow: Plant dormant roots with two or three eyes in fall, positioning eyes 1 to 2 inches below soil surface. Plant well-rooted, container-grown plants in spring. Slow to establish; new plants may need two or three years to bloom well. May not bloom if planted too deep. Division unnecessary, but may be done on mature plants in fall.

Double types need staking. Best to inconspicuously stake individual flower stems rather than using ring support, which may cut stems. Avoid overhead watering when in bloom. Cut blossoms when buds are just beginning to open, leaving two sets of leaves. Gray mold fungus can be serious. Practice good sanitation; apply fungicide if necessary. Ants on buds are harmless.
Cultivars and Similar Species: More than 500 cultivars available; too

numerous to list. *Paeonia tenuifolia* (fern-leaf peony), early red blossoms, finely divided leaves.

PAPAVER ORIENTALE
Oriental Poppy

Oriental poppy's 6- to 10-inch, crepe-paper-like blossoms sway atop tall, prickly stems, creating a spectacular display for about 10 days in early summer. Flowers of the species are flaming red, but cultivars

PAPAVER ORIENTALE

come in shades of pink, orange, red, salmon, raspberry-purple, or white, with showy, dark, velvety stamens filling their centers. Black splotches sometimes decorate the petal bases, and fancier hybrids may be bicolored or double. Plants have deep taproots and a basal rosette of coarse, thistlelike foliage, which goes dormant by midsummer, but produces an overwintering rosette in fall. Foliage clumps grow to 2 feet tall and 3 feet wide; flower stalks 3 to 4 feet tall.

Oriental poppies are striking in cottage gardens and informal plantings; plant in groups of no more than three to avoid large midsummer gap. Combine with later-blooming or leafy plants, such as baby's-breath, which fills in bare spots.   *continued*

PAPAVER ORIENTALE
(continued)

Site: Full sun; part shade in hot areas. Deep, fertile to average, well-drained soil. Moderate moisture. Zones 3 to 7; best with cool summers.

How to Grow: Plant bare-root plants 1 to 3 inches below soil surface in late summer or early fall, or plant container-grown plants in spring, spacing 2 feet apart. Needs no division for years, but plants can be divided if desired in fall. May rot in winter-wet soil. May need staking. Remove faded flower stalks unless you want to harvest seedpods. Usually pest-free.

Cultivars: Early: 'Doubloon', orange flowers with rosy spots; 'China Boy', white with orange edges; 'Helen Elizabeth', crinkled, light salmon-pink; 'Red Flame', fiery red; 'Glowing Rose', watermelon pink; 'White King', white with purple splotches.

Midseason: 'Harvest Moon', orange-yellow flowers, double; 'Carnival', white with orange edges and black splotches; 'Snow Queen', bright white with purple splotches; 'Raspberry Queen', raspberry pink with black splotches.

Late: 'Bonfire', intense red flowers with black splotches, double; 'Golden Promise', golden orange with purple splotches; 'Springtime', white with pink edges.

PEROVSKIA ATRIPLICIFOLIA
Russian Sage

This long-blooming perennial begins its show of two-lipped, lavender-blue flowers in midsummer and carries on into fall. Tiny flowers decorate 1- to 1½-foot-tall, loosely branched panicles that create a delicate vertical effect above the bushy plants. Woolly, white hairs cover the flower stems above gray-green leaves with coarsely toothed edges for an overall misty, fine-textured result. The foliage of this

PEROVSKIA ATRIPLICIFOLIA

mint family member releases a sagelike pungence when crushed. Grows 3 to 5 feet tall; 3 feet wide.

Russian sage creates a silvery effect combined with grasses and other large-scale perennials in informal and naturalistic gardens.

Site: Full sun. Average to sandy or gravelly, well-drained soil. Moderate moisture; drought-tolerant. Zones 5 to 9; heat-tolerant.

How to Grow: Plant container-grown plants in spring, spacing 3 feet apart. Take cuttings in summer; needs no division. Tends to lean toward sun. Loose staking may be needed; cultivars are stronger-stemmed. Cut back woody stems to 1 foot tall in fall or late winter. Usually pest-free.

Cultivars: 'Blue Spire', deep blue flowers, finely dissected leaves, upright growth; 'Longin', narrow and strongly upright.

PHLOX SPP.
Phlox

Wild blue phlox or blue phlox (*Phlox divaricata*) a graceful, native wildflower puts on a showy display of long-stemmed clusters of pastel blue, lavender, or white flowers in mid to late spring. Each five-petaled, 1½-inch-wide flower has a

contrasting eye and a light fragrance. Narrow, dark green leaves decorate the upright flower stems and the creeping nonflowering stems, which spread out on the soil surface, rooting as they grow. Grows 12 to 15 inches tall in bloom; spreads to form 24-inch-wide clumps. Lovely where allowed to spread in wildflower or shade garden. Combine with ferns and hostas to provide interest after bloom period.

Today's garden phlox or summer phlox (*P. paniculata*) is nothing like the muddy magenta wild plant found growing along woodland edges in eastern North America. Hybridizers have developed spectacular flower heads in vivid colors, including crimson, rose, purple, lilac, lavender, red, pink, white, and a rare pure orange. Blooming usually for a month in July, August, or September,

PHLOX PANICULATA

depending on the cultivar, garden phlox often reblooms if immediately cut back. Flower domes are a foot or more in diameter, made up of 1-inch-wide, five-petaled, honey-scented flowers often accented by contrasting eyes. The upright stems are unbranched with smooth, lance-shaped leaves. Plants grow 3 to 5 feet tall; 2 feet wide. Garden phlox is beautiful if well-grown and scattered in cottage gardens or massed in midground of formal borders.

Creeping phlox (*P. stolonifera*) is a magnificent woodland wildflower that blooms lavishly in shady gardens from early to mid spring. Clusters of five-petaled flowers with contrasting eyes bloom on leafless stems held 6 to 8 inches above the leaves. The most

PHLOX STOLONIFERA 'BRUCE'S WHITE'

fragrant of the phloxes, its flowers may be pink, lavender, blue, or white with yellow eyes. The shiny, oval leaves are evergreen and form a dense groundcover.

Plants are 6 to 8 inches tall in bloom; spread to form 24-inch-wide mats. Use as a groundcover in shade and wildflower gardens and under shrubs. Makes a pretty edging.

Moss pink or moss phlox (*P. subulata*), a common spring bloomer, is the easiest of the phloxes to grow. For a month or more in early spring, its dense mats of spiky, green, evergreen foliage are obliterated by 1-inch-wide, pink, white, blue, or purple flowers. Most often seen in garish pink, cultivars also come in subtler colors. Grows 4 to 6 inches tall and forms wide-spreading mats. Moss pink makes a nice evergreen edging

plant and bulb companion for beds and borders. Excellent in rock gardens and walls, and along paving.

Site: Plant wild blue phlox in light shade, garden phlox and moss pink in full to half sun, and creeping phlox in light to full shade. Wild blue phlox, garden phlox, and creeping phlox prefer humus-rich, fertile, moist soil with plentiful moisture. Creeping phlox does best in neutral to acid soil. Plant moss pink in average or sandy, well-drained, neutral to alkaline soil with moderate moisture. Wild blue phlox is hardy in zones 3 to 9. Garden phlox is hardy in zones 4 to 8; best with cool summers. Creeping phlox is hardy in zones 2 to 8, moss pink in zones 2 to 9.

How to Grow: Plant container-grown or bare-root plants in spring. Space wild blue phlox 15 inches apart, garden phlox 3 feet apart, creeping phlox 1 to 2 feet apart, and moss pink 2 feet apart. Divide wild blue, creeping, and moss pink phlox just after blooming or in fall, as needed. Divide garden phlox every four years in spring or fall.

Wild blue phlox spreads slowly by creeping rhizomes. Shear back if attacked by mildew and also after flowers fade to neaten appearance.

Garden phlox is difficult to grow well. Remove every second or third new stalk in early spring to encourage strong growth, large flowers, and good air circulation. For a fuller look, pinch tips of foreground stems in early summer so flowers will be lower than those on the stems behind. Loose staking may be necessary. Gently rub out dried flowers from flower head as they fade until no new blossoms appear; then cut off flower heads to prevent seed formation (seedlings do not come true) and to encourage branching and reblooming.

Mulch creeping phlox lightly to protect its shallow roots, but avoid smothering the evergreen leaves. Allow plants to set seeds, if desired, then shear off dried stems.

Moss pink is easy to grow. Shear it after blooming to neaten.

Wild blue phlox is somewhat susceptible to mildew and slug damage. Garden phlox is highly susceptible to mildew; provide good air circulation, avoid overhead watering and wetting foliage at night, and use fungicide if needed. Choose mildew-resistant cultivars. Mites are troublesome in full sun and if soil dries out. Creeping phlox is not troubled by mildew as are other phloxes. Moss pink may get spider mites if grown in a location that's too hot and dry, or root rot in a winter-wet site.

Cultivars and Similar Species: Wild blue phlox: 'Fuller's White', pure white flowers, notched petals, extremely floriferous, 10 inches tall; 'Dirigo Ice', pale blue, 8 to 12 inches tall; 'Chattahoochee', hybrid, deep violet-blue with purple eye, long-blooming.

Garden phlox: 'Blue Boy', near-blue flowers; 'Mt. Fuji', white, long-blooming, mildew-resistant; 'The King', deep purple, long-blooming; 'Sir John Falstaff', salmon-pink with deeper eye, long-blooming; 'Starfire', true red flowers, maroon foliage; 'World Peace', white, late-blooming; 'Bright Eyes', soft pink with rose eye; 'Eva Cullum', bright pink with red eye, disease-resistant; 'Orange Perfection', clear orange; 'Franz Shubert', lilac; 'Nora Leigh', white-edged foliage, lavender flowers; 'David', white flowers, highly mildew-resistant. *P. maculata* 'Miss Lingard', white, earlier blooming, but similar to garden phlox, mildew-resistant.

Creeping phlox: 'Blue Ridge', large, lavender-blue flowers; 'Bruce's White', large, white flowers with yellow eye; 'Home Fires', bright rose-pink; 'Pink Ridge', medium pink, fragrant; 'Sherwood Purple', rich pastel purple, fragrant.

Moss pink: 'Blue Emerald', medium blue-lavender flowers; 'Pink Emerald', rose-pink; 'Scarlet Flame', rose-red; 'White Delight', large, white flowers; 'Amazing Grace', white with rose centers; 'Atropurpurea', *continued*

Perennials

PHLOX SPP.
(continued)

wine red; 'Candy Stripe', pink-and-white flowers; 'Apple Blossom', pale pink; 'Coral Eye', white with coral eye, reblooms; 'Snowflake', compact, white star-shaped flowers.

PHYSOSTEGIA VIRGINIANA
Obedient Plant, False Dragonhead

Named obedient because its snapdragon-like flowers remain facing whichever way they're pushed, this native plant makes a bold addition to any garden. The lance-shaped, shiny, dark green leaves with toothed edges are arranged in two ranks, like a cross, around the upright

PHYSOSTEGIA VIRGINIANA 'ALBA'

stems. Tightly clustered, 1½-inch-long, tubular, two-lipped pink, magenta-pink, or white flowers also are arranged in ranks, forming striking spires above the leaves from late summer into fall. Plants grow 3 to 4 feet tall and form clumps up to 3 feet wide. Obedient plant is excellent for late-summer color in borders and naturalistic gardens.

Site: Full to half sun. Average well-drained soil. Moderate to plentiful moisture. Zones 2 to 9; tolerates heat and humidity.

How to Grow: Plant bare-root or container-grown plants in spring, spacing 2 feet apart. Divide in spring every two or three years. Spreads aggressively. Needs staking in fertile soil or shade. Cut back after blooming to encourage rebloom. Rust fungus may be troublesome.

Cultivars: 'Vivid', compact to 20 inches tall, bright orchid-pink flowers; 'Pink Bouquet', rose-pink, 3 feet tall; 'Bouquet Rose', 3 feet tall, rose-pink; 'Summer Snow', white, earlier-blooming, 2½ feet tall, less invasive; 'Variegata', pink flowers, 3½ feet tall, white-edged leaves.

PLATYCODON GRANDIFLORUS
Balloonflower

Balloonflower's 3-inch-wide, cup-shaped flowers open from beautiful, inflated flower buds that look like tiny hot-air balloons. Somewhat resembling bellflowers,

PLATYCODON GRANDIFLORUS 'DOUBLE BLUE'

balloonflower features petals with an intricate netting of dark veins surrounding white stamens. Usually rich purplish blue, the long-blooming,

mid- to late-summer flowers also may be pink or white and occasionally double. The upright, succulent stems emit a milky sap if broken and bear oval, blue-green leaves that turn golden yellow in fall. Plants grow 2 to 3 feet tall; 1½ feet wide.

Excellent for summer gardens, this plant combines well with daylilies, lilies, and Japanese anemones.

Site: Full sun in North; part shade in South. Deep, fertile to average, well-drained soil. Plentiful moisture. Zones 3 to 8.

How to Grow: Plant bare-root or container-grown plants in spring, spacing 2 feet apart. Needs no division, but fleshy roots may be carefully divided in spring.

Tall forms need staking to prevent floppiness. Emerges late in spring; avoid disturbing. Transplant deep taproots with care. Deadhead individual flowers every few days to promote long flowering; cut back to encourage second bloom flush after flowering ceases. Usually pest-free.

Cultivars: 'Mariesii', deep blue-lavender flowers, 30 inches tall, no staking; 'Shell Pink', pastel pink, 2 feet tall; 'Alba', white, 3 feet tall; 'Double Blue', double, violet-blue flowers, 3 feet tall; 'Fuji White', pure white, 20 inches tall; 'Misato Purple', purple, 15 inches tall, early; 'Hime Murasaki', lavender-blue, 12 inches tall; 'Fuji Pink', pink flowers, 20 inches tall; 'Hakone Blue', double, violet-blue flowers, 20 inches tall.

PRIMULA SPP.
Primrose

A candelabrum of 1-inch flowers arranged in five or six tiers characterizes the elegant, moisture-loving Japanese primrose (*Primula japonica*). Flowers may be purple, magenta, rose, pink, or white with light or dark eyes and bloom from mid spring to early summer. Plants self-sow where happily situated to create thick stands in a delightful assortment of color patterns. The rough-textured leaves form basal clumps reminiscent of romaine lettuce. Flower stalks grow to 2 feet tall; leafy clumps 8 to 10 inches tall and to 2 feet wide. This primrose is best grown in a naturalistic setting along a stream or in a bog.

PRIMULA × POLYANTHA

A favorite springtime florist plant, the polyanthus or English primrose (*P. × polyantha*) has ancient roots. It was cultivated and hybridized from several English wildflowers including *P. vulgaris* during Elizabethan times. Modern hybrids feature bunches of 2-inch, short-stemmed flowers in electric colors, including blue, purple, yellow, pink, and red, with yellow eyes. Blooming throughout spring, English primrose forms rosettes of small, heavily crinkled, oblong leaves that grow larger after flowering ceases. Flower stalks grow to 1 foot tall; leaf clusters grow to 6 to 7 inches tall and wide. Plant English primrose in drifts in a shade garden or along a woodland path.

Site: Give Japanese primrose light shade in moist site; part to full sun in wet or boggy site. English primrose is best in light shade. Both like humus-rich, fertile soil. Japanese primrose thrives in an acid pH and tolerates heavy soil; needs a constantly moist, wet, or boggy site. English primrose needs well-drained soil and plentiful moisture. Japanese primrose is hardy in zones 5 to 7; polyanthus primrose in zones 6 to 8, best with cool summers.

How to Grow: Plant container-grown Japanese primrose plants in spring, English primrose in early spring. Space Japanese primrose 3 feet apart, English primrose 1 foot apart. Plant English primrose in fall for winter bloom in mild-winter areas; plant florist plants in garden when soil warms. Divide Japanese primrose in fall as desired; divide polyanthus primrose every few years.

Mulch heavily to keep soil cool. Water during dry spells. Protect shallow roots of English primrose from heaving with winter mulch of evergreen boughs. Slugs and snails are troublesome; spider mites cause problems for English primrose if too hot and dry.

Cultivars and Similar Species: Japanese primrose: 'Album', white, 16 inches tall; 'Carmina', rose-red; 'Miller's Crimson', crimson; 'Redfield Hybrids', cold-hardy mix.

English primrose: 'Pacific Giants', seed-grown, large-flowered hybrids; 'Crescendo Hybrids', cold-hardy, large-flowered, tall-stemmed, seed-grown, may rebloom in fall. *P. veris* (cowslip), slender stems of tubular, bright yellow flowers in one-sided bunches, zones 3 to 8.

PULMONARIA SPP.
Lungwort, Bethlehem Sage

Valued by early herbalists as a cure for lung ailments because the leaves are lung-shaped and bear white spots like diseased lungs, common lungwort (*Pulmonaria officinalis*) is one of the earliest lungworts to bloom.

Bright pink, funnel-shaped flowers, which fade to bluish lilac, open along with the earliest bulbs. The bristly, white-spotted leaves are evergreen except during the harshest winters. Grows 1 foot tall; 1½ feet wide.

PULMONARIA SACCHARATA 'MRS. MOON'

The most ornamental lungwort, Bethlehem sage (*P. saccharata*) has rough-haired, elliptical evergreen leaves with variable spotting—in some types silver spots are distinct, in others, spots coalesce into allover silver. In early spring, coiled clusters of pink flower buds open to pink, funnel-shaped flowers which age to blue. Plants grow 1 to 1½ feet tall and 2 feet wide.

Both plants make an eye-catching groundcover in shade gardens; combine them with bulbs, hostas, ferns, and other tall perennials.

Site: Light to full shade. Humus-rich, fertile, well-drained, moist soil. Plentiful moisture. Hardy in zones 3 to 8.

How to Grow: Plant bare-root or container-grown plants in spring, spacing common lungwort 1 foot apart, Bethlehem sage 1 to 2 feet apart. Divide after flowering when needed. Remove faded flower stalks. Wearing gloves, remove older leaves as they fade in early summer to make room for new growth. Keep soil moist. *continued*

PULMONARIA SPP.
(continued)

Powdery mildew may occur if soil is too dry.
Cultivars and Similar Species:
Bethlehem sage: 'Mrs. Moon', silver-spotted leaves, pink flowers turn blue, hybrid; 'Margery Fish', vigorous; 'Sissinghurst White', white flowers, silver-spotted leaves; 'Pink Dawn', pink flowers don't change color, silver-spotted leaves; 'Janet Fisk', white-marbled leaves.

P. longifolia, nonaggressive, clump-forming, long, narrow, pointed leaves dappled with silver, purple-blue flowers; 'Roy Davidson', bright spots.

RODGERSIA AESCULIFOLIA
Finger-Leaf Rodgersia

A foliage plant par excellence, finger-leaf rodgersia bears huge, bronze-tinged, compound leaves resembling those of horse chestnut. The long-stalked leaves are divided into 7-inch-long leaflets like fingers on

RODGERSIA PODOPHYLLA

a hand. These form a large basal rosette of foliage, above which rises a flat, pyramidal cluster of feathery, creamy white or pinkish flowers in early summer. Coarse brown hairs cover the leaf veins, stems, and flower stalks. Foliage clumps grow 2 to 3 feet high and 3 to 6 feet wide; flower stalks 3 to 6 feet tall. Use single specimens in shade or bog gardens, along streams and ponds for dramatic contrasting size and texture. Allow plenty of growing space.

Site: Light to part shade best; full sun in constantly wet site. Fertile, humus-rich, moist to boggy soil. Plentiful moisture. Zones 5 to 6; performs poorly where hot and humid.
How to Grow: Plant container-grown plants in spring, spacing 4 to 5 feet apart. Divide in early spring after four or five years, if desired. Provide plenty of moisture; leaves scorch in too much sun or if too dry. Usually pest-free.
Similar Species: *Rodgersia podophylla*, similar with lobed leaf tips, foliage often bronze in spring and fall, zones 5 to 7. *R. pinnata* (feather-leaf rodgersia), leaves divided into five to nine 8-inch-long leaflets, rose-red flowers in late spring, zones 5 to 7; 'Superba', bronze-purple leaves.

RUDBECKIA SPP.
Coneflower

The prolific flowers of orange coneflower (*Rudbeckia fulgida*) resemble black-eyed Susan and consist of golden orange ray petals surrounding a raised, dark brown cone. The 3-inch-wide, daisy-type flowers bloom in branched clusters above coarse foliage from midsummer until frost. The broad, pointed leaves are dark green with a smooth texture. Orange coneflower grows 2 to 3 feet tall and spreads rapidly to form 2- to 3-foot-wide clumps. It is popular massed with grasses and perennials in low-maintenance landscapes; excellent for late color in informal, cottage, or cut-flower gardens.

Tall and dramatic, shining coneflower (*R. nitida*) provides late-season color with its 5-inch, daisylike flowers, which consist of drooping, bright yellow petals surrounding a greenish, columnar, raised disk. Dark green leaves are rounded with a few coarse teeth, forming a bushy base. Branched and sparsely leaved flowering stems rise above the base. Grows 3 to 4 feet tall and 3 feet wide.

RUDBECKIA FULGIDA 'GOLDSTURM'

Excellent back-of-border plant for informal gardens; naturalize in meadows; mass plant in easy-care gardens. Long-lasting cut flower.

Site: Full sun best; orange coneflower also tolerates half sun. Orange coneflower prefers fertile to average, humus-rich to clay soil. Plentiful moisture best; drought-tolerant once established. Give shining coneflower fertile, well-drained soil with plentiful to moderate moisture. Orange coneflower is hardy in zones 3 to 9; shining coneflower in zones 4 to 10, thrives in heat and humidity of South.
How to Grow: Plant container-grown plants in spring, spacing orange coneflower 1 to 2 feet apart, shining coneflower 3 feet apart. Divide in spring or fall every three or four years. Allow dried seed heads of orange coneflower to remain all winter; cut back in early spring. Individual stems of shining coneflower may need staking, especially in South or in part shade.

Deadheading encourages longer bloom. Usually pest-free; mildew may be troublesome at end of summer.

Cultivars and Similar Species: Orange coneflower: 'Goldsturm', compact, floriferous, cutting-grown plants superior and more uniform than seed-grown plants.

Shining coneflower: *R. laciniata* (green-eyed coneflower, cut-leaf coneflower), very similar, drooping lemon yellow petals surrounding raised olive green cones in late summer and fall, deeply cut leaves, 8 feet tall, zones 3 to 9; 'Golden Glow', double, lemon yellow flowers, 3 to 6 feet tall; 'Autumn Sun', 3 to 5 feet tall, needs no staking; 'Autumn Glory', 5 feet tall; 'Goldquelle', shaggy, double yellow, 2 to 3 feet tall.

SALVIA × SUPERBA
Hybrid Salvia

This hybrid sage is one of the showiest and longest-blooming of the cold-hardy salvias. Dense spikes of tubular, purple-violet flowers with wine red bracts bloom above

SALVIA × SUPERBA

woody-based mounds of pungent foliage in early summer. After flowers fade, the bracts remain showy, but if the old spikes are removed, another crop of fresh flowers develops. Oblong, gray-green, 3-inch-long leaves make a nice contrast to the rich-colored flowers. Grows 1½ to 3 feet tall, spreading to 3-foot-wide clumps. Offer vertical effect and violet color in informal and formal gardens.

Site: Full sun. Fertile to average, moist soil. Moderate moisture best, but tolerates drought once established. Zones 4 to 7. Best with cool nights; performs poorly in heat and humidity.

How to Grow: Plant container-grown plants in spring, spacing 2 to 3 feet apart. Divide in early spring every four or five years, being careful with woody base. Cut back hard after each flush of flowers to encourage repeat bloom. Tall types may need staking in hot areas. Usually pest-free.

Cultivars and Similar Species: 'Blue Hill', true blue flowers, 18 inches tall; 'Blue Queen', violet-blue, 18 inches tall; 'East Friesland', deep purple, 18 inches tall; 'May Night', deep indigo-blue, early-blooming, 18 inches tall; 'Rose Queen', rose-pink, 24 inches tall; *Salvia azurea* var. *grandiflora* or *S. pitcheri* (azure sage), 4 to 6 feet tall, stake with tall brush or allow to lean on nearby plants, zones 5 to 9.

SCABIOSA CAUCASICA
Pincushion Flower

Valued for its long-blooming blue flowers that begin appearing in midsummer, pincushion flower continues producing blossoms until fall. Its lance shaped, fuzzy, gray-green basal foliage forms evergreen clumps. Sparse, lobed leaves occur along slender, flowering stems, which are topped with solitary, flat, 3- to 4-inch-wide flower heads. Many tightly packed flowers with lobed petals and gray-tipped stamens make up the inflorescences; petals around the outside of the flower head are larger, giving it a lacy frame. Flowers

are most commonly light lavender-blue, but deep blue, white, and pink forms also are available. Flower stems grow 1½ to 2 feet tall; foliage clumps are 6 inches tall and 18 inches wide. Plant pincushion flower in groups in front of cottage, rock, and informal gardens.

SCABIOSA CAUCASICA

Site: Full sun in North, part shade in South. Fertile, humus-rich, moist soil. Plentiful moisture. Zones 3 to 7; best with cool summers.

How to Grow: Plant container-grown plants in spring, spacing 1 to 2 feet apart. Divide in spring every four years. Remove faded flowers to promote continual bloom. Mulch well in summer. Slugs may be troublesome.

Cultivars and Similar Species: 'Kompliment', deep lavender-blue flowers, 24 inches tall; 'Butterfly Blue', lavender-blue flowers blooming until frost, 12 inches tall; 'Perfecta', light lavender-blue flowers, 18 to 24 inches tall; 'Fama', intense sky blue flowers, 20 inches tall; 'Pink Mist', rose-pink flowers blooming until frost, 12 inches tall; 'Perfecta Alba', white flowers, 18 to 24 inches tall.

Perennials

SEDUM SPP.
(HYLOTELEPHIUM SPP.)
Stonecrop

A deciduous, ground-hugging plant, *Sedum cauticolum* features woody, purplish stems and round, succulent, 1- to 2-inch-wide, blue-gray leaves. Clusters of starry, rose-pink flowers bloom in late summer and fall. Plants grow 2 to 4 inches tall and 8 to 10 inches wide. Purple-leaved forms make excellent specimens for contrasting colorful foliage and late flowers in borders and rock gardens. Use low, spreading types for groundcovers and edgings.

SEDUM × TELEPHIUM 'AUTUMN JOY'

Autumn Joy sedum (*S. × telephium* 'Autumn Joy') creates a changing sight through much of the year. Its shoots poke through the ground in early spring, creating clusters of whorled, succulent, jade green leaves. By midsummer, pale green flower heads resembling broccoli top the stems. These turn pale pink in late summer, bright pink in fall, and rose-red with the onset of cold weather. Frost turns the whole plant rusty-bronze and the sturdy dried stems and seed heads stand all winter, adding an extra dimension to the garden. Plants grow 18 to 24 inches tall and wide. Mass-plant Autumn Joy in low-maintenance gardens or in groups in beds and borders. Attracts butterflies. Dried seed heads are attractive.

Site: Full sun best; Autumn Joy tolerates part shade. Average to sandy, well-drained soil. Moderate moisture. Autumn Joy is drought-tolerant. *S. cauticolum* is hardy in zones 5 to 9, Autumn Joy sedum in zones 3 to 10.

How to Grow: Plant bare-root or container-grown plants in spring, spacing *S. cauticolum* 8 inches apart, Autumn Joy 2 to 3 feet apart. Divide in spring, *S. cauticolum* when needed and Autumn Joy every four years.

S. cauticolum tolerates moist soil better than other sedums. Autumn Joy may sprawl in part shade; provide support or pinch in midsummer. Both are usually pest-free.

Cultivars and Similar Species: Groundcover types: *S. spurium*, mat-forming, dense, 1-inch semievergreen leaves, zones 3 to 9; 'Dragon's Blood', bronze leaves, blood red summer flowers; 'Tricolor', red-green-and-white leaves, pink flowers; 'Album Superbum', white flowers, bronze foliage. *S. kamtschaticum* (Kamtschatka stonecrop, golden stonecrop), pale green stems, succulent, scalloped, 2-inch rounded leaves, flat clusters of dark orange-yellow flowers in summer, as flowers die back, new rosettes of foliage form at bases, 4 to 9 inches tall, 12 to 15 inches wide; 'Variegatum', green-and-creamy white leaves with pink tinge; *middendorffianum*, needlelike leaves of red-bronze. *S. spathulifolium*, evergreen, groundcovering, dusty blue or red-tinged green leaves, yellow summer flowers, zones 3 to 8.

Tall sedums: 'Atropurpureum', bronze-purple leaves, weakly upright stems, cream-rose flowers. *S. spectabile* (showy stonecrop), similar, 18 to 24 inches tall, blooms earlier, less sturdy in winter; 'Brilliant', light lavender-pink flowers; 'Stardust', silvery pinkish white flowers; 'Meteor', carmine-red flowers, 18 inches tall; 'Variegatum', green-edged creamy yellow leaves; pink flowers.

SOLIDAGO HYBRIDS
Goldenrod

P rized in Europe as a late-blooming perennial, our native goldenrods have only recently found a place in North American gardens. Wrongly blamed for causing hay fever because they bloom at the same time as ragweed, goldenrod has an ill-deserved bad reputation. Garden-worthy hybrids, mostly bred in

SOLIDAGO 'PETER PAN'

Europe, bring large, feathery plumes of tiny, daisylike, golden yellow blossoms to gardens in late summer and fall. The toothed, dark green leaves form handsome clumps. Some types spread aggressively; other types are better behaved. Plants grow 2 to 3 feet tall and spread to form 3- to 4-foot-wide clumps. Goldenrod offers wonderful form and color to combine with ornamental grasses, coneflowers, and asters in fall gardens. A good cut flower.

Site: Full sun. Average to poor, well-drained soil. Moderate moisture; drought-tolerant. Zones 3 to 9.
How to Grow: Plant bare-root or container-grown plants in spring, spacing 2 feet apart. Divide every three years to control spreading. May grow rampantly and flop in fertile soil. Usually needs no staking. Pest-free.
Cultivars: Hybrids bred from several native species are compact and floriferous: 'Crown of Rays', yellow-gold flowers, late summer; 'Golden Dwarf', golden yellow, 12 inches tall; 'Peter Pan', bright yellow, 2 feet tall, midsummer and fall; 'Golden Baby', canary yellow, 2½ feet tall; 'Baby Sun', clear yellow, midsummer, 12 inches tall.

STACHYS BYZANTINA
Lamb's-Ears

With leaves the shape, size, and plushness of lamb's ears, this plant's common name is obvious. Forming groundcovering evergreen clumps of thick, 6- to 10-inch-long,

STACHYS BYZANTINA

silver-furred leaves, lamb's-ears makes an indispensable addition to almost any garden. The summer flower stalks are also silvery white, furred with odd-looking clusters of magenta flowers tucked at their tops. Some gardeners like the flowers; others cut them off as they form, admiring the

plant for its foliage alone. Foliage clumps grow 6 inches tall and 2 feet wide; flower stalks 2½ feet tall.

The silver foliage of lamb's-ears combines well with almost any color. Use it as edging or border in formal and informal situations and as groundcover under roses and tulips.

Site: Full sun. Fertile to poor, well-drained soil. Moderate moisture; drought-tolerant. Zones 4 to 8; tolerates hot, dry sites.
How to Grow: Plant bare-root or container-grown plants in spring, spacing 1 to 2 feet apart. Divide in spring or fall as needed to control spread. Gently rake out or hand-pull winter-tattered leaves in early spring to make room for new growth. Remove flower stalks as they fade, if not earlier. Avoid overhead watering. May be invasive. Crown and leaf rot may occur in humid or wet-summer areas.
Cultivars: 'Silver Carpet', nonblooming form, best choice for edging; 'Helene Von Stein', huge leaves twice as large as species.

STOKESIA LAEVIS
Stokes' Aster

Improved selections of this southeastern wildflower are fashionable, long-blooming garden subjects. Broadly lance-shaped, shiny green leaves with prominent white midribs form attractive evergreen rosettes. Flowering begins in early to midsummer when the loosely branched, hairy flower stalks bearing 3- to 5-inch-wide, flat, lavender-blue, pink, or white flower heads develop. Flowers have two rows of ragged-toothed petals surrounding fuzzy, creamy white centers. As long as faded stalks are removed, more flower stalks will form after the initial flush, extending the bloom season into fall and even winter where the climate is mild. Flower

STOKESIA LAEVIS

stalks grow 12 to 24 inches tall; clumps spread to 18 inches wide. Plant in groups in the foreground of informal flower gardens.

Site: Full sun to part shade. Average to sandy, well-drained, moist soil. Moderate moisture. Zones 5 to 9.
How to Grow: Plant container-grown plants in spring, spacing 15 inches apart. Divide in spring every three or four years. Deadhead regularly to prolong bloom. Provide winter mulch in North. Crown rot is troublesome if not well-drained in winter.
Cultivars: 'Blue Danube', deep blue flowers; 'Klaus Jelitto', 5-inch pale blue flowers; 'Wyoming', dark blue; 'Silver Moon', 5-inch, white flowers; 'Rosea', rosy pink.

TIARELLA CORDIFOLIA
Foamflower

A woodland wildflower native up and down the East Coast, foamflower is aptly named after its foamy clusters of creamy white flower spires. Flowers bloom above the foliage at the tips of straight, wiry stems for four to six weeks beginning in mid spring. Many woodland wildflowers die to the ground after flowering, but foamflower's sharply toothed, maple-shaped leaves are evergreen, often *continued*

Perennials

TIARELLA CORDIFOLIA
(continued)

TIARELLA CORDIFOLIA

decoratively marked with dark veins or mottling. Plants spread enthusiastically by runners and make a good groundcover. Foliage clumps grow to 6 inches tall and 3 feet wide; flowers to 18 inches tall.

Foamflower is a spectacular groundcover for shade and woodland gardens; use under taller plants and shrubs. Use clump forms near low, woodland wildflowers so they won't be overrun.

Site: Light to full shade. Humus-rich, fertile, moist soil. Plentiful moisture. Zones 3 to 9.
How to Grow: Plant container-grown plants in spring, spacing 2 to 3 feet apart. Divide every three or four years in spring or fall. May burn in cold, snowless winters. Rake away tattered leaves in early spring to make room for new growth. Shear off faded flower spikes to encourage repeat bloom. Usually pest-free.
Cultivars and Similar Species: 'Brandywine', pink-tinged flowers, leaves with wine-red centers. *Tiarella cordifolia* var. *collina/T. wherryi*, runnerless, forms clumps; 'Oakleaf',

profuse pink-tinged white flowers for six to eight weeks, new red leaves mature to dark green, then turn burgundy in fall and winter.

VERBENA SPP.
Verbena

Clump verbena or rose verbena *(Verbena canadensis)*, a perennial version of the popular bedding verbena *(V. × hybrida)* is native to the Southwest and Mexico. Plants form effective, cascading clumps whose creeping stems root as

VERBENA CANADENSIS 'HOMESTEAD PURPLE'

they go and form billowing masses of foliage and flowers. Showy circular clusters of small, hot pink or purple flowers blanket the plants from early summer until fall. The wedge-shaped, toothed leaves are evergreen, but take on burgundy hues in winter. Grows 8 to 18 inches tall; 3 feet wide. Plant to tumble over walls or slopes or in rock gardens. Also works well in containers or as foreground planting.

Site: Full sun. Average, well-drained soil. Moderate moisture; drought-tolerant. Zones 6 to 10; tolerant of seashore conditions, heat, and drought.
How to Grow: Plant container-grown plants in spring, spacing 3 feet apart.

Divide in spring or fall, every three or four years; take cuttings in spring. Cut back stems hard if plant becomes scraggly or grows out of bounds. Crown rot and mildew can occur in damp sites; spider mites if too dry.
Cultivars and Similar Species: 'Homestead Purple', dark purple flowers, early-blooming; 'Sissinghurst', deep pink flowers; 'Old Royal Fragrance', lavender-and-white, fragrant; 'Springbrook', rose-pink flowers. *V. tenuisecta* (moss verbena), 1 foot tall, 1½ feet wide, finely divided leaves, lilac-lavender flowers, zones 8 to 10, self-sows in colder areas or may be grown as annual; 'Imagination', violet-blue flowers.

VERONICA SPP.
Speedwell

Long-lived, easy-care Hungarian speedwell *(Veronica austriaca* subsp. *teucrium)* spreads slowly to form a weakly upright, spreading

VERONICA SPICATA 'MINUET'

mound of 1½-inch-long, somewhat-toothed leaves. Star-shaped, deep blue flowers blanket the plants for a month in late spring and early summer and may rebloom later in summer. Unlike most other speedwells, the spikes arise from along the sides of the branches rather than from their tips, creating a fuller, less vertical effect.

Plants form a mound 6 to 20 inches tall; spreads 3 to 4 feet wide. Pure blue flowers combine well with pastel yellow, pink, and white flowers.

Crowned in late spring and early summer with dense, 1- to 3-foot-long spikes of tiny, pure blue flowers with long, purple stamens, spike speedwell (*V. spicata*) may produce a second flush of bloom later in summer. Cultivars offer flowers in shades of pink, lavender, blue, and white. The evergreen plants form low clumps of scalloped, oval, dark green leaves, but one beautiful form is decorated with woolly, white, feltlike foliage. Grows 6 to 18 inches tall and 2 feet wide. Speedwells are wonderful massed for vertical effect in foreground of beds and borders.

Site: Full sun best; tolerates half shade. Humus-rich to average, slightly acid to alkaline, moist but well-drained soil. Moderate to plentiful moisture. Hardy in zones 3 to 8.
How to Grow: Plant container-grown plants in spring, spacing Hungarian speedwell 2 to 3 feet apart, spike speedwell 2 feet apart. Divide in early spring or fall every three to five years. Take stem cuttings in summer.

Cut back after flowering to neaten and encourage reblooming. Hungarian speedwell is usually pest-free. Spike speedwell may get root rot in winter-wet sites in South. Mildew and leaf spot occasionally troublesome.
Cultivars and Similar Species:
Hungarian speedwell: 'Crater Lake Blue', navy blue flowers, 12 to 15 inches tall; 'Trehane', bright blue flowers, golden foliage, 6 inches tall; 'Royal Blue', bright blue, 12 inches tall. *V. repens* (creeping speedwell), light blue flowers, rapidly spreading, ground-hugging mat.

Spike speedwell: 'Icicle', white flowers, 24 inches tall; 'Blue Peter', dark blue, 18 inches tall; 'Red Fox', deep rose-red, 15 inches tall, midsummer; 'Blue Charm', blue-violet, 18 inches tall.

Hybrids: 'Minuet', pale pink flowers, gray-green foliage; 'Barcarolle', rose-pink flowers, 10 inches tall, gray-green leaves; 'Sunny Border Blue', dark violet-blue flowers all summer into fall, rounded leaves, 18 inches tall; 'Foerster's Blue', dark blue, 18 inches tall; 'Rosea', pink, 3 feet tall.

VIOLA SPP.
Violet, Viola

Resembling a small pansy, the horned violet or viola (*Viola cornuta*) is a hardy perennial hailing from the Pyrenees Mountains. The 1- to 1½-inch-wide, rounded flowers have five petals, a short spur, and may or may not have pansylike faces. Blossoms form on single stems from the leaf axils, transforming the tufted mounds of egg-shaped leaves into a mass of color during spring and early summer and again when weather

VIOLA CORNUTA 'SCOTTISH YELLOW'

cools in fall. Grows 5 to 12 inches tall and as wide. Use horned violet as an edging or foreground plant; combines well with tulips and other spring-flowering bulbs.

Once grown for perfume, the sweet violet (*V. odorata*) produces fragrant, short-spurred purple blossoms on long stems that rise directly from the rootstocks. The irregularly shaped

flowers are made of five petals marked with dark veins and small beards near the flower's center. Blossoms peek just above the foliage from early to late spring. Semievergreen heart-shaped leaves have bluntly serrated edges and are covered with fine hairs. They also arise directly from the creeping rootstocks. Plants grow 8 inches tall; 15 inches wide. Plant sweet violet in naturalistic settings such as woodland gardens. A pretty cut flower.

Site: Light to part shade; horned violet tolerates full sun where cool, sweet violet takes full sun if constantly moist. Humus-rich, fertile, well-drained but moist soil. Plentiful moisture. Hardy in zones 6 to 9.
How to Grow: Plant bare-root or container-grown plants in spring, spacing 1 foot apart. Divide horned violet in spring or fall, sweet violet in fall when crowded.

Deadhead horned violet regularly to prolong bloom; cut back after first bloom flush to encourage rebloom in late summer and fall. Self-sown sweet violet seedlings may become weedy, and creeping plants may be invasive; diligent weeding necessary.

Spider mites sometimes trouble horned violet in hot sites; slugs and snails often troublesome. Leaf spot may bother sweet violet.
Cultivars: Horned violet: 'Chantreyland', large, faceless, apricot flowers; 'Jersey Gem', bright blue; 'White Perfection', pure white; 'Nellie Britton', lavender-pink flowers with face; 'Arkwright Ruby', deep red flowers with face; 'Baby Franjo', light yellow; 'Baby Lucia', sky blue; 'Blue Perfection', sky blue; 'Scottish Yellow', bright yellow, no face.

Sweet violet: 'Black Magic', black blossoms with yellow eyes; 'Czar', deep violet; 'White Czar', pure white; 'Rosina', mauve-pink; 'Queen Charlotte', dark blue; 'Royal Robe', large, long-stemmed, deep violet-blue flowers.

Ornamental Grasses

BRIZA MEDIA
Quaking Grass, Rattlesnake Grass

The flowers of this small, clump-forming, cool-season, evergreen grass resemble rattlesnake tails. Opening luminescent green and faintly striped with purple in spring

BRIZA MEDIA

and maturing to golden seed heads in summer, the tiny flower spikelets shake and quiver delightfully in the slightest breeze, but shatter by summer's end. Flower stalks rise above the dense clumps of soft-to-the-touch linear leaves. Cut flowers (both green and tan flowers) at various stages of maturity for fresh and dried arrangements. Foliage grows 12 to 18 inches tall; flowers 1 foot taller. Individual plants not very interesting; best used as groundcover in a meadow or naturalistic garden or in cut-flower garden.

Site: Full sun to part shade. Average to poor, moist to wet soil; becomes coarse in fertile soil. Zones 4 to 8; tolerates heat with regular water.
How to Grow: Plant container-grown plants in spring, spacing 2 feet apart, or sow seeds. Divide in spring or fall. Remove tattered flower heads. If plant looks ragged, cut back to several

inches from ground in summer to renew. Usually pest-free.
Similar Species: *Briza maxima* (annual quaking grass), 2 to 3 feet tall, loose, quaking spikes of large, light green spikelets in early summer; use in meadows or cut-flower gardens.

CALAMAGROSTIS × ACUTIFLORA 'STRICTA'
Feather Reed Grass

Stiffly upright, this cool-season clump grass changes alluringly through the seasons. Spring brings a fountain of light green leaves, which by early summer is topped with tall, feathery, pink inflorescences. These change to light purple in early summer and by midsummer ripen into golden wheatlike sheaves. The sterile

CALAMAGROSTIS × ACUTIFLORA 'STRICTA'

seed heads remain attractive into fall, when the green leaves turn gold and stand through winter. Grows 6 to 7 feet tall; 2 to 3 feet wide.

A handsome specimen in formal gardens; mass-plant as screening in low-maintenance landscapes or around ponds.

Site: Best in full sun; tolerates half shade. Average to heavy, well-drained to wet soil. Zones 5 to 9.

How to Grow: Plant container-grown plants in spring, spacing 3 feet apart. Cut back in late winter. Foliage rust disease is an occasional problem.
Cultivars: 'Karl Foerster', 5 to 6 feet tall, blooms two weeks earlier.

CAREX SPP.
Sedge

Forming a dense, arching mound of stiff, ½-inch-wide leaves, Japanese sedge (*Carex morrowii*) is a grasslike plant that thrives in shade, remaining evergreen or semievergreen

CAREX ELATA 'AUREA'

through most winters to add texture and color to the dull months. Flowers are insignificant, tucked among the leaves in summer. Variegated forms with gold or white stripes are most popular and are especially nice in shade gardens. Grows 12 to 18 inches tall; 2 to 3 feet wide. Use as specimen or groundcover in shade gardens.

Sending up light green shoots in spring, Bowles golden tufted sedge (*C. elata* 'Bowles Golden') brings welcome greenery to shady sites. The narrow, upright leaves of this cool-season, grasslike plant bend at their tips, creating a loose, vase-shaped mound of cascading foliage that turns luminous golden green or chartreuse with narrow, green margins in summer. Brightest yellow of all the grasses, Bowles golden tufted sedge retains color until a heavy frost. Flowers are not showy. Grows 20 inches tall. Creates the effect of sunlight in shade. Use with gold-variegated hostas. Does well in wet sites, such as beside a pond.

Site: Light to full shade; Bowles golden tufted sedge needs more shade in South than North. Fertile to average, humus-rich, well-drained but moist soil. Plentiful moisture. Japanese sedge is hardy in zones 5 to 9, Bowles golden tufted sedge in zones 7 to 9.
How to Grow: Plant container-grown plants in spring, spacing Japanese sedge 3 feet apart, Bowles golden 12 to 18 inches apart. Divide Japanese sedge clumps in spring, Bowles golden in spring or fall. Hand-pull winter-tattered leaves from clumps; don't cut back. Usually pest-free.
Cultivars: Japanese sedge: 'Variegata', green with thin, white leaf margins; 'Goldband', gold-striped leaf edges, zones 7 to 9; 'Aureo-variegata', broad, creamy-yellow-striped edges, floppy leaves with tips curling under.
　Bowles golden tufted sedge: *C. buchananii* (leatherleaf sedge), fine-textured cinnamon-bronze leaves; interesting contrast to green or blue plants, zones 6 to 9.

CHASMANTHIUM LATIFOLIUM
Sea Oats, Wild Oats

This warm-season native grass forms graceful, vase-shaped clumps of light to dark green foliage, which change to copper in fall and bleach to tan in winter. Arching spikes of flat, nodding flowers and seed heads look decorative and rustle in the wind. They start out purple-tinged green in mid- to late summer and finally age to bronze in winter. Grows 2 to 3 feet tall and wide. Cut sea oats for fresh and dried arrangements. Mass in meadows or along streams.

CHASMANTHIUM LATIFOLIUM

Site: Part shade best. Fertile to poor, well-drained to wet soil. Best with moderate to plentiful moisture, but tolerates drought. Zones 5 to 9; good seashore plant.
How to Grow: Sow seeds or plant container-grown plants in spring, spacing 18 inches apart. Divide in spring when crowded. Reseeds, but isn't weedy. Becomes light yellow-green in too much sun. Leaf tips brown if too dry. Usually pest-free.
Cultivars: Only the species is sold.

CORTADERIA SELLOANA 'PUMILA'
Dwarf Pampas Grass

A midget compared to the species, this smaller-growing selection of a normally 10-foot-tall-and-wide species fits better in most gardens. Razor-edge evergreen leaves form dense, weeping mounds that are topped in autumn with flamboyant shaggy plumes of creamy white flowers that resemble huge feather dusters. Flowers remain showy into winter. Foliage grows 3 feet tall; flowers 4 to 6 feet tall. Use dwarf pampas grass as specimen in large-scale garden; eye-catching near water and where highlighted from behind by sunlight.

Site: Full sun to part shade. Fertile, well-drained soil. Moderate to plentiful moisture. Zones 8 to 10; to Zone 7 in protected site. Use as annual elsewhere.
How to Grow: Plant container-grown plants in spring, spacing 5 feet apart. Divide with axe in early spring. Cut flowers for arrangements when freshly opened to avoid shattering. May rot in winter-wet site. Wearing protective clothing, cut back winter-damaged leaves or thin out old foliage in spring. Usually pest-free.

CORTADERIA SELLOANA 'PUMILA'

Cultivars: 'Argentea', silver plumes, 9 to 12 feet tall; 'Carminea Rendadleri', pink plumes, 8 to 9 feet tall; 'Silver Comet', variegated, 6 to 8 feet tall, zones 7 to 10.

DESCHAMPSIA CAESPITOSA
Tufted Hair Grass

This cool-season grass features low hummocks of rough-textured, narrow, pleated, dark green leaves. One of the earliest-blooming grasses, it sends up numerous stems of delicate, airy inflorescences that form a mist of silky green above the foliage in late spring. Flowers turn yellow to gold, then bronze or purple as they ripen. Seed heads *continued*

Ornamental Grasses

DESCHAMPSIA CAESPITOSA
(continued)

remain ornamental into late winter. Leaves are evergreen in mild climates and turn russet in winter in cool climates. Foliage grows 1 to 3 feet tall; flowers 2 to 3 feet taller.

Tufted hair grass is elegant planted in drifts against dark background in borders and shade gardens. Use as groundcover in moist sites.

DESCHAMPSIA CAESPITOSA

Site: Full sun to part shade. Average to fertile, well-drained to damp soil. Best with moderate water. Zones 3 to 9; flowers showiest in cool zones.
How to Grow: Sow seeds or plant container-grown plants in spring, spacing 3 feet apart. Divide in spring or fall. Cut back flower stalks when unsightly or in late winter; rake out winter-tattered foliage. May brown in hot, dry sites in summer. Flowers last longest if protected from winter wind. Rabbits may eat plants.
Cultivars: 'Bronzeschleier' ('Bronze Veil'), bronze-yellow seed heads; 'Goldschleier' ('Golden Veil'), bright yellow seed heads.

ELYMUS ARENARIUS 'GLAUCUS'

ELYMUS ARENARIUS 'GLAUCUS'

Blue Wild Rye, Blue Lyme Grass

Spreading by rhizomes to form stands of bright blue-gray leaves, blue wild rye creates an exquisite long-lasting accent in a flower garden. It's the largest of the blue-colored grasses and valued as a colorful foliage plant. The sturdy warm-season plant looks attractive all year, changing in late fall and winter from blue to yellow to bright beige in cold climates, but remaining evergreen or semievergreen in mild areas. The beige flowers that sometimes appear in summer are insignificant. Grows 1 to 2 feet tall; 2 to 3 feet wide.

Use blue wild rye as a specimen in flower gardens; it combines well with pink, white, yellow, and purple flowers. Mass-plant for erosion control on banks and at seashore.

Site: Full sun to light shade. Heavy to sandy, dry to wet soil; spreads less aggressively in heavy or dry soil. Zones 3 to 10; tolerates hot, dry sites and seashore conditions.
How to Grow: Plant container-grown or bare-root plants in spring, spacing 3 to 5 feet apart. Divide in spring, as needed, to control growth. Plant in bottomless container sunk in ground to

control spread in flower gardens. Mow or cut back in spring, even where evergreen, to stimulate brightly colored new growth. Usually pest-free.
Similar Species: Often mislabeled as *Elymus glaucus*, a less invasive blue species native to California, but rarely available, or sold simply as *E. arenarius*.

ERIANTHUS RAVENNAE (SACCHARUM RAVENNAE)

Ravenna Grass, Hardy Pampas Grass

This towering grass looks beautiful throughout the year. Clumps of narrow, arching, gray-green leaves turn multicolored blends of orange, brown, purple, and beige in autumn, then bleach tan in winter. The silvery flowers, which create a light-catching

ERIANTHUS RAVENNAE

arrangement above the foliage clumps in late summer, mature to fluffy cream-colored seed heads that last through winter. Foliage grows 4 to 5 feet tall; flowers 8 to 12 feet taller.

Ravenna grass is best as a specimen or mass planting in large gardens. Looks wonderful along ponds and seashores and in naturalistic gardens.

Site: Full sun. Best in fertile, well-drained, moist soil. Tolerates drought. Zones 6 to 10, tolerates seashore conditions, but showiest if protected from wind.

How to Grow: Plant container-grown plants in spring, spacing 3 to 4 feet apart. Divide clumps in spring. May self-sow in ideal growing conditions. Protect from wind to prolong seed heads in winter. Usually pest- and disease-free.

Cultivars and Similar Species: Only the species usually is sold.

FESTUCA OVINA VAR. GLAUCA (F. CINEREA, F. GLAUCA, AND F. ARVENSIS)
Blue Fescue, Blue Sheep's Fescue

Everyone's favorite, this petite cool-season grass forms cute hedgehoglike mounds of fine-

FESTUCA AMETHYSTINA

textured, pale silvery blue leaves. Its perfect symmetry and neat appearance gives blue fescue a pleasing character that endures throughout the year because the foliage is evergreen, retaining its lovely color through winter. Tall stalks of fine-textured, green flowers, which age to tan, wave above the foliage in summer, but aren't particularly showy. Plants grow

6 to 12 inches tall and wide. Blue fescue combines well with pastel pink, yellow, or white flowers, and purple foliage. Use as edging or groundcover or in rock gardens.

Site: Full sun. Average to poor, well-drained soil. Moderate moisture. Best in low fertility soils; tolerates drought Zones 4 to 9, but best in cool regions; suffers in heat and humidity.

How to Grow: Plant container-grown plants in spring, spacing 1 foot apart. Divide every three years in spring or fall to prevent dead centers and maintain best foliage color. May rot in winter-wet site or if heavily mulched in summer. Cut back to 3 to 4 inches in late winter. Crown rot may develop if plants are heavily mulched in summer.

Cultivars: 'Elijah's Blue', icy blue, retains color through summer heat, 10-inch mounds; 'Solling', blue-gray in spring and summer, red-brown in fall and winter, 8 inches tall, no flowers; 'Bluefinch', 6 to 8 inches tall, fine-textured; 'Tom Thumb', silver-blue in spring, green in summer, 4 inches tall, groundcover; 'Sea Urchin', silvery blue-gray, medium-textured, 12 inches tall. *Festuca amethystina* (sheep's fescue), fine-textured, 12-inch, blue-green mounds, 18- to 30-inch-tall flowers; 'Superba', showy flowers.

HAKONECHLOA MACRA 'AUREOLA'
Japanese Wind Grass, Hakone Grass

Low and slow-spreading, this cool-season grass displays elegant, bamboolike, yellow-green leaves with gold or cream stripes that cascade toward the light from short, wiry stems. Sprays of dainty flowers bloom among the leaves in late summer and fall, adding a soft mist around the leaves. Foliage turns an alluring pinkish red in fall and bleaches to bright tan in winter. The golden-variegated cultivar is more beautiful

HAKONECHLOA MACRA 'AUREOLA'

and more widely grown than the all-green species. Grows 1 to 2 feet tall.

Plant hakone grass to weep over a rocky slope or beside a waterfall. Use as specimen or groundcover in shade, rock, and woodland gardens. Combines well with hostas.

Site: Light to half shade. Humus-rich, fertile, well-drained but moist soil. Plentiful moisture. Zones 6 to 9.

How to Grow: Plant container-grown plants in spring, spacing 18 inches apart. Divide in spring when crowded. Leaves burn in too much sun. Cut back dried foliage in late winter. Usually pest-free.

IMPERATA CYLINDRICA 'RED BARON'
Japanese Blood Grass

The narrow, upright, grassy leaves of Japanese blood grass emerge green with red tips in spring and gradually become redder. By summer they create a stunning two-toned effect. Autumn transforms the foliage to flaming scarlet until frost turns it bronze and winter bleaches it straw colored. This warm-season grass doesn't bloom and spreads slowly by rhizomes to form attractive light-catching clumps. Grows 12 to 24 inches tall and wide.   *continued*

IMPERATA CYLINDRICA 'RED BARON'
(continued)

IMPERATA CYLINDRICA 'RED BARON'

Plant blood grass in ribbons in front of border or rock garden where sunlight strikes foliage from behind or side.

Site: Best color in full sun; grows well in light to part shade, but is less red. Provide some midday shade in hot regions. Fertile, humus-rich, well-drained, moist soil. Plentiful moisture. Zones 5 to 9, perhaps to Zone 4 with winter protection.
How to Grow: Plant container-grown plants in spring, spacing 1 to 2 feet apart. Divide in spring if crowded. Immediately pull stems that revert to all-green because they spread aggressively and are pernicious weeds. Blood grass performs poorly in hot, dry sites or heavy wet soil. Pest-free.
Cultivars: This is the only cultivar.

MELICA CILIATA
Hairy Millet, Silky-Spike Melic

This clump-forming, cool-season grass puts on a pretty show of flowers that are a flower arranger's dream. The silky, white spikes bloom in spring and early summer, gradually turning creamy yellow and then beige as they mature, but remaining showy well into fall. The flowers and seed heads bob alluringly over the loose clips of narrow, gray-green leaves. Grows 1 to 2 feet tall and wide. Locate melic where backlit by sun to enhance beauty of flowers. Plant it behind later-blooming flowers to obscure plant late in season.

MELICA CILIATA

Site: Light shade to half sun. Well-drained, fertile soil; tolerates alkaline soil. Keep moist. Zones 5 to 8.
How to Grow: Sow seeds or plant container-grown plants in spring. Divide in spring or fall. Flowers may need to be loosely staked. This cool-season grass may become unattractive by midsummer in hot climates. Usually pest-free.
Cultivars: None available.

MILIUM EFFUSUM 'AUREUM'
Golden Wood Millet

Golden wood millet, a cool-season evergreen grass, forms loose clumps of bright yellow-green leaves topped with a sparkling cloud of tiny golden yellow flowers in early summer. New spring growth is bright yellow and becomes yellow-green with maturity. Foliage clumps grow

MILIUM EFFUSUM 'AUREUM'

12 to 18 inches tall; flowers 12 to 18 inches taller. Plant golden wood millet as a specimen or in a group to brighten shade gardens and borders; useful on the edge of a woodland garden.

Site: Light shade best; tolerates full shade. Fertile, humus-rich, moist soil. Plentiful moisture. Zones 6 to 8; may die in hot summer weather in hot areas.
How to Grow: Sow seeds or plant container-grown plants in spring, spacing 2 to 3 feet apart. Divide when clumps become crowded, in spring. May self-sow; select the most golden seedlings to propagate. Usually pest-free.
Cultivars: The green species form is less eye-catching, but is an attractive, somewhat taller plant.

MISCANTHUS SINENSIS
Eulalia, Silver Grass

This outstanding warm-season grass brings gardeners a wealth of showy cultivars valued for foliage and flowers. Leaves of the species, which are 1 inch wide and dark green with a white midrib, form huge, vase-shaped clumps. Inflorescences begin in late summer as drooping purple-tinged fans. These open to long, silky spikelets that mature after frost to dazzling, curly plumes of silvery hairs.

MISCANTHUS SINENSIS 'ZEBRINUS'

The foliage and plumes bleach to the color of dried corn husks and stand proudly through winter's ice and snow. Cultivars are variations on the theme, featuring narrower leaves, variegated foliage, excellent fall color, or more silvery flowers in a variety of sizes. Plants grow 3 to 15 feet tall and 3 to 8 feet wide, depending on cultivar. Use miscanthus as specimen in mixed borders; mass-plant in low-maintenance gardens or as a screen. Excellent with evergreen background. Be sure to allow enough space.

Site: Full sun best; flops with shade. Average to heavy soil. Moderate to wet conditions; drought-tolerant. Zones 4 to 9.
How to Grow: Plant bare-root or container-grown plants in spring, spacing 3 to 6 feet apart according to size. Divide every five or more years, when centers become bare and plants flop open. Drought-resistant, but leaf tips may burn. Cut back to ground in late winter with hedge shears or string trimmer. Usually pest-free, but new mealybug pests are rapidly becoming serious problem.
Cultivars: 'Condensatus', broad leaves, white midribs, bronze seed heads, 6 to 8 feet tall; 'Gracillimus' (maiden grass, Japanese silver grass), 3 to 4 feet tall, silvery plumes, narrow leaves with white midrib, vase-shaped; 'Morning Light', narrow leaves with thin, white edges that make leaves appear gray-green, silvery plumes, 4 feet tall; 'Silver Feather', 6 to 7 feet tall, early plumes, silvery white; 'Zebrinus' (zebra grass), wide leaves banded horizontally with gold, tolerates wet soil, floppy; 'Strictus' (porcupine grass), gold horizontal bands, more stiffly upright; 'Gaziella', wide leaves with broad, silver midribs, deep burgundy fall color, 4 to 5 feet tall; 'Variegatus', wide leaves with creamy white vertical stripes, 5 to 6 feet tall, floppy, tolerates some shade; 'Cosmopolitan', wide, white stripes, 6 to 7 feet tall, not floppy; 'Purpurescens' (flame grass), 4 to 5 feet tall, narrow foliage turns orange-red in fall in sun and salmon, pink, or gold in part shade, early-blooming, needs moisture.

OPHIOPOGON PLANISCAPUS 'NIGRESCENS'
Black Mondo Grass

Not a true grass, but resembling ornamental grasses in appearance and behavior, this unusual

OPHIOPOGON PLANISCAPUS 'EBONY KNIGHT'

foliage plant is a standout in the garden, especially when contrasted with brighter flowers and foliage. It forms slowly spreading clumps of purple leaves that are so dark they are almost black. Pink-tinted white flowers bloom on short spikes among the leaves in midsummer, followed by clusters of black berries. Grows 6 inches tall and 12 inches wide. Use as contrast with light green, chartreuse, or blue-gray foliage plants. Good edging or paving plant.

Site: Full sun to part shade. Fertile, humus-rich, moist soil. Plentiful moisture. Zones 6 to 9.
How to Grow: Plant bare-root or container-grown plants in spring, spacing 12 inches apart. Divide in spring only when crowded. Slow-growing. Usually pest-free.
Similar Species: *Ophiopogon japonicus* (dwarf mondo grass), fine-textured, green leaves, lilac flowers, excellent groundcover, zones 7 to 9.

PANICUM VIRGATUM 'HEAVY METAL'

PANICUM VIRGATUM
Switch Grass

Deep-rooted, this native prairie grass makes an excellent display in fall and winter. Its blue-green leaves form an upright to narrow fountain, which turns bright yellow in autumn, although some cultivars become red. An airy cloud *continued*

PANICUM VIRGATUM
(continued)

of dark purple or pink flowers, which ripen to straw yellow, floats over the plants in midsummer. The dried grass persists well through winter, standing as a buff-colored spray of leaves. Foliage grows 3 to 6 feet tall, flowers 2 feet higher. Use as a specimen in flower borders; effective, especially in winter and fall, mass-planted in naturalistic gardens and along water.

Site: Full sun best; may flop in shade. Average to sandy, well-drained soil. Moderate moisture, tolerates drought and heat. Zones 5 to 9.
How to Grow: Plant bare-root or container-grown plants in spring, spacing 3 feet apart. May need staking in shade. Cut back in late winter. Usually pest-free.
Cultivars: 'Haense Herms', 3 to 4 feet tall, red fall color; 'Rotstrahlbusch' (red switch grass), best red fall color; 'Strictum' (tall switch grass), blue leaves, 5 to 6 feet tall; 'Heavy Metal', stiff, upright, metallic blue leaves, 4 to 5 feet tall.

PENNISETUM SPP.
Fountain Grass

O ne of the most useful grasses for including in flower gardens and mixed borders, fountain grass (*Pennisetum alopecuroides*) is a warm-season grass that looks wonderful throughout most of the year. The fine-textured, glossy, green leaves form a dense, wide-spreading, symmetrical mass that remains green well into fall and briefly changes to rose, apricot, or gold before bleaching to bright almond in winter. In late summer or fall, 9-inch-long, foxtail-like plumes, which open green and mature to rosy silver, purple, or white, stand out just above the foliage all over the plant. The flowers shatter by the end of fall, but the leaves remain attractive. Grows 2 to 4 feet tall and wide. Use as a specimen in mixed borders or mass-plant around water and for meadowlike effect. Especially useful for adding volume to otherwise empty winter garden.

PENNISETUM ALOPECUROIDES

From summer into fall, the showy, long-blooming Oriental fountain grass (*P. orientale*) becomes a mound of silky, 4-inch-long, pink foxtails, which mature to creamy light brown before shattering in late fall. Fine-textured, blue-green leaves form a dense, mounded clump that turns yellow-brown in autumn and bleaches to a handsome straw color in winter. Grows 1 to 2 feet tall and wide. An elegant grass for small gardens; use as specimen or mass-plant.

Purple fountain grass (*P. setaceum* 'Atropurpureum') is a tender, warm-season grass valued for its arching clumps of gorgeous, burgundy-bronze leaves and 12-inch-long, reddish purple foxtails, which bring a long season of color to mixed borders. The leaves are evergreen to semievergreen where the plant is hardy; elsewhere they bleach to straw color in winter, but look attractive until spring. Plants

PENNISETUM SETACEUM 'ATROPURPUREUM'

grow 3 to 4 feet tall; 2 to 2½ feet wide. Often used as a bedding plant along with flowering annuals. Makes beautiful accent in perennial border. Combines well with pink, blue, and pale yellow blossoms. Wonderful in containers combined with other annuals. Excellent cut flower.

Site: Give fountain grass full sun in North; full sun to light shade in South. Oriental fountain grass grows in full sun to part shade, purple fountain grass in full sun to light shade. Fountain grass prefers average to fertile, well-drained, moist soil. Moderate to plentiful moisture; tolerates drought in cool climates. Oriental fountain grass needs fertile, humus-rich, well-drained soil and plentiful moisture. Purple fountain grass needs humus-rich to sandy, moist soil; best with good soil and moderate moisture. Fountain grass is hardy in zones 5 to 9. Oriental fountain grass hardy in zones 7 to 9; tolerates seashore conditions if moist. Purple fountain grass hardy in zones 8 to 10, grows as annual elsewhere; adapts to seashore gardens.

How to Grow: Sow seeds of fountain grass in spring or fall or plant bare-root or container-grown plants in spring, spacing 2½ to 3 feet apart. Plant container-grown Oriental and purple fountain grasses in spring, 2 feet apart. Divide fountain grass in spring or fall if center flops open, usually every five to 10 years. Divide Oriental fountain grass only when dead centers develop; resents division. Cut back dried foliage to 6 inches in late winter. Fountain grass may self-seed and be invasive in natural landscape in moist, mild climates. Remove winter-killed purple fountain grass plants in early spring; flops in too much shade; plants are usually sterile and rarely self-sow. All usually are pest-free.

Cultivars: Fountain grass: 'Hameln', compact to 2 feet tall and wide, zones 5 to 8; 'Little Bunny', miniature to 1 foot tall and wide; 'Cassian', foliage to 10 inches tall, flowers to 2 feet tall.

Oriental fountain grass: Only the species is sold.

Purple fountain grass: Species has green leaves and pink-tinged flowers; may self-seed aggressively and is a pest in Southwest; 'Burgundy Giant', 1-inch-wide leaves, 6 to 7 feet tall.

PHALARIS ARUNDINACEA 'PICTA'
Ribbon Grass, Gardener's Garters

Rapidly spreading, ribbon grass features longitudinally striped, green-and-white leaves that produce a beautiful flash of white in the garden. May remain evergreen in mild climates, but turns beige with the first frost in cold climates. The lacy, white flowers are not significantly showy. Grows 3 feet tall and is wide-spreading. An excellent groundcover where its invasive nature is not a problem. Use 'Dwarf Garters' in formal and informal mixed borders.

PHALARIS ARUNDINACEA 'PICTA'

Site: Part to full shade. Average to poor or heavy soil; tolerates wet to standing shallow water as well as drought. Hardy in zones 5 to 9; to Zone 3 with snow cover. Heat-tolerant. Good seashore plant.

How to Grow: Plant bare-root or container-grown plants in spring, spacing 2 to 3 feet apart. Divide rhizomes every few years in spring to keep in bounds; sprouts from any tiny piece of root left in ground. Extremely invasive; needs impenetrable underground barrier, such as concrete or fiberglass, to keep in place in garden. Also can plant in bottomless container or choose noninvasive form. If plant becomes tattered during growing season, cut back to 4 inches from ground. Cut back dried stems in late winter. Weed out stems that revert to nonvariegated green. Pest-free.

Cultivars: 'Tricolor', pink-white-and-green; 'Luteo-Picta', creamy gold and green; 'Dwarf Garters', pink-tinged, green-and-white leaves, 12 to 15 inches tall, more upright, noninvasive, good in flower gardens; 'Feesey's Variety', 1½ to 2 feet tall, spreading, pink in spring, snow white in summer.

STIPA GIGANTEA
Giant Feather Grass

One of the showiest of all the grasses, giant feather grass forms a low fountain of extremely narrow, 2-foot-long, arching, gray-green, evergreen leaves. In early summer, golden oatlike flower spikes tower above the mounds of this cool-season

STIPA GIGANTEA

grass. The flower spikes remain as showy seed heads through fall. Foliage clumps grow 1½ to 2 feet tall and as wide; flowers 4 to 5 feet tall. Use giant feather grass as an accent or see-through screen in flower gardens and mixed borders. Best with dark background and where backlit.

Site: Full sun. Fertile, well-drained soil. Average to dry conditions; performs poorly in damp sites. Zones 7 to 9; tolerates seashore conditions and windy sites.

How to Grow: Plant container-grown plants in spring, spacing 1½ to 2 feet apart. In rainy areas, soil must be extremely well-drained or plants may die. Usually pest-free, but attractive to gophers.

Similar Species: *Stipa spartea* (porcupine grass), nodding flower clusters with stiff bristles, 2 to 3 feet tall, zones 3 to 8.

ADIANTUM PEDATUM

ADIANTUM PEDATUM
Maidenhair Fern

There's no mistaking this magnificent fern for any other—its fronds grow in an unusual pattern, forming layered, rounded fans 1 to 2 feet across and parallel to the ground. The translucent, bright green, wedge-shaped leaflets grow on wiry, shiny black stems, which further add to the fern's allure. Rusty brown fiddleheads emerge in early spring. The plant spreads slowly by rhizomes to form large patches. Grows 2 to 2½ feet tall. A graceful fern for shade and woodland gardens; elegant in shaded formal gardens.

Site: Deep to light shade. Deep, humus-rich, fertile, slightly acid to slightly alkaline, moist soil. Plentiful moisture. Hardy in zones 3 to 8.
How to Grow: Plant container-grown plants in spring, spacing 2 to 3 feet apart. Divide in early spring when fiddleheads are visible. Loses color and vigor in too much sun or in poor soil. Protect from wind. Slugs may be troublesome.
Similar Species: *Adiantum capillus-veneris* (southern maidenhair, rosy maidenhair), leaflets arranged in slender pattern, excellent groundcover, zones 7 to 8.

ATHYRIUM SPP.
Lady Fern, Japanese Painted Fern

Perhaps the most common wild fern, lady fern (*Athyrium filix-femina*) makes a graceful addition to wildflower or shade gardens, spreading by rhizomes to colonize large areas. Its feathery, 2- to 3-foot-

ATHYRIUM FILIX-FEMINA

long fronds are twice divided and emerge from the rhizomes at 6- to 12-inch intervals. Varying from light to dark green, leaves have red or green

ATHYRIUM NIPPONICUM 'PICTUM'

stems and feature characteristic crescent-shaped spore cases arranged in a herringbone pattern on the undersides of the fertile fronds. Grows

2 to 3 feet tall and wide. Best used in naturalistic shade or woodland gardens because it wanders.

The outstanding Japanese painted fern (*A. nipponicum* 'Pictum', syn. *A. goeringianum* 'Pictum') brings subtle color to the shade garden with maroon-splashed, silvery gray leaves. The gracefully tapered fronds are 12 to 18 inches long and feature maroon midribs. This deciduous Asian fern grows 1 to 2 feet tall and spreads slowly by rhizomes to form clumps 2 to 3 feet across. Japanese painted fern is spectacular planted with blue flowers and blue-leaved hostas.

Site: Lady fern grows best in light shade; tolerates full sun if constantly moist. Japanese painted fern thrives in part to full shade. Humus-rich, neutral to slightly acid, well-drained but moist soil. Plentiful moisture. Lady fern is hardy in zones 2 to 8, Japanese painted fern in zones 3 to 9.
How to Grow: Plant container-grown plants in spring, spacing lady fern 2 to 3 feet apart, Japanese painted fern 2 feet apart. Divide clumps in spring just as fiddleheads are visible; Japanese painted fern also may be divided in fall.

Lady fern may become tattered by summer's end if exposed to too much heat and wind. Keep well-mulched and constantly moist. Japanese painted fern emerges late, but new growth continues to appear until late summer. Keep well-watered during summer drought to prolong beauty through fall. Loses color in too much sun.

Fungal disease may attack base of lady fern; avoid watering at night. Slugs and snails may eat foliage. Japanese painted fern is usually pest-free.
Cultivars: Lady fern: Leaf shape and height may vary according to native habitat. 'Cristatum' (crested lady fern), contorted (crested) leaflets create fluffy-textured effect.

Japanese painted fern: No named cultivars, although leaf color can vary from one source to another.

CYRTOMIUM FALCATUM
Japanese Holly Fern

Once grown only as a houseplant, Japanese holly fern is an outstanding choice for southern gardens. Its bold-textured, 2½-foot-long arching fronds consist of 3- to 5-inch-long, pointed leaflets. Leaflets are dark green with a leathery texture and a shiny finish. This tough evergreen fern tolerates adverse

CYRTOMIUM FALCATUM

growing conditions. It grows 2 to 2½ feet tall and as wide. Japanese holly fern is excellent in shade gardens, under shrubs, and in mixed borders.

Site: Light to full shade. Well-drained, humus-rich, neutral to slightly alkaline soil. Plentiful to moderate moisture. Zones 8 to 11.
How to Grow: Plant container-grown plants in spring or fall. Divide scaly rhizomes and multiple crowns in spring. Cut off browned leaves when necessary. Usually pest-free.
Cultivars: 'Rochfordianum', leaf edges strongly toothed, resembles holly more than species does.

DENNSTAEDTIA PUNCTILOBULA

DENNSTAEDTIA PUNCTILOBULA
Hay-Scented Fern, Boulder Fern

Spreading rapidly in open locations, this fern gives off a fresh, sweet scent when brushed against. The lacy, fine-textured, bright to light green leaves are 2 feet long and 8 inches wide, tapering at the tips. This sun-tolerant, native fern grows around boulders in fields where the mower can't touch it, or colonizes clear-cut areas in forests. Grows 2 to 3 feet tall; spreads rapidly to form large colonies. Hay-scented fern looks lovely planted around boulders and at bases of stone walls. Use as groundcover to stabilize banks and along the edges of large-scale woodland gardens.

Site: Part shade best; tolerates full sun if constantly moist. Humus-rich to average, well-drained, moist soil. Plentiful moisture. Zones 3 to 8.
How to Grow: Plant container-grown plants in spring, spacing 2 to 3 feet apart. Divide rhizomes in early spring when fiddleheads are visible. Control aggressiveness by mowing in lawns or fields. Usually pest-free.
Cultivars: Only the species is available.

DRYOPTERIS SPP.
Japanese Autumn Fern, Marginal Shield Fern

Autumn fern (*Dryopteris erythrosora*) brings surprising color to a shade garden. In spring, its copper-pink crosiers unfurl into light amber or rust-colored fronds. The fronds deepen to rich green during summer and are decorated in autumn with brilliant red spore cases on the backside of each frond. Autumn fern is semievergreen and remains colorful well into winter. It grows 2 to 3 feet tall. Gorgeous in shade gardens combined with copper-tinged barrenworts and orange- or red-flowered primroses. Offers excellent contrast to green ferns.

DRYOPTERIS MARGINALIS

The fronds of the leathery-textured, evergreen, native marginal shield fern (*D. marginalis*) grow from a central crown, forming a tidy individual plant that doesn't spread. Dark blue-green and twice-cut, the fronds are 5 to 10 inches long. During late summer or early fall, a crown of brown crosiers forms just above the ground at the base of the fronds and overwinters until the new fronds unfurl in spring. Grows 1½ feet tall. Fronds can be cut for flower arrangements. *continued*

Ferns

DRYOPTERIS SPP.
(continued)

Dark green leaves look very attractive in fall and winter gardens. Plant in shade and woodland gardens.

Site: Light shade is best for autumn fern; tolerates sun in the morning or late afternoon; avoid midday sun. Plant marginal shield fern in light to full shade. Fertile, humus-rich, moist soil. Plentiful moisture; autumn fern tolerates drier soil than most ferns, but marginal shield fern tolerates wet soil. Autumn fern is hardy in zones 6 to 9, marginal shield fern in zones 3 to 8.
How to Grow: Plant container-grown plants in spring. Space autumn fern 2 feet apart, marginal shield fern 2 to 3 feet apart and keep crown at same level it was growing in the pot. Divide in spring, separating small crowns from alongside large crown, if desired. Keep marginal shield fern heavily mulched. Cut off old fronds of both species in late winter to make way for new growth. Pest- and disease-free.
Cultivars and Similar Species: Autumn fern: *D. erythrosora* var. *prolifica* (proliferous autumn fern), similar, but only 12 to 15 inches tall.
Marginal shield fern: *D. spinulosa* var. *intermedia* (spinulosa wood fern), 2½-foot-tall twice- or thrice-cut fronds, nearly evergreen. *D. filix-mas* (male fern), feathery, green fronds, tolerates dry site and half sun, suitable for flower borders.

MATTEUCCIA PENSYLVANICA (MATTEUCCIA STRUTHIOPTERIS)
Ostrich Fern

Bright green, feathery, twice-cut fronds of the ostrich fern arise from a central crown, forming an imposing tall vase. Leaves may be 4 or more feet long and are widest at the middle. Resembling ostrich

MATTEUCCIA PENSYLVANICA

feathers, fertile fronds emerge in the plant's center in midsummer and are half as long as the infertile fronds. The fronds are shiny bronze-green, eventually turning brown, and remaining attractive all winter. Ostrich fern spreads aggressively by underground runners, sending up vase-shaped clusters of leaves from its far-flung rhizomes. Grows 3 to 4 feet tall; 2 to 3 feet wide. Naturalize ostrich fern in moist woodlands, along streams and ponds, or in bog gardens. Spreads too exuberantly for small gardens.

Site: Half sun to light shade; more sun tolerant than many ferns. Humus-rich, slightly acid, moist soil. Constant, plentiful moisture; tolerates wet or swampy sites. Hardy in zones 2 to 9.
How to Grow: Plant container-grown plants in spring, spacing at least 4 feet apart. Divide rhizomes in spring every few years to control spread. Emerges late; take care not to injure. Leaves scorch if soil dries. Spreads aggressively. Usually pest-free.
Cultivars: Only the species is available.

OSMUNDA SPP.
Cinnamon Fern, Royal Fern

Cinnamon fern *(Osmunda cinnamomea)*, a stately native fern forms elegant, slow-spreading, vase-shaped clumps. Uncurling from woolly white crosiers, fertile fronds develop in early spring, emerging green and soon withering and turning cinnamon-brown. Soon after the fertile fronds appear, a ring of bright green,

OSMUNDA REGALIS

twice-cut, infertile fronds expands around them. Turning orange-yellow in fall with the first frost, cinnamon fern boasts the best fall color of any fern. Grows 2 to 5 feet tall; half as wide. The elegant formal shape works well in moist flower borders and foundation plantings, as well as in naturalistic sites.

Royal fern *(O. regalis)* is eye-catching planted in groups in bog gardens, along streams, and in moist, naturalistic gardens.

Site: Full sun to open shade in wet to swampy or constantly damp soil; part to light or full shade in drier, but moist conditions. Humus-rich, acid, moist soil. Constant, plentiful moisture. Cinnamon fern is hardy in zones 4 to 9, royal fern in zones 3 to 9.

How to Grow: Plant container-grown plants in spring, spacing 3 feet apart. Divide royal fern when center becomes bare, in spring. Cinnamon fern spreads slowly. Royal fern grows tallest in wet conditions. Both ferns are usually pest-free.

Similar Species: *O. claytonia* (interrupted fern), similar to cinnamon fern, but fertile, dark green leaflets form along portions of leaf stalks then wither and turn brown; tolerates deeper shade.

POLYSTICHUM ACROSTICHOIDES

POLYSTICHUM SPP.

Christmas Fern, Western Sword Fern, Soft Shield Fern

Christmas fern *(Polystichum acrostichoides)* is a tough, easy-to-grow native fern that forms an individual cluster of once-divided, 1- to 2-foot-long, 4-inch-wide, leathery fronds. Foliage emerges light green in early spring, maturing to leathery, dark green. It remains green all winter, but flattens to the ground under snow cover. Spores form on the undersides of the leaflets. Grows 1 to 2 feet tall; 2½ feet wide. Plant Christmas fern on slopes in open shade where soil is too fast-draining

POLYSTICHUM MUNITUM

for other ferns. It is lovely in shade and woodland gardens as well as borders.

Resembling a large, stiff Christmas fern, the western sword fern *(P. munitum)* features erect, once-divided, rough-textured fronds. The

POLYSTICHUM SETIFERUM

evergreen fronds of this West Coast native grow from 1 to 5 feet long and 2 to 10 inches wide, making a dramatic appearance. Use western sword fern as a focal point in a garden or mass-plant in naturalistic setting.

Soft shield fern *(P. setiferum)*, an evergreen European fern, forms

rosettes of softly spreading, twice-divided, lacy, lance-shaped fronds with rough, brown stems. Light green and velvety, fronds arch softly from the central clump, unlike other members of its genus. Grows 3 to 4 feet tall; 2 to 3 feet wide. Soft shield fern is lovely in naturalistic settings or in more formal gardens.

Site: Christmas fern and western sword fern prefer part to light shade; tolerate more sun in constantly moist site. Plant soft shield fern in light shade. Give Christmas fern average to humus-rich, neutral, well-drained soil; best in moist conditions, but tolerates some dryness. Western sword fern grows best in humus-rich, well-drained but moist soil; plentiful moisture. Soft shield fern prefers similar conditions, but tolerates some dryness. Christmas fern is hardy in zones 3 to 9, western sword fern and soft shield fern in zones 5 to 8.

How to Grow: Plant container-grown plants in spring. Space Christmas fern 2½ feet apart, western sword fern 3 or more feet apart, soft shield fern 2 to 3 feet apart. Divide clumps with multiple crowns when crowded; divide western sword fern in fall, soft shield fern in spring, Christmas fern in spring or fall. Christmas fern needs good drainage. Remove old brown foliage of all three species as new growth emerges, if desired. Keep western sword fern and soft shield fern well-mulched and moist. Usually pest-free.

Cultivars: Christmas fern: 'Crispum', ruffled leaves; 'Incisum', deeply cut leaflets.

Western sword fern: No cultivars available.

Soft shield fern: Many cultivars available with overlapping or deeply divided leaflets and in various heights.

Annuals

CHAPTER 7

ABOUT ANNUALS

Perky pansy faces fill in empty spaces when spring bulbs have ceased flowering. These old-fashioned favorites prefer light shade and plentiful water. The varieties shown here are 'Baby Lucia' and 'Maxim Blue'.

For a show of pure color in the garden, few plants can match the flash and glitter of a profusion of flowering annuals.

Planted in generous groups, pansies turn their appealing faces toward the sun, every flower smiling at the same time in the same direction. Impatiens catch and reflect the dappled light beneath tree branches, turning dimness into lightness with pretty, pastel blossoms. When it comes to sheer flower power, no other plants measure up to these prolific bloomers.

Many garden annuals bloom practically nonstop from late spring or early summer until fall's first frost. By definition an annual plant lives for only one year; it completes its entire life cycle in a single growing season. It germinates, develops into a mature plant, blooms, sets seed, and finally dies, all in a span of several months.

Some annuals, especially hardy ones such as sweet alyssum and larkspur, can reseed in your garden.

Delightful in bouquets, the airy Cosmos bipinnatus thrives in full sun and poor to average soil. It can be grown easily from seed.

They may come back the next year without your planting them again.

Most annual plants die because of a hormonal trigger set off by seed formation or ripening. Gardeners can subvert this natural phenomenon, at least for a while, by continually removing the faded flowers—a practice called deadheading. By preventing seed formation, deadheading encourages the annuals to continue blooming. Some modern annuals are sterile and do not set seed. They flower without deadheading until frost cuts them down.

BEYOND PETUNIAS

Impatiens, petunias, and marigolds are perhaps the most popular flowers around—perhaps too popular, because we see them everywhere. The world of annuals offers many other kinds that are just as easy to grow. Many less familiar annuals, such as Swan River daisy and blackfoot daisy, are delicate to look at, being dainty of both flower and form, and a snap to grow. Try these softer-looking flowers instead of the more flamboyant annuals when

DROUGHT-TOLERANT ANNUALS

Centaurea cyanus (bachelor's-button, cornflower)
Dianthus chinensis (China pink)
Eschscholzia californica (California poppy)
Felicia amelloides (blue daisy, blue marguerite)
Gaillardia pulchella (annual blanket flower)

Gazania rigens (gazania)
Gomphrena globosa (globe amaranth)
Helichrysum bracteatum (strawflower)
Melampodium paludosum (blackfoot daisy)
Pelargonium peltatum (ivy geranium)

Portulaca grandiflora (moss rose)
Sanvitalia procumbens (creeping zinnia)
Scaevola aemula (fanflower)
Tithonia rotundifolia (Mexican sunflower)
Tropaeolum majus (nasturtium)
Zinnia angustifolia (zinnia)

TYPES OF ANNUALS

Not all annuals are equal in temperament and growing needs. Annuals can be classified into several broad categories, all with different characteristics. Knowing what types of annuals you're growing helps you understand their habits and needs.

■ **TENDER PERENNIALS:** Many of the "annuals" sold at your garden center are actually tender perennials. These are long-blooming perennials in their native habitats. But the cold of winter, not their genetic makeup, kills them each year in your garden, so they behave like annuals. Some, such as zonal geraniums, are perennial in tropical or semitropical climates. Others, such as blue salvia, are perennial in temperate areas that receive only light frosts. Seed should be sown indoors, because the plants take so long to mature.

■ **WARM-SEASON ANNUALS:** Flourishing in heat and blooming best in summer, warm-season annuals, such as zinnia, marigold, and cosmos, cannot survive even a light frost. Freezing temperatures kill tender seedlings and sometimes seeds. Because plants take several months to mature and begin flowering, you may want to start seeds of warm-season annuals indoors. If you sow seeds outdoors, wait until the soil has thoroughly warmed.

■ **COOL-SEASON ANNUALS:** Nasturtium, sweet alyssum, pot marigold, and other cool-season annuals (and some tender perennials) flower best during cool weather and wither or die during summer's heat. Freezing temperatures usually do not harm seeds, which often self-sow and overwinter in the garden, sprouting in spring or summer. In temperate regions, early planting provides the best show from cool-season annuals, allowing them to bloom until the heat of summer arrives. Cut back heat-stressed cool-season annuals in midsummer to stimulate a new crop of flowers when cool weather returns.

Cool-season annuals benefit from light shade or afternoon shade in the Southeast. In warm climates, such as Florida or the Southwestern desert, plant transplants or seeds in late summer or fall for late fall and winter bloom. Cool-season annuals may be either hardy or half-hardy.

■ **HARDY ANNUALS:** This type of cool-season annual withstands the most cold. Sow the seeds in spring before frost danger has passed or in late fall for spring germination. Hardy annuals include Iceland poppy, pot marigold, and larkspur.

■ **HALF-HARDY ANNUALS:** Not as cold-hardy as hardy annuals, half-hardy annuals, such as Madagascar periwinkle, spider flower, and lisianthus, withstand cold weather in spring and fall, but are killed by outright frost. Sow their seeds outdoors in spring after all frost danger has passed, but you need not wait until the soil has warmed.

A cool-season annual, nasturtium grows in average to poor sandy soil and withstands drought.

you want to create a lovely texture in your garden that will complement—not compete with—other plants.

More than 60 different annuals are highlighted in the encyclopedia section starting on page 354. Many are not commonly grown, but are worth seeking out. If you can't find transplants of the more unusual types at your nursery, try growing them from seed either sown directly in the garden or started indoors. You'll find that growing something different adds more fun to your gardening endeavors.

Photo by Linda Joan Smith

Available in an array of colors, California poppies are long-stemmed beauties that thrive even when water is scarce. Bright yellow native wildflowers take center stage in this rock garden.

PLANTING AND CARING FOR ANNUALS

Garden annuals grow all over the world and in all types of climates, from rain forests to deserts, from meadows to seashores. Their origins dictate their preferred growing conditions. Most annuals, with a few notable exceptions, require more tending during the growing season than perennials. Annuals need to be replaced every year, and the soil needs to be improved annually.

You don't need a lot of skill to grow most annuals, but you will need to put in a fair amount of work to keep them looking attractive. Despite the high level of upkeep, their dependable, long bloom is a boon to keeping a flower border showy from early summer until frost.

This is how a healthy root ball looks when you slide it from a pot or cell-pack. Before planting, the root ball should be teased apart if the roots are more dense than this, so they will grow outward into the surrounding soil.

SHOPPING FOR ANNUALS

Young annuals usually come in divided plastic trays called cell-packs, either four, six, or eight in a pack. The little plants quickly can outgrow these containers, so select wisely. Choose seedlings with healthy, dark green foliage and only a few flower buds or open flowers. Avoid larger annuals that are tall and leggy with roots trailing from the container's drainage holes. These plants are overgrown and stressed and will transplant poorly.

Some garden centers rush the season with annuals, getting them out and ready for sale before the area is safe from frost. However, if you wait too long to purchase the little plants, they will be bursting from the cell-packs and be so stressed that they may not adjust well. Shop around for the best-looking plants at the proper planting time, or buy a bit early and look for younger seedlings.

PLANTING OUT

Choose a cool, cloudy day to plant, when the weather is expected to remain moderate for at least a few more days.

Water the cell-pack so the plants slide out. If they don't slide out, push the bottom of the cell with your thumb, and the root ball should pop out. Well-grown annuals will have a network of white roots around the soil ball. If a mat of roots obscures the soil, the seedling is old and overgrown and may not transplant well.

You need to break apart a matted root ball to encourage the roots to grow outward. If you don't, they will grow round and round as if confined to the pot. Gently split the matted root ball up the middle by pulling

with both hands in opposite directions and untangling as many roots as possible.

Install each plant in a small hole dug in prepared soil, spacing them so they'll fill in to form a beautiful mass. Be sure the transplant rests at the same level as it did in the container. If the root ball protrudes above the soil, it will dry out; if it is too low, it may rot. Apply mulch to discourage weeds and to keep the soil moist and the plants clean.

Water immediately after planting. Because the annuals are still small with relatively tiny root systems, you may need to water every day for several weeks until the plants get established. If annuals wilt at this stage, their vitality can be set back considerably.

Most annuals don't need staking. However, a few tall types are floppy and may need support.

SEEDS: SELF-SOWN AND OTHERWISE

You can start almost any annual from seed. Start seeds indoors in winter or sow them directly into the garden at the proper planting time. (See page 579 for frost maps.) A few annuals, notably morning glory, nasturtium, and zinnia, do best in most regions if sown directly in the garden. Seed starting is both an art and a science, and it brings great reward to people with the patience to try it. One major benefit of starting annuals from seeds is that your garden choices aren't limited by the offerings at the local nursery. Many specialty mail-order catalogs sell an alluring variety of annual seeds, offering gardeners a whole world of wonderful, uncommon plants. (See Chapter 12 for information on how to start plants from seeds.)

Some annuals reseed in the garden and come back the following year. You can let the seedlings grow where they will if you like a casual cottage garden look. Or, you may wish to thin or transplant the seedlings to meet your design needs.

Self-sown seedlings do not always resemble their parents. For example, self-sown sweet alyssum usually is taller and floppier than the hybrid parents, and the flowers may be a different color. In the right setting, these changes may not matter.

IN A PINCH

You can help annuals branch, grow stronger and bushier, and flower more by pinching the growing tips of young plants. Use your thumb and forefinger to remove this portion of the plant (see page 294).

Most annuals look and bloom best if regularly deadheaded, although some, notably impatiens, are self-cleaning, dropping their faded blossoms. Individual annual flowers last only a few days, so make it a point to pinch off the dead flowers

every few days. Be sure to remove the entire flower and its ovary so seeds won't form. If you pull off just the petals, the remaining ovary may fatten up and form seeds. If you notice this happening, pinch off the young seedpods, too.

For annuals that form tall flower stalks (such as flowering tobacco) or for large-flowered annuals (such as zinnia and marigold), remove the entire flowering stem, cutting just above a pair of leaves to encourage branching and blooming. Plants with numerous small flower heads (such

Sweet alyssum, a cool-season hardy annual, self-sows in this rock garden, returning year after year to create billowy white masses of flowers that weave among the rocks.

Bright pinks, purples, and white form a visual medley in this annual cutting garden. The flowers— salvia, cosmos, zinnia, and petunia—form delightful bouquets.

PLANTING AND CARING FOR ANNUALS

continued

as verbena and sweet alyssum) can be refreshed by clipping them with pruning shears or scissors.

If annuals get tired by midsummer, trim them back to reinvigorate them. (Most annuals tire by midseason in hot climates; cool-season annuals tire almost everywhere by midsummer.) Don't be afraid to cut stems back so they are only a few inches tall. If you allow some leaves to remain behind, and if you provide water and fertilizer when you cut them, the plants should rebound vigorously for a beautiful late-summer and fall bloom.

ANNUAL APPETITES

Because annuals bloom so prolifically, most benefit from heavy feeding. They need copious amounts of phosphorus to keep them flowering. Don't fertilize with too much nitrogen; it encourages foliage instead of flowers.

Annuals can be fertilized in a number of ways. Work a granular fertilizer designed for annuals, such as 5-10-10, into the soil at planting time and replenish it every month or according to package directions. An easier way to feed annuals is to apply timed-release fertilizer pellets to the soil around the plants at planting time. The pellets slowly release nutrients for three months, so you can forget about further fertilizing. In areas with long growing seasons, you may need to apply the pellets a second time. To fertilize organically, apply composted manure around the plants early in the growing season, and water with a solution of commercial fish emulsion or seaweed extract every week or two.

The ability of annuals to put on a seemingly inexhaustible show of flowers makes them popular among beginning and experienced gardeners. Whether you grow annuals for cut flowers, to decorate your deck, or to bring cohesiveness to a perennial border, you can expect them to provide splendid color and texture.

ANNUALS FOR EVERY REASON

▪ ANNUALS FOR CUTTING

The following annuals make excellent cut flowers. They look pretty in arrangements and often last a week or more when cut.

Antirrhinum majus (snapdragon)

Calendula officinalis (pot marigold)

Callistephus chinensis (China aster)

Celosia argentea (cockscomb)

Centaurea cyanus (bachelor's-button, cornflower)

Cleome hasslerana (spider flower)

Consolida ambigua (rocket larkspur)

Cosmos bipinnatus (cosmos)

Eustoma grandiflora (lisianthus)

Gaillardia pulchella (annual blanket flower)

Heliotropium arborescens (heliotrope)

Lathyrus odoratus (sweet pea)

Matthiola incana (stock)

Nigella damascena (love-in-a-mist)

Papaver species (poppy)

Pelargonium × *hortorum* (geranium)

Petunia × *hybrida* (petunia)

Salvia farinacea (mealy-cup sage)

Tagetes spp. (marigold)

Viola × *witttrockiana* (pansy)

Zinnia elegans (zinnia)

▪ ANNUALS FOR AIR-DRYING

These annuals make excellent dried flowers. After cutting, hang them upside down in a cool, dry place to dry.

Celosia argentea (cockscomb)

Gomphrena globosa (globe amaranth)

Helichrysum bracteatum (strawflower)

Limonium sinuatum (statice)

Lunaria annua (money plant, honesty) seedpods

Moluccella laevis (bells-of-Ireland)

Nigella damascena (love-in-a-mist)

▪ FRAGRANT ANNUALS

These flowers are attractive and smell good, too. Some perfume the air around them; others hide their charms, sharing their fragrance only when you come near.

Clarkia amoena (farewell-to-spring)

Cleome hasslerana (spider flower)

Dianthus chinensis (China pink)

Erysimum cheiri (wallflower)

Lathyrus odoratus (sweet pea)

Matthiola incana (stock)

Nicotiana alata (flowering tobacco)

Pelargonium spp. (scented geranium)

Petunia × *hybrida* (petunia)

Phlox drummondii (annual phlox)

Tagetes spp. (marigold)

▪ SELF-SOWING ANNUALS

The following annuals readily self-sow and perpetuate themselves in your garden. They are especially suited to cottage gardens.

Antirrhinum majus (snapdragon)

Browallia speciosa (sapphire flower)

Calendula officinalis (pot marigold)

Centaurea cyanus (bachelor's-button, cornflower)

Cleome hasslerana (spider flower)

Consolida ambigua (rocket larkspur)

Cosmos bipinnatus (cosmos)

Eschscholzia californica (California poppy)

Impatiens wallerana (impatiens)

Lobularia maritima (sweet alyssum)

Lunaria annua (money plant, honesty)

Moluccella laevis (bells-of-Ireland)

Myosotis sylvatica (woodland forget-me-not)

Nigella damascena (love-in-a-mist)

Papaver rhoeas (Shirley poppy)

Portulaca grandiflora (moss rose)

Torenia fournieri (wishbone flower)

Tropaeolum majus (nasturtium)

Viola tricolor (Johnny-jump-up)

AGERATUM HOUSTONIANUM
Flossflower

Ageratum is one of the purest blue flowers in the garden. Now it also is available in shades of pink and white. The furry-looking flowers of dwarf types nearly hide the rounded, dark green leaves. Plants grow 6 to 8 inches tall, forming a wide cushion. Taller varieties grow 12 to 30 inches tall and make lovely cut flowers.

Ageratum self-sows in warm, moist climates. Short varieties work best at front of borders, taller ones in midground or in cutting gardens.

AGERATUM HOUSTONIANUM
'ROYAL DELFT'

Site: Full sun; part shade where summers are hot. Rich, well-drained soil. Plentiful moisture. Half-hardy, warm-season annual in zones 2 to 11. In warm climates, replant in late summer for fall bloom.

How to Grow: Sow uncovered indoors at 64° to 70°F, eight to 10 weeks before last frost, or set out nursery transplants after last frost. Space plants 4 to 12 inches apart. Pinch young plants to encourage branching. Shear or pick off faded flowers. Southern blight, powdery mildew, two-spotted mites, whiteflies, gray mold, and snails can be troublesome.

Cultivars: Tall: 'Blue Mink', 12 inches, powder blue; 'Blue Horizon', 30 inches, medium blue; 'Capri', 12 inches, blue and white.

Dwarf to 6 inches tall: 'Hawaii' series, floriferous, compact, white and blue; 'Pink Powderpuffs', pale pink; 'Pinky Improved Selection', dusky pink.

ANTIRRHINUM MAJUS
Snapdragon

Children love to squeeze snapdragon flowers to see the "jaws" open. Some newer types have exchanged their snap for open blossoms, even open double ones. Flowers are purple, red, orange, pink, yellow, white, or bicolored, in dense spikes. Blooms summer to frost from spring planting, early winter to summer when planted in fall in mild-

ANTIRRHINUM MAJUS
'LIBERTY LIGHT PINK'

winter areas. Size varies from bushy dwarfs 7 to 12 inches tall to types that reach 3 feet. Use in front to middle of border in formal or cottage gardens. Tall types best for cut flowers.

Site: Full sun or partial shade. Average to rich, well-drained soil. Moderate water. Cool-season annual in zones 2 to 8. Annual or perennial in zones 9

to 11. Needs cool weather when young for best growth.

How to Grow: Sow seeds uncovered indoors at 55° to 75°F, six to eight weeks before last frost, or buy nursery transplants. In zones 9 to 11, plant in fall. Space 6 to 18 inches apart, depending on final size. Stake taller types. Cut back spent stems to stimulate rebloom. Snapdragon rust is a problem; seek resistant types, don't overhead water, and rotate in garden year to year. Downy mildew, aphids, and whiteflies also are problems.

Cultivars: 'Floral Carpet Mixed', 6 to 8 inches tall; 'Royal Carpet Mixed', 8 inches tall, 12 inches wide; 'Princess with a Red Eye', 20 inches tall, red-and-white bicolor; 'Coronette Mixed', 18 inches tall. Available as mixes or single colors: 'Liberty', 36 inches tall; 'Rocket', 36 inches tall; 'Little Darling', 12 inches tall, trumpet, nonsnap flowers; 'Madame Butterfly', 24 to 30 inches tall, double azalea-type flowers.

BEGONIA ×
SEMPERFLORENS-CULTORUM
Wax Begonia, Bedding Begonia

Whether called wax, fibrous, or bedding begonia, this popular annual blooms willingly in shade. Newer types form tight, compact mounds and often have larger flowers, which may be doubles or picotees. Colors include white and shades of pink, peach, and red. The glossy, rounded leaves may be bright green, bronze, or mottled. Most are 6 to 12 inches tall and as wide. Bronze-leaf types tolerate more sun. Use in beds, formal borders, and containers. Good in shade gardens.

Site: Full sun in cool-summer areas; part to full shade in warmer climates. Fertile, well-drained, organic-rich soil. Moderate water. Spring to fall annual in zones 2 to 8; short-lived perennial in zones 9 to 11, blooming most of year.

How to Grow: Press tiny seeds into surface of seedling mix and grow indoors, at 61° to 75°F, for four to six months, potting once. Or, purchase nursery transplants. Plant outdoors, 8 to 12 inches apart, when soil warms. Can be dug before first frost and brought in as houseplant. Usually problem-free, but sometimes affected by two-spotted spider mites, leaf rot, and whiteflies. Root rot occurs if overwatered.

BEGONIA × SEMPERFLORENS-CULTORUM

Cultivars: Many mixes and single colors available. 'Cocktail', 6 to 8 inches tall, bronze foliage; 'Thousand Wonders', 6 inches; 'Viva', 6 to 8 inches, white; 'Pizzazz', 10 inches, large blossoms; 'Wings', 12 inches tall, extra-large blossoms; 'Frilly Dilly', 10 to 12 inches, frilled petals; 'Bingo' series, bronze foliage, 8 to 10 inches, early flowering; 'Encore', deep bronze or green leaves, extra-large flowers, 12 inches, bushy, upright.

BRACHYCOME IBERIDIFOLIA
Swan River Daisy

A pretty Australian native, the Swan River daisy offers abundant, delicately fragrant, 1-inch-wide, daisylike flowers in blue, pink, violet, or white with dark or yellow centers. The flowers are held on branching

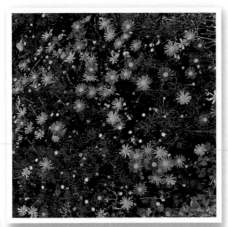

BRACHYCOME IBERIDIFOLIA

stems above fine-textured, gracefully sprawling mounds of needlelike leaves and bloom best in cool weather. Plants grow 8 to 18 inches tall and wide. Mass for informal effect in rock and cottage gardens. Use as edging in formal gardens. Swan River daisy looks beautiful cascading from window boxes or containers.

Site: Full sun. Rich, well-drained soil. Moderate water. Cool-season annual in zones 2 to 11.

How to Grow: Sow indoors, at 60° to 70°F, six weeks before last frost, or if winters are mild, sow in garden in early spring. Space plants 6 inches apart. Tends to burn out when weather turns hot; cut back to rejuvenate. Deadheading and successive plantings prolong bloom period in hot areas. Shear spent flowers to extend blooming. Usually problem-free, except for occasional botrytis and aphids.

Cultivars: Mixes provide several colors. 'Splendor' series, 9 to 12 inches tall, blue, purple, white flowers; 'Blue Star', quilled petals, dark centers.

BRASSICA OLERACEA
Flowering Cabbage and Kale

The spectacular foliage of flowering kale and cabbage is best in cool fall weather; light frost improves the color. Usually blue-green outer leaves surround white or brightly colored inner ones, but variegated leaves are common. Colors include cream, white, pink, rose-red, and purple. Leaves of ornamental kale are frillier than those of ornamental cabbage. Use the edible leaves to garnish salads. Grows 12 to 18 inches tall, 15 to 20 inches across. Plant to replace summer annuals for fall and early-winter display as edging, carpet bedding, or in containers.

BRASSICA OLERACEA

Site: Full sun. Average, well-drained soil. Moderate water. Tender biennial in zones 8 to 10; grown as hardy annual in zones 2 to 11. Showy into mild winters.

How to Grow: Sow in garden in late summer or indoors at 75° to 80°F, eight to 10 weeks before last spring frost. Space 12 inches apart. Purchase nursery plants in fall. Inspect often for pests: Imported cabbageworms, snails and slugs, cutworms, and clubroot.

Cultivars: Many variations. 'Osaka', wavy leaves, red, pink, or white centers; 'Dynasty', mix, semiwavy leaves, rose-red, pink, or white centers; 'Sparrow', dwarf kale, 10 to 12 inches diameter; 'Peacock', cutleaf kale, feathery.

Annuals

BROWALLIA SPECIOSA
Amethyst Flower, Star Flower, Sapphire Flower

A charming choice for shady gardens or window boxes, amethyst flower forms low mounds of bright green leaves studded with

BROWALLIA SPECIOSA
'BLUE BELLS IMPROVED'

starry blue, violet, or white flowers. Plants grow 12 to 18 inches tall and wide. They bloom from late spring through summer where summers are warm and may self-sow. Use as edging and foreground planting and in containers, window boxes, and hanging baskets.

Site: Light to part shade; full sun in cool areas. Fertile, well-drained soil rich in organic matter. Plentiful moisture. Mulch in cool areas. Warm-season annual in zones 2 to 11. May not flower in short, cool summers. May live through mildest winters.
How to Grow: Sow uncovered, at 64° to 75°F, eight weeks before last frost date. Set out, after last frost, 8 to 10 inches apart. Use as houseplant at summer's end. Whiteflies are common; botrytis strikes occasionally.
Cultivars: 'Blue Bells', lavender-blue flowers; 'Marine Bells', indigo-blue flowers; 'Blue Troll', clear blue flowers; 'White Bells' and 'Silver Bells', white

flowers. 'Starlight' series, dwarf to 6 inches tall, good basal branching, early and long blooming; 'Blue', 'Sky Blue'.

CALENDULA OFFICINALIS
Pot Marigold

This easy-to-grow annual is a pot herb often found in cottage or herb gardens. The 2- to 4-inch-wide, daisy-type flowers often are double and bloom on sturdy branched stems with small straplike leaves. Long available in orange and bright yellow, newer hues include white, cream, pale yellow, and apricot. The petals are edible in soup or salad. Calendula

CALENDULA OFFICINALIS

often self-sows. Plants grow 1 to 2 feet tall, 10 to 15 inches wide. Use in front or midground in borders or in cottage, herb, or cutting gardens.

Site: Full sun. Poor to rich, well-drained soil. Moderate water. Cool-season annual in zones 2 to 11. Has larger blossoms in cool weather.
How to Grow: Sow in garden in early spring to midsummer in zones 3 to 8, fall to spring in zones 9 to 11. Or, sow indoors at 70°F, six to eight weeks before planting outdoors. Set 10 to 15 inches apart. Remove spent blossoms to prolong bloom period. Troubled by powdery mildew, leaf spot, smut, cabbage loopers, and aphids.

Cultivars: 'Fiesta Gitana', 9 to 12 inches tall, mixed colors; 'Bon Bon', 1 foot tall, mixed or single colors; 'Pacific Beauty', 18 inches tall, mixed colors; 'Art Shades', 24 inches tall, mixed colors, including apricot and cream; 'Touch of Red', 16 to 18 inches tall, mixed colors with red picotee.

CALLISTEPHUS CHINENSIS

CALLISTEPHUS CHINENSIS
China Aster

The native Chinese plant produces single, daisylike purple flowers, but breeders have created blue, pink, peach, red, and white semidouble and double flowers with shapes varying from spidery to pompon. The midsummer-into-fall flowers are fine for cutting, but plants don't rebloom if cut. Plants are 6 to 36 inches tall. Dwarfs are as wide as they are tall; tall ones are 1 foot or more wide. Use dwarfs for edging and taller ones in middle of border or in cutting beds.

Site: Full sun or light shade. Rich, well-drained, neutral to basic soil. Moderate water. Warm-season annual in zones 2 to 11.
How to Grow: Sow in place when frost danger is past or indoors at 55° to 64°F, six weeks earlier. Thin to 6 to 12 inches apart. Replant every few weeks for continuous bloom. Stake tall

types. Wilt diseases and aster yellows virus are common; destroy affected plants, seek resistant types, rotate planting location. Aphids, mealybugs, rust, and gray mold may be problems.
Cultivars: Wilt-resistant: 'Ostrich Plume', 18 inches tall; 'Pastel Mixed', 30 inches tall; 'Dwarf Queen' and 'Carpet Ball', 8 to 10 inches tall.

Unusual: 'All Change', 15 to 18 inches tall, bicolored pompons; 'Florette Champagne', 20 to 24 inches tall, quilled, pale pink flowers.

CATHARANTHUS ROSEUS (VINCA ROSEA)
Periwinkle, Vinca

One of the most reliable annuals in summer heat, this glossy-leaved spreader is covered with 1½-inch-wide phloxlike blossoms from May until frost. Flowers may be white, light or deep pink, or bicolored, including white with a red eye. The

CATHARANTHUS ROSEUS

tidy foliage and pretty blossoms of this durable annual make it an excellent seasonal groundcover. Or, use as an edging or in containers and hanging baskets. Plants grow 4 to 24 inches tall and as wide or wider.

Site: Full sun or part shade. Any well-drained soil. Withstands drought; does better if kept moist. Annual in zones 2

to 8; perennial in zones 9 to 11. Thrives in heat.
How to Grow: Use nursery plants or sow indoors, at 70° to 75°F, eight to 12 weeks before last frost. Space 8 to 18 inches apart. Shear plants in mid- to late summer to force new growth and blossoms. Slugs are the only serious problem.
Cultivars: 'Carpet' series, 4 inches tall, 24 inches wide. 'Pretty In' series, 12 to 14 inches tall, large flowers. 'Cooler' series, 6 to 8 inches tall and wide, good where cool.

CELOSIA ARGENTEA 'APRICOT BEAUTY'

CELOSIA ARGENTEA
Cockscomb

Cockscomb flowers come in two forms: plumes resembling colorful hat feathers or convoluted, velvety crests resembling a rooster's comb. Both bloom in white, gold, pink, and shades of red and maroon, and are available in dwarf, medium, and tall forms, 4 to 36 inches tall with equal width. Plumed types also come in orange and apricot. Plants tolerate high temperatures, bloom from midsummer to frost, and make excellent cut or dried flowers. Use cockscomb in formal and informal gardens, bedding, containers, and cutting beds.

Site: Full sun. Rich, fertile soil. Moderate water. Warm-season annual in zones 2 to 11.
How to Grow: Sow seeds outdoors, barely covered, when soil is warm, or indoors, at 64° to 75°F, four weeks before last frost. Set out before plants bloom; space 4 to 18 inches apart. Harden-off transplants well before planting out. Spider mites sometimes troublesome; root rot may occur after transplanting if too wet.
Cultivars: Crested: 'Toreador' and 'Fireglow', both red, 20 inches tall; 'Jewel Box Mixed', 5 to 9 inches tall.

Plumed: 'Century Mixed', 24 inches tall; 'Geisha', 10 inches tall; 'Kimono', 4 to 6 inches tall, mixed and solid colors.

CENTAUREA SPP.
Dusty-Miller, Cornflower, Bachelor's-Button

The common name dusty-miller (*Centaurea cineraria, Chrysanthemum ptarmiciflorum*) refers to several similar-looking plants grown

CENTAUREA CINERARIA 'SILVERDUST'

for their magnificent silvery gray, felt-covered leaves. Leaves of *Centaurea cineraria* are bluntly lobed; the leaves of *Chrysanthemum ptarmiciflorum* are lacier. Plants grow 6 to 18 inches tall and as wide. Both enhance the colorful flowers of other plants when tucked between or planted in a *continued*

CENTAUREA SPP.
(continued)

drift. Plant dusty-miller in groups in beds and borders to form bold contrasts; use as edging or in window boxes and containers.

Cornflowers *(C. cyanus)* often provide the blue in a Fourth of July bouquet. They also bloom in mixtures that combine blue with white, pink,

CENTAUREA CYANUS

and purple. The 1½-inch-wide button-shaped flowers are vivid against their gray-green stems and small, narrow leaves. Cornflowers grow 1 to 3 feet tall and half as wide. They often self-sow. Cornflower is a delicate plant for weaving with other flowers in borders, cottage gardens, and meadow plantings; good cut flower.

Site: Full sun. Both plants prefer warm weather. Dusty-miller likes average to rich, well-drained soil. Moderate water. *Centaurea cineraria:* half-hardy annual in zones 2 to 4; perennial in zones 5 to 11, but best replanted each year and treated as annual. *Chrysanthemum ptarmiciflorum:* annual in zones 2 to 11. Cornflower does best in sandy loam with moderate moisture; tolerates poor soil and drought. Grow biennial cornflower as a warm-season annual in zones 2 to 8; grow as cool-season

annual in warmer parts of Zone 9 and in zones 10 and 11.

How to Grow: Sow dusty-miller uncovered indoors, at 75° to 80°F, 10 weeks before last frost, or use nursery starts. In zones 10 and 11, set out in fall. Space 12 to 18 inches apart. Remove flower stems in bud stage; cut back to keep compact. Root rot is common in wet soil; aphids, downy mildew, aster yellows, and rust sometimes cause problems. Sow cornflower in garden after last frost, or indoors, at 60° to 76°F, four weeks earlier for summer bloom. Sow in garden in late summer or fall for spring bloom. Space 6 to 15 inches apart. Deadhead after first flush of bloom to prolong bloom period. Aphids sometimes serious.

Cultivars and Similar Species:
Centaurea cineraria: 'Cirrus', less lobed than species; 'Silverdust', 7 inches tall, more finely cut.

Chrysanthemum ptarmiciflorum: 'Silver Lace', 7 inches tall, lacy.

Cornflower: Blue Boy', 2 to 3 feet tall, blue flowers; 'Jubilee Gem', 12 inches tall, deep blue flowers, dense; 'Polka Dot', 15 inches tall, white, blue, and crimson flowers.

CLEOME HASSLERANA
Spider Flower

Spider flower's tall, sturdy stems are tipped from midsummer to frost with 3-inch-wide rounded clusters of pink, violet, or white blossoms. Elongated stamens and long seedpods give plants an airy, spidery look. Leaves are large and have seven lobes. It makes a delightful cut flower, although its odor may be unpleasant up close, but is not overpowering. Spider flower grows 3 to 4 feet tall and 1 foot wide; may reach 5 to 6 feet tall. Use as back-of-border plant in informal or cottage gardens or in cutting beds. Group for bushier effect. Underplant with shorter plants to hide an eventually leggy base.

CLEOME HASSLERANA

Site: Full sun or partial shade. Average to rich soil. Moderate to plentiful water. Warm-season, hardy annual in zones 2 to 11; tolerates heat if well watered.

How to Grow: Chill seeds overnight and sow in garden after last frost or indoors, at 70° to 75°F, four to six weeks earlier. Set plants 1½ to 2½ feet apart. Stake plants in part shade or windy locations. Be careful of thorny stems. Often self-sows. Usually pest-free, but sometimes bothered by aphids, leaf spot, and rust.

Cultivars: 'Queen' series: pink, rose, violet, white or mixed colors. 'Helen Campbell', white flowers.

COLEUS × HYBRIDUS (SOLENOSTEMON SCUTELLARIODES)
Coleus

Multicolored foliage makes coleus a favorite shade-garden plant, providing color from early summer to frost. Tooth-edged leaves may be broad or narrow, crinkled or flat, and feature simple patterns or harlequin markings in combinations of green, red, pink, yellow, bronze, purple, and almost black. Named varieties provide mixes or same-patterned leaves. Plants propagated by cuttings are desirable for uniform color. Plants grow 6 to 24 inches tall, variable width. Use

COLEUS × HYBRIDUS 'BELLINGRATH PINK'

groupings of same color or pattern to avoid busy look. Purple and chartreuse forms are excellent color contrasts in foliage gardens.

Site: Partial to full shade. Rich, well-drained soil. Plentiful moisture. Warm-season annual in zones 2 to 11.
How to Grow: Sow uncovered indoors at 65° to 75°F, six to eight weeks before last frost, or buy nursery starts. Space 6 to 12 inches apart. Stem cuttings root easily. Some are basal branching; others will be bushier if pinched while small. Pinch older plants to reshape; remove blossom spikes early to keep plants attractive. May be attacked by mites, mealybugs, leafspot, and damping-off fungus.
Cultivars: Color mixes and cultivars available: 'Wizard', 10 to 12 inches tall, solid or mixed colors; 'Fiji Mix', 12 to 15 inches, fringed; 'Black Dragon', 12 inches, rose flowers with purple edge; 'Scarlet Poncho', 12 inches tall, red flowers with gold edge.

CONSOLIDA AMBIGUA (DELPHINIUM AJACIS)
Rocket Larkspur, Annual Delphinium

An annual cousin of the magnificent perennial delphinium, rocket larkspur bears similar tall stems of spurred blossoms. The blue, white,

lilac, pink, or peach flowers emit a light scent and are held above a mass of lacy, dark green foliage. At its best where summers are cool, this fine cutting flower is handsome when grouped in a border. May self-sow. Cultivars grow 9 inches to 4 feet tall. Charming in cottage or informal gardens. Excellent filler among bulbs; essential in cut-flower gardens.

CONSOLIDA AMBIGUA

Site: Full sun or light shade. Rich, well-drained soil. Plentiful water; avoid wetting leaves. Hardy, cool-season annual in zones 2 to 11. Warm weather shortens bloom period.
How to Grow: In zones 9 to 11, sow in fall for spring bloom. Otherwise, sow in early spring to summer. Chill summer-sown seeds one week before planting. May be started indoors at 60° to 65°F, six to eight weeks before setting out. Space 12 inches apart. May require staking. Cut spent stems for longer bloom. May be troubled by aphids, leaf miners, mealybugs, and southern blight; root rot or crown rot in wet soil.
Cultivars and Similar Species: 'Giant Imperial' series, 3 to 4 feet tall, mixed or solid colors; 'Imperial Blue Picotee', 3 feet, white with blue edge; 'Dwarf Hyacinth Flowered Mix', 12 inches, double; 'Blue Butterfly', 12 inches tall, long-blooming.

COSMOS SPP.
Cosmos, Yellow Cosmos

One of the easiest annuals to grow, the airy cosmos (*Cosmos bipinnatus*) has satiny, 3- to 4-inch-wide, yellow-centered daisy-type blossoms in bright magenta, shades of rose, pink, white, or bicolored. Older types grow 3 to 6 feet tall; newer strains, 2 to 3 feet tall. Cosmos is a good cut flower, and cutting prolongs its bloom period, which can last from July to frost. The plants often self-sow.

Yellow cosmos (*C. sulphureus*), a cousin of *C. bipinnatus,* blooms in

COSMOS BIPINNATUS 'SEASHELLS'

vibrant shades of gold, yellow, orange, and scarlet. Cut the 2- to 3-inch-wide flowers when freshly opened. Full-size types of yellow cosmos can reach 7 feet tall. Newer strains may be 3 to 4 feet or 1-foot-tall dwarfs.

Both types of cosmos are ideal for informal or cottage gardens or meadow plantings. Taller versions shine in back of borders or cutting gardens; use dwarfs in the middle of borders or in containers.

Site: Full sun. Poor to average, well-drained soil. Overfertilizing inhibits blooming. Somewhat drought-tolerant. Half-hardy, warm-season annual in zones 3 to 10. Yellow cosmos *continued*

COSMOS SPP.
(continued)

COSMOS SULPHUREUS 'SUNNY RED'

is heat-tolerant and does well in zones 2 to 11.

How to Grow: Sow outdoors in place in spring when soil is warm or indoors at 68° to 86°F, six to eight weeks before last frost. Space plants 1 to 1½ feet apart. Yellow cosmos does not transplant well; best sown in garden. For best blooming, pinch out plant tips when they're about 1½ feet tall. In windy locations, stake or interplant with sturdier plants. Usually pest-free, but sometimes troubled by bacterial wilt, powdery mildew, aster-yellows virus, aphids, and mites.

Cultivars: Cosmos: In short-season areas, plant early blooming 'Sensation' and 'Early Wonder' series. 'Purity', white flowers, 3 to 4 feet tall; 'Gloria', 5-inch pink-red flowers, 3 to 4 feet tall; 'Seashells', white, pink, or two-toned, 3½ feet tall; 'Red Versailles', fiery red flowers, 4 feet tall; 'Imperial Pink', deep rose-pink flowers, 3 to 4 feet tall; 'Sonata' series, early flowering in white or mixed colors, bushy, 2 feet tall.

Yellow cosmos: 'Bright Lights', 3 feet tall in mixed shades of yellow, orange, and red; 'Ladybird' series, 1 foot tall, mixed or solid colors, 1½- to 2-inch flowers; 'Sunny Gold' or 'Sunny Red', 12 to 14 inches tall.

DAHLIA × HYBRIDA
Annual Dahlia

These shorter versions of tuberous dahlias are also tender perennials, but because they bloom the first summer from seed, they're used as annuals. Although annual dahlia blossoms are smaller than their gigantic cousins, they come in the same brilliant colors—every color except blue—and include single, semidouble, double, and collarette

DAHLIA × HYBRIDA

(having a second row of larger petal-like rays in a second color) dahlia flower forms. Plants are 1 to 2 feet tall, about half as wide. Excellent plant in formal or informal gardens in foreground or midground. Also grow annual dahlia in cutting beds or in containers.

Site: Full or at least half-day sun. Fertile, moist soil. Cool-season annual in zones 3 to 11. May not thrive in extremely hot summer weather.

How to Grow: Sow indoors at 68° to 85°F, six to eight weeks before last frost. In areas with long growing season, sow seed outdoors in place. Plant 12 inches apart. Pinch tips early in season for bushier plants. Cut spent flowers for longer bloom. Occasionally aphids, powdery mildew, and spider

mites are problems. In West, earwigs may eat flowers and foliage.

Cultivars: 'Mignon Silver', 15 to 20 inches tall, white.

Mixed colors: 'Rigoletto', 13 inches; 'Redskin', 14 inches, reddish foliage; 'Collarette Dandy', 20 to 24 inches; and 'Sunny' series, red, rose, or yellow.

DIANTHUS CHINENSIS
China Pink

China pinks' 1- to 2-inch-wide, lightly scented flowers cover the low mounds of grassy, blue-green leaves from late spring to frost. Blossoms have fringed petals in white, pink, coral, red, crimson, or purple; bicolors often are intricately patterned. Plants grow 6 to 12 inches tall and spread to 1½ times as wide. They may self-sow. Use low types as edging in cottage gardens, as long-season color in rock gardens, or in containers. Use tall types in cutting beds.

DIANTHUS CHINENSIS 'TELSTAR PICOTEE'

Site: Full sun to light shade. Average, well-drained, neutral to alkaline soil and moderate water. Tolerates poor soil and drought. Hardy, cool-season annual in zones 2 to 11; tolerates light frost.

How to Grow: Sow outdoors after last frost or indoors, at 70° to 75°F, eight to

10 weeks before last frost. In mild-winter areas, sow outdoors in fall. Blossoms are usually self cleaning, but shearing in midsummer rejuvenates heat-stressed plants. Root rot occurs in heavy, wet soils; spider mites appear in dry climates.

Cultivars: 'Queen of Hearts', scarlet-red. Mixes of mostly solid colors: 'Charms', 6 to 8 inches; 'Princess', 8 to 10 inches.

Solids and picotees: 'Telstar', 8 to 10 inches, dark red "eyes"; 'Strawberry Parfait', 8 inches, early bloomer, rose with scarlet centers; and 'Raspberry Parfait', 8 inches, blush pink with crimson centers, early bloomer.

Solid and bicolor mix: 'Splendor Mixed', 8 to10 inches. 'Flash' series in pink or mix, heat-tolerant.

DYSSODIA TENUILOBA (THYMOPHYLLA TENUILOBA)
Dahlberg Daisy, Golden Fleece

A delicate-looking plant with a mass of ½- to 1-inch-wide, bright yellow daisies blanketing the finely divided dark green leaves, dahlberg

DYSSODIA TENUILOBA

daisy's perky blossoms continue from summer through fall and into early winter where mild temperatures permit. Plants grow 8 to 12 inches tall and sprawl. They often self-sow. The fine texture looks perfect in rock

gardens and planted in stone walls and gravel paths. Or, use to cascade over the edge of containers and in hanging baskets.

Site: Full sun. Any well-drained soil. Allow soil to dry between waterings. Tender annual in zones 2 to 11. May overwinter, but generally looks scruffy after winter. Drought- and heat-tolerant.

How to Grow: Purchase nursery plants or sow uncovered indoors at 65° to 70°F, six to eight weeks before last frost. Where winters are mild, sow in garden in fall or set out transplants in fall or early spring, spacing 6 inches apart. Takes four months to flower from seed; may prove difficult to start indoors. Usually pest-free.

ESCHSCHOLZIA CALIFORNICA

ESCHSCHOLZIA CALIFORNICA
California Poppy

The satiny, 2-inch-long blossoms of California poppy wave atop long, nearly bare stems above finely cut gray-green leaves. Wild versions are gleaming orange, yellow, or bicolored; new garden selections include cream, crimson, pink, and violet—some with fluted or doubled petals. Plants are 8 to 24 inches tall, often sprawling. California's state flower blooms in summer from a spring sowing or in spring if sown in fall. Flowers close in

shade or on overcast days. Plants often self-sow. California poppies are charming in rock gardens, cottage gardens, and low meadow plantings.

Site: Full sun to partial shade. Sandy, nonacid soil. Rich soil inhibits bloom. Needs ample water until past seedling stage, then drought-tolerant. Hardy, cool-season annual in zones 2 to 11.

How to Grow: Sow in garden in fall or in early spring. Thin to 6 inches. Cut spent flowers to prolong blooming. Usually pest-free; sometimes bacterial blight, leaf mold, powdery mildew, and aster yellows virus occur.

Cultivars: Single colors: 'Orange King', 'Milky White', 'Purple-violet', and 'Mikado', crimson-orange.

Mixes: 'Ballerina' and 'Mission Bells', semidouble and double. 'Thai Silk', 8 to 10 inches tall with fluted petals, pink shades or mixed.

Similar: *Eschscholzia caespitosa* 'Sundew', 6 to 10 inches tall, yellow, and scented.

EUSTOMA GRANDIFLORA (LISIANTHUS RUSSELLIANUS)
Lisianthus, Prairie Gentian

A native American wildflower, lisianthus is popular for its beauty and its ability to last as a cut flower.

EUSTOMA GRANDIFLORA

continued

EUSTOMA GRANDIFLORA
(continued)

The upturned cup-shaped blossoms, up to 3½ inches across, may be single or double, white, pale yellow, pink, violet, blue, or bicolored. Gray-green leaves meet in pairs on the stems. Plants grow 6 to 28 inches tall and half as wide. Plant in groups in informal gardens or containers.

Site: Full sun to partial shade. Average, well-drained soil. Keep moist. Biennial grown as a half-hardy annual in zones 2 to 11. Prefers warm climate.
How to Grow: Sow uncovered indoors at 68° to 77°F, three months before last frost, or purchase nursery transplants. Space 6 inches apart. Some types are basal branching; others will be bushy if pinched while small. Cut faded flowers. Usually pest-free, but occasionally root rot or leaf spot occurs.
Cultivars: 'Double Eagle Mixed', 18 to 24 inches tall, blossoms to 3 inches across. Mix or single color series: 'Echo', 24 inches tall, includes some picotees; 'Flamenco', heat-tolerant, includes some colored-rim types.
  Dwarfs: 'Mermaid', 6 to 8 inches tall, 'Little Bell Mixed', 9 inches tall, silver-veined leaves, double.

FELICIA AMELLOIDES
Blue Daisy, Blue Marguerite

This eye-catcher features flowers with blue petals and yellow centers on slender stems above a mound of small, oval, dark green leaves. Plants grow 1 to 2 feet tall and 4 to 5 feet wide if untrimmed. Flowers close at night and on overcast days. Effective in rock gardens, cascading over walls and embankments, and in window boxes and containers. Combines well with yellow flowers.

FELICIA AMELLOIDES

Site: Full sun. Fertile, well-drained soil. Drought-tolerant, but better with water. Cool-season annual in zones 7 and 8; perennial in zones 9 to 11, but difficult to keep looking healthy beyond the first year.
How to Grow: Set out nursery plants in spring in cold-winter areas, in fall where winters are mild. Or, sow indoors at 55° to 60°F, 10 to 12 weeks before last frost. Plant 9 inches apart. Pinch, shape, and deadhead frequently. Prune to control spread. Cut spent flowers to prolong bloom. Usually pest-free, but occasionally aphids, beech scale, scab, or caterpillars are troublesome.
Cultivars and Similar Species: Dark blue: 'George Lewis', 'Midnight', and 'Rhapsody in Blue'.
  Medium blue: 'San Luis', 'San Gabriel', and 'Santa Anita'.
  Dwarf: 'Astrid Thomas' (stays open at night). *Felicia bergeriana* is similar, 4 to 6 inches tall, with abundant ½-inch, turquoise blue flowers.

FUCHSIA × HYBRIDA
Fuchsia, Lady's Eardrops

The fanciful flowers of fuchsia feature prominent stamens and pistils dangling through the ring of petals, which is framed by decorative backswept sepals. Sepals and petals may be white, pink, red, or purple and are often two different colors.

FUCHSIA × HYBRIDA

A shrub where mild winters permit, fuchsia is grown as an annual elsewhere. It is 1 to 2 feet tall when grown as an annual. Often grown in hanging baskets or as a standard in a container. Use as a temporary low shrub in mild climates.

FUCHSIA × HYBRIDA

Site: Light shade or full sun. Average, neutral to acidic, well-drained soil and moderate water. Do not allow to dry out. Annual in zones 2 to 8; perennial in zones 9 to 11. Plant prefers cool, humid weather.
How to Grow: Set out nursery plants in the spring or use plants grown from softwood cuttings taken in summer. Some seed is available; sow indoors at

70° to 75°F. Expect germination in three to 13 weeks. Pinch tips of young plants to increase bushiness. Fuchsia mites, spider mites, whiteflies, and aphids are sometimes troublesome.

GAILLARDIA PULCHELLA
Annual Blanket Flower

A homespun flower of the American prairie, annual gaillardia looks right at home in informal gardens. Flowers are 2 to

GAILLARDIA PULCHELLA 'RED PLUME'

3 inches across, yellow, gold, cream, red, or crimson, often with bicolored petals, and have dark red centers. Newer double types resemble bright pompons and grow on more compact plants. This excellent cutting flower grows 10 to 24 inches tall and blooms from late spring to frost. Use in meadow gardens, informal borders, cutting beds, and containers.

Site: Full sun. Best in poor, sandy soil kept moderately dry. Drought-tolerant. Half-hardy, warm-season annual in zones 2 to 11.

How to Grow: Sow in garden after last frost or indoors at 70° to 75°F, four to six weeks before last frost. Barely cover seeds. Thin to 12 inches apart. Does poorly in cold, heavy soil. Deadhead to prolong bloom. Leaf spot, powdery

mildew, rust, and aphids are sometimes troublesome.

Cultivars: Species is single, to 2 feet tall with solid or bicolored petals. 'Double Mixed', 24 inches tall, double flowers in cream, gold, crimson, and bicolors; 'Red Plume', 12 to 14 inches tall, red pompon; 'Yellow Plume', 12 to 14 inches tall, yellow pompon.

GAZANIA RIGENS

GAZANIA RIGENS
Treasure Flower

Brightly splashed flowers stand on single stems, 6 to 12 inches tall, above mats of leaves 6 to 9 inches tall. Flowers are 2½- to 5-inch-wide daisies. Older types are solid yellow, orange, red, or bronze with black dots at each petal base. Newer ones may be boldly striped or ringed with contrasting colors. Flowers close at night, and most kinds close on dull days. The lobed leaves may be silvery on the undersides or both sides. Makes a good groundcover. Use for edging or in containers.

Site: Full sun; tolerates light shade. Poor to average, well-drained soil. Tolerates drought. Tender annual in zones 2 to 8; perennial in zones 9 to 11. Best in dry, hot climates where it blooms from three to four months after

seeding until frost; blooms year-round in mild areas.

How to Grow: Grow from nursery plants or sow indoors at 68° to 86°F, seven to nine weeks before last frost. Space 6 to 10 inches apart. Gazania can be overwintered as cuttings from favorite plants. Crown rot develops if overwatered.

Cultivars: 'Ministar', 8 to 9 inches tall, solids, including beige and pink, 2½-inch flowers; 'Sundance', 12 inches tall, darker colors and a red-and-yellow stripe, 5-inch flowers; 'Sunshine', 6 inches tall, rings and stripes, 4-inch flowers; 'Daybreak', 8 inches tall, large blossoms open earlier in the day. 'Chansonette Mix', 10 inches tall, compact, early flowering.

GOMPHRENA GLOBOSA
Globe Amaranth

This easy-to-grow everlasting adds a strong presence to a border because it forms a dense bushy plant sprinkled with colorful cloverlike

GOMPHRENA GLOBOSA 'BICOLOR ROSE GLOBOSA'

flowers. The 1-inch flower balls, formed of papery bracts, may be purple, red, lavender, pink, or white and are favorites for cutting or for dried bouquets. Plants are 8 to 24 inches tall to 12 inches *continued*

GOMPHRENA GLOBOSA
(continued)

wide. Charming in cottage or informal gardens. Essential in cut-flower beds.

Site: Full sun. Poor to average, well-drained soil; sandy soil best. Moderate water, but tolerates drought. Half-hardy, warm-season annual in zones 2 to 11. Grows best in hot, dry locations, but tolerates humidity.
How to Grow: Soak seed 1 to 4 days, then sow in garden after last frost or indoors at 70° to 75°F, six to eight weeks before last frost. Space 10 to 15 inches apart. Taller varieties may need staking. Cut when partly open for drying and hang in a shady place. Occasionally aphids, two-spotted spider mites, and red spider mites are troublesome.
Cultivars and Similar Species: 'Buddy' series, 6 to 8 inches tall, purple or white. All 18 to 24 inches tall; 'Lavender Lady', lavender-pink; 'Strawberry Fayre', light red; 'Innocence', white; 'Professor Plum', purple; 'Amber Glow', light orange; 'Blushing Bride', pale salmon-pink.

HELIANTHUS ANNUUS
Sunflower

While the tall sunflowers grown for their edible seeds make a striking appearance, newer, lower ornamental types offer more garden-worthy sizes, colors, and forms. Flowers vary from a few inches to more than a foot across and are borne singly or in groups on sturdy stems clothed in large heart-shaped leaves. Most have showy dark centers with bright yellow, cream, orange, maroon, or bicolored petals. Sunflowers grow 2 to 12 feet tall, 1 to 3 feet wide. Use sunflowers in informal and cottage gardens and in cutting beds or as temporary hedge or screen.

HELIANTHUS ANNUUS

Site: Full sun. Poor to average, well-drained soil; provide ample water. Hardy, warm-season annual in zones 2 to 11. Thrives in heat.
How to Grow: Sow in garden after last frost or indoors at 68° to 86°F, four to six weeks before last frost date. Space 1 to 3 feet apart. Stake taller types. To save seeds, wrap head in paper bag until mature.
   Verticillium wilt, powdery mildew, and beetles may be troublesome.
Cultivars: 'Mammoth', 12 feet tall, edible seeds; 'Sunburst', 4 feet tall, mixed colors, 4-inch heads; 'Italian White', 4 feet tall, cream and pale yellow, 4-inch heads; 'Sunspot', 18 to 24 inches tall, yellow, 10-inch heads; 'Sunbeam', 5 feet tall, green centers. 'Teddy Bear', dwarf, double, golden orange, 6-inch heads.

HELICHRYSUM BRACTEATUM
Strawflower

Strawflower's 1- to 2-inch-wide double blossoms grow in clusters on narrow plants and bloom in shades of orange, pink, yellow, red, white, bronze, and purple from July until the first hard frost. Plants are 1 to 4 feet tall, 6 to 10 inches wide. The dainty flowers are pretty in the cottage

garden, as cut flowers, or in dried arrangements.

Site: Full sun. Average to sandy, well-drained alkaline soil kept on dry side; drought-tolerant. Half-hardy, warm-season annual in zones 2 to 11.
How to Grow: In long-season areas, sow outdoors after last frost. Elsewhere, sow indoors at 70° to 75°F, six to eight weeks before last frost. Space 8 to 10 inches apart. May self-sow. Stake taller forms. For dried flowers, cut before central yellow eye is visible, strip leaves, wire stems, and hang in warm, dry room. Aster yellows virus and aphids may be troublesome.

HELICHRYSUM BRACTEATUM

Cultivars: 'Monstrosum', 3 to 4 feet tall, mix and single colors; 'Pastel Mixed', 3 to 4 feet; 'Bright Bikini Mix', 10 to 12 inches, bushy and showy; 'Frosted Sulphur/Silvery Rose', 30 to 36 inches, pale silvery yellow and pink.

HELIOTROPIUM ARBORESCENS
Heliotrope

Heliotrope is best loved for its intoxicating, vanilla-like scent, which is most intense in the evening. The small flowers are borne in dense heads 1 to several inches across, from

HELIOTROPIUM ARBORESCENS 'MARINE'

HYPOESTES PHYLLOSTACHYA
Polka-Dot Plant

This colorful tropical perennial has been grown for years as a houseplant, but has recently gained popularity as a garden annual. Older forms have small, pointed, dark green leaves spotted and streaked with pink polka dots. Newer strains have more color and less green, being splashed all over with white, pink, rose, or maroon. Plants are 8 to 24 inches tall and spreading. Colorful ground-covering plant for shade gardens; plant to tumble over edge of containers.

HYPOESTES PHYLLOSTACHYA 'WHITE SPLASH'

Site: Light shade. Rich, moist, well-drained soil; provide plentiful water. Warm-season annual in zones 3 to 10; perennial in Zone 11.
How to Grow: Sow indoors at 70° to 75°F, 10 to 12 weeks before soil is warm. Space 8 to 10 inches apart. Pinch to encourage branching and to shape; pinch out flower buds. Sometimes gray mold attacks.
Cultivars: 'Confetti' series, 18 to 24 inches tall, mixed or single, in burgundy, pink, rose, or white; 'Splash Select' series, 8 to 10 inches, pink, rose, or white.

IMPATIENS WALLERANA
Impatiens, Busy Lizzie

Admired for the carpets of care-free color it produces in the shade, impatiens is the number-one rated annual. Intensive breeding

IMPATIENS 'DECO ORANGE'

brings myriad varieties, including types that branch basally and need no pinching, ones that form a blanket of self-cleaning blossoms, ones with better sun tolerance, and an ever-expanding color range. The 1- to 2-inch-wide, open-faced blossoms have spurred petals and come in white, pink, rose, red, peach, salmon, orange, lavender, or purple and may be bicolored. A few produce double roselike blossoms. Leaves are usually bright green, but some types are bronze or variegated. Plants grow 6 to 15 inches tall, 10 to 18 inches wide. Best planted in single-color groups in shaded gardens, window boxes, or containers. Combines with ferns, hostas, and other shade-loving foliage plants. Pastel colors stand out best in shade.

Site: Part or full shade; tolerates full sun in cool-summer areas. Rich, sandy loam; plentiful moisture, especially when hot. Tender perennial grown as half-hardy, warm-season *continued*

early summer to frost, and may be purple, deep blue, lavender, or white. The leaves are deeply veined, lance-shaped, and dark green. Plants grow 1 to 2 feet tall and as wide. Heliotrope can be potted for overwintering inside. Use in cottage gardens or informal borders, containers, and cutting beds.

Site: Full sun, afternoon shade where summers are hot. Rich to average well-drained soil; moderate water, but not drought-tolerant. Half-hardy annual in zones 2 to 9; can be carried through with some protection in Zone 10; perennial in Zone 11.
How to Grow: Set out purchased plants when weather has settled or sow seed indoors at 65° to 75°F, 10 to 12 weeks ahead. Space 1 foot apart. Overwatering decreases scent. Aphids, thrips, mealybugs, and gray mold are sometimes troublesome.
Cultivars and Similar Species: 'Marine', 18 inches tall, violet-purple; 'Dwarf Marine', 14 inches tall; 'Fragrant Delight', 2 to 3 feet tall, deep lavender, richly fragrant; *Heliotropium* × *peruvianum*, 18 to 24 inches tall, lavender to purple, some with white eyes.

IMPATIENS WALLERANA
(continued)

annual in zones 2 to 10. Perennial in Zone 11 and mild parts of Zone 10.
How to Grow: Use nursery transplants or sow lightly covered indoors at 70° to 75°F, 10 to 12 weeks before last frost. Set 10 to 15 inches apart. Some types come true only from cuttings. If plants don't branch enough, pinch tips. Wilting at midday usually means too much sun, too little water. Occasionally subject to two-spotted spider mites, thrips, and damping-off fungus.
Cultivars: 'Super Elfin' series, 6 to 10 inches tall, 11-color mix and single colors, excellent in deep shade. 'Accent' series, 4 to 8 inches tall, 2-inch blossoms, 15 colors and 5 bicolors called 'Accent Star'; 'Rosette Hybrid Mix', 18 to 20 inches tall, doubles. 'Deco' series, red, orange, purple, or scarlet with bronze foliage. 'Blitz' series, 12 to 14 inches tall, 2-inch flowers. 'Dazzler' series, 8 to 10 inches tall, excellent shade performer, in more than 15 colors, including 'Cranberry' and 'Sky Blue' (pale lavender). 'Confection' series, 12 to 24 inches tall, double and semidouble flowers in light pink, orange, red, rose, or mixed.

Impatiens × hybrida (New Guinea impatiens), bushy 12 to 36 inches tall and wide, sun-tolerant plants, 3- to 4-inch vivid red, orange, pink, coral, purple, lavender, or white single, spurred flowers with brightly colored leaves in bronze or green bicolored or tricolored leaves with stripes and splashes of bronze, yellow, orange, and red.

I. balsamina (rose balsam), a Victorian favorite, 12 to 36 inches tall, blossoms tucked between the leaves along stems, flowers white or shades of pink, rose, salmon, scarlet, yellow, or purple; some are bicolored.

LANTANA CAMARA
Lantana

Lantana has 1½-inch-wide flat domes of small flowers arranged in a pinwheel and blooms nonstop in gardens from late spring to frost. Flowers start out yellow, turn orange

LANTANA CAMARA 'PINK CAPRICE'

or red, and finally turn to lavender, sometimes showing all colors at once. Other colors include white, orange, yellow, red and yellow, and white and lavender. Plants are 1½ to 4 feet tall and are wide-spreading. Lantana is an excellent groundcover in informal gardens and a graceful trailer for containers and window boxes.

Site: Full sun. Average to rich, neutral to acidic, well-drained soil; moderate water. Tropical shrub grown as an annual in zones 2 to 8; may survive winter in Zone 9. Grown as perennial in zones 10 and 11.
How to Grow: Set out nursery plants in spring or sow seed indoors at 70° to 75°F, eight to 10 weeks earlier. In areas where season is long, sow in garden. When planting, space plants 1 foot apart. If needed, cut plant back to shape attractively. Sometimes troubled by whiteflies, aphids, caterpillars, mealybugs, and mites.
Cultivars: 'Camara Mixed Hybrids', a dwarf strain, grows to 18 inches tall,

mixed color combinations. A trailing form with purple flowers also is available.

LATHYRUS ODORATUS
Sweet Pea

Short and bushy, or tall and climbing, sweet peas bear clusters of 1-inch-long pea-type flowers on long stems amid gray-green leaves. Many, though not all, are highly fragrant and make wonderful cut flowers. The blossoms may be white, pink, peach, creamy yellow, lavender, blue, red, purple, or bicolored. Sweet peas bloom beginning in winter in mild climates and elsewhere in early spring, lasting into summer in areas where temperature stays cool. New heat-resistant types bloom longer. Bushy forms grow 1 to 3 feet tall; climbers grow 3 to 8 feet tall on a trellis. Decorative on trellis or fence in cottage or informal gardens.

LATHYRUS ODORATUS

Site: Full sun. Fertile, well-drained soil and ample water; do not allow to dry. Hardy, cool-season annual in zones 2 to 11. Dies out with onset of hot weather.
How to Grow: Sow in deeply dug soil high in organic matter in early spring; if summers are cool, sow again in mid spring. Where winters are mild, sow in winter or fall. Thin bushy types to 6 to

12 inches, climbers to 4 inches apart. Provide netting, string supports, or trellis. Mulch ground to keep roots cool. Remove spent blooms immediately to encourage rebloom. Feed heavily. Sometimes troubled by powdery mildew in warm weather, anthracnose, black root rot, aphids, and spider mites.

Cultivars: Climbers: 'Spencer' strain, many colors, some well-scented; 'Royal Family', heat-tolerant, fragrant.

Bushy: 'Bijou Mix', to 12 inches tall, heat-tolerant; 'Cupid', 6 inches tall, 18-inch spread, mixed colors, fragrant.

Older varieties such as 'Antique Fantasy' and 'Painted Lady' also are fragrant.

LIMONIUM SINUATUM
Statice

One of the most useful flowers for fresh and dried arrangements, statice produces branched stems densely packed with papery blue,

LIMONIUM SINUATUM

rose, lavender, red, salmon, yellow, or white bracts. The everlasting's tiny white flowers, nestled in the bracts, fade fast, but the bracts remain showy. Lobed leaves form a ground-hugging rosette; stems are nearly leafless, but have flat wings. Plants grow 1 to 3 feet tall, 6 to 15 inches wide.

Put dwarf, bushy forms in borders, rock gardens, seaside gardens; put tall types in cutting beds.

Site: Full sun. Deep, sandy loam; allow to dry between waterings. Half-hardy annual in zones 2 to 11.

How to Grow: Sow outdoors after last frost or indoors in peat pots at 70°F, eight to 10 weeks before last frost. Space 12 to 18 inches apart. Cut often to increase blooming. For best results, clip flowers just after they open. Rust and leaf spot sometimes troublesome.

Cultivars: 'Fortress', 2 feet tall, single colors and mix; 'Mixed Art Shades', 2½ feet tall, pastel colors; 'Sunset Shades', 2 feet tall, orange, gold, rose, amber, and apricot; 'Azure', 2 feet tall, purest blue.

LOBELIA ERINUS
Edging Lobelia

A small plant best known for its vivid blue flowers, edging lobelia now also comes in pale blue, lilac, rose, and white. The tiny flowers are borne on thin upright or trailing stems in dense clusters amid narrow green

LOBELIA ERINUS

or bronze-green leaves. If high temperatures or humidity do not cause their decline, the plants bloom from spring to hard frost and much of

the year where winters are mild. Lobelia is poisonous if eaten. Plants grow 3 to 8 inches tall, as wide or wider. Use trailers to cascade from hanging baskets, containers, or walls. Plant compact forms as edging or in rock gardens.

Site: Full sun or part shade. Light, fertile soil rich in organic matter; keep moist. Tender perennial treated as hardy, cool-season annual in zones 2 to 11.

How to Grow: Set out nursery plants after last frost or sow indoors at 70° to 75°F, 10 to 12 weeks earlier. May sow outdoors when soil thaws. Space seedling clusters 6 inches apart. Pinch when young to promote branching. Shear after first bloom. May die out in hot weather if soil dries. Occasionally rust and leaf spot cause problems.

Cultivars: 'Crystal Palace', 6 inches tall, intense blue, bronze leaves; 'Cambridge Blue', 4 inches, sky blue; 'Sapphire', blue with white eye; 'String of Pearls', 4 inches, mixed; 'Cascade' series, trailing in mix or single colors—ruby, blue, crimson, and lilac.

LOBULARIA MARITIMA
(ALYSSUM MARITIMUM)
Sweet Alyssum

Blooming six weeks after seeding, sweet alyssum quickly forms a sweet-scented white, cream, lavender, rose, or purple carpet of flowers. Plants grow 3 to 6 inches tall, up to 24 inches wide. The dainty, 1-inch-wide, rounded flower heads all but hide the small, linear, gray-green leaves. Sweet alyssum self-sows readily, but seedlings tend to be taller and not true to color, so some gardeners hoe them out. An excellent paving and rock garden plant. Use to edge a bed, underplant tall flowers, or cascade from container. *continued*

LOBULARIA MARITIMA
(continued)

LOBULARIA MARITIMA

Site: Full sun or light shade. Average to poor, well-drained soil; moderate water. Hardy, cool-season annual in zones 2 to 9. Perennial in zones 10 and 11.
How to Grow: Sow in garden uncovered in early spring; thin 4 inches apart. Or, sow indoors at 65° to 70°F, four to six weeks earlier. Or, purchase plants, spacing seedling clusters 8 inches apart. Elongates and may stop blooming in hot weather; shear to reinvigorate. Downy mildew and caterpillars sometimes cause problems.
Cultivars: 'Carpet of Snow', 3 to 4 inches tall, white; 'Snow Crystals', 4 inches tall, larger white flowers, heat-tolerant; 'Violet Queen', deep violet; 'Rosie O'Day', 3 to 4 inches tall, deep rose; 'Oriental Night', purple, 3 to 4 inches tall; 'Apricot Shades', 3 to 4 inches tall, apricot to buff.

LUPINUS TEXENSIS
Texas Bluebonnet

A pretty wildflower that deserves more use in gardens, Texas bluebonnet produces spires of ¾-inch vivid blue-and-white flowers. The leaves are typical lupine, composed of five to six leaflets forming a rounded outline. Plants are 12 inches tall and as wide. Bluebonnets bloom from summer through fall from a spring sowing in cool climates and from spring until weather turns hot in hot climates. Use them in meadow, cottage, and informal plantings. Seeds are poisonous if eaten.

LUPINUS TEXENSIS

Site: Full sun or light shade. Poor to average soil and moderate water. Half-hardy, cool-season annual in zones 2 to 11. Blooms best in cool weather.
How to Grow: Sow indoors at 55° to 70°F, eight to 10 weeks before last frost, or in mild-winter areas, outdoors in fall. Set plants or thin to 1 foot apart. If planted too closely, branching and blooming suffer. Leaf blight, leaf spot, crown rot, powdery mildew, and rust may cause problems.
Cultivars: The species often is included in wildflower seed mixes. 'Pixie Delight', hybrid, 1 to 1½ feet tall, has flowers in white and various pastel shades.

MATTHIOLA INCANA
Stock

Grown for their strong, sweet-and-spicy scent, stocks are old-fashioned cut flowers. Double-flowered forms offer solid spires of

MATTHIOLA INCANA 'COLUMN MIX'

blooms, while single-flowered types are wispy. Both bloom in a variety of colors: white, pink, rose, lavender, purple, cream, red, and bicolors. The straplike, gray-green leaves cloak the bottoms of the plants. Column types reach 36 inches tall; dwarf bedding types reach 15 inches in height; both spread 12 inches. Use column types in cut-flower gardens and dwarf types in cottage gardens.

Site: Full sun or light shade. Well-drained, moderately rich soil. Keep moist; don't overwater. Biennial grown as half-hardy, spring annual in zones 3 to 8, as winter annual in zones 9 to 11.
How to Grow: In zones 3 to 8, sow seed of dwarfs indoors at 70°F, eight weeks before last frost. Space plants 9 to 15 inches apart. In zones 9 to 11, set plants outdoors in late fall. Column types of stock need five-month growing season below 65°F. Plants won't bloom if warmer than 65°F. Fertilize weekly. To select for doubles, lower to 45°F after germination and, after several weeks, transplant light green seedlings, discarding dark ones. Root rot occurs if plants are overwatered; downy mildew, powdery mildew, leaf spot, springtails, and diamond-back moths may cause problems.
Cultivars: 'Giant Imperial', 2½ feet tall, branched, single or mixed colors; 'Trysomic Ten Week', 18 inches tall,

blooms early; 'Cinderella', 8 to 10 inches tall, single or mixed colors; 'Midget', 8 to 10 inches, heat-tolerant.

MELAMPODIUM PALUDOSUM
Melampodium, Blackfoot Daisy

This bushy, free-flowering little plant produces small, daisy-type flowers with golden-yellow petals and orange centers. The plant is self-branching and self-cleaning, needing no deadheading or pinching. Light green leaves are rough to the touch

MELAMPODIUM PALUDOSUM 'SHOWSTER'

and perfectly set off the flowers. Blossoms appear abundantly from early summer right up until frost. Grows 12 inches tall and wide. Plant in groups as a path edging or in informal or rock gardens. Good in containers and window boxes.

Site: Full sun. Average to poor soil on the dry side. Drought-tolerant. Half-hardy, warm-season annual in zones 2 to 11. Thrives in heat.
How to Grow: Sow seed indoors six to 8 weeks before last frost date at 70°F. Plant outdoors after soil has warmed, spacing 8 inches apart. Seed may be sown outdoors when warm. Take cuttings in midsummer. Overfeeding

decreases flowers. Slugs are a problem in damp areas; occasionally aphids and red spider mites are problems.
Cultivars: 'Medallion', 18 inches tall, gold.

MOLUCCELLA LAEVIS

MOLUCCELLA LAEVIS
Bells-of-Ireland

This unusual plant provides a reliable source of striking green blossoms for the back of the border or cutting. Cut flowers turn a lovely pale beige after drying. The apple green "bells" actually are sepals that surround the tiny white flowers or "clappers." Plants grow 24 to 36 inches tall, with one to several stems, each 6 to 8 inches wide. Use for vertical effect in the middle of a border and include in cutting beds.

Site: Full sun. Average, well-drained soil and moderate water. Hardy, warm-season annual in zones 2 to 11. Best in warm summer weather.
How to Grow: Sow outdoors uncovered in very early spring (fall in mild-winter areas) or indoors at 55° to 60°F, eight to 10 weeks before last frost. Set 12 inches apart. Protect from strong wind. Hang cut stalks indoors in darkness to dry. Usually pest-free, but sometimes troubled by crown rot in wet soil.

Cultivars: Usually only the species is available.

NICOTIANA SPP.
Flowering Tobacco

These showy relatives of commercial tobacco bring white and colored flowers to the garden. The blossoms of the most common species, *Nicotiana alata* and *N. affinis* grow on erect stems and are 2- to 3-inch-long tubes with 1- to 2-inch-wide flared faces. Colors include white, cream, rose, red, purple, buff-salmon, wine, pink, chartreuse, and

NICOTIANA ALATA

chocolate. Flowers of the species open only from late afternoon until morning and are fragrant; modern hybrids remain open all day and may be scentless. Plants grow 12 to 36 inches tall and 8 to 15 inches wide.

Green-flowered tobacco, *N. langsdorffii* offers airy sprays of chartreuse bells on wiry stems above refined, narrow leaves. Inside each bell are eye-catching blue anthers. Hummingbirds are fond of the flowers. Blossoms appear from early summer to frost, and flowers are long-lasting when cut. Plants are usually 3 to 4 feet tall, but may reach 5 feet.

continued

NICOTIANA SPP.
(continued)

NICOTIANA LANGSDORFFII

Bold, tropical-looking leaves form a vase-shaped rosette at the base of the dramatic great-flowering tobacco, *N. sylvestris*. Tall, branched stems bear more leaves and starbursts of narrow, white, tubular flowers, each 4 to 5 inches long and tipped with a ½-inch-

NICOTIANA SYLVESTRIS

wide flared face. Up to 50 flowers form from one set of buds. Although the blossoms remain open all day, they do not release their sweet, heavy fragrance until evening. Blossoms appear from midsummer to frost.

Plants grow 2 to 6 feet tall and 18 to 24 inches wide.

Nicotiana is excellent for a vertical effect in gardens and containers. Green-flowered tobacco is useful for blending brighter flower colors and is stunning planted in groups before dark burgundy or dark green foliage plants. Use great-flowered tobacco in border background; it is valued for height and late-season flowers. *N. alata* and *N. langsdorffii* make good cut flowers.

Site: Light shade; full sun where humid or moist. All three types like fertile, well-drained soil high in organic matter; moderate water. *Nicotiana* is grown as a warm-season annual in zones 2 to 9. *N. alata* is perennial in zones 10 and 11, and the other two species also may winter over.

How to Grow: Sow seeds of *N. alata* barely covered and seeds of green-flowered or great-flowered tobacco uncovered outdoors after last frost. Or, sow indoors at 68° to 86°F, six to eight weeks earlier. Set *N. alata* 8 to 12 inches apart; *N. langsdorffii* 12 inches apart; and *N. sylvestris* 12 to 36 inches apart. Provide plenty of water when weather is hot. Remove spent flower stalks. Great-flowered tobacco may need staking where windy. Sometimes troubled by whiteflies, tobacco budworms, aphids, and virus.

Cultivars of *N. alata*: 'Nicki' series, 15 to 18 inches tall, free-flowering, mix or singles, light scent. 'Domino' series, 12 to 14 inches tall, bushy, fragrant, open all day, weather-tolerant, mix or singles, white eyes; 'Sensation', 4 feet wide, color range, open all day. 'Starship' series, 10 to 12 inches tall, compact, early flowering, several colors including 'Lemon-Lime'. 'Breakthrough Mix', 10 to 12 inches tall, nonhybrid, fragrant, open all day; 'Lime Green', 30 inches tall; 'Daylight White', 20 inches tall. The other two types are available only in species form.

NIGELLA DAMASCENA
Love-in-a-Mist

A halo of thin, branched filaments surrounding each pretty 1½-inch-wide flower and the airy, finely divided leaves inspired this plant's common name. Flowers are usually light blue, but also come in white, pink, and purple. Plants are 12 to 30 inches tall and as wide. The decorative seedpods dry well. This plant is pretty in cottage gardens and as a cover for spring bulbs. Flowers and seedpods are charming fresh-cut and dried.

NIGELLA DAMASCENA

Site: Full sun. Sandy loam or gravely soil; excellent drainage. Moderate water. Hardy, cool-season annual in zones 2 to 11. Dies out quickly in hot weather.

How to Grow: Sow in garden in early spring and in fall. Thin to 8 to 15 inches apart. Stake taller varieties. Dead-heading prolongs bloom, but delays seedpods. Short-lived, but as long as days are cool, may resow to prolong the show. For dried arrangements, cut stems with dried leaves because seedpods dry and split open. Readily self-sows. Usually problem-free.

Cultivars: 'Miss Jekyll', 18 inches tall, light sky blue; 'Persian Jewels',

15 inches, mixed lavender-blue, pink, and white. 'Dwarf Moody Blue', 6 to 0 inches, semidouble, compact

PAPAVER RHOEAS
Corn Poppy, Shirley Poppy, Flanders Poppy

Corn poppies add waving splashes of color to gardens and meadows from mid-June to early August and readily reseed. The species has four scarlet-, black-, or

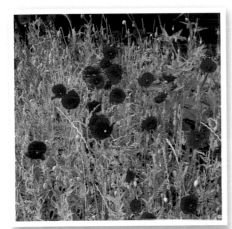

PAPAVER RHOEAS

white-spotted petals in a 2-inch-wide, cup-shaped blossom on downy, wiry stems clad with ferny, blue-green leaves. Cultivars have large flowers in red, purple, pink, white, pastel blue, lavender, and apricot. The strain called Shirley poppy has white petal edges and pink centers in shadings from red to apricot, in singles and doubles. Plants grow 1 to 2 feet tall and 6 to 12 inches wide. Corn poppies are graceful, airy plants for informal gardens and meadows.

Site: Full sun. Poor to average, well-drained soil and moderate water. Hardy annual in zones 2 to 11.
How to Grow: In mild-winter areas, sow in the garden in fall or very early spring. Elsewhere, sow outdoors in early spring and thin to 9 to 12 inches

apart. For bouquets, cut just before buds open; sear cut stems with a match. Occasionally aphids, whiteflies, bacterial blight, downy mildew, and leaf spot cause problems.
Cultivars and Similar Species: 'Shirley Mix', 24 inches tall, pink, white, rose, salmon, crimson, usually double; 'Mother of Pearl', 10 to 14 inches, pastel shades; *Papaver commutatum*, red with black splotch; *P. nudicaule*, Iceland poppy, perennial, often grown as a fall-planted biennial or annual.

PELARGONIUM SPP.
Geranium

Few annuals are simultaneously as neat and exuberant as zonal geraniums *(Pelargonium × hortorum)*. The clusters of 2- to 2½-inch flowers form bright balls above tidy, rounded leaves. Flowers may be white, red, salmon, pink, lavender, orange,

PELARGONIUM × HORTORUM

peach, bicolored, or even speckled. The leaves are softly hairy, often "zoned" with brown, yellow, red, or white rings. Cutting-grown cultivars are husky tetraploids with double flowers. Seed-grown cultivars have single flowers and are less stocky. Blossoms appear from early summer to mid fall, year-round in mildest climates. Use in bedding schemes, cottage gardens, informal borders,

containers, window boxes, and as a houseplant.

The trailing stems of ivy geranium *(P. peltatum)* are studded with glossy, bright green leaves shaped like ivy. Long-stemmed clusters of double red, pink, burgundy, lavender, or white

PELARGONIUM PELTATUM

flowers top plants from summer until frost, unless subjected to high heat and humidity. Stems grow 2 to 3 feet or more long. Excellent cascading from containers, hanging baskets, and window boxes.

PELARGONIUM × DOMESTICUM

Regal or Martha Washington *(P. × domesticum)* is the showiest geranium, with huge clusters of 2-inch-wide white, pink,   *continued*

PELARGONIUM SPP.
(continued)

red, lavender, or purple blossoms blotched with a darker color on the upper petals. The 2- to 4-inch-wide, heart- or kidney-shaped leaves have attractive, wavy edges. Flowers appear in spring, continuing as long as nights remain below 60°F. Excellent container plant.

Zonal and regal geraniums grow to 18 inches tall as annuals, to 3 feet as perennials; erect or somewhat spreading.

Site: Give zonal and regal geraniums full sun, light shade where hot. Ivy geranium needs partial shade in hot climates, full sun in cool climates. Geraniums like fertile, well-drained soil and moderate water; ivy geranium is drought-tolerant. Geraniums are grown as annuals in zones 2 to 9; will overwinter in zones 10 and 11. Ivy geranium is best in warm weather, but high heat with humidity causes decline. Regal requires cool nights, in the 50°F range or lower, to bloom well; performs well in the West.
How to Grow: Purchase plants. Seeds of zonals can be sown indoors at 55° to 65°F, three months before last frost. Set zonals 12 to 18 inches apart; set regals 2 feet apart. Ivy and regal can be started by stem cuttings. Pinch growing tips of young zonal and regals to promote branching. Cut spent blossom stalks of all types to extend bloom period. Occasionally bacterial leaf spot, edema, pythium, gray mold, aphids, geranium bud worms, whiteflies, spider mites, rust, and bacterial wilt may attack.
Cultivars: Zonal geraniums: Seed-grown—'Orbit' series, 12 to 16 inches tall, basal branching, many colors, zoned leaves; 'Elite' series, compact, basal branching, wide color range; 'Ringo' series, almost dwarf, intense leaf zone, range of colors; 'Breakaway', 9 to 10 inches tall, salmon

or red, spreading form for hanging baskets; 'Softly, Softly Mix', 12 to 15 inches tall, pastels. Cutting-grown— 'Tango', orange-red, dark foliage; 'Forever Yours', scarlet; 'Sincerity', semidouble scarlet; 'Appleblossom', pastel pink; 'Springtime Irene', deep salmon; 'Snow White', semidouble, white; 'Cherry Blossom', soft rose with white center.

Ivy geranium: 'Beauty of Eastbourne', cerise; 'Salmon Queen', light pink; 'Amethyst', lavender; 'Snow Queen', double white; 'Comtesse de Gray', pink semidouble; 'Galilee', cherry pink; 'Sugar Baby', dwarf bright pink. 'Balcon' series, single-flowered, heat-tolerant.

Regal: 'Allure', cameo pink with red center; 'Bollero', pink with black center; 'Crystal', white with vermilion center; 'Granada', apricot with white eye; 'Lily', violet-red with dark purple throat; 'Candy', pink with purple and lavender splotches.

PERILLA FRUTESCENS 'CRISPA'

PERILLA FRUTESCENS
Perilla, Beefsteak Plant, Shiso

Strongly resembling coleus, and used as a culinary herb in Japan and Korea, perilla is also handsome enough to grow as an ornamental. Most commonly grown is the purple-leafed form, valued for the excitement its dark color and metallic sheen

brings to a flower garden. Small white or red-tinged blossoms appear on the upper stems when the plant is mature. Plants grow to 3 feet tall and 12 to 15 inches wide. Use for foliage contrast in informal, herb, and fragrance gardens.

Site: Full sun or partial shade. Average to rich, well-drained soil and moderate water. Tender, warm-season annual in zones 2 to 11. Prefers warm weather.
How to Grow: Refrigerate seed in moist peat moss for 1 week. Then sow in garden after the last frost or sow indoors at 65° to 75°F, six to eight weeks before last frost. Space 6 to 12 inches apart. Stem cuttings root easily. Pinch to encourage branching. Often reseeds. Usually pest-free.
Cultivars: The species has green leaves. 'Atropurpurea', purple leaves. 'Crispa' and 'Laciniata', purple, crinkled or fringed leaves.

PETUNIA × HYBRIDA
Petunia

Well-grown petunias provide color from early summer to frost. The fragrant, funnel-form flowers bloom in white and shades of salmon, pink, red, magenta, lavender, purple, and, rarely, yellow. Flowers may be picoteed, striped, or dark-veined. Doubles that resemble carnations are best for containers.

Multiflora types are vigorous with numerous 2-inch, smooth-edged blossoms that recover well from rain and withstand heat. Grandiflora types have fewer, but larger, ruffled or fringed blossoms, to 4 to 5 inches across, and are not weather-resistant. Floribunda types are a cross between the two, with profuse 3-inch blossoms and good rain recovery. Milliflora, Surfina, and Supertunia types have numerous small flowers and do not need pruning. *Petunia integrifolia* spreads rapidly and blooms nonstop

PETUNIA × HYBRIDA

without deadheading; best sheared once or twice a growing season.

Petunias reach 8 to 18 inches in height and as wide or wider. Use grandifloras in containers and hanging baskets or to cascade over walls; use other types in beds and borders.

Site: Full sun. Fertile to poor, well-drained soil and moderate water. Tolerates alkalinity. Tender perennial grown as summer annual in zones 2 to 8; winter annual in deserts of zones 9 to 11. Performs poorly above 90°F.
How to Grow: Set out nursery plants when warm or sow uncovered indoors at 70° to 80°F, 10 to 12 weeks earlier. In zones 10 and 11, plant in fall. Space 6 to 12 inches apart. Avoid in-bloom nursery starts. Pinch when 6 inches tall, remove spent flowers, and shear flush after first bloom to encourage fullness. Whiteflies, botrytis, pythium, aster yellows virus, and ozone damage sometimes troublesome.
Cultivars: Multiflora: 'Merlin' series, solid colors and picotees; 'Joy' series, clear colors and bicolors; 'Plum' series, dark-veined, includes the bright yellow 'Summer Showers'; 'Carpet' series, compact, basal-branching, 2-inch flowers in pink, plum, red, rose, white, and mixed; 'Blue Lace', mid blue with violet veins; 'Flame', soft coral-orange with gold throat.

Grandiflora: 'Dreams' series, disease-resistant, 4-inch flowers in clear, bright colors such as midnight (violet-blue), pink, red, and white. 'Supercascade' series, more compact, trailing in many colors; 'Ultra' series, solids and stripes, compact and branched; 'Magic' and 'SuperMagic' series, heavy bloom, compact, branched plants.

Floribunda: 'Madness' series, solids, dark-veined and striped, doubles and singles.

Milliflora: 'Fantasy' series, dense plants with petite flowers. *P. integrifolia* 'Purple Wave', magenta-purple blossoms with dark centers, easy-care.

Surfina and Supertunia: new, heat-tolerant hybrids with good basal branching, purple, pale blue, light pink, lavender, or white.

PHLOX DRUMMONDII
Annual Phlox

Breeders have turned this deep rose, 18-inch-tall Texas wildflower into a low plant with large clusters of

PHLOX DRUMMONDII
'DWARF BEAUTY BLUE'

white, pink, red, blue, lavender, purple, salmon, and sometimes yellow flowers. Flowers are often bicolored with dark or light "eyes." The lightly scented flowers form mounds and are

long-lasting when cut. Dwarfs are 6 to 8 inches tall and spreading; tall types are 15 to 18 inches tall and upright. Use in informal and cottage gardens, in containers, and in cutting gardens.

Site: Full sun. Average to fertile, well-drained soil and moderate water. Half-hardy, cool-season annual in zones 2 to 11.
How to Grow: Sow in garden in very early spring or indoors at 55° to 65°F, eight to 10 weeks before last frost. Sow outdoors in fall for winter and spring bloom in mild climates. Space 6 inches apart. Water early in day at ground level to prevent disease. Remove spent flowers to stimulate rebloom. May decline in hot weather, but revives when cooler. Leaf spot, powdery mildew, rust, beetles, and two-spotted mites may cause problems.
Cultivars: 'Brilliant' series, 20 inches tall, eyed; 'Twinkle', 6 inches, star-shaped, often bicolored; 'Promise Pink', 8 to 10 inches, pink, semidouble.

PORTULACA GRANDIFLORA
Moss Rose

Few annuals have the firecracker brightness of the reds, oranges, yellows, purples, and pinks of moss rose. Petals reflect the sun with a luster that makes even white ones glow. The lush, 2-inch blossoms contrast with the sparse, ground-hugging plants and their narrow, dull green, succulent leaves. Plants grow 4 to 8 inches tall and spread to 2 feet. Old types opened at noon and closed at dusk and on overcast days; new types stay open longer. Flourishes in dry, hot sites that deter most flowers. May self-sow.

Excellent in dry sites as groundcover, in rock gardens, and between pavers. *continued*

PORTULACA GRANDIFLORA
(continued)

PORTULACA GRANDIFLORA
'SUNDIAL PEPPERMINT'

Site: Full sun. Average, well-drained soil; sandy soil best. Allow to dry between waterings. Drought-tolerant. Half-hardy, warm-season annual in zones 2 to 11. Best in hot, sunny climates.
How to Grow: Sow outdoors uncovered after last frost or indoors at 70° to 80°F, four to six weeks earlier. Space 12 to 24 inches apart. Once established, water only when plants seem near wilting. Aphids, thrips, and white rust are sometimes troublesome.
Cultivars: 'Sundial' series, 5 inches tall, mix or singles, remains open longer; 'Sundance Mix', 6 inches tall, open even when overcast; 'Minilaca Mix', 4 inches tall, upright.

RICINUS COMMUNIS
Castor Oil Plant, Castor Bean

Rapidly growing from seed to a person's height, castor oil plant makes a dramatic summer show. The large leaves have five to 11 lobes and measure 1 to 3 feet across. Foliage may be green, green-and-white, blue-gray, or various shades of reddish purple and brown. Flowers are usually insignificant, although the stems and spiny pods may be colorful. Some gardeners remove pods because the seeds are poisonous if eaten. Grows 3 to 6 or more feet tall, three-fourths as wide. Use for tropical look and architectural foliage in gardens; makes a quick screen or hedge.

RICINUS COMMUNIS 'CARMICITA'

Site: Full sun. Rich, deep, well-drained soil and moderate water. Tropical perennial grown as warm-season annual in zones 2 to 7, perennial in zones 8 to 11. Thrives in heat and moisture.
How to Grow: Soak seed 24 hours, then sow 1 inch deep outdoors in warm soil or indoors at 70° to 75°F, six weeks before last frost. Space 3 to 4 feet apart. Do not plant where young children might eat seeds. Do not nick seeds. Sap may cause allergic reaction. Bacterial leaf spot and bacterial wilt may be troublesome.
Cultivars: 'Sanguineus', bronze stems, red leaves; 'Impala', 3 to 4 feet, young growth maroon; 'Zanzibarensis', green leaves, white veins.

SALVIA
**Mealy-Cup Sage (*S. farinacea*)
Red Salvia (*S. splendens*)**

Mealy-cup sage has narrow spires of small, deep violet-blue, light blue, or white flowers that bloom all summer on leafless stems held above mounds of gray-green, straplike foliage. The short, whitish hairs covering much of this plant give it a "mealy" surface. Grows 15 to 36 inches tall and bushy. Cut the flowers for bouquets or drying, while enjoying this plant's sturdy good looks in your garden. Excellent for spiky shape in formal and informal gardens, containers, and cutting beds.

SALVIA FARINACEA

Despite its common name, red salvia is now available in not only the familiar scarlet but also in white, pink, dusky purple, and lavender. The 1½-inch-long flowers bloom on wide spires held above heart-shaped, medium to dark green leaves from summer to frost. It grows 6 to 36 inches tall, half to three-fourths as wide. Group plants in borders for spiky shape. Use reds carefully; try with white or green flowers or foliage. Attracts hummingbirds.

SALVIA SPLENDENS 'FLARE'

Site: Full sun, light shade in the South and Southwest for mealy-cup sage. Pastel varieties of red salvia best in partial shade. Average, well-drained soil with moderate water for mealy-cup sage and plentiful water for red salvia. Tender perennials grown as annuals in zones 2 to 7, perennial in zones 8 to 11. Best in warm weather, high humidity.

How to Grow: Sow indoors uncovered at 75°F, 10 to 12 weeks before last frost for mealy-cup sage, six to eight weeks before last frost for red salvia. Or, sow mealy-cup sage in garden in warm soil if summer is long and hot. Space mealy-cup sage 12 inches apart; space salvia 6 to 12 inches apart. Pinch older varieties of mealy-cup sage to encourage branching. Remove entire flower spikes on red salvia as they fade to stimulate more flowers. Damping-off fungus, leaf spot, rust, aphids, stalk borers, and leafhoppers are occasionally troublesome.

Cultivars: Mealy-cup sage: 'Victoria', 18 inches tall, violet-blue, uniform; 'Blue Bedder', 24 inches tall, deep blue; 'Porcelain', 15 to 18 inches tall, white; 'Silver White', 18 inches tall, white plumes, silvery foliage.

Red salvia: Bright red—'Red Fire', 12 inches tall; 'Bonfire', 10 inches; 'St. John's Fire', 12 inches; 'Red Hot Sally',

deep red, 10 to 12 inches, compact, and stocky; 'Laser Purple', 10 to 12 inches, resists fading; 'Phoenix Mix', 12 to 24 inches, includes salmon, pink, cream, lilac, and red; 'Empire' series, 12 to 15 inches, well-branched, dark or light salmon, lilac, deep purple, red, white, or mixture.

SANVITALIA PROCUMBENS
Creeping Zinnia

Cheerful miniature flowers in orange, gold, or lemon yellow with large black-purple centers bloom all summer on this ground-hugging plant. Flowers are ½ to 1 inch across and leaves are about 2 inches long. Plant grows just 4 to 8 inches tall,

SANVITALIA PROCUMBENS

trailing to 12 or more inches. The blossoms fall invisibly when spent, making it an easy-care annual. Use as edging in informal and cottage gardens; use in rock gardens, wall plantings, and hanging baskets.

Site: Full sun or part shade. Average, well-drained soil and moderate water. Drought-tolerant. Warm-season annual in zones 2 to 11. Tolerates heat and high humidity.

How to Grow: Sow uncovered in garden after last frost. Or, sow indoors in individual peat pots at 70°F, six to

eight weeks earlier. Space 4 to 6 inches apart. Avoid overhead watering. Performs poorly in wet soil. Somewhat resistant to zinnia mildew.

Cultivars: 'Gold Braid', 4 inches tall, gold; 'Mandarin Orange', 4 inches tall, vivid orange; 'Yellow Carpet', 4 inches tall, lemon yellow.

SCAEVOLA AEMULA 'BLUE WONDER'

SCAEVOLA AEMULA
Fanflower

The creeping habit of this vigorous annual makes it a perfect plant for a container, where its branches drape alluringly over the edges. Clusters of small flowers bloom nonstop at the tips of the elongating stems from early summer until frost. Petals are bright blue, although they may look lavender in a photograph, and are arranged like a fan around the yellow centers. Grows 6 to 8 inches tall, trailing to several feet. Excellent in containers or hanging baskets, or plant it in the ground to weave around taller plants. Combines well with silver foliage.

Site: Full sun. Average, well-drained soil. Drought-tolerant. Tender perennial grown as warm-season annual.

How to Grow: Plant transplants after the soil has warmed, *continued*

SCAEVOLA AEMULA
(continued)

spacing 8 to 12 inches apart. Cuttings from nonflowering shoots root readily and may be overwintered indoors. Pinch to promote branching. Cut back in midsummer if plant gets ungainly. Problem-free.
Cultivars: 'Blue Wonder', large blue flowers.

TAGETES ERECTA 'SUPER HYBRID MIX'

TAGETES SPP.
Marigold

Big and bold, African marigolds (*Tagetes erecta*) actually are Mexican in origin. Some catalogs call them American marigolds. The carnation-like blossoms are 3 to 6 inches in diameter and colored yellow, pale yellow, gold, or orange, rarely creamy white. Deeply cut, dark green, pungent foliage provides a nice contrast. Blossoms appear from summer through light fall frosts. Afro-French hybrids (between *T. erecta* and *T. patula*) are generally shorter, with profuse, long-lasting, large blossoms in all of the above colors, plus red and red-and-yellow bicolors. These triploid plants (triple the number of regular chromosomes, infertile, extra-large flowers) are not bothered by heat and humidity and do not set seed, so they need no deadheading to keep blooming. African marigolds grow 1 to 3 feet tall, 1 to 2 feet wide. Group plants in the midground of formal and informal gardens.

French marigolds (*T. patula*) are small, easy-to-grow, low plants with 2-inch-wide single or double flowers, which are usually bright yellow or gold and bicolored with red or mahogany. Some flower types are flat-headed with shingled petals; others are crested with a prominent central

TAGETES PATULA 'DISCO FLAME'

tuft of petals surrounded by flat petals; and still others are single with five petals surrounding a central button. Blossoms appear from early summer through light frosts. Plants grow 6 to 18 inches tall and as wide. The 6-inch-tall dwarf French marigolds make excellent edging annuals; use taller ones in cutting beds and containers.

Signet marigolds (*T. tenuifolia*) are delicate-looking plants with mounds of feathery foliage and masses of

TAGETES TENUIFOLIA 'GOLDEN GEM'

¾-inch-wide, single blossoms in colors and bicolors similar to those of French marigolds. They grow 6 to 12 inches tall and as wide. Less common than African or French marigolds, these dainty plants are favored by sophisticated garden designers. Edible petals are tasty in salads. Use these dainty plants in cottage and herb gardens, front of borders, window boxes, and containers.

Site: Full sun; part shade in hot-summer areas of the South and Southwest. Fertile to average, well-drained, sandy loam and moderate water. Warm-season annuals in zones 2 to 11. Flowering slows when weather is hot and humid.
How to Grow: Sow indoors at 65° to 75°F, four to six weeks before last frost. In long-summer areas, sow outdoors after frost. Set African marigolds 12 to 24 inches apart; set French and signet marigolds 6 to 10 inches apart. Pinch young plants to encourage branching and more bloom. Avoid overhead watering, which can rot blossoms. Botrytis, root rot, fusarium wilt, leaf spot, rust, Japanese beetles, and slugs may be troublesome.
Cultivars: African marigold: 'Toreador', 30 inches tall, rich orange; 'Inca Mixed', 12 inches, orange, bright yellow,

tangerine, and gold; 'Excel', 14 to 16 inches, gold, orange, primrose (pale yellow), yellow, or mix, blooms regardless of day length; 'Climax', 2½ to 3 feet; 'Snowdrift', 22 inches, white, give afternoon shade.

Afro-French hybrids: 'Solar', 12 to 14 inches, 3-inch blooms, gold, lemon, orange; 'Zenith', 15 to 18 inches, 2½- to 3-inch blooms in yellow, orange, or red and yellow bicolor.

French marigold: Singles—'Disco' series, 12 inches tall, 2-inch blossoms in golden yellow, yellow-and-mahogany, bronze-and-russet, and red. Broad-petaled—'Aurora' series, 10 to 12 inches tall, 3-inch double blossoms in orange and red, gold-yellow, light yellow, gold, or mixed; 'Sophia' series, 12 inches tall, double yellow, orange, red, or the red-and-gold 'Queen Sophia'; 'Safari' series, self-cleaning and disease-resistant, 12 inches tall, 3-inch blossoms in yellow, scarlet, orange, light yellow, maroon-and-gold, and red-and-gold. Dwarf crested—'Hero' series, 10 to 12 inches tall, 3-inch blossoms in yellow, orange, red, gold, red and gold, yellow, maroon-and-orange, yellow-and-mahogany, or mixed; 'Boy' series; 8 to 10 inches tall, 1½-inch flowers in gold, orange, yellow, or yellow and maroon; 'Little Devil' series, flat-crested 1½-inch double flowers, early flowering, in orange, yellow, yellow-and-maroon, and mixed; 'Bonanza' series, deep colors, 10 to 12 inches tall, 2-inch flowers in orange, gold, yellow, and bicolors.

Signet marigold: 'Gem' series, 9 inches tall; 'Lemon', 'Gold', 'Tangerine', 'Paprika', 6 inches tall, red-edged gold; 'Starfire', mix of orange and orange with gold edge.

TITHONIA ROTUNDIFOLIA

TITHONIA ROTUNDIFOLIA
Mexican Sunflower

The small, dahlia-like blossoms of this dramatically tall, heat-tolerant annual bloom from midsummer to frost and attract butterflies. The 2½- to 3½-inch-wide flowers were once available only in fiery red-orange with yellow undersides and yellow centers, but now also come in deep chrome yellow. The leaves are large, velvety, and often deeply lobed. Newer varieties grow 2 to 4 feet tall; the species grow to 5 feet or more, half as wide. Use in background of informal and cottage gardens. Good cut flower.

Site: Full sun. Average to poor, well-drained soil; light to moderate water. Half-hardy, warm-season annual in zones 2 to 11. Heat-tolerant.
How to Grow: Sow seeds in garden after last frost or indoors in peat pots, covered lightly, at 70°F, six to eight weeks earlier. Space 2 to 3 feet apart. Stake in windy sites. For cut flowers, sear stem ends in flame, plunge into warm water. Do not overfertilize. Slugs may be troublesome.
Cultivars: 'Torch', 30 inches tall, orange-red; 'Goldfinger', 24 to 30 inches tall; 'Yellow Torch', 3 to 4 feet tall, chrome yellow.

TORENIA FOURNIERI
Wishbone Flower

In a relatively cool, lightly shaded corner of an otherwise warm garden, this pretty annual forms rounded mounds of 1-inch-long funnel-shaped blossoms from spring to frost. Usually bicolored in shades of blue and purple, the flowers now

TORENIA FOURNIERI

come in pink, burgundy, and white, all with pale or white throats and yellow-spotted lower petals. The wishbone is the pair of arching stamens at each flower's center. Foliage turns reddish-purple in fall. Plants grow 8 to 12 inches tall, as wide as tall. Plants may self-sow. Excellent as edging in formal and informal gardens; use in containers.

Site: Light shade; full sun where day temperatures are below 75°F. Plant needs fertile soil, high in organic matter; plentiful water. Warm-season annual in zones 5 to 11. Thrives in high humidity.
How to Grow: Sow indoors uncovered at 70° to 75°F, 10 to 12 weeks before last frost. Space 6 to 8 inches apart. Root rot sometimes a problem in wet soil. *continued*

TORENIA FOURNIERI
(continued)

Cultivars: The species is 12 inches tall with sky blue flowers marked white and yellow; 'Clown' series, 8 to 10 inches, single colors and mix in burgundy, pink, lavender, and white marked with purple and pink; 'Pink Panda', 4 to 8 inches, white marked rose-pink; 'Blue Panda', 4 to 8 inches, light blue marked deep purple-blue.

TROPAEOLUM MAJUS
Nasturtium

Either tidy and dwarf or exuberantly trailing, nasturtiums bring the garden a cheerful combination of 1- to 4-inch-wide, nearly round leaves and 2½-inch-wide, bright flowers. The

TROPAEOLUM MAJUS 'CLIMBING MIX'

spurred blossoms are single, semidouble, or double in orange, yellow, gold, scarlet, mahogany, carmine, and sometimes bicolored. Leaves and blossoms are edible with a peppery taste. Dwarfs are 6 to 12 inches tall, mounded; trailers 18 inches high, trailing or climbing 6 feet or more. Use trailers as bank covers, in hanging baskets, and on trellises; dwarfs as edging in informal, cottage, and herb gardens.

Site: Full sun to part shade. Average to poor, well-drained sandy soil; tolerates drought. Tender, cool-season annual in zones 2 to 11.
How to Grow: Best started in garden. Sow after last frost. In mild-winter areas, sow in fall for winter or spring bloom. Often self-sows. Don't fertilize. Rich soil makes leaves taller and more abundant than flowers. Aphids, leaf spot, aster yellows, cabbage loopers, and two-spotted mites may be troublesome.
Cultivars: Dwarf: 'Double Dwarf Jewel', 12 inches, mixed; 'Whirlybird', 6 to 10 inches tall, showy, upward-facing, spurless blossoms in seven rich colors or mixed; 'Empress of India', 2 feet, dark scarlet, blue-green leaves; 'Alaska', 6 to 10 inches, mixed, white-splashed leaves.

Trailing: 'Climbing Mixed', 6 to 8 feet, all colors; 'Parks Fragrant Giants', varied colors, fragrant; 'Gleam', 3 feet tall, semitrailing, semidouble, and double, all colors.

VERBENA × HYBRIDA 'PEACHES AND CREAM'

VERBENA × HYBRIDA
Verbena

Verbena has charmed generations of gardeners with its 2- to 3-inch-wide, domed heads of small, fragrant, white-eyed blossoms. It blooms early summer to frost, in white, red, purple, blue, lavender, and peach. Leaves are dark green and lance-shaped with serrated edges. Plants grow 6 to 12 inches tall, up to twice as wide. Use as a groundcover and in rock gardens, wall cracks, and containers.

Site: Full sun; light shade where hot. Fertile, well-drained soil and moderate water. Drought-tolerant. Half-hardy, warm-season annual in zones 2 to 11. Also perennial in zones 9 to 11.
How to Grow: Sow indoors without cover (but keep dark until seeds sprout) at 65° to 70°F, 12 to 14 weeks before last frost. Improve germination by sowing in moist medium, then not watering until germination begins. Space 12 to 18 inches apart. Pinch young plants to encourage branching. Remove spent blossoms. Bacterial wilt, aphids, blister beetles, caterpillars, thrips, whiteflies, and mites may be problems.
Cultivars: Upright: 'Blue Lagoon', 9 inches tall, blue, mildew-resistant; 'Derby', 10 inches, mix, eyed; 'Armour' series, early flowering, balled heads.

Spreading: 'Peaches and Cream', 8 inches, peach-pink and cream; 'Sparkle', 6 inches, mix, some eyed; 'Trinidad', rose-pink, eyeless; *Verbena tenuisecta* 'Imagination', 1- to 2-foot spread, ferny leaves, violet flowers.

VIOLA × WITTROCKIANA
Pansy

The familiar flat-faced flower comes in single colors, bicolors, and tricolors, including red, white, yellow, peach, cream, orange, pink, mahogany, blue, lavender, purple, and almost black. Blossoms range from 2 to 7 inches across. Plants grow 4 to 9 inches high and wide. Pansies need cool weather; heat-tolerant types extend bloom somewhat. Use as a companion to spring bulbs in informal and cottage gardens; excellent in containers and cutting beds.

VIOLA × WITTROCKIANA

Site: Full sun to part shade. Fertile, well-drained, organic soil; plentiful water. Hardy, cool-season annual in zones 2 to 11; winter annual in zones 9 to 11.

How to Grow: Set out nursery plants several weeks before last frost. Or, sow seeds indoors at 65° to 70°F, 10 to 12 weeks earlier. In mild-winter areas, also plant in fall for winter bloom. Space 4 to 6 inches apart. Mulch to cool roots and prolong blooming. Remove spent flowers. Anthracnose, crown rot, downy mildew, botrytis, leaf spot, powdery mildew, and slugs may be problems.

Cultivars: 'Imperial' series, 6 inches tall, mostly bicolors, many pastels; 'Crystal Bowl' series, 7 inches tall, solid colors, heat-tolerant; 'Super Chalon Giants Mix', deep, rich bicolors and tricolors, ruffled; 'Floral Dance', 6 to 9 inches, many bi- and tricolors, cold-hardy. 'Universal', best for winter flowering, 11 colors; 'Bingo' series, enormous upward-facing flowers, many colors; 'Rally' series, upward-facing flowers, winter annual in the South.

ZINNIA SPP.
Zinnia

Common zinnia (*Zinnia elegans*), sturdy and bright, blooms steadily in warm gardens from early summer to frost. Plants and flowers vary from dwarf to tall, with blossoms from 1 to 6 inches across. Most are double, and these may be pompons or cactus-flowered. Blossoms include

ZINNIA ELEGANS

all the colors of the rainbow, in brilliant hues and pastels. Some types are bicolored, streaked, and speckled with other colors. Grows 6 to 36 inches tall, some bushy, others upright and narrower.

ZINNIA ANGUSTIFOLIA

Short and sweet, narrow-leaf zinnia (*Z. angustifolia*) is a delightfully sprawling plant quickly gaining in popularity because of its easy-care nature. Perky 1- to 2½-inch-wide single blossoms in burnished yellow, orange, or white, with prominent orange centers bloom freely all summer, blanketing the narrow, dark green leaves with brilliant color. Grows to 12 inches tall and sprawling.

Zinnias are easy-care plants for informal gardens, cottage gardens, and containers. Plant common zinnias in masses in foreground or midground of borders and cottage gardens and in cutting beds. Use narrow-leaf zinnia as a fine-textured edging.

Site: Full sun; part sun in hottest areas. Moderately fertile, nonalkaline, well-drained soil; give common zinnia richer soil. Both grow best with regular water, but narrow-leaf zinnias are drought-tolerant. Warm-season annuals in zones 2 to 11. Narrow-leaf zinnia thrives on heat.

How to Grow: Best sown in garden after last frost. Sow indoors in peat pots, at 75° to 80°F, six weeks earlier. Set 6 to 12 inches apart. Avoid wetting leaves. Narrow-leaf zinnia needs no deadheading. Cut common zinnia often to encourage blooming. Strip off leaves before adding to bouquets. Common zinnia prone to mildew, although many cultivars are now mildew-resistant; narrow-leaf zinnia is less troubled. Bacterial wilt, alternaria, root and stem rot, Japanese beetles, and mites may be troublesome for common zinnia.

Cultivars: Common zinnia: 'Thumbelina', 6 to 10 inches tall, 1½- to 2-inch flowers; 'Peter Pan', 10 to 12 inches, 4-inch flowers; 'Splendor', 22 inches, 5-inch flowers; 'Peppermint Stick Mix', 24 inches, streaked bicolors; 'Cut and Come Again', 3 feet tall, well-branched.

Narrow-leaf zinnia: 'Star' series: 'Orange', 'White', 'Starbright Mix', orange, white, and gold, 'Classic Orange', orange; 'Classic White', creamy white.

BULBS

CHAPTER 8

ABOUT BULBS

Our most beloved garden bulbs—sunny daffodils, elegant tulips, and fragrant Dutch hyacinths—bloom in spring well before most perennials and annuals. Some bulbs, such as snow crocus, Siberian squill, and glory-of the-snow, bloom even earlier, popping out of the ground on the edge of the melting snow. They bring lively blossoms to take the edge off the pallor of winter.

Summer- and fall-blooming bulbs are fewer and compete more for attention in the garden because so many things are happening around them. Nevertheless, the late bloomers fill a necessary garden niche.

Planted in quantity—as they should be—spring-flowering bulbs echo the overhead display on the shrubs and trees that bloom so generously at the beginning of the growing season. Bulbs make wonderful companions to these woody plants, creating a blanket of color beneath their limbs. If it weren't for bulbs, the ground would be rather bare in spring. Most bulbs live many years and even increase in number from year to year, so your initial investment in planting large numbers will be well-rewarded.

BULBS BY DEFINITION

The term "bulb" is used loosely to describe any underground storage structure that carries a plant through dormancy and contains its flower and leaf buds. These dormant structures may be true bulbs, corms, tubers, tuberous roots, or rhizomes. (See Types of Bulbs on page 385.) Bulbous plants are perennials that live for many years, but lie dormant underground for much of the year. Most bulbs are dormant during the frigid winter months and during the heat and drought of summer. They send up leaves and flowers for only a few months each year.

TENDER AND HARDY

Bulbs and their kin can be tender or hardy. Tender types survive winter only where the ground doesn't freeze as deep as the bulb. In cold climates, you can grow tender bulbs as annuals, discarding them at the end of the season. If you want to go to the trouble, however, you can dig them up before fall frost and store them in a cool, dry place during winter, then replant them when the soil warms up the next year. Gladiolus and dahlias commonly are dug up and stored over winter in the North, but left in the ground year-round in the South. Northerners can grow tender bulbs in a decorative container and bring the container indoors for the winter rather than having to dig and store the bulbs.

not to be overlooked. Now called special bulbs by the growers, these smaller plants aren't as widely grown or as well-known, but their lovely little flowers occur in such great numbers, and the bulbs spread so readily, that they can put on a major show. If you aren't familiar with special bulbs, the encyclopedia section starting on page 388 will introduce you to many of these wonderful little plants.

BULB SHOPPING

Mail-order suppliers are a good source for quality bulbs. Because bulbs are dormant when you buy them, they are easy to ship and they travel well. Bulb purveyors send out glossy catalogs in spring that make you wish all those pretty spring flowers were blooming right then in your garden. Use the color pictures in catalogs to select the best bulbs to complete your spring color scheme; order by mid- to late summer. The bulbs are shipped at the proper planting time in fall.

Some garden centers create beautiful displays of spring-blooming bulbs at fall planting time. Use the color photos that decorate the boxes to select the bulbs. Be sure to place a tag with a picture of the flower in the bag with the bulbs, so you'll remember what you purchased when you get home.

Select large, firm bulbs without blemishes or rotten spots and store them in a cold, dry place until planting time. Beware of bargain bulbs—both at the nursery and from catalogs; they are often of inferior quality or size and won't bloom well.

Like perennials, hardy bulbs are cold-hardy to different degrees and are recommended for specific hardiness zones. Most hardy bulbs do poorly in warm-climate areas, because they need a lengthy winter chill to break dormancy and spur them to grow in spring. In Florida and the Gulf Coast, you can plant cold-treated bulbs or dig up bulbs and store them in the refrigerator during winter, replanting them in spring. The wet winters of the Pacific Northwest cause some hardy bulbs to rot unless they are planted with care in gravelly soil.

MAJOR VS. MINOR

Large, showy bulbs that we all know and love—Dutch crocus, tulips, daffodils, Dutch hyacinths, dahlias, lilies, and gladiolus—often are called major bulbs. This term was coined by commercial growers because these bulbs are their major crops, and perhaps coincidentally because the flowers tend to be large and make a major contribution to the beauty of the garden.

The minor bulbs—snowdrops, Siberian squill, snowflakes, and checkered lily, to name a few—are

PLANTING AND CARING FOR BULBS

Bulbs, especially spring-flowering ones, are about the easiest flowers to grow. If you follow a few simple rules, most types bloom year after year, increasing in number each year.

PERFECT PLANTING

Plant hardy bulbs anytime in fall before the soil freezes, but it's best to plant them early enough so the root systems can grow before extremely cold weather arrives. In some climates, you can plant until Thanksgiving or Christmas. Late-planted bulbs will develop roots in spring and may bloom later than normal; they'll get back on schedule the following year. Water the bulbs after planting to stimulate the roots to grow.

As a general rule, bulbs should be planted with the bottom of each bulb at a depth that's 2½ times the diameter. Plant them deeper than that in light soil and shallower in heavy soil.

Positioning bulbs at their proper depth helps ensure their longevity. Generally bulbs should be planted so the bottom rests at a depth that's two and a half times the bulb's diameter. The chart below illustrates the planting depth for common bulbs. In well-drained or sandy soil, plant an inch or two deeper to increase longevity and discourage rodents.

Because bulbs look best planted in groups, you are better off using a garden spade instead of a bulb planter, which encourages you to plant bulbs singly. A spade makes it easier to set bulbs side by side in large groups. Plant groups of bulbs in holes no smaller than a dinner plate or dig wide, curving trenches and position the bulbs in the bottom.

Layer different types of bulbs from bottom to top in the same hole to create companion plantings or a succession of bloom in a given location. For example, dig a 6-inch-deep hole and place several Dutch hyacinths in the bottom, cover them with soil, then plant a handful of grape hyacinths at a 5-inch depth. The two types of hyacinths bloom at the same time in spring. The grape hyacinths create a softening skirt beneath the more massive Dutch hyacinths. As another benefit, the leaves of the grape hyacinth form in autumn and remain all winter, providing a marker for the dormant Dutch hyacinth bulbs, so you won't inadvertently plant on top of the hyacinths or dig them up.

Interplanting provides maximum flowers in the smallest space and eliminates bare spots when bulbs go dormant. To create a succession of bloom and foliage, plant perennials around the bulb holes. As the bulb foliage dwindles, the perennials will grow up, camouflaging the bulbs' yellowing leaves. This interplanting technique works in both formal and informal gardens.

BULB HOUSEKEEPING

Remove spent flowers of large-flowered bulbs, such as tulips and daffodils, as soon as they fade. The plants' energy is then channeled into forming large bulbs and offsets rather than into setting seeds. Allow the minor bulbs to set seed, so they self-sow and form ever-larger drifts.

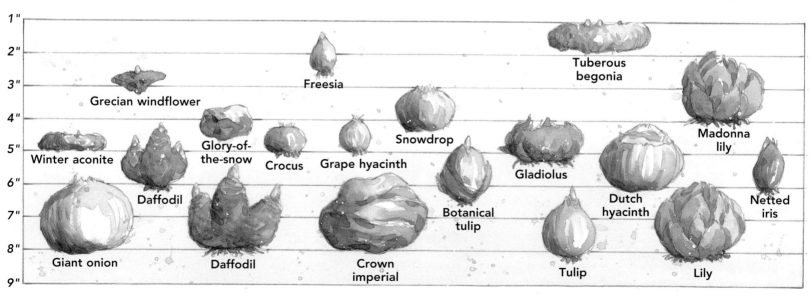

FORCING BULBS

Forcing bulbs enables you to enjoy the powerful fragrance of hyacinths, the sweet scent of paper-white narcissus, and the cheerful color of tulips and a host of other spring-flowering bulbs indoors in winter.

Forcing—planting bulbs indoors for extra-early bloom—is simple. In the fall, purchase bulbs that force well, such as paper-white narcissus, tulips, and hyacinths. Check catalog or display descriptions for cultivars that are well-suited to forcing.

To force paper-whites, place the bulbs in a container 2 or more inches deep and large enough to hold 2 to 12 bulbs. Fill the container partway with pebbles, then set the bulbs atop the pebbles. Add more pebbles to cover the bottom third of the bulbs. Add enough water to touch the bottom of the bulbs. (Check the water daily to maintain the level.) Place the container in a cool, dark location for two weeks or until shoots are a few inches high. Move the container to a bright, sunny place to encourage flowering. Discard bulbs after they bloom.

Other bulbs can be forced by planting them in a pot filled with commercial potting soil. Squeeze the bulbs close together with the smaller, pointed sides up. Barely cover with soil. Water well and put the pot in a dark, cool (35 to 50 degrees Fahrenheit) but not freezing place until shoots 1 to 2 inches high appear (in 10 to 14 weeks). Keep the soil moist. After shoots appear, move the pot to a sunny, warm spot, such as a south-facing window, to encourage further growth and blooming.

The bulbs may rebloom if planted outdoors.

Whatever else you do or don't do, resist removing bulb foliage while it is green; the green leaves nourish the bulb and next year's flower buds, which form during summer. Cut or pull off leaves only after they yellow. Also, don't braid leaves to get them out of the way. Braiding diminishes sunlight and hinders growth. It is safe to mow the green leaves of crocus and snowdrops naturalized in a lawn if you wait at least six weeks after blooming.

Major bulbs need fertilizer, but at the proper times. Work a high-phosphorus plant food, such as rock phosphate or superphosphate, into the bottom of the holes when you plant. Do not apply bonemeal, which attracts animals. Thereafter the bulbs need nitrogen. Fertilize with a balanced fertilizer in early spring when the shoots emerge and again after flowering to fuel foliage and bulb growth for next year's flowers. Or, apply bulb booster (a slow-release formula) to plantings in fall.

Bulb leaves suddenly may poke above ground during warm winter spells, causing gardeners to worry unnecessarily that later snow or freezing temperatures will kill the bulbs or destroy the flowers. Foliage and flower buds of spring-flowering bulbs usually can withstand freezing temperatures without harm. The flowers actually freeze, but they suffer injury only if the brittle stems are broken or if they thaw too quickly. If the flowers thaw slowly, they will not be adversely affected.

TYPES OF BULBS

- **Bulb:** A true bulb, such as a lily, is a round, pear-shaped, or oval structure consisting of modified, fleshy storage leaves and a flattened, compressed stem. Roots grow from the base of the stem plate, the bulb's bottom. Leaf buds and often flower buds are located on top of the plate between the fleshy leaves. Some bulbs, such as onions and tulips, have a protective, paperlike skin.
- **Corm:** A corm, such as a crocus, actually is a stem base that has swollen and modified itself to become a storage structure. A corm is rounded with a flattened top where the growth bud rests. Roots emerge from a concave bottom. A dry, papery tunic often covers the corm. Unlike bulbs, corms are solid and shrivel during growth. At the end of the growing season, they produce numerous new corms above the old one. The new corms are called cormels.

The term "bulb" loosely describes many plants with underground food storage parts, shown here.

Netherlands Flower Bulb Information Center

- **Rhizome:** A rhizome is a swollen, solid underground stem. Bearded iris grow from rhizomes. One tip of the horizontal rhizome houses buds for stalks, flowers, and leaves; roots grow along the bottom and at the other end of the rhizome. Mature rhizomes may be branched and have several growing points.
- **Tuber:** A tuber is a swollen, rounded stem covered with small scaly leaves and growth buds (eyes). Cyclamen and tuberous begonias are tuber plants. Although stems and roots grow from all sides of the tuber, it has a top and a bottom and should be planted correctly. The top is flat, and the bottom is concave.
- **Tuberous root:** A tuberous root is similar to a tuber, but is a swollen, rounded root, not a modified stem. Thus, it does not have buds on its surface. The growth buds are located at the base of the old stem where it attaches to the tuber. Dahlias are tuberous roots.

PLANTING AND CARING FOR BULBS

continued

Spectacular dahlias are grown from tender bulbs planted each spring and then dug up in fall and stored.

DIVIDE AND CONQUER

In cold climates, dig up tender bulbs, such as gladiolus and dahlias, in autumn after the first frost and before the ground freezes. Lift the bulbs with a garden fork and shake off all soil. Cut off topgrowth at 2 inches. Set the bulbs to dry in a dim, airy place for two weeks before storing.

Separate large gladiolus corms and similar "bulbs" from their tiny offsets, saving these for the nursery bed. Place the bulbs in a net bag or an old stocking and hang in a cool (50 to 60 degrees Fahrenheit), dark, airy place, such as a ventilated basement,

to discourage mold. Some gardeners dust corms with fungicide powder before storing.

Tubers and fleshy roots, such as dahlias, need to be kept slightly moist during storage. Bury them in a container of slightly moist peat moss

or vermiculite and seal in a plastic bag. Inspect the tubers from time to time to be sure they haven't dried out. If they shrivel, mist them lightly.

If you're growing tender bulbs in a container, you don't need to dig them up. Instead, cut off all topgrowth and

HOW TO DIVIDE DAHLIAS

Cut back foliage and lift tubers from ground. Wash off dirt. Divide tubers by cutting into groups of two or three.

Dust the cut tubers with sulfur to prevent disease.

Store tubers in trays of slightly damp peat moss or vermiculite and maintain at about 40°F. To retain moisture, seal tray with plastic.

Photo by Barbara Martin

Hot summer days coax Asiatic and Oriental lilies into a flamboyant display. Here lilies are paired with perennials in complementary colors and heights.

store the container in an unheated garage or shed where the temperature remains above freezing. Don't allow the soil to dry completely. In spring, empty the pot and replant the bulbs in fresh potting mix.

No garden can be complete without splashes of beautiful bulbs in spring. Plant bulbs in large groups, and in great quantities. You'll be rewarded for many years with their cheerful blossoms.

DIVIDING HARDY BULBS

Hardy bulbs sometimes need to be divided, too. Some daffodils, narcissus, and other bulbs produce offsets or small bulblets around the base of the bulb after a number of years in the garden. After the foliage dies back, you can dig up the bulbs and carefully separate the offsets from the parents to increase your plantings. Replant immediately or store them in a cool, dry place until bulb-planting time in fall. Plant the offsets twice as deep as their height; don't plant them as deep as mature bulbs. Small offsets will take a few years to reach blooming size.

Some corms, such as gladiolus, crocus, and freesia, produce small structures called cormels around their base. These can be divided the same as bulblets. When plants are dormant, remove the cormels. Replant cormels of hardy plants like crocus and colchicum. For tender plants like gladiolus, store the corms and cormels in a cool, dry place over winter and plant in spring.

For scaly bulbs like lilies, you can dig the bulbs in spring and remove the small scales that form around the outside. Replant immediately.

BULBS TO DIVIDE

Allium spp. (ornamental onion)
Alstroemeria spp. (Peruvian lily)
Colchicum spp. (autumn crocus)
Crocus spp.
Freesia × *hybrida*
Fritillaria spp.
Galanthus nivalis (snowdrop)
Gladiolus spp.
Iris reticulata (netted iris)
Leucojum spp. (snowflake)
Lilium spp. (lily)
Muscari spp. (grape hyacinth)
Narcissus spp. (daffodil, narcissus)

Bulbs

ACIDANTHERA MURIELAE
**Abyssinian Gladiolus,
Peacock Orchid**

More graceful than the florist's gladiolus, this native of Ethiopia features curving rather than stiff flower stems. The exotic-looking, creamy white flowers are 3 to 4 inches wide with chocolate, maroon, or red stars at their throats. They bloom for two months in late summer and fall. The plants grow 2½ to 3½ feet tall.

ACIDANTHERA MURIELAE

Plant in groups of 12 or more in formal borders or where the glowing white flowers and lovely fragrance can be enjoyed in the evening. Excellent in containers and cutting beds.

Site: Full sun. Deeply prepared, well-drained soil and abundant water. Cold-hardy in zones 7 to 11. In zones 3 to 6, dig up corms in fall when leaves yellow, store at 60° to 68°F. In Zone 7, apply winter mulch or dig and store corms.
How to Grow: Plant corms 4 to 6 inches deep and 6 inches apart after last frost. In Zone 6 and colder, start in cold frame or indoors in peat pots one month before last frost.
   Protect from wind. Remove spent flowers to promote continued bloom. Thrips, bacterial scab, and mosaic virus sometimes troublesome.

Similar Species: *Acidanthera bicolor,* only 1½ to 2 feet tall, white with chocolate star.

AGAPANTHUS HYBRIDS
Lily-of-the-Nile, African Lily

Agapanthus is a handsome, easy-care plant that blooms steadily throughout the summer. Dome-shaped clusters of 1- to 6-inch-wide blue or white lilylike flowers bloom atop bare stems 1 to 5 feet tall (depending on the cultivar), high above thick clumps of straplike leaves. Evergreen types are frost-tender; grow them in containers that overwinter indoors.

AGAPANTHUS AFRICANUS MINOR

Mass-plant in borders where cold-hardy, in containers where tender. Use dwarfs for edgings. Excellent in cutting beds and as houseplants.

Site: Full sun in the North; part shade where summers are hot. Fertile, well-drained but moist soil and abundant water during growth. Evergreen types hardy in zones 8 to 11; deciduous types to Zone 7 with winter mulch.
How to Grow: Plant tuberous roots just under soil surface, 1 to 2 feet apart. Blooms best when undisturbed for several years or if potbound. Snails and slugs troublesome; stem rot occurs if overcrowded.

Cultivars and Similar Species:
Evergreen: *Agapanthus orientalis* and *A. africanus* often are confused. The first reaches 5 feet tall; the second reaches 3 feet. Both are available in blue and white. Popular evergreen hybrids include 'Rancho Dwarf White', white, 24 inches tall; 'Peter Pan', deep blue, 18 inches; 'Lilliput', porcelain blue, 18 inches; 'Albidus', white, 36 inches.
   Deciduous: 'Headbourne Hybrids', 36 inches, in mixed shades of blue with an occasional white, or as selections such as 'Bressingham Blue', amethyst blue.

ALLIUM SPP.
**Persian Onion, Lily Leek,
Drumstick Allium**

Persian onion (*Allium aflatunense*) bears 2- to 4-inch-wide spherical clusters of small, violet flowers on bare stems that reach 2½ to 5 feet in height. The low, straplike leaves decline as the plant blooms in late spring to early summer, so place it among plants with summer foliage.

ALLIUM CHRISTOPHII

Star-shaped, ¾-inch, sunny yellow blossoms in 3-inch-wide heads top the charming and useful lily leek (*A. moly*). Each plant has two leaves, ½ to 2 inches wide and 12 inches long, which remain green throughout

ALLIUM MOLY

the bulb's late spring and early summer bloom period. The plant spreads and self-sows to form wide clumps, a feature some gardeners cherish and others find disagreeable. The plant grows 6 to 18 inches tall.

The ornamental *A. sphaerocephalum* (drumstick allium) produces eye-catching, egg-shaped, 2-inch-wide, reddish purple flower heads on slender stalks that grow to 3 feet in

ALLIUM SPHAEROCEPHALUM

early to midsummer. The green flower buds give the heads a bicolored look, and long stamens add an airy feeling. The blossoms dry in place to produce a long-lasting effect. Leaves, which are semi-cylindrical and hollow, are much shorter than the flower stalks.

Persian onion and drumstick allium make excellent cut or dried flowers. Plant Persian onion in groups of five or more in borders, rock gardens, or cutting gardens. Lily leek is charming between paving stones, tucked into rock gardens, massed in low groundcover plantings, or in cutting gardens. Plant drumstick allium in the midground of borders, meadow gardens, and cutting gardens. Plant in groups for best effect.

Site: Sun or light shade. Sandy, well-drained, moderately fertile soil and abundant water. Persian onion and lily leek are hardy in zones 4 to 8, drumstick allium in zones 3 to 9.
How to Grow: Plant bulbs in fall. Set Persian onions 5 to 8 inches deep and 10 inches apart, set lily leeks 4 inches deep and 3 to 4 inches apart; plant drumstick allium 6 inches deep and 6 inches apart. Divide when crowded and blooming diminishes; divide drumstick allium every five years.

Rodents may eat bulbs.
Cultivars and Similar Species: Persian onion: 'Purple Sensation', deep violet, 2 to 3 feet tall.

A. giganteum (giant onion) is tallest of the commonly planted alliums; ground-hugging clusters of 2-inch-wide blue-green leaves die back as flowers bloom; tall, bare flower stalks topped by 4- to 6-inch-wide, globe-shaped, reddish purple flower heads. 'Globemaster', hybrid with 10-inch-wide flower heads, foliage attractive during and after blooming.

A. christophii or *A. albopilosum* (star-of-Persia) has 6- to 12-inch-wide heads of pink or purplish white blossoms, 6 to 10 inches tall, broad, gray-green leaves; use in rock gardens or containers.

A. flavum is similar to lily leek but taller, with bell-shaped, yellow flowers.

ANEMONE BLANDA

ANEMONE BLANDA
Grecian Windflower

A common wildflower of lands bordering the Mediterranean Sea, the wild Grecian windflower has sky-blue flowers. Garden varieties bloom in sky blue and dark blue, white, pink, or red for a month beginning in early spring. The wheel-shaped, 2-inch-wide flowers have numerous narrow, silken petals surrounding clusters of yellow stamens. Each plant bears one or two low, finely divided leaves that last through spring. Grows 6 to 12 inches tall. Spreads readily.

Plant in groups of two dozen or more under trees and shrubs or along walks. Allow to naturalize in woodland and rock gardens.

Site: Full sun to light shade from deciduous trees in spring; avoid midday sun in hot areas. Fertile, well-drained soil. Abundant water during growth; drier conditions needed during summer dormancy. Hardy in zones 4 to 8; apply heavy mulch in zones 4 and 5; spreads best in zones 4 to 7.
How to Grow: In fall, soak tubers overnight in warm water, then plant 4 to 6 inches apart and 2 to 3 inches deep. In Zone 5 or colder, plant in spring. *continued*

ANEMONE BLANDA
(continued)

In very wet climates, dig up when dormant and store until fall. Tubers decay if they remain too moist after bloom.

Cultivars and Similar Species: Popular large-flowered cultivars include 'Blue Star', dark blue; 'Blue Shades', mixed blues; 'Pink Star', light pink; 'White Splendor', bright white. *Anemone coronaria* (poppy anemone), 6 to 18 inches tall with 2- to 5-inch red, pink, blue, or white blossoms that are dark-centered, sometimes double, zones 6 to 9; 'De Caen Hybrids', singles in mixed or separate colors.

ARISAEMA TRIPHYLLUM
Jack-in-the-Pulpit

The charming spring flowers of this woodland wildflower line a tall stalk (spadix) that rests inside a hooded cup (spathe), creating the so-called Jack-in-the-pulpit. Green with faint white or purple stripes, the

ARISAEMA TRIPHYLLUM

hooded cup is surrounded by several three-part leaves that rise directly from the ground. The leaves usually remain all summer, and the stalks ripen into showy wands of bright red berries in fall. Plants grow 1 to 3 feet tall and 18 inches wide.

Use in wildflower or shade gardens, where it will naturalize.

Site: Light shade. Moist to wet, fertile, humus-rich, slightly acid soil. Hardy in zones 4 to 9.

How to Grow: Plant container-grown plants in spring or plant corms 6 inches deep in fall. Do not dig from the wild. Easy to grow in the proper location and usually pest-free.

Similar Species: *Arisaema sikokianum* (Japanese Jack-in-the-pulpit), very showy with silver-green leaves, dark purple hood, and white-tipped spadix.

BEGONIA × TUBERHYBRIDA
Tuberous Begonia

Offering spectacular summer and fall blossoms in shady gardens, tuberous begonias thrive in areas with warm, humid days and cool nights.

BEGONIA × TUBERHYBRIDA

The flowers are as wide as 6 inches in white, yellow, red, and shades of peach and pink. Tuberous begonia blossoms may be bicolored or picoteed. They come in single or several distinct double forms, including rose, camellia, carnation, and ruffled. The glossy, succulent leaves point in the direction that blossoms will face. Plants are 12 to 18 inches tall, often trailing.

The flowers are showy in hanging baskets and containers, and excellent massed in shady borders.

Site: Light to medium shade. Humus-rich, fertile, moist soil. Provide extra fertilizer and abundant water during bloom; gradually withhold both for a few weeks as plants go dormant in late fall. Cold-hardy in zones 10 and 11; grow as tender bulb in other zones.

How to Grow: Plant tuberous roots indoors in early spring; position at soil level, indented side up. Move outdoors after nights are above 50°F. Or, plant outdoors, barely covered, 12 to 15 inches apart, when nights are warm.

Remove spent flowers to neaten and prevent disease. Where tender, dig tubers after dieback and store in dry peat over winter, at 40° to 50°F.

Whiteflies, mealybugs, powdery mildew, and gray mold troublesome.

Cultivars: Numerous cultivars. 'Nonstop' series is easy to grow, with large, rose-form double flowers in various colors.

CALADIUM

CALADIUM × HORTULANUM
Fancy-Leaved Caladium

Grown for its patterned tropical-looking foliage, caladium has 6- to 24-inch-long, arrowhead-shaped leaves that combine pink, rose, red, or white with green edges or centers.

The pink flowers are insignificant. Plant grows 1 to 3 feet tall.

Plant caladium in drifts of a single type in shade gardens, or use in containers indoors or out.

Site: Light to deep shade. Humus-rich, well-drained but moist soil with acid to neutral pH; plentiful moisture. Hardy in zones 10 and 11; tender elsewhere.

How to Grow: Plant tubers in garden, 2 inches deep, knobby side up, 12 to 18 inches apart when nights are above 60°F, or start indoors six to eight weeks earlier.

Store dormant tubers at 40°F in dry peat; overwinter potted plants indoors as houseplants or allow to go dormant in their containers.

Snails and slugs are troublesome.

Cultivars: Available as color mixtures or in dozens of named cultivars with predictable leaf colors and patterns. 'Postman Joyner', green-edged red; 'Little Miss Muffet', red-speckled white, dwarf; 'Candidum', green-veined white; 'Rosebud', bright pink, green-edged with white; 'White Queen', white with pink central veins, green outer veins.

CANNA × GENERALIS
Canna Lily

Boldly dramatic in both flower and foliage, cannas bring a lush, tropical appearance to a garden. Big, broad lance-shaped leaves vary from deep green to bronzy red or purple, or may be variegated green and yellow. Clusters of 4- to 5-inch-wide blossoms that resemble orchids or gladiolus appear atop the 1½ to 6-foot-tall plants from midsummer to frost. Blossoms may be white, cream, yellow, peach, pink, orange, red, or bicolored. The leaves are useful in cut-flower arrangements.

Best used in single-color groups to give a bushy effect in borders, or as accent plantings near pools and in large containers.

CANNA × GENERALIS 'STADT FELTBACH'

Site: Full sun. Adaptable, but prefers humus-rich, well-drained but moist soil. Water well in dry weather, but avoid overwatering. Hardy in zones 9 to 11; hardy to Zone 7 with winter mulch. Thrives in heat and humidity.

How to Grow: In zones 7 to 11, plant rhizomes in garden in spring, 2 to 4 inches deep and 1 to 2 feet apart; divide every three or four years. Elsewhere start indoors in peat pots a month before nights stay above 50°F, then plant outdoors. In zones 8 to 10, may leave in the ground over winter; elsewhere dig and store in dry peat above 40°F.

Snails, slugs, leaf-feeding insects, leaf-rolling caterpillars, and bacterial bud rot troublesome.

Cultivars: 'Pfitzer's Dwarf Hybrids', 30 inches tall, green leaves; 'Chinese Coral', coral-pink; 'Primrose Yellow', soft yellow; 'Salmon Pink', bright salmon pink; 'Pfitzer's Scarlet Beauty', early blooming, scarlet; 'Seven Dwarfs Hybrids', 18 inches, mixed colors, usually sold as seed; 'Red King Humbert', purple-red foliage, scarlet blossoms, 7 feet; 'Wyoming', light orange flowers, bronze-red foliage, 5 to 6 feet; 'Striatus', yellow-streaked leaves, orange flowers.

CHIONODOXA LUCILIAE
Glory-of-the-Snow

First discovered blooming at the snow's edge in the mountains of Asia Minor, glory-of-the-snow is among the earliest garden flowers to bloom. Each plant has two or three ribbonlike, dark green leaves and several arching stems with up to 10 star-shaped flowers arranged in a loose spike. The blossoms are usually bright blue to lavender-blue with white centers, but may be pink or white. Plants grow 3 to 6 inches tall.

CHIONODOXA LUCILIAE

Plant in groups of 50 or more in rock gardens or under shrubs. Allow to naturalize in lawn or meadow.

Site: Full sun; light shade in hot-summer areas. Humus-rich, fertile, well-drained soil. Water abundantly while growing, less when dormant. Hardy in zones 4 to 9; best in cooler climates.

How to Grow: Plant in fall, 2 to 3 inches deep, 1 to 3 inches apart. Divide during dormancy. This plant self-sows vigorously. Do not mow foliage for at least six weeks after blooming.

Nematodes may destroy bulbs; chipmunks and mice may eat bulbs.

Cultivars: 'Alba', white; 'Rosea', pink; 'Gigantea', larger, violet-blue; 'Pink Giant', larger, pink.

Bulbs

COLCHICUM AUTUMNALE
Autumn Crocus, Meadow Saffron

Resembling a long-stalked crocus without leaves (*Crocus* has three stamens, *Colchicum* has six), this gorgeous fall bloomer produces 4-inch-long, chalice-shaped, pink, pale lavender, or white flowers in early to midfall. The blooming plant has no leaves; flowers arise in clusters directly from the ground. Leaves are coarse-looking with prominent veins,

COLCHICUM CILICICUM 'PURPUREUM'

making unsightly clusters in spring when most bulbs are blooming. Plants grow 6 to 8 inches tall. Corms may bloom without being planted and sometimes are used as decorations.

Plant *Colchicum* where unattractive leaves go unnoticed and don't mask spring bloomers. Excellent massed in a groundcover; use in rock gardens or under shrubs in mixed borders.

Site: Full sun to light shade. Average, well-drained soil; abundant water when active. Suited to zones 5 to 9.
How to Grow: Plant corms before they bloom in mid- to late summer, 3 to 4 inches deep, 4 to 6 inches apart. To increase, divide after three or four years when dormant; otherwise leave undisturbed. Plants may self-sow.

All parts of plant poisonous. Corms allowed to bloom unplanted survive if planted, but temporarily weakened.
Usually pest-free.
Cultivars and Similar Species: 'Waterlily', 6 inches tall, lavender-pink water lilylike double. 'Album', 3 inches tall, white; 'Plenum', lilac, double peony form. *Colchicum byzantinum*, large rose-lilac flowers, leaves emerge after flowers fade and over winter. *C. speciosum*, raspberry-lilac, fragrant, later blooming; zones 3 to 9. *C. cilicicum*, star-shaped, fragrant, deep rose-lilac, later-blooming flowers; leaves grow in autumn.

CROCOSMIA × CROCOSMIIFLORA (TRITONIA × CROCOSMIIFLORA)
Montbretia

A valuable plant for its brilliant late summer and early fall blossoms, montbretia is an old garden favorite from South Africa. Its sword-shaped gladioluslike leaves measure up to 3 feet long and form upright to slightly arching clumps. Leafless

CROCOSMIA 'LUCIFER'

branched flower stems 1½ to 3 feet tall carry curving spikes of numerous lilylike, orange, red, gold, yellow, and sometimes bicolored flowers that are 1½ to 3 inches across.

Use as accent in midground of hot-color border, or mass in meadow gardens and with ornamental grasses. Good cut flower.

Site: Full sun or light shade. Average to humus-rich, well-drained soil. Drought-tolerant; best with moderate water. Hardy in zones 6 to 10.
How to Grow: Plant corms in spring, 2 inches deep and 3 inches apart. Where hardy, divide corms every third spring. Where not hardy, cut frosted tops in fall, dig up with soil attached, dry in shade, and store at 55° to 65°F in dry peat.
Usually pest-free.
Cultivars: 'Emily McKenzie', orange with deep-red central stars; 'Jenny Bloom', deep yellow; 'Lucifer', scarlet, hardy to Zone 5 with winter mulch.

CROCUS VERNUS

CROCUS SPP.
Dutch Crocus, Snow Crocus, Saffron Crocus, Fall Crocus

Dutch crocus hybrids (*Crocus × vernus*) are the most common and largest crocuses. These early-spring bloomers come in white, yellow, and various shades of lavender and violet, often streaked or veined in a contrasting color. Flowers have satiny petals, bright orange stamens, and measure up to 4 inches tall and 3 inches wide. The leaves,

CROCUS CHRYSANTHUS

which appear before or along with the flowers, are 2 to 8 inches long, upright, narrow, and dark green with central white stripes.

Snow crocus (*C. chrysanthus*) is smaller than Dutch hybrid crocuses, but blooms earlier and produces more flowers per corm. The species has bright orange flowers and bronze markings on the petal exteriors; hybrids may be white, cream, yellow, blue, and purple, and often are bicolored. The fragrant, long-lasting blossoms appear in late winter at the same time as the narrow, upright, spiky leaves, which elongate after blooming then die down. Flowers are 3 to 4 inches tall and leaves to 10 inches high. Corms increase rapidly.

The large, scarlet stigmas of saffron crocus (*C. sativus*) are the source of saffron, the world's most expensive spice. It takes at least six flowers to season one recipe. The 4-inch-long, fragrant, lilac-purple blossoms appear in autumn, along with short, spiky leaves, which elongate after blooming and last through winter. *C. sativus* corms often are available from sources that sell herbs.

Fall-blooming crocus (*C. speciosus*) is pretty, easy to grow, and the earliest of the fall-blooming crocuses. Less commonly sold than other autumn

bloomers, it is worth seeking out. The long-stalked, 5- to 6-inch-long flowers are lavender-blue with showy scarlet stigmas; cultivars come in blue, white, lavender, and bicolors. Blossoms appear in succession from late summer through early autumn; the 12-inch-long, 4 inch-wide leaves appear in spring and die back by summer.

CROCUS SATIVUS

Plant crocuses in groups for best effect at front of beds and borders, under shrubs, along walks, and in rock gardens; naturalize in lawn or meadow. Plant Dutch crocus in groups of 25 or more, snow crocus in groups of 50 or more. Plant fall crocus in groups in meadow, rock, or woodland gardens; interplant in low groundcovers in mixed borders.

Site: Full sun or light shade from deciduous trees. Dutch crocus thrives in average, well-drained soil with moderate water while growing. Snow crocus needs sandy to average, well-drained acid to neutral soil; requires water during growth, tolerates it when dormant. Give saffron crocus fertile, well-drained soil and moderate moisture when growing. Fall crocus best in average, well-drained soil; needs abundant water when growing.

Dutch hybrids hardy in zones 3 to 8 (best with cold winters); snow crocus in zones 3 to 11 (best in Zone 7 or colder); saffron crocus in zones 6 to 8 (Zone 5 with protection) and best with a long, hot summer; fall crocus in zones 4 to 8.

How to Grow: Plant corms of Dutch crocus and snow crocus in fall, Dutch crocus 5 inches deep and snow crocus 2 to 5 inches deep, both 2 to 3 inches apart; divide only when crowded, during dormancy. Plant saffron crocus in summer, 4 to 6 inches deep and 4 to 6 inches apart; divide every one to three years when leaves die in spring; replant in improved soil. Plant fall crocus in midsummer, 4 to 6 inches deep and 3 inches apart; divide only when crowded.

For earliest bloom, plant snow crocus where sun warms soil in late winter. Where naturalized in lawn, do not mow leaves until six weeks after blooming.

Mulch Dutch crocus in cold winters.

To harvest saffron, pick stigmas when flowers open, let dry, and store in a plastic or glass vial.

Fall crocus multiplies quickly by seed and offsets. Corms and seeds are poisonous. Flowers flop if corms are planted too shallowly.

Rodents may eat corms of Dutch and snow crocus; saffron and fall crocus not usually bothered. Birds may attack Dutch crocus flowers.

Cultivars and Similar Species: Dutch crocus: 'Peter Pan', white; 'Pickwick', silvery white with violet stripes; 'Yellow Mammoth', golden yellow; 'Purpurea', purple; 'Queen of the Blues', blue; 'Remembrance', silvery purple; 'Jeanne d'Arc', pure white.

Snow crocus: 'Prins Claus', white inside, purple blotched outside; 'Ladykiller', white inside, deep purple, white-edged outside; 'Blue Ribbon', light blue; 'Purity', white; 'Advance', yellow inside, lavender outside; 'E.A. Bowles', lemon yellow with bronze veins; 'Princess Beatrix', pale blue with yellow base; *C. tommasinianus*, lilac-mauve; 'Barr's Purple', large lavender-blue. *continued*

CROCUS SPP.
(continued)

Saffron crocus: *C. s.* var. *cartwrightianus albus*, white, rare; *C. medius*, similar.

Fall crocus: *C. goulimyi*, pale lavender with white throat, mid to late fall; *C. kotschyanus* (*C. zonatus*), pale lilac with dark veins and yellow throat.

CYCLAMEN HEDERIFOLIUM

CYCLAMEN HEDERIFOLIUM (C. NEAPOLITANUM)
Hardy Cyclamen

Blooming in late summer to fall, the hardy cyclamen may not bloom much its first year or two, but mature tubers can produce up to 50 flowers at a time. Undisturbed for a long time, corms produce a bounty of 1-inch, dark-eyed, pink or white flowers with backswept petals that resemble butterflies hovering over the foliage. Leaves are heart-shaped and more pointed than winter cyclamen; they measure up to 5½ inches across, are silver-marbled, and grow on leafless stalks 3 to 6 inches tall. Leaves begin to appear with or soon after the flowers, lasting all winter and spring.

Plant cyclamen along paths or in rock gardens, or naturalize in woodland and shade gardens.

Site: Light shade. Humus-rich, well-drained soil and plentiful moisture during growth. Hardy in zones 7 to 9 or possibly Zone 5 with winter mulch or snow cover. Best where summers are relatively dry with cool nights.

How to Grow: Plant container-grown plants in spring or fall, or plant tubers during dormancy, smooth side down with tops at soil surface, 6 to 12 inches apart. Best if undisturbed for many years and allowed to self-sow. After bloom ends, top-dress with 1 inch of compost or leaf mold. Do not divide corms; plant reproduces by seed.

Cyclamen mites a serious problem; leaf spot less so. Gray mold troublesome during humid weather.

DAHLIA PINNATA
Dahlia

One of the garden's most luxuriant flowers, dahlia offers late summer to early fall blossoms in every color but blue. Breeding transformed the original Mexican daisy-form flower into a variety of double forms, including ball-shaped

DAHLIA HYBRID

pompons and spiky-petaled, cactus-flowered types. Flowers are borne atop branched stems and vary from several inches across to dinner-plate size. The dark green compound leaves form bushy plants. Height varies from 1 to 7 feet, depending on cultivar.

Depending on size, locate in groups in front to back of formal borders. Excellent in cutting gardens.

Site: Full sun, midday shade in hot summer areas. Fertile, humus-rich, well-drained soil with abundant moisture. In zones 8 to 11, if soil is well-drained and unfrozen, may winter in ground or be dug. In colder zones, dig after dieback or the first frost and store, undivided, where cool, in dry sand or peat.

How to Grow: Plant tuberous roots horizontally in 6-inch-deep holes under 3 to 4 inches of soil in spring after soil has warmed. Divide stored roots two to four weeks before planting and set in moist sand. As shoots grow, gradually add 3 inches more soil. Space small types 1 to 2 feet apart, larger ones 3 to 4 feet apart. Usually grown from tuberous roots, but seeds started indoors in early spring bloom in one season and can be propagated from roots in subsequent years.

Stake tall types at planting with stout 5-foot stakes placed 2 inches from growth-eye end of tubers. Tie loosely beginning when 2 feet tall. For cut flowers, strip leaves from lower stems; dip ends in boiling water for one second before arranging.

Potato leafhoppers, mites, European corn borers, beetles, aphids, slugs, snails, virus diseases, and powdery mildew may be troublesome.

Cultivars: Hundreds of named cultivars. Specialty nurseries offer many, and local dahlia societies often sell.

ERANTHIS HYEMALIS
Winter Aconite

Blooming on the edge of the melting snow, the satiny, 1- to 2-inch, yellow flowers of winter aconite announce winter's end. Each plant bears a single stem with a ruff of lobed leaves that ring a single, 1-inch-wide, buttercup-like flower. Ground-hugging, lobed basal leaves develop right after the blossoms,

ERANTHIS HYEMALIS

going dormant by summer. Plants grow 2 to 8 inches tall. Best when planted in large groups and allowed to spread in naturalistic setting.

Site: Full sun to part shade. Average to humus-rich, well-drained but moist soil, with plentiful moisture even during summer dormancy. Zones 3 to 7; best where cold.

How to Grow: Plant tubers 3 inches deep and 3 inches apart in late summer or early fall after soaking overnight in warm water. Divide after three years by breaking tubers into pieces. Plant where tubers will not be disturbed for a long time. Plants self-sow freely and may invade lawns. Usually pest-free.

Similar Species: *Eranthis cilicia*, 2½ inches tall, bronzy leaves, blooms a bit earlier.

ERYTHRONIUM AMERICANUM
Trout Lily, Adder's-Tongue

In mid spring, this native woodland wildflower produces solitary 2-inch-long, lilylike, yellow flowers with backswept petals. These flowers nod on leafless stems 6 to 12 inches tall above ground-hugging leaves, which are mottled with pale green, darker green, and purplish brown. The tubers form stolons that enlarge the planting year after year. Naturalize them in woodland or shade gardens, or use as specimen plants in rock gardens.

Site: Light to medium shade from deciduous trees. Humus-rich soil, kept moist during growing season, drier in late summer and fall. Zones 3 to 8; performs poorly where summers are hot and dry.

How to Grow: Plant corms in early fall, 6 inches deep and 4 to 6 inches apart. Rarely needs division. Plant where it will be undisturbed for a long time. Foliage dies back in summer. Usually pest-free.

ERYTHRONIUM DENS-CANIS

Similar Species: *Erythronium californicum* (fawn lily), cream to white flowers, banded inside with yellow or orange. *E. dens-canis* (dogtooth violet), white, pink, or purple flowers, mottled leaves, needs more sun; 'Lilac Wonder', large, lilac. *E. tuolumnense* 'Pagoda', vigorous hybrid with one to four sulfur yellow flowers per stem; zones 5 to 8.

FREESIA X HYBRIDA
Freesia

Freesia's sweet fragrance is one of the most powerful floral scents, though not every modern hybrid is fragrant. Each leafless stem is sharply angled below the one-sided row of up to eight trumpet-shaped flowers, causing blossoms to point upward. Flowers may be white, yellow, pink, orange, lavender, red, purple, or bicolored. The two-ranked, sword-shaped leaves precede the flowers and die back after blooming. Plants grow 1 to 1½ feet tall. Plant freesia in single-color groups in front or midground of borders. Force as indoor plant. Excellent cut flower.

FREESIA

Site: Sun or part shade. Average, well-drained soil; water abundantly during growth, less during summer dormancy. Hardy in zones 9 to 11. In colder zones, lift corms; overwinter in cool, dark area.

How to Grow: In zones 9 to 11, plant corms in fall, 2 inches deep and 2 to 4 inches apart. Elsewhere, purchase corms specially treated to bloom in midsummer and plant in spring. When grown indoors, freesias do best at 68° to 72°F, with a drop to 55° to 60°F at night. Mosaic virus can be serious; remove infected plants.

Cultivars and Similar Species: 'Telecote Hybrids': large flowers, extremely fragrant, in 'Multi-Rainbow Mix'. Single colors: 'Matterhorn', white; 'Golden Melody', rich yellow; 'Oberon', red with yellow throat; 'Talisman', soft orange and pink; 'Adonis', double-flowered, rose-pink with cream throat; 'Silvia', blue-violet, semidouble. *Freesia alba (F. refracta alba)*, white flowered, scented parent of modern hybrids; naturalizes well in suitable climates.

FRITILLARIA SPP.

Crown Imperial, Checkered Lily

Blooming about daffodil time, crown imperial is an unusual-looking plant with a crownlike arrangement of flowers and foliage that accounts for its common name. A tightly packed whorl of 4-inch orange, red, or yellow blossoms topped by a spiky cap of green leaves forms a bold crown effect at the top of stout 2- to 4-foot stems. These are bare below the flowers, then covered to the ground with whorled, wavy-edged leaves that release a skunklike odor when crushed. Plant crown imperial in groups of a dozen or more to grow out of leafy plants such as hostas or ornamental grasses to hide conspicuous dying foliage in summer.

FRITILLARIA IMPERIALIS

Checkered lily or guinea-hen tulip, a graceful European wildflower, produces its unusual 2-inch-long, bell-shaped blossoms in early spring. The dainty flowers, which dangle from wiry stems, may be white or purple with a delicate two-toned brown or wine checkered pattern. Each plant has a few 3- to 6-inch-long, grasslike, blue-green basal leaves with a few smaller leaves scattered along the flowering stems. Grows 1 to 1½ feet tall. Plant in drifts for best visibility in rock, meadow, or woodland gardens. White flowers show up best.

Site: Full sun or part shade. Humus-rich, fertile, well-drained soil. Crown imperial needs regular water during growth, less while dormant; checkered lily needs moderate moisture. Crown imperial is hardy in zones 5 to 8. Checkered lily is hardy in zones 3 to 8 and does not adapt well to hot, dry summers or frostless winters.

How to Grow: Plant bulbs as soon as available in fall, 4 to 6 inches deep. Space crown imperial 8 to 12 inches apart; checkered lily 3 to 4 inches apart. Tip bulbs slightly to keep water from puddling in their tops. Divide every four to six years when dormant, if desired.

Apply deep mulch to crown imperial in fall. Be careful not to weed out delicate foliage of checkered lily.

Leafspot and mosaic virus sometimes trouble crown imperial; checkered lily is usually pest-free.

Cultivars and Similar Species: Crown imperial: 'Aurora', orange-yellow; 'Lutea Maxima', yellow; 'Rubra Maxima', red.

Checkered lily: 'Alba', white. In Pacific Northwest, plant better-adapted West Coast natives: *Fritillaria lanceolata*, brownish purple, checkered greenish yellow, and *F. recurva*, scarlet.

GALANTHUS NIVALIS

Snowdrop

Not even a light snowfall stops snowdrops from showing off their nodding white bells. Blooming in late winter and early spring when little else is in flower, the ½-inch flowers appear on single slender stems 4 to 8 inches tall, above two or three short, thin, gray-green leaves 3 to 8 inches tall. Green marks tip the three inner petals, while the longer outer ones are pure white. Bulbs spread to form dense stands of flowers and foliage, which die back in early summer.

GALANTHUS NIVALIS

Plant snowdrops in groups of 25 or more. They make charming drifts in lawns and woodland gardens and pair prettily with winter aconites.

Site: Full sun or part shade. Fertile, well-drained, constantly moist soil. Zones 3 to 8; best in cold-winter climates.

How to Grow: Plant bulbs 4 inches deep and 2 to 3 inches apart. Move or divide as flowers are fading, not when dormant. Do not mow foliage until at least six weeks after blooming. Usually pest-free. May rot in winter-wet Southern sites.

Cultivars and Similar Species: 'Flore Pleno', double. *Galanthus elwesii* (giant snowdrop), 1½-inch, earlier-blooming flowers, 12-inch stems, wider leaves; zones 4 to 8; better adapted to mild winter areas.

GLADIOLUS × HORTULANUS

Gladiolus

A popular cut flower, gladiolus offers tall, tightly packed spikes of gorgeous ruffled flowers with contrasting throats. The 2½- to 6-inch-wide blossoms open in sequence from the bottom up, all facing the same way. They come in solids or bicolors in all hues but true blue.

Flowering about two months after planting, gladiolus can be planted for blooming in late spring, summer, or fall. Each plant has one flower stem 3 to 6 feet tall and sword-shaped leaves.

In informal gardens, single plants or rows look stiff. For a more pleasing look, group in drifts with other plants. Plant in rows in cut-flower gardens.

GLADIOLUS

Site: Full sun. Average to humus-rich, well-drained soil. Plentiful water from shoot emergence until blooming ends, then reduced water. Hardy in zones 8 to 11, but best if stored over winter in all climates.

How to Grow: Plant corms after soil warms (beginning in mid winter in mild winter areas and early summer in the North), 4 to 6 inches deep and 4 to 6 inches apart. Stagger plantings at two-week intervals to produce full season of cutting flowers. Separate cormels from mother corms when digging and replant in nursery bed to mature.

Stake plants or mound earth to 6 inches around stems when 12 inches tall. Remove faded flower stalks immediately. Leave three or four leaves when cutting flowers to allow corms to mature for next year.

Thrips, spider mites, aphids, bacterial scab, mosaic virus, gray mold, corm rot, rust, and corn borers can be serious. Obtain clean stock, rotate site, and clean up debris.

Cultivars and Similar Species: Many cultivars in a range of colors and sizes. *Gladiolus nanus* (hardy gladiolus), 1½ to 2 feet; white, salmon, red, pink, and bicolors, zones 5 to 11 (to Zone 3 with winter protection). *G. byzantinus*, (Byzantine gladiolus), 2 feet, maroon, pink, white, or two-tone pinkish purple with white stripes, zones 7 to 11 (to Zone 5 with winter protection).

HYACINTHOIDES HISPANICA (ENDYMION HISPANICUS, SCILLA HISPANICA, AND SCILLA CAMPANULATA)
Wood Hyacinth, Spanish Bluebell

Botanists have renamed this pretty shade-loving bulb more than once. Although it is now called *Hyacinthoides hispanica*, catalogs may sell it by earlier names. The 1-inch-wide glossy, green, straplike leaves develop into vase-shaped clusters in early spring and are joined from late

HYACINTHOIDES HISPANICA 'BLUE QUEEN'

spring into early summer by sturdy spikes of 12 to 15 blue, pink, or white, ¾-inch, bell-shaped flowers. Plants grow 12 to 20 inches tall and 12 inches wide.

Wood hyacinth increases by self-sowing and offsets when well-situated.

Plants go dormant by midsummer. Allow the plants to naturalize in woodland or shade gardens.

Site: Half sun to light or full shade. Fertile, well-drained, acid to neutral soil. Plentiful moisture from fall until blossoms fade, then drier. Hardy in zones 4 to 8.

How to Grow: Plant bulbs in fall, 3 to 6 inches deep (deeper in cold-winter areas), 4 to 6 inches apart. Divide during dormancy only if crowded. Usually pest-free.

Cultivars and Similar Species: 'Excelsior', deep blue; 'Blue Queen', porcelain blue; 'Rosabella', pink; 'White City', white. *H. non-scripta*, or *Scilla non-scripta* (English bluebell), gracefully arching, fragrant violet-blue flowers, 8 to 12 inches tall, zones 5 to 8. See also *Scilla siberica*.

HYACINTHUS 'LORD BALFOUR'

HYACINTHUS ORIENTALIS
Dutch Hyacinth

Treasured for their showy flowers that have a heady fragrance which permeates the garden with a sweet and strong scent, Dutch hyacinths bloom in mid spring. Colors include pastel or vivid shades of yellow, pink, salmon, orange, blue, violet, and white. The 1-inch-long, tubular blossoms open to star-shaped faces and are tightly *continued*

HYACINTHUS ORIENTALIS
(continued)

packed around a 6- to 10-inch length of the 12- to 18-inch stems. Leaves are ¾ inch wide and straplike and form a stiff whorl beneath the flower stalk.

Best in informal drifts with underplantings of pansies or smaller bulbs to soften stiff appearance. Force for indoor bloom in pots or in water.

Site: Full sun or light shade. Humus-rich, well-drained acid to neutral soil and plentiful water during growth and bloom. Hardy in zones 3 to 7; elsewhere special treatment required. Winter mulch in zones 3 and 4. Poorly adapted where little or no freezing cold occurs, but can be grown as annual.
How to Grow: In zones 3 to 7, plant bulbs in early fall 4 to 6 inches deep, 6 to 9 inches apart. In zones 8 to 11, refrigerate bulbs for nine weeks and plant in mid to late fall. Plants persist, but multiply slowly and revert to an open blooming habit after the first year. Replace each year, or when flowers are no longer pleasing.

Fungal and bacterial rot may be serious; do not plant in infected soil for three years. Aphids troublesome.
Cultivars: 'L'Innocence', 'Mont Blanc', both white; 'City of Haarlem', 'Lemon Queen', yellow; 'Pink Pearl', 'Anna Marie', pink; 'Wedgewood', light blue; 'Delft Blue', medium blue; 'Blue Jacket', deep blue-violet.

IPHEION UNIFLORUM
(TRITELEIA UNIFLORA, BRODIAEA UNIFLORA)
Spring Starflower

This early-spring bloomer spreads rapidly to form great drifts of pale blue, fragrant, 1- to 1½-inch stars with bright orange stamens. Each flowering stem bears only one flower, but each bulb produces several stems over several weeks. The narrow, flattish leaves emerge in fall or spring

IPHEION UNIFLORUM

and die back in early summer. Starflower grows 6 to 8 inches tall and blooms best when crowded.

Allow it to naturalize in lawns, woodland and shade gardens.

Site: Full sun or part shade. Average well-drained soil with plentiful moisture during active growth, but drier during summer dormancy. Hardy in zones 7 to 9; hardy to Zone 5 with winter mulch.
How to Grow: Plant bulbs in mid- to late summer, 2 to 3 inches deep and 3 to 6 inches apart. Lift after flowering to divide. May be invasive. Snails and slugs sometimes troublesome.
Cultivars: 'Wisley Blue', large, deep blue blossoms.

IRIS SPP.
Reticulated Iris, Dutch Iris

Sometimes blooming with snow surrounding its feet, the violet-scented blossoms of reticulated iris (*Iris reticulata*) make a welcome display in late winter and early spring. Each plant bears a single, 3-inch, orange-splashed purple blossom on a stem 3 to 8 inches tall. Leaves, which are short when flowers bloom, but elongate to 18 inches later, are narrow, four-angled, and upright, disappearing by summer. Plant in groups of 10 or more in rock gardens or under shrubs along a walk.

Hybrid Dutch or Spanish irises (*I. xiphium*) are treasured as garden and cut flowers for their long stems and handsome blossoms. Plants bear one or two 4- to 5-inch flowers atop a single stem 1½ to 2 feet tall. The beardless mid-spring and early-summer blossoms may be blue, white, yellow,

IRIS RETICULATA

orange, bronze, or bicolored, often with contrasting blotches on the lower petals. The narrow, almost round leaves grow to 2 feet tall in winter and die back in summer. Plant Dutch irises in drifts in midground of beds and borders and in rows in cutting gardens.

Site: Full sun. Give reticulated iris average to rich, well-drained soil; moderate water while growing, dry during summer dormancy. Dutch iris needs humus-rich, well-drained soil with regular water during growth, less or none after leaves die. Reticulated iris hardy in zones 5 to 9; poorly adapted to wet-summer areas. Dutch iris hardy in zones 7 to 11 (to Zone 6 with winter mulch); treat as tender bulb in zones 3 to 5.
How to Grow: Plant bulbs in fall, setting reticulated iris 3 to 4 inches deep and 3 to 4 inches apart, Dutch iris 3 to 5 inches deep and 4 to 6 inches apart. Divide reticulated iris only when overcrowding reduces vigor. Divide Dutch iris after blooming, setting small

IRIS XIPHIUM

and interplanting with later-blooming perennials. Naturalize in a meadow, woodland, or informal garden.

LEUCOJUM AESTIVUM

LILIUM X AURELIANENSE 'THUNDERBOLT'

bulbs in nursery bed to mature. Replant immediately after dividing.

Where summers are wet, reticulated iris bulbs decline in a few years, but some may adapt and thrive. Bulb scale sometimes troublesome to reticulated iris; bulb rot, aphids, mosaic virus may attack Dutch iris.

Cultivars and Similar Species: Reticulated iris: 'Joyce', sky blue; 'Natascha', ivory with yellow blotch; 'Violet Beauty', deep purple; 'Harmony', royal blue; 'J.S. Dijt', reddish purple. *I. danfordiae* (Danford iris), green-marked yellow blossoms in late winter.

Dutch iris: 'Casablanca', white; 'Lemon Queen', two shades of yellow; 'Ideal', lobelia blue; 'Professor Blaauw', violet-blue; 'Purple Sensation', deep violet-purple with small yellow blotch.

LEUCOJUM VERNUM
Spring Snowflake

Flowering two weeks later than similar-looking snowdrops *(Galanthus nivalis)*, spring snowflake produces numerous stalks of several violet-scented, bell-shaped, ¾-inch, white flowers. Each of the blossom's six equal-length petals is tipped with a green spot. Leaves grow to 10 inches long and the flower stalk to about 1 foot tall. Excellent for mixed borders

Site: Full sun to part shade. Humus-rich, well-drained soil; regular water all year, especially while growing and blooming. Zones 3 to 8; better in the South than snowdrops.

How to Grow: Plant bulbs in fall, 3 to 5 inches deep, 8 to 10 inches apart. Do not divide for three years; may leave undisturbed for years. Usually pest-free.

Cultivars and Similar Species: *Leucojum aestivum* (summer snowflake), late spring to early summer, 12 to 18 inches tall, two to eight blossoms per stem, zones 4 to 9; 'Gravetye Giant', 1- to 1½-inch flowers, 18 inches tall.

LILIUM SPP.
Aurelian Hybrid, Asiatic Hybrid, Oriental Hybrid Lily

Derived from several Asiatic species, Aurelian hybrid lilies (sometimes called trumpet or Olympic lilies) offer up to 20 splendid, variously shaped blossoms atop tall stems 3 to 8 feet tall and whorled with narrow leaves. Blooming in July and August, between the earlier Asiatic and the later Oriental hybrids, these fragrant flowers are 6 to

8 inches long and up to 8 inches wide. Colors include white, greenish white, orange, yellow, peach, pink, and purple, often with yellow throats or maroon stripes. Most grow between 4 and 6 feet tall.

LILIUM 'ENCHANTMENT'

Asiatic hybrid lilies bring bright splashes of color to the early summer garden. Plants bear up to twenty 4- to 6-inch-wide flowers with flat or recurved petals. Flowers may be white, yellow, orange, pink, red, or combinations, often with small, dark spots; most face upward, but some face outward or downward. Upward-facing types, which include the popular Mid-Century Hybrids, are great for beds that will be viewed *continued*

LILIUM SPP.
(continued)

from an adjacent path or a second-story window. Outward-facing and pendant types show their faces from across the garden. Plants grow 2 to 6 feet tall, depending on cultivar.

Richly scented, voluptuously formed Oriental hybrid lilies bloom mainly in white and shades of pink and ruby red. Yellow is rare, though some have

LILIUM ORIENTAL HYBRID 'CASA BLANCA'

a yellow or coral band along the length of each backswept petal. Many have dark spots, bands of a second color, or a white picotee edge, and ruffled petal edges. Flower size varies from 6 to 12 inches across; plant height varies from 2 to 7 feet, with most 3 to 5 feet tall. Oriental hybrids bloom mainly in August, although a few newer, short hybrids bloom in late June or July.

Plant lilies in groups of three or more in midground of borders and meadow gardens.

Site: Best with tops in full or part sun and the bases shaded by other plants. Deep, fertile, humus-rich, well-drained soil. Regular water during growth and bloom; do not allow to completely dry, even when dormant. Aurelian hybrids

grow best in zones 4 to 7; in zones 9 and 10, dig bulbs and refrigerate for at least eight weeks before spring planting. Not well adapted to dry heat, but may perform if mulched heavily and grown in moist shade. Asiatic hybrids are best in zones 4 to 8, east of the Rocky Mountains. Oriental hybrids are suited to zones 5 to 8.

How to Grow: Plant bulbs in fall, before first frost, or when available in spring, 4 to 6 inches deep and 12 to 18 inches apart. Divide in late summer as they go dormant.

Stake individual stems. Spread 1 inch of organic matter around shoots in spring. Deadhead by cutting stems just below lowest spent flower. When leaves die, cut stem just above the ground to mark location. If blossoms are cut with many leaves, plants may die or fail to bloom the next year. Pollen from the flowers can stain skin and clothing.

Rodents may damage bulbs. Slugs, snails, aphids, gray mold, viruses, and bulb rot sometimes troublesome.

Cultivars and Similar Species: Aurelian hybrids: Trumpet—'Black Dragon', white inside, maroon reverse; 'Golden Splendor', buttercup yellow, maroon stripes on reverse; 'Pink Perfection', deep pink. Bowl-shaped—'Moonlight Hybrids', chartreuse yellow, scented in evening; 'Heart's Desire Hybrids', cream to white, golden orange center. Pendent—'Golden Showers', yellow, tinged maroon on reverse; 'Thunderbolt', deep apricot-orange. Sunburst—'Bright Star', white with orange-gold centers.

Asiatic hybrids: Upward—'White Swallow', pure white, a few dark spots, 3 feet; 'Snowy Owl', white, black-spotted, 4 feet; 'Dreamland', golden yellow with apricot centers, 3 to 4 feet; 'Malta', lavender-pink, 2 to 3 feet; 'Cream Puff', ivory, a few tiny spots, 2 feet; 'Lemon Custard', pastel yellow, dark dotted lines, 2 to 3 feet; 'Corsica', pink, pink-spotted ivory centers, 3 feet; 'Connecticut Yankee', bright yellow with golden centers, unspotted, 2 to

3 feet; 'Enchantment', nasturtium red, black spots, 3 feet. Outward—'Sally', orange-pink, burnt orange center, 6 feet; 'Sunny Twinkle', golden yellow, many black spots, 3 feet. Pendant—'Red Velvet', deep red, 4 feet.

Oriental hybrids: Bowl-shaped—'Fine Art', pure white with a touch of yellow in centers, 3 feet, July. Flat-faced—'Casa Blanca', pure brilliant white, 4 to 5 feet, August; 'Imperial' series, pinks and reds, 5 to 7 feet, August; 'Journey's End', magenta-rose with red stripes, 4 to 5 feet, August to September. Backswept—'Everest Hybrids', white, 4 to 5 feet, August; 'Jamboree', crimson with silver margins, 5 to 6 feet, August. Upward—'Stargazer', deep crimson with crimson-spotted white edges, 2 to 3 feet, July to August. Dwarfs—'Mona Lisa', white with pink spots; 'Mr. Ed', pink with pink-dotted white edges; 'Mr. Sam', white-dotted red. *Lilium aurantum* (gold-band lily), white with gold bands and red spots. *L. speciosum* 'Rubrum' (rubrum lily), white and crimson, fragrant.

LYCORIS SQUAMIGERA
Resurrection Lily, Magic Lily, Naked-Lady Lily

In late summer, resurrection lily bears a ring of fragrant, rose-lilac, trumpet-shaped flowers, each 3 inches long, around the top of its leafless 1½- to 2-foot flower stems. The leaves, 9 to 12 inches long and 1 inch wide, don't appear until flowers fade and remain green until spring. Plants are about 2 feet wide. Bulbs are dormant in summer and multiply freely, forming handsome clumps.

Plant in groups in midground of borders and naturalistic gardens; combines well with ornamental grasses. Looks best when interplanted with other plants whose foliage hides the naked stems.

LYCORIS SQUAMIGERA

Site: Full sun. Humus-rich, well-drained soil with regular water while growing, on the dry side while dormant. Hardy in zones 5 to 9; best when winter-chilled.
How to Grow: Plant bulbs in mid- to late summer, 5 to 6 inches deep, 6 inches apart. Divide bulbs during dormancy, only when crowded. Tolerates some summer water, if soil dries quickly. Bloom increased by crowding, so container culture is successful. Protect pot-grown plants from freezing. Root and bulb rot occur if overwatered.
Similar Species: *Lycoris radiata* (spider lily), red with spidery stamens, zones 8 to 10, to Zone 6 with winter protection. *L. aurea* (golden spider lily), yellow with spidery stamens, zones 9 to 11.
   Similar: *Nerine*, frost-tender, smaller, several pink-flowered species; *Amaryllis belladonna* or *Brunsvigia rosea* (belladonna lily, naked-lady lily), 4 to 12 sweetly fragrant, trumpet-shaped, 3- to 6-inch-long, lilylike rosy pink or white, blossoms in clusters atop 2- to 3-foot naked stems in late summer or early fall. In zones 9 to 11, plant bulbs with tops 1 to 2 inches below soil surface; in zones 5 to 8, plant 6 to 9 inches deep.
   Hybrids of *A. belladonna* with *Crinum* (× *Amarcrinum* or *Crinodonna*): evergreen in mild climates if watered, 3- to 4-foot stems of fragrant pink blossoms, zones 7 to 11, or Zone 6 with mulch.

MUSCARI BOTRYOIDES
Grape Hyacinth

This diminutive bloomer naturalizes easily in most gardens. It puts on a pretty show of tiny, urn-shaped, intense blue flowers—packed 20 to 40 to a stem—for a month or more from early to mid spring. The grasslike leaves emerge with the plum-scented flowers in spring and last all summer. The plants, which usually produce two spikes of grapelike clusters of buds and flowers, make charming drifts under daffodils and tulips. They grow 6 to 8 inches, sometimes to 12 inches. Cut spikes for small bouquets.

   Plant in groups of 50 or more as border edgings, in woodland, rock, or meadow gardens. Combine with daffodils, tulips, and Dutch hyacinths. Overwintering foliage of grape hyacinth may look messy, but serves as marker for other bulbs at fall planting time.

MUSCARI ARMENIACUM 'BLUE SPIKE'

Site: Full sun to light shade. Average to poor, well-drained soil; regular to plentiful water all year. Zones 2 to 8.
How to Grow: Plant bulbs in fall, 3 inches deep and 3 to 5 inches apart. Divide and transplant just after blooming. Spreads by seeding and increasing bulbs. Usually pest-free.

Cultivars and Similar Species:
'Album', white. *Muscari armeniacum*, white-tipped, cobalt-blue flowers, similar to *M. botryoides*, but blooms a bit later and leaves appear in fall and overwinter; zones 4 to 8; 'Blue Spike', double, sterile; 'Heavenly Blue', clear deep blue. *M. azureum*, bright blue, dense spikes. *M. comosum*, light and dark blue flowers in tassel-like clusters.

NARCISSUS SPP. AND HYBRIDS
Daffodils, Narcissus

Daffodils and narcissus are among the cheeriest flowers, blooming in early spring before tree leaves emerge. There are numerous types of narcissus, and some of the best are described here.

NARCISSUS CYCLAMINEUS 'TETE-A-TETE'

   The most familiar form are the trumpet and large-cup daffodils. The classic blossom is the long-trumpeted yellow, such as 'King Alfred', but many variations such as long-cup, short-cup, split-cup, and double abound. Colors include white, pale to bright yellow, and bicolors and tricolors with orange-red, peach, or pink. The strap-shaped leaves emerge before the flower stems and are usually somewhat shorter. Plants vary in height from about 14 to *continued*

NARCISSUS SPP. AND HYBRIDS
(continued)

20 inches tall. The sweetly fragrant blossoms make excellent cut flowers.

One of the parents of the charming hybrid daffodils is *Narcissus cyclamineus* (cyclamen daffodil), a 4- to 8-inch species with long, bright yellow trumpets and perianth segments that flare backward. Hybrids are generally taller and come in various colors and combinations; all have recurved perianths and long trumpets. They are the first daffodils to open, blooming from late winter through early spring, and bear one blossom per stem. They range in height from 5 to 16 inches, but most are 10 to 12 inches tall.

Jonquils (*N. jonquilla*) are the most fragrant narcissus, bearing sweet-scented, small-cupped, golden yellow flowers, up to six on a stem, in early spring. Leaves are narrow, rushlike, and dark green. Plants grow 12 inches tall. Jonquils like hot summer weather and are more likely than most narcissus to thrive in the South.

The sweetly fragrant pheasant's-eye or poet's narcissus (*N. poeticus*) blooms in mid to late spring and bears one flower to a stem. The perianth is purest white, surrounding a short, pale yellow cup edged in red. Cultivars retain the white perianth, but feature variously colored coronas. Leaves are narrow and blue-green. Plants grow 12 to 18 inches tall.

Hybrids of the paper-white narcissus (*N. tazetta*) possess a heady fragrance, small, shallow-cupped flowers borne several to a stem, and tall, slender grace. Flower color varies from white to deep yellow, with a smooth or ruffled, shallow corona, which is orange or the same color as the perianth. The bright white *tazetta*

NARCISSUS TAZETTA

hybrid 'Paper-white' is commonly forced in winter, bringing sweetly scented flowers indoors to the winter weary. They grow from 12 to 20 inches tall.

Native to Portugal and Spain, the delicate-looking angel's-tears (*N. triandrus*) bears white to pale yellow nodding flowers with backswept petals, blooming in late spring after most other narcissus have finished. The species usually has one flower per stem, but many of the cultivars have two or three flowers clustered at the tops of the stems. The narrow leaves are about a foot long, and plants are 10 to 18 inches tall.

Plant narcissus and daffodils in groups of 10 or more (12 or more for small types) in borders, woodlands, rock gardens, and meadows. Interplant larger hybrids with daylilies or hostas to hide fading foliage. Allow to naturalize under deciduous trees, or use small types like angel's-tears in groundcover plantings. Or, plant in containers.

Site: Full sun to light shade from deep-rooted deciduous trees; pink-flowered hybrids retain color best in part shade. Humus-rich, well-drained, neutral to slightly acid soil; regular water when growing and blooming, drier during

summer dormancy. Pheasant's-eye narcissus adapts better to poorly drained soil than most narcissus.

Trumpet and large-cup hybrids are hardy in zones 3 to 9; not well-adapted where summers are wet. Cyclamen daffodil is suited to zones 6 to 9 in the East, to Zone 11 in the West. Jonquils, pheasant's-eye narcissus, and angel's-tears grow best in zones 4 to 9 in the East, to Zone 11 in the West. *N. tazetta* is hardy in zones 7 to 11; some cultivars to Zone 5, others only to Zone 8; it is poorly adapted where summers are wet. *Tazetta* does better in the South than many narcissus because it does not need a long, cold dormant period.

How to Grow: In cold-winter areas, plant bulbs in late summer to early fall; in areas with warm autumns and mild winters, plant in November. Set trumpet and large-cup hybrids, jonquils, and pheasant's-eye narcissus 6 to 8 inches deep and 4 to 6 inches apart. Set cyclamen daffodils 5 to 8 inches deep and 3 to 6 inches apart. Plant *N. tazetta* in fall, 3 to 5 inches deep and 6 to 8 inches apart. Set angel's-tears 5 to 6 inches deep and 6 to 8 inches apart.

Do not remove foliage until it yellows and dies back. Do not braid foliage of large hybrids as sometimes advised to increase tidiness. Cut off faded flowers. For best reblooming, fertilize with high-nitrogen fertilizer when foliage emerges from the ground each spring.

Root and bulb rot, mosaic virus, and narcissus bulb flies occasionally troublesome. Bulbs not usually eaten by rodents.

Cultivars and Similar Species: Colors are given for perianth (flat petals) first, then for the cup or corona.

Trumpet hybrids: 'King Alfred', yellow/yellow, 16 to 20 inches; 'Mount Hood', both open creamy yellow, white when mature, 16 inches; 'Spellbinder', sulfur yellow/white, 16 to 18 inches.

Large-cup hybrids: 'Accent', white/salmon-pink, 14 to 16 inches; 'Rosy Wonder, white/pink, 16 to 18 inches, often two flowers per stem;

'Daydream', pale yellow/white, 14 to 16 inches; 'Carlton', yellow/yellow, naturalizes well, 18 to 20 inches; 'Ice Follies', creamy white/light yellow, naturalizes well, 16 to 19 inches; 'Fortissimo', golden yellow/orange-red, 16 inches.

Short-cup hybrids: 'Barret Browning', creamy white/orange, 16 inches, early. Double-flowered: 'Cheerfulness', white/creamy yellow, 14 to 16 inches; 'Ice King', both open creamy yellow, turn white, 16 to 18 inches.

Cyclamen daffodils: 'February Gold', yellow/yellow, 12 inches, good naturalizer; 'February Silver', white/yellow fading white, 12 inches; 'Tete-a-tete', yellow/yellow, 5 to 7 inches, two flowers per stem, not as backswept; 'Jack Snipe', white/yellow, 8 to 10 inches; 'Jenny', white/white, 10 inches; 'Peeping Tom', golden yellow/golden yellow, 10 inches.

Jonquils: 'Suzy', yellow/deep orange, 16 inches; 'Bell Song', creamy white/pink, 16 inches; 'Baby Moon', pale yellow/pale yellow, 7 inches; 'Pipit', light yellow/white, 7 inches.

Pheasant's-eye narcissus. 'Actaea', white/yellow with red edge, flowers 3 inches across, 15 to 18 inches tall; 'Pheasant's Eye' (*N. poeticus recurvus*), white/yellow, edged with green and with orange centers, 14 inches.

Tazetta narcissus: 'Paper-white', white/white, 16 inches; 'Soleil d'Or', yellow/orange, 16 inches; 'Minnow', pale yellow/yellow, 8 to 10 inches; 'Geranium', white/orange, 15 to 17 inches; 'White Pearl', white/white; 'Cragford', white/orange, 12 to 14 inches.

Angel's-tears: 'Thalia' (orchid narcissus), pure white with up to five pendent, lightly fragrant blossoms per stem, 18 inches; 'Ice Wings', ivory white, scented, 12 inches; 'Hawera', lemon yellow, fragrant, 10 inches; 'Liberty Bells', soft yellow, 12 to 14 inches; 'Tuesday's Child', clear white and yellow, 14 to 16 inches.

POLIANTHES TUBEROSA
Tuberose

These old garden favorites are found more commonly in florist's shops than in gardens. With at least four months of warm summer weather, however, it's easy to grow these headily fragrant flowers. From a fountain of grassy leaves that reach to 18 inches in length, several 2½- to 3-foot flower spikes—made up of some 30 waxy white, 2-inch-long, single or double, tubular flowers—appear in late summer and fall.

POLIANTHES TUBEROSA

Use tuberoses in groups in the midground of borders and in cutting gardens and containers.

Site: Full sun. Fertile, humus-rich, well-drained, acid to neutral soil. Water once at planting. Needs regular water after shoots emerge during growth and bloom, taper off when foliage declines. Zones 8 to 11; elsewhere treat as tender bulb, although usually dug and wintered indoors even where hardy.
How to Grow: Plant rhizomes in spring, after last frost, no more than 1 or 2 inches deep and 4 to 8 inches apart. Or, start indoors, four to six weeks before warm nights begin. Divide offshoots in fall when digging, but divisions may not rebloom for one or two years.

In short-season areas, start indoors or grow outdoors in containers. Keep containers indoors until spring warms and during early fall frosts. Where temperatures fall below 20°F, dig rhizomes, dry two weeks, and store in cool place in dry peat.

Aphids may damage buds.
Cultivars: 'The Pearl', double flowers, 15 inches; 'Everblooming', to 3½ feet, single, longer-lasting cut flower.

SCILLA SIBERICA
Siberian Squill

Dark, pure blue like the winter sky on a sunny day, Siberian squill forms wonderful eye-catching drifts in late winter and early spring, blooming soon after snowdrops. The nodding ½-inch flowers have flared petals. Although only three to five blossoms form a loose flower spike, each plant makes three or four stems.

SCILLA SIBERICA

The straplike leaves, which emerge with the flowers, are ½ inch wide, up to 6 inches long, and die back in summer. Siberian squills are small plants, just 4 to 6 inches tall.

continued

SCILLA SIBERICA
(continued)

Plant in groups of 50 or more in mixed borders, under shrubs, and in rock gardens. Naturalize in lawns, woodlands, and meadows.

Site: Full sun to light shade. Fertile, well-drained, acid to neutral soil. Keep moist from fall until plant declines after blooming; keep drier during dormancy. Zones 2 to 8.
How to Grow: Plant bulbs in fall, 3 to 4 inches deep, 4 inches apart. Plant where bulbs will be undisturbed for a long time. Siberian squill readily reseeds. Bulbs rot easily in storage; plant only healthy bulbs.
Cultivars: 'Spring Beauty', large flowers, 6 inches tall, multiplies more slowly than the species because it makes fewer seeds. 'Alba', white.

STERNBERGIA LUTEA
Winter Daffodil

Looking much like a large, deep yellow crocus, winter daffodil adds its surprising blossoms to the fall garden. Each bulb sends up one to

STERNBERGIA LUTEA

several flower stems, 4 to 9 inches high, each bearing a single, 1½-inch-long, chalice-shaped blossom that opens to a six-pointed star. The

¾-inch-wide leaves grow 8 to 12 inches high, emerge at the same time as or just after the flower stems, and last through winter.

Plant winter daffodils in groups at the front of gardens and under shrubs, in rock gardens, and on slopes where drainage is good.

Site: Full to half sun. Average, well-drained soil; moderate water during growth, drier during summer dormancy. Hardy in zones 6 to 11. Best where summers are hot and dry.
How to Grow: Plant bulbs in mid- to late summer, 4 inches deep and 6 inches apart. Divide in summer if crowded. Endangered in its native Iran. Buy only nursery-propagated bulbs.

Bulb rot occurs if drainage is poor.
Cultivars: 'Major' has large blossoms.

TIGRIDIA PAVONIA

TIGRIDIA PAVONIA
Tiger Flower

Blooming in brilliant hot colors, tiger flowers make a strong statement in the summer garden. Each 3- to 6-inch-wide flower is a widely flared, upward-facing tube with three large and three small petals. The small petals and the bases of the larger ones are speckled with bright or dark spots, while petal edges are solid. The palette includes red, orange, yellow,

pink, cream, and white. Each blossom lasts one day, but flowers open on the branched stems over many weeks from mid- to late summer. The ridged leaves form a fan beneath the blossoms. Plants grow 1½ to 2½ feet tall. Bulbs usually are sold as a mix of colors.

Plant tiger flowers in groups in beds and borders.

Site: Full sun, part shade in hot-summer climates. Fertile, humus-rich, well-drained soil; regular water during growth and blooming, none when foliage yellows. Hardy in zones 7 to 11; elsewhere treat as a tender bulb.
How to Grow: Plant corms in spring, 2 to 4 inches deep and 4 to 8 inches apart. Where hardy, divide every three or four years. Reseeds where hardy. May need staking. Gophers and red spider mites may be troublesome.

TRILLIUM GRANDIFLORUM
White Trillium

One of the showiest woodland wildflowers native to the East Coast, white trillium displays its gorgeous flowers for three or four

TRILLIUM GRANDIFLORUM

weeks in early to midspring. The 2- to 3-inch-wide flowers are solitary, opening atop a slender stalk that arises from the joint formed by three oval, pointed, 3- to 6-inch-long leaves. The upward-facing flowers are comprised of three wavy, pointed petals backdropped with three pointed, green sepals. They open white and gradually fade to pink. The foliage dies down in midsummer if soil dries. Plants grow about 1½ feet tall, forming 2-foot-wide colonies.

White trillium is gorgeous when naturalized in shade and woodland gardens.

Site: Full sun in spring followed by light shade cast by deciduous trees. Humus-rich, fertile, moist, neutral to acid soil; plentiful moisture. Hardy in zones 4 to 9.

How to Grow: In spring, plant rhizomes 4 inches deep or plant container-grown plants, spacing 2 feet apart. Do not dig up or purchase wild plants. Division not necessary, but roots of mature clumps may be separated when dormant. Seeds may be sown directly in the garden when fresh; seedlings will not flower for several years.

Keep moist and well-mulched. Usually pest-free.

Cultivars and Similar Species: 'Flore-pleno', double, very showy; var. *roseum*, pink. *Trillium erectum* (purple trillium), deep maroon flowers, acid soil.

TULIPA SPP. AND HYBRIDS
Tulip

Among our most familiar spring flowers are hybrid tulips with their elegant, long-stemmed, cup-shaped blossoms. As they age, the egg-shaped flowers open into wide bowls on sunny days, closing at night. The usually 2- to 3-inch-deep flowers may be single or double, fringed, pointed, or ruffled, blooming in mid to late spring. They come in all colors but true blue. Some are streaked, blotched with basal stars, or picoteed.

The broad gray-green leaves are generally much shorter than the flower stems. Most hybrid tulips grow 10 to 30 inches tall.

Modern hybrids and species/hybrid groups are classified by bloom time (early, mid, or late in the tulip season) as well as by flower type. Early bloomers include Single Early, Double Early, and Fosteriana tulips. Midseason hybrids include Triumph, Greigii, and Darwin Hybrids. Late bloomers include Lily-flowered, Darwin and Cottage (now classified together as Single Late), Parrot, Double Late or Peony-Flowered, Fringed, and Viridiflora tulips.

ANGELIQUE DOUBLE LATE HYBRID

In addition to the hybrid groups, there are numerous species tulips to consider for your garden. Bokhara tulip *(Tulipa batalinii),* a diminutive Asian wildflower, is buff yellow with a yellow-gray blotch at the base of each petal; cultivars come in shades of yellow, bronze, and red. The leaves are narrow and grasslike, forming along with the mid spring blossoms. Plants are 4 to 6 inches tall.

Lady tulip *(T. clusiana)* is especially easy to grow in mild-winter areas with hot, dry summers, where it often naturalizes. The graceful, fragrant blossoms are rosy red and white or

ESTELLA RIJNVELD PARROT HYBRID

creamy on the outside, with reddish purple bases, opening to reveal a white interior. When fully opened, the flowers are star-shaped. Leaves are narrow and few, folded lengthwise. Grows 12 to 14 inches tall.

GEORGETTE MULTISTEM HYBRID

Native to Asia Minor, dwarf Taurus tulip *(T. pulchella)* is painted red to purple on the inside of the petals with a bluish basal blotch, and gray or green on the reverse of the petals. Cultivars come in violet, violet-pink, and white. The 1½-inch blossoms open into flat stars on sunny days. Flowers bloom early, from a base of two or three strap-shaped leaves. Grows 4 to 6 inches tall. *continued*

TULIPA SPP. AND HYBRIDS
(continued)

Short of stature, water lily tulips (*T. kaufmanniana* hybrids) bloom early with flowers that resemble water lilies. The pointed petals open into wide stars on sunny days. The species includes creamy white insides with golden yellow bases and bright carmine exteriors. Cultivars may have flowers 3 inches across in shades of yellow, mauve-pink, deep red, violet, and white, often with a contrasting base, edge, or reverse. The leaves are broad and low-spreading, in one case striped with white. This easy-care tulip grows 4 to 10 inches tall and naturalizes readily.

Pretty Florentine tulip (*T. sylvestris*) blooms in mid spring and adapts better than most tulips to mild-winter areas. The 2-inch-long, fragrant, yellow blossoms often are borne several to a 6- to 12-inch stem. The straplike leaves are nearly as tall as the flower stems.

Kuenlun tulip (*T. dasystemon* or *T. tarda*) grows almost like a groundcover, with flat, bright green leaves and flowers that open to flat stars. Petals are yellow with white edges on the inside, white with hints of green and sometimes red on the outside. The 2-inch blossoms open several to a stem in early spring. Bulbs form on ends of stolons and spread where well-sited. Grows 4 to 6 inches tall.

Plant hybrid tulips in groups in midground of beds and borders; also excellent in cutting gardens. Combine with hostas to hide dying foliage. Plant species in groups in rock gardens and front of garden. Dwarf Taurus tulips are nice under shrubs.

Site: Full sun is best for most tulips. *T. batalinii, T. sylvestris,* and hybrid tulips also will grow in light shade, but the tall hybrids will lean toward light that doesn't come from overhead. Fertile, humus-rich, well-drained soil; regular water during growth and blooming, drier when leaves die back.

Hybrid tulips are hardy in zones 3 to 7. In zones 8 to 11, use them as annuals or dig bulbs when dormant and refrigerate in moist peat at 40° to 45°F until late-fall planting. Bokhara tulip is hardy in zones 4 to 8. Where summers are wet, dig dormant bulbs and store at 65°F until fall planting time. Lady tulip is adapted to zones 4 to 8 in the East, to Zone 11 in the West. Where summers are wet, dig and store as for Bokhara tulip. Dwarf Taurus tulip is suited to zones 5 to 8. Where summers are wet, dig and store as for Bokhara tulip. Water lily tulips are hardy in zones 3 to 8, Florentine tulips in zones 4 to 10, and Kuenlun tulips in zones 4 to 8.

How to Grow: Plant hybrid tulips in early fall in zones 3 to 7, 5 to 6 inches deep and 4 to 6 inches apart. In zones 8 to 11, refrigerate bulbs for eight weeks at 45°F, then plant in mid to late fall, 6 to 8 inches deep. Most hybrid tulips do not rebloom well after the first year, so often are treated as annuals even where hardy. To encourage reblooming in subsequent years, plant 10 to 12 inches deep, fertilize with nitrogen during leaf growth, remove spent blossoms, and allow foliage to die back naturally. If treating as annual, pull plants after flowers fade; otherwise, cut back foliage only when it yellows.

Plant species tulips in fall. Set Bokhara tulips, dwarf Taurus tulips, and water lily tulips 3 to 6 inches deep and 3 to 6 inches apart. Plant candystick tulip 4 to 7 inches deep and 3 to 6 inches apart. Plant Florentine tulips 4 to 6 inches deep and 3 to 6 inches apart. Plant Kuenlun tulips 5 to 6 inches deep and 3 to 6 inches apart.

Mulch dwarf Taurus tulips in cold climates.

Hybrid tulips may be troubled by fire (a disease similar to gray mold), mosaic virus, aphids, gophers, mice, and deer. Species tulips are usually pest-free.

Cultivars and Similar Species: Hybrid tulips: Single Early—'Couleur Cardinal', dark red, 13 inches; 'Dr. An Wang', lilac-blue, 15 inches; 'General De Wet', warm orange, fragrant, 13 inches. Double Early—'Schoonoord', white, light fragrance, 12 inches; 'Abba', bright red, 12 to 14 inches. Triumph—'Apricot Beauty', salmon and apricot, 18 inches; 'Bastogne', red, light fragrance, 18 inches; 'Boccherini', dark periwinkle blue, light scent, 20 inches; 'Hans Anrud', deep lilac, 22 inches; 'Orange Wonder', warm orange, fragrant, 18 inches; 'White Dream', white, 20 inches. Lily-flowered—'Ballerina', apricot-tangerine, fragrant, 24 inches; 'West Point', primrose yellow, 23 inches; 'White Triumphator', white, 26 inches. Single Late—'Bleu (or Blue) Aimable', lilac-blue, touches of lavender, 26 inches; 'Georgette', butter yellow, red edge, several to a stem, 18 inches; 'Sweet Harmony', lemon yellow, white edge, 24 inches. Darwin Hybrids—'Burning Heart', white flamed red, 28 inches; 'General Eisenhower', red, 26 inches; 'Golden Apeldoorn', golden yellow, 24 inches; 'Holland's Glory', orange-scarlet, 26 inches; 'Jewel of Spring', primrose yellow, red edge, 24 inches. Parrot—'Blue Parrot', lilac-blue, streaked lavender, 26 inches; 'White Parrot', white, streaked green, 25 inches. Double Late or Peony-Flowered—'Maravilla', violet, 22 inches; 'Mount Tacoma', white, 23 inches; 'Angelique', pale pink, lighter edge, 22 inches.

Bokhara tulip: 'Bright Gem', golden yellow, flushed orange; 'Bronze Charm', bronze; 'Red Jewel', red; 'Yellow Jewel', lemon yellow. *T. linifolia*, red, bluish base, pointed petals, red-edged leaves, 5 to 10 inches tall.

Lady tulip: *T. c.* var. *chrysantha*, crimson outside, deep yellow inside, 6 inches tall. *T. c.* var. *stellata*, yellow blotch inside.

Dwarf Taurus tulip: *T. p.* var. *humilis* (*T. humilis*), bright rose-pink. *T. p.* var. 'Violaceae', violet-purple, crocus-shaped blooms, 4 inches tall; 'Persian

Pearl', rosy red inside, silvery gray outside, 6 inches tall. *T. bakeri,* large wine-purple flowers, 4 to 6 inches tall; 'Lilac Wonder' rose-purple.

Water lily tulip: 'Cherry Orchard', scarlet, 8 inches; 'Heart's Delight', pink with pale pink edges, 6 inches; 'Alfred Cortot', deep scarlet, white-striped leaves, 6 inches; 'Gaiety', violet-edged in creamy white, 4 inches; 'Shakespeare', carmine exterior, salmon interior. *T. greigii* similar but blooms later, gray-green leaves striped with maroon; 'Red Riding Hood', red; 'Perlina', rose; 'Cape Cod', apricot-edged yellow.

Florentine tulip: *T. saxatilis,* suited to mild winter areas, forms bulbs at ends of stolons, fragrant rosy lilac flowers, one to three per stem, 12 inches tall; thrives in poor soil and hot summers.

ZANTEDESCHIA AETHIOPICA
Calla Lily

A large subtropical plant related to Jack-in-the-pulpit, calla lily shares that flower's unusual form. Tiny, petal-less flowers decorate the yellow spike, around which furls a graceful, showy, cone-shaped bract. The bract may be white, creamy white, or marked with green. The plant's large, arrow-shaped, glossy, dark green leaves emerge in late winter, and the slightly longer flower stems bear solitary 6-to 8-inch flower heads from early spring into early summer. Calla lilies grow 1½ to 4 feet tall. Where hardy, the plants naturalize and sometimes become weedy.

Plant calla lily in groups in midground to background of borders and naturalistic gardens. Excellent in boggy or damp sites and around garden ponds.

Site: Full sun or part shade. Average to humus-rich, well-drained to wet soil; ample water while growing and blooming. Tolerates wetness.

ZANTEDESCHIA AETHIOPICA

Hardy in zones 9 to 11; elsewhere best overwintered as a container plant. Rhizome may be dug and stored in peat, but it is never quite dormant, so it doesn't store well.

How to Grow: Where hardy, plant rhizomes in fall through early spring, 2 to 3 inches deep and at least 12 inches apart. In cold winter areas, rhizomes may be sprouted indoors and planted out after last frost. Cut off faded flower stalks. Leafspot may be troublesome; remove affected leaves. Virus, spread by sucking insects, and snails and slugs also cause problems.

Cultivars and Similar Species: 'Hercules', larger than species, broad, recurved bracts; 'Green Goddess', bracts green toward tips; 'Childsiana', 1-foot-tall, heavy-blooming dwarf. *Zantedeschia pentlandii,* deep yellow bracts, 16 to 18 inches tall; 'Golden Mikado Lily', a choice cultivar. Also available are hybrids in shades of pink, lavender, and orange, usually 1½ to 2 feet tall, often with spotted leaves.

ZEPHYRANTHES ATAMASCO
Rain Lily, Atamasco Lily

The rain lily earned its name from its habit of bursting into bloom after rain. Several species are summer to autumn bloomers. The most hardy is *Zephyranthes atamasco,* a Southeastern native that blooms for a

month or more beginning in early spring. The dainty, 3-inch, six-pointed, starlike, white or purple-tinged flowers are borne singly on slender stems above grasslike, dark green leaves. Grows to 12 to 18 inches tall. Naturalize in moist open woodlands and shade gardens. Plant in groups in borders. Excellent container plant. Bulbs are poisonous.

ZEPHYRANTHES ATAMASCO

Site: Full to part shade. Average well-drained soil. Alternate periods of wet and dry soil stimulate flowering. Best if drier for two months after blooming, but tolerates some water while dormant; should never be bone-dry.

Hardy in zones 7 to 11. Where not hardy, treat as tender bulb; overwinter in container or store in moist sand, keeping moist.

How to Grow: Plant bulbs in fall where hardy, in spring in colder areas, 1 to 2 inches deep and 3 to 4 inches apart. Divide when the number of blossoms declines. Usually pest-free.

Similar Species: *Z. candida,* 2-inch white flowers summer to fall, evergreen foliage, zones 9 to 11. *Z. grandiflora* (zephyr lily), 3-inch pink to red flowers in spring and summer, zones 9 to 11. *Z. rosea* (Cuban zephyr lily), 1-inch rose-red flowers in late summer and fall, zones 9 to 11.

FRUITS & NUTS

CHAPTER 9

ABOUT FRUIT

As bountiful as the harvest looks from this red 'Stayman Winesap' apple, the fruit would have been much larger had they been thinned to one apple every 4 to 6 inches along the branches.

Nothing is more sublime than biting into a freshly picked apple, its fragrance and crispness evoking memories of a brisk autumn day with a chill hanging in the air. Nothing except perhaps sinking your teeth into a fat, sun-warmed strawberry, its red juice staining your lips. Or maybe savoring the aroma and crunch of a walnut you cracked out of its hard shell. If a rose symbolizes love, fruits and nuts represent abundance overflowing with rich goodness.

As an attentive gardener who is willing to invest some time and effort into growing berries, tree fruits, and nuts, your homegrown harvest will be tastier than anything you can purchase at the market and will bring all kinds of rewards. If you love nuts and fresh fruits, a little planning will make this part of your gardening a fulfilling experience.

FRUIT TREE PARTICULARS

Choosing a well-adapted plant for the home garden has always been critical to gardening success, but when it comes to fruit trees, it can be life or death—literally. Whenever you have a choice, try new cultivars with outstanding hardiness, good disease resistance, and improved fruit quality.

Because your livelihood isn't dependent on garden yields, you may choose a lower-yielding cultivar for its exceptional flavor or disease resistance. Let the commercial growers wrestle with hard-to-grow 'Granny Smith' apples; you can grow 'Freedom' or 'Liberty', whose very names hint at how much easier they are to care for. Those big, old apple trees of yesteryear may be a sight that warms the heart on a fall day, but they're tough to prune, and pest control is a real challenge. It's much easier to harvest fruit from a tree that's not much taller than you are, so most home gardeners eschew standard fruit trees and turn to those grown on dwarfing rootstocks.

THE LONG AND SHORT OF DWARF TREES

With their naturally small size, dwarf fruit trees are much more manageable than standard-size trees and begin to bear at a much earlier age, sometimes when they are only three or four years old—half the time it takes a standard-size tree to bear fruit. Dwarf trees are easier to prune, spray, and harvest. And the fruit from a dwarf tree is as good as, or better than, the fruit of the same cultivar grown as a full-size tree. It's all a matter of care; because the tree is a manageable height, you can pay closer attention to it and deal with any problems as soon as they arise. Even pruning becomes easier. With proper pruning, more light reaches the inner branches of the tree, resulting in sweeter fruit.

Dwarfing characteristics come from grafting a desirable cultivar onto a rootstock that controls size. (The top part of the grafted tree is called the budwood, or scion.) There are several types of rootstocks, each named and each with its own particular set of idiosyncracies. A tree's size at maturity depends upon the dwarfing effect of its rootstock, the soil type, the care the tree receives, and the scion's own characteristics. A dwarf tree may reach only 8 feet at maturity; a semidwarf grows 15 to 18 feet tall.

The important thing to remember is that each rootstock has different traits that make it unique; these traits aren't limited to how short the tree will be. The rootstock does make a big difference in the tree's best location and care requirements. Don't try to make sense of the combination of numbers and letters that identify the rootstock; they were designated by researchers. In the case of apples, the research was done in England.

Before buying a dwarf tree, check with your nursery to see what they offer. If the description simply states "dwarf," find out which rootstock the trees grows on. If the nursery can't tell you, go to a nursery that can identify the rootstock so you can be sure how tall your plant will grow.

An interstem tree is a dwarf tree consisting of three grafted parts: the fruit-bearing cultivar; the interstem piece; and the rootstock, or understock. This practice combines the vigorous growth and good anchorage of a semidwarf rootstock with the superdwarfing effect of the interstem piece (both the interstem piece and the rootstock have a dwarfing effect). These grafted trees don't require much staking and don't have the other problems associated with dwarfing rootstocks. They may be better suited to certain sites.

An interstem tree is identified by its name, which includes two sets of letters and numbers, such as M.9/MM.111. Look on a young, bare-root tree to see the graft unions of the 6- to 8-inch-long interstem piece.

Dwarf apple trees have been around for a long time. Dwarf and semidwarf pear, peach, apricot, plum, and cherry trees are more recent introductions and may be available from some suppliers.

CHOOSING NURSERY STOCK: BIGGER ISN'T BETTER

When it comes to buying nursery stock, less is more. Keep in mind that medium-size, bare-root, one-year-old trees (called "whips") or two-year-old trees are actually preferable to larger, older trees. Small trees are much easier to transplant, train, and prune. Make every effort to get trees in the ground very early in spring, before they start growth. If you get caught short, you can always heel them in—that is, set them close together in a temporary trench in a cool, shady location and cover the roots with moist soil until you can plant.

Dwarf fruit trees, such as this apple tree, fit better into home gardens and are more productive and easier to care for than tall, standard trees.

TRAITS OF DWARF APPLE ROOTSTOCKS

Rootstock	Height	Characteristics
M.9	8 feet tall	Needs moist, well-drained soil; staking necessary; susceptible to fireblight.
M.26	11–14 feet tall	Cannot tolerate extra-dry conditions; needs well-drained soil; must be staked.
M.9/MM.106	14–16 feet tall	Strong-growing, well-anchored tree; subject to collar rot.
M.9/MM.111	14–16 feet tall	Requires staking when planted; vigorous; tolerant of a wide range of soil types.
M.7	15–18 feet tall	Needs deep soil to anchor roots; susceptible to root rot and crown gall.
MM.106	18–20 feet tall (almost standard size)	Needs well-drained soil; often grows late into fall, making tree susceptible to winter injury; subject to collar rot.
MM.111	19–24 feet tall (almost standard size)	Fairly tolerant of a wide range of soil types; less subject to collar rot than MM.106.

SUCCESSFUL FRUIT GROWING

Although berries, tree fruits, and nuts add to your eating pleasure, berries (small fruits) are generally the easiest to raise. Berry plants bear fruit quickly—you'll be picking plump strawberries the year after you've planted them. An apple tree, however, may not bear for three or four years after planting. Berry plants cost less, take up little space, and don't have as many pests. Most beginning gardeners like to start off small and easy by planting a berry patch and only two or three fruit trees.

REQUIREMENTS FOR EXCELLENT FRUIT SET

Several interacting factors influence fruit set and therefore the size of your harvest. When all these factors work together, your harvest will be bountiful.
- Good bloom
- Warm, sunny weather during flowering
- Freedom from extreme winter cold and late-spring frost, which can damage flower buds
- Healthy, disease-free plants
- Good plant nutrition
- Successful pollination

THE RIGHT SITE

Choosing a suitable site for tree fruits, nuts, and berries is the first step toward reaping a bountiful harvest. Most of these plants need a sunny location protected from wind, although gooseberries and currants do well in part shade. All grow best in well-drained soil. Even if your soil is not well-drained, you can still grow berries and dwarf fruit trees—plant them in raised beds. Otherwise these plants are forgiving and tolerate a broad range of soil types. Before planting, it's always best to have your soil tested to determine its pH and nutrient status.

All nuts and fruits, except blueberries, prefer a pH between 6.0 and 6.5; blueberries do best in acid soil with a pH of about 4.5. To lower the pH, mix sulfur into the soil before planting. Incorporate lime if you need to raise the pH for other crops. It takes about a year for the pH to change significantly, so do this well in advance of planting.

Low organic matter content, low fertility, and weeds are the nemesis of fruits and nuts. Because each of these can greatly hamper productivity, take steps to correct these problems before planting. Remember, these plants will be in the ground for many years to come, so start them off right.

STEPS TO A BOUNTIFUL HARVEST

To ensure a big harvest, start out with plants adapted to your climate, then take the necessary steps to help them get pollinated.

The intensity of the winter cold determines in part which crops will adapt to your garden. A plant's cold-hardiness reflects the lowest temperatures it can tolerate without dying from the cold in winter. Cold-hardiness is a big issue in the North, where cultivars that can withstand brutal winters must be chosen. In the South, where cultivars that need only a short winter do best, the chilling requirement is more of a concern. The chilling requirement is the number of hours of cool temperatures (about 32 to 45 degrees Fahrenheit) a plant needs during winter before it breaks out of dormancy and starts growing. Some plants need a longer winter than others to cause the hormonal changes that tell the plant

HOW EASY IS IT TO GROW?

Here's a general guide to help you decide which fruits and nuts to grow based on their simplicity or difficulty:

Easy care
- Blueberry
- Chestnut
- Currant
- Elderberry
- Gooseberry
- Hickory
- Pawpaw
- Persimmon
- Raspberry, fall-bearing
- Walnut

Moderate care
- Blackberry
- Fig
- Hazelnut
- Kiwifruit
- Pear
- Pecan
- Plum
- Quince
- Raspberry, summer-bearing
- Strawberry, June-bearing and everbearing

High care
- Almond
- Strawberry, day-neutral

that spring has arrived and it's safe to start growing.

Tried-and-true cultivars for particular regions are based on meeting the balance between these two factors. This balance is especially critical for tree fruits. A mismatch might be fatal. For example, northern gardeners might want to grow the 'Junegold' peach, but cannot because of its low chilling requirement; it breaks out of dormancy too soon and is subject to injury from spring frosts in northern gardens. In cold regions, choose high-chill cultivars, which remain dormant until frost is no longer a danger. On the other hand, it would be a mistake to grow an extra-cold-hardy plant with a high chilling requirement, such as a 'Cortland' apple, in Southern California; the tree would remain dormant until late spring, then produce weak shoots and might not even bloom at all. In this instance, it is best to plant a low-chill cultivar.

Bear in mind that matters are slightly complicated by local growing conditions. Temperatures in any given region can vary depending on elevation. Cold air settles into low areas, creating frost pockets. Even during an extended hard freeze, temperatures at the middle or top of a slope can be several degrees warmer than those at the bottom, making the higher spot a better choice for growing fruits and nuts.

POINTERS ON POLLINATION

In order for fruits, nuts, and berries to bear well, conditions must be right for pollination and fruit set to take place.

Pollination—the transfer of pollen from the male flower parts (anthers) to the female flower part (stigma)—occurs after the flowers have opened.

Most fruit trees need to be pollinated by another compatible tree to bear fruit. However, this 'Montmorency' sour cherry is self-fruitful and pollinates its own flowers for a rich summer harvest. The tree is beautiful enough to use as an ornamental in the front yard.

In some plants, such as walnuts, chestnuts, hazelnuts, pecans, peaches, and grapes, pollen is shed and falls by gravity or is carried by the wind. In strawberries, blueberries, apples, plums, and sweet cherries, insects transfer the pollen from one flower to another. Once pollen reaches the stigma, it fertilizes the egg in the pistil and fruit begins to grow—fruit set has occurred. Always locate fruiting plants of the same variety within 100 feet of one another for good pollination.

Strawberries, peaches, grapes, and raspberries are self-fruitful. This means they can set fruit with their own pollen or pollen from the same plant. You'll get fruit even if you grow a single variety of any of these fruits, making them appealing to gardeners with small yards. Apples, sweet cherries, pears, plums, elderberries, and most nut trees are self-unfruitful. They need to be cross-pollinated—one plant needs pollen from another plant, usually a different cultivar—to set fruit. Without at least two compatible cultivars, the trees will bloom year after year but won't fruit.

Of course, there are always exceptions to the rule. Blueberries produce well with only one cultivar, but yield bigger berries if cross-pollinated. The cherry 'Stella' and the plum 'Stanley' are self-fruitful. 'Gravenstein' and 'Rhode Island Greening' apples have ineffectual pollen; their pollen can't pollinate any cultivar. If you grow one of these apples, you'll need to plant three different cultivars so that all three trees will bear fruit.

After pollination occurs, fertilization stimulates a flower to turn into a fruit, which in turn forms seeds. Seed formation is important for the growth and development of most fruits and nuts. Apples with only a few seeds fall off the tree early or remain small and misshapen.

CARING FOR NEW FRUIT AND NUT TREES

Spring planting is best for fruit and nut trees, although many southern gardeners plant successfully in the fall. Planting in the spring gives the trees a jump on the season, allowing them to send out roots and become established before the stressful heat of summer.

PLANTING AND FERTILIZING

Plant fruit and nut trees as you would any other tree (see pages 128–131). Some nut trees, such as hickory, are infamous for their long taproots, so dig a large hole. Remove broken or injured roots and avoid exposing the roots to sun or wind during the planting process.

Unlike most ornamental trees, fruit and nut trees may have been grafted to a rootstock. Plant the tree so the graft union is about 2 inches above ground level. If the graft union is below the soil level, roots may develop on the base of the scion, or cultivar, and you'll lose the dwarfing effect. Plant an interstem tree so that only 2 to 3 inches of the interstem is above the soil line.

If you've prepared the soil well, you won't need to fertilize the trees during the first year. In subsequent years, your trees will benefit from fertilization. Always apply fertilizer in early spring, before growth starts. The amount of fertilizer required depends upon the species, age, and size of the plant, the soil pH, and the amount of organic matter in the soil. Spread the fertilizer around the entire root area and under the tree branches, but not adjacent to the trunk. Many home gardeners use a balanced fertilizer such as 10-10-10. This material is practical and easy to find, but it isn't always what your trees need. You can create nutrient imbalances this way—too much of one, not enough of another. It is well worth the cost of having a laboratory perform a leaf nutrient test to accurately determine which nutrients your trees need. With the test results in hand, you can feed each tree exactly what it requires.

GET RID OF GRASS

Keep the ground under the drip line of your fruit and nut trees (and berry bushes) free of grass and weeds. Grass is a strong competitor with the trees for soil nutrients and water. Apply an organic mulch to prevent weeds from growing and to conserve moisture. Grass clippings are one of the best mulches for fruit trees. Unlike heavy mulches, which can hold too much moisture and create a hiding place for bark-gnawing rodents, grass clippings are lightweight and decompose quickly. If you use a different mulch, pull it away from the tree trunks in fall to discourage mice and voles.

DON'T FORGET TO WATER

Trees seem so big and durable, it is easy to forget that they need water. Even more than ornamental trees, fruit trees need a steady supply of water, which can come either from rainfall or irrigation. In general, they use about ⅓ inch of water every day during summer. Although trees constantly use water, it's much better to give them a thorough, slow soaking once every week to 10 days than to sprinkle them lightly every day or so. Deep watering promotes a healthy, deep root system. During a dry spell, try to imitate a gentle, soaking rain by applying about an inch of water over several hours.

A DWARF APPLE HEDGE

Dwarf apple trees easily can be trained as a space-saving hedge. Grow them against a wire trellis made from sturdy posts set 8 feet apart and strung with two horizontal wires. String the first wire 2 feet above the ground and the other 4 to 5 feet up, depending upon the ultimate height of the tree. Larger dwarfs may need a third wire at 6 to 7 feet. Space young, well-branched trees 3 feet apart; start planting adjacent to an end post.

Prune trees so the scaffold branches form a horizontal plane of well-spaced branches at 45-degree angles from the trunk. Tie the scaffolds to the wires, but allow the side branches to grow away from the trellis and form a bushy hedge. Each year during dormancy, cut back the scaffold to four buds. Remove suckers and excessive growth as needed during summer, topping the hedge near the highest wire.

Espalier, an ancient way of training fruit trees, turns them into beautiful landscape features. Many elaborate patterns may be used. All are symmetrical designs with the branches trained in a single horizontal plane against a wall or support. The main idea is to head back the trunk and prune the side branches to create new branches where you need them to fill out the pattern. Tie the young, supple new branches—called cordons—to wire that is set into the wall.

PRUNING FRUIT AND NUT TREES

Knowledgeable pruning is the key to keeping fruit and nut trees bearing year after year. A properly trained and pruned tree is easy to care for. It is important to begin training and pruning the trees the day they go into the ground.

Take care when pruning not to remove the short spurs where fruit will grow.

Fruit trees require annual pruning throughout their lives for the best fruit production. In the years before your trees begin to bear fruit, focus on developing good tree structure. Your goal is to have limbs well-spaced along and around the trunk with wide angles where they attach to the trunk. Remove any competing leaders (forks in the main trunk where two stems of equal length and diameter arise at a common point). In time you'll notice spurs—short branches bearing fat clusters of flower buds—developing on fruit trees. Do not remove these or you'll eliminate future fruit.

Most nut trees are easy; prune them lightly for the first few years, then let them take off on their own.

Unless you're working with stone fruits, or unless otherwise indicated in the encyclopedia starting on page 428, always prune during the dormant season—that is, any time after leaves have fallen in autumn and before growth begins in spring. Pruning cuts on young trees stimulate vegetative growth and delay fruiting. That's why you should make only the cuts that are absolutely necessary for proper structure in a tree's early years.

PRUNING BASICS

How you prune a tree depends on what type of tree it is. Most fruit and nut trees, including apples and pears, do well when pruned to a single stem, or central leader. Stone fruits (cherry, apricot, peach, nectarine, and plum), hazelnuts, and almonds thrive when pruned as open-center trees. Many trees do well when pruned into a modified leader, a combination of the two methods.

TRAINING TO A CENTRAL LEADER

A single-stem or central-leader tree takes advantage of the natural growth habit of many fruit and nut trees; of the types described above, it's the easiest to work with.

After planting a new, dormant, one-year-old tree, cut back the unbranched tree to a height of about 30 inches. This pruning is critical, because it forces a flush of new growth that will be the tree's future scaffold limbs. If you cut back too far—say to a height of 24 inches—the resulting growth is too upright; if you don't cut back enough, the new growth is insufficient for a good scaffold structure. After the new shoots start to grow, remove the second and third side shoots nearest the top to encourage a strong central leader, or main trunk. The top shoot grows upright to form the new leader.

If you plant a dormant, two-year-old tree, remove all but a leader branch at the top and three or four well-spaced lateral branches below it. These branches become the tree's permanent framework, so be sure they are well-spaced around the trunk. After growth begins in spring, pinch out the second and third new shoots from the tip of the leader.

Training during the second year depends on the cultivar. Each cultivar has a slightly different growth habit, which becomes apparent with observation. For example, 'Granny Smith' apple trees are notoriously difficult to work with, but 'Golden Delicious' behave beautifully. The limbs on 'Golden Delicious' tend to grow in a naturally spreading manner; about all you need do is remove the crowding shoots and any fruit that sets on the leader of young trees.

The limbs on especially vigorous cultivars such as 'Granny Smith' grow too upright. You'll need to remove some of the lateral branches and spread the remaining ones to create a 45-degree angle with the trunk, either by using commercial wooden or plastic branch spreaders or by hanging a plastic sandwich bag filled with sand on each branch. Try to select scaffold limbs that are positioned around the trunk and are separated by at least 8 inches along the trunk's height.

PRUNING OLDER CENTRAL-LEADER TREES

A mature, central-leader tree has a cone shape, which most efficiently intercepts light. The cone shape—and its characteristic central leader—is a bit difficult to preserve as the tree ages. The top of the tree, which has the most vigorous growth, tends to spread and shade the lower limbs. To counteract this effect, avoid making small cuts, which have an invigorating effect. Each year,

during dormancy, make the following corrective pruning cuts; be sure to make all these cuts flush with the trunk:

■ Make one or two large, well-placed cuts; either remove an entire branch or cut back at least half of the limb to a vigorous, fruitful, lateral branch.

■ Remove all upright, vigorous water sprouts.

■ Remove limbs from the lower part of the tree that are shaded by other branches.

■ Take out older, less fruitful limbs. Young, fruitful limbs are in an upright to horizontal position. As they become older and less fruitful, they rotate to a drooping position.

■ Remove all broken and crossed limbs.

Use branch spreaders to train branches to a wider angle, if necessary.

METHODS OF PRUNING FRUIT AND NUT TREES

Central-leader method
Apple and pear trees respond well to training to a single leader, which follows their natural shape. This method also can be used for cherry and plum trees.

Open-center method
Apricot, peach, and nectarine trees produce best and are easiest to pick when trained into this vaselike shape. This method also can be used with almond, hazelnut, cherry, and plum trees.

Modified-leader method
A cross between the other two methods, this is often used for nut trees and also can be used for apple and pear trees.

Thin the dense inside shoots of open-center trees so sunlight can reach the ripening fruit.

PRUNING FRUIT AND NUT TREES
continued

TRAINING OPEN-CENTER TREES

An open-center tree, such as a stone-fruit tree, is vase-shaped, has no central leader, and has only three to five main scaffold limbs. Open-center pruning allows you to thin growth easily, which is necessary to ensure continuous cropping. It also allows a lot of light to reach the tree's interior.

At planting, prune back one-year-old trees to a height of 24 to 36 inches. Then cut back the length of all the laterals, leaving branch stubs a few inches long. After growth begins, strong shoots emerge from the bases of the remaining stubs. As soon as these shoots have grown a few inches, usually by early summer, select three to five of the strongest, best-positioned ones to become the primary scaffold branches. Choose shoots that are equally spaced around the trunk, with 4 to 6 inches between them along the length of the trunk. Equal growth and branching of these shoots results in the open-center tree structure. Remove all other shoots and shorten the stubs.

The following year, head back these main scaffold branches to outward-growing laterals to reinforce the open-center structure and create some secondary scaffolds. The resulting tree is low, strong, and spreading, which facilitates thinning, pest control, and harvesting. Leave some small shoots in the center; they will bear the first fruit.

PRUNING OLDER OPEN-CENTER TREES

During a tree's bearing years, you'll need to thin growth to ensure good cropping. Continue to prune to outward-growing laterals. Keep the center of the tree open by thinning dense interior shoots. After heading back all the main branches each year, thin and space the one-year-old shoots so they are about 6 to 8 inches apart. This spacing allows sunlight into the tree to ripen the coming year's crop.

Peach and nectarine trees require severe pruning; as the trees get to be full-size, heavy pruning maintains and renews the fruiting wood throughout the tree. For good fruiting, the tree must make 12 to 18 inches of new shoot growth each year. If the shoots are weak or the lower limbs become too long, cut back the branches to two- or three-year-old wood. Make these cuts to an outward-growing lateral branch.

Cherry and plum trees need fewer cuts. In most years, all that is necessary is to lightly head back to a strong lateral branch to keep the tree

Thinning fruit allows the remaining crop to grow larger and better.

in bounds. Then thin out branches to provide ample sunlight for the remaining limbs; remove any dead, broken, or diseased wood growth.

THINNING TREE FRUITS

After your efforts have finally produced small fruit that hold the promise of a bountiful harvest, it's time to pick some of the fruit off the trees and discard it. Although it might seem counterproductive, this thinning results in larger, better-colored, higher quality fruit. It also promotes return bloom the following year. Besides, trees usually self-thin if you don't help them; gardeners familiar with this process in apples often refer to it as "June drop." Thinning may take a little hand labor, but don't you want to be the one who decides which fruit comes off the tree? It doesn't take much time, and it encourages repeat bloom on the trees.

Young trees seldom set so much fruit that thinning is necessary, but it's different with older trees. Thin fruit within 30 days after the petals fall. Wherever fruit is clustered, remove all but one in each cluster. Get rid of small and insect- or disease-injured fruit first. As a general rule, space peaches 4 to 8 inches apart; early cultivars require wider spacing. Thin apples and European-type plums so the fruit is 4 to 6 inches apart. The other tree fruits rarely set so much fruit that thinning is warranted, unless you want extra-large fruit and are willing to take the time.

OPEN-CENTER PRUNING METHOD

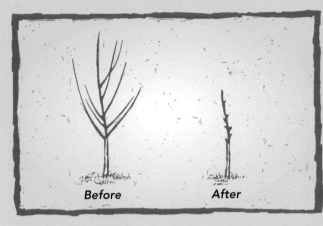

Before *After*

Right after planting, head the young tree to proper height. Cut back shoots.

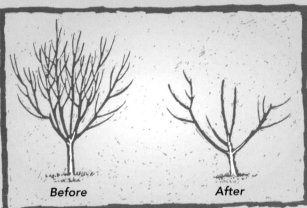

Before *After*

In the tree's second year, select the scaffold branches and prune to outward-growing laterals.

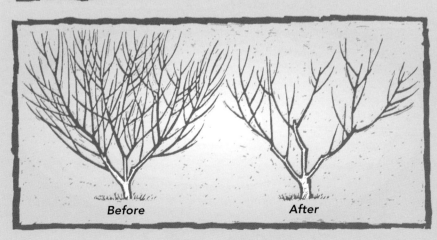

Before *After*

In the tree's third year, continue to thin. Head branches to outward-growing laterals.

GROWING SMALL FRUITS

Not all fruits grow on trees. Small fruits, especially berries, take up relatively little space and are just as sweet as large fruits.

Strawberries, grapes, raspberries, blackberries, currants, blueberries, and others are easy to grow and yet are among the most prized of garden produce. They're also excellent candidates for pies, jams, and other treats that bring the fresh taste of summer to our tables even on the coldest winter day.

A STRAWBERRY PRIMER

Strawberries are a gardener's joy. The small perennial plants sport pretty, white blossoms followed by luscious, red fruit. Most types have a runnering habit—that is, they propagate themselves by sending out runners at their tips that form daughter plants. Each daughter sends down roots and begins a whole new plant, which in turn sends out its own runners. Within a few years, without proper management, your neat rows of strawberry plants can turn into a dense, messy patch.

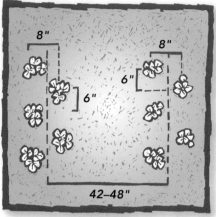

As a variation from straight rows, plant June-bearing strawberries in staggered rows.

Strawberry plants are usually day-length sensitive, forming blossoms during the short days in spring and fruit during the long days of summer. June-bearing types bear fruit in June in the North and in April or May in the South. Everbearing strawberries are also day-length sensitive; they produce berries over a longer period than the far more productive day-neutral strawberries. Day-neutral berries are not sensitive to day length at all. They flower and bear fruit as long as the temperature is between 35 and 85 degrees Fahrenheit. However, they aren't long-lived, because they exhaust themselves with so much fruiting.

Strawberry care depends on the type of berries you have and how much time you want to devote to them. You can space plants widely and allow them to runner freely to form a wide patch, or you can set them more closely in rows and regularly remove some or all of the runners that stray into the paths. Wide-spaced plantings are easier to care for, but the yield is higher with tighter spacing.

STRAWBERRY-GROWING METHODS

Planting Method	Spacing	Comments
June-bearing matted row system	15–18 inches within row; 48 inches between rows	Remove flowers the first year. Allow to runner freely. Easy to maintain, but produces lots of plants with small berries and low yields.
June-bearing spaced system	6 inches within row; 48 inches between rows	Remove flowers the first year. Leave 6-8 runners per plant, clipping all others. Labor-intensive, but large plant and fruit size, and easy harvest.
June-bearing ribbon system	4 inches within row; 36 inches between rows	Remove flowers the first year and clip all runners. Extra-productive with large berries, but labor-intensive and initially expensive because you need more plants.
Fall planting method for warm climates	9–12 inches between plants set in double or triple rows	Remove all runners for entire season.
Day-neutral strawberries	5–9 inches between plants; 42 inches between rows; plant in staggered double row	Remove flowers for 6 weeks after planting. Remove runners the first year. Treat as an annual or till under after second year. Labor-intensive, but bears fruit from early summer to fall frost.

As a general rule, in cold climates plant cold-stored, bare-root strawberry plants in early spring. In warm climates, fall planting is preferable. Wide spacing works best where summers are hot and winters are cold. Replant strawberries each year in warm climates or if you are growing day-neutrals. See the encyclopedia entries on pages 441–443 for specific information on particular types of strawberries.

TRAINING GRAPES

Homegrown grapes require a lot of care. Begin by planting the best kind for your climate (see encyclopedia section starting on page 428). Grapes need annual pruning to produce a full crop of fruit because they bear on one-year-old wood. If you avoid pruning, which stimulates new growth, yields suffer. Grapes can be pruned many ways. The following methods are popular and easy:

■ FOUR-ARM KNIFFEN METHOD: Perhaps the best way to prune grapes, this method uses a trellis made by stringing two lines of galvanized wire between heavy wooden posts. Set 8-foot posts 2 feet deep and about 18 feet apart. Use pressure-treated posts or locust posts made especially for this purpose. Make the top wire of the trellis about 6 feet above the ground and the lower wire about 3 feet above the ground. Train the grapes along the wires (see illustration below).

Sturdy arbors offer a delightful and decorative way to grow grapes.

FOUR-ARM KNIFFEN METHOD

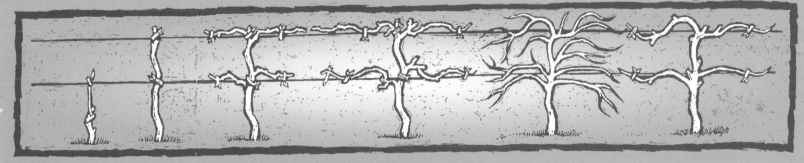

1. If the grape cane doesn't grow to reach the top wire during the first year, allow it to grow as a single cane the following year until it reaches the top wire.

2. Prune off side branches to encourage a strong single cane once the cane reaches the top wire.

3. In early spring of second year (or first year if the cane reaches the top wire), while the cane is still dormant, tie it to the top wire and cut it off just above the wire. Remove all but four to six buds on the cane near each wire.

4. As new shoots begin to grow from the remaining buds, remove any flower clusters that form.

5. In early spring of third year, before growth starts, select a total of four canes (side branches), two for each wire, and remove the rest. Tie one cane along each wire in each direction to create four arms.

6. Every year thereafter, cut the remaining four canes back to the stubs containing two buds each. Allow the four arms to flower and bear fruit up to the sixth bud along each arm.

GROWING SMALL FRUITS

continued

Blueberries produce best if the oldest canes are removed at ground level every year.

■ **PRUNING MATURE GRAPEVINES:** In early spring, remove all fruiting canes from the previous year. Tie one of the two canes from the stub to the trellis wire and cut it off after the tenth bud. Cut back the remaining cane to two buds to create next year's stub and arm. Most inexperienced grape growers leave too many buds, which results in poor fruit quality. A shortage of buds reduces the crop.

■ **TRAINING GRAPEVINES TO AN ARBOR:** Grapevines grown on an arbor or a pergola are attractive and provide shade as well as fruit. The principles that apply to the Kniffen method apply here: Renew fruiting wood annually, but with a modified method. The main differences between training on a trellis and training on an arbor or a pergola are in the number of buds, old wood, and fruiting canes retained.

Plant the grapevine beside one of the structure's sturdy posts and allow the vine to grow up beside it. (Be sure the structure is sturdy; old, gnarled grapevines are heavy.) Let the trunk grow tall enough to reach the top of the structure. Allow more fruiting canes and spurs to develop so they can spread across the top and supply shade. Train short, permanent arms from the trunk so the foliage will cover the arbor.

You won't need to take off as much wood each year, but annual pruning is necessary.

A WORD ABOUT SEEDLESS GRAPES

Nearly everyone enjoys the juicy sweetness of seedless grapes. Growing top-quality specimens of this fruit is time-consuming. Commercial growers coddle the plants from the start, spraying them with plant hormones to enlarge and elongate the berries and girdling the trunk to improve berry set and size. Growers also increase fruit size by thinning clusters and berries.

You can grow seedless table grapes without all this fuss by following the training method used for kiwifruit (see page 435). Unfortunately, this system also makes for easy harvesting by raccoons and birds.

TRELLISING SUMMER-BEARING RASPBERRIES AND BLACKBERRIES

Brambles, including blackberries, as well as red, purple, and black raspberries, perform best if trellised. Most brambles have a perennial root system and biennial canes, meaning the canes live for only two growing seasons. The first-year canes are called primocanes; second-year canes are called floricanes. The plants produce fruit from buds on their usually thorny floricanes. While the floricanes are flowering and fruiting, the primocanes are growing larger and can interfere with harvesting. They also shade the fruiting canes, reducing fruit quality. Trellising alleviates this predicament.

If you have only a few plants, plant them about 30 inches apart in a row and tie the floricanes to a single stake in the middle of each plant. Allow the primocanes to grow freely on the outside. Alternatively, you can tie the floricanes to a simple trellis consisting of a single wire 3 to 4 feet above the ground. These methods are inexpensive and easy, but you'll have to reach through all those thorny, new canes to harvest the fruit.

If you have a lot of plants, consider building a V-style trellis. Angle the posts so they are 3 feet apart at the top and 1½ feet apart at the bottom. Let the primocanes grow in the middle of the V; pull the floricanes up against the wires and tie them to the inside of both the top and bottom wires, where they'll be accessible. This will increase the yield and produce more attractive fruit. Berries that grow off the ground and have more air circulation tend to be cleaner and more disease-resistant.

PRUNING BERRY BUSHES

Although their fruits look and taste quite different, blueberry, gooseberry, currant, and elderberry plants are somewhat alike in their growth habits. Prune them in early spring, removing any branches that are broken, lying on the ground, or winter-injured. Thin them with proper pruning, but don't shear them, as shearing greatly reduces yields.

■ **PRUNING BLUEBERRIES:** The most productive blueberry canes are ½ to 1 inch in diameter at their bases. The ideal plant has about 16 canes—one or two for each year up to eight years of growth. Select two new canes each year, removing all other new growth from the time the bushes are planted until they are about eight years old and the oldest canes are about 1 inch thick. Early in the ninth year, remove the two largest canes and all but the two largest one-year-old canes. Repeat annually.

■ **PRUNING GOOSEBERRIES AND CURRANTS:** Gooseberries and currants begin to produce fruit on spurs at the

This tidy berry patch contains currants, blackberries, and raspberries, all trained to trellises to keep them neat and easy to care for.

base of one-year-old wood, but most spurs occur on two- and three-year-old wood. After the first year of growth, remove all but six to eight of the most vigorous new canes. At the end of the second growing season, leave several one-year-old canes and several two-year-old canes. By the fourth year, remove the oldest set of canes and allow the new ones to grow. A strong, healthy plant will have about eight bearing canes, with younger canes eventually replacing older ones.

■ **PRUNING ELDERBERRIES:** Elderberries send up many new canes each year. They usually reach full height in one season and develop lateral branches in the second year. To plan your pruning, remember that two-year-old canes are the most fruitful; three- and four-year-old canes are less productive. Remove all canes older than three years at ground level; leave an equal number of one-, two-, and three-year-old canes. Prune them in late winter while the plant is still dormant.

PRUNING BRAMBLES

Pruning and training brambles—raspberries, blackberries, and their relatives—vary with the type of bramble. After fruiting, the floricanes

begin to die and should be removed at ground level.

■ **PRUNING RASPBERRIES:** For red and purple raspberries, prune out winter damage in early spring, topping the canes as high as the trellis permits, but not cutting below the point of winter injury (severe cutting will decrease yield). Tie the canes loosely to the stake or top wire and remove all but three or four canes per linear foot of row. Remove all the previous year's expended floricanes.

Thin black raspberries in early spring, pruning one-year canes to two to three per foot of row and shortening laterals to remove winter-damaged wood. In summer, remove at least 4 inches from the tops of the primocanes when they reach about 2 feet tall. By season's end, primocanes will have long, lateral branches. Support them with trellis wires during winter to keep them from breaking.

■ **PRUNING ERECT BLACKBERRIES:** Remove the tips of the primocanes of erect blackberries in summer when they reach 3 to 4 feet tall. This stiffens their canes and promotes lateral branching. In early spring of the following year, thin canes to two per linear foot of row and shorten the laterals to between 12 and 16 inches.

■ **PRUNING TRAILING BLACKBERRIES:** In early spring, weave the floricanes around the trellis wire without cutting them back (or cut them back to the height of the trellis wire and tie them). Cut back the lateral branches on the floricanes to about 18 inches. Thin the new primocanes to six to eight per hill in northern regions, fewer in the South, and let these grow along the ground all season.

■ **PRUNING FALL-BEARING RASPBERRIES:** This type of raspberry produces fruit at the top of the first-year canes in late summer or fall and on the lower portion of these same canes in early summer of their second year. Either sacrifice the early summer crop in favor of a huge fall crop or enjoy two smaller crops each year.

For a large, fall-only crop, cut all the old canes to the ground in early spring each year before new canes emerge from the ground. Cut the old canes as close to the ground as possible so buds will break from below the soil surface. For two crops a year, prune in early spring, clipping off the tops of the year-old canes—the portion that fruited the previous fall. You'll harvest a second crop on these canes in early summer and a crop on the new primocanes in fall.

WARDING OFF PESTS

To protect a fruit tree from rodents, wrap the trunk with a cylinder of hardware cloth that extends down into the soil and up to the first scaffold.

Even though you've fed, pruned, weeded, and watered your fruit trees, a successful harvest still depends on how well you control diseases, insects, and animal pests. Most nut trees need pesticide treatments only during severe infestations. Infestations are more common in fruit trees, however, and can be serious enough to compromise your harvests.

If you are an ecologically minded gardener, try thinking differently about your harvest. Fruit doesn't need to be absolutely perfect to be tasty and enjoyable, and your tolerance for imperfection will be better for you and the environment. You'll also save money by not buying pesticides.

However, there may be times when you may want to use an insecticide or a fungicide. Even disease-resistant cultivars are troubled by insects, and some insects severely reduce the quality of the fruit harvest.

TIMING IS EVERYTHING

The most important thing to keep in mind when combating pests is timing—each pest has a unique life cycle. You'll need to target each one during its most vulnerable state. Different regions of the country vary greatly, both in terms of pest problems and the best times to control them.

A good way to find out which pests are problematic in your region is to contact your county Cooperative Extension Service or land-grant university. They can provide information about the common pests in your area and ways to treat them.

SPRAYING FRUIT TREES

If you choose to spray fruit trees, time the applications according to the developmental state of the flower or fruit. To control apple diseases and insects, spray three times: during dormancy, when the flower buds are filling out and showing color, and again when the petals fall. Never apply insecticide during full bloom when bees are pollinating the flowers, because it can kill the bees, resulting in poor pollination and little or no fruit set. Depending on the particular disease or insect, sprays may continue into summer.

Use a hand-operated pump-type sprayer to reach all tree branches. Always apply pesticides according to the label directions. Even plant-based

TIPS FOR REDUCING PESTS AND DISEASES

■ **INCREASE AIR CIRCULATION.** Close, crowded limbs and canes encourage many fungal diseases. Train trees and bush fruits properly. Grow brambles on trellises to increase air circulation among plants.

■ **CLEAN UP DEBRIS.** Keep your yard neat and clean. Many insects and diseases overwinter on weeds and around garden debris, such as brush and old boards.

■ **REMOVE DISEASED FRUIT.** When diseased fruit and leaves remain in the yard all winter, they can carry disease from one year to the next. Rake up and destroy fallen fruit. Remove dead twigs and branches during the dormant season.

■ **HARVEST FRUIT AS SOON AS IT IS RIPE.** Overripe fruit spoils and attracts insects.

■ **CONDUCT QUICK, FREQUENT CHECKS.** By looking for pests every day, you'll develop a sharp eye for potential problems. You'll also be able to treat small flare-ups before they get out of hand.

■ **PLANT RESISTANT CULTIVARS.** Avoid planting fruits that require pesticide sprays. If possible, plant cultivars that are resistant to any diseases in your area. For instance, 'Freedom' and 'Liberty' apples resist apple scab, the most serious disease of apples. They are preferable to 'McIntosh'.

which is notoriously susceptible. If you're planting nut trees, look for cultivars bred with hard shells to discourage pests.

■ **LEARN ABOUT LOCAL PROBLEMS.** Find out which insects and diseases are potential troublemakers in your area. Learn more about their life cycles from your local nursery or county Cooperative Extension Service.

■ **CHOOSE REGIONALLY ADAPTED CULTIVARS.** Some diseases prey on plants that have been weakened by cold weather or are otherwise poorly suited to their climate. To prevent this problem, select regionally adapted cultivars.

insecticides that are labeled organic can be toxic to people, pets, and wildlife. (See pages 546–551 for more information about safe pesticide use.)

PESTICIDE ALTERNATIVES

There are many things you can do to avoid using pesticides. All it takes is a little planning and careful attention to your plants.

For example, you can prevent disease by always preparing a new planting site a year in advance. Add all organic matter, nutrients, and any other amendments so the plants will be well nourished from the soil that will be their permanent home. Prune and train the plants to promote air circulation, thus avoiding fungal diseases. Most importantly, be sure to water deeply during dry weather.

To discourage insect infestations, try some physical control methods, including the following:
■ Place a paper bag over apples and pears in early summer while the fruit is still small. This acts as a barrier to insects such as codling moth and plum curculio. Remove the bag one to two weeks before you expect the fruit to ripen.
■ Float a row cover over strawberry plants to prevent strawberry bud weevil injury. Remove the cover when plants flower to allow bees to pollinate.
■ Lay a thick layer of mulch around strawberry plants to keep the fruit off the soil, thus avoiding leather rot.

BIOLOGICAL CONTROLS

Biological control involves introducing natural enemies of fruit pests into your garden or encouraging beneficial insects in the garden. Ladybugs, parasitic wasps, and praying mantises are all good guys in the garden, devouring harmful scales, aphids, and mites.

It's important to be alert to a pest's presence early on; then you can take measures only when necessary. Insect traps and sticky balls, for example, monitor populations of such pests as codling moths and Japanese beetles.

CONTROLLING LARGER PESTS

Rodents such as rabbits, moles, and mice are tricksters, hiding beneath the snow or mulch, nibbling away at tree bark, getting to the tasty inner cambium layer before you know it. Come spring, you'll find your fruiting plants stripped of their bark, and it is too late to save them.

To prevent rodent injury, loosely wrap the trunk base with a cylinder of ¼-inch hardware cloth or similar material. Encircle the trunk with the cylinder extending several inches below the soil and reaching the first scaffold branch. As an extra measure, add a 2- to 3-inch-deep, 6- to 12-inch-wide layer of fine stones or cinders around the trunk.

Other enemies of fruiting plants include deer, who love to nibble at buds and branches. Even mild deer browsing can be damaging, because it disrupts pruning and training efforts. (See pages 556–559 for information on deer control.)

Birds also are pests. They can gobble small berries and gouge larger fruits. Unfortunately, they quickly get used to scare devices, such as rubber snakes and scarecrows.

There are several options that will keep birds at bay. The first—covering trees with nylon netting when fruit begins to change color—is somewhat expensive, but it works. Make sure the netting has no holes; birds will find them. Secure the netting firmly

Cover grapevines (or other fruiting plants) with nylon netting when the fruit begins to ripen to keep birds from devouring the crop. Fasten the netting securely.

on a frame over the plants. This prevents it from tangling with branches, which enables birds to peck at nearby fruit.

You also can distract birds from your precious fruit with a mulberry tree. The mulberries ripen in midsummer at the same time as many other fruits. By enticing the birds, the mulberry tree acts as an effective decoy, allowing your other fruits and berries to mature in peace.

If you are a clever carpenter, you can build a walk-in cage made of hardware cloth or chicken wire to house several berry plants. This structure can be left in place permanently to keep out marauding birds, rabbits, and deer.

Nut trees, too, are susceptible to pests—especially squirrels, who begin their harvest before the nuts even fall from the trees. To discourage squirrels, prune the lower branches of nut trees, then purchase special collars to prevent the rodents from climbing. Also, position trees far enough apart to keep squirrels from jumping from tree to tree. Finally keep your eye on the maturing nuts so you can get to them first.

HARVESTING FRUITS AND NUTS

Harvest peaches when the fruit is fully colored and easily comes off the tree. Ripe flesh "gives" slightly when pressed.

The care you've put into growing fruits and nuts will be rewarded as you head out to the orchard with a basket or pail for harvesting. For details on testing the ripeness of different fruits, see the encyclopedia section starting on page 428. As a general rule, though, the best test is simply to try a fruit fresh from the vine or tree.

DETERMINING FRUIT RIPENESS

To prevent fruit from over-ripening, check it often as harvesttime nears. A fruit is probably ready when it has deepened in color, softened, lost its astringency, and taken on its familiar flavor.

Always harvest with care, handling fruits and berries gently to avoid bruising. Try to pick during the cool of the day; fruit keeps longer that way. Harvest berries every couple of days; overripe berries attract wasps and bees and won't taste good or keep long.

Don't stack berries too high in your picking container. A quart basket may be all right for blueberries, but it's too deep for ripe, fragile raspberries, which will be crushed beneath their own weight.

For the best flavor, allow fruit to ripen on the plant. However, if you plan to store tree fruits, try picking them just before they are fully ripe. For long-term storage, keep them in a refrigerated area or cold cellar. Store only fruit that is in excellent condition and of the highest quality. Use imperfect fruit immediately for cooking.

If refrigerated right after picking, berries will keep for several days. To

NUT TREE POINTERS

Take the following items into consideration if you plan to grow nut trees:

■ All nut trees prefer deep, fertile soil with good drainage, full sun, and a constant supply of moisture.

■ Some nut trees, such as the pecan, can grow as tall as 150 feet; others, including the Persian walnut, may reach only 30 feet tall. Choose the right tree for your site.

■ Most nut trees are not self-fruitful. For good pollination, plant more than one cultivar of each species within 100 feet of one another.

■ Nut trees don't demand the rigorous pest control that fruit trees do, however, squirrels will vie with you for the harvest. Be prepared to fend them off or plant enough so you can enjoy their playful antics.

■ Be careful where you plant a black walnut. Juglone, a substance exuded from the roots and in the hulls, inhibits the growth of many garden plants, including tomatoes and rhododendrons. Keep the tree far away from vegetable and flower gardens. Do not compost leaves or twigs.

prevent mold, refrigerate them without washing. Simply cover them loosely with plastic wrap. Then, before serving, allow the berries to reach room temperature with the plastic in place. This technique prevents condensation, which can encourage mold.

HARVESTING NUTS

Simply put, nuts are ripe when you can shake them off the tree. Hickories and pecans come out of their husks easily, but black walnuts and butternuts are more stubborn (see the encyclopedia section starting on page 443).

After you've gathered and removed the nuts from their husks, cure them in their shells by hanging them in mesh bags in a dry, dark place. Chestnuts need to cure for about a week; other nuts can cure for several weeks. Treat almonds differently (see the encyclopedia section starting on page 443). No matter what type of nuts you're curing, protect them from scavenging rodents.

Cured nuts keep for several months. If you want to store them for longer periods, crack them and refrigerate or freeze the nutmeats in airtight containers.

The hardest of the nuts—black walnuts, butternuts, and hickory nuts—may be tough to crack with traditional nutcrackers. Hitting them with a hammer on a hard surface works well; so does soaking them in hot water for 15 to 20 minutes before applying the nutcracker.

Different fruits require different harvesting containers. Apples might work well in large boxes, but fragile raspberries need gentle handling; use small boxes to prevent crushing.

EXPECTED YIELDS AT MATURITY

Crop	Expected Yield Per Plant
Apple on M.9	60 pounds
Apple on MM.106	300 pounds
Apricot	100 pounds
Blackberry	2–3 pounds
Blueberry	3–10 pounds
Cherry, sweet	300 pounds
Cherry, tart	100 pounds
Currant	6–8 pounds
Elderberry	8–10 pounds
Gooseberry	6–8 pounds
Grape, American bunch	20 pounds
Grape, vinifera type	10 pounds
Pear	100 pounds
Plum	75 pounds
Raspberry	2–5 pounds
Strawberry, day-neutral	2–3 pounds
Strawberry, June-bearing	1–2 pounds

APPLE
Malus domestica

Plant this deciduous tree for its fragrant spring flowers and crisp apples that ripen in late summer and fall. Dwarf trees are best in home gardens. Recently, heirloom varieties

STAYMAN DOUBLE RED APPLE

have become popular for their romance and taste. However, newer disease-resistant cultivars prove easiest to grow; choose such cultivars whenever possible. Dwarf trees grow 8×12 feet; semidwarf, 12×20 feet; standard, 20×30 feet.

Site: Full sun. Prefers deep, moist, well-drained soil with pH 5.5 to 7.0. Tolerates other soil types, but must be well-drained. Hardy in zones 3 to 9; choose cultivars suited to your area's cold-hardiness and chilling needs.
How to Grow: Plant one-year-old "whips" or two-year-old bare-root, grafted trees in early spring. Know which rootstock you have. Space dwarf trees 7 feet apart, 13 feet between rows; semidwarf, 10 to 15 feet apart and 15 to 20 feet between rows; standard trees, 18 to 24 feet apart and 24 or more feet between rows. Considerable annual pruning needed. Best trained with a single leader. May be espaliered.

Needs cross-pollination; plant compatible varieties.

Apple scab, powdery mildew, fireblight, cedar-apple rust, apple maggot, plum curculios, borers, codling moths, scale insects, mites, and others can be serious depending on the region. Damaged by deer, mice, and voles.
Harvest: Warm, sunny days and cool nights promote ripening; rainy, warm weather delays it. For long-term storage, pick a week or so before ripe; seeds will be dark in color, but flesh still slightly crisp. Take a bite: Fruit should taste good, with no astringency. For eating right away, allow to ripen fully for peak flavor and quality.
Cultivars: Hundreds of cultivars available with different characteristics for flavor, storage quality, winter-hardiness, and disease-resistance. For all but the warmest regions: 'Freedom', disease-resistant, large, red, crisp, juicy, all-purpose; 'Liberty', most disease-resistant, bright, shiny red stripe over yellow, crisp, juicy, all-purpose; 'Jonafree', red, slightly spicy, fragrant; 'Prima', yellow-green, with bright red areas, mildly acid, juicy; 'MacFree', mostly red stripe on green, tender, juicy, sweet; 'Golden Delicious', juicy, yellow-skinned fruit, not disease-resistant, but easiest to train. Regional favorites vary; check to see what thrives in your area. Choose low-chill varieties in warmest areas of the South.

APRICOT
Prunus armeniaca

With their reddish stems, lovely pinkish white flowers, and heart-shaped leaves, apricot trees make attractive additions to the landscape. Homegrown apricots taste infinitely better than store-bought ones. Trees bloom early in spring, and a late spring frost can ruin fruit set and prevent a harvest; don't expect a harvest every year.

APRICOT

Dwarf trees grow 6 to 12 feet tall; semidwarf, 12 to 18 feet tall; full-size, 24 feet tall.

Site: Full sun. Avoid warm southern exposure to prevent early bloom and frost injury. Moist, humus-rich, well-drained neutral to alkaline soil. Zones 4 to 9.
How to Grow: Purchase trees grafted on apricot seedling rootstocks. Plant 15 to 20 feet apart. Train as an open-center tree. Always prune after blooming. Bears on spurs which are productive for up to four years, so needs less pruning than peaches. Stake tree branches to prevent narrow crotch angles. Pinch tips of unbranched shoots that are more than 18 inches long to induce lateral branching.

Thin fruit lightly to 2 to 3 inches apart, only with a full crop. Although many cultivars are self-fruitful, plant two cultivars 20 feet apart to set more fruit. Same pests and diseases as peaches.
Harvest: Ripens over a two- to three-week period. Harvest fruit just before fully mature, when they turn a rich color and "give" slightly when pressed. Handle gently to prevent bruising.
Cultivars: Where spring temperatures are uneven, plant late-blooming cultivars.

Southeast and Southwest: 'Blenheim', medium-large, pale orange, juicy, freestone.

Northwest: 'Harcot', medium to large, orange, freestone, firm, early harvest; 'Jerseycot', small-medium, pale orange, good flavor, slightly soft, consistent cropper, early; 'Puget Gold', large freestone, good flavor, productive, firm, midseason; 'Sundrop', medium size, bright orange, soft, juicy, clingstone, midseason.

Midwest: 'Harcot' and 'Jerseycot'; 'Goldcot', medium size, round, yellow skin, juicy, freestone, slightly soft, midseason.

Northeast: 'Harcot'; 'Alfred', medium size, bright orange, pink blush, slightly soft, sweet, rich, early bloomer, midseason harvest; 'Harlayne', medium size, orange with red blush, freestone, good flavor, firm; 'Sundrop', medium size, bright orange, clingstone, moderately soft, consistent producer, midseason harvest.

CHESTER BLACKBERRY

BLACKBERRY, DEWBERRY
Rubus subgenus *Eubatus*

Like a raspberry, a blackberry fruit is actually a cluster of small fruits. But unlike a raspberry, the receptacle comes off when the fruit is harvested, giving it a solid center. Blackberries have stiffly erect, semierect, or trailing stems, depending on the cultivar. They tend to be extremely thorny and tolerate heat and drought better than raspberries. Thornless cultivars are available, but are not as cold-hardy. The name "dewberry" applies to any species or cultivar of trailing blackberry, such as boysenberry or loganberry. Many hybrids that result from crossing related *Rubus* species, such as red raspberry with blackberry, offer gardeners a wide selection. The hybrids tend to be more like blackberries than red raspberries, so they can be managed like a trailing blackberry. Most hybrids perform well only in the western states.

Erect blackberries have self-supporting canes up to 8 feet long. Trailing types can have canes to 15 feet long, which require support.

Site: Full sun. Prefers sandy, acid loam with pH 6.0 to 6.5, but tolerates drought and poorer soil. Hardy in zones 4 to 9, depending on type.
How to Grow: Set out dormant woody suckers in spring, planting 1 inch deeper than in the nursery and spacing 30 inches apart. Prune trailing types heavily and train to a trellis to control size and rampant growth; wrap trailing stems around wire of single- or double-wire trellis or tie to a stake. Erect types also need to be pruned.

Rabbits and other animals gnaw on bark of thornless varieties in winter. May get Phytophthora root rot in wet soil. May be troubled by verticillium wilt, spur blight, anthracnose, crown gall, botrytis fruit rot; and by raspberry cane borers, crown borers, raspberry fruitworms, spider mites, raspberry sawflies, and Japanese beetles.
Harvest: Harvest when fruit is glossy, soft, and deeply colored; receptacle should come off easily with the fruit.
Cultivars: Erect: North—'Darrow', early, medium-size fruit, good flavor; 'Illini', late, good flavor, vigorous plants. Southeast and Midwest—'Shawnee', excellent quality, large fruit,

productive; 'Cherokee', early, productive, firm fruit with good flavor; 'Cheyenne', early, large, firm fruit; 'Choctaw', productive, early, good flavor; 'Navajo', late, good flavor, thornless.

Semierect, thornless: North—'Dirksen', late, large fruit, vigorous and productive. Midwest and Mid-Atlantic—'Black Satin', late, large, firm, tart fruit; 'Chester', late, large, firm fruit; 'Hull', late, large, firm, sweet fruit. Lower Midwest—'Thornfree', late, firm, flavorful. Gulf Coast—'Flint', midseason, firm, flavorful, large fruit.

Trailing (includes hybrids between related species): Pacific Coast—'Boysen', early, large, soft, flavorful fruit, hybrid; 'Marion', late, firm, medium-large fruit, hybrid; 'Logan', early, large, soft, maroon-colored fruit with excellent flavor, hybrid; 'Sunberry', fruit similar in size to Logan, but more deeply colored, hybrid; 'Tayberry', early ripening, productive, large purple-red fruit, widely adapted, hybrid; 'Tummel-berry', close relative of Tayberry, but hardier, smaller, less purple, less fragrant fruit, hybrid. Florida and the Gulf Coast—'Flordagrand', early, large, soft, full-flavored fruit; 'Oklawaha', early, medium-size, soft, flavorful fruit.

BLUEBERRY, HIGHBUSH BLUEBERRY
Vaccinium corymbosum

These easy-to-raise bushes bear delicate, bell-shaped, pale pink blossoms in spring; the foliage is an attractive dark green all summer and turns red in fall. Select early, mid-, and late-season cultivars for a two-month harvest. Half-high hybrids (crosses with the lowbush blueberry, *Vaccinium angustifolium*) are winter-hardy in the far North because they are low enough to be protected by snow. Bushes reach 8 to 15 feet tall; half-high hybrids, 1½ to 3½ feet tall.

continued

BLUEBERRY
(continued)

JERSEY BLUEBERRY

Site: Full sun for at least 6 hours a day. Must have well-drained, moist, acid soil with a pH of 4.0 to 4.8. Best in sandy loam or sandy peat, but tolerates heavier soils with good aeration and drainage. Grow in containers where soil is not acid. Provide ample moisture during flowering and fruiting. Zones 4 to 9.

How to Grow: Buy only two- or three-year-old plants, since one-year-old cuttings have a high mortality rate. Soak roots for several hours before planting. Space 4 feet apart, in rows 10 feet apart. Set plants 1 inch deeper than their depth in the nursery and prune to half their original size.

Prune annually in spring. Use organic mulch to maintain soil moisture and control weeds. Fertilize each year with 4 ounces of ammonium sulfate (or organic equivalent); increase by one ounce each year until sixth year. After this time, use 8 ounces per application. Do not use fertilizer containing chlorides or nitrates. Use netting to keep out birds or enclose blueberry patch in a walk-in cage to also keep out deer and rabbits. Grow in containers where soil is not acid.

Blueberries occasionally are affected by fusicoccum canker, phlomopsis canker, and mummyberry; and also by blueberry maggots and stem gall. Nutrient deficiencies occur with a soil pH that's above 5.0.

Harvest and Storage: Blueberries turn blue a week before fully ripe; a red ring around the stem end indicates under-ripeness. Ripe berries fall into your hand when lightly brushed. Store unwashed in the refrigerator for several weeks or freeze.

Cultivars: Plant at least two cultivars for large berry size. Northeast and North: Highbush types—'Bluecrop', large fruit, excellent flavor; 'Blueray', ripens early to midseason, large with strong flavor; 'Patriot', vigorous, excellent taste; 'Herbert', ripens late, consistent producer, good flavor. Half-high hybrids—'Northblue', large fruit, dark blue, good quality; 'Northsky', early ripening, medium-size, light blue; 'North Country', early ripening, sweet, mild; 'St. Cloud', most upright of half-highs, so more susceptible to winter injury; firm, good flavor, light blue.

South: Grow low-chill highbush blueberries—'Blue Ridge', vigorous, large fruit, light blue; 'Cooper', medium-size fruit, good flavor and color; 'Cape Fear', productive, large fruit; 'Gulf Coast', moderately productive, medium-size fruit, good flavor; 'O'Neal', large, firm fruit.

CHERRY
Prunus spp.

Sweet cherry trees (*Prunus avium*) do quadruple duty in the ornamental arena: They produce gorgeous white blossoms in spring, have attractive summer foliage, bear beautiful gleaming fruit, and feature deep reddish, shiny, smooth bark. Cherries are one of the first tree fruits to ripen in summer. Standard trees are still available, but they're propagated mainly on Mahaleb and Mazzard rootstocks; Mahaleb is smaller, but Mazzard is less subject to damage by collar rot in poorly drained soils.

BLACK TARTARIAN SWEET CHERRY

Trees reach 10 to 50 feet tall, depending upon rootstock. Mahaleb rootstock, 15 to 18 feet tall; Mazzard, 24 to 28 feet tall. New dwarf rootstocks include Damil, 10 feet, and Gisela, 10 to 12 feet.

SOUR CHERRY

Sour cherries (*P. cerasus*), sometimes called tart or pie cherries, are easier to care for than their sweet cousins. They're self-fruitful, so you only need to plant one tree for abundant fruit, and they begin bearing at a younger age. Like sweet cherry trees, sour cherry trees look attractive in the landscape. Enjoy their juicy fruit in jelly and pie; some people love them out of hand despite the tart flavor. Typically available on Mazzard rootstocks; trees are smaller than sweet cherry. They grow 8 to 20 feet tall, depending on cultivar.

Nanking cherries *(P. tomentosa)* and bush cherries *(P. japonica × jaquemontii)* may be the gardening world's best-kept secrets. They can be planted as an ornamental edible hedge or screen. The bushy Nanking cherry grows 10 to 15 feet tall and as wide or wider. It has downy green leaves and profuse, showy white flowers that are pink in bud. Its

NANKING CHERRY

brilliant red, tartly sweet fruits ripen in summer. Orange-brown bark looks interesting in winter and begins to peel in strips on older plants. The bush cherry, a shorter plant 3 to 4 feet tall, is a low-maintenance alternative to the sour cherry, with beautiful blossoms and no brown rot. Its fruit is larger than Nanking, with smaller pits. The flavor in a pie is exquisite. They ripen in fall, so extend the fruit harvest later in the year, and are not eaten by birds.

Site: Full sun. Sweet and sour cherries prefer moist, fertile, well-drained sandy loam with pH 6.2 to 6.5. Mazzard and Maheleb rootstocks tolerate heavier soil. Nanking and bush cherries tolerate most well-drained soils. Sweet cherries

are hardy in zones 5 to 9; sour cherries in zones 4 to 9; neither tolerates extremely hot summers. Nanking cherries are suited to zones 3 to 6; bush cherries, zones 4 to 8.

How to Grow: Plant dormant bare-root trees in spring; set grafted trees 2 inches higher than in the nursery. Plant Nanking and bush cherries in early spring, spacing 8 to 10 feet apart. Cherries can be pruned as central-leader or open-center trees. Regular pruning, fertilizing, and pest control increase sweet cherry yields. Protect from birds by covering tree with netting when fruit begins to change color. Plant two sweet cherry cultivars for cross-pollination, except for 'Stella', which is self-fruitful. Sour cherries generally are easier to prune and maintain at a manageable height.

Thin branches of Nanking and bush cherries to remove crossing or broken limbs and enhance fruiting and appearance. Prune older plants like blueberries. Both species need cross-pollination; plant two cultivars.

Brown rot is a serious sweet cherry problem in areas with high heat and humidity. Other problems include: black knot, leaf spot, plum curculios, scale insects, and cherry fruit flies. Birds strip off ripe fruit; dark red cherries appeal to birds more than yellow or red-cheeked yellow fruit.

Sour cherries are not as troubled with insects and diseases, and Nanking and bush cherries even less so. Cover Nanking cherry with bird netting if necessary. Bush cherries tend to be less bothered by birds.

Harvest: Sweet cherries lose firmness, deepen in color, and sweeten when ripe. Pick as soon as ripe. Sour cherries ripen one to two weeks after sweet cherries; handle the same way. Pick fruit with stems on and handle gently to avoid bruising. Place in basket and do not stack too deeply. To avoid bruising, use a container no larger than peck basket. Refrigerate sweet cherries for up to a month if not bruised; sour cherries are more perishable.

Nanking cherries are about ½ inch across, too small to "pit" for preserves or pies, and too soft to store for any length of time. Best eaten out of hand. Pick as soon as ripe when fruit deepens in color and becomes soft. Pick bush cherries when ripe and sweet, or allow to dry on the bush into sweet raisinlike fruit and harvest in late fall and winter.

Cultivars: Sweet cherry: West—'Bing', dark red, meaty, purple flesh, excellent flavor, prone to cracking; 'Black Tartarian', early bearer, medium-large, heart-shaped, dark red fruit, rich, sweet flavor; 'Early Burlat', large, sweet, deep red, excellent flavor; 'Van', dark, early bearing, good flavor, firmer than 'Bing'; 'Lapins', large, firm, red fruit, excellent flavor, self-fruitful, heavy producer; 'Sweetheart', dark red, good flavor, late ripening. North—'Hedelfingen', large, firm, black fruit, excellent quality; 'Stella', large, heart-shaped, dark red, vigorous, self-fruitful; 'Emperor Francis', yellowish white with red blush, firm, meaty, excellent flavor; 'Schmidt', deep mahogany color, sweet, rich flavor, vigorous. Great Lakes—'Rainier', yellow with red blush, early ripening, good flavor. East—'Sam', medium-large, bright red, firm fruit; 'Ulster', large, dark red, good flavor, vigorous; 'Kristin', large, dark red, good flavor, vigorous; 'Royalton', large, exceptional flavor; 'Hudson', medium-large, black fruit, firm, sweet, crack-resistant.

Sour cherry: 'Montmorency', bright red fruit, most popular, widely adapted; 'North Star', large, red fruit, light red skin, red flesh, resists brown rot, vigorous, 8 to 12 feet high on Mazzard rootstock; 'Meteor', tart, juicy, meaty, red fruit, cold-hardy; 'Early Richmond', heavy producer, juicy, bright red fruit.

Nanking cherry: 'Drilea', Canadian cultivar, cold-hardy; 'Slate' and 'Monroe', tasty, large fruit; 'Orient', self-fertile, fairly large, tasty fruit.

Bush cherry: 'Jan' and 'Joy', glossy, red, tart, late-ripening.

CURRANT
Ribes spp.

Long-lived and a favorite fruit of the last century, currant bushes can be found around old homesteads and abandoned properties. They aren't widely grown commercially, so to enjoy them you have to grow your own. One of the few fruits that perform in part shade, currants are low-maintenance, adaptable shrubs with attractive flowers and foliage, which grant them ornamental status. Plant a row beside a building or shady arbor, or use as a foundation shrub, border, or hedge. The jewel-like round fruit of red currant (*Ribes silvestre* or *R. sativum*) is tart—few people enjoy currants out of hand—but the red or white berries make delicious jellies and preserves.

RED CURRANT

Black currants (*R. nigrum*) aren't as common in the United States as in Europe, because the shrub is an alternate host for white-pine blister rust disease, and some states have prohibited planting. The taste is strong and musky, unappealing to some and delicious to others. Black currants are similar in fruit and plant size to red currants and are used for liqueurs, juices, and jellies. Currants grow 4 to 5 feet tall.

Site: Full sun to part shade; protect from hottest sun in warm climates. Best in rich, moist, well-drained soil with a pH of 6.2 to 6.5. Hardy in zones 3 to 8.
How to Grow: Purchase strong, well-rooted one- or two-year-old plants. Incorporate plenty of organic matter before planting. Plant in early spring or fall, spacing 3 to 5 feet apart. Head back stems of new plants to 6 to 10 inches at planting. Prune lightly each year to keep fruitful.

Self-fruitful. Disbud the first year to establish a large, healthy planting. Apply organic mulch to keep soil moist. Fertilize annually with rotted manure or compost. Can be trellised.

Occasionally troubled by currant aphids and powdery mildew. Choose a location with good air circulation to discourage mildew.
Harvest: Currants ripen over a two-week period in early summer, but don't drop immediately upon ripening, so you can harvest in one or two pickings. Pick in clusters; strip fruit later.
Cultivars: Red currant: 'Red Lake', good quality, dark red, widely available; 'White Grape', good quality, white; 'White Imperial', white with pink blush, large, sweet, mild-flavored fruits.

Black currant: 'Consort', 'Coronet', 'Crusader', disease-resistant, black, unique musky flavor; 'Ben Lomand', 'Ben Nevis', 'Ben Sarek', not disease-resistant, productive, large fruit, black.

ELDERBERRY
Sambucus canadensis

These old-fashioned, fast-growing shrubs, 8 to 20 feet tall, have lush, compound leaves and display large, flat clusters of creamy white flowers in summer. These eventually fill out with tasty, shiny, purplish black berries, which ripen in mid- to late summer. Berries have a sweet, unique flavor. Grow them for their unusual taste in pies, jellies, jams, and wine. Naturalize the shrubs as a tall hedge.

NOVA ELDERBERRY

Site: Full sun. Best in moist, fertile, well-drained soil with a pH of 5.5 to 6.5, but tolerates most well-drained soils. Hardy in zones 3 to 9.
How to Grow: Plant rooted cuttings 6 to 10 feet apart in spring. Long, lanky canes lose productivity after third year and need to be pruned back to the ground. Prone to suckering; thin out unwanted growth in spring.

Fertilize in early spring with 2 ounces of ammonium nitrate (or organic equivalent) for each year of the plant's age, with a limit of 1 pound per plant. Mulch to control weed growth and keep well-watered, especially during the first year, since plants are shallow-rooted. Plant two cultivars for pollination. Usually pest-free, but birds can be troublesome.
Harvest: Harvest in late summer when fully ripe. Berries deepen in color to dark purple, become soft, may begin to drop individual berries from cluster when ripe. Remove the entire cluster, then strip off berries later. Use as soon as possible or refrigerate.
Cultivars: 'Adams No. 1' and 'Adams No. 2', large shrub to 20 feet, broad clusters, large fruit, vigorous, productive; 'York', bears early in second or third year, large fruit, productive; 'Johns', small shrub to 6 to 10 feet, large fruit; 'Kent', productive small shrub, large fruit; 'Nova',

productive, large shrub, early ripening; 'Scotia', good quality, large clusters, and large fruit; 'Victoria', moderately productive, excellent flavor.

FIG
Ficus carica

Ripe figs make a simple yet sublime desert. They are quite expensive in the market, so why not grow your own? Their soft fruit is plump, rich, and easy to cook with. The large, deeply lobed leaves turn

BLACK MISSION FIG

yellow in fall. The smooth, gray bark adds interest in the landscape, especially on old trunks, which become twisted and gnarled with age. Plant fig trees as specimens, hedges, or in containers. They reach 15 to 30 feet tall, but dwarf cultivars may be only 10 feet. In colder climates, grows more commonly as a 6- to 10-foot-tall, multistemmed shrub.

Site: Full sun for best fruit production; tolerates some shade. Average, well-drained soil best; does not need rich soil to perform well. Hardy in zones 8 to11; to Zone 7 if wrapped and protected during winter.
How to Grow: Plant bare-root or containerized trees before they leaf out

in spring; space 8 to 25 feet apart, depending on climate and cultivar.

Winter temperatures influence pruning methods. Train as trees in warm climates, as shrubs in cold areas. For a central-leader tree, train to four main branches with the first branch 2 or more feet off the ground. Make corrective cuts as needed. May be espaliered or allowed to grow naturally.

Grow against a warm wall in cold regions; avoid southwestern exposure.

Generally pest-free. Occasionally troubled by mites and in Florida by fig rust, but pests usually limited to birds.
Harvest: In warm regions, figs bear two crops of fruit each year—in summer and fall. In colder areas, they bear one crop in summer. Pick fruit when soft and stems break off easily; your finger will make an impression in the fig. Fruit is not ready if a thin, white sap comes from the stem when you pick. Allow to wither on the tree and harvest later if you prefer them dry.
Cultivars: 'Brown Turkey', widely grown, hardy, medium-large fruit, brownish violet skin.

California: 'Black Mission', large tree, sweet, rich, black fruit; 'Violette de Bordeaux', medium-size, violet-black fruit.

Northern California and Northwest: 'White Genoa', medium-large, green fruit; 'Desert King', large, green fruit with pale red flesh, sweet, rich.

Southeast: 'Celeste', small fruit with bronze skin, sweet, bland, pinkish flesh.

Gulf Coast: 'Tena', medium-size fruit with green skin and sweet, pale red flesh.

GOOSEBERRY
Ribes spp.

Gooseberries are an extremely thorny relative of currants, and the bushes make an unusual hedge or border. Some people are passionate about this juicy fruit, which used to be much more popular. The greenish or pink berries have a tart, juicy flavor reminiscent of rhubarb and grape, and

GOOSEBERRY

they look a bit like a small, veined table grape. Gooseberries may be small or as large as a small plum. Berries are much sweeter when dead ripe; if flavor is not good, you may be harvesting them too soon. Leaves are attractively lobed, and the red-fruited cultivars are particularly nice in the landscape. The European cultivars *(Ribes uva-crispa)* have larger fruit and better flavor, but are more susceptible to powdery mildew. The American cultivars *(R. hirtellum)* tend to be healthier, more productive plants, but otherwise, the plants look similar. The two have been crossed to develop hybrids. Plants grow 3 to 5 feet tall.

Site: Full sun to part shade; protect from hottest sun in warm climates. Best in rich, moist, well-drained soil with a pH of 6.2 to 6.5. Hardy in zones 3 to 5.
How to Grow: Grow as directed for currants, page 432.
Harvest: Pick individual fruit. Flavor improves and sweetens when fruit is ripe. After color deepens, try one. If it's still tart, leave on bush for another few days and try again. Fruit remains quite firm when ripeness approaches, so taste test is the best gauge for ripeness. Best cooked and made into pies and preserves, or eaten fresh if allowed to fully ripen. *continued*

GOOSEBERRY
(continued)

Cultivars: 'Downing', pale green fruit, used for commercial processing; 'Pixwell', fair tasting, green fruit, rosy when ripe, soft, juicy, productive, widely available; 'Poorman', distinctive, excellent flavor, pear-shaped, wine-red fruit; 'Fredonia', pinkish green, excellent when fully ripe, thorny; 'Oregon Champion', productive, small, pale yellowish green berries, rich flavor; 'Welcome', productive, light green turning pinkish red, sweet-tart flavor; 'Houghton', large, red skin, vigorous; 'Early Sulphur', pale golden yellow, sweet, rich flavor; 'Careless', large, white, sweet, tangy; 'Colossal', heavy-bearing, egg-shaped, green skin and flesh, mild flavor, tart skin; 'Whitesmith', fairly resistant to mildew, sweet, medium-size, greenish yellow fruit; 'Hinnonmaki Yellow', large, sweet, rich flavor, greenish yellow fruit.

STEUBEN AMERICAN GRAPE

GRAPE
Vitis spp.

Grapes hold the distinction of having the longest history of all cultivated fruits. Wine was made from grapes as long ago as 4,000 B.C. In the 1800s when European vines began to die of grape phylloxera, a root pest, the resistant American native grape *(Vitis labrusca)* saved the day. Growers grafted it by the thousands as a rootstock and saved the European wine industry. Eat homegrown grapes fresh and make juice, jelly, wine, and pie. The lobed leaves can be stuffed and cooked. Train the vines on an arbor to cast shade. The gnarled older vines are picturesque in winter.

American grapes taste "foxier" or more grapey than their European cousins, which is why American wine is typically more fruity. This type of grape is the most cold-hardy.

European grapes *(V. vinifera)* are recognized throughout the world for their wine-making superiority. However, the vines are lower-yielding and less cold-hardy. Several cultivars are derived from crosses between these two species. French-American hybrids offer the best of both worlds: They produce good wine, yet are much hardier and more disease-resistant than the *V. vinifera* parents.

Vines generally are trained to a 6-foot-tall trellis.

Site: Full sun; needs plenty of sunshine to produce sweet fruit. Prefers well-drained, deep, sandy loam, but not as sensitive to extremes in drainage as other fruit crops. Drought-tolerant once established.

American grapes are hardy in zones 4 to 10; European grapes in zones 6 to 10 (extremely sensitive to cold); hybrids in zones 5 to 10.

How to Grow: Purchase vines from a nursery, or take dormant hardwood cuttings. Plant 8 feet apart along a trellis or arbor in early spring as soon as ground can be worked. Train and prune heavily each year.

Fertilize in early spring of the second year with 2 ounces of 10-10-10. Increase by two ounces each year with a limit of 16 ounces or use organic equivalent. European grapes may be grown in the North if protected in

CONCORD GRAPE

winter: Lower and bury the canes each fall; tie them back to a trellis in spring.

Depending on location, grapes may be troubled by powdery mildew, black rot, downy mildew, and bunch rot. Grape berry moths, Japanese beetles, grape cane girdlers, and grape leafhoppers may cause problems. European grapes also troubled by grape phylloxera.

Harvest: Harvest only after fully ripe in fall, because sugar content doesn't increase after picking. Ripe when color deepens and berries soften and become sweet and juicy. In northern regions, often harvested after a frost, which greatly increases sweetness. Yield depends on climate and cultivar, but in general, vines may produce 5 to 10 pounds of fruit by the third year.

Cultivars: American: 'Concord', cold-hardy, productive, deep blue, excellent flavor, used for juice; 'Niagara', white, sweet, large, tight, compact clusters; 'Ontario', good early ripening white, sweet, loose clusters; 'Delaware', high quality for fresh eating and wine, red berries subject to cracking; 'Catawba', late-ripening, coppery red, full, sweet flavor; 'Steuben', spicy sweet, late, blue-black. Many excellent seedless cultivars available.

European: 'Chardonnay', outstanding vigor, dry white-wine grape; 'Riesling', fruity white-wine grape; 'Gewurztraminer', small, spicy, pinkish grape, produces distinctive, spicy white wine, moderately productive; 'Zinfandel', round, juicy, reddish black fruit, productive, makes good jelly and fruity wine; 'Merlot', round, deep blue-black grape, makes high-quality, full-bodied red wine; 'Cabernet Sauvignon', small round, purplish black berries, strong, distinctive flavor, makes red Bordeaux-type wine. Seedless cultivars available.

Hybrids: 'Baco Noir', long clusters, bluish black grapes, fine red wine; 'Dechaunac', bluish black fruit, vigorous, needs cluster thinning, high-quality red wine; 'Aurora', excellent white with pink blush, produces consistently; 'Seyval', white fruit, productive, crisp, quality white wine; 'Vignoles', tight cluster, white fruit, high-acid white wine; 'Horizon', white fruit, clean, neutral white wine; 'Cayuga', large, compact clusters, clean, neutral light white wine; 'Marechal Foch', black grape, full-bodied red wine; 'Cascade', bluish black fruit, productive, early ripening, used in blush wine; 'Chancellor', bluish black fruit, makes red wine with good body. Seedless cultivars available.

Muscadine: a native grape, strong, musky, aromatic flavor, for table use or wine, flavor doesn't appeal to all.

KIWIFRUIT, HARDY KIWI
Actinidia spp.

Hardy kiwi (*Actinidia arguta*) is related to the fuzzy kiwifruit so familiar in the market (*A. deliciosa* var. *deliciosa*), but its fruit is smooth, thin-skinned, lime green, and about 1 inch in diameter. Eat the smooth-skinned fruit like grapes, without peeling; peel the fuzzy type. Both are black seeded and have a pineapple-strawberry flavor. Vines of both provide ornamental value from their small white flowers with chocolate-colored centers and lily-of-the-valley scent. Nonfruiting male varieties make good ornamentals. The vigorous,

ANANASNAJA HARDY KIWI

heavy vines need a heavy-duty trellis or sturdy arbor or pergola.

Hardy kiwi vines can grow to 40 feet high, but generally are managed by the 6-foot-tall trunk.

Site: Full sun. Prefers moist, well-drained soil with pH 5.5 to 7.0. Tends to break bud in early spring and may be subject to frost injury; locate with a northern exposure to minimize risk.

Hardy kiwi grows in zones 4 to 8, but is sensitive to late spring frost injury if planted in exposed site. Kiwifruit is hardy in zones 7 to 9.

How to Grow: Add organic matter before planting. Set 10 feet apart after danger of frost; plant one male for every nine females and water faithfully in dry spells.

Must be heavily pruned each year; produces fruit on shoots that grow from one-year-old canes. At planting, prune plants back to one or two buds. After growth starts, select one vigorous shoot to train upward as a trunk and remove all others. Remove all basal shoots that break along the trunk. In the dormant season, head back trunk to wood that's ¼ inch diameter. In second growing season, develop two permanent arms along wire, in opposite directions, wrapping through the season to secure to the wire. Each dormant season thereafter, prune these two canes and their laterals back to

wood ¼ inch diameter or larger. T-bar system best; locate the top wire 7 feet from the ground.

Fertilize in early spring of the second year with 2 ounces of 10-10-10 (or organic equivalent) per plant; increase by 2 ounces each year until plants receive 8 ounces, then do not exceed this amount. Relatively pest-free.

Harvest: Fruit matures in fall, often after the first frost in northern regions, so may be injured. Handle gently to avoid bruising. If you harvest early, fruit ripens slowly in the refrigerator. Hardy kiwifruit doesn't store as long as kiwifruit, but flavor is better.

Cultivars: Hardy kiwi: 'Ananasnaja', light green flesh, sweet, spicy, pineapple aroma, good-size fruit, vigorous, fast-growing vine; 'Geneva', small fruit, late-ripening, good flavor, hardy; 'Meader', sweet, tasty, early ripening; also male plants by same name available; 'MSU', good-size fruit, excellent taste; '74 Series', all are cold-hardy, adaptable, vigorous, large fruit; 'Issai', self-pollinating, large fruit, sweet flesh, good keeper. Other males: 'Belfast', 'Dumbarton Oaks', 'Longwood'.

Kiwifruit: 'Hayward', standard grocery store cultivar, lime-green flesh with strawberry-like texture and sweet-tart taste; 'Chico Hayward', productive, sweet, green flesh, male plants by same name available; 'Kramer', similar to 'Hayward', outstanding quality; 'California' and 'Matua', good long-flowering male pollenizers.

PAWPAW
Asimina triloba

Often called "the poor man's banana," the pawpaw is perhaps our most underappreciated native fruiting tree. Bold leaves, maroon blossoms, and clear yellow fall color add interest to the landscape. Clusters of fruit turn from green to yellowish brown and liven up the fall menu in preserves and puddings. They are soft and custardy, several *continued*

PAWPAW
(continued)

PAWPAW

inches long, with a taste reminiscent of bananas; in fact, they look a little like a short, fat banana. The flavor also has been compared to pears or mangoes. Use this handsome, rounded small tree as an ornamental edible specimen in a small garden. Grows 20 to 30 feet tall.

Site: Part sun. Prefers a moist, well-drained, loamy soil and even moisture. Hardy in zones 5 to 8.
How to Grow: Purchase seedlings or grafted cultivars. Space with mature size in mind.

Water during dry spells and apply an organic mulch. Tends to sucker; train to a single stem, if desired. Generally no pest or disease problems.
Harvest: Trees bear early, often at three years of age. Harvest pawpaws in September or October when fully colored and slightly soft; pick fruit by hand to avoid bruising. Bring indoors to fully ripen.
Cultivars: 'Sunflower', large, thick, sweet, excellent-flavored fruit, blooms and bears late, productive; 'Taytwo', medium-size, fine-tasting fruit, prolific producer; 'Overlease', productive, large, roundish fruit.

PEACH, NECTARINE
Prunus persica

Sweet, juicy, and sensual, a ripe peach *(Prunus persica)* is the epitome of good summer eating. The tree's showy, pink flowers bloom in early spring before the long, gracefully drooping leaves emerge. Peach trees grow 20 to 25 feet tall, but may be kept to 10 feet with pruning. They are notoriously short-lived, declining in 10 to 15 years. If you don't like the fuzziness of peaches but like their taste, try nectarines (*P. persica* var. *nucipersica)*. They resemble their peachy sisters in nearly every way, except the furry skins.

REDHAVEN PEACH

Often sold on Lovell (cold-hardy), Siberian C, (cold-hardy), Halford, (cold-hardy to -10°F, adaptable to broad range of soils) or Bailey (sandy-loam soils) rootstocks. Nemaguard rootstock recommended in the Southwest and Deep South.

Site: Full sun. Prefers a moist, well-drained, sandy loam with pH 6.2 to 6.5. Hardy in zones 5 to 9; nectarines are not as cold-hardy as some peach cultivars bred for cold regions.
How to Grow: Trees grafted onto sand cherry or Nanking cherry rootstocks produce a short tree that tends to be short-lived. Instead, purchase standard stock and train to a manageable height. Plant one-year-old whips in early spring, 15 to 20 feet apart.

Needs extensive annual pruning. Train to an open-center, vase-shaped tree.

Some hand-thinning of fruit and spraying for pests is necessary for high-quality fruit. Water during dry spells; fertilize in early spring. Susceptible to peach leaf curl, brown rot, bacterial spot, and powdery mildew; also peach tree borers, scale insects, and plum curculios. Nectarines are more susceptible to disease than peaches.
Harvest: With good training, trees bear fruit in their second or third year. Fruit is ripe when fully colored and easily comes off the tree. The flesh of ripe fruit "gives" slightly when pressed. Handle carefully to avoid bruising. Fruit on a tree ripens over a period of two weeks.
Cultivars: Peaches: North—'Reliance', showy flowers, large, freestone, cold-hardy; 'Redhaven', good flavor, midseason, yellow flesh, widely adapted, good for areas with late spring frosts; 'Harrow', high quality, bright yellow with red blush, excellent flavor; 'Harson', freestone, firm, sweet, juicy, cold-hardy; 'Harcrest', firm, freestone, mostly red over yellow background, vigorous, productive; 'Canadian Harmony', yellow with red blush, firm, yellow freestone, flavorful, cold-hardy; 'Raritan Rose', excellent midseason, productive, tender, juicy, rich, white flesh. Mid-Atlantic and Midwest—'Fantastic Elberta', large, high quality, freestone, used for canning, double, pink blossoms; 'Glohaven', large, yellow, freestone, firm, tough skin mostly fuzzless, good for canning; 'Madison', medium-size, flavorful, soft flesh, freestone, spring frost-tolerant; 'Monroe', late season, bright red skin over yellow-orange background, firm, mild flavor, freestone, attractive flowers; 'Washington', large, high quality,

yellow, freestone, with showy flowers. Southwest—'Desertgold', early, firm yellow, semi-freestone, good flavor, self-fruitful. Southern California and the Deep South—'Flordaking', early, yellow flesh, firm, medium-size, clingstone, self-fruitful, heavy producer; 'Texstar', yellow flesh, heavy cropping, semi-clingstone, fair tasting, with good resistance to bacterial spot; 'La Feliciana', good flavor, yellow with red blush, freestone, fuzzy, resists brown rot; 'TropicSweet', excellent flavor, yellow flesh, freestone, moderate resistance to bacterial spot.

Nectarines: 'Cavalier', high quality, productive; 'Fantasia', large, mostly red over brilliant yellow, vigorous, productive; 'Redchief', good size, white flesh, late season, resistant to brown rot; 'Cherokee', midseason, highly colored yellow-red, firm juicy, resists brown rot; 'Independence', firm, yellow flesh, early season choice for areas with warm winters.

PEAR
Pyrus spp.

Pears *(Pyrus communis)* may be crisp and juicy, or soft and sweet.

HONEYSWEET PEAR

Enjoy them fresh with a slice of good cheese or in preserves and baked goods. Pear trees have showy white flowers, glossy, deep green leaves and are loaded with fruit in late summer

CHOJURO ASIAN PEAR

and fall. Pears may be green, yellow, brown, or bright red. Their skin is smooth as silk or rough and russeted. The flavor may be ambrosial, mild, or rich. Even the flesh varies, from gritty to buttery. Of course, the ones grown at home are the most luscious. Recommended rootstocks are those designated as OHXF, which provide a dwarfing influence, some fireblight-resistance, and cold-hardiness.

Crisp, crunchy and round, Asian pears *(P. serotina)* often are mistaken for apples—earning them the nickname "apple pears." Long-lived and productive, Asian pear trees provide gorgeous white blossoms in spring and refreshing fall fruit. If pear diseases are troublesome in your area, look for disease-resistant cultivars.

Standard pear trees grow 30 to 40 feet tall; semidwarf (OHXF 333 and OHXF 513), 15 to 20 feet; dwarf (OHXF 51), 12 to 15 feet.

Several rootstocks available for Asian pears; both scion and rootstock must be adapted to region. *P. communis* rootstock produces trees of a manageable size. Trees on standard 'Bartlett' rootstock may be highly susceptible to fireblight.

Site: Full sun. Best in deep, well-drained loam with a pH of 6.0 to 6.5; tolerates somewhat poorly drained soil better than other fruit trees. Pears are hardy in zones 4 to 9, Asian pears in zones 5 to 9; choose cultivars well-adapted to your region.

How to Grow: Plant one-year-old, unbranched whips in early spring; space standard trees 20 feet apart, semidwarf trees 10 to 15 feet apart, and dwarf trees 8 to 10 feet apart.

For both types of pears, plant two cultivars with overlapping bloom times to ensure a large crop.

Pears need annual pruning. Train to a single leader. After planting, cut back to 30 inches and remove branches with narrow crotch angles. Prune out excess fruiting spurs and weak wood each year to keep trees productive.

Water during dry spells and apply organic mulch to control weeds and keep in moisture. Some spraying, fertilizing, and hand-thinning usually needed for good-quality fruit. Needs cross-pollination; plant two cultivars.

Depending upon location and cultivar, may be troubled by pear scab, fireblight, pear decline, and collar rot; and pear psylla, pear root aphids, and codling moths.

Harvest: Harvest just before fully ripe, when fruit begins to soften, but not too early, or it will lack flavor and sweetness. Fruit allowed to fully ripen on trees often becomes mushy and brown. Refrigerate pears for a month or so (called after-ripening), then allow to fully ripen at room temperature when you're ready to eat them.

Asian pear trees usually begin to bear by third year. Fruit on a given tree ripens over two to three weeks. Let fruit ripen on tree; it is ready to pick when it changes color and becomes sweet and flavorful. Late-ripening fruit keeps longer.

Cultivars: Pear: Lower Midwest and West—'Harrow Delight', yellow with red blush, early, resistant to fireblight, excellent quality, smooth texture; 'Moonglow', yellow with *continued*

PEAR
(continued)

pink blush, midseason, resistant to fireblight, mild flavor; 'Seckel', brownish with russet-red cheek, late midseason, sweet with exceptional taste, moderate resistance to fireblight; 'Doyenne Gris', golden brown, midseason, smooth-textured russet, resistant to fireblight, good keeper; 'Maxine', golden yellow with white flesh, late midseason, firm, flavorful, good for canning, moderately resistant to fireblight. Pacific Northwest— 'Harrow Delight'; 'Clapp's Favorite', yellow with red cheek, early, excellent quality, smooth texture, resistant to fireblight; 'Orcas', yellow with red blush, large, flavorful, vigorous, resistant to pear scab; 'Flemish Beauty', clear yellow with marbled red blush, late season, firm texture, sweet, aromatic. Northeast and Upper Midwest—'Harrow Delight', 'Maxine', 'Magness', greenish yellow russet, late season, good quality, smooth texture, slow to bear, resists fireblight; 'Tyson', yellow, midseason, excellent quality, spicy sweet, resists fireblight; 'Honeysweet', late midseason, firm, smooth, good for canning, moderate fireblight resistance.

Asian pear: 'Hosui', Early bloom and harvest, medium-large russet, brownish, exceptional flavor, juicy; 'Shinseiki', early bloom and harvest, medium-large, yellow, mild flavor, sweet; 'Chojuro', midseason bloom and harvest, medium-size greenish brown, sweet, bland fruit; 'Twentieth Century', midseason bloom and harvest, medium-size, yellow, juicy, and crisp; 'Kosui', late bloom and harvest, medium-size, yellow with gold russet, sweet, and juicy; 'Shinko', late bloom and harvest, medium-large fruit, gold, russet, sweet, good flavor; 'Nitaka', blooms early, matures late, extra-large fruit, thick russet, coarse texture, moderate fireblight resistance. All are susceptible to fireblight unless indicated.

PERSIMMON
Diospyros spp.

The handsome native American persimmon (*Diospyros virginiana*) has lustrous green leaves, attractive rough brown bark, and beautiful yellow to orange golf-ball-size fruit that remains on the trees after the leaves fall. Fall color is clear yellow to deep red. Drooping branches give trees a graceful, tranquil appearance. Trees grow 30 to 45 feet tall in home landscapes (taller in the wild). Enjoy the smooth-textured, sweet fruit after fully ripened in persimmon pudding, a Midwestern specialty that is enjoyed each fall.

AMERICAN PERSIMMON

Like its native cousin, the Japanese persimmon (*D. kaki*) is a striking tree in the landscape, with heart-shaped leaves in summer, large orange fruit persisting well after the leaves drop in fall, and rough-textured black bark. Trees grow 25 to 30 feet tall. Fruit from the Japanese persimmon must be fully ripe before it is edible.

Site: Full sun. Tolerant of moderate to well-drained soils. American persimmon is hardy in zones 5 to 9, Japanese persimmon in zones 7 to 10.
How to Grow: Plant bare-root or containerized stock in spring. Difficult

FUJU JAPANESE PERSIMMON

to transplant because of taproot, so plant carefully and pamper with weekly waterings during dry spells. Space 15 to 20 feet apart. Plant two varieties for best crop.

Prune young trees to encourage a central leader that has wide-angled branches to provide a strong framework able to support a heavy load of fruit. Pruning is generally not necessary as the tree ages.

Pick up fallen fruit to deter insect pests. Occasionally troubled by anthracnose, scale insects or persimmon girdlers, but otherwise easy to maintain.
Harvest: Pick fruit while firm, yet fully colored, and allow to finish ripening indoors. Placing fruit in a bag with a ripe apple or banana speeds ripening. When fully ripe, fruit becomes soft and sweet; unripe fruit is extremely astringent.
Cultivars: American persimmon: 'Beavers', overall good quality; 'Craggs', yellow-orange skin with red blush, high quality; 'Florence', prolific, medium-size, excellent flavor; 'Wabash', excellent flavor; 'Weber', early ripening, large fruit, excellent flavor; 'Early Golden', large, sweet, large-seeded fruit, excellent flavor; 'Killen', productive, high-quality fruit; 'John Rick', large, late ripening, excellent flavor; 'Garretson', early ripening, productive, excellent-quality fruit with medium-size seeds; 'Meader',

early ripening, tomato-shaped fruit, sweet, excellent quality, productive, cold-hardy, self-fruitful; 'Pieper', small fruit, cold-hardy, early ripening.

Japanese persimmon: 'Fuju', large, reddish orange, glossy fruit, non-astringent, good keeper, self-fruitful, beautiful fall color; 'Tanenashi', large, light yellowish to light orange fruit of high quality, good flavor; 'Tecumseh', high-quality seedless fruit, self-fruitful, handsome ornamental; 'San Pedro', early fruiting, deep orange; 'Sheng', orange, medium-large fruit, dries well; 'Great Wall', small, flattened, sweet, orange fruit, productive, good for the northernmost range; 'Gailey', often used as a pollenizer.

JAPANESE PLUM

PLUM
Prunus spp.

If you've eaten only store-bought plums, try a juicy homegrown one to see what you're missing. Plums are wonderful eaten fresh and equally good cooked into desserts, dried or preserved. Trees grow 8 to 20 feet tall, depending on rootstock (Japanese plums grow faster than European plums). They have rough black bark and produce white flowers in spring.

European plums (*Prunus domestica*) have a thick, rich flesh and may be freestone or clingstone. They are divided into dessert types, eaten fresh and juicy, or prune types, which tend to be dry and sweet and are eaten fresh, dried, or cooked. The glossy, attractive fruit may be red, yellow, green, blue, or purple, with yellowish or reddish flesh. Damsons are a related species that bear small, tart plums, great for preserves.

Japanese plums (*P. salicina*) tend to be larger and juicier than their European cousins; fruit is 2 to 3 inches across and somewhat bitter-tasting around the pit. Skin color ranges from red to purple, black or yellow, and flesh is yellow or reddish. Some cultivars bloom so early in spring that they are susceptible to spring frosts; others bloom late enough to escape damage. Choose a cultivar adapted to your location.

Site: Full sun. Prefers deep, moist, well-drained soil with pH 6.2 to 6.8. Choose a site protected from late-spring and early fall frosts. European plum is hardy in zones 4 to 7 and zones 8 and 9 in the Pacific Northwest only, where summers are cool; performs poorly in the Deep South. Japanese plum is suited to zones 6 to 9, withstands southern heat better.

How to Grow: Plant bare-root, grafted trees. Space standard trees 15 to 20 feet apart; semidwarf, 12 to 15 feet; and dwarf trees, 8 to 10 feet.

Mulch to drip line with organic material; some spraying, pruning, fertilizing, and hand-thinning necessary for good-quality fruit. Most cultivars need cross-pollination. Fertilize Japanese plums cautiously; do not apply heavy amounts of nitrogen.

Not as prone to diseases as apples, but often troubled by black knot, brown rot, bacterial spot, and bacterial canker, as well as plum curculios. Plum leaf scald and root nematodes are problems in the Southeast and Southwest.

Harvest: Begins to bear in the third or fourth year. Tastes best if allowed to fully ripen on the tree, but perishable.

Ripe fruit is fully colored, juicy and sweet, and "gives" when pressed with a thumb. Harvest plums for drying when fully colored, yet still firm.

Cultivars: European: 'DeMontfort', small-medium, dark purple, sweet, juicy, rich-tasting, freestone; 'Golden Transparent Gage', large, round, golden yellow dotted with red, rich, sugary, clingstone; 'Seneca', large, reddish blue, sweet, dessert-quality, rich-tasting, clingstone; 'Green Gage', commonly grown, medium, oval, yellowish green, rich, sweet, high quality, but highly susceptible to bacterial canker and brown rot; 'Yellow Egg', large, oval, golden yellow, sweet, juicy, self-fruitful, productive, but highly susceptible to bacterial canker.

Good quality, oval-shaped, purplish blue prune types: 'Italian Prune', medium-large, oval, purplish black, reliable, early, cold-hardy, self-fruitful; 'Mount Royal', bluish black, large, freestone, meaty flesh, all-purpose, productive; 'Oneida', reddish black, self-fruitful, consistent producer; 'Earliblue', purplish blue, excellent flavor, self-fruitful, susceptible to bacterial canker, similar to 'Stanley', but softer; 'Stanley', self-fruitful, dark blue, large, freestone, reliable bearer, most cold-hardy.

Japanese: North—'Abundance', medium-size, dark red with purple blush, tender juicy flesh, fast growing; 'Early Golden', round, yellow with red blush; 'Shiro', medium-large, yellow with pink blush, sweet flesh, excellent all-purpose. South—'Burbank', large, purplish red, sweet, meaty flesh, excellent flavor, pick before fully ripe; 'Elephant Heart', large, heart shape, thick skin, reddish purple, juicy, blood-red flesh, rich flavor, good all-purpose; 'Methley', old favorite, medium-size, reddish purple fruit with sweet, amber flesh, heavy cropping; 'Ozark Premier', large fruit, tough, bright red skin with juicy yellow flesh, productive; 'Satsuma', medium-large, round, dark red, firm, meaty, sweet, excellent flavor, all-purpose.

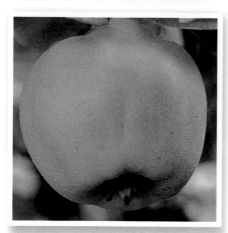

QUINCE

QUINCE
Cydonia oblonga

The quince tree is a four-season ornamental. Train it as an espalier to capitalize on all its good qualities, or plant as a hedge or screen. It grows 15 to 20 feet tall. Showy white or pink flowers bloom in late spring, and summer foliage is attractive. Handsome, fragrant fruit is borne abundantly in fall, while interesting gnarled trunks add winter interest. The fruit is bright yellow, green, or orange-yellow, firm, and about the size of an apple, but with a characteristic oblong shape more like a pear. Quinces are too astringent to enjoy fresh, but use them in jelly and chutney for a real treat. Quince fruit is a great source of pectin and can be added to firm up other jellies. A bowl of ripe quinces releases a heavenly fragrance.

Site: Full sun. Best in well-drained loam. Tolerates clay loam and somewhat poorly drained soil, but performs poorly in sandy soil. The quince tree is drought-tolerant with age. Hardy in zones 5 to 9.
How to Grow: Purchase bare-root and plant like an apple tree. Tends to be shrublike, but can be trained to a single stem, like an apple. Where fireblight is common, keep pruning cuts to a minimum to avoid the disease.

Occasional fertilization is adequate; avoid heavy applications of nitrogen.
Subject to same pests and diseases as apples.
Harvest: Harvest in fall after fruit has deepened in color and is fragrant. Handle carefully; flesh is firm, but bruises easily.
Cultivars: 'Orange', early-maturing large fruit with excellent aroma and flavor, smooth bright yellow skins and yellowish orange flesh; 'Pineapple', large, smooth, round, golden yellow, pineapple-scented, white-fleshed fruit, prolific; 'Smyrna', large pear-shaped, golden yellow fruit covered with fine brown hairs, excellent quality, good keeper.

RASPBERRY
Rubus spp.

Raspberries are the most popular bramble for fresh eating. Their sweet, fragrant berries come in many jewel-like colors. Although the root system is perennial, canes are biennial, living only two years. First-year canes are called primocanes. These winter over to become the next season's floricanes or fruiting canes. After fruiting, floricanes die. Their lanky stems may be thorny or nearly thornless, depending on the cultivar. Several to many new canes sprout from the ground at the plant base each year and need controlling. Canes are best managed with some type of trellis system. "Everbearing" or "fall-bearing" types bear fruit at the tips of first-year canes in late summer and again lower on those same stems in early summer. The norm, though, is the "summer-bearer," which bears fruit only during the summer on second-year canes.

A raspberry fruit, like its blackberry cousin, is actually a cluster of small, delicate fruits with seeds in them. The fruits cluster around a receptacle, which stays attached to the plant when the fruit is picked. Yellow raspberries (*Rubus idaeus*) taste extremely sweet. They are a mutation of the red raspberry (also *R. idaeus*) and should be grown like them. Both grow at least 5 to 7 feet tall.

ROYALTY PURPLE RASPBERRY

Black raspberries or "blackcaps" (*R. occidentalis*) ripen to a deep purplish blue and are borne on longer, more trailing, thorny canes than red raspberries. They don't withstand winter temperatures as well, get more diseases, and produce less abundantly, but gardeners passionate about their unique taste are willing to coddle them a bit. Black raspberries grow to 5 to 8 feet tall and are propagated in late summer by tip layering. Purple raspberries, a hybrid between the red and black species, grow 6 to 8 feet tall.

Site: Full sun for at least 6 hours. Blackcaps need some shade in hot climates. Prefer sandy acid loam with pH 6.0 to 6.5, but tolerate other well-drained soils. Red and yellow raspberries are hardy in zones 3 to 9; black raspberry (the most heat-tolerant) in zones 5 to 9; purple raspberry in zones 4 to 9. Best berry production occurs in regions with relatively cool summers and moderate winters. Excellent in the Pacific Northwest.

How to Grow: Purchase only certified virus-free plants. Do not propagate from older plantings because they may carry virus. Set out dormant woody suckers in spring, planting 1 inch deeper than in the nursery and spacing 30 inches apart. Best grown on a trellis to get fruit off the ground and promote air circulation, which reduces diseases. New canes must be thinned every spring and mature canes removed after bearing fruit. Fertilize each year in early spring; avoid using fertilizers containing chlorides. Apply no more than 5 pounds of 10-10-10 per 100 linear feet the first year and no more than 10 pounds in subsequent years. Apply organic mulch to prevent weeds and keep soil moist and cool; cultivating too deeply to control weeds injures shallow roots. Remove stray young primocanes that pop up nearby, to prevent the planting from becoming invasive.

Tends to get phytophthora root rot in wet soil. Occasionally troubled by verticillium wilt, spur blight, cane blight, anthracnose, crown gall, botrytis fruit rot; and by raspberry cane borers, crown borers, raspberry fruitworms, spider mites, raspberry sawflies, and Japanese beetles. Red raspberries can be symptomless virus carriers; don't plant susceptible black raspberries near reds of unknown virus status.

Harvest: When ripe, berries become soft, deepen in color, remove easily from plants, and taste sweet. Ripe berries don't keep well on the plant; harvest every few days. Expect a small crop the year after planting; production peaks in the third year.

Cultivars: Red raspberry: 'Heritage', excellent, widely adapted everbearer, adapts readily to single fall-crop culture or two-crop culture. Pacific Northwest—'Willamette', easy to harvest, rich-flavored, large fruit, vigorous plants; 'Meeker', excellent fruit size and quality; 'Chilcotin', productive, good quality, large fruit; 'Skeena', vigorous, productive, large fruit. East and Central—'Latham', old standard of average vigor, fruit size, and quality; 'Canby', excellent producer, good-

quality fruit, not thorny; 'Killarney', exceptionally beautiful fruit, high-yielding; 'Newburgh', large fruit, high-yielding; 'Boyne', high-yielding, average fruit size and quality; 'Taylor', excellent overall; 'Titan', unusually large, mild-flavored fruit.

Yellow raspberry: 'Amber', summer-bearing, widely adapted, excellent. 'Kiwi Gold', 'Fall-gold', and 'Goldie' all produce in late fall and are cold-hardy with good fruit size and quality.

Black raspberry: 'Black Hawk', late ripening, moderately productive; 'Bristol', excellent productivity, firm, glossy, sweet, rich-flavored berries; 'Cumberland', large, round, glossy, sweet, full-flavored berries, good productivity; 'Munger', early ripening, excellent-quality fruit; 'Allen', large fruit, productive, good flavor; 'Jewel', northeastern favorite, productive, large fruit.

Purple raspberry: 'Royalty', especially productive, large fruit; 'Brandywine', wonderful for jellies and jams, smaller berries than 'Royalty'.

EVITA JUNE-BEARING STRAWBERRY

STRAWBERRY
Fragaria spp.

Favorite fruit of the mythical goddess Venus, strawberries are a must for most home gardens. These small, herbaceous perennials, which send out lots of runners, don't require much space, and the explosion of berries is worth the after-harvest care. June-bearing strawberries (*Fragaria* × *ananassa*) more appropriately would be called "daylength sensitive" strawberries, since they fruit once a year when days are short—June in the North, much earlier in the South.

DAY-NEUTRAL STRAWBERRY

As their name implies, day-neutral strawberries (*F.* × *ananassa*) are not sensitive to daylength, and bear fruit throughout the growing season as long as temperatures remain between about 35° and 85°F. Day-neutral cultivars are resistant to soil diseases, hardy, and far more productive than the once popular "everbearing" types such as 'Ozark Beauty'. Plants are smaller than June-bearers, since more energy goes into fruiting. Fruit is smaller, too, but flavor is excellent. These berries are fussier than their June-bearing cousins. Plants are usually grown for only one or two seasons before being replaced, but the pleasure of picking strawberries in October makes coddling them rewarding.

Grow the tiny European alpine strawberry (*F. vesca*) for its pretty white flowers and intensely aromatic, wine red or creamy white fruit. The conical berries are petite *continued*

STRAWBERRY
(continued)

ALPINE STRAWBERRY

and form in small clusters above the pale green foliage. The flavor is similar to garden strawberry, but much more concentrated and wild, with notes of raspberry and even pineapple. A casual, every-other-day picking from spring through fall provides a light harvest of berries to top cereal or ice cream. If you neglect to pick them, berries simply dry up, so harvest isn't urgent. Plants are runnerless and small (6 to 8 inches high), and tend to be low-yielding, but self-sow readily to form pretty patches. Compact growth makes alpine strawberries well-suited to rock gardens and for edging paths.

Site: Plant June-bearing and day-neutral strawberries in full sun. Alpine strawberry grows best in part shade. All three prefer well-drained sandy loam with pH 6.2 to 6.5, but tolerate any soil that is not too heavy. Provide plentiful moisture during dry spells. Day-neutral types are most sensitive to drying out.

June-bearing strawberries are suited to zones 3 to 10, day-neutral berries to zones 3 to 8, and alpine strawberries to zones 4 to 10.

How to Grow: Purchase dormant, virus-indexed, June-bearing or day-neutral plants in bundles of 25. Plant as soon as possible in spring, taking care to avoid burying the crown.

Propagate alpine strawberries from seed or crown division. Start seed indoors, plant into rich, moist soil after danger of frost has passed.

Remove flowers and possibly runners (depending on system) from June-bearing and day-neutral strawberries the first year. Thin oldest alpine strawberry plants each year.

Renovate beds of June-bearers annually in the North after harvest, to keep the patch from overcrowding and to maintain productivity. Mow the plants with the lawn-mower blade set at a height of 3 inches and power-till the mulch into the alleys between rows. Don't worry about raking off what you've mowed; it breaks down rapidly. Reduce the width of matted rows to 12 inches and cover plants with 1 inch of soil to aid root development. Till under strawberry runners that stray into the alleys. Don't be timid! Wide matted rows are less productive than narrow rows filling the same space, so plan accordingly. Fertilize lightly when renovating or after harvest; apply 5 pounds of 10-10-10 (or equivalent) per 100 feet of row. Or, sidedress with compost, manure, or other organic fertilizer. Keep plants well watered if weather is dry. Stay on top of weeds the first year—mulch and cultivate to keep a clean bed. In the North, apply a layer of straw mulch over the entire bed in late fall to suppress weeds and protect the shallow-rooted plants from winter injury; be sure to wait until night temperatures dip between 20°F and 30°F or frost heaving may occur. Remove mulch as soon as possible in early spring. To accelerate flowering and fruiting, apply a lightweight, floating row cover over the bed after removing the mulch to let in light, but remove the cover before flowers open to allow in pollinating bees; be prepared to re-cover on frosty nights.

Do not renovate day-neutral strawberries and do not try to establish a matted row. Mulch them with straw after planting and provide a steady water supply, especially in hot, dry summers. Treat as an annual or leave in the ground for only two years and then replace with new plants. One month after planting, fertilize lightly each month of the growing season with 1 pound ammonium nitrate, or organic equivalent, per 100 linear feet. Productivity will decline after the second year.

Alpine strawberries benefit from weeding, fertilization, and winter protection in cold regions. Replant or divide every three or four years.

Depending on location and cultivar, strawberries may be affected by verticillium wilt, red stele, botrytis fruit rot (gray mold), leather rot, leaf spot, and leaf scorch; also tarnished plant bugs, strawberry bud weevils, spittlebugs, and spider mites. Slugs are especially troublesome. Gray mold and tarnished plant bugs are most problematic for day-neutral strawberries because the harvest season is longer.

Harvest: For maximum flavor, pick fruit a day or two after full color. Immediately remove any berries with a gray, fuzzy mold to avoid spreading the disease. Cool immediately after harvest. Store unwashed berries in refrigerator loosely wrapped in plastic; when you're ready to eat them, leave plastic on until berries come to room temperature.

Alpine strawberries are small and time-consuming to harvest; relatively flavorless until very ripe. Grow just a few and use for a pretty garnish.

Cultivars: June-bearing: Northeast, Mid-Atlantic and Midwest—'Earliglow', excellent flavor, early enough to avoid tarnished plant bug injury, resists red stele; 'Allstar', midseason, large, firm, orange-red color, resists red stele; 'Honeoye', midseason, bright red, good quality, firm; 'Jewel', midseason, large, attractive, excellent flavor; 'Scott', midseason, large, firm, good color;

'Bounty', late season, medium-large, bright red, good flavor, size decreases through season; 'Cavendish', late season, large, firm, good flavor, high-yielding, resists red stele; 'Delite', late season, good-yielding, glossy bright red, holds size well, large; 'Fletcher', late season, reliable, large, excellent flavor. Northwest—'Totem', excellent flavor, red throughout, good for freezing and jam; 'Puget Reliance', even better than 'Totem'; 'Shuswao', large, firm, glossy fruit; 'Redcrest', firm, medium-dark red fruit, good flavor, good for freezing and jam. South—'Cardinal', midseason, large, firm, bright red. Deep South and California—'Sweet Charlie', great flavor, resistant to anthracnose, large size; 'Chandler', widely adapted, productive, large fruit, firm.

Day-neutral: Lower Midwest, California and Florida—'Camarosa', 'Oso Grande' and 'Selva', all are large, firm-textured, mild-flavored berries that are raised commercially. North and East—'Tristar', medium-size, excellent flavor, resistant to red stele and verticillium wilt; 'Tribute', medium-large, firm, resistant to red stele and verticillium wilt.

Alpine: 'Pineapple Crush', creamy yellow berries, pineapple-strawberry flavor, bushy, earliest to bear, produces over long period; 'Alpine Yellow', pale cream to golden yellow, large, sweet fruit with intense flavor; 'Alpine White', tiny, white berries, runners, evergreen foliage; 'Improved Rügen', dark red, delicious, tangy flavor, heavy bearer; 'Baron Solemacher', deep red, about twice the size of wild berries, intense flavor, compact, bushy plants; 'Mignonette', excellent flavor, large red fruit, great edging or groundcover.

ALMOND
Prunus dulcis

Like their relatives, peaches and apricots, almond trees are covered with beautiful pink flowers in spring. The edible nut is a delicious oval seed or kernel contained in a hard shell

ALMOND

that's surrounded by a fleshy outer hull. Like apricot and peach seeds, almonds contain a substance called amygdalin, which provides the characteristic "almondy" flavor. (Peach and apricot seeds are inedible because they contain dangerously high levels of this bitter substance.) With proper care, almond trees can produce for 50 years or more.

Trees are vigorous. Dwarf and semidwarf trees reach 8 to 20 feet tall; standards, 20 to 30 feet.

Site: Full sun. Must have well-drained soil. Best in fertile site, but fairly tolerant of a range of soil types. Drought-resistant once established. Hardy in zones 6 to 9; best with warm summers and low humidity; performs consistently well in the central valleys of California and in some other areas of the Southwest.

How to Grow: Plant bare-root trees in early spring. Occasionally sold in late spring or early summer as containerized stock. Plant smaller trees 8 to 12 feet apart, standards 18 feet apart. Plant two cultivars for nut production.

Prune as an open-center tree.

Subject to same pests and diseases as peaches. Squirrels also are troublesome.

Harvest: Trees may begin to bear by the fourth year. Harvest nuts in summer by hand or by shaking the tree, after the leathery hulls begin to split. Dry the almonds in their hulls. Spread in a single layer; they'll rot if you pile them up. After two to three days, remove hulls and dry nuts in their shells for another week to 10 days. Store in an airtight container in a cool place or freeze the nuts.

Cultivars: 'Garden Prince', attractive genetic dwarf, showy pink blossoms, self-fruitful, early bearer, medium-size, soft-shelled, high-quality nuts; 'Hardy', large, easy-to-crack nuts, early bearing, cold-hardy; 'Hall's Hardy', attractive, fragrant, pink flowers, late-blooming, self-fruitful, heavy-bearer, large nuts with hard shells, cold-hardy; 'Nonpareil', widely grown commercial cultivar, smooth, broad, flat kernel with soft shell, excellent flavor, white flowers; 'Ne Plus Ultra', good pollinator for 'Nonpareil', white flowers, smooth, broad, flat nut with soft shell.

HAZELNUT, EUROPEAN FILBERT
Corylus avellana

A free-suckering shrub, the European species is the one grown most extensively for its filberts or hazelnuts. The flowers of this birch relative are long, dangling, yellowish catkins that bloom before the leaves appear in late winter or early spring. Plants grow 15 to 20 feet tall. The tasty, round, reddish brown nuts are enclosed by fringed, ornamental leafy bracts or husks, unlike the leathery husks of other nuts, and grow in clusters. They're delicious roasted and especially good in desserts and cookies combined with chocolate or coffee. Unfortunately, the plant is susceptible to Eastern filbert blight.

An alternative is the American hazelnut, a close relative, which is resistant and more cold-hardy. Its nuts are smaller than those of the European species and have closed husks, but taste delicious. *continued*

HAZELNUT
(continued)

HAZELNUT

Site: Full sun. Needs well-drained, deep, loamy soil. Choose a northern exposure to delay flowering in spring and escape late frosts. Hardy in zones 4 to 8; most widely grown in the Pacific Northwest, since spring frosts and hot, humid summers are limiting in other areas.

How to Grow: Plant bare-root plants in spring, spacing 10 to 15 feet apart, closer if grown as a screen. Transplants more easily than other nut trees. Plant two cultivars for cross-pollination.

Tends to develop a multistemmed, bushy habit. Bears on previous year's wood, so lightly thin each year during dormancy to encourage new growth. Protect from winter wind to reduce injury to catkins and wood. An organic mulch is beneficial.

Susceptible to eastern filbert blight, filbertworm, aphids, mites. Squirrels may devour the nuts, which are easily accessible; protect with netting.

Harvest: Pick up nuts as soon as they drop to the ground in fall. May bear heavily one year and not the next. Nuts are easy to crack.

Cultivars: 'Barcelona', widely grown, large nuts, susceptible to eastern filbert blight; 'Royal', large, soft-shelled, easy to crack, good quality, often planted as a pollenizer for 'Barcelona'; 'Du Chilly', slow-growing, large-size nuts may adhere to husks, distinctive flavor. Dwarf cultivars available.

Hybrids: Crosses with American hazelnut provide early-maturing, hardy plants resistant to eastern filbert blight, sold under the trade name Filazels: 'Gellatly', best-quality early filazel; 'Nut Washer Hazel', extremely thin shell that may crush during cracking, sweet flavor.

PECAN
Carya illinoinensis

This native tree has long been valued for its tasty nuts with a high protein and oil content. The pecan's native range extends from the Mississippi River basin into the Southeast. Trees may be large—75 to 150 feet tall—but still have a light, lacy quality. They leaf out early in spring and drop their golden brown leaves in early fall. The nuts are covered in husks; at maturity these split along four lines to release the delicious pecans. Pecans are thin-shelled, which makes them easy to crack, but also makes for voracious squirrel, jay, and crow feeding. Pecans make beautiful, stately shade trees. Plant on the south side of the house where they provide excellent shade in summer, but allow sun to filter through in spring and fall.

Site: Full sun. Deep, well-drained loam with pH 6.0 to 7.2 is best. Hardy in zones 5 to 9; needs long, hot summers with high night temperatures (rarely below 70°F) for good nut production.

How to Grow: Culture is like that of hickory. Trees may live for 200 years or more, so choose the location with care. Always plant two cultivars.

Occasionally troubled by anthracnose, leaf blotch, scab, and crown gall; scab is most common. Also

PECAN

bothered by weevils, scale insects, aphids, shuckworms, and, most seriously, squirrels.

Harvest: After the leaves fall, frost causes the husks to blacken and split, and nuts begin to drop. This can continue into winter; shake branches with poles to speed harvest and collect nuts immediately or squirrels will get them. A mature tree can bear up to 100 pounds of nuts each year.

Cultivars: Choose cultivars that start bearing at about the same age, as this can vary.

Lower Midwest and South: 'Cheyenne', medium-size nut with thin, soft shell, rich flavor; 'Pawnee', large, soft-shelled nut, excellent quality, productive, early bearing.

Midwest: 'Giles', medium-size, thin-shelled, well-filled nuts, good flavor, early bearing; 'Major, medium-size, easy-to-crack, excellent-flavored nuts, handsome ornamental.

Southeast: 'CapeFear', long-lived, early bearing, scab-resistant, kernels do not break during cracking; 'Sumner', large, high-quality nuts, early bearing, good scab resistance; 'Stuart', large, easy-to-crack, excellent-quality nuts, heavy bearer.

North: 'Colby', medium-large nuts, thick shell, good flavor, heavy bearer; 'Peruque', medium-size nuts with thin shells, excellent flavor, heavy bearer.

WALNUT, BUTTERNUT
Juglans spp.

Valued for its timber, attractive compound leaves, craggy branches, and distinctive, full-flavored nuts, black walnut (*Juglans nigra*) trees thrive in open areas where they

BLACK WALNUT

can't cause trouble to other plants. Locate trees far away from garden plants because roots and leaves exude juglone, an allelopathic compound that inhibits growth of plants such as tomato and rhododendron. Black walnut drops a lot of leaf litter and may not be suited to a groomed area. Trees grow to 100 feet tall.

The butternut (*J. cinerea*) is a beautiful native tree that develops large, heavy "tree-house" branching and can be used as a shade tree. Butternut contains less juglone than does the black walnut. Trees tend to be fast-growing and short-lived, reaching 80 feet high. Their nuts are a little easier to crack than black walnuts and taste much sweeter and milder. Butternuts are not widely grown because they are susceptible to butternut canker, a fungal disease that spreads through the branches and eventually kills the trees.

Mild-tasting and crunchy, Persian or English walnuts—and their cold-hardy relative the Carpathian walnut (all *J. regia*)—are delicious in baked goods and enjoyed right from the shell. The trees have their "roots" in Eastern Europe and grow to medium size, somewhat broad-spreading, handsome specimens. Trees reach 30 to 60 feet tall, depending on soil type and care. The large, rough-shelled nuts are contained in smooth, green husks.

Site: Full sun. Black walnut and butternut prefer a well-drained, rich, loam with pH 5.8 to 7.0. Water in dry climates.

English and Carpathian walnuts grow best in moist, deep, fertile, sandy loam, but tolerate poorer soil. Water deeply in dry areas, but don't overwater. Don't soak the trunk; crown rot may result.

Black walnut is hardy in zones 4 to 9, butternut in zones 3 to 9, English or Persian walnut in zones 6 to 9, and Carpathian walnut in zones 4 to 8. Sporadic winter weather and late spring frosts limit production of English and Carpathian walnuts in the South.

How to Grow: Purchase grafted or seedling trees. Taproot makes transplanting difficult, so dig a deep hole. Space 50 feet apart. Plant more than one cultivar for cross-pollination. Fertilize lightly each year. Water during dry spells. Black walnut and butternut can be planted from seed and still produce a bearing tree in 5 to 6 years.

Train to strong central leader with light annual shaping; don't prune from late winter into early spring because of inclination to "bleed." Trees are self-fruitful, but pollination is improved with two cultivars. Don't mulch with walnut leaves or other plant parts.

Walnut husk flies, walnut caterpillars, aphids, lacebugs, black walnut curculios, and weevils may be troublesome. English and Carpathian walnuts also are susceptible to codling moths, fruit tree

leaf rollers, filbertworms, and red-humped caterpillars. Anthracnose and blight are common.

Harvest: Gather nuts as soon as they drop in autumn to beat the squirrels, which love them. Black walnuts are covered by thick husks that stain hands; butternuts stain to a lesser degree. To easily husk tough-shelled black walnuts, pile nuts in the driveway and drive the car over them to remove the husks; this method doesn't break the hard shells. Or, tread on nuts with heavy boots. Handle husks with gloves to prevent staining. Cure in dry location for several weeks before storing.

Unlike black walnuts, Persians usually fall from their husks, but all nuts can be shaken from the tree when they first begin to split to avoid squirrel damage. Peel away remaining husk and wash to prevent stains. Cure in a cool, dry place for two to three weeks before storing.

Cultivars: Black walnut: 'Clermont', medium-size, thin-shelled nuts, excellent flavor; 'Rowher', easy-cracking, excellent quality; 'Thomas', large nuts with large, plump kernels, cracks fairly easily, rich walnut flavor.

Butternut: Watch for blight-resistant cultivars in the future. 'Kenworthy', large, easy-cracking, well-flavored nuts. 'Mitchell', medium-size, easy-cracking, well-flavored nuts; 'Craxeasy', medium-size, easy to crack, good producer.

English or Persian walnut: West—'Hartley', large nuts with thin shells, high quality, excellent flavor, good producer, self-fruitful; 'Chandler', large nuts with light-colored kernels, excellent flavor, small, late-blooming, heavy-bearing tree; 'Payne', medium-size nuts, early blooming, productive; 'Pedro', outstanding flavor, small self-fruitful, widely adapted tree. East—'Hansen', most widely planted, self-fruitful, medium-size, sweet, excellent-flavored nuts, early bearing. North—Plant hardy cultivars of the Carpathian race. 'Ambassador', high quality, plump buttery kernels, heavy bearer; 'Somers', medium-size, easy-to-crack nuts with mild, pecanlike flavor, early ripening.

VEGETABLES

CHAPTER 10

PLANNING YOUR VEGETABLE GARDEN

This vegetable garden is as beautiful as it is practical. The raised beds and vertical supports save space and foster healthier plants, while the neatly mulched paths keep the garden tidy and weed-free.

new area. An early start allows plenty of time to choose a good location, decide what and how much to grow, and work out a planting plan. But if you haven't made a plan, you still will have time to plant a garden

S tart small when planning your first vegetable garden. Excess ambition in spring often leads to exhaustion by late summer. Begin with a few favorites, then expand in later years as you gain confidence and skill. Experienced vegetable gardeners can save time and labor by adopting some of the intensive gardening techniques recommended in this chapter.

The best time to start planning a garden is in late winter, or even the previous fall if you need to dig up a

when you get inspired by all those tomato seedlings at the garden center in spring.

WHERE TO PLANT

B ecause most vegetables love sun, the ideal garden spot is an open area that receives eight to 10 hours of full sun each day. Some vegetables, especially leafy ones, tolerate part to light shade. (See Vegetables for Shady Places on page 449.) In the South, most vegetables appreciate a little shading from the hot late-afternoon

sun. Choose a location where the garden won't be an eyesore in the off-season or screen it with a low fence or hedge.

Watering is the most frequent chore vegetable gardeners face, so plant the garden close to an outside faucet or install one near the garden. Put the garden near the house, if possible. You're more likely to regularly check for pests, pull weeds, or pick beans when you have to take only a few steps outdoors. Your garden will be more productive for the attention.

CHOOSING YOUR CROPS

M ake a list of vegetables you'd like to grow, then read about them in the encyclopedia starting on page 462. Some vegetables are easier to grow than others. Lettuce and tomatoes, for example, are a breeze for beginners, but cabbage and celery are best reserved for experienced gardeners. Some vegetables require little space. Others, such as sweet corn and watermelon, demand a lot of room. Some vegetables prefer cool weather; others need a long, hot season. Cross off your list vegetables that are too demanding of your space, skill, and climate.

Remember, if you're new to gardening, keep the garden small and simple at first. It's more gratifying to grow four or five crops well than to watch a dozen limp along.

HOW MUCH TO PLANT

E xperience is the best way to gauge how much to grow of each vegetable. Check the Vegetable Planting Guide on page 457 to determine the average yield for each 10-foot row of a particular vegetable (when you space plants as indicated). Use that estimate to decide how much room you'll need for each crop. Weather and other factors can affect your yield from year to year. So can the planting method you use.

PLANTING METHODS

The traditional vegetable garden is a tilled plot with rows of crops separated by 2- to 3-foot-wide bands of empty soil, which serve as paths. Beginning gardeners often find this layout easy to work with, but it has several drawbacks. It wastes space that could be used for producing food. It leaves bare ground exposed, inviting weeds and allowing water to evaporate rapidly from the soil. It also promotes the spread of insects and diseases because each row contains the same type of plant.

A popular alternative is to arrange vegetables in small, dense plots, called beds. This technique, known as intensive gardening, has several distinct advantages. By growing vegetables close together in beds rather than in rows, you need less overall space to harvest the same quantity of crops. Densely planted vegetables shade the soil, discouraging weed growth and retaining moisture in the soil. The smaller beds are easier and less expensive to maintain. Intensive gardening prevents soil compaction and root damage to plants because you don't need to step into the garden to tend it.

Once you've selected a method of gardening, sketch a map of the garden's size and shape, and the crop locations.

RAISED BEDS

In soil that is full of clay or rocks, is highly alkaline, or is so shallow that root growth would be inhibited, gardening in raised beds lets you rise above the problem. A raised bed is an enclosed, thick layer of soil on top of the ground. Fill the bed with quality commercial soil or mix existing soil with compost or well-rotted manure.

A raised bed can be enclosed with boards, cinder blocks, bricks, landscape timbers, or railroad ties (ones not treated with creosote)—anything that gives it shape and holds the soil. Another option is to build a plateau of soil without walls. Then, at the end of the season, shovel any soil that washed from the sides back onto the mound.

A raised bed is usually 6 to 12 inches deep, which will accommodate the roots of most crops. Make the bed narrow enough so that you don't have to step into it: A width of 4 feet lets you reach into the bed from either side; if one side is against a fence or house, make the bed 3 feet wide. The bed should be at least 4 feet long. If you have multiple raised beds, build paths between them. Make the paths wide enough to accommodate a wheelbarrow—usually 3 feet is sufficient. Line the paths with a material such as grass, bricks, mulch, gravel, or wood chips to simplify maintenance.

The loose, rock-free soil in raised beds is perfect for root crops, which become stunted or deformed in heavy or rocky soils. Because raised beds drain well, they dry out and warm up quickly in the spring, allowing early planting. The only drawback is that they need more watering than flat ground during summer's hot, dry weather, especially in the South. Mulch to conserve water.

In regions such as the Southwest and the Rockies, where spring and fall can be windy and frigid and summer can be extremely hot, some gardeners reverse the raised-bed technique and garden in 1-foot-deep trenches. The soil stays cooler and damper in summer, and the trenches can be covered with protective plastic sheeting in spring and fall.

VEGETABLES FOR SHADY PLACES

Although most vegetables need at least six to eight hours of full sun each day, these vegetables do well with less sun.

PART SHADE
These plants produce well with two to six full hours of direct sun. They can tolerate shade from a building, hedge, or other structure.

Arugula	Cress	Pumpkin
Bean	Garlic	Radish
Beet	Kale	Rhubarb
Brussels sprout	Kohlrabi	Rutabaga
Cabbage	Leaf lettuce	Salsify
Cauliflower	Leek	Sorrel
Celery	Parsnip	Spinach
Chard	Pea	Summer squash
	Potato	Turnip

LIGHT SHADE
These vegetables produce well with two or fewer hours of direct sun, if the shade is bright or dappled or is cast from a faraway building or tree.

Chard	Endive	Radish
Cress	Leaf lettuce	Spinach

GETTING MORE VEGETABLES FROM LESS SPACE

A small garden doesn't have to mean a small harvest. Intensive growing methods can make the most of every inch of soil. Some techniques capitalize on spacing plants closely; others exploit differences in growing times. Fertile soil that is rich in organic matter is important for successful intensive gardening.

INTERCROPPING

Whether you garden in rows or in beds, you can increase your productivity from a small garden by intercropping, or alternating two closely spaced vegetables. The trick is to choose vegetables that complement rather than compete with each other. Combine short-season and long-season plants, tall and short plants, sun-loving and shade-tolerant plants, and above- and belowground plants. Intercrop radishes with beans or broccoli, for example, or intercrop peppers with onions.

To determine how far apart to space intercropped plants, add the recommended spacing for each vegetable and divide the sum by two. For example, onions should be spaced 2 inches apart and peppers should be spaced 12 inches apart, thus the distance between each onion and pepper plant should be 7 inches (2 plus 12 inches, divided by 2).

VERTICAL GARDENING

Another way to increase the number of plants in a small area is to train some to grow up rather than out. Vining crops such as squash and cucumbers take up less space when they grow up a trellis, lattice, or chain-link fence rather than spreading across the ground. Tall, weak-stemmed plants such as tomatoes and peas consume less space if they're staked rather than allowed to sprawl. Growing plants on supports also keeps them away from mud, rot, and small animals.

A trellis provides the best support for cucumbers, squash, chayote, vining peas, pole beans, and other tall climbers. For the frame, hammer tall posts or poles into damp soil at about 10-foot intervals. (Heavy steel fence stakes work well and are long-lasting.) Attach several cords or plastic-coated wires at 6-inch intervals horizontally between the posts, or stretch garden netting between the stakes. Gardeners with carpentry skills can build attractive wooden trellises or collapsible and movable A-frames, which last for years.

A tripod of tall stakes or bamboo poles can be used to support pole beans. Space three poles about 2 feet apart on the ground and bind them together at the top with twine. The twining vines coil up and around the poles.

Wire cages are commonly used to support tomatoes. Commercial tomato cages often are too short and flimsy

Intercropping, the close placement of plants with different needs, maximizes limited space. These lettuces have shallow root systems that don't compete with their neighbors, a row of scallions.

AUTUMN VEGETABLES

These crops ripen well in the autumn garden. Choose varieties recommended for planting from midsummer to fall.

Sow 6–8 weeks before the first fall frost.	Sow 8–10 weeks before the first fall frost.	Sow 10–12 weeks before the first fall frost.	Sow 12–14 weeks before the first fall frost.	Sow 15–17 weeks before the first fall frost.
Arugula Kale Leaf lettuce Mesclun Mizuna Mustard Spinach	Bok choy Radish Turnip	Beet Carrot Chinese cabbage Collards Pea Radicchio	Broccoli Cauliflower	Brussels sprout Cabbage

to support large plants. You can build sturdy cages using 4- to 5-foot-tall heavy fencing with a mesh that's wide enough to fit your hand through when harvesting. Surround a young plant with the cage; brace the cage with narrow wooden or metal poles if your garden is exposed to wind.

Bush peas need light support for their tendrils to grasp. Some gardeners push twiggy branches (called pea stakes) into the soil, stem end down and twiggy end up. Another method is to run twine at 6-inch intervals or use garden netting between 3-foot-tall stakes set at intervals along the row or in the bed.

RELAY PLANTING

Plant the following vegetables several times during the season, planting at two- to three-week intervals. Plant heat-sensitive vegetables, such as broccoli, early enough so that the last crop is harvested before hot days arrive.

Arugula	Kohlrabi
Beet	Lettuce
Broccoli	Pea
Bush bean	Radish
Carrot	Turnip
Corn	

SUCCESSION AND RELAY PLANTING

Succession planting and relay planting maximize yields by not allowing any part of the garden to lay fallow during the growing season. With succession planting, one crop follows another in the same garden spot, so you have spring, summer, and fall harvests of different crops.

You might plant a cool-season, short-season crop such as lettuce or peas in spring, then replace it with a warm-season, long-season vegetable such as tomatoes or beans. Or, you might follow a spring-planted crop that is harvested in midsummer, such as beets, carrots, or broccoli, with a short-season planting, such as lettuce or radishes, for fall harvest.

To maximize space and time, you often can sow seeds of the second crop beside or beneath the first crop before it is harvested.

Use the Vegetable Planting Guide on page 457 to plan a succession garden. Early spring vegetables are listed first. Check the days to harvest to determine if they'll be ready by early or midsummer in your region. Many of those vegetables also work in a fall garden. For summer planting, choose vegetables planted on or after the average date of the last frost.

Relay planting is a way to extend the harvest of a crop rather than have it ripen at the same time. Plant small quantities of the same vegetable every two to three weeks for a month or two. Make the next planting only after the first one is up and growing. Or, plant at the same time two varieties of the same crop with maturity dates that differ by at least two weeks.

Pea stakes support snow peas.

EXTENDING THE GROWING SEASON

By protecting plants from cold, you can plant a few weeks earlier in spring or harvest a few weeks later in autumn than you would ordinarily. Try one of these season-extending options:

■ COLDFRAMES. A coldframe is a bottomless box with a glass or plastic lid. Sunlight shining through the lid heats the air within. Protected by a coldframe, some cool-weather vegetables, such as lettuce, can grow early in spring or survive well into winter. The back of a coldframe usually is higher than the front and the window faces south to capture as much light as possible. On warm, sunny days, leave the lid ajar to keep plants from overheating.

■ HOT CAPS. Also called cloches, hot caps are glass or plastic covers that function as mini greenhouses to protect individual plants. For small plants, use inverted glasses or plastic cups, anchored with a rock on top if necessary. For large plants, use 1-gallon plastic milk jugs with the bottoms cut off. The opening at the top of a milk jug allows excess heat to escape. Use hot caps made of milk cartons or traditional clay cloches only at night to keep off frost; leave translucent plastic or clear ones on all day early in the season to warm the air around young plants.

■ ROW COVERS. Row covers can be sheets of clear plastic draped over hoops to form tunnels, or they can be lightweight spun-plastic fabric that's anchored on all sides and floats lightly on the plants. Both trap warm air over a row or bed, raising the temperature by 2 to 6 degrees Fahrenheit. Floating row covers are better ventilated and allow moisture to penetrate. They can stay in place longer into the season and also effectively protect plants from flying insects. Don't forget to remove the covers when plants bloom so pollination can take place.

■ PLASTIC MULCH AND LANDSCAPE FABRIC. Because dark colors absorb the sun, covering the soil with black plastic sheeting or landscape fabric warms the soil quickly in spring. You should be able to plant two to three weeks earlier than usual if you install the plastic or fabric a month before you would ordinarily plant. (Be sure to protect transplants from frost.) Black plastic also keeps the soil dry, and dry soil heats faster than wet. Remove the sheets before planting, or cut X-shaped slits in the material and plant through the slits.

Row Cover

Photo by Peter Krumhardt

Photo by Peter Krumhardt

Coldframe

Photo by Peter Krumhardt

Landscape Fabric

Photo by Peter Krumhardt

Plastic Tunnel

Photo by Peter Krumhardt

Hot Cap

PLANTING VEGETABLES

Fall is the best time to begin preparing the soil in anticipation of next spring's vegetable garden. Often, spring rains leave only a short period when the soil is dry enough to dig, but fall frequently offers a long dry spell. Moreover, working fresh animal manure or green manure into the soil in fall allows it to mellow over winter.

If you're beginning a new garden and need to remove existing lawn, see Easy Digging on pages 518–519. You also will find suggestions there for improving soil before planting, which is a good idea for almost every vegetable garden.

Gardeners planning to grow root crops or contending with soil that's clayey should consider double digging the first year they plant a garden. Double digging loosens the soil to a depth of 18 to 24 inches, making it easier to grow well-formed root crops and improving drainage in some clay soils. For more on double digging, see page 518.

For vigorous crops, add organic matter and fertilizer to your garden each year after you do the main digging, but before you plant.

ADDING FERTILIZERS

Vegetables need a good supply of nutrients to keep them producing well. You can fertilize in fall or spring. The type of fertilizer dictates when you need to apply it.

Once you've turned the soil in fall, add slow-release sources of phosphorus and potassium as well as other nutrients that a soil test shows to be deficient. Fall also is the best time to add lime or sulfur to soil that needs to have the pH adjusted. Don't add nitrogen in fall; it's water soluble and washes out before spring.

Gardens that were fertilized in fall should be treated with a slow-release source of nitrogen, such as bloodmeal, in spring. You don't need to apply additional phosphorus and potassium.

For gardens not fertilized in fall, apply a balanced, slow-release fertilizer in spring to supply nitrogen, phosphorus, and potassium.

PLANTING VEGETABLES

Before you plant, use a metal garden rake (not a leaf rake) to smooth the soil surface. A fine-textured bed enhances the contact between seed and soil that's necessary for good germination. Raking also removes any remaining rocks, twigs, soil clods, and other debris that can interfere with seed germination and root growth.

The soil you have carefully prepared now becomes the ideal home for your vegetable crops. Seeds of many vegetables can be sown directly into the garden, a method called direct seeding. Other vegetables more commonly are grown as transplants.

PLANTING METHODS

Make a row guide with stakes and string. Large seeds, such as corn, beans, and peas, can be sown individually. Make holes with a pencil or twig.

You also can use your finger or a tool called a dibble to make holes for large seeds.

Another way to plant seeds is to make a furrow, or drill, to the correct depth for the seeds you are sowing.

12"

Plant pumpkins, melons, and other warmth-loving seeds in mounds or hills. Make the mounds about a foot across.

DIRECT SEEDING

The Vegetable Planting Guide on page 457 identifies crops that usually are direct-seeded into the garden. Most seeds germinate a few days earlier than usual if you soak them in water or a weak solution of liquid seaweed for a day before planting. Don't soak bean or pea seeds, however, because they may split and not germinate.

The encyclopedia starting on page 462 specifies how deep to plant seeds of different crops; seed packets also give planting depths. As a rule, the bigger the seed, the deeper you plant it. For example, plant the large seeds of beans, peas, and corn 1 inch deep. Plant the tiny seeds of radishes and kale ¼ inch deep. For soil that's high in clay and dries slowly, plant a little shallower than recommended. For sandy soil that dries easily, plant a little deeper.

Gardeners use various methods to plant at the correct depth. Some scrape out a furrow with a trowel or hoe, then drop the seeds along the length of the furrow and push soil over the seeds. Others use a finger or a dibble (a pointed hand tool marked or notched like a ruler) to poke holes in the soil.

The best way to plant vining crops, such as squash, cucumber, and melon, is in hills. A hill is a cluster of six to eight seeds equally spaced within a 12-inch-diameter circle. The hill doesn't have to be a mound, but it can be. Mounded soil drains and warms quickly, encouraging seeds to germinate faster.

After planting seeds, sprinkle the garden gently with water to moisten the seeds and surrounding soil. Don't water deeply at this stage, because the seeds are near the surface. Keep the soil damp until the seeds sprout

SOWING SMALL SEEDS

Small seeds can be tricky to distribute evenly. Here are six ways to simplify the task:

■ Rub a pinch of seeds between your index finger and thumb while moving your hand along the row.
■ Put the seeds in an old salt shaker with a small amount of sand and sprinkle them on the soil mix.
■ Scatter seeds, then rake them in or cover them lightly with sand, potting soil, or vermiculite.
■ Mix the seeds thoroughly with white table sugar. Use a spoon to spread the mixture over the planting medium.
■ Fold a seed packet in half lengthwise, and align the seeds in the crease. Tap the packet to drop one seed at a time.
■ Run a strip of toilet paper down the furrow and drop the seeds on top so you can see them.

and the seedlings are several inches high and growing vigorously.

Beans, cucumbers, peas, and squash are an exception to the watering rule. They need extra-warm soil to germinate, and watering cools the soil. They sprout best in dry or barely damp soil, so plant them a little deeper than other seeds (about 1½ inches) and don't water until seedlings emerge.

When the weather is colder or wetter than normal, the germination time listed on the seed packet will double. If nothing comes up, dig in the soil with your finger. Do you see seeds sprouting? If not, they probably rotted, and you need to replant.

PLANTING IN BEDS

There are two methods for planting in beds rather than in rows. If you're sowing seeds of beans, beets, carrots, lettuce, peas, or spinach, you can broadcast the seeds—scatter them evenly over the entire area. Once seedlings emerge from the soil, thin them to the recommended in-row spacing on all sides. (Ignore the spacing between rows.)

For other vegetables, sow seeds or set transplants equidistantly in a staggered pattern. For example, for transplants spaced 12 inches apart, center each plant 12 inches away from the plants on all its sides. Space seeds as recommended for sowing; thin them once they emerge.

COVER CROPPING WITH GREEN MANURE

A cover crop or green manure is a plant—often a nitrogen-fixing legume—that's grown in the garden and then turned over into the soil where it rots and adds organic matter and nutrients.

You can broadcast seeds of a cold-hardy cover crop in fall. The seeds germinate and the crop remains green all winter, then continues to grow in spring until you cut it down. You also can grow the cover crop from one spring to the next, or through summer and plow it under in fall. If you leave the green manure on through summer, mow or cut it each time it begins to flower, letting the clippings fall to the ground. Otherwise it will go to seed and become a weed.

A few weeks before you plant your vegetable garden, mow or cut the cover crop. Let the cuttings dry on the surface for a few days, then turn them under with a spade or tiller. If you have a sturdy power tiller, skip the mowing step and churn the green cover crop directly into the soil.

Plants used as green manures include annual ryegrass, alfalfa, crimson clover, soybeans, winter wheat, buckwheat, sweet clover, vetch, ladino clover, winter rye, and Sudan grass.

PLANTING VEGETABLES
continued

A cover crop, also called green manure, adds organic matter and nutrients when it is tilled into the soil. Here, a fall-sown cover crop is cut and tilled into the soil with a power tiller.

Don't worry about spacing seeds perfectly when you plant. Thin out crowded seedlings to their recommended spacing once they emerge. Thinning is especially important for root crops, which become deformed if crowded. Remove small, spindly seedlings and leave the most robust. To prevent disturbing the roots of nearby seedlings, pinch off unwanted seedlings with your fingers or use a nail scissors to snip off "thinnings."

TRANSPLANTING

To give long-season vegetables a head start, especially in areas with a short growing season, plant small transplants directly in the garden rather than direct-seeding. You can buy transplants or start your own indoors. Shop for transplants that are compact, young plants without yellow or spotted leaves or overgrown roots. Set out transplants during cloudy weather to avoid wilting and transplant shock

Set most vegetable transplants at the same depth in the soil that they were in the pot. For cabbage and peppers, and tomatoes with short stems, bury the stem up to the lowest leaves; roots form along the buried stem. For leggy peppers and tomatoes with long stems, bury the stems at an angle to encourage more root growth.

GROWING TIPS

These vegetable-growing tricks will make your crops more bountiful and your garden more beautiful.

ROOT CROPS
■ Loosen the soil deeply before planting and remove all rocks, soil clumps, and other obstacles that can deform roots.
■ Sow radish seeds with seeds of other root crops. The quick-to-germinate radishes loosen the soil and are ready to harvest when the other crops are still small.
■ If root crops grow poorly, test the soil for phosphorus and potassium and fertilize as recommended.

LEAF CROPS
■ Provide enough water and nitrogen to keep leaf crops growing quickly.
■ Use floating row covers all season to deter insects and hasten growth.
■ Pick early in the day when leaves are crispest.

FRUITING CROPS
■ Don't overfertilize with nitrogen, or you'll get a lot of leaves but no fruit.
■ Remove floating row covers when flowers bloom to allow for pollination that results in fruit set.
■ Mulch to keep the soil evenly moist and to prevent blossom-end rot on peppers, squashes, tomatoes, and watermelons.
■ As the end of the season approaches, pinch off the tips of vining crops so their energy goes into existing fruit, not into producing new growth.

VEGETABLE PLANTING GUIDE

Vegetable	Planting	Thinning	Days to Harvest	Yield Per 10 Feet
SOW OR TRANSPLANT 4–6 WEEKS BEFORE LAST SPRING FROST DATE.				
Broccoli*	Transplants	12–24"	65–85	8 pounds
Brussels sprout**	Transplants	24"	100–150	6 pounds
Cabbage*	Transplants	18–24"	60–100	6 heads
Cauliflower*	Transplants	24–36"	65–100	5 heads
Chinese cabbage**	Transplants or direct-seed	12–24"	55–70	6 heads
Collards**	Transplants	18–24"	50–70	8 pounds
Kale**	Transplants	18–24"	50–70	8 pounds
Kohlrabi	Direct-seed	3–4"	40–60	5 pounds
Leek*	Transplants or direct-seed	6"	95–140	15 stalks
Lettuce*	Transplants or direct-seed	4–10"	45–80	20 heads
Onion**	Transplants or direct-seed	2–3"	110–130	10 pounds
Pea*	Direct-seed	2–3"	50–70	2 pounds
Rutabaga**	Direct-seed	4–6"	80–100	15 pounds
Spinach*	Direct-seed	2–3"	40–50	4 pounds
SOW OR TRANSPLANT 2–3 WEEKS BEFORE LAST SPRING FROST DATE.				
Beet	Direct-seed	3–4"	45–60	4 pounds greens, 10 pounds roots
Carrot***	Direct-seed	2–3"	55–110	10 pounds
Celery	Transplants	12"	75–90	10 bunches
Parsnip	Direct-seed	4–6"	100–120	8 pounds
Radish*	Direct-seed	1–1½"	28–36	100 roots
Turnip*	Direct-seed	4–5"	35–50	10 pounds greens, 5 pounds roots
SOW OR TRANSPLANT AT LAST SPRING FROST DATE.				
Bean (not lima)***	Direct-seed	2–3"	45–70	8 pounds bush, 15 pounds pole
Corn	Direct-seed	24"	60–100	6 ears
Tomato	Transplants	24–48"	50–85	15 pounds
SOW OR TRANSPLANT 2–3 WEEKS AFTER LAST SPRING FROST DATE.				
Bean, lima	Direct-seed	4"	70–90	1 pound shelled
Cucumber	Direct-seed in hills	36–48"	45–65	12 pounds
Eggplant	Transplants	18–24"	50–75	8 pounds
Melon	Transplants or direct-seed	12"	80–110	10 fruits
Pepper	Transplants	20–24"	50–70	5 pounds
Squash, summer	Transplants or direct-seed	16–24"	45–60	20 pounds
Squash, winter	Transplants or direct-seed	16–24"	85–110	20 pounds
Watermelon	Transplants	12"	70–85	7 fruits

*Suitable for late summer or fall planting in all regions **Usually a fall crop ***Planted in fall in the South
****Planted in spring and fall in the South

CARING FOR YOUR VEGETABLE GARDEN

After your vegetables are planted, loving care throughout the growing season will help them produce a good crop.

MULCHING THE GARDEN

One of the best things you can do for your vegetable garden is to mulch it. The effort spent mulching early in the season saves time on watering and weeding later and produces healthier crops. Mulching reduces evaporation from the soil and discourages weeds. Because you turn the soil in the vegetable garden each year, use an organic mulch—one that breaks down during the season and can be worked into the soil or one that can be removed easily.

Organic mulches for vegetable gardens include compost, composted apple pomace, composted manure, grass clippings, leaf mold, shredded leaves, and thin layers of newspaper. Mulches that are easy to remove at the end of the season include straw and thick layers of newspaper.

Mulch keeps soil from splashing onto vegetables. This benefit is especially valuable with low, leafy crops such as lettuce, spinach, and leeks, which must be washed free of dirt before you can eat them.

Wait to apply mulch until seedlings are several inches tall, to give the soil a chance to warm up and to avoid smothering tiny seedlings. If you're setting out transplants, mulch after the soil has warmed, but before weeds start. The mulch shouldn't crowd the plants. Keep the mulch about 2 inches from plant stems to prevent crown rot and stem rot.

The amount of mulch depends on the density of the material. For most mulches, a depth of 1 to 3 inches is sufficient. Less mulch doesn't suppress weeds and more mulch blocks oxygen from the soil.

Inorganic mulches for the vegetable garden include plastic sheeting and landscape fabric, which is a porous, clothlike plastic. See pages 522–525 for more information on mulches.

WATERING VEGETABLES

Most vegetables need about an inch of water each week, either from rain or irrigation. A rain gauge can help you monitor rain and irrigation amounts. But weather and soil conditions can affect the amount of water required. Vegetables require less water when the weather is cool and humid and more water when it's hot, dry, and windy. Sandy soil drains more quickly and needs more water than clay soil, which holds water longer—sometimes too long for healthy growth. Adding organic matter improves water retention in both types of soil.

Watch plants for signs that they need water. Water-stressed plants wilt in the heat, but perk up as night approaches. The leaves look dull and plants droop. Don't let plants become water-stressed because it stunts their growth and reduces production.

How often and how deeply you need to water depends on the crop. Shallow-root crops such as lettuce need fairly constant moisture from frequent, short waterings. Deep-rooted vegetables such as squash need less-frequent but deeper watering. The encyclopedia starting on page 462 identifies the moisture needs of individual vegetables.

See pages 542–545 for more information on watering systems and methods.

SUPPLEMENTAL FEEDING

During the growing season, most vegetables need feeding to boost the fertilizer you applied in fall or spring. Sidedress by applying a strip of balanced dry fertilizer beside the plants and raking it lightly into the soil surface. Take care not to damage roots. Another option is to apply a strip of rotted manure or compost. Sidedress leafy vegetables and root crops once, about midway between planting and harvest. Sidedress fruiting crops, such as tomatoes and peppers, when they begin to set fruit.

To feed with a liquid fertilizer, use manure tea, a diluted concentrate of seaweed extract, or liquid fertilizer according to label directions. Spray it onto leaves every three to four weeks (foliar feeding) or water it into soil around crops using a watering can.

Each feeding method has its advantages. Side-dressing lasts longer. Foliar feeding or watering with a liquid fertilizer is easier in densely planted gardens, and the nutrients from foliar feeding are available almost immediately. For soil that's infertile or has an extreme pH, foliar feeding also makes nutrients more readily available than other methods. See pages 512–517 for more information on types of fertilizers.

The pine straw mulch around this Swiss chard suppresses weeds and conserves moisture.

WEEDING

It's important to control weeds in the garden because they compete with crops, robbing them of nutrients, light, and soil moisture. Weeds also harbor insects and diseases.

The traditional method of controlling weeds in a vegetable garden is to use a garden hoe on the paths between the rows and a scuffle hoe between plants. This is a labor-intensive technique that must be repeated weekly for good control. Some gardeners use a minitiller to combat weeds in the rows. But you can save time and effort by mulching to prevent weeds and then hand-pulling the few that do appear.

CONTROLLING PESTS AND DISEASES

Although it's difficult, most gardeners learn to tolerate a little pest damage. A few holes or spots on lettuce leaves or a couple of blemishes on a tomato don't ruin the harvest. If the problem causes enough damage to decrease your yield more

An empty container serves as a collar on this red cabbage plant, stopping cutworms from girdling the stems.

than you can bear, be sure to identify the source of the problem before you treat it. For help identifying pests and diseases, check a reference book with good color photographs or take a sample of the crop damage to your county Cooperative Extension Service office or a reputable garden center.

After you identify the insect that is causing the damage, choose the least toxic control method. Hose off small insects with a hard stream of water. Pick off larger ones by hand. Stop cutworms from girdling stems of tender, young plants and dining on them by surrounding the stems with a collar made of newspaper, aluminum foil, or a small plastic container or by inserting nails into the ground on either side of the stem. Use insecticidal soaps or other insecticides only as a last resort and always use the least toxic product on your edible plants, following label directions explicitly.

Diseases are less prevalent than insects in vegetable gardens, but they can be more serious because many can't be treated. Disease prevention is critical. Environmental problems, such as excess water and air pollution, also can mimic diseases.

If only a few plants are affected, remove and destroy them. When many plants are affected, the symptoms are spreading rapidly, or the problem occurs year after year, have a laboratory analyze an affected plant. (Your county Cooperative Extension Service office can analyze affected plants or suggest a laboratory that can help.) See pages 546–555 for more information on controlling common insects and diseases.

Deer, raccoons, gophers, birds, and other varmints also can bother vegetable gardens. See pages 556–559 for more information on controlling animals.

DETERRING INSECTS AND DISEASES

Only a few insects and diseases seek out vegetable gardens. You can keep most of them from doing significant harm by following these simple guidelines:
■ Visit your garden often—daily if possible—and learn to look for trouble. That way, you'll catch problems before they become serious.
■ Grow plants adapted to your climate and soil. Fertilize and water when needed. Vigorous plants are better able to withstand insect and disease attacks.
■ When possible, choose plants bred to resist diseases. You'll find information on disease resistance in seed catalogs, on the seed packet, or on the label of the transplant.
■ Space plants widely in areas with poor air circulation and keep leaves dry, especially late in the day, by watering the soil with soaker hoses instead of sprinkling overhead. To prevent mosaic virus, don't smoke near plants. To avoid spreading diseases, don't work among wet plants.
■ Keep insects off plants by using floating row covers. Bury the edges of the covers to keep them from blowing off and to prevent pests from sneaking under.
■ Invite beneficial insects to your garden to prey on pests by growing a variety of flowering plants nearby. Don't use insecticides unless absolutely necessary.
■ Clean up and remove diseased and infested plants immediately.
■ Rotate crop families to break the cycles of diseases and insects. After a disease or insect problem, don't grow a susceptible member of the diseased family in the same area for two to three years. Create a small plot in a different part of the yard for that plant family.

HARVESTING AND STORING VEGETABLES

When you grow your own, you can enjoy a wonderful assortment of flavorful cherry and slicing tomatoes.

Vegetables are at their best—and tastiest—when they're picked in their prime. Harvest them too early and the texture and flavor are underdeveloped. Harvest them too late and they may be tough and bitter.

WHEN TO HARVEST

Harvest leafy crops, cucumbers, summer squash, and other watery vegetables in midmorning, after the dew dries, when they're most crisp. Harvest tomatoes, corn, peas, and other sugary crops in the afternoon, when their sugar content is highest.

PICKING AT THE PEAK OF FLAVOR

To tell when vegetables are at their best and are ready to harvest, follow these guidelines:
■ Check beans, beets, corn, cucumbers, peas, and zucchini daily.
■ Check eggplant, leeks, melons, peppers, and tomatoes every few days.
■ Check dried beans, Brussels sprouts, kale, parsnips, potatoes, and winter squash occasionally.

HOW TO STORE

Refrigerate harvested vegetables immediately or keep them cool by stashing them in a cooler or covering them with a damp cloth.

Don't wash vegetables before storing them because the dampness encourages rot. Instead, wash vegetables just before use. Leafy greens are an exception. Shake them in a basin of cool water and pat dry with a paper towel or spin-dry them before refrigerating.

Store most vegetables in plastic in the refrigerator's vegetable bin, which is somewhat warmer than other areas of the refrigerator. You can use plastic wrap or reusable plastic bags, but the best choice is a bag designed for vegetables. One type has a lining that absorbs the gas that makes vegetables ripen; another has tiny holes that release excess moisture. Both types maintain vegetables a little longer than regular plastic.

Store onions, potatoes, pumpkins, unripe tomatoes, and winter squash unwrapped and in a dry, cool place (55 to 65 degrees Fahrenheit). A root cellar is an ideal storage spot, as is an old-fashioned cellar with a hinged door that opens from the outdoors to steps leading into the cellar. Create storage in a window well or spread your vegetables on shelves in an unheated basement.

Daily checking and harvesting of green beans ensures capturing their peak of flavor and texture. Continual picking also makes the plants more productive.

ARTICHOKE, GLOBE ARTICHOKE
Cynara scolymus

Globe artichoke is a thistlelike, tender perennial with an edible flower bud. The 3- to 6-foot-tall plants

ARTICHOKE

yield well the second year, but decline after the fourth, at which time you should make a new planting. Artichokes are difficult to grow anywhere but in their ideal climate.

Site: Full sun. Rich, well-drained soil. Plentiful moisture. Best in a damp, mild, preferably frost-free area; may winter-kill in regions with freezing temperatures.
How to Grow: Add low-nitrogen fertilizer to soil before planting. Plant root divisions on average date of last frost. Space 2 to 3 feet apart in rows that are 3 feet apart.

After first season, remove thinnest, smallest plants. In cool regions, provide winter protection by cutting plants back to 10 inches high, covering with bushel baskets or rose cones, and burying with a pile of leaves or other mulch.

Remove aphids with hard stream of water from hose. No serious diseases.
Harvest: Cut off flower bud with 1 to 1½ inches of stem before it begins to open. Refrigerate in plastic for up to two weeks, or keep in cold, moist place for up to one month.

Cultivars: 'Green Globe Improved', 90 days from transplanting, productive, tasty, fleshy hearts, silver-green leaves; 'Imperial Star', 95 days from transplanting, high yields, thornless, early, mild flavor.

ARUGULA
Eruca vesicaria **var.** *sativa*

Arugula (also called rocket or roquette) is an easy-to-grow, leafy salad crop with piquant-tasting, lobed, dark green leaves. It tolerates cold—a fall planting can overwinter in most

ARUGULA

areas. The leaves develop a stronger bite in hot weather. Use in salads or sandwiches or steam as a green.

Site: Full sun to part shade. Tolerates poor, dry soil, but prefers fertile site and moderate moisture. Grows in a wide range of climates; best at temperatures below 80°F.
How to Grow: Sow seeds in spring four to six weeks before average date of last frost. For continuous harvest, sow at three-week intervals thereafter. Plant in late summer for fall and winter harvests. Sow seeds ¼ inch deep and 2 inches apart in rows spaced 12 inches apart. Thin to 8 to 10 inches when seedlings are a few inches tall.

Water during drought. Remove hairy flower stalks that form in center of rosette. No serious pests or diseases.

Harvest: Pick outer leaves while plants are still small, leaving inner leaves to keep growing, or cut off entire plant at soil surface. For free crop next season, let a few plants flower and set seed.
Cultivars: Usually sold as arugula or garden rocket. 'Sylvetta' is smaller and more bolt-resistant (see Bok Choy).

JERSEY KNIGHT ASPARAGUS

ASPARAGUS
Asparagus officinalis

A long-lived, cold-tolerant perennial, asparagus sports delicate, feathery leaves that are pretty enough for a flower border. Edible stems (spears) are a spring delicacy when young and tender. For highest yields and less effort, grow a cultivar that has only male plants. You can start asparagus from seed, but most gardeners find it easier to buy crowns. Pick your site carefully; a well-tended planting lasts for years.

Site: Full sun to part shade. Well-drained, deeply dug soil, high in organic matter; pH of 6.5 or higher. Moderate moisture. Most cultivars need a climate with a winter freeze.
How to Grow: If starting seeds indoors, plant 10 to 12 weeks before you plan to set outdoors. Sow seed ¼ inch deep and keep at 70° to 80°F.

Set out plants in spring two to three weeks after average date of last frost, spaced 10 to 24 inches apart. Plant crowns (dormant roots) four to six weeks before average date of last frost, spacing them 15 inches apart on top of loose soil, with roots spread out. Cover with 2 more inches of soil. If soil is poorly drained, plant in raised beds. Traditional method of planting crowns in trenches is no longer recommended. Remove perennial weed roots from bed before planting.

Water during first year if less than 1 inch of rain each week. Each spring and fall, apply 1-inch layer of compost or aged manure to soil surface. Mulch deeply with hay, straw, or leaves in midsummer to prevent weeds. Keep bed weeded. After stems brown in winter, cut back to 5 inches and remove cuttings. Apply winter mulch for protection; remove in spring so soil can warm.

To prevent asparagus beetles, remove brown stems in winter. Hand-pick beetles during growing season. Plant disease-resistant cultivars.

Harvest: If growing older male/female cultivars in cold climates, wait two years after planting to allow crowns to become established. In milder climates or if growing all-male cultivars, harvest lightly for two or three weeks one year after planting. Cut or twist tender, plump spears at base when 6 to 8 inches tall. Harvest season is about six weeks long for established plantings; stop harvesting when spears come up pencil thin. Store for up to one week in refrigerator, with stem bases in water.

Cultivars: Mostly male plants: 'Jersey Prince', thick spears, high yields; 'Jersey Knight', large, tender spears with purple bracts, resists fusarium and rust; 'UC 157', for mild regions such as California, the South, and the Northwest, high yields, good flavor; 'Larac', white spears when deeply mulched, tender, early, well-adapted, high yields; tolerates some cutting one year after planting.

BEAN
Phaseolus spp.

Once called string beans, snap beans (*Phaseolus vulgaris*) have had the "strings" bred out of them. They usually have thick, crunchy, blue-green pods, but also may be yellow (wax) or purple. Another type

GREEN CROP BUSH BEAN

is the French delicacy called filet or haricot bean, which is eaten when young and slender. Romano beans are flattened snap beans. Most beans grown as snap beans can be allowed

SCARLET RUNNER BEAN

to mature and develop ripe seeds for shelling. Beans bred for shelling and drying are diverse and lovely, including the dark red-brown kidney bean, gray-white navy bean, rose-pink pinto bean, and shiny, black turtle bean. Horticultural beans, which tolerate cool weather, have pink-and-cream pods. Eat the speckled seeds fresh from the pod or dried. Scarlet runner bean (*P. coccineus*), a favorite ornamental edible, is a quick-growing vine with red flowers that attract hummingbirds. Long green pods have pink-and-black seeds and can be eaten as snap, shell, or dried beans.

Snap and most shell beans come in two forms: bush or pole. Bush beans are 1 to 2 feet tall and stand upright. Pole beans are tall, twining vines that require support. Bush beans are ready for harvest earlier than pole beans, but pole beans produce a larger yield over a longer period.

Site: Full sun to part shade. Shading reduces yields. Well-drained soil with pH of 6.0 to 6.5; scarlet runner beans tolerate low fertility. Plentiful moisture. Beans grow in most climates; scarlet runner tolerates cooler weather than most and is excellent in the North.

How to Grow: For continuous harvest, plant every two weeks for four to six weeks. In the South, make another planting or two in mid- to late summer for fall harvest. Plant seeds 1 inch deep after last frost. Space bush beans 2 to 3 inches apart in rows 18 to 24 inches apart. Plant pole beans at base of a 6- to 8-foot-tall support, spacing seeds 2 to 3 inches apart in rows 3 to 4 feet apart, or plant six seeds at base of each pole and space poles 4 feet apart. Plant scarlet runner beans on average date of last frost, 1 to 2 inches deep and 3 to 4 inches apart; do not presoak or seeds may split. Thin to 6 inches.

Don't use high-nitrogen fertilizers, which can decrease yields. Pole and scarlet runner beans need support to climb, such as fence, trellis, or tripod made of poles.

Hose off aphids with hard stream of water. Control Mexican bean *continued*

BEAN
(continued)

beetles with pyrethrin. To prevent mildew, anthracnose, and bean mosaic virus, grow resistant cultivars. Prevent rust by not working among wet plants.

Harvest: Pick snap beans when pods are full size, but beans inside are still small. Daily picking keeps pods tender and increases yields for pole beans. Harvest French (filet) beans when pods are ⅛ inch thick and 4 to 6 inches long. Refrigerate in plastic for up to one week. Harvest horticultural beans when pod begins to feel rubbery and before seeds harden. For fresh shell beans, harvest when seeds are mature but still soft. For dried shell beans, pull plant when foliage turns yellow; let plants dry outdoors until beans are stone hard. Shell pods by hand or hold plant base and bang it against inside of box, pail, or fabric bag. Store in airtight jar in cool, dark place for up to one year.

Scarlet runner bean is usually ready to begin harvest in 13 weeks. Pick for snap beans before seeds have formed; may need to be stringed. Harvest for shell beans when desired size, and for dry beans when pods are crisp and brown. Dry as directed above.

Cultivars: Choose cultivars that mature before day temperatures stay above 80°F. Dozens of cultivars available. The following do well in most regions:

Snap bush: 'Contender', 40 to 50 days, 6-inch-long pods, tolerates heat, resists mildew; 'Venture', 55 days, long, tender, Blue Lake type, curved pod, high yields, resists mosaic virus, seed tolerates cool soil; 'Jumbo', 65 days, high yields, long, broad, flat pods, tolerates coolness; 'Royal Burgundy', 60 days, purple pod turns green when cooked, tolerates cool weather; 'Tendercrop', 55 days, round, tender pods, high yields, virus-resistant; 'Marbel', 54 days, filet type, purple-streaked, harvest when long and thin.

Snap pole: 'Kentucky Blue', 73 days, long, straight, deep green pods, extended harvest, tender even when large; 'Kentucky Wonder', 64 days, fleshy, tender 9-inch pods, also can be shelled fresh or dried; 'Romano', 70 days, long, wide pods, distinct taste, cans and freezes well.

Wax: 'Goldmarie', 67 days, pole type, intensely yellow Romano type, 10-inch pods, tender even when large.

Shelling: 'Pinto', 90 days, viney, can grow on pole, use dry or fresh shelled; 'Navy', 85 days, small semivining, white, oval bean; 'Red Kidney', 100 days, reliable, pods inedible, beans large, flavorful; 'Adzuki', 90 days, long, narrow pods, high yielding, can be eaten as snap bean when immature; 'Black Turtle', 85 days, dwarf bush type, high yields, not adapted to the extreme North, can be eaten as snap bean when immature.

Scarlet runner: Choose types sold as vegetables, not ornamentals, for best production; bush types aren't very productive. 'Scarlet Emperor', 70 days, large, flavorful pods; 'Red Knight', 70 days, 10- to 12-inch stringless pods.

BEET
Beta vulgaris

Growing beets gives you two vegetables in one: the fleshy taproot and the leafy tops. Taproots may be red, white, or yellow; round or carrot-shaped (carrot-shaped roots yield uniform slices). Most beet cultivars are all-purpose, but some are best for specific uses, such as salads, canning, pickling, or winter storage, so match the beet to your needs.

Site: Full sun to part shade. Loose, deep soil high in organic matter; poor to moderate fertility; ideal pH of near 7.0, tolerates alkalinity. Consistent moisture prevents "zoning," or rings, in taproot. Adapted to most climates; prefers cool weather.

How to Grow: Before planting, remove stones and soil clumps. Sow seeds two to three weeks before average date of last frost. For continuous harvest, plant every two to

ACTION BEET

three weeks through midsummer. In the South, also plant from late summer through mid fall. Plant seeds ½ to 1 inch deep and 1 inch apart, in rows 16 inches apart. Thin seedlings to 3 to 4 inches apart when 4 inches tall.

Keep soil moist. When seedlings are 4 to 5 inches tall, mulch to retain soil moisture and reduce temperature fluctuations, which can make beets pale. Hill soil over shoulders of carrot-shaped roots emerging from soil.

Prevent scab by keeping pH near 7.0. Leaf miners may tunnel within leaves; pull off and destroy affected leaves. Boron deficiency may make black, corky spots in roots; test soil before treating with borax.

Harvest: Harvest baby beets for fresh eating when roots start getting round. Red round beets are best when 1½ to 2 inches in diameter. White and yellow still are tender when 2 to 3 inches in diameter. Carrot-shaped beets are ready when shoulders of root push out of soil, but can be harvested later. Red beets "bleed" when cut, so twist off leaves instead of cutting. Steam leaves and eat like spinach. For winter storage, remove tops and keep roots in cool, humid place (don't allow to freeze). Refrigerate beets for five to seven months in perforated plastic bag filled with damp sawdust, peat moss, or sand, or store in root cellar. Refrigerate greens in plastic for up to one week.

Cultivars: Round: 'Action', 48 days, good for baby or mature beets, remains sweet with age; 'Early Wonder', 50 days, for greens or roots, roots suited to table, canning, or pickling; 'Red Ace', 50 days, early, uniform, for roots and tops; 'Detroit Dark Red', 58 days, spring or fall, for greens and roots, roots suited to table, storage, or canning; 'Lutz Green Leaf', 80 days, fall harvest, stores well.

Carrot-shaped: 'Cylindra', 60 days, dark red, 8 inches long, tender, for salads or pickling; 'Formona', 60 days, dark red, 8 inches long, sweet, for salads or pickling.

Baby: 'Kleine Bol' ('Little Ball'), 50 days, uniform, small, tender, for fresh or pickling; 'Pronto', 58 days, uniform color and shape, very sweet, doesn't become woody.

Unusual: 'Apoundina Vereduna', 58 days, white, nonbleeding, tender when large, for table or pickling; 'Burpee's Golden', 55 days, bright gold, nonbleeding, for roots and greens, use roots fresh or cooked, best small; 'Chioggia', 55 days, flat, pink-and-white candy-striped rings.

BOK CHOY, PAK CHOI
Brassica rapa (Chinensis Group)

The name bok choy can be confusing, because sometimes it is used for two other members of the cabbage family, Chinese cabbage and Michihli. Bok choy forms a loose head of leaves; the other two form tight, compact heads. Its thick, white, fiberless leaf stalks also have a milder flavor. Most cultivars need a short day length not to bolt (send up a flowering stalk without forming a head); a few tolerate any day length.

Site: Full sun to part shade. Fertile soil; tolerates sand and clay. Plentiful moisture. Adapts to most climates.

MEI QING CHOI BOK CHOY

How to Grow: Direct-seed daylight-insensitive cultivars in spring on average date of last frost or in mid- to late summer. Sow day-length-sensitive cultivars only in mid- to late summer. Plant seeds ½ inch deep and 3 to 4 inches apart in rows 2 to 2½ feet apart. Thin to 10 inches apart. Eat thinnings in salad or stir-fry. For continuous harvest, plant three to four more times at two-week intervals.

Keep soil moist. Needs nitrogen to grow quickly; side-dress with dry fertilizer every four weeks or apply liquid manure tea or seaweed every two weeks.

Use floating row covers to protect from cabbage worms, cabbage loopers, and flea beetles. Treat worms and loopers with BT and flea beetles with pyrethrin. No serious diseases.

Harvest: Pick outer leaves as needed, or cut whole head when large and weighing 3 to 4 pounds. Refrigerate in plastic for up to three weeks. Store in cool, moist place for up to six weeks.

Cultivars: 'Mei Qing Choi', 30 days for baby, 45 for full, mini heads 6 inches high, fast-growing, crisp stem, tender leaves, for spring or fall planting; 'Joi Choi', 45 days, white stems, glossy, dark leaves, for fall planting, frost-tolerant, resists bolting; 'Shanghai', 45 days, tolerates warm weather, for spring or fall planting, stems tinged green.

BROCCOLI
Brassica oleracea (Botrytis Group)

Growing your broccoli frees you from the constraints of commercial growers—they choose cultivars that produce tight, large main heads that ship and market well. Grow what tastes best to you, even if it has a small main head and many side shoots. Whatever type you grow, it will be nutritious—broccoli's stems and dense green heads of unopened flowers are vitamin-rich. Like other members of the cabbage family, broccoli prefers cool weather and endures a light frost. If the weather is too hot or cold, the plant may bolt (see Bok Choy).

GREEN GOLIATH BROCCOLI

Site: Full sun to part shade. Fertile soil with pH of 6.0 to 7.5. Plentiful moisture. Best where weather is cool (below 80°F) long enough for head to form (about 70 days).

How to Grow: If starting indoors, sow seed four to six weeks before you plan to set out transplants. Set out transplants in spring four to six weeks before average date of last frost or, for fall harvest, in midsummer in the North and late summer in the South. Mix ¼ to ½ cup of low-nitrogen *continued*

BROCCOLI
(continued)

organic fertilizer in the planting hole; too much nitrogen makes stems hollow. Space transplants 12 to 24 inches apart; closer spacing encourages more side shoots, wider spacing encourages larger main heads. In regions with long cool season (summer in the far North, winter in the Deep South), direct-seed outdoors four to six weeks before last frost. Plant seeds ½ inch deep and 3 inches apart, thinning to 18 inches when several inches high.

Mulch to keep soil cool and moist. Side-dress overwintering types with balanced dry fertilizer in midwinter.

To control cutworms, stick nail into soil beside young transplant's stem to block cutworm. Prevent cabbage worms and cabbage loopers by covering young plants with floating row cover; treat infestation with BT.

Harvest: Cut off central head when full size with plump flower buds, but before flowers open. Leave base of plant in ground. Smaller side stems will sprout for later small harvests. Refrigerate in plastic bag for up to two weeks.

Cultivars: Maturity times are from date of transplanting; add about 35 days from seed. 'Green Comet', 40 days, early, deep green heads 6 to 7 inches across, smaller heads after cutting, high yields; 'Packman', 55 days, early, large head, side shoots after cutting, tender, mild; 'Premium Crop', 58 days, early, firm, blue-green heads 9 to 10 inches across, delicate flavor, freezes well; 'Purple Sprouting', 125 days, long-season, fall-winter type (sow in late spring to summer for harvest in fall or winter), many small purple heads; 'Green Goliath', 55 days, heavy producer, many side shoots.

BRUSSELS SPROUT
Brassica oleracea (Gemmifera Group)

The small, round, cabbagelike sprouts of this favorite winter vegetable grow along the sides of a thick, 2- to 3-foot-tall stem. Like others in the cabbage family, Brussels sprouts require cool weather. In fact, a frost so improves their sweet, cabbagey flavor that some gardeners recommend planting late for a fall harvest. There are two types of Brussels sprouts: Tall types mature late and have long-stalked, teardrop-shaped sprouts that are easy to harvest. Dwarf varieties with closely spaced, tightly clinging, round sprouts mature early and are winter-hardy, but are more difficult to pick.

BRUSSELS SPROUT

Site: Full sun to part shade. Low fertility tolerated; ideal pH range is 6.5 to 7.5. Moderate moisture. Needs about 80 days of spring or fall weather below 80°F. Mature plants hardy to low 20s. Can sow in fall and overwinter for early spring harvest in mild climates.

How to Grow: If starting indoors, plant seed four to six weeks before you plan to set out transplants. Set out transplants in spring four to six weeks before average date of last frost. For fall harvest, plant in midsummer in the North and late summer after heat has passed in the South. Space transplants 15 to 20 inches apart in rows 24 to 30 inches apart.

Water if plants receive less than 1 inch of rain weekly. To increase size of upper sprouts and ensure all sprouts are ready to pick at one time, pinch off top 6 inches of plant when lower sprouts are ½ to ¾ inch in diameter.

Prevent cabbage worms and cabbage loopers by covering new transplants with floating row cover; treat infestation with BT.

Harvest: For best flavor, pick after light frost, when 1 to 2 inches in diameter, bright green, firm, and round. Unless you trim off plant top, sprouts mature from bottom of plant up. Pick lowest ones first, removing leaf below sprout before picking sprout itself. Refrigerate in plastic for up to two weeks. Or, harvest entire stalk and store in cool root cellar for three to four weeks. Flavor best immediately after harvest; cabbagey taste intensifies with storage.

Cultivars: Dwarf: 'Jade Cross E', 80 days, early, tolerates range of climates and soils, large, blue-green sprouts, long stalks, freezes well; 'Oliver', 90 days, very early, good for short growing season, large, medium-green sprouts.

Tall: 'Rubine', 125 days, lovely ruby red sprouts and leaves; 'Long Island Improved', 100 days, teardrop sprouts, high yields, freezes well; 'Valiant', 110 days, round sprouts on longer stems, good flavor, high yields.

CABBAGE
Brassica oleracea (Capitata Group)

Cabbage is easy to grow and tastes sweeter from the garden than the grocery. A cool-season crop like its relatives broccoli and cauliflower, cabbage tends to resist bolting (see Bok Choy) during warm weather. Early types (planted in early spring for a late-spring harvest) have round or pointed small heads, mature quickly, and are milder than other

RED ACRE CABBAGE

types. Midseason cultivars, medium to large heads, can be planted for spring or fall harvest. Late types have large, round or flat heads, mature slowly, keep well, and should be planted in summer for a fall harvest. Early-maturing cultivars store least well. Later types can stay in the garden for several weeks after reaching full size. Red cabbages keep well and resist insects; savoy cabbages have a strong flavor and thin, crinkled leaves.

Site: Full sun to part shade. Fertile soil with pH between 6.5 and 7.5; tolerates most soils. Plentiful, consistent moisture prevents heads from splitting. Needs about 60 to 90 days of spring or fall temperatures between 25° and 80°F.
How to Grow: Start spring plantings from transplants and fall plantings from seed. If starting indoors, plant seed four to six weeks before you plan to set out transplants. Set out transplants in spring four to six weeks before average date of last frost. Mix 1½ to 2 cups of complete fertilizer in each planting hole. Space transplants 18 inches apart for small cultivars and 24 inches apart for large cultivars in rows 18 to 34 inches apart. For fall harvest, direct-seed in midsummer in the North and late summer in the South. Plant seeds 1 inch deep and 3 inches apart in rows 24 to 36 inches apart, thinning to 18 to 24 inches when several inches high.

Water if plants receive less than 1½ inches of rain weekly in hot weather. Mulch to keep soil moist. If head begins to crack, give it ¼ rotation to break roots and decrease water uptake. You also can prevent splitting by harvesting immediately when mature.

Prevent cabbage worms, root maggots, and cabbage loopers by covering young transplants with floating row cover; treat infestation with BT. Red cabbages are less prone to insects. Prevent club root by applying lime to acidic soils.
Harvest: Thin out and eat young, crowded plants. Cut full-size heads before they split. Heads are ready to harvest when firm and solid. Cut head and a few leaves from stem. At 32°F and 98 to 100 percent humidity, early types keep for one to two months and late types for up to six months.
Cultivars: Early: 'Early Jersey Wakefield', 63 days, heirloom, 2- to 3-pound, pointed head, waxy, dark green, resists splitting; 'Julius', 75 days, savoyed blue-green leaves, round, 3- to 5-pound green head, resists splitting; 'Red Acre', 70 days, 3 to 4 pounds, resists splitting; 'Ruby Ball', 75 days, firm, 3- to 4-pound, red head, resists splitting; and 'Speedy Savoy', 75 days, dark blue-green, disease-resistant.

Midseason: 'Ruby Perfection', 85 days, round, 4-pound, red head, resists splitting, stores well; 'Chieftan', 88 days, flat, 4- to 6-pound, blue-green head, highly savoyed, summer crop.

Late: 'Stonehead', 100 days, tightly packed, blue-green, 5 pounds, disease-resistant, long keeper; 'Red Rodan', 140 days, tender, 3-pound, hard, round, red head; 'January King', 160 days, flat, 3- to 5-pound, green head with purple marks, cold-hardy.

CARROT
Daucus carota var. *sativus*

Grow supersweet carrots not adapted to commercial production in your garden. There are six types of carrots, classified by shape and length. Imperator types are 8 to 10 inches long, slender, and tapering. Danvers are 6 to 7 inches long, wide at the top and tapering to the tip; they store well, but can be dry and strong-flavored. Nantes are cylindrical and blunt, 5 to 7 inches long, sweet and juicy, best eaten fresh. Chantenay are 4 to 5 inches long, wide at the top and tapered to the tip, and do well in heavy soils. Amsterdam are 2 to 3 inches long, thin fingerlings. Paris Market are short and round, like radishes. Within each type are dozens of cultivars.

BERTAN CARROT

Site: Full sun. Deep, loose, cool soil high in organic matter, free of rocks, clumps, twigs, and other obstacles. Plentiful, consistent moisture. Needs cool season of at least 65 to 80 days between 40° and 85°F.
How to Grow: Before planting, till deeply to loosen soil, break up clods, and remove stones so roots grow straight. In the North, plant in spring two to three weeks before average date of last frost. Make subsequent plantings every two to three weeks until midsummer. In the South, plant from mid winter to early spring and again from midsummer to late fall. Plant seeds ½ inch deep *continued*

CARROT
(continued)

about ¼ to ½ inch apart in rows 12 to 16 inches apart. Thin seedlings to 2 to 3 inches so they have room to grow straight and thick. Repeat thinning two or three times during season, because carrots germinate over several weeks. Heavy or rocky soil can cause twisted or forked roots; grow short cultivar, or grow in raised beds or containers.

Keep soil moist, especially as seedlings emerge. To prevent cracking, water less as plants near maturity. Mulch to keep soil cool and moist, discourage crusting and weeds, and prevent exposed shoulders from turning green and bitter.

Prevent maggots and carrot rust flies by covering young seedlings with floating row cover. Prevent blight by removing carrot plants at season's end and by growing carrots in same area only once every three years.

Harvest: Pick anytime after full color develops, but while still tender. Large types wait better than short ones. Store in garden by laying carrots on surface and covering with thick layer of straw or other loose mulch. To store indoors, remove tops, then refrigerate in plastic. Or, layer in leaves, sand, or sawdust and keep cold and moist, but above freezing in cellar or garage.

Cultivars: Long types remain sweet longer than shorter types.

Hybrids: 'Bertan', 70 days, remains sweeter longer, resists splitting, 6 inches; 'Ingot', 55 days, extremely sweet, 8 inches.

Imperator: 'King Midas', 65 days, colors early, harvest when baby size or full size, nearly coreless, crisp, sweet; 'Blaze', 68 days, fresh taste, disease-resistant, stores well.

Danvers: 'Danvers', 70 days, tolerates heavy soil, high fiber, keeps well.

Nantes: 'Napoli', 60 days, sweet, tolerates crowding, resists forking; 'Rondino', 64 days, high yields, sweet, brittle, uniform; 'Nantes Half Long',

69 days, sweet, 8 inches long, good for heavy soil.

Chantenay:'Royal Chantenay', 70 days, dark orange, juicy, uniform; 'Chantenay Supreme', 70 days, deep orange, smooth skin, small core.

Amsterdam: 'Minicor', quick-rooting, uniform, good for canning.

Paris Market: 'Thumbelina', 60 days, 1- to 1½-inch diameter, good color and flavor, holds sweetness, tolerates crowding, container growing, and heavy soil; 'Planet', 68 days, orange-red, good flavor; 'Orbit', 50 days, sweet, resists splitting after maturity.

CAULIFLOWER
Brassica oleracea
(Botrytis Group)

Like others in the cabbage family, cauliflower is a cool-season crop. The edible head, or curd, is a collection of unopened flower buds. Besides the usual creamy white types, you can grow green or purple cauliflower.

WHITE CORONA HYBRID CAULIFLOWER

Cauliflower is finicky, dislikes bad weather, and requires pampering. It may be grown in spring, but warm temperatures make the curd ricey, so it does best as a fall crop. To increase success, try planting several cultivars with different maturity dates. In zones 8 through 10, plant overwintering types by August 1 for an early spring harvest.

Site: Full sun or part shade. Well-drained soil high in organic matter; pH of 6.5 to 7.5. Plentiful moisture. Needs two months of temperatures between 55° and 80°F. Performs poorly in extreme heat, cold, or dryness.

How to Grow: In regions without hot summers, direct-seed cauliflower outdoors. Plant about 10 seeds ½ inch deep in a clump, spacing clumps 2 feet apart. When seedlings come up, remove all but strongest one from each clump. Elsewhere use transplants. If starting indoors, sow seeds six weeks before you plan to set out transplants. In the North, set out transplants in spring four to six weeks before average date of last frost. For fall harvest, plant in midsummer in the North (60 to 90 days before average date of first hard fall frost) and late summer in the South. Mix ¼ to ½ cup of complete organic fertilizer in hole at planting time or apply a high-nitrogen fertilizer at planting, then once a month until harvest. Space plants 18 inches apart in rows 24 to 36 inches apart. If transplants are leggy, plant deeply—up to base of lowest leaves.

Mulch to keep soil cool and moist. Fertilize annual types monthly with liquid fertilizer. Fertilize overwintering types after late January only, using high-nitrogen fertilizer such as blood meal. Protect early plantings from frost. When small heads are visible on white cultivars, blanch them to prevent brown spots and keep them sweet; pull outer leaves over head and fasten with twist-tie, rubber band, or clothespin. Or, grow self-blanching types with leaves that cover heads, or colored cultivars.

Prevent cabbage worms, root maggots, and cabbage loopers by covering transplants with a floating row cover; treat an infestation with BT.

Harvest: Cut off head when it's full and still compact, usually one or two weeks after head first appears. The head loosens up as it passes its prime. Refrigerate in plastic for up to one week, or leave on stalk, place stalk end into pot of soil, and store in root cellar for up to one month.

Cultivars: 'Snow Crown', 55 days, rapid growth, mild sweet flavor, spring or fall; 'White Rock', 90 days, small plants, self-blanching; 'Alverda', 90 days, green head, uniform; 'Violet Queen', 70 days, large purple head turns green when cooked; 'Purple Cape', 200 days, overwinters, needs frost protection, bright purple, sweet; 'White Corona Hybrid', 30 days, 4-inch single-serving-size heads, heat- and mildew-resistant.

CELERIAC, CELERY ROOT, KNOB CELERY
Apium graveolens var. *rapaceum*

A type of celery grown for its large, swollen, white root, celeriac is a popular winter vegetable in Germany

MENTOR CELERIAC

and Eastern Europe. It tastes like sweet, starchy celery with a hint of parsley. Use it to flavor soups, juices, and stews, or shred it with carrots to make a slaw.

Site: Full sun to light shade. Fertile soil, high in organic matter. Constant moisture. Best in cool climates; grows poorly if there are long hot spells.

How to Grow: If starting indoors, plant seeds six to seven weeks before you set out transplants; seeds are slow to germinate. In the North, set out transplants on average date of last frost, spacing 6 to 8 inches apart in rows 24 to 36 inches apart. In the South, set out transplants in late summer or direct-seed in spring, sowing seeds ½ inch deep and ½ inch apart. When seedlings have two true leaves, thin to 6 to 8 inches.

Shallow-rooted celeriac requires regular watering; if soil dries, vegetable toughens. Mulch to keep soil moist and prevent weeds. Gently pull any weeds that appear. Clip off side roots.

No serious pests or diseases.

Harvest: Harvest in fall after first or second light frost, when tuber is 3 to 4 inches around; or leave in garden, protected with thick straw mulch. To store, cut off tops ½ inch above crown and refrigerate unwashed for up to one week, or keep in sawdust or straw in a cold, moist place for up to three months. Cook or use raw. Peel off brown skin before preparing.

Cultivars: 'Brilliant', 110 days, uniform, round, buff skin, white interior, stores well; 'Mentor', 110 days, high yields, tolerates frost, white interior; 'Dolvi', 150 days, white interior, good texture, stores well, disease-resistant.

VENTURA CELERY

CELERY
Apium graveolens var. *dulce*

Celery, a member of the parsley family, is finicky. It can be a challenge to grow because it doesn't like to be too cold or too hot. You can blanch it to make the stalks tender and sweeter for fresh eating, or leave it unblanched to give it a strong flavor that's good in soups and stews. Celery likes wet soil, so it's a good choice for a boggy spot.

Site: Full sun to part shade. Needs moist, fertile soil high in organic matter with an adequate supply of magnesium and calcium. Tolerates wet soil; best with even moisture. Best in long, cool growing season where temperatures stay between 55° and 85°F. Celery bolts (see Bok Choy) if conditions are too cold.

How to Grow: If starting indoors, plant seeds 10 weeks before you plan to set out transplants. Set out transplants two to three weeks before average date of last frost in the North and in late summer in the South. Space transplants 12 inches apart in rows 18 inches apart. In regions with long mild season (summer in the extreme North and winter in the Deep South), sow directly in garden. Create loose, moist area for seeds by removing soil from 3-inch-deep trench, then filling it with 2 inches of loose garden soil and 1 inch of vermiculite. Plant seeds ½ inch deep and 1½ inches apart. Gradually thin out weak plants until seedlings are spaced 12 inches apart.

Keep soil moist. Use liquid fertilizer every three weeks. If desired, blanch for two weeks before harvest to make stalks tender and sweeter. To blanch, shield stalks from sun with heavy paper, bottomless milk carton, soil, or other barrier. Leaves should be exposed.

No serious pests. To control diseases such as pink rot, black heart, and blights, make sure soil has adequate calcium and magnesium or spray plants with liquid seaweed.

Harvest: When head is 2 to 3 inches in diameter at base, cut off entire head at soil line. To prolong harvest in climates with mild winters, cut off outer stalks, leaving inner stalks to continue growing. Refrigerate in *continued*

CELERY
(continued)

plastic for up to two weeks. Store in cold, moist place for two to three months.

Cultivars: 'Golden Self-Blanching', 115 days, compact, stocky plants, tender nonfibrous hearts and stalks, requires no blanching; 'Ventura', 80 days, upright, well-developed heart, tall, crisp stalks, widely adapted, some disease resistance; 'Utah 52-70r Improved', 125 days, Green Pascal type, upright, compact, dark green stalks, tender, crisp.

CHARD, SWISS CHARD
Beta vulgaris (Cicla Group)

Grow this beet relative for its beautiful, glossy leaves. It doesn't develop a big edible root.

SWISS CHARD

Leaves are dark green with prominent creamy white or ruby red midribs and veins. Chard is so pretty and easy to grow that it's at home in the flower garden as well as the vegetable patch. Swiss chard is a cool-season crop, but it tolerates heat better than spinach.

Site: Full sun, part shade, or light shade. Fertile, loose soil, high in organic matter with pH of 7.0 or above. Plentiful, even moisture. Adapts to a

wide range of climates. Needs cool season of at least 60 days. Chard bolts (see Bok Choy) in hot weather and becomes inedible.

How to Grow: In the North, direct-seed in spring two to three weeks before average date of last frost. In the South, plant anytime, fall to early spring. Plant seed clusters 1 inch deep, 4 to 6 inches apart in rows spaced 18 to 24 inches apart. When seedlings are several inches tall, thin to 9 to 12 inches.

Keep soil moist. If plant becomes overly mature, cut back to 4 inches—it will send out tender new shoots.

Hose off aphids with hard stream of water. Control leaf miners by removing affected leaves. No serious diseases.

Harvest: Cut off at soil level. To prolong harvest, remove only outer leaves, leaving rest to continue producing. Refrigerate for up to two weeks, or can, freeze, or dry. Cook as for spinach, eating entire leaf and ribs.

Cultivars: 'Ruby Red', 55 days, also called 'Rhubarb Chard', bright red stalks and veins, crinkled, dark green leaves, sweet, bolts if sown too early; 'Large White Rib', 50 days, smooth, dark green leaves, silvery white stems, tender, fleshy; 'Fordhook Giant', 50 days, crinkled, medium green leaves, white stalk, very large, tolerates cold and heat.

CHICORY, BELGIAN ENDIVE, WITLOOF
Cichorium intybus

Chicory is a cold-hardy perennial grown for its long, fleshy taproot, which is used to make a coffeelike beverage, or for its sharp-tasting, lettucelike leaves, which are cooked as a green. Some cultivars resemble dandelions; others are upright and oval and resemble cos lettuce. Witloof chicory roots can be forced to sprout indoors, producing a sheaf of tightly wrapped, tender leaf stalks called Belgian or blanched endive. "Chicory" may be used for relatives, endive and escarole.

BELGIAN ENDIVE

Photo by Karen Bussolini

Site: Full sun to part shade. Tolerates many soils; best in loose, well-drained soil high in organic matter. Even moisture. Adapts to a wide range of climates.

How to Grow: If growing chicory for roots, remove all stones from soil. Sow seeds in garden two or three weeks before average date of last frost. Plant 1 inch deep in rows 2 to 3 feet apart; thin to 12 to 18 inches when several inches tall.

To force Belgian endive, dig up roots after a few light frosts or when plant stops growing. Only use roots 8 to 10 inches long. Cut off foliage to within 1 inch of crown and store roots in damp sand or sawdust in humid, 35° to 40°F place until ready to force. Closely pack roots upright in 12-inch-tall container with drainage hole. (Newer cultivars can be forced without soil in cool, dark area.) For older cultivars, cover with sand or clean soil 4 inches above tops of roots. Cover pot with plastic bag to hold humidity and keep in dark at 50° to 60°F, watering lightly but regularly. When head breaks surface in about three weeks, dig down to crown and cut off pale, compact, pointed, leafy head where it meets root. Return potted roots to dark—you should be able to get two more harvests. Start forcing routine every one or two weeks from winter through spring for supply of Belgian endive until early summer.

No serious pests or diseases.

Harvest: Harvest leaves for greens when 6 to 8 inches long. Taproot is ready about 120 days after planting; it will be about 5 inches in diameter at widest point, 10 inches long. Dig up roots before ground freezes. Roast and grind taproot to use like coffee or use it to force edible leafstalk or head. Refrigerate head for up to one week.

Cultivars: Nonforcing: 'Crystal Hat', 70 days, grown for leaves and roots, oval heads, tolerates heat and frost; 'Dentarella' ('Catalogna'), 65 days, also called asparagus chicory, succulent stems, tart dandelion-like leaves.

Forcing: 'Witloof Zoom', needs no soil to force, pale yellow stalks; 'Witloof Robin', needs no soil to force, pale pink stalks.

CHINESE CABBAGE, NAPA CABBAGE
Brassica rapa (Pekinensis Group)

Chinese cabbage has the crisp texture of iceberg lettuce and a flavor reminiscent of celery. In garden catalogs, it sometimes is lumped with bok choy, but the two are different. Chinese cabbage forms a tight head; bok choy is a loose-leaf vegetable. Chinese cabbage bolts (see Bok Choy) readily in hot weather: In the North, plant in summer for fall harvest; in the South, plant in fall for winter harvest. Some bolt-resistant cultivars have been bred for spring planting.

Site: Full sun to part shade. Fertile, well-drained soil high in organic matter; pH of 5.5 to 7.0. Plentiful moisture. Needs cool season lasting 70 days or more.

How to Grow: For fall or winter harvest, plant seeds or transplants when soil is 70°F—usually midsummer in the North and early fall in the South. Plant seeds ¼ to ½ inch deep. Thin seedlings to 12 inches for small or upright cultivars and 18 to 24 inches for large ones. Use same spacing when

JADE PAGODA CHINESE CABBAGE

setting transplants. For spring planting, choose early, bolt-resistant variety and set out transplants in April or May.

Water to keep soil moist. Side-dress with dry fertilizer every four weeks or apply liquid manure tea or seaweed every two weeks.

Hose off aphids with hard stream of water. Prevent cabbage worms and maggots by covering plants with floating row cover; treat infestation with BT. Treat flea beetles with pyrethrin.

Harvest: Harvest spring planting as soon as heads form; harvest fall planting before first hard freeze. Cut off heads at soil line and remove outer leaves. Refrigerate in plastic for up to two weeks or store four to six weeks in cold, moist place such as root cellar.

Cultivars: 'Blues', 50 days, large heads, bolt-resistant for spring; 'China Express', 65 to 80 days, tight dark green, barrel-shaped heads, resists bolting, can plant in spring; 'Spring A-1', 63 days, early, 4-pound, pale green heads, resists bolting, can spring plant; 'W-R Super 90', 90 days, barrel-shaped, 7-pound heads, disease-resistant, for fall planting, stores well; 'Jade Pagoda', 72 days, tall, cylindrical heads, slow to bolt; 'Summertop Napa', 43 days, big, solid, mild-tasting, bolt-resistant heads, disease-resistant; 'Wong Bok', 80 days, oval, tender heads.

COLLARDS
Brassica oleracea (Acephala Group)

A nonheading member of the cabbage family, collards is a biennial with thick, ruffly, blue-green leaves that are harvested during the plant's first year. Collards can withstand more cold and heat than most of its relatives. In fact, a light frost improves the distinctive, mild flavor of the leaves, similar to kale and cabbage. In milder regions, plants survive the winter, providing fresh greens through the dreariest months.

CHAMPION COLLARDS

Site: Full sun. Fertile soil, ideal pH of 6.5 to 7.5. Tolerates drought, but steady moisture makes leaves tender. Needs three-month cool season.

How to Grow: If starting indoors, sow seed four to six weeks before you plan to set out transplants. In the North, set out transplants in spring four to six weeks before average date of last frost; plant in late summer for fall harvest. In the South, plant in late winter for spring harvest and in early fall for late fall and winter harvest. Set transplants 12 inches apart in rows 18 to 24 inches apart. In regions with long cool season, direct-seed, sowing seeds 1 inch deep and 3 inches apart in rows 18 to 24 inches apart. Thin to *continued*

COLLARD
(continued)

12 inches when seedlings have four or five true leaves; transplant thinnings.

Some cultivars grow to be several feet tall; stake heavy plants that fall over. Mulch overwintering plants.

Prevent cabbage worms and cabbage loopers by covering plants with floating row cover; treat infestation with BT. Collards have no serious disease problems.

Harvest: Harvest individual leaves, starting at bottom, before they become tough. Collards withstand freezing temperatures, so in many regions you can harvest through winter. Refrigerate for up to one week or store in cold, moist place for two to three weeks.

Cultivars: 'Georgia Blue Stem', 80 days, tall stem, leaves widely spaced; 'Vates', 75 days, heavy, large, wavy, dark green leaves, best adapted to mild winters; 'Champion', 70 days, large, dark leaves, overwintering Vates type, retains quality two weeks longer than Vates in spring, resists bolting (see Bok Choy).

CORN
Zea mays

Corn eats up garden space; each 6- to-10-foot-tall plant yields only one or two ears, but if you have room, the vibrant taste of fresh corn is worth the effort. In addition to the traditional yellow, you can grow black, red, white, and bicolor sweet corn. You also can grow the delicious supersweet, sugar-enhanced types, which stay sweet longer after harvest because the sugar in the kernels converts to starch more slowly.

Site: Full sun. Deep, fertile soil, plentiful moisture. Thrives in regions with warm summers.

How to Grow: Plant seeds when soil reaches 60°F in the North, usually around average date of last frost. In the South, plant in early spring and again

SILVER QUEEN CORN

in early fall. Sow seeds 1 inch deep and 4 inches apart. To ensure good pollination, plant in blocks rather than in long rows. For example, four rows of four plants, rather than one row of 16 plants. To prolong harvest, plant block every two weeks, or plant early varieties in midseason, and late varieties at same time. When plants reach height of 2 to 4 inches, thin short varieties to 2 feet apart and tall varieties to 3 feet apart.

Keep soil moist. Mulch to hold soil moisture and prevent weeds. Fertilize with dry fertilizer before planting, again when corn is 8 inches tall, and again when 18 inches tall. Or, use liquid fertilizer every three weeks.

To control cutworms, place a nail in soil alongside each seedling, so cutworm can't wrap around stalk to feed. To control corn borers and earworms, apply a few drops of mineral oil to tips of silks after pollination, but while silks are still green to trap worms before they reach ear. Discourage overwintering insects by removing corn stalks after harvesting. To prevent smut, plant resistant cultivars; get rid of infected plants and don't plant corn in same part of garden for two years.

Harvest: Harvest after silks turn brown and kernels ooze milky sap when punctured. Most cultivars lose sweetness rapidly; eat corn as soon as possible after harvesting. To store,

wrap ear and husk in damp paper towels and refrigerate for up to one week or blanch and freeze ears.

Cultivars: Short cultivars are about 5 feet tall; tall ones are 7 to 10 feet. Tight husks protect ears from weather and insects.

Yellow: 'Earlivee', 65 days, 7-inch ears, good flavor and yield, short, for the North; 'Precocious', 70 days, buttery flavor, 7-inch ears, seed tolerates cool soil; 'Golden Bantam', 78 days, old-fashioned texture, starchy, 7-inch ears, medium stalks; 'Kandy Korn', 83 days, uniform 8-inch ears, seed tolerates cool soil, tall, strong, reddish stalks withstand wind, well-adapted, freezes and cans well; 'Jubilee', 85 days, 11-inch ears, tip kernels fill well, freezes and cans well.

White: 'Silver Queen', 94 days, tall, tight husks, 8-inch ears, needs warm soil; 'Platinum Lady', 86 days, slender 8-inch ears, tall.

Bicolor: 'Peaches and Cream', 80 days, yellow-and-white kernels, tall plants, 8-inch ears; 'Seneca Dawn', 80 days, yellow-and-white kernels, creamy texture, can stay on stalk for up to two weeks after ripe; 'Early Gold & Silver', 62 days, 8½-inch ears.

Supersweet: 'Northern Xtra Sweet', 63 days, seed tolerates cool soil, uniform 8-inch ears, tight husks, short, freezes and cans well; 'Early Xtra Sweet', 71 days, sweeter after picking, good texture, tight husk, widely adapted, tip kernels fill well, freezes and cans well.

CRESS, GARDEN CRESS
Lepidium sativum

For a quick-and-easy homegrown salad, try growing cress or peppergrass. This green is so easy, you can grow it on a windowsill indoors on a damp sponge. It takes only two to four weeks from planting to harvest—faster than watercress and upland cress. Curly cress has finely divided, curled leaves good for garnishes or chopping. Plain cress has slightly toothed leaves. Broad cress

CURLY CRESS

AMIRA CUCUMBER

has wide, flat leaves good for sandwiches. All have the same sharp, peppery flavor that's delightful combined with milder greens.

Site: Full sun, part shade, or light shade. Loose, well-drained soil. Consistent, even moisture. Tolerates hot and cold weather; frost sensitive.
How to Grow: Starting in early spring, plant every two weeks through fall for continuous harvest. In frost-free regions, plant year-round. In the North, grow inside in sunny area. Sow seeds ¼ inch deep and ½ inch apart in rows 18 to 24 inches apart.

Keep soil moist. When watering, take care to keep soil from splashing on leaves because washing it off after harvest may damage leaves. Soaker hose makes it easier to water soil only. No serious pests or diseases.
Harvest: Harvest cress when it's 2 to 4 inches tall. Cut at base with scissors and use fresh in salads or sandwiches. Refrigerate up to one week.
Cultivars: Usually sold under plant name. Check botanical name to ensure you're not buying different type.

CUCUMBER
Cucumis sativus

Cucumbers are either slicers or picklers. For fresh eating, grow slicing cucumbers, which have thick skins that most cooks peel. For both fresh eating and pickling, grow picklers, usually shorter with thin skins. Within both groups, there are semivining or bush types. Bush types need less room. You can find cultivars that are "burpless" because they lack the compound that make cukes bitter and hard to digest. You also have a choice of shape, color, and length. Most modern cultivars are gynoecious, with separate male and female plants. Seed companies include a few tinted male seeds in the packet that you must plant for a source of pollen. Some cultivars are parthenocarpic and don't require pollination.

Site: Full sun to part shade. Adapted to many soil types, but best in fertile, well-drained, slightly alkaline soil high in organic matter. Plentiful moisture. Grows in a wide range of climates; needs temperatures above 75°F for about three months.
How to Grow: Sow in garden when soil temperature reaches 70°F. In the North, plant three to four weeks after average date of last frost. In the South, plant in mid spring for summer harvest or during summer for fall harvest. If possible, plant in dry soil, which is warmer. Cover soil with black plastic in spring so it warms faster. Sow 1½ inches deep in hills, six seeds per hill. Space hills 3 to 4 feet apart in rows 3 to 4 feet apart if staking or trellising and 4 to 6 feet apart if not. When seedlings are several inches tall, thin out all but strongest, widest-spaced three plants. Or, set out transplants, using hill spacing.

Don't water until seedlings emerge, then keep soil moist to prevent bitterness. Protect from early frost. Mulch to keep soil moist and prevent weeds. Discourage insects and keep warm with floating row cover. Remove when flowering, unless cultivar is parthenocarpic. Trellis to save space.

Prevent spotted and striped cucumber beetles, which spread bacterial wilt, by keeping grass near garden mowed and by covering plants with floating row cover. Pick off beetles or treat with pyrethrin. To prevent diseases such as anthracnose, leaf spot, mildew, mosaic virus, scab, and bacterial wilt, plant resistant varieties, remove plants from garden at season's end, and destroy infected plants.
Harvest: Pull cucumbers from vine when they reach full size. If they hang on vine longer, seeds form and plants stop producing. After picking, quickly cool cucumbers by dunking in cold water. Refrigerate in plastic for up to two weeks.
Cultivars: Slicing: 'Amira', 56 days, Middle Eastern type with size between slicer and pickler, thin skin, good flavor, tolerates cool summers; 'Straight Eight', 65 days, straight 7- to 8-inch fruit; 'Marketmore 86', 56 days, earlier and shorter vine than 'Marketmore 76', straight, uniform, slight taper at ends, seldom bitter, tolerates poor weather, disease-resistant; 'Lemon', 70 days, yellow skin, apple-shaped, not bitter.

Pickling: 'H-19 Little Leaf', 70 days, fruit retains quality on vine, small leaves make harvesting easier, can pollinate or be parthenocarpic, disease-resistant; 'Lucky Strike', 52 days, blocky fruit on compact plants, tolerates cool weather, disease-resistant; 'Vert de Massy', 53 days, can harvest when tiny for French cornichon pickles.   *continued*

Vegetables

CUCUMBER
(continued)

Bush: 'Spacemaster', 60 days, crisp, smooth, 8-inch fruit, disease-resistant; 'Salad Bush', 60 days, uniform, tender, crisp, 8-inch fruit, good flavor, high yield, disease-resistant.

Burpless: 'Sweet Success', 55 days, 12- to 14-inch slicing fruit, seedless, needs staking, disease-resistant; 'Tasty Green', 60 days, pickling, high yield, disease-tolerant, tolerates cool soil; 'Suyo Long', 61 days, pickling, long Asian type, 15-inch fruit, widely adapted.

AGORA EGGPLANT

EGGPLANT
Solanum melongena var. *esculentum*

The popular purple eggplant is a fairly recent creation. Originally eggplant was small, white, and round, hence the common name. Today you can grow all kinds of eggplants: black, yellow, pink, orange, and striped. Whatever type you choose, it needs plenty of summer heat. In cool areas, choose a cultivar that tolerates lower temperatures. Warm the soil by covering it with black plastic one or two weeks before you set out transplants, or grow eggplant in a raised bed where soil temperatures are warmer.

Site: Full sun. Tolerates a range of soils, but best with well-drained soil high in organic matter. Moderate moisture. Needs daytime temperatures of 80° to 90°F and night temperatures of 70° to 80°F for about 75 days.
How to Grow: Grow from transplants; don't direct-seed outdoors. To start transplants indoors, sow seeds 10 weeks before you plan to set out seedlings. In the North, set out transplants two or three weeks after average date of last frost. In the South, set out transplants in mid to late spring for summer harvest, or early summer to midsummer for fall harvest. Space 18 to 24 inches apart in rows 24 to 36 inches apart.

Mulch to keep soil moist and soil temperature even. Cover to protect from frost. Stake plants that bend under weight of fruit.

For cutworms, set nail beside stem at planting time so cutworm can't wrap around it to feed. Pick off large insects such as hornworms. Check undersides of leaves for orange masses of potato beetle eggs and crush. Prevent flea beetles by covering young plants with floating row cover; remove when plants flower. Treat flea beetles with pyrethrin.
Harvest: Cut, don't pull fruit from stem when it's plump and firm and skin is still tender. Many cultivars can be picked before they reach full size. Keep picked to encourage highest yields. Store unrefrigerated, at about 50°F.
Cultivars: Maturity dates are from transplanting.

Purple: 'Black Beauty', 80 days, round to oval fruit, widely adapted, high yields; 'Dusky', 80 days, 8- to 9-inch oval fruit, can pick at 3 to 5 inches, tolerates cool summers, high yields, disease-resistant; 'Agora', 68 days, bears heavily under adverse conditions.

Baby: 'Bambino', 70 days, dark purple, walnut-size fruit, compact 12- to 18-inch plants good in pots.

Unusual: 'Neon', 65 days, cylindrical pink fruit, not bitter, tender; 'Snowy', 72 days, firm, ivory-white fruit; 'Easter Egg', 65 days, small, white, egg-shaped fruit, compact plant, high yields.

ENDIVE, ESCAROLE
Cichorium endiva

Leafy vegetables with a tart flavor, escarole and endive add a spark to salads that you can't get with plain lettuce. Endive has flat or curly, feathery leaves. Escarole is a different variety of the same plant with wider leaves and a more delicate flavor. Both prefer cool weather, although they tolerate heat better than lettuce.

SALAD KING ENDIVE

Site: Full sun to part shade. Loose, well-drained soil. Plentiful moisture. Adapted to a wide range of climates; needs cool season, 60° to 75°F, lasting about 100 days. Tolerates more cold and heat than lettuce. Becomes bitter in hot weather.
How to Grow: Sow seeds outdoors four to six weeks before average date of last frost. For fall harvest, plant in midsummer in the North, late summer in the South. For prolonged harvest, plant every two weeks over six-week period. Sow seeds ¼ inch deep in a band, in rows 18 to 24 inches apart.

Thin to 9 to 12 inches apart when seedlings are a couple of inches tall; thinning helps prevent bolting (see Bok Choy). If using transplants, set 9 to 12 inches apart in rows 18 to 24 inches apart.

Keep soil moist. You may blanch endive or escarole two or three weeks before harvest to make it less bitter. To blanch, bind leaves with rubber band or cover with flowerpot, plastic container, or other device to block light. Some are self-blanching.

Hose off aphids from spring plantings with hard stream of water.
Harvest: Harvest while young and tender, before it becomes too bitter. Cut off plant at base. Refrigerate in plastic for up to two weeks.
Cultivars: Endive: 'President', 80 days, deeply cut and frilled dark green leaves, pale yellow blanched core, cold-hardy; 'Salad King', 45 days, deep green leaves, creamy self-blanching center, bolt-resistant; 'Green Curled', 90 days, curled, self-blanching leaves.

Escarole: 'Perfect', 80 days, medium green, ruffled rosette, mild, blanched center; 'Batavian Full Hearted', 85 days, upright, broad leaves, outer leaves smooth and green, inner leaves blanch pale yellow; 'Nuvol', 60 days, wavy, dark green leaves, creamy self-blanching center; 'Grosse Bouclee', 50 days, broad, dark green leaves, self-blanching, creamy white heart.

FLORENCE FENNEL
Foeniculum vulgare var. azoricum

A relative of parsley, Florence fennel or finocchio forms lacy green tops that resemble dill, but it's valued for the thickened, fleshy, white leaf bases that form a dense, globelike "bupound" or bulb. The crunchy bupound—a delicacy in the Mediterranean—tastes like a nutty,

ZEFA FINO FLORENCE FENNEL

anise-flavored celery eaten fresh or sautéed. Grow this tender perennial as a cool-season annual.

Site: Full sun. Well-drained soil, high in organic matter; tolerates dry soil. Adapted to a wide range of climates; needs cool spring or fall season of about 90 days.
How to Grow: In the North, direct-seed in garden from two to three weeks before average date of last frost through late summer. In the South, plant in late summer. Sow seeds ¼ inch deep and 1 inch apart, in rows 2 to 3 feet apart. When seedlings are several inches tall, thin to 12 inches.

Water during drought. Stake plants that fall. No major pests or diseases.
Harvest: As soon as plant is growing steadily, pick a few leafy stalks to flavor soups and casseroles. Entire plant is ready to harvest when base is about 3 inches across. Cut off at soil level and cut off tall stalks. Refrigerate in plastic bag for up to one week. Store in cold, moist place for two to three months.
Cultivars: 'Zefa Fino', 65 days, nutty flavor, large bulb, widely adapted, resists bolting (see Bok Choy); 'Romy Fennel', 89 days, large bulb; 'Herald', 74 days, resists bolting, good for early planting.

GARLIC
Allium sativum

G arlic is grown from cloves, the same sort used for cooking. There are three types of garlic. Softneck has soft necks at maturity and can be braided. Its outer cloves are medium size; the inner ones are smaller. It has a strong flavor and stores well. Stiffneck or rocambole has four to six mildly flavored outer cloves, but no inner ones. The most cold-hardy and easy to peel, it sends up a coiled "scape" that should be cut

GARLIC

off to encourage larger cloves. Giant or elephant garlic (Allium scorodoprasum) produces huge, mild, easily peeled bulbs if well-fertilized.

Site: Full sun. Fertile, well-drained soil; tolerates dry soil. Adapted to a wide range of climates.
How to Grow: Plant in October in the North, from November through January in the South. Break bulbs apart and plant individual cloves tips up, with tips 1½ to 2 inches deep, spaced 4 to 6 inches. Plant elephant garlic 4 to 6 inches deep, spaced 6 to 8 inches.

In the North, mulch heavily in winter to keep bulbs from heaving out of the ground as they thaw and freeze. When topgrowth starts in spring, be sure plants get 1 inch of water   *continued*

GARLIC
(continued)

each week. Reduce watering as leaves turn yellow near harvest. Cut off woody seed stems. No serious pests or diseases.

Harvest: Gently dig bulbs in summer when half of the leaves are yellow and necks are soft. Cure by drying strung up or on screens in ventilated place. Store braided or with tops cut off in cool, dry place for up to eight months.

Cultivars: 'Italian Late', soft neck, good flavor, pungent, stores six to nine months; 'German Extra-Hardy', stiff neck, long roots resist heaving, winter-hardy, stores well; 'Elephant Garlic', mild bulbs 6 to 8 inches in diameter, 4- to 5-foot-tall plants.

JERUSALEM ARTICHOKE

JERUSALEM ARTICHOKE, SUNCHOKE
Helianthus tuberosus

This member of the sunflower genus is a 5- to 10-foot-tall, yellow-flowered perennial with tasty, potato-like tubers. Although it's easy to grow, Jerusalem artichoke is difficult to eliminate from the garden if you tire of it. It spreads invasively, forming larger plots each year unless you're diligent in digging up all the tubers. Consider planting it in an out-of-the-way spot where the plants can double as a screen or windbreak.

Site: Full sun. Tolerates a wide range of soil and moisture conditions. Adapts to a wide range of climates.

How to Grow: Plant tubers (sometimes found in grocery store's produce department) in spring two or three weeks before average date of last frost. You also can cut tuber into seed pieces, making sure each one has an eye. Plant 2 to 6 inches deep and 12 to 18 inches apart.

Water during dry periods. Remove flower stalks so plant's food energy goes to tubers. Tubers may rot in soggy soil. Remove infected plants.

Harvest: Dig up tubers with spading fork once leaves die back in fall, leaving a few behind for next year's crop, or leave them in ground to harvest throughout fall and winter. To store, refrigerate in plastic bags or freeze. Eat raw or cooked like potatoes.

Cultivars: 'Stampede', 90 days, extremely early, high yields, winter-hardy, large tubers.

KALE
Brassica oleracea (Acephala Group)

Kale is a firm, tasty, leafy green that's one of the most cold-hardy vegetables available. Even snow won't hurt it, so it can be harvested all winter as far north as Zone 5. For best performance, grow as a fall vegetable. In cool climates, spring plantings succeed if leaves are harvested when small, before warm weather makes them bitter. The 12- to 24-inch plants with intensely green, blue-green, or purplish ruffled leaves cheer the off-season garden. Ornamental kales in fall flower gardens also are edible.

DWARF BLUE CURLED VATES KALE

Site: Full sun to part shade. Fertile, well-drained soil with pH of 6.5 to 7.5. Plentiful moisture. Grow in regions with cool season that lasts about 60 days.

How to Grow: If starting indoors, sow seeds four to six weeks before you plan to set out transplants. Set out transplants in spring four to six weeks before average date of last frost. For fall or winter harvest, direct-seed or set out transplants in midsummer in the North and late summer in the South. Sow seeds ½ inch deep and 3 inches apart in rows 18 to 24 inches apart. Thin seedlings to 12 inches apart when several inches tall; transplant or eat thinnings. Space transplants 12 inches apart in rows 18 to 24 inches apart.

Keep soil moist. No serious pest or disease problems.

Harvest: Begin harvesting about 55 days after transplanting. Remove leaves as needed; let the rest of the plant grow.

Cultivars: 'Dwarf Blue Curled Vates', 55 days, finely curled, thick, blue-green leaves, compact plant, resists bolting (see Bok Choy), cold-tolerant; 'Red Russian', 50 days, tender, mild, oak-shaped leaves with purple stems and veins; 'Winterbor', 60 days, curled, medium green leaves, high yields, cold-tolerant; 'Verdura', 60 days, curled, dark blue-green leaves, compact plants.

EARLY WHITE VIENNA KOHLRABI

KOHLRABI

Brassica oleracea
(Gongylodes Group)

Easy-to-grow kohlrabi produces a crunchy, sweet-tasting aboveground bulb that can be white, green, or purple. Like other members of the cabbage family, kohlrabi loves cool temperatures and tolerates frost. If the weather is too hot, it becomes woody and hot-tasting.

Site: Full sun to part shade. Fertile, well-drained soil, ideal pH 6.0 to 7.5. Plentiful moisture. Suited to all climates; grows best in temperatures of 60° to 70°F.

How to Grow: In the North, sow seed outdoors in spring four to six weeks before average date of last frost for early summer harvest. In the South, plant in late summer or fall for fall or winter harvest. Sow seeds ½ inch deep and ¼ inch apart in rows 12 inches apart. When seedlings are several inches tall, thin to 3 to 4 inches.

Keep soil moist. To prevent cabbage worm and cabbage looper, cover young plants with floating row cover. Treat infestation with BT.

Harvest: For best flavor, slice off stem 1 inch below leaves, 40 to 60 days after planting when bulbs are 2 to 3 inches in diameter (except giant varieties). Cut off leaves. Refrigerate up to two weeks.

Cultivars: 'Early White Vienna', 55 days, white flesh; 'Early Purple Vienna', 55 days, purplish stems and bulbs; 'Kolpak', 40 to 50 days, light green bulbs stay tender when large; 'Superschmeltze', 60 days, tolerates dry areas, tender, giant 10-inch bulbs; 'Grand Duke', 45 days, disease-resistant.

LEEK

Allium ampeloprasum
(Porrum Group)

Leeks have a thick, edible stalk (composed of the tightly wrapped leaf bases) and leaves with a delicate onion flavor. Grow this cold-hardy crop for fall, winter, or overwintering

OTINA LEEK

spring harvest. Some cultivars can be direct-seeded outdoors; others do best as transplants. All should be blanched. Leeks are so easy to grow that some gardeners plant the roots of grocery-store leeks with only an inch of stalk.

Site: Full sun to part shade. Fertile soil. Plentiful moisture. Adapts to all climates; best where 60° to 70°F.

How to Grow: Direct-seed suitable cultivars outdoors in spring four to six weeks before average date of last frost. Thickly sow seeds ½ inch deep in rows 18 inches apart. When seedlings are a few inches tall, thin to 2 inches apart. Some cultivars should be started

indoors eight to 10 weeks before transplanting outdoors. Set 8- to 18-inch-tall transplants out on average date of last frost in spring (or in fall for an overwintering crop), in holes 6 inches deep and 6 inches apart, in rows 24 inches apart. Don't fill in holes; let rain wash soil into holes. With this method, blanching isn't necessary.

Blanch direct-seeded leeks to make stems white and tender by mounding soil around stems as they grow. Keep weed-free. To overwinter, mulch heavily to keep ground from freezing.

No serious pests and diseases.

Harvest: Pull up when stalk base is about 1 inch around. Refrigerate in plastic for one to two weeks. Wash grit from folds in leaves before using.

Cultivars: Summer leeks, frost-tender: 'Otina', 120 days, long, blue-green leaves; 'Varna', 80 days, tall, slender, self-blanching stalks, fast-growing; 'King Richard', 70 days, stocky, fast-growing, self-blanching.

Long-season, winter-hardy: 'Giant Musselburgh', 110 days, fat, juicy stalks, cold-tolerant, does well in the North and the South; 'Blue Solaise', mild flavor, overwinters well; 'Poncho', 100 days, short, stocky, disease-resistant, for summer and fall harvest.

LETTUCE

Lactuca sativa

One of the first vegetables you can plant in spring, lettuce is a snap to grow. Seeds sprout in soil as cool as 40°F, but best growth is in 60°F soil. Gardeners easily can grow three types: Leaf lettuce forms a loose head, grows fastest, and is best for poor soil and hot weather. Boston or butterhead has large, ruffly leaves outside and pale, delicately flavored leaves inside. Romaine, or cos, has long, broad, upright leaves that are thick, juicy, crisp, and strong flavored. Iceberg lettuce in groceries is difficult to grow for home gardeners because it has specific watering needs, *continued*

LETTUCE
(continued)

JERICHO ROMAINE LETTUCE

and in hot weather it won't form solid heads. If you live in the South or plant late, choose a bolt-resistant cultivar (see Bok Choy) to avoid bitter leaves.

Site: Full sun to light shade. Cool, loose soil with good supply of nitrogen and potassium. Plentiful moisture. Adapted to all climates; best in temperatures of 60° to 75°F.

How to Grow: Sow seeds outdoors as early as soil can be worked. For continuous harvest, plant every three to four weeks through summer and fall, using heat-resistant cultivars in summer. Sow seeds 1 inch apart in rows 12 to 18 inches apart. Cover with ⅛ inch of soil, firm soil gently, and water lightly. Thin leaf lettuce to 6 inches; cos and butterhead to 8 to 10 inches. For early spring start, begin indoors in cool room three to four weeks before you plan to set out transplants.

Keep soil moist, especially after planting and when seedlings are small. Spray every 10 to 14 days with liquid seaweed to hasten harvest. Mulch to keep soil cool and leaves clean.

Prevent cabbage loopers by covering with floating row cover. Treat with BT. Hot, dry weather can cause tip burn; plant resistant cultivars.

Harvest: Pick leaf and romaine types when outer leaves are 4 to 6 inches long. Cut off entire head at base or pick outer leaves and allow rest to continue growing. Harvest butterhead when heads are firm. Refrigerate in plastic bag for up to two weeks.

Cultivars: Leaf (45 to 50 days): 'Black-Seeded Simpson', early, extra large, with juicy, crinkled, light green leaves; 'Red Sails', reddish leaves, not bitter, resists bolting; 'Oakleaf', mild-tasting, smooth, lobed, green leaves, resists bolting; 'Red Salad Bowl, reddish oak-shaped leaves, slow to bolt.

Butterhead (65 to75 days): 'Bibb', crisp, delicate flavor; 'Buttercrunch', compact, crisp fan-shaped head, resists bolting; 'Summer Bibb', early, resists bolting; 'Anuenue', especially well-suited to warm conditions.

Romaine (75 to 85 days): 'Parris Island Cos', slow to bolt; 'Parris White Cos', upright , large head; 'Little Caesar', resists tip burn, flavorful, small head; 'Jericho', tall heavy heads remain sweet in hot weather; 'Balloon', large, pale green heads, heat-tolerant.

LIMA BEAN, BUTTER BEAN
Phaseolus lunatus (P. limensis)

Beautiful pearly green lima beans with their mealy, chestnut-flavored flesh can be eaten when fresh and tender from their shells or allowed to mature into a dried storage bean. Like green beans, lima bean plants come in two forms—bush or pole—but they require a warmer climate. Bush types bear two weeks earlier than pole types and don't need staking or trellising; pole types bear longer once they begin.

Site: Full sun. Well-drained soil with pH to 6.5. Plentiful moisture. Needs warmer climate than snap or dried beans.

How to Grow: Plant two weeks after average date of last frost. Plant seeds 1 inch deep in moist soil; don't water until they sprout. For bush limas, space

FORDHOOK 242 BUSH LIMA BEAN

seeds 3 inches apart in rows spaced 18 to 24 inches. For pole limas, space seeds 4 to 6 inches apart in rows spaced 30 to 36 inches, beside 6-foot trellis. May not set pods during high summer temperatures.

Mildew, anthracnose, mites, and bean beetles may be problems (see Beans).

Harvest: Harvest when beans are plump within pod for fresh eating. Refrigerate unshelled for up to one week. Harvest dried limas as you would dry shell beans.

Cultivars: Bush: 'Fordhook 242', 80 days, early, large-seeded, tender, high yields, adapted to the North; 'Burpee's Improved', 75 days, large flat pods in clusters, high yields; 'Baby Fordhook Bush', 70 days, small moist beans for eating fresh; 'Geneva', 85 days, cold-tolerant, can plant earlier; 'Jackson Wonder', 65 to 76 days, heat-resistant.

Pole: 'Dr. Martin', 90 days, high yields; 'Christmas', 80 days, speckled.

MELON
Cucumis melo

Few garden crops come close to the juicy sweetness of melons. Muskmelons (sometimes incorrectly called cantaloupe) have a netted, yellow-tan rind and salmon-colored flesh. Honeydew-type melons include honeydew, which has a smooth, white rind and pale green flesh; casaba, which is pointed at the stem end and has a yellow rind and white flesh when ripe; and crenshaw, which is oval with netted, tan skin and pinkish flesh. Charentais-type melons, a French true cantaloupe with a warty, ribbed rind, has sweet, bright orange fruit. Because melons grow on long vines, they commandeer more than their fair share of garden space. They also need a long, hot growing season, making them more difficult to grow in the North. Minimize the problem by growing early-maturing cultivars.

CANTALOUPE

Site: Full sun. Well-drained, warm soil high in organic matter with pH above 6.0. Plentiful moisture when vines are growing; less as fruit ripens. Long, warm summers best.

How to Grow: If starting indoors, plant in peat pots three or four weeks before you plan to set out transplants. Where warm season is 120 days or more, direct-seed outdoors or set out transplants two or three weeks after average date of last frost. Plant six to eight seeds in hills spaced 3 feet apart if trellised and 4 to 6 feet apart if not. Thin plants to strongest two or three after threat of cucumber beetles and shifting weather has passed. Or, plant seeds 1 foot apart in rows 5 to 6 feet apart, thinning to 3 feet if trellised and 4 to 6 feet if on ground. Use same spacing for transplants.

Warm soil in spring by covering with plastic sheet, then planting in holes in plastic. In the South, remove plastic once hot weather arrives and use organic mulch to keep soil temperature even. To save space, provide support for vines to climb. If melons hang heavily, support in net or pantyhose sling. If plants lie on ground, set melons on butter tubs or boards to prevent insect damage. Keep soil moist when vines are growing and flowers are being pollinated. As fruit ripens, water only if leaves wilt at midday.

To prevent cucumber beetles, cover with row covers; remove when female flowers appear (base of female flower is swollen). Treat infestation with pyrethrin. To prevent mildew, keep plants vigorous and plant resistant cultivars.

Harvest: Following are the signs of ripeness: muskmelon, stem separates from fruit with light pull, leaving round depression; honeydew, blossom end (opposite stem end) softens, rind smells faintly sweet, and skin turns creamy; casaba, blossom end softens and skin is yellow; crenshaw, green skin has yellow streaks; and charentais, fruit begins turning yellow and blossom end softens or cracks. Store in cool, dry place. Refrigerate if overripe.

Cultivars: Because cultivars vary greatly in their temperature and moisture adaptation, contact your county Cooperative Extension Service office for recommendations. Small cultivars generally are earlier than large ones.

Muskmelon: 'Earligold', 72 days, larger than most early types, tolerates mildew, flesh thick, juicy, and orange; 'Ananas', 100 days, does well in the South, pale gold flesh, sweet and aromatic.

Honeydew: 'Earlidew', 80 days, tolerates uneven weather, fruit is 6 inches in diameter, keeps well.

Casaba: 'Marygold', 80 to 85 days, very early, 3- to 4-pound fruit, thick, sweet, white flesh.

Charentais: 'Alienor', 80 days, small, oblong fruit, green-gray skin, bright orange flesh; 'Pancha', 80 days, small, intensely sweet flesh, vigorous vine.

MUSTARD GREENS
Brassica juncea

Fresh mustard greens add a pleasant bite to sandwiches, salads, and stir-fry dishes. Mustard grows best in cool weather and tolerates frost. As the days heat up, so does the flavor. The tall, leafy plants

OSAKA PURPLE MUSTARD GREENS

are so attractive, especially the purple-leaf types, that they often are grown for foliage effect in edible landscapes.

Site: Full sun to part shade. Loose, well-drained, fertile soil enriched with source of nitrogen, such as composted manure. Plentiful moisture. Any climate; prefers cool temperatures. Tolerates light frost.

How to Grow: Sow as early as soil can be worked. For continuous harvest, plant every two to three weeks until mid spring. In the South, plant in late summer for fall harvest. Sow seeds 1 inch apart and ½ inch deep in rows 8 inches apart. When seedlings are several inches high, thin to 6 inches.

Keep soil moist. To prevent flea beetles, cover with floating row covers. No serious diseases. *continued*

MUSTARD GREENS
(continued)

Harvest: Pick side leaves as needed, or cut entire plant at base. Refrigerate in plastic for up to two weeks.

Cultivars: 'Red Giant', 50 days, large, spicy, purple leaves; 'Miilke Giant', 80 days, crinkled, purple leaves, pungent flavor, very cold-hardy; 'Green Wave', 55 to 60 days, hot-tasting, frilly leaves, resists bolting (see Bok Choy); 'Osaka Purple', 40 days, deep purple leaves with green midribs.

OKRA
Abelmoschus esculentus

Heat-loving okra is a southern favorite, but its short season makes it suitable for northern gardens, too. A hibiscus relative, okra produces

LEE OKRA

large, hibiscus-like, yellow flowers on a strong, hairy, 3- to 6-foot-tall plant. The edible seedpod contains a liquid that adds body to gumbos and stews.

Site: Full sun. Warm, well-drained, dry soil; the ideal pH is 7.0 to 8.0. Adapts to any climate; prefers temperatures above 70°F.

How to Grow: Sow seeds four weeks after average date of last frost; in the South, plant anytime from early April to mid-August. Sow seeds ½ to 1 inch deep in rows 2 to 3 feet apart. Thin to 12 to 18 inches when plants are growing vigorously.

Overwatering reduces yield. Handle plants and pods carefully; they cause an allergic reaction in some gardeners.

Hose off aphids with hard stream of water. Spray flea beetles with pyrethrin. Prevent viral wilts by rotating crops and cleaning up garden after harvest.

Harvest: Pick pods when they're 4 to 6 inches long, about 50 days after planting. Refrigerate immediately.

Cultivars: 'Annie Oakley', 50 days, reliable in the North, pods tender and flavorful; 'Burgundy', 55 days, tender, reddish pods and stems, good yields; 'Clemson Spineless', 56 days, high yields, lacks irritating hairs, making it easy to pick; 'Lee', 50 days, compact 3-foot plants, spineless 6-inch pods.

ONION, SCALLION
Allium cepa

So many types of onions are available that choosing one to grow can be a pleasantly complicated decision. Onion bulbs can be white, red, or yellow and round or flattened. They can be strong-flavored storage onions, which have thick, darkish skins and keep well; mild-flavored fresh onions, also called sweet onions, which keep for only a few weeks in a cool, dark place; or pearl onions, fresh onions about 1 inch in diameter. Another choice is to grow green onions, or scallions, for their edible, strappy leaves. Scallions can be grown from nonbulbing or bulbing onions.

Site: Full sun. Drained, phosphorus-rich soil high in organic matter with pH of 6.5 to 7.5. More acidic soil causes more pungent flavor. There are onions suited to all climates; scallions prefer cool, moist conditions.

How to Grow: Grow onions from seed, transplants, or "sets" (small

ROSSA DI MILANO
RED STORAGE ONION

dormant bulbs). Plant four weeks before average date of last frost in the North and in fall in the South.

Sets: Plant bulbs 2 to 3 inches deep and ½ inch apart. For continuous harvest, plant sets weekly. Sweet onions cannot be grown from sets. Sets are sold as "white" or "yellow," not by variety name.

Seed: All types can be seeded. Sow indoors four to eight weeks before you plan to transplant outside or direct-seed outdoors. Sow seeds ¼ inch deep, one to three seeds per inch, in rows 12 to 18 inches apart. Thin to 2 inches apart when seedlings are 2 to 3 inches tall. Thin again to 4 inches apart when 6 inches tall. Eat thinnings.

Transplants: Set transplants about 1 inch deep and 2 to 3 inches apart with main crown partially covered.

Blanch scallions to tenderize them by hilling soil around the growing stems. If bulb onions begin to bolt (see Bok Choy), harvest immediately and eat soon. Usually pest- and disease-free. To prevent onion maggots, cover with floating row covers in spring. To control thrips, use insecticidal soap. To prevent pink root, grow resistant cultivars.

Harvest: Harvest scallions six to 10 weeks after planting when tops are about 1 foot tall. Harvest bulbs in late summer or fall when 2 to 4 inches in diameter and tops have fallen over. Harvest when soil is dry. To cure for storage, dry entire plant outdoors on flat surface with good air circulation. In the North, dry in full sun; in the South, dry in shade. Dry sweet onions for two to four days, and storage onions for 10 to 14 days. For sweet onions, cut leaves to within 1 inch of bulb and refrigerate unwrapped for a few weeks. For storage onions, cut off leaves as for fresh onions or braid dried tops together, and store at 33° to 45°F for six months or more.

Cultivars: Consider day length when picking a cultivar. Some produce bulbs when days are short, some when days are long, and some fall in between. Choose long-day cultivars for spring planting in the North, short-day cultivars for fall planting in the South, and intermediate cultivars for summer planting in central states.

Short day: 'Colossal PRR', 165 days, large, high yields, yellow, fresh type, mild flavor, resists pink root; 'Texas Grano Valley Sweet', 168 days, large, yellow, fresh type, resists pink root; 'Red Creole', 187 days, hot-tasting, medium, fresh, red; 'Red Burgundy', 98 days, red skin, white flesh, fresh type, mild flavor suited to eating raw; 'New Mexico White Grano', 185 days, large, mild, white, storage type.

Long day/intermediate: 'Walla Walla', 125 days spring-sown, 300 days summer-sown and overwintered, classic jumbo yellow, fresh type, mild, sweet, juicy; 'Mambo', 112 days, red storage type, pungent flavor; 'Ebeneser', 105 days, medium size, white, storage type, moderately hot flavor, harvest early for scallions; 'Rossa di Milano', 110 days, pungent, red, storage type, flat-top barrel shape.

Scallions: 'Evergreen White Bunching', 80 days, long, slender white stalks, tolerates severe cold; 'Red Beard', 80 days, tender and flavorful, red stem.

Pearl: 'Snow Baby', 57 days, round white bulbs 1 to 2 inches in diameter; 'Purplette', 60 days, changes from burgundy to pink when cooked, can harvest early as scallions.

PARSNIP
Pastinaca sativa

Parsnips are a biennial relative of carrots grown as an annual. The top is a rosette of stalky leaves, and the edible taproot resembles a creamy,

LANCER PARSNIP

thick-skinned carrot. Parsnips are easy to grow; all they ask is a long, cool growing season and deep soil free of rocks and other obstacles that might deform the root. A nip of frost sweetens the flavor.

Site: Full sun to part shade. Fertile soil loosened to about 15 inches deep. Average moisture. Adapted to all climates; best where 60° to 70°F.

How to Grow: Thickly sow seeds in spring two to three weeks before average date of last frost, ½ to 1 inch deep, in rows 18 to 24 inches apart. When seedlings have two true leaves, thin to 4 to 6 inches by cutting out crowding plants. (Pulling disturbs the roots of adjacent seedlings.) If soil is clay, grow in raised beds at least 15 inches deep.

Keep soil moist until seedlings are several inches tall. Keep well weeded when plants are small. Mulch to keep soil cool. Prevent root maggots by covering with floating row cover. No serious diseases.

Harvest: After frost, dig up individual roots as needed. Leave remainder in ground, deeply mulched in extremely cold climates. Finish harvesting before growth resumes in spring, or harvest and bury in sand with tops attached and store in root cellar. Refrigerate in plastic for up to three weeks or in cool, moist place for up to six months.

Cultivars: 'Harris Model', 120 days, white roots 12 inches long and 2 inches wide at top, very smooth; 'Gladiator', 105 days, early hybrid, fast germination, large, high-quality roots, smooth white skin; 'All American', 95 days, white flesh, small core, sweet.

PEA
Pisum sativum

Peas grown in your own garden taste sweeter and are more flavorful than store-bought peas. Peas require cool weather—they quit bearing when summer heat arrives. Grow green (shelling) peas for the

SNAPPY SNAP PEA

round seeds within the pod; snow peas (sugar peas) for the tender immature pods; and snap peas for the high yield and succulent sweet pods that stay tender even when mature. Most peas grow on weak vines that climb by tendrils and need support, although plants of short *continued*

PEA
(continued)

bush-type cultivars prop up each other. Peas, like other legumes, house nitrogen-fixing bacteria in their roots that improve the soil.

Site: Full sun to part shade. Well-drained soil, high in organic matter. Plentiful moisture. Matures earlier in sandy soil; yields more in heavy soil. Peas grow in all climates; require temperatures below 85°F, with 65° to 70°F ideal. Prefers damp weather.

How to Grow: To prevent splitting, don't soak seed before planting. In the North, plant as soon as soil can be worked in spring and again in fall. In the South, plant in fall and late winter. Sow seeds 2 inches deep, 2 to 3 inches apart, in rows 18 to 24 inches apart. Plant early and plant main-season cultivars for continued harvest or plant same cultivar at two-week intervals.

Keep soil moist. Wetting flowers can interfere with pollination. Provide trellis for vining types; string between two poles for low-bush types to lean on. Avoid high-nitrogen fertilizer. Cover with deer netting to discourage rabbits and other mammals. Hose off aphids with hard stream of water.

Harvest: Pick shell peas when pods are shiny and filled out. Pick sugar peas when pods are about 3 inches, still shiny, and seeds visible as small lumps, but not large and round. Pick snap peas when seeds start plumping within pods. Refrigerate immediately; store in plastic bag for up to 10 days.

Cultivars: Shelling: 'Knight', 56 to 60 days, large-podded, double-podded (two pods per node), medium-size peas, short vines need light support, disease-resistant; 'Maestro', 57 to 61 days, sweet, tender, disease-resistant, short vines don't need support, long-bearing; 'Bounty', 67 days, main season, high yields, short vines, double-podded, easy shelling, disease-resistant.

Snow: 'Ho Lohn Dow', 75 days, large pods, vining; 'Oregon Giant', 60 days, sweet, large pods, high yields, short vines don't require support, disease-resistant; 'Oregon Sugar Pod II', 70 days, high yields, long, wide pods, mild flavor, short vines don't need support.

Snap: 'Sugar Snap', 70 days, fat, crunchy, sweet pods, not disease-resistant, 6-foot vines; 'Snappy', 68 days, like 'Sugar Snap' but higher-yielding, earlier, and with some disease resistance; 'Sugar Ann', 59 days, short, no support needed, sweet.

PEANUT
Arachis hypogaea

Peanut plants are shrubby or vining annuals with pealike flowers that grow on long stems called pegs. After pollination, the pegs drop and push into the soil, producing peanuts on the

JUMBO VIRGINIA PEANUT

buried tips. Peanut roots, like those of peas and other legumes, host nitrogen-fixing bacteria that improve the soil.

Site: Full sun. Sandy soil high in organic matter. Plentiful moisture as vines grow; less after flowering. Peanuts require a long, warm growing season, so they're commercially grown in the South. By starting plants indoors, you can grow them in the North as

well. Peanuts are fun to grow, but aren't high yielders—expect 40 to 50 peanuts per plant.

How to Grow: If starting indoors, plant five weeks before you plan to set out transplants. Set out transplants or direct-seed outdoors two to three weeks after average date of last frost. Set transplants or shelled raw peanuts 6 to 8 inches apart in rows 12 to 18 inches apart. Plant raw peanuts 1 to 2 inches deep.

Don't use high-nitrogen fertilizer. Cover soil with loose mulch to prevent crusting. Keep soil moist until plants flower, then allow to dry. Wet soil causes hollow shells.

Few pests or diseases. Rodents can be a problem.

Harvest: Pull up entire plant when it shows frost damage. Let pods dry on plant in cool, dry, well-ventilated area. Store pods in dry, cool place for up to 12 months.

Cultivars: 'Valencia', 120 to 150 days, large plant, three small peanuts per shell, full flavored, adapted to many soils; 'Spanish', 110 days, compact plants, two or three small peanuts per shell, early; 'Jumbo Virginia', 120 days, compact plants, high yield, large peanuts.

PEPPER, BELL PEPPER, SWEET PEPPER, HOT PEPPER
Capsicum annuum

In their native Central America, peppers are woody shrubs that bear year after year. In North America, we grow fast-ripening cultivars as annuals and hope for a hot summer and a late frost. If the summer is long or if you live in the South, you have an easier time getting sweet peppers to mature from bland-tasting green to a sweet true color—yellow, orange, red, brown, purple, or black. Hot peppers develop the most heat in hot climates, but varieties bred for colder climates work well in the North. Hot peppers are hottest when they ripen from green to red or yellow.

IVORY HYBRID SWEET PEPPER

Site: Full sun. Well-drained soil, high in organic matter for sweet peppers; sandy soil for hot peppers. The ideal pH is 6.0 to 7.3. Moderate moisture. Prefers warm climates.

How to Grow: If starting indoors, plant ⅓ inch deep eight to 10 weeks before you plan to set transplants outdoors; germinates best at soil temperature of 80°F. Set out transplants in spring two to three weeks after average date of last frost, when soil is at least 60°F and night temperatures are at least 55°F. Space transplants at 20 to 24 inches.

Warm soil by covering with plastic. Protect new transplants from cold by covering with bottomless milk jugs or floating row covers for about five weeks; remove when flowering begins. Provide 1 inch of water every week. Mulch to conserve moisture. Spray with liquid seaweed one month after planting and again when fruit sets.

Control aphids and tarnished plant bugs with pyrethrin. Prevent blossom-end rot by mulching soil to keep it evenly moist. Prevent sunscald by covering fruit not shaded by leaves with cheesecloth.

Harvest: Cut from plant when full size and either green or mature color. Waiting for maturity can decrease yield in the North. Dry off and refrigerate in plastic bag. Freeze hot peppers whole.

Cultivars: Peppers vary in their regional adaptation; ask your county Cooperative Extension Service office for recommendations. Maturity dates below are from set-out date; add eight to 10 weeks from seeding date.

Sweet: 'California Wonder', 72 days, blocky, deep green fruit; 'Jingle Bells', 55 to 60 days, prolific, tiny, bell-shaped fruit, turns green to red, good for cold climates; 'Sweet Banana', 65 to 70 days, 6-inch cylindrical, waxy fruit, turns yellow to red, crisp and mild; 'Cubanelle', 68 days, smooth, frying pepper, yellow-green ripens red; 'Gypsy', 65 days, high yields, disease-resistant, yellow fruit turns to orange then red, good for cold climates; 'Ace', 50 days, early, reliable, bell-type, small to medium fruit, good for cold climates; 'Chocolate Beauty', 75 to 85 days, turns green to brown, reliable color, size, and taste; 'Purple Beauty', 65 to 75 days, reliable, turns green to purple then red, firm and tart fruit; 'Vanguard', 59 days, medium-large, three- to four-lobed green bells ripening to red, virus-resistant, resists heat and cold stress.

CAYENNE HOT PEPPER

Hot: 'Poblano', 90 to 100 days, mild, turns green to red, wrinkled when mature, called ancho when dried; 'Cayenne', 70 days, prolific, extra hot, long, thin, tapered, turns dark green to red, good dried for chili powder; 'Hungarian Hot Wax', 75 days, good for the North, hot, yellow, conical, three-lobed fruit; 'Jalapeño', 65 to 75 days, short, rounded, dark green with red tinge, hot, high yields; 'Serrano', 80 to 90 days, extra hot, short, tapered, red fruit; 'Habañero', 75 days, extra hot, green to pink-orange, short, bell-shaped, best in the South; 'Aji Habañero', 85 days, fruit ripens to gold, spicy, smoky flavor.

POTATO

POTATO

Solanum tuberosum

Growing potatoes allows you to sample exotic types of this staple tuber—blue or pink potatoes, or elongated fingerlings, for example. A potato crop is started from pieces of potatoes called seed pieces or eye sets. (A plant grows from each eye.) Don't plant eyes of grocery-store potatoes, which are chemically treated and won't sprout. Buy "seed potatoes" that are certified disease-free.

Site: Full sun to part shade. Light-textured, deeply loosened, well-drained soil high in organic matter with supply of potassium and phosphorus. Ideal pH 4.8 to 5.8. Raised beds often advised. Plentiful moisture. Best where summers are 60° to 70°F.

How to Grow: Before planting you can "chit" seed potatoes by *continued*

POTATO
(continued)

exposing them to light for a few weeks to induce sprouting. Where summers are cool, plant in spring as soon as soil can be worked. In the South, plant in fall or winter. Plant whole, small tubers, or seed pieces with at least one eye. Line planting holes with compost or source of phosphorus and potassium. Three planting methods are common; all protect tubers from sunlight, which causes greening.

Hilling: Plant in furrow 3 to 4 inches deep. Set seed pieces with the cut-side down and eye up at 10-inch intervals in rows 2 to 3 feet apart and cover with soil. When 6 inches of stem is above soil, loosely mound soil around stems. Repeat every time 6 inches of stem shows.

Black plastic: In cool regions, plant into holes in black plastic mulch, planting 3 to 4 inches deep and 9 to 12 inches apart.

Straw: In clay or waterlogged soils, lay pieces on ground and cover with 6 inches of straw or leaves.

To prevent scab, don't add manure to soil. Withhold water as storage potatoes begin to die down, to improve storage.

Use floating row covers to protect from Colorado potato beetle. Destroy orange clusters of potato beetle eggs hidden beneath leaves. Pull and destroy plants with blighted leaves that turn yellow, then brown and withered.

Harvest: Dig small, immature, new potatoes seven to eight weeks after planting. Take care not to disturb the plant by removing soil from side of hill to harvest. Potatoes are mature when full size or after tops die down. Dig by loosening soil with spade or fork and removing potatoes by hand. Let dry outdoors in shade for several hours. Brush off soil, but don't wash. Store in dry, cold, but not freezing, area. Cut off any green skin or sprouted eyes before eating; both can be toxic.

Cultivars: 'Dark Red Norland', early, red skin and white flesh, oval-oblong, summer harvest, stores well; 'Yukon Gold', mid early, yellow flesh and flaked skin, medium-large, oval-round, late summer harvest, all-purpose, good storage, disease-resistant; 'Kennebec', late, large, white, oval, good yield and flavor, fall harvest, stores well, drought-tolerant, disease-resistant; 'All Blue', late, deep purple skin and flesh, high yield, fall harvest; 'Rose Finn Apple', small fingerling, pink skin, waxy yellow flesh, late summer, good yield, stores well, disease-resistant.

RADICCHIO, RED CHICORY
Cichorium intybus

An old-fashioned cultivar of chicory, radicchio is a beautiful gourmet salad ingredient that tastes pleasingly bitter. There's a trick to

SILLA RADICCHIO

getting radicchio to form tight heads, composed of firm, purplish red leaves with creamy white midribs. During warm weather, the plant is a tall, hairy, green-leaved chicory. If cut back when cool weather arrives, however, the new growth becomes the gourmet red-leaf vegetable. Modern cultivars develop dense heads during warm weather without cutting back, then develop their distinctive color when cool weather arrives.

Site: Full sun to half shade. Humus-rich, moist soil. Plentiful moisture. Grows anywhere, but older cultivars bolt (see Bok Choy) quickly in warm weather.

How to Grow: Sow seed ½ inch deep in rows 1 foot apart, thinning to 1 foot in mid spring in the North and late summer in the South. Allow traditional cultivars to grow until date of first fall frost, then cut off green tops. Tightly packed red heads resprout and can be harvested in four to six weeks. In cold climates, plants overwinter, and red heads form in spring.

Can be forced like Belgian endive. Often unpredictable or not uniform. Usually pest-free.

Harvest: Harvest when heads feel firm to touch, cutting above crown so fall-harvested plants will resprout in spring for a second harvest. If heads fail to form, harvest loose leaves.

Cultivars: Traditional: 'Red Treviso', 100 days, slender leaves turn from green to deep burgundy, white veins, pointed heads; 'Red Verona', 100 days, round heads.

Modern: 'Giulio', 60 days, bolt-resistant, dense red heads, grow in cool season in frost-free areas, for fall harvest in other areas; 'Rossana', 75 days, round, dark crimson heads, bolt-resistant; 'Silla', 65 days, round, red, bolt-resistant heads.

RADISH
Raphanus sativus

When you're winter-weary, grow radishes. Plant early in spring and wait only about a month to harvest. Most radishes mature so quickly you can fit in several crops each season, skipping only the hottest part of summer and the iciest part of winter. Besides the traditional round radishes, try the long French types and the Daikon type popular in Asian and German cooking.

Site: Full sun to light shade. Loose, deeply worked soil, free of clods and rocks and high in organic matter.

CHERRY BOMB RADISH

Plentiful moisture. All climates; prefers cool, moist weather.

How to Grow: Make first sowing in spring two or three weeks before average date of last frost. For continuous harvest, plant every two or three weeks, except during hottest part of summer. Plant Daikon types about two months before average date of first fall frost. Sow seeds ½ inch deep and ½ inch apart in rows 1 foot apart. Thin seedlings to 1 to 1½ inches apart; Daikon types to 6 inches apart.

Keep soil moist so radishes don't become pithy and hot. Prevent flea beetles and cabbage root maggots by covering with floating row cover. No serious diseases.

Harvest: Pull up whole plant while root is still tender and not too hot. (Best harvest size varies with cultivar, so test a few.) Refrigerate in plastic bag for two to three weeks.

Cultivars: Round: 'Sparkler', 24 days, red on top, white at tip, crisp; 'Easter Egg', 25 days, multihued including white, scarlet, lavender, and pink, oval, crisp, not woody; 'Poker', 30 days, mild, bright red, tolerates close planting; 'Cherry Bomb', 25 days, bright red skin, juicy, crisp, white flesh, resists woodiness after reaches prime.

Long French: 'White Icicle', 27 days, long, white, crunchy, mild, best harvested young; 'D'Avignon', 21 days,

3 to 4 inches long, slender, red with white tip, pointed.

Daikon: 'Spring Leader', 60 days, resists bolting (see Bok Choy), for late winter to mid spring seeding, white, smooth, tapered; 'Summer Cross No. 3', 55 days, late summer and fall planting, 8 inches long, uniform, tapered roots, sweet, juicy.

RHUBARB
R. × cultorum

Rhubarb's tart, reddish leaf stalks are delicious in sauces and pies, but don't eat the green leaf blades, which can be toxic. Rhubarb doesn't always come true from seed, so it usually is started from root divisions. Instead of planting this attractive, long-lived perennial in the vegetable garden, which gets turned each year,

CANADA RED RHUBARB

plant it in a separate bed or in the back of the flower border, where its 2- to 4-foot-tall stalks can add color and bold texture. Three or four plants usually are sufficient.

Site: Full sun to part shade. Deep, loose, fertile soil, organically rich with supply of phosphorus and potassium. Plentiful moisture. Best in areas with cool, moist summers, freezing winters.

How to Grow: Plant as soon as you receive crowns in early spring so they don't dry out. Crowns should be dormant or just beginning to leaf out. Space 3 feet apart and cover with 1 to 2 inches of soil.

Keep soil moist. Mulch once plants are actively growing. Remove flower stalks, which are long stems growing from center.

Destroy plants with stalks and crowns infested by rhubarb curculios. Destroy nearby dock weeds, which shelter curculios. No serious diseases.

Harvest: Harvest by twisting and pulling stalks from plants. Don't harvest during first year. In spring of the second year, harvest a few stalks from each plant. In subsequent years, harvest for two months each spring; stop when new stalks come up slender. Remove no more than half the stalks from any plant during a season. Refrigerate stalks without leaves for up to three weeks in plastic bag.

Cultivars: 'Canada Red', large, red stalks retain color when cooked; 'Valentine', good quality, sweet, deep red; 'Victoria', green stalks with red shading.

RUTABAGA
Brassica napus
(Napobrassica Group)

Rutabaga, a biennial grown as an annual, is a cross between a turnip and a cabbage. Its deeply lobed, grayish leaves form a rosette that attaches to the large edible bulb. Most rutabagas have yellow bulbs with a purple top. Rutabaga likes cool weather with a distinct contrast between day and night temperatures and usually is grown in fall and winter. When it's too hot, the bulbs become stringy.

Site: Full sun to part shade. Well-drained soil, high in organic matter, with no rocks and lumps that can cause splitting, and a pH of 6.0 or above. Plentiful moisture. Grows in *continued*

RUTABAGA
(continued)

YORK SWEDE RUTABAGA

all climates, but requires 50° to 75°F weather.

How to Grow: In the North, plant in spring four to six weeks before average date of last frost. Make fall planting in late summer in the North, in fall in the South. Sow seeds ½ inch deep and 2 inches apart in rows 18 to 24 inches apart. Thin 6 to 8 inches apart.

Keep soil moist so roots don't get stringy. In cold areas, mulch deeply to prevent soil from freezing and to extend harvest.

Hose off aphids with hard stream of water or spray with insecticidal soap. To prevent clubroot, grow resistant cultivars. If interior has brown spot, test soil for boron deficiency.

Harvest: Dig root when 3 to 5 inches in diameter. Do not refrigerate. Store for up to six months in moist place near freezing.

Cultivars: 'Marian', 85 to 95 days, yellow flesh, purple bulb tops, stores well, resists clubroot, tolerates close spacing; 'York Swede', 95 days, sweet, cooks well, resists clubroot; 'Purple Top Yellow', 90 days, sweet, dense, turns from yellow to orange when cooked, stores well; 'Laurentian', 90 days, rich yellow flesh, good keeper.

SHALLOT
Allium cepa
(Aggregatum Group)

A staple of French cuisine, shallots are easy to grow: Stick the little bulbs in the ground and wait for them to multiply. A mild member of the onion family, shallots usually are started from sets (cloves of bulbs), but they also can be started from seed.

SHALLOTS

Site: Full sun to part shade. Tolerates poor, shallow soil; may be less flavorful in clay. Plentiful moisture. Grows well in any climate.

How to Grow: Plant sets in fall or in spring four to six weeks before average date of last frost. Fall planting best in the South. Divide cloves into individual bulbs and poke each bulb into ground so top is even with or just above soil. Space 6 to 8 inches apart in rows 12 inches apart, or sow seeds ½ inch deep and ½ to 1 inch apart in rows 10 to 18 inches apart.

Keep soil moist. Control weeds to reduce competition. No serious pests or diseases.

Harvest: For scallions, harvest tops from fall-planted bulbs in spring. For shallots, pull up when tops die back and dry in airy, dry place for up to two weeks. Store in cool, dry place.

Cultivars: Bulb sets not always sold by cultivar names.

Bulbs: 'Golden Gourmet', 77 days, crisp, brown skin, high yields, stores well; 'French Red', pink skins, pink cast to flesh, easy to grow, fall plant, doesn't store well.

Seed: 'Atlas', 90 days, early, pink flesh, widely adapted; 'Creation', 105 days, white flesh, yellow skin, stores well, adapted to the North.

SORREL, GARDEN SORREL
Rumex acetosa

Garden sorrel is a small perennial plant about 1 to 3 feet tall with arrow-shaped leaves that add a piquant lemony taste to soups and salads. It's extremely cold-hardy and grows almost anywhere—not surprising when you know that most

SORREL

of its relatives are considered weeds. You can harvest sorrel from early summer through fall for many years.

Site: Full sun to part shade. Well-drained, fertile soil. Abundant moisture. Perennial in zones 3 to 9.

How to Grow: Sow seeds three to six weeks before average date of last frost, thickly sowing seeds ½ inch deep in rows 18 to 24 inches apart. In six to eight weeks, thin to 12 to 18 inches apart. Keep soil moist to prevent tough leaves. Remove flower stalks as they form to encourage more leaf production. Divide mature plants every three or four years.

Hose off aphids with hard stream of water. No serious diseases.

Harvest: Cut off leaves as needed. Refrigerate in plastic bag for up to two weeks.

Cultivars: French sorrel (*Rumex scutatus*) is a similar 18-inch-tall plant cultivated in Europe, tastes tangier, can be difficult to obtain in United States.

SPINACH
Spinacia oleracea

Spinach loves cool soil and weather, so it's one of the first crops to plant in spring. You can make a fall planting too, but the seed doesn't germinate as well in the still-warm soil of the fall garden. In hot weather, spinach can bolt (see Bok Choy), which makes the leaves bitter.

SPUTNIK HYBRID SPINACH

Site: Full sun to light shade. Fertile soil with ideal pH of 6.5 to 7.5. Plentiful moisture. Grows in all climates; tolerates cold, but not heat.

How to Grow: Plant in early spring as soon as soil can be worked. For continuous harvest, sow every 10 days while soil is still cool. For fall and overwintering crop, plant in late summer in the North, in mid fall in the South. Sow seeds ½ inch deep, 1 inch apart, in rows 12 to 18 inches apart. Thin to 2 to 3 inches.

Keep soil moist. Mulch soil to keep leaves clean. Apply blood meal or other source of nitrogen beside plants to increase size and improve flavor.

Pick off leaves showing tunnels made by leaf miners. Prevent mildew by growing resistant cultivars.

Harvest: Harvest when leaves are 4 to 6 inches long, cutting entire plant or individual leaves. Refrigerate immediately without washing. Keeps up to two weeks.

Cultivars: 'Indian Summer', 40 days, high yields, flavorful, savoyed (crinkled) leaves, resists bolting, disease-tolerant; 'Space', 40 days, early, smooth leaf, high yields, large, mildew-resistant; 'Tyee', 42 days, upright, savoyed leaves, resists bolting, resists mildew; 'Olympia', 45 days, smooth leaf, resists bolting and mildew; 'Bloomsdale', 50 days, thick, savoyed, sweet leaves, good for fall and overwintering; 'Sputnik Hybrid', 60 days, dark green, slightly savoyed, mildew-resistant.

SQUASH, PUMPKIN
Cucurbita spp.

For convenience (rather than for any botanically significant reason), squashes (*Cucurbita pepo*) are divided into two groups: summer and winter. Summer squashes include scallop or pattypan, straightneck, crookneck, and zucchini. Winter squashes include acorn, banana, butternut, cushaw, delicata, golden nugget, hubbard, kabocha, spaghetti, and turk's turban. Pumpkins (*C. pepo* var. *pepo*) also are a type of winter squash.

Summer squashes can be eaten raw or cooked when immature and tender. The raw blossoms are edible, too. Winter squashes and pumpkins have a hard, mature skin and dark yellow flesh and are eaten when fully mature.

Some pumpkin cultivars are best for eating, others for decoration or jack-o'-lanterns. Winter squashes store for months if properly cured.

Squashes usually grow on long, twining vines, which can be trellised to save space, but some cultivars are compact bushes. Bush-type summer squashes are highly productive, but bush-type winter ones are not.

BUTTERNUT SQUASH

Site: Full sun to part shade. Fertile, well-drained, deeply loosened soil rich in organic matter. Plentiful moisture. Squashes hate frost, need warm soil to germinate, and thrive in warm weather. They prefer warm, dry, sunny conditions and are cold-sensitive.

How to Grow: If starting indoors, sow seeds in peat pots three to four weeks before you plan to set out transplants; sow pumpkins two to three weeks before transplanting. Sow seeds outdoors or set out transplants two to three weeks after average date of last frost or when soil is 65°F. Plant four or five squash seeds 1 inch deep in hills spaced 3 to 4 feet apart; plant six to eight pumpkin seeds 1½ inches deep.

When seedlings are several inches tall, thin to strongest two or three plants per hill. Or, sow squash seeds 2 inches apart in rows 2 feet apart for bush type and 4 to 6 feet apart for vines; thin seedlings to 16 to 24 inches apart. Thin pumpkins to *continued*

SQUASH, PUMPKIN
(continued)

BIG MAX PUMPKIN

3 feet apart, in rows 6 feet apart for compact types or 10 feet apart for vining types.

To prevent seed rot, especially in pumpkins, plant in moist soil; don't water again until seedlings are up.

In cool regions, use black plastic mulch to warm soil. Keep soil moist after seedlings are up, especially during hot weather. Trellis vines if space is limited.

To prevent cucumber beetles, which can carry wilt bacteria, cover with floating row covers until female flowers set (check for swollen base). For squash vine borers, slit open stem if wall is thin or has hole and kill borer within. Cover stem with soil at slit to encourage rooting. Prevent bacterial wilt, mosaic virus, and mildew by planting resistant cultivars.

Harvest: Pick crookneck or straightneck when it's 4 to 7 inches long, pale yellow, and skin is pliable; pattypan when it's small and still grayish or greenish white, and zucchini when it's 4 to 6 inches long. Refrigerate unwashed for up to two weeks. Cut off winter squashes and pumpkins, leaving 1 inch of stem, before heavy frost, when skin is hard and stems are brown and dry. For longest storage, cure in sun for 10 days (cover if frost is predicted) or indoors at 80° to 90°F for four days. Cure pumpkins at 80° to 85°F for 10 days. Dunk winter squash in solution of 1 part bleach to 10 parts water and dry. Keep in cool, dry place for up to several months.

Cultivars: In the North, choose early-maturing cultivars.

Summer squash: Crookneck—'Early Golden Summer', 50 days, tender, best when 6 inches long, freezes well; 'Supersett', 50 days, bright yellow, thick neck, high yields, long-bearing; 'Multipik', 50 days, disease-resistant bush, 7-inch, glossy yellow fruit. Straightneck—'Early Prolific', 50 days, light yellow, cylindrical, long, high yields, open bush; 'Goldbar', 53 days, early, light yellow, long, smooth, good quality and flavor, high yields, compact bush; 'Seneca Prolific', 51 days, bright yellow, high yields. Scallop—'Peter Pan', 50 days, early, meaty fruit, best small, long-bearing, high yields, compact bush; 'Sunburst', 50 days, compact bush, gold fruit, tender even when mature. Zucchini—'Cocozelle', 60 days, dark green with light green stripes, long, slender, high yields; 'Gold Rush', 50 days, early, compact bush, deep yellow, cylindrical; 'Green Magic', 51 days, compact bush, dark green, cylindrical, high yields.

Winter squash (some are sold by the type name, not as named cultivars): Acorn—'Table King', 100 days, high yields, high quality, deep green, stores well; 'Cream of the Crop', 105 days, cream-colored, nutty rather than sweet, compact bush. Buttercup—'Burgess Strain Buttercup', 100 days, turban-shaped fruit, 6½ inches across, dark green skin with white stripes, lighter cap, dry, orange flesh; 'Home Delite', 100 days, dark green, small fruit; 'Golden Debut', 105 days, skin turns from green to orange, moist sweet flesh, boiled skin edible. Butternut—'Ponca', 100 days, base 8×4 inches, small vine, nutty taste, stores well; 'Waltham', 100 days, large, 11×6-inch base, tan rind, orange flesh, vigorous, stores well.

Delicata—'Delicata', 105 days, 7 inches long, 3 inches wide, cream-colored with green stripes and flecks, sweet, light orange flesh, high yields, stores well; 'Sugarloaf', 112 days, fruit sweeter, drier, shorter, and blockier than regular Delicata; 'Sweet Dumpling', 110 days, small ½-pound fruit, sweet, high yields, stores well. Hubbard—'Golden Delicious', 100 days, heart-shaped, warty bronze skin, orange-yellow flesh, cans and freezes well; 'Blue Hubbard', 120 days, large, blue-gray, dry, sweet flesh. Kabocha—'Honey Delight', 95 days, large, flat, dark green fruit with light green stripes, sweet, flaky, orange flesh. Spaghetti—'Orangetti', 85 days, oblong, orange skin; 'Tivoli', 98 days, high yields, compact bush.

Pumpkin: 'Jack Be Little', 95 days, flat miniature, 3-inch diameter, for cooking or decoration, grow on trellis; 'Howden', 110 days, big, orange, ribbed Halloween pumpkin, good handle, large spreading vines, not for eating; 'Rouge Vif D'Etampes', 110 days, flat, red heirloom, for display and eating; 'Spirit', 100 days, compact semibush vine, high yields, 12-inch diameter, Halloween; 'Lumina', 115 days, 10- to 12-pound white pumpkin, 8 to 10 inches diameter, orange flesh, stores well; 'Atlantic Giant', 120 days, mammoth orange pumpkin can reach record-breaking sizes. 'Big Max', 120 days, can grow quite large.

SWEET POTATO
Ipomoea batatas

With their long growing season and sensitivity to frost, sweet potatoes traditionally have been a southern vegetable, but new early cultivars now make them a northern crop, too. Grow the plant—a vine with trumpet-shaped flowers—from a piece of tuber called a slip. You can buy slips or grow your own. (Don't use sweet potatoes from the grocery, which are chemically treated to prevent sprouting.) Sweet potatoes with moist flesh sometimes are called yams, although true yams are a different species.

VARDAMAN SWEET POTATO

Site: Full sun. Best in deeply worked, sandy soil free of rocks and lumps that can deform tubers. Needs 1 inch of water each week. Best in the South; in the North, grow early types.
How to Grow: Buy rooted slips or root your own indoors eight to 10 weeks before you plan to plant outside. To root slips, cut sweet potato into six to eight pieces, each with a bud or eye. Bury 2 inches deep in moist sand or vermiculite and keep at 70° to 80°F. When slip sprouts, add 1 inch of soil. Plant slips four weeks after average date of last frost, when soil is warm. Make 10-inch-high, 12-inch-wide mound of soil. Plant slips on top of mound, spaced 15 inches apart in mounds 2 to 3 feet apart.

Keep soil moist to prevent cracking. Use plastic mulch to warm soil and prevent vines from rooting, which can decrease yield. Avoid high-nitrogen fertilizers, which cause leafy growth, but smaller tubers.

No serious pests or diseases in the North. In the South, plant resistant cultivars to control wireworms, weevils, and fusarium wilt.

Harvest: Carefully dig up tubers at base of plant after first frost or before soil temperature drops below 50°F, whichever occurs first. Avoid breaking delicate skins. Dry in sun for two hours, place in paper bag, and let cure for 10 days in warm place. Remove from bag and store in cool, dry place for up to six months.
Cultivars: 'Georgia Jet', 90 days, dark red skin, orange flesh, high yields, adapted to the North and the South; 'Centennial Days', early, orange skin and flesh, sweet, tender, mashes well; 'Porto Rico', 120 days, copper skin, reddish orange flesh, bakes well, compact bush; 'Vardaman', 90 to 100 days, plant turns purple to dark green, compact bush, yellow skin, reddish orange flesh, high yields.

TOMATILLO
Physalis ixocarpa

Tomatillos, a traditional Mexican food, resemble green or yellow table-tennis balls with papery skins. The tart flesh resembles a cherry

TOMA VERDE TOMATILLO

tomato when cut open. Tomatillos are distant relatives of tomatoes; closer relatives of ground cherries or husk-tomatoes. Native to Central and South America, tomatillos are easy to grow in northern climates if protected from frost. Plants grow about 3 feet high

and 5 feet wide and bear so heavily and long that two or three are plenty.

Site: Full sun. Tolerates range of soil types; best in fertile, well-drained soil. Plentiful moisture. Grows in any climate during warm season; frost-sensitive.
How to Grow: If starting indoors, sow seeds eight to 10 weeks before you plan to set transplants outdoors. Transplant four weeks after average date of last frost. To save space, stake or cage as you would tomatoes. Pinch off tips to slow growth. Mulch to keep fruit clean and hold moisture in soil.

Plants usually outgrow insects. Control heavy infestations of cucumber beetles, bean beetles, and aphids with insecticidal soap. No serious diseases.
Harvest: Pick at any size. Best for cooking when papery skin begins to split. For eating fresh, use larger. Store in dry, ventilated area. If skin molds, wash and dry fruit, wrap in paper towels, refrigerate up to two months.
Cultivars: 'Toma Verde', 75 days, bushy plant 3 to 4 feet wide, large fruit, good for salsa; 'Golden Tomatillo', 70 to 80 days, low-growing, small, sweet, yellow fruit, eat fresh.

TOMATO
Lycopersicon esculentum
(L. lycopersicum)

Endless good options—that's what makes tomato-growing interesting and fun. First, there are myriad sizes, shapes, and colors. Do you want, cherry, plum, pear, or beefsteak, yellow, red, white, or pink tomatoes? Should you stake, cage, or allow plants to sprawl on the ground? Should you prune out suckers (those little branches at the leaf axils) or not? Do you want short, determinate cultivars with fruit that ripens about the same time (good for canning)? Or, tall indeterminate ones that flower and set fruit throughout the season (good for a steady fresh supply)? Should you plant early, midseason, or late *continued*

TOMATO
(continued)

NORTHERN EXPOSURE SLICING TOMATO

MILANO PASTE TOMATO

types, or all three? All these tomato decisions may leave you dizzy, but it's hard to go wrong with any decision you make or any tomato you select.

CHELLO CHERRY TOMATO

Site: Full sun. Well-drained soil, high in organic matter; ideal pH 5.5 to 6.5. Plentiful moisture. Grows in all climates during warm season. In the far North, choose early-maturing cultivars. In the South, choose early and heat-tolerant cultivars.

How to Grow: If starting indoors, sow seeds six to eight weeks before you plan to transplant outdoors. Set out two to three weeks after average date of last frost. For fall harvest in the South, set out transplants in mid- to late summer. Space supported plants 2 to 3 feet apart and unsupported ones 3 to 4 feet apart. Bury stem up to lowest leaves; set plant on its side if stem is long.

At transplanting, stake, trellis, or cage indeterminate varieties, which grow tall. Support is optional for determinate varieties, which are shorter. Prune staked plants (removing side shoots where branches meet stem) for larger, earlier fruit. Mulch to prevent weeds, hold moisture in soil, and keep unstaked plants clean. Keep watered early and during flowering; reduce watering as fruit sets. If air is calm during flowering, gently shake plants to distribute pollen. Avoid high-nitrogen fertilizers, which reduce fruiting.

Pick off tomato hornworms. To prevent most diseases, plant resistant varieties. To prevent blossom-end rot, mulch to keep soil moisture even.

Harvest: If possible, pick fully colored, firm fruit. Otherwise, pick full-size green or slightly colored fruit and ripen at room temperature out of direct sunlight. Store at room temperature unless they're very ripe, in which case refrigerate for up to one week.

Cultivars: Days to maturity is from set-out date.

Slicing: 'Early Girl', 52 days, indeterminate, flavorful, long-bearing; 'Celebrity', 70 days, midseason, determinate, medium-large, firm fruit, resists cracking, disease-resistant, well-adapted; 'Brandywine', 78 days, indeterminate, extra-large, pink fruit, spicy, moderate yields; 'Champion', 62 days, indeterminate, large, meaty, sweet fruit, disease-resistant; 'Beefmaster', 80 days, mid- to late season, indeterminate, extra-large, fleshy fruit, flavorful, high yields, disease-resistant; 'Better Boy' 72 days, midseason, indeterminate, extra-large fruit, disease-resistant; 'Northern Exposure', 67 days, excellent flavor, determinate, bears well in cool short-season areas.

Cherry: 'Sweet 100 Plus', 70 days, indeterminate, great taste, crack-resistant, extremely high yields, best staked; 'Tiny Tim', 50 days, determinate, good for containers, 18 inches tall, high-yielding; 'Chello', 63 days, semibush, indeterminate, golden-yellow fruit; 'Yellow Pear', 73 days, clusters of small, yellow, pear-shaped fruit; 'Camp Joy', 65 days, full-flavored, red fruit, indeterminate.

Paste: 'Roma', 76 days, determinate, meaty, high yields, disease-resistant; 'Milano', 63 days, determinate, disease-resistant, meaty pear-shaped fruit; 'San Remo', 76 days, indeterminate, meaty, high yields, disease-resistant; 'Viva Italia', 76 days, indeterminate, pear-shaped, high yields, disease-resistant.

Yellow: 'Taxi', 65 days, determinate, sweet, meaty, medium-large fruit, well-adapted; 'Lemon Boy', 72 days, indeterminate, large, mild, yellow fruit, disease-resistant, well-adapted, high yields, best staked.

TURNIP
Brassica rapa (Rapifera Group)

A hardy biennial, the turnip is grown as an annual for its root (actually a swollen stem base) and for its leafy, green tops. A cool-weather

DE MILAN TURNIP

Cultivars: 'Purple Top White Globe', 50 days, round bicolor with white base and purple top, smooth root, mild flavor, large-lobed greens, performs well throughout season; 'Shogoin', 70 days, good for root and greens, white skin, flat-topped root, tall, green, ready in 30 days; 'Gilfeather', 75 days, large, oval, white root with green top, sweet, grows large without losing quality; 'De Milan', 35 days, rose-red tops, use as baby turnip.

CRIMSON SWEET WATERMELON

crop, turnips become bitter if temperatures are too warm or if they don't get enough moisture. Turnips are a good source of amino acids and potassium.

Site: Full sun to part shade. Best in fertile, humus-rich, well-drained, soil; pH of 6.0 to 8.0. Tolerates poor fertility. Plentiful moisture. Adapted to a wide range of climates; needs short, cool season.

How to Grow: Plant when soil is at least 60°F, up to six weeks before average date of last frost. Plant in late summer for fall harvest, in fall for winter harvest in the South. Thickly sow seeds ¼ to ½ inch deep in rows 8 to 12 inches apart. Thin to 4 to 6 inches apart. Eat thinnings as greens.

Keep soil moist, watering deeply. Mulch to conserve moisture. Avoid high-nitrogen fertilizers, which encourage topgrowth and excessive root formation. Hose off aphids with hard stream of water. Control flea beetles with insecticidal soap.

Harvest: Dig or pull up when roots are 1½ to 2½ inches in diameter, before heavy frosts. Don't refrigerate; store in cool, moist place for up to five months. For greens, use thinnings or cut when harvesting roots. Refrigerate in plastic for up to two weeks.

WATERMELON
Citrullus lanatus

Older types of watermelons had extensive vines that required too much space for most home gardens to accommodate. Newer short-vine or bush-type cultivars take up less room—some as little as 3 square feet. Cultivars give you a choice of crunchy sweet melons, ranging in size from 5 to 100 pounds. Cultivars also provide a variety of colors—pink, red, yellow, or white flesh. Small-fruited icebox types (with fruit weighing 10 pounds or less) mature faster and grow better in northern gardens.

Site: Full sun. Warm, humus-rich, well-drained soil; pH of 6.2 to 6.8. Plentiful moisture. Best in the South; needs warm growing season.

How to Grow: If starting indoors, sow in peat pots two to three weeks before you set out transplants. Set out two to three weeks after average date of last spring frost, when soil is above 70°F. Plant in hills. For vining types, space hills 3 feet apart in rows 8 feet apart. For bush types, space hills 2½ feet apart in rows 3 feet apart. In warm areas, direct-seed five or six seeds in hills spaced as for transplants. Thin to strongest two or three seedlings per hill. Use plastic mulch to warm soil.

Water often while plants are growing, but let them dry out between waterings as fruit ripens. Mulch to hold soil moisture and keep fruit clean. Trellis vines to save space, supporting melons in net or pantyhose hammock.

Pick off cucumber beetles, which spread wilt. Prevent anthracnose and wilt by planting resistant cultivars.

Harvest: Pick when fruit is full size, surface is dull, tendril on stem turns brown and dry, and side on ground changes from white to pale yellow. Store for up to several weeks in refrigerator or other cool place.

Cultivars: Short vine or bush: 'Garden Baby', 70 days, short vine, sweet, red flesh, 7-pound fruit, green rind with light stripes; 'Yellow Doll', 76 days, short vine, sweet, yellow flesh, 5- to 8-pound fruit, light rind with dark stripes; 'Sugar Bush', 80 days, extra-compact, 6- to 8-pound fruit, red flesh, high sugar content, tolerates less fertile soil.

Standard vine: 'Crimson Sweet', 95 days, medium-large fruit up to 25 pounds, sweet, red flesh, round, hard dark green rind, resists wilt, dependable; 'Charleston Gray', 85 days, crisp, pink flesh, medium-large fruit up to 30 pounds, disease-resistant, won't sunburn; 'Sugar Baby', 80 days, sweet, red flesh, 8- to 10-pound fruit, resists cracking and keeps flavor in wet seasons, dark rind; 'Carolina Cross', 100 days, green-striped, extra-large fruit up to 200 pounds.

HERBS

CHAPTER 11

THE PLEASURES OF GROWING HERBS

No matter where you live—in the city or in the country—or how much space you have for gardening, you can enjoy growing and using herbs.

Your herbal harvests can be used in multiple ways. Herbal teas blended from dried leaves and flowers are easy to prepare. Savor a hot, fragrant brew at the end of a hectic day or relax on a summer afternoon with a cooling pitcher of iced herbal tea. You also may wish to research herbal remedies, of which herb teas are a mainstay. Plus, you can enhance your culinary creations with homegrown herbs and edible flowers, adding flavor without salt and fat.

Your home, too, can benefit from herbs. Follow tradition by fashioning wreaths and swags from herbs that were once thought to ward off evil spirits. Or, create a tussie-mussie, a Victorian herbal nosegay, in which each leaf and flower holds a special meaning. Potpourris, the original air fresheners, are fragrant mixtures of oils, spices, and dried petals and leaves. Extremely popular today, homemade potpourris make thoughtful gifts.

Getting started with herbs is easy, fun, and immediately gratifying. Herb gardening can fill many aspects of your life with beauty and pleasure. The rewards may be summarized by the popular saying among herbarians: "Herbs leave their fragrance on the hand that gathers them."

EASY HERB-GROWING TECHNIQUES

If you are new to raising herbs, you will be pleased to learn that most herbs are easy to grow. Many flourish with ordinary watering, require little special care, and suffer from few pests and diseases. Gray-leaved herbs and those filled with aromatic oils come from the Mediterranean area, so they thrive in well-drained soil and hot sun. In fact, most herbs grow best in full sun, but some also tolerate shade (see Herbs for Shady Places on page 495). Although many herbs grow reasonably well in poor soil, most prefer average fertility and a neutral to slightly alkaline pH.

When selecting a site for an herb garden, consider how you intend to use the harvest. If you want to use the herbs for cooking, choose a location close to the kitchen so it will be convenient for snipping a few leaves or sprigs to add to your favorite dishes.

Herbs, like most other flowering plants, may be divided into three categories: annuals, perennials, and biennials. Some herbs are woody shrubs; some are tender perennials that are treated as annuals in cold climates and grown year-round in warm climates. Tender perennials can be potted and overwintered in a coldframe, greenhouse, or cold, sunny window. Some gardeners keep herbs in pots all year, growing them outdoors during summer and bringing them indoors for the winter.

The lovely lavender-pink blossoms of chives mingle with irises, all rising above the crinkled green foliage of spearmint. Chive blossoms are tasty as well as decorative in vinegars and salads.

HERBS FOR WET CONDITIONS

Most herbs thrive in well-drained soil, but these prefer or tolerate moist conditions:

- Angelica
- Comfrey
- Lovage
- Marsh mallow
- Mint
- Pennyroyal
- Sweet woodruff
- Valerian

Position the herbs in your garden according to their size and growth habits. Creeping thyme, for example, never achieves any height, but spreads in a dense mat that can cover a large area. Lemon balm reseeds profusely; mints spread via underground runners.

There are ways to contain spreading herbs to prevent them from taking over the garden. Corral herbs that spread by underground stems or runners, such as mint, bee balm, lemon balm, tansy, and tarragon, by growing them in pots. Or, plant the spreaders inside chimney flue tiles or bottomless wooden boxes that have sides at least 12 inches high. Then bury the tiles or wooden boxes in the ground.

To control herbs that self-sow prolifically, such as chives, dill, catnip, and fennel, simply deadhead the flowers before they go to seed.

Mulch is invaluable in herb gardens. It slows weed growth, keeps the soil moist, and prevents soil from splashing onto edible plants. Cocoa hulls are favored in herb gardens because of their chocolate scent and lovely, fine texture. Wood chips also work well for mulch. In damp areas, a gravel mulch spread under moisture-sensitive herbs such as thyme and sage will prevent them from rotting.

Just a step or two takes the cook from the kitchen to this lush, fragrant herb garden. This back-door garden contains thyme, chives, sage, fennel, and lavender.

HERBS FOR SHADY PLACES

These herbs can tolerate some degree of shade:

- Angelica
- Chervil
- Chives
- Costmary
- Lemon balm
- Lovage
- Mint
- Parsley
- Sweet cicely
- Sweet woodruff
- Tarragon

BASIL, SWEET BASIL
Ocimum basilicum

No tomato sauce would be complete without basil. Basil and its delightful varieties also complete the herb garden. Basil's culinary uses are legendary and legion, with sauces, pestos, and vinegars the most popular. Foliage varies from tiny leaves on globe-shaped plants to bold, scalloped, or crinkled ones on tall stems. Leaf color may be bright emerald green or deep dusky purple,

BASIL

and plant size varies from 9 to 24 inches tall and wide. All versions are wonderfully aromatic. Graceful spires of small white to rose-pink flowers top plants in midsummer.

Use miniature basils as edgings and purple-leaved forms for contrast in borders, containers, and herb gardens.

Site: Full sun. Rich, well-drained soil. Plentiful water. Warm-season annual in zones 2 to 11.
How to Grow: Sow seed indoors at 70°F, eight weeks before last frost, or outdoors after soil is warmed. In long, warm-summer areas, resow in midsummer. Plant nursery transplants after soil is warm. Space 9 to 12 inches

apart. Pinch several times when young to encourage branching and prevent flowering. For culinary use, don't allow to flower. Often troubled by slugs, snails, and flea beetles.
Harvest: Sprigs of purple basil look lovely in bouquets and dry well for wreaths. Cut to use fresh as needed; best before flowering. Freeze whole leaves. Red and purple varieties make stunningly colorful, tasty vinegars.
Cultivars: 'Mini', 9 to 12 inches tall, small green leaves, white flowers; 'Anise' or 'Thai', 12 to 18 inches tall, young leaves purple, flowers pink, intense flavor; 'Green Ruffles', 12 to 18 inches tall, ruffled green leaves, white flowers; 'Purple Ruffles', deep purple, ruffled leaves, pink flowers; 'Opal Basil', deep purple foliage, pink flowers.

BEEBALM, OSWEGO TEA, BERGAMOT
Monarda didyma

One of the few herbs with remarkably showy blossoms, beebalm also attracts hordes of bees, as well as hummingbirds and

BEEBALM

butterflies. Originally red, garden versions now include bright red, salmon, pink, burgundy, or white flowers carried in clusters atop slender

3- to 4-foot stems. Beebalm is ideal for bee, butterfly, hummingbird, and tea gardens. Beautiful in perennial borders and cottage gardens.

Indigenous to North America, beebalm was prized both by Native Americans and later by the Shakers for its medicinal uses. The aromatic, lance-shaped leaves also are the flavoring in Earl Grey tea. Use the leaves and edible flowers to add a citrus tang to fruit salads.

Site: Full sun to part shade. Fertile, peaty soil. Plentiful moisture. Hardy in zones 4 to 9.
How to Grow: Divide in fall or spring, or use nursery plants. Space 2 feet apart. Can be invasive. Dig up 3-year-old clumps, discard centers, and replant sucker shoots. Mulch well in cold winters without snow cover. Cut back immediately after blooming for rebloom in fall. Easily susceptible to mildew, especially after flowering and if underwatered. Cut diseased stems to ground and new growth often will be disease-free.
Harvest: Harvest fresh leaves for tea as needed. Make two harvests for drying: one before flowering and one after. Cut to within 1 inch of ground when lower leaves yellow; repeat when resulting new growth matures. Strip leaves from stems and dry on screens in a warm, dark place for three days. Or, hang bunches of flower stalks upside down in a dry, dark place.
Cultivars and Similar Species: 'Snow White', pure white flowers; 'Croftway Pink', bright pink; 'Mahogany', deep red; 'Adam', deep red; 'Cambridge Scarlet', vivid red.

Mildew-resistant: 'Gardenview Red', rose-red; 'Stone's Throw Pink', bright pink; Marshall's Delight', pink; 'Violet Queen', magenta-violet. *Monarda citriodora*, pink-purple blossoms, strong lemon scent.

BORAGE
Borago officinalis

Bearing edible sky blue flowers with a cucumber taste, borage adorns herb and vegetable gardens as well as cottage gardens and edible landscapes. The coarse, somewhat prickly leaves form a basal rosette from which arises a hollow stalk topped with intense blue, starlike flowers. These open successively in midsummer for a month or more and look especially lovely when backlit by the sun. They also attract bees. Plants grow 2 to 3 feet tall and half as wide. Tea made from borage leaves is said to instill courage and good spirits.

BORAGE

Site: Full sun. Best in light but fertile, well-drained soil; don't allow to dry. Cool-season hardy annual in zones 3 to 8.
How to Grow: Sow seeds in fall or spring; plant nursery plants in spring. Thin to 2 feet apart. Self-sows to perpetuate itself. Cut back during flowering to promote bushiness and prolong life. Pull out plants after they shed seeds and begin to yellow. Self-sown plants are more robust than purchased transplants. Slugs may eat leaves.

Harvest: Pick tender young leaves for salads. Pick flowers for decorative and culinary use; freeze in ice-cube trays for summer punches.
Similar Species: *Borago laxiflora*, perennial in zones 5 to 9, blue flowers in late spring.

CHAMOMILE, ROMAN CHAMOMILE
Chamaemelum nobile (*Anthemis nobilis*)

This popular, apple-scented perennial herb adds a pretty note to cottage and herb gardens, with its

CHAMOMILE

mat of finely divided, downy leaves and tiny, white, daisylike blossoms, which appear from early summer to midsummer. With special care, chamomile forms a thick carpet that makes a fragrant lawn substitute. You also can grow it between pavers or stepping-stones. Plants grow 3 to 9 inches high and spread to 24 inches.

The oil from the flowers has medicinal properties: chamomile flower tea is reputed to aid the skin, help digestion, and calm the nerves. People sensitive to ragweed may suffer an allergic reaction to chamomile.

Site: Full sun. Average to rich, well-drained fertile soil; moist, but not wet. Perennial hardy in zones 3 to 8.
How to Grow: Plant container-grown plants in spring, spacing 6 inches apart as lawn substitute and 18 inches apart in gardens. Take cuttings in spring; divide in early spring. For lawn, mow high to prevent flowering. Include stepping-stones to prevent too much wear. Best where summers are cool. Usually trouble-free.
Harvest: Harvest flowers and young leaves when petals turn inward around centers. Hang bunches upside down in dry, dark place. Use dried flowers for potpourri, arrangements, and tea.
Cultivars and Similar Species: 'Flore-Pleno', showier double flowers; 'Treneague', nonflowering, forms mats, best choice for paving. *Matricaria recutita* (German chamomile), 2 to 3 feet tall, similar appearance, less fragrant, annual.

CHIVES
Allium schoenoprasum

The showy lavender blossoms of chives are the glory of the herb garden in early summer. These tightly

CHIVES

packed globes rise above dense clumps of tubular green leaves. Both leaves and blossoms are *continued*

Herbs

CHIVES
(continued)

edible, with a mild, sweet, oniony taste that makes a nice addition to cheese, egg, potato, and other vegetable dishes. When steeped in vinegar, the chive blossoms give the vinegar a pink color and an onionlike flavor. European colonists brought chives to America, where they hung bunches in their homes to ward off evil spirits. The plants grow 18 inches tall and wide, and spread over time.

Site: Best in full sun; tolerates part shade. Moderately rich, well-drained soil. Average moisture. Perennial in zones 3 to 9.

How to Grow: Sow seeds in flats indoors; allow two to three weeks for shoots to emerge. Plant outdoors in four weeks. Divide every three years in spring or fall. Reseeds prolifically unless deadheaded. Cut back to 1 inch from ground after flowering to stimulate new growth. Usually pest-free.

Harvest: Snip individual leaves any time after plants are 6 inches tall. Don't shear off entire clump. Pick blossoms at peak for vinegars and salads; separate blossoms into individual florets for salads.

Cultivars and Similar Species: 'Forsgate', rose-pink flowers. *Allium tuberosum* (garlic chives), garlic-flavored, flat leaves, large, white flower heads in late summer, used in Chinese cuisine.

CORIANDER, CILANTRO, CHINESE PARSLEY
Coriandrum sativum

Both the pungent, citrus-and-sage-scented leaves—called cilantro or Chinese parsley—and the sweet, citrusy seed—called coriander—of this aromatic herb have many culinary uses. Southwestern and Asian cuisines make wide use of both coriander and

CORIANDER

cilantro. The youngest leaves resemble flat-leaf parsley; as plants mature, new leaves on the flowering stalk are more finely divided. Plants grow 2 to 3 feet high and 1 foot wide. The small, flat, white to pale mauve flower heads appear in midsummer, followed by clusters of small, green, globelike seeds, which brown as they ripen. The flowers attract bees.

Site: Full sun; partial shade in hot areas. Average soil with good drainage. Plentiful water to keep lush. Grow as a cool-season annual in zones 2 to 11.

How to Grow: Sow seeds directly in garden in fall or very early spring for spring germination; dislikes transplanting. Thin to 4 to 8 inches apart. Needs plenty of room; close groupings cause stunting. Weed and mulch well early in season. Stake flowers to prevent toppling. If growing for leaves only, snip out flower stems as they form. Bolts quickly in heat, producing few leaves; plant early. Usually pest-free.

Harvest: Harvest entire young plant, using roots, stems, and leaves, or pluck individual young leaves as needed. Harvest seeds when leaves are brown, but seeds not yet scattered. Cut whole plant and hang to dry, gathering seeds as they fall. Undried seed tastes bitter.

Cultivars: 'Slo Bolt', slow to flower.

DILL
Anethum graveolens

Valued both for the piquant flavor of its feathery, blue-green leaves and its crunchy seeds, dill also makes a pretty addition to an edible landscape or cottage garden. Flat heads of lacy yellow flowers decorate the 3- to 4-foot-tall stalks of bright green, feathery leaves as this annual herb matures. Plants grow 1½ feet wide. The cut flowers add a delicate finery to summer bouquets. Greek and Roman warriors wore dill garlands to celebrate their homecomings from battle.

DILL

Site: Full sun. Rich, well-drained, acidic soil. Plentiful moisture. Cool-season annual in zones 2 to 11. Grow in spring and early fall.

How to Grow: In the South, sow seeds in garden in early spring and again in late summer. In cool climates, sow every few weeks from spring through summer. Thin to 6 to 18 inches apart. Will self-sow and perpetuate from year to year, if allowed to go to seed. Doesn't transplant well. Stake if strong winds threaten plants. Plants mature too quickly in hot weather. Parsley worms and carrot weevils may be troublesome.

Harvest: Harvest entire tender young plants or snip leaves from growing plants for cooking and freezing. Harvest seeds in fall for breads and pickling. When seed head turns brown, enclose in paper bag, secure around stem, and shake seeds into bag; store.

Cultivars: 'Aroma' and 'Dukat', leafy, good fresh and for seeds; 'Bouquet', 3 feet, slow to bolt; 'Fernleaf', 18 inches, compact and bushy, slow to flower.

FENNEL
Foeniculum vulgare

Like its relative dill, fennel is prized for flavorful, feathery leaves, young stems, and seeds, which have a nutty anise taste. It is a lovely addition

FENNEL

to herb, vegetable, and cottage gardens, and ideal in edible landscapes. The plants grow 3 to 7 feet tall and 2 to 3 feet wide. The large, flat, yellow flower umbels look pretty, then ripen to yield the fragrant seeds prized for flavoring Italian sausages, lentils, sauerkraut, cabbage, pickles, breads, and cheese. During the Middle Ages on Midsummer's Eve in the British Isles, fennel hung over doorways to ward off evil spirits.

Site: Full sun. Humus-rich, well-drained soil; avoid heavy clay. Even moisture; tolerates drought once established. Perennial hardy in zones 6 to 10, but usually grown as annual there and elsewhere.

How to Grow: Sow seeds directly where wanted in fall or early spring for spring germination; difficult to transplant. Thin to 1 to 2 feet apart. Readily self-sows. For continuous crop, make successive plantings through mid-August. Keep seedlings well-watered. Aphids may be troublesome.

Harvest: Snip leaves as needed for fresh culinary use. Freeze chopped leaves. Cut stems to use like celery just before bloom. Harvest seeds as for dill.

Cultivars and Similar Species: 'Rubrum' (bronze fennel), dark reddish bronze foliage, zones 5 to 10, often grown in flower gardens. *Foeniculum vulgare* var. *dulce* (Florence fennel, finocchio), annual vegetable with edible bulbous base, preferred for salads.

LAVENDER, ENGLISH LAVENDER
Lavandula angustifolia (*L. officinalis*, *L. vera*, and *L. spica*)

Lavender forms a compact, rounded, woody-based plant that's 3 feet tall and about as wide. The plant consists of upright, woolly, white stems clad in narrow, gray-green to gray, aromatic evergreen leaves. Tight spikes of small, fragrant flowers, ranging from deep to pale purple, bloom at the stem tips for a month in early summer.

Lavender is excellent for foliage contrast in the garden. Use it as a low hedge in herb or rose gardens, or grow it in rock gardens, borders, and Xeriscape gardens.

The stalks dry well for arrangements and sachets.

HIDCOTE LAVENDER

Site: Full sun. Average to poor, well-drained, neutral to alkaline soil. Highly drought-tolerant; don't overwater. Hardy in zones 5 to 8; best where hot and dry, especially in the West. Less winter-hardy in heavy, wet soil.

How to Grow: Plant container-grown plants in spring, spacing 1½ to 3 feet apart. Divide in fall. Take side-shoot cuttings in summer. Mulch after ground freezes. May rebloom after stalks are harvested. Severely cut back old woody plants after blooming. Sometimes bothered by root rot and caterpillars.

Harvest: Cut flower stalks just before full bloom, leaving stems long. Hang upside down in bunches in dry, dark place to dry. Use in crafts, potpourris, and arrangements.

Cultivars and Similar Species: 'Hidcote', silvery leaves, deep purple-blue flowers, 16 inches tall; 'Jean Davis', pale pink flowers, blue-green leaves, 15 inches tall; 'Munstead Dwarf', fragrant, early, violet-blue flowers, 12 inches tall; 'Baby White', white flowers, 12 inches tall; 'Alba', white, 3 feet tall, not as cold-hardy; 'Lavender Lady', 10 inches tall, flowers first year from seed, may be sold as bedding plants. *Lavandula stoechas* (Spanish lavender), showy flowers with large purple bracts, zones 8 to 10.

LEMON BALM, BALM
Melissa officinalis

Although somewhat ordinary looking, this bushy, mint family member has a delightfully intense lemony, and slightly minty, fragrance. It offers neat green leaves with scalloped edges, square stems, and tiny white flowers in summer and early autumn. Plants grow 2 feet high and 2 feet wide. Lemon balm is excellent in herb, bee, and lemon-scented theme gardens.

Bees love lemon balm, and so do cooks. Try the leaves in fruit and green salads, chicken and fish dishes, vegetables, iced tea, and punch. Lemon balm tea is used to calm the nerves and lower blood pressure.

LEMON BALM

Site: Full sun to part shade. Average, well-drained soil. Plentiful moisture. Perennial in zones 4 to 9.
How to Grow: Sow seed, uncovered, in garden; keep moist. Layer stems or take cuttings in summer. Divide plants in spring. Space 3 feet apart. Cut back and harvest in midsummer to prevent flowering and prolific self-seeding. Less aggressive spreader than other mint family member. Powdery mildew sometimes troublesome.

Harvest: Best used fresh before flowering; pick sprigs as needed. Or, harvest entire plant by cutting off 2 inches from ground; it will regrow. For tea, dry the stems and leaves on screens in the shade during hot, dry weather.
Cultivars: 'Aurea', gold-edged leaves.

LOVAGE
Levisticum officinale

Fast-growing lovage has broad, flat, deeply toothed bright green leaves and hollow stems that resemble a

LOVAGE

huge celery. It's an early spring perennial with flowers that emerge in June and July as pale yellow umbels. Plants grow 4 to 6 feet tall. The celery flavoring stands up to long cooking in soups and stews; seeds also taste of celery, making them a good ingredient in herbal seasoning blends.

Lovage adds height to herb or perennial gardens. Plant it in edible landscapes where height is desired.

Site: Full sun to part shade. Rich, deep, moist but well-drained soil. Plentiful moisture. Hardy in zones 3 to 8; best growth promoted by cold winters.
How to Grow: Sow seed in fall for spring germination. Divide in spring or fall; separate offshoots in fall. Space

3 feet apart. Cut flower stalks to prevent seeding, which keeps leaves usable. Since plant gets so big, only one or two are necessary. Aphids may be troublesome; control with garlic spray.
Harvest: Cut off fresh young stems and leaves to use as needed. Blanch and freeze chopped stems. Cut off stems and lay to dry on screens. Harvest seed as you would dill.

MARJORAM, SWEET MARJORAM
Origanum majorana

The fuzzy, pale gray-green leaves of marjoram are more prominent than its tiny, knotlike white or pink flowers, which bloom in August and September. Plants grow 1 foot tall and wide, and form a floppy mound. Called "joy of the mountains" by the Greeks, marjoram tastes like a sweeter, milder oregano with a touch of balsam and enjoys wide culinary use in France, Italy, and Portugal.

MARJORAM

Cluster the small, bushy plants in the herb garden or grow marjoram in containers, especially hanging baskets.

Site: Full sun. Light, well-drained, neutral to slightly alkaline soil.

Moderate moisture. Hardy in zones 6 to 10; grow as an annual elsewhere.
How to Grow: Start seeds indoors in midspring; set plants outdoors after frost. Take cuttings in early summer. Pinch back just before flowering to encourage bushiness. Slow-growing. Usually pest-free.
Harvest: Cut back no more than one-third of new growth. Dry in bunches upside down in dry, dark place; rub stems on screen to shred dry leaves. Use in fresh or dried wreaths.
Cultivars: Often confused with oregano. 'Aureum', golden leaves, spreading growth.

SPEARMINT, PEPPERMINT, APPLE MINT
Mentha spp.

Believed to be the oldest of all mints, spearmint (*Mentha spicata*) has hairy, pointed, toothed green leaves with a crinkly texture. Square

SPEARMINT

stems are green or reddish. From June to September, spearlike flower spikes, made up of clusters of tiny white or lavender flowers top the stems. It grows 2½ feet tall and spreads wide. Its taste is milder than peppermint. Spearmint is used in Middle Eastern cooking and mint juleps.

PEPPERMINT

Peppermint (*M.* × *piperita*) grows 3 feet tall, with smooth, dark green leaves and reddish purple stems. A rampant grower, it has a strong mint and menthol aroma and many medicinal qualities as a digestive aid; also used in confections.

Apple mint (*M. suaveolens*) features scalloped, rounded, pale green to silvery, wooly leaves with a delightful fruity fragrance. It grows 3 feet tall and spreads. A stand of apple mint with its white flower stalks looks

APPLE MINT

lovely in late summer. The variegated form—called pineapple mint—has light green leaves with creamy white variegations; its leaves change their

aroma from pineapple to apple as summer progresses. Leaves of these mints make an enticing addition to drinks and fruit salads.

Mints are good fillers for awkward spaces in the garden and also are excellent container plants.

Site: Full sun to part shade. Average to fertile, moist soil. Plentiful moisture. Spearmint is hardy in zones 5 to 8, peppermint in zones 4 to 11, and apple mint in zones 5 to 10.
How to Grow: Take cuttings in midsummer; divide in spring every few years. Doesn't come true from seed. Mints are aggressive spreaders. To control, surround with 10-inch-deep barrier or plant in 10-inch-deep, bottomless container sunk in garden. Rust fungus, verticillium wilt, spider mites, mint flea beetles, and aphids may be troublesome.
Harvest: Cut young sprigs and use fresh. To dry for cooking and tea, hang bunches of stems upside down in dry, dark place. Freeze blanched stems and leaves.
Cultivars and Similar Species:
Spearmint: 'Crispii' and 'Curly', curly leaves.
Peppermint: 'Chocolate', chocolate-mint flavored.
Apple mint: 'Variegata', variegated leaves, floppy growth to 1 foot, pineapple scent.
M. requienii (Corsican mint), tiny-leaved, creeping plant, intense mint aroma; use as paving plant in semishaded, damp sites; zones 6 to 8.

OREGANO, GREEK OREGANO
Origanum vulgare subsp. *hirtum* (*O. heracleoticum*, *O. hirtum*)

A stand of aromatic oregano puts on a show of dainty white flowers among its aromatic leaves from July to September.   *continued*

OREGANO
(continued)

OREGANO

Plants grow 1 to 2 feet tall and wide, and demand a place in every culinary herb garden. Greek oregano is widely believed to have the best flavor, but plants often are mislabeled. Buy from a reliable mail-order source or brush a leaf gently with your finger to test the scent when buying locally.

Every lover of Italian and Greek cooking knows the flavor and charm of oregano, which enhances tomato sauces and also bean, egg, and cheese dishes, many meats, marinated vegetables, and dressings. Its flavor combines well with garlic, thyme, basil, parsley, and olive oil.

Site: Full sun. Well-drained, average soil. Moderate water. Needs good drainage. Hardy in zones 5 to 9. Performs poorly in hot, humid weather.
How to Grow: Divide in spring. Take cuttings in early summer. Seeds may be sown indoors in spring, but plants do not always come true from seed. Pinch young plants to promote bushier growth. Root rot and fungus diseases may be troublesome in wet soil.

Harvest: Start snipping sprigs when plant is 6 inches tall to encourage bushy growth. Cut whole plants in June, dry upside down in bunches in dry, dark place. Cut back drastically in August.
Similar Species: *Origanum vulgare* (common oregano, wild marjoram): flavorless, looks similar except for pink or lavender flowers; 'Aureum', golden leaves.

PARSLEY

PARSLEY
Petroselinum crispum

Beloved for its emerald color and attractive leafy foliage, parsley makes a popular choice as an ornamental edible. Classically used as a garnish, it is a rich source of vitamins A, C, and B, and its flavor complements many foods. The low mounds of curly or moss-leaf types grow 6 to 12 inches high and work best as edging or tucked between low bedding plants such as pansies and marigolds. Flat-leaved or Italian parsley *(Petroselinum crispum var. neapolitanum),* which grows taller (to 18 inches) and more openly, looks pleasing in an informal border. Parsley grows well in containers and looks good with white or pastel flowers. Include some in butterfly gardens as food for larvae.

Site: Full sun to part shade. Fertile, well-drained soil. Plentiful water. Parsley is a biennial grown as a half-hardy annual in zones 2 to 11, but may be grown year-round in zones 9 to 11. Grows best in cool weather.
How to Grow: Soak seeds in warm water overnight, then sow indoors at 60°F, 10 to 12 weeks before last frost. Unless soaked, seeds may take at least three weeks to germinate. May sow outdoors in fall. Space 6 to 12 inches apart. Set out young nursery plants after last frost. Pull out and replace overwintered plants; they produce few leaves and quickly form seed heads. If allowed to self-sow, stand may perpetuate itself. Parsley worm, larvae of black swallowtail butterfly, often troublesome.
Harvest: Pick young sprigs as needed for garnish and fresh use. Dry thoroughly in shade to preserve color; store in airtight containers. Chop curly varieties and freeze.
Cultivars: 'Extra Curly Dwarf' and 'Moss Curled', both 10 to 12 inches tall, curly; 'Paramount', 6 inches tall; 'Decora', long, extra-curly leaves, resists heat; 'Gigante', large, flat, sweet leaves.

ROSEMARY
Rosmarinus officinalis

A flowering or topiary rosemary as the focal point of an herb garden is a memorable sight. This shrub has long, narrow, deep green leaves with fuzzy white undersides and a pungent, piney aroma. In mild climates plants produce dainty white flowers. Plants grow 5 to 6 feet tall and wide in warm climates, and 2 to 4½ feet tall in cold climates and

ROSEMARY

Harvest: Cut 4-inch pieces from branch tips for fresh use. Dry sprigs on screens, strip off leaves, and store in airtight containers. Use fresh or dried sprigs in culinary wreaths.

Cultivars: 'Beneden Blue', blue flowers; 'Pine Scented', especially strong scent. *Rosmarinus officinalis* var. *prostratus*, trailing, 2 feet tall, 4 to 8 feet wide.

RUE

How to Grow: Sow seed indoors in mid to late winter for spring transplanting; take cuttings in summer, root in shade, then move to sun. Space 18 inches apart. Provide good drainage. In cold climates cut off deadwood in spring. Root rot may occur in soggy soil. Oils from leaves may cause skin irritation.

Harvest: Pick leaves before flowers form; dry on screens in a dark place. Store in airtight containers for use as a strewing herb.

Cultivars: 'Variegata', white-edged leaves; 'Jackman's Blue', compact with rich blue foliage; 'Blue Mound', compact, good blue-green color.

SAGE

indoors. There are both upright and creeping forms of rosemary.

Rosemary is an excellent landscape shrub in arid climates. Use it as a specimen, hedge, or groundcover; grow it in herb gardens and to attract bees. Fine container plant. Unforgettable for culinary use, rosemary traditionally is served with lamb. It is included in *herbes de Provence*, a dried seasoning mix from southern France, where the scent of huge rosemary hedges permeates the air.

Site: Full sun. Light, average to poor, well-drained soil. Tolerates drought; don't overwater. Hardy in zones 8 to 10; grow as annual or overwinter indoors elsewhere. May overwinter in zone 7 if planted next to warm house foundation.

How to Grow: Take cuttings in late summer. Hard to grow from seeds. Set out nursery plants in spring. Apply lime to acidic soil. Can grow in porous container with cactus soil and perlite. In cold climates, grow all year in pot: bury pot in garden in summer; dig up and place in greenhouse, cold frame, or sunny, cold window in winter. Successfully overwinters indoors only with high humidity. Root rot a problem in wet soil.

RUE
Ruta graveolens

Once grown in monastery gardens as a medicinal herb and to ward off evil influences, rue today adorns herb gardens as a beautiful, aromatic edging or specimen plant. Plants grow 3 feet tall and 2 feet wide, with blue-green leaves that are finely cut into blunt lobes. In midsummer, airy bunches of tiny yellow-green flowers peek above the leaves. Rue is evergreen in warm climates and dies to the ground in colder zones. Its bitter leaves are best dried in bunches and never eaten. Hang up the leaves or strew them as an insect repellent.

Site: Full sun. Well-drained loamy soil best, but tolerates light or heavy soil. Moist soil produces prettiest leaf color. Evergreen in zones 7 to 9; dies back in zones 4 to 6.

GARDEN SAGE
Salvia officinalis

A sacred plant to Native Americans and thought in many cultures to prolong life and enhance memory, sage has a long history of medicinal use. It's now grown primarily for the culinary uses of its aromatic, silvery green foliage.

A network of prominent veins gives the velvety, blunt leaves a pebbly appearance. Tall, woolly, white spikes of violet-blue, two-lipped tubular flowers bloom above the *continued*

Garden Sage
(continued)

foliage in midsummer, making a striking display. Leaves grow 1 to 2 feet tall; flower stalks to 3 feet. Purple and variegated cultivars bring dramatic color to gardens; all retain the same lemon-camphor aroma that brings back vivid memories of Thanksgiving dinners.

Sage is indispensable in herb gardens. Plant it in cottage and formal gardens for foliage accent among green-leaved plants.

Site: Full sun. Fertile to average well-drained soil. Moderate moisture. Drought-tolerant once established. Hardy in zones 4 to 8.
How to Grow: Plant container-grown plants in spring, spacing 2 feet apart. Take cuttings in summer. Grows easily from seeds started indoors. Prune or cut back to near woody base in early spring to renew. Rots in winter-wet site. Slugs and spittle bugs sometimes troublesome.
Harvest: Pick leaves sparingly for culinary use. Harvest sprigs just before flowering and dry in upside-down bunches in dry, dark place. Store crumbled, dried sage in airtight container. Use whole dried bunches in wreaths.
Cultivars: 'Berggarten', silvery, round leaves; 'Compacta', 15 inches tall; 'Tricolor', gray-green leaves variegated with creamy white and purple; 'Aurea', gray-green leaves variegated with golden green, 18 inches tall; 'Purpurea', steely, purplish gray leaves, 18 inches tall.

Scented Geranium
Pelargonium spp.

Orange, rose, peppermint, lemon, coconut, ginger, apricot, and nutmeg are just a few of the many fragrances of scented geraniums.

Glands containing fragrant oils coat the leaves, releasing a sweet perfume whenever a leaf is brushed, crushed, or even warmed in the sun. Fifty or more types exist. Most have decorative leaves and small, unshowy

Chocolate-Mint Scented Geranium

flowers of pink or white; many kinds trail. Size varies by species. Most are 12 to 18 inches tall in pots; some grow to several feet tall in gardens.

Scented geraniums are essential in a fragrance garden. Or, plant in beds or

Peppermint Geranium

containers in herb and cottage gardens. These geraniums may be overwintered as houseplants. Use trailers in hanging baskets. Use the scented leaves in sachets, potpourris, and gourmet cooking.

Site: Full sun; light shade in hot areas. Average, well-drained soil. Hardy in zones 10 and 11; grow as annuals elsewhere.
How to Grow: Stem cuttings taken in summer are easiest. Some may be started from seed. Nursery stock is becoming increasingly available. Pinch to encourage branching. May become leggy and oversized when wintered over. Best to take new cuttings each year. Occasionally bacterial leaf spot, pythiums, gray mold, geranium bud worms, aphids, spider mites, rust, and wilt may cause problems.
Harvest: Pick young leaves sparingly for use in potpourris, cooking, and crafts.
Species: *Pelargonium tomentosum*, peppermint scent, large velvety leaves, trailing; *P. graveolens*, rose scent; *P. fragrans*, orange scent; *P. crispum*, lemon scent, small, crinkled leaves; *P. grossularioides*, coconut scent.

Tarragon, French Tarragon
Artemisia dracunculus var. *sativa*

This scraggly aromatic perennial isn't much to look at, but its distinctive, aniselike fragrance and taste make it a favorite with chefs. Borne on tall, unbranched, woody-based stems, shiny, narrow, deep green leaves are rounded at their bases and pointed at their tips. The tiny globe-shaped, white or yellow flowers are insignificant. Plants grow 2 to 3 feet tall and about a foot wide.

Tarragon is one of the French fines herbes, a classic ingredient in béarnaise sauce, veal, fish, and chicken dishes. The Romans, as well as medieval pilgrims, believed that tarragon placed in their shoes prevented fatigue.

TARRAGON

THYME

WOOLLY THYME

growing along the trailing semiwoody stems. Plants grow 1 foot tall and twice as wide. Tiny white or pale lavender flowers decorate thyme plants in summer and attract bees.

More than 40 species or varieties of thyme are grown in herb gardens; all have scented leaves, although the scent may vary from that of common thyme. Some species or varieties taste like lemon, caraway, or oregano. Some thymes form low mats and have showy flowers or brightly variegated leaves.

Site: Full sun to partial shade. Rich, sandy, well-drained loam. Moderate moisture. Fails in wet soil; tolerates drought. Hardy in zones 4 to 6.

How to Grow: Doesn't set seed. Set out nursery plants in spring. Take cuttings or divide in spring or autumn; may take two months to root. Pinch to promote bushiness. Divide every two or three years to assure vigor and flavor. Mulch well in winter to protect from heaving. Stake plants that start to sprawl. Root rot and mildew may be problems.

Harvest: Take two main harvests, one in early to midsummer and one before frost, or cut sprigs as needed. Leaves may be preserved in vinegar, frozen, or dried.

Similar Species: *Artemisia dracunculus* (Russian tarragon) sets seed, looks identical, but has inferior flavor. Be sure to buy French tarragon.

THYME

Thymus vulgaris

Common thyme is an indispensable kitchen herb. The pungent taste is prized by cooks for stews, meat, cheese, and egg dishes, and in breads and stuffings. Its gray-green leaves are tiny and pointed,

Thyme is beautiful in bee gardens, rock gardens, culinary gardens, containers, and hanging baskets. Plant creeping types as edging or paving plants.

Site: Full sun best; part shade in hot climates. Light, dry, well-drained soil. Moderate moisture; drought-tolerant. Hardy in zones 5 to 9; excellent in arid climates.

How to Grow: Take cuttings from new growth in midsummer. Divide in spring. Sow seed indoors in spring at 70°F. Cut back hard and harvest in mid- to late summer to keep plant from becoming woody and developing dead center. Don't cut back in fall as new growth

won't be winter-hardy. Replace plant if woody and unsightly. May rot in winter-wet site. Fungal diseases common in humid weather or damp soil. Mulch well to prevent winter-kill where temperatures drop below freezing.

Harvest: Take small sprigs for culinary use anytime. For drying, cut whole plant back to 2 inches above ground before midseason. Hang upside down in bunches in dry, dark place. Strip fresh leaves and dry on screen or freeze in airtight container.

Cultivars and Similar Species: 'Argenteus', silver edged; 'Aureus', gold edged. *Thymus herba-barona* (caraway thyme), shiny green leaves, lavender flowers, caraway scent, forms mats. *T. × citriodorus* (lemon thyme), dark green leaves, lemon scent, upright and spreading, 6 to 12 inches tall; 'Argenteus', white-edged leaves; 'Aureus,' gold-edged. *T. praecox* subsp. *arcticus* (mother-of-thyme), dark green leaves, strong aroma, forms dense mats to 4 inches tall; 'Coccineus', showy rose-pink flowers. *T. pseudolanuginosus* (woolly thyme), mat-forming, tiny, gray-green leaves, rapid spreader; excellent paving plant.

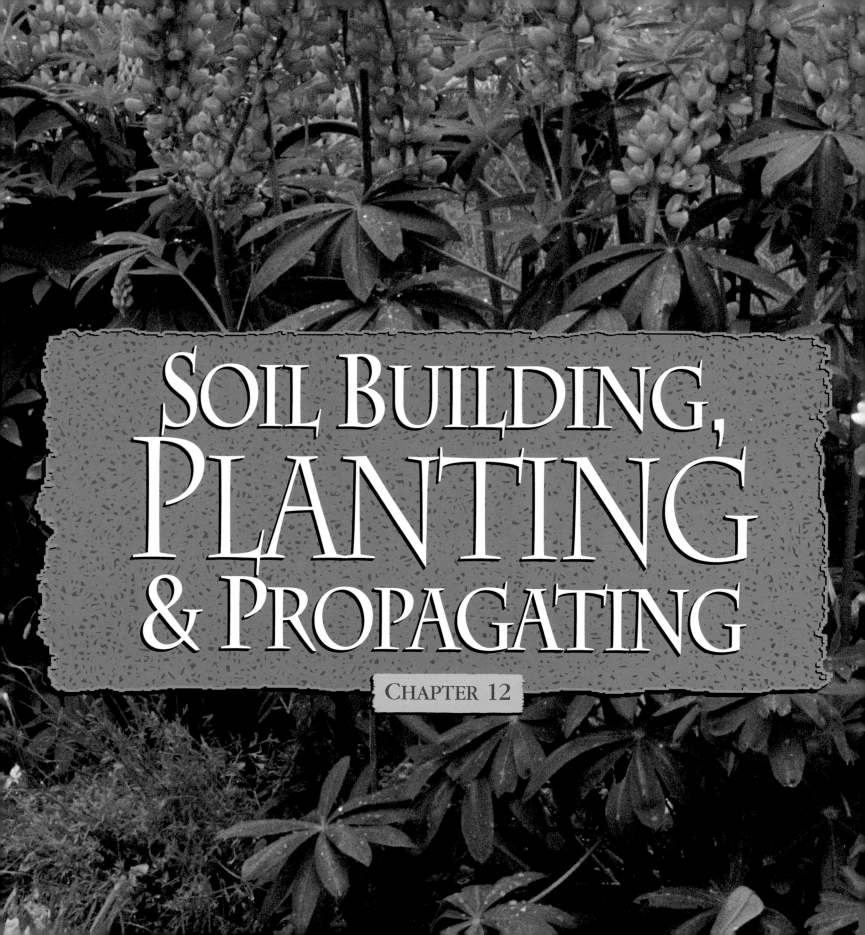

Soil Building, Planting & Propagating

CHAPTER 12

SOIL SCIENCE

Soil may look like simple dirt, but it's much more complex. The bulk of it is made up of rocks that have, over millions of years, crumbled into minuscule pieces. The largest particle is a grain of sand, with a diameter of 0.5 to 2 millimeters. A silt particle is 10 times smaller than a grain of sand. A clay particle, the smallest piece of soil, is 100 times smaller than sand.

Besides sand, silt, and clay, soil contains organic matter, mostly in the form of humus. Humus is a dark, crumbly substance composed of decayed leaves, dead insects, and other decomposed plant and animal material. As you will see, organic matter is beneficial to soil: It holds nutrients and water well, buffers the pH, and improves the soil structure. In most soils, about 2 to 5 percent of the soil solids are humus. That number is smaller for sandy soil and much greater for peaty soil.

When you scoop up a cup of soil, about half of it is soil solids—rock and humus—and half is small pores filled with water or air. Under ideal growing conditions, half the pores hold water, which contains dissolved nutrients. These pores are called the soil solution. The other pores hold air, which contains the oxygen that plant roots need for respiration. Soil that has enough air is said to be well-aerated. Most plants do best in well-aerated soil. Soil that lacks air pockets drains poorly and becomes soggy; only plants that thrive in wet areas will do well in such soil.

SOIL TEXTURE AND STRUCTURE

Soil texture is determined by the relative amounts of sand, silt, and clay in the soil. How a soil behaves depends on the percentage of each. Soil structure is the way the particles in the soil—be they sand, silt, or clay—clump together. Sandy soil, which has a loose structure, doesn't clump well. Clayey soil, which has a tight structure, has particles that adhere together too much.

Because sand particles are large and often irregularly shaped, they fit together loosely and are separated by large gaps—like marbles in a jar. Water drains easily through the gaps in sandy soil, making it dry. Nutrients dissolved in soil water quickly drain

You can have a flourishing garden in poor, sandy soil without adding a lot of soil amendments if you choose well-adapted plants. Here drought-tolerant plants beautify an infertile site. The gravel mulch is suited to the site and keeps the water-sensitive plants dry during rainy periods.

out, so sandy soil may be infertile. Because it is loose and dry, sandy soil is easy to dig. You may have heard it referred to as light soil.

Clay particles are so small that they pack tightly together. The tiny spaces between them hold water well—sometimes too well—making soil with a high clay content heavy, poorly drained, and difficult to dig. The close spacing also makes it difficult for roots to push their way through clay soil. And clay soil often swells when wet, then shrinks into hard clumps when dry.

Clay particles are the only soil particles that are negatively charged. For that reason, positively charged nutrients—and that's most of them, with the notable exception of nitrogen—cling to the surface of clay particles, making clay soil fertile. The negative charge also accounts for the gumminess, or the plasticity, of clay.

Silt particles are shaped like mini grains of sand. Because they are usually coated with clay, they behave like a weak clay and are sticky, plastic, and absorb water and nutrients. As with clay soil, air and water move slowly through silty soil.

The best soils for gardening have some sand, some silt, and a little clay. These soils, called loams, hold nutrients, drain adequately, are easy to work, and are easy for roots to penetrate. Loam is about 20 percent clay, 40 percent silt, and 40 percent sand. Loam with a bit more sand is called sandy loam; add more sand and it becomes loamy sand. Loam with more clay is called clay loam. Those same variations apply to silts and clays; thus, you can have a silty clay, a sandy clay, a silty clay loam, a sandy clay loam, and so on.

You can't do much to change soil texture, short of adding an impractical amount of sand or clay. But you don't have to give up gardening if you lack loamy soil, because you can compensate by improving the soil structure.

To encourage good soil structure:
■ **ADD ORGANIC MATTER**, such as compost or manure, each year. Organic matter helps bind soil particles together into good-size crumbs.
■ **DON'T OVERTILL THE SOIL.** Excessive rototilling or digging breaks down the structure, leaving you with a dusty powder or concrete.
■ **DON'T DIG SOIL THAT IS TOO WET OR TOO DRY.** This harms the structure. The soil is ready when you can form it into a loose ball that falls apart when you poke it.

NUTRIENTS, GLORIOUS NUTRIENTS

Plants need nutrients to grow. Those they use in large quantities—carbon, oxygen, hydrogen, nitrogen, phosphorus, potassium, sulfur, magnesium, and calcium—are called macronutrients. The micronutrients, or trace elements, are those elements that plants need only in small quantities. They include boron, hydrogen, iodine, iron, molybdenum, manganese, copper, nickel, and zinc. Too much of any trace element can be toxic. Plants absorb most nutrient elements from soil, where they dissolve in water as electrically charged ions. Exceptions are carbon and oxygen, which plants absorb from the air, and hydrogen, which they derive from water.

The amount of the macro- and micronutrients available to plants—that is, how fertile a soil is—depends on four factors. One is the mineral content in the rocks and plant litter that formed the soil. A soil that formed from limestone, for example, is high in calcium and magnesium. Another factor is the amount of rainfall a region gets, because minerals gradually wash out of the soil. In gardens, two other factors affecting soil fertility are how intensively plants were grown on the site in the past and whether fertilizer was applied.

THE pH EFFECT

Even if a nutrient is abundant in the soil, it may not be in a chemical form a plant can use. The soil pH—the measure of its acidity or alkalinity—plays a major role in determining which nutrients are available to the plants. The pH scale ranges from 1 to 14. A pH of 7.0 is neutral; that's the pH of pure water.

Acid soils, common in the rainy East and Pacific Northwest, usually have a pH between 5.0 and 6.9, although in some areas the pH dips to about 3.5. Acidic soils are sometimes called sour soils. Alkaline soils, prevalent in the dry West, Southwest, and parts of the Midwest, have a pH greater than 7.0 but usually below 10, although in some areas they may peak at 10.5. Alkaline soils often are called sweet soils.

The nutrient balance is best in soils with a pH between 6.0 and 7.5. In that range, macronutrients are abundant and micronutrients are limited enough to be nontoxic. That's why most plants grow best in soil with a nearly neutral pH, although a few plants, such as blueberries and azaleas, prefer acidic soils. Such "acid-loving plants" suffer nutrient deficiencies if the soil is not acid enough. They only can use iron or magnesium in the chemical form it takes in acid soil.

To determine the soil type in your garden, squeeze a handful of slightly moist soil. If it compacts into a tight ball, top, it's clay. If it holds its shape somewhat but crumbles around the edges, center, it's loam, which is best for most plants. Sandy soil, bottom, won't hold the balled shape at all.

PREPARING AND CARING FOR SOIL

Wild plants thrive in the type of soil that suits them and are scarce where the soil isn't to their liking. For example, plants that can tolerate dry, infertile soil grow at the seashore and those that need humus-rich, moist soil thrive at the edge of a woodland. Garden plants, however, are dependent on the soil you provide. So, for a healthy garden, you should match plant type to soil type. Or, you can make your soil more hospitable to most garden plants by adding organic matter, fertilizing, and turning the soil only when necessary.

Compost—decomposed garden waste and kitchen scraps—is a good source of organic matter for your garden. (To learn how to make your own compost, see Composting with Confidence on page 520.)

Organic matter provides another benefit to your garden soil: It encourages healthy populations of soil insects and microorganisms that break down the organic matter, releasing nutrients for plants to use. Earthworms ingest organic matter, and the tunnels they make through the soil improve the soil structure, aeration, and drainage.

Research indicates that it's best to improve the soil in an entire planting area, if you can, rather than just the planting hole. To add organic matter to bare soil that you're preparing for a vegetable garden, perennial or shrub border, or foundation planting, either fork compost into the top few inches of the soil or leave it on the surface for earthworms to take deeper. If you're applying compost four months or more before planting, add a 4- to 6-inch layer. If you plan to plant in one to two months, apply 2 to 3 inches of compost. Apply a 1-inch layer if you're planting sooner, and avoid material with large chunks that could create large air pockets near roots. How quickly organic matter blends into the soil varies. The process is fastest if the compost is already well-decayed and the weather is warm and damp.

You can improve the soil of established plantings, such as shrub borders or beds of perennials, without disturbing them. First rake back any long-lasting mulch such as river rocks or bark. Then spread a 2- to 3-inch layer of compost on the surface of the ground. Earthworms will do the rest of the work, taking the compost materials deep into the soil.

The nutrient content of soil can be improved by adding a variety of amendments, which are first spread on the soil surface.

Soil amendments should be worked deeply into the soil, where they benefit the plants' root systems.

SHAPING UP WITH ORGANIC MATTER

Few gardeners are blessed with perfect soil. Most have excess clay or sand and the accompanying drainage, aeration, and soil structure problems. Many gardeners must also cope with extremes of pH that limit nutrient availability.

Whether your soil has too much clay, too much sand, or too high or low a pH, the solution is the same: Add organic matter and plenty of it. Organic matter is dead-plant material, such as leaves, grass clippings, and manure from plant-eating animals.

Woodland wildflowers such as the trilliums at right do best in acidic soil—soil with a low pH. This soil occurs naturally where there is a lot of leaf litter to form it.

Prairie wildflowers such as these bluebonnets, winecups, and poppies, above, thrive in alkaline soil, which is common in areas of the West that have low rainfall.

SHIFTING THE pH

If you garden where the soil pH is extremely acidic (below 6.0) or extremely alkaline (above 7.5), have a soil-testing laboratory determine the exact pH. Ask them to provide specific recommendations for changing your soil pH to enhance the specific plants you intend to grow.

To raise the pH (decrease acidity), apply limestone. How much you apply depends on the pH and the soil type—some soils resist change—so follow the recommendations from the soil laboratory. As a rule, to raise the pH by one full point (for example, from 5.5 to 6.5), apply 20 pounds per 1,000 square feet to sandy soil, 40 pounds to loamy soil, and 60 pounds to clay soil.

The lab report will tell you whether to apply regular limestone, which supplies calcium, or dolomitic limestone, which supplies calcium and magnesium. The report also will suggest the grade of limestone to use. The size of the limestone particles affects how quickly the pH rises; fine particles work fastest. Retest the soil three to four months after applying limestone, telling the lab how much you applied. The lab can tell how much more, if any, is needed.

Lowering the pH of an alkaline soil to render it neutral or acidic is more difficult than raising it. You can apply elemental or garden sulfur, but it's an expensive material, and the results vary greatly depending on the soil type. Unfortunately, the soil improvements last only a few years. The best decision may be to choose well-adapted plants or plant in raised beds containing neutral soil.

If you do apply sulfur, the rate is usually 10 pounds per 1,000 square feet to lower the pH one full point. Don't apply more than 1 pound at a time; the rapid change may shock existing plants. If you want to use more, split the application between the spring and fall. Retest every two to three years.

TAKING A SOIL SAMPLE

To ensure reliable results from a soil test, take a sample from every area of the yard where the soil looks different, has a different slope, or has been fertilized differently. For each sample, collect soil from 10 to 15 different spots in each area.

Remove leaves, grass, and litter from the soil surface. Using a spade or trowel, remove a slice of soil that's about 3 inches deep for lawns and 6 inches deep for garden areas. Remove a 1-inch plug from the center of the slice. Place the plug in a dry plastic container.

Mix the 10 to 15 plugs thoroughly in the container, then remove 1 pint of soil. Pick out foreign material such as sticks, stones, and insects. Let the sample air-dry on a newspaper for two to three days, then mail it to the testing laboratory.

Take a soil sample by first cutting out a slice of soil. Remove a plug from the center of the slice (as indicated by the dotted line).

FERTILIZER FACTS

Whether or not you should fertilize your landscape and garden plants depends upon the fertility of the soil. A soil test provides a profile of the soil's nutrient content. Contact the local Cooperative Extension Service or a private soil-testing laboratory for instructions on collecting a soil sample (see box on page 511 for tips). You also can learn about your soil's fertility by observing how well plants grow year after year.

Photo by Stephen Cridland

Compost is one of the best and least expensive organic fertilizers. It feeds plants, improves soil structure, and costs nothing to produce.

TYPES OF FERTILIZER

Fertilizer labels list three numbers, separated by hyphens; for example, 12-8-10. The first number represents the percentage of available nitrogen (N), the second is available phosphorus (P), and the third is available potassium (K). Plants use these nutrients in large amounts. These numbers sometimes are called the NPK ratio or the nutrient analysis. A fertilizer may contain nutrients other than N, P, and K. Check the label; it will list all other nutrients the fertilizer supplies.

SHOPPING FOR FERTILIZER

A fertilizer that supplies nearly equal percentages of nitrogen, phosphorus, and potassium is a balanced fertilizer. Common formulas are 5-5-5 and 10-10-10. You can purchase fertilizers that supply only one nutrient; for example, bloodmeal supplies only nitrogen.

Organic fertilizers are derived from minerals, animals, and plants. They release nutrients slowly, through the action of soil organisms. Synthetic (chemical) fertilizers are more highly processed and are more concentrated and soluble. The nutrients are available more quickly, but they also leach from the soil more quickly. Because synthetic fertilizers are more concentrated, they are more likely to burn plant roots than organic fertilizers (although the nitrogen in fresh animal manure can damage roots). Synthetic fertilizers also can reduce the numbers of beneficial soil organisms and earthworms.

The nutrient analyses for organic fertilizers often are lower than those for synthetic ones. That's because labeling laws allow only immediately available nutrients to be listed, and the nutrients in organic fertilizers are released gradually. Over time, the total amount of nutrients released from organic fertilizers is higher than the label suggests.

THE BIG THREE NUTRIENTS

Nitrogen, phosphorus, and potassium are so important they are called The Big Three. Here's why: Nitrogen helps plants green up

SAVING MONEY ON SOIL TESTS

A soil test is a diverse tool. Depending on the kind of test you request, you can learn your soil pH, the organic matter content, and any deficiencies in nutrients. But soil tests can be expensive. Prices vary, but expect to pay about $25 per sample. Because soil varies from one part of your property to another, for the test results to be worthwhile, you should have separate tests done for a vegetable garden, lawn, and various flower beds.

To cut the cost of soil tests, try one of these ideas:

■ Test only areas where you plan to grow expensive plants, such as perennials, so you can correct deficiencies before planting.

■ Test established gardens where plants perform poorly year after year, even after you've applied a balanced fertilizer and plenty of organic matter.

■ Ask your extension agent what pH is common in your area; have the pH tested only if the norm is less than 6.0 or more than 7.5—indicators of extreme conditions.

■ Ask your extension agent if any nutrients are commonly deficient in your area and what the symptoms of deficiency are. Have the soil tested if your plants show signs of that deficiency.

Do-it-yourself soil-testing kits are accurate only if you follow the instructions exactly. Even then, it's a good idea to have a laboratory test conducted every so often to be sure the do-it-yourself tests closely match the professional test.

quickly and encourages stems and leaves to grow. Without it, plants are yellow and stunted. But too much nitrogen inhibits flowering and fruit formation in favor of leafy growth and encourages soft, weak stems, which are susceptible to insects and diseases. Unlike most nutrients, nitrogen dissolves in water and leaches out with rain, so a soil test can't gauge current nitrogen content.

Phosphorus is critical for flowering, fruiting, and seed formation. It's also a key element in root growth, so it's a good idea to use a high-phosphorus starter fertilizer when planting trees and shrubs or flower and vegetable transplants. Phosphorus helps plants fight some diseases.

Potassium encourages healthy, vigorous plants by playing a role in disease resistance and root formation. It is a key element in photosynthesis.

SIGNS OF NUTRIENT DEFICIENCIES

Diagnosing a nutrient deficiency can be difficult without testing the soil or the leaves of plants. That's because symptoms of deficiency are so general—stunting, poor growth, and lack of vigor. But some nutrient deficiencies produce symptoms that are easy to see.

■ **BORON:** Black spots on beets; black rot of turnips; corking of apples; bitter, discolored cauliflower; cracked celery stalks

■ **IRON:** Yellow leaves with green veins; curled leaves

■ **NITROGEN:** Yellow leaves; yellow veins on green leaves

■ **MAGNESIUM:** Thin, brittle leaves; bronzed leaves; purple-red leaves

■ **PHOSPHORUS:** Poor fruit development; purplish leaves and stems; leaves streaked with yellow

TELLTALE WEEDS

The weeds growing in your yard can provide a clue to your soil's fertility because they have soil preferences just as garden plants do. Avoid judging your soil by only one weed; instead, look for several indicators.

Poor soil: Yarrow, ragweed, shepherd's purse, dandelion, thistle, black medic, crabgrass, plantain

Fertile soil: Pigweed, lamb's-quarters, foxtails, common chickweed

Common Yarrow

Canada Thistle

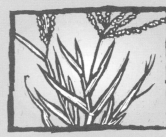
Large Crabgrass

Common Ragweed

Black Medic

Blackseed Plantain

Shepherd's Purse

Dandelion

Common Lamb's-Quarters

Redroot Pigweed

Giant Foxtails

Common Chickweed

FERTILIZER FACTS
continued

ORGANIC SOURCES OF FERTILIZERS

Fertilizer	Nutrients Supplied	How to Apply (rate per 100 square feet)	Comments
Alfalfa meal	5% nitrogen, 1% phosphorus, 2% potassium	2 to 5 pounds on surface, or work into soil.	Adds organic matter.
Bloodmeal (dried animal blood)	10% nitrogen	1 to 3 pounds. Rake into soil surface; leaches into root zone.	Quickly available; lasts 3 to 4 months. May repel rodents and deer.
Bonemeal (finely ground, steamed animal bones)	11% phosphorus, 1% nitrogen, 24% calcium, but analysis varies. Mainly used as phosphorus source	Broadcast before planting when soil temp. above 55°F. 1 to 3 pounds, depending on soil's phosphorus supply. Work into top 6 to 12 inches.	Moderately available; lasts 6 to 12 months, use only on acidic soils because calcium increases alkalinity.
Compost (decayed and partially decayed plant and animal waste)	0.5–4% nitrogen, 0.5–4% phosphorus, 0.5–4% potassium	Apply 1- to 4-inch layer in spring and/or fall on surface, or work into soil.	Adds organic matter.
Cottonseed meal	6% nitrogen, 2% phosphorus, 1% potassium	1 to 3 pounds, work into soil.	May contain pesticide residues.
Fish emulsion (liquid concentrate)	4% nitrogen, 1% phosphorus, 1% potassium, 5% sulfur	Dilute according to label directions.	May have odor.
Fish meal (dried ground fish parts)	6% nitrogen, 3% phosphorus, 3% potassium	1 to 3 pounds at planting, depending on soil fertility. If side-dressing, use the same rates per 100 feet of row.	Quickly available; lasts one season.
Granite meal, granite dust (ground granite rock)	3–5% potassium, 67% silica (sand), 19 micronutrients	Broadcast 10 pounds if soil is low in potassium, 5 pounds if moderate potassium, 2.5 pounds if adequate potassium.	Rake into soil surface. Slowly available; application can last 10 years.
Grass clippings	0.5% nitrogen, 0.2% phosphorus, 0.5% potassium	1- to 2-inch layer fresh, 2- to 4-inch layer dried.	Adds organic matter.
Greensand (glauconite)	5–7% potassium, 32 micronutrients, up to 50% silica (sand)	In autumn broadcast 10 pounds if soil is low in potassium, 5 pounds if moderate potassium, 2.5 pounds if adequate potassium.	Sand-based fertilizer mined from dried ocean deposits.

Fertilizer	Nutrients Supplied	How to Apply (rate per 100 square feet)	Comments
Gypsum, land plaster (calcium sulfate powder)	22% calcium, 17% sulfur	Broadcast 1 to 4 pounds.	Loosens clay and neutralizes excessive sodium or magnesium.
Kelp (seaweed, dry form)	NPK negligible, 60 micronutrients, plant-growth hormones	1 pound on surface, or work into soil.	Adds organic matter.
Kelp (seaweed, liquid form)	NPK negligible, 60 micronutrients, plant-growth hormones	½ tablespoon per gallon. Drench soil or spray on leaves every 2 weeks for leafy vegetables, every 3 to 4 weeks for other plants.	
Langbeinite (sulfate of potash magnesia)	22% potassium, 11% magnesium, 22% sulfur	No more than 1 pound on surface, or work into soil.	Quickly available. Sold as Sul-Po-Mag and K-Mag. Excess can burn plants.
Manure (solid animal waste, aged)	**COW:** 2% nitrogen, 2% phosphorus, 2% potassium **HORSE:** 1.7% nitrogen, 0.7% phosphorus, 1.8% potassium **POULTRY:** 4% nitrogen, 4% phosphorus, 3% potassium **SHEEP:** 4% nitrogen, 1.4% phosphorus, 3.5% potassium **PIG:** 0.5% nitrogen, 0.3% phosphorus, 0.5% potassium	10 to 20 pounds on surface, or work into soil.	Adds organic matter. High nitrogen in fresh manure can burn plants; compost first or dig into soil one season before planting.
Rock phosphate (crushed, washed rock)	33% total phosphorus (only about 3% available at any time), 32% calcium, 11 micronutrients	6 pounds if soil is low in phosphorus, 2.5 pounds if medium phosphorus, 1 pound if adequate phosphorus. Work into top 6 inches of soil or add to compost pile in autumn.	Slowly available. Do not use on alkaline soils because calcium raises pH.
Wood ash	About 7% potassium, 20% calcium, some micronutrients	No more than 2 pounds every 3 to 4 years, on surface or work into soil.	Do not use on soil with pH above 6.0 because calcium raises pH.
Worm castings (worm manure)	Not significant	Apply 25 pounds if soil is low in organic matter, 10 pounds if moderate organic matter, and 5 pounds if adequate organic matter. Spread on surface or work into soil.	Adds organic matter and improves soil structure.

APPLYING FERTILIZERS

You can apply organic and synthetic fertilizers as dry solids or as liquids. Dry fertilizers come as granules or powders. In an unplanted garden, broadcast dry fertilizer evenly over a large area, then fork it into the top few inches of soil. An alternative is to mix a small amount with the soil in the planting hole; the label should specify the recommended amount. In established vegetable gardens, place dry fertilizer beside each plant, a technique called side-dressing, then lightly scratch the fertilizer into the soil without nicking roots or stems. Fertilize permanent landscape plantings and perennial gardens by sprinkling the dry fertilizer over the soil or on top of an organic mulch.

Liquid fertilizers are powders that must be dissolved in water or liquid concentrates that must be diluted with water. Liquid fertilizers don't last as long in the soil as dry fertilizers, so you need to feed more often—every three to four weeks while plants are actively growing. Before applying a liquid fertilizer, follow the label instructions for dissolving or diluting it. Either drench the soil at the base of the plant, or spray it on the leaves, a method called foliar feeding.

Foliar feeding allows plants to make the most efficient use of nutrients and lets you bypass the nutrient-binding effect of extremely acid or alkaline soils. Because plants close down their leaf pores (stomata) when it's very hot or sunny, apply foliar fertilizers early or late in the day, or during a cloudy spell. Spray the tops and undersides of the leaves until the liquid runs off.

HOW MUCH FERTILIZER TO USE

Not all plants require the same amount of fertilizer. Some, such as roses and broccoli, are heavy feeders. Others, such as wildflowers and herbs, actually do best in suitable soil with no fertilizer. Use the plant encyclopedias in chapters 3 through 11 to learn about the nutrient needs of the plants you grow.

How much fertilizer to apply depends on a particular plant's needs, and also on your soil's fertility. That's why a soil test is helpful. In general, if your soil provides a balanced supply of nutrients, you need to replace only what's removed each year. In the spring, apply a balanced dry fertilizer, such as a slow-release packaged fertilizer, or aged manure or compost.

If a soil test reveals a nutrient deficiency, apply a fertilizer (or fertilizers) that supplies the missing nutrients. The soil test should specify the amount to apply. If your soil is particularly infertile or has an extreme pH, your best bet is to foliar-feed with a liquid fertilizer. Work organic matter and corrective fertilizers into the soil each year. In a few years, you should need to apply a balanced fertilizer only in spring.

For details on fertilizing specific types of plants, see the appropriate chapters and plant encyclopedias.

WHEN TO FERTILIZE

How often to fertilize depends upon the plants you're feeding and the kind of fertilizer you use.

■ **TREES AND SHRUBS:** Do not fertilize during the first three years after planting. After that, spread compost around the plant bases each spring. If you use a soluble synthetic fertilizer, don't apply it within three months of the average date of the first autumn frost, so that new growth can toughen up before cold weather comes.

■ **PERENNIAL FLOWERS:** Mix slow-release sources of potassium and phosphorus into the soil before planting. After that, apply a thin layer of compost or well-rotted manure to the soil surface when plants green up each spring, or apply a balanced, slow-release fertilizer. To encourage more growth, spray the leaves with a liquid fertilizer as often as every two weeks during summer, stopping two months before the average date of the first autumn frost to let roots prepare for winter.

■ **ANNUAL FLOWERS AND VEGETABLES:** Add fertilizer to the soil before or when you plant. For a boost, sidedress with a dry fertilizer when plants flower, or spray leaves with a liquid fertilizer as often as every two weeks.

■ **ROSES:** Feed roses one month after planting. Feed established modern hybrids every two to three weeks from spring through summer. Fertilize old garden roses once a year in spring.

■ **LAWNS:** Fertilize cool-season lawn grasses in spring and fall, and warm-season grasses in late spring, summer, and fall.

Photo by Balthazar Korab

FERTILIZER "TEA"

The same aged manure and compost that add nutrients to the garden in solid form also can be dissolved in water to form a liquid fertilizer. To make manure or compost tea, put about a cup of aged manure or rotted compost into a cloth bag or a perforated plastic bag designed for storing vegetables. Close the bag and place it in a gallon of water. Let it brew at least three days; longer steeping makes stronger tea.

Use the liquid brew full strength for occasional feedings, or dilute it for daily use. Apply it directly to the soil, not as a foliar feed, because it can burn leaves if it's too strong.

For best growth and profuse flowering, fertilize perennials each spring with compost or a balanced fertilizer.

EASY DIGGING

Here is good news for people with bad backs or tight schedules: Whether you're planting trees, shrubs, flowers, or vegetables, you may not need to do as much digging as you think. New techniques are replacing more strenuous ones.

GOOD REASONS TO DIG LESS

Garden books used to suggest a lot of digging. They suggested digging big and deep holes for trees and shrubs, then adding plenty of organic matter to the holes. They told readers to double-dig flower and vegetable gardens, and to turn the soil in beds of annual flowers and vegetables each spring and fall.

Although digging still has its place, researchers find that many gardeners overdo it—which can be hard on the soil as well as the spine. Research shows that digging too often can destroy soil structure. Small clumps of soil particles are pummeled when you dig, especially if you use a power tiller. Breaking apart the clumps too much turns the soil into a fine powder or a solid mass; either way, the right-size spaces between soil particles are lost. Those spaces are necessary for air and water to reach plant roots. Digging also floods the soil with oxygen, encouraging soil microorganisms to digest too much organic matter—the same organic matter that helps bind soil particles together to give the soil good structure. Another problem is that digging destroys worm tunnels that loosen and aerate the soil.

When planting trees and shrubs, arborists have found that digging deep holes, which used to be the common practice, can make the new tree or shrub settle excessively. If that happens, roots are buried too deeply and don't get enough air. Arborists now suggest digging a wide hole that is no deeper than the root mass to avoid soil settling. They also recommend that no peat or other soil enhancers should be added to the backfill soil. Research shows that roots may be reluctant to grow from the highly improved soil into the unamended soil beyond the hole. (For more on planting trees, see Chapter 3.)

WORKING THE SOIL SENSIBLY

How deeply and how often should you dig? That depends on what you're planting and what kind of soil you have. Deep-rooted perennials and clay soils require more effort than vegetables and loamy soil.

Double digging is a traditional technique that's well-suited to preparing a new bed for perennials. Once the perennials are in the ground, you won't have to work the soil again for years. Double digging isn't necessary for annual flowers or for most vegetables because their roots seldom go deeper than 12 inches. You might make an exception if you're growing root crops such as carrots. Because double-dug beds eventually settle, it may be better to grow root vegetables in raised beds.

To double-dig a bed, remove the top 8 to 12 inches of soil, then loosen the subsoil with a fork another 10 to

REMOVING SOD

There are many ways to create a new flowerbed in an existing lawn, but one tried-and-true method is to first remove the sod. This prevents grass from invading the new garden and becoming a weed.

With a spade, outline the new bed by cutting through the sod to a depth of 2 to 4 inches.

Working in strips, slide the spade under the sod and push it repeatedly with your foot to sever the grass roots. The sod can then be rolled and laid in other parts of the yard.

To double-dig a garden, first remove the top layer, then loosen and improve the lower layer. Replace the top layer of soil.

12 inches deep. Work organic matter and other soil amendments into the soil. Replace the top layer and work soil amendments into it also. To avoid removing the top layer from the entire bed at once and finding a place to store the topsoil, dig one strip of the garden at a time, temporarily storing excess soil in a wheelbarrow. Then shovel the top layer (see illustration above).

Limit double digging to once per bed, usually the first year you plant.

Many gardeners never double-dig their beds, not even perennial beds. Instead, they turn over only the top 8 to 12 inches of soil with a spade or spading fork, then use a metal rake to break up clumps before planting. You can use this single-dig method in an area intended for landscape plantings, a flower garden, or a vegetable garden.

In the past, it was common to single-dig vegetable patches and annual flower gardens in both spring and fall. However, we now know that turning the soil once a year, or even every other year, is sufficient in most soils for plantings of annuals and vegetables.

There is an advantage to turning the soil and working in organic matter in autumn. The freezing and thawing cycles of winter and the early spring rains break up most soil clumps and settle the soil. Thus, you should be able to get away with raking the ground smooth only before planting in spring.

NO-TILL GARDENING

You may wish to try the no-till method of gardening to prepare a vegetable garden, flower bed, mixed border, or foundation planting. To avoid tilling, cover lawn that you want to turn into a garden with about 8 inches of organic matter, such as shredded leaves, compost, or manure. The organic matter smothers and kills the grass. It also decays, allowing worms and other organisms to work the organic matter into the soil below. In a few months, you'll have a thick layer of rich, loose soil.

In areas with stubborn weeds, cut the weeds to the ground, then cover the soil with overlapping layers of corrugated cardboard or newspapers 12 sheets deep. Wet the paper mulch, then add several inches of organic matter to the top. Pull any stubborn perennial weeds that poke through. The plot should be ready to plant in three to six months. If you don't want to wait, create planting pockets for each plant by digging holes through the organic matter, through the paper mulch, and down into the soil.

GETTING RID OF LAWN

Gardeners always seem to be digging up the lawn to make new gardens. But there are right ways and wrong ways to remove grass. Do not power-till it under; the grass will come back to haunt your garden as weeds. Here are better ways to remove sod:

■ **APPLY A NONSELECTIVE HERBICIDE.** Choose a weed killer containing glyphosate, an herbicide that will not move in the soil and that breaks down quickly. Two weeks after application, you can plant in the dead sod, which acts as a mulch that breaks down gradually.

■ **STRIP OFF THE SOD.** Rent a power tool specifically made for stripping sod, or use a spade. When the soil is slightly damp, slide the spade just under the grass roots, cutting them free of the soil. You can roll up long strips like a carpet, but 2×2-foot squares are lighter and easier to handle. (See illustration on page 518.)

■ **SMOTHER THE SOD.** Cover the grass with black plastic, which will smother and cook the sod. How long you need to leave the plastic in place depends upon the temperature and the vigor of the grass. Check the grass every two weeks in warm weather, every four to six weeks in cool weather. Remove the plastic when the grass is strawlike.

■ **PLANT ON TOP.** Lay down thick layers of newspaper covered with a 3-inch-deep layer of commercial compost and soil mix. With this technique, you can plant immediately in the soil mix by cutting a hole through the paper and into the sod. The grass eventually smothers and dies. (See illustration below.)

Smothering grass with newspaper and mulch, then planting through the paper is a simple way to create a new garden.

COMPOSTING WITH CONFIDENCE

As more municipalities avoid hauling away grass clippings and other yard waste—or charge to do so—more gardeners are turning to composting to cut their trash bill and to create

Yard waste can be turned into good-quality compost, an invaluable substance that nourishes the soil and is called "black gold" by gardeners.

their own balanced fertilizer, mulch, and soil conditioner. Think of composting as controlled rotting. You toss yard waste and nonmeat kitchen scraps into a pile, and decay organisms turn them into humus, a crumbly, black substance rich in nutrients and organic matter.

COMPOSTING SECRETS

The secret to turning trash into compost as quickly as possible is to pamper the soil-dwelling microorganisms (fungi, bacteria, actinomycetes, insects, and other creatures responsible for decomposition). The more you cater to them, the more they'll reproduce, and the faster you'll get a finished product. You'll know that the organisms are active because the pile heats up and steam may rise when you turn it. This approach, sometimes called hot composting, should produce humus in a season or less.

Don't worry if tending a compost pile is at the bottom of your priority list. You can pile the materials and ignore them. The organisms will still digest the material, but they may take several years to finish the process. This method is called cold composting; the pile decays slowly and doesn't heat up as much or at all.

AVOIDING ODORS

Some compost piles smell bad. Avoid the problem by adding the right materials and by spending a little time to plan and care for the compost pile so it decomposes at a steady rate. Here are some tips for making sweet-smelling compost:

■ **PICK THE RIGHT SITE.** If you live in a cold region, situate the pile in full sun to warm it. In hot regions, site it in part shade so it doesn't get too warm or dry out. For your convenience, locate the compost where it's easy to get to and near a source of water.

■ **KEEP THE SIZE MANAGEABLE.** If the pile is too big, decomposition slows and odors increase. A 3- to 4-foot cube is a manageable size.

■ **TURN THE PILE.** Desirable decay organisms need oxygen, so fluff and turn the pile every week or so to speed decomposition.

■ **WATER THE PILE.** The organisms that break down compost work best if the compost pile is damp but not soggy.

■ **BALANCE THE MATERIALS.** Decay organisms balance their diets with carbon and nitrogen. Too much of either slows them down. To avoid this imbalance, try to mix carbon and nitrogen sources equally. A pile high in nitrogen-rich materials becomes slimy and smelly. High-nitrogen, or "green," materials include vegetable scraps, manure, grass clippings, green leaves, seaweed, and alfalfa hay. High-carbon, or "brown," materials include dried leaves, straw, newspaper, sawdust, and woody stems.

■ **SHRED THE MATERIALS.** It's easier for decay organisms to work on small, soft materials with a lot of surface area. Woody stems, thick leaves, and twigs and branches take a long time to break down, so either shred them before adding them to the pile or put them in their own pile.

In this setup, one bin holds new organic matter. When it breaks down, it's moved to a second, partially decomposed heap to break down more. The third pile is fully composted and ready for use.

There's plenty of room to turn and store compost in these bins.

This plastic insulated bin works for a small city garden.

Rotating bins, such as this one, create compost in just a week or two.

A large, sprawling heap works well for cold composting.

CONTAINING THE COMPOST

You can toss compost into a freestanding heap, but if you like things tidy, you may want to build a structure to house it. Consider creating two or even three piles, each composed of compost of different ages. That way you don't have to toss fresh material into compost that's almost ready to use.

Compost bins may be built at home or purchased at a store and can be minimalist or fancy. Choose a design that makes it easy for you to turn and to water the pile. Consider the following suggestions.

■ CINDER BLOCKS. Build a three-sided enclosure using cinder blocks. Set the blocks so the holes face into the pile to allow ventilation. Some compost may fall through the holes.

■ FENCING. Contain your compost in a wire cage that's open on one side. Use wooden fence posts at the corners or, most simply, use metal fence supports and let the fencing curl around them. Choose a fencing material with a small enough mesh to keep the compost from falling out.

■ WOODEN SLATS. Make a bin from boards spaced 2 to 4 inches apart. Attach a hinged or sliding door, or leave one side open. If animals are a problem, add a hinged lid.

■ TUMBLERS. Purchase a ready-made barrel-like tumbler. Turn the crank to rotate the bin and mix the compost. Tumblers make compost quickly if you turn them daily.

■ INSULATED BINS. Toss ingredients in the top of a ready-made plastic or metal insulated bin and remove the completed compost from the bottom. No turning is required. Such bins keep compost warm even in winter and protect it from animals.

USING COMPOST

Compost adds both nutrients and organic matter to the soil, improving its structure, drainage, and aeration. Each year, you can mix compost into the top few inches of the soil in a vegetable or annual flower garden, or apply it to the surface of a perennial garden or landscape planting and let worms do the mixing for you. Try to apply a 2- to 3-inch layer once a year.

Compost can be used before it completely breaks down into humus, if you don't mind a few eggshells in the garden—they'll decay eventually—or the animals they may attract. Avoid using unfinished compost with large amounts of undecayed, high-carbon material such as sawdust, because the decay organisms rob nitrogen from the soil to offset the carbon in their diets.

WHAT YOU CAN COMPOST

Lawn trimmings and kitchen scraps are best transformed into compost when the compost pile is a balanced mix of "green" (fresh) and "brown" (dry) ingredients. Here are the best and worst ingredients for your compost recipe:

Do compost:
Coffee grounds
Eggshells
Fruit and vegetable scraps
Grass clippings
Flower heads (before they set seed)
Leaves (preferably shredded)
Manure
Paper (preferably shredded)
Plant clippings
Sawdust
Soil
Weed tops (before they set seed)

Do not compost:
Bones
Meat
Diseased plants
Seed heads
Carnivore feces
Oils and fats
Weed roots

MULCHING

Mulch works magic in the garden. A mulch is simply a cover over the soil surface. It can be organic—a biodegradable plant material, such as shredded leaves, pine needles, bark chunks, manure, or newspaper—or a long-lasting inorganic material, such as gravel, plastic sheeting, aluminum foil, or even old carpeting. The type of mulch you choose depends upon which area of the garden you're mulching and which natural materials are available in your region.

A mulch, no matter what it's made of, has the following benefits:

■ **BLOCKS LIGHT**, inhibiting the growth of weed seeds and seedlings.

■ **SLOWS WATER EVAPORATION** from the soil, meaning the soil dries out more slowly.

■ **BREAKS THE IMPACT OF RAIN**, preventing soil from washing away or splashing onto plants.

■ **KEEPS SOIL COOL** in the heat of summer; plant roots aren't stressed.

■ **INSULATES THE GROUND** in winter so it freezes and thaws gradually, which prevents plants from "heaving"—popping out of the soil as it rapidly freezes and thaws.

■ **NOURISHES THE SOIL**, because organic mulch improves soil structure and nutrient content as it slowly degrades. Organic mulch also encourages earthworms, which aerate and feed the soil.

CHOOSING A MULCH

There are many mulching materials from which to choose. Some, such as bark chips, are widely available. Others, such as apple pomace and nut hulls, are byproducts of local industries and generally are sold only regionally.

When choosing a mulch, decide if one purpose is to look attractive. You probably want the bed of shrubs and flowers near your front door to look pretty, but you may be less concerned with the aesthetics of the vegetable garden. For areas with visual impact, choose an attractive mulch such as mini bark chips or cocoa hulls. Use shredded bark to prevent erosion on a slope, since it weaves together well. When you just want to get the job done and don't care how it looks, use grass clippings, newspaper, old carpet—just about anything.

HOW MUCH MULCH?

A 2- to-4-inch layer of mulch usually does the job. Using less allows weeds to grow through; using more prevents plant roots from getting enough oxygen. You can use more of lightweight mulches, such as straw, and less of dense mulches, such as carpet or newspaper. For complete information, see Mulch Choices on page 525.

WHEN TO MULCH

Organic mulches decompose slowly, so they need to be refreshed every year. Wait to renew the mulch until mid spring. Mulch blocks light and traps cool moisture, slowing the warming of soil in spring.

A generous layer of wood chip mulch does more than look attractive. It also keeps plants healthy and minimizes garden chores by preventing disease, suppressing weeds, feeding the soil, and conserving moisture.

SOLVING MULCH PROBLEMS

Mulches can create problems, but usually they can be easily solved.

■ **PROBLEM:** Slugs, cutworms, and earwigs may hide under mulch.

■ **SOLUTION:** Keep the mulch about 6 inches away from the plant to discourage pest feeding. Prevent slug damage by encircling valuable plants with a copper strip buried halfway into the ground. To thwart cutworms, wrap young stems with a collar of newspaper or cardboard, or push nails into the soil alongside stems. Reduce earwig populations by leaving a rolled newspaper in the garden overnight; in the morning, dump the earwigs hiding in the paper into a bucket of soapy water.

■ **PROBLEM:** Mulches high in carbon, such as straw and sawdust, create a nutrient imbalance that encourages soil organisms to take nitrogen from the soil.

■ **SOLUTION:** To compensate, apply bloodmeal or another source of nitrogen to the soil.

■ **PROBLEM:** Light-colored mulches prevent the soil from warming in spring.

■ **SOLUTION:** In early spring, rake aside any winter mulch; do not reapply it until a few weeks after plants begin growing.

■ **PROBLEM:** In the South, dark mulches such as black plastic heat the soil too much in summer.

■ **SOLUTION:** Replace or cover with a light-colored material.

■ **PROBLEM:** If too close to stems and crowns, organic mulch enhances moisture-loving diseases.

■ **SOLUTION:** Keep mulch 1 to 2 inches away from stems.

Timing is everything when it comes to mulching. This gardener applies mulch in mid spring to prevent weeds from germinating and keep the soil from splashing onto the flowers during spring rains.

Don't renew mulch until perennial plants send out new growth. Mulch can smother seedlings, so if you sow seed in the garden, wait until the seedlings are growing steadily before applying mulch.

Both black and clear plastic mulch make the soil warm faster in spring. Use either to warm annual flower and vegetable beds in the early spring, so you will be able to plant a few weeks ahead of schedule.

Apply a winter mulch to protect perennials after the soil freezes. Lay the winter mulch directly over the summer mulch. Use a 6- to 12-inch layer of a lightweight mulch such as straw or whole leaves. Rake off the winter mulch in early spring to allow the soil to warm.

MULCHING

continued

USING LANDSCAPE FABRIC

If weeds are a major problem around your trees and shrubs, consider using landscape fabric, also called weed barrier or weed cloth. This porous plastic covers the soil surface, but unlike plastic sheeting, it allows water and air to pass through the microscopic pores without allowing most weeds to penetrate.

Landscape fabric is a nearly impenetrable barrier for weeds, yet allows water to seep through. The fabric should be covered with a layer of mulch.

Photo courtesy Reemay, Inc.

You can spread the landscape fabric before planting. First dig the planting holes, then spread the fabric across the garden soil. Cut openings in the fabric to correspond to the planting holes. You also can put down landscape fabric after planting. Just cut slits in the fabric to fit around the bases of plants and shrubs. Or, you can overlap the fabric pieces around plant bases.

Conceal the fabric under a 2-inch layer of decorative mulch, to make the bed more attractive and to keep sunlight from reaching the fabric. The sun's ultraviolet light degrades the plastic material, causing it to disintegrate. Protected from sunlight, the cloth should last many years. As the decorative organic mulch degrades, however, weeds may germinate in it. Remove and replace the mulch when it becomes thin and sparse.

Aggressive perennial weeds, such as Bermuda grass and nut sedge, can break through landscape fabric from underneath. Pull the weeds when they're small to avoid damage to the fabric. Using a coarse-textured mulch, such as bark nuggets, discourages these invaders better than a fine mulch. Or, you may wish to lay down a double layer of the fabric.

Sometimes tree and shrub roots attach to the landscape fabric and can be damaged if you remove the fabric. To decrease that risk, use a tightly woven fabric, not the loosely woven kind. Don't remove the fabric unless it's absolutely necessary. Consider it a permanent addition to your landscape.

USING GRAVEL AND STONE MULCH

Gravel and small stones look natural and attractive in the right setting. Rock is particularly suitable in a dry-climate garden, but less at home in a cool, woodsy setting. Avoid bright white or light-colored gravel and stones; they reflect sunlight and heat onto plants that already may be stressed by sunny summer weather.

Gravel and small stones work their way into the soil in cold-winter regions where the soil freezes and thaws. This turns good soil into poor soil, creating large air pockets that cause roots to dry out. To avoid the problem, spread landscape fabric beneath the gravel or stones. Where a coarse texture looks appropriate, try mulching with large stones.

The mulch you choose should depend on the type of garden you have. This small stone mulch, for example, is perfect for a dry-climate garden.

MULCH CHOICES

Mulch	Where and How to Use	Thickness	Comments
Bark	Trees, shrubs, perennials, pathways. Apply anytime. Renew annually.	2 to 4 inches	May deplete soil nitrogen unless aged. Large nuggets long-lasting, suppress weeds better than smaller pieces. Small chips look most attractive.
Cocoa hulls	Trees, shrubs, perennials, herbs. Apply anytime.	2 to 4 inches	Adds nutrients. May contain pesticide residue. May mold, attract rodents, blow off. Lovely color.
Compost	Vegetables, flowers, fruit. Apply at any stage in the decay cycle, after soil warms.	2 to 4 inches	Good source of organic matter. Depletes nitrogen if partly decomposed and high in carbon.
Grass clippings	Vegetables, flowers, fruit. Apply after soil warms. Replenish as needed.	2 to 4 inches if dry	Good source of organic matter. Fresh clippings heat up, mold if too thick; use only 1 to 2 inches.
Hay	Vegetables, flowers, fruit. Apply after soil warms. Use as winter mulch for perennials.	Up to 6 inches	May contain weed seed.
Landscape fabric	Trees, shrubs. Easiest to lay out before planting and then cut holes for plants. Cover with 2-inch layer of mulch.	1 or 2 layers	Breaks down after several years if exposed to sunlight. Good weed barrier, but tough weeds may pop through.
Leaf mold	Flowers, vegetables, fruit. Apply after soil warms. Can turn under at end of season.	Up to 4 inches	Good source of organic matter. To make, compost leaves for 2 to 3 years. Or, shred leaves, add nitrogen, and keep pile moist and fluffed.
Leaves, shredded	Trees, shrubs, flowers, vegetables, fruit, natural landscapes. Apply in spring or fall. Use as winter mulch for perennials.	2 to 4 inches	Lasts 1 to 2 seasons. To shred, rake into windrows and mow with grass catcher attachment or use leaf shredder. Improves soil.
Manure, rotted	Vegetables, flowers, fruit. Apply after soil warms. Can turn under at end of season.	2 to 4 inches	Adds organic matter. Can supply nutrients; type and amount vary with type and age of manure.
Mushroom compost	Vegetables, flowers, fruit. Apply after soil warms. Can turn under at end of season.	2 to 4 inches	Good source of organic matter. May contain pesticide residues. May not control weeds well.
Newspaper	Shrubs, vegetables, flowers, fruit. Apply to garden after soil warms. Anchor with soil, stones, or mulch so won't blow away. For perennial weeds use 10 sheets.	Start with 3 sheets in dry regions, 6 in wet regions	Good weed barrier. May deplete soil nitrogen. Speed of breakdown depends on thickness; usually lasts one season.
Pine needles	Trees, shrubs, flowers, natural landscapes. Apply anytime.	2 to 4 inches	Regional. Lasts 2 to 4 seasons. May be fire hazard during drought. Don't collect from forest. May make soil more acidic.
Plastic sheeting	Trees, shrubs, vegetables, flowers, fruit. Apply before planting, then cut holes. Can disguise with thin layer of attractive mulch.	1 layer	Breaks down in 2 or 3 seasons if exposed to light. Good barrier. Raises soil temperature. Lay soaker hose underneath to water.
Pomace (pulp of apples)	Vegetables, flowers, fruit. If soggy, compost with leaves or hay before applying.	1 to 2 inches	Adds phosphorus and potassium. May contain pesticide residues, attract flies, and smell sour.
Sawdust	Pathways; vegetables, flowers, fruit if composted. Apply after soil warms.	2 inches	Regional. Depletes soil nitrogen unless composted.
Straw	Good for newly seeded lawns and as winter mulch for perennials.	6 to 8 inches for winter mulch; 1 to 2 inches for lawns	Lasts 1 to 2 seasons. May deplete soil nitrogen. May blow away. May be too loose for good weed control.
Wood chips	Trees, shrubs, and perennials. Apply anytime.	3 to 4 inches	Quality varies. Compost before using or add nitrogen to fresh chips.

Buying Plants

You can buy plants locally or through mail-order nurseries. Either source is a good choice. When you buy at a nearby garden center, you get the joy of immediate gratification. When you order by mail, you get the thrill of receiving a package brimming with surprise and promise.

For instructions on planting your new acquisitions, see the chapters that discuss the specific plants you're adding to your garden and landscape.

Shopping at Garden Centers

Before you jump into the car on a spring day with your checkbook in hand, ready to dash to the garden center, heed a word of caution: All garden centers are not created equal. They vary greatly in the quality, selection, and price of the plants they sell. Further, they vary in the amount of expertise their employees possess.

Do you want knowledgeable advice? Are you seeking a plant that's out of the ordinary? Head for the pricey place with the well-trained staff and an owner who's involved in the operation. You may pay more, but you'll probably get better quality. A reputable nursery guarantees its plants, stocks only plants adapted to the region, and takes good care of them. If you want five trays of ordinary petunias, consider going to a garden center that stocks only the most popular plants and sells them at low prices.

Nurseries stock plants year-round in mild regions and from spring through fall in colder ones. Although

Buying through mail-order companies is an excellent way to purchase hard-to-find plants, although they tend to be smaller than those purchased at local nurseries.

spring is a favorite planting time, fall is ideal in many regions because the soil is warm and the air is cool, giving transplanted plants a few stress-free months to adjust to the new location. Container-grown plants may be successfully planted in spring, summer, or fall if they are given the care they need, with special attention to watering in summer.

Wherever you shop, pay attention to the quality of the plants. When purchasing annuals or vegetable transplants, choose compact plants with deeply colored leaves. Avoid any plants that are spindly, pale, have splotches on the leaves, or show signs of insect damage or diseases. Flower buds, if present, should be closed or barely open.

If you're in the market for trees or shrubs, look for symmetry and deeply colored leaves with no evidence of insects or diseases. Avoid plants with roots growing out the drainage holes and those with tops that seem out of proportion to the root ball or container.

CHOOSING MAIL-ORDER NURSERIES

Shopping for plants by mail gives you a greater selection than any garden center can. However, the plants you receive by mail are generally younger and smaller than those from a retail center. Mail-order plants usually are shipped only in spring and fall, targeted to the proper planting time for your area. Armchair shopping with catalogs is an excellent way to discover and acquire unusual plants. But you can't examine the merchandise before buying, so be sure the mail-order company is trustworthy.

Ask friends to suggest mail-order nurseries they've found reputable.

Check gardening magazines, which are laden with advertising from mail-order sources. Some nurseries offer free catalogs; others charge a few dollars, which often can be deducted from your first order.

Send for several catalogs. Old, established nurseries are a good starting point; their catalogs often have color photographs, which are helpful to browse. Don't overlook the small nurseries; they may offer rare plants and often are owned and managed by dedicated plant lovers. If possible, get a few catalogs from nurseries headquartered in regions with a climate similar to yours.

While browsing mail-order catalogs, look for substantial information about growing conditions: details on how much sun, heat, and drought the plant tolerates; the type of soil it prefers; and recommended hardiness zones, the regional climate to which the plant is adapted. Read the information about how and when plants are shipped, whether planting instructions come with the order, and if the company guarantees its plants.

SUCCESSFUL TRANSPLANTING

Container-grown plants have adapted to confined quarters, and their roots may be growing in circles. To help them develop a healthy root system in the garden, untangle encircling roots and break up any network of fine surface roots. To do this, remove the plant from the container, then use a weeding claw and rake it over the root ball. If necessary, cut any thick roots that threaten to strangle the root ball. (For specific planting instructions, see the chapters on trees and shrubs, perennials, annuals, and other kinds of plants.)

GETTING READY FOR YOUR SPECIAL DELIVERY

Mail-order nurseries usually ship plants that are dormant—not growing—or plants that are just beginning to show growth. Perennials may arrive in a little pot of soil. Or, they may be unpotted with the roots wrapped in a water-retaining material, such as wet sawdust in a plastic bag. Such packaging saves on shipping costs.

Trees and shrubs usually are shipped when dormant and bare-root, although some nurseries ship them in soil and containers. Dormant, bare-root plants look like a tangle of dried roots wrapped in newspaper or wood shavings and sealed in a plastic bag.

Spring-blooming bulbs are shipped in early fall when they're dormant; summer- and fall-blooming bulbs are shipped when dormant, in late spring or summer. They arrive packed in net bags or wood shavings.

If the plants arrive before you can get them in the ground, take steps to keep them healthy. If plants are potted, provide light and water. The goal is to keep the soil moist but not wet.

Maintain bare-root plants in a cool and dark place until you can plant. Most mail-order companies recommend soaking the roots of bare-root plants in warm water for several hours before planting. If you can't plant for several days after your shipment arrives, the instructions may recommend "heeling in" the plants. To do that, lay the plants on their sides in the garden and cover the roots with moist soil.

MORE PLANTS FOR LESS MONEY

Starting plants from seed is less expensive than buying them from a nursery. Gardeners often use seeds for annual vegetables and flowers. They germinate quickly, and young plants are ready for the garden in weeks or months. You also can grow herbaceous perennials and woody plants from seed, but they can take years to be garden-ready.

For a small investment in a grow-light, seeds, and supplies, a gardener can start hundreds of seedlings, costing a fraction of the price of the more mature plants found in nurseries.

CONTAINERS AND SOIL

There are many types of containers for starting seeds. Choose plastic or wood-fiber flats, plastic cell-packs in various sizes, plastic pots, peat pots, or peat pellets. Or, recycle food containers into plant pots. Try yogurt and cottage cheese cups, paper cups, clear plastic take-out boxes, juice cartons—anything that's waterproof and holds its shape. Rinse them before using with a weak bleach solution to sterilize the container. Punch drainage holes in the bottom.

Seed flats and other containers in which seedlings are not in individual sections save space and are easy to carry. But they also pose problems. It's not practical to sow several types of seeds in the same flat because they may not germinate at the same time. And eventually you have to transplant seedlings from flats into individual containers so the seedlings grow. When you transplant, you risk damaging roots. Pots, cell-packs, peat pots and pellets, and food containers are ideal for seedlings that don't like to have their roots disturbed.

POTTING SOIL

Seeds sprout and grow best in a lightweight, moisture-retaining, well-drained growing medium. Most garden soil is too heavy and can harbor disease pathogens. Even many commercial potting soils can be too dense for tiny seedlings.

Soil-less mixes contain sterile materials such as peat, perlite, and vermiculite that provide bulk, improve aeration, and absorb water.

Buy soil-less mixes for starting seeds, or make your own by mixing equal parts of milled sphagnum peat, perlite, and vermiculite.

Plants that stay potted for a long time, such as perennials, shrubs, and trees, must eventually be transplanted into a mixture that contains some soil.

SOWING SEEDS

Seeds of most flowering annuals and vegetables should be sown from six to 12 weeks before the last frost date for your area.

Fill a container to 1 inch from the top with loose potting medium. Moisten and press down the mix.

Follow the technique of experienced seed sowers for delivering the right amount of seed to the container: Use a white 3×5-inch file card folded in the middle. Pour a few seeds into the crease of the file card, then with a toothpick gently push individual seeds from the card onto the soil. Put two or three seeds in each container because all may not germinate. Push the seeds into the soil with the eraser of a pencil. The rule of thumb is to bury a seed at a depth of two or three times its size.

You may find it easier to sow fine seeds in a community flat and, after they germinate, transplant the seedlings into individual pots. Sow the seeds in rows in the flats. Fine seeds need only a dusting of soil as a cover. Mist gently but thoroughly to moisten or water from the bottom.

Seeds that need light to germinate should not be covered with any soil. After tapping seeds onto the soil surface, gently mist to nestle the seeds into the potting mix. Bottom-water to keep the mix moist.

Cover the pots or flats with plastic film or a plastic humidity dome and set them under the grow-lights. Check daily and water as needed to keep the potting mix evenly moist but not soggy.

SEEDLING CARE

Newly planted seeds sprout faster if the growing medium is kept between 70 and 80 degrees Fahrenheit with bottom heat. Buy warming mats from garden centers and catalogs, or set containers atop a water heater or refrigerator. When the seeds sprout, move the containers to a cooler place in good light.

When the first leaves appear, gradually remove the cover: Open it slightly one day; then open a little more each successive day. Bottom-water when the soil surface is dry, usually several times a week.

Give seedlings eight to 12 hours of natural light each day; use a south-facing windowsill. If using fluorescent lights, leave them on 12 to 14 hours each day. The light must be 2 to 3 inches from the top of the plants.

Seeds and young seedlings need frequent, gentle, shallow watering to prevent drying out. Seeds warmed from below are especially vulnerable. Use a small watering can with a fine sprinkler head, a hose with a sprayer that makes a fine mist, or a pump spray bottle. Water with a balanced soluble fertilizer mixed at one-quarter the recommended strength.

Once seedlings develop their first set of true leaves—the characteristic leaves that form above the rounded seed leaves—they need to be transplanted or thinned. Transplant from community flats to individual 4-inch pots or cell-packs. Don't touch seedlings with your hands. Pick them up by the leaves with a wooden tongue depressor, notched at one end.

Seedlings growing in individual containers should be thinned to one seedling per container. To avoid disturbing its roots, cut out the weakest plants with small scissors.

Two weeks before you intend to plant vegetable or annual seedlings outdoors, start hardening them off by watering less frequently and by gradually exposing them to lower temperatures and outdoor light. Move the plants to a bright, unheated porch or set them outside in a shaded area protected from wind. Expose them to the new environment for 30 minutes the first day, and increase by 30 to 60 minutes each day. After a week, move the seedlings into an area with conditions similar to those they'll face after transplanting.

KEEPING WARM WITH A COLDFRAME

A coldframe is a rectangular bottomless box that rests on top of well-prepared garden soil (or firm ground if you're growing young plants in pots). The cover is clear glass, acrylic, or plastic; light passes through the top, warming the air inside. The warmer-than-outside temperature allows the coldframe to play numerous roles. You can start seeds of vegetables and flowers, grow cool-season vegetables early or late in the season, propagate new plants from stem or root cuttings, and harden off young transplants.

A coldframe doesn't have to be elaborate. You can build a permanent wooden structure with a lid of UV-resistant hard plastic. Or, you can make one with straw bales or stacks of cinder blocks covered with an old storm window. Many garden-supply catalogs offer convenient, ready-made models.

A coldframe can be any length, but it shouldn't be wider, front to back, than your reach. The depth is up to you. Deep frames shade plants slightly, but they allow you to grow tall plants. The air temperature doesn't fluctuate as much in a deeper frame. Regardless of the depth, the back usually is higher than the front, so the clear top is sloped. A slope helps the coldframe collect more light and allows rain to run off. The recommended slope is about 15 degrees in the South and up to 30 degrees in the North.

To gather as much light and heat as possible, position your coldframe with the top slanting southward. If possible, put the back against a wall to protect it from north winds. The site should be well-drained; a slight slope is ideal.

On very sunny days, even when it's cold, the air in the coldframe can become warm enough to damage plants. Keep a thermometer in the box, and when the air gets too hot (the ideal temperature varies with the plant), prop the lid open slightly. Or, install a solar-powered opener that automatically lifts the lid when the air reaches a specified temperature.

Coldframes are like mini greenhouses. They extend the gardening season and get seedlings off to a good start.

FREE PLANTS FROM YOUR GARDEN

If you covet a tree, shrub, or perennial flower and it's difficult to start from seed or you can't find one to buy, try propagating it vegetatively from an existing plant.

DIVISION

Eventually, most herbaceous perennials—and some woody perennials—send up side plants from the main plant, creating a clump. To get a new plant, just dig up and pull or cut apart the clump—making certain each piece has a shoot and roots—and replant the individual divisions. It may seem brutal, but in most cases dividing a plant helps it, because crowded plants lose vitality. Generally, plants are divided most successfully in early spring or fall.

How you divide the parent clump depends on the plant. For plants with relatively mild-mannered root systems, such as columbine and yarrow, separate a side plant by digging it out with a trowel. Tough root systems must be completely unearthed and cut apart with a knife; or they can be pried apart with your hands or two spading forks set back-to-back. Some ornamental grasses, such as pampas grass, are so tough they require an ax or chain saw.

CUTTINGS

Many plants produce roots from the cut end of a stem when it is planted in soil. You can take such stem cuttings from herbaceous perennials, such as coneflower and garden phlox, and from woody plants, such as azalea and boxwood. Woody plants root most readily in spring, when the bark is still soft; these are called softwood cuttings. But cuttings also can be taken later in the year, even in winter; these are called hardwood cuttings because the bark is fully developed. Hardwood cuttings root more slowly than softwood, but are less likely to dry out. Most cuttings are tip cuttings— taken from the end of the stem.

To take a cutting, snip off a section of stem containing a growing tip. For most plants, cut just below a node— the swollen area on a stem where a leaf or smaller stem grows. For plants that already have root buds on the stem, such as willow, and for stems densely covered with leaves, cut between two nodes. In both cases, the cutting should be 4 to 5 inches long and have about five nodes.

Strip the leaves from the end that you'll insert in the soil. Don't remove the immature leaves on the rest of the stem, but remove or cut in half most large leaves. (Keep only one leaf on plants with very large leaves.) The goal is to keep some leaves to photosynthesize, but reduce water loss from large leaves.

If you take a cutting from a woody plant between late summer and early spring, when the tissue is hard and woody, use a sharp knife to peel away a small, thin layer of bark at the stripped end of the stem. This helps the wounded area develop roots more readily.

Unless the plant roots easily, you can speed up the process by dipping the cut end into rooting hormone, which is sold as a powder at most nurseries. Use just a little—too much can harm plants. Insert the base of the stem into loose potting soil, water it well, and enclose it with a plastic bag to retain moisture.

Keep pots or trays of cuttings under grow-lights as you would seedlings. When the cuttings show signs of growth, test them for new roots with a gentle tug. After they are well-rooted, gradually acclimate the cuttings to a drier atmosphere by opening the plastic bag little by little. Water as needed.

Root cuttings are chunks of root removed from the parent plant and potted in loose, damp soil to encourage production of stems and leaves. Take root cuttings any time of year, choosing young, vigorous sections about as thick and long as your index finger. Iris, pulmonaria, and sedum are a few plants suited to this method of propagation. Many shrubs can be propagated from root cuttings too.

Place the root cuttings horizontally just below the soil surface. Or, position the cuttings vertically just below the soil surface; the end that was closest to the center of the parent should point upward. To help remember which end should point up, notch that end when you cut it from the plant.

Water stem or root cuttings lightly every week or two to keep the soil moist but not soggy. Roots form faster if the soil is 65 to 75 degrees Fahrenheit for cool-climate plants and up to 90 degrees Fahrenheit for warm-climate plants. Harden off the plants once roots form and the top shows new growth.

LAYERING

Layering is similar to making stem cuttings, with one important difference—the offspring stays attached to the parent until it's ready to live on its own. There are four techniques for layering (see the illustrations bottom right), all of which involve burying part of a branch in the soil. When dense roots develop on the buried portion, sever the new plant from the parent and transplant it.

■ TIP LAYERING: This method often is used for brambles such as raspberries and blackberries. In spring, when the branches are flexible, remove the leaves from the tip of a branch, bend the tip to the ground, and bury it. Pin the buried tip in place to keep it from popping out of the soil, or place a rock over it until roots form.

■ SIMPLE LAYERING: This method is similar to tip layering, but the middle of the stem, rather than the tip, is buried in the ground. Bury a section of the stem that's 6 to 12 inches away from the tip. For woody stems, nick the stem and prop the wound open with a toothpick; roots form near the wound.

■ SERPENTINE LAYERING: This layering method works for vines such as clematis and ivy. Bury the length of the vine at intervals; roots form readily at the buried sections. Cut rooted sections from the parent plant and transplant them.

■ MOUND LAYERING: Try this method for upright shrubs such as cotoneaster and hydrangea. A year before you plan to layer the shrub, cut all the branches back to about 2 feet from the ground. This encourages new shoots to grow from the base. Bury the base of the 2-foot-tall shrub in a mound of soil about a foot high. The new shoots will root in the mound below the soil and can be dug up and cut apart into individual plants.

DIVISION

1. Dig the entire plant out of the soil, maintaining as much of the root structure as possible.

2. With your hands, gently break apart the plant into two or more pieces.

3. Tough root systems may need to be cut apart.

4. Plant the division in its new home.

CUTTINGS

1. Cut off the tip of a healthy, growing stem.

2. Strip off the bottom leaves.

3. Dip the plant into rooting hormone, a substance that stimulates root development.

4. Place the plant in loose, damp soil.

5. Cover with plastic to conserve moisture while roots form.

6. Transplant to an individual pot when roots form.

LAYERING

Tip layering is rooting a plant at the tip of a stem.

Serpentine layering can create more than one new plant.

Simple layering creates roots in the middle of the stem.

Mound layering encourages a plant to send out new rooted shoots, which are then dug up.

GARDEN TOOLS
& MAINTENANCE

CHAPTER 13

EARTH-MOVING EQUIPMENT

When it comes to tackling tasks around the yard and garden, the standard advice about using the right tool for the job holds true—the correct tool makes the work easier and faster. But don't buy tools you won't use often enough to justify the price. Some power equipment is so expensive that it may be more economical to rent the tools you need only occasionally. Renting also is a good way to test a few tool models before buying.

Tools are available for controlling insects, weeds, and diseases in the garden—and most of them don't require using toxic pesticides. If you do need a pesticide, using the correct one and the correct equipment to apply it reduces your exposure to the chemical and the possibility of overapplying it. With any tool, but especially with power tools and pesticide equipment, read the instructions thoroughly and follow all safety precautions. Wear the recommended protective gear and maintain your equipment to keep it working properly.

Most gardening tools deal with dirt—digging in it, smoothing it,

Pitchfork

Spading fork

Garden fork

keeping it weed-free. Whichever soil-working tool you use, it's easiest to work if the soil is damp. Dry soil is as impenetrable as concrete, and wet soil is as heavy as bricks. Damp soil is just right. Working slightly damp soil also helps preserve the soil's structure. If need be, water a day or two ahead of digging.

SHOVELS, SPADES, AND A SECRET WEAPON

Shovels have long handles and concave blades or scoops that make them ideal for picking up soil, mulch, and other materials. Many gardeners use shovels for digging because the slightly pointed tip can pierce hard soil. Choose a shovel to fit your body; the scoop should be small enough so you can lift it when it's full, and the handle should be about shoulder height.

Spades resemble shovels, but they have flat-edge blades, which slice straight into soil that's not too dry or heavy, and make tidy holes with straight sides. Most spades have plastic or metal D-shaped hand grips. If you're tall, look for a 32-inch handle rather than the standard 28-inch one. Look also for a blade with a thick top edge, called a boot tread, where your foot pushes against the blade to drive it into the ground.

To dig with a shovel or spade, push your foot against the boot tread while bearing down on the handle. If the soil is

Round-point shovel

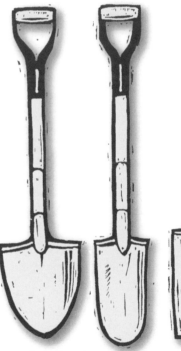

Mattock

hard, rock the blade slightly. The power for lifting the soil should come from your leg muscles, not your back.

Gardeners with very clayey or rocky soil often need a secret weapon: a mattock, or combination pick and hoe, which makes quick work of digging difficult soil. Use the pick end to break the soil, and the hoe end to dig. Both ends work well for prying rocks loose. To use, swing the blade sideways and over your shoulder, then drop it into the ground, in an "I've-been-

D-handle shovel   *Transplanting spade*   *Square-end spade*

working-on-the-railroad" motion. Mattocks come in different weights; choose one that you can swing easily. This tool requires more stooping than a spade or shovel, but it can make relatively light work of a heavy job.

FORKS AND TROWELS

To turn loose soil with less effort, try a spading fork, which has curved tines, or a garden fork, which has thick, straight tines. Because a fork doesn't have a solid blade, it weighs less than a shovel or spade, and it moves less soil. Push the tines into the soil with your foot, as you would a spade, then lift and turn the fork to the side. Buy a quality fork with tines that are thick enough to resist bending if you hit a rock or other obstruction.

Don't confuse these digging forks with pitchforks, which have thinner, curved tines that are designed for scooping and pitching lightweight materials such as hay and compost.

Trowels are ideal for small digging jobs, such as digging holes for flower and vegetable transplants. Trowels are used while you kneel or sit. These hand tools have various-size blades and handles. You may want several shapes. A transplanting trowel has an extra-narrow blade. Wide-blade types are multipurpose.

Choose a trowel that feels comfortable in your hand. Perhaps you want one with a bright handle that's easy to find if you lay it down while you're working. A trowel pressed out of a single sheet of metal is not durable.

To use a trowel, hold it with your knuckles wrapped around the back of the handle and your thumb pointed up, as if it were an icepick, and stab the blade into the soil.

Front-mounted tiller

Multipurpose trowel

Transplanting trowel

POWER TILLERS AND CULTIVATORS

If you have more soil to till than you can do by hand, a power rotary tiller, or rototiller, can master the job. Similar but smaller and simpler, a power cultivator tills weeds from established gardens. Both can be expensive to buy, so consider renting.

When you use a rototiller or power cultivator, avoid overworking the soil. Overworked soil loses its structure and consequently its drainage capacity and aeration. Be sure to add organic matter at least once a year to maintain the soil quality.

There are two types of power tillers. On front-mounted models, the tines are in front of the wheels and pull the machine along. The wheels provide balance. On rear-mounted models, the tines are behind the wheels; both the wheels and tines are powered, but the wheels drive the machine. Front-mounted models are smaller and lighter and perform well on loose soil and existing beds. Self-propelled, rear-mounted models are easier to use and the best choice for hard ground.

When shopping for a power tiller, determine if you're strong enough to control it. And be sure it stops when you take your hands off the control. Compare also the number of speeds, the width and depth cultivated, the engine size, and the warranty.

The smaller power cultivators

Rear-mounted tiller

usually have gas engines, although some models are electric. The handles connect to the engine, which connects to the tines. This no-frills design makes these tillers lightweight; most weigh less than 25 pounds. They tend to vibrate and are hard on the back. Less than a foot wide, a power cultivator can control weeds between rows of vegetables and cut flowers. However, don't use it in plantings of perennials and shrubs because it harms roots.

On some models, you can adjust the width of its path by removing tines. Some models have optional attachments, such as edgers and dethatchers.

Power cultivator

CLUES TO QUALITY

The handles of garden tools are attached to the business end in four ways. Solid-strap and solid-socket attachments are the best quality. Tools with open-socket or tang-and-ferrule construction are weaker.

■ Tang-and-ferrule, *far left.* A spike atop the blade inserts into the handle and is covered with a metal collar.

■ Open-socket, *center left.* The handle inserts into a metal tube that's open on the back.

■ Solid-socket, *center right.* The handle inserts into a closed metal tube.

■ Solid-strap, *far right.* A metal tongue extends from the blade and is screwed onto the handle.

TOOLS FOR WORKING THE SOIL

A n elaborate collection of garden tools is not necessary. The well-equipped gardener collects tools over a period of years. In the meantime, buy the tools you will use most often and buy the best quality you can afford.

GARDEN RAKES

M etal soil rakes—as opposed to leaf rakes—are meant for removing small rocks and clods from bare ground. Flip the rake over and use the back to level the soil before sowing seeds or setting out transplants. The tines of straight-back rakes attach to a straight metal bar. The tines on bow rakes attach to a curved bar. Bow rakes are more flexible and ride closer to the ground, but the curved back doesn't smooth the soil as well as a straight rake.

When purchasing a rake, look for one that's heavy enough to stay on the soil as you push and pull it. You also want one that's narrow enough to fit into small places. When the rake is held vertically, the handle should reach your nose.

HOES AND MORE HOES

H oes come in a surprising variety of designs, so it should be easy to find one that suits you. Most hoes are designed for slicing off weeds at the soil surface, but a few are made for digging. Eight types of hoes are illustrated on page 537.

Most gardeners use an American pattern hoe, which features a broad, straight blade about 6 inches long and 4 inches wide. An onion hoe is similar, but has a longer, narrower blade. Both move easily over the soil surface, skimming off weeds. A scuffle hoe—also called a hula, an oscillating, or an action hoe—has an oblong metal hoop hinged to the handle. The hoop moves back and forth, cutting weeds each time you push or pull. A swan-neck hoe has a long, curved neck that allows the blade to sit almost flat on the ground, saving you from bending. The scuffle hoe is a push hoe; you slide it in front of you as you walk forward.

Hoeing is easiest when the soil is slightly moist. The correct technique is to skim the blade just under the soil surface, not dig it in. If you use a pull hoe, sweep the blade toward you over the soil in short strokes. Scoot a

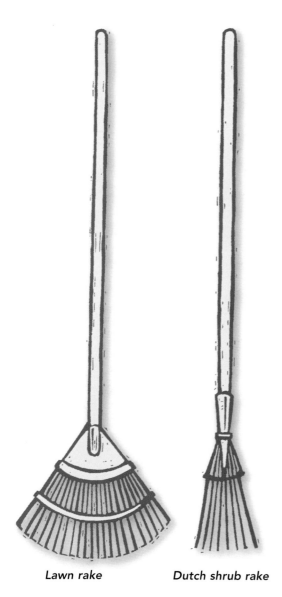

Lawn rake   *Dutch shrub rake*

Leaf rakes

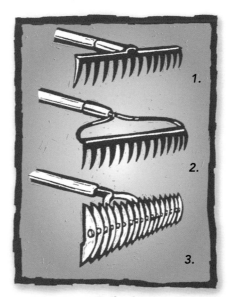

Soil rakes
1. Straight-back rake
2. Bow rake
3. Thatching rake

To battle weeds, skim a hoe just under the soil surface, so the sharp edge severs the weeds' roots.

push hoe in front of you, just under the soil surface, as you walk.

If you want to dig with a hoe rather than a spade or shovel, try an eye hoe, which has a large, heavy blade. For digging out large clumps of weeds, use a warren hoe, which has an arrow-shaped blade.

CARTS AND WHEELBARROWS

I t's difficult to get through a day in the garden without hauling something somewhere, so a wheelbarrow or garden cart—or both—is essential.

Wheelbarrows move on one wheel, which is in front. The legs and handles are in back. The single wheel makes a wheelbarrow easy to maneuver, but also easy to tip. Wheelbarrows vary in durability, depth, and price. Choose one solid enough for the kind of hauling you do.

Garden carts have wheels on each side, with the axle toward the front. They're more stable than wheelbarrows, but less maneuverable. On hills, carts are more likely to run away from you or run over you. Carts are deeper than wheelbarrows, so they hold bulky loads more securely. Some carts have a removable front end, making loading and dumping easier. You can upend the cart and roll or shove a heavy load into or out of it. You must lift the load into a wheelbarrow.

Whether you choose a cart or wheelbarrow, look for a model with wheels that are high enough so the bed will clear obstacles in your yard. For a cart, this probably means a 26-inch-diameter wheel. For a wheelbarrow, you'll want a 16-inch-diameter wheel.

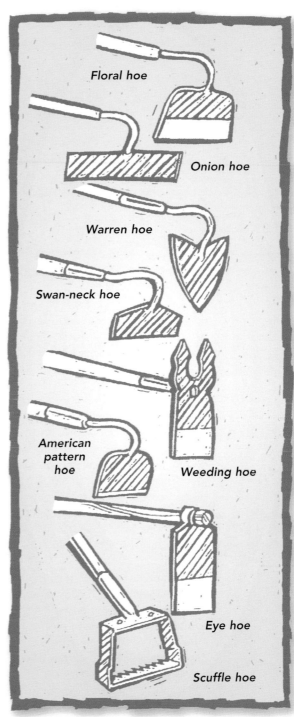

Floral hoe

Onion hoe

Warren hoe

Swan-neck hoe

American pattern hoe

Weeding hoe

Eye hoe

Scuffle hoe

Hoes

CUTTING TOOLS

Trees and shrubs are delightful features in our landscapes, but they do occasionally need pruning. Old or wayward tree limbs need to be cut back, flowering shrubs need to be rejuvenated, and hedges should be sheared into smooth walls. There are specific tools to tackle each task. When it's time to remove a branch from a tree or shrub, the tool you should reach for depends upon the size of the branch.

PRUNING SHEARS AND LOPPERS

Stems and twigs no bigger than your thumb (about ¾ inch in diameter) should be cut with pruning shears, also called secateurs. These handheld clippers come in anvil and bypass designs. The anvil style has one cutting blade that presses against a flat plane. It can crush stems if the blade isn't quite sharp. The bypass style has two offset cutting blades. Bypass shears give a closer, cleaner cut and are more widely used. Look for hardened steel blades with a high carbon content; the blades should be replaceable. You should be able to tighten the bolt, or pivot pin, that joins the blades. For secure closing, the latch should be near the blades, not at the end of the handles. In addition to these basics, shop for shears that feel comfortable in your

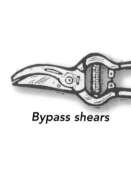

Bypass shears

hand. A wide range of handles, sizes, and weights are available.

For small shrub and tree branches up to about 2 inches in diameter, use lopping shears, which are similar to pruning shears except the blades are larger and the handles are about 18 inches long. It takes two hands to operate them. Long-reach loppers have handles up to 6 feet long and are designed for cutting high branches.

PRUNING SAWS

For larger stems and branches—from 1½ inches up to a foot across—use a pruning saw, also called a tree or an orchard saw. It's designed to work on both the push and pull strokes. Look for a pruning saw with a tricut blade, also called a Japanese or three-sided blade. The three-sided teeth enable the blade to cut through wood faster and easier than other blades and leave a smoother cut.

Pruning saws have

either straight or curved blades that are narrower at the tip than at the handle. Curved blades are easier to use. The blade is approximately 14 inches long. The handle may be banana- or D-shaped, wood or plastic. Some smaller models have a folding blade, allowing you to store the saw in your pocket until you need it.

Designed for sawing high in a tree, a pole pruner has extendable, long-reach handles and may have a lopping shear attachment. (Be sure the high branch you're cutting off doesn't fall on you.)

Pole saws

Pole pruner

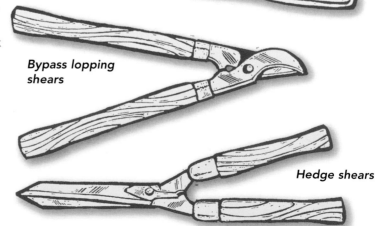

Blade-and-anvil lopping shears

Bypass lopping shears

Hedge shears

Straight pruning saw

Curved pruning saw

Folded-blade curved pruning saw

Bow-frame pruning saw

For cutting big limbs and whole trees, nothing works faster than a chain saw. Since the days when you had to be descended from a lumberjack to use one, chain saws have come a long way in both safety and ease of operation. They vibrate less, weigh less, and make less noise. New models have many safety features, such as shutting off the saw when you release the trigger or you hit something too tough to cut.

Shop for a chain saw with an engine volume that's 35 to 60 cubic inches and a blade that's 15 to 20 inches long. A blade can cut a branch twice its length. Shorter blades are easiest to use in tight spaces.

HEDGE TRIMMERS

A hedge trimmer is the tool of choice for manicuring a hedge, creating a topiary, or **Power hedge trimmer** quickly cutting back perennials. For small jobs, manual trimmers are adequate. But power models will prune a long, woody hedge quicker and easier.

The standard manual trimmer resembles a big scissors that requires two hands to use. Lightweight models work well for small, soft twigs and herbaceous plants; for woody stems, you need a heavy-duty model. Some come with wavy-edge blades that can cut through hard wood, but these blades are difficult to sharpen.

Power hedge trimmers are available in gas and electric models. Electric types are lighter and quieter than gas models. They operate by rechargeable batteries or by plugging them into an outlet. Trimmers that run on batteries have less power. The reach of the plug-in type is limited by the length of your extension cord and requires care and attention so you don't nick the cord.

Blade lengths vary, but 16 inches works well for most jobs and is short enough to handle easily. Most power hedge trimmers cut stems up to ¼ inch thick, although heavy-duty models can cut ½- to 1-inch branches.

If you can afford the higher price, choose a blade with cutting teeth on both sides, so you can swing the trimmer back and forth over the hedge. Stainless-steel blades are available, but forged steel works almost as well and costs considerably less. Shop for a hedge trimmer with a blade that can be easily replaced.

Look also for a style you find comfortable—one that fits your grip well and is designed for reduced vibration. Compare safety features, too; the blade on a power trimmer should stop moving if you take one hand off the machine.

HOW TO CARE FOR GARDEN TOOLS

■ Before storing tools for the day, wash dirt off shovels and other digging tools with the hose; leave in the sun to dry.

■ Before storing any tools, brush dried dirt off them with a wire brush, then wipe them with a rag moistened with household oil or spray with lubricating-and-penetrating oil.

■ Keep shovels, spades, and hoes sharp with a single-mill file. Give them a few quick push strokes with the file each time you use them for a major digging job.

■ Keep pruning shears sharp with a whetstone, taking care to follow the existing bevel as you sharpen.

■ Apply a lubricant such as household oil or lubricating-and-penetrating oil to tools with moving parts, such as shears and action hoes.

■ Use a bench grinder or a coarse grinding disk on a sander to remove nicks from shovels, axes, and mattocks. Wear protective goggles when grinding.

■ If wooden handles become rough, rub them down with sandpaper to remove cracked varnish. Then brush on boiled linseed oil and place in the sun so the oil absorbs into the wood. Repeat the application, then wipe off any excess oil.

■ Paint wooden handles with red oil-based or enamel house paint so the tools are easier to find in the garden.

Correct

Incorrect

The correct way to use pruning shears is demonstrated at top left. Position the shears so the cutting blade is closest to the permanent part of the plant; otherwise, you cannot cut closely enough to avoid leaving a scab.

TACKLING LEAF LITTER AND YARD WASTE

A mulching mower easily sucks up and shreds leaves that are on a lawn, returning them to the ground as an almost invisible soil-enriching mulch.

Depending upon where you live, leaf cleanup in fall is either an onerous task or a small chore. Either way, these tools and techniques will make the job easier. And a leaf-collecting tip: The job is easier if the leaves are dry.

LEAF RAKES AND SWEEPERS

A leaf rake, also called a fan or lawn rake, is a low-tech and affordable way to collect leaves. Leaf rakes range from 10 to 30 inches in width at the widest point of the fan. Don't get carried away and choose one too wide to handle comfortably; as a rule, smaller people need smaller rakes. You might find that owning two sizes is handy: a wide rake for the lawn and a narrow one for under shrubs. Tines are available in plastic, steel, or bamboo. The type of rake you choose is a matter of personal preference, but a quality rake should be springy, not stiff.

Leaf sweepers are higher on the technology ladder than rakes. These manually operated machines have a large roller brush in the front that tosses leaves backward into a cloth or nylon hopper. You push from the back. When the hopper is full, you flip the sweeper forward to empty it. Sweepers don't work well on grasses with runners on the surface, such as St. Augustine grass.

LEAF BLOWERS

Leaf blowers, whether gas or electric, are best used where rakes and sweepers can't go. Most types do not work well for removing leaves from a lawn, but they are ideal for sweeping a deck or driveway. Blowers vary in size. Most homeowners use small gas or electric handheld blowers. Landscape maintenance crews often use gas-powered backpack models or push models that resemble lawn mowers.

Shop for a well-balanced blower that's light enough for you to carry and that absorbs vibration. Some strain the back because they throw off your center of gravity. Look for one that's relatively quiet. Some communities have banned some types of leaf blowers because they violate noise ordinances. Before you buy, see whether such ordinances affect you.

The blower you choose should put out a strong enough blast of air—usually more than 300 cubic feet per minute—to do your toughest job. Buy a model that allows you to reduce the airflow so you don't damage plants with hurricane-force winds.

Wear earplugs when using a leaf blower, no matter how quiet it is. Add goggles to the ensemble for protection from flying dust and debris. Do not operate the blower when pets and people, who could be injured by flying debris, are in the vicinity. If you use an electric model, follow the precautions for using electrical equipment listed under Safety First on page 541.

LEAF SHREDDERS

Before full landfills and bans on burning leaves, it was easy to get rid of fallen leaves. Now the best solution is to recycle plant debris in your yard as mulch or compost. That's why a leaf shredder can be handy. Small models shred dry leaves only; heavy-duty types also handle small, soft twigs and stalks. None handle woody branches. For that you need a chipper or combination chipper/shredder. Decide what you need before you go shopping.

The small, inexpensive leaf shredders designed for shredding leaves only have a hopper that can stand alone or rest on top of a garbage can. Inside is a spinning nylon filament that does the shredding, then allows the shredded leaves to fall through a sifter that adjusts for fine or large pieces. Small twigs that piggyback with the leaves can wear out the filament quickly, requiring frequent changing. Debris can shoot out of the hopper like a missile, so wear safety goggles to protect your eyes.

Larger models have metal tines rather than a nylon filament. They can handle dry leaves, soft twigs, and branches up to about 1½ inches in diameter.

Select a shredder you can move around the yard easily; most types are electric and are light enough to carry. Also consider how the leaves are fed into the shredder. Some models have a hopper on top where you feed the leaves; others have a vacuum that sucks leaves from below.

Some gardeners use a lawn mower to perform the role of a shredder—it can do it very well. With a bagging mower you can "mow" the leaves along with the grass and collect the shredded leaves in the bagger. You also can collect leaves raked up from beds and other areas, dump them in piles on the driveway, and shred them with your lawn mower. You may need to mow them twice to get them as fine as you want. A mulching mower sucks leaves off the lawn as it mows, returning them to the lawn as a finely chopped soil enhancer.

CHIPPERS

Chippers designed for chopping twigs and branches into wood chips vary greatly in size, cost, mobility, and the size and type of material they can digest. Most are combination machines that chip wood through a chute and shred leaves through a hopper, although many don't shred leaves efficiently.

Chippers can be gas-powered or electric. Gas chippers work faster, but are louder, heavier, and harder to move around, and they vibrate more. Some have a power takeoff (PTO) attachment, which lets you power them with a garden tractor.

The most important point of comparison among chippers is

capacity—the branch size the chipper can handle. The manufacturer's literature usually gives the best-case scenario—a straight branch with all side branches trimmed off. Take about 25 percent off that number to find the size the machine handles readily. Check the width and angle of the chute to be sure it accommodates crooked branches. In most cases, you'll have to prune side branches.

Consider how easy the machine is to move and store and the safety of the design. Make sure you can't get your hand near the chopping blade. Other safety features should include a flap that blocks debris from blowing back into your face, a thermal overload that shuts off the machine if it gets too hot, and baffles that direct the chips into a pile.

When shopping for a chipper that includes a leaf shredder, check the position of the shredder. Is it easy to reach? On some models, the leaf hopper is high on top. And consider the volume of leaves it can handle at one time.

For safety's sake, observe a few commonsense practices. Always wear goggles, earplugs, and leather gloves. Don't wear loose-fitting or dangling

clothing that could be pulled into the machine. Shut off the chipper before trying to unclog a jam. Unplug an electric machine; disconnect the spark plug from a gas machine. Keep people and pets a safe distance away from the machine.

A good chipper/shredder has a wide chute that turns small branches into wood chips. Chips are collected in a heavy-duty bag.

SAFETY FIRST

When working around the yard, you may be tempted to get the job done as quickly as possible. But take time to work safely. Here are a few safety pointers:

■ Use equipment only as it's intended to be used. Read all directions before using power equipment the first time and reread if you have not used the equipment for a while.

■ When working on a ladder, don't overreach.

■ Wear eye protection when using a leaf shredder, chipper, or leaf blower or when pruning.

■ When digging, use your leg muscles, not your back, and take frequent rest breaks.

■ When using power equipment, wear eye and ear protection. Wear clothing that can't tangle in moving parts.

■ Don't use electrical equipment outdoors during or just after a rain. Always keep the cord away from moving blades. All outlets should have a ground fault circuit interrupter (GFCI).

■ Keep people and pets away from the work area when using power machinery or pesticides.

WATERING EQUIPMENT

Tools for watering plants can be as simple as a watering can or as complex as a multistation automated irrigation system. How elaborate your watering system is depends upon how many and what kind of plants you grow.

HOSES AND HOSE ACCESSORIES

Hoses carry large amounts of water long distances. Most are made of soft, flexible polyvinyl chloride (PVC); to prevent kinks that stop water flow, spend extra on reinforced or double-walled hoses. Hard plastic ones usually don't last as long. Black rubber hoses last longest, provided they are kept out of the elements in winter. Shop for metal couples for joining hose to faucet and hose to hose; plastic ones break readily.

Most hoses are ½ inch or ¾ inch in diameter. The smaller ones weigh less, but deliver less water. The most versatile hose lengths are 25 feet and 50 feet. With a long hose, you don't have to join shorter ones together to get to far-off corners, but it is heavier and there's more hose to trip over when you're working close to the water source.

To overcome the irritation of repeatedly screwing hoses onto the faucet and to each other, attach a

Wall-hung hose caddy

quick-coupler to the end of each hose; then you can just snap the two together. A Y-shaped connector lets you water two places at once. Use one to attach two hoses to the faucet or to attach two hoses to another hose for branching off. Choose brass not plastic connectors; brass lasts longer and is more drip-proof.

To avoid sprinting to shut

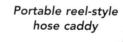

Portable reel-style hose caddy

off the faucet when you set down the hose, attach a pistol-style nozzle, which shuts off when you're not squeezing the trigger. Most nozzles feature a range of spray patterns, from a fine mist for watering seedlings to a full-blast stream of water for washing insects off plants.

A reel-style caddy keeps hoses out of the way when they're not in use. Choose one that lets water flow through the hose even when the hose is only partly unwound.

If you leave a hose outdoors, preserve its life by turning off the water at the faucet and draining the hose. Sun can heat the water inside a hose to such a degree that a full hose will burst. Drain hoses and store them indoors over winter.

SOAKER AND POROUS HOSES

Soaker hoses have small holes along their length. When the holes face up, the hose works like a long sprinkler; however, this is inefficent, as you lose a lot of water to evaporation. The right way to use a soaker hose is to face the holes down so the water soaks into the soil. A porous soaker hose is covered with pores, making the surface feel rough. Water slowly seeps from the pores.

Soaker hoses apply water along the entire length of the hose, so if plants are widely spaced, bare ground receives unnecessary water. These hoses apply water slowly and should be left on for a long time. You can

WATER-SAVING TIPS

■ Group plants that have similar water needs. As a rule, vegetables and annual flowers need more water than trees, shrubs, and perennials.

■ Use a rain gauge so you know how much of a deficit you need to make up.

■ Except for seedlings, water plants deeply and infrequently. Water seedlings shallowly and keep the soil moist.

■ If possible, water only the soil in the plant's root zone.

■ When watering overhead—with a sprinkler, for example—minimize evaporation by watering early in the day and when the air is calm.

■ Water slowly so the water has time to soak in. Shut off the water when it puddles or runs down the pavement.

Pistol-style nozzle

Mist nozzle

Barrel nozzle

Fan nozzle

cover these hoses with a decorative mulch. Inexpensive hoses spring leaks, but can be repaired. Be aware that thirsty animals may chew through your hose in search of water.

SPRINKLERS

Sprinklers are good for watering large areas densely covered with plants, such as lawns and flower beds. Different sprinklers are designed for different jobs. Here are the most common types:

■ STANDING: Stationary head; some are attached to a stake you push into the ground. Most spray in a circle, but some spray in rectangles, fans, or oblongs. Inexpensive. Use for lawns.

■ ROTATING: Spinning head with a few nozzles; applies water evenly in a circular pattern. Quality ones have brass nozzles. Moderately priced. Use for lawns.

■ PULSE-JET: Single jet on a spinning head that spurts water in a circular pattern. On some models, the head is mounted on a long stem that raises it a few feet to water beds and borders. Moderately priced. Use for lawns.

■ OSCILLATING: Many nozzles on a horizontal arm that moves back and forth. Applies water evenly in a rectangular pattern. Trees and other obstacles interfere with the watering. Quality types have brass nozzles. Inexpensive to moderately priced. Use for lawns.

■ RING: Doughnut-shaped tube with holes in the top. Inexpensive. Use for small areas.

■ TRAVELING: Moves along the length of a hose that's up to 100 feet long, so you don't have to move the sprinkler. Lay out the hose in a pattern to ensure even coverage. Delivers water in a rectangular pattern. Expensive. Use for lawns.

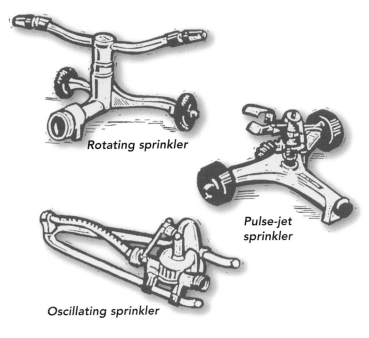

Rotating sprinkler

Pulse-jet sprinkler

Oscillating sprinkler

TIMERS

Timers are extremely convenient for gardeners. Attached to any watering system, they turn on water when you're not home and shut off water even if you forget. A timer fits between the faucet and the hose or irrigation pipe. With inexpensive timers designed for hose and sprinkler setups, you turn on the water, then turn the dial to the length of time you want the water to run.

Computerized timers designed for in-ground or drip irrigation systems allow you to program when and how long to water. Some types of timers control several areas of the yard, so the vegetable garden, lawn, and flowers can have their own watering schedules (different lengths of time).

WATERING EQUIPMENT
continued

IN-GROUND SPRINKLER SYSTEMS

In-ground sprinkler systems consist of a grid of buried PVC pipes fitted with aboveground or ground-level sprinkler heads. The system can be designed to cover lawns and adjacent ornamental beds and should be divided into zones. A good system allows you to water different parts of the yard separately, applying more water to lawns and less to shrubs, as needed.

Convenience is the biggest selling point; you don't have to move a sprinkler around all day. Price is the primary disadvantage, although prices have come down with the advent of PVC pipe. You can save money by designing or installing the system yourself. A local supplier of irrigation equipment may help with the design.

If you hire out the job, bear in mind that many installers know more about fitting pipes than about watering plants. Check an installer's references and ask a lot of questions when interviewing candidates for the job. A quality system, not the lowest price, should be your primary consideration when making comparisons. Be specific about how long and how often you want each area to be watered. A sprinkler system should include a timer or controller that allows you to water each zone on different days and for different lengths of time.

Remember to control the system; don't let it control you. Don't set the timer once and then forget it. The garden's need for water varies. It needs less during rainy or humid weather, more during hot, dry times. Shady areas usually need less and sunny areas more. Many skilled gardeners manually operate their automatic systems, making decisions based on recent or expected weather. They set the system on automatic only when on vacation. A moisture sensor is optional but wise, because it shuts off the system when it rains.

DESIGNING AN IN-GROUND SPRINKLER SYSTEM

The design goal for a sprinkler system is to distribute water uniformly with as few sprinkler heads as possible. (However, a little overlap is better than missing spots.) A variety of sprinkler heads is available. Some rotate, others are fixed, some send out long, pulsating jets of water, and some send out a fine mist. Low-volume heads deliver water slowly so it can sink in, preventing runoff. Matched-precipitation sprinklers decrease the amount of water applied if the sprinkler covers only a fraction of a circle. Pop-up sprinklers rise from the lawn when active, then retract when the job is done. Pop-ups are convenient for areas with foot traffic or that you mow. Where the spray must reach above tall plants, place sprinkler heads on risers.

Most in-ground sprinkler systems include a filter at the water source. If the plumbing connects to drinking water, a shutoff valve and backflow prevention valve are needed. If the ground freezes where you live, consider installing a drain valve so you can empty the pipes before winter. Or, you can blow compressed air through the pipes or hire a sprinkler service to do the job.

DESIGNING A DRIP IRRIGATION SYSTEM

In vegetable gardens, ornamental beds, orchards, container gardens, vineyards—almost everywhere but lawns—drip irrigation systems save water by slowly putting it on the soil near individual plants. They also solve the problem of tall plants blocking the spray from in-ground sprinklers. All plants thrive with drip irrigation because they get a steady, slow supply of water and the nutrients that dissolve in water.

Early-generation drip equipment had problems, notably emitters (the part the water comes out of) that clogged and complicated assembly. New equipment has in-line emitters that rarely clog and are easy to put together. If you aren't a do-it-yourselfer, buy a kit or hire a professional to do the job. Catalogs and dealers that sell equipment will provide how-to information and refer you to a skilled installer.

Drip irrigation systems have three main parts: the head, which includes valves and filters near the faucet; the lines, which carry water to plants; and the emitters, which put out water.

The head consists of a filter that catches particles before they clog the emitters; a pressure regulator, which lowers the pressure so water doesn't blow out your system; and an adapter that fits the head to the lines. Optional head equipment includes a fertilizer injector; a vacuum valve, or backflow prevention valve (a must if the hose connects to your drinking water supply, which is likely); and a timer or controller (see Timers on page 543).

The lines may be stiff PVC pipe or flexible poly tubing. The tubing is easier to install because you just push the sections together. PVC pipe requires glue or clamps. The main

WATERING METHODS

Drip emitters are highly efficient, delivering water directly to each plant. They can be covered with mulch.

Pop-up heads rise from the ground when the system goes on and retract to ground level when it goes off.

Soaker hoses are a good way to keep closely spaced plants watered without wetting the foliage.

A traveling sprinkler waters along the entire length of the hose. The spinning head applies water in a circle.

line carries the water to the garden. Lateral lines attach to the main line; they contain the emitters that deliver water to the plants. An end cap at the end of the lateral line keeps water from gushing out the end.

In early systems, the emitters were thin tubes with a metal head that clogged easily or flat circles that tended to pop out. New clog-free in-line emitters come installed, at spacings of 12 to 36 inches. Pressure-compensating emitters eliminate

pressure changes caused by hills and friction in the tubing.

The soil type and the depth of the plants' roots determine how far apart emitters should be installed. In sandy soil, water moves down, but does not spread wide; the reverse is true in clay soil. An emitter that covers 16 inches in sandy soil may cover 24 inches in clay. Plants with shallow roots, such as most vegetables, require more closely spaced emitters than plants with deep roots such as

trees. To determine how far water spreads in your soil, let a hose drip slowly on the soil for 30 minutes. Then dig into the soil to see how wide an area is moistened; that's roughly the spacing for the emitters.

Because different parts of your property have different watering needs, install independent controls for each zone. For example, the vegetable garden may represent one zone and the foundation plantings another.

PREVENTING AND CONTROLLING GARDEN PESTS

It's impossible to completely rid your garden of insects, plant diseases, and weeds; nor should you want to, because they form a natural part of a diverse ecosystem. Some bugs are good guys who prey on the bad guys, and it's sometimes difficult to get rid of those that damage your garden without harming the beneficial insects. But you can prevent pests from significantly affecting your yard's beauty and productivity. Controlling bugs, diseases, and weeds in your garden begins with prevention.

PREVENTION AND CONTROL

Observe your garden often (daily if possible) to catch problems when they begin. And remember that good gardening practices go a long way toward keeping your plants healthy. Vigorous plants can fight off pest attacks by producing natural pesticides. Encourage healthy plants by growing cultivars adapted to your climate and soil and by fertilizing and watering when needed. Where possible, rotate vegetable families from year to year to break the cycle of some diseases and insects. Either plant in a different area or don't grow those vegetables for two to three years after a disease or insect problem. For example, if you grow tomatoes in an area, don't grow them (or eggplants, peppers, or potatoes, which are in the same family) in the same spot for three years.

Many insects and mites disfigure plants and can carry disease

The bright-colored larvae of the monarch butterfly do eat garden plants, but most gardeners choose to tolerate some damage so they can enjoy the beautiful butterflies later in the season.

BENEFICIAL INSECTS

Just because it's a bug doesn't mean it's bad. Here are some insects you should encourage to reside in your garden to keep the bad bugs at bay. Planting a variety of flowering plants and avoiding insecticides encourages beneficial insects.

■ **GROUND BEETLES:** Large, shiny, black, green, or dark brown beetles with long, shallow grooves on their backs. They hide under rocks and in other dark places. They feed on snails, slugs, caterpillars, cutworms, and other beneficial insects.

■ **PRAYING MANTIS:** This insect has a thin, long body and holds its long, bent forelegs in a praying posture. The praying mantis eats large quantities of caterpillars, aphids, crickets, beetles, and leafhoppers as well as beneficial bees and wasps.

■ **LACEWING:** A small, green flying insect with thin, lacy wings. The larvae feed on red spider mites, thrips, leafhoppers, and aphids.

■ **LADYBUG:** More correctly called a ladybird beetle, this familiar friend has a round, red back with dark spots. The hungry larvae are harder to recognize—they resemble tiny, pale alligators. The larvae eat small pests such as aphids, mealybugs, mites, and scales.

■ **PARASITIC WASP:** This tiny wasp lays its eggs in the bodies of insects such as tomato hornworms and sawfly larvae or on the eggs of moths and butterflies.

■ **PREDACEOUS MITE:** It feeds on the eggs of mites and insects.

COMMON ORGANIC PESTICIDES

Common organic pesticides, derived mostly from plant sources, effectively control insects and diseases, but are considered less harmful to the environment than chemical pesticides. Organic pesticides quickly break down to harmless substances. Still, they are poisons and can harm people and pets when freshly or incorrectly applied. Follow all label instructions for when and how to apply these materials. Remember, most insecticides kill beneficial as well as harmful insects, so use them judiciously.

■ **BACILLUS THURINGIENSIS (BT):** This bacterium, which paralyzes the intestines of small chewing caterpillars, is applied in a spray. Caterpillars must be feeding for Bt to work. After the caterpillars reach a certain size, Bt is no longer effective, so it is best to treat them when they are young. It's not toxic to birds or mammals.

■ **CORN GLUTEN:** Derived from corn, this botanical herbicide kills crabgrass and other lawn weed seedlings.

■ **DIATOMACEOUS EARTH (DE):** Made of tiny shells of fossilized diatoms (one-celled animals), this fine, white powder cuts insects it touches, causing dehydration of fleas, pill bugs, slugs, and others. Don't use pool-grade DE.

■ **INSECTICIDAL SOAPS:** The salts of fatty acids can be applied as a spray to kill small insects on contact. The soaps are not toxic to mammals or birds. They can burn young plants or those with a thin cuticle (a waxy covering on the leaves). Soaps work on soft-bodied pests such as aphids, mites, mealybugs, and thrips. They have no residual action.

■ **NEEM:** The oil from the seeds of India's neem tree is applied as a spray. Low in toxicity, it controls many pests, including Colorado potato beetles, several nematodes, flea beetles, and gypsy moths.

■ **NICOTINE SULFATE:** The active ingredient in tobacco paralyzes insects on contact when they are feeding on treated plants. Apply as a spray. It is highly toxic to mammals.

■ **PYRETHRIN:** This is the active ingredient in pyrethrum, the common name for two species of chrysanthemum. Apply as a spray. It kills on contact only. It is moderately toxic to mammals and can cause hayfever in susceptible people. Use it to combat chewing and sucking insects such as Colorado potato beetles, flies, gnats, cabbage loopers, and others.

■ **ROTENONE:** This botanical insecticide, derived from the roots of several South American legumes, is applied as a dust or spray. It is very toxic to birds, fish, and some mammals and is more persistent than most botanicals. Use it to control pests, including flea beetles, spider mites, and many chewing insects.

■ **ULTRAFINE HORTICULTURAL OILS:** Lightweight oils applied in summer control mealybugs, spider mites, scales, and aphid eggs. Do not confuse with dormant oil.

■ **DORMANT OIL:** A heavy oil applied to woody plants in late winter or early spring. Dormant oil smothers overwintering insect eggs and larvae.

organisms. However, not all the insects you see in your garden are harmful. Sometimes the ones actually doing the damage are out of sight, either performing their work underground or emerging and feeding under cover of darkness. Harmful insects and mites injure plants by chewing on them or by sucking out the plants' juices. Some tunnel into leaves or stems.

If insect pests do appear, try hosing off small ones, such as aphids, with a hard stream of water before resorting to an insecticide. Repeat daily as needed. Pick off large insects, such as caterpillars, by hand. Protect stems of young plants from cutworms by wrapping newspaper around the stems or inserting a large nail into the soil on both sides of the stems.

PREVENTING INSECT INVASIONS

■ **USE FLOATING ROW COVERS.** A cover of lightweight spun-plastic fabric over a row of young vegetable or strawberry plants keeps flying insects from landing and feeding on the plants. To anchor the cover, bury the edges.

■ **ENCOURAGE BENEFICIAL INSECTS.** Invite beneficial insects—those that prey on harmful bugs—to your garden by growing a variety of flowering plants and using insecticides only when absolutely necessary.

■ **KEEP PLANTS HEALTHY.** Insects are particularly drawn to plants stressed by lack of water or nutrients, so keep your garden properly watered and fertilized.

■ **KEEP THE GARDEN CLEAN.** Remove dried plant parts and fallen leaves to eliminate overwintering insect eggs and larvae.

■ **CONTROL WEEDS.** Nearby weeds often are a source of insect pests, hosting them until crops are ready.

PREVENTING AND CONTROLLING GARDEN PESTS

continued

PESTICIDE SAFETY ESSENTIALS

■ Read the label before you buy. If the pest you want to control isn't listed on the label, don't buy the pesticide. And don't buy it if the directions and safety precautions seem like too much bother to follow.

■ Keep the product in its original container, so you always have the label directions and can't mistake the product for something harmless.

■ Keep pesticides locked up, away from children and pets.

■ Always follow label directions exactly; they explain the only way the material can be used legally.

■ Don't eat or smoke when mixing or applying pesticides.

■ Spray pesticides only on windless days so they won't drift onto edible plants or onto plants they can harm.

■ Apply sprays only when the temperature is below 80°F. Evaporation at higher temperatures can cause pesticides to drift onto plants they may harm; this is especially a problem with herbicides.

■ Stay out of treated areas for the recommended period and never walk through a treated area if it is still wet.

■ Wear the recommended protective clothing, which may include rubber boots and gloves, a brimmed hat, and a respirator.

■ The clothes you wear to spray in should be washed alone; don't mix them with other laundry. After washing, run your empty machine through a cycle.

■ Dispose of empty containers in a hazardous-waste disposal site, not with your day-to-day trash.

■ Don't pour an unused pesticide down the drain or sewer. Many towns have drop-off sites where residents can dispose of such chemicals (and herbicides).

IDENTIFYING PEST PROBLEMS

Often it's easy to identify a pest. You discover dozens of green inchworm-like loopers gnawing on your lettuce or find black spots on your rose leaves. Sometimes, however, identifying a pest is difficult because it isn't highly visible. What you think is a bacterial disease really may be symptoms caused by overwatering or a nutrient deficiency. The ugly insects covering the leaves on a shrub may be beneficial ladybug larvae eating harmful scale insects.

Because a vast number of pests trouble garden plants, it's impossible to include them all here. You may wish to acquire a few reference books with color photographs of insects, weeds, and diseases to aid in identification. You also can get help from a county Cooperative Extension Service specialist or from a local botanical garden.

SENSIBLE STEPS TO PESTICIDE USE

Most gardeners are concerned about the environment and their own health. That's why they keep pesticide use to a minimum and look for safer ways to control insects, diseases, and weeds in their gardens. By their nature, most pesticides are hazardous to plants, beneficial insects, birds, fish, and mammals, especially if they are used incorrectly. Follow package directions precisely, paying special attention to safety and disposal instructions.

Integrated pest management (IPM) is a sensible approach to managing pests that was developed for commercial agriculture. Gardeners can adapt the method to their own garden. IPM recommends forgoing routine pesticide applications in an attempt to prevent problems, as was once common practice. Instead, it suggests using pesticides only when a problem occurs, is serious enough to warrant treatment, and can't be controlled by any other means. When a pesticide is necessary, choose the least toxic one targeted to that pest; often this means using a botanical rather than a synthetic pesticide.

Professional growers use traps to monitor insect pests in their fields and orchards. You can do the same. A passive trap, such as a sticky ball or card, reveals an insect's presence by trapping it in glue. However, the trap itself may not sufficiently control an infestation. Some traps, such as pheromone traps that contain sex attractants, lure insects into them and provide good control if located to draw insects away from the crop.

The keys to IPM are observation and identification. By frequently observing your garden, you know when a problem starts and how fast it is progressing. After correctly identifying the problem—be it an insect, disease, or weed—you can choose the best and least toxic control method.

TOOLS FOR APPLYING PESTICIDES

Applying a pesticide with the right device gives the best control and protects you from exposure to the substance. Whichever applicator you use, wash it thoroughly afterward with soapy water and rinse several times. Do not use it for fertilizer or any material other than pesticides. Keep separate sprayers for insecticides and herbicides, labeling them with a marking pen. Herbicide residues can kill plants if inadvertently applied with an insecticide.

A Guide to Common Pests

Pest	Symptoms, Damage	Plants Attacked	Controls
Aphids	Tiny, green, yellow, pink, or black insects cluster on soft stems, new leaves, and flowers. Curled leaves, stunted new growth. Sticky honeydew coats plants, hosts sooty mold.	Vegetables, fruit plants, garden flowers, trees, and shrubs. Some aphid species are plant-specific; others attack a wide range of plants.	Wash off plants daily with strong stream of water, or spray insecticidal soap or pyrethrin. Use dormant oil to control overwintering eggs on fruits and landscape plants in late winter or early spring.
Bagworms	Brown caterpillars spin 2-inch-long bags where moths lay overwintering eggs. Caterpillars eat foliage; may permanently harm evergreens.	Deciduous and evergreen trees; serious on junipers and arborvitae.	Handpick bags in winter, clipping them off with pruner. Spray heavy infestations with Bt in early spring and early summer.
Black vine weevils	Brown or black beetles with apparent snouts chew leaf edges, leaving small, scalloped bites; not serious. Larvae are white grubs that seriously damage plant roots.	Serious on rhododendrons, azaleas, euonymus, camellias, yews, hemlocks, sour gums, blackberries, blueberries, grapes, and strawberries.	Control night-feeding weevils with sticky trap around trunks. Spread parasitic nematodes on soil to kill grubs. Apply pesticide to foliage in spring and early summer to stop beetles from laying eggs. Drench soil with pesticide to control grubs in early summer.
Borers	Adult beetles lay eggs on bark; larvae bore tunnels into bark and wood. Sap exudes from trunk, forming wet spots. Limbs or entire tree may die. Wilting of vines.	Almost any tree or shrub; especially dogwoods, birches, fruit trees, and shade trees. Squashes and melons.	Keep plants healthy; borers attack weakened plants. Avoid injuring bark. Remove dead limbs. Insert wire in borer hole to kill larvae.
Budworms	Larvae of various moths tunnel into flower and leaf buds, eating them from inside out, preventing opening. May tie leaves with silken threads.	Common on azaleas, roses, columbines, petunias, and verbenas. Serious on pines, larches, spruces, hollies, hemlocks, and fruit trees.	Handpick on small plants. Apply Bt to trees and shrubs when larvae are feeding. Use dormant oil and horticultural oil to reduce overwintering populations.
Cabbage loopers	Pale green caterpillars; night-flying white moths. (Day-flying white moths are imported cabbageworm.)	Cabbage-family vegetables, beets, lettuces, spinach, peas, tomatoes, and garden flowers.	Handpick caterpillars. Spray with Bt, pyrethrin, or rotenone. Watch for several generations a year.
Cankerworms (inchworms)	Small, green or dark caterpillars feed in spring on new leaves, hang from trees on thin threads.	Many deciduous trees and shrubs.	Apply dormant oil to control overwintering eggs. Spray Bt to control feeding larvae.
Codling moths	White to pink caterpillars with brown heads bore into core of fruits or disfigure surface. Infested fruits or nuts may drop off. Moths have coppery bands on wing tips.	Serious on apples, pears, and walnuts; less serious on plums, cherries, and peaches.	Pheromone traps. Bt for larvae according to when moths lay eggs. (Consult Cooperative Extension Service.) Control some larvae with sticky bands on trunks. Pick up and destroy all infected fruits.

A GUIDE TO COMMON PESTS *continued*

Pest	Symptoms, Damage	Plants Attacked	Controls
Colorado potato beetles	Yellow-orange beetles with black stripes and spots. Larvae humpbacked, dark red, with black spots on sides. Beetles and larvae eat leaves and stems; may defoliate, kill, or stunt plants.	Serious on potatoes, tomatoes, and eggplants. Also on petunias and other ornamentals in nightshade family.	Plant resistant cultivars. Mulch deeply with straw to prevent overwintering pests from emerging from soil. Cover plants with floating row covers. Spray with Bt or pyrethrin.
Cucumber beetles, corn rootworms	Yellow or green beetles often with black spots or stripes. Beetles chew off corn tassels, causing poor kernel formation, and eat foliage and flowers of other vegetables and flowers. Larvae eat roots, stunting plants. Beetles and larvae carry bacterial wilt and mosaic virus.	Serious on cucumbers, squashes, beans, sweet potatoes, and corn; also on asters, calendulas, chrysanthemums, zinnias, and sweet peas.	Practice good sanitation to eliminate overwintering sites. Protect seedlings with floating row covers. Handpick beetles by shaking into funnel secured to a bag. Plant resistant varieties. Spray weekly with pyrethrin or rotenone.
Cutworms	Fat, night-feeding, gray or brown caterpillars sever stems of seedlings near soil level or eat entire seedlings, in early to mid spring.	Almost any young vegetable or flower seedling.	Encircle each seedling with cardboard collar. Destroy larvae in soil near base of damaged plants. Transplant in late spring to avoid damage or plant larger transplants.
Fall webworms	Black-headed worms form silken nests over foliage and branch tips in summer and fall. Several generations per season.	Many deciduous trees and shrubs, including ashes, oaks, roses, and fruit and nut trees.	Spray Bt when webworms are young and unprotected by webs. Knock caterpillars from trees and destroy.
Flea beetles	Tiny, dark beetles chew numerous small, round holes in leaves, often killing plants. Beetles leap like fleas from leaf undersides. Larvae live in soil; eat roots. May spread virus diseases.	Eggplants, tomatoes, peppers, potatoes, spinach, cabbage-family crops, melons, lettuces, rhubarb, sweet potatoes, and petunias.	Till soil in fall or spring; remove debris. Control weeds. Cover plants with floating row covers. Use white sticky traps, pyrethrin, or rotenone.
Gypsy moth caterpillars	Fuzzy, gray-brown caterpillars with pairs of blue and red dots chew holes in leaves and may defoliate trees. Tan, 2½-inch male moths fly vigorously, mate with nonflying, white females on tree trunks. Lay overwintering fuzzy, tan egg masses.	Most trees and shrubs, including conifers, which may die. Serious on oaks.	Trap caterpillars in sticky band on tree trunk in early summer. Trap male moths in midsummer with pheromone trap to reduce next year's population. Have Bt professionally sprayed early during serious infestations. Natural fungus in wet years may help control.
Japanese beetles	Metallic, blue-green beetles eat holes in and skeletonize leaves and flowers. White grubs eat roots of lawn and field grass.	Many vegetables and ornamentals, especially rose family members.	Handpick beetles in early morning. Use pheromone traps. Apply milky spore disease to lawn to control grubs. Spray plants with rotenone.
Mealybugs	Clusters of bugs form cottony white masses on stems and leaf axils. Heavy infestations slow growth and cause dieback, fruit drop, and dead twigs. Honeydew hosts sooty mold.	Many different species attack fruit trees, grapes, potatoes, flowers, and ornamentals, including yews, cedars, cypresses, junipers, oaks, and willows.	Parasitic wasps may provide control. Hose off mealybugs or apply insecticidal soap. Apply horticultural oil spray on plants that tolerate it.

Pest	Symptoms, Damage	Plants Attacked	Controls
Nematodes	Microscopic, soil-dwelling eelworms infest plant roots, bulbs, stems, or leaves, causing stunting, dieback, yellow leaves, and reduced growth and yield. Root-knot nematodes cause root swellings.	Serious on many vegetables and flowers; less serious on trees and shrubs. Attack many weeds.	Plant resistant vegetables. Rotate crops and increase organic matter. Keep woody plants properly watered and vigorous. Replace infested plants with unsusceptible species. Effective pesticides highly toxic; apply only by professionals.
Rose chafers	Light brown, ½-inch beetles eat holes in and skeletonize flowers and leaves in early summer.	Roses, grapes, brambles, strawberries, fruit trees, peonies, hollyhocks, irises, and vegetables.	Handpick beetles; cover crops with floating row covers. Apply pyrethrin or rotenone.
Scales	Hard, round, shell-like insects adhere to stems and leaf undersides, sucking plant juices, stunting plants, and causing distorted growth.	Many different scales attack shade trees, shrubs, flowers, roses, fruit trees, and grapes.	Protective shell makes most contact insecticides ineffective, except for dormant oil and horticultural oil sprays, unless timed to kill shell-less, crawling stage of insect. Use systemic insecticide on ornamentals.
Slugs, snails	Night-feeding, soft-bodied, shell-less slugs and shelled snails leave slime trails and eat ragged holes in tender leaves and flowers. Most damaging in moist areas during wet years.	Most seedlings and young plants; foliage plants such as hostas and ferns with tender leaves.	Eliminate hiding places. Keep a clean garden. Hunt at night and destroy. Trap under flowerpots and destroy each morning. Edge garden beds with copper flashing to disrupt slug trails. Paint tree trunks with Bordeaux mixture. Apply slug bait every few weeks where serious.
Spider mites, mites	Tiny spiders may or may not form fine webs on leaf undersides and branch tips. Suck plant sap, causing pale, speckled, yellowish foliage. Stunt and may kill plants. Most serious during hot, dry weather.	Many vegetables, flowers, shrubs, and fruit and ornamental trees. Serious on eggplants, beans, roses, azaleas, fuchsia, hemlocks, pines, spruces, maples, sycamores, lindens, and fruit trees.	Keep plants healthy and well-watered. Apply dormant oil to trees and shrubs to kill overwintering eggs; horticultural oil where tolerated. Hose off undersides of infested leaves.
Thrips	Tiny, darting, black insects suck juices from flowers and young leaves; cause silvery streaks and spots, scarred fruits. May carry bacterial and viral diseases.	Many different thrips attack flowers, vegetables, fruit trees, ornamental trees and shrubs, and many weeds.	Reduce weeds. Destroy infested plant parts. Apply dormant oil. Use blue or yellow sticky traps. Apply insecticidal soap or pyrethrin.
Whiteflies	Tiny, white insects fly about when plants are moved. Cause leaf yellowing and mottling; stunt plants. Secrete sticky honeydew, which hosts sooty mold. May spread virus.	Serious on fuchsia, begonias, gardenias, squashes, tomatoes, peppers, cucumbers, melons, beans, grapes, blackberries, and many weeds.	Control weeds. Use yellow sticky traps and shake plants to encourage trapping. Apply insecticidal soap, pyrethrin, rotenone, or other pesticides; repeat for full control.

PREVENTING AND CONTROLLING DISEASES AND WEEDS

This zinnia has powdery mildew, a common fungal disease that flourishes in crowded gardens where air circulation is poor.

Whether it's a powdery gray coating on the leaves, strange black spots, or wilting plants, diseases can destroy a planting in just a few days. Before things get so bad you need to use chemicals, take some preventive measures to avoid the problems.

DISEASE PREVENTION

Plant diseases are caused by bacteria, fungi, or viruses. These diseases often are spread from plant to plant by hands and tools, droplets of splashing water, airborne spores, or through the soil. Many leaf diseases need a film of water and/or a broken surface to enter the plant and start an infection. Here are steps to help you prevent problems before they begin:

■ Choose resistant plants. Select species not prone to diseases and cultivars bred to resist serious diseases. Check the seed catalog, seed packet, or label of the transplant.

■ Provide air circulation. Air movement allows water to evaporate from leaves wet from dew or irrigation, thus preventing fungal and bacterial diseases that need a wet surface to get started. Avoid blocking air movement with shrubs, walls, and solid fences.

■ Do not crowd plants. In areas where you cannot improve air circulation, space plants widely so air can move betwen them.

■ Mulch the garden. Apply a mulch to control weeds and prevent soil, which may contain disease organisms, from splashing onto leaves.

■ Avoid overhead watering. Water the soil with drip irrigation instead of overhead sprinklers.

ORGANIC FUNGICIDES

Try these organic methods of controlling fungal diseases, which include powdery mildew, several types of wilt, and various leaf spots.

■ **BAKING SODA:** Controls black spot of roses and some other fungal diseases. Mix with water or ultrafine horticultural oil and apply as a spray. See page 275 in Chapter 5 for the formula.

■ **ANTITRANSPIRANTS:** These waxy sprays, available at garden centers, control powdery mildew.

■ **SULFUR:** Prevents fungal diseases if applied before the spores reach the leaves. Apply as a spray or powder. Must reapply after rain.

■ Water in the morning. If you must water overhead, leaves will dry quickly when watered in early morning. Avoid wetting plants late in the day or early evening because they may remain wet all night.

■ Do not take tobacco into the garden. Prevent mosaic virus by not smoking near plants and by washing your hands after handling cigarettes.

■ Work among dry plants. To avoid transferring diseases from one plant to another, do not work in the garden when plants are wet from dew, rain, or watering.

■ Remove diseased plants. Infected plants can spread infection to other plants, so remove them immediately. Don't let infected fruits and leaves fall to the ground and remain over winter, because that carries the disease from one year to the next. Do not compost diseased plant material.

PREVENTING AND CONTROLLING WEEDS

Weeds not only look unattractive, they compete with desirable plants for light, nutrients, and water. Eradicating them is good for your garden's health as well as its beauty. Garden soil is full of dormant seeds just waiting to flourish into unsightly weeds. Weed seeds may lie dormant for years, awaiting the opportunity to germinate. Usually they need to be close to the soil surface and receive the correct amount of warmth, light, and moisture to germinate. More weed seeds are continually entering the garden, carried by the wind and on soil from new plants, tools, and even your garden clogs.

To prevent weed seeds from germinating and competing with desirable plants, take these steps:

■ Apply a thick mulch. Mulch keeps weed seeds buried, cool, and dark so they don't germinate.

■ Keep weeds out of the compost. Don't throw weeds into the compost if they are in flower or have set seeds. The seeds may get carried with the compost back into your garden.

■ Use weed-free soil improvers. Manure and hay (not straw) may carry weed seeds, so compost manure and hay first to kill seeds before using them as a mulch.

■ Don't let weeds set seed. Pull or hoe weeds in your garden before they flower and set seed or the seeds produced will make the problem worse in later years.

Weed by hand first. When weeds appear, try eradicating them by hand before using a herbicide. Grasp the weed near its base and pull with a steady tug. This is easiest when the soil is moist. Pull as much root as possible because some weeds regrow from even a small piece of root left behind. Even if you leave the root, the plant is weakened, so pull it each time it regrows. You can hoe weeds in a vegetable garden. For lawns or waste areas, mow. Both methods kill or weaken weeds.

Heat kills weeds. Try waving the flame of a propane torch or weed flamer over weeds in a gravel driveway or walkway for just a few seconds—not long enough to crisp them, but long enough to damage them. They'll die within a few days. To eradicate weeds and unwanted greenery from a large area, you can solarize or heat-treat the area with the sun. See the box above for directions.

STERILIZE SOIL WITH THE SUN

Few diseases and insects survive heat—that's why we cook food. The same principle applies to soil. You can't put your garden in the oven, but you can take advantage of the sun's heat to solarize your soil.

For solarization to work, the soil must be bare. Because solarization is less effective along the outer 3 feet than toward the center, the area should be large enough to justify the effort. To solarize:

1. Hoe or till to clear all weeds.

2. Turn the soil with a garden fork or spade and water until the area is saturated.

3. Wait 24 hours, then cover the area with clear 3- to 6-mil plastic sheeting. Bury the edges to seal.

4. Leave the soil covered for four weeks if you're killing weeds or disease pathogens. If you're killing healthy lawn, leave the soil covered for two to three months.

5. Remove the plastic. Let the soil cool for a few days before planting.

PREVENTING AND CONTROLLING DISEASES AND WEEDS
continued

A GUIDE TO COMMON DISEASES

Disease	Symptoms, Damage	Plants Attacked	Controls
Anthracnose	Rotten spots on leaves, flowers, and fruits. Spots start yellowish, enlarge to brown or purple with dark edges. May kill twigs, cause early leaf drop, defoliate trees, and ruin fruits.	Beans, peppers, squashes, tomatoes, dogwoods, elms, hawthorns, lindens, maples, horse chestnuts, and sycamores.	Clean up infected debris. Avoid wetting foliage; increase air circulation. Keep trees healthy and free of drought stress. Plant resistant varieties. Apply Bordeaux mixture or other fungicide.
Apple scab	Gray spots that change to olive green, brown, then black on leaves and fruit. Leaves drop early. Cracked fruit with corky spots.	Apples, pears, crabapples, hawthorns, mountain ashes, and firethorns.	Clean up all fallen infected leaves and fruits. Space and prune for good air circulation. Apply sulfur spray or other fungicide before and after rainy, humid weather in spring through summer.
Bacterial wilt	Wilting and recovering of stems, then permanent wilting with yellow and brown leaves. May kill plants. Infected stems ooze slime when cut or show discolored rings.	Chrysanthemums, delphiniums, nasturtiums, petunias, dahlias, zinnias, beans, tomatoes, peppers, potatoes, eggplants, cucumbers, and squashes.	Practice good sanitation; sterilize cutting tools. Plant resistant varieties. Control insects that spread wilt.
Black spot	Round, black spots on upper and lower leaf surfaces. Yellow rings develop around spots; leaves drop off; plants are weakened.	Roses, especially hybrid tea, hybrid perpetual, polyantha, and tea.	Clean up infected leaves. Do not work among wet roses; avoid watering overhead. Plant resistant varieties. Apply new mulch in spring. Spray with baking soda or other fungicide.
Blight	Different fungal diseases of flowers, leaves, or stems; sudden and widespread wilting and browning. Worst in humid, moist weather.	Many flowers, vegetables, and woody plants.	Increase air circulation. Avoid overhead watering. Plant resistant varieties. Practice good sanitation. Apply fungicide.
Botrytis blight (gray mold)	Attacks flower buds, shoots, flowers, leaves, and fruits. Yellow or orange spots turn into masses of fuzzy, gray mold, then slimy rot. Prevalent during damp weather.	Dogwoods, rhododendrons, peonies, roses, marigolds, chrysanthemums, begonias, lilies, gladiolus, snowdrops, tulips, beans, lettuces, tomatoes, onions, berries, and others.	Remove aging flowers. Do not plant moldy bulbs or plants. Remove infected plant parts immediately. Increase air circulation. Apply fungicide.
Canker	Bark lesions can girdle stems, branches, or trunks, causing dieback. Wounds may exude gum.	Different species attack many types of woody plants, including conifers, shade trees, fruit trees, and shrubs.	Cut out infected branches; sterilize tools between cuts. Water and fertilize properly. Apply fungicide.
Crown gall	Soft, irregular growths (galls) on plant crown near soil line; yellowing and wilting of leaves and stems.	Fruit trees, grapes, berries, almonds, willows, cedars, junipers, honeysuckle, euonymus, asters, daisies, chrysanthemums, tomatoes, beets, and turnips.	Do not put new plants showing galls into the garden. Remove infected plants and surrounding soil. Avoid wounding stems and trunks, which admits bacteria.

Disease	Symptoms, Damage	Plants Attacked	Controls
Damping-off	Fungus rots seeds or girdles stems of seedlings at soil line.	Almost any young plant.	Do not overwater or crowd seedlings. Use sterile pots and growing medium.
Fireblight	Widespread browning and dieback of leaves, twigs, and branches. Infects flowers first, eventually blackens entire branches, and kills plant.	Serious on pears, quinces, apples, and rose family members.	Plant resistant varieties. Cut out infected branches; sterilize tools between cuts. Apply streptomycin or Bordeaux mixture to blooming fruit trees.
Fusarium wilt	Stunted, yellow plants that wilt and die. Infected stems reveal black streaks when cut.	Most flowers and vegetables.	Plant resistant varieties. Rotate crops. Water and fertilize properly. Use sterile pots and growing medium.
Leaf spot	Water-soaked spots on leaves; reddish brown spots with yellow halos and black spots during rainy or humid weather. Spots may enlarge to fill area between veins.	Many different types of specific leaf spot diseases attack vegetables, flowers, trees, shrubs, and roses.	Avoid splashing water and soil on plants. Practice good sanitation; rotate crops; do not handle wet plants. Plant resistant varieties. Apply copper or streptomycin sprays if indicated.
Mosaic virus	Curled leaves are mottled yellow and green. Plants are stunted and flower and fruit poorly, if at all.	Many flowers, vegetables, and weeds.	Control weeds and insect pests. Plant resistant varieties. Remove and destroy infected plants.
Powdery mildew	Powdery, white spots spread over leaf surface; leaves shrivel and die. Crop yield diminished. Fungal spores germinate in dew on leaves.	Cucumbers, squashes, melons, potatoes, lettuces, asters, zinnias, chrysanthemums, phlox, beebalm, lilacs, and roses.	Increase air circulation. Hose off leaves weekly. Spray both sides of leaves with fungicide when symptoms appear. Keep plants healthy and garden clean.
Rust	Raised rusty red, orange, or yellow lesions on undersides of leaves and on stems, flowers, and fruit. Weak, stunted plants; plants die.	Many different species of this fungus attack shade trees, conifers, fruit and berry plants, vegetables, roses, and flowers.	Avoid overhead watering and do not work among wet plants. Increase air circulation. Practice good sanitation. Apply sulfur or other fungicide.
Scab	Dark, raised lesions on leaves, then stems and fruit. Disfigures fruit and plants, but rarely kills.	Cucumbers, melons, squashes, beets, cabbages, carrots, eggplants, and root crops. Apple scab: apples, crabapples, hawthorns, pears, and mountain ashes.	Plant resistant varieties. Clean up fallen infected leaves and fruit to prevent reinfection. Spray with sulfur or other fungicide during rainy years.
Verticillium wilt	Lower leaves turn pale green, then yellow, then brown. Branches wilt and leaves drop. Stunted plants may die. Cutting into infected branches reveals yellowish streaks.	Tomatoes, eggplants, potatoes, maples, oaks, honey locusts, fruit trees, other trees and shrubs, and flowers.	Destroy infected plants. Remove wilted branches of trees and shrubs. Avoid wounding trunks. Plant resistant varieties.

PREVENTING AND CONTROLLING ANIMAL PESTS

Deer are tenacious, nimble, and bold, often leaping over fences and other barriers to munch plants, even those close to a house.

Insects, diseases, and weeds aren't the only pests that can plague gardeners. Four-footed pests pose problems, too. There are a variety of tactics you can take to prevent, repel, and control animal pests in the garden.

DEER

Deer cause the worst damage to home landscapes in late winter and early spring when their natural food supply is depleted. Deer feed on tender buds and shoots of trees and shrubs, sometimes eating them down to the ground. They browse on flower and vegetable gardens, eating the blossoms off tulips and trampling underfoot whatever they don't fancy for dinner.

Gardeners go to great lengths to control deer. Some gardeners swear by a method that others find useless. Such inconsistencies reflect the size of the deer population and the extent of their hunger, which in turn largely determine how brave they are, how far they will venture into your yard, and how finicky they are about what they eat. Once they've feasted in your garden, deer will return again and again.

REPELLING DEER

Several repellents that smell or taste bad seem to work well to protect landscape plants from deer. To be effective, these repellents must be sprayed on plants before deer begin feeding on them. They work best in areas where the deer population is low to moderate. However, research shows that at best repellents can reduce deer feeding only by about half.

Some gardeners hang mesh bags of unwashed human or dog hair every 3 feet in fruit and landscape trees to repel deer. However, hair works only where the deer population is low. Bars of soap—ones high in tallow—hung in trees also can repel deer, but soap can attract hungry rodents and dissolves in rain. Hot-pepper sprays are less effective than hair or soap.

The best repellents are commercial products containing putrescent eggs, tar oil, or ammonium soap; these repel deer with their odor. Repellents containing a fungicide called thiram, which can be sprayed on plants to make them taste bad, also effectively keep deer away, but leave a white residue on the foliage. Repellents must be reapplied regularly, perhaps every 10 days to two weeks. The product label gives exact instructions.

DEER-PROOF PLANTS

Deer prefer some plants and turn up their noses at others, but all gardeners who deal with them agree: When deer are hungry enough, they will eat anything. That's why lists of so-called deer-proof plants differ so much. In general, deer avoid fuzzy-leaved, aromatic plants, but thorns don't seem to deter them. In fact, rosebushes are a favorite meal.

Where the deer population is low, you often can prevent damage by carefully choosing what you grow. Avoid favorite deer plants, especially near the perimeter of your property. Instead, concentrate the plants they don't like near the edges of your property. This strategy may keep them from venturing closer to your home and garden.

DEER-RESISTANT PLANTS

These plants are not guaranteed to be deer-proof; however, they seem to be on the menu of last resort. The plants marked with * are not bothered by white-tailed deer, but are eaten by mule deer, which are common in the West.

ANNUALS
Ageratum houstonianum (flossflower)
Begonia × semperflorens-cultorum (wax begonia)

BULBS
Iris spp. (iris)
Muscari spp. (grape hyacinth)
Narcissus spp. (daffodil)

DECIDUOUS SHRUBS
Berberis thunbergii (Japanese barberry)
Buddleia davidii (butterfly bush)
Cotinus spp. (smokebush, smoke tree)
Forsythia spp. (forsythia)
Hibiscus syriacus (rose-of-Sharon)
Myrica pensylvanica (bayberry)
Philadelphus spp. (mock orange)
Potentilla fruticosa (shrubby cinquefoil)
Spiraea spp. (spirea, bridal-wreath)
Syringa vulgaris (common and French hybrid lilacs)

DECIDUOUS TREES
Amelanchier spp. (shadblow)
Betula papyrifera (paper birch)
Cornus florida (flowering dogwood)
Cornus kousa (Kousa dogwood)
Elaeagnus angustifolia (Russian olive)
Gleditsia triacanthos (honey locust)
Magnolia spp. (magnolia)
Pyrus spp. (pear)
Robinia pseudoacacia (black locust)

EVERGREENS
Abies fraseri (Fraser fir)
Buxus sempervirens (common boxwood)
Cryptomeria japonica (Japanese cedar)
Ilex cornuta (Chinese holly)
Ilex opaca (American holly)
Leucothoe fontanesiana (drooping leucothoe)
Lonicera nitida (boxleaf honeysuckle)
Picea abies (Norway spruce)
Picea glauca (white spruce)
Picea pungens var. *glauca* (Colorado spruce)
Pieris japonica (Japanese pieris)
Pinus aristata (bristlecone pine)
Pinus mugo (Mugo pine)
Pinus strobus (Eastern white pine)
Pinus sylvestris (Scotch pine)
Pinus thunbergiana (Japanese black pine)
Pseudotsuga menziesii (Douglas fir)
Rhododendron catawbiense (Catawba rhododendron)
Yucca smalliana (Adam's needle)

PERENNIALS
Achillea spp. (yarrow)
Aquilegia spp. (columbine)
Astilbe spp. (astilbe)
Coreopsis spp. (tickseed)
Digitalis spp. (foxglove)
Echinacea purpurea (purple coneflower)
Paeonia spp. (peony)
Stachys byzantina (lamb's-ears)

VINES AND GROUNDCOVERS
Epimedium spp. (bishop's hat)
Wisteria floribunda (Japanese wisteria)

FAVORITE PLANTS OF DEER

If deer are common in your area or often visit your garden, discourage them and reduce the damage they do by removing or not planting their favorite plants:

BULBS
Lilium spp. (lily)
Tulipa spp. (tulip)

DECIDUOUS SHRUBS
Cotoneaster spp. (cotoneaster)
Euonymus alatus (burning bush)
Rhododendron spp. (azalea)

DECIDUOUS TREES
Acer platanoides (Norway maple)
Cercis canadensis (Eastern redbud)
Cornus mas (Cornelian cherry)
Malus spp. (apple, crabapple)
Sorbus aucuparia (European mountain ash)

EVERGREENS
Chamaecyparis spp. (false cypress)
Euonymus japonica (evergreen euonymus)
Ilex spp. except *I. cornuta* and *I. opaca* (holly)
Juniperus spp. (juniper)
Kalmia latifolia (mountain laurel)
Rhododendron carolinianum (Carolina rhododendron)
Taxus spp. (yew)
Thuja occidentalis (arborvitae)
Tsuga canadensis (Canada hemlock)

PERENNIALS
Geranium spp. (cranesbill)
Hemerocallis spp. (daylily)
Hosta spp. (plantain lily)

ROSES
Rosa spp. (rose)

VINES AND GROUNDCOVERS
Euonymus fortunei (wintercreeper)
Hedera helix (English ivy)
Juniperus horizontalis (creeping juniper)
Vinca minor (myrtle, periwinkle)

PREVENTING AND CONTROLLING ANIMAL PESTS
continued

FENCING OUT DEER

The best way to control deer is to keep them out with a high fence—an expensive but long-term solution. Deer are high jumpers, not long jumpers, and can leap over most landscape fences. To be effective, a deer fence must be at least 8 feet high; in areas with a lot of pressure from deer, a 10- to 12-foot-high fence may be needed. Keep in mind that deer can jump over higher fences if they have an uphill takeoff. A low fence may be effective if pressure from deer is minimal or if the fence is a solid-board type that deer cannot see through or over. They do not like to leap into unknown territory.

Unfortunately, high fences can look unattractive and block your view. If you're concerned about aesthetics, use metal stakes painted black and wire mesh—or even black plastic bird netting—which disappear from view when seen from a distance. Plant shrubbery in front of the fence to camouflage it further.

Here are several effective deer fences recommended by the experts:

■ **WIRE-MESH FENCE.** Build an 8-foot-tall fence of woven wire mesh with posts tall enough to accommodate two additional high-tensile wire strands at 9 and 10 feet if the 8-foot height proves to be too low.

■ **LOW DOUBLE FENCE.** Build two 4-foot-tall wire mesh fences spaced 5 feet apart. Deer avoid tight spaces and will not jump this configuration. Although this solution will not block your view, it does take up ground

As cute and innocent as this rabbit may appear, it can wreak havoc in a garden, eating the leaves and flowers of many low-growing plants.

Photo by Elvin McDonald

space. However, you could consider using the space between the fences for a vegetable garden.

■ **ELECTRIFIED FENCE.** Enclose large properties with an electrified fence built from five high-tensile wire strands. String the first wire 10 inches from the ground. Add the others at 12-inch intervals, for a total height of almost 5 feet. Power the fence with a high-voltage energizer.

Although initially expensive, a quality fence provides excellent deer control that lasts for years. It's an important investment if you live where deer are a problem. Be sure to inspect your fence regularly to repair gaps where deer can crawl through. Be diligent about controlling weeds to avoid an unsightly fence line.

RODENT PESTS

Mice, voles (meadow mice), and gophers feast on bulbs and roots and gnaw on the bark of young tender trees, such as fruit trees. Moles, although they damage a lawn with mounds and tunnels, actually eat soil-dwelling insects, not plants.

Keep these pests from damaging young trees by encasing each trunk in a cylinder of hardware cloth that extends 18 inches up the trunk and is buried 2 inches deep. Control burrowing moles and voles, which use mole tunnels, by installing a 2-foot-deep hardware cloth barrier around garden beds and lawns. Gophers require a 2-foot-tall fence as well as the underground barrier to stop them.

You also can discourage mice and voles by removing piles of brush and debris where they might nest. Keep mulch pulled back from tree trunks and don't apply winter mulch to your garden until the soil is frozen; by then the rodents will have nested elsewhere.

Snap traps baited with peanut butter and placed in mole or vole runways can catch and kill these creatures. Gophers are larger and must be killed with harpoon-type traps. Although live traps may seem humane, they leave you with the problem of releasing the caught animal. Local laws usually prohibit transporting a live wild animal and releasing it, because it may carry parasites and diseases. Also, wild animals are territorial and if released far from home probably will starve or be attacked by other animals.

DEALING WITH OTHER CREATURES

Other four-footed animals, including rabbits and raccoons, also can bother gardens. Birds can be problems, too, especially for fruit. Chapter 9 includes suggestions for keeping birds away from fruit. Popular scare tactics to keep pests out of vegetable gardens include putting out replicas of owls; spreading soap shavings, human or dog hair, or bloodmeal around plants; or spraying plants with garlic, urine, or rotten eggs. You can create noise with radios and suspended pie tins or create motion with whirligigs and reflective tape. These methods sometimes work, but rarely for long. The most effective way to deter animal pests is to fence them out.

Rabbits jump and burrow. An 18- to 24-inch-tall fence buried 6 to 12 inches below ground will keep them out of the garden. Angle the buried section and a few inches of the aboveground section away from the garden so the rabbit sits on the

Many gardeners try scare tactics, such as erecting plastic owls, to frighten off birds, but these strategies seldom work for long.

buried fence while digging. Deer netting also works well, provided you anchor the edges so rabbits can't wriggle under it.

Raccoons are a tenacious pest— smart, nimble-fingered, able to climb,

and partial to sweet corn. Enclose your garden in a tall cage with a ceiling. Or, try interplanting squash or cucumber vines between other crops; the prickly leaves and stems annoy raccoons.

Starting & Maintaining Lawns

CHAPTER 14

ABOUT LAWNS

For beauty and ease of maintenance, consider reducing your lawn and planting shrubs and trees around the perimeter.

No outdoor surface is as resilient, beautiful, and inexpensive to install as a lawn. An expanse of grass shows off a formal flower garden and lends your home a sense of permanence and comfort. Lawns also improve the environment. A 2,500-square-foot lawn (smaller than average) releases enough oxygen annually to supply the breathing needs of a family of four.

But lawns pose challenges. Americans douse 40 million acres of turf with more than 70 million tons of chemical pesticides each year. The average homeowner uses 10,000 gallons of water each year—about half the consumption of a typical household—to water the lawn. Yet it is possible to enjoy the verdant look of a lawn to set off house and garden while keeping a keen eye fixed on environmental issues.

WORK- AND RESOURCE-SAVING TACTICS

You can have an environmentally friendly lawn by following savvy lawn-care practices.

To make your lawn easier to maintain and less demanding on the environment, consider reducing its size and reworking its shape. Round, oval, and square lawns are attractive and easy to mow; lawns with complicated, curved edges make mowing difficult. Avoid isolated trees, shrubs, and other obstacles; plant them in large beds where they will grow better, cause fewer mowing problems, and eliminate the need to hand-trim around tree trunks. (String trimmers cause serious wounds to tree bark.)

With a mulching mower, it's easy to recycle clippings back onto the grass as a natural fertilizer—and save labor. Lawn clippings are composed of what the lawn needs: 4 percent nitrogen, 0.5 percent phosphorus, and 2 percent potassium as well as all necessary minor nutrients. A year's worth of clippings returned to the lawn is the equivalent of

1 pound of nitrogen fertilizer. Not only can you skip hauling away clippings, you also can cut down on fertilizer applications.

Edge your lawn with a brick or stone mowing strip to prevent grass from creeping into planting beds and becoming a weed problem. Install the strip correctly to prevent grass roots from growing under it and rhizomes from creeping over it. You should be able to run the mower wheels over it, eliminating the need to use an edger.

A perfect lawn may cost too much in terms of energy and natural resources, but even with up to 15 percent weeds, a lawn still can be healthy and attractive. Clover, for example, takes nitrogen from air in the soil and turns it into a form that grass can use—a natural, no-cost nitrogen fertilizer. You also can incorporate short flowering plants in the lawn so it resembles a meadow.

The best protection from excessive weeds is healthy grass. Your lawn will be healthier and freer of weeds, pests, and diseases if you learn to mow at the right height, water properly, fertilize correctly, and choose the best-adapted type of grass for your growing conditions.

KNOW YOUR GRASSES

It is important to make the right match between grass type and location. Most lawn grasses are perennial species that live for many years; a few are annuals (usually nurse grasses that fill in until the perennial grasses become established, or weedy components of inferior, inexpensive mixtures), and live for only one growing season.

■ COOL-SEASON GRASSES grow most actively during spring and fall. They even may turn brown and go dormant during hot, dry summer weather. In winter, they may remain green (or yellow-green), even under snow. These grasses predominate in the northern part of the continent, but they must be watered to keep them desirably green during hot weather.

■ WARM-SEASON GRASSES take heat, growing most actively and exhibiting a rich, green color during summer.

They turn tan to brown in winter and may not green again until mid spring. Warm-season grasses tolerate summer drought in various ways. Some remain green; others lose color quickly. They flourish in the South and irrigated landscapes of the Southwest.

■ BUNCHGRASS AND CREEPING GRASSES. Some grasses grow in bunches that

never widen appreciably and may expose bare ground if not sown thickly enough. Other grasses have rhizomes or stolons that help them spread out aggressively to form a dense, thick cover, such as Kentucky bluegrass, the most beautiful lawn of all.

MAJOR LAWN-GROWING REGIONS

Each of the six major lawn-growing areas has different requirements. For the best-quality lawn, follow the first fertilization schedule. For a lower-maintenance lawn, follow the minimal fertilization schedule.

NORTHEAST AND UPPER MIDWEST

■ **BEST GRASSES:** Cool-season grasses (a Kentucky bluegrass blend or a mix of Kentucky bluegrass, perennial ryegrass, and fine fescue). For shade, use turf-type tall fescue in warmer regions or fine fescue and selected cultivars of Kentucky bluegrass in cooler regions.

■ **BEST FERTILIZATION SCHEDULE:** Feed three times a year, in late spring, late summer, and late fall.

■ **MINIMAL FERTILIZATION SCHEDULE:** Feed once a year, in late summer or late fall.

SOUTH AND GULF COAST

■ **BEST GRASSES:** In the upper South, cool-season, turf-type tall fescue. In the Deep South, warm-season hybrid Bermuda grass or zoysia grass, overseeding with ryegrass in winter. Along the Gulf

Coast and Florida, centipede grass, St. Augustine grass, and Bahia grass.

■ **BEST FERTILIZATION SCHEDULE:** Feed Bermuda grass five times a year, once every six weeks from mid spring through late fall. Feed St. Augustine grass four times a year, every eight weeks. Feed centipede grass, zoysia grass, and Bahia grass three times a year, in spring, summer, and fall.

■ **MINIMAL FERTILIZATION SCHEDULE:** Feed once in early summer and once in late summer.

PLAINS

■ **BEST GRASSES:** Cool-season grasses (Kentucky bluegrass, turf-type fescue, fine fescue, and perennial ryegrass) only with irrigation or 20 to 24 inches of rainfall a year. For sunny, natural landscapes and low-maintenance, unirrigated landscapes, grow buffalo grass or blue grama. In warmest irrigated regions, grow hybrid Bermuda grass.

■ **FERTILIZATION SCHEDULE:** Same as Northeast and upper Midwest.

MOUNTAINS

■ **BEST GRASSES:** Cool-season grasses (Kentucky bluegrass, perennial ryegrass, and fine fescue) in high-elevation areas. Where rainfall is less than 20 inches annually, grow buffalo grass in unirrigated areas.

■ **BEST FERTILIZATION SCHEDULE:** Feed in early spring and late fall.

■ **MINIMAL FERTILIZATION SCHEDULE:** Feed in late fall.

SOUTHWEST

■ **BEST GRASSES:** Grow buffalo grass in natural, low-maintenance, and unirrigated areas. For irrigated lawns above 7,000 feet, choose Kentucky bluegrass and turf-type tall fescue. For irrigated desert areas, choose zoysia grass or hybrid Bermuda grass.

■ **BEST FERTILIZATION SCHEDULE:** Feed warm-season irrigated grasses five times a year, every six weeks from spring through fall. Do not feed native grasses.

■ **MINIMAL FERTILIZATION SCHEDULE:** Feed once in fall and once in spring for irrigated warm-season grasses. Feed cool-season winter grasses once in fall.

NORTHWEST

■ **BEST GRASSES:** A blend of Kentucky bluegrass or a mix of Kentucky bluegrass, fine fescue, and perennial ryegrass. Choose turf-type tall fescue for shade. In drier, inland areas, try buffalo grass for unirrigated areas. Along the coast, try fine fescue in sandy soil.

■ **BEST FERTILIZATION SCHEDULE:** Feed three times a year, in late spring, late summer, and late fall.

■ **MINIMAL FERTILIZATION SCHEDULE:** Feed once in fall.

ABOUT LAWNS
continued

Where shade is a problem for Kentucky bluegrass, choose tall fescue instead. Many new cultivars of this once-upon-a-time pasture grass have fine-textured, deep green blades that make a beautiful lawn in tough growing situations.

Most bags of grass seed contain several types of grass. One labeled "Kentucky bluegrass" may be a blend of several improved cultivars, ensuring the best resistance to insects and disease. Other bags may include mixes of several types of grasses, as well as several cultivars of those grasses. Over the years, the grasses best adapted to your particular growing conditions will predominate. Mixes also provide a balance between bunch- and creeping grasses to produce the thickest turf. Sometimes a small amount of Kentucky bluegrass is added to a turf-type tall fescue blend to provide improved "knitting" of the lawn.

Some grasses grow best by themselves, unmixed with any others. Monocultures often are blends of several improved cultivars of that type of grass. For instance, turf-type tall fescue grows best as a monoculture, but it often is sold as part of a blend of three or more improved cultivars.

IMPROVED GRASSES

Lawn breeders and researchers have created many new and improved grass varieties. The latest named cultivars are more disease- or insect-resistant, more tolerant of drought, have an improved texture and appearance, or develop a better green color with less fertilizer. Always purchase quality seed with named cultivars. Don't skimp on price—you'll get what you pay for. An inexpensive grass seed may contain a lot of weed seeds or annual grasses.

Great strides have been made in turning coarse but hardy pasture-type grasses, such as tall fescue and perennial ryegrass, into candidates for lawns. Now called turf-type tall fescue, the new cultivars ('Falcon II', 'Houndog V', 'Jaguar', and 'Rebel Jr.') feature finer-textured, deeper green blades that approximate the lushness of Kentucky bluegrass. They also have deep roots, giving the grass its tolerance to shade, sun, and drought.

New ryegrass cultivars ('Pennant II', 'Imagine', 'Majesty', and 'Calypso II') exhibit a deep green color, not the yellow-green of former types. They also have a finer, denser texture.

Even Kentucky bluegrass—once a thirsty, nitrogen-greedy, sun lover—can be had in new varieties that perform well in shade and require less water and fertilizer. Cultivars ('Tifway', 'Midiron', 'Midlawn', and 'Tifgreen') have finer-textured leaves.

The latest innovations in grasses are slow-growing cultivars that need to be mowed less. The hard fescue 'Spartan', grows so slowly that it needs mowing only every other week during its fastest growth in spring. In summer, when growth slows, it needs mowing only once a month. 'Bonsai', a dwarf cultivar of turf-type tall fescue, needs mowing half as often as its tall cousin.

READING GRASS SEED LABELS

A high-quality grass seed will clearly state all the following specifications on the label.

■ Named varieties of grass types, not VNS (variety not stated).

■ Germination percentages of at least 85%.

■ The amount of weed seed no more than 0.5% for non-noxious weeds and 0% for noxious weeds.

■ The amount of inert matter. It should not exceed 1%.

■ The amount of other crop seed, such as annual bluegrass, bent grass, and rough bluegrass. It should be less than 1%.

■ Growing conditions to which the seed adapts.

■ A test date for freshness that is less than a year old.

Some grass seeds now host a beneficial fungus called an endophyte, which is poisonous to many insect pests. If your lawn has insect problems, look for these "endophyte-enhanced" cultivars:

■ **PERENNIAL RYEGRASS:** 'Repell II', 'Palmer II', 'Advent', 'Citation II', 'Express', and 'Yorkton III'

■ **FINE FESCUE:** 'Warwick', 'SR 5000', 'Jamestown II', and 'Reliant'

■ **TURF-TYPE TALL FESCUE:** 'Titan,' 'Tribute', 'Mesa', and 'Shenandoah'

The fungus won't remain alive in the grass seed for more than a year, so purchase seed with the present year's date on the label. Use the seed right away or store it for a short time in a cool, dry place out of direct sunlight.

NATIVE GRASSES AS LAWNS

If you're interested in a slow-growing lawn, you can sow selections of native, short-grass prairie grasses such as buffalo grass or blue grama grass. By mowing only several times a year, you can keep these grasses looking like a well-tended lawn. If you don't mind an 8-inch shaggy look, compatible with a natural landscape, you need not mow these grasses at all.

Buffalo grass and blue grama are blue-green to gray-green in color and look best with the rocks and gray-hued plants that predominate arid and mountainous regions.

Once established, a native-grass lawn is practically care-free, needing little or no irrigation or fertilization. It may go dormant and turn brown during prolonged dry spells in summer, but you can keep it green with one or two soakings.

Native-grass lawns also are tolerant of extreme temperatures. Buffalo grass withstands 120 degrees Fahrenheit in summer to below-40 degrees Fahrenheit in winter, but buffalo grass performs poorly in humid climates that receive more than 20 inches of rain a year.

Prairie grasses make tough, drought-tolerant lawns that thrive in difficult conditions. This lawn is an improved buffalo grass cultivar, '609'.

STARTING A LAWN

Turning a bare patch of ground into an expanse of fresh, green lawn is a rewarding endeavor that can bring out the gardener in anyone. Think of the lawn as a grass garden and pay as much attention to preparing the bed as you would a perennial bed.

SOWING SEED

Starting from seed is the most economical way to create a new lawn, and it isn't difficult if you time it right. Seed-grown lawns require more time to become established than sodded lawns, but in the long run they are often deeper-rooted and more durable. Also, seeds come in a wider choice of blends and mixes than sod, allowing you to meet the growing conditions in your yard.

In most regions of the country, the best time to start a lawn from seed is in fall, about six weeks before the first expected frost. In autumn, the soil is still warm, which speeds germination, the air is cool, and rain is frequent, keeping the tender, young grass blades from becoming too hot. In addition, fall-sown grass has many months to grow a healthy root system before stressful summer conditions arrive. Early spring is the second-best time to sow seed. Never sow grass seed in summer.

For the best results in sowing seed, follow these steps:

1. Prepare a smooth, level seedbed by removing existing plants or sod. (Use a sod stripper or herbicide containing glyphosate to kill an existing lawn.) Clear away all roots, rocks, clods, and debris.
2. Work a 3-inch layer of decomposed organic matter into the soil, then work in fertilizer and lime as recommended by a soil test.
3. Roll soil flat and level with a lawn roller half-filled with water. Rake just before seeding to fluff up the surface.
4. Choose a high-quality seed with named cultivars of grasses suited for your growing conditions.
5. Sow seed with a drop spreader. Walk back and forth across the area with the tracks of the spreader wheels overlapping 6 inches, spreading half the recommended amount of seed. Drop the second half of the seed while walking in a pattern at right angles to the first.
6. To cover the seed, rake it gently into a shallow (about ⅛ inch) layer of soil.
7. Firm the soil and press the seed into the seedbed with a roller one-third-filled with water. Protect it with a thin layer of chopped straw or other mulch to discourage birds.
8. Water once or more a day with a gentle spray of water, keeping the seedbed moist until seeds germinate. Thereafter, water every day or two, depending upon the weather, until the grass is 2 inches tall. Do not let the new grass wilt.
9. Mow for the first time when the grass reaches its usual recommended mowing height.

LAYING SOD

Putting down sod provides instant gratification. The lawn looks thick and lush immediately, and after a few weeks it will be well-rooted. The premier grasses—Kentucky bluegrass and hybrid Bermuda grass—and grasses that are difficult to propagate by seed often come as sod. Those that grow readily from seed, such as turf-type tall fescue, aren't available as sod.

Sod comes in strips 2 to 10 feet long and 1 to 2 feet wide and is sold by the square yard. Most nurseries will install sod, or you can lay it yourself.

To determine how many square yards of sod you need, calculate the number of square feet in your lawn by multiplying the length in feet by

Lay rows of sod tightly against one another, staggering them in a bricklike pattern. Cut them to fit and fill in any gaps with soil.

SUCCESSFUL SHADY LAWNS

Lawns often struggle in shade, becoming thin, unsightly, and invaded by weeds. With knowledgeable lawn management, you can encourage a shady lawn to perform better.

■ Sow a shade-tolerant grass: turf-type tall fescue or a mix of fine fescue and selected types of Kentucky bluegrass where cool-season grasses grow. Use St. Augustine grass for shady sites where warm-season grasses grow.

■ Mow grass ½ to 1 inch higher than normal, because a longer grass uses available sunshine more efficiently.

■ Apply half the usual amount of fertilizer, because shaded lawns grow more slowly than sunny lawns.

■ Water more if surface tree roots are competing with the lawn for moisture.

■ Thin overhanging tree branches to allow more light.

In mild-winter areas, grow shade-tolerant St. Augustine grass for a beautiful lawn in dappled sunlight.

the width in feet. Divide the square-foot area by 9 to determine the number of square yards in the lawn.

If you plan to lay the sod yourself, ask the nursery to cut the strips in sizes you can handle. Have the sod delivered the day you plan to lay it; it deteriorates rapidly once cut. If you can't lay it right away, unroll the pieces, lay them in the shade, and keep them moist with a covering of wet burlap. Sod left rolled heats up, harming the grass blades and roots.

The following are instructions for laying sod.

1. Prepare the ground by stripping off existing vegetation. Till the soil and work in organic matter, fertilizer, and lime as recommended by a soil test. Remove all roots, rocks, and clods and rake the surface smooth.
2. Lay the first row of sod end to end along the straight edge of a walk, driveway, or planting bed. If you have no straight edge, use a string pulled tight between two low stakes to mark a straight line.
3. Lay a wooden plank over the first row to kneel on without denting the newly laid sod. To access new areas, move the planks, making a plank path as you work.
4. Lay the next rows tightly against one another, but in a staggered, bricklike pattern, so joints do not line up with each other. Cut the sod, if needed, with a sharp bread knife.
5. Cut sod pieces to fit the curves of odd sections. Fill in any small gaps between sod pieces with soil.
6. Firm the sod with a roller filled one-third with water to ensure good contact between roots and soil. Roll first at a right angle to sod strips, then make a pass along their lengths.
7. Water immediately after laying all the sod to moisten the soil to a depth of 6 inches. Water regularly for about two weeks or until the grass is established. Pay special attention to sod laid near hot pavement; it will dry out quickly.
8. Stay off the lawn as much as possible for 3 weeks to allow the sod to root well and to keep it smooth and even.

SPRIGS AND PLUGS

Some cultivars of rapidly spreading southern grasses, such as Bermuda grass and zoysia grass, do not grow true from seed and are planted as sod, sprigs, or plugs. Sprigs are torn-up pieces of sod containing short stems with a few attached roots. Plugs are small pieces of sod containing roots, stems, and soil. You can buy them by the bushel or purchase sod and tear it yourself.

Starting a lawn from sprigs or plugs is more economical than using sod. Prepare the soil the same way as for sodding. To plant sprigs, have the soil lightly moistened and ready for planting when you pick up the sprigs or have them delivered. Keep the containers of sprigs cool, moist, and

out of direct sunlight as you work, or the grass may dry out and die. Evenly space the sprigs in shallow rows 4 to 12 inches apart. Water sections of the sprigged lawn as you plant. Keep the soil moist until the sprigs start filling in.

Plant plugs the same way in holes of the proper depth. Keep the lawn evenly moist. You may need to add a little topsoil and roll the lawn again after the plugs are established to prevent an uneven surface that results from soil shifting before the plugs fill in.

PLANTING SPRIGS

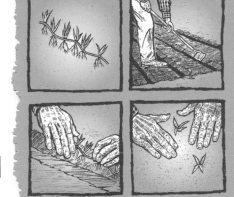

To plant sprigs, prepare shallow trenches. Lay the sprigs in place, then gently firm soil around them and water as you go.

PLANTING PLUGS

To plant plugs, use a bulb planter, trowel, or auger to make individual holes 6 to 12 inches apart. Place a plug in each hole. Roll the lawn or tamp the plug gently with your foot until it is even with the soil surface.

LAWN CARE

To patch the lawn, first remove areas of dead grass, rake out thatch, and pull or spot-spray perennial weeds with herbicide. Even out the soil, then broadcast seed and fertilizer where needed. Water thoroughly and keep moist until the seed germinates.

If your lawn is more than 10 years old, chances are it contains older types of grass that lack the advantages of modern cultivars. To update your lawn, renovate it in spring or fall by either killing the old lawn and replacing it with a new one or by overseeding it with improved cultivars. A shady patch might look better replanted with one of the new, improved turf-type tall fescues. A Kentucky bluegrass lawn will use less water if you overseed it with a more drought-tolerant bluegrass.

STARTING OVER

There are three ways to kill an old lawn entirely before sowing new seed or laying sod:

Whether you're fertilizing or spreading seed, cover the lawn in two passes, working at right angles to ensure even distribution.

■ Cover the lawn with sheets of black plastic weighted down at the edges with rocks and let it cook in the sun for several weeks.
■ Strip off the sod with a sod stripper; do not till it under, because the grass roots will resprout.
■ Spray carefully with a glyphosate herbicide, which does not move through the soil to harm other plants.

If you have cooked the lawn in the sun or killed it with herbicide, you can sow the grass seed in the dead grass, which will act as a natural mulch and soil improver. If you have stripped off the sod, see page 566 for directions on starting a lawn.

SMART WATERING PRACTICES

The best way to water a lawn if rainfall is insufficient is to give it a thorough soaking once a week. Water twice a week in arid climates or during extremely hot weather. Do not lightly sprinkle the lawn each day or every few days in an attempt to keep it green. It is better to water deeply at longer intervals; this encourages grass roots to penetrate farther into the soil in search of water. Deep-rooted grass withstands dry spells best.

Lawn grasses need an average of 1 inch of water a week during the growing season to keep them bright green. This rate varies with soil texture; for example, clay soil holds more water and sandy soil holds less. Hot, windy weather causes faster evaporation than cool, humid weather.

The easiest way to water a lawn is with an in-ground sprinkler system. To test the system, place small pet-food cans at different locations on the lawn, then run the system to determine how long it takes to collect 1 inch of water. If necessary, recalibrate or rearrange the sprinkler heads for a more even application.

Look also for areas where water puddles or runs off; these indicate that you are applying water too fast. If this happens, apply the designated amount of water in intervals spaced an hour or more apart to allow time for the water to soak in.

To determine when your lawn needs water, watch the weather conditions. Use a rain gauge near the edge of the lawn, then supplement weekly natural rainfall with enough irrigation water to equal 1 inch a week. Leave the system on automatic only in regions where there are extended periods of drought or when you are on vacation.

The best time to water is in the early morning. While the air is still cool and calm, water can soak in without evaporating, and the grass can dry during the day. Lawns watered in the evening have the greatest disease problems because they remain wet all night.

BROWN IS GOOD

When summer drought threatens to turn the lawn brown, don't worry. Cool-season grasses naturally turn brown and go dormant during dry spells. They will green up when the rains come.

To ensure that the dormant lawn will survive the drought, give it a little benign neglect:
■ Do not mow until the grass turns green again. Leave the grass 3 to 4 inches tall to prevent the roots from burning.
■ Do not fertilize in an attempt to turn the grass green.
■ Do not water lightly. Either water deeply or not at all.
■ Do not walk on a dormant lawn.

In the South, annual ryegrass is planted over zoysia grass for a beautiful lawn all year long.

FERTILIZER FACTS

A properly fertilized lawn grows vigorously and remains an attractive green. Without regular fertilizer, a lawn may become thin and susceptible to weeds, diseases, and insects. On the other hand, an overfertilized lawn will grow too quickly—demanding frequent mowing, developing thatch, and becoming more susceptible to diseases and winter injury.

During periods of active growth, a lawn needs plenty of nitrogen fertilizer. This is true during spring and fall for cool-season grasses and late spring, summer, and early fall for warm-season grasses. Nitrogen is usually in short supply in the soil and is easily leached from soil by water.

For slow, even growth rather than a spurt of excessive, fast growth, use a fertilizer containing organic sources of nitrogen or one with at least 30 percent of its total nitrogen in water-insoluble form. Look for slow-release forms: either urea-formaldehyde or sulfur-coated urea as major ingredients. These are water-insoluble and won't leach or burn the grass. Avoid ammonium sulfate, urea, and ammonium nitrate; these are water-soluble and leach quickly, encouraging quick growth before they leach out of the soil.

Lawn grasses also need potassium in large amounts, but the soil usually supplies this. Phosphorus, too, is needed for root growth, but in smaller quantities.

HOW MUCH FERTILIZER?

Each time you fertilize, apply about 1 pound of actual nitrogen for each 1,000 square feet of lawn. The actual amount of fertilizer depends on the concentration of nitrogen. A fertilizer with an NPK ratio of 3-1-2 is best for most lawns, although 6-2-1 or 2-1-1 are other common formulas for lawns. Follow the label directions for application.

Each grass variety has its own particular nitrogen needs. Some, such as Kentucky bluegrass, are heavy feeders; others perform well with less. If a particular grass needs 4 pounds of nitrogen for every 1,000 square feet each year and you are feeding it four times a year, apply 1 pound with each feeding.

RENOVATING

If less than 50 percent of your lawn needs renovating, scatter seed over the existing lawn after some easy preparation:

1. Remove areas of dead grass, raking out thatch and pulling or spot-spraying perennial weeds with herbicide. Fill in holes with topsoil to make the lawn smooth and even.
2. Mow the lawn to a height of 1 to 1½ inches. Then use a power rake to go over it in two passes at right angles, removing debris and exposing soil between remaining grass plants. Use a power aerator if the soil is compacted.
3. Apply fertilizer with a ratio of 3-2-1 according to the label directions or as directed by a soil test. If necessary, add lime at a rate of 50 pounds per 1,000 square feet.
4. Using a drop spreader, broadcast seed at half the recommended rate for a new lawn.
5. Water gently every day, keeping the lawn moist until the seed germinates. Water frequently thereafter until the grass is mature.

OVERSEEDING WARM-SEASON LAWNS

In the South, warm-season lawns go dormant from late fall to mid spring, turning brown or tan. To enjoy a green lawn all winter, overseed with a cool-season grass on top of the warm-season one in mid-September in the upper South, in late October in the lower South.

The cool-season grass will germinate and live through the winter, dying off in warm weather without harming the permanent lawn. You'll have a green lawn all winter and spring, and you will have to mow throughout the year. For successful overseeding, follow these steps:

1. Mow the warm-season lawn short, but do not scalp it. Bag the clippings from this mowing.
2. Broadcast the seed of annual or perennial ryegrass at a rate of 5 to 10 pounds of seed per 1,000 square feet. You can do this by hand for a small area or with a spreader for a large area.
3. Water in the seed thoroughly to wash it down between the grass blades so it makes contact with the soil. Keep it moist until it germinates and matures.
4. Mow the lawn short in mid spring. This will encourage the warm-season grass to grow faster, shading out the cool-season grass.

MOWERS AND MORE

Choosing a lawn mower is not simple; there is a range of prices, models, and options.

REEL MOWERS

Reel mowers have made a comeback, thanks to smaller lawns, concern about air and noise pollution, and improvements in the mowers. Most reel mowers lack an engine—you provide the power. As you push, the spiral blade attached to the wheels spins against a cutting bar.

Reel mowers make a clean cut, reducing stress on the grass. They also are inexpensive and easy to maintain; the blade only needs sharpening once a year. Although safer to use than a power mower, take care when clearing a jam—the freed blade is quite sharp.

Reel mowers do have some drawbacks. They don't cut thick, tall grass well and often leave clumps of cut grass behind. They jam easily on rocks, twigs, and even on grasses with stolons. On some models, the blade doesn't raise more than 1½ inches, but many grasses require a 2- to 3-inch cutting height. The cutting width is usually narrow, only 14 to 18 inches, which requires you to make more passes in the yard.

ROTARY POWER MOWERS

If you have a lawn larger than 1,000 square feet but less than half an acre, look into a gasoline or electric rotary mower. Basic models are not self-propelled. Self-propelled models cost more, but are useful on hilly property. Another effort-saving option is an electric starter. Choose a mower with adjustable height settings that can be changed easily. (You need a higher setting for summer than for spring and fall.)

Gas-powered mowers have four-cycle or two-cycle engines. Four-cycle engines have a separate chamber for the oil, which must be changed periodically. Two-cycle ones run on a gas-oil mix and require no oil change. They also weigh less. However, they pollute more, and are being phased out as emission standards for mowers become more stringent.

A removable bag for collecting clippings is a useful accessory if you let the grass get too long, want clippings for the compost pile, or shred leaves with your mower. The bag should be easy to attach, remove, and empty. Rear-bagging types cost more than side baggers, but hold more clippings, are better balanced, and allow you to mow closer to fences and other objects.

MULCHING MOWERS

Mulching mowers chop grass clippings and leaves and spread them evenly on the lawn, where they break down rapidly and add nutrients to the lawn. These clippings will not cause thatch. Mulching mowers with 5-horsepower engines or more do the best job; 4.5-horsepower engines are adequate. Mulching blades that fit nonmulching machines are available.

The 33-inch cutting width on a wide-cut mower is a foot greater than a conventional mower, so you can cut more grass with each pass.

RIDING MOWERS AND LAWN TRACTORS

For ½ to 1 acre, a riding lawn mower makes good sense. Most have rear-mounted engines with 12 or less horsepower and a 28- to 34-inch cutting width. Small tires and a short wheel base help them maneuver.

Test-drive a few to see if you prefer steering with a wheel or levers. Compare turning radii and find out how close you can get to obstacles.

MOWING HEIGHT

Grass Type	Best Mowing Height	Mow When This Tall
Annual ryegrass	2–2½ inches	3–3¼ inches
Bahia grass	2–3 inches	3–4½ inches
Common Bermuda grass	1½ inches	2¼ inches
Hybrid Bermuda grass	1–1½ inches	1½–2¼ inches
Buffalo grass	1½–2½ inches	3–3¼ inches
Centipede grass	1½–2 inches	2¼–3 inches
Fine fescue	1½–2½ inches	2¼–3¼ inches
Kentucky bluegrass	2½–3 inches	3¾–4½ inches
Perennial ryegrass	1½–2 inches	2¼–3 inches
St. Augustine grass	2–3 inches	3–3½ inches
Turf-type tall fescue	2½–4 inches	3¾–6 inches
Zoysia grass	1–2 inches	1½–3 inches

NOTE: During heat and drought, mow cool-season grasses when they're at the taller height.

(You may need a string trimmer or push mower to cut grass in tight spots.) For safety, be sure the machine shuts off when you get off it.

A lawn tractor is ideal for cutting 1 to 3 acres of grass. Most have 10- to 16-horsepower engines and a 32- to 48-inch cutting width.

GRASS SHEARS

Grass shears are like big scissors, helping you cut grass in areas a mower can't reach. Trimming grass by hand takes a lot of squeezes, so look for padded, hollow-metal handles. Be sure the padding material won't slip off the handle or rip. Forged steel is more durable than cast-iron. The best grass shears allow you to adjust the angle of the blades. If you don't like to stoop, try long-handled shears.

To spare your hands, consider rechargeable battery-powered shears. Most models come with a removable long handle, so you can operate them while standing or kneeling.

STRING TRIMMERS

For tougher jobs, use a gas- or electric-powered string trimmer. They spin a nylon string fast enough to cut grass and weeds. Gas-powered versions are heavier, louder, more expensive, and more powerful. Electric ones are fine for small yards, where an extension cord can reach all corners. Cutting widths range from 7 to 18 inches. Most models work as edgers when you turn them sideways. Some with 4-cycle engines have attachments such as cultivators, leaf blowers, and leaf vacuums.

Some models feed the string on their own. A few require that you dismantle part of the machine each time you add string. Less expensive models may lack an automatic

shutoff, which stops the string when you release the trigger.

String trimmers can nick tree bark badly enough to kill the tree. To avoid damaging trees, surround them with a lawnless area of mulch or groundcover, or trim with shears.

SPREADERS

Two types of lawn spreaders are available for applying fertilizer, grass seed, and other dry materials. A drop spreader drops material straight down, giving you good control over where it lands (important for weed killers). A rotary spreader distributes material in a wide arc, requiring fewer steps to cover the area, but making it more likely that material

Drop spreader

will scatter where you don't want it.

When using a drop spreader, cover the area as if you were mowing a lawn, aligning each pass with the edge of the previous one, but not overlapping it. For even coverage,

Rotary spreader

apply half the material in one direction and the rest perpendicular to the first direction. To ensure even coverage with a rotary spreader, set the spreader so it applies half the recommended amount. Then make a pass at half the width the spreader covers—if the spreader covers 4 feet, make each pass 2 feet from the previous one.

MOWING CORRECTLY

Most lawn problems result from mowing too short with a dull blade. Each type of grass has a best height for mowing. If mowed to that height (not allowed to grow too tall or be clipped too short), the grass grows thickly, squeezing out weeds.

Mowing grass too short shocks it and weakens the roots. A dense, tall lawn keeps the soil cool and moist, shading weed seeds that need light and warmth to germinate.

Mow when the grass needs it, not according to a schedule. In periods of rapid growth, such as spring and fall for cool-season grasses, mow twice a week. Your mower should have an easy-to-adjust blade-height mechanism. Change it as necessary so you don't cut the grass too short.

The following mowing tips work for any type of grass:

■ Remove no more than a third of the length of the grass blades at each mowing, no matter how tall the grass is. If it's extra tall, mow in stages. Cut a third of the length, then lower the blade at the next mowing to cut another third; repeat as necessary.

■ During extreme heat or drought, after insect or disease problems, or after the lawn has been weakened by heavy use, cut ½ inch higher than usual to allow it to recover.

■ Sharpen the mower blade every few months during mowing season. A dull blade tears grass blades, leaving them ragged and ugly and allowing insects and diseases easy entry.

■ Remove long clippings, but allow short ones to remain to nourish the soil.

■ Don't mow wet grass; it clogs mowers and doesn't cut evenly.

■ Mow flat lawns in a straight path at one end of the lawn, turning at the end and overlapping the wheels about 6 inches on the next pass.

■ Mow slopes at a right angle to the slope.

■ If your mower has a discharge chute, direct it toward the center of the lawn, away from walks and flowerbeds.

DETHATCHING AND AERATING

Sometimes a lack of fertilizer, underwatering, insects, or disease is blamed for the mysterious decline of a lawn, when in actuality the culprit is either a buildup of thatch or compacted soil. Both conditions can deprive the turf of water and nutrients, resulting in an unhealthy lawn.

THATCH FACTS

Thatch is a buildup of dead, undecomposed, fibrous roots, stolons, and rhizomes just above the soil surface. It is not a buildup of undecayed grass clippings, nor is it caused by clippings left on the lawn. Thatch results from an imbalance between lawn growth and

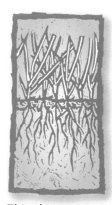 

This shows a healthy lawn with a normal amount of thatch.

The thatch here is too deep, inhibiting root growth.

decomposition of old grass parts. Grass clippings decay rapidly, but old stems and stolons break down slowly.

If the lawn grows too fast due to overfertilization with water-soluble nitrogen, the older parts of the grass plants die off faster than normal and more quickly than they can decay; the result is thatch buildup. Compacted soil also slows down decomposition; so does the use of pesticides, which kill soil organisms. Some grass varieties, such as Kentucky bluegrass, Bermuda grass, and zoysia grass, tend to produce thatch more than others.

To determine if you have a thatch problem in your lawn, use a spade to remove a small sample of turf about 6 inches deep. Look carefully to distinguish the thatch layer from the soil and living plant material. Thatch will look like a layer of spongy, compressed peat moss, but will have live grass roots penetrating it. Measure the depth of the thatch.

A thin layer of thatch on a lawn is beneficial because it cushions the turf from wear and tear, insulates the soil from heat and cold, and holds in moisture. Too deep a layer (more than ½ inch thick) prevents air, water, and fertilizer from penetrating the soil. The grass roots actually may not grow much beyond the thatch layer, so they don't penetrate the soil to reach nutrients and moisture.

A lawn with a heavy thatch buildup is difficult to mow. The mower wheels sink in and the blade scalps the living parts of the lawn, which are too high. Thatch is difficult to wet and dries out quickly, so a lawn with a heavy buildup suffers from lack of nourishment during drought and heat. As a result, it is more susceptible to diseases and insects.

HOW TO DETHATCH

To improve the lawn's health, remove a moderate layer of thatch (½ inch to 2 inches deep). On a small lawn, use a dethatching rake—a hand rake with sharp, convex blades that cut through the thatch and soil as you push and pull it over the lawn. This is heavy work; on large areas, rent a power dethatcher.

Thatch that has been allowed to grow deeper than 2 inches poses a real problem. Use a power dethatcher to remove much of the thatch. Then follow up with a power aerator, which helps to spur decomposition of the remaining thatch. Finally overseed with an improved grass cultivar. You may have to dethatch each year for several years before the lawn is in prime condition.

In the short run, dethatching is traumatic for the lawn, because it cuts and tears the grass roots. To allow the injured grass to recuperate during mild weather, dethatch in late summer or early fall for cool-season grasses, and in late spring or early summer for warm-season grasses. Be sure to water the lawn well after dethatching to keep the newly exposed roots moist. Fertilize the lawn about a week after dethatching.

AERATING COMPACTED SOIL

Experts estimate that 70 percent of all lawns are compacted. When the top 4 inches of soil become compressed due to heavy use, the pore spaces in the soil are reduced, preventing water and nutrients from penetrating. The compacted soil also lacks oxygen because air spaces are absent.

Lawns gradually compact over the years even when walked on only lightly. When used for sports or lawn

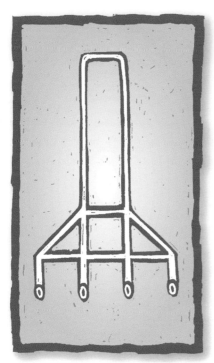

A manual aerator has a U-shaped base with hollow tubes at the end.

parties, the ground can become seriously compacted in a year or two. Sometimes just one part of a lawn—such as a frequently used path between the front of the house and a gate to the rear—becomes compacted. The ground around newly constructed homes is certainly compacted from heavy machinery. No matter what the cause of compaction, you can rehabilitate the lawn with proper aeration.

First test your lawn to see if it is compacted by using a probe to remove plugs of grass and soil. Plunge a ¾-inch-diameter, hollow, metal conduit pipe into the moist lawn. Push the plug of lawn from the pipe and examine it closely. The grass roots may be only 1 inch deep in compacted soil. In a healthy lawn, they should be 6 or more inches deep, depending on the grass type.

Removing cores, or plugs, of soil every 6 inches across the compacted lawn can bring it back to health. You can leave the soil plugs on the lawn surface, where they'll eventually fall apart, or break them up with a rake. For cool-season grasses, remove the plugs about 4 to 6 weeks before the first expected frost in fall; for warm-season grasses, aerate in midsummer.

For a large lawn, rent a power-operated aerator. For a small lawn, use a manual sod-coring tool, which has a U-shaped base with hollow tubes at the ends of its legs. Plunge this long-handled device into the ground, rock it back and forth a bit, and pull it out. Tap it if necessary until the plugs fall out.

CONTROLLING WEEDS, INSECT PESTS, AND DISEASES

A properly sown and tended lawn will not suffer unduly from weeds, insects, or diseases. If you see brown patches or other problems in your lawn, first evaluate your lawn-care practices. The lawn's troubles may result from improper mowing or watering, or from compaction and thatch. By correcting your mower height, fertilizer applications, and watering amounts—and overseeding bare patches—you can probably restore your lawn to its former beauty without resorting to pesticides.

If you decide to use a lawn service, make sure they will customize the treatment of your yard. Many companies routinely apply the same chemicals to every lawn, whether or not the grass has a problem. This may actually encourage problems by harming beneficial soil organisms.

It's possible to have a picture-perfect lawn without resorting to weed killers and pesticides if you mow it high, use a mulching mower, fertilize once or twice a year, and water deeply once a week when it doesn't rain.

Examine the plugs you have removed from your lawn for signs of compaction, such as shallow roots.

Hardiness Zone and Frost Date Maps

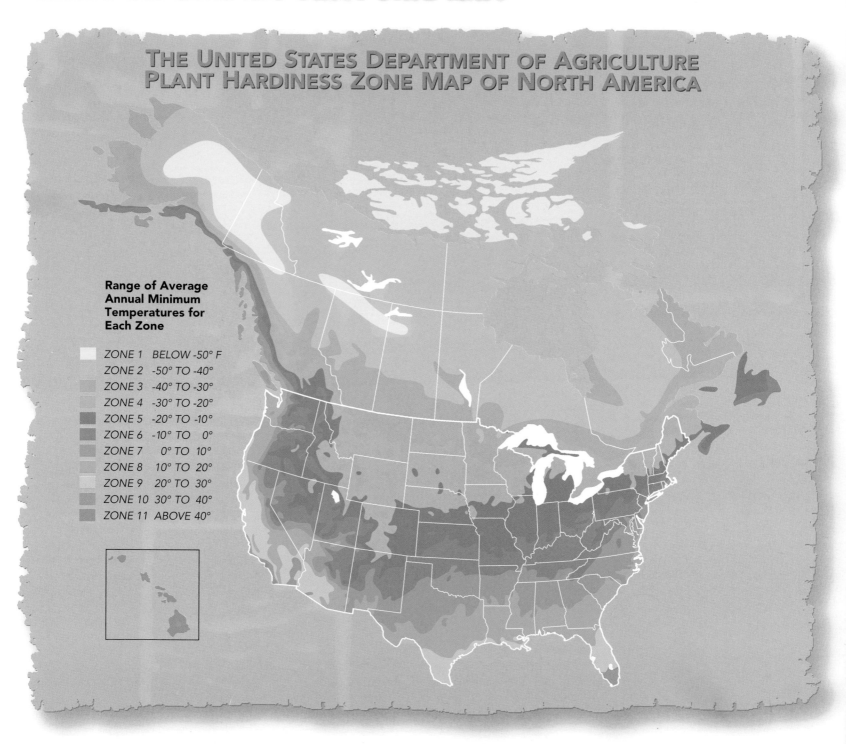

The United States Department of Agriculture Plant Hardiness Zone Map of North America

Range of Average Annual Minimum Temperatures for Each Zone

ZONE 1 BELOW -50° F
ZONE 2 -50° TO -40°
ZONE 3 -40° TO -30°
ZONE 4 -30° TO -20°
ZONE 5 -20° TO -10°
ZONE 6 -10° TO   0°
ZONE 7   0° TO 10°
ZONE 8   10° TO 20°
ZONE 9   20° TO 30°
ZONE 10 30° TO 40°
ZONE 11 ABOVE 40°

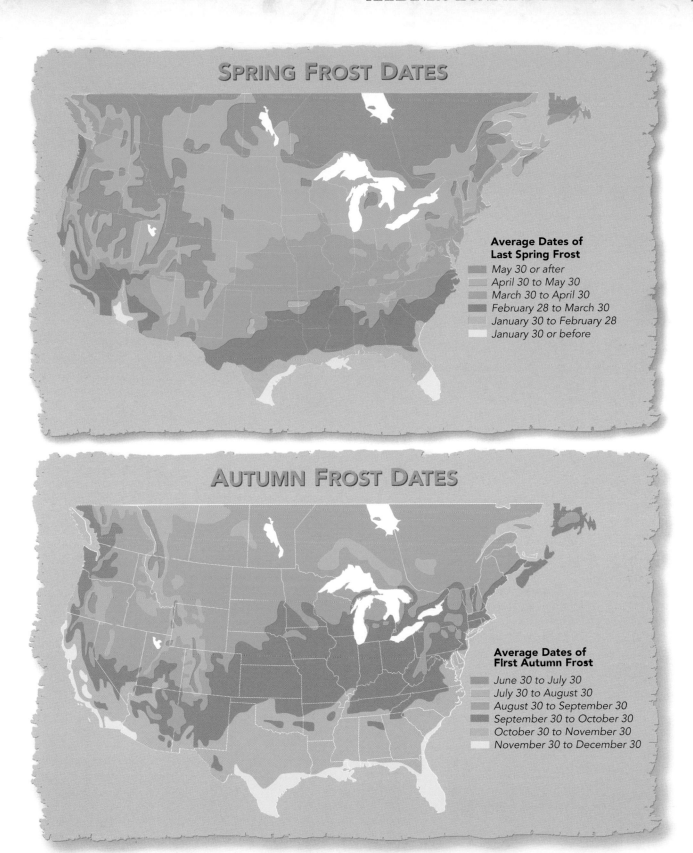

SPRING FROST DATES

Average Dates of Last Spring Frost

- May 30 or after
- April 30 to May 30
- March 30 to April 30
- February 28 to March 30
- January 30 to February 28
- January 30 or before

AUTUMN FROST DATES

Average Dates of First Autumn Frost

- June 30 to July 30
- July 30 to August 30
- August 30 to September 30
- September 30 to October 30
- October 30 to November 30
- November 30 to December 30

576

INDEX

Boldface numbers indicate pages with photographs related to the topic.

A

Abelia
Abelia × grandiflora, 41, 79, 88, 96, 117, **170–171**
glossy, 41, 79, 88, 96, 117, **170**–171
Abelmoschus esculentus, **480**
Abies concolor, 88, 203–204
Acanthus
A. mollis, 97
A. species, 91
A. spinosus var. spinosissimus, **296**
Accessories, garden, **54–55**, 65, 100–101
Acer
A. buergerianum, 38
A. campestre, 38, 91, 142–143
A. circirnatum, 34
A. × fremanii, 34, 144
A. griseum, 34, 37, **142–143**
A. japonicum, 142
A. negundo, 93
A. palmatum, **24**, 34, 89, 142
A. p. 'Aoyagi', 37
A. p. 'Bloodgood', 34
A. p. 'Ornatum', **142**
A. p. 'Sango-Kaku', 37
A. p. var. dissectum, 142
A. platanoides, 34, 74, 143–144
A. rubrum, 34, 38, 93, 143–144
A. saccharinum, 91, 93, 123, 143–144
A. saccharum, 34, 143–144
A. species, 85, 113, 142–145
A. tataricum, 38
A. t. subsp. ginnala, 38, 75, 96, 142–143
A. truncatum, 34, 38
Achillea
A. filipendulina, 296
A. f. 'Coronation Gold', 46, 102, **296**
A. millefolium, 102, 296
A. m. 'Appleblossom', 47
A. m. 'Fire King', 47
A. m. 'The Beacon', **296**, 297
A. × 'Moonshine', 46, 296–297
A. species, 91, 97, 117

Acidanthera murielae, **388**
Aconite, winter, 394-**395**
Aconitum
A. carmichaelii , 103, 297
A. fischeri, 297
A. napellus, **297**
A. species, 89, 107
Actinidia
A. arguta, 435
A. kolomikta, 89, 236, **242**
A. species, 435
Adam's needle, 71, 91, 97, **233**
Adder's-tongue, **23**, 107, 395
Adiantum pedatum, 89, 107, **342**
Aegopodium podagraria 'Variegatum', 89, 97, **242**
Aesculus
A. × carnea, 38, **145**
A. glabra, 89, 96, 115, 145
A. parviflora, 35, 41, 88, **171**
African lily, 88, 388
Agapanthus hybrids, 88, 388
A. africanus minor, **388**
Ageratum
A. houstonianum, 111, 354
hardy, 89, **312**
Ajuga reptans, 19, 44, 61, 89, 97, **240**–243
A. r. 'Burgundy Glow', **242**–243
Akebia quinata, 43, 89, 236, **243**
Alba rose, 268, 276
Albizia julibrissin, 115, **145**–146
Alcea rosea, 115, 117, 289, **297**–298
Alchemilla
A. mollis, 89, **298**
A. species, 19, 44
Allium
A. aflatunense, 103, 388–389
A. ampeloprasum, Porrum Group, 449, 457, **477**
A. cepa, **450**, 457, **480**
A. cepa, Aggregatum Group, **486**
A. christophii, **388**–389
A. moly, 388–**389**
A. sativum, 449, 451, **475**–476
A. schoenoprasum, **494**, **495**, **497**–498
A. scorodoprasum, 475-476
A. species, 96, 110, 117, 387, 388–389

A. sphaerocephalum, **389**
drumstick, **389**
Almond, **443**
Alpine currant, 79, 96, **195**–196
Alpine plants, **110–111**
Alstroemeria species, 103, 387
Althaea officinalis, 495
Alyssum
A. saxatile, 91, 97, 110, 117, **302, 382**
sweet, 19, 22, **30, 48–49**, 61, 88, 91, 110, **111**, 117, 348–349, **351**–353, 367–**368**
Amaryllis belladonna, 103
Amelanchier
A. arborea, 93, **146**
A. canadensis, 146
A. species, 34, 89, 96, 113, 146
Amethyst flower, 353, **356**
Ampelopsis
A. brevipedunculata, 43
A. b. 'Elegans', **243**–244
A. quinquefolia, 260
A. species, 236
variegated Amur, **243**–244
Amur chokecherry, **37**, 162–163
Amur cork tree, 387, **161**
Anemone
A. blanda, **389**–390
A. × hybrida, 36, 89, 117, 298
A. × h. 'Margarette', **298**
Japanese, 36, 89, 117, **298**
Anethum graveolens, 117, **498**–499
Angelica, 495
Angel's-tears, 403
Animal pests, 425–426, 459, **556**–559
Anise, Florida, 88
Annuals
in container gardens, 48
for cutting, 353
deadheading, 348, 351
defined, 348
drought-tolerant, 348
as edging plants, 19
encyclopedia of, **354–379**
feeding, 352, 516
fragrant, **49**, 353
for off-season color, 36
planting, **350**
seeds and seedlings, 350–351, 528–529

self-sowing, 351, 353
shopping for, 350, 526–527
types of, 349
unusual, **49**
using in the landscape, **48–49**
Anthemis
   A. nobilis, 497
   A. tinctoria, 298–**299**
     A. t. 'E.C. Buxton', 47, 299
Antirrhinum majus, 36, 103, 115,
   117, 353, 354
   A. m. 'Liberty Light Pink', **354**
Apium graveolens
   A. g. var. *dulce,* 448, 449, 457,
     469–470
   A. g. var. *rapaceum,* **469**
Apple, **53, 410–411,** 414, **428**
Apple mint, **501**
Apricot, **428**
Aquatic plants, **108–109**
Aquilegia
   A. canadensis, 105
   A. flabellata, 110
   A. × *hybrida,* 33, 299
     A. × *h.* 'McKana Hybrids',
     46, **299**
Arabis
   A. albida, 110, 299–300
   A. caucasica, 110, 299–300
     A. c. 'Snowcap', **299**–300
Arachis hypogaea, **482**
Arbors and pergolas, 14, **42, 44, 45,**
   65, **101, 421–**422
Arborvitae, 78–**79,** 93, **140, 231–**232
   giant, 78, 88, 231–232
Arctostaphylos uva-ursi, 89, 91, 93,
   97, **244**
Arisaema triphyllum, **390**
Aristolochia
   A. durior, 244
   A. macrophylla, 117, 236, **244**
Armeria maritima, 97
Aronia
   A. arbutifolia, 41, 93, 171–172
     A. a. 'Brilliantissima', **171**–172
   A. melanocarpa, 41
   A. species, 35, 41
Artemisia
   A. dracunculus var. *sativa,* 495,
     504–**505**
   A. ludoviciana, 102

A. l.. var. *albula,* 300
A. × 'Powis Castle', **300**
A. schmidtiana 'Silver Mound',
   44, 300
A. species, **90**
Artichoke, globe, **462**
Arugula, 449, 451, **462**
Asarina
   A. barclaiana, 245
   A. scandens, 236, **245**
Asarum
   A. canadense, 245
   A. caudatum, 89, 245
   A. europaeum, **245**
   A. shuttleworthii, 245
Asclepias tuberosa, 91, 97, 103,
   105, 115, 117, 300
   A. t. 'Hello Yellow', **300**
Ash
   green or red, 34, 38, 75, 91, 96, 153
   Korean mountain, 34, 38, 166–**167**
   white, 34, 38, **153**
Asiatic sweetleaf, 41, **199**
Asimina triloba, 435–**436**
Asparagus
   A. officinalis, 462–463
     A. o. 'Jersey Knight', **462**
Asperula odorata, 252
Aster
   A. × 'Alma Potschke', 46, 301
   A. frikartii, **47,** 301
     A. f. 'Monch', 47, **301**
   A. novae-angliae, 46, 103, 300–301
   A. novi belgii, 300–301
   A. × 'September Ruby', 47, 301
   A. species, 36, 105, 113, 117, 294,
     300–301
   China, 103, 353, **356–**357
   New England, 46, 103, 300–301
   Stokes', 47, **331**
Astilbe
   A. × *arendsii,* 103, 301, 302
     A. × *a.* 'Glow', **301**–302
   A. × *rosea* 'Peach Blossom', **25,** 302
   A. species, 33, **84,** 89, 294, 301–302
   A. taquetti, 301–302
Athyrium
   A. filix-femina, 107, **342**
   A. goeringianum 'Pictum', **342,**
     343

A. nipponicum 'Pictum', 57, 89,
   342, 343
Aubretia deltoidea, 117
Aucuba japonica, 41, 88, **204**
Aurinia saxatilis, 91, 97, 110, 117,
   302, 382
Azalea
   coast, 93, **193**
   Cumberland, 194
   evergreen, **32,** 124, 227–228
   Exbury rhododendron hybrid,
     194–195
   flame, 35
   Florida flame, 193
   Knap Hill rhododendron hybrid,
     194–195
   Korean,35, 41, **194**
   Mollis rhododendron hybrid,
     194–195
   native, 35, 41, 79, 88, 117, 124–**126,**
     135, 141, 193–194, 227–229
   pink-shell, 35, 193–194
   pinxterbloom, 193
   plum-leaved, 193–194
   royal, 194
   Southern Indica, **227**
   swamp, 41, 193, 194
   sweet, 35, 41

B

Baby's-breath, 91, 97, 102, 103, **314**
Bachelor's-button, 91, 103, 348,
   353, **358**
Backyards
   play areas in, **11–12, 73**
   seating, 72–**73**
   utility areas in, **72–73**
Baking soda spray, 275, 552
Balloonflower, 47, 294, **326**
Balm, lemon, 54, 495, **500**
Baptisia australis, 105, 117, **302–303**
Barberry, 41, 96, 172
   dwarf red, 71
   Japanese, 35, 79, **172**
   Korean, 35, 79, 172
   wintergreen, **205**
Bark color, 23, **37**
Barrenwort, **250**
Basil, **496**

Basket-of-gold, 91, 97, 110, 117, **302, 382**
Basket willow, 88, 93, **196**
Bay
bull, 88, 93, **217**
sweet, 93, 217
Bayberry, 41, 79, 91, 96, 113, **191**
Bean
scarlet runner, 115, **463**–464
snap, 449–451, **461,** 463–464
Bearberry, 89, 91, 93, 97, **244**
Beautyberry, 41, 88, 113
Japanese, 41
purple, 71, 93, 173
Beautybush, 96, 115, **189**
Beds
island, 28–**29**
raised, **448**–449
shapes of, **18**
vegetable, **448**–449, 455
Beebalm, 46, 115, 117, **496**
Beech
blue, 89, 93, **147**
European, **152**–153
Beefsteak plant, 49, **372**
Beet, 449, 451, 457, **464**–465
Begonia
bedding, 19, 88, 354–**355**
B. grandis, 89
B. × *semperflorens-cultorum,* 19, 88, 354–**355**
B. × *tuberhybrida,* 57, 88, 385, **390**
hardy, 89
strawberry, 89, **263**
tuberous, 57, 88, 385, **390**
wax or bedding, 19, 88, 354–**355**
Belamcanda chinensis, 97
Belgian endive, 451, **470**–471, **484**
Bellflower
Carpathian, 46, 61, 303, **304,** 305
clustered, **304,** 305
Dalmatian, 47, 110, **304**–305
milky, 294, 304, 305
peach-leaf, 304, 305
Bells-of-Ireland, 49, 102, 353, **369**
Benches, 28, 60, 65
Berberis
B. julianae, **205**
B. koreana, 35, 79, 172
B. species, 41, 96, 172
B. thunbergii, 35, 79, 172

B. t. 'Rose Glow', **172**
B. t. var. *atropurpurea* 'Crimson Pygmy', 71
Bergamot, 46, 115, 117, **496**
Bergenia, 288
B. cordifolia, 303
B. c. 'Silver Light', **303**
B. species, 93
Berms, 78–79
Berries
brambles, 422–423
for color, 23, 37
growing, 420–422
harvesting, 426–**427**
patches, **423**
pruning and training, 422–423
trellising, 422
Beta vulgaris, 449, 451, 457, **464**–465
B. v. (Cicla Group), 449, **459, 470**
Bethlehem sage, 19, 89, **327**–328
Betula
B. alba, 147
B. nigra, **37,** 38, 93, 146–147
B. n. 'Heritage', **20,** 147
B. papyrifera, 146–147
B. pendula, **146**–147
B. species, 34, 37, 113, 146–147
Biennials, 288–**289**
Bignonia
B. capreolata, 89, 93, 236, 245–**246**
B. radicans, 246
Birch, 34, 37, 113, 146–147
canoe, 146–147
European white, **146**–147
paper, 146–147
river, **20, 37,** 38, 93, 146–147
Birds
attracting, 108, **112–115**
deterring, **559**
food and water for, **112–113**
Bishop's hat, **250**
Bishop's weed, 89, 97, **242**
Bittersweet
American, 236, **246**
Oriental, 43
Blackberry, **429**
Blackberry lily, 97
Black-eyed Susan vine, 57, 89, 97, 236, **263**

Blackfoot daisy, 49, 57, 91, 110, 348, **369**
Black haw, 201–202
Black spot, 274–275, 554
Blanketflower, 47, 105, 117, **313**
annual, 91, 96, **105,** 110, 117, 348, 353, **363**
Blazing-star, 91, 97, **320**
Bleeding heart
common, 103, **310**–311
fringed, 47, 107, 288, 310
Bloody cranesbill, 46, 314
Blowers, leaf, 540
Bluebeard, 41, 91, 96, **174**
Bluebells
Spanish, 397
Virginia, **106**–107
Blueberry
highbush, 429–430, 509
lowbush, 429–430
Bluebonnet, Texas, 91, 105, **368, 511**
Blue daisy, 117, 348, **362**
Blue gamma, 105
Blue lyme grass, 97, 105, **336**
Blue marguerite, 117, 348, **362**
Blue wild rye, 97, 105, **336**
Bok choy, 451, **465**
Boltonia
B. asteroides, 105, 303
B. a. 'Pink Beauty', **303**
white, 105, 303
Borage, 117, **497**
Borago officinalis, 117, **497**
Border forsythia, 79, **182**–183
Borders
double, 16, 28–**29**
English-style, 16, **28**
herbaceous, **28**
mixed, **26–27,** 29, **40**
for privacy, **74**
shapes of, **18**–19
Bottlebrush buckeye, 35, 41, 88, **171**
Bouteluoa gracilis, 105
Box
dwarf sweet, **262**–263
Korean, 71
littleleaf, 71
Boxwood, 28, 45, 79, 88, 124, **205**

Brachycome iberidifolia, 49, 57, 61, 91, 96, 110, 348, **355**
Brambles, 422–423
Brassica juncea, **53, 479**–480
Brassica napus, Napobrassica Group, 449, 457, 485–**486**
Brassica oleracea
   Acephala Group, 49, 449, 451, 457, **471**–472, **476**–477
   Botrytis Group, 57, **355**, 449, 451, 457, **465**–466, **468**
   Capitata Group, 448, 449, 451, 457, 466–**467**
   Gemmifera Group, 449, 451, 457, **466**
   Gongylodes Group, 449, 451, 457, **477**
Brassica rapa
   Chinensis Group, 451, **465**–466
   Pekinensis Group, 451, 457, **471**
   Rapifera Group, 449, 451, 457, 490–**491**
Briza media, 102, 105, **334**
Broccoli, 451, 457, **465**–466
Brodiaea uniflora, 398
Broom, 41, 91, 96, **179**
Browallia speciosa, 353, 356
   B. s. 'Blue Bells Improved', **356**
Brussels sprouts, 449, 451, 457, **466**
Buckeye, 35, 38, 41, 88, 89, 96, 115, **145, 171**
Buddleia
   B. alternifolia 'Argentca', 41
   B. davidii, 41, 115, 117, 172–**173**
   B. globosa, 41
   B. species, 96
   silver fountain, 41
Bugleweed, 19, 44, 61, 89, 97, **240**–243
Bulbs
   bloom times, **382,** 385, **387**
   buying by mail, 527
   caring for, 384–385
   combinations of, **50**
   corms and cormels, 385, 387
   defined, 382, **385**
   dividing, 386–387
   encyclopedia of, **388**–**407**
   fertilizing, 385
   forcing, 385
   interplanting, **50**–51, 384, **387**

in lawns, **51**
major and minor, 383, 385
naturalizing, 50–**51**
for off-season color, 36
offsets (bulblets), 387
planting and interplanting, 384, **387**
rhizomes, 385
shopping for, 383
tuberous roots, 385
tubers, 385–386
types of, 385
winter protection for, 382–383, 385–387
Burning bush, 35, 79, 88, **182**
Bush clover, 41, 71, 91, **189**–190
Busy Lizzie, 19, 26, 57, 88, 348, 351, 353, **365**–366
Butterflies, **116**–117, **546**
Butterfly bush, 41, 96, 115, 117, 172–**173**
   globe, 41
Butterfly plant, 117
Butterfly weed, 91, 97, 103, 105, 115, 117, **300**
Butternut, 445
Buttonbush, 88, 93, **174**–175
Buxus
   B. microphylla, 71
      B. m. var. *koreana,* 71
   B. sempervirens, 28, 45, 79, 88, 124, **205**

C

Cabbage, 448, 449, 451, 457, 466–**467**
   Chinese, 451, 457, **471**
Caladium
   C. × *hortulanum,* 57, 88, **390**–391
   fancy-leaved, 57, 88, **390**–391
Calamagrostis × *acutiflora* 'Stricta', **334**
Calamint, 97
Calamintha nepeta, 97
Calendula officinalis, 36, 91, 96, 103, 349, 353, **356**
Calla lily, 93, 103, **407**
Callicarpa
   C. dichotoma, 71, 93, 173
      C. d. 'Issai', **173**
   C. japonica 'Leucocarpa', 41
   C. species, 41, 88, 113

Calliopsis tinctoria, **105**
Callistephus chinensis, 103, 353, **356**–357
Calocedrus decurrens, 78, 88, 205–**206**
Caltha palustris, 109
Calycanthus floridus, 41, 88, 93, **174**
Camas, 107
Camassia leichtlinii, 107
Camellia
   C. japonica, 88, 124, 141, **206**
   C. sasanqua, 206
Campanula
   C. carpatica, 46, 61, 303, **304**, 305
   C. glomerata, 304, 305
      C. g. 'Joan Elliot', **304**, 305
   C. lactiflora, 294, 304, 305
   C. persicifolia, 304, 305
   C. portenschlagiana, 47, 110, **304**–305
   C. poscharskyana, 47
   C. species, **111**
Campsis radicans, **42,** 89, 91, 93, 97, 115, 236, 238, **246**
Canby paxistima, **261**
Candytuft, edging, 19, 44, 110, 117, **317**
Canna × **generalis,** 22, 57, 115, **391**
   C. × *g.* 'Stadt Feltbach', **391**
Canna lily, 22, 57, 115, **391**
Cantaloupe, 457, 478–**479**
Capsicum annuum, 457, 482–**483**
Cardinal climber, 91, 236, **254**
Carex
   C. elata 'Aurea', **334**
      C. e. 'Bowles Golden', 89, 334–335
   C. morrowii, 89, 334, 335
      C. m. 'Variegata', 19
Carolina allspice, 41, 88, 93, **174**
Carolina jasmine, 89, 236, **253**
Carolina silverbell, 89, 155
Carpet bugle, 19, 44, 61, 89, 97, **240**–243
Carpinus
   C. betulus 'Fastigiata', 38
   C. caroliniana, 89, 93, **147**
Carrot, 451, **457, 467**–468
Carts, 537
Carya illinoinensis, **444**

Caryopteris × *clandonensis,* 41, 91, 96, **174**
Castor bean, 49, **374**
Castor oil plant, 49, **374**
Catalpa
  C. bignonioides, 89, 93, 147–**148**
  common, 89, 93, 147–**148**
Caterpillars, **116**–117
Catharanthus roseus, **357**
Cathedral bells, 89, 91, 97, 236, **249**
Catmint, 44–45, 47, 321–**322**
Cauliflower, 449, 451, 457, **468**–469
Cedar
  Alaska, 208–209
  Atlantic white, 93, 110
  Atlas, 88, 206–207
  Deodar, **206**–207
  Eastern red, 75, 78, 91, 97, **214**–215
  Eastern white, 78–**79**, 93, **140,** **231**–232
  incense, 78, 88, 205–**206**
  Japanese, 78, 88, 209–**210**
  -of-Lebanon, 207
  Western red, (See also *Juniperus scopulorum; Thuja plicata),* 71, 78, **88,** 91, 97, 110, 214–215, 231–232
Cedrus
  C. atlantica, 88, 206–207
  C. deodara, 206–207
    C. d. 'Aurea', **206**
  C. libani, 207
  C. species, **32,** 206–207
Celandine poppy, **106**
Celastrus
  C. orbiculatus, 43
  C. scandens, 236, **246**
Celeriac, **469**
Celery, 448, 449, 457, **469**–470
Celery root, **469**
***Celosia argentea,* 32,** 57, 102, 103, 353, 357
  C. a. 'Apricot Beauty', **357**
Celtis occidentalis, 89, 93, 96, **148**
Centaurea
  C. cineraria, 357–358
    C. c. 'Silverdust', **357**–358
  C. cyanus, 91, 103, 348, 353, **358**
  C. montana, 46, **305**
  C. species, 46, 57

Cephalanthus occidentalis, 88, 93, **174**–175
***Cephalotaxus harringtonia,* 88,** 207–208
  C. h. 'Prostrata', 71, **207**–208
Cerastium tomentosum, 44, 46, 61, 91, 97, 110, **305**–306
Ceratostigma plumbaginoides, 44, 89, 246–**247**
Cercidiphyllum japonicum, 34, 89, **148**–149
Cercis canadensis, 89, **149**
***Chaenomeles speciosa,* 41, 115
  C. s. 'Chajubai', **175**
Chamaecyparis
  C. lawsoniana, 71, 208–209
  C. nootkatensis, 208–209
  C. obtusa, 71, 208–209
    C. o. 'Aurea', **208**–209
  C. pisifera, 71, 110, 208–209
  C. species, 37, 78, 88, 208–209
  C. thyoides, 93, 110
Chamaemelum nobile, **497**
Chamomile, **497**
Chard, 449, **459, 470**
Chasmanthium latifolium, 89, 102, 105, **335**
Chaste tree, 96, **203**
Checkberry, 89, 252–**253**
Chelone
  C. glabra, 105
  C. lyonii, **306**
  C. species, 93
Cherry
  bush, 431
  Higan, 163
  Nanking, **431**
  Okame, 34, **162**–163
  Oriental, 34, 163
  ornamental, 37, 162–163, 430–431, 439
  sour, **413, 430**–431
  sweet, **430**–431
  weeping, 163
Cherry laurel, 71, 88, **225**
Chervil, 495
Chickabiddy, 236, **245**
Chicory, 451, **470**–471, **484**
Children and gardening, **118**–119
Chimonanthus praecox, 41, **175**–176

Chionanthus
  C. retusus, 37
  C. virginicus, **149**–150
Chionodoxa luciliae, 50–**51**, 382, **391**
Chippers, **541**
Chives, **494, 495, 497**–498
Chocolate vine, 43, 89, 236, **243**
Chokeberry, 35, 41
  black, 41
  red, 41, 93, **171**–172
Chokecherry, Amur, **37**, 162–163
Chrysanthemum (See also *Dendranthema* species)
  C. leucanthemum, 105
  C. × *morifolium,* 309
  C. ptarmiciflorum, 357–358
  C. species, 36, 293–295, 308–309
  C. × *superbum,* 293, 319–320
  hybrid, 47, 309
Chrysogonum virginianum, 89, 107, **247**
Cichorium
  C. endiva, 449, **474**–475
  C. intybus, 451, **470**–471, **484**
Cilantro, **498**
Cimicifuga
  C. simplex, 107, **306**
  C. species, 46, 89, 93
Cinquefoil, shrubby, 41, 71, 91, 96, **192**–193
Citrullus lanatus, 448, 457, **491**
Cladrastis
  C. kentukea, **150**
  C. lutea, 34, **150**
Clarkia amoena, 49, 353
Clay soil, 508–**509**
Clematis
  C. armandii, **248**–249
  C. dioscoreifolia, 248–249
  C. × *hybrida,* 89, 247–248
    C. × *h.* 'Ville de Lyon', **247**
  C. maximowicziana, 89, 248, 249
  C. montana, 248, 249
    C. m. var. 'Rubens', **248**–249
  C. paniculata, 248, 249
  C. species and hybrids, 43, 44, 236, 238, 247–249
  C. tangutica, 248, 249
  hybrid, 89, **247**–248
Cleome hasslerana, 49, 57, 96, 103, 105, 349, 353, **358**

Clethra alnifolia, 35, 41, 79, 88, 93, **176**
  C. a. 'Hummingbird', 71
Climate control, landscaping for, 80–83
Cloches, 452
Cobaea scandens, 89, 91, 97, 236, **249**
Cockscomb, **32**, 57, 102, 103, 353, **357**
Colchicum
  C. autumnale, 36, 392
  C. cilicicum 'Purpureum', **392**
  C. species, 387
Coldframes, 452–**453**, **529**
Coleus × *hybridus*, **56**–57, 88, 358–359
  C. × *h.* 'Bellingrath Pink', **359**
Collards, 451, 457, **471**–472
Color
  analogous, 31
  of bark, 23, **37**
  of berries, 23, **37**
  in borders, 28
  combining, **22–25, 27**, 31, **32–33**
  in container gardens, **56**
  as design element, **22–23, 30–33**
  foliage, **23, 32–33**
  off-season, **34–38**, 39
  schemes, 30–31, **32**
Color wheel, 30–31
Columbine
  hybrid, 33, 46, **299**
  wild, 105
Comfrey, 495
Compost, 510, **512**, 514, 517, **520–521**, 525
Coneflower
  orange, 46, 91, 97, 103, **328**, 329
  purple, 46, 91, 97, 103, 105, 113, 117, **311–312**
  shining, 47, 328–329
Confederate jasmine, 89, 236, 263–**264**
Conifers, **39, 123–125**, 135–**138, 140**
Consolida, 348, 349
  C. ambigua, 103, 105, 115, 117, 353, **359**
Container gardening, 48, 54, **55–59**
Convallaria majalis, 89, 103, 249–**250**

Coralbells, 316
  purple-leaf, 19, 57
Coreopsis
  C. grandiflora, 47, 103, **307**
  C. rosea, 44
  C. species, 105, 113, 117, 307
  C. tinctoria, 117
  C. verticillata, 22, 46–47, 91, 97, 288, 307
  pink, 44
  thread-leaved, 22, 46–47, 91, 97, 288, 307
Coriander, **498**
Coriandrum sativum, **498**
Corkscrew hazelnut, 41, **177**
Corms and cormels, 385, 387
Corn, 448, 451, 457, **472**
Cornelian cherry, 89, 150–151
Cornflower
  annual, 91, 103, 348, 353, **358**
  perennial, 46, **305**
Cornus
  C. alba, 79, 93
  C. alternifolia, 150–151
  C. florida, 27, 89, **150**–151
  C. kousa, 150–151
  C. mas, 89, 150–151
  C. sericea, 35, 37, 79, 93, **176**–177
  C. species, **23**, 34, 37, 113, 122, **135**
  C. stolonifera, 176–177
Cortaderia selloana 'Pumila', 97, **335**
Corydalis lutea, 89, 110, **307**–308
Corylopsis
  C. glabrescens, **177**
  C. species, 41, 88
Corylus avellana, 177, 443–**444**
  C. a. 'Contorta', 41, **177**
Cosmos
  C. bipinnatus, 57, 103, 105, 117, **348**, 353, 359–360
    C. b. 'Seashells', **359**–360
  C. species, 96, 113, 349, **352**, 359–360
  C. sulphureus, 105, 359–360
    C. s. 'Sunny Red', **360**
  yellow, 105, 359–**360**
Costmary, 495
Cotinus coggygria, 35, **40**, 41, 177–178
  C. c. 'Royal Purple', 177–**178**

Cotoneaster
  bearberry, 71, **209**
  C. adpressus, 71
  C. apiculatus, 71, 178–179
  C. dammeri, 71, **209**
  C. divaricatus, 35, 71, 178–179
  C. horizontalis, 71, **178**–179
  C. lucidus, 35, 79
  C. multiflorus, 79, 178–179
  C. salicifolius, 71, 209
  C. species, 35, 41, 113, 178–179
  cranberry, 71, 178–179
  creeping, 71
  hedge, 35, 79
  many-flowered, 79, 178–179
  rockspray, 71, **178**–179
  spreading, 35, 71, 178–179
  willowleaf, 71, 209
Country cottage gardens, 17, 44, 62, **100–101**
Cover cropping, 455–**456**
Crabapple, Japanese flowering, 27, 115, 158–**159**
Cranberry bush
  American, 113, **201**–202
  European, 41
Crape myrtle, 34, 96, **156**
Crataegus
  C. phaenopyrum, 115
  C. species, 38, 113
  C. viridis 'Winter King', **151**–152
Creeping Charlie, 19, 89, **258**
Creeping Jenny, 19, 89, **258**
Cress, 449, 472–**473**
Crimson starglory, 236, **259**
Crocosmia
  C. × *crocosmiflora,* 392
  C. 'Lucifer', **392**
Crocus
  autumn, 36, 392
  C. chrysanthus, 36, 50–51, 91, 382, **393**
  C. sativus, 36, **393**
  C. species, 50, 96, 110, 385, 387, 392–394
  C. speciosus, 393
  C. × *vernus,* 50, 383, **392**
  Dutch, 50, 383, **392**
  fall, 393
  saffron, 36, **393**
  snow, 36, 50–51, 91, 382, **393**

Crop rotation, 459
Cross vine, 89, 93, 236, 245–**246**
Crown imperial, 383, **396**
Cryptomeria japonica, 78, 88,
   209–**210**
Cucumber, 457, **473**–474
Cucumis
   C. melo, 457, 478–**479**
   C. sativus, 457, **473**–474
Cucurbita pepo, 449, 457, **487**–488
   C. p. var. *pepo,* 449, 487–**488**
Cultivators, 535
Cup and saucer vine, 89, 91, 97,
   236, **249**
× *Cupressocyparis leylandii,*
   78–79, **210**
Cupressus arizonica* var. *glabra,
   78, 211
   C. a. var. *glabra* 'Blue Ice', **211**
Currant
   alpine, 79, 96, **195**–196
   black, 432
   red, **432**
Cutting gardens, **51, 102**–103
Cuttings, 530–531
Cyclamen
   C. hederifolium, **394**
   C. neapolitanum, 394
   C. species, 110
   hardy, **394**
Cyclamen daffodil, **401**, 402, 403
Cydonia oblonga, **440**
Cynara scolymus, **462**
Cyperus isocladus, 109
Cypress
   bald, 93, 123, **168**
   Leyland, 78–79, **210**
   Russian, 71, **259**
   Siberian, 71, **259**
   smooth Arizona, 78, **211**
Cyrtomium falcatum, 28, 89, **343**
Cytisus
   C. × *praecox,* 91, **179**
   C. species, 41, 96

D

Daffodil, 26, 50–51, 103, **382**–384,
   387, 401–403
   cyclamen, **401**, 402, 403
   winter, 36, 110, **404**

Dahlberg daisy, **48**–49, 57, 61, **361**
Dahlia
   annual, 117, **360**
   D. hybrid, **394**
   D. × *hybrida,* 117, **360**
   D. pinnata, 103, 115, 382–383,
      385–**386,** 394
Daisy
   blackfoot, 49, 57, 91, 110, 348, 369
   blue, 117, 348, **362**
   Dahlberg, **48**–49, 57, 61, **361**
   fall, 46, 103, 300–301
   Frikart's, **47, 301**
   Michaelmas, 300–301
   Shasta, 103, **319**–320
   Swan River, 49, 57, 61, 91, 96, 110,
      348, **355**
Damask rose, 268, 278
Daphne
   Burkwood, 88, 179–180
   D. × *burkwoodii,* 88, 179–180
      D. × *b.* 'Carol Mackie', 179–**180**
   D. cneorum, 71, 88, 211
   D. mezereum, 180
   D. odora, 71, 211
      D. o. 'Variegata', **211**
   D. species, 41, 71, 179–180
   February, 180
   winter, 71, **211**
Daucus carota* var. *sativus, 451,
      457, 467–468
   D. c. var. *sativus* 'Bertan', **467**–468
Daylily, 46–47, 50, **295, 315**–316
Deadheading, **141,** 294, 348, 351
Deciduous shrubs, 40, **124**–125
   (*See also* Shrubs)
   encyclopedia of, **170**–203
   pruning, 138–139
   siting, 126–127
Deciduous trees, 81, 122–**123**
   (*See also* Trees)
   encyclopedia of, **142**–170
Decks, **58, 60**–61
Deer, **556**–558
Delphinium
   D. ajacis, **359**
   D. × *elatum,* 103, 288,
      293–294, **308**
Dendranthema
   D. × *grandiflorum,* 103, 308–309
      D. × *g.* 'Red Headliner', **308**
   D. × *rubellum,* 47, 309

Dennstaedtia punctilobula, **343**
Deschampsia caespitosa, 335–**336**
Deutzia
   D. gracilis 'Nikko', 35, 71, **180**
   D. species, 41, **140**
Dewberry, 429
Dianthus
   D. barbatus, 103, 115, 309–310
   D. chinensis, 49, 91, 110, 117, 348,
      353, 360–361
      D. c. 'Telstar Picotee', **360**–361
   D. deltoides, 309–310
   D. plumarius, 110, **309**–310
   D. species, 117, 309–310
Dicentra
   D. eximia, 47, 107, 288, 310
   D. species, 89, 115
   D. spectabilis, 103, **310**–311
Digging tools and techniques,
   518–519, 534–537
Digitalis purpurea, 89, 103, 115, **289,**
   293, **311**
Dill, 117, **498**–499
Diospyros
   D. kaki, **438**
   D. virginiana, **438**
Dirca palustris, 88, 93, 180–**181**
Diseases
   black spot, 274–275, 554
   guide to, 554–555
   of lawns, 573
   organic fungicides for, 552
   powdery mildew, 275, **552,** 555
   preventing and controlling, **552**
   of roses, 274–275
   vegetables and, 459
Division of plants
   bulbs, 386–387
   perennials, 294–**295,** 530–531
Dogwood, 23, 34, 37, 113,
      122, **135**
   flowering, 27, 89, **150**–*151*
   Kousa, 150–151
   pagoda, 150–151
   red-osier, 35, 37, 79, 93, **176**–177
   Tartarian, 79, 93
Double digging, 454, 518–519
Douglas fir, 78, 225–226
Downy serviceberry, 34, 89, 96,
      113, 146

Drainage and drain pipes, 92
Drifts of plants, 24–**25**, 29, 48
Drip irrigation systems, 544–**545**
Drought-tolerant plants
    lawn grasses, 563, **565**, 568
    for Xeriscapes, 94–97
Dry-climate gardens, **524**
Drying flowers, 102
Dryopteris
    D. erythrosora, 343–344
    D. marginalis, 89, 107, **343**–344
    D. species, 93
Dusty-miller, 19, **357**–358
Dutchman's pipe, 117, 236, **244**
Dyer's greenweed, 41, 91, 96,
    183–**184**
Dyssodia tenuiloba, **48**–49, 57,
    61, **361**

E

Earth-moving equipment, 534–535
Eastern redbud, 89, **149**
Echinacea purpurea, 91, 97, 103,
    105, 113, 117, 311–312
    E. p. 'Bright Star', 46
    E. p. 'Magnus', **311**–312
Echinops ritro, 113
Edging, **19,** 54
Edible landscaping, **52–55,** 118–119
Eel grass, 109
Eggplant, 457, **474**
Eichhornia crassipes, 109
Elaeagnus
    E. angustifolia, 96, **152**
    E. umbrellata, 91, **181**
Elderberry, 113, **432**
Elm
    American, 93, **169**–170
    Chinese, 34, 37–38, 75, 97, 169–170
    White, 93, **169**–170
Elymus arenarius 'Glaucus', 97,
    105, **336**
Endive, 449, **474**–475
Endophytes, 564
Endymion hispanicus, 397
Energy-conserving tips, 83
English gardens, 16, **28,** 65
English ivy, 57, 89, 236, 239, 240,
    241, 253–254
English laurel, 88, **225**

English lavender, 44–46, 91, **94–95,**
    97, 102, **495,** 499
Enkianthus
    E. campanulatus, 35, **181** 182
    E. perulatus, 35
    E. species, 41
    red-vein, 35, **181**–182
    white, 35
Entry landscaping, **68–70,** 71
Environmental issues
    groundcovers, 43
    lawns, 562
    pesticides, 117, 548
    water conservation, **94–95,** 543
Epimedium
    E. species, 89, 91, 288
    E. × *versicolor* 'Sulphureum', **250**
Eranthis hyemalis, 394–**395**
Erianthus ravennae, **336**–337
Erica
    E. carnea, 250–251
    E. c. 'Silberschmelze', **250**–251
    E. herbacea, 250–251
Erosion, 99
Eruca vesicaria var. *sativa,* 449,
    451, **462**
Erysimum cheiri, 49, 353
Erythronium
    E. americanum, **23,** 107, 395
    E. dens-canis, **395**
Eschscholzia californica, 61, 91,
    96, 105, 110, 113, 348–**349,**
    353, **361**
Espaliers, **53, 415**
Eulalia, 102, 293, 338–339
Euonymus
    E. alatus, 35, 79, 88, **182**
    E. atropurpurea, 182
    E. europaeus, 41
    E. fortunei, 97, 113, 236, 241, 251
        E. f. var. *radicans,* **251**
        E. f. 'Silver Queen', **251**
    E. japonica, **32,** 88, 211–**212**
    evergreen, **32,** 88, 211–**212**
    winged, 35, 79, 88, **182**
Eupatorium
    E. coelestinum, 89, **312**
    E. fistulosum, 312
    E. purpureum, 93, 105, 117, 312
Euphorbia polychroma, 97
European red elder, 196–**197**)

Eustoma grandiflora, 103, 105, 349,
    353, **361**–362
Evergreens (*See also* Conifers;
    Shrubs; Trees)
    broad-leaved, 124, 126–127, **135,**
        137, **141**
    for climate control, 80, 81, 82
    encyclopedia of, **203–233**
    pinching, 137
    shrubs, 40, **124**
    trees, 122–**123**
    using in landscape, **10**
Exotic love, 236, **259**

F

Fagus
    F. grandiflora, 113
    F. sylvatica, **152**–153
False cypress
    Hinoki, 71, 208–209
    Lawson, 71, 208–209
    Nootka, 208–209
    Sawara, 71, 110, 208–209
False dragonhead, 46, 105, **326**
False holly, 41, 79, 88, 218–219
False rockcress, 117
Fanflower, **49,** 57, 348, **375**–376
Farewell-to-spring, 49, 353
Feather grass, giant, **341**
Feather reed grass, **334**
Felicia amelloides, 117, 348, **362**
Fences
    building codes for, 77
    choosing, 75
    as deer deterrents, 558
    as design elements, **20, 64–65**
    installation tips, 77
    and outdoor rooms, 14–**15**
    for privacy, 65, **75**–77
    styles of, **76–77**
Fennel, 117, **495, 499**
    Florence. **475**
Fern
    autumn, 343–344
    boulder, **343**
    Christmas, 57, 89, 107, **345**
    cinnamon, 89, 93, 107, 344, 345
    hay-scented, **343**
    Japanese holly, 28, 89, **343**
    Japanese painted, 57, 89, **342,** 343

lady, 107, **342**
maidenhair, 89, 107, **342**
marginal shield, 89, 107, **343**–344
ostrich, 93, 107, **344**
royal, 93, 107, **344**–345
soft shield, 107, **345**
western sword, 89, **345**
Ferns
caring for, 295
for color, **33**
defined, **288**
encyclopedia of, **342–345**
planting, **290**
Fertilization
annuals, 352, 516
bulbs, 385
container plants, 58–59
fruit and nut trees, 414
lawns, 516, 563, 569, 571
perennials, 516–**517**
roses, 271, 516
trees and shrubs, 134, 516
vegetables, 454, 458, 516
Fertilizers
applying, 458, 516–517
NPK ratio, 512–513
organic, 512, 514–515
sources of, 514–515
"tea", 517
types of, 512, 516
Fescue
blue,19, 57, 97, 293, 337
blue sheep's, 19, 57, 97, 293, 337
Festuca
F. amethystina, 97, **337**
F. arvensis, 337
F. cinerea, 337
F. glauca, 337
F. ovina, 105
F. o. var. *glauca,* 19, 57, 97, 293, 337
Fetterbush, **221**
Ficus
F. carica, **433**
F. pumila, 89, 236, **251**–252
F. repens, 251–252
Fig, 433
climbing, 89, 236, **251**–252
creeping, 89, 236, **251**–252
Filipendula rubra, 93, 105, 312–**313**
Finger-leaf rodgersia, 328

Fir
Douglas, 78, 225, 226
white, 88, 203–204
Firethorn, 41, 97, 113, 236, 238, 261–262
Florida anise, 88
Flossflower, 111, 354
Flowering tobacco, 49, 57–**58,** 351, 353, **369**–370
Foamflower, 331–**332**
Foeniculum vulgare, 117, **495, 499**
F. v. var. *azoricum,* **475**
Foliage
of bulbs, 50
for color, **23, 32–33**
designing with, **33**
Forget-me-not, 44, **321**
woodland, 89, 93, 353
Forks, 534–535
Formal gardens, **16**–17, 45, 62, 65
Forsythia
F. × intermedia, 79, **182**–183
F. species, 41
Fothergilla
dwarf, 71, 88, **183**
F. gardenii, 71, 88, **183**
F. species, 35, 41
Foundation plantings, 70–71
Fountain grass, 102, **340**–341
Oriental, 340–341
purple, **340**–341
Foxglove, 89, 103, 115, **289,** 293, **311**
Fragaria
F. × ananassa, **441**–443
F. species, 441–443
F. vesca, 441, **442**–443
Franklinia alatamaba, 34, 36, **153**
Franklin tree, 34, 36, **153**
Fraxinus
F. americana, 34, 38, **153**
F. pennsylvanica, 34, 38, 75, 91, 96, 153
Freesia × hybrida, 103, 387, **395**
Fringe tree
Chinese, 37
white, **149**–150
Fritillaria
F. imperialis, 383, **396**
F. meleagris, 50
F. species, 110, 387, 396

Front yards
and entry landscaping, **68–70,** 71
foundation plantings and, 70–71
Frost pockets, 82
Fruits and fruit trees
buying nursery stock, 411
chilling requirements, 412–413
disease prevention, 424
dwarf and semidwarf, 410–**411**
encyclopedia of, **428–445**
espaliers for, **53, 415**
fertilizing, 414
four-arm Kniffen method, 421
fruit-set requirements, 412
grapes, **421**–422, **425**
harvesting, **426**
hedges, 414
interstems, 410–411
maintenance requirements, 410, 412
pest control, **424–425**
pH requirements, 412
planting, 414
pollination, 412–413
pruning and training, 414, **416–419**
rootstock characteristics, 410–411
seed formation, 413
strawberry growing, 420–21
thinning, **410, 418**–419
using in landscape, **52–53**
Fuchsia × hybrida, 57, **115, 362**–363
Fungicides, organic, 552

G

Gaillardia
G. × grandiflora, 47, 105, 117, **313**
G. pulchella, 91, 96, **105,** 110, 117, 348, 353, 363
G. p. 'Red Plume', **363**
Galanthus nivalis, 36, **50**–51, 88, 383, 387, **396,** 399
Galax
G. aphylla, 252
G. urceolata, 89, **252**
Galium odoratum, **23, 43**–44, 107, **252,** 495
Gallica rose, 268, 279
Gardener's garters, 97, 291, **341**
Gardenia jasminoides, 71, 88, **212**

Gardens, special
bird-attracting, **112–115**
butterfly-attracting, **116–117**
for children, **118–119**
country cottage, **100–101**
cutting, **51, 102**–103
meadow and prairie, **104–105**
rock, **110–111**
water, **108–109**
woodland, **106–107**
Garland flower, 71, 88, 211
Gaultheria procumbens, 89, 252–**253**
Gaura
    G. lindheimeri, 22, 25, 47, 91,
        313–314
    white, 22, 25, 47, 91, **313**–314
Gay-feather, 91, 97, **320**
Gazania rigens, 91, 348, **363**
Gelsemium sempervirens, 89, 236, **253**
Genista tinctoria, 41, 91, 96, 183–**184**
Gentian, prairie, 103, 105, 349, 353,
    361–362
Geranium
    G. endressii 'Wargrave Pink',
        46, **314**
    G. × 'Johnson's Blue', 46
    G. sanguineum, 46, 314
    G. species, 19, 44, 110
    hardy, 46, 314
    ivy, 57–**58**, 115, 348, **371**–372
    Martha Washington, **371**–372
    scented, 49, 353, **504**
    zonal, 57, 103, 115, 353, **371**–372
Giant feather grass, **341**
Giant redwood, 78, 229–230
Giant sequoia, 78, 229–230
Ginger
    British Columbia wild, 89, 245
    Canada wild, 245
    European wild, 245
Ginkgo biloba, **34,** 38, 75, **154**
Gladiolus
    Abyssinian, **388**
    G. × hortulanus, 51, 382–383,
        386–387, 396–**397**
    G. hybrids, 103, 115
Gleditsia
    G. triacanthos 'Sunburst', **154**
        G. t. var. *inermis,* 38, 96, 154
Globe amaranth, 91, 102, 348, 353,
    363–364

Glory-of-the-snow, 50–**51**, 382, **391**
Golden-chain tree, 37, **156**
Golden fleece, **48**–49, 57, 61, **361**
Golden marguerite, 47, 298–**299**
Golden-rain tree, 38, 96, **155**–156
Goldenrod, 36, 105, 113, 117,
    330–331
Goldenstar, 89, 107, **247**
Gomphrena globosa, 91, 102, 348,
        353, 363–364
    'Bicolor Rose', **363**
Gooseberry, 433–434
    American cultivars, 433–434
    European cultivars, 433–434
Gophers, 558–559
Gordonia alatamaha, 153
Goutweed, 89, 97, **242**
Grape
    American, **434**
    European, 434–435
Grape hyacinth, **50,** 91, 384, 387, 401
Grasses, lawn (*See also* Lawns)
    Bahia, 563, 570
    Bermuda, 563, 566–567, 570
    blue grama, 563, 565
    buffalo, 563, **565,** 570
    centipede, 563, 570
    drought-tolerant, 95, 563, **565,** 568
    endophyte-enhanced, 564
    fine fescue, 563–564, 566, 570
    Kentucky bluegrass, 563–564, 566,
        568, 570
    lawn-growing regions and, 563
    prairie, **565**
    ryegrass, 563–564, **569**–570
    St. Augustine, 563, 566–**567,** 570
    seeds, 564, 566
    shade-tolerant, 566–**567**
    slow-growing, 564–**565**
    turf-type tall fescue, 563–564, 566,
        568, 570
    zoysia, 563, 567, **569**–570
Grasses, ornamental (See Ornamental
        grasses)
Grecian windflower, **389**–390
Green-and-gold, 89, 107, **247**
Green manure, 455–**456**
Groundcovers
    as edging plants, 19
    encyclopedia of, **242–265**
    environmental issues, 43

planting and caring for, 236,
    240–241
on slopes, 99
using in landscape, 35, 42–**43**
Gum
    black, 34, 38, 89, 93, 113, **160**
    sour, 34, 38, 89, 93, 113, **160**
    sweet, 34, 38, 75, 113, **157**
Gymnocladus dioica, 38, 96, 154–**155**
Gypsophila
    G. paniculata, 91, 97, 102,
        103, **314**
    G. repens, 110

H

Hackberry, common, 89, 93, 96, **148**
Hakonechloa macra 'Aureola', 89,
        289, **337**
Hakone grass, 89, 289, **337**
Halesia
    H. carolina, 89, 155
    H. monticola, **155**
    H. tetraptera, 155
Hamamelis
    H. × intermedia, 35, 184
        H. × i. 'Arnold Promise', **184**
    H. mollis, 36, 184
    H. species, 41, 88, 184
    H. vernalis, 93
    H. virginiana, 35, 184
Harry Lauder's walking stick, 41, **177**
Hawthorn, 38, 113, 115
    Indian, 71, 88, **226**–227
    Washington, 115
    winter king green, **151**–152
Hazelnut, 177, 443–**444**
    corkscrew, 41, **177**
Heart-leaf bergenia, **303**
Heath
    spring, **250**–251
    winter, **250**–251
Heavenly bamboo, 41, 71, 88, 91, **218**
Hedera helix, 57, 89, 236, 239–241,
        253–254
    H. h. 'Goldheart', **253**
Hedges and screens
    evergreen, 78
    for herbaceous borders, 28
    planting, **133**
    plants for, **78–79,** 414

for privacy, **78–79**
pruning, **138–139**
Helenium autumnale, 105, **315**
Helianthus
    H. angustifolius, 91, 97, 105
    H. annuus, 91, 96, 105, **364**
    H. species, 117
    H. tuberosus, **476**
Helichrysum bracteatum, 91, 96, 102,
    117, 348, 353, **364**
Helictotrichon sempervirens, 97
Heliopsis helianthoides, 46, 91, 97, 105
Heliotrope, 49, 57, 103, 117, 353,
    364–**365**
Heliotropium arborescens, 49, 57,
    103, 117, 353, 364–365
    H. a. 'Marine', **365**
Helleborus
    H. niger, 46, 89
    H. orientalis, **315**
    H. species, 103
Hemerocallis
    H. fulva, 89
    H. hybrids, 46–47, 50, **295,**
    315–316
    H. 'Stella de Oro', 47, **315**–316
Hemlock, Canadian or Eastern,
    88, **232**
Herbaceous plants and borders,
    22, **28**
Herbs, 494–495
    in container gardens, 54–**55**, 56
    as edging plants, 19
    encyclopedia of, **496–505**
    garden design, **54–55**
    using in landscape, **52–53**
Heuchera
    H. micrantha 'Palace Purple',
    19, 57
        H. m. 'Rachel', **316**
    H. sanguinea, 316
    H. species, 25, 44, 110, 115
Hibiscus
    H. moscheutos, 22, 316–317
        H. m. 'Disco Belle', **316**
    H. syriacus, 35, 79, 96, 115,
    184–185
        H. s. 'Aphrodite', **185**
Hoes, 536–537
Holly, 35, 41, 88, 113, 124, 135,
    187–188, 212–214

blue, 71, 113, 213–214
Chinese, 212–213
deciduous, 88, 91, 93, **187**–188
English, **212**–213
Japanese, 79, 213–214
Meserve, 71, 113, 213–214
yaupon, 213–214
Hollyhock, 115, 117, 289, **297**–298
Holly osmanthus, 41, 79, 88, 218–219
Honesty, 89, 102, 353
Honeysuckle, 79, 96, 113, 115, 236,
    238, 257–258
    boxleaf, 79, 88, 216–217
    fragrant, 88, **191**
    goldflame, 89, 238, **257**–258
    Japanese, 43, 239, 257–258
    trumpet, 97, 115, **257**–258
    winter, 88, **191**
Hornbeam
    American, 89, 93, **147**
    fastigiate European, 38
Hoses and accessories, 542–543, **545**
Hosta
    H. 'Golden Tiara', **317**
    H. medio-picta, **25**
    H. species and hybrids, 19, 22, **33,**
    57, **84,** 89, 295, 317
    H. Thomas Hoag', **87**
    H. undulata variegata, **87**
Hot caps, 452–**453**
Hummingbird gardens, 114–**115**
Hyacinth
    Dutch, 50–51, 382–384, 397–398
    grape, **50**, 91, 384, 387, 401
    water, 109
    wood, 88, **397**
Hyacinthoides hispanica, 88, 397
    H. h. 'Blue Queen', **397**
Hyacinthus
    H. 'Lord Balfour', **397**
    H. orientalis, 50–51, 382–384,
    397–398
Hydrangea
    climbing, 43, 89, 236, 238, **254**
    French, 71, 88, 185–186
    H. anomala subsp. *petiolaris,* 43,
    89, 236, 238, **254**
    H. arborescens 'Annabelle', **185**–186
        H. a. 'Grandiflora', 185–186
    H. macrophylla, 71, 88, 185–186

    H. paniculata 'Grandiflora',
    185–186
    H. quercifolia, 35, 37, 88, 185–186
    H. species, 185–186
    oakleaf, 35, 37, 88, 185–186
    peegee, 185–186
    smooth, 185–186
Hylotelephium
    H. 'Autumn Joy', **36, 46**–47,
    102, **330**
    H. species, 330
Hypericum
    H. frondosum, 91, 186–**187**
    H. species, 71, 41
Hypoestes phyllostachya, 49,
    57, 365
    H. p. 'White Splash', **365**

I

Iberis sempervirens, 19, 44, 110,
    117, **317**
Ilex
    I. aquifolium, **212**–213
    I. cornuta, 212–213
        I. c. 'Burfordii Nana', 71
    I. crenata, 79, 213–214
        I. c. 'Hetzii', 71, **213**–214
    I. decidua, 88, 91, 93, **187**–188
    I. glabra, 79, 93, 213–214
    I. × *meserveae,* 71, 113, 213–214
    I. species, 35, 41, 88, 113, 124, 135,
    187–188, 212–214
    I. verticillata, 41, 79, 88, 93, 113,
    187–188
    I. virginica, 35
    I. vomitoria, 213–214
Illicium floridanum, 88
Impatiens
    I. 'Deco Orange', **365**–366
    I. wallerana, 19, 26, 57, 88, 348,
    351, 353, 365–366
Imperata cylindrica 'Red Baron',
    337–**338**
Incense cedar, 78, 88, 205–**206**
Indian bean, 89, 93, 147–**148**
Indian hawthorn, 71, 88, 226–227
Indigo
    blue false 105, 117, **302**–303
    kirilow, 41, **188**
    wild blue, 105, 117, **302**–303

Indigofera kirilowii, 41, **188**
Informal gardens, 16–**17**
Inkberry, 79, 93, 213–214
Insecticides (*See* Pesticides)
Insects (*See also* Pesticides)
　beneficial, 459, 546–547
　controlling, 547–551
　guide to, 549–551
　identifying, 548
　in lawns, 564, 573
　preventing, 546–547, 549–551
　on roses, 274–275
　traps for, 548
　on vegetables, 459, 546
Integrated pest management
　　(IPM), 548
Intensive vegetable gardening,
　　449–**450,** 451
Ipheion uniflorum, 50, **398**
Ipomoea
　I. batatas, 488–**489**
　I. lobata, 259
　I. × *multifida,* 91, 236, **254**
　I. species, 115, 236, 254–255
　I. tricolor, 91, 97, 117,
　　236–**237, 254**
Iris
　bearded, 97, 103, 318–319
　crested, 107, **318–319**
　Dutch, 398–**399**
　I. cristata, 107, **318**–319
　I. danfordiae, 110
　I. ensata, 93, **318**–319
　I. × *germanica,* 97, 103, 318–319
　I. kaempferi, 318–319
　I. laevigata, 93
　I. pseudacorus, **92**–93, 109
　I. reticulata, 50, 110, 387, **398**–399
　I. sibirica, 93, 318–319
　I. versicolor, 109
　I. xiphium, 398–**399**
　Japanese, 318–319
　reticulated, 50, 110, 387, **398**–399
　Siberian, 93, 318–319
Ironwood, 89, 93, **147**
Irrigation systems, 544–**545**
Island beds, 28–**29**
Itea
　I. japonica, 88
　I. virginica, 35, 41, 71, 93, **188**
　　I. v. 'Henry's Garnet', 35, 188

Ivy, English, 57, 89, 236, 239–241,
　253–254
Ivy geranium, 57–**58**, 115, 348,
　371–372

J

Jack-in-the-pulpit, **390**
Jacob's ladder, 107
Japanese blood grass, 337–**338**
Japanese laurel, 41, 88, **204**
Japanese plum yew, 88, 207–208
Japanese rose, 37, 41, 88, 96, **189**
Japanese skimmia, 41, 71, 88, **230**
Japanese snowbell, 89, **167**–168
Japanese wind grass, 89, 289, **337**
Jasmine
　common, 255
　Confederate, 89, 236, 263–**264**
　poet's, 236, 255
　star, 89, 236, 263–**264**
　winter, 89, 91, 255
Jasminum
　J. nudiflorum, 89, 91, 255
　J. officinale, 255
　J. polyanthum, **255**
　J. species, 236, 255
Jerusalem artichoke, **476**
Jessamine, yellow, 89, 236, **253**
Joe-Pye weed, 93, 105, 117, 312
Johnny-jump-up, 353
Jonquil, 402, 403
Juglans
　J. cinerea, 445
　J. nigra, **445**
Juniper
　Chinese, 71, 78, 91, 214–215
　creeping, **43,** 71, 91, 97, 110,
　　255–**256**
　dwarf Japanese garden, 71, 110
　Pfitzerana Chinese, 97
　Rocky Mountain, 71, 78, 91, 97,
　　110, **214**–215
　savin, 97, **256**
　shore, 71, 89, 91, 97, 110, **255**–256
Juniperus
　J. chinensis, 71, 78, 91, 214–215
　J. conferta, 71, 89, 91, 97, 110
　　J. c. 'Blue Pacific', **255**–256
　J. horizontalis, **43,** 71, 91, 97, 110,
　　255–**256**

J. × *media,* 214–215
　J. × *m.* 'Pfitzerana', 97
J. procumbens var. 'Nana', 71, 110
J. sabina, 97, **256**
J. scopulorum, 91, 97, 214–215
　J. s. 'Skyrocket', 110, **214**–215
　J. s. 'Welchii', 71, 78
J. species, **95**, 113, 214–215
J. squamata, 97
J. virginiana, 75, 78, 91, 97,
　214–215

K

Kale, 49, 449, 451, 457, **476**–477
Kalmia latifolia, 88, 141, **215**
Kamschatka bugbane, 107, **306**
Katsura tree, 34, 89, **148**–149
Kentucky coffee tree, 38, 96, 154–**155**
Kerria japonica, 37, 41, 88, 96, 189
　K. j. 'Picta', **189**
Kinnikinick, 89, 91, 93, 97, **244**
Kiwi, hardy, 435
Koelreuteria paniculata, 38, 96,
　155–156
Kohlrabi, 449, 451, 457, **477**
Kolkwitzia amabilis, 96, 115, **189**
Kolomikta vine, 89, 236, **242**
Kudzu, 239

L

Laburnum × ***watereri,*** 37, 156
　L. × *w.* 'Vossii', **156**
Lace shrub, 35, 71, 79, **198**–199
Lactuca sativa, 448–449, **450**–451,
　457, 477–**478**
Lady's eardrops, 57, **115, 362**–363
Lady's-mantle, 898, **298**
Lady tulip, 405–406
Lagerstroemia indica, 34, 96, 156
　L. i. 'Tuskegee', **156**
Lamb's-ears, **19,** 44, 91, 97, **331**
Lamium maculatum, 19, 44, 89, 319
　L. m. 'Pink Pewter', **319**
Landscape design elements
　axes, 20, 28
　balance, **24**
　beds and borders, **18**–19
　color, **22–23,** 24, **30–37**
　contrast, **22–23,** 24, **33**

edging, **19**
focal points, 20–**21**, 100, 101
foliage, **33**
hardscape, **20**, 24
harmony, 24
house style and, 17
outdoor rooms, **14–15**
plant combinations, **22–29**
rhythm, 24–**25**
shady gardens, **87**
shape, **18**–19, 22, **54**
for small spaces, 15
structure, 20–21, 54, **64–65**
style, **16–17**
texture, **22–23**
visual weight, 12–29
and Xeriscapes, **94–95**
Landscape fabric, 452–**453**, **524**–525
Landscape planning
assessing site and needs, 8–9,
  10–11
building codes and, 12
climate considerations, 8–9, 80–83
drawings, **8–9**, 13
for energy conservation, 83
maintenance considerations, 10–11
professionals for, 13
vegetable gardens and, **448**–449
Lantana
  L. camara, 57, 366
    L. c. 'Pink Caprice', **366**
  L. species, 115, 117
Larch, 123
American, 93
European, **157**
golden, **163**
Japanese, 156–157
Larix
  L. decidua, **157**
  L. kaempferi, 156–157
  L. laricina, 93
  L. species, 123
Larkspur, 348, 349
rocket, 103, 105, 115, 117, 353, **359**
Lathyrus odoratus, **49**, 103, 353,
  366–367
Laurel
cherry or English, 71, 88, **225**
Japanese, 41, 88, **204**
mountain, 88, 141, **215**

Lavandula
  L. angustifolia, 44–46, 91, **94–95,**
    97, 102, **495,** 499
    L. a. 'Hidcote', 44, **499**
    L. a. 'Munstead Dwarf', 19
  L. officinalis, 499
  L. spica, 499
  L. vera, 499
Lavender, 499
English, 19, 44–46, 91, **94–95,** 97,
  102, **495, 499**
Lavender cotton, 44–45, 91
Lawns (*See also* Grasses, lawn)
aerating, 572–573
for climate control, 81
compacted, 572–573
disease prevention, 573
edging, **19,** 562
environmental issues, 562
fertilizing, 516, 563, 569, 571
growing regions, 563
lower maintenance, 563, 565
mowing and trimming, 562,
  570–571
native grasses as, **565**
overseeding, **569**
reducing, **562**
removing, 518–519, 568
renovating and patching, **568**–569
in shade, 29, **566–567**
starting, **566**–567
thatch in, 572
watering, 568
weeds in, 562, 573
in Xeriscapes, 95
Layering methods, 530–531
Leadwort, 44, 89, 246–**247**
Leaf cleanup tools, 540–541
Leatherwood, 88, 93, 180–**181**
Leek, 449, 457, **477**
Lemon balm, 54, 495, **500**
Lenten rose, **315** (See *Helleborus
  orientalis*)
Lepidium sativum, 449, 472–**473**
Lespedeza thunbergii, 41, 71, 91,
  189–190
  L. t. 'Gibraltar', **189**–190
Lettuce, 448–449, **450**–451, 457,
  477–**478**

Leucanthemum × *superbum,* 103,
  319–320
  L. × *s.* 'Marconi', **319**–320
Leucojum
  L. aestivum, 88, **399**
  L. species, 383, 387
  L. vernum, 399
Leucothoe
drooping, 37, 88, 215–**216**
  L. fontanesiana, 37, 88, 215–**216**
  L. species, 71
Levisticum officinale, 495, **500**
Leyland cypress, 78–79, **210**
Liatris
  L. species, 105
  L. spicata, 91, 97, 320
    L. s. 'Kobold', **320**
Ligularia species, 89
Ligustrum
  L. japonicum, **216**
  L. ovalifolium, 190
  L. species, 28, 79, 113, **133**
  L. vulgare 'Lodense', **190**
Lilac, 41, 79, 96, 199–200
common, 199–**200**
Japanese tree, 38, **168**
Meyer or dwarf, 71, 199–200
summer, 41, 115, 117, 172–**173**
Lilium
  L. × *aurelianense* 'Thunderbolt',
    399–400
  L. canadense, 93
  L. 'Enchantment', **399**–400
  L. martagon, 88
  L. Oriental hybrid 'Casa
    Blanca', **400**
  L. species and hybrids, 26, 51, 103,
    117, 383, 384, 385, **387,**
    399–400
Lily
African, 88, 388
atamasco, **407**
Asiatic and Aurelian hybrids,
  399–400
blackberry, 97
calla, 93, 103, **407**
canna, 22, 57, 115, **391**
checkered, 50
magic, 88, 400–**401**
naked-lady, 88, 400–**401**
Oriental hybrids, **399**–400

Peruvian, 103, 387
rain, **407**
resurrection, 88, 400–**401**
trout, **23**, 107, 395
water, **108–109**
Lily leek, 388–**389**
Lily-of-the-Nile, 88, 388
Lily-of-the-valley, 89, 103, 249–**250**
Lily-of-the valley bush, 71, **124,** 221
Lilyturf
  blue, 89, 320–321
  creeping, 89, 97, 241, 257
Lima bean, 457, **478**
Limonium sinuatum, 102, 353, **367**
Linden
  littleleaf, 38, **169**
  silver, 38, **169**
  small-leaved, 38, **169**
Lindera benzoin, 35, 88, 113, 117,
  190–191
Liquidambar styraciflua, 34, 38,
  75, 113, **157**
  L. s. 'Burgundy', 34
Liriodendron tulipifera, 34, 38, 115,
  117, **157**–158
Liriope
  L. muscari, 89, 320–321
    L. m. 'Variegata', 19, 57, **320**–321
  L. spicata, 89, 97, 241, 257
Lisianthus, 103, 105, 349, 353,
  361–362
Loam, **509**
Lobelia
  edging, 19, 36, 57, 61, 110,
    115, **367**
  L. erinus, 19, 36, 57, 61, 110,
    115, **367**
Lobularia maritima, 19, 22, **48–49**,
  61, 88, 91, 110, **111,** 117,
  348–349, **351**–353, **367–368**
  L. m. 'Wonderland', **30**
Locust
  black, 75, 91, 97, 115, 117, **165**–166
  thornless honey, 38, 96, 154
London plane tree, 38, **161**–162
Lonicera
  L. fragrantissima, 88, **191**
  L. × heckrottii, 89, 238, **257**–258
  L. japonica, 43, 239, 257–258
  L. nitida, 79, 88, 216–217
    L. n. 'Baggesen's Gold', **216**–217

L. sempervirens, 97, 115, **257**–258
L. species, 79, 96, 113, 115, 236,
  238, 257–258
Lovage, 495, **500**
Love-in-a-mist, 49, 96, 102, 103, 105,
  110, 353, **370**–371
Low-maintenance landscaping, 10, 43,
  95, 563, 565
Lunaria annua, 89, 102, 353
Lungwort, 327–328
Lupine, 103, 105, **321**
Lupinus
  L. hybrids, 103, **321**
  L. species, 105
  L. texensis, 91, 105, **368, 511**
Lycopersicon esculentum, 448, 450,
  457, 460–**461,** 489–**490**
Lycoris squamigera, 88, 400–**401**
Lyme grass, blue, 97, 105, 336
Lysimachia nummularia, 89, 258
  L. n. 'Aurea', 19, **258**

M

Magnolia
  M. grandiflora, 88, 93, **217**
  M. × *soulangiana,* 89, **158**
  M. species, 217
  M. stellata, 158
  M. tomentosa, 158
  M. virginiana, 93, 217
  saucer, 89, **158**
  Southern, 88, 93, **217**
  star, 158
Mahonia
  leatherleaf, 97, **217**–218
  M. aquifolium, 88, 97, 217–218
  M. bealei, 97, **217**–218
  M. species, 41
Maidenhair fern, 89, 107, **342**
Maidenhair tree, **34,** 38, 75, **154**
Mail-order nurseries, **526**–527
Mallow
  marsh, 495
  rose, 22, **316**–317
Malus
  M. domestica, **53,** 410–**411,**
    414, **428**
  M. floribunda, 27, 115, 158–159
    M. f. 'Snowdrift', **159**
  M. species, **38, 113,** 122

Maple, 85, 113, 142–145
  Amur, 38, 75, 96, 142–143
  coral-bark, 37
  cutleaf, 142
  Freeman, 34, 144
  full moon, 142
  hedge, 38, 91, 142–143
  Japanese, **24,** 34, 37, 89, 142
  Norway, 34, 74, 143–144
  paperback, 34, 37, **142**–143
  red, 34, 38, 93, 143–144
  Shantung, 34, 38
  silver, 91, 93, 123, 143–144
  sugar, 34, 143–144
  Tatarian, 38
  trident, 38
  vine, 34
Marigold, 32, 96, 103, 117, 348–349,
  351, 353, **376**–377
  African, 113, **376**–377
  French, 57, **376**–377
  marsh, 109
  pot, 36, 91, 96, 103, 349, 353, **356**
  signet, 19, **376**–377
Marjoram, **500**–501
Marsh mallow, 495
Marsh marigold, 109
Matteuccia pensylvanica, 93,
  107, **344**
Matthiola incana, 49, 103, 353,
  368–369
  M. i. 'Column Mix', **368**
Mattocks, 534
Mazus reptans, 89, 93, **258**–259
Meadow gardens, **104–105**
Meadow saffron, 36, 392
Mealy-cup sage, 57, 103, 353,
  374–375
Melampodium paludosum, 49, 57,
  91, 110, 348, 369
  M. p. 'Showster', **369**
Melic, silky-spike, **338**
Melica ciliata, **338**
Melissa officinalis, 54, 495, **500**
Melon, 457, 478–**479**
Mentha
  M. × *piperita,* **501**
  M. requienii, 61, **501**
  M. species, 119, 501
  M. spicata, **494, 501**
  M. suaveolens, **501**

Mertensia virginica, **106**–107
Metasequoia glyptostroboides, 78, 123, **159**
Mexican sunflower, 49, 91, 117, 348, **377**
Mice, 558–559
Michaelmas daisy, 300–301
Microbiota decussata, 71, **259**
Microclimates, 80–81
Milium effusum 'Aureum', **338**
Millet
golden wood, **338**
hairy, **338**
Mimosa, 115, **145**–146
Mimulus × hybridus, 93
Mina lobata, 236, **259**
Mint, 119, 501
Apple, **501**
Corsican, 61, 501
Miscanthus sinensis, 102, 293, 338–339
M. s. 'Zebrinus', **339**
Mist flower, 89, **312**
Mock orange, 41, 96
Molina caerula, 105
Moluccella laevis, 49, 102, 353, **369**
Monarda
M. didyma, 46, 115, 117, **496**
M. species, 105
Mondo grass, 240–241, **257**
black, 339
Money plant, 89, 102, 353
Moneywort, 89, 258
Monkey-flower, 93
Monkshood, 89, 103, 107, 297
Montbretia, 392
Morning glory, 91, 97, 117, 236–**237, 254**
Moss pink, 61, **106**, 110, 325, 326
Moss rose, **48,** 61, 91, 96, 113, **283,** 348, 353, 373–**374**
Mother-of-thyme, 61, 505
Mountain bluet, 46, **305**
Mountain laurel, 88, 141, **215**
Mountain snowbell, **155**
Mowers, **540,** 562, 570
Mugwort, 300(
silver mound, 44, 300
Mulch
choosing and using, **522–524,** 525
for disease prevention, **522,** 552

gravel and stone, **508, 524**
organic, 458
plastic, 452–**453**
for trees and shrubs, 134–**135**
in vegetable gardens, **448,** 458–**459**
for weed control, **522,** 553
Mum, garden, 103, 308–309
Muscari
M. armeniacum 'Blue Spike', **401**
M. botryoides, **50**, 91, 384, 387, 401
Mustard greens, **53, 479**–480
Myosotis
M. scorpioides, 44, **321**
M. sylvatica, 89, 93, 353
Myrica
M. cerifera, 79
M. pensylvanica, 41, 79, 91, 96, 113, **191**
Myriophyllum
M. aquaticum, 109
M. species, 109
Myrtle, 89, 240, **241, 264**
wax, 79

N

Nandina domestica, 41, 71, 88, 91, **218**
Narcissus
N. cyclamineus, 402
N. c. 'Tete-a-tete', **401,** 403
N. jonquilla, 402, 403
N. poeticus, 402, 403
N. species and hybrids, **26,** 50–51, 103, **382–384,** 387, 401–403
N. tazetta, 385, **402**–403
N. triandrus, 403
paper-white, 385, **402**–403
poet's, 402, 403
Nasturtium, 57, 348, **349,** 353, 378
Natural gardens, 16–**17,** 62
Nectarine, 436–437
Nepeta
N. × faassenii, 44–45, 47, 321–**322**
N. species, 91, 97
Nicotiana
N. affinis, 369
N. alata, 49, 57–**58,** 351, 353, **369**–370
N. langsdorffii, 369–**370**
N. species, 57, 115, 69–370
N. sylvestris, **370**

Nigella damascena, 49, 96, 102, 103, 105, 110, 353, **370**–371
Non-native vines, 239
Nurseries and garden centers, 526–527
Nutrients in soil, 509, 510, 512–513, 516, 521
Nut trees (*See also* Fruits and fruit trees)
growing tips, 426
harvesting nuts, 427
pruning and training, 416–419
using in landscape, **52**–53
Nymphaea species, **108–109**
Nyssa sylvatica, 34, 38, 89, 93, 113, **160**

O

Oak, 34, 38, 113, 164–165
Burr, 96
live, **226**
native willow, 165
Northern red, 165
pin, 93, **164**–165
possum, 75, 93, 164
sawtooth, 164–165
swamp white, 93
water, 93
white, 93
Obedient plant, 46, 105, **326**
Ocimum basilicum, **496**
Odessa, **200**–201
Oenothera
O. berlandieri, 97, 322, 323
O. fruticosa, 322, 323
O. speciosa, 46, 91, **322,** 323
O. tetragona, 46, 105, **322,** 323
Ohio buckeye, 89, 96, 115, 145
Okra, **480**
Old-man's-beard, **149**–150
Olive
autumn, 91, **181**
Russian, 96, **152**
Onion, 457, **480**
Persian, 103, 388–389
Ophiopogon
O. japonicus, 240–241, **257**
O. planiscapus 'Ebony Knight', **339**
O. p. 'Nigrescens', 339
Orange, hardy or trifoliate, 37, 162

Orchid, peacock, **388**
Oregano, 501–**502**
Oregon holly grape, 88, 97, 217–218
Organic matter, 90, **456,** 508–509, **510,** 521
Origanum
   O. majorana, **500**–501
   O. vulgare subsp. *hirtum,* 501–**502**
Ornamental grasses, 113, 269
   caring for, **293**
   encyclopedia of, **334–341**
   in meadows and prairies, **104**–105
   for off-season color, 35, **36**
   planting, 291
   types of, 289
   using in landscape, **47**
Osmanthus
   O. heterophyllus, 41, 79, 88, 218–219
      O. h. 'Gulftide', **218**–219
Osmunda
   O. cinnamomea, 89, 93, 107, 344, 345
   O. regalis, 93, 107, **344**–345
Oswego tea, 46, 115, 117, **496**
Outdoor rooms, **14–15**
Oxeye
   daisy, 105
   sweet, 46, 91, 97, 105
Oxydendrum arboreum, 34, 89, **160**

P

Pachistima canbyi, 261
Pachysandra terminalis, 89, **240,** 241, **259**–260
Paeonia
   P. lactiflora, 103, **288,** 289, 294, **323**
   P. suffruticosa, 88, 191–**192**
Pagoda tree, Japanese, 38, 97, **166**
Pak choi, 451, **465**–466
Pampas grass
   dwarf, 97, **335**
   hardy, **336**–337
Panicum virgatum, 97, 105, 339–340
   P. v. 'Heavy Metal', **339**–340
Pansy, 36, **53,** 57, 88, 103, **348,** 353, 378–**379**

Papaver
   P. orientale, **323**–324
   P. rhoeas, 105, 353, **371**
   P. species, 91, 96, 103, 353, **511**
Paper-white narcissus, 385, **402**–403
Papyrus, 109
Parrotia persica, 34, 37, 89, **160**–161
Parrot's-feather, 109
Parsley, 53, 55, 117, 495, **502**
   Chinese, **498**
Parsnip, 449, 457, **481**
Parthenocissus
   P. quinquefolia, 89, 97, 113, 260
   P. tricuspidata, 97, 113, 236, 239, **260**
Passiflora, 236
   P. alata, **260**
   P. caerulea, 260
Passion flower, blue, 260
Pastinaca sativa, 449, 457, **481**
Paths, **46,** 54, 62–**63,** 100
Patios, **14,** 60–**61, 68,** 101
Paving materials, **14–15,** 61–**62,** 63, 101
Pawpaw, 435–**436**
Paxistima canbyi, **261**
Pea, 449–**451,** 457, **481**–482
Peach, **436**
Peanut, **482**
Pear, 437–438
   Asian, **437**–438
   Bradford, 34, **164**
   Callery, 34, **164**
Pecan, **444**
Pelargonium
   P. domesticum, **371**–372
   P. × hortorum, 57, 103, 115, 353, **371**–372
   P. peltatum, 57–**58,** 115, 348, **371**–372
   P. species, 49, 353, **504**
Pennisetum
   P. alopecuroides, 102, **340**–341
      P. a. 'Atropurpureum', **340**–341
   P. orientale, 340–341
   P. setaceum 'Rubrum', 57, 340–341
Pennyroyal, 495
Penstemon species, 115

Peony
   Chinese, 103, **288,** 289, 294, **323**
   garden, 103, **288,** 289, 294, **323**
   tree, 88, 191–**192**
Pepper; bell, sweet, or hot, 457, 482–**483**
Pepperidge, 34, 38, 89, 93, 113, **160**
Peppermint, **501**
Perennials
   buying by mail, 25, 527
   caring for, 292–295
   cutting back, 295
   defined, **288**–289
   dividing, 294–**295,** 530–531
   double digging of beds, 518–519
   as edging plants **19**
   encyclopedia of, **296–333**
   fertilizing, 516–**517**
   interplanting with bulbs, 384, **387**
   longest-blooming, **46–47**
   mulching of beds, 523
   for off-season color, **36,** 46
   planting, 25, 290–291
   tender, 349
   winter protection for, 295
Perilla frutescens, 49, 372
   P. f. 'Crispa', **372**
Periwinkle, 357
   common, 89, 240, **241, 264**
   large, 57
Perovskia atriplicifolia, 47, **55,** 57, 91, 97, **324**
Persian parrotia, 34, 37, 89, **160**–161
Persimmon
   American, **438**
   Japanese, **438**
Peruvian lily, 103, 387
Pesticides
   and fruit trees, 424–425
   organic, 547
   safety precautions with, 534, 541, 548
   tools for applying, **135,** 548
   for tree pests, **135**
   using, 548
   and wildlife, 117
Pests, animal, 425–426, 459, **556**–559
Pests, insect (See Insects)
Petroselinum crispum, **53, 55,** 117, 495, **502**

Petunia
  P. × *hybrida,* 49, 57–**58,** 91, 103, 115, 117, 348, **352–353,** 372–**373**
  P. × *integrifolia,* **48**
Phalaris arundinacea 'Picta', 97, 291, **341**
Phaseolus
  P. coccineus, 115, **463**–464
  P. limensis, **478**
  P. lunatus, 457, **478**
    P. l. 'Fordhook', 457, **478**
  P. species, 449–451, **461,** 463–464
  P. vulgaris, **463**–464
Phellodendron amurense, 38, **161**
Philadelphus
  P. coronarius, 88, **192**
  P. species, 41, 96
Phlox
  annual, 49, 105, 115, 117, 353, 373
  blue, 103, 324, 325
  Carolina, 46
  creeping, 89, 107, 325
  garden, 46–47, 103, 288, **324**–325
  moss, 61, **106,** 110, 325, 326
  P. divaricata, 103, 324, 325
  P. drummondii, 49, 105, 115, 117, 353, 373
    P. d. 'Dwarf Beauty Blue', **373**
  P. maculata, 46
  P. paniculata, 46–47, 103, 288, **324**–325
  P. pilosa, 107
  P. species, 117
  P. stolonifera, 89, 107, 325
    P. s. 'Bruce's White', 325
  P. subulata, 61, **106,** 110, 325, 326
  wild blue, 103, 324, 325
pH of soil, 509, **511**–512
Photinia
  Chinese, **219**
  Fraser, 79, 88, 219
  P. × *fraseri,* 79, 88, 219
  P. serrulata, **219**
  P. species, 41
  red-tip, 79, 88, 219
Physalis ixocarpa, **489**
Physostegia virginiana, 105, 326
  P. v. 'Alba', **326**
  P. v. 'Vivid', 46

Picea
  P. abies, 110, 219–220
  P. glauca, 88, 91, 110, 219–220
  P. omorika, 219–220
  P. orientalis, 91, 110, 219–220
    P. o. 'Aurea-Spicata', **219**–220
    P. o. 'Whittgold', **123**
  P. pungens var. *glauca,* 110, **220**–221
  P. species, 37, 113, 219–221
Pickerel rush, 109
Pieris
  Japanese, 71, **124,** 221
  P. floribunda, **221**
  P. japonica, 71, **124,** 221
  P. species, 88, 141, 221
Pincushion flower, 47, 110, 113, 117, **329**
Pine, 37, **39,** 78, 113, 137, 221–224
  Austrian, 97, 223–224
  bristlecone, 97
  dragon's eye, **223**–224
  dwarf white, 71, 110, **125**
  Eastern white, 71, 221–**222**
  Himalayan, 222
  Jack, 97
  Japanese black, 75, 223–224
  Japanese red, 223–224
  Japanese white, 75, 221–222
  Korean, 221–222
  lace-bark, 37, **222**–223
  limber, 75, 88, 97, 221–222
  loblolly, 93, 222–223
  longleaf, 223
  mountain, 71, 97, 110, 223–224
  Mugo, 71, 97, 110, 223–224
  pinyon, 97
  pitch, 91, 97
  Ponderosa, 97
  red, **123,** 223–224
  Scotch, 97, 110, 223–224
  slash, 93, 223
  umbrella, 88, **229**
  Virginia, 223–224
Pink
  China, 49, 91, 110, 117, 348, 353, 360–361
  cottage, 110, **309**–310

  garden, 117, 309–310
  maiden, 309–310
Pinus
  P. aristata, 97
  P. banksiana, 97
  P. bungeana, 37, **222**–223
  P. densiflora, 223–224
    P. d. 'Oculis-Draconis', **223**–224
  P. edulis, 97
  P. elliottii, 93, 223
  P. flexilis, 75, 88, 97, 221–222
  P. koraiensis, 221–222
  P. mugo, 71, 97, 110, 223–224
  P. nigra, 97, 223–224
  P. palustris, 223
  P. parviflora, 75, 221–222
  P. ponderosa, 97
  P. resinosa, **123,** 223–224
  P. rigida, 91, 97
  P. species, 37, **39,** 78, 113, 137, 221–224
  P. strobus, 71, 221–**222**
    P. s. 'Soft Touch', 71, 110, **125**
  P. sylvestris, 97, 110, 223–224
  P. taeda, 93, 222–223
  P. thunbergiana, 75, 223–224
  P. virginiana, 223–224
  P. wallichiana, 222
Pipe vine, 117, 236, **244**
Pistachio, Chinese, **161**
Pistacia chinensis, **161**
Pistia stratiotes, 109
Pisum sativum, 449–**451,** 457, **481**–482
Pittosporum
  Japanese, 88, 224–225
  P. tobira, 88, 224–225
    P. t. 'Variegata', **224**–225
    P. t. 'Wheeler's Dwarf', 71
Plaintain lily, 19, 22, **33,** 57, **84,** 89, 295, 317
Platanus
  P. × *acerifolia* 'Bloodgood', 38, **161**–162
  P. occidentalis, 93, 162
  P. species, 37
Platycodon grandiflorus, 47, 294
  P. g. 'Double Blue', **326**
Plum, purple-leaf, 162–163
Plumbago, 44, 89, 246–**247**
Plum yew, Japanese, 88, 207–208

Podocarpus macrophyllus, 78–79, 88, **225**
Polemonium caeruleum, 107
Polianthes tuberosa, 103, **403**
Polka-dot plant, 49, 57, **365**
Polygonum
    P. aubertii, 89, 97, **261**
    P. biflorum, 107
Polystichum
    P. acrostichoides, 57, 89, 107, **345**
    P. munitum, 89, **345**
    P. setiferum, 107, **345**
Poncirus trifoliata, 37, **162**
Ponds and pools, **108–109,** 113, **114**
Pontederia cordata, 109
Poplar, 37
    white, 91
    yellow, 34, 38, 115, 117, **157**–158
Poppy, 91, 96, 103, 353, **511**
    California, 61, 91,96, 105, 110, 113, 348**–349,** 353, **361**
    Celandine, **106**
    corn, 105, 353, **371**
    Flanders, 105, 353, **371**
    Oriental, **323**–324
    Shirley, 105, 353, **371**
Populus
    P. alba, 91
    P. species, 37
Porcelain-berry, tricolor, **243**–244
Portulaca grandiflora, **48,** 61, 91, 96, 113, **283,** 348, 353, 373–374
    P. g. 'Sundial Peppermint', **374**
Possum haw, 88, 91, 93, **187**–188
Potato, 449, **483**–484
    sweet, 488**–489**
Potentilla fruticosa, 41, 71, 91, 96, 192–193
    P. f. 'Goldfinger', **192**–193
Pot marigold, 36, 91, 96, 103, 349, 353, **356**
Potting soil, 58–59, 528
Powdery mildew, 275, **552,** 555
Prairie gardens, **104–105**
Prairie gentian, 103, 105, 349, 353, **361**–362
Primrose, 89, 117, 326–327
    English, **327**
    evening, 46, 91, **322,** 323
    Japanese, 93, 326–327

polyanthus, **327**
showy, 89, 97, 117, 326–327
Primula
    P. japonica, 93, 326–327
    P. × *polyantha,* **327**
    P. species, 89, 117, 326–327
    P. vulgaris, 327
Privacy
    berms for, 78–79
    fences for, 15, 65, **75–**77
    hedges and screen plantings for, **78–79**
    options for creating, **74–75**
    for outdoor rooms, 14, 15
Privet, 28, 79, 113, **133**
    California, 190
    Japanese, **216**
    wax-leaf, **216**
Propagating plants, 530–531
Prunus
    P. armeniaca, **428**
    P. avium, **430**–431
    P. × *cerasifera* 'Atropurpurea', 162–163
    P. cerasus, **430**–431
        P. c. 'Montmorency', **413,** 431
    P. domestica, 439
    P. dulcis, **443**
    P. japonica × *jaquemontii,* 431
    P. laurocerasus, 88, 225
        P. l. 'Otto Luyken', 71, **225**
    P. maackii, **37,** 162–163
    P. × 'Okame', 34, **162**–163
    P. persica, 436
        P. p. 'Redhaven Peach', **436**
        P. p. var. *nucipersica,* 436–437
    P. salicina, **439**
    P. serrulata, 34, 163
    P. species, 37, 162–163, 430–431, 439
    P. subhirtella var. *pendula,* 163
    P. tomentosa, **431**
Pruning
    fruit and nut trees, **416–418,** 419
    roses, 272–273
    safety precautions, 136
    shrubs, 137, **138,** 139–141
    thinning, 136
    tools and techniques for, 538–539
    trees, 136, **137**–138**, 140**
    vines, 238–239

Pseudolarix
    P. amabilis, 163
    P. kaempferi, **163**
Pseudotsuga menziesii, 78, 225–226
    P. m. 'Glauca', **226**
Pulmonaria
    P. officinalis, 327–328
    P. saccharata, 19, 89, 327–328
        P. s. 'Mrs. Moon', **327–**328
    P. species, 115, 327–328
Pumpkin, 449, 487**–488**
Purple coneflower, 91, 97, 103, 105, 113, 117, 311–312
Purple-leaf plum, 162–163
Purple osier, 88, 93, **196**
Pussy willow, 93, 196
Pyracantha
    P. coccinea, 41, 97, 113, 236, 238, 261–262
    P. × 'Mohave', **41, 261**–262
Pyrus
    P. calleryana 'Bradford', 34, **164**
        P. c. 'Redspire', 34
    P. communis, 437–438
        P. c. 'Honeysweet', **437**–438
    P. serotina, 437–438
        P. s. 'Chojuro', **437**–438

Q

Quaking grass, 102, 105, **334**
Queen-of-the-Prairie, 93, 105, 312–**313**
Quercus
    Q. acutissima, 164–165
    Q. alba, 93
    Q. bicolor, 93
    Q. macrocarpa, 96
    Q. nigra, 75, 93, 164
    Q. nuttallii, 93, 165
    Q. palustris, 93, **164**–165
    Q. phellos, 165
    Q. rubra, 165
    Q. species, 34, 38, 113, 164–165
    Q. virginiana, **226**
Quince, 440

R

Rabbits, **558**, 559
Raccoons, 559
Radicchio, 451, **484**
Radish, 449, 451, 456–457, 484–**485**
Railroad ties, **98, 99**
Rain lily, **407**
Rakes, 536, 537, 540
Raphanus sativus, 449, 451, 456–457, 484–**485**
Raspberry
  black, 440–441
  red, 440–441
  yellow, 440–441
Rattlesnake grass, 102, 105, **334**
Ravenna grass, **336**–337
Redbud, Eastern, 89, **149**
Red horse chestnut, 38, **145**
Redleaf rose, 284
Redwood
  dawn, 78, 123, **159**
  giant, 78, 229–230
Rhaphiolepsis indica, 71, 88, **226**–227
Rhizomes, 289, 385
Rhododendron
  Carolina, 71, 228–229
  Catawba, 228–229
  evergreen, 5, 41, 79, 88, 117, 124–**126, 135, 141,** 193–194, 227–229
  Korean, 35, 41, **194**
  R. arborescens, 35, 41
  R. atlanticum, 93, 193
    R. a. Choptank River strain, **193**
  R. austrinum, 193
  R. calendulaceum, 35
  R. carolinianum, 71, 228–229
  R. catawbiense, 228–229
  R. hybrida, 124, 227–228
    R. h. 'Fashion', **32**
  R. hybrids, **26,** 88, 194–195
  R. × indicum, **227**
  R. maximum, 228–229
  R. mucronulatum, 35, 41, **194**
  R. periclymenoides, 193
  R. prunifolium, 193–194
  R. schlippenbachii, 194
  R. species, 35, 41, 79, 88, 117, 124–**126, 135, 141,** 193–194, 227–229

R. vaseyi, 35, 193–194
R. viscosum, 41, 93, 194
R. yakusimanum, **228**–229
rosebay, 228–229
yaku, **228**–229
Rhubarb × cultorum, 449, **485**
Rhus
  R. species, 35, 41, 96, 113
  R. typhina, 195
    R. t. 'Laciniata', **195**
Ribbon grass, 97, 291, **341**
Ribes
  R. alpinum, 79, 96, **195**–196
  R. hirtellum, 433–434
  R. nigrum, 432
  R. sativum, **432**
  R. silvestre, **432**
  R. species, **433**–434
  R. uva-crispa, 433–434
Ricinus communis, 49, 374
  R. communis 'Carmicita', **374**
Robinia pseudoacacia, 75, 91, 97, 115, 117, **165**–166
Rockcress
  false, 117
  wall, 110, **299**–300
Rock gardens, **110–111**
Rodgersia
  finger-leaf, 328
  R. aesculifolia, 328
  R. podophylla, **328**
  R. species, 33, 93, 117, 328
Roots, 122, **130**
Rosa (*See also* Rose)
  R. alba, 268, 276
  R. banksiae, 97, **281**
  R. chinensis, 283
  R. damascena, 268, 278
  R. gallica, 268, 279
    R. g. 'Camaieux', **270**
    R. g. 'James Mason', **275**
  R. glauca, 284
  R. multiflora, 283
  R. moschata 'Plena', **273**
  R. rubrifolia, 284
  R. rugosa, **91, 95,** 96, 113, 284–**285**
  R. species, 41
Rose (See also *Rosa*)
  Bourbon, 44, 276
  Canadian, 276–277
  centifolia, 277

'Charles de Mills' gallica, **279**
China, 277
climbing, 44, 236, 238, 269, 272, **273**–274, **282**
damask, 268, 278
'Dortmund' shrub, **285**
English, 269, 278
floribunda, 45, 269, 278–279
gallica, 268, 279
'Gene Boerner' tree, **285**
'Graham Thomas', **45**
grandiflora, 45, 269, 279–280
hybrid musk, **268**, 280
hybrid perpetual, 44, 45, 280
hybrid tea, 45, 269, 280–281
'Jacques Cartier' Portland, **283**–284
'James Mason' gallica, **275**
'John Cabot' Canadian climber, **276**–277
'Kathryn Morley' English, **278**
Lady Banks, 97, **281**
landscape, 281–282
large-flowered climbing, 272, **282**
love grandiflora, **279**
'Madame George Staechelin' large-flowered climber, **282**
'Madame Hardy' damask, **278**
'Madame Isaac Pereire' bourbon, 45, **276**
'Meidiland' pink landscape, **281**–282
miniature, 282–283
modern, 44, 269–270, 272, 274
'Moderna' hybrid tea, **281**
moss, 283 (See also *Portulaca grandiflora*)
'New Beginning' miniature, **282**
'Old Blush' China, **277**
old garden, 44, 268–270, 273
'Paul Ricault' centifolia, **277**
polyantha, 269, 283
Portland, 283–284
rambler, 236, 269, 272–274, 284
redleaf, **284**
'Red Moss', **283**
rugosa, **91, 95,** 96, 113, 284–**285**
semi plena, **276**
'Showbiz' floribunda, **279**
shrub, 41, 45, 285
'Silver Charm', **44**
tea, 277

'The Fairy' polyantha, **283**
tree, 285
'Ulrich Brunner Fils' hybrid
    perpetual, **280**
'Vanity' hybrid musk, **280**
'Veilchenblau' rambler, **284**
Rosemary, 55, 502–**503**
trailing, 57, 97
Rose-of-Sharon, 35, 79, 96, 115,
    184–185
Roses
blooming season, **269**
companion plants for, **44**–45
encyclopedia of, **276**–**285**
feeding, 271, 516
formal gardens for, 45
fragrant, **45**
modern, 44, 269
old garden, 44–45, 268–269
pests and diseases of, 274–275
planting, 270–271
pruning and training, 272–273
using in the landscape, **44**–45
watering, 271
winter protection for, 274
Rosmarinus officinalis, 55,
    502–**503**
R. o. var. *prostratus,* 57, 97
Rototillers, 535
Row covers, **452,** 459
Rubus
creeping, **262**
R. calycinoides, **262**
R. idaeus, 440–441
R. occidentalis, 440–441
R. pentalobus, 262
R. 'Royalty', **440**
R. species, 440–441
R. subgenus *Eubatus,* **429**
Rudbeckia
R. fulgida, 91, 97, 103, 328, 329
   R. f. 'Goldsturm', 46, **328,** 329
R. nitida, 328–329
   R. n. 'Autumn Glory', 47
R. species, **32,** 105, 113, 117,
    328–329
Rue, **503**
Rumex acetosa, 449, **486**–487
Rutabaga, 449, 457, 485–**486**
Ruta graveolens, **503**
Rye, blue wild, 97, 105, **336**

S

Saccharum ravennae, **336**–337
Safety precautions, 136, 534, 541, 348
Sage, 58, 117, **352**
Bethlehem, 19, 89, 327–328
garden, **54,** 57, **495, 503**–504
hybrid, 47, **329**
mealy-cup, 57, 103, 353, **374**–375
Russian, 47, **55,** 57, 91, 97, **324**
Sagina subulata, **262**
St.-John's-wort, golden, 91. 186–**187**
Salix
S. alba 'Tristis', 37, 93, 166
   S. a. var. 'Vitellina', 166
S. discolor, 93, 196
S. purpurea, 88, 93, **196**
S. species, 196
Salvia
red, 115, 374–375
S. farinacea, 57, 103, 353,
    374–375
S. officinalis, **54,** 57, **495,**
    503–504
S. species, **58,** 117, **352**
S. splendens, 115, 374–375
   S. s. 'Flare', **375**
S. × *superba,* 47, **329**
Sambucus
S. canadensis, 113, **432**
S. racemosa, 196–197
   S. r. 'Plumosa-Aurea', 197
Santolina chamaecyparissus,
    44–45, 91
Sanvitalia procumbens, 49, 96, 110,
    117, 348, **375**
Sapphire berry, 41, **199**
Sapphire flower, 353, **356**
Sarcococca hookeriana var. *humilis,*
    262–263
Saucer magnolia, 89, **158**
Saws, pruning, 538–539
Saxifraga
S. sarmentosa, 263
S. stolonifera, 89, **263**
Scabiosa caucasica, 47, 110, 113,
    117, **329**
***Scaevola aemula, 49,** 57, 348,
    375–376
   S. a. 'Blue Wonder', **375**–376
Scallion, **450,** 457, 480

Schizanthus pinnatus, 117
Scholar tree, Chinese, 38, 97, **166**
Sciadopitys verticillata, 88, **229**
Scilla
S. campanulata, 397
S. hispanica, **50,** 397
S. siberica, 36, 50–51, 110, 382–383,
    403–404
Scotch moss, **262**
Sea oats, 89, 102, 105, **335**
Sea thirft, 97
Seating
in backyards, 72–**73**
in country cottage gardens, **101**
on decks, 60–61
for double border garden, 28–**29**
and garden style, 65
space requirements for, 61
Secateurs, 538
Sedge
Bowles golden tufted, 89, 334–335
Japanese, 89, 334, 335
Sedum
S. acre, 61
S. cauticolum, 330
goldmoss, 61
S. kamtschaticum, 110
S. maximum atropurpurea, **90**
S. species, 91, **94,** 97, 117, 330
S. × *telephium* 'Autumn Joy', **36,**
    46–47, 102, **330**
Seeds and seedlings
coldframe for, **529**
grass, 564, 566
lawns from, 566
plants from, **528**–**529**
potting soil for, 528
vegetables, 454–456
wildflowers, 104–105
Senecio cineraria, 19
Sequoia, giant, 78, 229–230
Sequoiadendron
S. giganteum, 78, 229–230
S. sempervirens, **230**
Serviceberry, 34, 89, 96, 113, 146
Shadblow, 34, 89, 96, 113, 146
Shade
and compacted soil, 85
lawns in, 29, 566–**567**
modifying, 85
plants for, **84,** 86–**87,** 88–89

tree position and, 81, 87
types of, 84
vegetables in, 449
Shallot, **486**
Shasta daisy, 103, 319–320
Shears, **138**–139, 538–539, 571
Sheds, garden, **72**–73
Shellflower, 109
Shiso, 49, **372**
Shovels, 534
Shredders, 540–**541**
Shrub althaea, 35, 79, 96, 115,
    184–**185**
Shrubby cinquefoil, 41, 71, 91, 96,
    192–193
Shrubs (*See also* Deciduous shrubs;
        Evergreens)
    bark of, 23, 37
    caring for, 134–**135**
    choosing, **127**, 130, 527
    deadheading, **141**
    dwarf conifers, 124–**125**
    fertilizing, 134, 516
    in foundation plantings, 70–71
    in mixed borders, **40**
    for off-season color, **34–35**, 36–37,
        40–**41**
    planting, 128–130, **132–133**, 135
    for privacy, 14–15, 40, **74**
    pruning and thinning, 137, **138,**
        139–141
    rejuvenating, **140**–141
    with showy berries and flowers, **41**
    siting, 126–127
    types of, **124–125**
    using in landscape, 21, **40**–41
    watering, 134
    winter protection for, 134
Silk tree, 115, **145**–146
Silky-spike melic, **338**
Silt, 508–509
Silver grass, 102, 293, 338–339
Silver fleece vine, 89, 97, **261**
Silver lace vine, 89, 97, **261**
Skimmia japonica, 41, 71, 88, **230**
Slopes, **98–99, 110–111**
Smokebush, 35, **40,** 41, 177–178
Smoke tree, 35, **40,** 41, 177–178
Snapdragon, 36, 103, 115, 117,
        353, **354**
    climbing, 236, **245**

Sneezeweed, 105, **315**
Snowberry, 41, 91, 199
Snowdrop, 36, **50–51**, 88, 383, 387,
    396, 399
Snowflake, spring, 399
Snow-in-cereum, 44, 46, 61, 91, 97,
    110, **305**–306
Sod
    installing, **566**–567
    removing, 518–519, 568
Soil
    amending and improving, **510**–511
    compacted, 85
    composition of, 508
    digging and working, 518–519,
        534–537
    drainage, 92–93
    erosion, 99
    fertility, 512–513
    improving, 90, 106, 509
    nutrients in, 509, 512–513, 516, 521
    pH of, 509, **511**–512
    poor, **90–91**
    potting, 58–59, 528
    sandy, 90, 508–**509**
    sterilizing (solarizing), 553
    testing, 511–512, 516
    for trees and shrubs, 135
    types of, 508–**509**
    wet, **92**–93
Solanum
    S. melongena var. *esculentum,*
        457, **474**
    S. tuberosum, 449, **483**–484
Solenostemon scutellariodes, **56**–57,
        88, 358–**359**
Solidago
    S. hybrids, 36, 117, 330–331
    S. 'Peter Pan', **330**–331
    S. species, 105, 113
Sophora japonica, 38, 97, 166
    S. j. 'Regent', **166**
Sorbaria sorbifolia, 88, **197**
Sorbus
    S. alnifolia, 34, 38, 166–**167**
    S. aucuparia, 97
    S. species, 113
Sorrel, 449, **486**–487
Sorrel tree, 34, 89, **160**
Sourwood, 34, 89, **160**
Spades, 534

Spanish bluebell, 88, **397**
Spanish flag236, **259**
Spearmint, **494, 501**
Speedwell
    Hungarian, 332–333
    spike, 333
Spicebush, 35, 88, 113, 117, **190**–191
Spider flower, 49, 57, 96, 103,
        105, 349, 353, **358**
Spinach, 449, 451, 457, **487**
Spinacia oleracea, 449, 451, 457, **487**
Spindle tree
    European, 41
    winged, 35, 79, 88, **182**
Spiny bear's breeches, **296**
Spiraea
    blue, 41, 91, 96, **174**
    S. × *bumalda,* 26, 35, 197–198
    S. japonica 'Anthony Waterer',
        125, 198
    S. nipponica 'Snowmound', 71
    S. sorbifolia (See *Sorbaria*
        sorbifolia)
    S. species, **40**–41, 79, 197–198
    S. thunbergii, **197**–198
    S. × *vanhouttei,* **133,** 198
Spirea
    bridal-wreath, **133,** 198
    Bumald, 26, 35, 197–198
    Thunberg, **197**–198
    Ural false, 88, **197**
Spotted dead nettle, 19, 44, 89, 319
Spreaders, 571
Sprinklers, 543, 544, **545**
Spruce, 37, 113, 219–221
    Colorado, 110, **220**–221
    Norway, 110, 219–220
    Oriental, 91, 110, 219–220
    Serbian, 219–220
    white, 88, 91, 110, 219–220
Spurge, Japanese, 89, **240,** 241,
        259–260
Squash, 449, 457, **487**–488
Squill, Siberian, 36, 50–51, 110,
        382–383, **403**–404
Stachys byzantina, **19,** 44, 91,
        97, **331**
    S. b. 'Silver Carpet', 19, 97
Staghorn sumac, 195

Staking
ornamental grasses, **293**
perennials, 292–293
using in landscape, 40–41
vegetables, **448, 451**
Star flower, 353, **356**
Starflower, spring, 50, **398**
Star jasmine, 89, 236, 263–**264**
Star magnolia, 158
Statice, 102, 353, **367**
Statuary, **21,** 65
Stephanandra
cutleaf, 35, 71, 79, **198**–199
S. incisa 'Crispa', 35, 71, 79,
198–199
Steps, **99, 111**
Sternbergia lutea, 36, 110, **404**
Stewartia
Japanese, 34, 37, 89, **167**
S. pseudocamellia, 34, 37, 89, **167**
Stipa gigantea, **341**
Stock, 49, 103, 353, **368**–369
Stokes' aster, 47, **331**
Stokesia laevis, 47, **331**
Stolons, 289
Stonecrop, 91, **94,** 97, 117, 330
Strawberry, 441–443
Alpine, 441, **442**–443
barren, 107, **264**–265
day-neutral or June-bearing,
441–443
Strawberry begonia, 89, **263**
Strawberry geranium, 89, **263**
Strawflower, 91, 96, 102, 117, 348,
353, **364**
Styles, garden
cottage, 17, 44, **100–101**
country, 17, 44, 62, **100–101**
English, 16, **28,** 65
formal, **16**–17, 45, 62, 65
informal, 16–**17**
natural, 16–**17,** 62
Stylophorum diphyllum, **106**
Styrax japonicus, 89, **167**–168
Sumac, staghorn, 195
Summer snowflake, 88, **399**
Summer-sweet, 35, 41, 71, 79, 93, **176**
Sunchoke, **476**
Sundrops, common, 46, 105, **322,** 323

Sunflower, 91, 96, 105, **364**
fall, 91, 97, 105
Mexican, 49, 91, 117, 348, **377**
Sweet alyssum, 19, 22, **48–49,** 61, 88,
91, 110, **111,** 117, 348–349,
351–353, 367–**368**
Sweet bay, 93, 217
Sweet box, dwarf, **262**–263
Sweet cicely, 495
Sweet gum, 34, 38, 75, 113, **157**
Sweet pea, **49,** 103, 353, **366**–367
Sweet pepperbush, 35, 41, 71, 79, 93,
176
Sweet potato, 488–**489**
Sweet shrub, 41, 88, 93, **174**
Sweet William, 103, 115, 309–310
Sweet woodruff, **23, 43**–44, 107,
252, 495
Switch grass, 97, 105, 339–340
Symphoricarpos
S. albus, 41, 91, 199
S. a. var. *laevigatus,* **199**
S. × chenaultii, 41
S. species, 88, 96, 113, 115
Symplocos paniculata, 41, **199**
Syringa
S. amurensis var. *japonica,* 168
S. meyeri, 71, 199–200
S. reticulata, 38, **168**
S. species, **41,** 79, 96, 199–200
S. vulgaris, 199–**200**

T

Tagetes
T. erecta, 113, 376–377
T. e. 'Super Hybrid Mix', **376**
T. patula, 57, 376–377
T. p. 'Disco Flame', **376**–377
T. species, **32,** 96, 103, 117,
348–349, 351, 353, 376–377
T. tenuifolia, 19, 376–377
T. t. 'Golden Gem', **376**–377
Tamarisk, five-stamen, **200**–201
Tamarix
T. ramosissima, **200**–201
T. species, 96, 201
Tarragon, 495, 504–**505**
Taxodium distichum, 93, 123, **168**

Taxus
T. baccata, 230–231
T. b. 'Repandens', 71
T. cuspidata, 71, 230–231
T. c. 'Capitata', **230**–231
T. × media, 230–231
T. species, 28, 37, 78–79, 88, **138,
140,** 230–231
Terraces, **98**–99
Texas bluebonnet, 91, 105, **368, 511**
Thatch, 572
Thornless honey locust, 38, 96, 154
Thrift, sea, 97
Thuja
T. occidentalis, 78–**79,** 93, **140,
231**–232
T. plicata, 78, 88, 231–232
T. species, 231–232
Thunbergia alata, 57, 89, 97,
236, 263
T. a. 'Susic Orange with Black
Eye', **263**
Thyme
common, **54–55, 495, 505**
lemon, **55,** 505
wild, 97
Thymophylla tenuiloba, 361
Thymus
T. × citriodorus, **55,** 505
T. herba-barona, 505
T. praecox subsp. *arcticus,* 61, 505
T. pseudolanuginosus, 61, 110, **505**
T. serpyllum, 97
T. species, 91, **94**
T. vulgaris, **54–55, 495, 505**
T. v. 'Argenteus', 19
Tiarella
T. cordifolia, 331–**332**
T. species, 107
Tickseed, 22, 44, 46–47, 91, 97, 103,
105, 113, 117, 288, **307**
Tiger flower, **404**
Tigrida pavonia, **404**
Tilia
T. cordata, 38, 169
T. c. 'Greenspire', **169**
T. tomentosa, 38, 169
Tillers and tilling, 509, 519, 535
Timbers, landscape, 99
Tithonia rotundifolia, 49, 91, 117,
348, **377**

Tobacco, flowering, 49, 57–**58**, 351, 353, **369**–370
Tomatillo, **489**
Tomato, 448, 450, 457, 460–**461**, 489–**490**
Tools (*See also* specific tools)
    caring for, 539
    for cutting and pruning, 538–539
    for earth-moving, 534–535
    handles of, 535, 539
    for pesticide application, 548
    safety precautions with, 534, 541
    storing, **72**–73
    for yard cleanup, **540–541**
Torenia fournieri, 49, 88, 353, **377–**378
Trachelospermum jasminoides, 89, 236, 263–**264**
Transplantation, 527, 529
Treasure flower, 91, 348, **363**
Trees (*See also* Conifers; Deciduous trees; Evergreens; Fruit trees)
    anatomy of, 122
    animal pests and, 557–558
    bark of, 23, **37**
    caring for, 134–**135**
    choosing, 127, 130, 527
    for climate control, 80–83
    fertilizing, 134, 516
    insect pests and, **135**
    mulching, 134–**135**
    for off-season color, 34, 36–**39**
    planting, **128**, 129, **130–131**, 135
    pruning and thinning, 136, **137,** **140,** 141
    rejuvenating, **140,** 141
    road-salt-tolerant, 75
    roots, 122, **130**
    shade and, 38, 81, 87–89
    siting, **39,** 80–83, 126–127
    on slopes, 98, 99
    staking, 129–130, **131**
    using in landscape, **38–39**
    watering, 134
    winter protection for, 134–135
Trellises, 422, 450
Trifolium pratense, 117
Trillium
    T. grandiflorum, 106–**107,** **404**–405, **511**
    white, 106–**107,404**–405, **511**

Trimmers, 539, 571
Triteleia uniflora, 398
Tritonia × *crocosmiflora,* 392
Tropaeolum majus, 57, 348, **349,** 353, 378
    T. m. 'Climbing Mix', **378**
Trout lily, **23,** 107, 395
Trowels, 535
Trumpet creeper, **42,** 89, 91, 93, 97, 115, 236, 238, **246**
Trumpet vine, **42, 89,** 91, 93, 97, 115, 236, 238, **246**
Tsuga
    T. canadensis, 88, **232**
    T. species, 78
Tuberose, 103, **403**
Tuberous begonia, 57, 88, 385, **390**
Tub gardens, 108
Tufted hair grass, 335–**336**
Tulbaghia species, **90**
Tulip, 51, 96, **102,** 103, 110, **382–383,** 384–385, 405–406
    Bokhara, 405–406
    dwarf Taurus, 405–407
    Florentine, 406–407
    Kuenlun, 406
    lady, 405–406
    water lily, 406–407
Tulipa
    'Angelique' double late hybrid, **405**–406
    'Estella Rijnveld' parrot hybrid, **405**
    'Georgette' multistem hybrid, **405**–406
    T. batalinii, 405–406
    T. clusiana, 405–406
    T. dasystemon, 406
    T. kaufmanniana hybrids, 406–407
    T. pulchella, 405–407
    T. saxatilis, 91
    T. species and hybrids, **51,** 96, **102,** 103, 110, **382–383,** 384–385, 405–406
    T. sylvestris, 406–407
    T. tarda, 406
Tulip tree, 34, 38, 115, 117, **157–**158
Tupelo, 34, 38, 89, 93, 113, **160**
Turnip, 449, 451, 457, 490–**491**
Turtlehead, 93, 105
    pink, **306**

U

Ulmus
    U. americana, 93, **169**–170
    U. parvifolia, 37–38, 75, 97, 169–179
        U. p. 'Athena', 34
    U. pumila, 97

V

***Vaccinium,* 430**
    V. angustifolium, 429–430
    V. corymbosum, 429–430, 509
Valerian, 495
Vallisneria americana, 109
Vegetable gardening
    in beds, 449, 455
    birds and, 559
    in children's gardens, 118–119
    cover cropping, 455–**456**
    crop rotation, 459
    crop selection, 448
    direct seeding, 454–455
    disease control, 459
    fertilizing, 454, 458, 516
    green manure, 455–**456**
    growing tips, 456
    guide to planting, 457
    harvesting and storing, 460–461
    intensive growing methods, 449–**450,** 451
    intercropping, **450**
    landscape design and, **52–53**
    mulching, **448,** 458–459
    pest control, **459,** 546
    picking, 460–**461**
    planning, **448–**449
    planting methods, 449, 454
    relay planting, 451
    season-extending methods, **452–453**
    from seeds, 528–529
    in shade, 449
    succession planting, 451
    transplanting, 456, 527
    vegetable encyclopedia, **462–491**
    vertical supports, **448**
    watering, 458
    weed control, **459**
    winter protection, **452–453**

Verbena
bedding, 57, 96, 110, 117, 332,
352, 378
Brazilian, 47
clump, 97, 332
rose, 97, 332
V. bonariensis, 47
V. canadensis, 97, 332
V. c. 'Homestead Purple', **332**
V. × hybrida, 57, 96, 110, 117, 332,
352, 378
V. × h. 'Peaches and Cream', **378**
Veronica
V. austriaca subsp. *teucrium,*
332–333
V. longifolia, 47
V. spicata, 333
V. s. 'Minuet', **332,** 333
Viburnum
double file, 88, 201–202
Korean spice, 201–202
laurustinus, 88, 233
leatherleaf, 88, 233
linden, 113, 201–202
V. carlesii, 201–202
V. dilatatum, 113, 201–202
V. d. 'Erie', **201**–202
V. nudum, 93
V. opulus, 113
V. o. 'Xanthocarpum', 41
V. plicatum forma *tomentosum,* 88,
201–202
V. prunifolium, 201–202
V. rhytidophyllum, 88, 233
V. r. 'Roseum', **233**
V. species, **26, 35, 40,** 41, 79,
201–202, 233
V. tinus, 41, 233
V. trilobum, 93, 113, 201–**202**
withe-rod, 93
Vinca
V. major, 57
V. minor, 89, 240, **241, 264**
V. rosea, 357
Vines
for cottage gardens, 100
encyclopedia of, **242–265**
as garden walls, 14–**15**
pruning, 238–239
training and supporting, 236–**237,**
238–239

undesirable, 43, 239
using in landscape, **42**–43
Viola
V. cornuta, 44, 333
V. c. 'Scottish Yellow', **333**
V. odorata, 333
V. species, 107, **111,** 117
V. tricolor, 353
V. × wittrockiana, 36, **53,** 57, 88,
103, **348,** 353, 378–**379**
V. × w. 'Admiration', **30**
Violet, 107, **111,** 117
horned, 44, 333
sweet, 333
Virginia creeper, 89, 97, 113, 260
Virginia sweetspire, 35, 41, 71,
93, **188**
Vitex agnus-castus, 96, **203**
Vitis
V. labrusca, 434
V. l. 'Concord', **434**
V. l. 'Steuben', **434**
V. species, 434–435
V. vinifera, 434
Voles, 558–559

W–X

Waldsteinia fragarioides, 107,
264–265
Walkways, **62**–63, **68,** 69, 71
Wallflower, 49, 353
Wall rockcress, 110, **299**–300
Walls
choosing, 75, **76**
as design elements, 64–65
and outdoor rooms, 14, **15**
for privacy, 75–**76**
Walnut, black, **445**
Washington hawthorn, 115
Water conservation, **94–95,** 543
Water gardens, **108–109**
Water hyacinth, 109
Watering
container plants, 59
disease prevention and, 552
in dry shade, 85
equipment, 542–544, **545**
and poor soil, 90
seeds and seedlings, 529

trees and shrubs, 134, 414
vegetable gardens, 458
Water lily, **108–109**
Watermelon, 448, 457, **491**
Water milfoil, 109
Weeds, **459,** 513, **524,** 547, 553
Weeping willow, golden, 166
Weigela
old-fashioned, **40,** 41, 88, 91,
115, 203
W. florida, **40,** 41, 88, 91, 115, 203
W. f. 'Variegata', **203**
W. rosea, 203
Wet soils, 92–93
Wheelbarrows, 537
Wildflowers, 87, **104–107, 511**
Wild ginger
British Columbia, 89, 245
European, 245
Southern, 245
Wildlife, attracting, **108, 112–117**
Wild oats, 89, 102, 105, **335**
Windbreaks, 80–83
Winged euonymus, 35, 79, 88, **182**
Winged spindle tree, 35, 79, 88, **182**
Winterberry, 41, 79, 88, 93, 113,
187–188
Wintercreeper, 97, 113, 236, 241, **251**
Wintergreen, 89, 252–**253**
Winter hazel, 41, 88, **177**
Winter King green hawthorn,
151–152
Winter protection
frost pockets and, 82–83
for perennials, 295
for roses, 274
for trees and shrubs, 134–135
wind and, 80–83
Wintersweet, 41, **175**–176
Wishbone flower, 49, 88, 353,
377–378
Wisteria
Chinese, 97
Japanese, 91, 117, **265**
W. floribunda, 91, 117, 265
W. f. 'Violacea-Plena', **265**
W. sinensis, 97
W. species, 43, 236, **238–239**
Witch hazel, 35, 41, 88, 93, **184**
Chinese, 36, 184
Witloof, 451, **470**–471

Woadwaxen, common, 41, 91, 96, 183–**184**
Wood, pressure-treated, 99
Woodbine, 89, 97, 113, 260
Wood hyacinth, 88, **397**
Woodland gardens, **106–107**
Woody plants, 22
Woolly thyme, 61, 110, **505**
Wormwood, 102
Xeriscapes, 90, **94–95,** 96–97

Y

Yarrow, 47, 91, 97, 117
   common, 102, 296
   fern-leaf, 296
   moonshine, 46, 296–297
Yellow corydalis, 89, 110, **307**–308
Yellow flag, **92**–93, 109
Yellowwood, 34, **150**
Yew, 28, 37, 78–79, 88, **138, 140,** 230–231
   English, 230–231
   hybrid, 230–231
   Japanese, 71, 230–231
Yew pine, 78–79, 88, **225**
Yucca
   Y. filamentosa, 233
   Y. smalliana, 71, 91, 97, **233**

Z

Zantedeschia aethiopica, 93, 103, **407**
Zea mays, 448, 451, 457, **472**
Zelkova, Japanese, 38, 91, 170
Zelkova serrata, 38, 91, 170
   Z. s. 'Green Vase', **170**
Zephyranthes atamasco, **407**
Zinnia
   common, 103, 113, 353, **379**
   creeping, 49, 96, 110, 117, 348, **375**
   narrow-leaf, 57, 96, 110, 348, **379**
   Z. angustifolia, 57, 96, 110, 348, **379**
   Z. elegans, 103, 113, 353, **379**
   Z. species, 117, 349, 351–**352**

ACKNOWLEDGEMENTS

Thanks to the following garden and landscape designers whose work appears in this book:

Barbara Berend (page 26)
Duncan Callicot (14, 76, 564 bottom)
Conni Cross (7, 18, 27, 40, 48 bottom, 51 bottom, 56 right, 57, 61, 62, 68, 70, 73, 77 bottom, 84, 86, 99, 102, 132, 351, 382, 522, 523)
Billie Gray (77 top, 87)
Caroline Marsh Lindsay (29)
Ben Page Associates (22, 69, 74, 77 middle, 78, 268)
Tom Pellett (43, 85)
Bill Smith (569)

Special thanks to the following gardeners, garden owners, and public gardens who offered assistance or whose gardens are pictured in this book:

David & Elizabeth Abbott
Louise Allen
Gail Barnard
Geof Beasley
Mr. & Mrs. Coleman P. Burke
Beth Chatto
Candy Cleveland
Andrew & Mitsuko Collver
Tony & Fran Constabile
Barrie Crawford
Joseph & Joanna D'Angelo
Leonna & Gerald Duff
Pam & Angus Duthie
Lewis A. Ellis
Kay Erikson
Mr. & Mrs. Herbert Ernest
Erwin & Yolanda Evert
Sally R. Geist
Jimmy Graham

Patricia & Troy Haltsman
Mary Jeanne Harris
The Headlands Inn
John & Leith Hill
Maurice Isaac & Ellen Coster
Domingo Jimenez
Jim Knopf
Sharon & Bud Koehler
Janet & Milton Lodge
Joyce Manzo & Jimmy Quinn
Katherine Follin Maxwell
Bob Maybeck & Lee Reed
Mr. & Mrs. Robert McCallum
Mary McDonnell
Louise & Wayne Mercer
Irma Merrill
Vern Nelson
Judy Ogden
Dudley & Carole Philhower
Ben & Joan Rechter
David & Margaret Riggs
Barbara Paul Robinson
Joanna Saccucci
Mark Schneider
Paul & Laurie Seigel
Jodi Slaymaker
Virginia Smith
Sandy Snyder
Vivian E. Sweeney
Ken Twombley
Ron Wagner & Nani Waddoups
Cynthia Wadelton
Jan Waltemath
Jim & Betty Warner
Margaret Willoughby

Brookside Gardens
Callaway Gardens
Chicago Botanical Gardens,
Denver Botanic Gardens
Longwood Gardens
Minnesota Landscape Arboretum
New York Botanical Garden
Old Westbury Gardens
Planting Fields Arboretum
Shady Acres Herb Farm
U.S. Botanic Garden
Winterthur Gardens